W9-AZV-015

2nd EDITION

Tools & Techniques of INVESTMENT PLANNING

STEPHAN R. LEIMBERG
ROBERT T. LeCLAIR
ROBERT J. DOYLE, JR.
THOMAS R. ROBINSON

The A Unit of Highline Media
National
Underwriter
Company

*The Leader in Insurance and
Financial Services Information*

P.O. Box 14367
Cincinnati, Ohio 45250-0367
800-543-0874

www.NationalUnderwriterStore.com

ISBN 0-87218-689-X

Library of Congress Control Number: 2006934881

THE NATIONAL UNDERWRITER COMPANY

Copyright © 2004, 2006
The National Underwriter Company
P.O. Box 14367
Cincinnati, Ohio 45250-0367

Second Edition

Printed in the United States of America

DEDICATION

Stephan R. Leimberg

To Bob LeClair
My co-author, partner, and dear friend – to whom I owe so much!

Robert T. LeClair

To Bion B. Howard, friend and teacher

Robert J. Doyle, Jr.

To Steve, Brother and Lifetime Best Friend!

Thomas R. Robinson

To Linda

iii

ABOUT THE AUTHORS

Stephan R. Leimberg

Stephan R. Leimberg, JD, is CEO of Leimberg Information Services, Inc., an e-mail and database service providing information and commentary on tax cases, rulings, and legislation for financial services professionals, CEO of Leimberg and LeClair, Inc., an estate and financial planning software company, and President of Leimberg Associates, Inc., a publishing company.

The 1998 Edward N. Polisher Lecturer of Dickinson School of Law and 2004 recipient of the National Association of Estate Planners and Councils Distinguished Accredited Estate Planner award, Leimberg was awarded Excellence in Writing Award of the American Bar Association's Probate and Property Section. He is Editor, Keeping Current of the Society of Financial Service Professionals, former Lecturer-in-Law in the Masters of Taxation Program of both Villanova and Temple University Schools of Law, and is on the Editorial Board of Estate Planning Magazine.

Professor Leimberg has addressed the Heckerling Tax Institute, Notre Dame Law School Tax Institute, ALI-ABA's Sophisticated Estate Planning Techniques Course, ALI-ABA's Planning for Large Estates Course, the NYU Tax Institute, the National Association of Estate Planners and Councils National Conference, the AICPA's National Estate Planning Forum, and Duke University Law School's Estate Planning Conference.

Leimberg has been frequently quoted in the Wall Street Journal, New York Times, Forbes, Fortune, Business Week, Standard and Poors' Outlook, The Christian Science Monitor, Bloomberg's Financial, Kiplingers, The Washington Post, Smart Money, and Money Magazine. Leimberg has been Estate Planner of the Year of the Montgomery County Estate Planning Council, Distinguished Estate Planner of the Philadelphia Estate Planning Council, recipient of the President's Cup of the Philadelphia Life Underwriters, a two time Boris Todorivitch Lecturer, and the First Ben Feldman Lecturer.

He is author or co-author of many books on estate, financial, and employee benefit and retirement planning and a nationally known speaker and creator and principal author of the entire nine book **TOOLS AND TECHNIQUES** series including **THE TOOLS AND TECHNIQUES OF ESTATE PLANNING**. He is co-author, with Howard Zaritsky, of **TAX PLANNING WITH LIFE INSURANCE**, with Charles K. Plotnick and Daniel Evans of **THE BOOK OF TRUSTS**, with Charles K. Plotnick in **HOW TO SETTLE AN ESTATE**, and with Morey S. Rosenbloom and Joseph Yollin in the **BUY-SELL HANDBOOK**. Leimberg is co-creator of many software packages for the professional including **NumberCruncher** (estate and financial planning), **ESTATE PLANNING QUICKVIEW** (instant calculations & flow charting), and the turnkey client-oriented PowerPoint seminar presentations, **TOWARD A ZERO ESTATE TAX**, **LONG TERM CARE**, and **GIFTS THAT GIVE, GIFTS THAT GIVE BACK** (Charitable Planning).

Dr. Robert T. LeClair

Robert T. LeClair, Ph.D., is Associate Professor of Finance at Villanova University, Villanova, Pennsylvania. He is a graduate of the Wharton School of the University of Pennsylvania and received his MBA and Ph.D. degrees from Northwestern University's Kellogg Graduate School of Management. Prior to joining the faculty at Villanova, Dr. LeClair served on the faculties of The American College, Bryn Mawr, Pennsylvania, and the University of Illinois at Champaign-Urbana, Illinois.

Dr. LeClair is also on the faculty of John Cabot University in Rome, Italy. In Rome, he has been a speaker for various United Nations organizations including the Food and Agriculture Organization and the World Food Program. He has also presented courses on accounting and finance developed by the American Management Association for Italian business executives.

Dr. LeClair is a frequent speaker for business groups and professional organizations in the areas of finance, investment, retirement planning, taxation, and personal financial planning. He has also been active as a consultant for numerous banks, thrift institutions, insurance companies, and professional associations. These include: Commerce Clearing House, Shenandoah Life

Insurance Co., Jewel Companies, Inc., CNA Financial Corp., Continental Bank, America's Community Bankers, the Pennsylvania Credit Union League, the National Board of Medical Examiners, National Liberty Corporation, Eagle Software Publishing, Fidelcor, Inc., and the Archdiocese of Philadelphia.

Robert J. Doyle, Jr.

Robert J. Doyle, Jr. is an independent financial economist/consultant, writer and speaker, and software developer specializing in executive compensation, retirement planning, investment and insurance tax planning, business valuation, and business continuation planning. He has been affiliated with Surgent McCoy CPE, Inc. in Devon, Pennsylvania, for approximately 12 years as a writer and speaker. Surgent McCoy CPE, Inc. is a CPA firm and publisher of continuing professional education courses for CPAs. It is the largest vendor in the United States of continuing professional CPA education courses in the topic areas of taxation and advisory services.

Prior to his affiliation with Surgent McCoy CPE, Inc., Mr. Doyle was Senior Vice President of Mandeville Financial Services, Inc., a diversified insurance, real estate, employee benefits, and executive compensation consulting firm and life insurance agency. Before joining Mandeville Financial Services, Mr. Doyle spent 15 years as Associate Professor of Finance and Insurance at The American College where he was responsible for courses in investments, insurance, retirement and wealth accumulation planning in the College's CLU and ChFC professional designation programs as well as Graduate School of Management and Financial Services. Mr. Doyle also has served as Adjunct Professor of Taxation in the graduate tax program of Widener University Graduate School of Management where he has taught courses in taxation of investments and taxation for financial planning.

He is an author or co-author of over a dozen books and monographs including *The Tools & Techniques of Financial Planning*, *The Tools & Techniques of Life Insurance Planning*, *Can You Afford to Retire?*, *Solutions Handbook For Personal Financial Planning*, *Business Planning*, *Employee Benefits*, *Estate Planning*, *TIAA's Retirement Planning Review Workbook*, *Life Insurance in Asset Accumulation and Preservation*, and *An Educator's Guide to Investments*. He has written and presented numerous professional education courses for CPAs for Surgent McCoy CPE, Inc. on tax, retirement, investment, business, and other financial planning topics. Beyond his book and education courses, Mr. Doyle has published nearly fifty articles in the academic, professional, and trade press and he has appeared as a financial planning expert on radio and television talk shows around the country.

Mr. Doyle has developed a number of tax, insurance, and financial planning software packages, including *IRS Factors Calculator*, *RETIRE*, *Roth IRA Analyzer*, *The Excizer*, and *Applications in Wealth Accumulation Planning*. He has also consulted in the design and development of a number of commercial software products, such as the *The Vanguard Retirement Planner*, *WealthBuilder*, *Softbridge Financial Planner*, and *NumberCruncher and Toolkit*.

Over the years, Mr. Doyle has been retained as a consultant to assist many of the nations' leading accounting firms, brokerage firms, insurance companies, and other financial services organizations develop their own financial planning programs. He has worked with Fortune 500 companies and smaller companies and nonprofit organizations in the development and implementation of nonqualified deferred compensation programs and other employee benefit programs for their key employees. He has also consulted as an expert witness in court cases involving deferred compensation programs, valuations of life insurance agencies and general agency contracts, and other life insurance disputes.

In addition to speaking at dozens of conferences sponsored by The American College and at several hundred CPA continuing education seminars, Mr. Doyle has addressed audiences in regional and national conferences sponsored by The Widener Tax Institute, The International Association of Financial Planners, The Institute of Certified Financial Planners, Commerce Clearing House, The American Society of CLU & ChFC, TIAA-CREF and a number of state CPA Institutes. He has spoken before dozens of chapters of The American Society of CLU & ChFC and numerous regional Estate Planning Councils as well as various community groups and charitable organizations.

Mr. Doyle did his graduate study as a Huebner Fellow at the Wharton School of the University of Pennsylvania. He holds the MA and MBA degrees from Wharton, a

In addition to magazine and journal articles, his other publications include *Money and Retirement*, *A Consumer's Guide to Personal Investing* and *Financial Planning Software Tool Kit*. He has also co-authored and published *NumberCruncher* (estate and financial planning software).

BA from Macalester College, is a CLU and a Chartered Financial Consultant (ChFC).

Mr. Doyle resides in Wayne, Pennsylvania with his wife, Kathryn, and their three children.

Thomas R. Robinson

Thomas R. Robinson, Ph.D., CPA, CFP, CFA is an Associate Professor of Accounting at the University of Miami where he primarily teaches Financial Statement Analysis and Valuation. He is also managing Director of Robinson, Desmond & Zwerner, a Florida registered investment advisory firm. Professor Robinson received his B.A. in Economics from the University of Pennsylvania and Master of Accountancy from Case Western Reserve University. He practiced public accounting for ten years prior to earning his Ph.D. in Accounting with a minor in Finance from Case Western Reserve University.

Professor Robinson has won several teaching awards, including Outstanding Educator from the Florida Institute of CPAs, and has published regularly in academic and professional journals. He is also a co-author of *Analysis of Equity Investments: Valuation*, published by the Association for Investment Management and Research and *Financial Statement Analysis: A Global Perspective*, published by Prentice Hall. He has served as a consultant on financial statement analysis and valuation issues for investment management firms, law firms, accounting firms and governmental agencies.

Professor Robinson is active locally and nationally with the CFA Institute and has served on several committees including the CFA Institute's Financial Accounting Policy Committee and the Council of Examiners. He is a past-president and board member of CFA Miami (formerly the Miami Society of Financial Analysts).

PREFACE

This was the 7th book we created in the very popular 9 book *Tools and Techniques* series – and there's no question in my mind – it was one of the most challenging to complete and remains one of the most difficult to keep up-to-date. The topics it covers are both broad and complex, offering a mental steeplechase course for even the most brilliant of authors. Fortunately, we have just that, a team of both pragmatic and creative authors – and editors – practitioners and scholars – who are more than equal to the Herculean task. This team includes Robert T. LeClair, Robert J. Doyle, Jr., Thomas R. Robinson, William J. Wagner, Deborah A. Miner, Sonya E. King, Joseph F. Stenken April K. Caudill, and John H. Fenton, each of whom is among the brightest minds in the field.

We wanted *Tools and Techniques of Investment Planning* to be readable by novices but useful to experts. Above all, our goal was not merely to educate – but to provide knowledge for performance – to help you turn information into real-world intelligence. So you'll find more formulas and numbers here than in most of the other texts in this series – and in fact – more than in almost all other texts on investment planning.

We welcome your comments, suggestions, and constructive criticism. Have you found this resource well organized? Is it physically easy to read? Does it cover the areas of investment planning you need to know? Is the scope of coverage deep and broad enough? What topics are we missing that you'd like to see covered? Please let us know what we can add or how we can change the next edition so we can better help you help others make a positive difference.

We think you'll find *Tools and Techniques of Investment Planning* to be your learning, review, and reference source of first resort for both information and insight into both traditional and state-of-the-art theory and practice in this most exciting field.

Stephan R. Leimberg

CONTENTS

Appendices

Chapter 1

CASH AND CASH EQUIVALENTS

WHAT IS IT?

Investments in "cash" are not just the physical currency, but typically include investments in bank certificates of deposit, bank savings accounts, short-term United States Treasury issues, and money market mutual funds.

A certificate of deposit is a debt instrument issued by a commercial bank, savings and loan, or other thrift institution (herein collectively referred to as "bank") in exchange for a deposit made by an investor. "CDs" are usually issued in minimum amounts of $5,000, but often are available in smaller denominations. The term of these certificates can range from seven days up to ten years. Interest rates on these certificates are frequently tied to the rate paid on United States Treasury investments of comparable maturity range.

A money market fund is a mutual fund that invests solely in short-term debt instruments. The term "money market" is applied to high quality, short-term debt instruments that mature within one year. These debt instruments include:

1. *United States Treasury Bills* – short-term certificates issued by the federal government that typically mature in three months to one year.

2. *Certificates of Deposit (CDs)* – These may include certificates of foreign banks as well as domestic institutions. Although the risk associated with foreign CDs is somewhat higher, they pay a slightly greater rate of return. Most money market funds will tend to diversify their portfolios by holding both foreign and domestic issues.

3. *Commercial Paper* – short-term debt of major industrial corporations that matures in 60 days to one year.

4. *Bankers Acceptances* – short-term (30 to 360 days) "drafts" drawn on a major bank that are typically used to finance international import/export transactions.

5. *Municipal Paper* – issued by state, county, or local governments or agencies, where the interest is exempt from federal income taxes and state and local income taxes depending on the investor's residency.

6. *Eurodollar Investments* – time deposits denominated in United States dollars, but held in banks headquartered outside the United States, or in foreign branches of United States banks. The minimum investment is typically $1,000,000, and trading is very active in maturities up to six months. The term "Eurodollar" is used on a worldwide basis, not just for deposits held in Europe.

WHEN IS THE USE OF THIS TOOL INDICATED?

1. When an investor desires a high degree of "liquidity" and the ability to convert an investment into cash quickly with little or no cost involved. This is an ideal vehicle for those investors who find themselves with large amounts of idle cash to invest for a short time period.

2. When there is a need or desire for a high degree of safety of principal. Security is provided by the combination of short maturities and the high quality of the issuers of money market securities.

3. When an investor desires a higher rate of return than is available from a passbook-type account, yet desires more flexibility than would be found in longer-term investments.

4. When immediate access or availability of the funds is desired. (However, the premature redemption of a CD will generally result in the imposition of some type of penalty–for example, the forfeiture of a portion of interest earned to date.)

ADVANTAGES

1. CDs are generally insured by various agencies of the federal government up to a maximum of $100,000 per account ownership title. Individuals who wish to invest more than this amount in their own name should open accounts with different account titles (such as husband only and wife only) or at different banks or affiliates of a parent bank to maximize the government insurance protection on their funds. Some banks participate in "networks" of other banks wherein a customer can deal with only one bank but have the money spread among other banks so as to not exceed insurance limits of any one bank. Note however, that mutual fund money market funds are not guaranteed by any federal agency.

2. An investment in a money market fund can be converted easily and conveniently into cash. Also, almost all banks will redeem their CDs prior to maturity on demand.

   However, there are penalties for early withdrawal of funds from a CD. First, there may be a withdrawal penalty. For example, an investor who wishes to redeem a 6-month certificate after only three months may be charged the equivalent of one month's interest as a penalty. A second penalty is a reduction in the rate of interest earned on the certificate to the level of passbook rates. (This assumes that CD rates are higher than passbook rates.)

3. As opposed to bonds and common stocks, which are typically longer-term investments, CDs may be purchased with maturities that match investors' short-term needs. In addition to formal certificates of deposit, some institutions may offer certificate-like accounts with maturities as short as seven days. The interest paid on these accounts will normally be very similar to that paid on short-term certificates. The availability of these accounts is particularly advantageous for investors who need a safe, liquid, and reasonably profitable "parking place" for cash while considering other investments.

   Investors may purchase a portfolio of certificates with differing maturities or simply roll over short-term CDs on an ongoing basis. For example, an investor with $100,000 could purchase four $25,000 CDs, one maturing at the end of each of the next four years. Alternatively, the entire $100,000 could be invested in a single 6-month certificate that would mature and automatically be reinvested (rolled over) in another 6-month certificate.

4. Most money market funds offer shareholders personalized check writing services as well as the ability to wire transfer money from the fund to the investor's bank account.

5. Due to the financial strength of the issuers of the underlying assets held by money market funds, they provide a secure investment. The investor knows that there will be little or no fluctuation in the market value of the investment and the return of capital is virtually assured.

6. The rate of return offered by money market funds is highly sensitive to changes in short-term interest rates. This means that if rates increase, the return provided by the fund will quickly follow. This is because the holdings of the average fund will "turn over" (i.e., will mature and be reinvested) typically within 20 to 90 days.

7. Most money market funds do not impose a sales charge on purchases of the fund or a redemption fee when shares are sold. (However, there are management fees of approximately 0.2% to 0.7% of the fund that are applied annually. An administrative charge may apply to accounts with balances below a certain level, such as $10,000, and is typically $10.00 per account per year.)

8. Certificates of deposit may be "laddered" in maturity dates to manage interest rate risk. Since there is normally a positively-sloped yield curve with higher interest rates on longer maturities, an investor can get a higher interest rate on longer term CDs. But if liquidity is needed or interest rates rise, staggering an investment into 6-month, 12-month, 18-month, 24-month and 30-month maturities will give a higher interest rate than simply a 6-month maturity, plus give the opportunity to reinvest at higher rates as each 6-month CD matures and is re-invested 6 months beyond the longest maturity or "last rung on the ladder."

9. Money market mutual funds are available for tax-exempt investors, both in national funds that are diversified in many states and are exempt from federal tax but subject to state tax or funds that are invested in a single state (less diversified) and exempt from federal and state tax for state residents.

DISADVANTAGES

1. The rate of return on CDs is lower than rates typically available on higher risk alternatives. For example,

1. CDs typically pay a rate of interest below that paid on long-term government bonds. A greater spread would be available from an investment in corporate bonds.

2. A substantial penalty is charged if the investor redeems the certificate prior to maturity. This penalty can significantly reduce the overall rate of return on the investment.

3. Normally, money market funds do not pay as high a rate of return as longer-term investments such as bonds.

4. All of the income generated by a money market investment CDs will be taxed as ordinary income. The investor has no control over the timing of income received and must report all income currently.

5. As mentioned above, investments in money market funds are not insured or guaranteed by any federal agency. Unlike banks that have federally mandated reserve requirements, money market funds are relatively unregulated.

TAX IMPLICATIONS

1. All of the income from CDs and money market funds is fully taxable and subject to ordinary income tax rates. Money fund "dividends" actually are considered to be interest payments for tax purposes.

2. Unlike other investments that are subject to price changes, CDs will be redeemed at maturity for their original investment value. This, together with the fact that there is no market for CDs, means that there can be neither capital gain nor loss with this type of investment. For example, Suzanne Carnes recently invested $50,000 in 6-month certificates of deposit. At maturity, the bank will pay her $50,000 for the certificates. Thus, there is no capital gain or loss.

3. Penalties paid by investors who redeem CDs prior to the maturity date are deductible for federal income tax purposes. For instance, in the example above, if Suzanne Carnes redeemed her CDs two months before they were to have matured, the penalty paid to the bank (actually deducted from the interest and/or principal she otherwise would have received) is deductible.

The taxpayer must report on his tax return the gross amount of interest paid or credited to his account during the year without subtracting the penalty. He then deducts the penalty in calculating adjusted gross income (i.e., regardless of whether deductions are itemized). The taxpayer may deduct the entire penalty even if it exceeds his interest income. Both the gross interest and the penalty amount will be reported to the taxpayer on Form 1099-INT by the financial institution issuing the certificate.

4. The foregone interest in the event of a premature redemption is not deductible. For instance, in the example above, Suzanne Carnes did not earn as much interest as she would have had she kept the certificate until its maturity date. The tax law does not allow a deduction for the loss of interest that might have been earned.

5. There are money market funds that specialize in short-term, tax-exempt investments. The payments received by investors from these funds would retain this tax-free status and are therefore federal income tax free, subject to the effects of the alternative minimum tax (see Chapter 43, "Taxation of Investment Vehicles"). Some mutual fund money markets specialize in state tax free investments to be exempt from federal and state income tax for state residents. These are common in high income tax states such as New York, California, and Ohio.

6. Because money market funds are mutual funds, they are exempt from the requirement that certain pass-through entities report to shareholders (as income) their shares of expenses of the fund, which would be miscellaneous itemized deductions if incurred by the shareholders individually.

ALTERNATIVES

1. Direct purchase of Treasury bills is another investment similar to certificates of deposit. The timing of maturities, safety of principal, and amount of required investment are comparable to investing in bank CDs. Interest on United States Treasury investments is exempt from state income tax. Most individuals find it easier to deal with their local banks than to purchase Treasury bills through the Federal Reserve system. United States Treasury investments can be purchased online at www.treasurydirect.gov. Banks offer a slightly higher return on CDs than that available from Treasury bills. United States Treasury bills, notes, and bonds are the very safest investments available and hence typically pay slightly

lower rates of interest than bank savings accounts or certificates of deposit.

2. Some corporations, especially financial service firms, offer short-term "investment notes" to individual investors. These typically have maturities ranging from three months up to one year. Rates paid on these notes are generally much higher than on CDs of comparable maturity, but corporate notes vary widely in terms of quality, and are not federally or otherwise insured.

3. Many commercial banks, savings and loans, and mutual savings banks offer "money market deposit accounts." The interest rate paid on these accounts is normally less than that paid by money market mutual funds. However, money market deposit accounts are convenient because they can be obtained at the same location where the investor banks and is known. These accounts are also insured subject to insurance limits and account ownership titles by various agencies of the federal government.

4. The direct purchase of Treasury bills, commercial paper, or other similar instruments. However, such an approach may not provide the diversification or professional management available from a money market fund.

WHERE AND HOW DO I GET IT?

Certificates of Deposit

Certificates of deposit are offered by virtually all commercial banks, savings and loans, mutual savings banks, credit unions, and similar financial institutions. To purchase a CD, the investor simply walks into the bank, deposits his or her funds, and receives a certificate in exchange. An investor already dealing with a bank may call the institution, obtain rate quotations, and decide on the maturity date of the certificate and the amount to be purchased. The customer's account will be charged, the CD will be issued and held in safekeeping by the bank, and the need to actually visit the bank has been avoided.

Typically, the investor will be notified two to three weeks prior to the maturity of the certificate. If no action is taken, the CD will simply be "rolled over" into another certificate with a similar maturity, but at the bank's current rate of interest. The investor also has the option of redeeming the certificate for cash or making an additional investment.

It is usually recommended that individuals with large amounts to invest in CDs purchase multiple certificates rather than one large certificate. This would make it possible to redeem part of the investment without disturbing the other certificates or paying the premature withdrawal penalty on the entire amount. For example, an investor with $100,000 should purchase ten certificates of $10,000 each rather than one certificate for $100,000.

Diversification of the CDs by bank and geographic location also enhances safety of principal as well as convenience. For additional protection of principal and interest against loss due to troubled savings and loan institutions, it may be desirable to spread investments among several institutions in more than one state. Individuals who live or work a significant part of the time in states other than their legal domicile might consider purchasing CDs in more than one state.

Money Market Funds

Almost all major brokerage firms make money market funds available to their customers. Customers are encouraged to leave on deposit in such funds the proceeds of any security sales or any dividends or interest received in the account.

Many brokerage firms also offer special accounts that provide a comprehensive package of investment services to customers. A money market account is typically included in the system in order to keep excess cash balances fully invested at all times.

Virtually all mutual fund organizations include a money market fund among their offerings. This enables a mutual fund investor to move assets within a "family of funds" conveniently, quickly, and with minimal cost. Money market mutual funds are purchased from the fund sponsor itself, either in person or by phone or mail. Direct mail and newspaper ads will provide the address and phone number of organizations offering money market funds.

WHAT FEES OR OTHER ACQUISITION COSTS ARE INVOLVED?

There are normally no specific fees or other acquisition costs associated with the purchase of CDs or money market funds. However, it is important to note that a premature redemption fee is assessed by most banks on CDs, and that a lower interest rate may be paid for the period of the investment. Even those mutual fund organizations that typically charge a "load" (i.e., a fee) will not do so in the case of a money market fund. Brokerage firms also do not charge a sale or redemption fee when funds are added to or removed from a money market account. However, there is a management fee based on the total value of the assets owned by the money market fund. This fee, which averages 0.2% to 0.7% of the value of the fund, is deducted from the assets of the fund and is not paid directly by the shareholders. In addition, most funds will deduct an annual account fee of about $10 for low balance accounts below about $10,000.

HOW DO I SELECT THE BEST OF ITS TYPE?

1. For CDs, the investor should compare the interest rates offered by several institutions for a given maturity. Higher rates are often available from banks and thrift institutions in other parts of the country. For this reason, investors, particularly those with larger amounts to invest, should shop around for the most attractive rates. Information on interest rates offered by out-of-state institutions may be found in *Barron's*, *The Wall Street Journal*, *The New York Times*, *The Investor's Business Daily*, and other major financial newspapers and various websites (see below).

2. For money market funds, investors should compare the yields offered by various funds. These returns are generally stated in terms of the average yield paid by the fund during the past seven days or during the past 30 days. If the funds are comparable in other respects, choose the fund that offers the highest yield. Also, funds should be selected with short average maturities. For example, assume Fidelity Cash Reserves and T. Rowe Price Prime Reserve Fund are both yielding 4.75%. If the average maturity of the Fidelity portfolio is 30 days and that of the Rowe Price fund is 40 days, investors may prefer the Fidelity fund because of its shorter maturity. Finally, check the rating services that evaluate the quality of securities in a money market fund's portfolio. Investors who have substantial amounts invested in these funds may wish to obtain these ratings as a means of comparing the safety of individual funds.

WHERE CAN I FIND OUT MORE ABOUT IT?

1. The leading source of information on investments in CDs would be the various financial institutions themselves. All of these sources provide information on rates offered, length of maturity, and any early withdrawal penalties.

2. Financial newspapers and magazines such as *The Wall Street Journal* (www.wsj.com), *New York Times* (www.NYTimes.com), *Barron's* (www.Barrons.com), and *Investor's Business Daily* (www.Investors.com) provide information on money market funds and CDs offered by major financial institutions throughout the country. Local newspapers will also carry ads from regional banks and thrift institutions. These newspapers and magazines also typically show the average maturity of assets held by each money market fund and its most recent yield.

3. Various sources on the Internet provide information on rates available on money market funds and bank CDs. Among these are:

   • Bankrate (www.bankrate.com)

   • Bloomberg (www.bloomberg.com)

   • iMoneyNet, Inc. (www.ibcdata.com)

   • MSN Money Central (www.moneycentral. com)

   • Yahoo Finance (www.finance.yahoo.com)

4. Investors interested in obtaining more information on money market mutual funds can also contact:

   Investment Company Institute
   1401 H Street, N.W.
   Washington, D.C. 20005
   (www.ici.org)

5. Treasury Direct (www.treasurydirect.gov) – a website operated by the United States Treasury, which allows investors to buy and sell Treasury bills and other Treasury issues, including Treasury Inflation-Protected Securities (TIPS) over the Internet. All transactions are processed electronically through a bank account linked to the investor's Treasury Direct account.

QUESTIONS AND ANSWERS

Question – Are all CDs insured by the federal government?

Answer – No, not all CDs are insured by the federal government and there is a limit to the amount of insurance on those that are covered. Some institutions are insured by state organizations rather than the federal government. These state insurance arrangements are not as secure as federal insurance. This was evidenced by the failure of certain savings and loans during the mid-1980's. It is recommended that investors place their funds with those institutions that do have federal deposit insurance. Also, amounts in excess of $100,000 per account are not covered. This indicates the need to diversify an ultra large investment among a number of different accounts or institutions. For instance, Lara Leimberg wishes to invest a million dollar gift she has recently received from her father. She should consider the purchase of certificates using not only her own name, but also the names of her husband and children (jointly with her own, or separately) so that no one certificate exceeds the federal insurance limit of $100,000. (Note that there may be gift tax implications where certificates are purchased in the names of other individuals.) Another alternative would be for Lara to purchase ten individual certificates in her own name from ten different banks.

Question – How do money market funds compare with the money market deposit accounts offered by banks, savings and loans and mutual savings banks?

Answer – The yields available from these two investments generally will be similar, though banks and thrift institutions offer rates that are generally lower than those provided by money market funds. The most important difference between the two investments is that the accounts offered by banks and thrift institutions are insured by various agencies of the federal government. Investors are protected against loss on these accounts up to a maximum of $100,000. Investments in money market funds are not insured by any government agency, though they are generally considered safe due to the high quality of their assets.

Question – Can a CD be used as collateral for a loan?

Answer – Yes. An investor can pledge a CD as security for a loan from the issuing institution or another lender. Banking law (Regulation Q) requires that a bank lending money to customers who use their own CDs as collateral must charge at least 1% over the rate of interest being paid on the CD. This does not apply, however, when an investor is borrowing money from a bank other than the one that issued the CD.

Question – When does the purchaser of a CD receive his interest income?

Answer – The timing of payment of interest varies with maturity range of the CD and is disclosed upon purchase. For CDs that mature in less than one year, interest is usually paid upon maturity. For CDs longer than one year, interest may be paid monthly, quarterly, semi-annually, annually, or at maturity, depending on the specific CD.

Question – Is there any practical way for an individual located in the United States to make relatively small investments in foreign currencies?

Answer – Yes, through Everbank (www.everbank.com) a unique banking organization located in Florida that offers both CDs and bank accounts denominated in a wide range of foreign currencies.

Chapter 2

UNITED STATES GOVERNMENT SECURITIES

WHAT IS IT?

United States government securities are issues of the United States Treasury and various government agencies used to finance the activities of the federal government. Government securities include direct issues of the Treasury such as bills, notes, and bonds, as well as bonds of governmental agencies such as the Government National Mortgage Association (GNMA) and the Federal Land Bank.

A Treasury bill ("T-bill") is a short-term debt security with a maturity of either 4, 13, or 26 weeks. (The Treasury began offering 4-week T-bills in July 2001. The Treasury discontinued the 52-week T-bill in February 2001). Treasury bills are purchased in minimum amounts of $1,000. These bills are issued on a "discount basis" (i.e., sold at less than their par or face value) and redeemed at face value without interest on their maturity date.

A Treasury note is a medium-term debt security, paying interest semi-annually. Notes have a fixed maturity date greater than one year and can extend for up to 10 years from the date of issue. The minimum face value denomination for a Treasury note is $1,000.

A Treasury bond is a long-term debt security, which, like Treasury notes, also pays interest on a semi-annual basis. Bonds have a fixed maturity of more than 10 years. (The United States Treasury temporarily discontinued issuing new 30-year bonds in 2001, but resumed offering them in the spring of 2006.) The minimum denomination for a Treasury bond is $1,000, and interest is paid semi-annually.

Another unique group of securities issued by the United States Treasury are Treasury Inflation-Indexed Securities, often called Treasury Inflation-Protected Securities, or TIPS. Interest payments and the principal value of these bonds are adjusted every six months to reflect changes in inflation as measured by the Consumer Price Index (CPI). These securities were first issued in 1997, and the United States Treasury auctions new 10-year notes four times each year in January, April, July, and October.

WHEN IS THE USE OF THIS TOOL INDICATED?

1. When the individual desires a high quality investment that has little or no risk of default. The United States government has never defaulted on even one of its obligations in more than 225 years. To only a slightly lesser degree, the securities of United States government agencies, such as the World Bank, Postal Service, and the Federal Home Loan Bank, offer low risk and high quality.

2. When an investor needs certainty of income. Because the Treasury can simply print money or raise taxes to pay interest on its obligations, an investor can be sure that payments will be timely made in the amounts promised.

3. When an investor seeks an investment with unquestioned utility as collateral. Due to the low risk of loss of capital and certainty of income, United States government securities are readily accepted by lenders as security for loans.

4. When an investor desires a security with the highest degree of marketability. Government securities are traded daily in very large volume by thousands of individuals and institutions. This insures a ready market and the availability of information on prices and returns.

5. When the investor is either unable or unwilling to accept the uncertainty and risk inherent in equity, tax sheltered, and corporate fixed income investments.

6. TIPS may be useful when an investor is particularly concerned with the potential loss of purchasing power due to the long-term effect of inflation.

ADVANTAGES

1. United States government securities are virtually free of the risk of default.

2. The income from government securities is assured.

3. Government securities are readily accepted by virtually every financial institution as collateral for loans.

4. The securities of the federal government and its agencies are easily and quickly convertible to cash.

5. Government issues provide a high degree of security and comfort for risk conscious investors.

6. Because of the variety of government issues, purchases can be tailored to meet the investor's goals and objectives.

7. The interest earned on Treasury securities is not subject to state and local taxation. This can be of considerable advantage to an investor in a high tax bracket.

8. TIPS provide long-term inflation protection through the semi-annual adjustment of interest payments and principal values to reflect changes in the Consumer Price Index (CPI).

DISADVANTAGES

1. United States government securities provide a rate of return that is generally lower than other fixed income securities.

2. Long-term government issues, like any long-term, fixed income investment, are subject to a high degree of interest rate risk. Therefore, the prices of United States government and agency bonds fluctuate substantially with changes in interest rates.

3. With the exception of TIPS, the purchasing power of the fixed amount of dollars paid by these issues will be eroded over time by the effects of inflation. This problem can be particularly acute if the instruments are long term.

TAX IMPLICATIONS

1. All interest from T-bills, notes, and bonds is subject to federal income tax. This income is taxable at ordinary income rates.

2. Interest from United States government securities is entirely exempt from all state and local taxes.

3. Interest from a Treasury bill is not reportable until the year that the T-bill matures. Therefore, if an investor purchased a 13-week T-bill in November 2006 and the bill matured in February 2007, the interest earned on this bill will be declared on his 2007 federal income tax return.

4. If an investor sells a T-bill on the open market prior to its maturity, he must report as ordinary income the difference between the price he paid and the selling price. If the bill is sold for more than he paid, the gain will be ordinary income. If the bill is sold for less than he paid, the loss is treated as a capital loss.

5. A Treasury note or bond may be subject to capital gains treatment. If a note or bond is sold before maturity on the open market, gain or loss is treated as capital gain or capital loss. (If the gain includes original issue discount or market discount, it may be necessary to treat part of the gain as ordinary income.)

6. In any year when the principal value of a TIPS bond increases due to the inflation adjustment, that gain is considered reportable income for the year even though the investor won't receive the inflation-adjusted principal until the security matures.

ALTERNATIVES

1. Short-term certificates of deposit issued by banks and savings institutions are comparable to Treasury bills. The interest rate paid on CDs is usually the same as or slightly higher than the current T-bill rate. Many institutions will pay up to a quarter of a percentage point premium over the T-bill rate in order to attract investors away from government securities.

2. Longer-term certificates of deposit, also issued by banks, savings and loans, and mutual savings banks, are competitive with Treasury notes and bonds and the securities of other government agencies.

3. High quality corporate bonds (for example, Standard & Poor's ratings of AA or AAA) should be considered as an alternative to long-term government securities such as notes and bonds. Corporate issues involve greater risk, but also provide considerably higher rates of return.

WHERE AND HOW DO I GET IT?

T-bills are offered according to a regular schedule. Thirteen and twenty-six week bills (3 and 6 month maturities) are offered every week by the Treasury. Every Thursday the offering is announced publicly in major newspapers such as *The Wall Street Journal* or *The New York Times*. The bills are auctioned the following Monday. Four-week T-bill auctions are announced on Monday and auctioned on Tuesday. You can find out the date of the next scheduled offering of notes and bonds by calling 1-800-722-2678 or by logging onto the Internet (www. publicdebt.treas.gov).

Federal government securities, including TIPS, can be purchased: (1) directly from the United States Treasury through a Federal Reserve bank (on issue); (2) from a commercial bank; (3) through a brokerage firm; or (4) by using the Treasury Direct system on the Internet.

An investor who wants to purchase a new issue directly from the United States Treasury submits a standardized form known as a "tender" either by mail or in person at the appropriate Federal Reserve Bank or one of its branches. (The investor should send a certified personal or cashier's check drawn on a bank in the same Federal Reserve district.)

Many individual investors prefer the convenience of purchasing United States government securities from their local bank or brokerage firm. They merely call their banker or broker and indicate the amount they desire to invest and the particular security they desire to purchase. The bank will then send the security to the investor, while a broker may offer to hold the security in the customer's account.

Individual investors can also purchase United States Treasury securities over the Internet through the Treasury Direct system (www.treasurydirect.gov). To open a Treasury Direct account, the individual must first submit a paper form that links the account to an investor's checking account.

Once the Treasury Direct account is opened, the individual can purchase new issues of bills, notes, and bonds by computer in amounts as small as $1,000. The amount of the purchase will be automatically deducted from the investor's checking account on the day the securities are issued. Similarly, when the security matures, the par value will be deposited to the same checking account. In addition to the convenience of the Internet, purchases made through Treasury Direct are free of commissions or other fees.

WHAT FEES OR OTHER ACQUISITION COSTS ARE INVOLVED?

When an investor purchases a security directly from the United States Treasury, there are no charges or commissions.

Making a purchase through a bank or broker will typically be more expensive. Banks may charge a commission as well as a premium on purchases under $100,000. Since these charges may vary considerably, it is wise for an investor to compare the fees and premiums charged by a number of banks and brokers.

Aside from commissions, an investor's cost in purchasing government securities from a bank or broker will be different from the cost of a direct purchase from the federal government. First, the bank or broker will either purchase the securities on the open market or will sell the investor issues from their inventory. This means the investor must pay the "asked" market price, which may be higher or lower than the price at which the note or bond was originally issued.

Another consideration is the amount of interest accrued on the note or bond since the last interest payment date. The investor is entitled only to the interest beginning with the date of his purchase. Therefore he must pay the seller of the security the amount of interest accrued since the last payment date in addition to the price of the note or bond itself. Of course, on the next payment date the investor will receive the full amount of interest for the period.

HOW DO I SELECT THE BEST OF ITS TYPE?

Unlike most other investments, all government securities with similar maturities have the same risk and reward characteristics. Therefore, selecting the "best of its type" will depend on the investor's goals and objectives. Planners should focus on the investor's needs for liquidity, income, and tax deferral in selecting among T-bills, notes, and bonds.

Example: Anne Lewis desires to have a high degree of liquidity since she feels interest rates are likely to increase sharply in the months ahead. Clearly, she should not purchase long-term notes or bonds since they will decline in value as rates increase. Anne should concentrate any investments in short-term issues such as T-bills that mature relatively quickly and that will enable her to reinvest at the higher interest rate.

WHERE CAN I FIND OUT MORE ABOUT IT?

1. Financial publications such as the *Wall Street Journal* (www.wsj.com) and *Barron's* (www.barrons.com) regularly quote prices for bills, notes, and bonds issued by the federal government.

2. Banks and brokerage firms will also provide investors with information on available issues and current prices.

3. Investors may also contact the Treasury itself for information concerning the purchase of government securities on issue. Inquiries should be addressed to: Bureau of the Public Debt, Department W, Washington, DC 20226. Purchase information can also be found on the Internet (www.publicdebt.treas. gov).

4. Information on government securities transactions may also be obtained through electronic data networks such as *Dow Jones Newswires* (www.dowjones. com).

QUESTIONS AND ANSWERS

Question – How is interest paid on United States Treasury bills?

Answer – Treasury bills do not pay interest in the same way as other securities. Bills are sold on a discount basis, which means they are offered at a price below their face value or redemption value. The difference between the offering price and the maturity value represents the interest earned by investors. For example, a Treasury bill may be offered at a price of $9,800 with the face value of $10,000 to be paid in thirteen weeks, or 91 days. This represents a rate of return to the investor of 8.2%, as shown in Figure 2.1.

Question – What is the difference between a Treasury "note" and a "bond"?

Answer – The difference is in the length of time until maturity. Notes generally mature in one to ten years. Bonds, on the other hand, typically have maturities of ten years or more. The Treasury Department discontinued issuing 30-year bonds in 2001, but resumed offering them in the spring of 2006.

Question – Are there any mutual funds that specialize in Treasury securities?

Answer – Yes, a mutual fund may restrict its portfolio to issues of the United States government. Although these funds are not insured, they are fully invested in Treasury securities and that gives them a high degree of security. Such mutual funds provide the same services as money market funds and investors can make automatic withdrawals and redemptions by telephone, check, or wire.

Figure 2.1

RATE OF RETURN ON A U.S. TREASURY BILL		
INPUT: Enter face value of Treasury Bill $10,000		
INPUT: Enter current price of Treasury Bill .... $ 9,800		
Enter date information:		
	Year	Month	Day
INPUT: Maturity	98	12	15
INPUT: Current	98	9	15
Number of Days to Maturity 91		
Annualized rate of return 0.082		

Reprinted with permission from *NumberCruncher*, Leimberg & LeClair, Inc.

Treasury mutual funds should be compared with money market funds that may invest in T-bills and other government securities, but also place funds in other short-term obligations such as bank certificates of deposit. Investors will typically receive higher yields from money market funds since their underlying assets are securities bearing higher risks than comparable Treasury securities.

Question – What is the "Treasury Direct" system the Treasury uses to issue bills, notes, and bonds?

Answer – In July of 1986, the United States Treasury Department changed the way it issues bills, notes, and bonds as well as the way it handles investor accounts. The familiar engraved certificates were replaced with a book-entry securities system that operates alongside the commercial system already in place.

Investors under the system called "Treasury Direct" receive a statement of account instead of engraved certificates. Statements provide a record of the investor's entire portfolio of Treasury securities (much like the system that has been in place for years with T-bills). All holdings (unless maintained under different registration options or with different payment instructions) are held under a single master account for simplified record keeping and flexibility. The account statement is similar to the statements issued by securities dealers to purchasers of stocks and bonds.

Treasury Direct provides more security to clients because it eliminates the possibility of certificates being lost or stolen. Clients also receive simplified and more accurate records, a broad choice of registration options, direct deposit of Treasury payments, and an automatic reinvestment option.

Investors can obtain information and conduct transactions on their accounts at Federal Reserve Banks or the United States Treasury. There are 37 locations that have been designated as Treasury

Direct servicing centers at which investors can purchase Treasury bills, notes, or bonds, transfer securities from one account to another, or request detailed information on their accounts.

Question – How can a lost United States Savings Bond be replaced?

Answer – Write to the Bureau of Public Debt, Department of the Treasury, P.O. Box 1328, Parkersburg, WV 26102. Request Form PD-1048. The form will request information about the:

1. name the bond was registered in;

2. issue date;

3. address given at time of issue;

4. current address; and

5. serial numbers.

Question – How is the semi-annual interest payment on a Treasury Inflation-Protected Security (TIPS) calculated?

Answer – Like other United States Treasury notes and bonds, TIPS pay a fixed rate of interest. But this fixed rate of interest is applied not to the par amount of the security, but to the inflation-adjusted principal. Each semi-annual interest payment is calculated by multiplying the inflation-indexed principal by one-half the interest rate set when the security was issued.

For example, suppose that you invested $100,000 in January on a new, 10-year, inflation-indexed note paying 4% interest. At mid-year, the Consumer Price Index (CPI) measures that inflation has increased by 1% during the first six months of the year. The principal value of your note would be increased to $101,000, and the investor's interest payment would be $2,020 ($101,000 x .02).

Chapter 3

CORPORATE BONDS

WHAT IS IT?

A bond is the legal evidence of a long-term loan made by the bondholder to the corporation that issued the bond. Typically the loan must be repaid as of a specified date, referred to as the "maturity date." Until the bonds are redeemed (i.e., paid off by the corporation), interest at a stated rate is paid, generally every six months, by the corporation to the bondholder. The interest rate paid on the bonds is usually fixed when the bonds are issued and does not change during the life of the bond.

An important subset of corporate bonds consists of so-called "high yield" issues, those that generally do not qualify for "investment grade" ratings by the major credit rating agencies. In Wall Street jargon, such issues are sometimes referred to as "junk" bonds.

WHEN IS THE USE OF THIS TOOL INDICATED?

1. When a primary concern of the investor is safety of principal.

2. When a relatively high current return on the investment is desired.

3. When a secure and consistent flow of income is necessary. ("Zero coupon" corporate bonds, which pay no current interest, may be suitable for investors who do not need additional income; see Chapter 7.)

4. When an investor anticipates holding the investment for a minimum of three to five years.

5. When an investor's cash flow and capital needs can be planned to coincide with scheduled bond interest payments and maturities.

6. For high yield issues, when an investor desires a substantial cash flow and return on investment, but also has the financial and psychological capacity to bear the added risk and volatility of lower-rated issues.

ADVANTAGES

1. Income and principal are relatively safe. Semiannual interest payments and eventual repayment of the principal on an unsecured corporate bond (a "debenture") are guaranteed by the general credit of the issuing corporation. Obviously, the security of both interest and principal are in direct proportion to the financial strength of the issuer. Income and principal payments on a secured bond are backed by specified collateral, such as real property owned by the corporation, as well as by the earning power and other assets of the firm.

Payment of both interest and principal to bond-holders takes precedence over payment of dividends on either preferred or common stock. In the event of corporate insolvency or bankruptcy, holders of secured bonds generally will receive better treatment than unsecured creditors, general creditors, or stockholders.

2. Bonds normally pay interest income on a regular basis. Once issued, the amount and timing of bond payments cannot be changed by the issuing corporation regardless of its financial condition (unless it files a petition under the bankruptcy code). Unlike the payment of dividends on stocks, which is made at the discretion of the board of directors, interest payments on bonds are a nondiscretionary legal obligation. Because of this fixed commitment, it is possible for an investor, through careful selection of individual issues, to be assured of a regular income. For example, by selecting six bonds, each with a different semiannual payment date, an investor can receive an interest check every month.

3. Gain on the sale of a bond held for more than one year is eligible for long-term capital gain treatment. Likewise, if the bond is held to maturity, and the maturity value (par value) exceeds the price paid for a bond purchased on the market, the difference would be treated as a long-term capital gain. For example, if an investor had purchased an AT&T bond in 2006 at a price of $900, and the bond matures in 2012 at its par value of $1,000, the

difference of $100 would be treated as a long-term capital gain.

The Tax Reform Act of 1984 changed the treatment of market discount on bonds issued after July 18, 1984 or purchased after April 30, 1993. When such a bond is purchased at a price less than the original issue price, the difference between the purchase price and the original issue price must be treated as interest income rather than capital gain. That income can be recognized on an annual basis, when the bond is sold, or when it matures. The law also provides for certain limits on the deductibility of interest expense incurred to purchase or carry market discount bonds.

In addition, if the original issue price of the bond is less than the maturity value, the excess of the maturity value over the original issue price must be included as interest income (i.e., original issue discount) as it accrues over the life of the bond.

4. Compared to many other investments, corporate bonds provide a high current rate of return on capital. Historically, the current yield on corporate bonds has ranged from 2% to 8% higher than the dividend yield on common stocks. In late 2003, the current yield on the Dow Jones Corporate Bond Index was approximately 6.13%, while the dividend yield on the Standard & Poor's 500 Stock Average was 1.8%, and many public utility stocks paid dividends yielding about 4%.

5. High yield bonds provide a higher level of current income when compared to investment grade bonds (those issues rated BBB or higher by Standard & Poor's, or Baa by Moody's). They also have the potential for significant capital appreciation if a bond's rating is upgraded at some future point in time.

DISADVANTAGES

1. While the interest payments on bonds are fixed as to the amount and almost certain to be paid, their purchasing power may be eroded by inflation. The longer the period of time to maturity, the more likely that the purchasing power of each fixed dollar payment will decline.

For example, assume that an inflation rate of 3% annually exists and that an investor purchases a bond paying $80 each year. His "inflation-adjusted" interest income would be equivalent to $69.01 after five years and only $59.53 after 10 years. Examined another way, the investor's income after five years would have to be $92.74 and after 10 years $107.51, to keep pace with a 3% annual inflation rate.

2. Interest payments are fixed when the bonds are issued. The dollar amount of these payments will not change even if the financial condition of the company or the economy improves. Since bondholders are creditors and not owners of the corporation, they do not share in the growth or prosperity of the company. This means that the fixed interest on bonds may be unattractive when compared with potentially increasing payments available from alternative investments. For example, dividends from common stocks and rental income from real estate investments can increase substantially over time.

3. Inflation will also reduce the purchasing power of a bondholder's principal. The longer the period of time the bondholder has to wait for repayment of principal, the more significant that effect may be. Assume that an investor purchases a bond for $1,000 and that the bond will mature in 10 years. At a 3% rate of inflation, the $1,000 repayment he will receive in 10 years would be equivalent to only $744.09 in current dollars.

4. Bond prices fluctuate with changes in current market interest rates. If interest rates paid on newly issued bonds increase, older bonds paying lower rates of interest will be less attractive to investors. In order to sell older bonds having lower interest rates, their price must be reduced. The effect of this decline in price is to make old bonds competitive with new ones in terms of their "yield to maturity." (Yield to maturity is the average annualized rate of return that an investor will earn if a bond is held until it matures.)

For example, if market interest rates increase from 8% to 10%, a 20-year bond paying 8% will fall in price from $1,000 to $828. Why? Because, by purchasing new bonds investors can now earn 10% on every $1,000 they invest rather than 8%. Therefore, the price of the 8% bond must be lowered until it produces a yield to maturity equivalent to the yield on the new 10% bond.

Of course, the reverse is also true. If market interest rates fall, the price of previously issued bonds will rise. In this situation bondholders will demand a higher price for their bonds since they are more attractive than new issues with lower interest rates.

5. If the overall financial condition of the issuing corporation deteriorates, the resale price of their bonds is likely to fall. A decline in the financial strength of the corporation would be reflected in a lower credit standing for the firm and, therefore, a lower quality rating for the bond issue. The lower quality rating results in a perception of increased risk and diminished worth in the minds of investors. In return for this increased risk, potential buyers will demand a higher rate of return. Since interest payments cannot be increased, the only way to satisfy a potential buyer's demand for a higher rate of return is for the seller to lower the price. An improvement in the issuer's financial condition and credit rating will typically result in higher bond prices.

6. An investor's ability to sell his bonds at a given time may be adversely affected by any one or more of the following factors:

   (a) The smaller the size of the issue, the less likely the bonds are to be actively traded.

   (b) The issue may be owned in large blocks by only a few large institutions, such as banks and pension funds, resulting in low levels of trading activity and a relatively restricted market.

   (c) If the quality rating of the issuer has declined since the bond was purchased, there may be fewer interested buyers. This, of course, makes a sale more difficult.

7. Today, most corporate bonds are issued as general credit obligations ("debentures"). Although such bonds provide a greater degree of security for investors than an equity (stock) investment, they still involve a greater degree of risk than a "secured" debt obligation, such as a mortgage. Bonds backed by real assets of the corporation provide an investor with the specific security of the mortgaged property.

Corporate bonds also are often issued in the form of "subordinated debentures," which generally have security preference over only the equity of the issuing company. Such debentures are subordinated in security to all other creditors, including general creditors. Because of the higher risk associated with subordinated debentures, they usually will pay a higher interest rate than general credit obligations, and often are issued with warrants for the purchase of common stock of the issuing company, or are convertible into such stock.

8. High yield bonds typically involve additional risks, such as: (a) greater price volatility than investment grade bonds with similar maturities; (b) increased risk of default (failure to pay principal and/or interest as stated in the bond indenture); and (c) less liquid markets with higher bid-ask spreads than for ordinary bonds.

TAX IMPLICATIONS

1. Interest income paid on a regular basis is generally taxable when received at ordinary income rates.

2. Profits or losses on the sale or maturity of corporate bonds are treated as capital gains or losses (see the discussion of capital gains and losses in Chapter 43, "Taxation of Investment Vehicles").

   Long-term capital gains are generally taxable at a maximum rate of 15%. Capital losses may be used to offset only capital gains and up to $3,000 of ordinary income per year. Unused losses may be carried forward by individuals and applied against future income.

3. If a bond is sold at a loss and then repurchased, the investor may be subject to the "wash sale" rules.

4. Bonds held at death in the sole name of the investor will be subject to both federal estate tax and state death tax. (Under EGTRRA 2001, the estate tax is repealed for decedents dying after 2009. However, EGTRRA 2001 "sunsets" (i.e., expires) after 2010.[1] Fifty percent of bonds owned jointly between spouses will be includable in the gross estate of a decedent but will generate no federal estate tax upon the death of the first spouse because of the unlimited marital deduction.

5. Bonds issued with "original issue discount," such as "zero coupon bonds," yield taxable income to the bondholders with respect to the discount over the life of the bond. This occurs even though the discount "income" will not be received until the bond matures. (Original issue discount is discussed in detail in "Questions and Answers," below.)

6. Special rules apply where bonds are purchased at a "market discount" (i.e., at a price below the original issue price and the maturity or face value). Generally, the amount of market discount need not be recognized as income until the bond is sold or matures. However, there is a limit on the deductibility

of interest expense on debt incurred to purchase or carry market discount bonds. Such interest expense can be deducted to the extent there is interest income on the bond (including original issue discount) that is includable in income. Beyond that amount, interest expense may be deducted only to the extent it is more than the market discount allocable to the days the bond was held in the year. The amount of interest expense not currently deductible may be deducted in the year the investor disposes of the bond. (The interest disallowance rules do not apply if the investor elects to recognize a prescribed portion of the market discount as income each year until the bond matures.)

7. High yield bonds are treated similarly to other corporate debt instruments for income tax purposes. Interest income is subject to both federal and state income taxes and is taxed as "ordinary income," such as wages. Gains and losses on high yield bond sales are also taxed like other capital transactions.

ALTERNATIVES

1. Municipal bonds generating a comparable or higher after-tax yield.

2. Single-premium deferred annuities providing a fixed annual payment.

3. Certain preferred stocks with a fixed dividend.

4. Intermediate or long-term securities of the federal government or federal agencies that provide a comparable or slightly lower after-tax yield.

5. Investors who do not need current income may want to consider "zero coupon" bonds, which pay no interest until maturity, but offer a comparable overall yield.

6. In the high yield area, most mutual fund organizations offer one or more high yield funds. These funds invest in a widely diversified portfolio of lower-quality bonds, which reduces the impact of default risk from any one issue.

7. Foreign bonds may be an attractive option for more sophisticated, risk-oriented investors. These bonds include offerings of foreign governments, including emerging markets, and foreign corporations. In order to achieve a desirable level of risk management and diversification, most investors should probably participate through purchases of foreign bond mutual funds.

WHERE AND HOW DO I GET IT?

Corporate bonds can be purchased directly by calling any brokerage firm as well as many banks and other financial institutions. Bond prices are established through dealers on the basis of supply and demand. Most bonds are traded on the "over-the-counter" (OTC) market rather than on an organized stock exchange. However, many of the most active and largest bond issues are traded on the New York Stock Exchange (NYSE).

Information on new bond issues will generally appear in the form of "tombstone ads" in the business section of major newspapers. The example shown in Figure 3.2 at the end of this chapter indicates the issuer of the bond as well as the size of the issue, its maturity date, and interest rate. Also shown are the "underwriters," the brokerage firms who originally purchased the bonds from the issuing corporation. The bonds are available from other brokerage firms, but there is a big advantage in purchasing them from one of the original underwriters—there is no commission payable on the purchase.

In periods of changing interest rates, bonds will frequently trade at a "premium" (i.e., sell above par value) or at a "discount" (i.e., sell below par value).

The prices of bonds are also influenced by their maturity date. The period of time to maturity can range from a few days to more than 30 years. Price volatility is directly related to the length of time to maturity. Long-term bonds tend to fluctuate more in price than short-term bonds.

The majority of bonds are held by institutional investors who tend to trade in "round lots" (i.e., large blocks of securities amounting to $100,000 or more). Individual investors typically make smaller purchases referred to as "odd lots."

The selection of a particular broker or bond dealer can affect the price an investor pays for the bond for the following reasons:

1. The commission or fees charged by different brokers can vary considerably, as noted below.

2. Some brokers may be willing to sell bonds at a lower price in order to reduce their inventory of a particular issue.

Some investors prefer to achieve safety of principal and income through the diversification available from a mutual fund of corporate bonds. These bond funds are managed portfolios holding a large variety of corporate bonds of different maturities and issuers.

There are two common ways of purchasing a corporate bond fund—directly from the fund itself ("no-load") or through a brokerage firm ("load"). A "no-load" fund is generally advertised in the newspaper, carries out its transactions by mail, and charges no sales commission on the purchase of its shares. A "load" fund is typically distributed through brokerage firms and the purchaser is charged a sales fee in addition to the value of the fund's shares. The price of a bond fund's shares will be determined by changes in the value of bonds in the fund's portfolio.

WHAT FEES OR OTHER ACQUISITION COSTS ARE INVOLVED?

The investor will pay no commission on the purchase of a new issue; the corporation selling the bonds or the underwriter absorbs the sales costs. In all other cases, buyers and sellers can expect to pay a brokerage fee ranging from $2.50 to $20.00 per bond. Some brokers will charge a minimum fee of $30 regardless of the number of bonds being bought or sold.

HOW DO I SELECT THE BEST OF ITS TYPE?

1. Investors interested in buying corporate bonds should consider the following:

a) *Quality Rating of the Bond* – as assigned by a professional appraisal service such as Standard & Poor's Bond Guide or Moody's Investors Service. These run from "AAA" (highest rating) to "D" (default), though conservative investors probably should not consider bonds rated lower than BBB. This rating is a current assessment of the creditworthiness of the issuer and is based on information furnished by the company or obtained by the rating service. The ratings take into consideration the nature and provisions of the obligation, likelihood of default, and protection afforded the holder in the case of bankruptcy.

b) *Current Yield* – the rate of return based on the current market price of the bond. This is obtained by dividing the annual interest amount by the current purchase price of the bond.

c) *Yield to Maturity* – the rate of return on a bond held to its maturity date and redeemed by the issuer at its par value. Yield to maturity includes any gain (or loss) if the bond was purchased below (or above) its par value.

2. A maturity date should be consistent with the investor's projected cash flow or capital needs objectives.[2]

3. It may be desirable to coordinate maturities with potential shifts in tax brackets. In other words, an investor should select maturities that delay the gain until he or she will be in a lower tax bracket or can utilize offsetting deductions.

4. Preference should be given to the larger issues of strong, well-managed corporations. The bonds of such firms are likely to be actively traded. This increased marketability will make the bonds easier and less costly to sell in a short time.

5. Bonds with shorter maturity dates will generally have greater price stability than longer-term bonds with the same quality rating (although the tradeoff may be a lower yield).

6. For high yield bonds, investors would be wise to: (a) diversify their holdings across issuers and industry sectors—concentrating in only a few issues greatly increases the risk of holding junk bonds; (b) adjust their portfolios over economic cycles—increasing holding during periods of economic expansion and reducing them as the economy slows or contracts; and (c) monitor the rating agencies, which often put companies on a "credit watch" list prior to downgrading an issue.

WHERE CAN I FIND OUT MORE ABOUT IT?

1. Standard & Poor's (www.standardandpoors.com), Moody's Investors Service (www.moodys.com), and other statistical rating agency reports are available on the Internet and at most libraries. Such services provide information on the issuers of bonds as well as price and yield information on the bonds themselves. Their ratings are based on past performance, present financial condition, and potential strength of the company. The rating represents a judgment as to the degree of protection for both interest and principal payments to bondholders.

2. *The New York Times* (www.NYTimes.com), the *Wall Street Journal* (www.wsj.com) and many other newspapers quote bond prices daily.

3. Additional information on specific issues and current market conditions can be obtained by calling major brokerage firms or banks.

4. There are many Internet sites that provide useful information on corporate bonds. Among the best are Bondsonline (www.bondsonline.com) and Investinginbonds.com.

QUESTIONS AND ANSWERS

Question – Why do corporations issue bonds?

Answer – A bond is a debt obligation of a corporation. The corporation issues a certificate that states the terms of the issue including the specified rate of interest. Corporations use bonds to raise funds for capital improvements or expansion. The interest paid by a corporation is tax deductible by the corporation as a business expense.

Question – What is an "indenture"?

Answer – An indenture is the legal document that authorizes a corporate bond issue. It contains the terms and features of the issue such as the amount of bonds, the rate of interest, the maturity date, and interest payment dates. The indenture will also provide a description of the company and its business, a listing of the major corporate officers, and the intended use of the funds to be raised through the bond issue.

Question – What is the most important factor in determining the price of a bond?

Answer – The level of interest rates and the direction in which they are moving (up or down) are the key factors in determining bond prices. Bond values go up when interest rates go down and prices fall when rates increase. Typically, long-term bonds (10 years or more to maturity) will fluctuate much more in price as rates change than will short-term issues (1-3 years).

Question – Why do the prices of long-term bonds fluctuate more than those of notes or short-term issues?

Answer – The reason is that a change in interest rates that extends over only a few months will require a smaller price change than the same interest rate change when projected far into the future. For instance, if interest rates decrease by 1%, a $1,000 short-term issue may drop in value by only $10. However, a bond with 20 years to maturity may lose as much as $100 in its price because investors recognize the compounding effect of the interest rate change.

Question – What is the difference between a corporate "bond" and a corporate "note"?

Answer – This distinction is more a matter of terminology than anything else. A debt security that is issued with a maturity date of more than 7-10 years generally is referred to as a bond. If the debt has an original maturity date less than 7-10 years into the future, it is frequently called a note.

Question – What is an "original issue discount" bond?

Answer – When bonds are originally sold by a corporation at a price below their eventual maturity value they are said to have original issue discount (OID). For example, if a 20-year bond with a maturity value of $1,000 is issued for only $950, the $50 difference between the maturity value and the issue price is original issue discount. (The extreme example of an OID bond is a "zero coupon" bond. A zero coupon bond pays no periodic interest. The purchaser's total return is the price appreciation.)

For federal income tax purposes, original issue discount on bonds issued after May 27, 1969 is taxable to the bondholder over the life of the bond even though no cash is received until the bond is sold or matures. With respect to OID bonds issued after July 1, 1982, the amount of OID income that is taxable each year is computed based on the bond's yield to maturity. Annual compounding is used if the bond was issued before January 1, 1985 and semiannual compounding if issued on or after January 1, 1985. Consequently, the amount of OID income will be lowest in the first year of the bond, but will increase each year as the prior year's OID income is added to the value of the bond for interest computation purposes.

For example, assume that on January 1, 1984 a corporation issued a 20-year, zero coupon bond priced at $7.60 per $1,000 that will be redeemed for $1,000 at maturity. The yield to maturity for anyone who purchases the bond for $7.60 on the issue date will be 13.31%. Assume an investor purchased $10,000 face amount of the bonds (paying a total of $760. In the first year of the bond, the OID income, taxable to the bondholder as ordinary interest income, would be $101.16 (13.31% x $760). In the second year, the $101.16 of income recognized in the prior year would be added to the original purchase price of $760, resulting in an $861.16 value for computing income at a 13.31% rate. The second year taxable income would be $114.62 (13.31% x $861.16).

For OID bonds issued on or before July 1, 1982, the annual amount of the OID income is computed by dividing the total amount of the discount by the period from issuance until maturity. Thus, in our example, the annual OID income for the 20-year period of the bond would be $460 ($10,000 - $760 = $9,240, divided by 20 years). As this example illustrates, the newer OID rules provide an advantage for investors over the older rules since the total OID income is recognized at a slower rate. However, it should be remembered that even under the newer rules, OID still results in taxable income without the receipt of any cash to pay the resulting tax. For this reason, OID bonds (especially zero coupon bonds) are most often purchased by tax-exempt entities such as pension trusts.

Question – What is a "mortgage bond"?

Answer – A mortgage bond is a corporate debt security backed by a claim against property, such as land or buildings owned by the corporation. In the event of default on payments of principal or interest, the bondholders can claim the assets, sell them, and use the proceeds to pay their claims.

Question – What is a "debenture"?

Answer – A debenture bond is a corporate obligation that is not secured by any property. Its only backing is the general credit of the corporation. Some investors prefer the additional security of a claim on corporate assets and will not purchase a debenture issue unless it offers a somewhat higher yield than a mortgage bond.

Question – What is the difference between "bearer bonds" and "registered bonds"?

Answer – At one time, most bonds were issued in "bearer" form. That meant the bonds were negotiable by the person holding them. Interest coupons were attached to these bonds. Interest, payable twice a year, was claimed by removing the coupons from the bonds

and presenting them to a paying agent. (This is where the phrase "clipping coupons" came from.)

Although there still are some bearer bonds outstanding, long-term corporate debt must be in the form of "registered bonds" in order to avoid certain adverse tax treatment. Registration is designed to assure the basic security of the bond. A bond may be registered as to principal to protect the owner from loss. This means the name and address of the bondholder are recorded with the issuing company. A registered bond is transferred in the same way as common stock is exchanged. Interest is paid to bondholders by mail and, because the names of the owners are recorded, they will automatically receive notices of redemption. The major advantage of registration is that if the bonds are lost, stolen, or destroyed, the owner is protected against loss.

Question – What is meant by "nominal yield" and how is it different from the current yield on a bond?

Answer – Nominal yield (also called "coupon yield" or "stated yield") is the interest rate stated on the bond. For example, the bond may indicate that it will pay 8%. The percentage is multiplied by the par value of the bond to arrive at the actual dollar amount of interest to be paid. Since almost all bonds have a par value of $1,000, an 8% nominal yield represents $80 per year (8% x $1,000) in actual interest received by the bondholder.

The current yield earned by an investor is based on the purchase price rather than the par value of the bond. If the bond is purchased below par value, at $800, for example, the actual rate of return will be higher than the nominal yield. Conversely, if the bond is purchased at a premium (i.e., above par) the actual yield will be lower than the nominal yield.

The example shown in Figure 3.1 shows yield calculations for a bond paying a coupon rate of 8.75% and selling for $980. Since the bond is selling at a slight discount, the current yield is 8.9% ($87.50/$980) and the yield to maturity is 9.1%.

Question – Are there any bonds for which the interest rates are not fixed and that pay interest based on changing market rates?

Answer – Yes, there are "floating rate" bonds (also called "adjustable rate bonds") on which the rate of interest will vary with changes in a specified market index, such as the yield on Treasury bills or Treasury bonds.

Figure 3.1

COMPREHENSIVE BOND CALCULATOR

INPUT:	FACE VALUE OF BOND	$1,000.00
INPUT:	ORIGINAL PURCHASE PRICE	$ 890.00
INPUT:	CURRENT MARKET PRICE	$ 980.00
INPUT:	COUPON INTEREST RATE	0.0875
INPUT:	YEARS TO MATURITY	7

BOND CALCULATIONS:

ANNUAL INTEREST PAID	$	87.50
GAIN (OR LOSS)	$	90.00
ORIGINAL ACCRETION (OR AMORTIZATION)	$	110.00
CURRENT YIELD		0.089
APPROXIMATE YIELD TO MATURITY		0.091

Reprinted with permission from *NumberCruncher*, Leimberg & LeClair, Inc.

For example, a floating-rate bond may adjust its rate every six months and pay 1% more than the rate on 5-year Treasury notes. Floating rate bonds provide greater stability of principal since their price tends to return to near par whenever the rate is reset.

Question – What is the definition of a "junk" bond?

Answer – The term "junk bond" is generally applied to the debt offerings of companies rated BB or lower by credit rating agencies. They generally pay a higher rate of interest than investment grade or higher-rated bonds due to their greater risk of default on interest and principal payments.

Question – What is the meaning of "currency risk," and how does it affect the purchase of a foreign bond?

Answer – Currency risk refers to the potential gain (or loss) on an investment denominated in a foreign currency due to fluctuations in exchange rates. For example, suppose an investor purchased a British bond maturing in five years for its par value of £1,000 when the exchange rate between the British pound (£) and the U. S. dollar was £1 = $1.80. The

cost of the bond in dollar terms is $1,800 (£1,000 X $1.80).

Now, assume that when the bond matures in five years, the exchange rate between the pound and the dollar is £1 = $1.60. The investor would receive £1,000 from the British government, but could only convert the pounds to $1,600 (£1,000 X $1.60). The loss of $200 is due entirely to currency risk. Note also that, if the exchange rate at maturity were £1 = $2.00, the investor would have a gain of $200.

CHAPTER ENDNOTES

1. IRC Sec. 2201; Sec. 901, EGTRRA 2001.

2. Before 2006, an investor seeking to provide college education funds in 10 years might have selected an issue with a similar maturity date. Such an investor might have considered whether purchasing the bonds under the "Uniform Gifts to Minors Act" (UGMA) or a "2503(c) trust" would shift income taxation to the child's relatively lower bracket. However, under the Tax Increase Prevention and Reconciliation Act of 2006—TIPRA), the "kiddie tax" age was raised from 14 to 18; consequently, this income shifting strategy has effectively been nullified. IRC Sec. 1(g)(2)(A), as amended by TIPRA 2005.

Figure 3.2

MOCK TOMBSTONE AD

This announcement is neither an offer to sell nor a solicitation of an offer to buy any of these Securities. The offer is made only by the Prospectus and the related Prospectus Supplement which may be obtains in any State from only such of the undersigned as may legally offer these Securities in compliance with the securities law of such state.

$100,000,000

ABC-XZY CORPORATION

5.25% Convertible Senior Debentures Due 2032

Price 100%

Managers:

First Capital, Inc.

Last Capital, Inc.

Big Bank Securities, Inc.

Dollars and Cents Financial Co.

More Money Securities, Inc.

July 26, 2002

Chapter 4

CONVERTIBLE SECURITIES

WHAT IS IT?

Typically, convertibles are bonds or preferred stocks that may be converted at a specified conversion price (per share) or conversion ratio (number of shares) into the common stock of the firm issuing the securities. However, there are many other variations. They allow a holder to exchange, trade in, or convert the security being held into another type of security. Convertible securities are hedge-type instruments that allow investors to enjoy much of the upside potential of a riskier investment while bearing the smaller downside risk more commonly associated with investments offering less upside potential.

WHEN IS THE USE OF THIS TOOL INDICATED?

1. When the investor would like to combine an element of certainty (through a fixed interest or dividend rate and a known payment schedule) with the opportunity for significant capital gains.

2. When the investor needs current cash flow that provides a higher rate of return than available from the dividends on common stock.

3. When the investor at the same time is willing to accept a somewhat lower rate of current income than might be available on bonds and preferred stocks that do not have the conversion feature.

ADVANTAGES

1. Such issues provide the investor with a relatively high degree of security for both principal and income. The general credit of the issuing corporation stands behind payments to convertible bondholders. Preferred stockholders are protected by the cumulative nature of most preferred dividends. This means that if the issuing corporation fails to pay the stated dividend on the cumulative preferred shares, the dividend accumulates and must be paid at some future time. Until preferred dividends are fully paid,

no payment of dividends can be made to common stockholders.

2. Convertible securities offer the potential for capital growth through ownership of the common stock. Convertible securities provide two opportunities for this appreciation. The first is through conversion and actual ownership of the common stock of a corporation. The second is through the appreciation in the market value of the convertible bond or preferred stock that occurs as a result of an increase in the price of the common stock. If the underlying stock price rises above the value of the convertible as a fixed income security, the convertible's price will move in almost direct relation to the price of the common stock.

   Example: A bond convertible into 50 shares of common stock that sells for about $1,000 as a fixed income security will sell for at least $1,500 if the common stock increases in value from $20 per share to $30 per share.

3. The basic form of a convertible bond or preferred stock offers some protection in the event that common stock prices decline. If the price of the company's common stock falls below the convertible's value as a fixed income security, the investor would still have a bond or preferred stock with a price determined by its intrinsic worth as a bond or preferred stock. This concept is often referred to as providing a "floor" under the price of the convertible security.

4. A company's convertible securities, whether bonds or preferred stock, typically pay a higher rate of return in the form of interest or dividends than is available from its common shares. (Many companies that issue convertible securities pay no current dividends on their common stocks.)

5. The investor controls the form of investment and the timing of the conversion. (Note, however, that in some cases a corporation may effectively force conversion by exercising the call feature common to almost all convertible securities.)

6. The change in the nature of the investment can be effected quickly and with little or no cost to the investor. The investor merely sends the convertible security to the issuer and requests the change. Typically there are no fees or charges associated with this transaction.

DISADVANTAGES

1. Until the conversion has been made, the investor is relatively unprotected from the effects of inflation. This is due to the fixed nature of interest payments on convertible bonds and the fixed dividend rate on convertible preferred stocks.

2. The yields provided by convertible securities often are significantly below the yields of alternative investments. Since convertibles provide both upside potential and downside protection, investors must pay a premium for these securities. For example, it would not be unusual for convertible bonds to pay yields one to two percentage points below the rate paid on comparable bonds without a conversion feature.

3. If the price of the underlying common stock does increase substantially, the value of the convertible will never increase as much as the value of the underlying common stock because of the premium paid for the convertible. Consequently, investors who buy convertibles will generally receive lower cash yields than they would have gotten from nonconvertible securities, and less appreciation than they would have gotten from outright purchase of the underlying stock. However, they also generally receive higher cash yields than they would have received from the underlying stock, and higher appreciation than they would have received from the nonconvertible securities.

4. Convertible bonds, like regular bonds, typically are callable by the issuing corporation at a price slightly above their par value. Companies can use this feature to force conversion if the price of the bond has appreciated to a point well above the call price.

Example: A bond convertible into 50 shares of common stock will sell for at least $1,500 if the stock is trading at $30 per share. The same bond may have a call price of only $1,080. If the issuer were to call the bond, investors would be forced to convert their bonds into common stock or face the loss of $420 per bond.

If the price of the underlying stock increases quickly, conversion may be forced earlier than the investor planned. In that case, the investor will not have recovered the premium paid to purchase the convertible, making the return less than if the underlying common stock had been purchased outright.

5. Convertible bonds are subject to many of the disadvantages of regular corporate bonds, often referred to as "straight bonds" (see Chapter 3). Likewise, convertible preferred stocks have some of the same weaknesses as other preferred stocks (see Chapter 11).

6. Many convertible issues tend to be of relatively small size when compared with regular bond and stock issues. With relatively few convertible bonds or preferred shares outstanding, trading is less active and may result in a lack of liquidity when buying or selling a particular issue.

7. Convertible bonds are generally subordinated to all other debt issued by the firm. Therefore, default risk is higher than for other nonconvertible debt.

8. Because of the complex nature of convertibles as hybrid securities, a more involved and detailed selection process is necessary. The multiplicity of factors that must be considered includes the financial condition of the issuing company, the trend of current interest rates, and estimates of future stock prices.

TAX IMPLICATIONS

1. Income received from a convertible bond or preferred stock is subject to ordinary income tax rates.

2. Appreciation is not taxable until the investor sells the bond, preferred stock, or the common shares received on conversion. (However, original issue discount on a convertible bond may be includable as it accrues.)

3. Conversion itself is not a taxable event. A deferral of taxation is allowed because the investor takes as his cost basis the price paid for the original investment. If the conversion feature is not detachable, there is

no allocation of basis to the two components of the security. That basis is carried over to the common shares acquired in the exchange.

Example: Nancy Manzi purchased a convertible bond for $800. She later converted the bond into 40 shares of the issuing company's common stock. Nancy's cost basis for those 40 shares of common stock is $800, a carryover of her original investment. This results in a cost basis for the common stock of $20 per share ($800 ÷ 40 shares).

4. Profits or losses on the sale of a convertible bond or preferred stock, or on the maturity of a convertible bond, are treated as capital gains or losses. (Market discount and original issue discount realized on sale or maturity of a bond may have to be treated as interest. See Chapter 43, "Taxation of Investment Vehicles.") Long-term capital gains are generally taxable at a maximum rate of 15%. Capital losses may be used to offset only capital gains and up to $3,000 of ordinary income per year. (See "Capital gain" in the Glossary and the discussion of capital gains and losses in Chapter 43.)

stock purchase warrants or call options with straight bonds.

A "stock purchase warrant" is an option to buy stock at a stated price for a given period of time. Warrants pay no income but do allow the investor to determine the timing of his purchase and offer the opportunity for appreciation. Warrants also provide leverage in that the exercise price of the warrant is generally fixed in the same manner as the conversion price of a convertible bond or convertible preferred stock.

Example: The illustration in Figure 4.1 assumes a warrant selling for $5 that enables the holder to purchase the common stock of a company at a price of $52 per share. If the current price of the company's stock is $46 per share, there is no reason to exercise the warrants and obtain the stock; it would be cheaper to simply purchase the shares directly rather than use the warrants and pay a price of $52 per share. However, if the price of the stock were to go up to $69, a gain of 50%, the value of the warrants would increase to at least $17 ($69 - $52), or an increase of 240%.

The package of a stock purchase warrant and a straight bond satisfies the investor's twin objectives of capital gain potential (through the warrant) and current income (through the straight bond). The major advantages of this strategy are the leverage and capital gains potential of the warrants coupled with the one to two percentage points of additional return provided by straight bonds.

Because listed calls are short-term in nature, the investor who combines straight bonds with listed call options would have to roll over the call position continuously and the premiums paid for the calls will vary over time and will not necessarily match the income given up by investing in the convertible. Furthermore, the exercise of the artificially created conversion feature (sale of bonds and exercise of call) will generally be a taxable event.

WHERE AND HOW DO I GET IT?

Convertible bonds may be purchased directly by calling a full service brokerage firm and placing an order. They may also be purchased through discount brokerage

ALTERNATIVES

1. Convertible bonds with a premium put are convertibles with additional downside protection. They are generally issued at their face value and include a put option that allows the investor to redeem the bonds for cash at a premium relative to the bonds' face value at a future date. Because of their added safety, they typically pay even lower interest than nonconvertibles, all else being equal. These convertibles are especially attractive when investors wish to protect themselves from potential bond price declines if interest rates rise.

2. Mutual funds specializing in convertible securities are another alternative.

3. Bond issues with equity warrants are essentially just convertible bonds with a detachable conversion feature. If the warrant is detachable, generally the bond and warrant will be treated for tax purposes as separate instruments. Also, sale of the bond and exercise of the warrant will typically be a taxable transaction.

4. Investors considering convertibles could also "package" their own form of convertible by combining

Figure 4.1

COMPUTING WARRANT VALUE, PREMIUM, AND LEVERAGE

TO COMPUTE VALUE:
INPUT: MARKET PRICE OF STOCK $46.00
INPUT: SUBSCRIPTION PRICE OF STOCK $52.00
INPUT: NUMBER OF SHARES PER WARRANT 1
          THEORETICAL WARRANT VALUE .... $ 0.00

TO COMPUTE PREMIUM:
INPUT: MARKET PRICE OF WARRANT .... $ 5.00
          PREMIUM .... $ 5.00
          PERCENT PREMIUM 0.000

TO COMPUTE POTENTIAL LEVERAGE:
INPUT: PROJECTED MARKET PRICE OF COMMON
          PROJECTED VALUE OF WARRANT $69.00
          GAIN IN MARKET VALUE $17.00
                                                                                                                    240.00%

Reprinted with permission from *NumberCruncher*, Leimberg & LeClair, Inc.

---

firms or through the discount brokerage services offered by many banks and thrift institutions.

In addition to a direct purchase, convertible bonds may also be acquired indirectly by investing in one of several mutual funds that specialize in convertibles. These funds offer the benefits of diversification and professional management that can be particularly advantageous to the small investor. A mutual fund also eliminates the need for the investor to analyze various bonds and to select the most attractive at any given time.

WHAT FEES OR OTHER ACQUISITION COSTS ARE INVOLVED?

Brokerage fees on the purchase of convertible bonds will be very similar to those paid in buying regular bonds. You can expect to pay from $5 to $20 per bond depending on the total value of the transaction, the number of bonds purchased, and whether or not a discount broker is used. Some firms will charge a minimum fee of $30 regardless of the number of bonds being bought or sold.

HOW DO I SELECT THE BEST OF ITS TYPE?

Evaluating the purchase of a convertible bond is more complicated than buying either bonds or stocks separately. Buyers are purchasing a combination of features that may look like a bond today but be converted into

common stock tomorrow. The following suggestions may be helpful in selecting convertible issues:

1. Look for a record of increasing earnings for at least the past five years and assets well in excess of the face value of the bonds.

2. For a new issue, the investment banking firm that underwrites the issue and offers it to the public should be a member of a major stock exchange.

3. Investors may prefer convertibles that are offered by companies in growth industries. Eventually, buyers will want to convert their bonds into stock or sell the bonds at an appreciated value. Companies that are experiencing growth in earnings per share are likely to have their stock price increase as well. This gain in value will be reflected in a higher price for the firm's convertible bonds.

4. The investor should calculate the "payback period" or how long it will take the investor to recoup the premium paid for the bond over its conversion value from the added yield of the convertible security.

    Example: Assume that ABC Company has a $1,000 face value bond with a stated rate of 5.25% that is convertible into its common stock at $32.50. The bond is selling at $1,084.20 in the market. The common stock is selling for $32.25 and does not pay a dividend. Annual interest on the bond is $52.50 ($1,000 x 5.25%).

Step 1. Find the conversion ratio: Divide the face value of the bond by the conversion price of the stock ($1,000 ÷ $32.50 = 30.769).

Step 2. Calculate the conversion value: Multiply the conversion ratio by the current market value of one share of stock (30.769 x $32.25 = $999.30).

Step 3. Calculate the conversion premium – the amount the convertible price exceeds the conversion value ($1,084.20 - $992.30 = $91.90; $91.90 ÷ $992.30 = 9.3%).

Step 4. Calculate the yield advantage: The amount by which the current yield on the bond exceeds the yield on the common. Current yield on the bond equals the annual interest divided by its current price ($52.50 ÷ $1,084.20 = 4.8%). Since the common pays no dividend, the yield advantage is 4.8%.

Step 5. Calculate the payback period: Divide the premium by the yield advantage (9.3% ÷ 4.8% = 1.94 years).

In this example, the investor will recoup the premium over conversion value paid for the bond in less than two years. As long as she has call protection for longer than two years, the convertible is more attractive than the common.

5.   The interest paid on the convertible bond should be within two percentage points of the rate paid on similar quality, nonconvertible bonds. If nonconvertible issues are yielding 10%, then an attractive convertible bond should be paying no less than 8%. Investors should not sacrifice too much in terms of current income in exchange for the speculative feature of converting to common stock in the future.

WHERE CAN I FIND OUT MORE ABOUT IT?

1.   *Standard & Poor's* (www.standardandpoors.com), *Moody's Investors Service* (www.moodys.com), and other statistical rating agencies provide information on convertible as well as regular bonds. These

services should be available at most local libraries and on the Internet.

2.   Various publications specialize in providing investors with information on convertible bonds. These include:

   Value Line Convertible Survey
   Arnold Bernhard & Company, Inc.
   711 Third Avenue
   New York, NY 10017

3.   Most brokerage firms offer some coverage of convertible issues through various publications and can supply basic information on companies that have convertible bonds outstanding.

4.   While most convertible bonds are traded on the over-the-counter market, some of the larger issues of better known companies are listed on the New York Stock Exchange. The *Wall Street Journal*, the *New York Times*, and many other metropolitan newspapers will carry daily listings of their trading activity.

5.   There are several Internet sites that provide information and calculations on convertible bonds. Among the most useful are:

   www.bondsonline.com
   www.convertbond.com

QUESTIONS AND ANSWERS

Question – Are convertible bonds rated in the same way as bonds that are not convertible?

Answer – Yes. Rating agencies such as Standard & Poor's evaluate convertible issues and assign quality ratings in much the same manner as regular bonds. Generally speaking, convertible bonds will be awarded a rating one notch lower than the same company's non-convertible debt. Also, since most convertible issues are somewhat speculative, their ratings tend to be relatively low. There are very few convertible bonds with ratings of AAA, AA, or even A. Most convertibles have a rating in the B or even C range.

Question – Should a convertible bond always be exchanged for common stock when the stock price goes above the conversion price of the bond?

Answer – Generally speaking, investors should not convert their bond into common stock until the yield on the common exceeds the yield on the bond, or until the bond is called. As noted above, once the stock price goes above the conversion price of the bond, the bond will move in almost direct proportion to the common stock. Rapidly growing companies that have a history of increasing their dividend regularly will reach a point where the dividends from the shares received in the conversion will exceed the bond interest. For example, suppose an investor owns $10,000 face amount of a 5.0% convertible bond. The interest income would amount to $500 a year. If the bond is convertible into 50 shares of common stock, a conversion would result in ownership of 200 shares. Therefore at the point where the common dividend goes over $2.50 per share, the investor would receive more money in dividends than in interest.

Question – What is "Exchangeable Debt"?

Answer – Exchangeable debt combines a long-term bond issue with an option (sometimes detachable) to exchange the bonds not for common stock of the issuing company but rather for common stock in a third company, which is typically held by the company issuing the bonds. For investors, exchangeable debt serves essentially the same function as regular convertible bonds—reasonable and predictable cash flow and upside appreciation potential with downside loss protection.

As with regular bonds, investors generally receive less interest than they would on nonconvertible bonds and, consequently, the risk that the overall yield on the exchangeable bond will be lower than they could receive on other types of debt.

Exchangeable debt may be less risky than regular convertible bonds because default risk on convertible bonds generally increases when the underlying firm's stock price falls. Since the firm issuing the exchangeable bond is different from the firm issuing the stock, there would generally be little relation between the stock price and the default risk on the exchangeable bond.

The exchange of the debt for the common stock is generally a taxable event, which is not the case with most conversions of regular convertible bonds into the underlying stock of the same company. If the option is detachable, basis should be allocated between the debt instrument and the option to buy the stock. Otherwise, the entire basis should be allocated to the debt.

Question – What are "Flip Flop Notes"?

Answer – They are debt instruments that allow investors to convert to and from two (and sometimes more) types of securities. Typically, they will allow investors to convert a long-term variable rate bond into a short-term or intermediate-term fixed-rate bond and back again, if desired.

These notes allow investors to invest long-term and to receive variable rate interest only slightly lower than on nonconvertible long-term variable rate debt, while retaining the flexibility of switching to short-term (and less price volatile) debt when funds may be needed for some potential expenditure on relatively short notice. For example, this type of instrument might be suitable for the portfolios of older investors since they would be converted to their short-term form at death, leaving them much less subject to interest-rate risk and price fluctuations while the estate is being settled.

In whatever form the notes are held, they have the same risk characteristics as regular bonds of the same type and quality. The principle risk is that the value of the conversion feature does not warrant the lower interest rate typically paid on these bonds because of their conversion features. Also, there may be some uncertainty regarding maturity dates and interest rates on flip flop notes.

Investors who convert from a floating-rate bond to a fixed rate bond may have to treat the conversion as a taxable event.

Question – What are LYONs?

Answer – LYONs (Liquid Yield Option Notes) are zero-coupon notes convertible into a fixed number of shares of common stock of the issuer. They are discussed in Chapter 10.

Chapter 5

MUNICIPAL BONDS

WHAT IS IT?

A municipal bond, also known as a tax-exempt bond, is a debt instrument issued by a state, county, city, or other non-federal governmental agency. Like corporate bonds, these issues typically pay a fixed rate of interest. Interest from these bonds generally is exempt from federal income tax and may also be exempt from state, county, and local taxes as well. (Some so-called private purpose or private activity municipal bonds are issued in taxable form.)

Municipal bonds include basically three types of bonds:

1. *General Obligation Bonds* – General obligation bonds are backed by the full faith and credit of the issuer's taxing authority. These bonds are typically issued to finance the general operations, functions, and programs of the issuing authority. These bonds have a strong claim on the tax revenues of the taxing authority and are generally considered the safest form of municipal bonds.

2. *Revenue Bonds* – Revenue bonds are generally issued to finance municipally owned toll roads, toll bridges, and other public capital projects or public services (such as sewage treatment plants or public transportation systems) where user fees or specific assessments are intended to repay the debt. Therefore, bondholders must rely upon the adequacy of the fees or assessments received by the municipality to pay interest on the bonds. The issuing municipality frequently may promise to pay interest from general tax revenues if fees and assessments are inadequate. However, revenue bonds are generally junior to the issuer's general obligation bonds, so revenue bondholders bear greater risk of default if the revenues prove insufficient and the municipality's general tax receipts cannot cover the deficit.

3. *Private Purpose Bonds* – Private purpose or "private activity" bonds are issued to finance certain

activities that do not constitute the normal activities or functions of government. These bonds generally are used in the trade or business of persons other than state or local governments. The interest on these bonds is not tax-exempt for federal income tax purposes (although it is usually exempt from the issuing state or local government's income tax). However, within limits, certain private activity bonds used for qualified purposes such as industrial development, student loans, qualified mortgages and veterans' mortgages, and waste disposal facilities may be exempt from federal income tax.

WHEN IS THE USE OF THIS TOOL INDICATED?

1. When the investor's tax bracket (including any state and local taxes) is high enough that the lower yield of a tax-exempt instrument results in a higher after-tax rate of return than would be produced by a comparable taxable investment (see below).

2. When a steady and consistent flow of income is desired.

3. When a secure and relatively conservative investment is indicated.

4. When an investor anticipates holding the investment for a minimum of three to five years.

ADVANTAGES

1. Income from these bonds is exempt from federal income tax. Compared to an alternative investment producing taxable income, municipal bonds may provide a higher after-tax return. For example, a tax-exempt yield of 6.00% is equivalent to an 8.96% taxable yield assuming the investor is in a 33% (in 2006) tax bracket. IRC Sec. 1(i), as amended by JG-TRRA 2003. Of course, the higher an investor's tax bracket, the greater the advantage of tax-exempt income.

If the investor were in a lower bracket, the benefit of the tax-free bond would be reduced. For instance, if the investor described above were in a 15% rather than a 33% bracket, a tax-exempt yield of 6.00% would be equivalent to only a 7.06% taxable return.

To compare tax-free with taxable yields, use the following formula:

$$\frac{\text{Tax Free Return}}{(100\% - \text{Tax Rate})} \times 100\% = \text{Taxable Equivalent Yield}$$

For example, if a tax-exempt bond yields 3.5% and the investor is in a 28% tax bracket, the taxable equivalent yield is:

$$\frac{3.5\%}{100\% - 28\%} = \frac{3.5\%}{72\%} = 4.86\%$$

The "Tax Exempt Equivalents" tables in Appendix G show the relationship between taxable and tax-free income for individuals in various tax brackets.

2. Income from municipal bonds may also be exempt from state, county, and city income taxes. Generally, the income is exempt from taxation only within the state where the bond was issued. The chart in Figure 5.1 shows the tax status of municipal bond income in the various states.

3. Principal and income are relatively safe. This is because a "general obligation" municipal bond is a debt obligation that has a strong claim on tax revenues. Payment on most tax-exempt municipal bonds has priority over many other government obligations. However, some bonds, known as "revenue bonds," must be paid from specific revenues rather than from general taxes. Examples would be bonds issued for the construction of toll roads or sewage treatment plants. Such bonds are considered riskier than general obligation bonds and pay a higher yield.

DISADVANTAGES

1. As with any fixed income investment, municipal bonds provide minimal protection against inflation. For example, the fixed income may not keep pace with an increasing cost of living. Similarly, the bond principal may not provide the purchasing power at maturity or sale that would have been available through an alternative investment.

2. Bond prices may fluctuate with changes in market interest rates. When interest rates rise, bond values typically decline (of course, if interest rates drop, bond prices generally rise).

3. There may be a limited market for municipal bonds, particularly those issued in small amounts that are not traded actively. The result is that an investor who wants to sell an issue quickly may have to accept a lower price. (This may be advantageous to buyers.)

4. Tax-free bonds can seldom be purchased directly for less than $5,000.

5. Bid-ask spreads (the difference in the price a broker is willing to pay a seller and the asking price for the same bond) is often quite large and can have a significant effect on the total return to the investor.

TAX IMPLICATIONS

1. The exemption of interest income from federal income and often state and local taxation has been explained above. Note that in calculating the relative advantage of a tax-exempt bond, the tax rate applicable after all allowable deductions and adjustments should be used rather than the rate shown for gross income.

2. Capital gains (or losses) realized on the sale of these bonds are subject to normal capital gain (or loss) treatment. (See "capital gain" in the Glossary and the discussion of capital gains and losses in Chapter 43, "Taxation of Investment Vehicles.") Special rules apply to municipal bonds having original issue discounts and bonds purchased in the secondary market at a price other than par. While often ignored—even by many practitioners—investors are required to amortize any discount from par that they paid for a bond over its remaining life and include this amount *in their return as ordinary income!*

3. Although municipal bonds are loosely called "tax-exempt," gifts of these bonds are generally subject to federal (and in many cases state) gift taxation. A bequest of municipal bonds is subject to the federal estate tax as well as applicable state death taxes.

4. Interest paid on certain private purpose bonds (such as industrial development bonds and private activity bonds) and arbitrage bonds issued by or on behalf of state or local governments is not tax-

exempt. For tax purposes, such nonexempt issues are government bonds taxed like Treasury bonds. However, interest on certain categories of private activity bonds is tax-exempt. In general, the interest earned on these qualifying private activity bonds is a tax preference item. (See the discussion of the alternative minimum tax in Chapter 43, "Taxation of Investment Vehicles.")

ALTERNATIVES

1. Taxable bonds generating a comparable, or higher, after-tax yield.

2. Single premium deferred annuities providing a fixed annual payment.

3. Certain preferred stock with a fixed dividend.

WHERE AND HOW DO I GET IT?

Municipal bonds can be purchased by calling a brokerage firm or contacting a bank (in some cases the bank will take an order over the phone), savings and loan, or savings bank.

Each dealer in bonds establishes a price based on cost and demand. Larger dealers set prices based on the amount for which similar lots of the same bonds can be sold or acquired. The point is that there is no national auction for municipal bonds as there is for stocks.

When comparing bonds, be sure to check the yield to maturity of each bond. For example, a 10-year, 3.5% bond selling at par ($1,000) and paying interest semi-annually will have the same yield as a 6% bond selling at $1,209 that also pays interest semi-annually and matures in 10 years. Both will yield 3.5% if held to maturity.

Rather than purchase bonds on their own, some investors prefer the greater diversification available through municipal bond unit trusts while others utilize municipal bond mutual funds. A "unit trust" is a fixed portfolio, which means that the underlying bonds do not change and are not "managed" (i.e., there is no continual buying and selling). Small investors find this approach appealing because of: (1) the increased safety through diversification; (2) professional selection; (3) security (the unit trust safeguards the securities themselves); and (4) convenience (interest and principal are collected by the unit trust and paid out on a regular basis or automatically reinvested).

Therefore, unit trusts are best for long-term holdings when a certain fixed income is desired. As the unit trust's holdings mature (or as the bonds are paid off through sinking funds), fund holders are paid on a pro rata basis. Unit trusts are "self liquidating," which means that when assets drop approximately 20% of the original investment, the fund ends and unit holders receive their share of the current price of the portfolio.

A municipal bond mutual fund is similar to a unit trust except that its underlying portfolio is "managed" (i.e., there is a regular sale and purchase of bonds to take advantage of changing market conditions). Shares of a municipal bond mutual fund are bought and sold on the open market. The prices fluctuate with the changing value of the underlying securities. If an investor expects to sell in a relatively short period of time (e.g., within three years), a managed tax-exempt fund is a better choice than a unit trust.

WHAT FEES OR OTHER ACQUISITION COSTS ARE INVOLVED?

When a municipal bond is purchased directly from a broker or a bank there is a sales charge or brokerage commission. These fees will vary depending on the amount invested and the number of bonds purchased. Some institutions charge fees based on the number of bonds while others calculate fees on the total dollars invested. These costs range from $5 to $10 per bond.

If municipal bonds are purchased through a unit trust, a "load" (i.e., sales charge) of 3.5% to 5.0% is typically added to the value of the purchase. For example, an investor may pay $40 per unit (units are generally valued at $1,000). This means less money is at work and penalizes an investor who liquidates holdings quickly.

Purchasers of municipal bond mutual funds may pay a sales charge (in what is known as a "load" fund), or may select a fund with no sales charge (in what is known as a "no-load" fund). Both of these types of funds charge an annual management fee, which will usually range from 0.5% to 1.0% of net asset value. This annual management fee is deducted from the assets of the fund itself and is not paid directly by individual investors.

HOW DO I SELECT THE BEST OF ITS TYPE?

1. Investors contemplating a direct purchase of municipal bonds should compare:

(a) *The quality rating of each bond.* Bond ratings can be found on the Internet or in your local library through services such as Standard & Poor's (www.standardandpoors.com), Moody's (www.Moodys.com), and Fitch's (www.fitchratings.com). Ratings of AAA or Aaa indicate the highest quality bonds, while those rated CCC or lower are quite speculative. An "A" rated bond will be safer and yield only slightly less than a lower quality issue.

(b) *Current yield.* Current yield means the coupon amount divided by the investor's cost. For example, a bond paying $90 per year in interest that costs $850 will have a current yield of 10.6%.

(c) *Yield to maturity.* "Yield to maturity" means coupon return plus gain or minus loss at maturity. For example, the bond described above, maturing in 10 years, will have a yield to maturity of 3.5% when the loss of $209 is included with the current yield. (See Chapter 34, "Measuring Yield" for a more detailed explanation of the yield to maturity calculation.)

2. Purchasing a bond issued in the investor's state of residence may result in a higher after-tax yield. For example, if the investor lives in Pennsylvania, which has an income tax, the income from Pennsylvania Turnpike Bonds would be exempt. The income would be exempt from both federal and state (and sometimes city) income taxes.

3. Select a maturity date of 10 years or less. For two bonds with the same quality rating, the bond with the shorter maturity date will typically have greater price stability (though perhaps a lower yield as well).

4. Schedule maturities according to projected cash flow or capital needs. An investor planning to retire in 10 years should select a discount bond maturing in a decade.

5. Search for large issues of general obligation bonds of state governments, and revenue bonds of large, well known authorities. These bonds are more marketable and will be easier and less costly to sell quickly.

WHERE CAN I FIND OUT MORE ABOUT IT?

1. Your local library should have Moody's Municipal Bond Guide, Standard & Poor's Bond Guide, or

Fitch's rating service. These are services that list large numbers of bonds and give quality rating, coupon rate, current yield, and yield to maturity. These sources are also available on the Internet as follows: Moody's (www.Moodys.com); Standard & Poor's (www.standardandpoors.com); Fitch's (www.fitchratings.com).

2. Major brokerage firms and banks can provide information on specific issues and current market conditions.

3. Another source of fixed income investing information is BondsOnline at (www.bondsonline.com).

QUESTIONS AND ANSWERS

Question – What is the difference between a general obligation bond (a "GO") and a "revenue" bond?

Answer – A general obligation bond is backed by the "full faith and credit" of the issuing entity. These bonds are generally considered safer than revenue bonds and, therefore, have a lower rate of return.

A revenue bond is issued for a particular project (e.g., Florida Pollution Control bonds). The interest and principal of these bonds are paid out of solely the income of the particular enterprise and may be less secure than general obligation bonds. For that reason, they generally sell at lower prices to yield a higher return.

Question – Can a tax-exempt bond be purchased in "bearer" form?

Answer – Since December 31, 1982, long-term obligations (maturing in more than one year) of state and local governments must be in registered form. This means that the right to principal and interest is transferable only through an entry on the books of the obligation's issuer or holder. The book entry system requires that any person or his agent holding an obligation in a "street name" account or for safekeeping must make it possible to identify the beneficial owner by creating ownership records.

Most bonds issued prior to January 1, 1983 are fully negotiable, meaning that title passes with possession. They are obviously prime targets for theft or misappropriation and should be kept in a safe deposit box or with a broker.

Question – Is a municipal bond an appropriate investment for a pension plan?

Answer – Qualified retirement plans such as a pension or profit sharing plan have many advantages. Among these is the fact that income earned by plan assets is free of all current income taxes. Therefore, bonds providing additional exemption are unnecessary and should not be held in such portfolios.

Question – What is the advantage of a "serial" maturity?

Answer – "Serial" maturity means that a portion of the bond issue comes due each year until the final redemption. This regular payment schedule makes it easier for the borrower to handle its cash flow obligations. This serial feature is also beneficial to the investor who can purchase bonds that will be redeemed as cash flow is needed. For example, bonds from a single issue may be purchased to mature in the same year or years that college tuition comes due or retirement income is needed.

Question – Can an investor buy a tax-exempt bond on margin?

Answer – Technically, an investor can borrow up to 80% of the current market price of a municipal bond. But, the interest an investor pays to buy such bonds (or previously purchased tax-exempt securities) will not be deductible for federal income tax purposes because the income produced by the bonds is non-taxable.

Question – Is there any given time during the year when it is better to buy tax-exempt bonds?

Answer – Late in the tax year many investors are trying to set up tax losses that can be used against earned income. They may "swap" (i.e., exchange) bonds to realize capital losses. This activity may temporarily "flood" the market and, consequently, lower prices. The end result may be a higher yield for the individual who buys at the end of the year.

Question – Is there such a thing as a short-term, tax-exempt bond?

Answer – It is possible to purchase municipal obligations with a maturity of less than 270 days. An investor

in a high tax bracket who would like to put funds to work for a short period of time will find this an excellent way to invest.

There are also short-term, tax-exempt bond funds—in essence, a type of money market fund. The cash received from the sale of shares is invested in municipal bonds with an average maturity of about 180 days. Chances of a capital loss are slight because of the short maturities, although the tradeoff for this safety is a yield slightly lower than those of regular funds.

Question – What are the advantages of tax-exempt bond funds?

Answer – There are six major advantages of tax-exempt bond funds:

1. *Ease of investing* – most bond funds allow an investor to begin with as little as $1,000 and then add amounts as low as $100.

2. *Diversification* – fund managers purchase different types of bonds, select issuers in widespread geographic location, and pick bonds with varied maturities.

3. *Automatic reinvestment* – interest and capital gains are immediately and automatically reinvested. This maximizes the potential of compound interest.

4. *Ability to exchange funds* – a single fund management group may offer many different types of funds. An investor could exchange shares in a tax-exempt fund for shares of a stock fund or a taxable bond fund paying higher returns.

5. *Convenience* – funds provide safekeeping of securities and may be selected on the basis of whether they pay interest monthly, quarterly, or semiannually.

6. *Tax reports and records* – detailed reports are provided to investors covering the purchase and sale of shares making it easy to determine any capital gain or loss for tax purposes.

Figure 5.1

STATE INDIVIDUAL INCOME TAX OF MUNICIPAL BOND INTEREST

State	Resident State Interest	Nonresident State Interest
Alabama	Exempt	Taxable
Alaska	No Income Tax	No Income Tax
Arizona	Exempt	Taxable
Arkansas	Exempt	Taxable
California	Exempt	Taxable
Colorado	Exempt (exceptions)	Taxable
Connecticut	Exempt	Taxable
Delaware	Exempt	Taxable
D.C.	Exempt	Exempt[1]
Florida	No Income Tax	No Income Tax
Georgia	Exempt	Taxable
Hawaii	Exempt	Taxable
Idaho	Exempt	Taxable
Illinois	Taxable (limited exceptions)	Taxable
Indiana	Exempt	Exempt[2]
Iowa	Taxable (limited exceptions)	Taxable
Kansas	Some taxable[3]	Taxable
Kentucky	Exempt	Taxable
Louisiana	Exempt	Taxable
Maine	Exempt	Taxable
Maryland	Exempt	Taxable
Massachusetts	Exempt	Taxable
Michigan	Exempt	Taxable
Minnesota	Exempt	Taxable
Mississippi	Exempt	Taxable
Missouri	Exempt	Taxable
Montana	Exempt	Taxable
Nebraska	Exempt	Taxable
Nevada	No Income Tax	No Income Tax
New Hampshire	Exempt	Taxable
New Jersey	Exempt	Taxable
New Mexico	Exempt	Taxable
New York	Exempt	Taxable
North Carolina	Exempt	Taxable
North Dakota	Exempt	Taxable
Ohio	Exempt	Taxable
Oklahoma	Some taxable[3]	Taxable
Oregon	Exempt	Taxable
Pennsylvania	Exempt	Taxable
Rhode Island	Exempt	Taxable
South Carolina	Exempt	Taxable
South Dakota	No Income Tax	No Income Tax
Tennessee	Exempt	Taxable
Texas	No Income Tax	No Income Tax
Utah	Exempt	Exempt
Vermont	Exempt	Taxable
Virginia	Exempt	Taxable
Washington	No Income Tax	No Income Tax
West Virginia	Exempt	Taxable
Wisconsin	Taxable	Taxable
Wyoming	No Income Tax	No Income Tax

[1] taxable if purchased after 1991
[2] taxable only for gross income tax purposes
[3] specified issues exempt

Chapter 6

STRIPPED BONDS

WHAT IS IT?

Stripped bonds are artificially "manufactured" zero-coupon bonds (see Chapter 7). These zero-coupon bonds are "manufactured" when investment bankers buy blocks of coupon-paying bonds (typically long-term government Treasuries) and separate them into two components: (1) the coupons (which have been "stripped" from the bond); and (2) the principal (the "stripped" bond). Each component is sold separately. The principal is sold at enough of a discount to provide a competitive market yield to maturity.

WHEN IS THE USE OF THIS TOOL INDICATED?

1. When investors want to be assured of reinvestment at the yield to maturity (unless the bond is called or sold before maturity).

2. Because of the certainty of the reinvestment rate, investors can better predict and plan for specific accumulated values at the maturity date.

3. Taxable strips are very suitable conservative investments for retirement plans.

4. Tax-exempt strips are an excellent vehicle for children under age 18 who are subject to their parents' tax rate on unearned income.

5. Strips are suitable when a known lump sum is needed at a specific future time.

ADVANTAGES AND DISADVANTAGES

1. Prices of stripped bonds are more sensitive to interest rate changes than prices of coupon-paying bonds of the same quality and maturity. Specifically, the market price of stripped bonds will fall (rise) when market interest rates increase (decrease) much more than the market price of comparable coupon-paying bonds. In addition, the size of the move in the market price associated with a given change in market

interest rates will be greater the longer is the term until maturity of the bond. Consequently, in periods of historically low interest rates, such as in the early years of the 2000-2010 decade, investors bear considerable risk of sustaining large capital losses in the event market interest rates rise and they are forced to sell the stripped bonds before they mature.

2. Many stripped bonds are callable at the discretion of the issuer. If a strip is called before maturity—which is more likely to occur when interest rates have fallen—the investor will generally not be able to reinvest the proceeds at the yield to maturity he enjoyed on the stripped bond. However, some strips are issued with call protection to assure investors that the bond will not be called for a specified period or not at all. Corporate and municipal strips are more likely to be callable than United States Treasury-based strips.

TAX IMPLICATIONS

1. Unless the bond is a tax-exempt municipal issue, interest is subject to tax as it accrues even though no cash is paid until the bond matures or is called. However, in the case of a tax-exempt bond stripped after June 10, 1987, a portion of the original issue discount may be treated as if it comes from a taxable obligation.

2. The original issue discount (OID) rules generally determine the amount of interest that accrues each period for tax purposes. In a nutshell, for bonds issued after April 4, 1994, OID must be accrued at a constant rate, effectively equal to the yield to maturity. The accrued interest each period is added to the investor's basis in the bond. Gain or loss, if any, upon disposition of the bond prior to maturity is equal to the difference between the sale price and the original issue price plus the accrued interest to the date of sale. The rules for computing the taxable interest for stripped bonds issued before April 4, 1994 differ somewhat, depending on when they were issued.[1]

3. If the underlying securities are federal government issues, there is some question as to whether the interest is exempt from state taxation. If the interest is United States government interest, the interest is exempt from state tax. If the interest is from the investment banker who "manufactures" the strip, the interest would be subject to state taxation.

ALTERNATIVES

1. Stripped federal government securities have many different names, depending on the investment banker that "manufactures" the stripped bond, including:

(a) CATs – Certificates of Accrual on Treasury Certificates

(b) COUGRs – Certificates of Government Receipts

(c) STAGs – Sterling Transferable Accruing Government Securities

(d) STRIPs – Separate Trading of Registered Interest and Principal of Securities

(e) TIGRs – Treasury Investment Growth Certificates

(f) ZEBRAs – Zero-Coupon Eurosterling Bearer or Registered Accruing Certificates

2. Stripped tax-free municipal bonds have one very important advantage over original issue zero-coupon municipals (which have been available for years): most of the tax-free strips are not callable while virtually all of the zero-coupon municipals are callable. Consequently, investors who buy tax-free strips have much more certainty about the holding period and their reinvestment yield.

Furthermore, some of the new tax-free strips are guaranteed by "pre-refunding." In other words, they are backed by United States Treasury bonds that have been purchased to guarantee payment if the municipality goes bankrupt, or is slow in paying investors when the bonds matures.

3. Another way to purchase zero-coupon instruments is through a target-maturity mutual fund. These open-end, no-load mutual funds—which typically require $2,500 as a minimum investment—specify a particular termination date. These funds invest in STRIPS and coupon-paying Treasury bonds that match the specified termination date, pay little or no interest during the life of the fund, and pay out a lump sum at the fund's termination date.

Some care should be exercised in the selection of target-maturity mutual funds. Some of the funds listed as target-maturity mutual funds (for instance, some of those offered by Kemper) are actually hybrid funds that combine STRIPs maturing at specified dates with investments in equities or other assets. The objective of these funds is to assure that investors will receive at least a "minimum" value at a specified future date together with the earnings and appreciation, if any, on the other assets. Although these hybrid funds may have a place in satisfying investors' objectives, they will not have the same risk, return, and tax features as pure target-maturity mutual funds.

CHAPTER ENDNOTES

1. See IRC Secs. 1271 through 1273, and the related regulations for a discussion of the rules as they apply to stripped bonds issued before April 4, 1994 and for certain other special rules as they apply to stripped bonds.

Chapter 7

ZERO–COUPON BONDS

WHAT IS IT?

Zero-coupon bonds are sold at a deep "original" issue discount (see Chapter 43) from their face value. Investors receive the face value at maturity rather than periodic interest payments. Corporations and governmental entities issue zero-coupon bonds. Some zero-coupon bonds issued by state and municipal governments are tax-exempt. For example, a zero-coupon bond issued at $500 and maturing in 10 years at $1,000 provides a yield of 7.18%.

WHEN IS THE USE OF THIS TOOL INDICATED?

1. With zero-coupon bonds, investors know their exact yield to maturity since they do not have to worry about reinvesting cash flows at, perhaps, lower rates of interest than they are receiving on the bond. If the bond is held to maturity and does not default, the return is guaranteed. Consequently, zero-coupon bonds are especially appropriate when investors wish to "lock in" a rate of return and be assured of a specified accumulation at a given future date (i.e., the maturity date).

2. Taxable zeros are very attractive conservative investments for retirement plans. The tax shelter feature of the retirement plan allows the unpaid, but otherwise taxable accruing interest to be tax deferred.

3. Tax-exempt zeros are suitable conservative investments for high-tax-bracket investors who wish to accumulate wealth, have little need for current cash flow, and who do not desire to worry about reinvestment of cash flows.

4. Zero-coupon securities are frequently used to meet specific financial or investment goals, especially when the date of a future need is known well in advance.[1]

ADVANTAGES AND DISADVANTAGES

1. Although investors are assured that they will receive a reinvestment rate equal to the yield to maturity

if they hold the bond to maturity, they derive this certainty by foregoing the opportunity to reinvest at higher rates if market interest rates rise.

2. Prices of zero-coupon bonds are much more sensitive to changes in interest rates than coupon bonds of comparable term and quality. Consequently, if an investor has to sell a zero-coupon bond before maturity, there is no assurance that he will realize the anticipated yield.

3. Many zero-coupon bonds are callable at the discretion of the issuer. If a zero-coupon bond is called before maturity—which is more likely to occur when interest rates have fallen—the investor will generally not be able to reinvest the proceeds at the yield to maturity he enjoyed on the zero-coupon bond.

TAX IMPLICATIONS

The investor must generally include accruing interest in his taxable income (unless it is a tax-exempt issue) even though no cash is received until the bond matures, is sold, or is called.

ALTERNATIVES

Deep-discount, low-coupon (market discount) bonds. Investors may acquire low-coupon bonds at substantial discounts from their face values, depending on the coupon rate and the remaining time to maturity. Investors are assured that the portion of the interest that is cash deferred until the bond matures will be effectively reinvested at the original yield to maturity, similar to zero-coupon bonds. (See Chapter 3 for an explanation of the tax treatment of market discount bonds.)

QUESTIONS AND ANSWERS

Question – What are LYONs (Liquid Yield Option Notes)?

Answer – LYONs are zero-coupon convertible notes. Corporations issue zero-coupon bonds that are convertible into a fixed number of shares of common stock of the issuer. Investors who choose to convert forfeit all accrued interest on the bonds.

These bonds are generally less valuable as convertibles than as zero-coupon bonds because it becomes more expensive to convert as time passes (because the investor must forego accrued interest).

Question – What are "bunny bonds" or multiplier bonds?

Answer – A "bunny bond" or multiplier bond is a bond in which investors reinvest the income into bonds with the same terms and conditions as on the original bond (thus, the term "bunny" bond because they multiply like bunnies). This reinvestment feature makes bunny bonds very similar to zero-coupon bonds.

These bonds eliminate the reinvestment problem characteristic of all income-producing assets—namely, the uncertainty of the rate of return at which the income can be reinvested. These bonds are especially well suited for retirement funds and other tax-sheltered vehicles or for tax-exempt entities, since investors must include interest in taxable income even though they receive no cash until the bonds mature.

The principal risk is that interest rates will rise and the investor will be "locked" into reinvesting at the lower specified rate. Because of the automatic reinvestment feature, the price of these bonds is more sensitive to interest rate changes than the price of a conventional bond of similar quality and maturity. The price will tend to fall more than conventional bonds of comparable quality and maturity when interest rates rise. On the other hand, if interest rates fall, the investor reinvests at the higher rate and the price of the bond will rise more than conventional bonds of similar quality and term to maturity.

Bunny bonds can be compared to bonds issued with detachable or nondetachable warrants. A warrant is like a long-term call option (see Chapter 41) that allows the investor to acquire more bonds of the same issue or a new issue at a specified price and yield.

CHAPTER ENDNOTES

1. Before 2006, an investor seeking to provide college education funds in 10 years might have selected an issue with a similar maturity date. Such an investor might have considered whether purchasing the bonds under the "Uniform Gifts to Minors Act" (UGMA) would shift income taxation to the child's relatively lower bracket. However, under the Tax Increase Prevention and Reconciliation Act of 2006—TIPRA, the "kiddie tax" age was raised from 14 to 18; consequently, this tax favored strategy has effectively been nullified. IRC Sec. 1(g)(2)(A), as amended by TIPRA 2005.

Chapter 8

PROMISSORY NOTES

WHAT IS IT?

A promissory note is a deceptively simple legal document that can be used in a wide range of lender-borrower relationships (See Figure 8.1, Promissory Note). Signed by both parties, it acknowledges that a loan has been made and sets out the terms under which it is to be repaid. These terms generally include not only how and when the original principal amount of the loan is to be repaid, but also the way in which interest on the loan, if any, is to be calculated and paid. In the case of a private mortgage, it includes clauses specifying the parties' interests in the real property securing the mortgage.

Promissory notes (sometimes simply called "notes") are often used by businesses, especially small businesses and startup companies, to raise capital. Because a promissory note is a private transaction without any regulatory oversight, it should not be viewed as an "investment" in the same sense as low-risk alternatives, such as CDs or money market funds. Occasionally, however, a planner

might need to advise a client who is contemplating such a transaction and wishes to view it as an investment. In this case, the client should, at the very least, be advised to see that the loan transaction is clearly documented in writing and signed by both parties. For guidance on seeing that the loan is properly documented and guidelines as to provisions that should be included, see Figure 8.1 for a sample form, and further discussion at "How Do I Select the Best of Its Type," below.

In addition to protecting the lender's interests and communicating the terms of the loan to each party, the promissory note will help reduce some of the many pitfalls inherent in private loans. Without a properly executed written document, both parties also risk the possibility that the IRS will classify the loan as a gift. Finally, the lender should be cautioned that even if the terms of the note are communicated and followed, personal loans carry the potential for conflicts of interest, mismanagement claims, and personal misunderstandings between borrowers and lenders.

Figure 8.1

PROMISSORY NOTE

___(borrower)___, referred to herein as "MAKER," agrees to pay to the order of ___(lender)___ referred to herein as "HOLDER," the sum of $100,000, (one hundred thousand dollars), at ___(lender's street address, city, state, zip)___, with interest thereon at the rate of ___% per annum, simple interest.

The full amount of principal and interest due herein shall be payable on ___(due date)___.

This note is payable in U.S. Dollars. At any time, the maximum rate of interest applicable to this transaction shall not exceed the legal maximum rate of interest for a note of this type. Any sums paid in excess of any lawful limitation shall be applied to principal.

After default herein, this note will bear interest at the highest legal rate for this type of note until paid in full. Upon any default, MAKER agrees to pay a reasonable attorney's fee for any and all services of an attorney, whether in or out of court, and for appeal and post-judgment collection legal services.

Dated: _____

_____
MAKER

WHEN IS THE USE OF THIS TOOL INDICATED?

1. When an individual or company finds it difficult or impossible to borrow from conventional sources, such as commercial banks and finance companies. Also, such companies would typically not be able to sell securities in the organized capital markets.

2. When an individual desires to invest in a local business--particularly one in which he or a family member may be an officer or director.

3. When acquaintances or members of a family wish to enter into a formal debtor-creditor relationship with each other, as may be the case when loans are made for education purposes, the purchase of a home, medical costs, or emergency needs.

ADVANTAGES

1. *Flexibility* – The terms and conditions under which a loan is made can be negotiated directly between the two parties. While legal and accounting support may be helpful, the two parties are generally free to arrange the conditions of the loan as they see fit.

2. *Simplicity*--Most loans that involve promissory notes are relatively straightforward, though some may be much more complex. They tend to be relatively short-term, generally involve a monthly payment schedule, and have few if any extra complicating provisions beyond the repayment terms.

DISADVANTAGES

1. *High Risk* – Promissory notes generally support personal loans in circumstances where the likelihood of default is quite high. For example, friends or relatives may advance funds for someone to start a new business, make a down payment on a house, or purchase a car. Repayment of the loan is almost entirely dependent on the ability and willingness of the borrower to comply with the terms of the note.

2. *Lack of Collateral* – In most cases where promissory notes are involved, whether the loans are made to a corporation, or to an individual, there is no collateral pledged to support the loan. The notes are simply an unsecured IOU (i.e., a promise to pay) without any property, securities, or other assets that could be attached or claimed in the case of default.

---

3. *Lack of Liquidity* – Once a loan of this nature is made, there is only a remote possibility that the lender will be able to liquidate or sell this loan at anything other than a "fire sale" price discount. Consequently, the loan precludes the use of the loaned funds for some other purpose, such as a more favorable investment opportunity or the for lender's own needs.

TAX IMPLICATIONS

1. All of the income from promissory notes is fully taxable to the investor at ordinary income tax rates.

2. Promissory notes pledge the return of the original investment at maturity and most corporate issuers do not allow them to be resold or transferred. This means that there will be no capital gain or loss on these instruments.

3. In the event that the loan fails to provide for interest, or provides for interest below certain market rates, interest may be imputed to the lender and considered paid by the borrower under the below market loan rules.[1]

4. Certain debts that become partially or wholly worthless may be deductible; however, for noncorporate taxpayers, the deduction is subject to very stringent limitations.[2]

ALTERNATIVES

1. Certificates of Deposit (CDs) are debt instruments issued by commercial banks, savings and loans, and other thrift institutions. While they are frequently issued with six-month maturities, some have longer terms of three to five years. The return is commensurate with the investment risk: while returns on CDs are obviously much lower than those of promissory notes, CDs are at one end of the risk spectrum (i.e., they are federally insured) while promissory notes are at the opposite end (i.e., relying merely on the credit standing and good faith of the borrower).

2. The direct purchase of shares in a money market fund should be compared as a low-risk alternative when a promissory note is being viewed as an investment option.

3. If the promissory note is implemented in the context of a personal loan, the investor may wish instead to co-sign on a note to the borrower by a lending

institution. While the co-signer may still end up being held responsible for the debt, the degree of risk is less than if he has made the loan himself.

WHERE AND HOW DO I GET IT?

Typically, promissory notes document a loan that has been privately negotiated between family members, friends, or business associates. In the case of promissory notes to corporations, advertisements are sometimes published in financial or business sections of local newspapers.

WHAT FEES OR OTHER ACQUISITION COSTS ARE INVOLVED?

There are generally no fees or other acquisition costs associated with an investment in promissory notes. When used by business firms to acquire capital, any transaction costs are typically paid by the borrowing firm. However, if the transaction involves large sums, is for a lengthy period of time, or requires a complicated note agreement, both parties may wish to have an attorney review the documents. This service would require the payment of fees.

HOW DO I SELECT THE BEST OF ITS TYPE?

Clear documentation in the form of a written and signed promissory note is essential, whether the loan is for personal or business purposes. There are some essential features of any loan agreement that must be included in the written note. These include:

- proper identification of the parties;

- basic repayment terms – interest, payment date, place of payment, etc.;

- optional default and confession of judgment provisions; and

- repayment ledger

Since individual state laws can vary somewhat in these areas, it is a good idea to have a local attorney at least review the document before it is signed by the parties.

While the formality of a note may seem unnecessary in the case of personal lending, it can prevent misunderstandings as to whether the money is a loan

or a gift, when it is to be repaid, and how much interest is owed. It can also be an effective tool for making a gift in excess of the annual exemption. When there is a written record of the transaction, the lender who wants to forgive a portion of the loan equal to the allowance each year can document such amounts until the entire note is forgiven. Documentation of an adequate rate of interest can prevent the parties from running afoul of the rules for below-market loans.

Because promissory notes are a highly individualized type of investment, they are likely to be customized to suit the particular circumstances of a specific borrower and lender. The repayment schedule is probably the most important aspect of the loan terms, and an investor should be familiar with the many possible types of repayment schedules that can be designed. These would include:

- *Equal Monthly Payments* – The borrower makes the same payment each month for the life of the loan. Part of each payment represents interest charges and the remainder is applied toward the amount of the outstanding principal. In legal terms, the loan is said to be "fully amortized" over the number of payment periods.

- *Equal Monthly Payments with a Final Balloon Payment* – This type of repayment schedule requires equal monthly payments of principal and interest, but for a shorter time period than would be required to fully pay off, or amortize, the loan. That leaves a remaining principal balance—referred to as a "balloon"—which must be paid off in a lump sum.

For the borrower, this type of repayment schedule means lower monthly payments initially, but it entails the obligation to pay a large sum at the end of the overall repayment period. Many borrowers plan in advance to make the final balloon payment by taking out another loan (from the same or a different lender), but this has additional risks associated with it. For example, lenders may not have funds available, or the interest rate on the new loan may be considerably higher if overall interest rates have increased.

A balloon payment loan also involves additional risks for the lender. For one, the periodic payments received during the life of the loan are smaller, and secondly, there is increased risk that the borrower will not be able to make the large balloon payment required at the end of the loan.

- *Interest-Only Payments and a Final Balloon Payment* – Under this arrangement, payments made by the borrower to the lender are for interest only. Since no principal is included in the payments, they are smaller than if some or all of the principal balance were also being repaid periodically. The full amount of the loan is represented by a balloon payment at the end, however.

  The borrower under such an arrangement will pay considerably more interest than under a plan where part of the loan is paid off each month. At the same time, the lender has the added risk that the borrower will be unable to pay off the full amount of the loan at maturity.

- *Single Payment of Principal and Interest* – With this type of promissory note, there are no periodic payments of either principal or interest. The entire amount of the loan principal is repaid at the end of the loan period, along with all of the accrued interest. Such arrangements are typically made only for short-term loans—typically less than one year in duration—and involve the greatest risk for the lender (investor).

Another important consideration in the use of promissory notes is whether the contract (note) can be sold, or transferred by the lender to a third party, without the approval of the borrower. This should be carefully spelled out in the instrument and clearly understood by both the borrower and lender. While there is no organized secondary market in such notes, there are some companies, and even some individuals, who may offer to purchase these instruments, at a discount, prior to maturity.

A promissory note agreement should also specify whether the borrower has the right to repay some or all of the outstanding principal balance in advance. This can be a valuable feature for the borrower, and substantially lower the total interest cost of the loan, in the event the borrower is able to repay it earlier than the agreement requires.

The lender might not wish to have the loan paid off in advance, especially if interest rates available on new loans would be lower than the original loan. One possible arrangement here is to specify a minimum period for which the loan will be outstanding. This allows the lender to receive some significant portion of the inter-

est income before the borrower can completely pay off the debt.

WHERE CAN I FIND OUT MORE ABOUT IT?

Companies that wish to borrow using unsecured, promissory notes may advertise in business newspapers, such as the *Wall Street Journal* (www.wsj.com), or in local newspapers where they are headquartered or operate. Larger organizations may also promote this type of financing on their Internet sites.[3]

Information on the availability of individual promissory notes is very sparse. There is no organized secondary market for the types of loans that involve such notes. For private lenders, the acquisition of these loans is done primarily on a "word-of-mouth" basis.

Commercial lenders, such as banks and finance companies, rarely sell these types of loans, though they may have the legal right to do so under the terms of the loan contract. Most loans are simply held to maturity.

The actual loan forms, such as the one illustrated in this chapter, on the other hand, are readily available. Most libraries, bookstores, and office supply stores will carry collections of legal forms that include promissory notes. They are also easily available over the Internet from various providers of legal and other business forms.

QUESTIONS AND ANSWERS

Question – When does an investor in a promissory note receive the interest income?

Answer – For shorter-term notes, those with maturities up to one year, interest is typically paid at maturity along with the return of principal. For longer-term notes (e.g., up to five years), the investor generally has the option to have interest either paid out in cash, or reinvested at the same initial interest rate, on an annual basis.

Question – Are all loans subject to the below-market loan rules?

Answer – For certain loans between individuals, if the total of all loans does not exceed $10,000, a *de minimis* rule may exempt the loan from the below-market loan rules.[4] However, if the below-market loan rules do apply, and the rate of interest is below the *applicable federal rate*, the transaction is essentially recharacterized as: (1) an arm's length loan requiring payment of interest at the applicable federal rate (see below); and (2) an imputed transfer of funds by the lender to the borrower.[5]

Question – Where are the applicable federal rates published?

Answer – The applicable federal rates (AFRs) are published by the Secretary of the Treasury on a monthly basis. The published AFRs include short-term, mid-

term, and long-term rates, and in July of each year, a "blended annual rate" is published.[6]

CHAPTER ENDNOTES

1. See IRC Secs. 7872(e), 7872(f).
2. See IRC Sec. 166.
3. For an example, see www.advanta.com.
4. See IRC Sec. 7872(c)(2).
5. See Prop. Reg. §1.7872-1(a).
6. See IRC Sec. 1274(d).

Chapter 9

GUARANTEED INVESTMENT CONTRACTS (GICs)

WHAT IS IT?

In a traditional guaranteed investment contract (GIC), an insurance company receives deposits from a benefit plan or other institutional customer, and then issues a fixed-rate contract. GICs are frequently offered as one of several investment options in 401(k) plans.

The deposits paid to the insurer are used to purchase investments that are held in the insurance company's general account. Fixed-income investments—typically mortgages and private placements—are the most common type of purchases, but equity investments may also be acquired. The benefit plan is a creditor of the issuing company and therefore has credit risk, although generally the GIC issuers have high credit-quality ratings.

The insurer offering the GIC is contractually obligated to repay the principal and specified interest guaranteed to the 401(k) or other benefit plan. The plan's provisions typically permit the participant to withdraw funds from the fund at book value (also referred to as account or contract value) for reasons such as

- loans,

- hardship withdrawals, or

- transfers to other investment options offered by the plan.

Companies can choose between two types of GICs: *participating* and *nonparticipating*. Participating GICs offers the investor a variable rate of return based on interest-rate fluctuations. Nonparticipating GICs, on the other hand, earn fixed rates of return.

WHEN IS THE USE OF THIS TOOL INDICATED?

1. When a company or other organization wishes to have secure funding for its obligations under various qualified retirement plans such as a 401(k) or 403(b)(7) plan.

2. When an organization does not wish to have the responsibility of investing and managing assets under a retirement plan, and elects to transfer those responsibilities to an insurance company.

ADVANTAGES

1. *Rate of Return* – GICs typically offer a higher rate of return than other relatively low-risk investments, such as money market funds or certificates of deposit.

2. *Moderate Risk* – Since GICs guarantee a specified rate of return, they are backed by the insurer's contractual obligation. Most insurers are credit-worthy, making the risk of nonpayment of interest or principal low.

DISADVANTAGES

1. *Lack of Federal Insurance* – As indicated above, GICs can be compared as a higher-yielding alternative to CDs and money market funds. But unlike CDs, GICs are not guaranteed or insured by the Treasury or any other government agency. Therefore, despite the use of the term "guaranteed," they are riskier than any federally insured investment.

2. *Moderate Risk* – Although insurance company insolvencies are unusual, in certain instances defaulting insurers have failed to make promised payments of interest or principal. Investors choosing a GIC alternative in a 401(k) plan should recognize that they assume some degree of credit risk.

TAX IMPLICATIONS

1. Income earned on a guaranteed investment contract and paid into a qualified plan account is not taxed to the participant or the plan until distributions begin.

2. All of the income attributable to a GIC is fully taxable to the investor at ordinary income tax rates to the extent that a distribution is made from the plan,

unless the participant elects to roll over part or all of the distribution.

ALTERNATIVES

1. Certificates of deposit are debt instruments issued by commercial banks, savings and loans, and other thrift institutions. While they are frequently issued with six-month maturities, some have longer terms of three to five years. One important distinction with these instruments is that they are federally insured while GICs rely on the credit standing of the issuer.

2. U.S. government bonds, money market funds or corporate debt instruments, if offered by the plan, are another option when considering a GIC as a 401(k) investment. For an accurate comparison, instruments of similar maturity should be compared. But it is important to note that while government bonds are backed by the full faith and credit of the United States, corporate debt, like insurers' creditworthiness can vary in quality. Investors considering corporate bonds should determine the credit quality of the issuers by looking at ratings provided by Moody's and Standard & Poor's. Returns should be commensurate with the degree of risk assumed by the investor.

WHERE AND HOW DO I GET IT?

Guaranteed investment contracts are issued by most major insurance companies. Firms wishing to fund 401(k) and other retirement plans should solicit quotes from a number of issuing companies before an investment decision is made.

WHAT FEES OR OTHER ACQUISITION COSTS ARE INVOLVED?

The commissions and fees involved in the issuance of a GIC are likely to vary considerably from one insurance company to another. It is suggested that a firm wishing to purchase these contracts solicit competitive bids from at least three different insurance companies before making a decision.

HOW DO I SELECT THE BEST OF ITS TYPE?

In trying to choose between participating and non-participating GICs, the potential investor or purchaser of a GIC should evaluate the current level of interest rates and estimate the likelihood of future rate fluctuations. If rates are considered "high" by historic standards, it may make sense to purchase a non-participating contract and "lock in" the attractive rate. If the sense is that rates are historically "low" and likely to increase in the future, then a participating contract may be appealing.

WHERE CAN I FIND OUT MORE ABOUT IT?

1. The *Wall Street Journal* (www.wsj.com) publishes a daily table of rates quoted for GIC contracts. The rates quoted represent the best quote for a $2 million to $5 million immediate lump-sum deposit with annual interest payments. The table also includes an index of GIC rates prepared by the T. Rowe Price organization.

2. The accounting regulations that apply to GIC contracts are presented in Financial Accounting Standards Board (www.fasb.org) Statement No. 97, *Accounting and Reporting by Insurance Enterprises for Certain Long-Duration Contracts and for Realized Gains and Losses from the Sale of Investments.*

QUESTIONS AND ANSWERS

Question – Are GICs insured by the U.S. government?

Answer – No; there is no federal insurance for GICs issued by insurers. The investor relies on the credit standing and financial performance of the company.

Question – How should an investor decide between a participating and a nonparticipating GIC contract?

Answer – This choice will depend on the investor's expectation of interest rates over the term of the investment. If the investor believes that interest rates are at historic lows and will most likely increase over the term of the investment, then the choice of a participating GIC would make sense. But if rates are at moderate or higher levels and, thus, more likely to drop, then a nonparticipating GIC with a fixed rate of return might be preferable.

Question – How do the rates paid on GICs compare with the interest rates available on certificates of deposit (CDs) of comparable maturity?

Answer – In general, a non-participating GIC contract will pay a rate of interest about 1% higher than a comparable maturity CD.

Chapter 10

COMMON STOCKS

WHAT IS IT?

Common stock represents an ownership interest in a corporation. Each shareholder is entitled to a proportionate share of the control, profits, and assets of the corporation. Stockholders exercise control through voting rights and receive a share of corporate profits through dividends. In the event the corporation is sold or liquidated, owners of common stock will share the net proceeds.

WHEN IS THE USE OF THIS TOOL INDICATED?

1. When an investor is willing to accept the risk of fluctuating share prices in return for potential capital growth and increasing dividend income.

2. When the investor is concerned that the purchasing power of fixed income securities may not keep pace with inflation.

ADVANTAGES

1. Over the long run, common stocks have provided an average annual rate of return almost twice that of fixed income investments. Returns on stocks have averaged 9% to 10% over the past 50 years while fixed income securities such as corporate bonds and government securities have averaged only 4%. From 1996 through 2005, the Standard & Poor's 500 Stock Index averaged a compound annual rate of return of 9.02%.

2. Common stocks are highly marketable. This means that they can quickly and easily be converted to cash if necessary. This liquidity itself enhances their value.

3. The huge number of common stocks available makes it possible for investors to select securities that are compatible with their own particular investment requirements and risk-taking preferences. For example, public utility stocks have traditionally been

selected by investors with a preference for security and stable income while growth stocks may be more attractive to those who are willing to accept greater risk and do not need current income.

4. Unlike many real estate investments, common stocks do not require personal involvement in the day-to-day management of the enterprise. How much time the investor spends on managing his or her portfolio is another matter and depends on many variables including: personal preference and investment style; availability of time; and the degree of knowledge and skill of the investor.

DISADVANTAGES

1. The market price of stocks can fluctuate widely over time. Day-to-day changes in share prices are inevitable and beyond the investor's control. Even over fairly long time periods, stock prices can decline. For example, the S&P 500 Stock Index fell by 9.1% in 2000 and declined another 11.9% in 2001, and by 22.1% in 2002. However, this was the first consecutive three-year decline since the late 1930's. This volatility may be unsettling to conservative investors for whom preservation of capital is a high priority.

2. The prices of individual securities may be adversely affected by factors unrelated to the financial condition of the business itself. These may include political events, changes in tax laws or interest rates, and general economic conditions.

3. It is possible that an investor could lose all or a significant portion of his investment. For instance, if an individual were forced to sell shares during a depressed market, the result might be a permanent loss of capital.

4. Payment of dividends on common stock is not guaranteed. Although many corporations have traditionally paid regular dividends, declaration of a dividend, as well as the specific amount, is at the discretion of the corporation's board of direc-

tors. Thus, dividends may vary with changes in the general financial condition of a company. This would be a potential problem for investors who desire a regular income.

TAX IMPLICATIONS

1. Dividends on common stock are generally taxed as ordinary income. However, under JGTRRA 2003, "qualified dividend income" (generally, dividends paid by domestic corporations and certain foreign corporations to shareholders) is treated as net capital gain and is, therefore, subject to lower tax rates. For taxpayers in the 25% income tax bracket and higher (28%, 33%, and 35%), the maximum rate on qualified dividends paid by corporations to individuals is 15% in 2003 through 2010. For taxpayers in the 15% and 10% income tax brackets, the tax rate on qualified dividend income is reduced to 5% in 2003 through 2007, and all the way down to 0% in 2008 through 2010. The preferential treatment of qualified dividends as net capital gains will "sunset" (expire) on December 31, 2010, after which time the prior treatment of dividends will, once again, be effective.[1] In other words, dividends will once again be taxed at ordinary income tax rates.

2. Capital gains are taxable at various rates depending on the holding period of the investment. Short-term gains (12 months or less) are taxable at ordinary income tax rates up to a maximum of 35% (in 2006). Long-term gains (more than 12 months) are taxable at only a 5% rate for investors in the 10% or 15% brackets (in 2003 through 2007; 0% in 2008 through 2010), and 15% for investors in all other brackets in 2003 through 2010. On December 31, 2010, the lower capital gain rates (15%/0%) will "sunset" (i.e., expire), at which time the capital gain rates will return to pre-JGTRRA levels (i.e., 20%/10%).[2]

3. Losses on the sale of common stock will be short-term or long-term depending on how long the stock was held (see "Capital gain" in the Glossary for the necessary holding period). Capital losses are deductible dollar-for-dollar against short-term capital gain, long-term capital gain, and finally, to a limited degree, against ordinary income. Assume Dick Goldman had a capital "paper loss" of $8,000 and an actual realized short-term gain of $5,000 in the same year. If he sold the depressed shares and recognized the $8,000 loss, $5,000 of the loss would be used to wipe out the entire short-term gain. This would leave a $3,000 loss that could be used to re-duce his ordinary income. (The maximum amount of ordinary income that may be offset in one tax year is $3,000; any excess capital loss may be carried over to the succeeding tax year.) Qualified dividend income, which is treated as net capital gain under JGTRRA 2003, is *not* eligible to offset capital losses.

4. Year-to-year appreciation in share prices is not taxable unless and until the investor realizes the gain by selling the stock or otherwise disposing of it in a taxable transaction. This makes it possible to defer the gain until a tax year in which the investor is in a lower tax bracket. For example, Bob Norton might deliberately delay the sale of highly appreciated stock until after retirement when he will be in a lower tax bracket.

It may be possible to avoid taxation on the gain entirely. Generally, if an investor holds appreciated stock until his death, the gain is never taxed. This is because the "basis" of the stock is "stepped-up" to its fair market value for federal estate tax purposes. However, EGTRRA 2001 provides that for an individual dying in 2010, the basis of the property will generally be the lesser of (1) the basis of the decedent, or (2) the fair market value of the property at the time of death; although a stepped-up basis can be allocated to a limited amount of property. For individuals dying after 2010, the basis of inherited property will once again be the "stepped-up basis."

Example: Bob Norton purchased stock for $30 per share, and it is worth $130 per share at the time of his death. The new basis of the stock in his executor's hands would be "stepped-up" to $130. If the executor sold the stock the next day for $130 there would be no gain. This is because the "amount realized" ($130) minus the adjusted basis ($130) would be zero and, therefore, there would be no taxable gain.

ALTERNATIVES

1. Certain types of real estate investments offer similar features in regard to capital gain potential, deferral of taxation, and the opportunity for increasing income over time.

2. Convertible bonds (see Chapter 4) are often thought of as an alternative to more direct investments in common stock. Interest income will generally be greater than the dividends paid on common shares of equal value. The conversion feature offers the

potential for bondholders to share in the future appreciation of common stock.

3. Securities options ("puts" and "calls") give the investor the right to sell (in the case of puts) or buy (in the case of calls) a certain number of shares of stock at a fixed price for a limited period of time. Options provide the opportunity for substantial leverage based on a relatively small capital outlay. (See "Questions and Answers," below.)

WHERE AND HOW DO I GET IT?

Common stocks are typically purchased through a stock brokerage firm. Once an account is established by providing certain personal and financial information, brokers will transact orders for the purchase or sale of shares. These orders may be submitted in person but are commonly transacted over the telephone.

It is also possible to buy and sell securities directly through many banks, mutual funds, and other financial institutions. Although these institutions may not provide the full range of services offered by the typical brokerage firm, they generally charge substantially lower commissions to buy and sell shares.

Recently, investors have been able to buy and sell securities using personal computers and the Internet. Such electronic trading, often through discount brokerage firms or electronic communication networks (ECNs), is growing rapidly. One factor contributing to this growth is the very low cost of such transactions. Fees paid on these trades can be as low as $4, which is a small fraction of the regular brokerage commission charge.

Once stock has been bought or sold, the investor is notified by mail in the form of a written confirmation. The confirmation will show the date of the transaction, the name of the company involved, the number of shares, the transaction price per share, the total value of the transaction, and the commissions or fees charged.

The ownership of stock is evidenced by certificates.

Investors can have their broker send them the actual stock certificates or they can ask the broker to hold them for safekeeping. This relieves the investor of the expense and trouble of providing security for the shares and makes it easier and faster to sell the shares at a later date.

When shares are held by the broker on behalf of the investor, they are registered in the name of the broker. This is commonly referred to as holding shares in "street name." As long as shares are held in street name, any dividends paid on the stock are remitted to the brokerage firm that will pay them to the investor or retain them in the investor's account.

Many investors prefer to own common stocks indirectly through mutual funds. These funds provide a number of advantages such as: (1) diversification; (2) professional management; (3) automatic reinvestment of dividends; and (4) ease of record keeping. (See Chapter 16 for a more detailed discussion of mutual funds.)

WHAT FEES OR OTHER ACQUISITION COSTS ARE INVOLVED?

When common stocks are purchased directly from a broker or a bank, there is a sales charge commonly called a brokerage commission or fee. The amount of the fee will be dependent upon the amount invested and the number of shares purchased.

Commission charges will vary widely and investors should compare the rates charged by various sources when buying or selling shares. However, transaction costs are not the only factor to consider in buying or selling shares of stock. The information, advice, and other services that are provided by a firm may easily justify a higher commission rate.

HOW DO I SELECT THE BEST OF ITS TYPE?

1. Professional security analysts rate common stocks according to their (1) overall quality, (2) security, and (3) growth potential. The process involves an analysis of various factors such as product and industry position, corporate resources, and financial policy. Among the rating services that can be found in your local library (or on the Internet) are Standard & Poor's (www.standardandpoors.com), Moody's (www.moodys.com), the Value Line Investment Survey (www.valueline.com), and Morningstar (www.morningstar.com). Standard & Poor's and Moody's issue quality ratings for common stocks. These rankings do not take into account the current price of a stock, which is a critical factor in making a particular purchase or sale. A highly rated stock may be overpriced while a stock with a low rating may be attractively priced and a good buy. Standard & Poor's also publishes research that attempts to evaluate the prospects for a particular stock based on their proprietary research.

"The Value Line Investment Survey" contains a number of useful ratings. Each stock covered is rated for timeliness, safety, and technical analysis, and is also issued a financial strength rating, price stability score, growth persistence score and earnings predictability score. Conservative investors usually avoid those stocks rated "B" or lower by Standard & Poor's or those with a Value Line safety ranking lower than "3."

2. Extensive information and investment advisory services are offered by most brokerage firms. They can provide recommendations on specific industries or individual companies in the form of research reports by their own analysts. Brokerage firms also make available information that they in turn purchase from one or more professional research firms.

3. A wealth of information can be obtained at no cost by writing to the headquarters of a company and requesting a copy of its "annual report." This report contains information on the company's activities, its financial condition, products or services, general outlook, management personnel, dividend payments, and future prospects. A more detailed version of this report, known as a "10-K report," can also be obtained by writing to the company or to the Securities and Exchange Commission, Washington, D.C. Free annual reports are provided by the Wall Street Journal on the Internet at: http://wsjie.arwilink.com/asp/WSJ3_search_eng.asp.

4. Investors seeking current income should examine the dividend payment record of the stock in question. The services listed above will indicate the current dividend being paid on the stock, if any, and the amounts paid in prior years. Brokerage firms can provide lists of companies that have paid dividends consistently for many years and those firms that have increased their dividends regularly. The Value Line Investment Survey ranks stocks according to their current dividend yield percentage. This ranking would enable an investor to quickly select those stocks providing the highest level of dividend income per dollar of investment.

WHERE CAN I FIND OUT MORE ABOUT IT?

1. As noted above, your local library can provide a wealth of information on common stocks. In addition to receiving rating services such as Standard & Poor's or Moody's, many libraries will have a variety of books on investment, security analysis, portfolio management, and related topics. Periodicals such as Barron's, Business Week, Forbes, and Fortune regularly carry reports on various industries and individual companies. Larger libraries may have collections of annual reports received from individual companies, particularly those with headquarters located in the immediate area.

2. The Wall Street Journal (www.wsj.com), New York Times (www.NYTimes.com), and most major newspapers carry daily listings of the trading activity on the larger stock and bond exchanges. Virtually all of these newspapers have accompanying Internet sites with search capacities that can be used to gather investment information.

3. Research reports and other information on specific issues and current market conditions can be obtained by calling major brokerage firms and the trust departments of many banks.

4. A great deal of investment information is now available on the Internet using a personal computer. Most larger companies and many smaller ones provide their annual reports, press releases, and other useful information electronically. Additional information is available from the Securities and Exchange Commission (SEC) though its Electronic Data Gathering, Analysis, and Retrieval (EDGAR) website (www.sec.gov/edgarhp.htm).

5. There are many Internet sites offering a wide range of business information that can be used to analyze and evaluate common stocks. Among the most widely used are those maintained by the Bloomberg organization (www.bloomberg.com) and Yahoo (www.finance.yahoo.com).

QUESTIONS AND ANSWERS

Question – Of what value is a stock's "price/earnings ratio" in deciding whether or not it is a good buy?

Answer – The "P/E ratio" is simply the stock's current market price divided by the company's earnings. For example, a stock selling at $50 per share, with earnings of $2 per share, has a P/E ratio of 25 (50÷2). The investor should be careful to note which period's earnings are being used. Most often (e.g., a P/E from Yahoo or Bloomberg) the most recent 12-month's earnings will be used. In other cases, the investor will see P/E's based on calendar year earnings or the consensus of analysts' estimates for the next calendar year. The ratio can be compared with that of other similar companies to determine the relative value of various companies' earnings. An investor interested in a particular company could also compare the current P/E ratio with the historic high and low ratio for the same company. Larger, slow growing companies tend to trade at a more modest P/E than smaller, rapidly growing companies. For more information, please see Chapter 35 "Security Valuation."

Question – Why do some companies "split" their common stock?

Answer – The main reason for stock splits is to lower the stock's price per share. For example, if a stock were selling for $75 per share before a 3:1 split, after the split each shareholder would have three times the number of shares held previously but the price per share would now be $25. Many companies desire to maintain a relatively low stock price, between $20 and $50 per share, so that small investors can buy one hundred share lots. The purchase of one hundred shares of a stock is often called a "round lot." Unsophisticated investors typically love stock splits, and in fact, the stock will often respond favorably to such an announcement in the market. It is important to remember, however, that the owner is in exactly the same position as before—their ownership percentage is identical. They will own more shares, but each share will represent a correspondingly smaller percentage of the company.

Question – What is a "stock dividend"?

Answer – A stock dividend is a dividend paid in additional shares of stock rather than cash. Since all common stockholders receive their proportionate share of the dividend, the total value of all the common stock of the company is unchanged, while at the same time the value of each share is proportionately reduced.

Question – Will I receive dividends if I purchase a call option on a particular stock?

Answer – No, option holders are not entitled to receive dividends during the option period since they do not actually own the stock. Only the actual owner of the stock is able to receive dividends.

Question – When would it be desirable to buy a call option on a stock rather than the stock itself?

Answer – Investors utilize this tool because with a minimal outlay of funds they have the potential for greater capital gains than if they purchased the shares directly. This is a very high risk alternative which should only be attempted by sophisticated investors. Options expire at various points in time and the interplay between the option price and the underlying common stock fluctuates dramatically as the time to expiration approaches. (For a more complete explanation, see Chapter 13, "Stock Options," Chapter 41, "Hedging and Option Strategies," and Chapter 42, "Leveraging Investment Assets.")

Question – What is "selling short" and how does it work?

Answer – Selling short is a technique used by both aggressive and conservative investors. The aggressive investor who feels the price of the stock will fall can earn money by selling short. The conservative investor can use short selling to defer the tax on gains. Short selling means that you sell shares you "borrow" from a broker with the hope that the stock will decline in price in the near future.

Short selling works like this:

1. The client calls the broker and says, "Sell X number of shares of Y stock short."

2. The broker tells the client that the stock is currently selling for $U dollars per share. In a short sale the client must sell on an "uptick." That means he can sell only if the last sale was at a price higher than the sale preceding it. The client can specify a target price for the sale (this is called a "limit' order) or the client can specify that the stock is to be sold "at market" or on the next uptick.

3. Assume the stock "ticks up" to the sell price and the trade is executed. The broker will borrow shares from one of its customer's holdings to deliver to the buyer. (When the client signs the new account agreement with his or her broker, the investor is agreeing to let them do this.) The client will be charged the standard commission for selling the stock.

4. The purchaser of the stock pays the broker and in return receives the stock certificates.

5. The client must put up 50% of the value of the borrowed stock in cash (or 100% of the value of the borrowed stock in securities) since this is a credit transaction. The money or securities are placed in the client's margin account. Interest is typically not charged on the transaction since the broker has the proceeds from the short sale as well as the initial margin.

6. The client must then decide when to close out the short sale by buying the stock back. As long as the stock is falling, the investor can continue to compare the price with the company's prospects to time the buy-back. If the stock begins to rise, however, the investor has to calculate the risk of catastrophic loss. A buyer can only lose his or her investment. If they buy $10,000 worth of XYZ, they can lose $10,000 if the stock drops to zero. A short seller who sells short $10,000 can lose a theoretically infinite amount. If the shorted stock was selling at $10 per share and subsequently goes to $100 per share, it will cost the investor $100,000 to buy it back—10 times their original "investment." This is not a silly example. Ask anyone who shorted internet stocks in 1999. Their judgment regarding the ultimate viability of the company might have been precisely correct, but they went broke before they were vindicated!

Selling short is highly risky because if the stock goes up instead of down, the client will have to buy back the stock at its higher price. The leverage that increases the client's gain if he is right also increases his loss if he is wrong. If the stock increases rapidly in value, the stock brokerage firm will issue the client a "maintenance call" or "margin call." This is a notice from the firm that the client must put more money into his margin account. This call will typically be issued when the margin account balance (the sum of what the client put into the account plus the proceeds from the short sale) falls below 130% of the current market value of the stock. The broker will automatically close out the client's position if the additional call money is not added to the account. (Most experts advise that it is better to take the loss than to put up more margin and lose more money).

Selling short should be considered only if the client has: (1) researched the particular stock and the state of its industry group thoroughly; (2) checked the volume of short sales of that stock (if many others have also shorted the stock, when they begin to buy the stock to cover their positions, it may drive the price of the stock back up); (3) considered the tax implications (all gains from short sales will be taxed at ordinary rates regardless of when the short sale is covered); and (4) has sufficient resources to ride out an adverse environment.

Question – How can an investor evaluate new issues of stock?

Answer – New issues should be evaluated very much the same as seasoned stocks—very carefully, and according to a standard procedure. That procedure should include studying the prospectus. Specifically, look for positive answers to:

1. What does the firm do?

2. What is its major product?

3. Who are the firm's major competitors? Look for businesses with a unique product that cannot be quickly or easily copied by major competitors.

4. How long has the firm been in business and has it survived major economic downturns?

5. How stable and experienced is the management of the company and what exceptional talent or experience does it possess?

6. What is the size of the company's profit and what is the trend?

7. How large is the company?

8. What is the source of the company's revenues and how dependent is it on any one source?

9. What is unique about the company—not only from the positive side but also from the negative side (e.g., what unusual down side risks or liabilities does it have)?

10. Has the firm been audited by a national accounting firm and, if so, has the firm qualified its endorsement?

11. What is the expected dividend per share for the issue? (Find price/earnings ratio by dividing

net earnings for the latest 12-month period by the number of shares the company intends to issue.) Divide the expected offering price by the company's past earnings per share to estimate the price/earnings for the new issue. Most new growth-oriented companies have P/E ratios higher than the average S&P.

12. What are brokers and statistical studies saying about the stock? Independent services that can be found in public libraries or that can be purchased directly include: (a) *Standard and Poor's*

Emerging Markets Insight; (b) *The IPO Reporter;* and (c) *New Issues* (www.ipofnonline.com).

CHAPTER ENDNOTES

1. IRC Secs. 1(h)(1), 1(h)(11)(A), 1(h)(11)(B); Sec. 102, Tax Increase Prevention and Reconciliation Act of 2005, *amending,* Sec. 303, JGTRRA 2003.

2. IRC Sec. 1(h)(1); Sec. 102, Tax Increase Prevention and Reconciliation Act of 2005, *amending,* Sec. 303, JGTRRA 2003.

Chapter 11

PREFERRED STOCK

WHAT IS IT?

A preferred stock is a security that combines some of the features of both bonds and common stocks. Most preferred stocks do not carry voting rights under normal circumstances. Preferred stocks, as their name implies, have a preferred position with respect to the earnings of a corporation. Dividends on preferred stocks must be paid before any dividends can be paid to holders of common shares. Owners of preferred stock have precedence over common stockholders with respect to the assets of the corporation in the event of a sale or liquidation of the company.

WHEN IS THE USE OF THIS TOOL INDICATED?

1. When a current rate of return on investment at a rate higher than that available from the same company's common stock is desired.

2. When a fixed amount and steady flow of income is needed. Most preferred stocks pay a fixed dollar amount of dividend, or a dividend based on a stated percentage of the preferred stock's par value. For example, assume Citigroup has a 7% preferred stock issue outstanding. The stock pays a quarterly dividend of 44 cents per share in January, April, July and October.

3. When the purchaser of the stock is a corporation. Generally, a corporation is entitled to deduct 70% of the dividends it receives from other domestic corporations from its taxable income. Therefore, only 30% of the dividends received by a corporation are subject to federal income tax.

   If a corporation owned 500 shares of a $6 preferred stock, it would receive $3,000 (500 x $6) annually in dividends. The receiving corporation would have to declare 30% of those dividends, or $900 (30% x $3,000) as income. The remaining $2,100 would be excluded from federal income taxes.

   Current law allows accumulations of up to $250,000 ($150,000 for most professional corpora-

tions) even if the corporation is used to avoid personal income tax by allowing preferred dividends to accumulate at favorable corporate rates.

4. When there is no particular date on which the investor must have his capital returned. Unlike bonds, preferred stocks have no specified maturity date. In order to regain their capital, investors must sell their preferred shares. Preferred stocks give investors more control over the timing of their recovery of capital than they have with bonds.

ADVANTAGES

1. Income from preferred shares is relatively certain, especially when compared to dividends on common stock. Typically, dividends on preferred shares are paid on a quarterly basis. While preferred dividends are not a fixed, legal obligation (in the sense that interest on bonds must be paid to avoid default), they must be paid before any common shareholders can receive dividends. Although preferred stockholders typically cannot vote and demand payment of dividends, pressure from common shareholders who want dividend payments will make preferred dividend payments more likely.

   Perhaps even more important than pressure by common shareholders is the generally "cumulative" nature of preferred dividend payments. This means that any preferred dividends that are "passed" (not paid quarterly as anticipated) must be accumulated by the corporation and eventually paid before any dividends can be paid to common stockholders. For example, if Citigroup skipped payments of a quarterly dividend of 44 cents per share for one year on an issue of preferred stock, it would be required to make up the arrearage of $1.76 before resuming payment of common stock dividends.

2. The investor's capital is relatively secure. This is because after bondholders and other creditors, preferred shareholders take precedence over common stockholders in the event of a corporate sale or liquidation. If XYZ Corp. were to be liquidated,

for example, any assets remaining after creditors had been paid would be first allocated to preferred shareholders in proportion to the value of their interests. (In some cases, a corporation may have more than one preferred stock issue outstanding. Each of these issues would be assigned an order of priority in terms of sale or liquidation.)

3. The prices of preferred stocks tend to be more stable than those of common stocks. Common stock prices are affected most directly by changes in corporate earnings, which can be highly erratic. Preferred stock prices are more likely to reflect changes in interest rates, which are relatively less volatile than changes in the earnings of a corporation. This is especially true for high quality preferred stocks issued by financially sound companies.

However, when interest rates do decline, the prices of preferred shares tend to increase. Obviously, the opposite result occurs when interest rates rise; the price of preferred stocks will typically decline because investors can obtain higher rates on new issues of preferred stock or newly issued bonds. Moreover, since most preferred stocks do not have a maturity date, they have the characteristics of very long-term bonds and will fluctuate significantly more than a shorter-term, fixed income investment for any given change in rates.

4. Some preferred stocks are "convertible." This means that they may be exchanged at a predetermined rate for common stock of the same corporation at the discretion of the preferred stockholder. This will be advantageous when the price of common shares is increasing due to the fixed rate of exchange. Therefore, the preferred stock investor will be able to participate in the equity growth in a manner similar to common stockholders while retaining the relative security afforded the preferred shareholders.

DISADVANTAGES

1. The purchasing power of future fixed preferred stock dividends may be eroded by inflation. The longer the holding period of the investment, the more likely that the purchasing power of each fixed dollar payment will decline. For instance, assume inflation takes place at a 3% annual rate. A preferred dividend of $10.00 per year will have the purchasing power equivalent of only $7.37 ten years later.

2. Dividend payments on preferred stock will not increase even if the financial condition of the company

or the economy improves. Preferred shareholders do not participate in the growth and prosperity of their company in the same way as do common stockholders.

Some preferred stocks are "participating" issues. This means that preferred stockholders may be entitled to payments above the normal level of dividends in certain situations. This would occur once common stockholders had received dividends of a specified amount.

For example, the terms of the preferred stock issue may provide that once common shareholders have received dividends amounting to $5.00 per share, both common and preferred stockholders will share equally in any further dividend payments.

3. Preferred stocks do not provide much opportunity for capital growth. The fixed nature of the dividend payments and the lack of voting rights limit the market's enthusiasm for these issues. (As noted above, however, the convertibility feature of certain preferred stocks may offset this disadvantage and provide the opportunity for significant capital appreciation.)

TAX IMPLICATIONS

1. Dividends received on preferred stocks are generally taxable at ordinary income rates. However, under JGTRRA 2003, "qualified dividend income" (generally, dividends paid by domestic corporations and certain foreign corporations to shareholders) is treated as net capital gain and is, therefore, subject to lower tax rates. For taxpayers in the 25% income tax bracket and higher, the maximum rate on qualified dividends paid by corporations to individuals is 15% in 2003 through 2010. For taxpayers in the 15% and 10% income tax brackets, the tax rate on qualified dividend income is reduced to 5% in 2003 through 2007, and all the way down to 0% in 2008 through 2010. The preferential treatment of qualified dividends as net capital gains will "sunset" (expire) on December 31, 2010, after which time the prior treatment of dividends will, once again, be effective.[1] In other words, dividends will once again be taxed at ordinary income tax rates.

It is important to note that qualified dividend income does *not* include certain preferred stock dividends where the "dividend" paid on the preferred stock is structured and treated as debt by the company.

2. Profits on the sale of preferred shares are long-term or short-term capital gains depending on how long the stock has been held by an investor. (See "Capital gain" in the Glossary for an explanation of the holding periods.) *Net capital gains* (i.e., the excess of long-term capital gains over short-term capital losses) are generally taxable at a maximum rate of 15% (under JGTRRA 2003) through 2010.[2]

3. Losses on the sale of preferred stock are subject to capital loss rules. Certain limits are imposed on the utility of capital losses in offsetting ordinary income. Unused capital losses may be carried forward by individuals and applied against future income.

4. If a share of preferred stock is sold at a loss and then repurchased within a given time period, the investor will be subject to the so-called "wash sale" rules discussed in Chapter 43, "Taxation of Investment Vehicles."

5. Dividends received on preferred stocks of domestic corporations are subject to the "dividends received" deduction if the dividends are received by a corporate investor. Up to 30% of the dividend will be subject to corporate tax rates.

6. Preferred stocks held at death in the sole name of the investor will be subject to both federal and state death taxes. Fifty percent of preferred stocks held jointly between spouses will be includable in the gross estate of the first joint owner to die but will generate no federal estate tax because of the unlimited marital deduction.

ALTERNATIVES

1. Government, municipal, or corporate bonds generally will provide many of the same characteristics of high quality preferred stocks. Investors should consider bonds that generate a comparable or higher after-tax yield.

2. An investor considering convertible preferred stocks may wish to explore convertible bonds of the same or similar companies.

3. Single premium deferred annuities providing a fixed annual payment. (Until the annuity payout period begins, this alternative may not be suitable. In addition, unless the annuity has a guaranteed payout or a joint and survivor provision, the value of the annuity, unlike preferred stock, will terminate at the owner's death and provide no benefit to heirs.)

WHERE AND HOW DO I GET IT?

Preferred stocks may be purchased directly through a brokerage firm much like common stock, bonds, or other investments. They may also be purchased through banks which offer brokerage services and through discount brokerage houses.

Quite a few preferred stocks are listed on the organized stock exchanges such as the New York or American stock exchanges. Their listings are shown immediately below the listings for the same company's common stock. However, the majority of preferred issues are unlisted and trade on the over-the-counter market.

The trading in preferred stocks is dominated by corporations and other institutional investors. This is due to the dividends received deduction (discussed above) and tends to work against individual investors. Also, the market for preferred stocks is not as active as the market for common shares and trading volume is relatively low.

Individuals may also invest in preferred stocks indirectly through the purchase of shares in a mutual fund. Income funds, which emphasize a high rate of current return on investment, frequently purchase large blocks of preferred stock. The mutual fund approach offers the added attractions of diversification and professional management in addition to high yield and relative price stability.

WHAT FEES OR OTHER ACQUISITION COSTS ARE INVOLVED?

When preferred stocks are purchased through a broker, a regular sales commission is added to the price of the preferred shares. Typically, this brokerage commission will be 2 to 3% of the value of the shares purchased. Banks and discount brokers may charge a flat fee of $10 to $40 for buying shares or a fee based on the number of shares purchased regardless of price. For example, one discount brokerage house advertises that it will charge a fee of $0.10 per share no matter what the price of the stock, with a $30 minimum charge.

If shares are purchased indirectly through a mutual fund, the fund's regular sales fee will apply in the case of a "load" fund. If a "no-load" fund is used, there will be no sales charge added to the purchase price of the shares. Both types of funds will normally charge a management fee and an account maintenance fee in addition to any sales fees.

HOW DO I SELECT THE BEST OF ITS TYPE?

1. Since preferred stockholders are mainly interested in security and a high yield, the financial condition of the issuer is of primary concern. Investors should evaluate the soundness of the company or rely on the published ratings of firms such as Standard & Poor's or Moody's Investors Services. The following factors will be important in evaluating the company's financial condition:

(a) The company's earnings record, particularly the growth of earnings or at least a pattern of stable earnings during the past 10 years.

(b) Earnings available to pay preferred dividends should be several times the amount actually required. Preferred stockholders do not have first claim on a company's earnings. Earnings are first used to pay any interest due to bondholders. Then, preferred dividends are paid before any payments are made to common stockholders. The company should have enough earnings to pay interest and dividends even if earnings should decline for a year or two.

This concept of a "margin of safety" is important due to the limitations placed on the dividends from preferred issues. One prominent investment text states preferred stocks should be selected "on a recession or depression basis." Since preferred dividends will not be increased no matter how prosperous the firm may be, the investor must be more concerned with the payment of those dividends under the worst of circumstances.

(c) Since preferred dividends are paid from cash, investors should review the liquidity of the company before they invest. An attractive company will have a substantial cash position as well as large amounts of short-term assets.

(d) The preferred stock issue should be relatively small compared with the other capital of the firm. This means that the amount of preferred dividends will be a small obligation compared with bond interest or even common dividends. This relatively small size generally adds to the overall security of the issue.

2. Investors should compare the dividend yield available from a preferred stock with other issues of apparent similar quality. If one issue offers a rate of return substantially higher than other similar issues, it may be an indication of excessive risk and the stock should be avoided.

3. Depending on their own risk preferences, investors may want to compare the yields available from bonds as an alternative to a preferred stock. Bonds do provide a greater degree of security than preferred stocks because the interest payments on bonds must be made in order for the firm to avoid bankruptcy. Preferred dividends can be passed, or deferred, even if they are cumulative. This may be difficult for some investors, particularly those who are dependent on a regular flow of investment income.

WHERE CAN I FIND OUT MORE ABOUT IT?

1. Publications from Standard & Poor's and Moody's Investors Services are available at most local libraries. These will provide information on the issuing companies as well as the historical record of any preferred stocks.

2. Major brokerage firms can usually provide information on specific issues as well as current market conditions that may or may not make preferred stocks attractive for investment.

3. An investor interested in an issue of a particular company can write to the president or treasurer of the firm and request an annual report. This financial statement will provide details on the issue itself as well as the overall financial condition of the company.

QUESTIONS AND ANSWERS

Question – What does it mean when a preferred stock is "cumulative"?

Answer – The cumulative feature is common among preferred stocks. It means that any preferred dividends that are not paid as scheduled must be accumulated by the company and paid at some future date. No specific date is stated, but if any preferred dividends have not been paid the company is normally prohibited from paying any dividends to common stockholders. This feature puts management under pressure to maintain preferred dividends and provides greater security for preferred stockholders.

Question – When would a "convertible" preferred stock be a desirable investment?

Answer – A convertible preferred would be attractive when the price of the company's common stock is expected to go up. The price of the preferred will increase along with the common, but not necessarily in direct proportion. Rather than convert their stock, preferred shareholders may continue to hold it, particularly if the preferred dividend yield is higher than that on the common stock.

Question – Does preferred stock have voting rights?

Answer – Generally not. In exchange for their preferred status in regard to dividends and liquidation, preferred shareholders give up voting control of the corporation to common stockholders. However, if preferred dividends are in arrears, preferred stockholders may be given the same voting rights as common stockholders.

Question – Are preferred dividends taxable if the company has no earnings but continues to pay dividends?

Answer – If a company has no accumulated or current earnings, any "dividends" paid to stockholders, whether common or preferred, are really a return of capital and are not taxable as income to the shareholder. Under these circumstances dividends are not considered taxable income, but shareholders must reduce the cost basis of their stock to reflect the pay out of capital. This will result in a larger amount of taxable capital gain when the stock is eventually sold.

CHAPTER ENDNOTES

1. IRC Sec. 1(h); Sec. 102, Tax Increase Prevention and Reconciliation Act of 2005, *amending*, Sec. 303, JGTRRA 2003.

2. IRC Sec. 1(h); Sec. 102, Tax Increase Prevention and Reconciliation Act of 2005, *amending*, Sec. 303, JGTRRA 2003.

Chapter 12

WARRANTS AND RIGHTS

WHAT IS IT?

Warrants and rights are essentially long-term and short-term call options, respectively, to purchase shares of the stock of the corporation issuing the warrants or rights. That is, similar to regular call options, they give the owner the right for a specified period of time to purchase a specified number of the company's shares of stock at a specified price (the exercise, subscription, or strike price).

In contrast with listed call options, which typically give the owner the right to purchase 100 shares of the underlying stock, each right typically gives the owner an option to buy a fraction of a single share of the company's stock. Consequently, it generally requires several rights to purchase one additional share of the stock. Similarly, warrants generally do not give the owner the right to buy 100 shares of the stock. Warrants may give the owner the right to buy one or some other number of shares. In addition, in some cases the exercise price may not remain level throughout the term until expiration, but rather increase at scheduled times and in scheduled amounts throughout the term until it expires. Finally, in-the-money warrants may be callable. Corporations may sometimes call the warrants to force their exercise before the end of the specified term.

WHEN IS THE USE OF THIS TOOL INDICATED?

1. Corporations typically issue *rights* (sometimes called subscription rights) when the corporation plans to raise funds by selling additional shares of common stock to the public. Every current stockholder is typically given one right for each one share of stock they own (although, as mentioned above, each right may in turn only allow the purchase of a new partial share). These rights give the current stockholders the opportunity to buy shares of the new stock issue at a predetermined price for a very short period of time. Typically, the life of a right is just a few weeks and the exercise price is virtually always set "in the money," or somewhat below the subscription price of the new shares to the public, to encourage the purchase of additional shares.

2. Shareholders who wish to maintain their proportionate ownership of the firm can exercise their *rights* and purchase new shares at the price specified by the rights. Stockholders who do not wish to exercise their rights may sell them for cash before they expire (if there is an open market for them—this is usually, but not always, the case). If they do not sell them before they expire and do not exercise them, they expire worthless, similar to other options.

3. Corporations sometimes issue *warrants* in conjunction with new bond issues or preferred stock issues. These warrants give the bond or preferred stock purchaser what is sometimes called "an equity kicker," making the bond or preferred issue more attractive to buyers by allowing the owner the opportunity to someday exercise the warrant and enjoy the potential appreciation of the underlying stock. In addition, issuing the bonds or preferred stock with warrants will usually lower the interest rate or dividend rate necessary to sell the issue (because prospective purchasers will accept a slightly lower interest rate because of the extra income potential of the equity kicker). This lowers the company's cost of debt service or the payments required on the preferred stock. Therefore, it is an especially useful borrowing technique for young, potentially fast-growing companies whose current cash flow is clearly needed for their current operations and growth. The warrants are generally issued with an out-of-the-money exercise price and an expiration date ranging from three to five years (sometimes longer). As a result, in contrast with rights, the warrants have a speculative premium that is valuable to the owner, but they cannot be immediately exercised profitably. Consequently, there is no immediate dilution of the stock (or the concomitant dilution of control of the corporation).

4. Corporations, especially young, start-up firms or fast-growing firms, will sometimes issue warrants in lieu of cash payments for investment banking, legal, and other services. Once again, this is a technique that permits the firm to acquire needed services while preserving current cash flow for growth and operations. In addition, if the firm is growing successfully as time passes, the warrants provide a future source of equity financing.

5. For investors, *warrants* have virtually all the same characteristics and may serve most of the same objectives as call options or Long-Term Equity Anticipation Securities (LEAPS—options with expiration terms as long as 2 years and 8 months):

a) When they wish to speculate on an upward movement in the value of the stock;

b) When they wish to create a leveraged situation, since the price of the warrant will virtually always be less than the current value of the stock into which it can be converted;

c) When they have limited funds, but still wish to participate in the potential gains in a firm's stock; and

d) When an investor has sold the stock short, but wishes to hedge his position in the event the stock appreciates in value.

ADVANTAGES

1. Rights provide current shareholders with the opportunity to retain their proportionate ownership and control of a firm.

2. Rights help to increase the likelihood for the corporation that the new issue of stock will be fully subscribed.

3. Warrants provide the owner with the opportunity to participate in the potential appreciation of the stock with a small investment relative to the cost of purchasing the number of shares into which it may be converted.

4. The low unit cost of warrants, relative to the price of the firm's stock, creates leverage and enables an investor to magnify potential gains for a given level of investment.

5. Like other securities, warrants can be sold short to take advantage of an anticipated decline in the value of the underlying stock. This is somewhat analogous to writing a call option, except that the transaction is subject to the short-sale margin requirements.

DISADVANTAGES

1. The administration of the rights offering may slightly increase the corporation's cost for a new stock issuance.

2. In a similar manner to call options, warrants offer no current income; they pay no dividends.

3. Although warrants enable the owners to purchase shares of stock, they carry no voting rights (until the warrants are exercised and the underlying stock is acquired).

4. If the warrant has an expiration date, the risk of being stuck with a valueless asset increases as that date approaches.

5. Leverage is a two-edged sword. Especially if a warrant is in-the-money (the exercise price is less than the current market value of the stock into which it may be converted), downside moves by the stock price will result in a more than proportional percentage downward move in the value of the warrant.

6. In some cases, in-the-money warrants may be called by the company to force exercise before the scheduled end of the term of the warrant.

TAX IMPLICATIONS

Stock Rights

When stock rights are distributed to an investor, the investor is generally not required to recognize the receipt of the stock rights as a taxable event.[1] But if the stock rights are exercised or sold, the investor must refigure his tax basis in the stock by allocating part of the basis in the existing stock to the stock rights (providing cost basis if the rights themselves are sold). The allocated basis of the stock rights is in turn added to the cost of the stock acquired at exercise (if the investor chooses to exercise the rights). The allocation is based on the relative fair market values of the stock and the stock rights at the time the stock rights are distributed. The basis of the stock rights is increased, and the basis of the existing stock is decreased, by the proportional value of the existing stock and the stock rights to the total value of the existing stock and the stock rights.

Example 1: An investor owns stock in a company and receives a distribution of stock rights to purchase additional shares at $36 per share. At the time of the distribution, the fair market value of the stock is $36 and the fair market value of the rights is $9. The basis allocation is determined by examining the relative value of the rights ($9) to the total value of the existing stock and the rights ($9 + $36 = $45). Therefore, the basis allocation ratio for the stock rights is $9 / $45 = 20%, and the remaining 80% of the basis would be allocated to the existing stock. Thus, if the existing stock had a basis of $20, it would be reduced to $16 ($20 x 80% = $16). The basis of the rights would be $4 ($20 x 20%). If the rights were exercised, the cost basis of the rights would be added to the delivered new shares, for a total cost basis of $40 ($36 + $4 = $40).

If the fair market value of the rights is less than 15% of the fair market value of the underlying stock on the date of distribution, investors do not make any basis allocation (and the basis of the stock rights is $0) unless they take action and make an irrevocable IRC Sec. 307(b)(2) election to do so. They must file this election with their tax returns for the year of the stock rights distribution.

Example 2: An investor owns stock in a company and receives a distribution of stock rights to purchase additional shares at $36 per share. At the time of the distribution, the fair market value of the stock is $36 and the fair market value of the right is $4. There is no basis allocation because the value of the right ($4) is less than 15% of $36 ($5.40). The cost basis of the rights will be $0.

Example 3: Continuing the previous example, the investor makes an irrevocable 307(b)(2) election to allocate part of his stock basis to the stock rights. Assume the investor's stock basis is $20 per share. The investor allocates 10% or $2 ($4/($4 + 36)) per share to the stock rights and 90% or $18 per share to the existing stock. The investor's total basis in each share of stock acquired through the exercise of the stock right will be $38 per share.

Long-term or short-term capital-gains treatment depends on the holding period.

- If investors sell their rights, the holding period for that gain begins with the date they acquired the original stock.[2]

- If investors exercise their rights and then sell the new stock they acquire, they have a short-term gain, because the holding period for the stock begins on the date of the exercise of the rights and the acquisition of the new shares.[3]

Example 4: An investor owns stock purchased in June 1998. In June 2004, the investor receives stock rights to purchase additional shares. If the investor sells the rights two weeks later, she has a long-term gain or loss based on a holding period of six years (and based upon the cost basis determination as explained above). If she exercises the rights and then sells the stock she acquired from the exercise a month later, she has a short-term capital gain or loss based on a holding period for the new stock of one month.

If investors foolishly permit stock rights to expire unexercised, they recognize no gain or loss.[4] Thus, a right that is about to expire out-of-the-money leaves an investor with a choice: 1) to sell, allocate basis away from the stock to the right (facing a larger gain or smaller loss upon future sale), and take a loss on the sale of the rights immediately; or 2) to allow the right to expire worthless, and maintain a higher basis in the existing stock. Note that if the existing stock had already been held for more than one year (thus becoming eligible for long-term capital gains treatment), then a sale of the worthless right for a loss will be a long-term capital loss, subject to the capital loss restrictions. But in most situations, even a current long-term capital loss that may be carried forward is likely better than simply retaining higher basis in the existing stock, which may not be sold until the distant future.

Warrants

Warrants are taxed under the same general rules as options, when acquired other than as employment compensation or as compensation for services:

1. No gain or loss is recognized when a warrant is acquired.

2. The warrant holder recognizes gain or loss when (a) the warrant period ends and the warrant expires unexercised; or (b) when the option is exercised, usually there is no taxable event. If the warrant is exercised, usually there is no taxable event.

3. When a warrant is sold or expires, the character of gain or loss is generally as a capital asset (although this can vary depending upon the underlying property that is the subject of the warrant, and is not applicable if the holder is a dealer in securities).

4. When warrants are issued in conjunction with a bond offering (or preferred stock offering), the investors who purchase the bonds (or preferred stock) generally must allocate their basis in the bonds (or preferred stock) and the warrants in proportion to their respective market values when purchased or received (in a similar manner to that determined above for stock rights).

5. When a warrant is exercised, the stock basis is the exercise price increased by the premium paid (or basis allocated per item 4 above) for the warrant, if any, and transaction/commission costs. The stock's holding period begins on the date of acquisition.[5] The taxpayer cannot tack on the holding period of the warrant prior to its exercise.

6. Warrants received as compensation for employment or as compensation for services for the company are generally taxable as ordinary income at their fair market value on the date of receipt. This value then constitutes the basis in the warrants.

WHERE AND HOW DO I GET IT?

1. Rights are originally issued to the current shareholders of the company planning to raise new funds through a new stock offering. But the investment banker or underwriting syndicate handling the new issue usually makes a secondary market for the rights to permit existing shareholders who prefer not to exercise their rights to sell them to other current shareholders or to outside investors.

2. Warrants are originally issued along with new issues of bonds or preferred stock, as an "equity kicker." In addition, depending upon the size and strength of the issuing company, where its stock is listed or traded, and the number of the specific warrants in the market place, warrants may be listed on organized stock exchanges, listed on the NASDAQ, or traded over the counter. For small companies with relatively small numbers of warrants issued, the investment banking firm that originally assisted with the issuance generally makes a market for the warrants.

WHAT FEES OR OTHER ACQUISITION COSTS ARE INVOLVED?

1. Rights are given to existing shareholders at no direct cost. There is also no commission paid upon the exercise of rights to purchase new shares of stock. There is a relatively small commission paid to sell or buy the rights in the secondary market created by the investment banker or syndicate handling the new issue of stock.

2. Warrants received along with a purchase of new bonds or preferred stock have no additional cost—they are simply acquired as an attachment to the purchased bonds or stock. Warrants bought or sold on listed exchanges, on the NASDAQ, or over the counter are subject to the same types of commissions as other securities.

HOW DO I SELECT THE BEST OF ITS TYPE?

Obviously, since warrants are essentially equivalent to long-term call options, the criteria for selecting the best warrants are similar to those for selecting the best call options. Warrants for stocks of companies with strong growth potential and low dividend payout ratios offer the most promising returns. For trading purposes, warrants with longer terms until expiration and for companies whose stocks are more volatile offer a greater chance of significant movements in the value of warrant.

ALTERNATIVES

1. Although much shorter in duration, call options otherwise have virtually the same characteristics as warrants. They enable the owner to purchase a certain number of shares of stock at a fixed price for a given period of time. They also provide similar leveraging opportunities and the ability to participate in the "action" of the stock at less than the full cost of buying the shares outright.

2. LEAPS (Long-Term Equity Participation Securities) are long-term listed options with expiration terms up to 2 years and 8 months—closer to the usual term of warrants. These instruments have characteristics quite similar to warrants and other call options.

3. With the advent of single-stock futures (SSFs), certain combinations of long and short positions in SSFs, straddles, or spreads, permit investors to create a "package" or "synthetic" investment with the risk, return, and leverage characteristics comparable to that of options or warrants on individual stocks.

4. If the primary interest of the investor is simply to maintain proportionate ownership in the underlying stock for investment or control purposes, he can (generally) always purchase the underlying stock itself on the open market.

Likewise, since rights are very similar to short-term call options, the criteria for selecting the best rights are similar to those for selecting the best short-term calls. Because of their short-term nature, rights purchased in the secondary market are usually purchased as a leveraged mechanism to speculate in the short-term movements of a stock. Rights that were originally distributed directly to an investor might be sold to enjoy a slight premium for the speculative value of the rights (although, because of the short-term nature of rights, this speculative premium will likely be very small, or simply non-existent), over and above the in-the-money exercise value, if they can be sold at a higher after-expenses/after-commission cost. In addition, the rights can be exercised at any point to acquire the underlying stock for its future growth potential, or to receive the stock for immediate sale.

WHERE CAN I FIND OUT MORE ABOUT IT?

Warrants are somewhat of a niche area of specialization within the investment community and there is generally much less information available regarding warrants than options and other types of securities. But the large brokerage firms have specialists who concentrate on warrants (and generally options and LEAPS) and they occasionally publish reports on warrants.

Stockwarrants.com (http://www.stockwarrants.com) advertises on its home page that it "is the internet's only coverage/analysis service for American warrants. In fact, you won't find better overall coverage of the stock warrant universe in any media."

QUESTIONS AND ANSWERS

Question – What is the value of a right?

Answer – If a firm that currently has 18 million shares of stock outstanding wants to issue and sell an additional two million shares, it might initiate a rights offering. The firm issues 18 million rights, one for each share of currently outstanding common stock. There is no charge to the shareholders to receive rights. Under the terms of the rights offering, it would take 9 rights in addition to a set price for the stock to buy one share of the newly issued common stock.

Suppose the firm's common stock is currently selling for $60 a share and each right gives the owner the opportunity to purchase one-ninth of a new share of common stock at $55 a share. It then takes 9 rights plus $55, the subscription or exercise price, to

purchase a share of the newly issued common stock. The rights have an expiration date, say two weeks after they are issued, during which the owners have the opportunity to exercise the rights.

Since the time until expiration is generally very short, rights typically have little or no speculative premium like other options. Consequently, the value of a right can be determined by the following approximation formula.

$$\text{Value of a right}^6 = \frac{\text{Market price of the current stock} - \text{subscription price of the new shares}}{\text{Number of rights required to purchase one new share of stock} + 1}$$

$$\text{Value of a right} = \frac{\$60 - \$55}{9 + 1} = 50 \text{ cents}$$

As long as the price of the firm's stock remains at $60 a share, the value of each right will be 50 cents. For each 9 rights the investor has, the investor can add $55 and buy a share of stock currently worth $60 a share. If the investor chooses not to exercise the rights, it pays to sell them to other investors who will then buy shares of stock in the corporation.

Due to their short life span, rights do not offer much in the way of trading possibilities. But sale of the rights in the secondary market may allow the investor to harvest the value of the rights received, without actually having/using the cash that would be necessary to exercise the rights (e.g., $55 per 9 rights in the example above).

Question – What happens to a warrant if the company announces a stock split or pays a major stock dividend?

Answer – The exercise price of the warrant would be adjusted to reflect the stock split or stock dividend. If the warrant gave the holder the right to purchase one share of common stock for $100 a share before the two-for-one stock split, the holder would have a right to buy two shares of stock for $50 a share after the split. Just as the underlying total value of a stock does not change after a stock split, the underlying total value of a warrant will not change as well. But a change in the average share price (due to the stock split or stock dividend) could affect the overall liquidity or trading tendencies of the stock, which may ultimately affect the speculative premium associated with the warrant.

Question – How is the fundamental value of a warrant determined?

Answer – As with all stock derivatives, warrants derive their value from the price of the underlying stock. Similar to options, warrants possess what is called a fundamental (or intrinsic) value. In addition to this, warrants (and other options) also possess a time (or speculative) value, which is often called the warrant premium. Whenever the market price of the underlying common stock is equal to or higher than the warrant's exercise price (the warrant is in the money), the fundamental or intrinsic value of the warrant is positive and can be determined by the following equation:

Fundamental value of a warrant =
$(M - E)$ x N

The terms in the equation are defined as follows:

M = The current market price of the common stock.

E = The exercise price of the warrant.

N = The number of shares of common stock that the holder can acquire with one warrant.

For example, suppose that a corporation's common stock has a current market price of $80, the corporation has warrants outstanding with an exercise price of $74, and that it takes one warrant to purchase one share of common stock. Using these numbers in the equation above, we can see that the fundamental value of a warrant equals $6 ($80 - $74) x 1.

In other words, at the current price of the common stock, $80 per share, each warrant (with an exercise price of $74) is worth $6; that is, it has a fundamental value of $6.

Notice that as the market price of the underlying stock increases, the value of the warrant goes up dollar for dollar with the stock price. This happens as long as the current market price of the stock at least equals or exceeds the exercise price of the warrant and that one warrant can be exchanged for one share of common stock. If the price of the common stock goes from its current level, $80 a share, to $86 a share, the stockholders will receive a 7.5% increase in the value of their investment. But the fundamental value

of the warrant will go from $6 to $12, a doubling in its value. It is immediately apparent that there is a much greater potential for gain in the warrants than in the common stock.

In addition to the fundamental value of the warrant, as determined above, bear in mind that the warrant will also have some additional value attributable to the speculative value, or warrant premium.

Question – What is a warrant premium?

Answer – The equation in the previous question was used to show how the fundamental value of a warrant is computed. In the market place, But warrants are rarely priced that way. The market price of a warrant usually exceeds its fundamental value. For instance, a warrant with a negative fundamental value will always trade for some positive price until it expires. Also, warrants with positive fundamental values often trade at much higher market prices than their fundamental value. This difference between the fundamental value of a warrant and its market price is known as warrant premium.

Question – Why do warrants trade at a premium?

Answer – The reason warrants trade at a premium is that warrants have speculative value. The size of the premium is directly related to the time the warrant has until expiration and the volatility of the underlying common stock. For the most part, the longer the time a warrant has to expiration and the more volatile the underlying common stock, the greater will be the size of the warrant premium. Usually the amount of the warrant premium decreases as the fundamental value of the warrant increases. That is, as warrants increase in price, the speculative premium they command generally declines. This is because, as the fundamental value increases, the relative leverage of the warrant decreases—a $1 price increase has a lesser relative impact on a warrant with a $20 fundamental value (a 5% increase) than on one with a $5 value (a 20% increase). This decrease in the impact of price changes when fundamental value is high reduces the speculative value and, accordingly the speculative premium, of the warrant (because for a given level of price volatility, one cannot earn as large a relative profit through price speculation).

The value of a warrant (and many other publicly traded options) is commonly measured by the Black-Scholes method. This formulation incorporates the value of the warrant's (or other option's) fundamental and speculative value. Although there are many criticisms to the Black-Scholes method, particularly regarding options that are not publicly traded (such as many types of restricted employee stock options), it is still the most common method used to evaluate publicly-traded options, including warrants.

Question – Why buy the warrant instead of the stock?

Answer – Investors buy warrants instead of the stock for the following reasons:

- Lower unit cost;

- Greater price volatility (for speculative leverage); and

- Potential for higher rates of return on investment.

For example, assume the current price of the common stock of XYZ Corporation is $70; the exercise price of a warrant to purchase one share of XYZ is $65; and the current price of the warrant is $10 (selling at a $5 premium).

	XYZ COMMON	XYZ WARRANT
Current price	$70	$10
Price after the common increases by $10	$80	$20
Change in market price	+$10	+$10
Percentage change in price	$10 / $70 = 14.3%	$10 / $10 = 100%

The rate of return provided by the warrant is substantially higher than provided by the common stock. If the investor is confident in the long-term prospects of XYZ (within the term limit of the warrant), his rate of return is potentially higher by purchasing an XYZ warrant rather than XYZ common stock. In addition, if the investor seeks to speculate on short-term price movements in XYZ common stock, he can earn a substantially higher short-term return through the "leverage" obtained by purchasing an XYZ warrant.

But it is critically important to bear in mind the possibility for an adverse result. If XYZ common stock were to decline, rather than increase, by $10 / share, the results are dramatically different.

	XYZ COMMON	XYZ WARRANT
Current price	$70	$10
Price after the common *decreases* by $10	$60	$0
Change in market price	-$10	-$10
Percentage change in price	-$10 / $70 = -14.3%	$10 / $10 = -100%

In this case, a $10 decline in the price of XYZ common stock could result in a 14.3% loss for an investor in XYZ common stock, but a 100% loss (the investor's ENTIRE investment amount) for the holder of XYZ warrant.

In point of fact, the investor would not likely experience an entire loss, because the warrant may still have a slight speculative value remaining, but the increased risk of warrants, as illustrated in the above scenario, should be evident.

Question – How do investors trade with warrants?

Answer – In general, warrants can be traded by aggressive investors to take advantage of the embedded leverage and magnify returns. For example, an investor wants to invest $7,000 to enjoy an expected rise in the price of XYZ common stock. If the investor purchases 100 shares of common stock with the $7,000 and the price of the stock rises by $10/share to $80, he will have a $1,000 capital gain for a 14.3% return on his investment. On the other hand, the investor could use the $7,000 to purchase 700 warrants. In this case a $10 increase in the price of the common stock will cause the warrants to go from $10 each to about $20 each. This gives the investor a 100% increase in his original investment—a total return of $7,000 on his $7,000 investment (final proceeds = $14,000). So instead of receiving a $1,000 return, the investor receives a $7,000 return on the original $7,000 investment, for the same price increase. (NOTE: the warrant values in reality would likely be slightly higher than reflected here, as the warrant would have some speculative value as well—but the underlying point of leveraged investing still applies).

Question – What are the drawbacks of using this aggressive approach?

Answer – Warrants pay no dividends and the gains must be made before the warrants expire. Consider the potential exposure to loss of the investor described above. Instead of assuming the price of the stock increases by $10, suppose instead it decreases by $10. This slight decrease in price will wipe out the entire $7,000 of the warrants' fundamental value (and thus, aside from some small remaining speculative value, will wipe out the investor's entire $7,000 investment). But the $7,000 invested in the shares of the firm's stock will decrease only by $1,000. The market value of the investor's 100 shares would now be down to (only) $6,000.

Question – How can conservative investors use warrants?

Answer – Conservative investors can use warrants to reduce the amount they invest and to limit their potential losses, because of the reduced unit cost of warrants. For instance, instead of investing $7,000 to buy 100 shares of the common stock, the investor invests only $700 to buy 100 warrants. The $10 increase in the price of the common stock will give the investor who bought the stock a $1,000 capital gain. But the investor who purchased 100 warrants for $700 will also have a $1,000 capital gain on the same increase in the price of the underlying stock. On the down side, the conservative investor could lose no more than the investor's initial investment of $700. A person who invested $7,000 in the stock, however, could lose much more than $700 if the price of XYZ common stock decreases below $63 per share.

Question – I have a warrant that seems to fit the description of a stock right. Which is it?

Answer – The market occasionally intermixes the terms of warrant and stock right. In practice (and for tax purposes), the controlling factor is generally how the option was actually obtained. If it was received as compensation or as part of the purchase of a corresponding debt instrument or preferred stock, it is a warrant. If the options were distributed to existing shareholders as an opportunity to purchase additional shares, they are stock rights. Occasionally individuals will receive stock rights that are "labeled" as warrants.

CHAPTER ENDNOTES

1. Generally, stock rights distributions are nontaxable. But in rare instances a rights distribution will be taxable—this is the case if the investor is given the choice between receiving rights or other property, such as cash. In this case, the rights distribution itself is treated as a dividend to the extent of the fair market value of the rights (and subject to certain restrictions based upon the earnings and profits of the corporation).

2. IRC Sec. 1223(5).

3. IRC Sec. 1223(6).

4. Rev. Rul. 74-501, 1974-2 CB 98.

5. IRC Sec. 1223(6); *Weir v Comm.* 10 TC 996 (1984) *aff'd per curiam,* 172 F.2d 222 (3d Cir. 1949).

6. The denominator must equal the number of rights required to purchase a new share + 1 in order to adjust for the effects of dilution. The current market value of the company's shares is 18 million × $60 = $1.08 billion. If 2 million shares of stock are issued with a subscription price of $55 per share, the additional value of this new capital to the firm equals 2 million × $55 = 110 million. Therefore, the total market value of the firm should be close to $1.19 billion. If $1.19 billion is divided by 20 million shares, the resulting market value per share should be $59.50. In other words, the value of the shares after the rights expire have to equal the value of the shares before the rights expire less the value of the expired rights, assuming that all rights are exercised.

Chapter 13

STOCK OPTIONS

WHAT ARE THEY?

An *option* is a contract that is bought and sold—it gives the buyer and holder a right (but not a requirement) to force the seller of the contract to complete a certain transaction. The transaction is generally for a certain amount of goods (i.e., shares of an underlying stock) at a specified price at a certain point in time when the contract is set to expire (or for some contracts, anytime in the specified period of time before the contract expires). Options are a form of *derivative* instrument—so named because their value is a derivative of the price of the underlying stock (or other property) that they are associated with.

A *call option* is a contract that gives the holder the right to purchase a specified number of shares of common stock at a fixed price for a stated period of time. For example, an investor who anticipated an increase in the price of ABC stock could purchase a call option for 100 shares instead of the stock itself. The call option might have a term of nine months and would have a fixed exercise price. At any time during the period of the contract, the holder could exercise his option and purchase 100 shares of the stock at the stated price regardless of how high the actual price of ABC had risen.

A *put option* is a contract that gives the holder the right to sell a specified number of shares of common stock at a set price for a given period of time. For example, if an individual owned 100 shares of ABC and expected the price of the stock to decline, he could purchase a put option giving him the right to sell his shares at a stated price any time during the term of the option contract regardless of the actual market price of ABC stock (the benefit being that, if the market price in fact rose instead of declining, the individual would still own the stock).

Most investors typically think of either buying or selling the stock itself. But, since both puts and calls are property, these may be bought or sold independently of the underlying stock. Investors may buy or sell either (or both) of these contracts depending upon their own investment strategies. For instance, Charlee Leimberg expects ABC to increase in value and therefore buys a call that gives her the right to purchase 100 shares of the stock at a fixed price, say $65, for the next six months. Assume that the current market price of ABC is $62 per share. The cost of her call option might be $2 per share, or $200 for the contract ($2/share x 100 share bundle).

If the market price of ABC stock were to jump to $70 per share, the value of her call would also increase. The minimum value of the contract would be $500 (the difference between the market price of $70 and her exercise price of $65 times the 100 shares associated with the contract). The value of her contract could actually be higher than $500 if the contract still had a significant amount of time until the expiration date. That is because investors might anticipate further appreciation in the value of the stock, which in turn would be reflected in the price of the call option.

Charlee's sister, Lara, might have an entirely different opinion about the price of ABC stock. If she expects the price to decline, she may decide to sell a call on 100 shares of the stock. This means that Lara would be on the "other side" of her sister's transaction—she would receive $200 in return for agreeing to sell 100 shares of the stock at a price of $65 per share any time during the next six months. If the price of ABC remains below $65 per share, Charlee will let her option to buy the stock expire (since it would not behoove her to utilize the option to purchase the stock at $65/share from Lara when she could purchase it outright in the market for less), and the right that she never used will have cost her $200. Lara, on the other hand, will have a profit of $200 from the transaction and will not have to deliver the stock.

Put options work as a natural opposite to call options. An investor would buy a put if he expected a stock's price to decline. The put would give him the right to sell at a fixed price higher than the actual market price of the stock. If John Mullen expects ABC to decline from its current price of $62 per share, he could purchase a put option that would give him the right to sell the stock at a price of $60. If the share price were to fall to $58, he could exercise his option and receive $60 per share instead of the lower market price.

The seller of a put contract expects the market price of the stock to remain stable or to increase. John's associate, Mike Dunleavy, feels that the price of ABC will not go below $60 per share and offers to sell a put at that price for $1 per share. If he is correct, then the option will not

Tools & Techniques of Investment Planning

be exercised, he will not have to purchase the stock, and he will have a profit of $100. If the stock's price does decline, the option will be exercised, and Mike will have to purchase the stock for $60 per share even though the actual market price may be significantly less—he might pay $60/share (as required by the put option) for a stock that might only be valued in the open market for $55/share. However, his "loss" of $500 (100 shares x $5/share of "excess" purchase price above the current market value) will be offset by the $100 premium he received for selling (also called *writing*) the contract.

WHEN IS THE USE OF THIS TOOL INDICATED?

1. When investors wish to speculate on a movement in the stock market—either up, down, to stay within a certain range, or to move outside a certain range—without actually buying or selling stocks themselves.

2. When an investor wishes to create a leveraged situation in his investment portfolio. In this case the leverage comes about due to the fixed price at which either a put or a call contract is exercised. This price, referred to as the *exercise price* or *strike price*, does not change during the life of the contract regardless of the movements in the price of the underlying stock.

   Example: Assume a stock is currently selling for $60 per share. A call option is available on that same stock and has an exercise price of $55 per share. The option alone will sell for at least the $5 per share difference between the stock price and the exercise price (and possibly for more). If the price of the underlying stock were to double to $120 per share, the investor who merely purchased the stock would have a gain of 100% (($120 - $60) / $60 = 100%). If the stock did increase to $120 per share, the value of the option would increase to at least $65 per share ($120 - $55 = $65)—however, the original purchase price of the option was only $5! This is an increase of 1300% (($65 / $5 = 1300%), a return that is 1200% higher than that earned with the purchase of the stock.

3. When an investor has limited funds but still wishes to speculate with some of his investments. Puts and calls are generally traded at small fractions of the price of their underlying stocks. For example, if IBM Corp. stock were selling at $70 per share, a call option to purchase 100 IBM shares at an exercise price of $70 might trade for $200 to $300, whereas the purchase of 100 IBM shares at $70 per share would be $7,000.

4. When an investor wishes to generate additional income from a stock portfolio without initially selling any of the positions. By selling call options on shares in his portfolio to speculators, the writer of these options can receive a fee or "premium" for taking part in the contract. For instance, Lara Leimberg, in the example above, received $200 for selling a call contract, and if the call option wasn't exercised, she would still be able to keep her underlying stock as well. Note, however, that if the stock price does rise such that the call option is exercised, the call writer will be required to provide stock to the option buyer at the specified strike price.

5. When an investor desires to "hedge" a stock or his entire portfolio against unexpected declines or other unfavorable moves in the price of the stock. John Mullen, in the example above, was protecting himself against a substantial decline in the value of his ABC shares by buying a put contract. The option guaranteed him a right to sell his stock at a minimum price of $60 per share, which might turn out to be much higher than the actual stock price in the event of a decline (thus hedging and preserving his account against the decline).

ADVANTAGES

1. The fixed exercise price of these option contracts creates a *leverage* factor that may be advantageous to the investor. For example, if a common stock were to double in value, a 100% increase, the value of a call option on the same stock might increase as much as 500% or more.

2. Option trading requires a relatively small investment on the part of the investor.

3. Income earned from the sale of either put or call contracts is paid to the investor immediately no matter what the term of the contract may be.

4. An investor can substantially hedge the risk of most or all of her potential portfolio losses without actually selling the underlying stock positions until desired.

Stock Options

DISADVANTAGES

1. Leverage operates in both directions, and a decline (rise) in the price of a stock will typically result in a much larger percentage loss for the buyer of a call (put) option. For example, if stock purchased at $60 per share were to drop to $30, the result is a 50% decline in market value. If an investor purchased an option to buy the stock at $55 per share when the market price was $60 per share, the call would have been worth at least $5 per share. But, when the stock drops to $30 per share, the value of the option will become almost nil—a 100% loss!

2. Both puts and calls have a relatively short life span—typically not more than nine months. In recent years, a new form of options have become available called LEAPS (Long-term Equity Anticipation Securities)—these long-term options generally have terms extending as far as 2 years and 9 months from issue. In either case, options are sometimes referred to as "wasting assets" because they will be of no value after a particular point in time, the expiration date—unless the stock price does in fact move (or not move) as desired.

3. Call options, though they enable the holder to purchase shares of common stock, have neither voting rights nor are they entitled to receive any dividends declared and paid during the term of the option. Even though the life of an option is relatively short (no more than nine months) this lack of income can be an important (and/or costly) disadvantage.

TAX IMPLICATIONS

1. Options generally are classified as capital assets for tax purposes[1], though they are subject to some special rules because of their unique nature. See the discussion of capital gains and losses in Chapter 43, "Taxation of Investment Vehicles."

2. Investors who buy call options will have a capital gain or loss if the option is sold in a "closing" transaction. Gain or loss is calculated by subtracting the sale price of the option from the purchase price (including any brokerage fees included in either transaction).[2] Because exchange-traded call options are issued for a term of only nine months, any capital gain or loss will be short-term.

3. No gain or loss is realized upon the exercise of a call option. A capital gain or loss is realized only when the stock acquired through exercise of the call is

sold.[3] The cost of the call is added to the purchase price of the stock in computing the gain or loss for tax purposes. The holding period is measured from the day after the call option is exercised, not from the date the call was purchased.[4]

4. Investors who write calls or purchase put options and then close out their positions by repurchasing them will recognize any capital gain upon the closing. However, since dispositions involving options are subject to the wash sale rule, loss on the sale of a call option within 30 days before or after the date of purchase of substantially identical stocks or securities may not be recognized. Instead, such a loss will generally increase the basis of the replacement stock or securities. It is important to note that an option to acquire or sell an underlying stock, and the underlying stock itself, are considered substantially identical property for the purposes of the wash sale rules.[5] If the option expires unexercised, the investor will realize a short-term capital gain.

5. An investor who writes a call option that is exercised will realize a capital gain or loss upon exercise. The capital gain or loss is actually realized on the underlying stock that must be sold/delivered to the call option buyer—the premium the investor received for writing the call is added to the selling price of the stock in calculating the amount of capital gain or loss.[6]

6. Exercising a put option constitutes a sale of the stock and is a taxable event. The cost of the put is subtracted from the selling price of the stock in computing capital gain or loss for tax purposes. The date of exercise of the put option is treated as the sale date of the stock.[7]

7. Investors who write puts and repurchase their put obligations will realize a short-term capital gain or loss on the closing. If the option expires unexercised, the investor will realize a short-term capital gain, because exchange-traded call options are issued for a term of only nine months.

8. When a put option is exercised, the writer is required to purchase the stock put to him. However, this is not treated as a taxable event for the writer of the put contract. Instead, the put writer deducts the premium received for writing the put from the purchase price of the stock.[8] The holding period for the stock is measured from the date of exercise of the put.[9]

9. The tax consequences of many options structures become more complicated when multiple options are held at once, and/or including positions in the underlying stock. See Chapter 41, "Hedging Option Strategies," for further tax consequences of more complex options strategies.

ALTERNATIVES

1. Stock purchase warrants have many of the same features as call options. They enable the owner of the warrant to purchase a certain number of shares of stock at a fixed price for a given period of time. The original term of the warrant is generally much longer than a put or call option, frequently lasting for several years. However, warrants are offered by corporations and are frequently issued in connection with the sale of other securities such as bonds or preferred stock. Some warrants are listed on the organized securities exchanges, but the majority are traded in the over-the-counter market. The fixed exercise price of warrants creates the same type of leverage provided by options. Additional information on stock warrants can be found in Chapter 12, "Warrants and Rights."

2. Stock "rights" are another form of option that enables existing shareholders to purchase new stock being issued by a corporation. Generally one right is issued for each share of stock an investor owns, and the rights entitle the stockholder to purchase additional shares at a stated price (or often fractional shares—sometimes it will take multiple rights to purchase a single share of stock). Rights have an extremely short life span and generally must be exercised within a month or so of the new stock offering. Additional information on stock rights can be found in Chapter 12, "Warrants and Rights."

WHERE AND HOW DO I GET IT?

Put and call stock options are traded on several organized exchanges, most of which are related to stock exchanges. The first exchange to be organized especially for trading of options was the Chicago Board Options Exchange (CBOE), which began operating in April, 1973. The CBOE was an extension of the Chicago Board of Trade that had a long history of trading options on agricultural commodities. Since 1973, trading in puts and calls has extended to the American Stock Exchange, the Pacific Coast Stock Exchange, the Philadelphia Stock Exchange, and the New York Stock Exchange. Several firms oper-

ate as market-makers at the various exchanges to help maintain liquidity and fair pricing for all traded options. Options traded through all of these exchanges are ultimately issued and maintained by the Options Clearing Corporation (OCC). Today these options may be traded on more than 1,500 different underlying stocks.

The formal organization of options contracts has brought tremendous popularity to the options markets because of the fact that all exchange-traded options contracts are standardized (i.e., all based upon the same terms). This allows all buyers and sellers to know exactly what they are receiving in the options contract (aside from their possibly differing beliefs about the underlying stock), which makes the contracts easier to evaluate, and far more liquid.

Buying or selling puts and calls is very similar to buying or selling the underlying stocks. However, option trades must be made through a "margin account" that allows a customer to buy securities with money borrowed from a broker. Transactions are made through brokerage firms that relay the orders they receive to the trading floors of the options exchanges. Orders are carried out by the exchange and the results of the trade are reported back to the brokerage firm, which in turn notifies its customer.

To execute a transaction an investor can merely call his broker and state, "Please purchase 5 ABC April-60 call option contracts for my account." A written record of the trade automatically will be sent to the buyer or seller of the trade option contract confirming the transaction. This is the only evidence of the purchase or sale that the investor will receive. This is due to the fact that the option is a contract to buy or sell rather than an actual security.

Once a trade has been made, the position of the buyer or seller remains "open" until one of three events occurs:

1. *The option may expire without being exercised.* Expiration of an option series will "close out" all positions open at that time. This is the result frequently desired by sellers of call options who hope to keep the premium they received and to keep their shares of stock as well.

2. *The option may be exercised and the underlying shares of stock will have to be transferred.* For example, if a call option is exercised, the seller will have to deliver shares of stock at the exercise price to be paid by the buyer of the call.

3. *The buyer or seller of the option may close out his original position.* This is done simply by entering an order opposite to the first order. For instance, assume Greg Murphy had purchased a put option allowing him to sell GM stock at a price of $70 per share. Greg now wishes to close out his position and may do so by *selling* the exact same option contract. The two option contracts offset each other and, at that point, Greg has neither an option to buy or sell. He may have had a profit or loss on his original position. The amount of the gain or loss will depend upon the change in price of the initial option contract from the date of purchase or sale until the position is closed. For example, Greg may have paid $5 per share, or $500 in total, for the original put option. If the contract were selling for $300 when he closed out his position, he would have a loss of $200 on the transaction.

WHAT FEES OR OTHER ACQUISITION COSTS ARE INVOLVED?

Commissions on the purchase or sale of option contracts are similar to those paid on other security transactions. Brokerage firms typically charge a percentage of the value of the transaction with a minimum commission of $25 or $30. For example, a single contract trade amounting to $250 may involve a commission of $25. Ten contracts amounting to $2,500 may result in a commission of $150.

HOW DO I SELECT THE BEST OF ITS TYPE?

1. Since investors can buy or sell puts or calls (while buying, selling, or holding the underlying security) there are a great many different option strategies available at any given time. Perhaps the first decision that must be made is an estimate of whether the stock market as a whole, or any one stock, is likely to advance or decline. If the market is moving upward, investors are more likely to want to buy calls or sell put options. If the market or a stock is weak, then a strategy of buying puts or selling calls may be in order.

2. The volatility of the underlying stock has a lot to do with the movement of both put and call options. The more active a particular issue, the more likely the option will have a wide swing in price. Speculators should look for stocks that experience fairly rapid movements, either up or down, over a relatively short period of time. More conservative investors may want to concentrate on options where the underlying stock is relatively stable in price.

3. The period of time to expiration of the option should be considered before any purchase or sale is made. The longer the term of the option, the more likely the price of the stock to change significantly, and the greater the volatility of the option. Again, investors who wish to speculate will tend to prefer longer-term options, while conservative investors will prefer shorter maturities.

4. The dividends paid on the underlying stock have a significant impact on the value of an option. Option holders do not receive any dividends, which are paid only to holders of actual stock. Therefore, options on high dividend-paying stocks will tend to be less valuable than those on issues with low dividends, or none at all.

WHERE CAN I FIND OUT MORE ABOUT IT?

1. Each of the option exchanges publishes a variety of booklets dealing with the mechanics of option trading and various strategies for investors. These booklets generally are also available through most brokerage firms or on the Internet. One such publication is *Characteristics and Risks of Standardized Options*, published by the Options Clearing Corporation. This booklet can be viewed or downloaded at www.cboe.com.

2. Larger brokerage firms have specialists who concentrate on options and may even manage option funds for their clients. Such firms frequently publish their own reports and recommendations.

3. Several of the major investment advisory services include information on options in their publications. Both Standard & Poor's and Value Line collect data on puts and calls although they do not make recommendations or assign a quality rating as they do with stocks and bonds.

4. For further information on options, see the Chicago Board Options Exchange at www.cboe.com.

QUESTIONS AND ANSWERS

Question – How long does an option contract last?

Answer – Option contracts can have maturities up to several months. Most exchange-traded options contracts expire on the Saturday after the third Friday of each month (although some types of options only have contracts that expire every three months). Most trading activity takes place on those options that will expire within the next two or three months. New options are introduced by the various exchanges as old options expire.

Question – Are options available for all stocks?

Answer – No, options are available on a relatively limited number of stocks. The five options exchanges trade puts and calls on about 1,500 issues, but this is only a portion of the thousands of listed stocks and the many thousands more that are traded on the over-the-counter market. Options are generally available on those issues that are widely held or that are very actively traded. The exchanges review their lists on a regular basis and add new issues from time to time.

Question – Do I have to own a particular stock before I can trade its options?

Answer – No, you may trade options—both puts and calls—without actual ownership of the underlying stock. This is referred to as trading "naked" or "uncovered" as opposed to owning the stock and being "covered." The additional risk in naked trading is the possible need to buy the stock for delivery if the option is exercised. This can be particularly expensive since double commissions are involved as well as the cost of purchasing the underlying stock.

Question – If I acquire stock by exercising a call option, what is the actual cost basis of my shares?

Answer – The cost basis of the stock for tax purposes will be the exercise price paid for the shares plus the premium paid for the call option. For example, if an investor paid $500 for a call on 100 shares of stock (i.e., $5/share), and later exercised the option at a price of $50 per share, the cost basis of the stock would be $50 + $5 = $55 per share.

Question – If I buy an option and let it expire without being exercised, is my loss on the transaction a capital loss?

Answer – Yes, if the option expires, it is treated as if it were sold on the expiration date. The premium that was paid to acquire the option is treated as a short-term capital loss.

Question – How is the premium income received by option writers taxed?

Answer – First, there is no tax due at the time the option is written and the premium is paid to the seller. For tax purposes, the premium is considered to be deferred until the transaction is completed, even though the writer actually receives the funds immediately. If the option expires without being exercised, the premium is recognized as a short-term capital gain and is included in the writer's income for the tax year in which the option expired. If the option is exercised, the writer adds the premium to the striking price to calculate the total amount received. This amount is compared with the writer's cost basis to determine whether a taxable gain or loss has been realized. Any gain or loss that results from a "closing purchase" is considered short-term capital gain or loss.

Question – What are LEAPS?

Answer – LEAPS, or Long-Term Equity AnticiPation Securities, are long-term options that generally have expiration dates up to 2 years and 9 months (issued in April and expiring in January in the 3rd subsequent year). They are available on a limited number of equities (approximately 450) and indexes (approximately 10). Fundamentally, LEAPS operate in the same manner as any other options—the primary difference is the increased utility (either for speculators or hedgers) available because of the increased term until expiration.

Question – What is the difference between an American option and a European option?

Answer – The difference between these two options types is the timing of when they can be exercised. American options can be exercised anytime between issue and expiration—this form of option is typical for most equity options traded on any of the exchanges. European options can only be exercised at (or in a short time window immediately before) expiration—these are occasionally used with some forms of cash-settled index options. Note that although there may be limitations on when they can be exercised, European options (like all options) can still be traded to close out a position at any time.

CHAPTER ENDNOTES

1. IRC Sec. 1234A.
2. Rev. Rul. 58-234, 1958-1 CB 279.
3. Ibid.
4. IRC Sec. 1223(6).
5. IRC Sec. 1091(a).
6. Rev. Rul. 58-234, 1958-1 CB 279.
7. Ibid.
8. Ibid.
9. IRC Sec. 1223(6).

Chapter 14

FINANCIAL FUTURES

WHAT IS IT?

Financial futures are standardized contracts calling for future delivery of a specified number or notional value of a specified financial instrument, for a specified price, at a designated future date. The price at which delivery will be made is determined at the present time, but delivery is scheduled for some future date.

Example: An investor may trade through the Chicago Board of Trade (CBOT) on June 15 to purchase a futures contract in GNMA certificates for actual delivery on November 26. The price and the number of contracts to be traded are set at the time of purchase or sale (June 15), and not at the time of delivery (November 26).

The financial futures market includes:

1. *Currency Futures* – contracts on foreign currencies;

2. *Interest-Rate Futures* – contracts on U. S. Treasury bonds, notes, bills, GNMA bonds, foreign government bonds, and other interest-related notional instruments, or benchmarks based upon such things as the Federal Funds Rate or the LIBOR (London Inter-Bank Offered Rate);

3. *Index Futures* – contracts on broad-based domestic or foreign stock indexes (e.g., the S&P 500 Index or the EAFE Index), or contracts on indexes of interest-related instruments (e.g., Treasury bonds);

4. *Narrow-Based Index (NBI) Futures* – contracts based on a small basket of stocks from a narrow sector of the market (e.g., airlines or chemicals); and

5. *Single Stock Futures* – contracts on individual stocks.

In addition, the futures markets are introducing creative new contracts all the time, and some of these

contracts do not fit easily within the five financial futures categories listed above or within the traditional commodity futures categories. For instance, the Chicago Board Options Exchange (CBOE) Futures Exchange (CFE) has introduced several futures contracts that are based not on the performance of the S&P 500 Index or the Dow Jones Industrial Average, per se, but rather just on the volatility or variance of these indices over various investment horizons. The Chicago Mercantile Exchange (CME) also lists futures contracts based not directly on financial instruments or commodities, as such, but rather on broad economic factors such as U.S. gross domestic product and the U.S. international trade balance. Also, investors may now trade futures on the CME based upon a home price index or a number of other contracts based on weather.

Two distinct trading arenas comprise the financial futures market – exchange-traded futures and over-the-counter futures. Exchange-traded futures are contracts listed on organized exchanges, such as the Chicago Mercantile Exchange (CME), New York Futures Exchange (NYFE), Chicago Board Options Exchange Futures Exchange (CFE), and other exchanges. These contracts have standardized features with respect to the amount of the product involved in each contract, the margin requirement, the settlement dates, etc. In addition, these contracts are subject to the "mark-to-market rule" that essentially settles differences in the long and short positions daily to assure that parties to the contracts maintain adequate margin.

The inter-bank, over-the-counter (OTC) futures market is essentially a negotiated private placement market, generally involving contracts on millions of dollars of financial instruments. In this market, contracts are much less standardized than in the exchange-traded futures market; terms and amounts can vary depending upon the desires of each party, and the contracts generally are not marked-to-market every day. Whereas virtually any investor who has the financial wherewithal to qualify for margin trading can invest in exchange-traded futures, the principal participants in the OTC futures market are large financial institutions and international corporations, professional traders and arbitrageurs, and governments. Since the vast majority of individual investors do not participate in the OTC futures market, the principal focus of this chapter will be on exchange-traded futures.

Most investors in the financial futures market do not plan to take delivery of the item purchased (or make delivery in the case of a sale). Less than 3% of contracts traded are settled by the buyer's receiving, or the seller's making delivery of the actual instrument on which the contract is based. The real purpose of the transaction is to transfer the risk (and potential reward) of price fluctuations from the hedger to the speculator, not to take actual possession of the asset.

Most investors "close out" their sale or purchase positions by entering into an "offsetting transaction" instead of taking or making delivery. This is accomplished by simply reversing their original position. For example, if an investor buys a futures contract on Treasury bills, he can close out the position by selling the identical contract prior to expiration.

Like all markets in "derivatives" (i.e., instruments that "derive" their value based upon some other financial instrument), the futures market is a "zero-sum" market. What this means is that for each investor who gains one dollar in this market, another investor must lose one dollar; for each long position in the futures market there is an equal, but opposite, short position. In contrast with the stock market, where most investors are long in the market and the average investor gains if the market rises or loses if the market falls, the "average" investor in the futures market must always earn zero. In fact, the average investor actually does worse than earn zero, since commissions and transaction costs reduce the average net return to below zero—and that's *before* taxes!

WHEN IS THE USE OF THIS TOOL INDICATED?

Why would anyone invest in a market where the average net return is negative? Financial futures can be employed in ways that range from highly speculative to ways intended to manage and limit price risks. In general, investors have one of three objectives when investing in financial futures: (1) speculating, (2) hedging, or (3) arbitraging (see below). Therefore, these tools are indicated when investors want to:

1. Speculate on anticipated increases or decreases in the price of the underlying financial instrument, or to speculate on a particular stock, bond, currency, or other financial instrument's performance relative to another's performance.

Such individuals can take large risks (which hopefully will result in similarly large returns) by purchasing financial futures contracts at a fraction of the price of actually owning the underlying securities or currencies.

2. Hedge current holdings of a particular position in a financial instrument against the risk of an adverse price change. For example, large financial institutions (e.g., banks and life insurance companies) typically hold large portfolios of mortgages and long-term securities that can fluctuate significantly in price as market conditions change. Such investors can use long or short positions in financial futures to better match the duration of their assets and future liabilities as market conditions or the nature of their liabilities change.

3. Establish, in advance, a definite purchase or selling price for a financial instrument that actually will not be bought or sold until some time in the future. For instance, a person who has contracted to purchase an expensive foreign product (say a Rolls Royce) with a specified payment due in the foreign currency (pounds) at a future date (say 3 months) faces the risk that the dollar may fall in value relative to the foreign currency (pounds or Euros) in the intervening time. In that case, although the contract price is fixed in the foreign currency, the dollar cost of the product would increase. But this person can buy a currency future today to lock in the future price of the foreign currency without having to put up the entire purchase price in dollars to purchase the foreign currency today.

4. Temporarily alter a stock portfolio's composition—as, for example, between different industry sectors—without having to acquire or liquidate shares of stock. This strategy may be employed for speculative and hedging purposes. For instance, speculators who are trying to time the business cycle through sector-rotation techniques can own a core portfolio that essentially matches the overall stock market. But as they anticipate changes in the business cycle, they can use broad-based equity index futures and narrow-based index futures to increase their effective investment in those sectors they expect to do better, and reduce their effective investment in those sectors they expect to do worse. In contrast, an investor may be bullish on the market for the long term, but is fearful that the current

political, economic, or international environment is such that the market may react badly in the relative short run. This investor could take the sell side of broad-based equity futures and reduce the risk associated with a market downturn without the hassle and expense of liquidating or rebalancing a large portion of his stock portfolio.

5. Create investment portfolios with specific risk and reward characteristics by combining stock futures with exchange-traded equity options (i.e., puts and calls). Such strategies can be used for speculative, hedging, or arbitraging purposes. One of the theoretical purposes of the derivatives markets is to make the markets for the underlying securities more efficient. Various combinations of derivatives have risk and return characteristics that are theoretically equivalent to owning the underlying security directly. Consequently, arbitrageurs watch the derivative markets and the underlying security's market to quickly take advantage of any differential between the price of the underlying security itself and the price of the combination of derivatives that is its theoretical equivalent.

ADVANTAGES

1. The terms of futures contracts are standardized by the various exchanges where they are traded. The coupon rate, maturity, issuer, and other terms are the same for each contract of a particular type. For example, a contract for Treasury bills will state the value of the underlying bills (typically $1,000,000), the maturity date of the contract, and the exchange where it is traded. These terms are identical for all similar contracts, and they remain fixed for the life of the contract. The only item that varies is the price of the contract, making for ease of quotation and trading.

2. Financial futures offer investors a high degree of "leverage" on their investments because of the low margin requirements involved. For example, the initial margin for the Chicago Board of Trade contract on $100,000 of Treasury bonds is only $2,000. This leverage offers speculators the opportunity for large returns on the relatively small investment they want to make. Low margins also make it possible for institutions to hedge their portfolios at a reasonable cost.

3. The financial futures market is highly liquid. On any given day billions of dollars of futures contracts will be traded on the various organized exchanges. New positions can be created and old ones closed out with little difficulty, and at relatively low cost in terms of commissions and fees.

4. All futures contracts are "guaranteed" by the clearinghouse that processes the transactions. In actuality, the clearinghouse becomes the other side of every trade—the buyer from every seller and the seller to every buyer. This arrangement improves market performance by eliminating concern over the creditworthiness of the opposing parties, assuring delivery of the underlying securities, and adding to flexibility in closing out positions.

DISADVANTAGES

1. Financial futures are an extremely volatile investment area where substantial price changes can take place in a very short period of time. Investors must have both the financial and emotional capacity to operate in this area where gains and losses are settled on a daily basis.

2. Since all accounts are settled on a daily basis, investors are subject to frequent margin calls, and must be prepared to invest additional funds or risk having their futures positions closed out by the brokerage firm.

3. Trading strategies in financial futures tend to be complex arrangements compared to many other kinds of investments, such as the simple purchase of a stock or a bond. This is due to the fact that a futures transaction generally accompanies some other investment rather than being carried out in isolation. For example, an investor in GNMA bonds may "hedge" that investment with a GNMA futures contract. Keeping track of these multi-part investments requires much more time and energy than most other investments.

TAX IMPLICATIONS

1. Financial futures generally are considered to be so-called "executory contracts" (i.e., contracts that require performance at some future date). Gains and losses on regulated futures contracts are capital gains and losses, regardless of the nature of the underlying property.

management and the additional management fees and organizational or administrative expenses that may reduce the amount available for investment in futures contracts.

2. Any gain or loss required to be reported by an investor on a futures contract is treated as if 40% of the gain or loss is short-term and 60% is long-term gain or loss. *Net capital gains* (i.e., the excess of long-term capital gains over short-term capital losses) are generally taxable at a maximum rate of 15%.

3. Under the "mark-to-market" tax rules, gains and losses on futures contracts owned by an investor at the end of the tax year, or at any time during the year, must be reported annually, even if the investor has not realized such gains or losses. A contract that is still in existence at the end of the year is, therefore, treated as if it were sold for its fair market value on the last business day of that year.

ALTERNATIVES

1. Investors can use put and call stock options to accomplish some of the same purposes as financial futures. Investors with large portfolios of common stocks can use options to hedge their stock positions while increasing the income from those portfolios. Similarly, speculators can purchase calls (puts) in anticipation of an increase (decrease) in stock prices, and invest a relatively small sum compared with the cost of actually buying (or selling) the underlying stock.

2. Stock purchase warrants also offer some of the same advantages in terms of leverage and relatively low investment that make financial futures attractive. Warrants are particularly attractive to speculators who hope to profit from a much larger percentage increase in the value of a warrant if the underlying stock increases in value.

3. Another alternative method of participating in futures is through a managed financial futures account, which is similar in concept to a common stock mutual fund. It is the only method of participation in which the investors do not have their own individual trading accounts. Instead, the investor's money is combined with that of other pool participants and, in effect, traded as a single account. Gains or losses are shared in proportion to each participant's investment in the pool. The advantages of this arrangement are that it offers potentially greater diversification of risks, participants' losses are generally limited to their investment in the pool (because most pools are formed as limited partnerships), and the individual participants are not generally subject to margin calls. The disadvantages include the risk of bad

WHERE AND HOW DO I GET IT?

Financial futures are traded on several organized exchanges, most of which are located in either Chicago or New York. These include the Chicago Board of Trade (CBOT), the Chicago Board Options Exchange (CBOE) Futures Exchange (CFE), the Chicago Mercantile Exchange (CME) and the New York Futures Exchange (NYFE) which is a subsidiary of the New York Board of Trade (NYBOT). Futures contracts on the Value Line Index are also traded on the Kansas City Board of Trade (KCBOT).

Buying or selling financial futures is quite similar in many ways to buying or selling stocks or bonds. Transactions must be carried out through a "margin account" with a brokerage firm that sends orders to the trading floors of the various futures exchanges. Orders are executed on the exchange floor, and the results of the trade are reported back to the brokerage firm, and in turn to the customer.

To execute a transaction an investor can call his broker and state, "Buy a Treasury note futures contract for my account at 79." This represents a contract for $100,000 face value of U.S. Treasury Notes. The price paid by the investor is 79, or $79,000. But only a relatively small margin position ($2,000) will typically have to be deposited by the investor. A written record of the transaction will be sent to the buyer confirming the transaction. This is the only evidence of the purchase that the investor will receive. This is due to the fact that the futures transaction involves a contract to buy or sell, rather than an actual security.

Once an investor initiates the trade the position of the buyer or seller remains "open" until one of two events occurs. One possibility is that the buyer will accept delivery of the underlying instruments (T-bills, GNMAs, etc.) on the settlement date. The seller of the contract is obligated to make delivery to the buyer. As noted above, less than 3% of futures contracts are settled in this fashion.

Much more common will be a "closing out" of the buyer's or seller's position by executing another trade that is the opposite of the first transaction. The buyer sells or the seller buys, and the original positions are offset and eliminated. Continuing our example of the buyer of a Treasury note contract, he may decide to close out his position when the price of the contract reaches 81, or $81,000. At that point he would sell the identical contract and recognize a profit of $2,000, the difference between the purchase price of $79,000 and the sale price of $81,000. (This example does not include commission costs and is intended for illustration purposes only.)

WHAT FEES OR OTHER ACQUISITION COSTS ARE INVOLVED?

Commissions on the purchase or sale of financial futures contracts are similar to those paid on other security transactions. Brokerage firms typically charge a percentage of the value of the transaction with a minimum commission of $25 or $30. Brokerage charges are relatively high on single unit trades, and most active investors will trade in multiples of five or ten contracts at a time.

HOW DO I SELECT THE BEST OF ITS TYPE?

1. An accurate forecast of interest rates is an essential part of an effective financial futures strategy. Estimating the direction of interest rate changes and the amount of change is critical to establishing profitable contract positions. For example, buyers of financial futures contracts will generally benefit if interest rates fall. When this happens the value of securities such as T-bills and GNMA certificates will increase, and so will the value of contracts to take delivery on these issues in the future. Sellers of futures contracts will tend to lose money under these circumstances. Conversely, when interest rates rise, buyers of futures contracts will see the value of their contracts decline while sellers will benefit from the fall in value of the underlying securities.

2. Individuals and institutions seeking to hedge their portfolios should determine the appropriate maturity structure of those portfolios in selecting the best financial futures contract. The portfolio hedged by the futures contract should be of approximately the same maturity as the securities underlying the futures contract. For example, an investor with a long-term bond portfolio would hedge that portfolio by using a futures contract on Treasury bonds rather than one based on short-term Treasury bills.

3. The period of time until settlement of the futures contract should be considered before any purchase

or sale is made. The longer the term of the contract, the more risk is generally involved for sellers and the more advantage for buyers. These conditions are reflected in the price of the contract along with the volatility of the underlying securities.

WHERE CAN I FIND OUT MORE ABOUT IT?

1. Major brokerage firms can usually provide brochures on the financial futures market as well as an analysis of current market conditions that may or may not make financial futures attractive for investment purposes.

2. Each of the futures exchanges publishes a number of booklets that explain the nature of futures trading, the contracts that are available, and various strategies for investors. You may contact the various exchanges at the following addresses, numbers, and web sites:

Chicago Board of Trade
141 West Jackson Boulevard
Chicago, IL 60604-2994
(312) 435-3500
www.cbot.com

CFE
CBOE Futures Exchange
400 South LaSalle Street
Chicago, IL 60605
(312) 786-7428
http://cfe.cboe.com/

Chicago Mercantile Exchange
20 S. Wacker Drive
Chicago, IL 60606
(312) 930-1000
http://www.cme.com

Kansas City Board of Trade
4800 Main Street
Suite 303
Kansas City, Missouri 64112
(816) 753-7500
http://www.kcbt.com/
v1_futures_options.html

The New York Board of Trade
World Financial Center
One North End Ave. 13th Fl.
New York, NY 10282-1101
(800) HEDGE-IT
http://www.nybot.com

3. Larger brokerage firms generally have specialists who concentrate on financial futures and may even manage discretionary accounts for their clients. Such firms often publish their own reports and recommendations.

QUESTIONS AND ANSWERS

Question – What is the meaning of the term "hedge"?

Answer – "Hedging" an investment refers to balancing the risk of a position in the current or cash market with an offsetting position in the futures market. For example, an investor who owns (i.e., is "long") long-term debt, and who is concerned that interest rates may rise (and, consequently, that bond prices fall), may sell (go "short") financial futures to hedge that risk. If bond prices decline, the profits from the short position in futures will offset, or at least partially offset, the losses on the long-term debt position.

Question – What is the usual length of time of a futures contract?

Answer – While it is possible to enter into a futures contract that covers two or three years, the vast majority of activity takes place in contracts that require settlement (i.e., mature) within 12 months. Therefore, investors who maintain permanent portfolios may enter into a series of contracts, "rolling over" or entering into new contracts when the old ones are settled or closed out.

Question – What does the phrase "marked-to-market" mean in regard to trading futures contracts?

Answer – "Marked-to-market" means that brokerage accounts trading financial futures, like all commodity trading accounts, are settled at the end of each day based on the closing prices of those futures contracts. Any paper gains or losses are recognized immediately and posted to the investor's account rather than when a security is bought or sold. This procedure, coupled with the small margin required on such accounts, may subject investors to daily margin calls if futures prices move against them.

Question – What are "index futures"?

Answer – "Index futures" are contracts to purchase a given index of stocks at a pre-specified price at some specified time in the future (i.e., the delivery date). The purpose is to use a futures contract as a substitute for the dollar amount of stock that otherwise would have been purchased. The purchasers typically pay about 10% of the specified price at the time they purchase the contracts and pay the remainder at the time the contracts expire. Since they will owe 90% of the price when the contracts come due, this is a "leveraged," and hence speculative, position. If the index rises by the delivery date, the holders will receive an index whose value is higher than the price they have agreed to pay. Conversely, if the market drops, they will receive an index whose value is below their purchase price. Figure 14.1 lists index futures contracts.

Question – What are "E-mini" stock index products?

Answer – "E-mini" stock index products are the fastest growing products in the history of Chicago Mercantile Exchange (CME). The E-mini S&P 500 and E-mini NASDAQ-100 are products that were pioneered by the CME and launched in 1997 and 1999, respectively. At one-fifth the size of their standard counterparts, the S&P 500 and NASDAQ-100 futures contracts, these mini contracts are designed to be more suitable for smaller professional and individual investors. The list of E-minis offered on the CME has continued to grow and includes contracts on the S&P Midcap 400 Index, the NASDAQ Biotechnology Index, The NASDAQ Composite Index, The Russell 2000 Index, the Russell 1000 Index, the MSCI EAFE Index, and the S&P Asia 50 Index.

The success of the CME E-mini contracts has led other exchanges to follow suit with their own similar contracts that are typically about one-fifth the size of the standard contracts. The CFE offers mini-contracts on the Russell 1000 and 2000 indexes, the NYFE offers mini-contracts on the NYSE Composite Index and the Russell 1000 Index, and the KCBOT offers a mini-contract on the Value Line Index.

Question – What are the advantages of trading mini stock index futures and options?

Answer – Trading mini stock index futures offers investors many advantages, including:

- *Exposure to the Leading U.S. and Foreign Stocks* – Investors now can have exposure to the S&P 500, S&P 400 Midcap, S&P Asia 50, NASDAQ Composite, NASDAQ-100, NASDAQ Bio-technology, Russell 1000, Russell 2000, NYSE Composite, MSCI EAFE, and Value Line Indexes with just one trade.

Figure 14.1

INDEX FUTURES

Contract	Market	Underlying Index
DJIA	Chicago Board of Trade	The DJIA is a price-weighted index of 30 large "blue-chip" stocks. The CBOT offers the DJIA contracts in three sizes: the regular contract has a contract price of $10 times the DJIA; the Big Dow contract, $25 times the DJIA; and the Mini-Sized contract, $5 times the DJIA.
China Index	CFE[1]	The China Index, created by CBOE, is a broad-based, equal-dollar weighted index composed of securities that are American Depository Receipts (ADRs), New York Registered Shares (NYSs) or NYSE Global Shares (NGSs) traded on the NYSE, Nasdaq or the AMEX.
DJIA Volatility Index	CFE	The DJIA Volatility Index (VXD), which is based on real-time prices of options on the Dow Jones Industrial Average, is designed to reflect investors' consensus view of future (30-day) expected stock market volatility, and provides investor with a tool to hedge changes in the volatility of the market.
Volatility Index	CFE	The Volatility Index (VIX), which is based on real-time prices of options on the S&P 500 Index, is designed to reflect investors' consensus view of future (30-day) expected stock market volatility, and provides investor with a tool to hedge changes in the volatility of the market.
S&P 500 Three-Month Variance Index	CFE	The S&P 500 Three-Month Variance contract is similar in concept to the (30-day) Volatility Index except that it measures variance (volatility) over three months rather than 30 days.
S&P 500 Twelve-Month Variance Index	CFE	The S&P 500 Twelve-Month Variance contract is similar in concept to the (30-day) Volatility Index except that it measures variance (volatility) over twelve months rather than 30 days.
PowerPacks Indexes	CFE	Twelve sector or industry indexes including Banking, Technology, Pharmaceuticals, Gold, Biotechnology, Semiconductors, Internet, Oil, Oil Service, Telecom, Retail, and Iron & Steel, each composed of 25 stocks that are among the largest and most actively traded in their respective industries.
Russell 1000	CFE	The Russell 1000 is a capitalization-weighted index designed to measure the performance of the top 1,000 companies from a universe of the 3,000 largest U.S. stocks traded on the NYSE, NASDAQ, or the AMEX.
Mini-Russell 1000	CFE	The Mini-Russell 1000 contract is the same in all respects as the regular Russell 1000 contract, except that the Mini contract is one-fifth the size of the regular Russell 1000 contract.
Mini-Russell 2000	CFE	The Russell 2000 is a capitalization-weighted index designed to measure the performance of the top 2,000 companies from a universe of the 3,000 largest U.S. stocks traded on the NYSE, NASDAQ, or the AMEX.
CME CPI	Chicago Mercantile Exchange	This contract is designed to track the market's expectation of future three-month inflation as measured by the U.S. city average for all urban consumers (CPI-U).
S&P 500 Index	Chicago Mercantile Exchange	The S&P 500 index is based on the market-weighted stock prices of 500 large-capitalization companies. The market value of the 500 firms is equal to about 80% of the value of all stocks listed on the New York Stock Exchange.
CME E-mini S&P 500	Chicago Mercantile Exchange	The E-mini S&P 500 contract is the same in all respects as the regular S&P 500 contract, except that the E-mini contract is one-fifth the size of the regular S&P 500 contract.

[1] The Chicago Board Options Exchange (CBOE) Futures Exchange uses "CFE" as the shorthand version of the exchange name.

Tools & Techniques of Investment Planning

Figure 14.1 (cont'd)

INDEX FUTURES

Contract	Market	Underlying Index
CME S&P MidCap 400	Chicago Mercantile Exchange	The S&P MidCap 400 Index represents the "middle" of the market. Like the S&P 500, the S&P MidCap 400 is market weighted, but it tracks the market performance of the stocks of medium-sized firms with market capitalizations of approximately $2 billion to $10 billion.
CME E-mini S&P MidCap 400	Chicago Mercantile Exchange	The E-mini S&P MidCap 400 contract is the same in all respects as the regular S&P MidCap 400 contract, except that the E-mini contract is one-fifth the size of the regular S&P MidCap 400 contract.
CME S&P 500/ Citigroup Growth & Value Indices	Chicago Mercantile Exchange	Each S&P 500 stock is assigned to the Growth or Value Index so that the two indices "add up" to the S&P 500. The indices are rebalanced twice a year based on a variety of factors so that each represents about 50% of the S&P 500 capitalization.[2]
CME S&P SmallCap 600	Chicago Mercantile Exchange	The capitalization-weighted S&P SmallCap 600 Index was launched in 1994 and has become the standard measurement of performance in the small-capitalization segment of the U.S. stock market.
CME Technology SPCTRs	Chicago Mercantile Exchange	These contracts are based upon the capitalization-weighted S&P 500 Technology and Telecom Sector Indexes underlying the S&P 500 Composite Index.
CME Financial SPCTRs	Chicago Mercantile Exchange	These contracts are based upon the capitalization-weighted S&P 500 Financial Sector Index. This index tracks companies such as banks, brokerage firms, insurance companies and real estate companies.
CME NASDAQ-100	Chicago Mercantile Exchange	The NASDAQ 100 Index comprises 100 of the largest domestic, non-financial common stocks listed on the NASDAQ Stock Market. It is a market-weighted index that has about a 94% correlation to the NASDAQ Composite Index.
CME E-mini NASDAQ-100	Chicago Mercantile Exchange	The E-mini NASDAQ-100 contract is the same in all respects as the regular NASDAQ-100 contract except that the E-mini contract is one-fifth the size of the regular NASDAQ-100 contract.
CME E-mini NASDAQ Composite	Chicago Mercantile Exchange	The E-mini NASDAQ Composite Index measures all listed NASDAQ common stocks. This contrasts with the NASDAQ 100 index which includes only the top 100 non-financial stocks listed on the NASDAQ Stock Market.
CME E-mini NASDAQ Biotechnology	Chicago Mercantile Exchange	The E-mini NASDAQ Biotechnology Index tracks approximately 150 companies classified by the FTSE™ Global Classification system as either biotechnology or pharmaceutical, and that have met other eligibility criteria set by NASDAQ for inclusion in the Index.
CME Russell 2000	Chicago Mercantile Exchange	The Russell 2000 Index, based on 2,000 stocks, is the most widely recognized market-weighted small-capitalization U.S. benchmark.
CME E-mini Russell 2000	Chicago Mercantile Exchange	The E-mini Russell 2000 contract is the same in all respects as the regular Russell 2000 contract, except that the E-mini contract is one-fifth the size of the regular Russell 2000 contract.
CME E-mini Russell 1000	Chicago Mercantile Exchange	The Russell 1000 is a capitalization-weighted index designed to measure the performance of the top 1,000 companies from a universe of the 3,000 largest U.S. stocks traded on the NYSE, NASDAQ or the AMEX.
CME E-mini MSCI EAFE	Chicago Mercantile Exchange	The Morgan Stanley Capital International EAFE (Europe, Australasia, and Far East) Index, is a leading barometer for international equity performance that measures the equity performance for all developed markets (in 21 countries) excluding the U.S. and Canada.

[2] These indices and the associated contracts were introduced in 2005 and were previously known as the S&P 500/Barra Growth and Value Indices and contracts.

Figure 14.1 (cont'd)

INDEX FUTURES

Contract	Market	Underlying Index
CME NIKKEI 225	Chicago Mercantile Exchange	The Nikkei 225 Stock Average is Japan's most widely followed and most frequently quoted equity index. The Nikkei is price-weighted and comprises the 225 top-tiered (the "bluest" chip) of Japanese companies. The contracts come in two varieties denominated in either U.S. dollars or Japanese yen.
CME S&P/TOPIX 150	Chicago Mercantile Exchange	Investors seeking to participate in one of the world's largest economies, Japan, have access to the Japanese counterpart to the S&P 500 Index, a yen-based futures contract on the S&P/TOPIX 150 Equity Index.
CME E-mini S&P Asia 50	Chicago Mercantile Exchange	The S&P Asia 50 Index is the first Pan-Asia index, tracking the region as a whole. The index is composed of some of the largest and most liquid issues from four markets: Hong Kong, Taiwan, Korea, and Singapore.
CME GSCI	Chicago Mercantile Exchange	The Goldman Sachs Commodity Index (GSCI) represents every major commodity group: energy, livestock, grains and oil seeds, food, and fiber and metals. The GSCI comprises 22 liquid, exchange-traded physical commodity futures contracts. It is a world production-weighted index, similar to a market-weighted stock index.
CME$INDEX	Chicago Mercantile Exchange	The contracts are based upon a geometric index of of seven foreign currencies weighted to reflect the relative competitiveness of U.S. goods in foreign markets. It provides investors with an instrument for foreign exchange market participation and risk management.[3]
CME TRAKRS	Chicago Mercantile Exchange	TRAKRS (Total Return Asset Contracts) are exchange-traded non-traditional futures contracts designed to provide market exposure to various TRAKRS Indexes, a series of market-based total-return indexes of stocks, bonds, currencies, commodities and other financial instruments.
KC Value Line Index	Kansas City Board of Trade	Approximately 1,650 stocks comprise the equally-weighted Value Line Arithmetic Index of stocks compiled by Value Line Investment Services.
KC Mini Value Line Index	Kansas City Board of Trade	The Mini contract is like the Value Line in all respects but the size of the investment. A Mini contract is one-fifth the size of a Value Line contract.
NYSE Composite	New York Futures Exchange[4]	The NYSE Composite Index is a market-weighted measure of the changes in the aggregate market value of all NYSE common stocks, adjusted to eliminate the effects of capitalization changes, new listings and delistings.
Mini NYSE Composite	New York Futures Exchange	The Mini NYSE Composite Index is the same in all respects as the regular NYSE Composite contract except that the Mini contract is one-tenth the size of the regular NYSE Composite contract.
Russell 1000	New York Futures Exchange	The Russell 1000 Index measures the performance of the 1,000 largest companies in the Russell 3000 Index of the total equity market and represents approximately92% of the total market capitalization of the Russell 3000.
Mini Russell 1000	New York Futures Exchange	The Mini Russell 1000 contract is the same in all respects as the regular Russell 1000 contract, except that the Mini contract is one-tenth the size of the regular Russell 1000 contract.

[3] The seven currencies comprising the index include the European Union Euro, Japan Yen, United Kingdom Pound, Switzerland Franc, Australia Dollar, Canada Dollar, and Sweden Krona.

[4] The New York Futures Exchange *NYSE) is a wholly owned subsidiary of The New York Board of Trade (NYBOT).

Figure 14.1 (cont'd)

INDEX FUTURES

Contract	Market	Underlying Index
Russell 1000 Value	New York Futures Exchange	The Russell Value Index measures the performance of those Russell 1000 companies (large cap U.S. equities) with lower price-to-book ratios and lower forecasted growth values. Value companies characteristically sell at lower prices in relation to a company's earnings and net worth than growth companies.
Russell 1000 Growth	New York Futures Exchange	The Growth Index measures the performance of those Russell 1000 companies (large cap U.S. equities) with higher price-to-book ratios and higher forecasted growth values. Growth companies characteristically sell at higher prices in relation to a company's earnings and net worth than value companies.
Russell 2000	New York Futures Exchange	The Russell 2000 Index measures the performance of the 2,000 smallest companies in the Russell 3000 Index of the total equity market and represents approximately 8% of the total market capitalization of the Russell 3000.
Russell 2000 Value	New York Futures Exchange	The Russell 2000 Value Index measures the performance of the value segment of the Russell 2000 companies (small- and mid-cap U.S. equities) with lower price-to-book ratios and lower forecasted growth values. Value companies characteristically sell at lower prices in relation to a company's earnings and net worth than growth companies.
Russell 2000 Growth	New York Futures Exchange	The Russell 2000 Growth Index measures the performance of the growth segment of the Russell 2000 companies (small- and mid-cap U.S. equities) with higher price-to-book ratios and higher forecasted growth values. Growth companies characteristically sell at higher prices in relation to a company's earnings and net worth than value companies.
Russell 3000	New York Futures Exchange	The Russell 3000 Index measures the performance of the 3,000 largest U.S. companies and represents approximately 98% of the investable U.S. equity market.

- *Affordability* – Mini stock index futures (generally) require one-fifth the margin of the standard futures contracts, enabling investors to control a large basket of stocks for a fraction of the cost.

- *Opportunity* – These futures contracts provide a variety of investment opportunities, including: the choice of taking a bullish or bearish position; the ability to increase or hedge portfolio exposure; and the ability to "spread" against other index products.

- *Accessibility* – Mini stock index futures provide investors with online opportunities to take advantage of market moves virtually 24 hours a day (see: www.cme.com/products/index/eminieducation.cfm).

- *Integrity* – CME customers and members are protected from default on futures and options contracts by the exchange's sophisticated risk management and surveillance processes. The CME Clearing House acts as guarantor to each of its clearing members, thus ensuring the integrity of all trades. CME's system has proven to be outstandingly effective, even under the most stressful market conditions. The other exchanges have similar measures to insure the integrity of the transactions on their exchanges.

Question – How do the mini stock index futures work?

Answer – Mini stock index futures contracts are legally binding agreements to buy or sell the cash value of the underlying index at a specific future date. Each of the mini stock index products has a different value. To determine a contract's value, you need to know its multiplier and the current index futures level.

For example, the CME's E-mini S&P 500 multiplier is $50. If the S&P 500 futures index level is 1300, multiply that by $50 (1300 x $50 = $65,000). If you buy one E-mini S&P 500 contract at 1300, you are trading an instrument with an underlying value of $65,000. The CME's E-mini NASDAQ 100 multiplier is $20. If the NASDAQ-100 index level is 2100, multiply that by $20 (2100 x $20 = $42,000). If you buy one E-mini NASDAQ-100 contract at 2100 you are trading an instrument with an underlying value of $42,000.

Futures contracts move in minimal increments called "ticks," and the value of the tick is different for each product. For example, the E-mini S&P 500 futures tick value is 0.25 futures index point, or $12.50 per contract. Thus, a move of one tick, from 1300.00 to 1300.25, equals $12.50. With this move, a long (buying) position would be credited $12.50, and a short (selling) position would be debited $12.50. A move of one entire E-mini S&P 500 futures index point—the equivalent of four ticks—would equal $50, and so on.

The E-mini NASDAQ-100 futures tick value is 0.50 futures index point, or $10 per contract. Thus, a move of one tick, from 2100.00 to 2100.50, equals $10. With this move, a long (buying) position would be credited $10, and a short (selling) position debited $10. A move of one entire E-mini NASDAQ-100 futures index point—the equivalent of two ticks—would equal $20, and so on.

Stock index futures are cash settled, just like their standard contract counterparts; thus, there is no delivery of the individual stocks. Likewise, mini stock index futures' daily settlements and quarterly expirations use the same price as the standard index futures. Identical daily settlement prices allow mini contracts to benefit from the liquidity of the larger contracts. Like the standard index futures contracts, which are settled using a Special Opening Quotation (SOQ), all mini stock index futures positions are settled in cash to the respective standard index contract on the third Friday of the quarterly contract month. The final settlement price for S&P 500 futures is based on the opening prices of the component stocks in the index, or on the last sale price of a stock that does not open for trading on the regular scheduled day of the final settlement. The final settlement price for NASDAQ-100 futures is based on a 5-minute, volume-weighted average of each component stock's opening prices on expiration day.

Question – Is there a way investors can reduce the leveraged and speculative nature of index futures?

Answer – Investors can "unleverage" (i.e., reduce the leverage of) the index contract and, consequently, reduce its speculative nature by buying a futures contract and simultaneously investing in Treasury bills in an amount equal to (or in some proportion of) the entire amount that will be due when the contract expires.

This strategy is economically equivalent to buying the index of stocks outright except that the investor

1. receives the T-bill interest rate rather than the dividends on the stocks (T-bill interest would typically be greater than the dividend income) and

2. pays any premium that the futures contract has over the actual index (typically there is a premium).

Arbitrageurs keep the premium very close to the difference between T-bill interest and dividends.

There are three advantages to this approach over outright purchase of the stocks in the index:

1. The bid/ask spread, which is a significant part of the transaction's cost, is narrower. For blue chip stocks the typical round-trip spread is about 1%, versus 0.1% for a futures contract. Assuming that futures contracts will have to be traded 3 times as often because they expire, the spread differential is still 0.3% to 1%.

2. The average commission costs are lower. For an equivalent portfolio of stocks with a discount broker the commission is about 13 times greater than the commission on a futures contract.

3. The speed and ease of trading the futures contracts and T-bills is an advantage over the stock portfolio.

The market risks are essentially the same as investing in the stocks of the underlying index.

Premiums on index futures will increase in busy up or down markets so there is some risk that the premium, as well as the basic index, will change. But this difference should be neutral over the long-term.

For contracts traded on domestic exchanges, gain or loss is capital in nature and is deemed to be 60% long-term and 40% short-term, regardless of the actual holding period. The contracts are marked-to-market at year-end so that all unrealized gains and losses are recognized at that time. Furthermore, taking or making delivery under the contract is a taxable event. The timing and characterization of gains or losses may be affected if the futures contracts are part of a straddle.

Two alternatives to index futures are purchasing the stocks in the index outright, or through an index mutual fund. The unleveraged index futures contract technique requires the investor to put up an amount equal to the striking price (i.e., price for the index) at the time the contract is purchased. For instance, an S&P 500 futures contract covers about $160,000 of stock. On the other hand, an investor can acquire shares in Vanguard's 500 Index Fund (based on the S&P 500 portfolio) with an initial purchase of only $3,000.

Any of the exchanges that make markets in index futures have informational brochures on index futures. Most brokerage firms have similar information.

Question – What are "single stock futures" and "narrow-based stock index futures"?

Answer – Single stock futures and narrow-based stock index futures are relatively recent inventions for exchange-traded futures markets. *Single stock futures* are futures contracts on individual stocks. Currently, several hundred well-known stocks, such as IBM, eBay, Philip Morris, Microsoft, Pfizer, General Electric, Citigroup, Time Warner, Johnson & Johnson, Yahoo!, and JetBlue Airways are traded in the single stock futures market. Many more stocks are expected to join the ranks in the near future. These futures products provide investors with a cost-effective and highly leveraged vehicle for participating in U.S. equities markets. Speculative traders who wish to leverage the action are the principal targets for this market since they can control bigger blocks of stock with less outlay than with margined purchases of the underlying stocks.

Also, investors now may trade futures contracts on *Narrow Based Indexes* ("NBI"). NBI are small groups of stocks in a concentrated area of the equities market (e.g., airlines, pharmaceuticals, semiconductors, biotechnology, energy, automotive, banking, etc.). Each NBI typically includes about five to eight companies in a given sector. Similar to single stock futures, these contracts should appeal largely to traders and market timers looking for high leverage and relatively low costs for their transactions.

With margin requirements of 20%, single stock futures provide a highly capital efficient way to participate in equities. In contrast with trades involving the underlying stocks, no uptick is required to establish a short position. Also, market participants initiating a short position should benefit from eliminating the costs and inefficiencies associated with the stock loan process.

Keep in mind, however, that futures contracts are highly leveraged vehicles and futures trading involves a considerable risk of loss, including the possibility of losing more than one's initial investment.

Question – What are "TRAKRS"?

Answer – TRAKRS are Total Return Asset Contracts, a line of non-traditional futures introduced in 2004 by CME in collaboration with Merrill Lynch & Co., Inc. These futures are non-traditional exchange-traded futures contracts designed to provide market exposure to various TRAKRS Indexes. The TRAKRS Indexes are a series of market-based indexes of stocks, bonds, currencies, commodities and other financial instruments. All TRAKRS futures products are cash settled and trade electronically on the CME Globex electronic platform from 8:30 a.m. to 3:00 p.m. (Chicago time) each business day, with orders matched continuously on a price-time priority basis (first-in, first-out).

What makes these contracts "non-traditional" is that the indexes on which TRAKRS futures are based differ from most financial indexes. They are calculated on a total return basis, with declared dividends and other distributions included in the index values. In other words, they are calculated to approximate the return to a strategy of investment in the index assets together with reinvestment of dividends and/or other cash flows from the investment back into the index assets.

The commodity TRAKRS track the value of the Dow Jones-AIG Commodity Index Total Return Index. The Dow Jones-AIG Commodity Index currently is composed of the prices of twenty exchange-traded futures contracts on physical commodities.

Euro Currency TRAKRS are designed to provide investors with an effective way to gain exposure to the euro/U.S. dollar exchange rate. Euro Currency TRAKRS futures track the Euro Currency TRAKRS Index, a total return index designed by Merrill Lynch, Pierce, Fenner & Smith Incorporated ("Merrill Lynch").

LMC TRAKRS are designed to provide investors with a cost-effective way to invest in a strategy that allocates assets between select value and growth stocks of companies with market capitalizations within a range of $325 million and $6 billion as of the end of 2001. LMC TRAKRS are designed to track the LMC TRAKRS Index, also a total return index designed by Merrill Lynch.

Chapter 15

COMMODITY FUTURES

WHAT IS IT?

A commodity purchase represents ownership of a definite physical item such as sugar, wheat, corn, lumber, or pork bellies. Other commodities include orange juice, cotton, cocoa, coffee, and eggs. The purchaser is buying—not a paper ownership right—but the actual item itself. The units of purchase are measured by given weights, sizes, or shapes. For example, a wheat contract may be described as "No. 2, soft red winter wheat" and each contract represents a 5,000 bushel purchase.

Most investors purchasing commodities buy a contract to either make or accept a delivery of a specified commodity on a given future date—thus the term "futures contract." If the contract runs to its termination, the investor must complete the contract by either making a delivery of the commodity or paying cash in acceptance of the commodity.

Despite stories of carloads of wheat or corn being dumped on someone's lawn, the vast majority (96%+) of commodity futures contracts are "closed out" before they mature.

WHEN IS THE USE OF THIS TOOL INDICATED?

1. When the investor is willing to take very high risks. Although the potential rewards of commodities trading are extremely high (it is possible for an investor to double his money in only a few days), over 70% of commodities speculators will lose money, and aggregate losses are typically five to six times greater than gains. If a commodities contract is allowed to expire (for example, because the price of soybeans plummets from $13 to $5, and the investor's contract allows him to purchase soybeans at $10 per bushel), the investor has no equity, his entire position is eliminated, and the value of his contract is zero.

2. When the investor is able to risk at least $10,000 of capital. This amount is the suggested minimum necessary to allow reasonable diversification of positions, and to respond to "margin calls." *Margin* is an amount of money deposited by both buyers and sellers of futures contracts to ensure performance of the terms of the contract. A brokerage firm may "call" for additional margin to bring the funds in a customer's account up to the required level.

3. When the investor desires a very high degree of leverage in his investments. This leverage comes from the low margin requirements on commodities investments. Compared to margins of 50% when investing in common stocks, margins on commodity investments are extremely low. An investor can finance 90% to 95% of the value of the contract at the time of purchase. (The actual cash required will vary according to the commodity and the standards of the broker handling the transaction.) The margin for commodities is considered a security deposit. Therefore, unlike margins for securities that are interest bearing, the investor pays no interest on the unpaid balance in a commodities contract.

4. When the investor has the emotional stability to accept frequent and possibly significant losses. Clearly, commodities trading is not for the fainthearted.

5. When the producer of a particular commodity would like to "hedge" one risk by taking an offsetting one. For example, assume a farmer plants winter wheat. He has calculated that he must receive a price of $ X.XX per bushel to break even. Yet, he has no assurance of what the price will be when he is ready to bring the wheat to market. To assure himself of at least a minimum price he enters into a futures contract guaranteeing a price of $ Y.YY per bushel upon delivery of the wheat.

If the cash market price is below the price guaranteed in the futures contract, the farmer will exercise the contract, deliver the wheat, and obtain his expected profit. Conversely, if the cash price is above the contract price, the farmer will likely sell his wheat in the cash market, buy back his futures contract, and presumably increase his profit.

In essence, the commodities exchange serves the function of finding someone to complete the opposite side of the contract. That someone is the investor (speculator). This individual assumes the risk because he feels he can profit from price movements on wheat before the delivery date of the contract. For example, the speculator may feel that wheat prices will rise sharply in the next few months, and that there will be a corresponding increase in the value of his contract (because the contract gives him the right to buy wheat at a fixed price below the expected market price).

ADVANTAGES

1. A speculator in commodities has the potential of making enormous profits in a relatively short period of time. Assume corn is selling at $2.90 per bushel and an investor purchases one 5,000 bushel contract. Instead of putting up $14,500, he is allowed to deposit only $1,000. If the price of corn rises to $3.19 (a price change of only 10%), he will have made a profit of $1,450 ($0.29 × 5,000 bushels), less commissions. But, if we compare his profit of $1,450 to his outlay of $1,000, the percentage return is 145% (lowered slightly by commissions).

2. For a given investment budget, the extremely low margin requirements for commodities permit more diversification than would be possible in the stock and bond markets.

3. Producers of various commodities can transfer the risk of price changes to speculators and lock in a particular price when they bring their commodity to market.

DISADVANTAGES

1. An investor's position can be completely wiped out by a relatively small change in the price of the commodity. This is due to the very low margin requirements of the contract, and the inherent volatility of the commodity markets. In the example above, the investor purchased a 5,000-bushel contract for corn selling at $2.90 per bushel. Instead of putting up $14,500 ($2.90 × 5,000), his broker allows him to deposit only $1,000. If the price of corn were to drop by twenty cents per bushel, the value of the contract would have declined by $1,000 and his margin would have been eliminated. This would result in a call from his broker for additional margin in order to maintain his position.

   It is very likely that an investor who puts up small amounts of margin will often have that margin eliminated. Unless the investor is willing to put up additional margin, his position will be "closed out" and the contract terminated. This may occur a number of times before the investor will be able to discern and follow a trend in the market.

2. Unlike other securities markets, positions in commodities are "marked-to-the-market" on a daily basis. This means that at the close of trading each day, the clearinghouse for the exchange calculates the gains and losses on all open positions and transfers those gains or losses into or out of all margin accounts. Profits may be withdrawn by an investor, but losses are deducted immediately from the investor's account. If the remaining margin declines below the level of the required maintenance margin, a "margin call" will be issued asking that additional funds be added to the account to bring it back to the minimum margin level. Should the investor fail to do so, his position will be "closed" by the firm handling his account. In other words, the brokerage firm will terminate the investor's interest in the contract. It does this by either buying or selling an offsetting contract.

3. Each commodity has a daily price limit, and once that limit is reached trading stops for the day. For example, the maximum daily price movement for soybeans, one of the most active commodity markets, is twenty cents per bushel. This represents a value of $1,000 per contract on a 5,000 bushel contract. The purpose of this limit is to protect the commodity markets from severe price fluctuations that could result from news of crop damage, weather reports, and other natural or market occurrences. This restriction on trading can cause the investor to be "locked in" to a position when the market is unavailable to buy or sell the commodity.

   For instance, Mary Satin owns a futures contract for wheat. A newly issued crop report indicates a tremendous surplus that causes a panic in the market. Prices fall sharply, and before Mary can act, the drop in price has reached the maximum daily limit. That causes all trading in wheat to stop and Mary is forced to hold her contract until trading resumes. By that time it may be even more difficult to close out her position.

TAX IMPLICATIONS

1. Net gains on all speculative commodity futures contracts are taxed at a maximum effective rate of 23%.

Chapter 15 – Commodity Futures

This is due to the fact that net gains on all speculative transactions are treated as though they are 40% short-term capital gains and 60% long-term capital gains. Applying the maximum tax rate of 35% (in 2004) and a 15% capital gains rate results in a 23% overall rate ((35% × 40%) + (15% × 60%)).[1] The usual holding period rule for determining whether a gain or loss is short-term or long-term is ignored.

2. All "open" positions (those that have not been closed out, exercised, or that have expired) at the end of the tax year are treated as if they had been closed on the last day of the year. In other words, any gain or loss inherent in a futures contract at the end of the year (or at any time during the year) must be reported annually, even if the investor has not actually realized those gains or losses. Therefore, if a contract has not been terminated or transferred before the end of the tax year, it is artificially treated as though the investor had sold it for its fair market value on the last business day of the year. Profits or losses from these open positions are combined with those positions that were actually closed during the rest of the year.

3. Net futures trading losses may be applied against the investor's other capital gains. If a net loss on futures transactions still exists, these may be carried back three years. If any loss still remains it may be carried forward into succeeding years.

ALTERNATIVES

1. Rather than buying commodities directly, an investor may purchase shares in a mutual fund that specializes in these investments. This alternative is especially attractive for the individual who does not have the expertise or time necessary to watch his investments on a day-to-day basis. Such attention is absolutely essential in the commodities area due to the rapid price movements and low margin positions. Commodity funds offer professional management and the constant attention demanded by this volatile market.

2. A "commodity pool" is an alternative to mutual funds, but has many of the same characteristics. For instance, in order to participate in a diversified portfolio of commodity futures with professional management, individuals will purchase units in the pool. Their money is combined and invested in a number of active commodities. In many cases the pool will be closed out when 50% of the original

capital is lost. These are normally structured as limited partnerships requiring a minimum investment of $5,000 or more. In addition to a minimum investment, these pools typically require that investors have a minimum income and wealth position.

WHERE AND HOW DO I GET IT?

Investors may trade contracts on commodities through their brokerage firms in much the same way as they buy and sell securities. A separate margin account is required and settlement on this account will be made on a daily basis as described above.

An investor may also take part in a so-called "managed account" program with a particular commodities broker or trading firm. Under this arrangement, the commodities broker has the discretionary power to trade for the investor's account. An added characteristic of these managed accounts is that the broker may participate in the profits earned on the account in addition to any commissions that may be generated by the trading activity.

Investors may also invest in commodities through mutual funds that may be purchased through a broker or, in the case of some funds, directly from the fund itself. Minimum investments generally range from $1,000 up to $10,000. An advantage of these funds is that they enable individuals to participate in a portfolio of commodity contracts that provides a degree of diversification that the small investor may not be able to achieve otherwise.

WHAT FEES OR OTHER ACQUISITION COSTS ARE INVOLVED?

A commission or service charge is applied to a commodities trade in much the same fashion as the buying or selling of stocks and bonds.

HOW DO I SELECT THE BEST OF ITS TYPE?

1. Investors should concentrate their attention on a few commodities rather than spread their investment over a large number of different contracts. More time and effort will be needed to follow commodity positions than similar investments in stocks and bonds, and the average investor will generally be less knowledgeable about commodity markets.

2. Select markets that are active and that have a large "open interest" (i.e., the number of contracts in a

commodity that have not been closed out, exercised, or allowed to expire). The level of open interest is reported daily in newspaper commodity pages. Conversely, beginning investors should avoid "thin" markets that are especially prone to volatile price swings because of the relatively low number of active traders. Some of the more active commodities are soybeans, wheat, cocoa, and copper.

3. Inexperienced traders should begin with a conservative position of one or two contracts that mature in a distant month. This will require a relatively small investment and give the investor time to study the market and get better acquainted with its characteristics before making greater commitments. Also, buying contracts in distant months will reduce the amount of trading and the amount of commissions charged.

4. It is generally a good idea to put in a "stop-loss order" 5% below the market price when buying a commodity, and 5% above the market for a short sale. This approach will limit the investor's losses while allowing for continued gains if the market moves in the anticipated direction.

5. Never put up additional margin to maintain a contract. If you are asked to do so it means that the market is moving against you and will likely continue to do so. It is better to liquidate your position and take a small loss rather than continue to increase your investment and risk a major loss of capital.

6. This is an area where an experienced broker can be invaluable. Investors should look for a firm with a strong background in commodities, and deal with a broker who is a specialist in the field. It is not likely that a broker whose area of expertise is stocks and bonds will also be knowledgeable in the area of commodities. Diversified investors may want to maintain a separate brokerage account for their commodities trading activity.

WHERE CAN I FIND OUT MORE ABOUT IT?

1. Daily price quotations on various commodities can be found in the *Wall Street Journal* (www.wsj.com) and other major financial newspapers.

2. Most of the major brokerage firms have departments that specialize in trading commodities. They can be a source of reports and charts on the various commodity contracts.

3. Serious traders may wish to subscribe to the monthly *Technical Analysis of Stocks and Commodities Magazine* published by Technical Analysis, Inc., 800-832-4642 (store.traders.com).

4. The Chicago Board of Trade (www.cbot.com) publishes a reference book entitled, *Commodity Trading Manual*. The Chicago Board of Trade web site has a wealth of information on both physical commodities and financial products, like Treasury bond futures contracts. It includes basic information on all contracts, as well as beginning and advanced commodity trading strategies.

QUESTIONS AND ANSWERS

Question – Why are the margins on commodity contracts so low in comparison with those on stocks and bonds?

Answer – The margin on a commodity contract is a security deposit to ensure performance on the contract. It is not a down payment on the commodity itself or a payment of equity as in the case of stocks and bonds. A similar concept applies in the field of real estate where a security deposit is typically paid to the seller of a house by the buyer to ensure that final payment will be made at the time of closing.

Question – Is commodities trading regulated?

Answer – Yes, the Commodity Futures Trading Commission (CFTC), an agency of the federal government, regulates the trading of all domestically traded commodities. The CFTC sets price fluctuation limits, prohibits excessive market positions, oversees the handling of investors' funds by brokers, and allows trading only on designated exchanges.

Question – Where can an investor obtain information on the commodities themselves?

Answer – A commodities investor must be concerned with a number of fundamentals and their relationship to each other. These include (1) the amount produced, (2) the surplus from prior years, (3) the amount that must be saved and is, therefore, not available for current use, and (4) the amount that is currently needed.

The United States Department of Agriculture (USDA) makes public announcements of most of this information. Until the public release, this information is a closely guarded secret.

Other factors that will directly or indirectly affect the price of various commodities are the weather, crop and animal blights and diseases, political influences, technological changes, and the expectations of farmers and other commodity producers.

CHAPTER ENDNOTES

1. The 15% rate applies to long-term capital gains realized on or after May 6, 2003 (under The Jobs and Growth Tax Relief and Reconciliation Act of 2003). The rate for long-term capital gains realized before May 6, 2003 was 20%.

Chapter 16

MUTUAL FUNDS

WHAT IS IT?

A mutual fund is a company (or a trust) that sells shares of its own stock and utilizes the proceeds to make other investments. These investments may include the stocks of publicly traded companies, corporate or municipal bonds, real estate, or short-term money market instruments. By purchasing shares in a mutual fund, the investor obtains a number of benefits that would otherwise be unavailable.

WHEN IS THE USE OF THIS TOOL INDICATED?

1. When an investor has limited capital to work with and cannot afford to purchase a broad enough range of securities to achieve adequate diversification.

2. When the investor is unwilling or unable to select, manage, or keep records on a large number of securities.

3. When the investor wants to be able to sell shares or increase his holdings at any time.

4. When an investor would like to hire a skilled, professional investment manager, but does not have enough assets to meet the usual minimum asset size for most money management firms.

5. When an investor would like to invest "passively" and capture market returns for a particular asset class, such as large cap U.S. stocks.

ADVANTAGES

1. Mutual funds can be an excellent vehicle to carry out a well-conceived investment plan (see Chapter 39). Once an investor has a disciplined, well thought out strategy, there are many choices available in the mutual fund universe to execute the investment plan with reasonable costs.

2. Mutual funds can provide a high degree of security of principal and income through diversification of

securities. Few individuals could afford to buy as many different types of stocks or other investments as the typical mutual fund holds. This spreading of risk makes it unlikely that poor performance by any one security will result in financial disaster.

3. The purchase of shares in a mutual fund allows an investor to hire top notch investment management expertise, thus freeing the investor from the responsibility of managing the portfolio of securities on a day-to-day basis.

4. Most mutual funds "maintain a market" in their own shares. Such funds are referred to as "open-end" investment companies. This means that the mutual fund company has obligated itself to buy back its shares from investors. An investor can require the fund to redeem its shares at any time. This requirement provides the purchaser of fund shares with a high degree of liquidity.

A small category of funds, referred to as "closed-end" funds, do not buy and sell their own shares. Instead, their shares are traded on the open market much like the shares of publicly traded companies. These funds may be listed on the organized stock exchanges or traded on the over-the-counter market. (Although closed-end funds technically are not mutual funds, the shareholders of a fund that qualifies and makes the necessary election to be taxed as a regulated investment company will be taxed like mutual fund shareholders.)

5. Several large discount brokerage firms have created "fund supermarkets" where an investor can have a wide mix of funds, from hundreds of separate fund groups, all in one brokerage account. This makes it easy for an investor to put together a diversified portfolio of funds from different fund families, with top-notch management and low costs. Investors can easily rebalance and make changes within the one brokerage account.

6. Mutual fund organizations have promoted the concept of a "family of funds." A company will sponsor a number of funds with different investment objectives

and underlying assets. The investor can decide to switch assets back and forth from one fund to another. The advantage is that the investor can quickly, conveniently (and typically without any additional sales charges) move assets into one or more funds that better meet his investment needs or desires.

7. From time to time—typically after down periods in the market—mutual funds may have significant realized capital losses that can be used to offset taxable capital gain distributions in the future. Further, the fund may have significant unrealized depreciation in assets. This means that future appreciation, up to the original cost basis of the security, is "tax free" within the fund itself. These two factors can make some funds more tax efficient, at least in the short run, than if the investor had purchased the same securities themselves.

DISADVANTAGES

1. Purchasing shares from many mutual funds involves payment of a sales charge, commonly called a "load." This charge covers the cost of marketing the fund through brokerage firms and certain other fees. Sales charges can be as high as 8.5% of the original investment, but this is very unusual. Market forces have reduced the typical front end load down to an average of about 4.75% for bond funds and 5.75% for stock funds. There are now many share classes, and the fees and commission structure can be very confusing (front load, back load, level load, etc). There are many "no-load" funds that market their products directly to the public by mail and through newspaper advertising. These funds do not charge a sales fee.

2. Annual management fees and administrative charges can reduce the overall return on the investment. Management fees can range from 0.5% to 3% or more of the value of the investment. Administrative charges may be imposed in addition to management fees and frequently cost from $5 to $25 annually per account. These small administrative charges are frequently waived for accounts that reach a minimum balance. These fees can eat up a significant portion of the return to an investor. For example, a bond fund earning 5% on Treasury notes with a 2% expense ratio will only return 3% to the investor. The expenses are eating up 40% of the returns.

3. While professional management relieves the investor of certain obligations and responsibilities, it also eliminates his personal involvement in the manage-

ment of the fund. The purchaser of a mutual fund cannot control the selection of specific assets or the timing of purchases and sales. Unlike the investor who buys stock directly and who can select the time to sell and recognize a gain or loss, the mutual fund shareholder has no choice. He cannot control the amount of any capital gain distribution, or when it must be reported. Capital gain distributions are paid annually and must be reported each year on the shareholder's tax return.

TAX IMPLICATIONS

1. Ordinary income distributions from mutual funds are generally taxed to individual shareholders at ordinary income tax rates. However, under JGTRRA 2003, "qualified dividend income" (generally, dividends paid by domestic corporations and certain foreign corporations to shareholders) is treated as net capital gain and is, therefore, eligible for the 15%/5% tax rates, instead of the higher ordinary income tax rates. Ordinary income dividends paid by mutual funds are eligible for the 15%/5% tax rates *only if* the income being passed from the fund to shareholders is qualified dividend income in the hands of the fund, and not short-term capital gain or interest from bonds (both of which continue to be taxed at ordinary income tax rates). Mutual funds will report on Form 1099-DIV the nature of the dividend being distributed to shareholders (i.e., whether the dividend is qualified dividend income subject to the 15%/5% rates, or nonqualifying dividend subject to ordinary income tax rates). Unless designated by the mutual fund as net capital gain, all distributions to shareholders are to be treated as ordinary income dividends.[1] See the "Questions and Answers," below for a description of tax strategies to consider when acquiring and disposing of shares.

2. Capital gain distributions are generally treated as long-term capital gain, and are taxable in the year in which the distribution is declared. (See the discussion of capital gains and losses, including the lower rates (15%/5%) for long-term capital gains incurred on or after May 6, 2003, in Chapter 43.)

3. The income paid from municipal bond funds is not subject to federal income tax, but is normally taxed at the state level. Capital gains, however, are fully taxable.

4. Every time a "switch" is made within a family of funds, shares of one fund are technically sold and

shares of another fund are purchased. These sales are taxable events and result in a gain or loss. Of course, if the funds are purchased through an IRA, Keogh, or qualified corporate pension or profit-sharing plan, tax is deferred until an actual or constructive distribution occurs.

5. The sale or other disposition of less than all of an investor's shares (or of shares acquired on various dates at various prices) can cause difficulty in determining the basis of the shares sold. Several methods are available for establishing the basis of shares and, thus, for determining the amount of taxable gain. These are explained in "Questions and Answers," below.

6. Some funds are set up as limited partnerships in order to allow investors an exemption from state and local taxes on interest from U.S. government securities; however, this exemption does not apply in all states.

ALTERNATIVES

1. A variable annuity has many of the characteristics and features of a mutual fund. Typically, these include ownership of a large portfolio of securities and management by professional investment advisers. See "Questions and Answers," below for more information on variable annuities.

2. Exchange-traded funds (ETFs) are baskets of securities traded on an exchange, like stocks. ETFs can be structured as unit investment trusts holding a fixed basket of stocks or other investments, or as open end mutual funds tracking a market index. ETFs are discussed fully in Chapter 17.

3. Real estate investment trusts (REITs) are similar to mutual funds in many respects, but differ mainly in the nature of their underlying assets. REITs generally have the majority of their assets invested in shopping centers, apartment buildings, office buildings, and other large-scale real estate ventures. Some investors have a preference for real estate as opposed to securities for investment purposes. REITs are discussed fully in Chapter 21. There are a number of mutual funds that specialize in REIT securities.

WHERE AND HOW DO I GET IT?

Most load funds are sold through brokerage firms that receive part of the load charge as a fee for selling shares

in the fund. Many brokerage firms are affiliated with particular fund groups or have their own set of mutual funds that they market to their clients. These funds will generally include a money market fund (see Chapter 1), one or more common stock funds, bond funds, and a fund that specializes in tax-exempt securities. Orders to buy and sell fund shares are treated like any other transaction and require that the investor have an account with the brokerage firm. Investors will receive confirming receipts of any trades, and activity will be shown on the monthly statement received from their broker.

Investors should realize that some brokers may be biased toward selling their own funds rather than those of other mutual fund organizations. Also, brokers typically will not sell shares in no-load funds for which they receive no commissions. Investors should be careful to review the recommendations of brokers to see that they are conforming to the investor's particular needs and desires.

As noted, no-load mutual funds are rarely sold through traditional brokerage firms. These funds are bought and sold directly through the funds themselves. Additionally, they are sold through "fund supermarkets" at the large discount brokers. No-load funds are widely advertised in the newspapers and most carry on an active campaign of direct mail advertising and solicitation. Investors interested in a specific fund or a particular group of funds can call, write, or visit the fund's website for additional information or the forms needed to open an account.

Once an account has been established with a no-load mutual fund organization, it is relatively easy to purchase additional shares, to switch investments from one fund in the group to another, or to sell shares. Most of these transactions can be done on the telephone, by mail, or via the fund's website. After a transaction is made, the fund will send a confirming receipt to the investor within a few days.

WHAT FEES OR OTHER ACQUISITION COSTS ARE INVOLVED?

The sales charge for purchasing a load fund generally ranges from 3% to 5.75% of the net asset value of the fund. Net asset value is the total value of the fund's assets, minus any liabilities, divided by the number of outstanding shares of the fund. For example, assume that Consolidated Fund, a hypothetical mutual fund, charges a 5% load to purchase its shares. If the fund's shares had a net asset value of $10.00 per share, the sales charge would be $0.50, and the purchase price of a share for investors would be $10.50.

The load fee for mutual funds may be as high as 8.5%; however, the vast majority of load funds charge less than this amount. Investors should be cautious in purchasing these funds since some also charge a redemption fee that may be as high as 5% of the value of any shares sold. This fee is assessed whenever the investor sells shares of the fund and is subtracted from the amount the investor is paid. This redemption fee may be waived if the investor sells shares of the fund but reinvests the money in another fund of the same group. The load, plus the "12b-1 fee" (see below), plus the redemption charges cannot exceed 8.5%.

The entire fee structure of "load funds" is now quite complex. Over the past 10 years, there has been a shift away from front end load funds (commonly called "A" shares) to back end load funds ("B" shares) and level load funds ("C" shares) and a number of variations. It's imperative that prospective investors understand what they are buying, and what the annual fees are, including 12b-1 fees and surrender charges.

The costs of buying and selling shares of so-called "closed-end" funds are similar to those of buying and selling any shares of stock. The transaction cost will be determined by the number of shares traded and the total value of the transaction. Typically this cost will be 2% to 3% of the total value of the shares purchased or sold.

As their names implies, no-load funds do not charge a fee for the purchase or sale of their shares. These funds may be identified in newspaper listings of mutual funds by the indication of "N.L." in the column of offering prices. These funds may be purchased or sold at their indicated net asset value with no additional sales charges. However, investors should be aware that while these funds do not charge a sales fee, they do assess administrative charges and management fees, and may charge "12b-1 fees" to cover the costs of marketing and advertising (typically on an annual basis). These fees can range from 0.2% to 1.25%. Further, service charges of 0.5% to 3% of the investment may be charged when shares are purchased or dividends reinvested.

HOW DO I SELECT THE BEST OF ITS TYPE?

Today there are more than 15,000 different mutual funds available to investors. These funds have a wide variety of investment objectives and vary considerably in terms of size, fees, management, performance, and services offered to investors. Selecting the right fund for a particular investment situation may not be easy and should be given a great deal of thought. Described below are some of the important factors to consider in making such a decision:

1. The selection process should begin with an evaluation of the fund's investment objective. This information can be found in the fund's "prospectus," which can be obtained from a brokerage firm or from the fund itself. In addition to describing the fund's investment objectives, the prospectus will provide some data on its historical performance. While there are a great many mutual funds, their objectives can be grouped into a few common categories:

   Growth Funds – more aggressive than common stock funds, these funds concentrate on long-term capital gains and high future income; generally invest in more speculative issues that provide little or no current income; most of their investments are in common stocks, and possibly a few convertible bonds. The most aggressive funds—with above-average growth potential, high portfolio turnover, high degree of leverage, and high risk—are called performance or "go-go" funds.

   Income Funds – specialize in securities that pay higher-than-average current rates of return from either dividends or interest by investing in securities not generally favored by the investment community; frequently invest a high percentage of their assets in bonds rather than common stocks.

   Balanced Funds – the most conservative of the funds investing in common stock; these funds have as their primary objective the preservation of capital and moderate growth of income and principal; secondary consideration is capital gains; generally diversify their investments among both stocks and bonds; during bear markets typically offer the best investor protection.

   Tax-Exempt Funds – operate principally to provide investors with high after-tax returns on their investments; generally limit their investments to municipal securities or other types of issues that offer tax-sheltered income.

   Index Funds – these funds are designed to track a particular market index, such as the S&P 500, with very low annual expenses. The idea is to give an investor a vehicle to achieve "market performance" in a particular asset class, be it large U.S. stocks, small U.S. stocks, REITs, international stocks, or certain categories of bonds. This is also known as "passive investing." The primary advantage of this form of mutual fund investing is the lower costs (both annual expenses and transactional) that give an inherent advantage, and the ability of an investor to eliminate the risk of manager underperformance and be assured of "market" performance. See "Questions and Answers," below for more information on index funds.

Sector Funds – restrict investments to a particular sector of the market, such as energy, electronics, chemicals, or health care; these funds tend to be more volatile than a more diversified portfolio. See "Questions and Answers," below for more information on sector funds.

Diversified Common Stock Funds – concentrate principally on long-term capital growth, with current income being a secondary consideration; a majority of the assets are invested in good quality common stocks with the balance in cash or short-term government notes. These funds follow a more conservative approach.

Specialty Funds – seek to achieve their objectives by concentrating their investments in a single industry, in a group of related industries, in an industry within a specific geographic region, or even in non-security assets such as real estate investment trusts that purchase real property or loans secured by real property.

Hedge Funds – use the most aggressive techniques, including high leverage, short sales, and the purchase of put and call options to achieve maximum growth of capital; for the most speculative investor.

Money Market Funds – typically no-load funds that invest exclusively in money market instruments such as Treasury bills, CDs, and corporate commercial paper, providing current income and relative safety of principal; offer competitive services such as check writing privileges and free conversion privileges to other types of funds managed by the same investment group.

Commodity Funds – designed to bring the small investor into the commodities market; organized as limited partnerships, these funds offer an inflation-hedge in an inflationary environment and an opportunity for large gains, but with a high degree of risk.

Bond Funds – possess several advantages over direct bond investing, provided expenses are kept low; offer a variety of portfolio types, and proven track records; allow an investor to indirectly participate in the bond market without acquiring the expertise necessary to invest in the market directly. See "Questions and Answers," below for more information on bond funds.

Foreign Stock And Bond Funds – open-end and closed-end funds that invest in foreign stocks and bonds; some invest exclusively in the securities of one nation while others invest more broadly in foreign regions, or in all foreign markets.

Asset Allocation Funds – in essence, these funds offer one-stop shopping for a complete investment portfolio and offer a substitute for the investor's own allocation of investment dollars among several different traditional funds. These funds offer diversification not only within asset classes but among asset classes, and they may include nontraditional asset classes, such as commodities and real estate. See "Questions and Answers," below for more information on asset allocation funds.

2. Another important selection factor is the fund's historical performance. Relatively few funds have outperformed the market as a whole over long periods of time, but some have consistently done better than others. Each fund's prospectus will give some indication of its rate of return during the last five or 10 years. Most funds will show what a typical investment would have returned in the form of dividends and capital gains. Various investment sources (see below) will also provide comparative information on large numbers of mutual funds. Investors should use this information to select those funds that have regularly been above average in their investment performance.

In analyzing the performance of mutual funds, it is important to note that many funds perform quite differently in bull markets as compared to bear markets. Growth funds, especially those that concentrate in speculative issues, tend to do well when economic conditions are good and the general trend of the stock market is up. However, these same funds have been relatively poor performers when market conditions are weak and the economy is in a decline. In contrast, income funds and some balanced funds tend to do better than growth funds when the market is weak. Few funds have been able to turn in better than average performance under all market conditions.

3. Investors should concentrate on those funds with low sales charges, management fees, and expense ratios. As noted above, funds differ considerably as to the cost of purchasing their shares. This should not be the only consideration, but high sales charges can sharply reduce an investor's overall rate of return on investment. Similarly, funds that charge high portfolio management fees have to provide better than average returns to compensate for those charges. Funds also have normal business expenses and these charges, referred to as a fund's "expense ratio," should be a factor in selecting a particular mutual fund for investment.

4. The range of services offered by the fund is another important consideration in making a selection. Most funds will provide for automatic reinvestment of dividends into additional shares of the fund. Another common feature is automatic payout of a specified amount on a monthly, quarterly, or annual basis. This feature is especially important to older investors who may be using the fund to provide retirement income. In addition, many offer convenient methods for purchasing shares at the day's net asset value, either by telephone, by wire transfer, or by logging onto the Internet.

5. It is desirable that a fund be a part of a "family of funds" that provide the investor with flexibility in terms of diversification and the opportunity to alter his investment objective. As noted above, few funds have done well under all market conditions, and the investor should be prepared to transfer investments when market conditions change. Also, it is not unusual for one person to have a variety of investment needs, and the opportunity to make investments in a number of funds within the same management group is attractive.

6. A sample worksheet for evaluating mutual funds is included in Figure 16.1. It is designed to allow an investor to systematically evaluate data to arrive at an investment decision. A fund's prospectus can supply most of the required information.

   (a) The first section, beyond requesting basic information, requires the investor to focus on his investment objectives as they relate to risk, return, and portfolio diversification.

   (b) The second section examines a fund's performance for five years, both on its own and relative to an index and the average for its investment category. The Treasury bill rate is a reference

point for examining riskless return. Returns should include any reinvestments of capital gains and income distributions.

   Comparison of a fund's performance to an index is an indication of the performance of the fund's management. An index is unmanaged (i.e., no management fees or expenses). Fund performance greater than the index indicates that the fund manager is doing a good job and is, essentially, worth his fees.

   Comparison of a fund's performance to the average for its category is an indication of how well a fund is performing relative to its counterparts with the same investment objectives and fees. If a fund performs worse than the average, it typically should not be considered for a portfolio.

   (c) The next section examines risk. The first differentiation concerns diversified versus non-diversified funds. Diversification is important because non-diversified funds are more risky than diversified funds due to their unlikeliness to follow the market and their tendency to exhibit more variation in return.

   The worst annual performance in the past five years is an indication of how much risk an investor can withstand without ruining long-term investment plans. Although overall performance is more important, if poor performance signifies more risk than the individual investor can tolerate, this figure is significant.

   The stock and bond fund sections focus on the risk involved with each. For example, sector funds and small stocks are riskier than equity funds and large stocks. The risk associated with bonds focuses on the creditworthiness of the issuer and the maturity of the bond. The federal government is more creditworthy and, hence, less risky than a corporate issuer. Likewise, bonds with longer average maturity dates are more risky as interest rates fluctuate than bonds with shorter average maturity dates.

   (d) The mutual fund expense section focuses on the expenses and fees associated with the fund's operation. Annual fees charged for the administration of the fund, management fees, and sales fees can grow to substantial amounts

Figure 16.1

MUTUAL FUND WORKSHEET

Fund Name _____

Address _____

Telephone _____

Minimum Initial Investment $ _____

Minimum Subsequent Investment $ _____

Telephone Exchange? ____ Yes ____ With money market fund?
____ No

Investment Objective

____ Aggressive Growth Stock
____ Growth Stock
____ Growth and Income Stock
____ Balanced, Stock and Bond
____ Bond
____ Tax-Exempt Bond
____ International Stock
____ International Bond
____ Other: _____

Performance

Total Annual Return for Most Recent 5 Years (%)

	1	2	3	4	5
Fund	___	___	___	___	___
Index*	___	___	___	___	___
Average for Category	___	___	___	___	___
Fund Return Less Index*	___	___	___	___	___
Fund Return Less Category Average	___	___	___	___	___
Treasury Bill Rate	___	___	___	___	___

*Stock index for stock funds; bond index for bond funds
Consistency of Performance:
In how many years did the fund outperform the average for its category? _____

Portfolio Manager: _____   No. of years in position: _____

Risk

____ Diversified   ____ Non-Diversified   Worst annual performance over last five years: _____ %

Stock Funds:

____ Yes
____ No
Industry: _____

Investments:
____ Large Stocks
____ Small Stocks

Bond Funds:

Investments:
____ Governments
____ High-Quality Corporates
____ Low-Quality Corporates
____ High-Quality Municipals
____ Low-Quality Municipals
____ Mortgages

Average Maturity:
____ Short-term (less than three years)
____ Intermediate-term (three to 10 years)
____ Long-term (over 10 years)

Figure 16.1 (cont'd)

Expenses

12b-1 annual charge: ____%	Greater than 0.50% ____ Yes ____ No
Annual expense ratio: ____%	Greater than:
	1.1% for bond funds? ____ Yes ____ No
____ No-Load	1.4% for stock funds? ____ Yes ____ No

Load: Front-End ____%	
Back-End or Redemption ____%	Disappears after 6 months? ____ Yes ____ No

Taxes

Distribution dates: Income _____

Capital gains _____

Net investment income as a percentage of average net asset value: _____%

Portfolio turnover rate: ____%   Greater than 50%   ____ Yes   ____ No

Tax-exempt interest: ____ Federal   ____ State   ____ Local

Account Status: IRA, Keogh, Simplified Employee Pension, or 403(b)   ____ Yes   ____ No

---

that reduce the overall return of the fund. Although it is unwise to judge a fund solely by its cost structure, excessive expenses are a very important factor in evaluating a mutual fund's attractiveness.

(e) The final section examines taxes so as to avoid paying them unnecessarily. To approximate required taxes, the ratio of net investment income to average net asset value of the fund is useful. This calculation estimates interest or dividend yield. The higher the yield, the greater the tax potential. Also useful is the portfolio turnover rate. This measure indicates how often the fund buys or sells securities during the year. The greater the number of transactions, the greater the potential for capital gains and subsequent distributions that are taxable. A benchmark portfolio turnover figure of 50% or less is usually desirable.

WHERE CAN I FIND OUT MORE ABOUT IT?

1. An excellent source of information on mutual funds is Morningstar (www.morningstar.com), 225 W. Wacker Drive, Chicago, IL 60606. Morningstar is generally considered the best source of unbiased mutual fund information.

2. Another source is CDA/Weisenberger's *Investment Companies Yearbook*, a reference book on mutual funds that is available from most libraries. This manual provides information on the investment objectives of several hundred mutual funds as well as a record of their past investment performance. It also includes the address of the fund where investors may write for additional information.

3. *Forbes* (www.forbes.com) magazine publishes an annual survey of mutual funds in one of its August issues. This survey is unique in evaluating the per-

formance of funds in both up and down markets. Investors can quickly see how well a fund has done under various conditions and match that performance to their own assessment of current market circumstances.

4. Most brokerage houses will be happy to provide information on the mutual funds that they offer to their customers. They are also required by law to provide a current prospectus on a fund before they solicit an investor to buy shares in that fund.

5. The funds themselves are good sources of investment information. In addition to a prospectus, funds publish quarterly reports that indicate their performance during the period and the investments currently in their portfolio. They may also make available information in the form of booklets that describe the various funds available, the objective of each fund in the group, and how those funds can be used to meet investors' needs.

6. Investment Company Institute (www.ici.org), 1401 H Street, N.W., Washington, DC 20005.

7. *Barron's* (www.barrons.com); Dow Jones and Company, 200 Burnett Road, Chicopee, Mass. 01020; weekly; separate listing of selected funds and listing of prices by exchange.

8. *The Wall Street Journal* (www.wsj.com); Dow Jones and Company, 200 Liberty Street, New York, NY 10281; daily.

9. *Moody's Bank and Finance Manual* (www.Moodys.com); Moody's Investors Service, 99 Church Street, New York, NY 10007; annual; financial details and summaries of selected funds.

10. *The Value Line Investment Survey* (www.valueline.com); Arnold Bernhard & Company, 711 Third Avenue, New York, NY 10017; closed-end fund industry summary and evaluation of selected funds.

QUESTIONS AND ANSWERS

Question – How do I compare one mutual fund with another?

Answer – Some of the factors that apply to the selection of mutual funds are:

1. fund objective;

2. management style and discipline;

3. fund size;

4. performance record;

5. sales charges (if any);

6. expense ratio; and

7. special services.

Fund objectives should match the investor's personal goals. Each fund states its objectives in its advertising and provides a more detailed explanation in its prospectus.

An investor should review a fund's performance record over a period of at least five years. This information can be found in most local libraries. Some of the more common sources are Morningstar, CDA/Weisenberger's *Investment Companies Yearbook, Forbes* magazine, and publications from the Investment Company Institute (www.ici.org) and the Mutual Fund Education Alliance (www.mfea.com).

"Load" and "no-load" are terms used to indicate whether or not a fund levies a direct sales charge. Such charges can range from 3% to 8.5% of the initial investment. It would appear that investors would always be better off by purchasing no-load funds, but this is not necessarily the case. The overall performance record of a good load fund can offset the absence of a sales charge in a mediocre no-load fund.

While all funds charge an advisory fee, these vary considerably from fund to fund. Investors should search for those funds with good performance records and relatively low advisory fees. These fees are reported in the fund's prospectus or annual report.

Some funds charge a management fee in addition to any sales charges and investment advisory fees. These fees are typically $5 to $25 per account per year.

Investors should select funds from those organizations that provide a wide range of special services to fund holders. These services include: (1) the ability to transfer from one fund to another; (2) automatic reinvestment of dividends; (3) automatic payments from the fund (this typically requires a

Tools & Techniques of Investment Planning

minimum investment); (4) service and information provided with respect to Keogh and IRA accounts; (5) a toll-free "hot line" for information and service (provided by customer service representatives); (6) direct access to accounts through an investor's touch-tone telephone (through which the investor can obtain 24-hour account information, and even make transactions by phone); or (7) access to account information via the Internet.

Question – What is a "beta coefficient" and how can it be used to measure how well a mutual fund will do in a bull market?

Answer – A beta coefficient measures the fund's relative volatility against a well-known market index such as the Standard & Poor's Index of 500 common stocks. The index selected would be assigned a beta of 1. If the fund tends to rise (or fall) twice as high (or low) as the selected index, then the fund would be given a beta of 2.

A fund that rose or fell only half as much as the selected index would be given a beta coefficient of .5. The beta of a fund will change according to the time period over which it is analyzed. High volatility does not assure that the fund will skyrocket in an up market. But in general, funds with the highest betas tend to go up further and faster in up markets than those with a lower beta.

Question – How can an investor determine the number of additional shares that have been purchased when a distribution is reinvested in additional shares of the fund?

Answer – Divide the amount of the distribution by the fund's "net asset value" (NAV) on the date of the distribution. For example, suppose the shares in a mutual fund have a NAV of $8.17. The fund pays a capital gains distribution of $0.30 per share and a dividend of $0.38 a share. Divide $0.68 (.30 + .38) by $8.17. That equals .083231 additional shares.

Question – What are "sector funds?"

Answer – Sector funds are mutual funds that restrict their investments to a particular sector of the market. For example, a health care sector fund would confine its investments to those industries related to that segment of the market—drug companies, hospital management firms, medical suppliers, and biotech concerns. The portfolio would consist of promising growth stocks from these particular industries. Among the more popular sector funds are those that concentrate their investments in energy, financial services, gold, leisure and entertainment, natural resources, electronics, chemicals, computers and peripherals, telecommunications, utilities, and health care.

The underlying investment objective of a sector fund is generally growth. The idea behind the sector fund concept is that the really attractive returns come from small segments of the market. Rather than diversifying widely across the market, the philosophy is to put your money where the action is. These funds should be considered only by aggressive investors who are willing to take on the added risks that often accompany these funds. Since sector funds are, by design, not well diversified, investors face greater price volatility than with more broadly diversified portfolios.

Some investors use sector funds to implement a market timing investment strategy. Because various sectors of the economy tend to "peak" and "trough" at different times within the business cycle, market timers shift from one sector fund to another as they anticipate the economy moving from one phase of the business cycle to another. This is an extremely risky technique; since (1) investors may poorly time the business cycle and shift their portfolios at incorrect times and (2) any given sector fund may not behave in the same manner as the entire sector in each business cycle. Research does not suggest that many, if any, investors have been able to consistently predict changes in the business cycle. If anyone can predict the way various industries will perform, that individual should be able to predict the entire market. There is more to be gained from knowing when to shift from stocks to Treasury bills than there is from knowing when to shift from health care to leisure and entertainment.

If the fund's managers do not select appropriate stocks for the fund, it may not truly reflect the performance of the sector it is supposed to mimic.

Question – What are variable annuities and how do they compare as an alternative to mutual funds?

Answer – A variable annuity allows the holder of an annuity contract, usually issued by an insurance company, to invest in a family of mutual funds with the purpose of accumulating savings, usually for retirement. The accumulated balance is then disbursed as a series of payments or a lump-sum payment upon retirement (or other planned event). The amount available for distribution is contingent on the performance of the mutual funds selected.

As an alternative to mutual funds, variable annuities offer the advantages of tax-deferral for any dividends or capital gains earned until the income is withdrawn, and a waiver on taxes normally required for fund transfers between mutual funds. Generally, variable annuities also guarantee that a beneficiary will never receive less than the sum of the contributions if the annuity holder dies before the annuity starting date.

On the other hand, money in variable annuities is tied up for long periods of time, which can be a disadvantage if the investment strategy is not long-term in focus. Additionally, to the extent the gain on the funds inside the annuity are from long-term share appreciation, this "capital gain" is converted to ordinary income at the time of withdrawal and does not receive any favorable tax treatment, as do long-term capital gains from mutual funds. Variable annuities are also illiquid because the IRS imposes a 10% penalty tax on premature distributions (generally before age 59½) and insurance companies also impose surrender charges. Expenses, too, are usually high—typically 2% of total assets versus a 1% charge for mutual funds. Finally, declining back-end surrender charges are frequently imposed over a 7-year period, whereas no-load mutual funds carry no such levy. Load mutual funds, however, impose a sales charge up to 8.5% that is paid up-front and does not decline if no withdrawals are made during the first few years.

Overall, variable annuities perform similarly to mutual funds. Specifically, though, variable annuities exhibit lower levels of stock market and total risk than the market as a whole.

On the whole, variable annuities present better investment opportunities when:

1. the investor's tax rate is higher during the accumulation phase and lower during the payout phase;

2. the accumulation period is longer;

3. the rate of return is higher;

4. the annual expense differential is smaller; and/or

5. payments will be taken from the annuity contract in the form of one of the annuity options rather than as a lump sum.

Also, a variable annuity is more likely to be the better investment if you are comparing it to a load mutual fund rather than a no-load mutual fund.

Figure 16.2 compares the after-tax accumulation of a variable annuity with a no-load fund over various accumulation periods assuming: a $25,000 initial investment; a 9% pre-tax rate of return (after investment management expenses); a 1% annual charge in excess of the annual mutual fund expenses; a 34% combined federal and state income tax rate; annuity payments/withdrawals that commence

Figure 16.2

COMPARISON OF VARIABLE ANNUITY VERSUS MUTUAL FUND

End of	No-Load Mutual Fund After-Tax Value		Variable Annuity After-Tax Value		
	Total	Total Retirement Payouts Over 20 Years	Total	Lump-Sum Surrender	Total Retirement Payout Over 20 Years
5 Years	$33,361	$57,880	$36,733	$32,744	$57,880
10 Years	44,518	77,240	53,973	44,122	81,060
15 Years	59,407	103,080	79,304	60,841	115,120
20 Years	79,276	137,560	116,324	85,406	165,160

after age 59½ (no 10% penalty); and no surrender charges on the annuity after year five.

The comparison shows that the variable annuity breaks even with the mutual fund in 12 years and outperforms the mutual fund for every holding period beyond 12 years. The annuity builds to over $85,406, versus the $79,276 an investor would receive from the mutual fund if he were to invest for 20 years before taking a lump-sum withdrawal. The advantage would be even greater if the investor were to take distributions from the annuity over 20 years. In this case, the investor would break even after waiting only five years to begin distributions, receiving a total of over $165,000 after tax, about 20% more than if the investor had systematically withdrawn funds from the mutual fund during the 20-year retirement period. If the investor's tax bracket were to drop to 25% after retirement (down from 34% before retirement), the retirement payout would increase to over $184,000.

The annuity break-even period is quite sensitive to changes in some assumptions, so comparisons should be run using assumptions applicable to each investor's situation. It should be noted that variable annuities are taxable as ordinary income, while mutual funds may be taxable at capital gains or ordinary income rates.

Question – Is the better strategy to invest in bonds directly or through a mutual fund?

Answer – With a diversified portfolio, an investor can reap the benefits provided by both bonds and funds. However, bond mutual funds possess several advantages over direct bond investing (provided expenses are maintained at low levels). In addition to diversification and professional management, mutual funds offer a variety of portfolio types, and proven track records. Furthermore, as an individual investor it is becoming somewhat more difficult and costly to deal directly in the bond markets due to their professional orientation. Therefore, by investing in bond mutual funds an individual can realize transaction cost economies by allowing the professionals to make the investments. Bond mutual funds offer greater liquidity, too, because an investor can take money out of a no-load fund without incurring transaction costs or unfavorable prices. Selling bonds before their maturity date carries penalties. Finally, direct bond investors rarely realize a bond's promised yield because rates of return are highly unpredictable. Bond mutual fund investors have a

greater chance of realizing returns due to their ability to reinvest any distributions as they are received and by having their interest compounded.

Overall, bonds, whether invested directly or through mutual funds, generally realize lower total returns than stocks. Therefore, it is necessary to maintain low costs in order to offset this disadvantage.

Question – What are "index funds?"

Answer – Index funds are mutual funds that try to match the performance of some market index by creating a portfolio that replicates the index (to the extent possible). For example, the Vanguard 500 Index (formerly known as the Vanguard Index Trust, the first publicly offered index fund), seeks to provide investment results that correspond to the price and yield performance of publicly traded stocks as represented by the Standard & Poor's 500 composite stock price index. The S&P 500 Index is a "value-weighted" index (i.e., the weighting of stocks in the index are in proportion to their value in the market relative to all the stocks in the index), which studies indicate is one of the best measures of overall market performance.

Index funds are useful when the investor wants to achieve "market performance." If you believe—as many studies indicate and general factors suggest—that it is nearly impossible to consistently outperform the market on a risk-adjusted basis, index funds provide a means to closely match the market, or given segments of the market, at low cost with broad diversification and convenience. On average, about 75% of the common stock mutual funds classified as either growth or aggressive growth fail to beat the S&P 500 Index in any given year.

Index funds offer several advantages, including:

1. *Diversification.*

2. *Low Initial Investment Requirements.*

3. *Lower Transaction Costs*—On average, the typical common stock fund incurs about a 4% transactions cost on a round-trip trade. The average common stock fund turns over about 80% of its portfolio each year. Therefore, even if the performance of a fund matches the market, annual average returns would be reduced by about 3.2% relative to the market. The portfolio

turnover rate for the Vanguard 500 Index has historically averaged about 5 to 6% per year (since it trades only when necessary to keep the fund in line with the S&P 500 Index). Consequently, the Vanguard 500 Index has averaged 13 times lower transaction costs than the average common stock mutual fund.

4. *Lower Management Fees and Expenses* – These fees have averaged about 1.5% per year for the average common stock mutual fund. Index funds that passively match a specified index charge no (or very low) management fees. Consequently, fees and expenses for index funds are many times lower than for the average common stock mutual fund. For example, over a 5-year period, the Vanguard 500 Index has averaged about 0.20%, or about 7.5 times less than the average stock fund.

5. *More Consistent Performance* – On average, any common stock mutual fund that "beats" the market one year has about a 50-50 chance of underperforming the market in the subsequent year. Index funds tend to closely match the specified index year after year.

However, index funds also possess several disadvantages. Investors bear essentially the same market risk as the underlying index. Also, some of the newer entries into the index fund market are, in reality, actively managed rather than passively (most notably, the Gateway Fund—formerly known as the Gateway Option Income Fund). Therefore, their performance can deviate substantially from the ideal. When selecting an index fund, read the prospectus carefully to determine the degree of latitude the management has in the active management of the fund.

Several tax-related issues are relevant when considering index funds. The principal tax consideration is that index funds, like all other mutual funds, must declare and pay both regular and capital dividends at least once annually. Investors do not have the same degree of latitude in the timing of sales of specified securities within the funds as they would if they held the underlying portfolio directly. Consequently, they may have to recognize gains when they would otherwise choose not to do so. However, investors may choose when to buy and sell shares in the funds and gains will be treated as long-term if they have held the shares for the required period (even if some of the underlying stocks in the portfolio have not been held for the long-term holding period).

Index funds can be effectively incorporated into a mutual fund portfolio by utilizing a core portfolio approach. This approach splits a stock portfolio into two portions: (1) a passively managed portion; and (2) an actively managed portion. The passive portion focuses on index funds and should account for at least 50% of the total stock portfolio. It should track a broad-based index like the Standard & Poor's 500. The active portion focuses on specialty funds or a particular market segment not covered by the index fund, or one that offers the potential for undiscovered market value. Although the active management of some of the new entries is classified as a disadvantage of index funds, active management in this instance works to the advantage of the investor.

Question – What accounts for the differences in returns among mutual fund rankings?

Answer – Although mutual fund rankings take into account both return and risk, this question focuses on the variations in returns reported by various organizations providing mutual fund rankings. A number of factors are responsible. They include:

1. *The Time Period Covered* – Not all mutual fund ranking services use the same time period for their calculations (due to publication deadlines). Some use a calendar year while others use only certain quarters of the year. Trying to compare time periods that are not exactly the same will distort data as extraordinary or unusual events occurring during those time periods take effect. A related problem occurs when some ranking sources provide returns for bull and bear markets while others do not. The definition of a bear or bull market is intuitive and varies with the individual. In addition, not all funds were in existence during all the bear and bull markets to-date.

2. *Return Figure Composition* – Total returns consist of capital gains *plus* income *minus* the operating expenses of the fund, brokerage costs, and commissions. Fund load charges and redemption fees are not normally included, although this is where the problem arises. Some sources include these load charges, but this distorts the short-term performance of the fund.

3. *Reinvestment of Fund Distributions* – Although almost all sources include the reinvestment of distributions of the fund, not all report these reinvestments at the same time period. Some

report reinvested distributions at the end of the month in which the reinvestment occurred. Others report reinvested distributions on the exact day of reinvestment, which may not be the end of the month. If the fund prices differ when reinvestments are made, the returns will subsequently differ.

4. *How Return Performance Is Reported* – Three reporting formats are common: reporting by dollar returns, annualized returns, or unannualized returns. Each will report a different return since the calculations for each differ, and since different time periods are used for the calculations.

Question – What tax strategies should be considered when acquiring mutual fund shares?

Answer – Several strategies are useful. These include:

1. *Timing Purchases Wisely* – For the investor, the purchase of mutual fund shares carries the extra burden of the fund's untaxed dividends and capital gains to date. When distributions are received, the shareholder is taxed on those previously accumulated dividends and gains.

   By timing purchases wisely, the investor can reduce his tax liability. Purchasing shares on, or soon after, the "ex-distribution date" (i.e., the date a shareholder is no longer entitled to the distribution) relieves the investor of this added tax because there is no taxable income to report. This factor is very important if very large capital gains are expected because they carry a large tax burden.

2. *Taking Advantage of Tax Deferrals* – Taxes on unrealized gains on stocks are deferred until the shares are sold. Because these gains are compounded on a pre-tax basis, tax deferral on the gains results in a lower effective tax rate. The longer the deferral, the lower the tax rate.

   Likewise, a stock mutual fund investor obtains the same advantages for as long as the fund holds the appreciated shares. Therefore, the lower the portfolio turnover rate, the better the opportunity for tax deferral.

3. *Trying to Time the Dispositions of Fund Shares* — so that short-term capital gains can be used to offset long-term capital losses, rather than

being treated as ordinary income. A fund's turnover rate is a good indicator of potential short-term gains. A high turnover may mean a greater potential for short-term gains, while a low turnover would indicate a lower proportion of short-term gains.

4. *Maximizing Mutual Fund Capital Loss Carryovers* – Because capital losses are not passed on to shareholders, but are offset against capital gains, a carryover loss can be used to reduce capital gains and subsequent taxes.

Question – What tax strategies should be considered when disposing of mutual fund shares?

Answer – The cost method used when calculating gains and/or losses on partial share purchases and redemptions affects the individual's taxable income. Four methods can be used:

1. *Average cost method*. An investor whose mutual fund shares are held by a custodian can use this method. The choice of the single-category or double-category method is up to the investor and affects the characterization (i.e., long-term or short-term) of the gain as well as the amount of taxable gain. The double-category method (i.e., where shares are divided based on whether they have been held for more than one year, or for one year or less) gives taxpayers greater control over the amount of gains or losses recognized.

2. *Specific identification method*. This is a more flexible method that allows shareholders to choose the specific shares sold in a partial redemption. Identification of shares to be sold must be done at the outset.

3. *FIFO method*. This method states that when a sale is made, the shares sold are those purchased earliest. If the price per share has risen since acquisition, then use of this method results in the largest overall gains.

4. *LIFO method*. This method assumes the most recently purchased shares are sold. If prices have gone up, gains are reduced.

Investors should choose wisely the cost method used in order to reduce their tax liability.

Question – What are "asset allocation funds"?

Answer – In recent years, a number of mutual funds referred to as "asset allocation funds" have been created to create diversification in asset categories not traditionally offered by conventional mutual funds. Specifically, these funds invest in traditional asset categories of domestic stocks, bonds, and money market instruments. However, they also invest in the nontraditional asset categories of foreign stocks and bonds, real estate securities, precious metals securities, commodities, and natural resources. Although mutual funds that invest in one of these nontraditional asset categories have proliferated in recent years, balanced mutual funds, which invest in some mix of common stocks, previously fixed-income securities (e.g., bonds and preferred stocks), and money market instruments, were generally the only types of funds that offered a limited kind of asset allocation in the past.

Asset allocation funds attempt to use the imperfect correlations between the nontraditional asset classes and the traditional asset classes to provide either higher returns for a given level of risk or lower risk for a given level of return relative to traditional mutual funds.

However, the term "asset allocation" is used by asset allocation mutual funds in both its strategic and its tactical sense. In other words, some asset allocation funds employ strategic asset allocation to broadly diversify with relatively fixed-mix asset proportions invested in traditional as well as nontraditional asset classes. Other asset allocation funds employ tactical asset allocation to time the market and to shift investments among both the traditional and nontraditional asset classes, depending on their manager's forecast of economic and market trends.

Thus, asset allocation funds differ from one another in a number of important ways:

1. *By the Asset Classes That Are Included or Permitted Within the Portfolio* –

- Some funds permit investments in virtually all asset classes.

- Others restrict investments to a subset of all asset classes and, by doing so, may better be described as hybrids between traditional balanced mutual funds and genuine asset allocation funds.

However, for practical reasons of cost and efficiency, even the asset allocation funds that have virtually no restrictions on the asset classes in which they may invest usually restrict their investment to a subset of all the major asset classes. It is possible to create "efficient portfolios" (i.e., the highest potential returns for a given level of risk) while limiting investments to a subset of all asset categories.

2. *By Investment Strategy and Philosophy* –

- Some asset allocation funds employ strict strategic asset allocation by applying a fixed-mix asset allocation scheme to their asset categories. In other words, the proportion of the portfolio invested in each asset class remains fixed in all economic and market environments.

- Some asset allocation funds employ unrestricted tactical asset allocation and set no minimum limit on the amount that must be invested in any one asset class. Fund managers are given the flexibility of investing virtually all or none of the fund's assets in any asset class depending on their assessment of the current economic and market environments.

- Most asset allocation funds set a restricted high/low range on the amount that must be invested in any given asset class. Managers are given limited discretion to shift funds among asset classes when, in their judgment, current economic and market conditions so warrant.

- Some asset allocation funds employ dynamic hedging or portfolio insurance strategies, or permit the use of put and call options, short selling, or stock index futures trading to limit downside risk.

When selecting an asset allocation fund, determine whether a fixed-mix strategic asset allocation strategy or a variable-mix tactical asset allocation best fits your own personal investment philosophy and select from those funds that match your philosophy. Review the fund's prospectus for the following information:

1. *The Permitted Asset Classes* – In general, more is better.

2. *The Asset Classes in Which the Fund Has Actually Invested* – Although some funds may permit investments in a broad range of asset classes, they may, in fact, not invest in many or most of those categories. Some of the funds are virtually nothing more than glorified balanced funds with their investments predominantly in U.S. stocks and bonds.

3. *The Limits or Restrictions on the Portfolio Weights in Each Asset Category* – If the investor wants tactical asset allocation and market timing, more flexible and broad limits may be better. However, if the investor wishes to assure at least some diversification among nontraditional asset classes, look for more restricted ranges or limits on the required investments in each asset class.

4. *Minimum Initial and Subsequent Investments* – Some funds have very low or minimal initial investment requirements, and permit additional investment of nominal sums. Others require quite sizable initial and subsequent investments.

5. *Expense Ratios* – Look at the history (which in many cases may be quite limited) of the fund's expense ratio as a percent of assets being managed. The expense ratio is an indicator of efficiency of management. However, expect expense ratios for asset allocation funds to be higher on average than for traditional mutual funds. Diversification into more asset classes and into nontraditional asset categories will entail some additional expense.

6. *The Use of Dynamic Hedging Techniques or Portfolio Insurance Strategies* – The prospectus should explain whether the fund will employ strategies to limit downside performance through various hedging or portfolio insurance techniques. These techniques may be beneficial for investors with a relatively short-term planning horizon. However, for investors with a longer-term planning horizon, the cost of such techniques will generally outweigh the benefits.

Question – What is a "lifecycle fund"?

Answer – A lifecycle fund is a diversified mutual fund—one that automatically shifts towards a more conservative mix of investments as it approaches a particular year in the future, known as its "target date" (hence, these funds are also sometimes referred to as "target-date funds"). Lifecycle funds are becoming increasingly popular as Baby Boomers plan for retirement. The primary decision when investing in a lifecycle fund is picking a fund with the right target date based on the investor's particular investment goal. Once that decision has been made, the managers of the fund then do the rest (i.e., they make all the decisions about asset allocation, diversification, and rebalancing). Some prefer to think of this as investing on "cruise control." It is easy to identify a lifecycle fund because its name likely will refer to its target date (e.g., "Portfolio 2015," "Retirement Fund 2030," or "Target 2045").[2]

CHAPTER ENDNOTES

1. See IRC Sec. 854(b), as amended by JGTRRA 2003. See, generally, IRC Sec. 852.

2. See "Lifecycle Funds," United States Securities and Exchange Commission at: http://www.sec.gov/rss/your_money/life-cycle.htm.

Chapter 17

EXCHANGE–TRADED FUNDS (ETFs)

WHAT IS IT?

On the simplest level, an "exchange-traded fund" is a security representing a basket of stocks or bonds, like a mutual fund. However, like individual stocks, ETFs are traded on a stock exchange. They are something of a hybrid security, combining features of both closed-end and open-end mutual funds, as well as other unique features.

ETFs represent shares of ownership in funds, unit investment trusts, or depository receipts that hold portfolios of common stocks or bonds that closely track the performance and dividend yield of specific indexes. They give investors the opportunity to buy or sell an entire portfolio of stocks in a single security, just as easily as they can buy or sell a single share of stock. They also offer a wide range of investment opportunities.

ETFs bear brand names such as Qubes, SPDRs ("spiders"), HOLDRs, iShares, VIPERs, StreetTracks, and Diamonds. All of them are passively managed, tracking a wide variety of sector-specific, country-specific, and broad-market indexes. Since May of 2002, the number of ETFs traded on exchanges in the United States and overseas has grown from about 80 to several hundred. In addition, new ETFs covering various market sectors, market indexes, or international markets are being created nearly every day.

Broad-based exchange-traded funds track a broad group of stocks from different industries and market sectors. For example, iShares S&P 500 Index fund (symbol IVV) is a broad-based ETF that tracks the S&P 500 Index. Sector funds track companies represented in related industries; one such fund is the iShares Dow Jones U.S. Healthcare Sector Index Fund (symbol IYH), a sector fund that tracks the Dow Jones Healthcare Sector Index. International funds track groups of stocks from specific countries or a broad index of international stocks, such as the MSCI - EAFE Index (Morgan Stanley Capital International Index - EAFE). For example, iShares MSCI-Australia (symbol EWA) tracks the Morgan Stanley Capital International index for Australian stocks.

Although ETFs are similar to index mutual funds in some respects, they differ from index mutual funds

in significant ways. Unlike index mutual funds, ETFs are priced and can be bought and sold throughout the trading day using market, limit or stop-loss orders. Furthermore, ETFs can be sold short and bought on margin. Essentially, anything investors might do with an individual stock, they can do with an ETF.

HOW DOES IT WORK?

An ETF is a portfolio of stocks or bonds, made up of "creation units" or shares of the fund. Currently, all ETFs are based on indexes as opposed to actively managed funds. Each day, a portfolio composition file (PCF), which indicates the portfolio constituents and their respective weights, is distributed via major data vendors. This transparency facilitates the process of creating and redeeming creation units.

As indicated in the PCF, an ETF offers investors units in a specific portfolio for a specified amount of cash or securities. This unit is then traded like an ordinary stock in the secondary market, the most important of which is the American Stock Exchange (AMEX).

When redeeming a creation unit, an institutional or large investor receives a basket of the underlying securities and a small amount of cash, as determined by the PCF. Because of this redemption for securities, the ETF managers do not have to sell stock, and thus no capital gains are realized. Typical individual retail investors sell their shares on the secondary market for cash.

On the other hand, mutual fund shareholders cannot sell their shares in the secondary market. Their only option is to receive cash when the mutual fund redeems their shares. When the mutual fund managers receive requests for redemption, they may be forced to sell stocks if not enough cash is available to pay the redeeming shareholders. As a consequence, capital gains may be realized by the remaining shareholders. Therefore, ETFs are far more advantageous than mutual funds in that ETFs can distribute stock, not cash, in the event of redemptions.

WHEN IS THE USE OF THIS TOOL INDICATED?

1. ETFs should be considered by investors who seek to invest in an industry sector or index and who do not want to acquire and manage a multitude of equity stocks in their portfolio. Investors can benefit from the low expense ratios and management fees incurred by ETFs. Index-oriented investors can also use ETFs as an easy and cost effective means of re-balancing their portfolio towards a specific sector or country and facilitate tax-based trading strategies.

2. Traders who want to try to capitalize on anticipated daily movements of broad market baskets of securities, market sectors, or international stocks now have the exchange-traded vehicle with which to conduct their speculative trading.

3. ETFs are appealing to participants in employer retirement plans who do not have a large selection of mutual fund options to buy passively managed funds or low cost funds, but may have a self-directed brokerage option to buy passively managed ETFs.

ADVANTAGES

1. *Diversification* – ETFs are designed to provide a single investment value for the aggregate performance of a number of companies representing specific industries, market sectors, or broad market indexes. Diversification is intended to reduce the risk inherent in particular securities. By incorporating several stocks in an index, an investor has a broader number of companies that gives a degree of protection in case the price of one company in the index goes lower.

2. *Liquidity* – Unlike open-end mutual funds that can only be redeemed at the end of the day, ETFs are priced throughout the day and, thus, can be bought or sold any time like stocks. They enable investors to easily rebalance their portfolios at a low cost and to take advantage of market trends. In a falling market, investors can sell sooner than they could with a mutual fund; likewise, in a rising market, investors can also buy sooner than they could with a mutual fund.

3. *Redemption Feature* – ETF shares are usually redeemed for the underlying securities. Generally, only large institutional investors or very wealthy investors can avail themselves of this feature since the minimum in-kind redemption is generally at least 50,000 shares.

This creates an arbitrage opportunity if prices in the market differ significantly from the net asset value. Consequently, in contrast with closed-end mutual funds, market arbitrage generally keeps ETFs trading close to their net asset values. Although the trading price for ETFs do not always equal their net asset values, they rarely, if ever, trade for very long at the significant discounts and premiums from net asset value that characterize market prices for closed-end funds. This characteristic also permits ETFs to be more tax-efficient, since shares can be distributed in-kind when a change occurs in an index, compared to an index mutual fund which must sell shares when an index changes, hence potentially triggering a capital gain.

4. *Low Cost* – ETFs generally do not have a manager or analyst actively managing the portfolio; thus, management fees are lower. The turnover of the portfolio is limited to changes in the underlying index (or corporate action in the underlying stocks); hence, transaction costs are lower.

5. *Trading Orders* – Similar to stocks, investors can place various types of orders, such as stop-loss orders, limit orders, and the like to automatically buy or sell units based on price movements or other criteria.

6. *Choice* – When investors purchase ETFs, they instantly get exposure to portfolios composed of stocks of their choice. They can choose a fund that either represents a broad-based market index, a specific industry sector, or an international sector.

7. *Tax Efficiency* – The legal design of ETFs provides them with the ability to avoid distributing capital gains to investors who are not selling their shares. Both ETFs and open-end mutual funds provide low stock turnover, which in itself is tax efficient because capital gains are not realized. However, ETFs provide a tax advantage not available with mutual funds. Whereas mutual funds must sometimes sell securities to cover redemptions, (thereby creating capital gains), ETFs can transfer securities out to redeeming shareholders instead of selling the securities (thus minimizing taxable capital gains). This benefit also applies when stocks are removed from an index.

8. *Margin* – Investors are able to buy ETFs on margin and "leverage" their investment, something they generally cannot do with mutual fund shares.

9. *Short Sales* – Investors can sell ETFs "short" to take advantage of anticipated declines in the market,

which they cannot generally do with mutual fund shares.

10. *Sales Loads* – ETFs involve no sales loads, but brokerage commissions generally apply.

11. *Management and Sponsorship Fees* – Expense ratios are very similar between ETFs and index mutual funds. Usually, they range from 0.09% of the value of the fund to 0.84%, with broad market ETFs being less expensive than international ETFs and U.S. sector ETFs. Since ETFs are passively managed, active management costs are absent. Since ETF shares are traded through broker-dealers, there is no need for the cost of mutual fund shareholder services. As a result, ETF expense ratios are generally less than comparable index mutual fund fees.

12. *Cash Flow* – ETF's, compared to index mutual funds, do not have cash flows from new investors coming in or out daily that must be managed to enable the mutual fund to track an index. Consequently, ETFs do not have a "cash drag" from uninvested cash in a rising market.

DISADVANTAGES

1. *Market Risk* – Because ETFs are based on an underlying basket of stocks or an index, they are subject to the same market fluctuations as the underlying securities.

2. *Commissions* – Investors purchasing ETFs in the secondary market are subject to regular stock commissions. If investors are making small or periodic investments or frequently rebalancing their portfolios, ETFs can be relatively costly because the commission costs may ultimately exceed the expense of investing in no-load mutual funds.

3. *Bid/Ask Price Spread* – Like any individual stock, ETF's are sold at the bid price and bought at the ask price. The bid price is below market price and the ask price is above market price. This spread represents a trading cost in addition to broker commissions.

4. *Market Price* – An ETF can trade at a premium or discount from its net asset value (NAV). Consequently, the ETFs' price might vary slightly from the true underlying values of the securities in the fund. In contrast, open-ended mutual funds are always bought and sold at the net asset value (but only at the end of the day and based upon market closing prices). Closed-end funds trade all day, similar to ETFs, but since they offer no redemption feature to permit arbitrage, they often are priced at large discounts or premiums from their net asset values.

5. *Automatic Reinvestment* – Most mutual funds permit investors to have income dividends automatically reinvested in the fund; ETFs offer no such option. However, most brokerage firms permit investors to direct that certain income dividends be used to automatically purchase additional shares of stock or ETFs for their account at no cost.

6. *Strategies to Offset Operating Expenses* – Index mutual funds can lend securities on margin to earn income that will offset the fund's expense ratio and use futures contracts to track an index more accurately when futures pricing inefficiencies exist. These strategies can result in a mutual fund tracking error even less than the expense ratio. ETFs generally do not employ either strategy.

7. *Dividend Cash Drag* – ETF's structured as unit investment trusts can have a lower return because of the accounting treatment for income dividends.

8. *Investing an Exact Dollar Amount* – Since ETFs must be purchased in share amounts rather than dollars, and odd-lot share amounts (less than 100 shares) or uneven increments may be more expensive to trade, an individual may not be able to fully invest 100% of the cash they have available.

TAX IMPLICATIONS

Stock can be distributed to ETF shareholders for redemption and the transaction does not cause the realization of any capital gains. Further, the ETF managers can assign low-cost stocks to the redeeming shareholders, leaving high-cost stocks in the portfolio holdings. When these high-cost stocks are later sold, smaller capital gains will be realized. Thus, ETFs provide an exit strategy for their managers to minimize capital gains. In either case, ETFs end up with lower capital gain distribution and less tax burden on the investors versus a comparable index mutual fund.

In contrast, mutual funds do not have such flexibility. The managers can distribute only cash to the investors who redeem their shares. In order to minimize the capital gain, the managers might be able to sell the high-cost basis stocks, leaving the low-cost basis stocks in holdings. Unfortunately, these low-cost basis stocks must eventually be sold. One way or the other, the managers cannot avoid the capital gain distributions that produce a high-tax burden on the investors. Investors buying into an index mutual fund may be buying into a pending unrealized tax liability. Investors buying an ETF establish their cost basis as the original purchase price plus commission, with no pending unrealized tax liability.

Nontaxable Entity – A company qualifies as a "regulated investment company" for tax purposes if it (1) derives at least 90% of its taxable income from dividends, interest, and capital gains from sales of securities, and (2) invests at least 50% of its total assets in cash or securities, but no more than 25% of its total assets are invested in the securities of any one issuer.[1]

A regulated investment company is not subject to federal income tax to the extent its taxable income has been distributed to its shareholders in a timely manner. The "required distribution" is 98% of the taxable income.[2] Therefore, the difference between the "required distribution" and the income actually distributed is subject to income tax plus a 4% excise tax.[3] In other words, in order to avoid any tax liability, the ETF managers must distribute at least 98% of its taxable income.

All current ETFs qualify as regulated investment companies and pay no federal income tax. Therefore, if managed well, an ETF is practically a nontaxable entity.

Capital Gains/Losses – An ETF may receive cash dividends or interest on account of the securities they own. The trust may also sell the securities for short-term capital gains or losses if held for one year or less, or for long-term capital gains or losses if held for more than one year. The short-term capital gains and losses offset each other to arrive at net short-term gains or losses. The long-term capital gains and long-term capital losses offset each other to arrive at net long-term capital gains or losses. If the netting results in a situation where there are net short-term capital gains and net long-term capital gains, these gains are passed through and taxed to the investor. Whether a gain or loss is long- or short-term when passed through to investors depends on how long the securities have been held by the trust, regardless of the length of time the shareholders have held the creation units of the ETF. The tax treatment also depends on whether the ETF unit holder (investor) is a corporation or not.

Individual Taxpayer – A similar netting process applies at the investor level. If the result is a net *short-term* capital gain or loss, it is treated as ordinary income tax-

able up to the maximum rate for ordinary income for that taxable year, or as an ordinary loss deductible up to $3,000 per year until it is used up. If the result is a net long-term capital gain, which is termed "net capital gain" or "capital gain dividend" when distributed, it is taxed at the preferential long-term capital-gain tax rate (the maximum rate is currently 15%). If it results in a net long-term capital loss, it is deductible up to $3,000 per year until it is exhausted. However, if both the short- and the long-term netting produce losses for an individual taxpayer, no more than $3,000 of these losses may be deducted per year. Any excess losses are carried forward every year until used up, with net short-term capital losses being used first before the net long-term capital losses.

Corporate Taxpayer – For a corporate taxpayer, both short- and long-term capital gains are taxed at ordinary income tax rates, but not to exceed 35%. Both short- and long-term capital losses are nondeductible; however, they can be carried back for three years and carried forward for five years to offset capital gains, but not ordinary income. If the ETF trust distributes cash dividends to a corporate taxpayer, the corporation may be entitled to a dividends-received deduction.[5]

Distributions from income and capital gains are taxable only to the extent of the ETF's current and accumulated earnings and profits. If the ETF distributes taxable income of more than the trust's current and accumulated earnings and profits, the excess distribution is treated as a return of investment capital. It thus reduces the shareholder's adjusted basis. If a shareholder's adjusted basis is reduced to zero, any additional distribution is treated as capital gain.

In-Kind Redemptions – After the initial investment, the shareholders may request redemption from the ETF. The trust may distribute securities and cash approximating the proportion of the entire portfolio holdings. These securities might have been purchased some time ago, and their market values may have changed. The most important question of the ETF operation is whether the gains or losses from these securities should be recognized by the distributing trust.

Under the general rule, if a corporation distributes property to a shareholder, and the fair market value of such property exceeds its adjusted basis, the gain must be recognized to the distributing corporation as if such property had been sold to the distributee at its fair market value.[6] This means that, generally, gains are taxable and losses are not deductible with respect to the trust making the redemption. Fortunately, there is an exception that provides that the general rule will not apply to any distribution by a regulated investment company if that distribution is in redemption of its stock upon the demand by a shareholder.[7]

As a result of this exception, gains from the securities distributed to the ETF shareholders are not taxable (and losses are not deductible on the part of the distributing trust). The redemption in the form of securities is termed an "in-kind redemption" and is tax-free. This special treatment makes ETFs very tax efficient because redemptions do not result in recognition of capital gains. It encourages the ETF managers to distribute securities rather than sell them. Mutual fund managers, on the other hand, cannot enjoy this special feature. Because mutual fund shareholders receive cash in redemption, fund managers may have to sell securities in order to raise the cash, resulting in recognition of capital gains.

When an ETF shareholder receives securities in a redemption, his adjusted basis in the securities received is the same as his adjusted basis was for his prior interest in the distributing trust. Gains or losses are recognized only when the securities are sold. Consequently, the ETF's old gains or losses are not avoided, only deferred. The gains follow the investor who redeems the units, rather than being currently recognized and distributed among all the remaining shareholders (as would be the case with a mutual fund capital-gain distribution).

Redemptions can also be employed in another way to minimize the realization of capital gains. To qualify as a regulated investment company, the composition of the ETF is limited such that at least 50% of its total assets must be invested in cash or securities, and no more than 25% can be invested in one single company. It is possible that ETF mangers could be forced to sell securities to meet this requirement. (Index providers are aware of this regulation and often produce a modified version of the index, which incorporates such restrictions into its methodology and adjusts the index constituents' weightings accordingly.) However, when shareholders request redemption, the managers can distribute the securities in a way that will help the ETF satisfy the above regulated investment company requirements and, thus, prevent the ETF from having to sell securities and produce capital gains.

ALTERNATIVES

1. *Open-End Mutual Funds* – Literally hundreds of index mutual funds track the same broad-market indexes, market sectors, and international markets and indexes tracked by ETFs.

2. *Closed-End Investment Companies* – Although not as numerous as the mutual fund offerings, many closed-end funds trading on exchanges track broad-market indexes, market sectors, or broad international indexes or single-country indexes similar to ETFs.

3. *Futures Contracts* – Investors may acquire futures contracts on many of the indexes and sectors tracked by ETFs. For aggressive investors who would like to invest in highly margined ETFs, futures contracts on the same indexes tracked by the ETFs would give them the highest potential margin and the highest potential gain, but with correspondingly high risk. Since ETFs are traded on exchanges and may be "shorted," investors who desire greater margin than is permitted when going long in ETFs, but less margin and risk than when investing long in futures contracts, can combine a long position in the futures contracts and an appropriate short position in ETFs. This combination permits them to create an intermediate position of risk and margin between that of the most highly allowed margin position in the ETFs long and the naked position in the futures contracts.

4. *Portfolio Management* – Individual investors with very sizable investment balances and institutional investors can buy the underlying securities of their desired index directly in the market in proportion to their weight in the index and reproduce the index fund in their own portfolio.

WHERE AND HOW DO I GET IT?

Similar to common stocks and other listed securities, ETFs can be purchased through any brokerage account.

WHAT FEES OR OTHER ACQUISITION COSTS ARE INVOLVED?

Most ETFs charge lower annual expenses than even the least costly index mutual funds. However, as with stocks, investors must pay a commission to buy and sell ETF shares, which can be a significant drawback for those with small sums to invest, who trade frequently, or invest sums of money on a regular basis.

Management Fees – Since the "creation units" (see below) of ETFs can be traded in the secondary market like a stock, many unit holders do not have to ask for redemption. They can simply sell all or some of their shares in the secondary market. Creation units are exchanged in large multiples of shares (e.g., the SPDR 500 creation units are traded in multiples of 50,000 shares).[8]

As a result, the fund itself usually experiences only a few high-value transactions. Accordingly, since most ETFs are passively managed, ETF fund managers' operations are greatly reduced. As a result, the management fees are much lower than a typical mutual fund's fees.

In one study, ETF management fees were about 0.18%, while mutual fund management fees were 0.23%.[9] In another study, ETF management fees were about 0.12% while mutual funds were 0.18%.[10] In yet another study, ETF management fees were 0.0945% while mutual funds were 0.95%.[11] The *Wall Street Journal* reported that the management fees for the SPDR 500 and the NASDAQ-100 were 0.12% and 0.18%, respectively, and the weighted average for the 31 largest ETFs was 0.1727% in 2001.[12] These numbers are quite consistent, and the ETF management fees are always lower than those for the mutual funds.

HOW DO I SELECT THE BEST OF ITS TYPE?

The real key to selecting the best ETF is to pick a type that meets the investor's objectives. Many ETFs track major market indexes (such as the S&P 500 Index, the S&P MidCap Index, the Wilshire Index, the Dow Jones Industrial Average), and permit investors to track indexes of large or small capitalization value or growth stocks as well as international stock indexes. To the extent these types of ETFs are used to create and rebalance a portfolio, they can be very beneficial to the investor.

However, a large number of the ETFs are not broadly diversified and focus on a particular sector of the market (e.g., technology, health care, or particular securities of a single foreign country). For most investors, unless they feel they have exceptional skill and knowledge in some particular sector, these would generally not be considered appropriate investments.

Although some ETFs have been in existence for a number of years (e.g., the SPDR 500), many are very new and have very little history with which to judge their efficacy. Although expenses have so far generally been quite low for ETFs, they do vary by ETF. Thus, it is important to check expense ratios because when several different investment vehicles are essentially tracking the same index or sector, any difference in expenses is simply a "dead-weight" loss to the vehicle with the higher expenses. Since they are tracking the same index

or sector, there is essentially no way for the ETF with the higher expenses to "catch-up" by offering superior investment performance. (Although ETFs seem to offer certain tax benefits relative to index mutual funds, the track record is really not long enough to know whether the results will pan out in the long run.)

Finally, it is important to consider all costs (e.g., fund expenses, commissions and other transactions costs like bid/ask spread) as well as the investor's investment style. Even taking into consideration the greater tax efficiency – and perhaps lower average management expenses – that ETFs provide, for investors who are making regular periodic investments for the long run, the commission costs can potentially cancel out any gains from the other factors.

WHERE CAN I FIND OUT MORE ABOUT IT?

Brokerage houses have extensive literature describing the various ETFs and how they operate, as well as expense and performance data. Most also have archives of articles and educational primers on ETFs available on their web sites.

Morningstar has an entire section of their web site dedicated to ETFs (http://www.morningstar.com). Potential investors can look for ETFs by investment style by clicking on the Morningstar style box in the research section of the page. They also have links to view international ETFs. Similarly, NASDAQ has extensive coverage on its web site at http://quotes.nasdaq.com/asp/ETFsHome.asp.

Finally, each of the creators of ETFs has their own web site on the topic. Check the following addresses:

http://www.Amex.com
http://www.HOLDRS.com
http://www.iShares.com
http://www.spdrindex.com/spdr/express.asp
http://www.streettracks.com
http://flagship2.vanguard.com/VGApp/hnw/FundsExTradedFunds

QUESTIONS AND ANSWERS

Question – Why do ETFs track indexes or index funds rather than actively-managed portfolios?

Answer – Their passive nature is a necessity. ETFs rely on the potential arbitrage mechanism of the redemption feature to keep the prices at which they trade roughly in line with the net asset values (NAV) of their underlying portfolios. For the mechanism to work, potential arbitrageurs need to have full, timely knowledge of a fund's holdings so they can measure the market value of the underlying securities directly and then compare that with the market value of the ETF. If the ETF is selling at a discount from its NAV, the arbitrageurs can buy a creation unit of shares, redeem the creation unit, and capture the difference in values. If the ETF is selling for a premium, they can short the ETF shares, buy the underlying stocks in the market, and then deliver the stocks to cover the short position, once again, capturing the difference in profit.

Question – Can ETFs be sold short?

Answer – Yes. All ETFs may be "sold short," representing the sale of borrowed shares in anticipation of lower prices when the borrowed shares must be replaced. Certain ETF products are also exempt from the rule that requires shares to be sold short only on an "up-tick" (i.e., the last sale price higher than a security's preceding last sale).

Question – Can ETFs be purchased on margin?

Answer – ETFs may be purchased on margin, generally subject to the same terms that apply to common stocks. Brokers have all the relevant information regarding initial and maintenance margin requirements.

Question – Is there a sales load on ETFs?

Answer – ETFs, unlike some mutual funds, are not subject to sales loads. However, investors must pay ordinary brokerage commissions for purchases and sales, similar to common stocks. Similar to mutual funds, ETFs have small expense ratios for management fees, and transactions costs that are almost universally less than the expense ratios for even the most efficiently managed index mutual funds.

Question – Do ETF investors get paid dividends and/or capital gains?

Answer – ETF holders are eligible to receive their portion of dividends, if any, accumulated on the stocks held in trust. In many cases few, if any, dividend distributions can be expected on certain stock portfolios based on the dividend history of the underlying stocks.

Question – Is the value of an ETF equivalent to 100% of the value of the underlying index?

Answer – Not necessarily. The share price of many ETFs is set at a percentage of the index upon which they are based. The chart below illustrates the relationship between the price of an ETF and the level of the underlying index. As an example, if the NASDAQ-100 Index were at 4200 then the share price of the NASDAQ-100 Index Tracking Stock (QQQ), at approximately 1/40th the value of the Index, would be approximately $105 per share.

Exchange Traded Funds	Approximate relationship to underlying index
QQQ (NASDAQ-100 Index Tracking Stock℠)	1/40
SPDRS (Standard & Poor's Depository Receipts)	1/10
MidCap SPDRs™ (Standard & Poor's MidCap 400 Depository Receipts™)	1/5
Select Sector SPDRs® (Select Sector SPDR Funds)	1/10
DIAMONDS® (The Dow Industrials)	1/100
iShares - Barclays Global Investors	varies
HOLDRs - Merrill Lynch	varies

Question – Where do ETFs initially come from?

Answer – ETFs are "created" by large investors and institutions in block-sized units of shares (or multiples thereof) known as "creation units." A unit of 50,000 shares (or multiples thereof) is required to create SPDRs, NASDAQ-100 Index Tracking Stock, Select Sector Funds and DIAMONDS, while a unit of 25,000 shares is required to create MidCap SPDRs.

To create a unit, the investor or institution must deposit: (1) a specified number of shares of a portfolio of stocks that closely approximates the composition of a specific index; and (2) cash equal to accumulated dividends. Some of these institutional investors hold the creation units in their own portfolios. Others (generally broker-dealers) break-up the creation units and offer the ETF shares on exchanges where individual investors can purchase them from brokerage firms just as they would any other listed security.

Similarly-sized units of ETFs can be redeemed in return for a portfolio of stocks approximating the index and a specified amount of cash.

Question – Where are ETFs listed in the newspaper?

Answer – ETFs are listed in the financial section of most major newspapers under the stock exchange market on which the ETF is listed.

Question – What are the trading hours for ETFs?

Answer – ETFs based on broad-based indexes trade until 4:15 p.m., Eastern Standard Time. Select Sector SPDR Funds trade until 4:00 p.m. Eastern Standard Time. iShares Sector Funds trade until 4:15 p.m. Eastern Standard Time. ETFs based on foreign stock indexes trade until 4:00 p.m. Eastern Standard Time. HOLDRS, which are depository receipts, trade until 4:00 p.m. Eastern Standard Time.

Question – Where can investors get up-to-date price information?

Answer – The pricing of ETFs is continuous during normal trading hours. Investors can obtain this information from their broker, stock quotation systems, or on a delayed basis from NASDAQ InfoQuotes. The closing prices are also published in major newspapers on the following business day.

Question – How can investors use ETFs in managing their portfolios?

Answer – The diversity of ETFs matches the diversity of the market. By using ETF offerings (to replicate either the total market, value, growth, large stock indexes, small stock indexes, sector-specific offerings, or single-country, regional and international offerings), investors can fully diversify the equity part of their portfolio solely by using ETFs.

Question – What does it mean to say ETFs are more "tax efficient" than mutual funds?

Answer – ETFs appear to have many potential tax advantages over mutual funds. But just how much of a tax advantage do they enjoy? Below is a comparison of the SPDR 500 exchange-traded fund and the Vanguard 500 mutual fund.[13] The former accounts for over 40%[14] of the ETF market share, and the latter is easily the most popular index fund with over $1 billion invested. The comparison is based on two elements:

1. components of taxable income; and

2. tax liability and tax savings.

Components of Taxable Income – The analysis is based on empirical data of annual taxable income per share *from 1993 to 2000* for SPDR 500 and Vanguard 500, respectively. The investors-taxpayers are assumed to be individual, noncorporate investors. The income generated by the funds is classified into three categories:

(a) *Ordinary income* consisting of dividends and interest, which was taxed at a maximum rate of 39.6%. (*Note:* Under current law, the top rate on ordinary interest income and non-qualifying dividends is 35%. The top rate on qualifying dividends is 15%.)

(b) *Short-term capital gains* encompassing the sales of securities held for 1 year or less, which were also taxed also at a maximum rate of 39.6% (for the years examined).

(c) *Long-term capital gains* from the sales of securities held for more than 1 year, which were taxed at a maximum rate of 20%.

The calculations involve figuring out the relative weights of these three components (i.e., ordinary income, short-term capital gains, and long-term capital gains) as percentages of the taxable income. Then each component is calculated for the eight years from 1993 to 2000. After that, the difference between the SPDR 500 and the Vanguard 500 funds is determined. For further comparison, the annual average taxable income per share was determined for the eight years.

Because the NAV is different from one year to the other – ranging from $45.93 in 1994 to $128.39 in 1999 for SPDR 500, and from $43.11 in 1994 to $134.31 in 1999 for the Vanguard 500 – the average taxable income per share per year may be misleading. Therefore, the difference in annual taxable income per share was converted into a percentage based on Vanguard 500 fund's taxable income per share per year. Only after that adjustment was made was the average of these percentages calculated for these eight years again. The results are shown in Figure 17.1.

As Figure 17.1 shows, the SPDR 500 fund's annual average total taxable income per share is $1.29. This amount is made up of 99.24% ordinary income, zero short-term capital gains, and only 0.76% long-term capital gains. In comparison, the Vanguard 500 fund's average taxable income per share per year is $1.596875, of which 82.57% comes from ordinary income, 2.67% from short-term capital gains, and 14.78% from long-term capital gains.

Unexpectedly, the SPDR 500 fund's annual ordinary income per share, as compared with the Vanguard 500 fund, is actually increased by $0.014059 or 16.67% of its taxable income. In contrast, the SPDR 500 fund's short-term capital gains per share per year, as compared with the Vanguard 500 fund's, are reduced by $0.048125 or 2.67% of its taxable income. Furthermore, the SPDR 500 fund's long-term capital gains per share per year are reduced by a sizable $0.267537 or 14.00% of its taxable income. Overall, SPDR 500 fund's annual taxable income per share per year is reduced by $0.301603 or 16.30%.

These results show that the SPDR 500 was able to shift taxable income from long-term capital gains to ordinary income and still reduce the total taxable income. It demonstrates that the SPDR 500 is able to maneuver its income position in such a way that the decrease in long-term capital gains is more than enough to offset the increase in ordinary income. The SPDR 500 does not have much of an edge in terms of ordinary income, but it does have a great deal of advantage in the area of long-term capital gains. The key implication of this result is that SPDR 500 can benefit long-term investors more than short-term investors.

Question – So which is the better investment — a mutual fund, or an ETF?[18]

Answer – ETFs offer many advantages over mutual funds, but there are some drawbacks as well. Investors should ask themselves the following questions when choosing between an ETF and a mutual fund:

Is it really necessary to have a fund that trades like a stock? For rapid traders and day traders, minute-to-minute quotes and trading opportunities are necessary. For them, the fact that ETFs trade just like stocks can be appealing. For the many investors who are looking for long-term investments, however, this characteristic is probably not a very important factor.

How cost-conscious is the investor? At first glance, ETFs may appear much more cost effective than mutual funds. For example, the SPDR (Standard & Poor's Depository Receipt) (SPY), which tracks the S&P 500 Index, charges 0.12% in expenses.

The iShares S&P 500 Index (IVV) exchange-traded fund is even cheaper at 0.09%. That is just $0.09 for each $100 invested — a small fraction of the typical mutual fund expense ratio. Even the extremely efficient Vanguard 500 Index Fund (VFINX) charges more, with 0.18% in annual expenses. In addition, Vanguard charges a $10 annual maintenance fee for account balances below $10,000. On a $3,000 investment, that effectively boosts the annual expense ratio from 0.18% to 0.51%.

However, the ETFs do not have all the advantages. First, not all ETFs have low expenses; it is important to check the expense ratio. In addition, as with stocks, trading boosts the cost of investing in any ETF. Investors have to pay a broker's commission when they make a trade. Investors who (1) use inexpensive discount brokers, (2) invest large amounts of money, and (3) hold stocks for the long term, may come out ahead. Otherwise, an exchange-traded fund is not likely to have a cost advantage over a typical index fund.[19]

Will the investor be investing a lump-sum or a series of investments? Investors who like to dollar-cost average or to make regular periodic investments should probably favor mutual funds over ETFs. Mutual fund investors can enroll in an automatic investment plan typically at no cost. However, if an investor buys a modest amount of ETF shares every month, the commissions add up quickly. For example, if a broker charges $8 per transaction and an investor is buying $250 of shares per month, the commissions cost the investor 3.2% of the investment, considerably more than the cost for investing periodically in a mutual fund. Assuming the ETF and the mutual fund are tracking the same index or sector, there is virtually no chance that an investor can recoup these costs through the superior performance of the ETF. These fees are just a "dead-weight" loss.

Are taxes an important factor? One return advantage for exchange-traded funds is that they tend to be more tax-efficient than mutual funds. When mutual fund investors redeem shares, the fund manager may have to sell stocks to meet the cash redemption requirements. If the fund manager incurs taxable gains by selling all of the remaining shareholders in the mutual fund may end up paying taxes on these gains. In contrast, when investors sell ETFs, they are not redeeming shares — instead, they are actually selling them to other investors.

Figure 17.1

ANNUAL TAX DISTRIBUTION PER SHARE
SPDR 500 TRUST FUND VERSUS VANGUARD 500 MUTUAL FUND

Year	Ordinary Income		Short-Term Capital Gains		Long-Term Capital Gains		Total Taxable Income	
SPDR Trust Fund								
1993	$1.135	(100.00%)	$0.000	(0.00%)	$0.000	(0.00%)	$1.135	(100%)
1994	1.128	(100.11%)	0.000	(0.00%)	0.000	(0.00%)	1.128	(100%)
1995	1.300	(100.00%)	0.000	(0.00%)	0.000	(0.00%)	1.300	(100%)
1996	1.383	(93.91%)	0.000	(0.00%)	0.090	(6.09%)	1.472	(100%)
1997	1.377	(100.00%)	0.000	(0.00%)	0.000	(0.00%)	1.377	(100%)
1998	1.416	(100.00%)	0.000	(0.00%)	0.000	(0.00%)	1.416	(100%)
1999	1.445	(100.00%)	0.000	(0.00%)	0.000	(0.00%)	1.445	(100%)
2000	1.090	(100.00%)	0.000	(0.00%)	0.000	(0.00%)	1.090	(100%)
Average	$1.284	(99.24%)	$0.000	(0.00%)	0.000	(0.86%)	$1.284	(100%)
Vanguard 500 Mutual Fund								
1993	$1.130	(97.41%)	$0.000	(0.00%)	$0.030	(2.59%)	$1.160	(100%)
1994	1.170	(85.40%)	0.040	(2.92%)	0.160	(11.68%)	1.370	(100%)
1995	1.220	(90.37%)	0.030	(2.22%)	0.100	(7.41%)	1.350	(100%)
1996	1.280	(83.66%)	0.010	(0.65%)	0.240	(15.69%)	1.530	(100%)
1997	1.320	(69.11%)	0.145	(7.59%)	0.445	(23.30%)	1.910	(100%)
1998	1.330	(76.00%)	0.085	(4.86%)	0.335	(19.14%)	1.750	(100%)
1999	1.410	(58.63%)	0.075	(3.12%)	0.920	(38.25%)	2.405	(100%)
2000	1.300	(100.00%)	0.000	(0.00%)	0.000	(0.00%)	1.300	(100%)
Average	$1.270	(82.57%)	$0.048	(2.67%)	$0.279	(14.76%)	$1.597	(100%)
Difference: SPDR 500 - Vanguard 500 Mutual Fund								
1993	$0.005	(+2.59%)	$(0.000)	(-0.00%)	$(0.030)	(-2.59%)	$(0.025)	(-2.19%)
1994	0.042	(+14.60%)	(0.040)	(-2.92%)	(0.160)	(-11.68%)	(0.242)	(-17.66%)
1995	0.080	(+9.63%)	(0.030)	(-2.22%)	(0.100)	(-7.41%)	(0.050)	(-3.72%)
1996	0.103	(+10.25%)	(0.010)	(-0.65%)	(0.150)	(-9.60%)	(0.058)	(-3.77%)
1997	0.057	(+30.89%)	(0.145)	(-7.59%)	(0.445)	(-23.30%)	(0.533)	(-27.90%)
1998	0.086	(+24.00%)	(0.085)	(-4.86%)	(0.335)	(-19.14%)	(0.334)	(-19.00%)
1999	0.035	(+41.37%)	(0.075)	(-3.12%)	(0.920)	(-38.25%)	(0.960)	(-39.93%)
2000	(0.210)	(+0.00%)	0.000	(-0.00%)	0.000	(-0.00%)	(0.210)	(-16.15%)
Average	$0.014	(+16.67%)	$(0.048)	(-2.67%)	$(0.268)	(-14.00%)	$(0.302)	(-16.30%)

Source: State Street Global Advisors.

Chapter 17 – Exchange-Traded Funds (ETFs)

ETFs can (and do) make taxable distributions. For example, ETFs may receive dividends on securities held by the ETF, or may recognize gains when the fund manager buys and sells securities to continue to track the index. In general, though, the taxable distributions have tended to be fairly minimal, and are often less than distributions from comparable index funds.

Are there no index fund options available whatsoever? In some cases investors may favor a particular market sector (e.g., health care or telecommunications) for which there are few, if any, index fund alternatives available, whereas there are many ETFs that do track these sectors. Similarly, there are many more ETFs than mutual funds that focus on single foreign countries. Although investing a large portion of one's overall portfolio in such sectors is generally not considered good investment management for the long-haul, ETFs do permit traders and sector rotation timers to shift significantly between sectors when they feel it is warranted. These sector ETFs also permit more conventional investors who want to "shade" their portfolio towards certain sectors with the opportunity to do so while maintaining broad diversification within that sector.

CHAPTER ENDNOTES

1. IRC Sec. 851(b).
2. IRC Sec. 4982(b).
3. IRC Sec. 4982(a).
4. IRC Sec. 1211(b).
5. IRC Sec. 243.
6. IRC Sec. 311(b).
7. IRC Sec. 852(b)(6).
8. American Stock Exchange, Prospectus for Standard & Poor's Depositary Receipts, SPDR Trust, Series I, January 26, 2000, p. B-32.
9. Budny, Hosker, and Chan, "Exchange Traded Funds: Where the Market is a Stock," Lehman Brothers Report, September 15, 2000, p. 9.
10. Traulsen, "Exchange-Traded Funds: Are They Right for You?," at www.news.morningstar.com, November 9, 2000.
11. McNally, Emanuel, and Chiu, "Fundamental Ideas for Exchange-Traded Funds," Solomon Smith Barney Report, October 18, 2000, p. 4.
12. *Wall Street Journal*, March 5, 2001.
13. Drawn and adapted from "Fresh Alternative to Mutual Funds Offers Tax Benefit," 67 *Practical Tax Strategies*, 2001.
14. Budny, Hosker, and Chan, "Exchange Traded Funds: Where the Market is a Stock," Lehman Brothers Report, September 15, 2000, p. 11.
15. Adapted from Di Teresa, "Should You Buy an ETF or a Mutual Fund?," at www.news.morningstar.com, March 1, 2002.
16. Morningstar.com has a Cost Analyzer tool that investors can use to make cost comparisons between mutual funds and ETFs.

Chapter 18

LIFE INSURANCE

WHAT IS IT?

A life insurance policy is a contractual promise by an insurance company or beneficial association to pay a specified amount of money to a designated beneficiary when the insured person dies. The contract is between the insurance company and the policyowner who pays premiums in exchange for the promised death benefits. Frequently the policyowner is the person insured, but the policy can (and often should) be owned by someone, or some entity, other than the insured.

There are many variations on the theme but classically, the insurance company charges a premium for the contract that is combined with premium payments on other contracts into a general account of the insurance company. This general account, in addition to growth/earnings on the investments, is designed to provide adequate funds to pay the promised death benefits as they come due and also cover insurance company expenses (and profits). Because a relatively small percentage of insureds actually die in any particular year, most of the policyowner premiums are collected in the general account and are saved (with accumulated growth) for payment as a death benefit in the (possibly distant) future. In addition, since most individuals will live many years before a claim must be paid, the insurance company will not only accumulate a large number of premiums over time, but will have a great deal of time to accumulate additional growth on the invested premiums. Consequently, the death benefit is almost always larger than the cumulative premium(s) paid for the individual policy (sometimes quite significantly so). Although on an individual basis, this could be a substantial loss for a company (in theory, a policyowner might make a single $1,000 payment, have the insured die, and $1,000,000 death benefit will be paid to the beneficiary), when the insurance company applies this pricing structure to a *large* number of policyowners, the individual fluctuations tend to offset each other and the inflows and outflows become extremely predictable when averaged over the aggregate.

There are different types of life insurance policies and they can be classified in different ways. The primary method of differentiating life insurance policies is as either term or permanent insurance. Term insurance

is generally purchased for a certain (and limited) term of time, such as 5, 10, 20, or 30 years, or until age 70. Permanent insurance, on the other hand, is generally meant to be "permanent" – i.e., it can be kept in force as long as the insured lives, however long that may be. One defining characteristic of permanent insurance is that there is a "cash value" associated with the policy, and it may be available to some extent to the policyowner, either via a loan from the insurance company, or outright when the policy is surrendered.

Permanent insurance policies are typically separated into four distinct categories:

1. Whole life;

2. Interest-sensitive or current-assumption whole life;

3. Universal life; and

4. Variable life.

Each of these types of permanent life insurance (as well as term insurance) is discussed in detail in the Question and Answer portion of this chapter.

Another method of classification is by the number of lives insured. Most policies cover only one life, but policies are available that cover two or more lives. A *joint life* policy covers two individuals and pays a death benefit at the first death only; a *joint survivorship* (also called a 2nd-*to-die* or *last-to-die*) covers two individuals and is not payable until the death of the second (or last) of the insureds.

WHEN IS THE USE OF THIS TOOL INDICATED?

1. When an individual wants to provide income (or create an asset base to fund a stream of income) for dependent family members (e.g., spouse, children, elder parents) after the head of the household dies, typically until they become self-supporting.

2. When an individual wants to liquidate consumer or business debts or mortgages, or to create a fund that will enable his or her family to do so, at the individual's death.

3. When an individual wants to provide large amounts of cash at death for college expenses or other capital needs.

4. When an individual wants to create an estate (or a larger estate) for surviving heirs.

5. When cash is needed as a liquid source to pay federal and/or state death taxes.

6. When an individual wants to provide funds for remaining (or successor) business partners or owners to buy out the estate's (or spouse's) share of the business at the death of the owner/partner under a "buy-sell" agreement. In this case, the insurance may be owned by and payable to the other/successor business partners, or the business itself, or perhaps a trust depending upon the particular structure of the buy-sell agreement.

7. When a business seeks economic indemnification for the loss of a key individual (which may be because of the individual's impact on sales, production, management, or any other "key" aspect). This is known as "key person" life insurance. In this case, the insurance is owned by and payable to the business, and insures the lives of employees or owners whose deaths could result in serious financial loss to the firm. This may also be helpful for a business that is seeking to secure a loan for a small company that is highly dependent on a key employee—sometimes a lending institution will own insurance coverage directly on the key employee for its own protection.

8. When an employer seeks to recruit, retain, or retire one or more key employees through a salary continuation plan that will pay benefits to a spouse and/or dependents of a deceased owner or key employee, and desires to transfer the risk of its obligations under that plan.

9. When a client is seeking an inexpensive and effective way to transfer large amounts of liquid capital to children, grandchildren, or others without the erosion often caused by probate costs, inheritance taxes, income taxes, federal estate taxes, transfer fees, or the generation-skipping transfer tax.

10. When a client wants to provide greatly enhanced charitable gifts. Although there are many ways life insurance is used in charitable gift planning, the two most common involve the use of policies owned by the charity and the naming of the charity as beneficiary or co-beneficiary of new or existing policies or riders.

ADVANTAGES

1. Life insurance provides a guarantee of large amounts of cash payable immediately at the death of the insured. The amount of the death benefit payable is almost always significantly greater than the premiums paid for the policy. This is particularly true when the insured individual dies at a younger age – which is often the very situation in which insurance is needed the most in the greatest amount.

2. Life insurance proceeds are not part of the probate estate when policy proceeds are payable directly to a specific beneficiary other than the insured's estate. Only when the estate is named as the beneficiary of the policy (or the proceeds are paid for the estate's benefit) are the proceeds subject to probate. Therefore, the proceeds can be paid to the beneficiary without expense, delay, and aggravation caused by administration of the estate.

3. There will be no public record of the death benefit amount or to whom it is payable.

4. Life insurance policies offer protection against creditors of both the policyowner and of the beneficiary. The amount of protection varies from state to state but in many states it is significant.

5. Life insurance cash values provide virtually instant availability of cash through policy loans. The interest rate for policy loans is almost always lower than the rate on loans from other sources.

6. The death benefit proceeds from a life insurance policy are generally not subject to federal income taxes. (See the discussion of the transfer-for-value rules below for the exception of this general case.)

7. The increases in the cash value of a life insurance policy enjoy favorable federal income tax treatment. Interest earned on policy cash values is not taxable unless or until the policy is surrendered for cash. (See the discussion of the modified endowment contract rules below for the exception to this general rule.)

8. Life insurance proceeds are often exempt from state inheritance taxes. In Pennsylvania, for example, proceeds are exempt, even if payable to the insured's estate. (But aside from a relatively small amount, life insurance proceeds paid to the insured's estate is not recommended).

9. The guarantees and risk management provided by life insurance often brings peace of mind to the policyowner.

10. Permanent life insurance, with its cash value accumulations, can provide a method of "forced" savings (because premiums must be paid anyway or the policy may lapse) that aid individuals in long-term savings. However, it is important that life insurance "savings" not be made to the detriment of other, more appropriate, savings plans.

DISADVANTAGES

1. Life insurance is often not available to persons in extremely poor health. Individuals in moderately poor health can almost always obtain insurance if they are willing to pay higher premiums. These extra charges, to take into consideration the extra risk assumed by the insurance company, are called "ratings."

2. Life insurance is a complex product that is hard to evaluate and compare. The time required to gather policy information, decipher it, and compare it with other policies discourages purchasers from engaging in comparison shopping for many types of insurance.

3. The cost of coverage reduces the amount of funds available for current consumption or investment for the future.

TAX IMPLICATIONS

1. In general no tax deduction is permitted for premium payments on life insurance policies. The notable exception is that the premium payment on group term life insurance provided by an employer to employees is income tax deductible.[1]

2. Dividends received by the policyowner on a mutual policy are considered a return of premium – repayments of this nature are generally not subject to federal income taxation.[2] Dividends will not be taxable income unless the aggregate of dividends paid (and other amounts withdrawn) exceeds the aggregate of premiums paid by the policyowner. However, income tax free dividend distributions do reduce the cost basis of the life insurance policy for future gain/loss determinations.[3]

3. The cash value increases on an in-force life insurance policy resulting from investment income are not taxable income. The cash value build-up in a life insurance policy enjoys deferral from taxation while the policy remains in force and is exempt from income tax if the policy terminates in a death claim.[4] However, if the policy is surrendered for cash, the gain on the policy is subject to federal income taxation. The gain on a surrendered policy is the amount by which the sum of the net cash value payable and policy loan forgiveness exceeds the owner's basis in the policy. The character of any gains are ordinary income rather than capital gains.[5] Because life insurance policies are personal property that are not held for investment, losses are not deductible.[6]

Basis in the policy equals the premiums paid less policyowner dividends and less any other amounts previously withdrawn. For example, a policy on which $35,000 has been paid in premiums and $7,000 has been received in dividends would have a basis of $28,000 ($35,000 – $7,000 = $28,000). If that policy were surrendered for $10,000 in cash and a policy loan of $50,000 canceled (as if a total of $60,000 was received at the time of surrender), there would be an ordinary income taxable gain of $32,000 ($60,000 – 28,000 = $32,000).

4. The death benefits payable under a life insurance policy are generally free from federal income taxation.[7] Proceeds from corporate-owned life insurance policies can increase "adjusted current earnings" (ACE), a portion of which may be taxed under the corporate "alternative minimum tax" (AMT).[8] In a worst case scenario, this tax amounts to roughly 15% of the total policy proceeds paid to a corporate beneficiary. The AMT system is basically an alternative tax system that calculates taxes due under a separate tax structure – in any particular year, the corporation pays the higher of the regular tax bill or the AMT system tax bill. The AMT system does not allow tax deductions or exclusions for certain items that receive preferential treatment under the regular income tax rules. The AMT is generally applicable only if there are large amounts of preferentially treated items relative to the regular corporate income tax. Consequently, it is possible

that the AMT will not apply if the death benefit proceeds are paid in a year when there are few other preference items. Additionally, after 1997, corporations meeting the definition of a "small corporation" are exempt from the AMT. A small corporation is generally one which has average annual gross receipts for the previous three years that do not exceed $7,500,000 ($5,000,000 for a new small corporation's first three years, and never applicable in the first year of a corporation's existence).[9]

In addition, the Act imposes new reporting requirements on all employers owning one or more employer-owned life insurance contracts. These provisions regarding employer-owned life insurance are effective for life insurance contracts issued after August 17, 2006, except for contracts issued in a 1035 exchange where there was not a material increase in the death benefit or other material change.

6. Life insurance policies that have been transferred by one policyowner to another may be subject to the *transfer-for-value* rule.[11] Under this rule, the death proceeds of a policy transferred to certain non-exempt parties for a valuable consideration are taxed as ordinary income to the extent the death proceeds are greater than the purchase price plus premiums and certain interest amounts relating to policy indebtedness paid by the transferee.

In other words, if an existing life insurance policy or an interest in an existing policy is transferred for any type of valuable consideration in money or money's worth, all or a significant portion of the death benefit proceeds may lose income-tax-free status. However, policies can be transferred safely to certain parties that are exempt from the transfer-for-value rules, including:[12]

a) The insured;

b) A partner of the insured;

c) A partnership in which the insured is a partner;

d) A corporation in which the insured is a shareholder or officer; or

e) Any party whose basis is determined by reference to the original transferor's basis (e.g., a gift transfer).

7. The proceeds of a life insurance policy will be included in the estate of the insured for federal estate tax purposes if the insured held any "incident of ownership" at death or at any time during the three years prior to death, or if the proceeds from the policy were payable to or for the benefit of the estate of the insured.[13] Incidents of ownership include such things as the right to: (a) change the beneficiary; (b)

purchase an equity interest from a family member, beneficiary, trust, or estate, the proceeds will not be included in the employer's income.

5. Unless certain requirements are met, the death benefits payable under an employer-owned life insurance contract will be included in the employer's income to the extent the death proceeds exceed the amounts that were paid for the policy (including premiums).[10] One set of requirements is that before an employer-owned life insurance contract is issued the employer must meet certain notice and consent requirements. The insured employee must be notified in writing that the employer intends to insure the employee's life, and the maximum face amount the employee's life could be insured for at the time the contract is issued. The notice must also state that the policy owner will be the beneficiary of the death proceeds of the policy. The insured must also give written consent to be the insured under the contract and consent to coverage continuing after the insured terminates employment.

Another set of requirements regards the insured's status with the employer. The insured must have been an employee at any time during the 12-month period before his death, or at the time the contract was issued was a director or highly compensated employee. A highly compensated employee is an employee classified as highly compensated under the qualified plan rules of Code section 414(q) (except for the election regarding the top paid group), or under the rules regarding self-insured medical expense reimbursement plans of Code section 105(h), except that the highest paid 35 percent instead of 25 percent will be considered highly compensated. Alternatively, the death proceeds of employer-owned life insurance will not be included in the employer's income (assuming the notice and consent requirements are met) if the amount is paid to a member of the insured's family (defined as a sibling, spouse, ancestor, or lineal descendent), any individual who is the designated beneficiary of the insured under the contract (other than the policy owner), a trust that benefits a member of the family or designated beneficiary, or the estate of the insured. If the death proceeds are used to take out a policy loan; (c) surrender the policy for cash; or (d) pledge the policy for a loan.[14]

8. Distributions such as cash withdrawals or policy loans from a life insurance policy classified as a *modified endowment contract* (MEC) may be taxed differently than if the policy is not so classified. If a policy entered into after June 21, 1988, falls into this category by failing the *seven-pay test*, distributions from the policy will be taxed less favorably than if the seven-pay test is met.[15]

A policy fails the seven-pay test if the cumulative amount paid at any time during the first seven years of the contract exceeds the net level premiums that would have been paid during the first seven years if the contract provided for paid-up future benefits.[16] If a material change in the policy's benefits occurs, a new seven-year period for testing must begin, which can potentially cause a policy to fail the MEC test, despite initially being exempt as a policy issued before June 21, 1988.[17] Once a life insurance policy becomes a modified endowment contract, it remains so for the duration of the policy.

Distributions, including policy loans, from modified endowment contracts are taxed as income at the time received to the extent that the cash value of the contract immediately before the payment exceeds the investment in the contract. In effect, this means that policy distributions are taxed as income first and recovery of basis second, much as distributions from annuity contracts are taxed.[18] Additionally, a penalty tax of 10% applies to distribution amounts included in income unless the taxpayer has become disabled, or reached age 59½ or the distribution is part of a series of substantially equal payments made over the taxpayer's life.[19] However, proceeds from a MEC paid as a death claim still enjoy the tax-exempt status of life insurance.

For the purpose of determining the amount includable in gross income, all modified endowment contracts issued by the same company to the same policyholder during any calendar year are treated as one modified endowment contract.

ALTERNATIVES

There are no good alternatives to life insurance for providing large amounts of tax-free cash upon death, and for ensuring that a set amount of assets will be available for beneficiaries regardless of when an individual might

die. If an individual is uninsurable and, therefore, cannot obtain life insurance, the best alternatives are accumulation funds, tax-deferred investments, certain forms of guaranteed issue life insurance (direct or through certain group arrangements that do not require underwriting), and alternative investments that incorporate some type of life insurance benefit without underwriting (such as certain types of annuity riders). But as noted above, almost any individual who is not terminally ill can purchase *some* amount of insurance with the payment of the appropriate additional premium.

WHEN AND HOW DO I GET IT?

There are about 1,000 life insurance companies actively marketing coverage in the United States. In addition to direct purchase from commercial insurance companies and some fraternal organizations and savings banks, coverage is offered indirectly through professional associations, membership organizations, and employer group benefit packages. Insurers are generally represented by agents, brokers, and financial planners or agents.

For persons having difficulty finding coverage because of health problems, there are agents who specialize in what is called the "substandard" market. They know which insurance companies are likely to write coverage for people with specific health, occupation, or avocation problems. Life insurance coverage can be obtained for people who cannot obtain it in any other way through "credit life insurance." This is a form of "group insurance" associated with loans for the purchase of automobiles, furniture, and even homes. This coverage is extremely expensive because it is priced to cover all ages and health conditions for the same premium, but it is available to anyone who qualifies for the loan. Likewise, insurance may be available through membership in an association that may be unavailable if purchased individually.

WHAT FEES OR OTHER ACQUISITION COSTS ARE INVOLVED?

Life insurance is generally sold on a specified price basis. Life insurance companies are free to set their premiums according to their own marketing strategies. All but a few states have statutes prohibiting any form of "rebating" by the agent (sharing the commission with the purchaser, or reducing the cost of the insurance for the buyer via the agent giving up a portion of the commission). The premium set by the insurance company includes a "loading" (a specified part of each premium payment) to cover such things as commission payments to agents, premium taxes payable to the state government, operating expenses of the insurance company such as rent or mortgage payments and salaries, any other applicable expenses, and a profit margin for the insurance company.

There are some life insurance companies that sell "no load" life insurance policies. These policies do not provide a commission to the selling agent. However, these companies tend to price in a cost premium that approximates the charge by those companies who do pay commissions to agents – the additional cost premium is generally used to cover other marketing costs which are necessary to secure sales to consumers when commissioned insurance agents are not used. These costs often bring the total loading up by an equal amount to the reduction in costs from commission savings – thus, the total loading (and thus the total cost) tends to be similar, whether using a "no load" insurance policy or not. However, for individuals who seek not to work with a commissioned individual, this still provides an alternative (although not necessarily cheaper) life insurance purchase experience. There are also opportunities for direct negotiation of premiums with the insurance company in the case of a private placement ultra large ($10,000,000 or greater) policy.

The bulk of an insurance company's expenses for a policy are incurred during the year the policy is issued. It may take an insurance company five to nine years or even longer to recover all of its front-end costs. These front-end costs include not only the commission paid to the insurance agent, but also the internal costs for the entire underwriting process (such as ordering the medical evaluation and physician statement and examining records and the insurance application) and the administrative work necessary to add the new policyowner to the system.

The state premium tax applicable to all life insurance premium payments is an ongoing expense. The average level of this tax (which varies from state to state) is about 2½% of each premium payment.

With most cash value policies, the aggregate of commissions payable to the selling agent is approximately equal to the first year premium on the policy. About half of it is payable in the year of sale and the other half will be paid on a renewal basis over a period of three to nine years. On single premium policies (where the entire cost for the policy is paid at once rather than over time) the commission payable usually ranges between 2 to 8% of the premium. Commissions are usually paid in

a similar manner on term insurance policies as they are on cash-value policies, but the premium/commission amounts tend to be significantly smaller (resulting in a smaller total commission per sale), and the commission is often even more front-loaded (possibly 75% to 100% of the first-year premium paid as a commission with no renewals in subsequent years).

HOW DO I SELECT THE BEST OF ITS TYPE?

Policy selection should be broken down into two components. In the first stage the planner should find the appropriate type or combination of types of policies suitable for the needs of the client. The second stage of policy selection should focus on the selection of the specific policy that "best" solves the client's needs (i.e., the exact product the client should purchase).

Appropriate Types of Policies

There is often no such thing as a single "best" policy or type of policy for a particular client since there may be many policies that will be appropriate and competitively priced. But the policies that the planner should consider should meet certain criteria. Factors to consider include:

1. Total death benefit required;

2. Duration of the need;

3. The preferences of the client as to living benefits;

4. The amount of premiums the client can afford and the client's cash-flow abilities and timing preferences;

5. The type and amount of investment and other risk the client is willing to assume (or guarantees the client demands or is willing to give up) in return for potential enhanced cash value, dividend, and death benefits.

Some generally accepted rule-of-thumb guidelines in policy selection are:

1. For durations of 10 years or less, term insurance is usually appropriate;

2. For durations between 10 and 15 years, both term insurance and cash value coverage should be evaluated;

3. For durations in excess of 15 years or when it is impossible to ascertain how long coverage will be needed, cash value forms of coverage are usually more cost effective than term;

4. Clients who prefer maximum premium flexibility and death benefit flexibility will want to consider some form or combination of universal life and variable universal life;

5. Clients preferring to direct the investments behind the policy and who are willing to assume the investment risk will want to consider variable life insurance (such as variable universal life or variable whole life); and

6. Clients desiring a maximum of guarantees and a minimum of risk assumption will prefer the more traditional contracts such as whole life and level term.

Individual preferences relative to "pre-funding" (paying higher payments at the beginning in order to avoid payment increases in later years) or "pay-as-you-go" (paying the lowest possible price initially subject to substantial increases with age) will influence the premium paying pattern appropriate for the client. Clients willing and able to pre-fund totally may consider single premium policies, while those who are willing to pre-fund only partially generally prefer level premium payments for a specified period. Clients not willing to pre-fund life insurance will purchase annual renewable term insurance and pay increasing premiums at each renewal of the term coverage. Pre-funding of life insurance may result in increased policy cash values. The tax-deferred earnings on those cash values help defray or eliminate the future premium needs of the policy.

Specific Policies

Selecting a specific policy involves a combination of factors that include:

1. An evaluation of the insurance company's financial soundness; and

2. A comparison of policy guarantees and projections (benefit promises).

The company should generally have one of the highest ratings from one or more of the following companies: A.M. Best Company, Standard & Poor's, Moody's Investor's Service, Fitch, Inc., or Weiss Research, Inc.

The company should also have a reputation for prompt and courteous service in handling policy changes and claims. It is important to give close attention to the full name and city of domicile for insurance companies as many of them have very similar names. Companies that do business in New York State are generally subject to more comprehensive consumer protection laws than companies that are not licensed there.

The agent should have experience with life insurance, as it is used for the particular needs situation of the client, a minimum of 3 years experience, and be well versed in both insurance knowledge and tax knowledge at the federal and state levels. He or she should have, or be working on obtaining, a CFP®, CLU, or ChFC designation.

WHERE CAN I FIND OUT MORE ABOUT IT?

1. Leimberg, Stephan R., and Doyle, Robert J., *The Tools & Techniques of Life Insurance Planning*, 3rd ed. (Cincinnati, OH: The National Underwriter Company, 2004).

2. *Tax Facts on Insurance & Employee Benefits* (Cincinnati, OH: The National Underwriter Company, revised annually).

3. Kenneth Black, Jr., and Harold Skipper, Jr., *Life and Heath Insurance*, 13th ed. (Upper Saddle River, NJ: Prentice Hall Incorporated).

4. Joseph M. Belth, *Life Insurance: A Consumers Handbook* (Bloomington, IN: Indiana University Press).

5. *Best's Insurance Reports* (Oldwick, NJ: The A.M. Best Company).

6. *Journal of Financial Service Professionals* (Society of Financial Service Professionals, Bryn Mawr, Pennsylvania).

7. Zaritsky and Leimberg, *Tax Planning with Life Insurance*, 2nd ed. (RIA, 2006).

8. Baldwin, Ben, The Lawyer's Guide to Insurance, (ABA, 2004).

QUESTIONS AND ANSWERS

Question – What is Term Insurance?

Answer – Term life insurance is insurance that can be maintained for a specified period of time such as

1 year, 5 years, 10 years, or to a specified age such as age 70. At the end of the specified period, the contract typically expires – it may either be contractually nonrenewable beyond the term, or may become *extremely* cost prohibitive to maintain. For a slightly higher premium, many term contracts allow term coverage to be "renewed", i.e., continued beyond the stated term for another successive period (generally annually). For 1-year term insurance (also called "YRT" – yearly renewable term – or "ART" – annually renewable term), the premium will increase every year if the contract is renewed for a new 1-year period of coverage, based upon the new attained age of the insured. For some term policies with longer intended periods, such as 5-year, 10-year, or 20-year term, the premium payment may be priced at the same level for the entire term. Some companies impose an upper age limit (such as age 70) on the renewability of term insurance – however, term policies are generally guaranteed renewable up until that point, without additional evidence of insurability, for whatever premium is set by the company. Because of the relatively short durations of coverage, these policies do not typically provide cash surrender values or provide for any policy loans.

Most term insurance policies can be converted - up to a specified age or time - to whole life or other cash value forms of permanent life insurance that do not limit the upper age of renewability or coverage. Therefore, planners should compare not only term insurance rates but also the rates and quality of the whole life policies into which the term insurance may be converted. There is usually an upper age limit (such as age 65) on the privilege of conversion. A conversion privilege allows the insured to exchange the type of coverage without undergoing a physical examination or otherwise showing evidence of insurability or good health. Sometimes there is a separate premium charged for the convertibility and the renewability features of term life insurance contracts. Other policies automatically include these provisions without charging a separate premium for them (in either event, the total cost is still generally the same if the features are all included). There are also term insurance policies that do not include convertibility and renewability privileges. These coverages can neither be converted to another form of coverage nor can they be renewed once they expire. Planners should utilize nonconvertible nonrenewable term policies only in very special circumstances, as they lack flexibility for a largely unknown future.

Question – What is Whole Life Insurance?

Answer – Whole life insurance is the "traditional" permanent life insurance policy, with level premium payments designed to remain in force over the entire lifetime of the insured individual. Premium payments in the early policy years are deliberately higher (often much higher) than would be required to cover the pure cost of insurance alone (i.e., the cost associated with the probability of death in that particular year). This excess charge in early years makes it possible for the insurer to build up a "reserve." These reserves will be needed, and are used – together with interest earned on them and continuing premiums – to cover the necessary cost of insurance charges in years when the insured is older and more likely to die. In other words, the reserve established in early years makes it possible to keep the premium level in later years when the insurance costs might otherwise make the premium prohibitively high.

As a result of the reserves, the whole life contract builds up internal "cash values" – portions of the insurer's general account, earmarked for that particular policy, that can be borrowed from the insurer or obtained by surrendering the policy while the insured is still alive and releasing the insurer from any future liability. Cash values enable life insurance companies to make policy loans available to the policyowner, usually within a few days after the policyowner requests them. The amount available for such loans is usually 90% or more of the existing cash value in the policy. The interest rate charged will be set forth in the life insurance contract as either a specific flat rate, such as 8%, or a fluctuating rate with limitations imposed by a specified index, such as Moody's average yield on seasoned corporate bonds.

Although the premium on whole life policies is usually payable as a level amount for the lifetime of the insured, it can be based on a shorter premium-paying period such as 10 years, 20 years, or to some specified age such as 65. These policies are known as "limited-pay" or "limited-payment whole life policies" (the premium is payable with level premium payments for a given "limited" period only). The ultimate limited-payment policy is the "single premium whole life policy" which is discussed in more detail below.

The premium paying period influences the cash value buildup in the policy. The shorter the time period that premiums will be made into the policy to build up a reserve adequate for future years, the greater the necessary premium payment amount and the higher the early reserve amounts (since there will be no premium payments to supplement reserves in later years). A single premium policy starts off with a relatively high cash value which continues to grow with policy duration and will eventually equal the "face amount" (contractually promised death benefit) of the policy if the insured lives to age 95 or 100 (depending upon the particular policy).

The level premium whole life policy, on the other hand, starts with a much lower cash value that builds up more gradually (because premium payments are spread out over a longer period of time) to reach the face amount of the contract, typically at age 95 or 100. For any type of cash value life insurance policy, the cash value will build up more rapidly during the premium paying period (when the reserves receive premium payments and investment earnings) than it does after the end of the premium paying period (when the reserves increase only due to investment earnings). Ultimately, if the insured lives long enough, the cash values will build up to the same amount, regardless of how premiums are paid (i.e., the face amount at age 95 or 100). Cash value buildup is fastest for a single premium whole life policy and slowest for a "continuous-pay" (level premium over life) policy.

As mentioned above, cash values are merely the residual effect of level premium payments used to pay for a long-term contract that has increasing costs with increasing duration of that contract. In essence, the cash values represent some pre-funding of the future death benefit obligation. Each insurance company is free to adopt its own approach with respect to the degree of advanced funding it incorporates into the policy design. There are statutory limitations on both minimum and maximum cash values relative to a given death benefit. However, there is a wide latitude of acceptable values within the statutory upper and lower limits. In general, companies charging a higher premium for the same level of death benefit will provide higher levels of cash value in their policies than those for policies with lower premiums and the same death benefit.

Whole life policies are designed to provide protection for the "whole life" of the insured. The death benefit will be payable whenever the insured dies and may be payable before death for the especially long-lived, since the full death benefit is typically

payable at age 95 or 100. However, benefits may not be tax-exempt when paid from a contract that matures, not due to death, but because the insured has reached the maturity age (e.g., 95 or 100). Instead they are taxed as ordinary income as the maturation of a tax-deferred contract.[20] Consequently, thanks to the increased longevity of the general population, many companies are adjusting old or new policies to mature at later points, such as age 115, to avoid this unfavorable tax result.

Question – What is Universal Life?

Answer – Universal life insurance is a variation of whole life insurance. Universal life differs from traditional whole life in several major ways. First, policyholders have a great deal of flexibility as to the premiums they pay. Second, policyholders may, within limits, change the death benefit levels of the policies. In addition, universal life contracts provide separate disclosure about expenses, mortality charges, and interest rates and allow policyholders access to cash values either through policy loans or through direct withdrawals. Similar to traditional whole life policies, standard universal life policies provide certain interest, mortality, and expense guarantees (although costs may in the end be more favorable, albeit on a non-guaranteed basis). Also similar to whole life policies, the cash value of a universal policy is actually just an "earmarked" partition of the insurance company's general account.

The first year of premium is the only required premium under a universal life policy. After the first policy year, the policyowner is free to make whatever premium payments he or she desires, if any, as long as there is enough cash value to keep the policy in force. Policyowners may contribute extra premiums at any time as long as they do not result in high enough aggregate premiums or cash value to violate the definition of life insurance set forth in Internal Revenue Code section 7702.

Alternatively, policyowners may reduce the level of premium payments or even skip premium payments as long as there is a sufficient cash value to cover the charges. Technically, the only requirement for a universal life policy to remain in force each month, after the first year, is that there be adequate cash value (net of loans) to cover that month's costs, which generally include administrative costs and mortality charges (i.e., the actual cost of insurance protection based upon the amount at risk and the insured's attained age).

The amount of premium payments made into the policy relative to the policy charges will determine whether it develops high or low cash values over any particular duration. Because the actual cost of insurance increases with time (as the probability of death increases as an individual ages), cash value build-up is easier for younger insured individuals, and is more difficult when policies are started in later years. Policyowners who choose to make low premium payments and keep the cash value at a level that barely covers insurance charges are treating the policy as if it were term insurance; policyowners who choose to make high premium payments are treating it as cash-value life insurance. Functionally, universal life insurance provides an individual an opportunity to make deposits into a tax-deferred "insurance account" to cover the monthly cost of insurance; the more that the individual pays into the "insurance account," the more potential tax-deferred growth to cover future insurance costs.

Universal life policyowners have access to the cash value amounts through policy loans or partial withdrawals. Partial withdrawals are not policy loans and therefore do not involve any borrowing or interest charges. Partial cash withdrawals do not have to be repaid and are not deducted from the death benefit of the policy when the death proceeds are paid, as are policy loans. However, they do reduce the cash value that is part of the death benefit of type B universal life policies. In addition, partial withdrawals reduce the cost basis of the policy, and may be taxable once they (in the aggregate) exceed the cost basis of the contract.

Policyowners may choose between two different death benefit designs for universal life policies. One design, typically called type-A or option-A (also called type-1 or option-1), has a level death benefit until the insured reaches a relatively advanced age, regardless of the underlying cash value. The other death benefit design, typically called type-B or option-B (also type-2 or option-2), provides the policy cash value *plus* a fixed level amount of protection as the death benefit. This second design results in an increasing death benefit at successive durations of coverage which are tied directly to the cash value increases.

Under either design, the amount at risk is the difference between the face amount of the coverage and the cash value in the policy. Consequently, the amount at risk decreases over time under an option-A policy (as cash value increases towards a level death benefit) but remains level with an option-B policy (as the amount at risk is a fixed level amount, and the death benefit increases or decreases directly by changes in the cash value). The insurance company deducts a mortality charge for the cost of insurance from the cash value every month. That mortality charge is based on the amount at risk and the mortality rate for the attained age of the insured. Consequently, the mortality charge increases every year under an option-B policy (where the amount at risk remains level but the attained age of the insured increases), whereas under an option-A policy the mortality charge may increase more slowly, or even decrease, as the amount at risk declines (while the attained age of the insured still increases).

Universal life policies specify a maximum mortality rate that can be charged at each attained age. However, the mortality rate actually charged is a discretionary amount and is set by the insurance company management based upon the company's mortality experience. Policyowners actually bear some of the mortality risk in that the rates actually charged could be increased all the way to the guaranteed maximum (although, in actuality, this is a rare occurrence). Of course, policyowners of traditional participating whole life policies similarly bear some mortality risk since the dividends they receive will similarly reflect the company's mortality experience and are not guaranteed.

Universal life insurance expenses incurred by the insurance company are treated in many different ways depending upon the individual insurance company policy design. Policies from some companies explicitly identify a front-end expense loading that will be deducted out of each and every premium payment (with the after-expense net amount actually being credited to the policy cash value). Other life insurers do not provide for any explicit disclosure of insurer overhead expenses. Instead they rely on surrender charges (a form of back-end expense), and on the spread between the portfolio earnings of the insurance company's general account and the lower rate of interest credited to the "earmarked" cash value of the policy, to cover overhead expenses.

The cash value of any universal life policy is explicitly increased by premium payments and monthly interest earnings and decreased by various charges for mortality and administrative expenses each month. The insurance company must provide the policyowner with a summary of the cash value account transactions at least on an annual basis.

This requirement is expensive because it mandates individualized computer processing and accounting for each policy.

Like traditional whole life policies, universal life insurance policies guarantee a minimum interest rate (often 4%) on the cash value of the policy. However, the interest rate actually credited to the cash value is a discretionary decision of the insurance company management that is made at least annually and is generally higher than the guaranteed rate. Many companies tie their current rate to some well-known index of interest rates, such as the average rate on U.S. government bonds with 5 years to maturity, so that prospective buyers have a standard for comparison. However, much life insurance marketing focuses only on the current interest rate applicable to cash values. This can be misleading if no attention is paid to the level of mortality charges and other expense loadings (high interest crediting and high expenses may net out to the same result as a lower interest and lower expense policy). Also, universal life policy illustrations may sometimes be misleading because they have been based on interest rates in excess of what can realistically be expected over the full duration of the policy – this problem was particularly common during the late 1970s and very early 1980s, when interest rates were well into the double-digits and even a long-term projection of "only" 9% proved to be well in excess of the actual crediting rate for the past two decades.

The interest rate credited to the cash value typically will be affected by outstanding policy loans. A lower interest rate is credited to a portion of the cash value equal in amount to the outstanding policy loan (i.e., the policy loan "collateral"). This lower interest rate may be, for example, 2% lower than the current rate being paid on the non-borrowed portion of the cash value. In some cases, the minimum guaranteed interest rate specified in the policy is the rate credited to the "borrowed" portion of the cash value. The obvious purpose of the differential is to discourage policy loans when investment returns are significantly higher than policy loan interest rates. However, this "net" loan rate (the difference between the current crediting rate and the rate applied to the "collateral" portion) may still be lower (i.e., 2%) than alternative borrowing sources for any particular policyowner.

Universal life policies are applicable for almost any situation where whole life policies are appro-

priate. The outstanding flexibility of these policies makes them adaptable to the changes in economic circumstances during an individual's life cycle. A single policy can be reconfigured constantly to suit changing needs. Generally, new evidence of insurability is required only in those cases where a significant increase in the amount at risk for the insurance company is involved. (Typically, this occurs when the death benefit amount is substantially increased).

However, universal life policies do not offer the level of guarantees that whole life policies provide – this is due to the fact that if actual investment or mortality experience is less favorable than originally projected, a whole life policy reduces or ceases dividends (but premium payments remain level), whereas a universal life policy may actually require higher-than-expected premium payments simply to avoid lapse.

Question – What is Interest-Sensitive Whole Life?

Answer – Interest-sensitive or current-assumption whole life policies are variations on the traditional whole life insurance contract. All whole life policies promise a certain minimum interest rate on cash value accumulations and use that rate to determine the premium. With traditional whole life policies, the premium and cash value schedule are fixed. If the insurance company earns a rate of return that is higher than that assumed, the policyholder may receive dividends back, which may be used to reduce the fixed premium. However, the nominal premium remains the same and cash values continue to build as presented in the contract.

Interest-sensitive policies rely on a higher assumed interest rate and typically do not have a fixed required premium or fixed cash value schedule. However, these policies do guarantee that the premium payments necessary to keep the policy in force will never exceed the amount guaranteed at issue. Required future premium payments may be less than the guaranteed maximum if investment experience warrants such a reduction. The investment earnings in excess of the minimum interest guarantee under these policies, called "excess investment return," gives rise to an "accumulation fund." The "accumulation fund" supplements the "scheduled cash value" (which is based on the minimum interest guarantee). The policyholder's aggregate cash value is equal to the "scheduled cash value" plus the "accumulation fund."

Rather than pay dividends, these policies make premium adjustments or cash value adjustments. If the investment performance is better than assumed when computing the required premium, the policyholder may either pay a lower premium, or continue to pay the premiums at the initial value and accumulate greater cash values. However, in the event that favorable performance does not actually occur, the required premium payment as guaranteed at issue may actually be slightly higher than it would have otherwise been under a comparable traditional whole life policy. This is the risk associated with having a possibility for favorable investment or mortality experience.

These policies generally subject the cash value to a surrender charge in the event of early policy termination.

Question – What is Variable Life?

Answer – Variable whole life insurance, which is sometimes simply called "variable life," is like a traditional whole life insurance contract in that it has fixed premiums and a minimum guaranteed death benefit. The difference is that the investment risk and return is shifted to the policyowner. Much like selecting among mutual funds, the policyowner is able to direct the funds backing the policy into one or more of a group of segregated investment accounts made available through the life insurance company (as opposed to being retained in the insurance company's general account, like a traditional whole life or universal life policy). The number and types of accounts available differs from one company to another and may be as few as three or, as choices have ballooned in recent years, as many as forty or more – one or two dozen investment options is typical. Generally, the policyowner is able to allocate assets among at least a stock fund, a bond fund, and a money market fund. Because the policyowner picks the portfolio of investments in which the cash value of the policy is invested, there is no minimum cash value guarantee.

When the performance on the portfolio of funds chosen by the policyowner is good, both the cash value and the death benefit of a variable life policy increase proportionately. However, when the portfolio performance is below expectations, the death benefit may drop–although never below the original amount of coverage when the policy was issued. The principal advantage of a variable life policy to policyowners is that they enjoy the benefit of

good portfolio performance. However, the major drawback is that they also must bear investment losses (or at least, bear the constant risk of investment loss). By transferring the investment risk and potential investment returns to the policyowners, the insurance company greatly reduces the incentive for policyowners to withdraw funds from the policy as they would with traditional whole life policies when opportunities elsewhere are better.

Variable life policies are particularly suitable for policyowners who desire to choose how the portfolio backing the life insurance policy (in general terms) will be invested and are willing to assume the investment risk that goes with that responsibility. If invested in equities, for instance, which have substantially outperformed inflation over the long term, these policies may provide a substantial cash value for future use that will help protect the policyowner against loss of purchasing power in retirement. However, for shorter periods in particular, the policyowner must bear some risk that the portfolio performance may not correspond to increases in the level of inflation in the economy. Consequently, these policies may not be appropriate for persons who become anxious over short-term fluctuations in stock and bond prices. Since most companies offer a short-term money market account option, policyowners generally may select a conservative investment strategy. However, even this strategy is riskier than traditional whole life policies since money market rates, theoretically and actually, can fall below the minimum guaranteed rates on traditional policies.

Question – What is Variable Universal Life?

Answer – Variable universal life (VUL) insurance, a variation of a permanent life insurance policy, is a hybrid of universal life and variable life insurance. Like a universal life policy, it provides policyowners with the ability to adjust premiums and to reconfigure the death benefit level. In addition, both investment risk and mortality risk (risk that mortality rates will be increased from current rates to less favorable contractually guaranteed rates) are shifted to the policyowner under this contract. As in the variable life contract, the policyowner who owns a VUL contract chooses the investment sub-accounts under this contract and there are no guarantees as to cash value levels or growth. Most of these policies give the policyowner the option of deciding whether favorable investment results will increase the death benefit level or will be directed only to cash value growth (i.e., the universal life choice between death benefit options A and B).

Variable universal life insurance saw a tremendous growth in use during the bull market of the 1990s. The reason for this is the tax-favored nature of life insurance – the fact that the growth of the internal cash value grows tax-deferred, that loans can be made without taxation (as long as the policy is not a MEC), and that the income and gain on the internal build-up will never be taxed if the policy matures as a death benefit. Policy proceeds can be used to repay the loan. Because of these benefits, individuals that needed life insurance anyway often purchased a VUL contract and sought to accumulate substantial assets in the contract over time. Substantial market returns at the time suggested that aggressive investing could provide tremendous tax-deferred growth that would be available during life through loans but would ultimately be tax-free. In fact, the benefits of this could be so substantial, given an assumption of high growth rates, and under the tax rates in place at the time, that sometimes individuals would consider the purchase of a VUL contract even if they had (or perceived they had) no life insurance need. This was potentially beneficial because the tax benefits of investing-and-borrowing-and-holding-until-death a VUL policy could be so substantial that they would exceed all of the costs and fees of the insurance contract.

Conceptually, this is potentially still a viable strategy. However, there have been three complications to this initial plan for many investors: 1) inadequate fundings; 2) less-than-projected market performance; and 3) the effect of market declines on policy charges.

Inadequate funding is a problem in many cases, because many VUL policies were not funded with adequate amounts in excess of the basic cost of insurance charges to truly accumulate substantial assets. If the policy is only funded to accumulate a small or moderate internal accumulation, the high fees associated with VUL policies generally make this an inferior investment tool in the long run if the insurance coverage is not otherwise needed. Ideally, any policy that is in place for accumulation should be funded as close as possible to the limit available without causing the policy to become a MEC. The reason is that many of the internal VUL charges are fairly fixed, regardless of the cash value – particularly in the early years of the contract. As a result, once the internal charges are covered

by the premium deposits, any "excess" deposits above this amount go directly towards the ultimate accumulation of funds. The greater the "excess" deposits, the better the long-term performance of this investment strategy.

Because of the (sometimes irrational) exuberance of market investors in the 1990s, many policyowners had an unrealistic expectation of market returns when they purchased their policies. Even if the market returns projected are realistic long-term amounts, they certainly have not been achieved over the past several years of bear market returns. As a result, many of these policies already have substantially less cash value than originally projected.

The third complicating factor is related to how insurance charges are calculated in a universal life policy. Cost of insurance charges is generally deducted monthly, and is based on the amount at risk – the difference between the death benefit and the current cash value. When the policy has been in place for many years and has accumulated a substantial cash value and then experiences a severe market decline, the amount at risk can increase substantially in a short amount of time. This results in a substantially higher cost of insurance charge, because cost of insurance is always based upon the amount at risk and a mortality rate based upon the age of the insured in that particular year. Although the market may potentially recover over time, the higher cost of insurance charges that occur in the meantime can severely and permanently damage the long-term projected results of the policy.

A VUL contract remains an excellent tool for an individual that is willing to invest in the stock market and fund the policy heavily to allow for future growth, either to offset and/or defray future premium costs, or to provide for an asset base against which loans can be made in the future. For very aggressive investors that have exhausted alternative tax-advantaged savings opportunities and have the adequate cash flow to substantially "over-fund" these policies above the cost of insurance charges and up to the MEC limit, VULs can be excellent pure-investment tools. But *extreme* caution should be exercised, as a policy with substantial loans that lapses before the death of the insured can cause a severe tax bill for the policyowner, who must declare as income all loans received from the policy (including accrued interest) in excess of the policy's cost basis. Because of overly-optimistic projections, inadequate funding, and the effect of market declines on the amount at risk and cost of insurance charges, this may be the eventual outcome for numerous policies in the future – a virtually certain point of litigation for those insurance companies and agents that improperly or inadequately advised clients about the risks or allow clients to make unreasonable assumptions as to the rate of underlying investments.

Question – What is Joint Life?

Answer – Joint life insurance is a life insurance policy (usually of a permanent variety) that insures two or more lives rather than just one. There are two basic types: first death and second (or last) death joint life. With a "first death" policy, the policy pays the face amount and terminates after the first death with no benefits remaining for the surviving insured. It is also called a "first-to-die" policy, or sometimes simply a "joint life" policy – a confusing moniker because the term is often used to refer generally to the category of multiple-insured-life policies and also to this particular variety of policy in the category. Because the policy provides only one death benefit, it is a less expensive way of providing insurance for a pair of individuals than purchasing separate policies on each life. This policy is often used for business buy-sell agreements and for estate taxes when the husband and wife intend to pay some estate taxes after the first death.

The "second death" variation of joint life also covers more than one life and pays only one death benefit. It is often known as "second-to-die," "last-to-die," or "joint survivorship" life because the death benefit is paid upon the last death of two (or occasionally more) insureds. Since the death proceeds are paid only once and only after *all* insureds have died, the premium burden for such a policy is significantly lower than that for two or more separate policies, and is also lower than the cost of a first-to-die policy (because one insured may accidentally die in a short period of time, but it is generally a much longer period of time before *all* insured individuals under the policy perish). This type of policy has increased in popularity under the current estate tax structure with its unlimited marital deduction, which permits married couples with large estates to defer estate tax liabilities until the second death – but may have a need for substantial cash to pay a very large tax bill at that second death.

Question – What are dividends?

Answer – Certain policies are called "participating" policies because their policyowners participate to some extent in the favorable experience of the insurance company. Policies in which the policyowners do not share in such experience are called "nonparticipating" or "nonpar." Dividends payable on participating whole life policies are considered a return of premium. Therefore they are not taxable income until the aggregate of all dividends and other amounts actually received exceeds the entire value of all premiums paid. The dividends payable on some life insurance policies exceed the premium payment after the policy has been in force for several years. Policyowner dividends effectively decrease the final cost of coverage for the policy.

Traditionally, participating policies were issued by mutual insurance companies, which are technically owned by their policyowners – policy dividends were literally dividends paid to the owners of the company. On the other hand, stock insurance companies are owned by their stockholders, and policyowners are simply owners of the corporation's products (but not the corporation itself) – as a result, stock insurance companies traditionally issued nonpar policies. Over the years, mutual companies have occasionally issued nonpar policies, and stock companies have experimented with issuing participating policies (where dividends are paid out of excess accumulated assets associated with the set of participating policies as accounted for by the stock company). However, in the overwhelming majority of cases, mutual insurance companies continue to issue whole life policies that participate, and stock companies continue to issue nonpar policies. Generally, only whole life policies are ever participating (where an outright dividend is paid), because under other types of permanent insurance, such as universal life, the favorable experience of the pool of policies is reflected directly in the more-favorable non-guaranteed rates that are charged by the insurance company in any particular month.

Dividends are influenced by three factors: (1) the mortality experience of the insurance company; (2) the "loading" (overhead costs and profit margin) experienced by the insurance company; and (3) the investment return on the insurance company portfolio. The more careful and conservative the underwriting and the fewer deaths in relation to those anticipated, the higher the dividends, assuming that the other two factors remain equal. The lower the business expenses compared to those anticipated when the premium rates were constructed, the higher the dividends. Finally, the higher the investment returns are over those anticipated, the greater the dividends. Dividends tend to increase with increasing policy duration and provide an incentive for the policyowner to retain the policy (which in turn helps the insurance company recover its costs over a longer period of time and therefore reduce its loading costs).

Most insurance companies that issue participating policies provide policyowners several options on how their dividends may be used, including: (1) receipt as outright cash; (2) deposit into a savings/accumulation side account that is credited interest; (3) reduction of next premium payment (where the dividend is effectively used to pay the next premium as it comes due); and (4) purchase of paid-up additional insurance (based upon the insured's attained age at the time of the dividend but without any underwriting or evidence of insurability required). This last option is very favorable to the policyowner because it provides additional coverage at net (no commission and little or no loading charges) rates and regardless of the insured's health.

Question – Since my state has a life insurance guarantee fund, should I be concerned about the rating of the insurance company?

Answer – Many states have established special funds called "life insurance guarantee funds." These are intended to pay policy benefits in case of an insurance company failure. However, these funds are usually designed to rescue policyowners and beneficiaries of a weak or troubled company by charging assessments against other insurance companies. Competitive forces in recent years have whittled away at the safety margin of many companies and there is a greater danger that the financial guarantee mechanism may prove inadequate in the face of multiple life insurance company failures. Even if the guarantee mechanism does provide protection, it is a slow and inefficient bureaucracy that could delay settlement, such as accessibility of the cash value or payment of a death benefit, for years. The best way to avoid such problems is to deal only with insurance companies that are financially sound and likely to remain so throughout the desired period of coverage. Further safety can be obtained by diversifying coverage with more than one insurer and through more than one type of policy.

Question – Is "single premium whole life" a good investment?

Answer – Single premium whole life is a fully pre-funded life insurance policy. Purchasing this type of policy entails paying mortality charges that may or may not be explicitly identified. Most of these policies have an initial cash value equal to the full single premium payment. This cash value grows year by year. This cash value buildup escapes income taxation if the policy terminates in a death claim. In any case, it enjoys tax deferral until the policy is terminated either by death or surrender prior to a death claim.

These policies can provide a respectable return to policyowners even after mortality charges and other expenses. However, single premium whole life policies are often subject to significant surrender charges in the early years of the contract. These surrender charges can drastically reduce the investment performance if the policy is surrendered for cash while they are applicable. These policies are not strictly an investment and should not be purchased for that purpose alone – although when held to maturity as a death claim, internal rates of return on investment are frequently 6% - 8% (and potentially may be much higher if death occurs well before life expectancy).

There are limits to the favorable taxation of policy distributions (including loans) from single premium whole life contracts, as they will be deemed a modified endowment contract at issue (See number 7 under "Tax Implications"). No deduction is allowed for policy loan interest on single premium whole life policies.

Question – Is there a difference between a single premium whole life policy and a universal life policy paid for by a single premium payment?

Answer – Yes. There is a guarantee that the single premium whole life policy is adequately funded and no further premium payments will be required. Under a universal life policy, the single premium payment will be adequate only if the interest assumptions and mortality assumptions are matched or exceeded by future actual experience under the policy. There is a risk that investment performance has been overestimated and/or that mortality expenses have been underestimated. If this is true, the premium paid could eventually turn out to be inadequate to sustain the policy under death. Under these circumstances, the policyowner would need to pay additional premiums to maintain the policy benefits or reduce the face value of coverage to keep the policy in line with the premium actually paid.

Question – Why do insurance premiums vary?

Answer – There are three main cost elements to life insurance policies: (1) mortality charges; (2) insurer expenses; and (3) investment performance. Each insurance company has varying degrees of efficiency associated with each of these factors.

Contrary to popular belief, there are many different mortality tables applicable to insurance products. Insurance companies tend to charge mortality rates based on the experience of their own policies. Standardized mortality tables such as the "1980 CSO (Commissioners Standard Ordinary) Mortality Table" are used for reserve purposes (i.e., for the insurer to create a reserve under the policy large enough to meet potential future claims, as these mortality rates are generally higher than those actually experienced by current insurance companies with proper underwriting departments) but are rarely used in setting the premium for the policy, for the sake of competitiveness. Part of the variation in premiums from company to company is explained by differences in mortality rates used. An even larger portion of the variation is explained by differences in assumed investment return.

Insurance company expenses vary significantly from one company to another. Part of that difference is a function of the amount of services provided to policyowners. Some variation in expenses is due to the differing efficiencies of the insurance company and its procedures.

One of the most important factors explaining variation in life insurance premiums is the investment return. Relatively small changes in the rate of investment return can result in sizable changes in the premium that must be charged. The decrease in life insurance policy premiums over the past decade is mainly the result of increased investment earnings for life insurance companies.

It is also important to note that even if policy A appears to be more expensive than policy B based upon the quoted rates, adjustments of non-guaranteed factors (i.e., crediting rates and/or mortality charges) and the payment of dividends (for participating policies) could result in more favorable and less costly insurance coverage over the long run under policy A than policy B. Insurers may offer quoted rates that are less expensive in the short run, but make adverse adjustments (within the guidelines set in the policy) over the long run, after the policy has been in force for several years, to make up for the initially aggressive pricing. Consequently, it is important to examine, as much as possible, the underlying assumptions used in any policy comparisons. This is helpful in the examination of permanent policies (term policies often have rates that are guaranteed for the entire term, making this a moot point), and is particularly important in the comparison of whole life policies – unfortunately, full disclosure of assumptions is not currently required of insurance companies and consequently is often unavailable. When otherwise lacking, an investigation of an insurance company's reputation and history of maintaining originally projected dividend scales and non-guaranteed factors on currently in-force policies may be helpful in the evaluation process.

Question – What is the difference between a "limited payment" policy and a "vanishing premium" policy?

Answer – A limited payment policy guarantees that a specified number of fixed premium payments will be sufficient to fully pay for the life insurance policy – although the policy cash value will continue to grow with investment returns over time, the policy is guaranteed to remain in force until maturity without any future premiums. This guarantee is not present in vanishing premium policies. Vanishing premium policies have fixed premiums but project the utilization of non-guaranteed policy dividends to pay anticipated premiums after the policy has been in force the prescribed period of time. If the dividends are as large as expected (or larger), the policyowner will not have to pay premiums beyond the specified policy duration. However, there is the possibility that dividend experience will fall short of expectations since they are not guaranteed. Consequently, the policyowner may have to make additional premium payments to supplement the dividends and cover the entire premium due. All too often, this has been the case and is the trigger for many lawsuits against both agents and insurers.

With some life insurance companies the dividend expectation is very conservative and it is highly unlikely that future dividends will not be adequate to cover premium payments. On the other hand, there are some insurance companies using such aggressive estimates of future dividends that it is unlikely future dividends will live up to these expectations. Policyowners with these companies may be both surprised and perturbed in the future to find that their vanishing premium does not vanish, or worse that it has suddenly reappeared as dividends are adjusted downwards (which is always possible, as dividends are completely non-guaranteed and can increase, decrease, or cease completely in any particular year). Planners should review past dividend records and compare the actual experience with the company's original projections to obtain some idea of how conservative or aggressive the company has been with respect to its dividend projections.

In addition, it is notable that numerous insurance companies and agents settled class-action lawsuits with policyowners around the turn of this millennium for vanishing premium policies that were sold in the late 1970s and early 1980s. These policies were sold when interest rates were extraordinarily high, and they were projected to remain (what turned out to be unrealistically) high over the subsequent years. In many cases, policyowners had not received adequate disclosure or been properly warned of the possibility that in fact occurred – interest rates declined dramatically, dividends underperformed the original projections, and, in many cases, premiums did not in fact "vanish," or vanished and then re-appeared.

Question – What is the purpose of a delay clause in the beneficiary designation?

Answer – Sometimes both the insured and the beneficiary die within a short time of each other. If the beneficiary survives the insured for a very short period of time, the proceeds of the policy will be payable to the beneficiary and flow through the beneficiary's estate when the beneficiary dies. A delay clause makes payment of the death proceeds contingent upon the beneficiary surviving a stated period of time, such as 90 days after the insured dies. If the beneficiary does not survive the specified period of time, the proceeds are payable to a contingent beneficiary specified in the beneficiary designation. Hence, the death benefits completely bypass the primary beneficiary's estate, avoiding unnecessary taxes and other estate expenses. It is notable, though, that the entire distributive schema of the estate plan may be altered by this – the contingent beneficiary of the insurance policy is not necessarily the same party that would have received the insurance proceeds had they been paid to the original beneficiary and then shortly thereafter been distributed according to the deceased beneficiary's estate plan. If the delay clause exceeds 180 days, the policy proceeds will not qualify for the federal estate tax marital deduction.

Question – What is private placement VUL (PPVUL)?

Answer – Private Placement VUL (PPVUL), a variation on VUL, is available only as a non-registered product to those who qualify. Generally, the buyer is a high-net worth individual willing to invest at least $500,000 either initially or over a relatively short period of time. PPVUL is insurance which, as its name implies, is coverage obtained by direct (and often vigorous) negotiation with the insurer to bargain costs and charges to a minimum. These contracts are appealing to high-net worth individuals and corporations because of the income tax treatment and investment flexibility (including dynamic hedging strategies) that make it a prime vehicle for capital accumulation and wealth transfer vehicle. Advantages include impressive internal performance through lower policy charges and institutional pricing, surrender fees, fund asset charges, and reduced (or no) sales loads. Special investment management design as well as a wider array of investment options, insurer responsiveness, privacy, confidentiality, and access to non-registered asset allocations (e.g., hedge funds) behind the insurance contract are additional benefits.

These contracts are typically issued either as a modified endowment contract (MEC) on a single premium basis or with limited payment periods to produce a non-MEC. Sold as private placements by both domestic and international insurers, provided on a policy-by-policy basis, they thus avoid SEC registration. Purchasing the policy through an offshore insurer results in a high degree of creditor protection, freedom from state regulation, and a reduction in costs due to the absence of the insurer's obligation to pay either state premium taxes or federal income taxes. (It is important to note, though, in any given case, the performance of offshore PPVUL may not be as favorable as a vehicle available domestically due to the policy-specific insurance charges in some offshore vehicles. Further, policy ownership structures, or indeed laws around assets within a policy itself, may also provide attractive asset protection without going offshore.) To avoid U.S. regulatory and tax jurisdiction, these offshore carriers must market and issue coverage while remaining offshore. Domestic insurers, on the other hand, can market their products directly to U.S. customers, a distinct marketing advantage.

For all flexible-premium insurance contracts (UL, VUL, PPVUL), in most cases, the best performance of the policies occurs when the premium is approaching, or at, the upper limits allowable by the various

Figure 18.1

COMPARING UL, VARIABLE, AND VARIABLE UNIVERSAL LIFE

FEATURE	UL	VL	VUL
Death Benefit Guaranteed While Policy in Force?	Yes	Yes	Yes
Premium Amounts Flexible?	Yes	No	Yes
Policy Owner Chooses How Premiums Invested?	No	Yes	Yes
Policy Owner Can Vary Frequency or Amount of Premiums Paid?	Yes	No	Yes
Policy Owner Can Increase or Decrease Death Benefits?	Yes	No	Yes
Death Benefit Options A and B Available?	Yes	No	Yes
Cash Values Fluctuate Depending on Performance of Underlying Asset?	No*	Yes	Yes
Interest Rate on Cash Values?	Yes	No	No
Partial Withdrawals Allowed from Cash Values?	Yes	No	Yes
Interest Rate on Cash Values Guaranteed?	Yes	No	No
Cash Value Grows on Tax-Deferred Basis?	Yes	Yes	Yes
Annual Statements Detail Monthly Deductions for Costs and C.V. Growth?	Yes	No	Yes
Considered a Security?	No	Yes	Yes

Note: The current interest credited to cash values of UL contracts fluctuates with the performance of the insurer's general portfolio, but cash values, once accumulated, do not fluctuate in value with fluctuations in the market value of the assets in the general portfolio.

threshold tests called for by government regulation. It should also be noted that prospective illustrated performance is, in almost all cases, heavily dependent upon a number of non-guaranteed factors.

Question - What is No-Lapse Guarantee Universal Life (NLGUL)?[21]

Answer - NLGUL provides relatively inexpensive permanent death benefit guarantees at the expense of cash value performance. Analytically, NLGUL policies typically offer very attractive guaranteed death benefit internal rates of return (IRR) up to, and a bit past, life expectancy. It is not uncommon to see these death benefit IRRs approach, and go beyond, an after-tax rate of 7% even beyond life expectancy. WL and UL death benefit returns may be (or may not be, depending upon the case) projected to be as favorable, but the illustrated WL and UL death benefit returns will assuredly carry the assumption of performance risk by the policyowner.

Some argue that it is prudent to think of NLGUL policies as largely illiquid. This is because it is unlikely that these contracts will have a cash value that is attractive for any other possible uses in the future due to the projected underperformance of the cash value. While the lack of a significant cash value is clearly a disadvantage should scenarios requiring a cash value rollover to another new product innovation be desired in the future, most who use NLGUL are not uncomfortable with the illiquidity given the relatively certain shifting of permanent death benefit risk to the insurance carrier third party. Further, proponents argue, in many trust-owned situations, the existence of a notable cash value is, at best, a secondary bonus to a family given that the cash is likely to have been tied up in trust anyway.

On the other hand, the lack (or non-existence) of cash value within a NLG contact creates a "last stop on the train" phenomenon – that is, the policyowner's options to perhaps make a change in stations in the future will be very much limited, if not precluded. The policyowner needs to be *permanently* comfortable with those death benefit returns of the NLG policy – because once the policyowner gets on this train, the reality is that they cannot (economically) get off.

NLGUL also bears the solvency risk of the carrier issuing it, especially since the low cash value and attractive death benefit guarantee create a situation where it is less likely to result in a policy's risk being transferred elsewhere in the future. Those who are comfortable with this point out that this risk does, to at least some degree, exist with any insurance, and there are some protection mechanisms to mitigate the risk. Some authorities, however, argue that these policies increase the solvency risk of carriers that issue them, particularly those who have underpriced their NLG products. The greatest risk to policyholders is the possibility that in an insolvency, the rehabilator would "reform the contract" Most state guarantee funds only provide that limited death benefits and cash value will be paid. This risk is more than theoretical; contracts were reformed in several large insurance company failures.

Finally, the last potential disadvantage of NLGUL is that while the death benefit is likely to have relatively little downside, it is also less likely than alternative contracts to have a notable performance upside in the event of a rising interest rate market place, or bull equity markets (which could positively drive the VL, UL, and VUL market places, respectively). Again, those who favor NLGUL would counter that the lack of upside is a fair trade-off for the very attractive "locked-in" IRR at death. Obviously, the NLGUL contract is most appealing and appropriate for clients seeking to assure the financial security of future generations through the most cost and tax effective and economically certain wealth transfer mechanism possible.

Aside from the issue of proper reserving (which in itself is a complex, difficult to determine, highly controversial, and very important issue), planners should give special attention to suitability (e.g. Is the client better served by a product flexible enough to meet life's inevitably changing circumstances than by the features of a policy that guarantee the sufficiency of the premium?) and fitting this type of contract to a buyer's circumstances. It is essential that clients be informed – in writing – of how these products really work, what is required to maintain the guarantee, and what happens to the product if the client fails to meet those requirements. It is also essential that the products considered for purchase are compared with a current assumption product and tested for relative premium flexibility, cash values, and potential to benefit from higher interest rates. In other words, would some other type of product be more suitable for the client's particular facts and circumstances? It is essential that the client be presented with an array of choices allowing for an informed decision.

Diversification, not one but two or three different life insurance contracts, across more than one carrier, may provide the best answer on product selection. For some people the assurance of a death benefit at a certain level with no future volatility, especially if they have an otherwise well-diversified financial picture, would indicate that a heavy concentration of NLG could be desirable. However, in most cases, because of its illiquidity and consequent lack of flexibility, it will best serve clients to utilize NLG as a relatively modest portion of an insurance portfolio that is carefully diversified across carriers, products, and cash value / death benefit performance projections.

CHAPTER ENDNOTES

1. IRC Sec. 79(a).
2. IRC Sec. 72(e).
3. IRC Sec. 72(e)(6).
4. IRC Sec. 101(a)(1).
5. IRC Sec. 72(e).
6. IRC Sec. 165.
7. IRC Sec. 101(a)(1). See Brody and Leimberg, "Avoiding the Tax Trap of the Transfer for Value Rule", *Estate Planning*, October, 2005, Vol. 32, No. 10, Pg. 3 and Brody and Leimberg, "Using a Transactional Analysis to Avoid the Transfer for Value Rule", *Estate Planning*, November 2005, Vol. 32, No. 11, Pg. 3.
8. IRC Sec. 56(g)(4).
9. IRC Sec. 55(e)(1).
10. IRC Sec. 101(j), as added by PPA 2006.
11. IRC Sec. 101(a)(2).
12. IRC Secs. 101(a)(2)(A), 101(a)(2)(B).
13. IRC Secs. 2042, 2035(a).
14. Treas. Reg. §20.2042-1(c).
15. IRC Sec. 7702A(a).
16. IRC Sec. 7702A(b).
17. IRC Sec. 7702A(c)(3).
18. IRC Sec. 72(e)(10).
19. IRC Sec. 72(q).
20. Treas. Reg. §1.72-11(d)(1).
21. Malarkey and Leimberg, "Innovative Planning With 'No Lapse Guarantee' Life Insurance", *Estate Planning Journal*, July 2005.

Chapter 19

ANNUITIES

WHAT IS IT?

Annuities are the only investment vehicles that can guarantee investors that they will not outlive their income, and they do this in a tax-favored manner. In addition, annuities are available with a host of features to meet a wide variety of investor needs. The income taxation of annuities is governed by IRC Section 72.

Technically, annuities are contracts providing for the systematic liquidation of principal and interest in the form of a series of payments over time.[1] However, this really refers to the "payout" phase of an annuity; in point of fact, annuities can (and often do) have an accumulation phase that also lasts for a substantial period of time.

An annuity is established when the investor makes a cash payment to an insurance company, which invests the money – this may be a single large cash payment or a series of periodic payments over time. The money remains invested with the insurance company and is periodically credited with some growth factor – this is the accumulation phase of the annuity. In return for making a deposit into an annuity, the insurance company ultimately agrees to pay the owner (or owners) a specified amount (the annuity payments) periodically, beginning on a specified date – this is the payout phase of the annuity.

If the specified date for payouts to begin is within one year of the date the contract is established (i.e., a single cash payment is made and the insurance company begins a systematic liquidation of the payment back to the owner within one year), the annuity is called an "immediate annuity". If, alternatively, the specified date for payouts to begin is at least one year later, the annuity is called a "deferred annuity" (because deposits are made now, but the payout is deferred). An immediate annuity only has a payout phase; a deferred annuity has both an accumulation and a payout phase.

If the payout phase of the annuity is a *life annuity*, the company promises that payouts will continue for as long as the annuitant (or annuitants) live; the income stream can never be outlived (NOTE: although often

the same, technically the owner of the annuity does not necessarily need to also be the annuitant; occasionally these *are* different individuals). If the payout phase is a *fixed period annuity* (also called a *term-certain annuity*), the company promises to pay stipulated amounts for a fixed or guaranteed period of time independent of the survival of the annuitant. An annuity payout can also utilize a combination of the life and fixed period options, such as "for the greater of 10 years or the life of the annuitant(s)."

In addition to differentiating between immediate and deferred annuities, and fixed and term-certain payouts, annuities are also categorized as to whether they are fixed or variable (be careful not to confuse a "fixed annuity" with a "fixed period payout"). Classification as a fixed or variable annuity refers to the underlying investments during the accumulation phase of the annuity; a fixed annuity is invested in the general fixed account of the insurance company, while a variable annuity is invested in separately managed sub-accounts (that function similarly to mutual funds) selected by the annuity owner. Variable annuities often have additional features to help manage the risk of their underlying investments, such as guaranteed death benefits or newer "living benefits" that provide company-guaranteed payments for owners or beneficiaries even if (or especially if) they would be higher than actual investment performance would provide for.

Newer annuities may also offer a variable option during the payout phase (whether for a fixed or term-certain period). A "variable annuitization" has payments that may fluctuate up or down depending upon the performance of the underlying sub-account investments; a "fixed annuitization" has payments that remain the same through the payout phase (or occasionally increase by some set rate to keep pace with inflation; however, this rate is pre-determined and contractual, is still invested in the insurance company's general account, and is thus still considered a "fixed payout").

Annuities purchased from an insurance company are called "commercial annuities" while those purchased from a person or entity that is not in the business of selling annuities are called "private annuities."[2]

Tools & Techniques of Investment Planning

Annuities grow tax-deferred during the accumulation phase, although withdrawals during this phase are taxed on a LIFO (last in, first out) basis – meaning that withdrawals during the accumulation phase are considered to be withdrawals of growth first (fully taxable) and principal second.[3] Payouts during the annuitization phase are split; a portion of each payment is considered principal and a portion is deemed interest/growth. The proportion of each is determined at the annuity's beginning payment date and is based upon the already-accumulated growth, an assumed internal growth factor for the payout period, and the expected length of the payout period. All amounts distributed that are considered interest/growth are taxed as ordinary income, regardless of the phase or timing of the withdrawal. In addition, certain withdrawals before the age of 59½ may be subject to an additional 10% tax penalty.

Although annuities have tax-deferral features that can be quite advantageous, the primary reason annuities should be purchased are for their risk management features. Annuities can provide a variety of guarantees, whether protecting against interest rate risk, reinvestment risk, market volatility risk, or the risk of living too long and outliving one's assets. Annuities are first and foremost a risk management tool.

WHEN IS THE USE OF THIS TOOL INDICATED?

There is such a fundamental difference in the risk and return characteristics of fixed and variable annuities that each type is more or less suitable for various purposes. However, some form of annuity would be indicated in the following circumstances:

1. When a person wants a retirement income that can never be outlived.

2. When an individual (often retired) wants a monthly income equal to or higher than other conservative investments and is willing to (or especially if he/she *wants* to) have principal liquidated.

3. When the person would like to avoid probate and pass a large sum of money by contract to an heir to reduce the possibility of a will contest.[4]

4. When a tax-deferred accumulation of interest is desired. The interest earned inside an annuity grows income-tax free and is not taxed until it is withdrawn.[5]

5. When an investor wants to be free of the responsibility of investing and managing assets (in the case of a fixed annuity or an annuity payout; this is not applicable to a variable deferred annuity, as the owner still retains the burden of making all investment selections).

6. As a supplement to an IRA. With limited opportunity for pre-tax contributions to IRAs, many clients are seeking opportunities of making regular after-tax contributions to an investment vehicle after reaching the IRA contribution limits. The annuity may be a good choice because contributions are not limited.

7. Fixed annuities, in particular, would be indicated: (1) when safety of principal is paramount consideration (this can be particularly important in some retirement planning scenarios); (2) when an investor wants a guarantee that a given level of interest will be credited to his investment for a long period of time; or (3) when a conservative complement to other investment vehicles is desired.

8. Variable annuities, in particular, would be indicated: (1) when an investor wants more control over his or her investment and is willing to bear the risk associated with his or her investment selections; or (2) when a person is looking for potentially increasing retirement income.

9. When an individual would like to be invested in variable sub-accounts, but desires some aspect of risk management, such as the guaranteed death benefits or living benefits offered by most insurance companies.

ADVANTAGES

1. The guarantees of safety, interest rates, and particularly lifelong income (if selected) give the purchaser peace of mind and psychological security.

2. An annuity protects and builds a person's cash reserve. The insurer guarantees principal and interest (in the case of a fixed annuity; a variable annuity is subject to the performance of the underlying selected sub-accounts), and the promise (if purchased) that the annuity can never be outlived. This makes the annuity particularly attractive to those who have retired and desire, or require, fixed monthly income and lifetime guarantees.

3. An annuity allows a client to invest in the market while moderating risk. The insurer may provide guarantees of death proceeds or a certain annuitization amount (if purchased) within a variable annuity, thus providing guarantees that would otherwise be unavailable to a client that purchased the underlying investments directly. This makes a variable annuity particularly attractive to those who have retired or are nearing retirement and need (or want) to hold risky investments while trying to moderate risk.

4. A client can "time" the receipt of income and shift it into lower bracket years. This ability to decide when to be taxed allows the annuitant to compound the advantage of deferral.

5. Because the interest on an annuity is tax-deferred, an annuity paying the same rate of interest (after expenses) as a taxable investment will result in a higher effective yield.

6. Because of the risk-management factors available, especially in variable annuities, a client may be able to take on greater risk in the underlying investment options (e.g., equities, smaller-capitalization equities, high-yield bonds, etc.) while still maintaining a reasonable overall risk exposure due to the underlying guarantees.

7. Adjusted Gross Income (AGI) may be reduced in years where the annuity is held with no withdrawals (thanks to the tax-deferral features of the accumulation phase). In addition, lower taxable income may be recognized during the payout phase, due to the partial recovery of basis associated with each payment. A reduced AGI can bring tax savings, as many other income tax rules are calculated based upon AGI and generally a lower AGI results in lower taxation (and vice versa). A reduced AGI can create tax savings by lowering the amount of Social Security includable in income, reducing the floor threshold for deduction of medical expenses (7.5% of AGI) or miscellaneous itemized deductions (2% of AGI), and avoiding the threshold for phase-out of exemptions and itemized deductions.

DISADVANTAGES

1. Receipt of a lump sum (either at retirement, or to a beneficiary at death) could result in a significant tax burden because income averaging is not available (however, this can be moderated if the proceeds are annuitized).

2. The cash flow stream of a fixed payout may not keep pace with inflation, particularly for longer-term payout phases such as a life annuitization.

3. A 10% penalty tax is generally imposed on withdrawals of accumulated interest during the accumulation phase prior to age 59½ or disability (this may also apply to the annuitization phase if the annuity was not an immediate annuity and certain short payout terms are selected).[6]

4. With a few limited exceptions, if an annuity contract is held by a corporation or other entity that is not a natural person, the contract is not treated as an annuity contract for federal income tax purposes. This means that income on the contract for any taxable year is treated as current taxable ordinary income to the owner of the contract regardless of whether or not withdrawals are made.

5. If the client is forced to liquidate the investment in the early years of an annuity, management and maintenance fees and sales costs could prove expensive. Total management fees and mortality charges can run from 1% to 2½% of the value of the contract (occasionally as high as 3% in the case of variable annuities with a number of underlying guarantees). There may be a "back end" surrender charge if the contract is terminated within the first few years to compensate the insurer for the sales charges that are not typically levied "up front."

6. Investment earnings are taxed at the owner's ordinary income tax rate when the owner receives payments, regardless of the source or nature of the return. Consequently, investment earnings attributable to long-term capital appreciation (typically in variable annuities) do not enjoy the more favorable long-term capital-gain tax rate that would otherwise generally apply. This has become even more disadvantageous with the reduction of the maximum long-term capital-gain rate to 15% (or even 5% for lower-income taxpayers). Furthermore, investment earnings attributable to dividends on stocks that would qualify for the 15% maximum tax rate if the stocks were held outside an annuity will also be taxed at the owner's ordinary income tax rate (although these dividends will not be taxed until withdrawal). Consequently, variable annuities where the annuity owner is inclined to invest in equities are much less attractive than previously. (See the question and answer section for a discussion of mutual funds versus variable annuities.)

TAX IMPLICATIONS

1. A client's investment in an annuity is returned in equal tax-free (return of capital) amounts during the payout phase. Any additional amount received is taxed at ordinary income rates. This means each payment consists of two parts – the first is considered return of capital and is therefore nontaxable, while the second part of each payment is considered return on capital (income) and is therefore taxable at ordinary rates.

The amount of each period's payment that will be considered nontaxable is determined by the following ratio, called the "exclusion ratio":[7]

<u>Investment in Contract</u>[8]
Expected Return[9]

The "exclusion ratio" is expressed as a percentage[10] and applies to each annuity payment equally through the payout phase. For instance, assume a 70-year-old purchases an annuity. He pays (the investment in the contract is) $12,000 for the annuity. Assume his expected return through the payout phase is $19,200.

The exclusion ratio is $12,000/$19,200, or 62.5%. If the monthly payment he receives is $100, the portion that can be excluded from gross income is $62.50 (62.5% of $100). The $37.50 balance of each $100 monthly payment is ordinary income.

The full amount of each annuity payment received would be tax free if the investment in the contract exceeds the expected return (i.e., when the exclusion ratio would be greater than or equal to 100%).[11]

The excludable portion of any annuity payment may not exceed the unrecovered investment in the contract (unless the annuity started before January 1, 1987).[12] The "unrecovered investment in the contract" is the policyowner's premium cost, reduced by any dividends received in cash or used to reduce premiums, and by the aggregate amount received under the contract on or after the annuity starting date to the extent it was excludable from income. Thus, the unrecovered investment in the contract is reduced each time an annuity payment is made, by the amount of the payment that is excluded from income by the exclusion ratio. This rule limits the total amount the policyowner can exclude from income to the total amount of his contribution. Once an annuitant has fully recovered his investment in the contract (which generally occurs at

the end of the *expected* payout term),), 100% of each subsequent payment will be taxable. Payments can continue beyond the expected payout term when the annuitant actually lives longer than his or her life expectancy.

Some annuities provide a refund if the annuitant dies before recovering his entire cost. The present value of the refund option must be ascertained by government tables and subtracted from the investment in the contract.[13] This would also apply if the annuity payout phase incorporated a combined life expectancy and term-certain structure.

2. The "expected return" is the total amount that the owner (or owners) should receive given the payments specified (which include an assumed internal growth rate) multiplied by the certain term or life expectancy according to the government's tables (currently Table V for single lives and Table VI for joint and survivor annuities). For instance, under Table V, a 70-year-old has a life expectancy of 16 years. If he (or she, since the life expectancy tables are unisex) receives $100 a month, the expected return would be $19,200 ($1,200 a year x 16 years).

When an annuitant dies before receiving the full amount guaranteed under a refund or period certain life annuity, the owner or beneficiary receiving the balance of the guaranteed amount will have no taxable income (unless the amount received by the beneficiary plus the amount that had been received tax free by the annuitant exceeds the investment in the contract).

If the refund or commuted (present) value of the remaining installments is applied by the owner or beneficiary to purchase a new annuity, payments received will be taxed under the annuity rules to the beneficiary. The refund amount will be considered the beneficiary's investment in the new contract and a new exclusion ratio must be determined. This option is often selected if the guaranteed refund amount will exceed the unrecovered investment in the contract and would otherwise create a partially taxable lump sum payment.

3. If the owner was receiving payments under a joint and survivor annuity, the surviving owner excludes from income the same percentage of each payment that was excludable by the first annuitant (assuming that the joint annuitants were joint owners). An income tax deduction may be available to the

survivor owner/annuitant to the extent inclusion of the annuity in the estate of the first to die generated an estate tax (under the rules for income in respect of a decedent).

4. When an owner makes a partial withdrawal from the contract and takes a reduced annuity for the same term, a portion of the amount withdrawn will be subject to income tax.

5. When an owner makes a partial withdrawal from the contract (allocable to an investment in the contract made after August 13, 1982) and chooses to take the same payments for a different term, to the extent the cash surrender value of the contract exceeds the investment in the contract, gain will be realized in the form of a taxable withdrawal of interest.

6. The purchase of a variable annuity (see Questions and Answers below) is not taxed on income during the accumulation period. No tax will be payable until the earlier of: (a) the surrender of the contract; (b) withdrawal from the contract; or (c) the time payments under the annuity begin (annuitization). To obtain annuity treatment, however, the underlying investments of the segregated asset account must be "adequately diversified."[14]

Payments made as an annuity under a variable annuity are not subject to the same exclusion ratio as is a regular fixed annuity. This is because it is impossible to determine the expected return. Instead, the following formula is used:[15]

Investment in Contract
Number of Years of Expected Return

If there is a period certain or refund guarantee, the investment in the contract is adjusted accordingly. If payments are made for a fixed number of years without regard to life expectancy, the divisor is that fixed number of years. If payments are made for a single life, use IRS Table V. If payments are to be made on a joint and survivor basis, use Table VI. As in the case of a fixed annuitization, the exclusion ratio no longer applies once an annuitant reaches his life expectancy and has fully recovered his investment in the contract.

If payments drop below the excludable amount in any given year, the annuitant can elect to redetermine the excludable amount in the next tax year in which he receives an annuity payment. The loss in exclusions is divided by the number of years remaining (in the case of a fixed period annuity).

In the case of a life annuity the loss is divided by the annuitant's life expectancy computed as of the first day of the first period for which an amount is received as an annuity.[16]

For instance, assume a 65-year-old taxpayer purchased an annuity for $20,000. The contract provides variable monthly payments for life. Since his life expectancy is 20 years (Table V), he may exclude $1,000 of each annuity payment from income ($20,000 /20). Assume on his 70th birthday he receives only $200, $800 less than his excludable amount. At age 70 his life expectancy is 16 years. He may elect to add $50 ($800/16) to his $1,000 exclusion, a total of $1,050 which he may exclude that year and in subsequent years.

7. If an annuitant dies before the investment in the contract has been recovered, a loss deduction can be taken by the owner for the amount of the unrecovered investment, provided the annuity starting date was after July 1, 1986. So if a wife purchases a single premium nonrefundable annuity (whether on her own life, or alternatively on the life of her husband), and the annuitant dies before all costs have been recovered, a loss deduction will be allowed.

The deduction for the unrecovered investment in the contract is an itemized deduction, but not a miscellaneous deduction.[17] Therefore, it is not subject to the 2% floor. It is taken on the decedent's final return, and will be treated as a business loss, eligible to be carried back if the loss exceeds the income shown on the decedent's final return. In addition, these deductions can ultimately be taken by the estate or any other beneficiary that receives post-death payments.[18]

8. Amounts payable under a deferred annuity contract at the death of an annuitant (prior to the contract's maturity) will be partially taxable as ordinary income to the beneficiary. The taxable amount is equal to the excess of (a) the death benefit (plus aggregate dividends and any other amounts that were received tax free) over (b) total gross premiums.

Beneficiaries can elect to delay reporting of the gain in the year of the annuitant's death if the beneficiary applies the death benefit under a life income or installment option within 60 days of the annuitant's death. The beneficiary will then report income according to an exclusion ratio. The beneficiary's investment in the contract will be the same as the annuitant's investment in the contract.

The expected return is based on the income the beneficiary will receive and the beneficiary's life expectancy.[19]

9. The owner of an annuity often takes dividends, makes cash withdrawals, or takes other amounts out of the annuity contract before the annuity starting date. Such amounts are taxable as income to the extent that the policy cash value exceeds the investment in the contract – this results in a LIFO (last in, first out) type of treatment where all interest/growth is taxed before any tax-free return-of-capital payments can occur.[20]

This "interest-first" rule was imposed to discourage the use of annuity contracts as short-term investment vehicles. Under this rule, a loan is considered a cash withdrawal.

Likewise, to the extent the contract is used as collateral for a loan, amounts borrowed will be taxable (to the extent that the amount received is less than or equal to the gain inherent in the contract). If the amount received exceeds the built-in gain, the excess of what was borrowed over potential gain is considered a tax free return of the contract owner's investment. With respect to contracts entered into after October 21, 1988, amounts borrowed increase investment in the contract to the extent they are includible in income under these rules.

In applying the interest-first rule, all contracts entered into after October 21, 1988 and issued by the same company to the same policyholder during any 12-month period are treated as one contract.

10. "Premature" distributions (those made before certain dates listed below) are subject not only to the normal tax on ordinary income but also to a penalty tax of 10%. The 10% penalty applies only to the amount of the distribution that is included in income.

The penalty for premature distributions will not apply to any of the following:[21]

a) Payments that are part of a series of substantially equal periodic payments made for the life (or life expectancy) of the taxpayer or the joint lives (or joint life expectancies) of the taxpayer and his beneficiary (unless the series of payments is modified under certain circumstances);

b) Payments made on or after the time the contract owner becomes age 59½;

c) Payments made on account of the contract owner's disability;

d) Payments made from qualified retirement plans and IRAs (but these are subject to other similar premature distribution requirements);

e) Payments made to a beneficiary (or annuitant's estate) on or after the death of an annuitant;

f) Distributions under an immediate annuity contract;

g) An annuity contract purchased on the termination of certain qualified employer retirement plans and held until the employee separates from service;

h) Payments allocable to investment in the contract before August 14, 1982.

11. If an annuity owner dies before the starting date of the annuity payments, the cash value of the contract must either be distributed within 5 years of death or used within one year of death to provide a life annuity or installment payments payable over a period not longer than the beneficiary's life expectancy. However, if the surviving spouse is the beneficiary, the spouse can elect to become the new owner of the contract instead of selecting one of the above options.[22]

The 10% premature distribution penalty tax does not apply to required after-death distributions.

If the annuity contract is transferred by gift, the tax deferral on the inside build up that was allowed to the original contract owner is terminated. The donor of the gift is treated as having received non-annuity income in an amount equal to the excess of the cash surrender value of the contract over the investment in the contract at the time of the transfer. The recipient of the gift will take a new basis in the contract equal to the donor's investment in the contract, plus the amount of gain recognized on the gift (note that the new basis, the sum of the donor's basis and the donor's investment in the contract, is generally equal to the fair market value of the contract).

12. Tax free build-up within the contract is allowed only to "natural persons."[23] If an annuity contract is held by a person who is not a natural person, then the annuity contract is not treated as an annuity and the income on the contract is treated as ordinary income received or accrued by the owner during that taxable year.

Corporations are not "natural persons." Neither is the typical trust, although a trust acting as the agent for a natural person would itself be considered a natural person. But if an employer is the agent for its employees, the contract will be considered as if owned by the employer. The employer will therefore be taxed on the inside build up. This means annuities are no longer appropriate tax advantaged investments for nonqualified deferred compensation agreements. Exceptions from the "natural persons" rules allow tax-free build up of the following annuities:[24]

a) Annuities received by the executor of a decedent at the decedent's death,

b) Annuities held by a qualified retirement plan or IRA,

c) Annuities considered "qualifying funding assets" (used to provide funding for structured settlements and by property and casualty insurance companies to fund periodic payments for damages),

d) Annuities purchased by an employer on termination of a qualified plan and held until all amounts under the plan are distributed to the employee or his beneficiary,

e) Annuities which are "immediate," i.e., those which have a starting date no more than one year from the date the annuity was purchased and provide for a series of substantially equal periodic payments to be made at least annually over the annuity period.

ALTERNATIVES

1. *Municipal Bond Funds* – These funds are an attractive option for retirement savings. The income they produce is exempt from federal and in many cases state income tax (although the sale of the bonds may result in taxable capital gains or losses, and some municipal bonds may be subject to the alternative minimum tax).

If a municipal bond fund's average yield is 6%, the equivalent taxable yield is almost 8.6% if the investor is in the 30% personal tax bracket. Money can be withdrawn from a municipal bond fund at any time without a tax penalty. A drawback of municipal bond funds as compared with annuities is the lack of a guaranteed return (bond rates may go down in future years, resulting in a lower yield on reinvestments of interest and matured bonds), and the potential for capital losses (if interest rates rise and bonds must be sold before maturity).

2. *Single Premium Life Insurance (SPLI)* – This type of life insurance offers many of the same advantages of annuities, but incorporates a death benefit at issuance that is higher than the cash deposit (whereas, for annuities that contain a death benefit feature, the guarantee is usually *equal* to the amount of the cash deposit). However, there are important differences between an SPLI policy and other types of life insurance.

Generally, no income tax or penalties are payable until or unless the policy is surrendered. However, single premium life insurance policies issued after June 21, 1988 are modified endowment contracts (MECs). Distributions from MECs are taxed under essentially the same rules as annuity contracts. This means that any policy distributions, including loans, will be taxed at the time received to the extent that the cash value of the contract immediately before the payment exceeds the investment in the contract. Additionally, a 10% penalty tax may apply to certain distributions. In effect, the MEC rules remove the tax-free borrowing possibilities otherwise associated with life insurance policies.

A client should not be directed to a product – any product – merely for its tax advantages, since these are at the mercy of a voter-conscious Congress, as demonstrated by the effect of legislation passed in 1988 on SPLI, discussed above (although Congress generally provides some level of grandfathering provisions for most tax law changes, as it did for the new MEC rules in 1988). Certainly, if a client doesn't need the leverage that life insurance provides, the costs and restrictions make SPLI less attractive as there is a cost for the death benefit which, in turn, leaves less capital available for investment growth.

3. *Mutual Funds* – During the accumulation period, variable annuities offer investment options that are essentially the same as mutual funds. Mutual funds do not enjoy the tax-deferred accumulation associ-

ated with variable annuities. However, tax on the capital appreciation of the assets in a mutual fund is deferred until the gains are realized. In addition, the realized gains are taxed as either long- or short-term capital gains, depending on the holding period. In contrast, all gains and income on the assets in the separate accounts of a variable annuity are taxed at ordinary income tax rates when paid. Also, mutual funds receive a step-up in basis at death in the hands of the heir.[25] There is no step-up in basis in annuity values in the hands of the beneficiary when the annuity contract owner dies.

WHERE AND HOW TO GET IT

Almost all life insurance companies offer annuities, and these companies distribute annuities to customers through life insurance agencies, many stock brokerage firms, independent insurance agents and financial planners, independent insurance brokerage firms, and direct to consumers through the mail and the internet. In addition, many banks now offer annuities (often through internal broker-dealers).

Variable annuities are considered securities under the federal securities laws. Consequently, they may be offered only by agents who are licensed and who have passed the applicable securities examinations. In addition, prospective buyers must be given a prospectus. The prospectus must describe the product and its features and the company offering the product. The prospectus must also explain and detail expense charges, contract options, investment options, and related information.

WHAT FEES OR OTHER ACQUISITION COSTS ARE INVOLVED?

There are five typical fees or charges that are usually incurred when purchasing annuities, particularly variable annuities. These include:

1. *Investment Management Fees* – These fees run from a low of about 0.25% to a high of about 1%.

2. *Administration Expense and Mortality Risk Charge* – This charge ranges from a low of about 0.5% to a high of about 1.3%. However, additional riders and features can increase this cost to as high as 2.0%.

3. *Annual Maintenance Charge* – This charge typically ranges from $25 to $100. However, it is often waived once total investments exceed a specified amount, such as $25,000.

4. *Charge per Fund Exchange* – This charge generally ranges from $0 to $10, but most funds will permit a limited number of charge-free exchanges per year. In addition, automatic rebalancing programs usually do not count towards this limit.

5. *Maximum Surrender Charge* – Surrender charges vary by company and policy and generally phase-out over a number of years. If the charge is lower, the phase-out tends to be longer. For example, typical charges and phase-out periods are 5% of premium decreasing to 0% over 10 years or 8% of premium decreasing to 0% over 7 years.

Items 1 through 4 in the above list must be explicitly stated in the prospectus for a variable annuity. In a fixed annuity, these costs are generally incorporated into the management of the insurance company's general account and are simply netted out of the return credited to annuity-holders. Thus, when comparing fixed annuities, cost comparisons (although other non-cost aspects are also analyzed) are generally restricted to an evaluation of the comparable crediting rates of the general account and the surrender charges.

HOW DO I SELECT THE BEST OF ITS TYPE?

1. Compare, on a spreadsheet, the costs and features of selected annuities. Consider all of the five costs discussed above as well as how much can be withdrawn from the contract each year without fee. Be certain to fully read through the *full* details of costs / charges, guarantees, riders, and special features in the prospectus of a variable annuity.

2. Compare the total outlay with the total annual annuity payment in the case of fixed annuities. Be certain to incorporate the time value of money if the payment schedules are different.

3. In an analysis of variable annuities, evaluate the total return for the variable annuity sub-accounts over multiple time periods (Lipper Analytical Services, Inc., and Morningstar, Inc., both have information to help assess this).

4. Compare the relative financial strength of the companies through services such as A.M. Best.

Insist on a credit rating of A+ (or at the very least, thoroughly discuss with the prospective buyer the risks involved in purchasing from a company with a lesser rating).

WHERE CAN I FIND OUT MORE ABOUT IT?

Information on annuities can be obtained in newspapers (especially the *Wall Street Journal's* quarterly report on mutual funds and variable annuities) and in three major statistical sources: (a) A.M. Best Co., (b) Lipper Analytical Services Inc., and (c) Barron's. Substantial comparative information, particularly for fixed annuities, can often be obtained from insurance brokerage firms that deal with multiple annuity product providers.

QUESTIONS AND ANSWERS

Question – What are the different ways that annuities can be categorized?

Answer – Annuities are classified according to: (1) How premiums are paid; (2) What residual values, if any, are paid upon the death of the annuitant; (3) When benefit payments begin; (4) How many lives are covered; (5) What investment options are available to the owner of the annuity contract; and (6) How benefits are calculated. It is important to bear in mind that a change in almost any of the above classifications results in an adjustment in the payout the annuity provides to maintain an actuarially equivalent benefit.

Figure 19.1 shows how annuities are classified.

1. *Premium Paying Method – Single premium annuities* are often the ideal vehicles for people who have come into large cash sums. A single premium annuity will convert such amounts, for example, from an inheritance, from the sale of a business or a large piece of real estate, or from a qualified pension or profit-sharing plan lump-sum distribution, into a lifetime or certain fixed period stream of payments. Immediate annuities are virtually always single-premium annuities (clients with subsequent investment amounts would simply purchase another immediate annuity). Single premium structures also occur sometimes with deferred fixed annuities that provide for guaranteed interest crediting rates for a specified period (to prevent subsequent investments at these guaranteed rates if

general interest rates decline in the future). Single premium structures are fairly rare amongst deferred variable annuities.

Fixed premium annuities are favored by investors who do not have large cash sums to invest but who desire a regular investment program with a "forced saving" feature. Typically, fixed annual (semiannual, quarterly, monthly or even weekly) premium payments are required and continue until the desired annuity starting date (the date when payouts begin). Since the periodic premiums are fixed, the total accumulation, and therefore the ultimate annuity payout, is very predictable. Fixed premium annuities are now fairly rare, having been replaced instead by flexible-premium annuities.

Flexible-premium annuities allow the contract owner to invest (make premium contributions) at any time and in any amount desired. In rare instances, the insurance company requires certain minimum annual contributions within the first few years, but after this initial period (or from the start in most cases) there are generally no restrictions or requirements that apply with regard to the timing or amount of further contributions.

2. *Disposition of Proceeds* – A *life annuity* with no refund feature continues annuity payouts only as long as the annuitant (or one of the annuitants) survive, with no final payment or refund at the death of the last annuitant, even if the total paid out of the annuity is less than the amount invested in the contract. This can involve a high amount of risk, as the death of a lone annuitant shortly after contract issuance could result in a forfeiture of virtually the entire original deposit.

For example, if Mr. Smith purchases an immediately annuity for $50,000 that provides for payments of $300/month for life, and dies after only receiving two payments, his total return out of the contract will be only $600. The remaining $49,400 of his original deposit will be forfeited to the insurance company, which will use the proceeds to help offset the payments due to annuity-holders that outlive their life expectancies.

Insurance companies also offer annuity contracts with minimum payback guarantees, since many investors are reluctant to forfeit a portion of their investment in the event of the premature death of the annuitant – particularly if there are heirs that will ultimately inherit all assets not consumed by the individual during his/her life. These guarantees take two forms.

Refund annuities promise to pay the difference between the amount invested in the contract (generally the total of the premiums paid) and the annuity payments actually paid out before the death of the annuitant. This refund takes the form either of lump-sum cash payments or of installment payouts. *Period certain annuities* promise to make payments for a stipulated period, such as 5, 10, or 20 years, or for the annuitant's life, whichever is longer. It is important to bear in mind that, due to the time value of money, this guarantee still does not make the annuity-holder entirely "whole" in comparison to having invested the assets in an alternative to begin with (where they would have ostensibly been *growing* during this time period, not merely preserving the original principal amount).

The payout period may also be shorter term – that is, for a specified period generally shorter than the expected life (or lives) of the annuitant(s). *Term-certain annuities* operate similarly to the amortization of a loan. Payments continue for a specified term only, regardless of when the annuitant dies. A *temporary annuity* is a variation on the period certain annuity concept. However, rather than paying a specified amount for the *longer* of the annuitant's life or the specified term, a temporary annuity continues payments only for the *shorter* of the annuitant's life or the specified term.

3. *Date Benefits Begin* – An *immediate annuity* begins annuity payments within one year after all premiums are contributed. Immediate annuities are commonly used when a person wishes to convert a large lump-sum amount, such as a substantial distribution from a qualified pension or profit-sharing plan, the settlement proceeds of a lawsuit, or simply a sizeable amount of cash, into an immediate income stream. As the name suggests, payments from

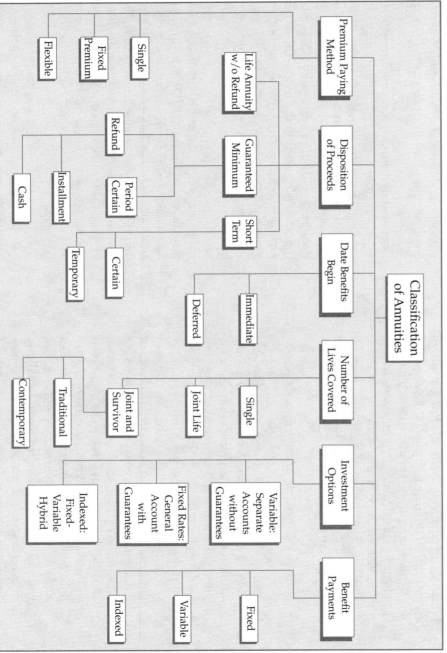

Figure 19.1

Chapter 19 – Annuities

deferred annuities are delayed or deferred for a period of time (the "accumulation phase") after the premiums or contributions have been completed. Deferred annuities are frequently used when a person has cash to invest before retirement and wishes to postpone the beginning of the annuity payments until retirement or later.

4. *Number of Lives Covered* – The annuity payout period may depend on one or two lives, or, less commonly, more lives. A *single life annuity* (with no refund feature) makes payments until the single covered life (the sole annuitant) dies. In the case of annuities based on two or more lives, payouts may continue until the last annuitant dies or only until the first annuitant dies (depending upon the exact terms of the contract). Annuities whose payments continue until the last death of the covered lives are called *joint and last survivor annuities*, or just joint and survivor annuities. Those annuities whose payments cease upon the first death are called *joint life annuities*. Currently, joint and survivor annuities are more common than joint life annuities.

A joint and survivor annuity may pay one amount while both annuitants are alive and the same, or another (lesser) amount, after the first death. The surviving annuitant often receives some specified percentage (called the survivor benefit ratio) of the amount payable before the first death. Survivor benefit ratios typically range from 50% to 100%, with 50, 66, 75, and 100% the most common. For example, a joint and 75% survivor annuity paying a $50,000 annual joint benefit would pay $37,500 per year to the survivor after the first death. The amount of the survivor benefit ratio is generally selected at the inception of the payout phase (annuitization) of the contract.

The benefit payable to the survivor may also depend on which annuitant dies first. The *traditional joint and survivor annuity* has a principal annuitant and a secondary annuitant or beneficiary. The survivor benefit ratio applies only to the benefit payable to the surviving secondary annuitant after the principal annuitant's death. If the principal annuitant outlives the secondary annuitant, the benefit payments are not reduced. These types of payment structures are particularly common in joint and survivor

annuity payments from defined benefit pension plans (where the former employee is the principal annuitant). In recent years an alternative form of the joint and survivor annuity has become popular. This *contemporary joint and survivor annuity* pays the reduced benefit to the survivor regardless of which annuitant dies first. These types of payment structures are most common from commercially available joint and survivor annuities. For a given total investment, insurance companies can afford to pay relatively higher joint and survivor benefits on these annuities than on traditional joint and survivor annuities.

5. *Investment Options* – Fixed rate annuities are similar to universal life policies in that amounts credited to cash values are based on the insurer's current declared rate, subject to a minimum guarantee of about 3% to 4.5% (varying by annuity contract and insurance company). Rates paid on new money (current contributions) may be guaranteed for one to five years (or occasionally as long as ten years). The currently declared rate depends on the performance of the insurer's general investment portfolio or general account, which is largely invested in fixed income investments such as bonds and mortgages. Although interest credits to the annuity depend on market rates on these types of fixed-income investments, the cash value itself is not market valued. Similar to a savings account, once interest is credited, the cash value will not decline if the market value of the underlying assets in the insurer's general account declines (however, some annuities levy a market-adjustment to the contract value based upon interest rate changes in the event of early surrender). The insurer bears the market risk.

Analogously, variable annuities are similar to variable insurance policies. The annuity owner may choose to invest contributions and cash values in a broad spectrum of investment options or separate accounts, which are similar to mutual funds (although the investor is limited to the selection of investment choices that are offered within the annuity contract). The investment options usually include diversified stock, bond, and money market funds and frequently include specialized stock funds, foreign stock and bond funds, real estate equity and mortgage funds, and even asset allocation funds (a type of or more annuitants frequently include a minimum payment guarantee. In other words, many annuities include both life and fixed period or refund elements so that if death occurs prematurely, the annuitant and the annuitant's survivors will recover a total of at least a minimum amount. Therefore, each annuity payment where a minimum guarantee has been purchased is composed of (a) return of principal, (b) interest or earnings on invested funds, and (c) a survivorship element.

If an annuitant dies before having recovered the full amount guaranteed under a refund or period certain life annuity, the balance of the guaranteed amount is not taxable income to the refund beneficiary - until the total amount received by the annuitant plus the total amount received tax free by the beneficiary equals the investment in the contract. From that point on, all additional amounts received are ordinary income.[26]

Question – What is the difference between a "fixed" annuity and a "variable" annuity?

Answer–Although annuities are classified in many other ways, the major distinguishing factor of annuities sold today is whether they are fixed or variable. About 90% of all outstanding annuity contracts fall into the fixed rate category, but variable annuities are becoming increasingly popular (variable annuities are also fairly *new* compared to the long history of fixed annuities). The investment account in a fixed rate contract operates much like the cash value account of a universal life policy. The annuity investment earns a fixed rate, which is often guaranteed for the first one to five (occasionally as many as ten) years of the contract. After that time, the rate depends on the investment success of the insurer's general portfolio (subject to a guaranteed floor, typically about 3 to 4.5%). The fixed rate contract gives the contract owner no choice or say in the underlying investments.

In some fixed rate contracts, there is a "bailout" provision. If the contract return falls below a certain rate (the "bailout rate"), the contract owner can terminate the contract without cost (ie., without surrender charges).

Variable annuities are becoming increasingly popular because, in return for the assumption of greater risk, the contract owner may obtain both greater investment flexibility and a (potentially) higher return. The contract owner can select from

balanced fund where the insurer's investment manager allocates investments among the other funds). In contrast with fixed rate annuities, cash values depend on the market value of the underlying assets in the selected separate accounts. Variable annuity owners bear the market risk of investment and forego minimum interest rate guarantees (although some limited guarantees may be available, subject to additional costs and substantial restrictions). However, they have the flexibility to choose their investment portfolio and the potential to earn far greater total returns than they would earn on fixed rate annuities.

Equity-index annuities (EIAs) are sometimes described as a hybrid of fixed and variable annuities. The returns on EIAs are linked to an equity index, such as the S&P 500 index. However, the annuity is not actually invested in the stocks making up the index. Rather, like fixed annuities, the returns to EIAs are paid from the insurance company's general account. However, the amount allocated to the EIA is based on some percentage, for example, 85%, of the appreciation in the reference index (often subject to annual caps and/or interest spreads). If the index declines in value, a minimum guaranteed amount (which may be 0%, but is generally never negative) is credited to the EIA. In this way, EIAs attempt to provide investors with some of the upside potential of the equity markets with the downside protection of more conservative general account investments.

6. *Benefit Payments* – The annuity benefit may be fixed or variable. Fixed benefit annuities guarantee a minimum annuity benefit payment per dollar of accumulated value, similar to settlement options under life insurance policies. Variable benefit annuities make no guarantees. Annuity benefit payments depend on the market value of the assets in the separate accounts.

Question – What happens to the money paid to the insurance company when the annuitant dies?

Answer –A "pure life annuity" is one in which the continuation of payments by the insurer is contingent upon the continuing survival of one or more lives. The remaining consideration (premium) paid for the annuity that has not been distributed (including accrued interest) is fully earned by the insurer immediately upon the death of the annuitant. This is why annuities payable for the life or lives of one among a number of separate accounts that are similar to mutual fund investments. The investment options typically include diversified stock, bond, and money market funds. Most insurers also now offer a broad array of alternative funds such as specialized stock funds (sector funds, small-capitalization stock funds, index funds), foreign stock and bond funds, junk bond funds, real estate equity and mortgage funds, GNMA-type funds, and asset-allocation funds (where the company's investment manager selects portfolio weights allocating investments among the other funds). It is important to note that although there is a great deal of latitude in investment selection, the investor is limited exclusively to the selection of investment choices that are offered within the annuity contract.

Question – What is the difference between a joint annuity and a joint and last survivor annuity?

Answer – A joint life annuity is a contract that provides a specified amount of income for two or more persons named in the contract. Income ends upon the first death. A joint and last survivor contract is much more popular because payments continue until the last death among the covered lives. Obviously, this form of annuity is more expensive than other forms because, on average, it will pay income for a longer time. This increased cost is reflected in a lower annuity payment than would be paid under a single life annuity at either of the two ages, or under the joint life annuity structure.

Clients can purchase the joint and survivor annuity on either a pure life basis (ending at the later death) or with a certain number of payments guaranteed. Most insurers offer a form of joint and survivor annuity that pays the full amount while both annuitants are alive and then two-thirds or one-half of that income when the first annuitant dies. This is called a "joint and two-thirds" or "joint and one-half annuity."

Question – How does the variable annuity work?

Answer – The variable annuity was the product of a search for a tool that would provide a guaranteed lifetime income that could never be outlived and also provide a relatively stable purchasing power in times of inflation by allowing for returns that may keep pace with (or even exceed) inflation. This can be contrasted with the level payments generally received from fixed annuities, whose purchasing power will be eroded over time by inflation.

The variable annuity is based on equity investments. Premiums are paid to the insurance company during the "accumulation phase." That money is placed into one or more separate accounts. The funds in these accounts are invested separately from the other assets of the insurer. Each year, some money is taken out of the contract owner's premium (or deducted from the account value) for expenses. The balance is applied to purchase "units of credit" in the separate accounts.

The number of credits purchased depends on the current valuation of a unit in terms of dollars. For example, if each unit was valued at $10 a unit based on current investment results, a $100 level premium (after expenses) would purchase 10 units. If the value of a unit dropped because of investment experience, the premium would purchase more units. If the value of a unit increased, the same premium would buy fewer units. The price of a unit of a separate account is analogous to the NAV price of a share of a mutual fund. This unit purchasing continues until the "maturity" of the contract.

At the transition to the payout phase (annuitization) of the contract, the insurer credits the value of the contract owner's total accumulation units to a retirement fund. A value of a given number of accumulation units will purchase so many retirement income units (based on actuarial principles). Note that a variable annuitization does not promise to pay a fixed number of dollars each month but rather a fixed number of retirement income units. In other words, the dollar amount of each payment depends on the dollar value of a retirement income unit (also called an annuity unit) when the payment is made. The dollar value of an annuity unit is in turn based on the investment results of the separate accounts. For example, assume an annuitant was entitled to a payment based on 10 annuity units each month. If the dollar value of an annuity unit varied from $12.10 to $12.50 to $12.80, the annuitant would be paid $121, $125, and $128, respectively.

Question – What are the risks assumed by the contract owner under a variable annuity?

Answer – Under a variable annuity, the insurer assumes only the risk of fluctuations due to mortality and expenses (guaranteeing that the annuitant will not outlive his or her income and that internal expense fluctuations will be absorbed). This means the contract owner is assuming the entire investment risk. If the separate accounts are invested poorly or in the wrong investments, the annuitant could receive fewer dollars of income than would have been paid under a fixed annuity.

Question – Why, if payments from variable annuities depend on the market value of the underlying assets, do variable annuities have an assumed investment rate (AIR)?

Answer – Under most variable annuity contracts there is an assumed investment rate (AIR) that the investment portfolio must earn in order for benefit payments to remain level. If the investment performance exceeds the AIR, the level of benefit payments will increase. On the other hand, if the selected investments underperform the AIR, the level of benefit payments will decrease.

For example, assume a variable annuity contract is issued with a 6% AIR and a beginning unit value of $20. The contract is issued with a payout of 100 units per month (providing an initial monthly payment of $20/unit x 100 units/month = $2,000/month). The investment yield during the first month of the contract was 10%; during the second month the investment yield was 4%. The monthly benefit can be calculated by monitoring the changes in the unit value and by comparing the actual performance with the assumed 6% interest rate. During the first month, the 10% return on the portfolio exceeds the assumed 6% AIR by 4% – which leads to a 4% increase in the $20 unit value. The new unit value is now $20.80 ($2,080 per month). During the subsequent month, because the actual return is only 4%, which is 2% less than the AIR, there will be a 2% reduction in the unit value to $20.38 ($2,038 per month). The unit value could actually drop below the beginning $20 value ($2,000 per month) if investment performance remains below the assumed 6% level for an extended period of time. However, for an increased cost, some annuities provide a guarantee that the monthly payment will never drop below the initial monthly payment, regardless of adverse investment performance.

Question – Can a person select the assumed interest rate (AIR) used to determine the payments from a variable annuity and, if so, what impact will it have on the level of benefit payments?

Answer – Under some contracts, the purchaser is able to select the AIR from a narrow range of possible rates (such as 3, 5, or 7%). It is much easier to receive an increasing stream of benefit payments by selecting a lower AIR – however, this can be initially more expensive (meaning the starting monthly payment will be reduced). The effect of choosing a different AIR can be demonstrated by returning to the example of the previous question.

If an AIR of 8% rather than 6% is chosen, the benefit increase in the first month will be 2% instead of 4%. The unit value changes to $20.40 instead of $20.80. The next month's decrease in benefits is more drastic, a 4% reduction rather than the 2% reduction. The unit value decreases to $19.58 instead of $20.38 from the lower AIR. Choosing the less costly higher AIR will start with a higher initial benefit (i.e., with an 8% AIR, the starting payment in the above example would likely have been higher than $2,000) but will increase the likelihood that benefit payments increase less rapidly and decrease more rapidly.

Keep in mind that although variable annuity contracts are intended to provide a hedge against inflation and protect the purchasing power of the benefits through positive market returns, the increases in market value have not always occurred at exactly the same time that prices increase. Often prices go up significantly before the market provides high returns and increases the level of benefits. These temporary mismatches between price increases and benefit increases are inevitable and can lead to a temporary loss of purchasing power.

Question – Although the investment options in variable annuities are similar to mutual funds, mutual funds are taxed differently than annuities and annuities charge higher fees and loads to cover various guarantees within the annuity contract. How can one determine if and when a variable annuity is a better investment than a mutual fund?

Answer – Conceptually, variable annuities are simply mutual funds wrapped in an instrument that permits tax on all income, whether ordinary or capital gain, to be deferred until monies are distributed. If annuitized, distributions are taxed under the rules of Internal Revenue Code Section 72, which essentially prorates the recovery of basis over the distribution period. In addition, and *more importantly*, the investor may enjoy any number of a myriad of contractual guarantees in a variable annuity contract (although the details of these guarantees are *highly* variable across various contracts). However, an investor must pay a price for these advantages.

First, the amount of each annuity payment in excess of the amount of basis recovery is taxed at ordinary income tax rates, regardless of whether it is attributable to ordinary investment income (i.e., interest or dividends, including the potentially tax-favored qualifying dividends) or capital apprecia-tion. Since an investor's marginal ordinary income tax rate always equals or exceeds the applicable capital gains rate (depending upon whether the gains are short-term or long-term), he/she will forfeit the favorable lower tax treatment on the por-tion of payments that is attributable to previously unrecognized capital gains. In addition, the taxpayer will be unable to take advantage of capital losses as they accrued (although capital losses will still offset gains within the contract, ultimately reducing the amount of growth taxed as ordinary income at withdrawal).

Second, variable annuities incur mortality and expense (M&E) charges (for other various riders and guarantees) that range from about 0.5%, up to 1.25% (occasionally as high as 2.0% with additional riders, features, and guarantees) in addition to the usual fund expenses which average from about 0.6% to 1.25% on equity funds (occasionally as high as 2.25% for small-cap equity or international equity funds), depending on the type of fund.

Third, most variable annuities impose surrender charges if money is withdrawn within the first five to nine years. The charge typically declines to zero in steps of 1% per year. As a general rule, variable annuities are less attractive than mutual funds if there is any possibility the contract will be sur-rendered within the first five to seven years. The period of tax deferral will generally be insufficient to overcome the additional fees and surrender charges. It is notable that in recent years, an increasing as-sortment of variable annuities are being offered to the public that allow for substantially reduced periods of surrender charges (as short as three years, or even one year) or no surrender charges. However, these contracts have increased M&E charges to compensate for the higher risk (to the insurance company) of an early liquidation.

Fourth, and potentially more problematic, is the 10% early withdrawal penalty on distributions from annuities before age 59½. Distributions that are not part of a series of substantially equal periodic payments for the life (or joint life) expectancy of the annuitant(s) are in most cases subject to a 10% penalty tax on the taxable amount withdrawn from the annuity, in addition to the ordinary income tax due.

Keep in mind that although equity mutual funds do not enjoy the same degree of tax deferral as vari-able annuities, they are, nonetheless, tax-favored investments. Although the tax on ordinary dividend and interest income earned by a fund is paid by the shareholders in the year the income is earned, the tax on capital gains is deferred until the gains are recognized, either through buy and sell transactions within the mutual fund portfolio or when the inves-tor sells his shares in the fund.

Therefore, when trying to decide whether vari-able annuities or mutual funds are more appro-priate for a particular client situation, the results (particularly the analysis of comparable returns) depend on certain critical assumptions regarding the size of the differential in fees and loads, the rate of return, tax rates on ordinary income, quali-fying dividends, and long-term capital gains, the turnover rate of the underlying investments, the length of accumulation period, and whether annu-ity distributions will be subject to a 10% penalty. In addition, the relative merit depends on how the variable annuity will be liquidated. Variable annuities are relatively more attractive if proceeds will be annuitized rather than taken in a lump-sum (because longer time periods generally favor the annuity's tax-deferral benefits).

For any combination of assumptions regarding the fee differential, tax rates, and rates of return and distribution options, there is a "break-even holding period" after which an investor can withdraw the accumulated value in a variable annuity, pay the regular income tax and, if applicable, the 10% penalty, and still be left with at least as much as he would have accumulated in a taxable mutual fund.

Figure 19.2 compares the effective after-tax rates of return of a variable annuity with a no-load mu-tual fund over various accumulation periods and a range of assumed pre-tax and before-expense rates of return. Since the maximum tax rate of 15% for long-term capital gains and qualifying dividends is scheduled to expire after 2010, the break-even periods are first computed as if they have already expired. This places the variable annuities in the most favorable light possible at this time. Sub-sequent analyses apply the current law rates for long-term gains and qualifying dividends assum-ing instead that the current law rates are extended indefinitely beyond 2010. Additional assumptions include that:

- Both the mutual fund and variable annuity are invested in common stocks;

- There are no front-end loads on either the mutual fund or the variable annuity;

- The variable annuity has surrender charges that grade to zero after year seven;

- The investor's marginal tax rate for current taxable (ordinary) income is 35% and for deferred gains is 20% (applicable state and local taxes are ignored);

- Regarding the mutual fund, 40% of the total returns are attributable to dividends and 60% to capital gains;

- The investor will be age 59½ or older at the end of the investor's variable annuity holding period (i.e., withdrawals from the variable annuity will not be subject to the 10% early-withdrawal penalty);

- All of the earnings from the variable annuity will be deferred until distributions are made;

- Total annual expense charges for administration and management of the mutual fund are 1%;

- Total annual expense charges for the variable annuity are 2% (1%, comparable to the administrative and management charges for the mutual fund, plus a 1% annual mortality charge); and

- The average annual turnover rate (for the calculation of taxes on gains recognized when the fund buys and sells securities) for the mutual fund is 20% (i.e., the average holding period for securities within the mutual fund is five years).

Figure 19.2 shows the effective after-tax and after-expense rate of return for the investment in the mutual fund and the variable annuity for the assortment of accumulation periods and the various assumed pre-tax and before-expense rates of return. The values are computed by assuming that both the mutual fund and the variable annuity are liquidated at the end of the specified accumulation period and that all taxes on the tax-deferred gains

and tax-deferred income, respectively, are paid at that time. The vehicle with the largest effective return is the one that would provide investment with the largest effective return; that is, it is the one that would provide the investor with the greatest after-tax balance at the end of the accumulation period.

Figure 19.2 shows that even if the total pre-tax and before-expense average annual compound rate of return on the investment is as great as 12%, the variable annuity becomes the better accumulation vehicle only if the accumulation period approaches 20 years. That is, under the assumptions listed above, if an investor is planning to accumulate funds for a period shorter than about 20 years, the mutual fund would be the better accumulation vehicle.

The period of years until the variable annuity becomes the better accumulation vehicle is even longer for lower assumed total rates of return. For instance, the average annual compound rate of return on the S&P 500 index since 1926 has been just slightly over 10%. Using this rate of return as a general guideline for a broadly diversified portfolio of stocks, an investor would have to wait almost 27 years before the variable annuity would provide the greater after-tax accumulation. If the rate of return is expected to be 8% or less, even 40 years is not a sufficient accumulation period for the variable annuity to outperform the mutual fund after taxes and expenses. In addition, it is important to note that most of the assumptions used in this exercise favor the variable annuity, and alternative assumptions could extend the break-even period even further.

In most cases, investors who accumulate substantial sums for retirement, either inside or outside of an annuity, do not take a lump-sum distribution, which would then trigger the immediate recognition and taxation of all deferred income or accumulated gains. Instead, they make periodic withdrawals (and/or outright annuitize the contract) which enables them to continue to enjoy the benefits of tax deferral on the remaining balance over the distribution years. This continuation of tax deferral increases the relative benefit of the variable annuity as compared to the mutual fund.

Assuming a distribution period of 20 years, Figure 19.3 shows the effective annual compound after-tax and after-expense rates of return for the entire accumulation and distribution period and the number of years in the accumulation period (the crossover

Figure 19.2

EFFECTIVE AFTERTAX RATE OF RETURN
Mutual Fund v. Variable Annuity

Lump-Sum Distribution at End of Accumulation Period

Accum Period		Total Before-Tax and Before-Expense Rate of Return					
		7%	8%	9%	10%	11%	12%
5	MF	4.22	4.93	5.65	6.37	7.09	7.82
	VA	3.36	4.05	4.76	5.47	6.19	6.91
	Dif	0.86	0.88	0.89	0.90	0.90	0.91
10	MF	4.26	4.99	5.72	6.46	7.20	7.94
	VA	3.49	4.24	5.00	5.78	6.57	7.37
	Dif	0.77	0.75	0.72	0.68	0.63	0.57
15	MF	4.28	5.01	5.75	6.50	7.25	8.00
	VA	3.61	4.40	5.21	6.05	6.89	7.50
	Dif	0.67	0.61	0.54	0.45	0.36	0.50
19	MF	4.29	5.03	5.77	6.52	7.27	8.03
	VA	3.70	4.52	5.37	6.23	7.12	8.01
	Dif	0.59	0.51	0.40	0.29	0.15	0.02
20	MF	4.29	5.03	5.77	6.52	7.28	8.04
	VA	3.72	4.55	5.40	6.28	7.17	8.07
	Dif	0.57	0.48	0.37	0.24	0.11	-0.03
22	MF	4.30	5.04	5.78	6.53	7.29	8.05
	VA	3.76	4.60	5.47	6.36	7.26	8.18
	Dif	0.54	0.44	0.31	0.17	0.03	-0.13
23	MF	4.30	5.04	5.78	6.53	7.29	8.05
	VA	3.78	4.63	5.51	6.40	7.31	8.23
	Dif	0.52	0.41	0.27	0.13	-0.02	-0.18
26	MF	4.30	5.04	5.79	6.54	7.30	8.06
	VA	3.84	4.71	5.60	6.51	7.44	8.38
	Dif	0.46	0.33	0.19	0.03	-0.14	-0.32
27	MF	4.30	5.04	5.79	6.54	7.30	8.07
	VA	3.85	4.73	5.63	6.55	7.48	8.42
	Dif	0.45	0.31	0.16	-0.01	-0.18	-0.35
33	MF	4.31	5.05	5.80	6.56	7.32	8.08
	VA	3.96	4.87	5.79	6.73	7.69	8.65
	Dif	0.35	0.18	0.01	-0.17	-0.37	-0.57
34	MF	4.31	5.05	5.80	6.56	7.32	8.08
	VA	3.98	4.89	5.82	6.76	7.72	8.68
	Dif	0.33	0.16	-0.02	-0.20	-0.40	-0.60
40	MF	4.31	5.06	5.81	6.56	7.33	8.09
	VA	4.07	5.00	5.95	6.91	7.88	8.85
	Dif	0.24	0.06	-0.14	-0.35	-0.55	-0.76
Crossover Yr.		62.2	43.6	33.3	26.9	22.5	19.4

year) until the variable annuity would outperform (provide greater annual after-tax distributions than) the mutual fund. These crossover years were calculated using the same assumptions as listed above plus the following assumptions with regard to the taxation of distributions during the 20-year distribution period:

- Distributions from the annuity are assumed to be level and taxed under the rules of IRC Section 72. Under these rules, basis is recovered in a pro rata fashion over the distribution period. For example, if the basis is $100,000 and the distribution period is 20 years, 1/20 of the basis, or $5,000 of each annual payment is treated as a nontaxable recovery of basis. The remaining portion of each annual payment is taxable as ordinary income. Given the assumptions of a level 35% tax rate on ordinary income and level annual distributions, the after-tax payments from the annuity will also be level each year over the distribution period;

- The amount withdrawn in any given year from the mutual fund is the amount necessary to provide equal after-tax annual distributions over the 20-year distribution period. It is assumed that the after-tax dividend income each year is the first money withdrawn. If, in a given year, the after-tax dividend income is less than the desired after-tax distribution, shares in the mutual fund must be sold to make up the difference. It is assumed that gain is recognized and taxed on the sale of such shares in the same proportion as the ratio of the total accumulated gains within the portfolio to the total value of the portfolio. For example, if

the total value of the portfolio is $100,000 and the built-in gain is $40,000, a sale of $5,000 worth of securities would result in the recognition and taxation of $2,000 of gains. The remaining $3,000 would be tax-free recovery of basis.

The variable annuity becomes relatively more advantageous when the continuing benefits of tax deferral over an extended payout period are also included in the analysis. However, even if funds are to be liquidated over a 20-year period, the variable annuity becomes the better alternative (under the listed assumptions) only if the accumulation period is still quite long.

For example, assume an investor expects to invest at a total pre-tax and before-expense rate of return of about 10% (matching the long-term compound average annual rate of return on the S&P 500 index). The investor can expect the variable annuity to outperform a mutual fund only if the investor plans to accumulate money in the variable annuity for about 20.4 years before beginning distributions over a 20-year payout period. Stated another way, an investor who plans to retire at age 65, for instance, would gain by making contributions to a variable annuity before age 45. However, any further investments made after age 44 would be better invested in the mutual fund outside the variable annuity. The after-tax payments associated with a systematic liquidation of the mutual fund for a twenty year period starting at age 65 for contributions after age 44 would be greater than for comparable contributions to the variable annuity.

Although the new preferential tax rate provisions for capital gains and dividend income are scheduled to expire after 2010, many experts expect that these

Figure 19.3

MUTUAL FUND VERSUS VARIABLE ANNUITY 20-Year Annuitization			
Total ROR	Effective Aftertax ROR		Crossover Year
	MF	VA	
12%	8.0920%	8.0920%	13.8
11%	7.3265%	7.3265%	16.5
10%	6.5683%	6.5683%	20.4
9%	5.8156%	5.8156%	26.4
8%	5.0670%	5.0670%	36.3
7%	4.3235%	4.3235%	54.5

provisions may become permanent or be extended beyond 2010. Figures 19.4 through 19.7 show break-even periods assuming the new tax rates for capital gains and qualifying dividend income will continue indefinitely into the future for taxpayers in the 35%, 30%, 25%, and 15% tax brackets, respectively.

Since dividend income is now taxed differently than interest income, the tables compute break-even periods by assuming that the income component of the return on the underlying mutual fund is composed of equal shares of dividend and interest income. Therefore, the preferential dividend income tax rate applies to half of the fund's income and the taxpayer's ordinary tax rate applies to half of the fund's income.

In addition, given the change in tax rates, it is assumed that variable annuities will have to reduce their mortality charges and expenses to have much chance to compete with mutual fund investments. Consequently, the additional variable annuity mortality charge is assumed to be just 0.75% rather than 1% as in the analyses above.

Otherwise, the analysis remains essentially the same, except that the new tax rates are used and the crossovers or break-even periods are computed for a number of different capital-gain proportions. That is, the break-even periods are shown not just for a

mutual fund with 60% of the return attributable to capital appreciation but for capital-gain proportions ranging from 0% to 95% of the return. All other assumptions remain the same as those used in computing the values in Figures 19.2 and 19.3. The charts find the number of years that money must be invested in the variable annuity before payouts commence in order for the after-tax payouts from the annuity over the 20-year payout period to exceed the after-tax payments the investor could obtain from the mutual fund.

Not surprisingly, the crossover or break-even period is longer uniformly than under the previous tax regime. For example, Figure 19.4 assumes the taxpayer is in the 35% tax bracket, just as was assumed when computing the values in Figure 19.3. Capital appreciation comprised 60% of the return in Figure 19.3. The grayed cells of Figure 19.4 show the corresponding values using the new tax rates for long-term gains and qualifying dividends for a taxpayer in the 35% bracket. The crossover or break-even period under the new tax rules until an amount invested in the variable annuity could provide the same after-tax payout over a 20-year period as the investment in the mutual fund outside the annuity is over 60 years until the rate of return exceeds 9%. At a 10% rate of return, the crossover occurs after 54 years. This is about 24 years longer, or more than twice as long, as the crossover period of 20.4 years

Figure 19.4

	MUTUAL FUND VERSUS VARIABLE ANNUITY BREAK-EVEN YEARS FOR TAXPAYER IN 35% BRACKET													
	Assumed Return													
	6%	7%	8%	9%	10%	11%	12%	13%						
0%	60+	47+	33+	24+	19+	15+	12+	10+						
15%	60+	60+	41+	30+	24+	19+	16+	14+						
30%	60+	60+	53+	39+	31+	25+	21+	18+						
45%	60+	60+	60+	51+	40+	33+	28+	24+						
60%	60+	60+	60+	60+	54+	44+	37+	32+						
75%	60+	60+	60+	60+	60+	60+	52+	45+						
90%	60+	60+	60+	60+	60+	60+	60+	60+						
95%	60+	60+	60+	60+	60+	60+	60+	60+						

Assumptions: 0.75% variable annuity mortality charge; 1.00% management and operating expense rate of both mutual fund and VA; 35% tax rate on ordinary income; 15% tax rate on long-term capital gain; 15% tax rate on dividend income; 25.0% averaged tax rate on mutual fund dividend and interest income; 20% portfolio turnover rate (portion of built-up gain taxed each year as a result of portfolio turnover); 50% dividend income portion of mutual fund income; 20-year payout period; **Capital Gain Portion:** the proportion of the fund's total return attributable to capital appreciation

Figure 19.5

MUTUAL FUND VERSUS VARIABLE ANNUITY
BREAK-EVEN YEARS FOR TAXPAYER IN 30% BRACKET

	Assumed Return							
	6%	7%	8%	9%	10%	11%	12%	13%
0%	60+	50+	32+	24+	18+	14+	12+	9+
15%	60+	60+	41+	30+	23+	18+	15+	13+
30%	60+	60+	52+	38+	29+	24+	20+	17+
45%	60+	60+	60+	49+	38+	31+	25+	22+
60%	60+	60+	60+	60+	50+	40+	34+	29+
75%	60+	60+	60+	60+	60+	55+	46+	40+
90%	60+	60+	60+	60+	60+	60+	59+	60+
95%	60+	60+	60+	60+	60+	60+	60+	60+

Key: 0.75%: variable annuity mortality charge; 1.00%: management and operating expense rate of both mutual fund and VA; 30%: tax rate on ordinary income; 15%: tax rate on long-term capital gain; 15%: tax rate on dividend income; 22.5%: averaged tax rate on mutual fund dividend and interest income; 20%: portfolio turnover rate (portion of built-up gain taxed each year as a result of portfolio turnover); 50%: dividend income portion of mutual fund income; 20-year payout period; **Capital Gain Portion:** the proportion of the fund's total return attributable to capital appreciation.

Figure 19.6

MUTUAL FUND VERSUS VARIABLE ANNUITY
BREAK-EVEN YEARS FOR TAXPAYER IN 25% BRACKET

	Assumed Return							
	6%	7%	8%	9%	10%	11%	12%	13%
0%	60+	56+	35+	24+	17+	13+	10+	8+
15%	60+	60+	43+	30+	22+	18+	14+	11+
30%	60+	60+	54+	37+	28+	22+	18+	15+
45%	60+	60+	60+	47+	35+	28+	23+	19+
60%	60+	60+	60+	60+	46+	36+	30+	25+
75%	60+	60+	60+	60+	60+	49+	40+	34+
90%	60+	60+	60+	60+	60+	60+	57+	48+
95%	60+	60+	60+	60+	60+	60+	60+	55+

Key: 0.75%: variable annuity mortality charge; 1.00%: management and operating expense rate of both mutual fund and VA; 25%: tax rate on ordinary income; 15%: tax rate on long-term capital gain; 15%: tax rate on dividend income; 20%: averaged tax rate on mutual fund dividend and interest income; 20%: portfolio turnover rate (portion of built-up gain taxed each year as a result of portfolio turnover); 50%: dividend income portion of mutual fund income; 20-year payout period; **Capital Gain Portion:** the proportion of the fund's total return attributable to capital appreciation.

Figure 19.7

MUTUAL FUND VERSUS VARIABLE ANNUITY
BREAK-EVEN YEARS FOR TAXPAYER IN 15% BRACKET

	Assumed Return							
	6%	7%	8%	9%	10%	11%	12%	13%
0%	60+	60+	60+	60+	60+	60+	44+	33+
15%	60+	60+	60+	60+	60+	60+	60+	49+
30%	60+	60+	60+	60+	60+	60+	60+	60+
45%	60+	60+	60+	60+	60+	60+	60+	60+
60%	60+	60+	60+	60+	60+	60+	60+	60+
75%	60+	60+	60+	60+	60+	60+	60+	60+
90%	60+	60+	60+	60+	60+	60+	60+	60+
95%	60+	60+	60+	60+	60+	60+	60+	60+

Key: 0.75%: variable annuity mortality charge; 1.00%: management and operating expense rate of both mutual fund and VA; 15%: tax rate on ordinary income; 5%: tax rate on long-term capital gain; 5%: tax rate on dividend income; 10%: averaged tax rate on mutual fund dividend and interest income; 20%: portfolio turnover rate (portion of built-up gain taxed each year as a result of portfolio turnover); 50%: dividend income portion of mutual fund income; 20-year payout period; **Capital Gain Portion**: the proportion of the fund's total return attributable to capital appreciation

under the old tax rules. If the investment earns 12%, the crossover occurs under the new rules after 37 years, or about 23 years longer than under the previous tax rules.

As Figure 19.7 shows, the crossover point is over 60 years in almost all circumstances for taxpayers in the 15% bracket. This is primarily because taxpayers in the 15% tax bracket pay long-term capital gains tax rates of only 5% (rather than 15% in all prior scenarios).

Figures 19.4 through 19.7 also show the crossovers if it is assumed no portion of the return (0%) is attributable to capital gains. This could conceivably be the case if the portfolio were invested in preferred stocks and bonds (it would also be applicable in a high-turnover portfolio, where all capital gains are taxed as short-term capital gains). Even if a taxpayer in the 35% bracket could earn 10% on such a portfolio, the crossover still does not occur for 19 years. For taxpayers in the 30% or 25% tax brackets, the crossover is only a year shorter for each step down in the tax bracket.

Figure 19.8 presents the results for a taxpayer in the 35% tax bracket assuming that the variable annuity assesses **no mortality** charge at all. In other words, it assumes the variable annuity and the mutual fund have exactly the same expenses. The table shows that if investors can find annuities with very low mortality charges, and the investors are planning

to invest in assets with low appreciation potential, the annuities could be viable alternatives. However, based upon current rates of return for fixed-income investments, a 6% return would probably be an aggressive assumption, at least for the first few years of the investment. At 6%, investors still need to invest in the annuities for at least 14 years before they plan to start taking distributions to make the investment profitable compared to investing outside the annuity.

Basically, what all of this means is that if investors anticipate that the new tax regime for dividends and capital gains are more likely than not to remain in effect beyond their current sunset date of 2011, then it appears that it is hard to justify any investment in variable annuities *on the basis of returns alone*. Even if the tax rates revert to the pre-2003 rules in 2011, taxpayers investing in variable annuities now will still find their break-even periods for investments in variable annuities considerably longer than under the prior rules. **However, the above charts have not taken into account the value provided by the annuity guarantees.**

Our entire analysis up to this point has assumed a level annual return. However, in point of fact, we know that annual returns are *not* level. Although the S&P 500 index has had a long-term compound average annual rate of return of approximately 10% over the past 75 years or so, individual year returns have ranged dramatically, and substantial losses in

Figure 19.8

MUTUAL FUND VERSUS VARIABLE ANNUITY
BREAK-EVEN YEARS FOR TAXPAYER IN 35% BRACKET

No Variable Annuity Mortality Charge

	Assumed Return							
	6%	7%	8%	9%	10%	11%	12%	13%
0%	14+	12+	10+	8+	7+	6+	5+	5+
15%	19+	15+	13+	11+	10+	8+	7+	7+
30%	23+	20+	17+	14+	13+	12+	10+	10+
45%	30+	25+	21+	17+	16+	15+	14+	13+
60%	36+	30+	26+	23+	21+	19+	17+	17+
75%	44+	38+	33+	29+	27+	24+	22+	21+
90%	54+	46+	41+	36+	33+	31+	29+	27+
95%	58+	49+	44+	39+	36+	34+	33+	30+

Key: 0.00%: variable annuity mortality charge; 1.00%: management and operating expense rate of both mutual fund and VA; 35%: tax rate on ordinary income; 15%: tax rate on long-term capital gain; 15%: tax rate on dividend income; 25%: averaged tax rate on mutual fund dividend and interest income; 20%: portfolio turnover rate (portion of built-up gain taxed each year as a result of portfolio turnover); 50%: dividend income portion of mutual fund income; 20-year payout period; **Capital Gain Portion**: the proportion of the fund's total return attributable to capital appreciation

a particular year are possible. If withdrawals need to be made from the investment, either on account of retirement (or other) spending needs, or because of a death of the account-holder, the guarantees provided by the annuity may become highly relevant. A severe market downturn shortly before a substantial withdrawal can provide an *immense* savings to the annuity-holder as the contractual guarantees are exercised. Over the long run, if the annuity is properly priced, individual fluctuations will average out and will approach the long-term averages (and concomitant long-term-based results) shown in the charts contained herein. However, on an individual basis, the guarantees may be vitally important to an individual client.

In addition, the provision of underlying guarantees may allow an investor to otherwise take a higher level of risk than he/she may otherwise be comfortable with. Consequently, an annuity investor might potentially earn an average rate of return of 10% in an S&P 500-like investment, while the mutual fund holder might only earn an average rate of return of 8%, due to a more conservative investment in light of the lack of underlying guarantees. The potential for a higher rate of return to an annuity-holder in light of higher investment risk taken on (mitigated by reduced total risk due to annuity contractual guarantees) can substantially shorten the break-even period necessary.

Because the appropriate amount of risk can vary tremendously on an individual basis, and risk characteristics can change over time, the primary factor in the decision to select a variable annuity should be its value as a *risk management* tool, not merely as a tax-deferral method. Because of the tremendous variety of contractual guarantees, with varying costs, available through commercial variable annuity providers, full analysis of the relevant options, and the client's needs and concerns, is *vital* to the decision to utilize a variable annuity and the appropriate selection of a particular contract.

Question – What is an FPDA?

Answer – An FPDA is a flexible premium deferred annuity. As the last two words indicate, the contract provides for the accumulation of funds to be applied at some future time designated by the contract owner to provide an income based upon the life of the annuitant(s) (or for a certain term). Premium payments are flexible – they can be paid as frequently or infrequently as the owner desires. They can be paid monthly, annually, or one or more years can be skipped as there is no specified contribution amount or required payment frequency. Most insurers do set a minimum payment level for administrative purposes – typically this runs from $25 to $50 for most companies.

Most FPDA contracts have no "front-end" load. Annual loads vary but many are under $50 a year. Some companies charge loads based on a percentage of each contribution, as a percentage of the annuity fund balance, or as a percentage of both. The insurer often does charge a "back-end" load (a surrender charge) when a cash withdrawal in a year exceeds a stipulated percentage of the fund balance – typically the annual "free withdrawal" amount is 10% of the premium deposits or contract value. The surrender charge will typically reduce year by year to 0 % by the 7th or 8th contract year.

With fixed FPDAs, insurers guarantee minimum interest rates (typically 3 to 4.5%) but usually pay much higher rates. The actual rate will depend on the earnings rate of the insurer. Current rates have ranged from 5 to 11% in recent years but are subject to rapid change as interest rates trend upward or downward (although the crediting rate is often set on the contract anniversary date and is valid for the entire year). Focus should be placed on the net (after loads and charges) return earned, over the entire expected holding period, when comparing fixed annuities.

Most variable annuities are FPDAs. Fixed annuities are often FPDAs, but some types do not have flexible premiums, or are immediate annuities. Equity-indexed annuities are virtually always deferred annuities, but often do not have flexible premiums.

Question – What is an SPDA?

Answer – An SPDA is a single premium deferred annuity. It provides, as its name implies, a promise that an annuity will begin at some time in the future in return for a single premium.

For fixed annuities (variable annuities are rarely single-premium contracts), a minimum stated rate of interest is guaranteed but most insurers pay competitive market rates. The actual rate paid is a function of: (a) the current investment earnings of the insurer, and (b) how competitive the insurer is determined to be. The rate is subject to change by the insurer.

The SPDA, like the FPDA, is back end loaded. No front-end charges are imposed. Surrender charges are graded and partial withdrawals are often allowed without charge. Bailout provisions allow the contract owner to withdraw all funds without

the imposition of a surrender charge if the interest rate actually credited falls below the "bailout rate" (typically set at the inception of the contract as 1 to 3% below the rate being credited at that time). Keep in mind that on any withdrawal both an ordinary income tax and a penalty tax may apply.

Question – What is a "temporary life annuity"?

Answer – A temporary life annuity is one which provides for fixed payments until the earlier of the death of the annuitant(s) or the end of a specified number of years. To compute the annuity exclusion ratio, expected return is found by multiplying one year's annuity payments by a multiple from the appropriate IRS annuity table.[27]

Question – In recent years, a new product, called an "equity-indexed annuity," has burst on the scene. What is it and what is the attraction?

Answer – Equity-indexed annuities (EIAs) are annuities with a crediting rate (return) that is tied to an index such as the S&P 500 stock index. But they are not the same as a variable annuity that invests directly in the securities of a market index (such as the S&P 500) through the use of sub-accounts. Rather, the assets deposited under an EIA are held directly by the insurance company, which invests the funds as necessary to apply a certain unique, formulaic crediting rate. EIAs promise to credit to the annuity-holder some percentage of the amount by which the underlying index has increased, subject to annual caps, if the index goes up, and to cut the investor's losses at zero (or even guarantee a slight positive return), if the index goes down.

The fundamental point is this: If the market goes up, the investor is happy because the value of the annuity will increase by some partial amount of the market increase. If the market goes down, the investor is happy because the annuity still has an underlying guarantee against loss.

However, the gain on the index does not include dividends, if any, earned by the companies making up the index. The loss of dividend income, a cap on market gains, and the possibility that the investor will only receive a percentage (such as 40, 60, or 80%) of the market return, can be a major drag on performance.

Question – Are equity-indexed annuities (EIAs) a good buy for astute individual investors?

Answer – EIAs issued by one company will differ (possibly quite dramatically) from EIAs issued by another company, but the annual investment returns generally are tied to a percentage (which could easily range from 40% to 80% or higher, and may be subject to periodic adjustments) of the S&P 500's gains (or occasionally other indexes such as the NASDAQ 100), not including dividends. The percentage (usually less-than-100%) of market returns and cap on gains is offset by protection against market losses.

It is not possible to compare historical fixed annuity, variable annuity, and EIA results because EIAs have only been available for several years. But, it is possible to construct a theoretical comparison by using the Vanguard Index Trust 500 portfolio and fixed annuity yields from August 1, 1976, to December 31, 1995. The results are shown in Figure 19.9.

As suggested by the data in Figure 19.9, "does not include dividends" can be a drag on an EIA's

Figure 19.9

THE VANGUARD INDEX TRUST RETURNS AND FIXED ANNUITY RATES: 1976-1995

Vanguard Index Trust 500*

Year Ended (%)	Capital Return (%)	Income Return (%)	Total Return (%)	Fixed Annuity Rates**
1976	4.1	1.2	5.3	2.1
1977	-11.7	3.7	-8.0	7.0
1978	0.8	5.0	5.8	7.3
1979	12.1	5.9	18.0	7.8
1980	25.5	6.4	31.9	8.4
1981	-9.8	4.6	-5.2	9.5
1982	14.8	6.1	20.9	11.0
1983	16.2	5.1	21.3	11.5
1984	1.5	4.7	6.2	12.0
1985	26.1	5.1	31.2	12.1
1986	14.0	4.0	18.0	11.2
1987	2.3	2.4	4.7	9.8
1988	11.6	4.6	16.2	9.5
1989	26.7	4.6	31.3	9.0
1990	-6.8	3.4	-3.4	8.4
1991	26.3	3.9	30.2	7.8
1992	4.4	3.0	7.4	7.5
1993	7.1	2.7	9.8	6.5
1994	-1.5	2.6	1.1	6.2
1995	34.4	3.0	37.4	6.1

* Vanguard Index Trust - 500 portfolio data from its inception August 1, 1976, to December 1995. Includes reinvestment of income dividends and any capital gains distributions and is adjusted for account maintenance fees.

** Representative fixed annuity rates for the period August 1, 1976, to December 1995.

performance. Dividends accounted for about 29% of the total return for the Vanguard Index Trust 500 (an S&P 500 index fund), over the 20 years from 1976 to 1995. Giving up dividends plus imposing a cap on market capital gains can be a severe penalty to pay for protection against periodic market losses, as will be shown below. In many cases, consumers may not even realize that dividends are not included in the index performance measure used by EIAs.

Figure 19.10 simulates the results for a fixed annuity, variable annuity, and indexed annuity, had they been purchased August 1, 1976. The table shows results through the end of 1995, in five-year increments, using the data from Figure 19.9.

Figure 19.11 shows the same simulation, but for the period January 1991 through the end of 1995. Isolating these five years is interesting because fixed annuity rates were much lower, while equity returns were robust, which are the market results that motivated insurance companies to develop the hybrid EIA.

Please note that Figures 19.10 and 19.11 are not an attempt to predict possible future results for fixed, variable, or indexed annuities. The only purpose of these tables is to show how the EIA formulas affect results relative to fixed and variable annuities.

If these 20 years offer any guidance (as shown in Figures 19.10 and 19.11), EIAs are a poor substitute for a variable annuity invested in the S&P 500 index. The benefit of eliminating periodic market losses is simply overwhelmed by the deficits of giving up reinvested dividend income and placing a limit on the capital gains in figuring the index. When the proper choices are identified, most astute investors will conclude that variable annuities are a better choice than EIAs.

Figure 19.10

VARIABLE VS. FIXED VS. INDEXED ANNUITIES: A THEORETICAL HISTORICAL COMPARISON (BASED ON A $100,000 INVESTMENT, AUGUST 1976 - DECEMBER 1995)

Time Period	Variable Annuity Vanguard 500* Projected		Fixed Annuity Projected		Company A Indexed** Projected		Company B Indexed** Projected	
	Value ($)	Return (%)	Value ($)	Return (%)	Value ($)	Return (%)	Value ($)	Return (%)
8/76-12/80	152,340	10.3	136,980	7.6	125,190	5.4	131,050	6.5
8/76-12/85	282,310	11.8	233,073	9.5	181,310	6.6	193,930	7.4
8/76-12/90	491,520	11.8	368,187	9.5	278,980	7.4	273,320	7.4
8/76-12/95	1,005,300	12.7	512,018	8.8	480,320	8.5	396,170	7.4

* Vanguard Index Trust-500 portfolio total returns reduced by 100 basis points to simulate variable annuity expenses.

** Company A computes the cash value every five years by taking 83% of the highest S&P 500 market value, not including dividends, during the five-year period. For example, if the starting investment is $100,000 and the five-year high point is $130,353, the fifth-year cash value is $125,190 — 83% of the highest capital gain for the five years. Each five years the equity-indexed annuity policyowner can decide to cash it in, convert to a traditional fixed annuity or lock into the equity-indexed annuity for another five years. Company B allows for 85% of the S&P 500 market gain (not including dividends), capped at 14% in any one year, but treats market losses as zero. For example, if the S&P 500 went up 10% (without dividends) went up 10% in year one, Company B would recognize 8.5%; if it went up 20% in the second year Company B would recognize 14%; and if the index went down 5% in year three, Company B would recognize 0%.

Figure 19.11

	VARIABLE VS. FIXED VS. INDEXED ANNUITIES: THE LAST 5 YEARS (BASED ON A $100,000 INVESTMENT, JANUARY 1991 - DECEMBER 1995)							
Time Period	Variable Annuity Vanguard 500* Projected		Fixed Annuity Projected		Company A Indexed** Projected		Company B Indexed** Projected	
	Value ($)	Return (%)	Value ($)	Return (%)	Value ($)	Return (%)	Value ($)	Return (%)
1/91-12/95	213,283	16.4	139,065	6.8	172,169	11.5	140,712	7.1

However, these conclusions do not mean to imply that EIAs have no use whatsoever. In certain circumstances, investors in their 50s and 60s who are making their final investment push to retirement may wish to consider EIAs because their investment time horizon might be just five to 10 years. As they have so little time to earn back any losses caused by market setbacks or investment mistakes, new investments and the repositioning of equity-invested assets might now be considered with an eye on conservation. If fixed-income yields are low and expected to remain so, an EIA can be a reasonable investment product for this investor. It will allow for the potential of outperforming fixed-income returns while not being fully exposed to market risk.

Question – What is the difference between an owner-driven and annuitant-driven contract?

Answer – The differentiation between owner-driven versus annuitant-driven contracts addresses the consequences of the death of an annuitant during the accumulation phase of a deferred annuity.

In the past, almost all contracts were annuitant-driven, but because of changes in the Internal Revenue Code, all contracts issued after January 18, 1985 must be owner-driven. It is important to read the details of the annuity contract to determine which type of contract is being evaluated or is in force.

Under the classic model of an annuitant-driven contract, if the annuitant were to pass away during the accumulation phase, the contract would pay the death benefit to the primary beneficiary of the contract. Any special death benefit provisions of the contract apply at the death of the annuitant. In situations where the owner and annuitant of the contract are the same person, this is not consequential. However, this can have substantial impact if the owner and annuitant are different people.

For example, let us assume that John Doe owns an annuitant-driven contract on his wife, Jane Doe. John Doe is the primary beneficiary, and John's son Daniel is the contingent beneficiary. The annuity contract has a current value of $120,000, and the death benefit is $150,000. In the event that Jane dies, the enhanced death benefit of $150,000 will be paid to John. However, it is important to remember that all annuities issued after January 18, 1985, whether owner- or annuitant-driven, must pay out at the death of the owner.[28] Therefore, we must contrast this with the result in the event that John Doe dies. If John Doe were to pass away, under an annuitant-driven contract, the enhanced death benefit would not be paid; the current value would be paid out, and Daniel would receive $120,000, *not* $150,000.

Alternatively, the results of an owner-driven contract reverse these results. Under an owner-driven contract, the death of the owner, John Doe, will cause a payout of the enhanced death benefit. A death of the annuitant, Jane Doe, simply creates an annuitant-less contract, and the owner will have the option of assigning a new annuitant.

Because of the radical differences in potential payouts at the death of the owner or annuitant, it is critical to understand whether a contract is owner-driven or annuitant-driven when structuring the setup of owners, annuitants, and beneficiaries.

Question – Where can I obtain additional information?

Answer – This chapter has still only lightly covered some of the complexities of annuities. The broad range of choices and the numerous changes in tax law as applied to annuities necessitates a thorough understanding for anyone wishing to seriously delve into this investment tool. For further reading on annuities, see *The Annuity Handbook: A Guide to*

Non-Qualified Annuities, by Darlene Chandler (Cincinnati, OH: The National Underwriter Company) and *The Annuity Advisor*, by John Olsen and Michael Kitces (Cincinnati, OH: The National Underwriter Company).

CHAPTER ENDNOTES

1. The term "annuity" encompasses all periodic payments resulting from the systematic liquidation of principal. A payment of interest only would not be an annuity payment. See Treas. Reg. §1.72-1.

2. See Leimberg, Stephan R., et al., *The Tools and Techniques of Estate Planning* (Cincinnati, OH: The National Underwriter Company).

3. Except for FIFO for withdrawals from contracts that have not been substantially modified and were entered into prior to August 14, 1982.

4. This only applies to annuities purchased *outside* a retirement plan; investments purchased *inside* a retirement plan already pass by beneficiary designation and are not subject to probate. Annuities provide no additional probate avoidance benefits *inside* a retirement plan that are not already provided by the underlying plan.

5. This only applies to annuities purchased *outside* a retirement plan; investments purchased *inside* a retirement plan are already tax-deferred by virtue of the retirement plan. Annuities provide no additional tax-deferral benefits *inside* a retirement plan, and thus should be purchased for other reasons, such as risk management.

6. Annuitization of a deferred annuity during the accumulation phase will be subject to the pre-59½ penalty unless the IRC Section 72(q)(2)(D) requirements for substantially equal periodic payments are met.

7. IRC Sec. 72(b)(1).

8. Investment in the contract is defined as the consideration paid for the contract (i.e., the premium) less any amounts received back from the insurer that were income tax free. IRC Sec. 72(c). Premium cost does not include any premiums paid for (1) waiver of premiums, (2) disability income, or (3) accidental death ("double indemnity"). Rev. Rul. 55-349, 1955-1 CB 232.

9. Expected Return is defined as the aggregate payments the annuitant can be expected to receive under the annuity contract. In other words expected return is:

   * If payments are for a fixed period:

   The sum of the guaranteed payments. IRC Sec. 72(c)(3)(B). See also Treas. Reg. §1.72-5(c).

   * If payments are of a fixed amount (with no life expectancy):

   The sum of the guaranteed payments. IRC Sec. 72(c)(3)(B). See also Treas. Reg. §1.72-5(d).

   * If payments are for the life (or lives) of the annuitant(s):

   Sum of one year's annuity payments multiplied by the life expectancy of the live or lives involved. IRC Sec. 72(c)(3)(A).

10. Round the quotient to 3 decimal places. See Treas. Reg. §1.72-4(a)(2).

11. Treas. Reg. §1.72-4(d)(2).

12. If the "annuity starting date" (first day of first period for which an amount is received as an annuity) is after December 31, 1986, the exclusion ratio applies to all payments received until the annuitant has fully recovered his or her investment in the contract. Once the annuitant's investment is fully recovered, further payments are subject in full to ordinary income tax. IRC Sec. 72(b)(2). But if the annuity starting date was prior to January 1, 1987, the amount tax free under the annuity exclusion ratio remains income-tax-free for as long as the annuitant receives payments, no matter how long he or she lives. IRC Sec. 72(b)(4)(A), before amendment by Sec. 1704(I)(1), PL 104-188, 8/20/1996.

13. See IRC Sec. 72(c)(2).

14. Rev. Rul. 2003-91, 2003-33 IRB 347.

15. Treas. Regs. §§ 1.72-2(b)(3), 1.72-4(d)(3).

16. Treas. Reg. § 1.72-4(d)(3)(ii).

17. IRC Sec. 72(b)(3)(A).

18. IRC Sec. 72(b)(3)(B).

19. IRC Sec. 72(h).

20. Different rules apply to contracts purchased on or before August 13, 1982, allowing withdrawal of principal first and interest/growth second. IRC Sec. 72(e)(5).

21. IRC Sec. 72(q)(2).

22. IRC Sec. 72(s)(3).

23. IRC Sec. 72(u).

24. IRC Sec. 72(u)(3).

25. This is only true until 2009. In 2010, under EGTRRA 2001, new rules repeal the current estate tax system, but also remove the across-the-board, step-up-in-basis rules at death, replacing them with a new set of rules for basis increase at death with limitations. After 2010, Pre-EGTRRA rules go back into effect.

26. IRC Sec. 72(e)(2).

27. Table IV or VIII of Treas. Reg. §1.72-9. See also Treas. Reg. §1.72-5(a)(3).

28. IRC Sec. 72(s)(1).

Chapter 20

REAL ESTATE

WHAT IS IT?

Real estate is land and the buildings and improvements on land. Real estate, by definition, includes natural assets, such as minerals, under the land. Because of the obvious limited supply of land, especially in "desirable" locations, real estate has long been viewed as an attractive investment alternative.

Real estate can be classified into four major categories:

1. land;

2. residential;

3. commercial; and

4. industrial.

"Land" can be subdivided into five categories: (a) unimproved; (b) farm land; (c) recreational; (d) ranches; and (e) subdivided lots.

"Residential" can be subdivided into three categories: (a) single family dwellings; (b) multiple family dwellings (such as apartments and condominiums); and (c) hotels and motels (transient dwellings).

"Commercial" can be subdivided into five categories: (a) residential rental; (b) office buildings; (c) retail stores; (d) shopping centers; and (e) specialty buildings (such as banks, movie theaters, stadiums, and bowling alleys).

"Industrial" can be subdivided into four categories: (a) factories; (b) warehouses; (c) industrial parks; and (d) utility facilities (such as power plants).

An investor should select the type of real estate that will best meet the specific objectives of the investment plan. For example, unimproved land can provide substantial, long-term appreciation, but cannot be looked to for a significant current flow of income.

WHEN IS THE USE OF THIS TOOL INDICATED?

1. When an investor desires an investment with tax shelter potential.

2. When a long-term hedge against inflation is needed.

3. When a relatively constant cash flow is required.

4. When an investor is looking for long-term appreciation.

5. When the investor would like a tangible investment. Many investors – for psychological reasons – are more comfortable with an asset that they can see, touch, and physically possess.

6. When the investor wants to make maximum use of leverage. Lenders are willing to advance large sums of money on the security of real estate for long periods of time at relatively low interest because real estate is not only tangible and stationary, but is also reasonably stable in value.

ADVANTAGES

1. Real estate has numerous different tax related advantages:

a) Expenditures that are considered ordinary and necessary in the production or collection of income or in the preservation of its value as an investment are deductible.

b) The costs of supplies, labor, and other components necessary to keep the property in good repair can be deducted.

c) Real estate property taxes are deductible.

d) A tenant leasing business property may deduct reasonable rental costs.

e) Interest on the unpaid balance of the mortgage is deductible (subject to limitations imposed by the tax law).

f) The full cost of buildings and real estate improvements (i.e., cost *excluding* land) is depreciable.

g) Gain on the sale of real estate can be reported over more than one taxable year. This may allow the investor to defer the payment of tax until cash proceeds from an "installment sale" of the property are received (although interest payments may be due on certain deferred tax liabilities).

h) Losses incurred on the sale of real estate are deductible (subject to limitations discussed below).

i) One parcel of real estate can be exchanged for another without the immediate recognition of taxable income. Tax on appreciation can be postponed an indefinite number of times (and for an indefinite period of time) if each trade meets the strict requirements of the tax-free exchange rule of the Internal Revenue Code (IRC Section 1031).

j) Upon the "involuntary conversion" of real estate (such as through fire or condemnation), the investor does not have to pay any tax upon the receipt of cash from insurance or condemnation award, so long as the cash is reinvested in "qualified property" (essentially property of similar use) having equal or greater value.

k) Liquidity (cash) can be obtained from real estate, including any appreciation, without paying taxes, through a mortgage on the property. (Of course, upon sale of the property, the investor is taxed upon the entire appreciation.)

l) The cost of rehabilitating certain buildings or structures may qualify for a special investment tax credit.

However, real estate is also subject to special "passive activity" tax rules that may limit the ability to use real estate losses to offset income from other sources. The "passive activity" rules are discussed in Chapter 43, "Taxation of Investment Vehicles."

2. Real estate is tangible. As mentioned above, many investors prefer an asset that can be seen, touched, fenced in, and built upon. It feels more "real" than intangible investments, such as life insurance or common stocks, which do not exist in a physical sense.

3. Real estate has historically proven itself as an excellent hedge against inflation. Real estate tends to increase in value while prices are rising and the value of the dollar is declining.

4. Each parcel of real estate is unique. Because no two parcels can share the same location, no two can be exactly alike. The "monopoly" each real estate owner has on each individual location is itself of value.

5. Because of its great value as security for a loan, real estate enables an investor to obtain maximum potential leverage.

DISADVANTAGES

1. Real estate is almost always relatively illiquid. Because there is no organized market on the national or local level for real estate comparable to the stock or commodity exchanges, real estate is difficult to convert to cash quickly.

   Other reasons that real estate is not as liquid as other investments include: (a) the usual difficulty in finding a "willing buyer" at the desired selling price (because the property must suit the buyer with respect to a multiplicity of factors, including location, financing, timing, potential income, etc.); (b) the length of time involved in the "closing" process (typically 30 to 90 days); and (c) the need for the purchaser to obtain financing in most cases.

2. Some degree of management is necessary with all real estate investments. For example, a properly managed real estate investment requires that someone maintain the physical premises, collect rents, and pay bills. If investors do not possess the requisite expertise (or have the time or inclination to obtain or exercise that expertise), they must hire a professional manager. This makes many small real estate investments impractical.

3. Typically the investment in real estate is large in amount and will require the commitment of investable funds for a long period of time. Compared to stocks, which can be purchased for as low as pennies per share and can be sold within a matter of hours, real estate requires many thousands

of dollars (not all of which need be put up by the investor, but can be leveraged) that may remain "locked in" for many years.

4. Costs related to the purchase or sale of real estate reduce its value as an investment that can produce a short-term gain. Such costs, which include transfer taxes, title insurance, appraisals, financing fees and "points," title recording and notary fees, and sales commissions, may run as high as 10% to 15% of the cost of the real estate itself.

5. Real estate, by definition, cannot be moved. This immobility can become a distinct disadvantage when the investor moves to a new location and can no longer properly manage the investment personally.

6. Once land has been improved with a building, that "improvement" is often difficult and expensive to modify or remove. For instance, a building designed as a warehouse can be converted to an apartment house to meet a shift in market demand, but only at great expense and considerable trouble. This disadvantage is often referred to as "fixity" of investment.

7. It is often difficult or impossible to assess the economic risks and projected return on a real estate investment with exactness. This is because unpredictables (such as changes in consumer demand, levels of maintenance and repair expenses, changes in tax laws) are involved in the analysis.

8. Because the investment return on real estate is significantly affected by the available tax benefits, such investments are most susceptible to the risk of challenge by the IRS.

TAX IMPLICATIONS

1. All the ordinary and necessary expenses paid or incurred by a real estate investor during the taxable year in carrying on a trade or business are deductible. Deductible expenses include costs incurred in the production or the collection of investment income. Expenditures for the management, conservation, or maintenance of real estate property held either to produce income or for appreciation are also deductible.

   Typical deductible expenses that a real estate investor might incur include utilities such as electric and gas, rental commissions, trash removal, and insurance.

2. Routine repair and maintenance expenses – those that do not appreciably add to the value of the property or significantly add to its life span but merely keep it in efficient running order – are deductible in the year the outlay is incurred.

   The cost of improvements must be "capitalized." This means that the cost of an item that increases the longevity or the value or alters the use for which the property is suitable cannot be deducted currently. However, such expenditures can be added to the investor's basis in the property. They are then recovered through depreciation deductions.

3. Amounts paid for real property taxes (subject to a limitation for certain taxes incurred during construction) are deductible when paid. An investor is allowed to deduct real estate taxes paid in the year property is acquired. However, those taxes must be allocated on a day-by-day basis between the buyer and the seller according to the number of days each owns the property.

   Certain "taxes" are in fact improvement assessments that add to the value of the property and, therefore, must be capitalized rather than currently deducted. Examples of such "taxes" include assessments for sidewalks and sewers. The cost of these items is deductible over a period of years according to a cost recovery schedule provided in the Internal Revenue Code.

   Construction period taxes must be capitalized and then amortized as part of the basis of the constructed property. Such taxes may therefore only be depreciated over the life of the property (generally 27½ years for residential real estate and 39 years for other real estate).

4. Rental expenses for the use of business property are deductible currently. This deduction by the lessee of property enables the owner/investor of the property to charge a higher rental, thus increasing the value of the property.

5. Interest paid to finance the purchase of investment real estate may be deductible currently. Certain special rules, however, must be considered by the investor. These rules may limit the deductibility of:

   a) construction period interest;

b) "investment interest;"

c) prepaid interest;

d) "points;" and

e) "passive losses."

Construction period interest must be capitalized and added to the basis of the property being constructed. For example, if an investor incurred $10,000 of interest expense during a one-year construction period, the entire amount could not be currently deducted. Instead, the investor could depreciate the interest as part of the cost of the constructed property.

Financing through debt is almost universal in real estate investment. This makes it critical that the advisor and the client be aware that there are limitations on the deduction of interest expense.

The applicable "passive activity" rules as they relate to interest expense are discussed in Chapter 43, "Taxation of Investment Vehicles."

Real estate investments are subject to the "at risk" rules, which may limit the deductibility of losses from real estate that is leveraged. The "at risk" rules are discussed in Chapter 43, "Taxation of Investment Vehicles."

Land is not depreciable. But improvements upon the land are eligible for depreciation deductions. In fact, in most cases the "tax losses" generated by depreciation deductions are the most important part of the tax shelter afforded by real estate. However, such "tax losses" are subject to the "passive activity" rules.

The key to the tax shelter value of real estate lies in the fact that depreciation is a "non-cash" charge against income. Depreciation creates an artificial loss enabling an investor to recover the cost of the asset over a specified period of time. In many cases, this tax benefit precedes any actual cost (resulting from reduction in the value of the property due to wear and tear or obsolescence). In addition, by financing (i.e., using leverage), the investor may depreciate the full cost of the building and improvements even though (a) most of the costs have been borrowed from the mortgagee, (b) the investor may have no personal liability on the mortgage debt, and (c) the actual cash outlay to repay the debt may not be paid for many years.

6. Tax on the gain upon the sale of real estate can be deferred. Subject to certain limitations, the "installment sale rules" of IRC Section 453 permit an investor to delay reporting any gain or paying any tax until money is received. For example, an individual in a high tax bracket this year could agree to sell the property before year-end but defer receipt of any sales proceeds until next year. In fact, installment sales rules are so flexible that a seller does not need to accept any cash proceeds for five, or ten, or even fifteen years. The law does not set a limit as to how long the parties can agree to extend the payment period. As long as at least one payment will be received by the seller after the close of the taxable year in which the disposition occurs, installment sales treatment is available.

7. Installment sales are often used as a vehicle for financing the sale, rather than (or in addition to) third party financing, such as from a bank. However, just as a bank requires the payment of interest for the use of the unpaid balance of the loan, tax law "expects" that the parties will provide for interest on the loan inherent in an installment sale. Tax laws cannot dictate the stated interest rate agreed to by the parties or even that there be interest actually charged. But, if an interest obligation is not stated in the installment sale agreement, or if the stated rate is insufficient under the law, IRC Section 483 will treat a portion of the sales price as built-in interest.

This imputation of interest on the unpaid balance of the sales proceeds has the effect of reducing the potential capital gain on the sale of the property, and increasing the ordinary income to the seller.

Example: Alex Benjamin sells a parcel of unimproved land to Sara Gail for $500,000. He paid $100,000 for the land five years ago. Alex agrees to accept $200,000 in cash at closing, with the balance in installments of $100,000 each on January 1 of each of the next three years.

It appears the sales price is $500,000. But when interest is imputed on the $300,000 unpaid balance, it becomes obvious that if part of that $300,000 is treated as interest, then the real sales price must be significantly less than $500,000. In this example, if the Internal Revenue Service were to impute a 10% interest rate on the $300,000 unpaid balance, the effect would be to treat approximately $51,314 of the total installment payment as interest (taxable to the seller and deductible by the buyer) and only $248,686 of the installment payments as principal. For tax purposes, the total sales price would be only $448,686 ($200,000 received at settlement plus the $248,686 principal payments on the installments). The adjusted capital gain would be $348,686 ($448,686 adjusted sales proceeds less $100,000 basis).

The benefits of installment sales of real estate may be limited if the seller pledged the installment receivable as security for a loan. This limitation, as well as other restrictions on the use of the installment method, is discussed in Chapter 43, "Taxation of Investment Vehicles."

In addition, the purchaser of real estate that is financed by seller-provided installment sale debt, will be subject to the "at risk" rules, which may limit the deductibility of certain loss.

8. Losses on the sale of real estate held for investment or used in a trade or business are generally deductible in the year incurred. Such losses are measured by the excess of (a) the investor's adjusted basis (generally cost less accumulated depreciation) in the property over (b) the proceeds from the sale of the property.

    Losses incurred upon the sale of personal use realty, such as an individual's residence, are not deductible (even if the owner expected the property to appreciate).

    The tax treatment for losses incurred on the sale of real property held purely for investment (such as unimproved land) will be different from the treatment of losses from the sale of real property used in a "trade or business" (such as a manufacturing plant).

    Real estate held purely for investment is treated as a capital asset. If all capital losses exceed all capital gains, they offset ordinary income dollar-for-dollar up to a maximum of $3,000 per year. Any unused losses may be carried forward.

    Real property used in a trade or business is not a capital asset. Such property, if held for the long-term holding period before being sold, is called "Section 1231 Property." A loss from the sale of real estate that is Section 1231 property is totaled with all other losses and gains from the sale of Section

1231 property recognized during the year. If the net of all Section 1231 gains and losses is a gain, the net gain will be treated as a capital gain. If the net of all Section 1231 gains and losses is a loss, the total loss will be treated as an ordinary loss.

9. It is possible, under certain circumstances, for an investor to trade (exchange) properties with another party and postpone all or a portion of the gain that would normally have to be recognized on a sale. This postponement or partial avoidance of taxation is known as a "like-kind" exchange. (Although this is sometimes referred to as a "tax-free" exchange because no tax is payable at the time of the transaction, it is more proper to refer to it as a "tax deferred" exchange; the tax on the exchange is usually paid when the property received in the transaction is subsequently sold.)

10. Tax deferral may also be available upon what is known as an "involuntary conversion." Involuntary conversion is the destruction of property by fire or other casualty. It may also be caused by the condemnation of property by a governmental body utilizing its right to take private property and convert it to the use of the public.

    When the investor receives payment through insurance or governmental compensation for property involuntarily converted, tax law treats that money as if it were the proceeds from a sale. Fortunately, any gain realized on that "sale" can usually be deferred if the investor reinvests the full proceeds in similar ("like kind") property within three years from the end of the year in which the proceeds are received. If less than the entire proceeds are reinvested, only a proportionate amount of the gain can be deferred.

11. An investor can convert part of the appreciated value of property into cash without either selling it or otherwise triggering a tax on any gain. This can be accomplished by using the property as security for a loan. However, there may be limitations on the deductibility of the loan interest.

12. The cost of constructing or rehabilitating certain buildings or structures may qualify for a special investment tax credit. The properties eligible for this credit include: (a) qualified low-income housing; (b) certified historic structures; and (c) buildings that were first placed in service before 1936.

ALTERNATIVES

Few investments are comparable to real estate because of its unique characteristics, location, potential for significant tax shelter benefits and relatively constant cash flow, and psychological comfort. Other investments, such as stocks, do provide a long-term hedge against inflation, the possibility of substantial appreciation, and the potential to maximize the use of leverage. However, no other investments possess all these characteristics to the extent of real estate.

WHERE AND HOW DO I GET IT?

Real estate may be held by an investor in any of the following forms:

a) outright ownership;

b) general partnership or joint venture;

c) limited partnership;

d) corporate ("C" corporation);

e) S corporation; or

f) real estate investment trust (REIT).

Each of these forms of ownership has advantages and disadvantages with respect to the liability incurred, management efforts required, income tax implications, transferability, and continuity of the entity upon the death of the investor.

Outright Ownership

Outright ownership of real estate does not protect the individual investor from full personal liability relating to the ownership and operation of the property. For example, an investor can be held financially accountable for negligent acts resulting in injury to a visitor on the property. Debts incurred with respect to the investment typically require the personal guarantees of the outright owner and therefore subject all his other assets to the claims of creditors.

An individual will typically purchase real estate in his own name directly from the seller or through a real estate broker or agent. However, most real estate acquired for tax shelter investment purposes is acquired by purchasing an interest in a partnership or other investment entity.

An outright owner has full management responsibility. Agents can be hired, however, to assume such tasks as maintenance, rental collection, and paying the bills.

All the tax benefits and costs of outright ownership are personal to the investor. The investor's individual tax return will reflect the taxable income and deductible expenses of the property.

An outright owner can convey the title to all or a portion of the property at any time without restriction.

The death of an individual owner results in the termination of the individual ownership form. The property will then pass through the investor's estate to his heirs or by operation of law to his joint owners.

General Partnership

A general partnership is one in which two or more individuals join together for investment purposes. Usually, a general partner is jointly and severally liable for all the debts and any obligations incurred by the partnership.

If a partner cannot pay his part of the obligations of a partnership, the remaining partners are liable to the total extent of their financial resources. Suppose Howard and Jonathan form a partnership and each invested $30,000 in cash that is used to buy real estate. A visitor slips on the doorstep and successfully sues the partnership for $80,000. Howard has no assets other than his investment in the partnership. Jonathan has other investments totaling $500,000. Assuming there is no insurance, the injured party would first take over the partnership property (worth $60,000) and then look to Jonathan for the remaining $20,000.

Although all the general partners may be held responsible by law for the management of the property, usually only one or a few partners are actively involved in operations. Subject to specific exceptions included in the partnership agreement, each general partner has the authority to bind the partnership (and therefore the other partners) to any contracts or commitments.

Partnerships are not taxed as separate entities. Income, deductions, and credits flow through to the partners according to their proportionate ownership. Each partner reports his or her share of partnership income, deductions, and credits as if each owned that percentage of partner-

Chapter 20 – Real Estate

ship losses is deductible only to the extent of his basis (investment) in the partnership.

A partner's rights to transfer his or her interest in the property are limited by the terms of the partnership agreement. Such agreements generally preclude the sale or gift of an individual's partnership interest without approval of the other partners or without first offering that interest to the other partners.

The death of an individual partner may cause the termination of the partnership unless the terms of the partnership agreement provide otherwise. In most cases, the partnership agreement provides for the purchase of the deceased partner's interest by the remaining partners.

Limited Partnership

A limited partnership permits certain partners (so-called "limited partners") the benefit of limited liability. (Such partnerships must have at least one general partner with full liability.) For this reason, limited partnerships are quite popular as a means of owning real estate. In fact, most tax shelter real estate investments are syndicated in this form.

Many limited partnership investments are heavily leveraged. Where the limited partners are not "at risk" to pay a proportionate amount of the debt in the event the partnership activities cannot generate enough cash to pay off the loans, the limited partners may not be able to fully deduct partnership losses.

Limited partners are passive investors and cannot actively participate in daily management without risking full personal liability. (Limited partners may participate in general policy decisions concerning the long-term goals of the venture.) Management authority in a limited partnership is vested solely in the general partner.

As in the case of a general partnership, income, deductions, and credits of a limited partnership flow through to the partners according to their proportionate ownership. Each partner, whether general or limited, reports his or her share of partnership income, deductions, and credits as if each owned that percentage of the property individually. A limited partner's share of partnership losses is deductible only to the extent of his basis (investment) in the partnership.

A limited partner's rights to transfer his or her interest in the property are limited by the terms of the partner-

ship agreement. Limited partnership agreements are generally more restrictive than general partnership agreements in precluding the transferability of an individual's partnership interest.

The death of an individual limited partner generally will not cause the termination of the partnership. In most cases, the partnership agreement provides for the deceased partner's heirs to succeed to his interest. However, the death of the sole general partner who is an individual may cause the dissolution of the partnership, unless the partnership agreement provides for a successor general partner. This is one reason why many general partners are corporations.

The most common form of tax shelter-oriented real estate investment ownership is a limited partnership. Interests in such a partnership are generally sold by real estate syndicators.

A syndicated partnership consists of two types of owners, the syndicator-promoters (sometimes referred to as developers) and the investors. A promoter will typically acquire a property (sometimes the promoter will merely obtain an option to buy the property) and then attempt to sell it to a group of investors. In addition to fees, the promoter will retain an ownership interest as a portion of the compensation for its efforts. Alternatively, promoters may form an investment group, raise cash, and then seek to obtain suitable property on behalf of the investors.

An interest in a syndication can be obtained through a representative of a registered broker-dealer. An offering brochure (usually called an "offering memorandum") is provided to potential investors and describes the objectives, benefits, and risks of the venture.

Corporation

A major benefit of investing in corporate form is the limited liability it provides. (This applies whether the corporation is being taxed as a regular ("C") corporation or has elected to be taxed as an "S" corporation.) Specifically, the investor is not personally liable for negligent acts of the corporation and its employees and officers. Unless the investor has been personally negligent (outside his role as a corporate employee), full liability stops with the corporation.

Limited liability also applies to corporate borrowing; technically, a creditor can look only to the corporation for payment of a debt and may not reach through to the

Tools & Techniques of Investment Planning   177 assets of the individual shareholders. But, as a matter of practice, many lenders will not make loans to closely-held corporations unless the individual shareholders personally cosign or guarantee payment of the debt. Once a shareholder does sign as an individual, the lender can look to that person for payment if the corporation defaults on its obligations.

Centralized management is another feature of the corporate form. The responsibility to manage and authority to run a corporation rests with the board of directors elected by the shareholders. These directors, who typically in closely-held corporations are the controlling shareholders, select officers to handle the day-to-day operations. (Often these officers are also shareholders and members of the board of directors. But it is also common for shareholders to be purely passive investors who do not participate in any way in the operation or management of the company.)

Continuity of life is another feature of the corporate form. A corporation does not terminate at the death of one or more of its owners. Legally, the corporation has an indefinite life. This continuity enhances the corporation's ability to raise large amounts of capital for long-term investment.

Finally, enhanced transferability of interests is another feature of the corporate form. A shareholder in a regular corporation (unless restricted by corporate bylaws or a shareholders' agreement) can transfer any number of shares to any party at any time. A shareholder in an S corporation has similar freedom of transferability. However, the transfer of shares to certain restricted parties (see below) will terminate S corporation status.

A regular ("C") corporation is treated for tax purposes as a tax entity entirely separate from its owners. A C corporation must file its own tax return and its income is subject to a special corporate income tax rate schedule. Because the corporation is considered a separate tax entity, once it earns and pays tax on the income, the net remaining after taxes belongs to the corporation itself, and not its shareholders. Those net corporate earnings can generally be distributed to the shareholders only as a dividend, which is then taxable to them upon receipt.

Note that corporate earnings paid to shareholders will typically be taxed twice, once to the corporation and then again to the shareholders when paid out to them. This means that the real estate investor operating in corporate form suffers two disadvantages; first, the earnings of the investment are taxed twice and, second, if the corporation operates at a loss, that loss can be utilized only by the corporate entity and cannot be passed through to the investor.

S Corporation

An S corporation is treated essentially the same as a C corporation except for taxation. (S corporations are also subject to certain shareholder limitations designed to insure that income is still taxed at the shareholder level – the corporation may not have more than 100 shareholders, all of whom are individuals or certain trusts, none of whom are nonresident aliens, and with not more than one class of stock.) An S corporation in many respects is taxed similarly to a partnership. Although it provides the corporate benefits of limited liability, centralized management, continuity of life, and free transferability of interests, its profits, losses, deductions, and credits are passed through the entity to the tax returns of the individual shareholders. Essentially, the corporation pays no federal income tax. The shareholders are taxed on the net income of the S corporation, whether or not it is distributed to them.

The obvious advantage of an S corporation to investors is this ability to enjoy the benefits of partnership-like flow-through taxation. The total of the deductions for interest, depreciation, and other expenses of operating and maintaining the investment property is netted against the corporation's operating income. A shareholder's share of losses is deductible only to the extent of the shareholder's (a) basis in the stock, plus (b) the amount of any loans which may have been made by the shareholder to the corporation. Any losses disallowed in a given year as a result of this limitation can be carried forward to future years.

REITs

A real estate investment trust (REIT) is a vehicle specifically designed to facilitate large-scale public participation in real estate investments. In many respects, a REIT operates similarly to a mutual fund. Having many investors (called the beneficiaries or shareholders), each contributing relatively small amounts of capital, enables the management of the REIT to make diversified and large-scale investments on their behalf. See Chapter 21, "REITs (Real Estate Investment Trusts)" for more details.

WHAT FEES OR OTHER ACQUISITION COSTS ARE INVOLVED?

An investor purchasing real estate on his own can expect to pay a number of acquisition costs. These include broker's commissions, legal fees, title examination and registration fees, title insurance, and state and/or local transfer taxes.

The costs of investing in a syndicated real estate venture will be higher than an investment where the owner finds, develops, and manages the property because these responsibilities are assumed by the developer/promoter. An investor can expect to pay more when investing through a public offering than a "private placement" (one that is not required to meet certain state and/or federal securities commission disclosure standards). This is because a private placement does not involve all the costs associated with full SEC registration.

Total fees and commissions in a typical public syndication will range from 16% to 26% of the amount invested. In the case of a private offering, total costs generally range from 13% to 25%. Obviously, the actual total costs will vary considerably with each investment. It is therefore critical that the investor thoroughly review the offering materials and factor the estimated costs into any investment analysis.

HOW DO I SELECT THE BEST OF ITS TYPE?

Because of the unique nature of real estate, "best" is a relative term – at best. An investor should study each of the following major criteria:

1. Location of the property. This is the most important single factor and will determine present and future market demand.

2. Soundness of construction and appropriateness of design for intended use. Maintenance costs will be higher with poor construction and rental income may be lower than anticipated if the project is not suited for its intended use.

3. Cost of capital. The interest rate that must be paid on the purchase debt will significantly affect the ultimate profitability of the venture.

4. Financing fee. Requiring payment of "points" has become a prevalent practice. These are paid to the lender on both the construction financing and the permanent mortgage. Each point is 1% of the borrowed amount.

5. The cost of operating and maintaining the property. A review of the track record of the promoter/manager in similar projects is particularly helpful.

6. Organization and offering expenses.

7. Sales commissions.

8. Construction costs. (Check to see if the general partner's fee will be reduced if costs of construction are higher than projected.)

9. Fees paid to the general partner for managing the partnership and the underlying investment property.

10. Projected cash flow and tax results from operations.

WHERE CAN I FIND OUT MORE ABOUT IT?

1. *Tax Facts on Investments* (Cincinnati, OH: The National Underwriter Company, published annually).

2. David F. Windish, *Tax-Advantaged Investments* (New York, NY: New York Institute of Finance, 1989).

3. Jack Crestol and Herman M. Schneider, *Tax Planning For Investors* (Chicago, IL: Commerce Clearing House, 1991).

4. The real estate industry offers many educational programs and courses. Some of these include:

   a) The National Marketing Institute of the National Association of Realtors.

   b) The CCIM (Certified Commercial Investment Member) designation for those interested in commercial and investment property.

   c) MAI (Member of the Appraisal Institute) for advisors interested in real estate appraising.

   d) FLI (Farm and Land Institute) for those interested in farm and ranch brokerage.

   e) GRI (Graduate of a Real Estate Institute).

f) CRB (Certified Residential Broker).

Related courses and certificate programs are also available by calling state and local realtor associations. Many universities and graduate schools also include real estate in their higher education programs.

QUESTIONS AND ANSWERS

Question – What deductions, if any, are available to an investor who purchases unimproved real estate?

Answer – Land is purchased for its future development potential. This investment is suitable mainly for upper income investors who are able to bear the risk of a long-term investment while realizing no immediate return.

Tax deductions are available only for interest, real estate taxes, and maintenance expenses. Alternatively, an investor may have the option of capitalizing certain expenditures, foregoing current deductions, and using the increased basis to reduce the gain at sale.

When unimproved land is sold, it is subject to capital gains treatment if the owner is not considered a "dealer." An individual's gain will be taxed as ordinary income if the property was held "primarily for sale to customers in the ordinary course of trade or business." This "dealer" treatment may apply once the individual has bought and sold a number of parcels of land and then subdivided that land or participated actively in its sale.

In making the distinction between an investor and a dealer, courts focus on the following factors:

1. The purpose and use for which the investor purchased and held the property.

2. The length of time between the acquisition and disposition of the property.

3. The number and frequency of sales.

4. The degree of active participation of the investor (or his agents).

5. The developments and improvements made by the investor to place the property on the market.

6. The manner in which the individual advertises in newspapers and telephone directories, and the presence or absence of (a) a business office to sell the property, and (b) memberships in professional realty associations.

7. The percentage of income derived from sales of developed and promoted real estate in comparison to the investor's other income.

It is possible for an individual to be considered an investor with respect to some properties while treated as a dealer with respect to others.

Question – Why might an investor exchange rather than sell a real estate investment?

Answer – The tax benefits of exchanging rather than selling real estate have been discussed above in the "tax implications" section: All or a portion of the tax that otherwise would be paid currently on the gain from the sale of property may be postponed. But there are several non-tax reasons for exchanging rather than selling real estate. One reason is that it may not be possible for the potential buyer to obtain adequate financing. A second reason is that the investor may want to acquire land in another location from a person who does not want to recognize a gain on the sale of that property.

Question – What are some of the sources for financing the purchase of real estate?

Answer – Approximately 60% to 70% of the value (as much as 80% for multiple family residential property) of investment real estate to be acquired can be borrowed from various financial institutions. The conventional financing sources include savings and loan associations, commercial banks, mortgage banking companies, and most life insurance companies.

Less conventional sources of real estate financing include mortgage brokers, private lenders, pension funds, REITs, and seller financing ("purchase money" financing).

Question – What are some of the techniques for financing the purchase of real estate?

Answer – Historically, most real estate purchases have been financed by use of long-term (15 to 30 year) fixed rate mortgages. For example, an investor could finance 80% of the cost of purchasing a $1,000,000 building by obtaining a 30-year bank loan of $800,000, bearing a fixed rate of interest on the unpaid balance. However, because of uncertainties in interest rates and the effects of inflation, other techniques of structuring the financing of real estate have become more popular. These techniques include:

1. *Adjustable Rate Mortgages (ARMs)* – The applicable interest rate payable is adjusted periodically (usually annually) as the "money market" dictates.

2. *Equity Participation Loans* – The lender agrees to a fixed or only moderately adjustable interest rate on the condition that upon the sale of the property he will share in the gain realized.

3. *Lease with Purchase Option* – Typically, a third party purchases the property and leases it to the user. The user is given an option to purchase the property at the end of the lease period. The option price is either predetermined or established by the fair market value at the date of the sale. This technique is employed when the user does not have either the immediate ability to purchase the property from the seller or a high enough tax bracket to utilize the tax benefits of ownership.

Question – What marginal tax bracket must an investor be in before real estate makes sense as a tax shelter?

Answer – There is no special breakpoint formula or number at which a real estate (or any other investment) does or does not make sense. The psychological as well as financial character of the investor must be matched to the attributes of the investment.

There is a formula that can be used to help answer the ultimate question with regard to the numbers involved: Will the "bottom line" of this investment increase the client's wealth more than any alternative investment?

The following formula will help regardless of the marginal tax bracket of the investor:

(1) State total cash invested ..... $ _____
(2) Subtract total tax savings .. $ _____
     After Tax Cost ...... $ _____

(3) State cash anticipated
     upon disposition ...... $ _____
(4) Subtract total tax due ...... $ _____
     After Tax Return ...... $ _____

(5) Subtract After Tax Cost
     from After Tax Return
       NET GAIN (LOSS) ...... $ _____

Will the end result of a particular real estate investment increase wealth significantly more than any appropriate alternative? Let's try an example:

Assume

(1) State total cash invested $100,000
(2) Subtract total tax savings .... $ 18,000
     After Tax Cost .... $ 82,000

(3) State cash anticipated
     upon disposition $250,000
(4) Subtract total tax due .... $ 50,000
     After Tax Return $200,000

(5) Subtract After Tax Cost
     from After Tax Return
       NET GAIN (LOSS) .... <u>$118,000</u>

It is important for the financial planner to recognize that this type of analysis is over simplified. It does not take into account such factors as: (1) the time value of money (see Chapter 16 and 17); (2) the investor's personal cash flow needs; (3) the investor's liquidity needs; and (4) the investor's personal investment preferences and risk-taking propensity.

Chapter 21

REITS (REAL ESTATE INVESTMENT TRUSTS)

WHAT IS IT?

A Real Estate Investment Trust (REIT) is essentially a publicly-traded closed-end investment company that invests in a managed, diversified portfolio of real estate or real estate mortgages and construction loans rather than in financial securities such as stocks and bonds. Although REITs are corporations or trusts, they are not subject to tax at the corporate level if they distribute at least 90% of their net annual earnings to shareholders and meet certain other requirements (discussed below). Investors must pay the tax on the REIT's earnings as the earnings are distributed. Therefore, REITs allow investors to share, with limited liability, the financial and tax benefits of real estate while avoiding the double taxation inherent in corporate ownership.

Investors have three types of REITs to choose from:

(1) *Equity REITs* – acquire ownership interests in commercial, industrial, or residential properties. Income is primarily received from the rentals of these properties.

(2) *Mortgage REITs* – invest in real estate indirectly by lending funds for construction and/or permanent mortgages. In some cases mortgage REITs invest in mortgage-backed securities such as "Ginnie Maes" or other mortgage-backed obligations.

(3) *Hybrid REITs* – combine the features of both equity and mortgage REITs.

WHEN IS THE USE OF THIS TOOL INDICATED?

1. When an investor has limited capital and cannot afford to purchase real estate properties or mortgages directly.

2. When an investor wants the added safety that a broadly diversified portfolio of real estate investments or mortgages provides.

3. When an investor does not have the skill or inclination to manage his own real estate investments.

4. When an investor desires a long-term hedge against inflation, equity REITs are indicated.

5. When an investor desires an investment that provides potentially increasing cash flows and the possibility for long-term capital appreciation, equity REITs are indicated.

6. When an investor desires high current income, mortgage REITs are indicated.

7. When an investor desires an investment combining the features of equity REITs and mortgage REITs, hybrid REITs are indicated.

ADVANTAGES

1. *Limited Liability* – REIT shareholders are treated like holders of common stock in a regular corporation. Thus, the liability of REIT shareholders is limited to the amount of their investment.

2. *No Corporate-Level Tax* – If the REIT distributes 90% of its income to shareholders (and meets certain other requirements described under "Tax Implications," below), there is no corporate-level tax. Therefore, REIT shareholders enjoy limited liability while avoiding the double tax of corporate ownership.

3. *Pooling of Resources.* – REITs pool individual investors' funds to acquire real estate interests and provide small investors with access to real estate investment opportunities not normally available to them through direct investment in real estate.

4. *Knowledgeable Professionals.* – REITs use the services of knowledgeable professionals who provide expert management and have a proven track record. Management compensation represents only a small portion of the overall expenses of these trusts. Thus, the major portion of the REITs' profits flows directly to the investors.

5. *Record-Keeping* – The REIT keeps detailed records of transactions, income and losses, distributions, expenses, and reports such information regularly to investors, sparing them the responsibility and inconvenience of record-keeping.

6. *Small Denominations* – Most REITs sell for less than $50 a share and, as with other stock investments, there is no minimum number of shares an investor must buy. However, because of the transaction costs involved, it is generally best to purchase shares in multiples of 100.

7. *Ability to Leverage Investments* – Many REITs use both short-term and long-term debt to finance their asset purchases. If the returns on the REIT's investments exceed the interest paid on the debt, the investor's returns are enhanced. However, the use of debt increases the investor's risk because actual returns may not be adequate to pay the interest on the debt.

8. *Utility as Collateral* – An investor's shares in a REIT may also be used as collateral for loans from the investor's bank or broker, subject to limits set by the Federal Reserve.

9. *Liquidity* – REITs are easily marketable and are widely traded on the various exchanges. In contrast, direct investments in real estate are generally extremely illiquid. In addition, if an investor sells a direct investment in real estate, he must typically sell the entire asset. On the other hand, the REIT investor may sell as few shares as the situation requires and continue holding the balance.

10. *Discounts from Book Value* – REITs generally have sold at discounts ranging from 5% to 20% of their book values. In other words, the price paid for a share has typically been less than an investor would have to pay to buy a pro rata share of the assets in the REIT portfolio directly. This discount in effect creates positive leverage for the investor.

Example: Assume a mortgage REIT is selling at a 10% discount from book value and the mortgages are yielding 10% inside the REIT. Since the REIT investor is in essence acquiring interests in the mortgage pool at 90 cents on the dollar, his pro-rata share of interest is ten cents for every 90 cents invested. This translates into a yield of 11.1%.

11. *High Dividend Payouts* – This is based on the requirement that REITs distribute 90% of their income.

12. *Automatic Dividend Reinvestment* – Most REITs allow investors to automatically reinvest dividends (similar to the reinvestment option allowed by mutual funds).

13. *Diversification in a Real Estate Portfolio* – REITs can provide investors with a high degree of risk reduction through diversification because the investment policy of many trusts requires them to spread their investments over wide geographical regions as well as among various property types.

14. *Inflation Hedge* – Real estate has historically proven itself as an excellent hedge against inflation. Equity REITs should provide the same inflation-hedging potential as direct real estate investments. In contrast, mortgage REITs, because they invest in mortgages and other loans where interest rates and principal balances are fixed, will tend to be poor inflation hedges. However, mortgage REITs that invest in variable-rate mortgages and loans will provide some inflation-hedging potential because interest rates will tend to move in concert with inflation.

15. *Diversification Beyond Stocks and Bonds* – By including real estate investments in their portfolios, investors can reduce their risks and enhance their expected returns beyond what they would enjoy with a portfolio containing only stocks and bonds, or only real estate. In some years when stocks and bonds perform poorly, real estate performs well; in other years, the opposite is often true. Consequently, the returns on a portfolio that includes stocks, bonds, and real estate will tend to fluctuate less severely than returns on portfolios containing only one of these asset categories.

DISADVANTAGES

1. *Loss of Control* – Professional management makes the investment easier for the investor, but it also reduces the investor's control and flexibility in the management of the investment. With direct investments, the investor can choose to buy and sell specific assets when it is advantageous for tax or other reasons to do so. With an investment in a REIT, assets are bought and sold at the discretion of the REIT management. Since 90% of the income from both rents or interest and gains on sales of assets must be distributed to

investors, the timing of such transactions may be disadvantageous to the investor.

2. *Lower Potential Returns* – Although diversification reduces risk, it also reduces the potential for substantial gains. An investor who can afford to invest directly in real estate, and who is knowledgeable enough to manage his own real estate portfolio, can expect to do better by investing directly than he could with REIT investments.

3. *Management Fees and Administrative Charges* – Although management fees are small relative to the overall amount of money involved (typically 0.5% to 1.5% of the value of the investment), they are still an additional expense that an investor may not incur if he manages his own investments. However, these fees are at least partially offset by economies of scale that reduce other transaction costs (e.g., legal fees, loan origination charges) that would typically be higher for an individual investor.

4. *No Flow-Through of Tax Benefits* – Only tax-sheltered income can be passed through to the investor; losses cannot be passed through. In contrast, losses may be passed through to investors with direct investments in real estate or with interests in limited partnerships (other than those taxed as corporations).

5. *Discounts from Book Values* – As described earlier in the discussion of advantages, REIT shares have generally sold at a discount from their book values. Purchase at a discount enhances an investor's yield; however, since these discounts vary considerably over time an investor might be faced with the additional risk that share values may decline. If the discount increases after investors have acquired shares in a REIT, they may suffer a capital loss when they sell their shares.

6. *Considerable Risk* – REIT share prices can be just as volatile as stock prices. The amount and sources of risk vary considerably depending on: (a) the type of REIT; (b) the management philosophy; and (c) its actual asset/liability makeup. (See "How Do I Select the Best of Its Type?" below for a further discussion of risk.)

7. *Poor Inflation Hedge* – Mortgage REITs, which have investment characteristics similar to bonds, are not likely to be good inflation hedges. If inflation rises and causes interest rates to rise, the value of the underlying mortgages and loans will typically fall. Consequently, in inflationary times, share values in mortgage REITs are likely to decline. However,

mortgage REITs that invest in variable-rate mortgages and loans will provide some inflation-hedging potential because interest rates will tend to move in concert with inflation.

TAX IMPLICATIONS

1. REITs will not be subject to federal income tax if they satisfy several Internal Revenue Code provisions that require that:

a) distribution of 90% of net annual earnings be made to shareholders;

b) at least 75% of gross income be derived from real estate – usually rents, mortgage interest, and gains for selling real estate;

c) at least 75% of the REIT's portfolio be invested in real estate, loans secured by real property or mortgages on real estate, shares in other REITs, cash or cash items, or government securities;

d) there be at least 100 shareholders and that no more than half the outstanding shares may be owned by five or fewer individuals at any time during the second half of each taxable year; and

e) the REIT to be managed by one or more trustees or directors.

2. Although REITs invest in real estate (which is generally subject to the passive activity rules), distributions are treated as investment income, like dividends on stock, and not as passive activity income. (See Chapter 43, "Taxation of Investment Vehicles," for a discussion of the passive activity rules.)

3. Shareholders pay taxes on distributions (i.e., dividends paid) from the REIT's earnings. Unlike a real estate limited partnership (which is not taxed as a corporation), REITs cannot offer flow-through tax benefits; however, some trustees pass on cash flow in excess of income as a nontaxable return of capital. Consequently, distributions may include portions that are treated as ordinary income, capital gains or losses, and return of capital.

Distributed income is *generally* taxed as ordinary income to shareholders. However, under JGTRRA 2003 "qualified dividend income" (generally, dividends paid by domestic corporations and certain foreign corporations to shareholders) is treated as net capital gain and is therefore eligible for the lower 15%/5% tax rates, instead of the higher ordinary income tax rates (25%, 28%, 33%, and 35% – see Chapter 43, "Taxation of Investment Vehicles"). Because REITS generally do not pay corporate income taxes, *most* ordinary income dividends paid by REITS do *not* constitute qualified dividend income, and, consequently, are not eligible for the 15%/5% rates. However, a small portion of dividends paid by REITS may constitute qualified dividend income – for example, if the: (a) dividend is attributable to dividends received by the REIT from non-REIT corporations, such as taxable REIT subsidiaries; or (b) income was subject to tax by the REIT at the corporate level, such as built-in gains, or when a REIT distributes less than 100% of its taxable income. Unless designated by the REIT as qualified dividend income, all distributions are ordinary income dividends.

Capital gains and losses on the sale of assets in the REIT's portfolio retain their character and are taxed as gains or losses to the investors when distributed. (New lower rates (15%/5%) apply to certain long-term capital gains incurred on or after May 6, 2003 and before January 1, 2011; see Chapter 43, "Taxation of Investment Vehicles.") For tax purposes, depreciation (which is a noncash expense) is subtracted from net operating income to derive the REIT's taxable income. Therefore, cash distributions may exceed net income. Distributions in excess of net income are treated as a nontaxable return of capital. Shareholders must reduce the basis in their shares by any such excess distributions.[1]

4. Gains or losses realized when investors sell their shares in a REIT are treated as capital gains or losses. The cost basis for determining gain or loss on sale is the original cost of the shares less cash distributions received in excess of the REIT's net income.

5. REITs are exempt from the requirement that certain pass-through entities report to shareholders, as income, their shares of expenses of the fund, which would be miscellaneous itemized deductions if incurred by the shareholders individually.

ALTERNATIVES

1. REITs allow investors to enjoy many of the benefits of direct investments in real estate; however, by investing through a REIT, investors give up many of the potential advantages of direct real estate investments. One of the major distinctions is that distributions are treated as investment income, and not passive activity income as they would be if the real estate were held directly. Furthermore, taxable losses on REIT properties do not flow through to shareholders as they would if the properties were held directly. Consequently, REIT shareholders cannot use taxable losses (income) on REIT properties to offset taxable income (losses) from other real estate investments or other passive activities.

2. Many real estate limited partnerships offer investors a pooled real estate investment similar to an equity REIT. However, similar to direct real estate investments, real estate limited partnerships (other than those taxed as corporations) have the flow-through characteristic that is lacking in a REIT.

3. Mutual funds that invest in mortgages or mortgage-backed securities offer an investment opportunity that is very similar to a mortgage REIT. One important distinction is the leveraging potential. Most mutual funds that invest in real estate mortgages or mortgage-backed securities limit the amount of borrowing the fund may employ to leverage its investments. Although the amount of borrowing allowed varies from one mortgage REIT to another, many mortgage REITs employ substantial borrowing to finance their asset acquisitions. This feature has both pros and cons, since such leverage can either enhance or depress returns to investors, depending on whether the returns generated by the assets acquired with the debt exceed the interest that must be paid on the debt. Other advantages associated with real estate mutual funds include a high level of diversification, professional management, and ease of ownership.

4. Mortgage-backed pass-through certificates, mortgage-backed bonds, collateralized mortgage obligations (CMOs) and real estate mortgage investment conduit (REMIC) bonds are all investments in pools of mortgages that are similar to mortgage REITs.

Except for pass-through certificates (such as Ginnie Maes), mortgage-backed securities are typically treated as debt for tax purposes whereas shares in mortgage REITs are treated like common stock. From the investor's perspective, in many cases this may be a distinction without a difference. However, certain items are treated differently for tax purposes at the investor level such as original issue discounts and market discounts on the underlying mortgages, as

Chapter 21 – REITS (Real Estate Investment Trusts)

well as the timing of recognition of principal repayments. In these respects mortgage REITs are much less complicated investments for investors.

Also, most mortgage-backed securities are backed by a fixed pool of mortgages; the pool is liquidated as the mortgages are repaid. Most mortgage REITs have indeterminate lives. They continue to acquire additional mortgages as the older mortgages in the pool are paid off. However, some REITs, called "finite-life REITs," or "FREITs," liquidate their holdings by a given date and distribute the proceeds to investors. FREITs are also unincorporated trusts, while REITs are incorporated.

Some mortgage REITs invest in mortgage-backed securities. Investors who buy shares in these REITs are essentially buying a pool of mortgages and are getting the ultimate in diversification.

5. Although residual interests in REMICs have generally been privately placed and are not available to the general public, if the market for these instruments grows as anticipated, residual interests will become publicly traded. Such interests will have characteristics very similar to hybrid REITs, such as cash flow and appreciation potential similar to a combined investment in equity and mortgage REITs.

WHERE AND HOW DO I GET IT?

Many REITs are listed on the national and regional exchanges. Others are traded in the over-the-counter market. Like common stocks, shares can be acquired from stock brokerage firms, discount brokers, and through many banks and other financial institutions.

WHAT FEES OR OTHER ACQUISITION COSTS ARE INVOLVED?

A commission is commonly charged when shares are purchased or sold. The fee will depend on (1) the amount invested, (2) the number of shares purchased, (3) whether the shares are purchased through a full-service broker or a discount broker, and (4) the market in which the shares are traded.

Like common stocks, REIT shares trade in round lots of 100 shares, with odd-lot transactions (less than 100 shares) involving higher commissions. Regular full-service commissions typically range from 2% to

3% of the dollar value of the shares purchased or sold. Discount brokerage fees range from about 15% to 70% of the regular full-service rate. In either case, there is typically a minimum fee of about $30.

The fee paid to acquire shares that are traded over-the-counter is essentially the "bid-ask spread." Market makers in the OTC market maintain a bid price at which they will purchase shares and an ask price at which they will sell shares. The bid price is always lower than the ask price. The difference, or "spread," is the broker's profit for making a market in the shares. The size of the spread depends on how many shares are outstanding and the volume of trading in the shares. The spread is smaller for very actively traded shares with a large number of shares outstanding.

HOW DO I SELECT THE BEST OF ITS TYPE?

There are over 300 REITs available to investors. These REITs have a wide variety of investment objectives and vary considerably in terms of (1) size, (2) fees, (3) management performance, (4) investment philosophy, (5) capital structure, and (6) asset characteristics. The selection process for REITs is at least as involved as that for stocks or mutual funds since REITs share many of the characteristics of each. Investors should consider many factors when making their selections. When selecting a REIT:

1. *Ascertain the type of REIT that best meets the investor's objectives with regard to income versus growth and tolerance for risk.* Equity REITs generally provide moderate income and opportunities for increasing cash flows and capital appreciation. Mortgage REITs generally provide higher income, but less opportunity for growth. Hybrid REITs provide a combination of both types of REITs. As a group, equity REITs are considered riskier than mortgage REITs, but in individual cases the opposite is often the case. Risk factors are discussed below.

2. *Determine whether the management's investment philosophy is consistent with the investor's.* The prospectus that accompanies an initial offering always includes a section describing the proposed activities of the trust. Read that section to see if the fund's objective and methods are consistent with the client's. Investors who buy REIT shares in the market after the original offering should obtain a copy of the original prospectus from their broker, if possible. They should also look at the annual reports for the most recent several years to confirm that the REIT management

is maintaining a consistent investment philosophy. Among the items that should be considered are:

a) *The types of assets that the REIT will invest in* – The type of assets the REIT acquires is critical in determining the risk and return characteristics of the REIT and the relative emphasis on income versus capital growth. For example, mortgage REITs that provide construction and development loans will be significantly riskier, and potentially much more profitable, than REITs that invest in government-insured mortgage-backed securities. However, since the default experience on construction and development loans is much higher than on other types of mortgage financing, cash flows from REITs that invest in these loans may fluctuate year to year much more than from REITs that invest in more secure mortgages.

Investors seeking stable income should avoid REITs that direct their investments to construction and development loans. In contrast, these types of REITs are recommended for investors who are looking for high yields and are less concerned with yearly fluctuations.

Some equity REITs focus on new construction and recently completed properties that have not yet been fully rented. Others invest only in "proven" properties that have a well-established rental history. The REITs that focus on new properties typically provide low cash flows from rents, but considerable growth potential and substantial capital gains when properties are sold. REITs that invest in proven properties generally provide higher and more predictable cash flows from rents, but less potential for growth and only moderate capital gains when properties are sold. Investors should seek out those REITs whose investment focus will provide the income and growth characteristics they desire.

b) *Whether leverage will be employed and, if so, whether there are limits on the amount of debt it can employ* – Leverage can increase investor's returns, but only with a corresponding increase in risk and potentially greater fluctuations in annual returns. In the early 1970s, many REITs had dismal performances, in large part because they were over-leveraged and managed their debt poorly. Since then REITs generally have been more conservative in the use of debt to finance their asset acquisitions. However, many REITs still employ debt to leverage their investments. Investors should look at what limits, if any, are placed on the use of leverage. In general, only the most aggressive and risk tolerant investors should consider REITs that use debt extensively.

c) *Whether the trust will provide broad diversification or concentrate its investments in a particular type of real property (such as motels, health care facilities, or apartments)* – Some REITs restrict their investments to specific segments of the market, such as health care facilities or motels or residential construction loans. The advantage of such segmentation is that the managers typically know the chosen market segment better than other market segments and can use their expertise to select the better opportunities within that market segment.

The disadvantage is that the REIT is less diversified and, therefore, is exposed to additional economic risk. For example, if a REIT specializes in motels, a general downturn in travel and tourism or overbuilding may adversely affect its returns. However, at the same time, demand for health care facilities, or new office space may be booming.

REITs that invest across many market segments will be less affected by economic and business factors that are detrimental to any one segment of the market. Unless an investor feels that one particular market segment offers exceptional opportunities, he will often be better off selecting a REIT that invests in many market segments.

d) *Whether the trust will diversify geographically* – Some REITs also limit their diversification by investing within one geographical region. The advantage of regional specialization is that managers are closer to their market. Successful real estate investing requires a great deal of hands-on management and local knowledge. REIT managers that invest within a region they know well are less likely to make poor investments. Consequently, many of the smaller REITs are limited in their geographical scope. However, such regional specialization exposes the REIT to the same kind of risk as market segmentation. One geographical region may be suffering adverse business conditions while other regions are booming. Investors who invest in REITs that are geographically diversified reduce their exposure to this kind of risk.

e) *Whether the trust will limit the placement of assets in any one project* – One last aspect of diversification should not be ignored. REITs may limit the proportion of their total assets that may be invested in one project. Clearly, if a major portion of a REIT's total investment is in one or two projects, the REIT essentially lives or dies by those projects. Unless an investor holds considerable assets elsewhere and, thus, provides his own diversification, he should generally look for REITs that limit the proportion of their total investment that may be placed in any given project.

f) *Whether the trust will emphasize income or capital appreciation when selecting its investments* – To a great extent, the type of assets the REIT acquires will dictate its policy regarding income and capital appreciation. Clearly, mortgage REITs will typically emphasize income, while equity REITs will typically seek at least some capital appreciation. However, how the management directs the portfolio and, in particular, its policy regarding when it sells properties will affect cash flows and growth potential.

Equity REITs that pursue essentially a "buy-and-hold" philosophy will often provide relatively stable, but increasing, cash flows. As the values of the properties in the REIT's portfolio increase, the REIT's share value should also appreciate. Equity REITs that specialize in new construction will often hold properties until they are rented to capacity, and then sell those properties (presumably for substantial gains). Since 90% of the REIT's net income (including gains on sales) must be distributed, investors have to recognize and pay taxes on the gains to the extent cash is distributed. Consequently, such REITs may earn substantial gains on their properties, but the net effect to investors is higher (and more volatile) cash flows, and less potential appreciation in their share value. Therefore, the management's philosophy and policy regarding how they direct their portfolio will greatly affect the degree to which returns are realized (i.e., as cash flows or as appreciation in share value).

3. *Evaluate the historical performance of those REITs that match the investor's investment objectives and philoso-*

phy – The S&P 500 REIT Composite Index tracks the market performance of U.S. REITS. The index consists of 100 REITS chosen for their liquidity and importance in representing a diversified real estate portfolio. The index covers 80% of the securitized U.S. real estate market.

a) The single most important factor in selecting a REIT is the quality of management. Some of the personal data about management personnel can be found in *Who's Who in Business, Who's Who in America,* or *Dun's Reference Book of Corporate Managements.* Investors should also try to evaluate the management's experience by looking at the performance of previous real estate ventures managed by the team. Success in the past does not guarantee success in the future, but a history of poor performance does suggest less than average prospects for future success.

b) The critical factors that reflect on the quality of management and the potential performance of a REIT are as follows: (i) dividend payout record; (ii) expense ratios; (iii) vacancy rates; (iv) length of time the REIT management has been in business; (v) the quality or value of the properties in which the REIT invests; and (vi) the percentage of ownership held by the managers of the company.

Historical information regarding earnings, dividends, assets, liabilities, expense ratios and the like can be obtained for many REITs from reports issued by investment advisory services such as Value Line, Moody's, and Standard & Poor's. Additional information is presented in the REITs' annual reports. REITs are also rated by the advisory services. Conservative investors should generally avoid REITs that are rated "B" or lower by Moody's or Standard & Poor's, as well as those with a Value Line rating lower than "3."

4. *Project future performance* – This, of course, is the most difficult step in the selection process. Growth will depend on the future income from the REIT's holdings. Income will depend on the rent and, sometimes, the sales level of the REIT's properties. Some reliance may be placed on professional appraisals of the REIT's properties to estimate future income growth and appreciation potential. But appraisals do not always reflect the same standards and may be derived using different assumptions regarding rent multipliers or capitalization rates (which are techniques used to

value the projected rental stream from a property). In addition, vacancy rates, poor regional economic growth, and overbuilding in the geographic region or the particular market segment favored by the REIT can all affect REIT income. High levels of debt may also cause shareholder dividends to be low.

Given the complexity of selecting the "best" REIT of its type, investors should consider buying shares in several REITs that have the basic investment characteristics and investment philosophy the investor is seeking. By diversifying among several REIT holdings rather than buying just one REIT, investors can expect about average performance, but they will also minimize downside exposure.

WHERE CAN I FIND OUT MORE ABOUT IT?

1. A pamphlet published by the National Association of Real Estate Investment Trusts (NAREIT) is a good place to start finding out more about REITs. The pamphlet titled, *Frequently Asked Questions About REITs*, can be viewed on the Internet at: http://www.nareit.com/aboutreits/faqtext.cfm.

2. In addition, the investment advisories listed below provide information not only about industries and companies but also about the outlook for the national economy. The investment advisory services cost several hundred dollars per year, but they are available for use in most libraries.

a) *Value Line Investment Survey*, 220 East 42 Street, New York, NY, 10017 212-907-1500, (www.valueline.com).

b) *Realty Stock Review*, a twice-monthly newsletter that tracks the performance of 100 REITs ($269/year). To subscribe, contact: Rainmaker Publications Group, LLC, Box 240, Oakhurst, NJ 07755, 732-493-1999, ext. 115, (www.realtystockreview.com/contact.html).

c) *Moody's Handbook of Common Stock*, Moody's Investment Services, 99 Church Street, New York, NY, 212-553-1653 (www.moodys.com).

d) *Stock Reports*, Standard & Poor's Corporation, 345 Hudson Street, New York, NY, (www.standardandpoors.com).

3. The *Wall Street Journal* (www.wsj.com), *New York Times* (www.nyt.com), and most major newspapers

will carry daily listings of the trading activity and prices for REITs listed on the major exchanges.

4. Articles on REITs appear periodically in various financial magazines and journals such as *Barron's* (www.barrons.com), *Forbes* (www.forbes.com), *Fortune* (www.fortune.com), the *Wall Street Journal* (www.wsj.com), and *Money* magazine (www.money.com).

5. Research reports and other information on specific REITs and current market conditions can be obtained by calling major brokerage firms, especially those firms that make a market in various REIT issues.

QUESTIONS AND ANSWERS

Question – How have REITs performed historically?

Answer – Figure 21.1 shows annual total returns (dividends and gains (losses) in share value) for the various types of REITs from 1972 through February 2006. In the early to mid-1970s REITs performed poorly, along with the general stock market. Economic conditions were partly responsible, but many of the trusts themselves were shaky. The period from 1987 through 1990 was also one of relatively weak returns.

REITs have enjoyed renewed popularity over the past few years due to a strong real estate market, falling interest rates, and a vibrant commercial rental market. Figure 21.2 compares the annualized total returns on equity REITs to those of the S&P 500 stock market index (figures shown are for periods ending December 31, 2005). Figure 21.2 shows that Equity REITs have outperformed S&P 500 Stocks, U.S. Small Stocks, and Long-Term Government Bonds over the prior 1-, 3-, 5-, 10-, and 20-year periods (except for U.S. Small Stocks for the 20-year period – 12.8% for Small Stocks versus 12.4% for Equity REITs).

Question – Are REITs sensitive to the stock market?

Answer – No, REITs do not normally react substantially to changes in the stock market. REITs are more sensitive to interest rate fluctuations. Generally, the behavior of REITs is opposite that of the behavior of interest rates; as interest rates rise, REITs decline, and as interest rates fall, the cash flow of REITs increases. In this instance, they provide a better source of current income than bonds.

Figure 21.1

REAL ESTATE INVESTMENT TRUSTS
RETURNS (%) 1972 - 2006 (*THROUGH FEBRUARY)

Year	All REITs			Equity REITs			Mortgage REITs			Hybrid REITs		
	Total Return	Price Return	Income Return	Total Return	Price Return	Income Return	Total Return	Price Return	Income Return	Total Return	Price Return	Income Return
1972	11.19	3.84	7.35	8.01	1.08	6.93	12.17	4.34	7.83	11.41	4.33	7.08
1973	(27.22)	(33.11)	5.89	(15.52)	(21.78)	6.26	(36.26)	(42.05)	5.79	(23.37)	(29.05)	5.68
1974	(42.23)	(49.55)	7.32	(21.40)	(29.33)	7.92	(45.32)	(53.96)	8.64	(52.22)	(57.78)	5.56
1975	36.34	22.20	14.13	19.30	8.34	10.96	40.79	24.51	16.28	49.92	34.49	15.43
1976	48.97	36.53	12.44	47.59	36.21	11.38	51.51	38.41	13.30	48.19	35.52	12.67
1977	19.08	10.10	8.98	22.42	13.97	8.45	17.82	8.16	9.67	17.44	8.43	9.01
1978	(1.64)	(9.42)	7.78	10.34	2.66	7.68	(9.97)	(17.86)	7.89	(7.29)	(14.98)	7.69
1979	30.53	19.35	11.18	35.86	25.49	10.37	16.56	4.26	12.31	33.81	22.57	11.23
1980	28.02	11.07	16.95	24.37	1.95	22.42	16.80	3.29	13.51	42.46	30.44	12.01
1981	8.58	(1.02)	9.60	6.00	(2.03)	8.03	7.07	(5.54)	12.61	12.23	2.80	9.43
1982	31.64	19.19	12.46	21.60	11.49	10.11	48.64	31.27	17.38	29.56	18.15	11.41
1983	25.47	15.11	10.36	30.64	21.01	9.63	16.90	5.56	11.34	29.90	20.10	9.81
1984	14.82	3.53	11.29	20.93	9.30	11.63	7.26	(4.54)	11.80	17.25	7.37	9.88
1985	5.92	(3.52)	9.44	19.10	9.62	9.48	(5.20)	(15.33)	10.13	4.32	(3.60)	7.93
1986	19.18	9.24	9.93	19.16	10.56	8.59	19.21	7.64	11.58	18.75	8.96	9.79
1987	(10.67)	(19.01)	8.34	(3.64)	(10.31)	6.67	(15.67)	(25.70)	10.03	(17.58)	(26.65)	9.07
1988	11.36	1.24	10.11	13.49	4.77	8.72	7.30	(5.12)	12.42	6.60	(2.87)	9.47
1989	(1.81)	(12.06)	10.25	8.84	0.58	8.26	(15.90)	(26.19)	10.28	(12.14)	(28.36)	16.22
1990	(17.35)	(28.49)	11.15	(15.35)	(26.45)	11.10	(18.37)	(29.18)	10.81	(28.21)	(38.88)	10.67
1991	35.68	23.10	12.58	35.70	25.47	10.22	31.83	13.93	17.91	39.16	27.08	12.08
1992	12.18	2.87	9.31	14.59	6.40	8.19	1.92	(10.80)	12.72	16.59	7.21	9.38
1993	18.55	10.58	7.96	19.65	12.95	6.70	14.55	(0.40)	14.95	21.18	12.44	8.75
1994	0.81	(6.41)	7.22	3.17	(3.52)	6.69	(24.30)	(33.83)	9.53	4.00	(5.95)	9.95
1995	18.31	9.12	9.19	15.27	6.56	8.71	63.42	46.80	16.62	22.99	13.10	9.89
1996	35.75	26.52	9.23	35.27	26.35	8.92	50.86	37.21	13.65	29.35	19.70	9.65
1997	18.86	11.85	7.01	20.26	13.33	6.93	3.82	(3.57)	7.40	10.75	2.79	7.96
1998	(18.82)	(23.82)	5.00	(17.50)	(22.33)	4.83	(29.22)	(34.29)	5.07	(34.03)	(42.16)	8.13
1999	(6.48)	(14.06)	7.59	(4.62)	(12.21)	7.59	(33.22)	(40.12)	6.90	(35.90)	(43.43)	7.53
2000	25.89	15.91	9.98	26.37	16.51	9.86	15.96	3.33	12.63	11.61	(1.88)	13.50
2001	15.50	7.05	8.45	13.93	5.85	8.08	77.34	46.37	30.97	50.75	40.58	10.17
2002	5.22	(2.15)	7.36	3.82	(3.12)	6.94	31.08	14.23	16.85	23.30	12.36	10.94
2003	38.47	29.34	9.13	37.13	28.48	8.66	57.39	38.19	19.20	56.19	44.85	11.34
2004	30.41	22.87	7.54	31.58	24.35	7.23	18.43	7.92	10.52	23.90	15.69	8.21
2005	8.29	2.51	5.78	12.16	6.67	5.49	(23.19)	(30.88)	7.69	(10.83)	(17.16)	6.33
2006*	8.54	7.88	0.67	9.22	8.53	0.69	0.25	(0.28)	0.53	5.92	5.92	0.00
Statistics												
Simple Ave.	13.72	4.51	9.21	15.82	7.15	8.68	10.68	(1.30)	11.98	12.73	3.19	9.54
Compound Ave.	10.81	1.51	9.18	13.62	4.84	8.41	6.72	(4.97)	12.24	8.56	(1.28)	9.95
Std. Dev.	20.96	20.09	2.60	17.85	17.41	2.99	30.03	26.22	5.02	26.74	25.88	2.90
Historical Returns (Compound Annual Rates Through End of May 2002)												
1-Year	24.82	18.09	6.74	29.76	23.34	6.42	(16.04)	(24.51)	8.47	1.15	(6.03)	7.18
3-Year	29.04	21.54	7.50	30.84	23.66	7.18	12.96	1.65	11.31	21.90	13.37	8.53
5-Year	20.83	13.13	7.70	21.33	13.98	7.35	22.89	7.71	15.18	22.26	13.43	8.83
10-Year	14.50	6.86	7.64	15.19	7.79	7.40	10.95	(0.91)	11.86	8.47	(0.87)	9.34
15-Year	14.38	6.32	8.05	15.14	7.58	8.55	10.87	(1.51)	12.38	11.34	1.86	9.48
20-Year	10.70	2.05	8.65	12.50	4.57	7.93	6.73	(5.34)	12.07	6.61	(3.50)	10.11

Figure 21.2

ANNUALIZED TOTAL COMPOUND RETURNS
EQUITY REITS VERSUS S&P 500 STOCK INDEX, U.S. SMALL STOCKS, U.S. LT GOV'T BONDS (As of 2005 Year End)

Investment	1 year	3 year	5 year	10 year	20 year
S&P 500	4.9%	14.4%	0.5%	9.1%	11.9%
U.S. Small Stocks	5.7%	26.2%	16.4%	13.6%	12.8%
LT Gov't Bonds	7.8%	5.9%	7.7%	7.6%	9.7%
Equity REITs	12.2%	26.5%	19.1%	14.5%	12.4%

Source: National Association of Real Estate Investment Trusts (www.nareit.com) and SBBI 2006 Yearbook, Ibbotson Associates, Chicago, Illinois.

Figure 21.3

DECLINING EQUITY REIT CORRELATION
CORRELATION OF REIT TOTAL RETURNS TO OTHER TYPES OF INVESTMENTS

Investment	1972-2003	1970s*	1980s	1990s	1993-2003
Small Stocks	0.63	0.74	0.74	0.58	0.26
Large Stocks	0.55	0.64	0.65	0.45	0.26
LT Bonds	0.2	0.27	0.17	0.26	0.16

* 1972-1979

Source: REITs - NAREIT Equity Index; Small Stocks – Ibbotson U.S. Small Stock Series; Large Stocks – S&P 500; LT bonds – 20-year U.S. Government Bonds.

A recent study shows that returns on REITs have become less correlated with returns on equities and long-term bonds.[2] Specifically, Ibbotson found that the correlation of REIT stock returns with the returns of other common stocks declined significantly over a 30-year time frame from the 1970s to the period from 1993 to 2000 Figure 21.3 shows the results of this study updated for the period through December of 2003. The correlation of equity REIT returns with those of small stocks (represented by the Ibbotson U.S. Small Stock Series) declined 65%, from 0.74 in the 1970s to 0.26 for the decade ending in 2003; large stock (Standard & Poor's 500) correlation declined 59%, from 0.64 to 0.26. The correlation of REIT returns with those of long-term bonds (20-year U.S. Government Bond) declined 41%, from 0.27 to 0.16 during the same span. These lower correlations together with favorable returns provides investors with an opportunity to enhance their overall portfolio performance by investing some portion of their portfolio in equity REITs.

Question–How can diversification be achieved with REITs?

Answer–REIT portfolio diversification is possible in several ways.

1. *Diversification through the Real Estate Portfolio* –This is accomplished in two ways. Investments can be made in a variety of property sectors, such as hospitals, hotels, or office buildings, rather than in one specific sector. Second, investments can be spread over a wide geographical area that may include foreign countries.

(2) *Diversification beyond Stocks and Bonds*—By investing in real estate in addition to stocks and bonds, an investor can enjoy greater returns with less risk. The balance created between the three investment options reduces the fluctuations of returns and risks associated with investments in just one of the assets. The Ibbotson study (discussed in the

previous question) suggests that as the publicly traded real estate industry evolved in the 1990s, real estate stocks demonstrated characteristics and provided returns that differed from those of other common stocks as well as fixed-income securities. Ibbotson found that the behavior of REITs makes a strong case for their inclusion in portfolios as a hedge against the volatility and underperformance of other securities.

Over time, real estate stocks have provided meaningful diversification benefits by boosting returns or reducing risks. A sample portfolio prepared by Ibbotson consisting of 40% bonds, 50% stocks and 10% Treasury bills provided an average annual return of 11.8% and a risk level of 11.2% between 1972-2000. When the asset mix was adjusted to include 35% bonds, 45% stocks, 10% T-bills and 10% REITs, the average return increased to 12% and the risk level declined to 10.9% over the same period. A third portfolio, adjusted to include 30% bonds, 40% stocks, 10% T-bills and 20% REITs saw the average return increase to 12.2% and the risk level decline to 10.8%.

Adding REITs to the portfolio boosted the average annual return by almost half a percentage point over the non-REIT portfolio, while reducing portfolio risk by that same amount. Based upon these statistics, a $10,000 investment in the non-REIT portfolio in 1972 with dividends reinvested would have grown to $219,049 by 2000. The second portfolio, including a 10% REIT allocation, would have gained $227,000 over the same period. And the third portfolio, which included 20% REITs, would have accumulated $238,349, an increase of more than $19,000 over the non-REIT portfolio.

Ibbotson found that REIT stocks registered a compound annual total return of 12.4% from 1981 to 2000, compared with 12% for government bonds, 13.3% for Ibbotson's Small Stock Index, and 15.7% for the S&P 500.

Question – How do REITs and RELPs differ?

Answer – Real Estate Limited Partnerships (RELPs) offer an alternative to REITs. As explained below, they differ in operational structure, tax treatment, and liquidity:

1. *Operational Structure* – A REIT is managed by a board of directors that is accountable to shareholders. A RELP is managed by an autonomous general partner.

2. *Tax Treatment* – REITs are categorized as portfolio investments. Income dividends are generally taxed as ordinary investment income; capital gain dividends are taxed as short- or long-term capital gains, depending on the REITs holding period; and gains or losses on sales of REIT interests or shares are taxed as short- or long-term capital gains, depending on the investor's holding period. RELPs on the other hand, are "passive activity" investments. Accordingly, different tax laws apply regarding gains and losses. (See Chapter 43, "Taxation of Investment Vehicles," for further discussion of the passive activity rules.)

3. *Liquidity* – REITs are very liquid due to their active trading on most stock exchanges. RELPs, with the exception of a small group of publicly traded partnerships, are generally illiquid.

CHAPTER ENDNOTES

1. See IRC Sec. 857(c), as amended by JGTRRA 2003. See also National Association of Real Estate Investment Trusts, Policy Bulletin, (5-28-2003).

2. The study was commissioned by the National Association of Real Estate Investment Trusts and was conducted by Ibbotson Associates, a leading authority on asset allocation. See NAREIT Press Release, "REITS Low Correlation to Other Stocks and Bonds is Key Factor for Portfolio Diversification," (contact Jay Hyde, NAREIT, (202) 739-9400 or Alexa Auerbach, Ibbotson Associates, (312) 616-7353).

   With respect to the industry as a whole, the National Association of Real Estate Investment Trusts (NAREIT) sponsors the NAREIT Real-Time index, which includes all REITs currently trading on the New York Stock Exchange (NYSE), the NASDAQ National Market System, and the American Stock Exchange (AMEX). It is the first index to include monthly historical statistics from 1972. The NAREIT Real-Time Index provides a standard with which to measure the REIT industry's growth and performance on a real-time basis. In addition to being the most statistically comprehensive real-time index currently available, the NAREIT index features: (1) total returns; (2) price returns; (3) dividend yields; (4) market capitalization weightings (5) monthly reweightings; and (6) monthly reconstitutions.

Chapter 22

REAL ESTATE MORTGAGE INVESTMENT CONDUITS (REMICs)

WHAT IS IT?

A Real Estate Mortgage Investment Conduit (REMIC) is a limited-life, self-liquidating entity that invests exclusively in real estate mortgages or in securities backed by real estate mortgages.

REMICs may issue two types of securities: "regular interests" and "residual interests." The REMIC may issue multiple classes of regular interests (REMIC bonds), but only one class of residual interests. REMIC bonds are treated for tax purposes as debt securities. Investors who hold REMIC bonds receive a specified cash flow from the underlying pool of mortgages. In this respect, REMIC bonds are very similar to collateralized mortgage obligations (CMOs). They are essentially a hybrid security combining features of conventional bonds and mortgage-backed participation certificates (PCs) such as Ginnie Mae pass-through certificates. Residual interests are treated for tax purposes much like interests in a partnership or grantor trust. As such, they are roughly comparable to the equity interest in the REMIC entity. Residual interest holders take into account all of the REMIC's net income that is not taken into account by the REMIC bondholders.

A REMIC is typically exempt from federal income tax. In other words, it is a flow-through entity, similar to a partnership; thus, it acts as a conduit and holders of REMIC securities must report any taxable income from the underlying mortgages. A REMIC terminates when its mortgages are repaid.

Eventually, REMICs are intended to be the exclusive means for issuing multiple-class real estate mortgage-backed securities. This means they will eventually replace all collateralized mortgage obligations. In addition, they may become the favored vehicle for issuing securities similar to mortgage-backed participation certificates such as Ginnie Maes.

WHEN IS THE USE OF THIS TOOL INDICATED?

1. When an investor is interested in an income-producing investment with risk and return characteristics similar to conventional bonds, regular interests in REMICs would be indicated.

2. When an investor desires a potentially high-yielding investment with risk and return characteristics similar to common stocks or partnership interests, residual interests would be indicated. Most residual interests have been privately placed and are not generally available to the investing public. However, if the REMIC market grows as anticipated, residual interests will become available to the general public.

3. When an investor wants the added safety provided by pooling a number of mortgages into one investment.

4. When an investor desires a relatively high rate of return on a debt-type instrument. The holders of REMIC bonds should receive a competitive yield on mortgage-backed securities that is generally higher than on other bond-type investments of similar quality and maturity.

5. When an investor wants to diversify beyond holding stocks, traditional corporate bonds, and government bonds. By investing in REMICs, an investor is expanding his portfolio into real estate and capturing the additional protection such diversity provides.

6. When an investor wants liquidity. Because of their specialized nature, REMIC bonds may not enjoy the same breadth of market as conventional bonds. However, the growth of this market is expected to be significant. It is anticipated that secondary markets will develop for REMIC bonds that will be similar to those that currently exist for Ginnie Maes, Fannie Maes, and other mortgage-backed participation certificates. In many cases, the issuers guarantee to maintain a secondary market in these securities. Also, some REMICs are structured to permit REMIC bondholders to redeem their holdings at par value before maturity (subject to limits and other restrictions).

7. When an investor wants a relatively secure type of investment. Regular interests are treated like

debt and will have risk characteristics similar to comparably rated traditional bonds. Some REMICs offer a senior and a subordinated class of interests. Investors who desire low risk may acquire the senior class, which receives all payments of interest and principal before the subordinated class. Investors who are willing to subordinate their interests to the senior class of security holders can expect to receive higher returns for bearing the slightly higher risk.

8. When an investor wants more predictability regarding prepayments of principal than is available with other mortgage-backed securities such as Ginnie Mae pass-through certificates. Since REMICs may issue multiple classes of regular interests, many are structured to offer a short-term class that matures in three to five years, intermediate-term class(es) that mature(s) in five to 15 years, and long-term class(es) that mature(s) in 15 to 30 years. Consequently, investors can invest in classes that match their investment horizons and avoid a great deal of the uncertainty regarding when principal will be repaid.

ADVANTAGES

1. Taxation of REMIC interests is established by statute without regard to their form, provided such interests qualify as regular or residual REMIC interests. Consequently, although regular interests may be issued as stock, bonds, or interests in trusts, they will always be treated as debt (bonds) for tax purposes.

2. Regular interests in many REMICs are virtually risk-free in terms of return of principal and certainty of income. The quality of the mortgages in the pool determines the quality of the issue. Many REMICs invest in mortgages guaranteed by the Government National Mortgage Association (GNMA), the Federal National Mortgage Association (FNMA), or the Federal Home Loan Mortgage Corporation (FHLMC). In addition, many REMICs have received triple A ratings from one or more of the bond rating companies (Moody's, Standard and Poor's, or Fitch's). However, the use of REMICs to pool residential and nonresidential mortgages that are not guaranteed by government agencies is expected to grow considerably. In these cases, the risk will depend on (a) the reputation of the issuing agency, (b) the quality of the mortgages in the pool, and (c) the existence and nature of the private insurance (if any) behind the mortgages.

3. REMICs offer investors a way to minimize the "prepayment risk" inherent in a mortgage pool.

4. REMICs combine the predictable cash flow of bonds with the relatively high yields of mortgage securities. Interest rates on mortgages are typically higher than short-term money market rates or even long-term corporate bond rates. Each class of REMIC bonds will usually yield more than bonds of comparable maturity. Also, since each successive class of securities receives principal repayments only after the prior class has been fully repaid, the cash flow is more predictable than for traditional mortgage-backed participation certificates and more closely resembles the cash flows for traditional bonds. For example, assume a REMIC creates a Class A security paying 8% and a Class B security paying 10%. Holders in Class A must be paid in full before principal may be paid on the Class B securities. A third class might be paid an even higher rate, but only after the Class A and B holders are paid.

5. By segregating the cash flows to create issues with different maturities, investors who have little desire to hold 30-year mortgages in their portfolios can still participate in the high yields associated with mortgage-secured investments by purchasing one of the shorter-term issues.

Prepayment risk arises because the mortgages in the underlying pool may be paid off sooner than anticipated. When prepayments exceed expectations, investors may be forced to reinvest the proceeds at lower current interest rates. When prepayments are slower than expected, investors may lose the opportunity to reinvest at higher current rates. Investors in regular mortgage-backed securities (e.g., Ginnie Mae pass-through certificates) share the prepayment risk in proportion to their ownership of the pool. Because prepayments tend to increase when interest rates fall (because people are more likely to refinance their mortgages), prepayments force investors to reinvest more of their capital when yields on reinvestment opportunities are less.

REMICs can issue different classes of REMIC bonds with different maturity dates, different interest rates, etc., enabling them to appeal to investors with different purposes (e.g., safety, yield, long-term or short-term investments). Certain investors have claim to predetermined principal repayment cash flows. As a result, the prepayment risk is not shared equally; rather it is borne sequentially by specific subgroups of the overall investors in the mortgage pool. Consequently, REMICs offer some protection against prepayments to investors who acquire the later maturing classes.

6. As the number of these issues grows, the secondary market will also grow. For larger issuers, secondary markets have arisen to provide liquidity if investors need to sell their securities. In some cases, issuers promise to maintain a secondary market or to provide limited redemptions at par value before maturity.

7. The price volatility of REMIC bonds tends to be less than for bonds of similar quality and maturity. Bond prices generally fall when interest rates increase and rise when interest rates decrease. The longer the term of the bond, the more sensitive the bond price is to a given change in interest rates. The prices of REMIC bonds move in the same general manner, but the velocity of the move is dampened by changes in the rate of prepayments. Prepayments on mortgages tend to accelerate when interest rates decline and homeowners find it advantageous to refinance. As prepayments increase, the average maturity of a given class of regular interests decreases. Consequently, the price of the regular interests will not tend to rise as much as the price of bonds with a similar maturity before the interest rate increase. Prepayments may also slow down somewhat when interest rates increase because there are fewer refinancings. However, the slowdown in prepayments caused by increases in interest rates is rather limited because mortgagors must still make their required mortgage payments of principal and interest. In other words, they cannot extend the maturity of their mortgages when interest rates increase. Since some principal is usually repaid on REMIC bonds before the ultimate maturity, even when interest rates rise, the price of REMIC bonds will tend to fall less than the price of bonds of similar maturities when interest rates rise.

8. Although many REMICs have been issued with minimum purchase requirements of $10,000 or more, the minimum purchase requirement is still less than the $25,000 minimum for Ginnie Maes. Most REMICs issue regular interests with smaller denominations that will attract smaller investors. In most cases, REMIC bonds are issued in $1,000 units, similar to conventional corporate bonds.

9. REMICs allow a great deal of flexibility in the forms of the securities they may issue. REMICs may soon offer such features as coupon-stripping, adjustable and variable rates, and other innovative forms of securities.

10. REMIC bonds with variable interest rates may provide some inflation-hedging protection since interest rates typically move in concert with inflation.

11. REMICs provide a number of advantages to the issuers, who ultimately will permit a more efficient (i.e., less costly) method for packaging and selling multi-class securities and, therefore, provide better returns and features for investors. First, there will no longer be the need (as in the case of CMOs) to follow debt format and substance. Second, there will be no need for excess equity capital to build in a minimum investment risk for the residual holders. Consequently, more capital will be used to acquire high-yielding mortgages rather than to fund excess reserve accounts paying low money-market rates. Third, the risk that the REMIC may be taxed as a corporation, rather than a flow-through entity, is eliminated if the REMIC rules are followed. Fourth, REMIC regular and residual interests are qualifying assets for thrift institutions and REITs. Residual interests may also be acquired by pension plans without the income being taxed as unrelated business taxable income (with some restrictions). This will broaden the original issue and secondary markets for these securities. Fifth, residual interests are freely transferable, which means more institutions are likely to create REMICs and further expand the market.

DISADVANTAGES

1. As with other interest-sensitive investments, the price of regular interests in REMICs will tend to fall when market interest rates rise. Investors who must sell their interests before maturity may have to sell them at a loss.

2. The actual yield an investor will realize on a REMIC bond is uncertain, mainly because of the unpredictability of prepayments on the underlying mortgage pool. (See "How Do I Select The Best of Its Type" for an explanation of quoted and realized yields.)

3. Secondary markets are expected to grow significantly as the number of REMIC offerings increases. However, because of their specialized nature, secondary markets for REMIC bonds may never be as well developed as for conventional bonds. For example, except for very large issues with standard features, REMIC bonds will not typically be listed on organized security exchanges. Consequently, investors who must sell their securities before maturity may have to sell at a sizable discount. The size of the discount will depend on the size of the issue, the reputation of the issuer, and the quality of the mortgages backing the security. In some cases, the underwriters and other investment banking firms

and financial institutions have promised to maintain secondary markets in the securities. Also, some mortgage-backed securities have been issued with put or redemption features that allow investors to redeem the bonds before maturity at face value, subject to limits and restrictions. Some REMIC issues may include similar features.

TAX IMPLICATIONS

1. There is a great deal of flexibility in the form of entity that may be used for a REMIC. A trust, partnership, corporation, association, or merely a segregated pool of mortgages is suitable. Once the entity elects REMIC status at startup, the initial form of the issuing entity is ignored and the entity is taxed under the special REMIC rules. REMICs are taxed as pass-through entities – that is, there is no entity-level tax. Except for certain prohibited transactions, REMIC taxable income or loss flows through to the holders of residual interests on a pro rata basis.

2. **REGULAR INTERESTS**

   a) A regular interest is treated as debt, regardless of its form.

   b) REMIC bonds have two unique features for tax purposes. First, holders of REMIC bonds must

4. REMIC bonds with fixed interest rates, similar to fixed-rate bonds and other mortgage-backed debt-type securities, are subject to two types of inflation risk: (a) the risk that the purchasing power of income will be eroded over time; and (b) the risk that the purchasing power of capital received at maturity will have diminished. The second risk is somewhat less than with conventional bonds because principal is recovered over a period of years and can be reinvested or consumed. It is somewhat higher for the later-maturing classes of REMIC bonds than with pass-through certificates because principal recovery is delayed on these securities until the early-maturing classes have been completely repaid.

5. Similar to many conventional corporate bond issues, many REMIC bonds are callable at the discretion of the issuer. Others are issued with a sinking fund feature, which requires that a specified number of securities be redeemed at specified dates. Random lot typically determines the bonds that are redeemed. Consequently, like conventional callable corporate bonds, REMIC bonds may be redeemed before the holder would otherwise choose to redeem them.

use the accrual method to report income on their bonds, even if they are cash-basis taxpayers for other purposes. Second, a special rule requires that a part of the gain on sale or exchange of a REMIC bond be taxed as ordinary income.

On a sale or exchange, the owner of a REMIC bond recognizes gain if the amount received exceeds the adjusted basis of the bond (or loss if the amount received is less than its adjusted basis). The adjusted basis will generally equal the investor's cost, *increased* by any "original issue discount" (see below) or "market discount" (see below) that has been included in income, and *reduced* by (i) any previous principal payments received, and (ii) premium amortization. The gain or loss, adjusted by any unrecognized market discount and the part of the gain subject to the special rule cited above, will be taxed as a capital gain or loss. The portion of gain attributable to market discount is taxed as ordinary income.

The portion of the gain on the sale or exchange of a REMIC bond that is treated as ordinary income under the special rule is an amount equal to the *excess* of the amount that would have been includable on the bond if its yield were 110% of the Applicable Federal rate (AFR) in effect when the holder's holding period began, *over* the amount actually included by the holder in gross income during the time the bond was held.

For example, assume a REMIC bond paying 8% interest per year is acquired for $1,000. The AFR at the time of acquisition is 9%. In three years, the bond is sold for $1,100. The gain, assuming no payments of principal have been received, is $100. The amount of interest actually included in income is $240. The amount that would have been includable in income if the yield were 110% of the 9% AFR is $297 (9.9% times $1,000 times 3). Therefore, $57 ($297–$240) of the $100 gain on sale is treated as ordinary income and the remaining $43 is treated as long-term capital gain.

   c) Each investor is required to report as ordinary income the interest paid or accrued on the indebtedness, and the "original issue discount" or "market discount," if applicable. The amount that must be reported as ordinary income is decreased by "premium amortization," if applicable.

Original issue discounts (OIDs), market discounts, and premiums arise when there is a difference between the acquisition price of a debt instrument and the total principal amounts that will be repaid on the security when it matures. If a debt instrument is acquired for a price that is greater than the total principal payments that will be repaid on the security, the difference is called a "premium." A premium typically arises when the coupon rate on a debt instrument is greater than the market rate of interest for comparable debt securities. For example, a regular $1,000 face-value bond with a 10% coupon rate and 25 years to maturity would sell for, perhaps, $1,100, or a $100 premium, if the market rate of interest on comparable bonds is 9%.

Conversely, if the purchase price in the after-original issue (secondary) market of a debt instrument (originally issued at par) is less than the total principal payments, the difference is called a "market discount." Market discount typically occurs when market interest rates rise above the coupon rate on the debt instrument. Original issue discount is essentially the same as market discount, except that it arises when a debt instrument is acquired from the original issuer, rather than in the secondary market. Despite the similarity, OID and market discount are accounted for separately because they are treated differently for tax purposes.

Original issue discounts in REMICs may arise in two ways: (i) the mortgages in the pool are acquired with OID (which is not typically the case); or (ii) the class of regular interests is structured so that the issue price is less than the redemption price (which is more common). If OID arises in the second way, and the term of such indebtedness is in excess of one year, OID must be reported as ordinary income by each investor as it accrues, in accordance with a constant-rate method that takes compounding into account, and in advance of the cash attributable to such income.

A special rule exists for calculating OID on debt instruments that have a maturity that is initially fixed, but may accelerate based on prepayments. In general, OID on such indebtedness is calculated and included in the holder's income by: (i) accruing the discount using the original yield to maturity for the instrument, assuming that a certain level of prepayments will occur;

(ii) increasing the amount of income recognized as more frequent prepayments occur; and (iii) decreasing the amount of accrued income (but never below zero) if there is a reduction in prepayments.

If OID arises because the mortgages in the pool are acquired with OID, the residual interest holders – not the regular interest holders – must report the OID. In these cases, the residual interest holders will typically have reportable income in excess of the cash income on the mortgages, and in excess of the deductible interest payments on the regular interests. (The original issue discount rules are discussed in more detail in Chapter 3, "Corporate Bonds.")

Market discount may also arise in two ways: (i) mortgages in the pool are acquired at a market discount from the total of the principal payments that will be paid on the mortgages; or (ii) the investor acquires the REMIC bond for a price that is less than the unpaid principal balance on the bond. In the second case, investors have an option as to when the market discount will be taxed and at what rate it will accrue. Market discount will accrue: (i) at a constant rate; or (ii) in proportion to original issue discount accrual (if there is such discount), or ratably in proportion to stated interest on regular interests. These two market discount accrual methods can best be understood by the example, below.

Example: Assume a 5% coupon bond ($50 per year in interest) that matures in three years for $1,000 is selling for $875, a $125 discount). The market rate of interest is 10%. Using the straight-line method, the investor would accrue one-third of the discount, or $41.67, each year. Adding this together with the $50 coupon amount, the investor would report and be taxed on $91.67 ($50 plus $41.67) of interest each year. Using the constant-rate method, the investor would report interest at the rate of 10% each year based on the outstanding principal balance on the bond. The principal balance in the first year is $875. Therefore the taxable interest is $87.50. Of this amount, $37.50 ($87.50 taxable interest minus $50 cash interest) is attributable to recovery of the discount. Because the investor receives no cash for the discount until the bond matures, it is added to the outstanding principal balance. In the second year the outstanding principal balance is $912.50 ($875 original price plus $37.50 accrued discount). Therefore, the investor must report $91.25 as taxable interest. The amount of the discount accrued in the second year is $41.25 ($91.25 taxable interest minus $50 cash interest), which is added to $912.50 to determine the $953.75 principal balance outstanding in the third year. At the end of the third year when the $1,000 face value of the bond is repaid, the investor reports $96.25 of taxable interest ($50 cash interest plus the remaining $46.25 of unrecovered discount).

In summary, the two methods provide the cash flows and taxable interest each year shown in Figure 22.1.

Since the amount of market discount that accrues before the maturity of the debt instrument is always less with the constant-rate method than with the straight-line method, investors are always better off for tax purposes if they elect to use the constant-rate method to compute accrued market discount.

Investors may choose not only the method for computing the accrued market discount, but may also decide when they will recognize the accrued market discount for tax purposes. Unless the investor elects otherwise, the accrued market discount will generally be recognized upon receipt of payments treated as principal payments. Alternatively, investors may elect to recognize market discount currently as it accrues, but before principal payments are actually received. In most cases, investors are better off deferring recognition of market discount until principal payments are received.

If mortgages in the pool are acquired at a market discount, the residual interest holders

– not the regular interest holders – will take the discount into income and pay any taxes that might be due. The residual holders have the same elections available to them for timing of recognition of market discounts as the regular interest holders do for their market discounts.

If the unpaid principal balance on a debt instrument is less than the investor's cost, the excess purchase price is deemed to be premium. Premium may be amortized and deducted by the investor over the life of the debt instrument using the constant-rate method.

d) Principal payments received are considered nontaxable return of capital to the extent of the investor's basis in the security, except to the extent of any market discount. (Payments of principal in excess of basis would typically arise only in circumstances where the investor contributed property instead of cash to acquire the securities, and the investor's basis in the contributed property was less than the fair market value.)

3. **RESIDUAL INTERESTS**

a) Residual interest holders must compute their taxable income from the REMIC on an accrual basis even if they are cash basis taxpayers for other purposes. In essence, they are taxed as if they owned a pro-rata partnership interest in the REMIC's taxable income. "REMIC taxable income" generally means the REMIC's gross income, including:

(i) interest;

(ii) original issue discount income;

(iii) accrued market discount income on the qualified mortgages owned by the REMIC; and

Figure 22.1

Year	Cash Interest	Straight-line				Constant-rate			
		Accrued Discount	Taxable Interest	Accum'd Discount	Accrued Discount	Taxable Interest	Accum'd Discount	Accrued Discount	Taxable Interest	Accum'd Discount
1	$50.00	$41.67	$91.67	$41.67	$37.50	$87.50	$37.50
2	50.00	41.67	91.67	83.34	41.25	91.25	78.75
3	50.00	41.66	91.66	125.00	46.25	96.25	125.00

(iv) income on reinvestment of cash flows and reserve assets;

minus deductions, including:

(i) interest and original issue discount expense on the REMIC bonds;

(ii) premium amortization;

(iii) servicing fees on qualified mortgages; and

(iv) bond administration expenses.

b) Taxable losses are limited to the residual holder's adjusted basis. (In other words, residual interest holders cannot take losses in excess of their investment in the interest.) However, losses may be carried over indefinitely and used to offset future income generated by the same REMIC.

c) An individual investor is allowed to deduct certain expenses, including expenses for the production of income (e.g., mortgage servicing fees and possibly administrative expenses of REMICs), but only to the extent that his miscellaneous deductions in the aggregate exceed 2% of the investor's adjusted gross income.

d) As a result of the multi-class structure of the regular interests, a REMIC's taxable income may include what is called "phantom income." Phantom or non-cash income arises as a result of timing differences between the recognition of accrued income on the underlying mortgages and the corresponding interest deductions for payments on the regular interests. It results, in part, from the fact that the interest deductions accrue at a rate that *increases* over time as the typically lower-yielding classes of REMIC bonds are retired, whereas the interest income on the underlying mortgages accrues at a *constant* rate. This phantom income in the early years will generally be recovered by offsetting "phantom losses" in the later years (when cash income exceeds taxable income).

e) Residual holders are also subject to a complicated set of rules that limit the deductions that may be passed through the REMIC to reduce their taxable income from the REMIC. In general, these rules provide that a residual holder's taxable income shall in no event be less than

what is called the "excess inclusion," which arises because of the phantom income problem described above.

f) In addition to reporting the taxable income of the REMIC, residual holders will have taxable income to the extent cash distributions from the REMIC exceed their bases in their residual interests. Basis is equal to the amount of money paid for the interest *increased* by the amount of taxable income reported by the holder, and *decreased* by the amount of loss reported by the holder. Cash distributions paid to the holder reduce the basis.

g) Gains or losses on the sale or exchange of residual interests or liquidation of the REMIC generally will be treated as capital gains or losses. However, certain losses on dispositions of residual interests will be disallowed or deferred if the seller of the interest, during a 6-month period before or after the disposition, acquires any residual interest in any REMIC that is economically comparable to the residual interest that was sold.

ALTERNATIVES

1. Many large mutual fund families offer funds that invest in mortgage-backed securities such as participation certificates (PCs) issued by GNMA, FNMA, FHLMC, private issuers, and CMOs. Minimum required investments are usually less than $2,500, which is considerably less than the $25,000 required for direct investment in participation certificates, and less than the minimum investment required for many REMIC bonds. They also allow investors to automatically reinvest interest, principal, or both, if desired. These mutual funds hold a broadly diversified portfolio of mortgage-backed securities with various maturities and yields. Therefore:

a) the yield uncertainty with mutual funds is typically less than with direct investments in PCs, CMOs, or REMIC bonds; and

b) the price volatility of a mutual fund generally will be less than with these instruments if the average maturity of the fund's portfolio is less than the maturity of these instruments.

However, mutual fund investors are not able to get the prepayment protection available to REMIC bond investors who acquire classes of REMIC bonds that do not repay principal until classes with shorter maturities are fully repaid.

2. Ginnie Maes, Fannie Maes, Freddie Macs and other PCs offered by private institutions possess many of the features of REMIC bonds, but without the flexibility to match the maturity to the desired holding period, and without the prepayment protection of the longer-maturity REMIC bonds. (Chapter 23, "Asset-Backed Securities," discusses the characteristics of PCs in more detail.)

3. Real Estate Investment Trusts (REITs) offer some of the same features as REMICs. In fact, some REITs may be organized as REMICs. (Chapter 21, "REITs (Real Estate Investment Trusts)," discusses the features of this investment vehicle.)

4. Expect to see mutual funds offering REMIC funds before long. These funds will provide investors with double diversification by pooling REMIC interests which themselves hold a pool of mortgages.

5. Collateralized mortgage obligations (CMOs) are mortgage-backed securities with features very similar to REMIC bonds.

WHERE AND HOW DO I GET IT?

Interests in REMICs can be acquired from a brokerage firm in much the same fashion as stocks and bonds. Thrift institutions and banks that offer investment services offer some issues.

WHAT FEES OR OTHER ACQUISITION COSTS ARE INVOLVED?

The fees or acquisition costs depend on how the investor acquires the security. Investors will pay no commission on new issues since the issuer or underwriter absorbs the initial sales costs. If the security is acquired in the secondary after-issue market, an investor can expect to pay a fee ranging from $2.50 to $20 per unit, depending on how many units are acquired. In most cases, the fee will not be less than $30.

HOW DO I SELECT THE BEST OF ITS TYPE?

REMICs are complex vehicles. To select the best of its type, an investor must evaluate the underlying mortgages backing the security and the characteristics of the security itself. Some of the distinctions an investor should consider when evaluating a REMIC include:

1. *The Identity of the Issuer of the Underlying Mortgages* – Mortgages guaranteed or backed by a U.S. government agency provide the highest degree of safety of principal. Those insured by private institutions, though still quite secure, are somewhat less safe than government-backed mortgages.

2. *The Types of Guarantees on the Underlying Mortgages* – Guarantees may assure that interest and principal are paid in a timely manner, or they may simply guarantee that interest is paid in a timely manner and that principal will ultimately be paid (perhaps up to a year after it is due). Some issues include hazard insurance as well, covering such risks as earthquakes and floods.

3. *The Risk-Return Tradeoff* – The safest mortgages with the most prompt payoff are those guaranteed by GNMA. They trade at a lower yield than other types of mortgages. Mortgages insured by private institutions trade at higher yields because of the slightly higher risk of default or delay in payment of principal. Mortgages insured by FNMA or FHLMC represent a middle ground with yields slightly higher than on GNMAs, but lower than on privately insured mortgages.

4. *The Quoted Yield and the Assumed Prepayment Rate on the Underlying Mortgages* – The return actually realized by an investor may differ substantially from the quoted yield if actual prepayments on the underlying mortgages differ substantially from the assumptions used to compute the quoted yield. (See "Questions and Answers," below, for a discussion of how the yield is computed.)

5. *The Characteristics of the Mortgage Pool that Serves as Collateral for the REMICs* – FHA and VA mortgages tend to prepay more slowly than conventional loans because they are often assumable and are not due on sale. Also, conventional mortgages tend to have higher original principal balances (because of the ceiling on the amount the FHA and VA will guarantee), which means they also imply higher-income homeowners who have a greater tendency to "trade up" or to relocate.

6. *The Similarity in the Coupon Rates and Maturity Dates of the Mortgages in the Pool* – Some REMICs

are issued from pools of mortgages that all have the same coupon rate; others may have mortgages having coupons spanning a range of rates. A pool of mortgages with a weighted average coupon rate of 10%, where individual mortgages within the pool have coupon rates ranging from 8% to 12%, is likely to have a different prepayment rate than a pool where all the mortgages in the pool have a coupon rate of 10%. Similarly, pools with varying final maturity dates on individual mortgages are likely to have a different prepayment pattern than pools where all the mortgages have the same final maturity date, even though the weighted average life is the same in both pools.

7. *The Pool Size and Diversification* – A larger, geographically diversified pool of mortgages is more likely to experience "average" prepayment experience than a smaller, less geographically diversified pool. However, it may be easier to estimate actual prepayment experience for a smaller, geographically isolated pool of mortgages.

8. *The Relative Size and Number of Classes of REMIC Bonds in the Issue* – A particular class has protection from prepayments as long as a faster-paying class exists. If the first few classes are small relative to the size of the overall issue, they could be paid off quickly if the actual prepayment rate is higher than expected.

9. *The Return on Collection Accounts and Reserve Funds* – Payments of interest and principal on the underlying mortgages may not correspond with the timing of payments to REMIC bondholders. Consequently, the issuer must place cash flows from the underlying mortgages in a collection account invested in high-grade, money-market instruments until the funds are paid to REMIC bondholders. In some cases, the REMIC has reserve funds that serve as additional collateral for the regular interests. The bond rating agencies require that the issuer assume a conservative below-market reinvestment rate (3% to 5%) on these short-term investments. That assumption is built into the quoted yield. Some issuers use the excess earned on these funds over the assumed rate to pay off principal on the earliest maturing classes. This shortens the effective maturity of the REMIC bonds and raises the realized yield over the quoted yield. Other issuers pay the excess cash flow to the residual interest hold-

ers. Factors affecting the quoted yield and the potential yield investors can expect on REMIC bonds include: (a) the size of the collection and reserve funds; (b) the rate assumed to be earned on these funds; and (c) whether the issuer uses the excess earned on these funds to pay off the REMIC bonds.

10. *The Existence of a Secondary Market in the Securities or the Presence of a Put or Redemption Feature for the REMIC Bondholder* – Liquidity varies considerably among REMIC offerings. In some cases, issuers, together with the underwriting syndicate of investment bankers, agree to make a secondary market in the securities to make the offering more attractive to potential investors. Also, some issues have a put (i.e., sell back) feature that allows bondholders to redeem their bonds before maturity, subject to certain limits and restrictions. This additional liquidity comes at a price. Typically, REMICs with such features will yield less than those without them.

WHERE CAN I FIND OUT MORE ABOUT IT?

Investment bankers and brokerage firms that have underwritten these offerings have brochures available that describe the basic operation of these types of securities. Since REMICs are complex instruments and each offering has its own characteristics, the only thorough description of any given REMIC is the initial offering prospectus, which can be acquired from brokers who participate in the offering. Also, brokerage firms making a secondary market in these securities should be able to provide bid and ask price quotes and yield information.

For a broad discussion of REMICs consider the following articles:

1. Robert A. Rudnick and Joseph R. Parise, "Real Estate Mortgage Investment Conduits: An Introduction," *The Journal of Taxation of Investments* (Summer 1987), pp. 238-257.

2. Michael Hirchfeld and Thomas A. Humphreys, "Tax Reform Brings New Certainty to Mortgage-Backed Securities," *The Journal of Taxation* (May 1987), pp. 280-286.

3. Arnold C. Johnson, "Real Estate Mortgage Investment Conduits – A Flexible New Tax Structure for Issuers and Investors," *Tax Notes* (March 2, 1987), pp. 911-918.

4. Charles M. Levitin, "REMICs: Removing Tax Obstacles to More Efficient Trading of Mortgage-backed Securities," *Real Estate Review* (Summer 1987), pp. 26-34.

For a discussion of all types of loan-backed securities, including mortgage-backed securities and securities backed by non-mortgage loans, consider: Christine Pavel, "Securitization," *Economic Perspectives*, Federal Reserve Bank of Chicago, Vol. 10, No. 5 (July/August 1986), pp. 16-31.

QUESTIONS AND ANSWERS

Question – How is the yield on a REMIC bond determined?

Answer – To determine the actual yield on a REMIC bond an investor must analyze and assess two key factors: (1) the probability of realizing the quoted yield; and (2) the probability of realizing the expected maturity. Both the yield quotation and the projected maturity depend on the specific prepayment assumption. Realized prepayment depends on the demographic, financial, and contractual nature of the underlying mortgage assets as well as on the structure of the REMIC issue itself.

1. The quoted yield on a REMIC bond is the "internal rate of return" (IRR) of all cash inflows (i.e., the interest and principal payments) and cash outflows (i.e., the price paid for the security). Simply stated, the IRR can be viewed as follows: if the investor placed the purchase price of the REMIC bond in an interest bearing savings account paying interest equal to the IRR, he could withdraw cash from the account exactly matching the projected cash flows from the security with no balance left over. The quoted yield (IRR) depends critically on when prepayments of principal are assumed to occur. The problem is that yields have been quoted in different ways by different dealers, making comparisons based on quoted yields all but impossible.

2. The yield actually realized by an investor may vary significantly from the quoted yield depending on when prepayments of principal actually occur compared to the assumed prepayments that were used to calculate the quoted yields.

Investors who buy REMIC bonds at a "premium" (i.e., when the promised interest

rate exceeds current market rates of return for comparable securities) will realize yields that are less than the quoted yields if actual prepayments are faster than assumed prepayments. Conversely, realized yields will be higher than quoted yields if actual prepayments are slower than assumed prepayments.

Investors who buy REMIC bonds at a "discount" (i.e., when the promised interest rate is less than current market rates for comparable securities) will realize yields that are less than the quoted yields if actual prepayments are slower than assumed prepayments. Realized yields will be greater than quoted yields if actual prepayments are faster than assumed prepayments.

Investors who buy REMIC bonds at "par" (i.e., when the promised interest rate is equal to current market rates for comparable securities) will realize yields equal to the quoted yield, regardless of when prepayments occur.

In addition, regardless of whether investors purchase their interests at a premium, at a discount, or at par, the timing of actual prepayments will significantly affect their potential total return, including reinvestment. Specifically, if actual prepayments are faster than assumed and interest rates have fallen, reinvestment return will be lower than expected. If interest rates have risen, reinvestment return will increase. Conversely, if actual prepayments are slower than assumed, reinvestment return will be either higher or lower than expected depending on whether interest rates have risen or fallen, respectively.

3. The quoted yield will not accurately reflect an investor's potential realized yield unless actual prepayments equal assumed prepayments. The larger the difference between assumed and actual prepayments, the greater the difference between the quoted and realized yield will be. Consequently, to compare potential investments in mortgage-backed securities and to determine a realistic estimate of the potential yield, investors must understand the types of prepayment assumptions that are used to compute quoted yields.

The weighted average life (WAL) is commonly used in the secondary mortgage market as a measure of the effective maturity of a mortgage pool. The slower the assumed payments, the longer the WAL. Likewise, the shorter the WAL, the faster the assumed prepayments. A number of conventional specifications of assumed prepayment rates have been used.

The first and simplest specification is to assume the "standard mortgage yield." This specification assumes there are no prepayments whatsoever until year 12 on 30-year mortgages, when all the mortgages in the pool are assumed to prepay entirely. Of course, some prepayments are inevitable before year 12. Therefore, a quoted yield based on this "standard" prepayment assumption seriously understates the potential yield on a security trading at a deep discount, and overstates the potential yield on one selling at a premium.

A second prepayment specification bases assumed prepayments on FHA experience. The FHA compiles historical data on the actual incidence of prepayments on the mortgage loans it insures. The quoted yield is determined by assuming some ratio of FHA experience. For example, if prepayments are expected to be slower than historical FHA experience, a ratio of 75% of the FHA experience might be used. The benefit of this method is that it uses historically validated assumptions, including in particular

the tendency to have higher prepayments in the first few years of the mortgage pool than in later years. The problem with this method is that it incorporates information on a variety of market conditions and mortgages that may not reflect the attributes of the underlying mortgage pool. Figure 22.2 shows the annual FHA prepayment rates based on 1981 experience.

A third prepayment specification is the constant prepayment rate (CPR). This specification assumes that the percentage of the principal balance that is prepaid during a given year is a constant, such as 6%. Because of its simplicity, the CPR method has often been used to determine quoted yields. Figure 22.2 shows the annual prepayment rates based on a 4% constant assumed rate.

Finally, many quoted yields are now based on the standard prepayment experience offered by the Public Securities Association (PSA), an industry trade group. The PSA's goal is to bring some standardization to the marketplace. Essentially, the PSA standard is a combination of the FHA experience method and the CPR method. The first 30 months of the PSA standard calls for a steadily rising prepayment rate. After that, the rate is assumed constant at 6%. Figure 22.2 shows the assumed annual prepayments using the PSA

Figure 22.2

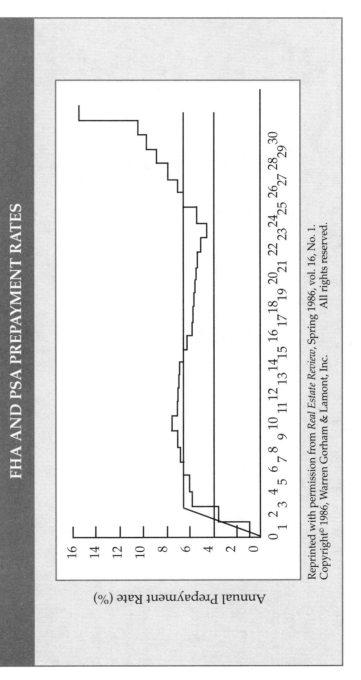

FHA AND PSA PREPAYMENT RATES

standard method. Similar to the FHA method, the quoted yield may be computed using some ratio of the PSA standard if prepayments are expected to be faster or slower than the normal. For example, 150% of the PSA standard would project prepayment rates that are half as great as under normal conditions.

Question – How do REMICs operate to reduce the prepayment risk inherent in other mortgage-backed securities, such as pass-through participation certificates?

Answer – One problem investors have with mortgage-backed participation certificates (PCs), such as Ginnie Maes, is that their maturity is uncertain due to the unpredictability of prepayments. PCs on a given mortgage pool are all identical, have a single stated maturity, and pass through a pro rata share of all cash flows to all participants in the mortgage pool. REMIC bonds are debt instruments, not pass-through securities. Consequently, instead of having a single stated maturity, they bear maturities that are staggered or "fast-pay, slow-pay." In other words, some classes of interests (technically called "tranches") receive all the principal that is repaid on the underlying mortgages before others. Within each tranche, cash flow is distributed in a pro rata fashion. By packaging a mortgage pool in such a way, investors have the opportunity to acquire securities with short-term, intermediate-term, or long-term characteristics, even though the mortgages backing the securities may have 25-year or 30-year maturities.

Figure 22.3 shows how a REMIC backed by a pool of 30-year mortgages and with three tranches of securities would operate. Panel A of Figure 22.3 shows the cash flows of a typical PC based on a pool of 30-year mortgages assuming a 6% annual prepayment rate. The height of the bars indicates the relative magnitude of the anticipated cash flows each year. The dark section of each bar represents the principal repayment portion of each cash flow and the remaining portion represents interest. The weighted average life (WAL) is 11.57 years. If prepayments materialized as assumed, a PC holder would receive decreasing payments of interest and principal over the life of the certificate.

Panel B shows the cash-flow pattern of the Class A securities that receive all scheduled and unscheduled principal payments on the pool until that class is entirely paid off. The WAL of the Class A securities is just over three years. The Class B securities (panel C) are paid interest only until the Class A securities are paid off and then all principal payments are allocated to the Class B securities. The WAL of the Class B securities is about 10½ years. Finally, the Class C securities (Panel D) are paid interest only until the Class B securities are paid off and then all principal payments are allocated to class C securities until the mortgage pool is liquidated. The WAL of the Class C securities is about 21 years.

Question – May issuers of REMICs offer a redemption feature?

Answer – Yes, issuers may offer a redemption feature to make the offering more attractive to investors and enhance marketability. These securities include a "put" (i.e., sell back right) that allows holders to redeem their securities at par value before maturity, subject to limits. In this manner investors are even better able to pick their desired maturity. This put option is usually combined with a "call" (i.e., buy back) provision and a "sinking fund" provision that allows the issuer to redeem some or all of the securities before maturity. In these circumstances, the redemption fund is equal to the amount that has built up in the sinking fund. Security holders who wish to redeem their bonds may do so to the extent funds are available in the redemption fund. If desired redemptions exceed the amount in the redemption fund, redemptions are usually allowed on a first-come, first-served basis within a specified priority schedule. For instance, priority may begin first to deceased bondholders for up to $100,000 each; second, to all other holders for up to $10,000 each; third, to any remaining bonds for deceased bondholders; and finally, to any other redemption requests in the order received.

Typically, if desired redemptions do not exceed the amount in the redemption fund on specified dates, the issuer will "call" (i.e., redeem) additional bonds, determined by random lot, until the redemption fund is depleted.

Question – Can one class of REMIC bonds be subordinated to another class?

Answer – Yes. An interest in a REMIC will still be considered a regular interest even if the payments of principal are subordinated to other regular interests. Issuers may use this arrangement to make the senior class more attractive to investors. If cash flows are insufficient to pay principal and interest on all securities, the senior class will be paid first.

Figure 22.3

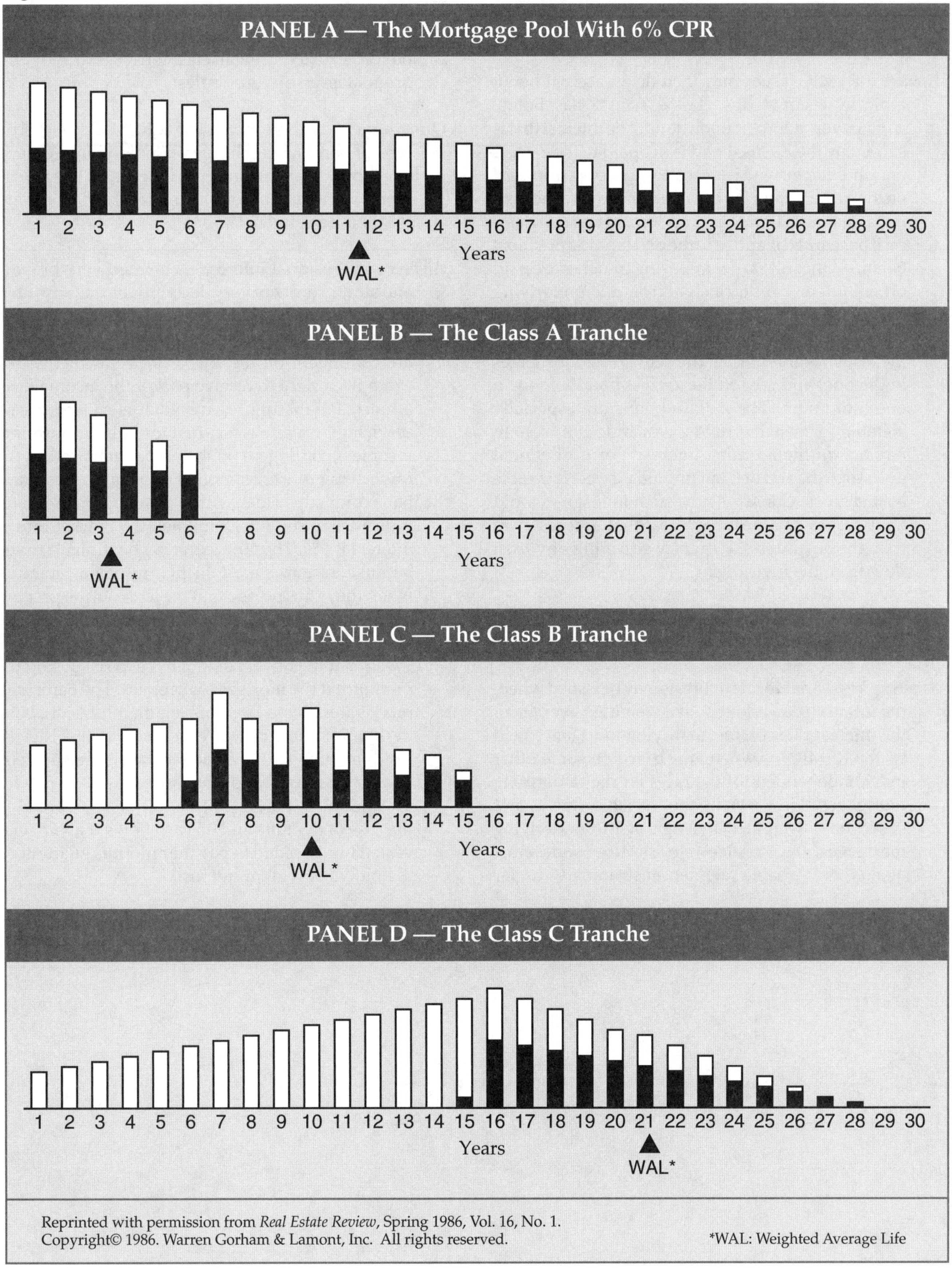

PANEL A — The Mortgage Pool With 6% CPR

Years

WAL*

PANEL B — The Class A Tranche

Years

WAL*

PANEL C — The Class B Tranche

Years

WAL*

PANEL D — The Class C Tranche

Years

WAL*

*WAL: Weighted Average Life

Reprinted with permission from *Real Estate Review*, Spring 1986, Vol. 16, No. 1.
Copyright© 1986. Warren Gorham & Lamont, Inc. All rights reserved.

Question – What is a "full accrual bond" (also called a "Z-class bond")?

Answer – REMIC issues may include an accrual bond, typically designated as "class Z." The "Z class bond" is effectively a zero-coupon bond. The interest that is earned by the Z-class bond is not paid to the Z-class bondholder; instead it is used to pay down principal on the earlier maturing tranches, effectively shortening their maturities. The compounded accrued interest that has earned is added to the outstanding principal balance. Once all earlier maturing tranches are paid off, all interest and principal from the underlying mortgage pool is paid to the Z-class bondholders. Often, when all other tranches have been paid off, the issuer will liquidate the remaining mortgages in the pool and pay off the Z-class bondholders in one lump sum. The Z-class bonds are especially suitable for pension funds, which do not have to pay tax on the accruing interest. For unsheltered investors, the accrued but unpaid interest is taxable as it accrues. Consequently, such investors would have to pay tax on the interest that accrues even though they are not currently receiving any cash flow from the investment.

Question – May REMICs issue REMIC bonds with variable interest rates?

Answer – Yes. Variable rate interests may be issued where the interest paid is based on a weighted average of the interest rates on the qualifying mortgages held by the REMIC, or where it is based on some other index independent of the rates on the underlying mortgages. However, if the variable rate is not based on a weighted average of the underlying mortgages, the variable rate REMIC bonds must qualify as "variable rate debt instruments" under regulations dealing with original issue discount. These regulations insure that the variable rates are not constructed in such a fashion so as to avoid the original issue discount rules.

Question – A regular interest in a REMIC is clearly a type of bond where the owner looks to interest and principal payments in return for his or her investment. But what do residual interest holders receive for their investment?

Answer – A "residual interest" is defined very broadly and simply (but not very descriptively) as any interest that is not a regular interest. Generally, residual interests are meant to be rights to payments that are contingent on the speed of prepayments. For example, a right to receive part of the income from a mortgage that represents what is called "excess servicing" may be a residual interest because that income is contingent on the prepayment rate of the underlying mortgage pool. For instance, assume a bank originates a loan with a 10% coupon rate. Later it decides to sell the loan when the market rate of interest is 9%. The 10% loan may be difficult to sell because investors are reluctant to pay a premium when they run the risk that the loan will be prepaid before the premium is amortized. Therefore, the bank therefore sells the loan at a lower price to yield 9% so that the buyers do not have to risk losing the premium if the mortgage is prepaid. The bank then retains the excess 1%. This retained interest above the market rate is called "excess servicing." REMIC residual interests may also receive the earnings on qualified reserve funds that are set aside to pay for unexpected expenses or as additional collateral in the case of defaults and on cash flows that are reinvested until needed to pay the amounts guaranteed to holders of regular interests.

Chapter 23

ASSET-BACKED SECURITIES

WHAT IS IT?

Asset-backed securities (ABS) are debt-type securities that are secured by a pool of similar debt obligations or receivables. The market for these securities arose in the early 1980s with the advent of mortgage-backed securities (MBS). Now virtually all forms of debt obligations and receivables have been securitized in the United States: residential mortgages; home equity loans; manufactured housing loans; timeshare loans; auto, truck, RV, aircraft and boat loans and leases; credit card receivables; equipment loans and leases; small business loans; student loans; trade receivables (of just about any type – e.g., airline tickets, telecommunications receivables, toll road receipts); and lottery winnings. Although the basic concepts – many based upon tax and accounting effects and desired results – are essentially the same, each asset class presents unique structuring considerations, and the players are constantly looking for ways to improve structures to achieve higher ratings (and thus lower costs) and to reduce expenses. Securitizations outside the United States have been more limited, but the market is growing. In Latin America the principal asset class to be securitized has been trade receivables (primarily the "future flow" from trade receivables).

For most non-corporate or non-institutional investors, mortgage-backed securities are the most familiar and accessible class of asset-backed securities. Mortgage-backed securities are simply ownership of an interest in a pool of residential mortgages. A trustee is assigned to hold the titles to all mortgages in the pool and to see that all mortgages and properties are in acceptable form and that payments are properly made.

Three of the best-known sources of these instruments are the Government National Mortgage Association (GNMA), the Federal National Mortgage Association (FNMA), and the Federal Home Loan Mortgage Corporation (FHLMC). GNMA is a wholly-owned U.S. government corporation within the Department of Housing and Urban Development. FNMA is a government-sponsored corporation owned entirely by private stockholders, though it is regulated by the Department of Housing and Urban Development. FHLMC was created by Congress and is owned by the twelve Federal Home Loan Banks. The securities they issue are appropriately

nicknamed, "Ginnie Maes," "Fannie Maes," and "Freddie Macs." State and local government agencies, as well as institutions in the private sector, such as the Bank of America, also issue various types of mortgage-backed securities. These privately issued securities are known collectively as "Connie Macs."

Although the markets and types of non-mortgage asset-backed securities are growing rapidly, the principal market for non-institutional investors is still mortgage-backed securities. Consequently, this chapter will focus on mortgage-backed securities.

WHEN IS THE USE OF THIS TOOL INDICATED?

1. When an investor desires a relatively secure type of investment that in most cases is guaranteed by the United States Treasury or a federal agency. Large money center banks that also offer a high degree of security generally offer private issues. Another factor contributing to the safety of these issues is the broad geographical distribution of the underlying mortgages. Many mortgage-backed securities obtain their underlying mortgages from throughout the country and, therefore, are not overly influenced by economic conditions in any one state or region.

2. When the investor desires a relatively high rate of return. The competitive yield on instruments such as GNMAs is generally higher than other long-term government securities.

3. When the investor requires a high level of cash flow. These instruments typically provide monthly payments that consist of both interest and the return of some portion of the loan principal. Payments to investors in the pass-through type of instrument may vary somewhat from month to month because some mortgages within the pool may be paid off before maturity and others may be partially prepaid.

4. When the investor desires a high level of liquidity. There is a very active secondary market for these issues because they are bought and sold through

investment bankers, and their price and yield quotations are easily found in the financial sections of most major newspapers.

5. When the investor seeks to diversify his portfolio beyond stocks and corporate bonds. Mortgage-backed securities are essentially an investment in real estate and, therefore, provide an alternative to money market funds and other income-oriented corporate securities.

ADVANTAGES

1. Mortgage-backed bonds are virtually risk-free in terms of return of principal and certainty of income.

2. Because interest rates on residential mortgages are usually higher than short-term money market rates or even long-term corporate bond rates, these issues provide one of the highest rates of return available from debt instruments. GNMAs, for example, offer the highest yield of any actively traded, federally guaranteed security. They have tended to yield 15% to 20% more than the yield on intermediate Treasury bonds. They have also outperformed AAA-rated corporate bonds over the period from 1985 through 2005 by about 5%.

3. Holders of mortgage-backed securities are usually guaranteed a monthly payment of interest and principal, whether or not the issuer has actually collected these sums. (In the case of "straight pass-through" certificates, GNMA guarantees only the proper performance of the mortgage servicing and the payment of only that interest and principal actually collected. In the case of "modified pass-through" certificates, GNMA guarantees the timely payment of principal and interest, whether or not collected by the originating association.)

4. Payments are generally made by the fifteenth day of the calendar month following the month in which collections on mortgages are made. Monthly principal payments to investors may actually increase at times because homeowners may voluntarily pay off their mortgage loans (e.g., when they sell their homes), or accelerate payments of principal (e.g., to reduce the term of their mortgage and the overall amount of interest paid on the loan.)

5. There is a well-developed secondary market for mortgage-backed securities, especially for those issued by federal agencies. In the private sector,

the larger the issuer, the more active the market for mortgage-backed securities of that issuer. This means that investors will have little or no difficulty in selling their securities if the need arises.

However, the selling price of an issue is not guaranteed and is subject to change as the level of mortgage interest rates changes. For example, if mortgage rates rise, the price of previously issued securities tends to decline because more attractive rates are available in the marketplace. Likewise, if rates fall, the price of existing issues will tend to increase.

6. Early repayments of mortgage loans may be subject to prepayment penalties. This operates to the advantage of the investor since these amounts are passed through and added to his monthly income.

DISADVANTAGES

1. Like other interest-sensitive assets, the price of mortgage-backed securities will tend to fall when market interest rates rise. This potential for capital depreciation could seriously affect the investor who is forced to sell his investment before it matures.

2. Mortgage-backed securities are subject to two types of inflation risk: (1) the risk that the purchasing power of their income will be eroded over time; and (2) the risk that the purchasing power of capital received at maturity will have diminished. This second risk is minimized to a degree by the very nature of the instrument itself – the investor constantly recovers principal that is available for reinvestment or current consumption.

3. A direct investment in mortgage-backed securities is difficult for many investors because a high minimum investment is required. For instance, a GNMA certificate has a principal value of $25,000 at its inception. (The actual amount an investor pays may be less than $25,000 if the pool of mortgages has been in existence for some time and some of the original principal has been repaid.) However, this disadvantage may be overcome by investing in mutual funds that specialize in mortgage-backed securities. These funds are discussed in more detail below.

4. Mortgage-backed securities carry the risk that the underlying mortgages will be paid off more quickly than anticipated and, thus, the holder will receive the stated interest for a shorter time period than desired.

Figure 23.1

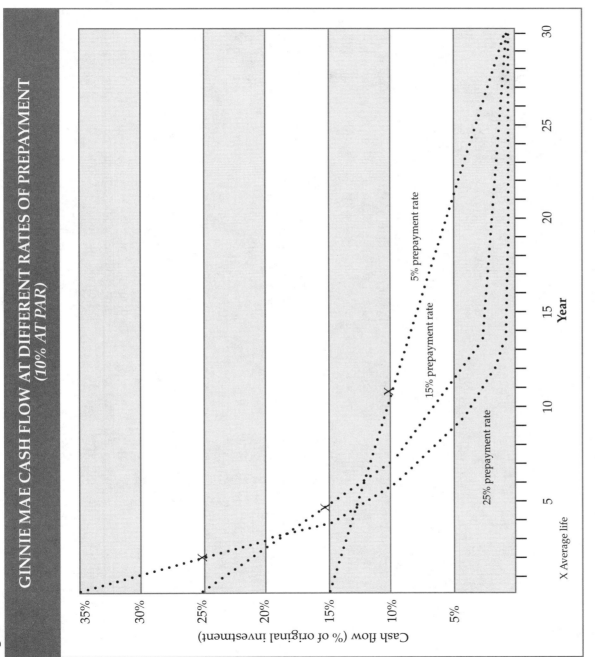

GINNIE MAE CASH FLOW AT DIFFERENT RATES OF PREPAYMENT
(10% AT PAR)

Mortgages are prepaid for a variety of reasons as homeowners relocate and refinance. The prepayment experiences on mortgage-backed securities vary depending on the underlying mortgages, and there is no way of accurately predicting an individual security's life. However, the general level of interest rates will affect prepayments because refinancing becomes more or less economically advantageous. For example, a new 30-year mortgage would have an average life of 21 years based on the scheduled amortization included in the monthly payments. When a large group of these mortgages are aggregated, however, about 10% of these mortgages on average are pre-paid when interest rates and housing conditions remain constant. If you assume an annual prepayment rate of 10%, a mortgage pool's average prepayment rate of 10%, a mortgage pool's average life is reduced to about 8 years. This average life could

be even shorter, though, if market interest rates decline substantially below the existing mortgage rates, leading more homeowners to refinance. Conversely, when interest rise substantially above the existing mortgage rates, fewer homeowners refinance and mortgage-backed securities will tend to be paid off more slowly than otherwise anticipated.

Figure 23.1 shows the cash flow patterns for three mortgage securities in which the underlying mortgages are prepaid at annual rates of 5%, 15%, and 25%. The mortgage securities with prepayments running at about 15% provide annual cash flows (both interest and principal) of 20% to 25% of one's initial investment in the first few years, with declining rates of cash flow as the years pass. In contrast, the mortgage security that is experiencing 5% in prepayments has a much steadier cash flow. The security experiencing 25% prepayments has even higher cash flows in the initial years. As the figure illustrates, owning a portfolio of mortgage securities is like owning a substantial portion of bonds with a relatively short maturity, a moderate portion of bonds with an intermediate maturity, and a small portion of bonds with a long maturity. This helps explain why mortgage securities generally experience less dramatic interest-rate-related price changes than most 10-year-or-longer maturity bonds.

5. Since the periodic payments from mortgage-backed securities include both interest and a return of principal, mortgage-backed bondholders face greater reinvestment risk than regular bondholders. The periodic payments must be reinvested and if interest rates have fallen, that money will be reinvested at lower rates, thus, lowering future total return. Also, prepayments generally accelerate when it is least desirable from the mortgage-backed security holder's point of view. If market interest rates decline substantially below the existing mortgage rates, more homeowners are likely to refinance, forcing the mortgage-backed security holder to reinvest the payments at lower yields. Conversely, prepayments are generally delayed when it is most desired (i.e., under conditions of higher interest rates).

Investors who purchase mortgage-backed securities at a premium in the secondary market are especially high risk from early prepayment. Rapid payoffs will reduce their realized yield. This occurs because investors are unlikely to fully amortize (i.e., recover) the premium before the bonds are repaid.

TAX IMPLICATIONS

1. The interest income from mortgage-backed securities is reportable as ordinary income in the year received. Each investor will receive from the issuer a monthly statement indicating what part of the distribution represents (1) scheduled amortization of principal, (2) interest, and (3) unscheduled collection of principal.

2. The portion of each monthly payment that represents the return of principal is a nontaxable repayment of the original investment. However, in some cases, principal payments may represent a discount on the purchase of the mortgages in the past or, if the bond is acquired in the secondary market, a market discount, and to this extent must be included as ordinary income. The investor must therefore report as ordinary income his ratable share of any discount income realized on the purchase of each of the mortgages in the pool under the "original issue discount" and "market discount" rules. These rules are discussed in more detail in Chapter 43, "Taxation of Investment Vehicles."

3. Prepayment penalties, assumption fees, and late payment charges passed through to the investor are ordinary income reportable in the year received.

4. Gains on the sale of these issues are typically capital gains. But, if an investor purchased a new issue at a discount (called "original issue discount" – see Chapter 43), the remaining unrecognized portion of the discount will be taxed as ordinary income. Similarly, any remaining unrecognized market discount will be taxed as ordinary income.

5. Amounts withheld from the investor by the issuer of the certificate to pay servicing, custodian, and guarantee fees are expenses incurred for the production of income and as such are deductible as miscellaneous itemized deductions. However, these miscellaneous items must be combined with certain miscellaneous items from other sources, and the total is deductible only to the extent it exceeds 2% of the investor's adjusted gross income.

ALTERNATIVES

1. Many large mutual fund organizations sponsor funds that specialize in mortgage-backed securities. They invest shareholders' funds in a diversified portfolio of securities issued by GNMA, FNMA, the Federal Home Loan Mortgage Corporation, and private issuers such as the Bank of America. These funds are particularly attractive to small investors who may not be able to invest $25,000 directly in mortgage-backed securities. They also offer automatic monthly reinvestment of interest, principal, or both, for investors who do not need additional income. In some cases mutual funds employ financial futures as well as put and call options to hedge against changes in interest rates that affect the rate of prepayments. This provides investors with some additional protection against the prepayment risk and reinvestment risk inherent in direct ownership of mortgage-backed securities.

2. Real Estate Investment Trusts (REITs) offer some of the same features as mortgage-backed securities

even though they are quite different in form. Investors in REITs purchase common shares in the REIT instead of bonds. These funds are then invested by the investment trust in a diversified portfolio of real estate such as apartment buildings, shopping centers, office complexes, and real estate mortgages. In order to qualify as a real estate investment trust under the Internal Revenue Code, 90% of the entity's income must be obtained from rents, dividends, interest, and gains from the sale of securities and real estate properties. REITs are discussed in Chapter 21.

3. Collateralized mortgage obligations and Real Estate Mortgage Investment Conduits (REMICs) are quite similar in many respects to pass-through participation certificates and other mortgage-backed-bonds. These are discussed in Chapter 22.

WHERE AND HOW DO I GET IT?

An investor can call a brokerage firm and purchase mortgage-backed securities in much the same fashion as stocks and bonds. Also, these issues may be purchased through those banks and thrift institutions that offer their customers investment services.

WHAT FEES OR OTHER ACQUISITION COSTS ARE INVOLVED?

Investors can expect to pay a modest commission or service charge to the brokerage firm or bank handling the transaction. This fee is typically $15 to $25 for each thousand dollars invested, and the fee may be included in the total cost of the securities purchased rather than shown separately as a commission or service charge.

HOW DO I SELECT THE BEST OF ITS TYPE?

At first glance it may appear that all mortgage-backed securities are similar. Yet there are a number of distinctions an investor should consider in the selection process. These include:

1. *The Identity of the Issuer* – A United States government guarantee assures the investor of the highest degree of safety of principal. A guarantee by a private mortgage issuer (e.g., the Bank of America) may be safe, and yet an investor should not have quite the same level of confidence that those payments of principal and interest will be made.

2. *The Age of the Mortgages in the Pool* – The payments received from older mortgages are made up of larger amounts of mortgage principal and smaller amounts of interest. This is because the early payments made on a mortgage are almost all interest and only a small amount is used to reduce the outstanding principal of the loan. Principal amounts in excess of basis will be taxed as capital gains, while interest will be taxed as ordinary income.

3. *The Nature of the Underlying Mortgages Included in the Pool* – Safety of principal and certainty of income payments depend upon: (a) the quality of the mortgages; (b) the number and size of the mortgages; (c) the distribution of mortgage maturities; and (d) the geographic distribution of mortgages. These factors will affect the amount of monthly cash flow and the breakdown between principal and interest as well as the regularity, predictability, and certainty of payment.

4. *The Guarantees on the Security and the Mortgages* – There are four types of guarantees that are given by issuers in order to enhance their creditworthiness. These include the following: (a) guarantees on interest payments; (b) guarantees on principal payments; (c) mortgage guarantee insurance; and (d) hazard insurance (covering such risks as earthquakes and floods). Because not all of these guarantees will apply to every issue, the investor should select the issues that provide those guarantees that are most important to him.

5. *The Risk-Return Tradeoff* – The securities that provide the lowest level of risk and that offer the most prompt payment (i.e., GNMAs) trade at a lower yield than other mortgage-backed securities. Conversely, various private issues trade at much higher yields because of their somewhat higher risk. A compromise is the Freddie Mac issue, which provides a level of security and guarantee of timely payment only slightly lower than a GNMA, but that may trade at a yield ranging from 15 to 40 basis points higher.

The table in Figure 23.2 illustrates the various factors that should be considered by an investor with respect to each of the major types of mortgage-backed securities.

Figure 23.2

TYPES OF MORTGAGE-BACKED SECURITIES

	Ginnie Mae	Freddie Mac PC	Freddie Mac GMC	FNMA CMBS	Mortgage-Backed Bond
Payment Stream	Monthly; guaranteed 15-day delay; Periodic prepayments.	Monthly; guaranteed 44-day delay; Periodic prepayments.	Semi-annually; annual principal payments.	Monthly; guaranteed 25-day delay; Periodic prepayments.	Semi-annually; principal at maturity or sale.
Underlying Asset	FHA/VA mortgages.	Conventional mortgages.	Conventional mortgages.	Conventional mortgages.	General assets.
Guarantee	Full faith and credit of U.S. Treasury.	Freddie Mac net worth; private mortgage insurance on mortgages with LTV over 80.	Freddie Mac net worth; private mortgage insurance on mortgages with LTV over 80.	Freddie Mac net worth; private mortgage insurance on mortgages with LTV over 80.	Overcollateralized by 150-200% with mortgage portfolio.
Liquidity/ Secondary Market	Active market due to high volume of issue, risk-free status.	Active market due to high volume of issue, low-risk status.	Less active due to high volume of issue, lower issue volume.	Unknown at this time.	Same as Institution PC.
First Issued	1970	1971	1971	1981	1975
Rating/Risk Equivalent.	Government security; no rating required.	Considered nearly equivalent to a government security; no rating.	Same as Freddie Mac PC.	Same as Freddie Mac PC.	AAA due to continuous maintenance of overcollateralized position.

WHERE CAN I FIND OUT MORE ABOUT IT?

1. Listings of mortgage-backed securities issued by GNMA and FNMA are carried daily in the *Wall Street Journal* (www.wsj.com) and other major newspapers. These listings show the securities available, current prices, and the yield on each issue.

2. The larger brokerage houses and mortgage banking firms publish a variety of booklets on mortgage-backed securities. Two of the best sources of information are First Boston Corporation and Salomon Brothers, both located in New York City. An excellent guide to mortgage-backed securities and other U. S. government issues is the *Handbook of Securities of the United States Government and Federal Agencies* published by First Boston Corporation.

QUESTIONS AND ANSWERS

Question – What are the two major types of mortgage-backed securities?

Answer – The two general types of mortgage-backed securities are: (1) pass-through certificates, and (2) mortgage-backed bonds. In the pass-through arrangement, investors actually own a share of the pooled mortgages. The stream of income generated by payments of principal and interest on mortgage loans is passed through to the investor. Mortgage-backed bonds are general obligations of issuing institutions and do not constitute a sale of assets as is the case with the pass-through arrangement. This debt is collateralized by a pool of mortgages that is held by a trustee representing the bondholders. Payments of principal and interest on mortgage-backed bonds are made out of the institution's overall asset earnings generated primarily through mortgage loans.

Question – How does a pass-through certificate work?

Answer – There are several variations of pass-through certificates. A *straight pass-through* pays principal and interest as they are collected from the mortgage pool. If payments on the underlying mortgages are delayed, payments to holders of pass-through investors are similarly delayed. A *partially modified pass-through* guarantees that monthly principal and interest payments will be made to a certain extent, even if not collected from the mortgage pool. For example, the issuer might guarantee payments up to 5% of the original or current principal amount of the certificate. A *modified pass-through* guarantees

Chapter 23 – Asset-Backed Securities

payment of the scheduled monthly principal and interest payments, irrespective of the amounts that are collected from the mortgage pool.

Question – What types of mortgage-backed bonds are there?

Answer – There are essentially four types of mortgage-backed bonds:

1. *pay-through* bonds;

2. *straight mortgage-backed* bonds;

3. *collateralized mortgage obligations (CMOs)*; and

4. *Real Estate Mortgage Investment Conduit (REMIC)* bonds.

Pay-throughs (also called "cash-flow" bonds) are designed so that the required amortization from the pool of mortgages will at all times be at least equal to the payments of both interest, at the coupon rate, and scheduled principal on the bonds. Additional payments of principal are made to bondholders when there are prepayments on the mortgage pool. Therefore, the life of the bonds is determined by the life of the mortgage pool. Although these instruments are treated differently than pass-throughs from the issuer's standpoint (because they are considered the debt of the issuer rather than a sale of claims on the underlying mortgage pool), they are functionally equivalent to pass-throughs from the investor's perspective. (Some pay-throughs are not fully amortizing; some may have balloon payments due at maturity.)

Straight mortgage-backed bonds are similar to conventional corporate bonds, except that a mortgage pool rather than the general assets of a regular corporation secures them. They feature scheduled interest payments on a monthly, quarterly, semi-annual, or annual basis. Principal is typically not scheduled to be repaid until the bonds mature, although interim principal repayments are not uncommon. The issuer is often required to maintain a specified amount of mortgages in the mortgage pool. If a mortgage is prepaid or foreclosed, the issuer usually must substitute similar mortgages into the pool. Many straight mortgage-backed bonds are callable at the discretion of the issuer, similar to most conventional corporate bonds. In many cases these issues have a sinking fund feature that requires the issuer to deposit principal

received on the underlying mortgages in an escrow account and to call (i.e., buy back) a specified portion of the outstanding bonds at specified intervals or when the sinking fund reaches certain levels. The bonds are generally called by random lot. In other words, some bondholders, determined at random, are periodically required to redeem their bonds before the maturity date.

Collateralized mortgage obligations (CMOs) and *REMIC bonds* (i.e., regular interests in REMICs) are more complicated hybrid securities combining features of pass-through certificates and conventional corporate bonds. These bond issues typically have several classes of interests (technically called "tranches") with differing rights to interest and principal from the underlying mortgage pool. They are designed to give investors the benefit of the high yields characteristic of other mortgage-backed securities without the same degree of uncertainty as to when principal will be repaid. Because of their importance as well as their unique and complex features, CMOs and REMICs are discussed in Chapter 22 and will not be discussed further in the remainder of this chapter.

Question – What is the minimum investment in a GNMA or FNMA certificate?

Answer – Initially these certificates have a principal value of $25,000. The amount actually paid may be less depending on whether the certificate is being sold at a lower amount due to amortization of principal (which may have occurred after the establishment of the particular pool). In such cases, the certificates may be purchased for substantially less since the original mortgage pool is actually lower in value. Increments above the $25,000 initial minimum are $5,000 for GNMA issues. There are no similar restrictions above the $25,000 minimum on FNMA issues.

Question – What if one or more of the mortgages in a pool goes into default?

Answer – In most cases, the issuer of the mortgage-backed security, such as GNMA or FNMA, must continue to pay the full amount of principal and interest payments even though a mortgage may be in default. As a matter of fact, the security holder will not be aware of any defaults and is not affected by them.

Question – What is the average maturity of a mortgage-backed security?

Tools & Techniques of Investment Planning

215

Answer – Most of the residential mortgages that make up the pools behind these issues are 30-year mortgages. However, homeowners may pay off their mortgages in advance (which typically occurs when a home is sold), make partial prepayments (which reduce the average life of the pool), or go into default. Taking all of these factors together, the average life of most mortgage-backed securities tends to be about 8½ years in length. However, older pools with lower interest rate mortgages are not likely to be paid off as quickly and will have a longer average life. Mortgage pools of VA and FHA mortgages tend to have longer average lives than other mortgage pools. Mortgage-backed bonds are typically issued with maturities ranging from five to 12 years.

Question – Can the yield on these issues be compared to those available on corporate bonds?

Answer – Yes, but there are some important differences. Mortgage-backed securities lack a definite maturity date and their average life can only be estimated. This uncertainty can have a major impact on the actual rate of return earned on such an investment. Also, most corporate bonds pay interest semiannually, while the interest on GNMAs and FNMAs is paid monthly. This means that interest on mortgage-backed securities can be compounded monthly rather than just twice each year. Over the course of six monthly payments, the effective rate of return earned on the mortgage-backed bond will be higher than one paying interest semiannually even though the stated rate on each issue is the same.

Question – How is the yield on a mortgage-backed security determined?

Answer – The yield an investor will actually receive on mortgage-backed securities depends critically on the rate of prepayments on the underlying mortgages. Both the yield quotation and the projected maturity depend on the specific prepayment assumption. Realized prepayment depends on the demographic, financial, and contractual nature of the underlying mortgage assets, as well as on the structure and guarantees of the mortgage-backed security issue itself.

Question – How is the quoted yield on mortgage-backed securities determined?

Answer – The quoted yield on a mortgage-backed security is the "internal rate of return" (IRR) of all cash inflows (i.e., the interest and principal payments) and cash outflows (i.e., the price paid for the security). Simply stated, the IRR can be viewed as follows: If the investor placed the purchase price of the security in an interest-bearing savings account paying interest equal to the IRR, he could withdraw cash flows from the account exactly matching the projected cash flows from the security with no balance left over. The quoted yield (IRR) depends critically on when prepayments of principal are assumed to occur. Yields have been quoted in different ways by different dealers, making comparisons based on quoted yields extremely difficult, and often irrelevant.

Question – What prepayment assumptions are used to determine quoted yields?

Answer – The "weighted average life" (WAL) is commonly used in the secondary mortgage market as a measure of the effective maturity of a mortgage pool. The WAL will be longer if the assumed prepayments are slower but shorter if the assumed prepayments occur faster. A number of conventional specifications of assumed prepayment rates have been used.

The first and simplest specification is to assume the "standard mortgage yield." This specification assumes there are no prepayments whatsoever until year 12 on 30-year mortgages, when all the mortgages in the pool are assumed to prepay entirely. Of course, in reality some prepayments are inevitable before year 12. Therefore, a quoted yield based on these "standard" prepayments assumption seriously understates the potential yield on a security trading at a deep discount, and it overstates the potential yield on one selling at a premium.

A second prepayment specification bases assumed prepayments on FHA experience. The FHA compiles historical data on the actual incidence of prepayments on the mortgage loans it insures. The quoted yield is determined by assuming some ratio of FHA experience. For example, if prepayments are expected to be slower than historical FHA experience, a ratio of 75% of the FHA experience might be used. The benefit of this method is that it uses historically validated assumptions, including in particular the tendency to have higher prepayments in the first few years of the mortgage pool than in later years. The problem with this method is that it incorporates information on a variety of market conditions and mortgages that may not reflect the attributes of the underlying mortgage pool. Figure 23.3 shows the annual FHA prepayment rates based on 1981 experience.

Figure 23.3

FHA AND PSA PREPAYMENT RATES

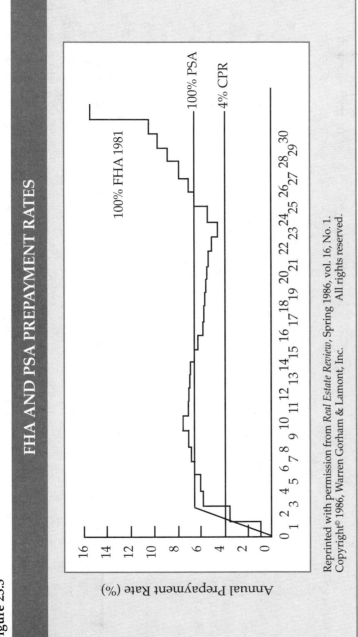

A third prepayment specification is the "constant prepayment rate" (CPR). This specification assumes that the percentage of the principal balance that is prepaid during a given year is a constant, such as 6%. Because of its simplicity, the CPR method has often been used to determine quoted yields. Figure 23.3 shows the annual prepayment rates based on a 4% constant assumed rate.

Finally, many quoted yields are now based on the standard prepayment experience offered by the Public Securities Association (PSA), an industry trade group. The PSA's goal is to bring some standardization to the marketplace. Essentially, the PSA standard is a combination of the PSA experience method and the CPR method. The first 30 months of the PSA standard calls for a steadily rising prepayment rate. After that, the rate is assumed constant at 6%. Figure 23.3 shows the assumed annual prepayments using the PSA standard method. Similar to the FHA method, the prepayments may be expected to be faster or slower than normal. For example, 150% of the PSA standard would project prepayment rates that are, again, half as great as under normal conditions.

Question – How are the yields an investor will actually realize related to the quoted yield and the rate at which prepayments occur?

Answer – The yield an investor actually realizes may vary significantly from the quoted yield if the ac-

tual rate of prepayments of principal differs from the assumed rate of prepayments that was used to calculate the quoted yield.

Investors who buy mortgage-backed securities at a premium (i.e., when the coupon rate paid on the security exceeds the current market rate of return for comparable securities) will realize yields that are less than the quoted yields if actual prepayments are faster than assumed when computing the quoted yield. This general principle can be demonstrated with a simple example. A regular bond maturing in two years with a face value of $1,000 and paying an annual coupon of $100 is priced at $1,017.59–a $17.59 premium over the face value. The quoted yield (IRR), assuming the bond is not "called" (i.e., prepaid) before the end of the second year, is therefore 9%. In other words, bonds of similar quality selling at their face values of $1,000 carry coupon rates of 9%. However, if the bond is called for $1,000 after the first year, the actual yield is 8.1%. (The $100 coupon less the $17.59 loss in value on the bond divided by the original investment of $1,017.59 equals 8.1%.) Consequently, the realized yield when principal is prepaid after year one (rather than after year two as assumed when computing the quoted yield) is less than the quoted yield of 9%. Although assumed and actual principal repayment schedules for mortgage-backed securities are more involved than in this simple example, the same general relationship between quoted and realized yields holds.

Conversely, realized yields on mortgage-backed securities purchased for premiums will be higher than quoted yields if actual prepayments are slower than assumed. This relationship can be demonstrated by simply reversing the example described above. An investor who purchases the bond for $1,017.59 and anticipates that it will be called after one year for $1,000 expects a yield (quoted yield) of 8.1%. If the bond is not called as expected after one year, the actual realized yield will be 9%.

Similarly, investors who buy mortgage-backed securities at a discount (i.e., when the promised interest rate is less than current market rates for comparable securities) will realize yields that are greater than the quoted yields if actual prepayments are faster than assumed prepayments. For example, an investor who buys a $1,000 face-value bond with an 8% annual coupon and a 2-year maturity for $982.41 (a $17.59 discount) has an expected yield to maturity (quoted yield) of 9%. If the $1,000 face value of the bond is prepaid at the end of the first year, the realized yield is 9.93%. (The $80 coupon plus the $17.59 appreciation on the bond divided by the $982.41 purchase price equals 9.93%.) Therefore, when actual prepayments of principal are faster than assumed, the realized yield on debt instruments purchased at a discount is greater than the quoted yield based on the assumed prepayments. Conversely, realized yields will be lower than quoted yields if actual prepayments are slower than assumed prepayments.

Investors who buy mortgage-backed securities at par (i.e., when the promised interest rate is equal to current market rates for comparable securities) will realize yields equal to the quoted yield, regardless of when prepayments occur.

In addition, regardless of whether investors purchase their securities at a premium, a discount, or at par, the timing of prepayments will also significantly affect their potential total return, including reinvestment. Specifically, if actual prepayments are faster than assumed, reinvestment return will be lower than expected if interest rates have fallen. If interest rates have risen, reinvestment return will increase. Conversely, if actual prepayments are slower than assumed, reinvestment return will be either higher or lower than expected depending on whether interest rates have risen or fallen, respectively.

The greater the difference between the assumed prepayments and the actual prepayments, the greater the difference will be between the quoted and realized yield. Consequently, to compare potential investments in mortgage-backed securities and to determine a realistic estimate of the potential yield, investors must understand the types of prepayment assumptions that are used to compute quoted yields.

Question – Are there any tax-free issues of mortgage-backed securities?

Answer – Yes, a small number of tax-exempt issues are available through the municipal bond departments of investment banking and brokerage firms. These securities are designed to raise funds for low-income housing construction and subsidized low interest mortgage loans. They are generally issued by state and local housing authorities.

Question – Are there marketable securities backed by other types of loan agreements?

Answer – Yes, in recent years investment bankers have been extremely creative and have come up with new marketable securities backed by every kind of loan agreement imaginable. Securities have been issued that are backed by auto loans, computer leases, and even credit card charge accounts.

Some lesser-known loan-backed securities come close to the record that Ginnie Mae 30-year home mortgage securities have experienced for high yields and safety. Specifically, the Student Loan Marketing Association (Sallie Mae) is a government-chartered corporation that creates a market in federally guaranteed student loans. It buys the loans from lending institutions and finances those purchases by issuing bonds to the public. Unlike mortgage pass-throughs, which are set up so that both interest and principal payments are "passed through" to investors each month, these bonds, called Sallie Maes, are in the form of conventional bonds. They pay interest semiannually, have set maturity dates, and return all principal when they mature. Although the bonds don't carry an explicit government guarantee, they are virtually risk-free because the underlying student loans are federally guaranteed. Sallie Maes, which are issued in minimum denominations of $10,000, yield about 0.25% more than Treasury bonds of comparable maturities.

Few investors realize that the same agency that issues Ginnie Maes also issues pass-through securities backed by mobile-home loans. These high-yielding, government-guaranteed securities have shorter maturities than conventional Ginnie Maes and tend to have less prepayment risk. That's a plus for investors seeking high-yield securities that sell at a premium. The securities are sold in four maturities: 12-years, 15-years, 18-years, and 20-years.

Question – Are Ginnie Maes subject to state taxation?

Answer – Federal statues provide that all Treasury bonds, notes, and other obligations of the federal government are not subject to state income taxation; however, Ginnie Maes are not direct obligations of the federal government. They are issued by private financial institutions, and the timely payment of interest and principal is guaranteed by the Government National Mortgage Association. Even though Ginnie Maes are backed by the full faith and credit of the federal government, the securities are *not* direct federal government obligations. Therefore, Ginnie Maes are subject to state income and personal property taxes as well as local taxation. The United States Supreme Court made this determination in June 1987.[1] This decision also extends to other privately issued securities guaranteed by the federal government.

CHAPTER ENDNOTES

1. *Rockford Life Insurance Company v. Illinois Department of Revenue,* 107 S.Ct. 2312 (1987).

Chapter 24

OIL AND GAS

WHAT IS IT?

Exploration for and production of oil and natural gas involves a high degree of risk, large amounts of capital, a great deal of technical expertise and offers, in return, incredible rewards.

The combined efforts and capital of many groups of individuals in the form of corporations (including S corporations), trusts, general and limited partnerships, and joint ventures are necessary to achieve profitable exploration and production.

There are four basic types of oil and gas investments:

1. exploratory drilling (the search for oil or gas in new areas);

2. development (the search for oil or gas near previous successful wells);

3. income (investment in the production of oil or gas reserves already located and drilled); and

4. diversified (a combination of the first three).

WHEN IS THE USE OF THE TOOL INDICATED?

1. When the investor is in a high income tax bracket and in need of tax shelter.

2. Where an investor desires additional diversification of his/her investment portfolio into an asset class that is not positively correlated to the equity and bond markets.

3. When the investor is psychologically willing and able to take relatively high risks in return for possible large rewards.

4. When the investor desires a completely passive role and does not wish to be actively involved in the operation of the investment.

ADVANTAGES

1. There are a number of major tax advantages associated with an investment in oil and/or gas. These result in both high front-end deductions (often exceeding 60% of the initial investment) and a continuing deferral of tax. These tax advantages include:

a) A deduction is allowed for the depletion of the oil or gas reserves in the ground. There are two types of depletion and an investor must generally use the method that generates the largest deduction. "Percentage depletion" allows for a deduction of a specified percentage of the gross income derived from the property (after reduction for any rents or royalties the investor must pay with respect to that property). The alternative to percentage depletion is "cost depletion," which essentially bases the deduction on proration of the investor's basis in the property between the number of oil or gas units sold during the year and the number of estimated units remaining. Stated as a formula, cost depletion for the tax year is computed as follows:

$$\frac{\text{Investor's Basis}}{\text{Barrels of oil (1,000's} \atop \text{of cubic feet of gas)} \atop \text{remaining}} \quad X \quad \genfrac{}{}{0pt}{}{\text{Barrels (cubic feet)}}{\text{sold during the} \atop \text{taxable year}}$$

The percentage depletion allowance can be a major tax advantage since it generally will permit a deduction greater than the amount computed on a cost depletion basis and the investor may continue to use it even when the right to use cost depletion has been exhausted. There is an overall annual limitation to the percentage depletion allowance. The annual deduction is generally limited to 100% of the taxable income (calculated before the depletion deduction) derived from the property.

b) Intangible Drilling Costs (IDC) incurred in exploratory and development programs (as well as any small amount of IDC associated with an income program) are deductible.

c) Investors may elect to take an "enhanced oil recovery credit" in lieu of deductions for depreciable property and IDCs equal to 15% of the investor's qualified enhanced oil recovery costs for certain projects begun after December 31, 1990 (the credit is phased out as the price of crude oil exceeds a certain level). The credit is a component of the general business credit; thus, it is subject to the general limitations and carryback and carryforward rules of the general business credit itself.

d) The interest expenses on funds borrowed to finance the investment are deductible, subject to limitations discussed in Chapter 43, "Taxation of Investment Vehicles."

e) Losses are currently tax deductible, subject to the "passive activity" limitations discussed in Chapter 43, "Taxation of Investment Vehicles," except so-called "working interests" in oil and gas properties.

f) The investor has the potential to receive long-term capital gain treatment upon the sale of his or her interest.

g) If an investor has purchased an interest in the form of a limited partnership unit, within certain limitations, participants (the general and limited partners) can agree to divide up income, deductions, and credits in a manner disproportionate to their ownership interests.

2. The investment required is relatively small when compared with the potential profit. A successful exploratory well could easily produce a return of $10 for every $1 of capital invested. Even development wells have the potential for returning profits that double the taxpayer's investment in a short period of time.

3. Since most investors becoming involved in an oil and gas venture do so as limited partners, their liability is limited to the extent of (a) their capital contributions to the partnership, (b) any contributions investors contractually agree to make in the future, and (c) any partnership debts the investors agree to guaranty in order to leverage their tax benefits.

DISADVANTAGES

1. An investor in oil and gas assumes an extremely high degree of risk if the investment is in exploratory drilling. An investor may lose 100% of capital since only one out of ten "wildcat" wells is successful.

However, by participating in only developmental or income drilling, the degree of risk can be reduced. But even with productive wells, success is not guaranteed. Many wells never produce reserves of sufficient quantity to enable a recovery of drilling costs. For these reasons, many advisors recommend that an investor split the total investment among two or three different types of drilling programs.

The chance of drilling a "dry hole" is not the only risk assumed by the investor. Since most investors do not live near enough to the drilling site to constantly inspect operations or monitor costs, the risk of mismanagement and/or fraud is high.

2. The tax advantages of investments in oil and gas are offset by the "at risk" and "passive loss" rules. The current deductibility of "losses" generated by the exploration and exploitation of oil and gas reserves is limited to the amount that the investor stands to lose in the economic sense. This amount that the investor has "at risk" consists of his actual (cash or property) investment in the property plus the amount of partnership debt incurred that the investor may personally be called upon to repay. In other words, a person is at risk to the extent he is not protected against the loss of the money or other property actually contributed or that he may be called upon to contribute.

To the extent the investor may not deduct the loss in the current tax year, the excess may be carried over indefinitely. The excess loss may be deducted in a subsequent year, when the investor has a sufficient amount "at risk" to absorb it.

In addition, investments in oil and gas are subject to the "passive activity" loss limitations (except so-called "working interests" in oil and gas properties).

A second disadvantage of investments in oil and gas is the possibility of paying the alternative minimum tax because of preference items. However, for tax years beginning after 1992, these preference rules apply only to integrated oil companies rather than to "independent producers." Because most oil and gas investments qualify as independent producers, the alternative minimum tax should affect fewer investors. For those few affected, two of tax advantages of investments in oil and gas – the deduction for IDC on productive wells and the percentage depletion allowance – are considered preference items and may result in the required payment of the alternative minimum tax. Only a portion of the intangible drilling cost is considered a preference item. This preference amount is computed using a very complex formula. The amount by which percentage depletion on a property exceeds its tax basis is also a preference. Investors subject to this rule may therefore recover the basis of the property through depletion allowances, but then subject all subsequent percentage depletion to the alternative minimum tax.

3. The "time line" of the investment varies, but is often long term (3 to 5 years).

4. The value of an investor's interest can quickly drop due to the volatility of energy prices.

5. The value of an investor's interest can drop in the long run due to conservation efforts, new technology, or alternative energy sources.

TAX IMPLICATIONS

The implications of oil and gas as a tax shelter investment have already been described above. Specifically, the investor may hope to achieve three results:

1. a deduction for intangible drilling costs;

2. a deduction for percentage depletion; and

3. a credit for enhanced oil recovery costs.

The investor's tax benefits may be reduced by:

1. the limitations on the depletion deduction;

2. the "at risk" and "passive loss" rules; and

3. for certain producers and royalty holders, the impact of the alternative minimum tax.

ALTERNATIVES

1. "Exotic" tax shelters, such as leasing "masters" (plates or recordings) for stamps, recordings, and lithographs as well as movie deals and cattle feeding programs, are all very high risk with possible high return.

2. On the basis of potential tax shelter, certain rental real estate investments would be appropriate for upper-middle to high-income investors who are able to take significant risks. (In general, rental real estate is less risky than oil and gas.)

WHERE AND HOW DO I GET IT?

Few investors buy a direct interest in oil or gas drilling operations. Those who do acquire a fractional, undivided working interest in a co-owned oil or gas property. Such investors participate in every item of income and expense attributable to the operation in accordance with their fractional ownership interest. Each co-owner signs an operating agreement that names one of the co-owners as the "operator" of each property. The co-ownership arrangement is often considered a partnership for tax purposes and co-owners are taxed as partners. (There are provisions allowing co-owners to "opt-out" of partnership taxation. If they are willing to take their share of production "in kind" and meet certain other requirements, co-owners can be treated under the tax law as individual owners.)

The advantage of co-ownership over the more popular limited partnership method of investing in oil and gas is that a co-owner's interest is more transferable and has a greater collateral value than a partnership interest. A co-owner may also make his own elections with regard to various tax matters and is not restricted by elections made by the partnership.

The major disadvantage of co-ownership is liability. When compared with the limited partner, the co-owner bears a significantly broader level of risk. Co-ownership involves an investment of more than merely a greater amount of funds than a limited partnership investment; a co-owner must be willing to invest a considerable amount of personal time and effort. Another disadvantage is that co-owners cannot allocate costs with the same flexibility as limited partners, who can make "special" allocations of deductions and credits among themselves.

Most investors prefer the limited partnership as the vehicle for participating in an oil and gas venture. They generally perceive the advantages of limited liability as outweighing the disadvantages of not participating in the operating decisions.

Revenues and costs are shared by partners according to an agreement appropriately termed the "sharing arrangement." Usually, capital costs are allocated to the general partners and tax deductible expenditures are allocated to the limited partners. There are many types of sharing agreements. Most fall into one of the following four categories:

1. *Functional Allocation of Costs* (*also known as Tangible-Intangible Allocation* – The general partner participates in revenues from the beginning of the venture. The percentage of that participation

is decided by agreement among the partners and is often higher than 35%.

This arrangement is very popular because it maximizes the tax deductions of the limited partners. (Limited partners pay costs that are deductible when incurred, while the general partner pays costs that must be capitalized.) The disadvantage of the functional allocation is that limited partners bear both the full cost of drilling unproductive wells and the majority of the cost of drilling productive wells.

2. *Promoted Interest* – In this type of sharing agreement, the general partner arranges to participate in revenues in excess of his participation in costs. In more simple language, this means that the general partner pays for (say) 8% of costs for a 22% participation in revenues. The 14% difference is the "promoted interest."

3. *Carried Interest* – Here, limited partners "carry" the general partner with respect to costs. The general partner participates in revenues from the beginning of the venture while paying a relatively minimal share of costs. For example, the general partner may receive more than 10% of the operation's revenues while paying perhaps only 1% or 2% of its costs. The general partner's income will typically increase a few more percentage points once the limited partners have recovered their investment from their share of production.

4. *Reversionary Interest* – The general partner in this method of sharing receives only a small percentage of the revenues and pays only a small portion of the costs until the limited partners have recouped their investment from revenues. At that point the general partner's interest becomes significant. For example, the general partner may begin with a minimal participation in both costs and revenues of only 1%. But after the pay out to the limited partners of their costs, the general partner may share costs and revenues at a level of 20% or greater.

WHAT FEES OR OTHER ACQUISITION COSTS ARE INVOLVED?

There are numerous fees a typical investor in an oil and gas syndication can expect to pay. These include:

1. sales commissions;

2. management fees (sometimes given exotic names such as "drilling overseeing fees");

3. broker-dealer fees;

4. loan origination fees and points;

5. guarantee fees (generally paid to the general partner for such commitments as providing a guaranteed minimum cash flow from the investment); and

6. other "syndication" fees paid to promoters or syndicators.

These fees will generally range from 13% to 20% of the equity invested in the partnership by the limited partners.

HOW DO I SELECT THE BEST OF ITS TYPE?

As is the case with any other tax shelter, oil and gas sharing arrangements should be measured by the investment standards of risk and cost versus economic reward. Six helpful guidelines in analyzing alternatives are:

1. Compare the "track records" of the sponsors. Give top rating to a sponsor with established programs (one that has been in business at least seven or eight years) and a history of consistently returning the investors' capital. A lower rating should be given to a program that has been in operation for four to six years and in which the limited partners have received a return of at least 20% of their original investment. Programs that have been in operation for less than four years should typically be considered only by investors with an ultra high risk taking propensity.

2. Determine the sponsor's success ratio. Compare wells completed and producing to wells drilled. Be careful to look not only at the ratio of success but also the location of the drilling. In certain areas of the country (Pennsylvania, West Virginia, and Ohio) the success ratio should be relatively high. A percentage of 80% to 90% should be expected. In other parts of the country (such as Oklahoma and Alaska), a lower ratio can be expected. A 15% to 20% ratio is considered successful. Of course, it is not only the percentage of completed and producing wells to wells drilled that is important; the amount of

oil lifted from the ground and the cost of doing so, measured on a "per well" basis, are equally as important.

3. Use "time value of money" measurements in the analysis process. In comparing sponsors' histories, check to see how quickly investors' money was returned as well as the amount of each payment. The more quickly the sponsor was able to return investors' money, the better. Also, the financial advisor should consider not only alternative drilling programs, but also alternative investments, other than oil and gas.

4. Ascertain the location of the wells to be drilled. The reliability of past history is directly proportionate to the location of the wells to be drilled. The sponsor that has been successful in one state or region may now be seeking funds for exploration in an entirely different type of geological formation.

5. Measure one sponsor's financial participation against another's. Give top grade to the sponsor with the greatest identity of interest with the limited partners. Identity of interest is reflected in a greater commitment of money and a larger share of the cost. Check to see if the sponsor is compensated merely for each well drilled. Higher scores should go to those sponsors who are in the business of finding oil or gas rather than to those who are in the business of just drilling wells.

Many sponsors will contribute land they already own to the oil or gas partnership. Higher marks should go to sponsors who place that acreage into the venture at their cost. The sponsor should not have the right to pick and choose which acreage will be drilled for its own account. Give low grades to general partners who reserve the right to be selective in the choice of which land they will drill and which land the limited partners' money will be sunk into. An examination should be made of each sponsor's prospectus or offering memorandum for a section describing these and other possible conflicts of interest.

6. Compare the cost/return ratios. The cost of finding and selling oil and gas entails more than merely finding it and pumping it from the ground. For example, once the oil is removed, it must be transported through pipeline hook-ups and held in storage facilities until it can be shipped. The investor should compare the cost information provided in the offering materials of the alternative sponsors.

WHERE CAN I FIND OUT MORE ABOUT IT?

1. *Tax Facts on Investments* (Cincinnati, OH: The National Underwriter Company, published annually).

2. John Orban, *Money in the Ground*, (Oklahoma City, OK: Meridian Press, 1997).

4. Lewis D. Solomon, *Taxation of Investments* (Clifton, NJ: Prentice Hall Law & Business, 1994).

QUESTIONS AND ANSWERS

Question – What is the difference between a "wildcat," a "step out," and a "deeper test" exploratory program?

Answer – Exploratory programs are organized to drill in areas with no known production. Pure wildcat programs are those that drill in completely unproven territory.

Step out programs involve drilling in unproven areas that are near producing fields. The step out is really an extension of the proven field and serves to test its boundaries.

Deeper test are those programs that extend the limits of a known field in terms of depth rather than surface boundary.

Question – Why are assessments often levied against the investors in oil and gas programs?

Answer – Additional capital is often required of investors to provide funds for drilling costs. An assessment provision in an oil or gas program requires that limited partners must put up more money if called upon to do so by the general partner. Investors who fail to make additional contributions are typically subject to certain penalties that can significantly reduce the viability of the investment. Obviously, the presence or absence of an assessment provision (more likely to be present in development programs) must be considered in the comparison of various ventures and in the overall decision of whether to invest in oil and gas at all.

Question—What items are involved in "intangible drilling and development costs?"

Answer – Intangible drilling costs include labor, fuel, repair, hauling, supply, and other expenditures incurred in the following:

1. ground clearing;

2. road making;

3. surveying and geological work needed to prepare a site for drilling; and

4. construction of physical structures such as derricks, tanks, and pipelines.

Expenditures to acquire tangible property that has a salvage value are not considered intangible drilling costs. Therefore, the costs incurred to obtain the following items would not be considered intangible drilling costs (although depreciation deductions may be available):

1. drilling tools;

2. pipes;

3. casings;

4. tubings;

5. tanks; and

6. other machinery or materials used in the construction of the wells or on the well sites.

Question – What is the tax treatment of an intangible drilling cost?

Answer – An investor with an interest in oil or gas property has two choices with respect to intangible drilling and development costs. He can (1) capitalize the intangible drilling costs, or (2) deduct them currently in the taxable year the expense is paid or incurred.

In actuality, the election to capitalize or expense intangible drilling costs is made by the general partner. This is another reason that a potential investor should examine the prospectus because the general partner's intent as to this election is stated there. Where the investment is marketed as a tax shelter,

the general partner will typically elect to expense the intangible drilling expenses.

Each limited partner can recover his share of capital expenditures on his personal income tax return through depletion or depreciation if the limited partnership elects to capitalize intangible drilling and development costs. On the other hand, if the partnership elects to expense intangible drilling costs, each partner has two choices as to how to treat his allocated share of intangible drilling costs: (1) take a current deduction for the allocable share, or (2) elect to amortize such costs ratably over a 60-month period.

Question – What is a "swap deal?"

Answer – A swap deal is an innovation designed to make oil or gas tax shelter investments more marketable. A newly organized public corporation exchanges shares of its stock for the oil and gas interests of the partnership's investors. Procedurally, after the exchange, the limited partnership is terminated and the individual investors own stock in the new corporation. If properly structured, the swap should be tax free to both the investors and the corporation. Because the investor now owns stock in a publicly traded company, the liquidity of his investment is significantly improved.

Perhaps even more appealing than the increased liquidity, the investor now owns stock that if sold at a profit may give rise to long-term capital gain. The transaction has eliminated the exposure of recapture of IDC and depreciation previously deducted individually by the investor. It therefore successfully converts what would have been ordinary income upon the disposition of the investment into capital gain.

A successful swap deal requires that both parties come to terms as to the value of the investor's oil or gas interest. Its major drawback is that the value of the investor's new interest (the stock) now fluctuates according to the vagaries of the stock market. The future price of the stock may be much more or much less than the value of an investor's share of the underlying oil or gas reserves held by the partnership prior to the exchange.

Question – What is the difference between a "royalty" interest and a "working" interest?

Answer – A landowner owns both the right to the surface of the land and the minerals beneath its surface. It is possible to sever these two rights and sell or lease one without the other. Therefore the owner of the land can retain the surface rights and sell or lease the rights to the minerals under the land.

The owner of the mineral rights in turn can lease or assign either a royalty interest or a working interest. The owner of the mineral rights may grant an operator the right to exploit that interest in return for a fraction of the total production. For instance, an operator who believes a farmer's pasture land may have high oil or gas potential will bargain with the farmer for the right to drill and extract any oil or gas. In return for a lease allowing the operator to drill and extract any oil or gas found, the farmer will be given (technically he reserves) a royalty interest. The exact percentage depends on the operator's

expectations as well as the farmer's bargaining abilities. The fraction may be as small as 1/8 or as large as 1/4 of production revenue.

An operator who acquires the right to exploit the minerals under the land has generally acquired a working (operating) interest in the mineral rights. This involves not only the benefits but also the burdens (the operating costs) of extracting the oil or gas.

Few owners of a working mineral interest have the capital to undertake the large and risky task of exploiting the minerals under the land. Therefore, the working owner may assign most of his rights and all of his obligations under the lease to another party. That other party is often a syndicated limited partnership.

Chapter 25

GOLD AND OTHER PRECIOUS METALS

WHAT IS IT?

Gold, silver, and platinum are the most common of the precious metal investments. They are valued primarily because of their scarcity and, to a lesser extent, because of their utility for scientific and industrial purposes.

WHEN IS THE USE OF THIS TOOL INDICATED?

1. When the investor anticipates instability in traditional capital markets. Historically, when stock and bond markets have fallen, the price of gold and other precious metals has tended to increase.

2. When the worldwide economic or political outlook is one of uncertainty and fear, precious metals tend to be viewed as a more stable and secure investment.

3. When the investor anticipates that the purchasing power of the dollar will be eroded by high rates of inflation.

4. When the value of the investor's dollars is declining because of international currency fluctuations. For example, when the value of the U.S. dollar declines, the price of gold and other precious metals generally increases.

5. When the investor desires to diversify a portfolio that already contains significant amounts of stocks, bonds, and real estate.

ADVANTAGES

1. Gold and the other precious metals offer a potentially high return (gold increased from $434 an ounce in August 2005 to more than $633 per ounce in August 2006).

2. Since precious metals are tangible, or physically possessable assets, they provide a degree of psychological security matched by few other investments.

3. Precious metals can be purchased in relatively small quantities and in a variety of forms. For instance, an investor can purchase gold by the bar or purchase an ounce (or even less) at a time by buying a coin such as the Canadian Maple Leaf. Such coins are available in amounts as low as one-half or one-quarter ounce.

4. Since all of the precious metals have some utility for scientific and industrial purposes, there is an underlying demand for them as a commodity in addition to their speculative or investment value. Silver, for example, is used extensively for jewelry and photographic purposes.

5. Historically, precious metals held over a very long period have proven to be a relatively safe and stable form of investment. Many investors have purchased gold, for example, as a long-term hedge against inflation.

DISADVANTAGES

1. Precious metals are a highly speculative form of investment. For example, the price of gold is determined more by international, political and psychological factors than by normal economic factors of supply and demand.

2. Historically, the prices of precious metals have been highly volatile and the investor is subject to a high risk of significant loss of capital. Panic buying of gold could quickly reverse itself. For instance, the price of gold dropped from $522 an ounce in December of 1987 to $360 an ounce in December of 1988.

3. Precious metals have frequently been controlled by various governments. For instance, the United States government hoarded gold in its vaults for many years and forbade U.S. citizens from owning and selling gold privately for investment or speculation until 1975.

4. Direct investments in precious metals typically yield no current income. This makes gold relatively

"expensive" when alternative investments are yielding high rates of return in the form of dividends or interest. (But the prices of metals do not always follow a logical or consistent pattern.)

5. Precious metal investments involve storage costs, either directly or indirectly. These costs may amount to more than a dollar per ounce on an annual basis. There may also be shipping and insurance charges.

6. Sales tax may be payable.

7. There may be assay costs involved in the purchase.

TAX IMPLICATIONS

1. Taxable gain is realized and must be recognized (i.e., reported) to the extent an investor receives more upon disposition than he paid. Therefore, to the extent that the selling price exceeds the investor's tax basis, he must realize a gain.

2. No gain is reportable until the investment is disposed of in a taxable transaction. Therefore, the appreciation on a precious metals investment will remain untaxed until the asset is sold. This can be particularly advantageous to high tax bracket investors.

3. A loss from a precious metals transaction is allowable to the extent an investor paid more for the asset than he received from the sale. To the extent that the investor's basis exceeds his selling price, he has a deductible loss.

4. Gain or loss on a precious metals transaction is a capital gain or capital loss assuming the metal is held as an investment, rather than by a dealer for trading purposes. The length of time the metal was held prior to disposition will determine whether the capital gain or loss will be long-term or short-term.

5. No gain or loss must be reported if one precious metal is exchanged solely for another. This favorable rule applies only if the metal received is of the same nature and the same character as the metal given up in the exchange. Therefore, if an investor exchanges gold coins for gold bullion, or trades gold bullion for certificates of gold, no gain or loss is recognized on the transaction. Likewise, if bullion-type coins of one country are exchanged for bullion-type coins of another country, no taxable income or loss would be generated.

Note that the tax-free exchange rules are strictly construed. A gain or loss would be triggered by the exchange of a "numismatic" coin for a "bullion-type" coin. (A "numismatic coin" such as the $20 U.S. gold piece is valued for its rarity and condition; its metal content is only one of many factors contributing to its value. Conversely, a bullion-type coin, such as the Canadian Maple Leaf, is valued solely for its metal content and the type of metal, purity, and weight are the primary value determinants.)

An exchange of any two different types of metals will trigger the recognition of gain or loss. For instance, gain or loss would be triggered by the exchange of a silver bullion-type coin for a gold bullion-type coin.

6. The exchange of a precious metal for property other than a similar type of precious metal will result in a reportable gain or loss.

7. Coins acquired in a taxable transaction must be valued for tax purposes at their fair market value rather than at their face value. For instance, a Fifty Peso Mexican coin with a gold content of 1.2057 ounces may be worth a lot more than fifty pesos.

ALTERNATIVES

1. From the standpoint of an investment, alternatives to precious metals would include speculative real estate (e.g., raw land), collectibles, diamonds and other gemstones, and art.

2. From a risk-return standpoint, alternatives would include speculative stocks, "junk bonds" (see Chapter 3) securities options (see Chapter 13), commodity futures (see Chapter 15), limited partnerships (see Chapter 27), and other capital gain-oriented investments.

WHERE AND HOW DO I GET IT?

There are a number of ways to invest depending on the type of metal. Gold or silver can be purchased as: (1) coins of the bullion-type, such as the U.S. Gold Eagle, the Canadian Maple Leaf, or the Mexican Peso; (2) bars (i.e., ingots of one or more ounces); or (3) certificates, which certify that a specific warehouse is holding a given amount of that metal for the investor.

Investors who wish to buy small quantities of gold should consider coins. They are easy to purchase, store, and resell. The most popular bullion-type coins – including the South African Kruggerand and the Canadian Maple Leaf – have a fine gold content of exactly one troy ounce. These coins generally have no numismatic value. This means that the value of an investor's holding can be figured by multiplying the price of gold for immediate delivery (the so-called "spot" or cash price) by the number of ounces held.

Many investors prefer to purchase gold in the form of small wafers called "ingots." Ingots are sold in standard weights that range from as little as one gram (0.0322 oz.) to as much as 400 troy ounces. The typical investor will purchase ingots in 1-ounce quantities.

Gold should be purchased only from a recognized dealer. Its fineness (the maximum is 0.999) should be stamped on the ingot. Investors should not purchase a bar with a lesser fineness. The ingot should be stamped with the name of a recognized refiner and should be accompanied by an assay certificate. This assures the purchaser of its purity and authenticity, and will typically save the cost of another assay when sold.

There are dealers, such as International Precious Metals (www.preciousmetals.com), who specialize in precious metals. Investors can establish accounts and obtain a firm, binding quote over the telephone. Payment may be made by cashier's check or wired funds typically postmarked by noon of the day after purchase.

WHAT FEES OR OTHER ACQUISITION COSTS ARE INVOLVED?

Gold, silver, and platinum are purchased at the market value plus a premium. That premium generally ranges from 2% to 3% and covers the dealer's profit and the cost of fabricating the metal. Premiums decline with the quantity of the metal purchased and may be less than 2% for a 100-ounce bar.

An investor who desires to take physical possession of a precious metal must pay insurance and shipping costs in addition to possible sales taxes. A representative shipping and insurance charge for six ounces of gold is $18.

Many investors prefer not to accept the risk and the expense involved in taking physical possession of a precious metal. Rather than accept delivery, such investors may utilize the certificate programs offered by a number of large dealers, banks, and brokerage firms. The investor will receive a certificate stating that he owns a specified number of troy ounces in an independent bank depository. This bank may be located in Delaware or in Switzerland. The investor can sell his holding at any time or take delivery of the bullion.

The obvious advantage of storage certificate programs is the savings in delivery costs. But, the investor also may save sales taxes and fabrication charges by using an independent bank depository. In general, the minimum investment required for these certificate programs is $1,000. Some dealers may allow additional investments of amounts as small as $100. A typical commission is 3% on orders up to $1,000; 2% to $10,000, and 2% to $50,000. Annual storage charges are 0.5% of the value of the investor's holdings and a 1% commission is paid upon the sale of the metal.

A number of banks act as an agent for their customers who choose to purchase precious metals. As an accommodation, the bank will "bulk" the orders of a number of smaller investors together. For instance, Citibank has generally accepted a minimum investment of $1,000 from a number of its customers. It then goes to the New York Commodity Exchange (COMEX) and purchases gold in 400-ounce bars of 0.995 fineness or better, and silver in 5,000-ounce bars of 0.999 fineness or better. This is the equivalent of buying wholesale since there is no markup. Citibank's customers have thus received the advantage of a bulk purchase and the best price available on the New York COMEX.

HOW DO I SELECT THE BEST OF ITS TYPE?

1. In making a selection among the various types of precious metals, an investor should consider the following factors:

a) *The price of one metal compared with another.* For instance, if silver were trading at $8 per ounce and gold were trading at $340 per ounce, and if other factors were equal, the small investor might opt for an investment in silver because it is more "affordable."

b) *The position of the price relative to recent highs and lows of the metal.* An optimistic investor might choose platinum at $370 per ounce if its recent high was $1,040 per ounce over gold selling at $400 per ounce with an expected high of $600 per ounce.

c) *The potential downside risk.* One metal may be used for many more scientific and industrial purposes than another and, therefore, may have a higher "floor" than the other.

QUESTIONS AND ANSWERS

Question – How are gold prices established?

Answer – The price of gold and other precious metals is determined by prevailing market forces of supply and demand. This takes place at three major exchanges; in London, New York and Hong Kong. The price is "fixed" at various times in each of these locations by selected gold specialists and bank officials representing individual investors and commodity traders throughout the world. Reports of these prices are published daily in major newspapers and broadcast by television and radio stations and on the Internet.

Question – Should an individual invest directly in gold mining stocks?

Answer – At certain times, gold shares have been among the most profitable equity investments from the standpoint of return. Gold stocks typically follow the price of gold, but at times may be even more volatile than the price of the metal itself. Investing in gold stocks may be more convenient than buying gold directly. The purchaser can also avoid the cost of shipping, insurance, and storage.

An investor should distinguish between the purchase of shares of gold mining companies in North America and those in South Africa. First, the size and quality of the mines is much higher in South Africa than in the United States. For instance, one South African mine alone produces more gold than the total U.S. production. Second, profits earned by South African mining companies are paid out more rapidly than those of U.S. concerns. Third, these advantages may be offset by the potential risk associated with the political and social unrest of South Africa. These threaten to disrupt production and may even endanger the investor's capital.

Question – Are there any mutual funds that invest in gold or other precious metals?

Answer – Yes, there are a variety of funds that concentrate their investments in the stocks of gold mining and other precious metals companies. Such investments provide the opportunity for relative safety through diversification of mine locations, accessibility of ore deposits, and remaining years of life. They also offer investment management expertise not available to the typical small investor.

Question – How does silver compare with gold as a precious metals investment?

d) *Other value determinants such as sensitivity to political changes and supply and demand influences.* For instance, an individual anticipating a major gold mining strike might prefer to invest in gold rather than silver or platinum.

2. Compare the premium charge imposed by a number of dealers. Premiums can vary significantly from one dealer to another.

3. Deal only with reputable dealers who are willing to ship within 48 hours of payment, if delivery is requested, and who are willing to exchange gold for cash.

4. When storing gold, deal only with a firm that has been in business for a minimum of five years and that is periodically audited by an independent certified public accountant. Gold should be stored in a segregated account and should not be subjected to the claims of the dealer's or the custodian's creditors. If an investor's bullion is mingled with that of other registered holders, his holdings should be clearly identified and available for delivery after the payment of any appropriate charges.

WHERE CAN I FIND OUT MORE ABOUT IT?

1. Newspapers such as the *Wall Street Journal* (www.wsj.com), *New York Times* (www.nytimes.com), and *Barron's* (www.barrons.com) carry the daily price "fixings" for gold and the other precious metals as well as stories and reports on market activity.

2. *American Metal Market* (www.amm.com), printed by Fairchild Publications of New York, is also a respected source of information for metals investors.

3. *Financial Times* (www.ft.com), an English publication, offers an international perspective, which can be important due to the global nature of these markets.

4. Statistics on precious metals production and use can be found in *Mineral Commodities Summaries* published by the U.S. Bureau of Mines and in an annual review of markets published by Handy and Harman. The multinational mining concern of Consolidated Goldfields Limited publishes an annual review of the statistics on gold.

5. Major brokerage firms and commodity trading houses also publish reports on metal markets and related investments.

Answer – Silver has always been considered a less valuable commodity than gold. Its price has swung even more widely than gold in recent years and is influenced by many of the same market factors that determine the price of gold – inflation, interest rates, and political tensions. However, silver has a value independent of its rarity. It is used in large quantities in film manufacturing and in the production of electronic products, and is therefore stockpiled for its use in national defense. Silver is also used in the production of coins, jewelry, and works of art. The world actually consumes more silver than it produces each year. This deficit is made up by recycling many of these same coins, jewelry, and artwork.

Question – How does an investor buy silver?

Answer – Like gold, silver can be purchased through brokers in many forms. These forms include silver bars (or ingots), bags of silver coins, silver forward contracts, silver futures contracts, silver options, and silver shares. Silver bars are purchased and sold in weights of 1,000 ounces. Purchasers must pay a premium of 5% to 8% over the "spot" price of the metal in addition to sales taxes in many states, if the bullion is actually delivered. There also may be assay and warehousing expenses. For these reasons, many owners choose to store silver bullion in warehouses and accept warehouse receipts as evidence of ownership.

Purchasers can obtain bags of silver coins. These coins are standard U.S. issue and are 90% pure silver. Each bag has a weight of about 65 pounds and the price of a bag is determined by daily spot quotations for silver. They are popular among speculators as an investment even though they are difficult to move and store.

Forward contracts are arrangements for future delivery of the actual metal made on the London Metal Exchange (LME). Silver futures are contracts for future delivery on the New York COMEX and Chicago Board of Trade (CBOT) that serve primarily as a device for hedging or speculation rather than for trading in physical silver. Silver options consist of put and call contracts that give the holder the right to sell or buy a certain amount of silver at a stated price for a given period of time.

Investors can also purchase the stock of silver producers on organized exchanges or the over-the-counter market. The prices of these companies' shares will typically follow the rise and fall of silver metal prices.

Question – What are some of the major factors an investor should consider before purchasing platinum?

Answer – Platinum is the rarest of the major precious metals, with world production less than one-fifth the amount of gold produced. South Africa is one of only two major sources of the metal, the other being the Soviet Union. The metal has commercial uses as well as being valued as a precious metal. There is only a small, unmined stock of platinum as compared with relatively large inventories of gold and silver. As a result, prices tend to respond quickly to changing market conditions. The same disadvantages present in the purchase of gold and silver (e.g., assay charges, shipping, storage, and insurance costs) are present in owning platinum. The price of platinum has tended to parallel the price of gold. It is affected by many of the same political, social and psychological forces that influence the price of gold, and also reacts to factors stemming from its industrial uses.

Chapter 26

COLLECTIBLES

WHAT IS IT?

An investment quality collectible is any item of property that meets the following three criteria:

1. rarity;

2. popularity; and

3. ready marketability.

The specific value of a particular collectible will depend on its history, aesthetic qualities, condition, position, and the number of similar items in existence.

Examples of popular investment quality collectibles include rare coins, art, stamps, gems, oriental rugs, antiques, and certain wines.

WHEN IS THE USE OF THIS TOOL INDICATED?

1. When the investor has little or no need for immediate income and desires long-term capital appreciation.

2. When the investor has a particular knowledge of factors affecting the value of a specific type of collectible. For instance, an artist or art historian may have a unique insight into the quality, rarity, and marketability of Middle Eastern or Oriental art. This sophistication gives such an individual a significant advantage in buying and selling such items.

3. When an investor has unusual access to the sources of supply and demand for a particular type of collectible. For example, an investor with political or social connections in a country famed for its Oriental rugs might be told of a collection coming to market or be given favored status in bargaining for a particular item.

4. When an investor wishes to combine the potential for capital appreciation with the psychological pleasure of owning a collectible. For instance, a stamp collector can derive many hours of personal

satisfaction from his "hobby" at the same time that it provides a source of financial security. A comic book collector can be entertained, amused, and possibly even rewarded.

5. When an individual is looking for an investment with relative capital stability. Many investors, because of their personal attachment to the items collected, are reluctant to sell. Because collectibles are not controlled by individuals who must sell continually, many items are not freely circulated and that adds to their value. The likelihood of a panic sell-off is minimal because collectible investors really wish to own the objects they have collected.

ADVANTAGES

1. Collectibles have the potential for long-term capital growth.

2. Investors with specialized knowledge or information can realize above-average returns.

3. Collectibles are fun!

4. Collectibles have proven to be a relatively stable form of investment with steady appreciation.

DISADVANTAGES

1. Collectibles generally provide no current income for the investor.

2. Most individuals are not expert enough in a particular area to judge the specific quality of the item they are purchasing. Therefore, they are dependent upon the dealer and any appraiser they may employ. An independent appraisal will add to the cost of purchasing the item.

3. Collectibles are subject to swings in popularity. Fads come and go, and even if the number of collectors increases, the price of a particular item may fall, or may not appreciate as rapidly as expected.

4. The absence of an organized market puts both buyers and sellers at a disadvantage; neither is likely to have adequate knowledge of supply, demand, or what is a "fair price" for a particular item. Recently, however, the availability of Internet auction sites, such as Ebay (www.ebay.com) have lessened, but not eliminated, this problem.

5. Investors must take the risk that an item will be damaged, stolen, or destroyed. For example, the pages of a rare book may be torn, wine may turn to vinegar, or a fine old toy bank may rust. Safekeeping, storage, and insurance costs will reduce the overall rate of return on these types of investments.

6. The value of a particular collectible may drop precipitously if a supply previously unknown to the market is discovered.

7. More than in any other area of investment, the potential for fraud and forgery must be considered. Although few experts will be fooled and copying may be difficult, this is a risk that cannot be discounted. (Investors should insist that sellers verify or guarantee the authenticity of a particular item.)

TAX IMPLICATIONS

1. With the exception of dealers, an individual who invests in collectibles is typically purchasing a capital asset. Therefore, any gain realized on the sale of such an item will be subject to long-term capital gain treatment, assuming that it is held for the requisite period of time. The long-term capital gain on a collectible is taxed at a maximum rate of 28% (see "Capital gain" in the Glossary and the discussion of capital gains and losses in Chapter 43, "Taxation of Investment Vehicles"). Likewise, any loss will be treated as either long-term or short-term capital loss. Most collectibles are held for at least one to two years, and therefore will usually result in either a long-term gain or a long-term loss.

2. Since there is no fixed maturity date on collectible investments, the individual can control the timing of any gain or loss. Obviously this makes it advantageous to delay any sale of an investment until a year when the investor's income is low, deductions are high, or a year in which tax brackets have dropped.

3. The increase in value of collectibles occurs on a tax-deferred basis year after year. The investor pays no tax until he chooses to sell.

ALTERNATIVES

1. The investor may switch from one area of collectibles to another as personal tastes and interests change. For example, a stamp collector may turn to rare coins. A collector of ancient Japanese woodcuts may decide to acquire rare and historically valuable photographs.

2. Gold, silver, platinum, and other precious metals share some of the same characteristics as collectibles. These include their tangible nature and emphasis on capital appreciation.

WHERE AND HOW DO I GET IT?

Specialty stores typically offer the finest investment grade collectibles. Such stores will usually concentrate in a particular area of collectibles such as antique furniture or clocks. The investor can expect to pay a premium in doing business with such establishments due to their relatively high overhead.

Auctions are another important source of fine collectibles. They provide the investor with useful pricing information, an opportunity to meet other investor-collectors, and they add to the psychological pleasure of buying, selling, and owning collectibles.

Internet auction sites are more impersonal, but offer access to a huge marketplace of traders and collectors (see "Where Can I Find Out More About it?" below).

Collector conventions are gathering places for large groups of buyers and sellers. They offer many of the same opportunities as auctions, but in a somewhat less formal setting.

Local newspapers are a source of information on estate sales. The pressure to pay taxes and other estate settlement expenses—or to dispose of unwanted assets—often makes valuable items available at favorable prices.

Many general interest newspapers carry advertisements for collectibles. Collectors' magazines such as The Antique Trader are directed at collectors in general. Other sources of market information are the very specific and narrowly focused periodicals – for example, there are magazines directed exclusively at antique gun collectors.

Flea markets are an important source of collectibles for the modest investor. These carnival-like gatherings provide an opportunity to view a large array of items

Chapter 26 – Collectibles

on sale at what are often bargain prices. The investor has an opportunity to negotiate the price, or just plain haggle, with the seller.

Fellow collectors may provide one of the most important sources of information as well as supply and demand for collectibles. Many collectors develop expert knowledge in a particular field and may maintain personal contact with a large number of individuals who share similar interests.

WHAT FEES OR OTHER ACQUISITION COSTS ARE INVOLVED?

Typically, there are no commissions or fees associated with the purchase of collectibles. One important exception would be the formal auction where a percentage of the bid price is added and paid to the auction house by both the buyer and seller of the item.

As with all tangible investments, shipping, storage, and insurance costs must be factored into the investment equation. Appraisal costs may also add significantly to the purchase price of an item.

HOW DO I SELECT THE BEST OF ITS TYPE?

1. There are authoritative (but not always totally accurate) price guides in the collectibles marketplace. These serve as useful tools for investors, but fall far short of being as indicative of value as are the transactions of buyers and sellers on an organized exchange.

2. Wealthy investors may wish to hire authorities and experts in a particular area of collectibles. For instance, an individual could employ an appraiser or art consultant to locate and negotiate the price for a specific painting.

3. Dealers in collectibles can provide access to information as well as share their expertise with valued customers.

4. As much as in any other investment, if not more so, the purchase of collectibles requires knowledge on the part of the investor. Specifically, this means knowledge of the particular characteristics that make the investment valuable. This insight can be obtained through courses given through colleges or adult continuing education programs. There are also programs available through museums and

galleries. These educational experiences enhance the collector's psychological enjoyment as well as increase the potential for investment gain.

WHERE CAN I FIND OUT MORE ABOUT IT?

1. There are many reference books for the collector available in libraries and local bookstores. Such references include *The Encyclopedia of Collectibles, The Concise Encyclopedia of American Antiques, Investments You Can Live with and Enjoy,* and *A Guide to the Grading of U. S. Coins.*

2. Periodicals are available for almost every type of collectible. Examples include *Antiques, Antique Toy World* (www.antiquetoyworld.com), and *Antique Trader.* Potential investors may want to browse through several of these magazines in their particular areas of interest before making an investment.

3. Clubs, museums, and auction houses often publish newsletters, articles, and catalogs of interest to the collector-investor.

4. Internet search engines such as Google (www.google.com) or Yahoo (www.yahoo.com) provide a powerful tool for collectors. By entering an item such as "Roseville Pottery" into the search engine, a collector can be directed to a variety of resources in his or her area of interest. These may include reference sites, catalogs, or auctions where collectibles are bought and sold. Auction sites provide a realistic measure of the current market value of a collectible.

QUESTIONS AND ANSWERS

Question – How do you determine a fair price for a painting?

Answer – A number of factors must be considered before purchasing a painting (or any other art) for investment purposes. These include: (1) the identity of the artist (an artist whose works are traded in the international art market will bring a higher price than one who is not so well known); (2) the time in the artist's life when the particular work was done (certain styles adopted either early or late in an artist's life may be more sought after and, therefore, bring larger sums than others); (3) the quality of the art (a top quality work will bring a higher price than work by the same artist that is executed in a less professional manner); (4) the condition of the art (scratches, chips, other damages, overcleaning and overpainting may all adversely affect the value of the art); (5) the subject (ugly scenes are less in demand than pleasant ones and certain subjects have a higher popularity than others); (6) the size (very small works of art may be worth more-or-less-than larger versions, and the size must be suitable for use or display); (7) exhibitions (if the work was ever exhibited in a prominent museum or gallery, its quality is presumed to be higher and it is considered more authentic and prestigious); (8) the pedigree (if the past ownership can be traced, the authenticity and quality of the art work are easier to establish); (9) whether there is a genuine signature (the signature of a recognized artist enhances the value); (10) the artist's price history (the various prices the artist has received in the past are indicators of current value); and (11) the identity of the seller (many large and reputable auction galleries will guarantee the authenticity and pedigree of the art).

Question – What should the collector-investor look for when purchasing stamps?

Answer – The first factor in stamp investing is scarcity. The condition of the stamp or stamps is the second major characteristic that should be examined. The shading of the color and the design "centering" are also key factors in determining value. If a stamp is canceled lightly or is unused it will be more valuable. (A "mint" stamp is one that is both unused and in perfect condition while an "unused" stamp is one that has never been used for postage, but is not in perfect condition.) A stamp that is interesting, easily understood, and physically attractive will have stronger appeal, and therefore greater value. Another factor is the country of origin of the stamp. Stamps of countries with a stable government and sound currency that also have wealthy stamp collectors are likely to be more valuable than stamps from countries that do not. A stamp is likely to increase in value at a greater rate if its "topic" is of considerable interest. For instance, a stamp depicting the first moonwalk will have greater value – other things being equal – than a similar stamp carrying the picture of Colonel Arthur Young.

Question – What are the factors that affect the price of a rare coin?

Answer – The four major factors that affect the price of a rare coin are: (1) quality (the condition of the coin); (2) the available supply; (3) the historical significance; and (4) the coin's attractiveness and physical appeal.

Question – Why do so few people become investors in collectibles if the potential for high return is so great?

Answer – It is a good rule of thumb when it comes to collectibles (and perhaps also to investments in gems) to invest in only what can be enjoyed without sacrificing measured income or liquidity needs. There are many reasons for this position:

1. Collectibles, precious metals, and gems are costly to own, store, and insure – yet they produce no income to help purchase or carry those costs.

2. Acquisition costs, markup, and commissions are high relative to the alternatives.

3. Market value fluctuations are common and often significant.

4. Price changes are often due to unpredictable and uncontrollable forces.

5. Perhaps most importantly, it is difficult to find reputable, trustworthy, experienced, and knowledgeable advisers whose income is related to results.

Assets such as gold, diamonds, or platinum are often called "hard assets" and are often purchased as a defensive measure against political instability and inflation.

Chapter 27

LIMITED PARTNERSHIPS

WHAT IS IT?

A limited partnership is a specialized form of business organization. It is an association or combination of one or more "general" partners with at least one or more "limited" partners. In many cases, there is a single general partner and a substantial number of limited partners.

In a typical limited partnership, one general partner manages and operates the business, while the limited partners contribute capital and share in the profits. The general partner's major contribution is frequently in the form of management expertise, not capital. Also, general partners are personally liable for the debts of the partnership.

Limited partners, on the other hand, have no liability beyond their contributions of capital to the partnership. Indeed, limited partners cannot participate in the management of the enterprise or they risk losing their limited-liability protection. The limited partnership form of business encourages individuals to invest without risking more than the capital they have contributed.

Since a general partner in a limited partnership has such a unique role and set of personal responsibilities, his participation in the organization and running of the business is critical. The death, disability, or withdrawal of a general partner normally dissolves the partnership, unless the partnership agreement provides otherwise, or all partners agree, in writing, to substitute a new general partner. Unlike the case with a general partner, the death or incapacity of a limited partner has no effect on the partnership.

There are a variety of different forms of limited partnerships. These include:

- *Private Limited Partnerships* – limited partnerships having no more than 35 limited partners, which allows them to avoid registration with the U. S. Securities and Exchange Commission.

- *Master Limited Partnerships* – an investment that combines the tax benefits of a limited partnership with the liquidity of publicly traded securities.

- *Public Limited Partnerships* – a limited partnership that is registered with the SEC and which is offered to the general public through broker/dealers.

- *Venture Capital Limited Partnerships* – limited partnerships that are formed to invest in small startup businesses.

In the case of larger enterprises, a corporation may be formed to serve as the general partner. This has the advantage of spreading the risk among the shareholders of the corporation acting as the general partner rather than concentrating the risk in a single individual.

WHEN IS THE USE OF THIS TOOL INDICATED?

1. When an investor wants to participate in an enterprise but does not want the responsibility and legal liability of a general partner.

2. When an individual wants to invest in a business but lacks the knowledge or experience to take an active role in the management of the business.

3. When an investor has limited capital and desires the investment diversification that a limited partnership can provide.

ADVANTAGES

1. *Limited Liability* – Similar to the purchase of stock in a publicly-traded corporation, the limited partners in an limited partnership are at risk only for the amount of money they have invested in the business. It is the general partner who has unlimited liability.

2. *Pooling of Resources* – Limited partnerships offer a means by which investors can combine their resources and achieve a level of diversification and risk reduction that they would not be able to enjoy individually. For example, the partnership may be able to invest in several parcels of real estate in

various areas where an individual might be limited to a single investment.

3. *Professional Management* – Investing in real estate, energy resources (oil and gas properties), equipment leasing, and other specialized assets requires a degree of professional knowledge and experience that most investors do not have. Thus, a limited partnership, employing a qualified general partner, permits individuals to take advantage of a wider range of investment opportunities than they might be willing to consider on a personal basis.

4. *Investment Income* – Limited partnership investors normally receive periodic payments from the cash flows of their investment. The amount of these payments is proportionate to their share of the partnership, and the payments are taxable to the limited partners as ordinary income. Also, while the general partner's management fee is normally paid prior to these distributions, the general partner will frequently earn a reduced fee until the limited partners have recovered their initial investment.

5. *Capital Gain Potential* – An additional source of return for limited partnership investors is the possibility of capital gain, or appreciation of the partnership's assets. Capital gains are typically shared with the general partner according to a clearly defined formula in the partnership agreement.

6. *Leverage* – The use of borrowed funds to finance a significant part of the limited partnership's investments can add significantly to the returns earned by the limited partners. The partnership may be able to borrow more money than any single individual. However, this is a two-edged sword that can increase the risk of the investment as well (see "Disadvantages," below).

DISADVANTAGES

1. *Lack of Control* – This is the trade-off that investors make when they engage a general partner to operate and manage the enterprise. Limited partners must rely on the management abilities, experience, and ethics of the general partner. While collectively the limited partners generally have the ability to terminate the general manager and/or sell their interests in the partnership, doing so may require lengthy and expensive legal procedures.

2. *Lack of Ready Marketability* – Unlike publicly traded stocks, bonds, or mutual funds, an interest in a

limited partnership may be difficult to sell or liquidate. Some partnerships have arrangements whereby investors can offer their interest for sale to other partners (or the general partner), but there is no guarantee that others will be interested in buying it. Also, in some states, a limited partnership interest may not be salable prior to the dissolution of the partnership.

The lack of liquidity in a limited partnership can be overcome to some extent through the use of a *master limited partnership* (MLP), which is a limited partnership that is publicly traded on a major stock exchange. Another vehicle to improve liquidity is the emerging secondary market in these programs. There are a number of well-known public limited partnerships where secondary market quotes are available.

3. *Leverage* – As noted earlier, the use of borrowed funds to finance the limited partnership's activities can magnify both potential gains and potential losses for the limited partners. More importantly, limited partners may be liable for their proportionate share of any loans taken out in the name of the partnership. Before taking part in such an investment, the investor should clearly understand whether or not the partnership has the authority and intends to use borrowed funds and what legal liability the investor may have as a limited partner to repay such loans.

4. *Investment Suitability* –In general, limited partnerships tend to be relatively risky investments, and as noted above, can be highly illiquid. Those two features make them unsuitable for the average investor, especially those who lack expertise in the area where investments are to be made. For these reasons, limited partnerships often restrict potential investors to persons with a certain level of income, wealth, or both, or to those subject to a certain federal income tax bracket. These criteria are intended to filter out those individuals who may not be capable of understanding or accepting the risks involved with this type of investment.

TAX IMPLICATIONS

Limited partnerships may be taxed either as corporations or partnerships. If the limited partnership is a publicly-traded partnership it will be taxed as a corporation, and the owners of the limited partnership interests will be taxed as if they were holding stock in a corporation (see Chapter 10, "Common Stock"). A publicly-traded partnership is generally a partnership that is traded on an established securities market or is readily tradable on a secondary market or a substantial equivalent.[1]

A limited partnership that is *not* treated as a corporation for tax purposes is treated as a "pass-through" entity. The limited partnership itself does not pay taxes on its income.[2] Instead, the income (or loss) of the limited partnership "passes-through" to the general and limited partners. Generally, the partnership agreement determines how the income (or loss) is allocated among the general and limited partners. However, if the allocations specified in the partnership agreement do not have "substantial economic effect," the partners' income (or loss) will be based on the partners' interests, based on all the facts and circumstances.[3] In many cases, the partnership agreement will provide for allocations to the limited partners until their contribution to the limited partnership is recovered. For example, the agreement might allocate 90% to the limited partners and 10% to the general partner; after the limited partners have recovered their investment, the allocation might change so that the new allocation will be 50% to the limited partners and 50% to the general partner.

The amount of loss that a limited partner is able to take may be limited. The limitation could come in one of three ways: due to the partner's basis in the partnership, the at-risk rules, or the passive loss limitation. Almost by definition, an investor in a limited partnership is engaging in a passive activity. See Chapter 43 for discussion of the passive activity loss rules and the at-risk rules. A partner's basis is generally the amount that was paid for the partnership interest, with adjustments. The basis is increased by any further contributions to the partnership and by his distributive share of taxable income, tax-exempt income, and the excess of the deductions for depletion over the basis of the property subject to the depletion. A partner's basis is reduced by distributions from the partnership and by his distributive share of losses the partnership may suffer.[4] A limited partner may not deduct partnership losses in excess of his basis in the limited partnership as of the end of the year. Any excess losses may be carried forward to future years.[5]

The generic definition of a passive activity is one in which an investor does not "materially participate" in its management or activity. Rental investments involving real estate, equipment, and other property are treated as passive activities regardless of whether or not the taxpayer materially participates. There are certain exceptions to the passive loss restrictions for investors actively participating in real estate rental activities. These involve the amount of time and personal service that the taxpayer

spends in the activity. These exceptions are gradually phased out for higher-income taxpayers.

ALTERNATIVES

1. Real estate investment trusts (REITs) typically operate as publicly-traded, closed-end investment companies. In the real estate area they generally own and operate a diverse portfolio of investments that may include assets such as shopping centers, apartment complexes (including low-income housing), and construction loans. REITs offer investors certain tax advantages (the avoidance of double taxation at the corporate level, for example) and also the benefit of limited liability similar to limited partnerships.

2. Mutual funds offer investors many of the same advantages of limited partnerships, including diversification, professional management, and certain tax benefits. Mutual funds raise capital by selling shares in the fund and then use the money to purchase a diversified portfolio of common stock. The funds are managed by experienced investors, and they themselves are not taxed as long as they pass on virtually all of their income and capital gains to the fund's shareholders.

WHERE AND HOW DO I GET IT?

1. Financial newspapers such as the *Wall Street Journal* or *Barrons* and major daily newspapers like the *New York Times* regularly carry announcements concerning limited partnerships.

2. Information on large-scale master limited partnerships or publicly traded limited partnerships is available from the SEC or the exchange where the partnership's shares are traded.

3. Publicly traded partnerships are sold by stockbrokers and other licensed securities dealers. Potential investors must be given a copy of the partnership's prospectus with information such as financial data, management information, transaction costs, and legal costs associated with the offering.

WHAT FEES OR OTHER ACQUISITION COSTS ARE INVOLVED?

An individual who purchases an interest in a limited partnership can expect to pay the promoters of the partnership a sales commission as well as various legal and management fees. These charges should be carefully spelled out in the partnership agreement, and investors should examine them carefully. The greater the amount of these fees, the less money is available to invest in the enterprise and the smaller the potential return.

Another concern in this area is that some limited partnerships are structured so that a large proportion of their gains go to the management and the general partners, rather than to the limited partners.

HOW DO I SELECT THE BEST OF ITS TYPE?

Investors considering an investment in a limited partnership should evaluate the following factors:

1. *Nature of the Investment* – Limited partnerships are formed to invest in a wide range of business fields with varying degrees of risk. Three of the most common areas are real estate, energy resources, and equipment leasing.

   Even within each of these three areas risk levels can be quite different. For example, a partnership that invests in quality real estate such as a fully-rented shopping center may have a low level of risk, while another that speculates on raw land investments may have a very high degree of risk. An investor should be familiar and personally comfortable with the types of investments that the partnership has made in the past and plans to make in the future.

2. *Partnership Terms and Conditions* – A careful reading of the partnership agreement is essential, and an investor should rely on legal and accounting expertise if needed. The purpose of the partnership and the relationship between the general partner and the limited partners are critical factors that need to be specified in detail and understood by all participants.

   Especially important is a clear understanding of how and when payments are to be made by the limited partners, and how the cash is to be handled. Can the limited partners be assessed for additional contributions, and under what circumstances? When and how are distributions to the limited partners to be made? What fees and other charges are involved, including promoter's fees and expenses? Can the general

partner be terminated or replaced, and how is the partnership to be disbanded?

3. *Track Record of the General Partner* – In general, limited partners are passive investors who only contribute funds to the partnership. The real success or failure of the enterprise depends almost exclusively on the skill and expertise of the general partner. Every investor should be familiar with the general partner's background, his ability to engage in the proposed business activities, and his prior experience in similar partnership arrangements. Is the general partner an individual or a corporation? Is there depth of management in case one person dies or becomes incapacitated?

WHERE CAN I FIND OUT MORE ABOUT IT?

Unfortunately, due to the unique nature of each limited partnership, there is very little information available to potential investors beyond the partnership agreement itself. This is especially true when the general partner is an individual rather than a corporation.

However, investors can ask to see the partnership agreements and financial records of the general partner's previous operations. They can ask for both personal and bank references, and to be put in contact with investors in previous limited partnerships operated by the general partner.

In those relatively rare circumstances where a master limited partnership or a publicly-traded partnership is involved, the investor can request information from the Securities and Exchange Commission or the exchange where shares in the partnership may be traded.

QUESTIONS AND ANSWERS

Question – How does a limited partnership differ from a real estate investment trust (REIT)?

Answer – One important distinction is that the REIT is typically organized as a corporation rather than a partnership. Another major difference is that a board of directors elected by investors governs and operates a REIT. A limited partnership that invests in real estate is managed by a general partner. Also, the majority of REITs in the U.S. are publicly traded.

Question – What's the difference between a public and a private limited partnership?

Answer – A public limited partnership is registered with the SEC and is offered to the general public through broker/dealers. Private limited partnerships can have no more than 35 limited partners in order to avoid the requirement of SEC registration.

CHAPTER ENDNOTES

1. IRC Sec. 7704.

2. IRC Sec. 701.

3. IRC Sec. 704.

4. IRC Sec. 705(a).

5. IRC Sec. 704(d).

Chapter 28

PRIVATE PLACEMENTS AND VENTURE CAPITAL

WHAT IS IT?

Private Placements

A *private placement* occurs when new securities (stocks or bonds) are sold directly to a single buyer, or a small group of buyers, without going through the process of a public offering. In most cases, the buyers of these issues are banks, mutual funds, insurance companies, pension funds, foundations, hedge funds, and other institutional investors.

More than 30% of the debt instruments sold in the United States each year are placed privately, with only an announcement ("tombstone ad") made in the financial press. The strong interest in private placements is due to a variety of benefits available to buyers and sellers of such issues.

Firms that sell securities using private placements can generally do so at lower costs than if the securities were registered and sold to the public. Legal expenses, accounting fees, and investment banking charges will generally be much less than if an issue has to be registered with the Securities Exchange Commission (SEC) and sold to the public. For example, a private placement does not require the preparation of a prospectus as is necessary with a public offering.

Another benefit for the issuer is the fact that private placements do not have to meet the SEC's normal standard of disclosure for public offerings of securities. The assumption behind this exemption is that the institutional investors participating in the private placement market are experienced and knowledgeable enough to assess the risks involved with these types of investments.

There are advantages for the buyers in a private placement as well. In exchange for all of the seller's gains, buyers typically can earn a return that is 50 to 75 basis points higher from a private issue than from a public offering. Higher yields are justified, not only because of the cost savings available to the seller, but also because of the limited marketability of the securities involved.

When the private placement involves equity, it is fairly common to use the device of "lettered stock" (also referred to as "restricted stock" or "legend stock"), which is subject to certain restrictions. Under SEC Rule 144, such stock can only be sold after a 2-year holding period, and the shares have to be sold gradually so as not to disrupt public markets.

The buyer and seller in a private placement both benefit from the ability to personally negotiate the terms and conditions of the issue. They may have more flexibility in designing the features of an issue than if they were constrained by conditions in the public securities markets.

Venture Capital

Venture capital (VC) is a source of funding typically made available to startup firms and small businesses with strong growth potential. The capital is generally in the form of an equity (stock) investment provided by venture capital funds, though convertible debt may sometimes be used. These organizations are generally private partnerships or closely held corporations. In the limited partnership form of organization, the venture capital firm serves as the general partner.

Venture capital firms obtain capital from a variety of sources, including

- private and public pension funds,
- endowment funds,
- foundations,
- corporations,
- wealthy individuals, and
- foreign investors.

Since venture capital investing has a high degree of risk, VC firms carefully screen companies before making an investment, and they generally invest in only a small percentage of the companies that they review. Venture

245

Tools & Techniques of Investment Planning

capital firms also try to reduce risk by spreading their investments over a portfolio of companies, and sometimes combining with other venture capital firms in providing financing to a business.

Venture capital firms are rarely passive investors. They normally take an active role in the businesses they finance, performing some or all of the following activities:

- assisting in the development of new products and services,

- contributing management expertise, or

- sharing experiences from other venture capital investments.

Venture firms generally do not see their investments as being permanent in nature. Most seek to exit their investment in three to seven years, and move on to investing in other new companies. During that period, however, the venture capital firm's investment is relatively illiquid.

WHEN IS THE USE OF THIS TOOL INDICATED?

Private placements and venture capital investments are attractive to investors who

1. are willing to commit relatively large amounts of capital for a significant period of time (three to seven years);

2. generally have no need for current income from their investments;

3. are able to accept a relatively high degree of risk in their investment portfolio in anticipation of substantial capital gain potential;

4. in the venture capital area, may be able to contribute some significant managerial or business expertise to the new venture; or

5. desire the relative secrecy and flexibility of negotiating the sale and purchase of securities privately.

ADVANTAGES

1. The greatest advantage of a private placement, from the issuer's and buyer's point of view, is that it does not have to be registered with the Securities and Exchange Commission (SEC) since it is not a public offering. In order to qualify for this exemption, the securities must be purchased for investment purposes rather than resale. If the buyers subsequently wish to sell the securities to the public, they must go through the normal registration process with the SEC.

2. Privately-placed debt issues normally offer a higher yield than publicly offered debt. Buyers can negotiate a higher rate of return in exchange for the cost savings and convenience of a non-public offering.

3. For individuals with specific business expertise in areas like management, marketing, engineering, or finance, a venture capital investment may offer them the opportunity to actively participate in running one or more business organizations.

DISADVANTAGES

1. *Lack of Investment Liquidity* – Private placement and venture capital investments should be considered long-term in nature. For example, many VC funds are organized as fixed life partnerships, usually having a term of ten years. In the case of private placements, possible restrictions on the sale of stock ("letter stock") and the lack of SEC registration may severely limit the ability to sell an investment.

2. *Lack of Current Income* – Startup firms and small businesses generally need to retain most if not all of their earnings to reinvest in the business. As they mature, they typically need new or expanded facilities, additional equipment, and more inventories to support rapidly growing sales. Dividends to shareholders are a luxury most such firms cannot afford in the early stages of their development.

3. *High Degree of Investment Risk* – A very large percentage of new businesses fail for many different reasons. For every successful firm, there are likely to be several that do not succeed. And, even those that do survive must be successful enough to offset the loss of capital from the failed firms. Venture capital investing is not for the faint-hearted.

It should be noted, however, that some private placements are fairly conservative investments, such as a debt (bond) issue with a well-established firm. These would be much less risky than the typical VC investment, and may provide some degree of current income as well.

4. *Lack of Management Control* – Many venture capital and private placement investments are structured as limited partnerships with a single general partner and a number of limited partners. However, the general partner may be a corporation, which helps to spread the risk associated with having full legal liability for the partnership's activities.

    The limited partners in these arrangements typically provide capital, but have very little control or influence over the organization's affairs or day-to-day operations. An exception to this general rule may be in the venture capital area where an investor may be able to contribute significant managerial experience gained during his business career.

5. *Uncertainty of Investment Timing* – Participating in a venture capital fund generally subjects the investor to a series of "capital calls," which occur when the fund actually begins to invest in various businesses and collects the needed funds from its partners. The timing of these requests may be somewhat uncertain and extend over a substantial period of time.

6. *Size of Required Investment* – The typical size of these investments is quite large, making them generally impractical for the average individual investor. Private placements are almost always done with institutional investors, and venture capital funds normally restrict investors to those with substantial wealth and high levels of income. It would not be unusual for a venture capital program to require a minimum investment of $1,000,000, or more.

TAX IMPLICATIONS

Private Placements – In a private placement, stocks or bonds are sold directly to a single buyer (or a small group of buyers). For the tax consequences of sales of stock, see Chapter 10, "Common Stock." (Note that under SEC Rule 144, restricted stock can only be sold after a 2-year holding period.) For the tax consequences of sales of corporate bonds, see Chapter 3, "Corporate Bonds."

Venture Capital – Venture capital firms generally "invest their capital through funds organized as limited partnerships in which the venture capital firm serves as the general partner." See Chapter 27, "Limited Partnerships," for the tax consequences applicable to limited partners.

Depending on the investment focus and strategy of the venture firm, it may seek to exit the investment in a company within three to five years of the initial investment through (1) an initial public offering (IPO), or (2) a merger or acquisition.

In a public offering, the venture firm receives stock in the company; however, the venture firm is regulated and restricted in how that stock can be sold or liquidated. Once the stock is freely tradable (usually after about two years), the venture fund distributes the stock or cash to its limited partner investors, who may then manage the public stock as a regular stock holding, or liquidate it upon receipt. Mergers and acquisitions are the most common type of successful exit for venture investments. In a merger or acquisition, the venture firm receives stock (or cash) from the acquiring company, and then distributes the proceeds from the sale to its limited partners.

If the transaction qualifies as a "tax-free" (or more accurately "tax deferred") reorganization under IRC Section 368(a)(1), the tax is deferred until the stockholders sell their new shares.[1]

ALTERNATIVES

Private placements and venture capital funds (partnerships) are somewhat unique in nature and they do not have many comparable alternative investments. Some that may be considered are

1. mutual funds, which may be an option to venture capital investing—especially those closed-end funds that concentrate their capital in one particular sector of the economy—and

2. Real Estate Investment Trusts (REITs), which offer some of the same advantages and disadvantages of private placements and venture capital in the area of real estate and construction financing.

WHERE AND HOW DO I GET IT?

Private placements are available to institutional investors and "accredited" individual investors (i.e., an individual whose net worth exceeds $1,000,000 or whose income exceeds $200,000 for the past two years). Venture capital funds are sometimes marketed through major brokerage firms and investment bankers, but the minimum initial investment is usually very large and not really practical for the average investor.

WHAT FEES OR OTHER ACQUISITION COSTS ARE INVOLVED?

If an individual were able to participate in a venture capital operation, they could expect to pay the promoters of the fund a sales commission as well as various legal and management fees. These charges should be carefully spelled out in the partnership agreement, and investors should examine them carefully. The greater the amount of these fees, the less money is available to invest in the enterprise and the smaller the potential return.

Also, as noted in Chapter 27, "Limited Partnerships," another possible concern in this area is that some venture capital limited partnerships are structured so that a large proportion of their gains go to the management and the general partner(s), rather than to the limited partners.

HOW DO I SELECT THE BEST OF ITS TYPE?

Private Placements

Since private placements are almost always negotiated between the issuing firm and one or more institutional investors, individuals rarely have the opportunity to participate. Only very wealthy individuals would be solicited for this type of investment. Those individuals would have to consider

1. the nature of the investment (i.e., debt vs. equity);

2. the terms of the particular offering (e.g., the interest rate, or yield for a bond issue, or the dividend paid on common stock, if any); and

3. the risk factors associated with the specific investment.

Venture Capital

Since so many venture capital funds are organized as limited partnerships, they share most of the same selection criteria (see Chapter 27, "Limited Partnerships"). These include:

1. *Nature of the Investment* – VC funds are established to invest in a wide range of business areas with varying degrees of risk. Investors should be familiar with the economic areas the fund plans to enter and the degree of risk they can expect to encounter.

2. *Partnership Terms and Conditions* – A careful reading of the partnership agreement is essen-

tial, and an investor should rely on legal and accounting expertise if needed. The objectives of the partnership and the relationship between the general partner(s) and the limited partners are critical factors that need to be specified in detail and understood by all participants.

Especially important is a clear understanding of how and when payments are to be made by the limited partners, and how the cash is to be handled. Can the limited partners be assessed for additional contributions, and under what circumstances? When and how are distributions to the limited partners to be made? What fees and other charges are involved, including promoter's fees and expenses? Can the general partner be terminated or replaced, and how is the partnership to be disbanded?

3. *Track Record of the General Partner(s)* – In general, limited partners are passive investors who only contribute funds to the partnership. The real success or failure of the enterprise depends almost exclusively on the skill and expertise of the general partner. Every investor should be familiar with the general partner's background, his (its) ability to engage in the proposed business activities, and his (its) prior experience in similar partnership arrangements. Is the general partner an individual or a corporation? Does depth of management exist in case one person dies or becomes incapacitated?

WHERE CAN I FIND OUT MORE ABOUT IT?

1. Due to the unique nature of private placements, there is generally little information available to individual investors. As noted earlier, one way that individuals can participate in this area indirectly is through certain mutual funds, typically so-called "closed-end funds." Information on such funds is available through the Investment Company Institute in Washington, DC (www.ici.org).

2. The National Venture Capital Association, NVCA, (www.nvca.org) provides a wide range of information on venture capital investing including (1) an industry overview, (2) NVCA members, (3) NVCA publications, and (4) a calendar of NVCA events.

3. The Investment Company Institute, Washington, DC, also offers a publication entitled, "A Guide to

Closed-End Funds" as part of its Investor Awareness Program" (www.ici.org).

QUESTIONS AND ANSWERS

Question – Does the federal government regulate venture capital-oriented mutual funds?

Answer – Yes, like the more common open-end type, closed-end funds are also governed by the Investment Company Act of 1940, which specifies how all publicly offered mutual funds must be organized and managed. All closed-end funds must meet certain operating standards, observe strict antifraud rules, and disclose complete information to current and potential investors. These laws are designed to protect investors from fraud and abuse.

Question – What is "letter stock"?

Answer – Letter stock, or a letter security is a stock or bond that is not registered with the Securities and Exchange Commission (SEC) and, therefore, cannot be sold in the public market. When an issue is sold directly by the issuer to the investor, registration with the SEC can be avoided if a letter of intent (investment letter) is signed by the purchaser establishing that the securities are being bought for investment, and not for resale.

Question – Does the federal government provide support for start-up companies in any way?

Answer – Yes, the federal government provides funds through the Small Business Administration (SBA – www.sba.gov), which promotes venture capital programs through the licensing and financing of corporations organized as Small Business Investment Companies (SBICs).

Question – What is "mezzanine financing"?

Answer – *Mezzanine financing* is an intermediate stage of the venture capital process. It comes after the initial stage of venture capital funding, and generally just prior to the firm going public. Venture capitalists entering at that point have a lower risk of loss than at previous stages, and can look forward to early capital appreciation as a result of an IPO.

CHAPTER ENDNOTES

1. See National Venture Capital Association, *The Venture Capital Industry* at www.nvca.org/def.html. See also Kenneth Rind and Martin Mushkin, Esq., *Exiting by Disposition – Negotiating an Acquisition of Your Portfolio Company*, 22nd Annual Venture Capital Institute, at www.ncva.org.

Chapter 29

AMERICAN DEPOSITARY RECEIPTS

WHAT IS IT?

American Depositary Receipts (ADRs) are simply receipts issued by a U.S. bank on foreign securities purchased by the bank through a foreign correspondent bank and held in trust for the benefit of the ADR holder.

ADRs were introduced as a result of the complexities involved in buying shares in foreign countries – primarily the difficulties associated with trading at different prices and currency values. The depositary bank sets the ratio of United States ADRs per home country share. This ratio can be anything less than or greater than one. The banks do this to price the ADR high enough to show substantial value, yet low enough so that individual investors can still afford to purchase these shares. Many investors try to avoid investing in penny stocks; thus, many would shy away from a company trading for, say, 50 Russian Rubles per share (which equates to about $1.50 US per share). As a result, the price range for the majority of ADRs is between $10 and $100 per share. If the shares are worth considerably less in the home country, then each ADR may represent several real shares.[1]

ADRs are priced in U.S. dollars and investors can buy or sell ADRs in the same way they trade American stocks. ADRs can be listed on any of the U.S. exchanges, such as the New York Stock Exchange (NYSE) and the American Stock Exchange (AMEX), and may be quoted for trading on the National Association of Securities Dealers Automated Quotation System (NASDAQ), the NASD's over-the-counter market, or the pink sheets. ADRs can also be privately placed and traded as Rule 144A securities. The average daily trading volume of ADRs in U.S. dollars has risen from under $200 billion in 1992 to over $2 trillion in 2003. The concept of the ADR has been extended to other geographical markets, resulting in structures known as Global Depositary Receipts (GDRs), International Depositary Receipts (IDRs), and European Depositary Receipts (EDRs), which are generally traded or listed in one or more international markets.[2]

Dividends on the stocks underlying an ADR are received by the depositary bank, which turns over the proceeds – net of foreign withholding taxes, and in U.S. dollars – to the ADR holder. The depositary bank acts something like a U.S.-based international mutual fund,

performing all the functions that individuals investing directly in foreign securities might not be able to perform. Essentially, ADRs permit investors to purchase whole and selected individual foreign company shares, rather than pro-rata shares, of a portfolio of foreign securities.

WHEN IS THE USE OF THIS TOOL INDICATED?

1. ADRs allow investors to buy foreign stocks and diversify internationally without the difficulties and restrictions of direct foreign investments.

2. ADRs internalize the costs of foreign currency exchange for U.S. dollars with every dividend or interest payment. They also eliminate the costs of buying and selling securities in a foreign currency.

3. Many studies indicate that investors can increase overall returns and reduce overall risk (as measured by volatility) by including foreign investments in their portfolios.[3] Most Americans are woefully underinvested in foreign securities. According to the Investment Company Institute, $6.97 trillion dollars was invested in U.S.-based mutual funds as of the end of 2001.[4] Of that total, only $429 billion was invested in international funds, which amounts to 6.14% of the mutual fund total.

ADVANTAGES AND DISADVANTAGES

1. International diversification can increase average returns for a portfolio while reducing the overall volatility of the portfolio.

2. It is possible that political or economic turmoil could cause the country of an investor's foreign security to restrict capital flows. Therefore, receipt of interest, dividends, and, perhaps, principal could be delayed or – in the extreme – forfeited altogether.

3. Currency differences can have a major effect on ADR performance. One could actually lose money on the stock and end up making money because of currency fluctuations, or vice-versa.

4. Financial information on foreign securities is generally less available and less reliable than what Americans have come to expect for domestic securities.

TAX IMPLICATIONS

1. Foreign taxes are generally withheld before interest and dividends are passed through to the ADR holder. U.S. treaties can result in partial reclamation of withholdings in some countries.

2. Foreign taxes paid can be offset, to some extent, against federal income taxes.[5]

3. There is often no capital gain tax imposed by foreign governments, but the United States government taxes such gains.[6]

4. Special rules apply to 10% or more ownership of a foreign corporation.

5. The 15% maximum tax rate for qualified dividends is generally applicable to U.S. individual investors in ADRs issued by entities that satisfy the Internal Revenue Code's definition of "qualified foreign corporations." For those ADRs issued by entities that do not meet the definition, dividends will be taxed at the taxpayer's tax rate for ordinary income.

Generally, the term "qualified foreign corporation" includes any foreign corporation that (a) is eligible for the benefits of a comprehensive income tax treaty with the United States, or (b) has issued stock that is readily tradable on an established securities market in the United States.[7] The term does not include passive foreign investment companies, foreign investment companies, and foreign personal holding companies.[8]

In order to be considered as a "qualified foreign corporation" under the treaty test, a foreign corporation must be eligible for benefits of one of the U.S. income tax treaties deemed satisfactory by the U.S. Treasury. Thus, the foreign corporation must be a "resident" within the meaning of such term under the relevant treaty and must satisfy any other requirements of that treaty, including the requirements under any applicable limitation on benefits provision.[9]

The United States Treasury has determined that a non-U.S. corporation's American Depositary Receipt (ADR) is considered to be readily tradable

on an established securities market in the United States if it is listed on a national securities exchange that is registered under Section 6 of the Securities Exchange Act of 1934" (e.g., the NYSE, AMEX), or on the NASDAQ stock market (i.e., collectively known as the "qualified exchanges").[10]

ALTERNATIVES

1. Alternatives to investing in ADRs include international or global mutual funds, passive foreign investment companies, international exchange-traded index funds, and single-country index funds.

2. Investing in multinational corporations listed on the U.S. stock exchanges is another alternative to investing in ADRs.

WHERE CAN I FIND OUT MORE ABOUT IT?

1. *Morgan Stanley Capital International Perspective*, Morgan Stanley, 1251 Avenue of the Americas, New York, NY; a publication with information about the stocks of over 2,100 companies located worldwide; primarily for institutional investors; price $5,000 annually; can be viewed at Morgan Stanley offices in major cities around the country.

2. ADR prices are listed in the *Wall Street Journal* and other newspapers as well as in electronic databases.

3. *Dessauer's Investor's World*, Phillips Investment Resources, LLC, 7811 Montrose Road, Potomac, MD, 20854 (www.investorplace.com).

4. *Worldwide Investment Notes*, 7730 Carondelet Avenue, St. Louis, MO 63150.

5. J.P. Morgan sponsors a site that is described as "the central source for information on ADRs and international equities" at www.adr.com.

CHAPTER ENDNOTES

1. *ADR Tutorial*, p. 2, at: www.investopedia.com/university/adr/.

2. *About ADRs*, at www.ADR.com.

3. See, e.g., Jeff Troutner, *Are You Giving Up on Global Diversification?*, TAM Asset Management, Inc., at: www.indexfunds.com.

4. Investment Company Institute, *Mutual Fund Fact Book*, pp. 38, 47 (2002 Edition), at: www.ici.org.

5. The foreign tax credit is intended to relieve investors of the double tax burden when foreign source income is taxed by both the United States and the foreign country. Alternatively, investors may opt to claim an itemized deduction for foreign taxes. Taken as a credit, foreign income taxes reduce U.S. tax liability; taken as a deduction, foreign income taxes reduce U.S. taxable income. IRS Publication 514 (Foreign Tax Credit for Individuals), pp.1-2, at: www.irs.gov.

6. The tax rate generally applicable for long-term capital gains incurred after May 5, 2003 is 15%. IRC Sec. 1(h)(1).

7. IRC Sec. 1(h)(11)(C).

8. Passive foreign investment companies (PFICs) are essentially investment companies based in foreign countries. Since these investment companies are not directly subject to U.S. tax law and organizational rules, PFIC investors who reside in the United States are subject to special tax rules to assure they do not avoid any U.S. tax on the investment income and capital gains they earn in PFICs. The discussion of these tax rules is beyond the scope of this chapter.

9. To qualify as an approved treaty, such treaty must be comprehensive, the Secretary of the Treasury must determine it is satisfactory, and it must provide for the exchange of tax information. IRC Sec. 1(h)(11)(C)(i)(II); Notice 2003-69, 2003-42 IRB 851.

10. For further detail on the "readily tradable" definition, see Notice 2003-71, 2003-43 IRB 922. The Treasury Department and the IRS are considering – for years after 2003 – having the favorable dividend rate extended *only* to stock or ADRs traded *only* on the Over-the-Counter Bulletin Board (OTCBB) or the electronic pink sheets. They are presently soliciting comments on the "readily tradable" definition for applicability for future taxable years.

Chapter 30

INVESTMENT RISK

WHAT IS IT?

Most people think of investment risk as the potential for loss. They envision the dollar value of their hard-earned assets shrinking due to forces beyond their control.

Since investments are purchased with the expectation of gain, focusing on the potential for loss alone is insufficient in explaining investment risk.

The notion of investment risk must take into account the possibility that the return may be positive (but greater or less than expected), zero, or negative. There can be wide variations in the magnitude of either positive or negative returns. When all possibilities (positive or negative returns and the variations in the magnitude of each type of return) are examined, investment risk can be more accurately defined as the variability in the expected return from an investment. The greater the potential variation in the investment's expected return, the greater is the actual risk of owning the investment.[1]

Causes of Variability in an Investment's Expected Return

Investors must examine each investment separately because the various forces affecting return have a different impact on each type of investment. For example, if interest rates increase, the prices of electric utility stocks may be adversely affected since many investors purchase utility stocks for the income they provide.

Investors, who would normally be in the market for income-producing stocks such as utilities, would be attracted to newly issued bonds offering a higher current return. Some holders of utility stocks will sell and invest the proceeds in bonds offering more attractive returns. The lack of buyers and the increase in the number of sellers will drive down the prices of utility stocks until their current dividend yield is competitive with the newly issued, higher paying bonds.

However, the prices of growth stocks such as those in the computer industry will be largely unaffected by rising interest rates. Investors purchase growth stocks

for their long-term capital gains potential and show little concern with current dividend yield.

The total investment risk for a particular asset depends on the combined effect of many forces. Before investing in certain products, it is important to understand the various risks that are associated with them. Investments may be exposed to a number of different types or sources of risk.

TYPES OR SOURCES OF RISK

Actuarial Risk – Risk an insurance underwriter covers in exchange for premiums, such as the risk of premature death.

Agency Risk – Agency risk is the risk associated with delegating decisions to an agent who may not always act in the client's best interest if the objectives of the client and the agent conflict. This is a widespread area of research in economic and financial theory involving the design of agency incentive and compensation systems that tend to correlate the agent's rewards with the achievement of the client's objectives. The problem arises in the control, regulatory, legal, and incentive arrangements for government agencies, professional management of firms, professional portfolio and money managers, financial advisers, and many other areas. However, whatever the compensation arrangement, conflicts will always inevitably arise.

For instance, basing a money manager's compensation on the rate of return earned by the fund he manages may seem to match investors' objectives for higher returns with the agent's incentive compensation. However, since money managers rarely have to pay investors if they happen to lose money in a given evaluation period (unless investors can prove malfeasance or fraud), the money manager has an incentive, perhaps, to take on greater risks in the search for exceptional gains than is consistent with the risk level the investors wish to bear. In addition, the investors and the manager may have different time horizons. The manager may be inclined to engage in transactions that enhance measured performance over the current evaluation period, but at the potential loss of future performance.

Tools & Techniques of Investment Planning

Asset Class Risk – Stocks, bonds, and cash are the three major asset classes (but certainly not the only ones). If investors allocate a disproportionate amount to any of the three main categories, or totally ignore one or two of them, they are subject to asset class risk. It is prudent to diversify across all major asset classes even when investors want to give primary emphasis to, say, stocks.

Bid-Ask Spread Risk—Securities sold over-the-counter by investment banking houses that make a market in the shares are subject to the risk that the bid-ask price spread will change. Dealers charge one price, the ask price, when they sell these securities and another lower price, the bid price, when they buy. The spread, or difference, is the profit the market maker gets for making the market in the security and helps to cover the market makers cost in maintaining an inventory of the securities. Depending upon supply and demand conditions in the security or the entrance or exit of market makers in a particular security, the spread may change over time. For example, investors buying a security when the spread is narrow may think that they will later be able to sell the security at only a small discount from the ask price. However, if the spread increases, the effective cost of the round-trip transaction will go up.

Business (Company) Risk – Business risk is an economic or operating risk reflected in the variability of a firm's earnings. Changes in earnings or the variability of earnings may result in changes in the investing public's perception of the company and sudden changes in the price of the stock. In worst case scenarios, companies may fail, leaving their stocks or bonds worthless. The best defense against this particular risk is to invest in more than one company and in companies engaged in different lines of business. Business risk is composed largely of four risk subcategories:

Management risk – Financial difficulties can arise from management's inability to handle change or failure to adapt to changing competitive conditions. Some companies are slow to take advantage of cost-cutting technologies and gradually become high-cost producers who are unable to survive in a highly competitive marketplace.

Product or obsolescence risk – Shifting demand or changes in consumer tastes and preferences can quickly leave companies with the capacity to produce the unwanted. Sometimes this risk is termed **technological or innovative risk**, as new innovations or technologies make a company's products or processes no longer state-of-the-art.

Legislative/regulatory/tax risk – Changes in the law can affect a company's fortunes. For example, if the federal government abandons protectionist policies that artificially raise the price of sugar in the United States to over 20 cents a pound and allow U.S. companies to purchase sugar on world markets at world prices (around 10 cents a pound), the makers of corn sweeteners would suddenly find themselves unable to compete. They would be stuck with production facilities they could no longer use. Their earnings would decline, their prospects would deteriorate, and the prices of their stocks would suddenly decline. Other companies such as Coca Cola and Pepsi, who purchase sugar in large quantities, would see a dramatic decrease in the price of a major raw material. The market would immediately recognize their higher earnings potential and bid up their stock prices.

Financial risk – This is the risk related to the mix of debt and equity used by a firm to raise capital. The more debt is in a firm's capital structure, the greater is its financial risk. Debt financing, as opposed to equity financing, obligates a firm to make periodic interest payments and to repay the amount borrowed at some future date. Before a firm can distribute dividends to its common stockholders, it must meet its fixed-payment obligations. Failure to meet these obligations when they are due will result in insolvency or bankruptcy.

Call (Prepayment, Redemption) Risk—Many bonds and some preferred stocks are issued with what is known as a call feature. The call feature gives the issuer the right to call the bond – to retire it after a certain date or on several dates before maturity. Having the right to call the bond does not mean that the issuer has a duty or obligation to exercise the call. Generally, bonds will be called only when it is profitable for the issuer to do so. This occurs when interest rates have declined since the bonds were issued. The high interest issue is then called and replaced with a new issue that is sold at a much lower interest rate. So call risk inherently includes **reinvestment risk** as well.

Suppose an investor purchases a bond with a 9% coupon, and expects it to pay that rate for the next 10 years. Suddenly, the bond is called. The investor receives the principal amount of the bond, but when the investor attempts to reinvest the funds in the bond market, the investor finds the interest rate is now 7% for similar issues. Suddenly the investor's interest income drops from $90 to $70 on a $1,000 bond – a 22% decline. This is what call risk is all about.

Country Risk – This refers to the risk that a country will not be able to honor its financial commitments. When a country defaults, it can harm the performance of all other financial instruments in that country, as well as other countries with which it has relations. Country risk applies to stocks, bonds, mutual funds, options, and futures that are issued within a particular country. In addition, this danger is associated with single-country mutual funds or closed-end funds and ADRs sold or traded in the United States. This type of risk is most often seen in emerging markets or countries that have a severe deficit. Investing overseas introduces many potential risks — including currency fluctuation, the potential for diplomatic and political instability, regulatory and liquidity risks, foreign taxation, and differences in auditing or other financial standards. Investing in foreign stocks can deliver great rewards, but investors must be aware of the risks and plan accordingly.

Credit or Default Risk – This is the risk that a government, company, or individual will be unable to pay the contractual interest or principal on its debt obligations. This type of risk is of particular concern to investors who hold bonds within their portfolio. Government bonds, especially those issued by the federal government, have the least amount of default risk and the lowest interest rates among bond issuers, while corporate bonds tend to have the highest amount of default risk, but also the higher interest rates. Bonds with lower chances of default are considered to be investment grade, and bonds with higher chances are considered to be junk bonds. Bond rating services, such as Moody's Investor Services or Standard and Poor's, allow investors to determine which bonds are investment grade, and which bonds are junk.

Currency (Foreign Exchange) Risk – Foreign holdings may change in value as the value of currency changes. If the U.S. dollar grows stronger relative to foreign currencies, investors will experience a currency loss on their foreign securities. As an example, assume American investors invest in some Canadian stock in Canadian dollars. Even if the share value appreciates, they may lose money if the Canadian dollar depreciates in relation to the American dollar. Conversely, if the U.S. dollar weakens relative to foreign currencies, investors who invest in the foreign securities will enjoy a bonus.

Fluctuating exchange rates are of particular concern to single-country investors. Currency fluctuations can be devastating for individuals who hold funds for short periods. Some foreign-stock fund managers may try to hedge their portfolios against adverse currency moves with currency futures or forward contracts. However,

hedgers are fallible and lose money when the currency goes opposite their predictions. In addition, a hedge costs money. Currency risk is generally not too much of a problem for long-term investors in well diversified international funds.

Depth of Market Risk – Depth of market risk is related to bid-ask spread risk and is related to securities that are relatively thinly capitalized. An investor trying to sell a relatively sizeable position in a thinly capitalized stock may find that there are not enough willing buyers at the current price to absorb his entire sale. Consequently, the very act of selling may depress the price and reduce the investor's gain or increase his loss.

Discount or Premium Risk – Closed-end investment companies listed on organized exchanges or sold over the counter typically trade at values different from their net asset values (NAV). The NAV is the value at which the securities underlying a share in the fund would trade if they were purchased directly in the market, rather than through the closed-end fund.

More often than not, closed-end fund shares trade at a discount from NAV, which can be a boon for investors. For instance, assume a closed-end stock fund is trading at a 10% discount from NAV and the underlying stocks are paying a 3% dividend yield relative to their market values as independently traded stocks. Investors who buy the stocks through the closed-end investment company essentially get to purchase $100 worth of action for only a $90 investment. Consequently, the dividend yield on their investment is 3.33%. In addition, if the underlying stock values increase 20%, the closed-end fund investors' share will increase by 20% if the discount remains steady at 10%.

Discounts and premiums on closed-end funds vary over time. Suppose the discount from NAV increases from 10% to, say, 15% at the same time the underlying securities increase in value by 20%. The closed-end fund investors will earn a respectable 13.33%, but that is still about 6.67% less than the 20% they otherwise would have earned by investing directly in the underlying stocks. But there can be more negative effects as well. If the value of the underlying securities had fallen by 20% while the discount also increased by 5%, the closed-end fund investors would have lost 24.44% as compared with only a 20% loss on a direct investment in the underlying stocks.

But suppose the discount from NAV decreases from 10% to 5% at the same time the underlying securities increase in value by 20%. The closed-end fund investors would have gained 26.67% as compared with only a 20% gain on a direct investment in the underlying stocks. If the value of the underlying securities had fallen by 20% while the discount also decreased by 5%, the closed-end fund investors would have lost 15.56% as compared with a 20% loss on a direct investment in the underlying stocks.

Although most closed-end funds usually sell at a discount from NAV, some frequently sell for premiums above NAV, especially among those funds investing in foreign stocks. The reason for this phenomenon is that individual investors often would find it extremely difficult to trade directly in all the underlying foreign securities of the fund, so they are willing to pay a premium to include these assets in their overall portfolio for diversification and asset allocation purposes.

Documentation Risk – The risk of loss due to an inadequacy or other unforeseen aspect of the legal documentation behind the financial contract.

Event Risk – Mergers, acquisitions, and other major occurrences can significantly affect a specific investment asset. For example, when one firm announces its intention to acquire another, the share prices of both companies are affected. This risk applies to bonds to some extent as well, but is not a consideration for other assets such as savings accounts and U.S. Treasury securities.

Financial Risk – This is the risk related to the mix of debt and equity used by a firm to raise capital. The more debt is in a firm's capital structure, the greater is its financial risk. Debt financing as opposed to equity financing obligates a firm to make periodic interest payments and to repay the amount borrowed at some future date. Before a firm can distribute dividends to its common stockholders, it must meet its fixed-payment obligations. Failure to meet these obligations when they are due will result in the company's insolvency or bankruptcy. The market's perceived level of this risk affects not just the company's cost of borrowing for bond issues and the value of its stock, but also the availability of lines of credit and financing for inventories and working capital, its credit terms with suppliers, and, ultimately, much of its cost of doing business.

Geographical or Location Risk – This is the risk associated typically with real estate, where the old saw goes: the three most important elements are location, location, and location! However, it is a broader concept, as well, relating to regional economic factors. In that sense, it is a smaller-scale version of **country risk**. For instance, certain regions of the U.S., such as Texas, Oklahoma,

and Colorado are heavily involved in the oil business. If the oil industry has a serious downturn, the regional economies will suffer, affecting other companies and industries within the region such as financial institutions, real estate, and retail sales. Similarly, many companies have their headquarters in Delaware because of its favorable tax and regulatory environment. However, if state government policies would change, these companies could be adversely affected.

Industry or Sector Risk – This risk relates to uncertainties caused by particular features of the industry sector in which a company operates.

These risks can vary dramatically. New technologies, for example, are always going to expose investors to higher uncertainty of future returns than the market average – because of the inherent uncertainty of their new products and new markets – and they will certainly be more uncertain than food retailers. (Food will never go out of fashion).

So industry risks can be identified and differentiated on a scale from low to high, relative to the market average. As investors need rewarding for taking on higher risk, investors can expect that all stocks in the technology sector will offer higher returns than stocks in food retailing – but those returns are less likely to appear than the lower, more certain returns in foods. But it is not conclusive. A really efficient company in the electronics sector may suffer less than an inefficient food retailer.

Inflation (Purchasing Power) Risk – The purchasing power of the dollar declines during periods of inflation. Inflation has been moderate in recent years; however, during certain times it has been quite substantial. For example, in the early 1980s, inflation rose to over 14%. Assets that are most susceptible to this risk include fixed income assets such as corporate and municipal bonds, and cash assets such as savings accounts and CDs. Generally speaking, real estate and equity investments such as common stocks tend to increase in value and pay higher dividends over time. However, it is not unusual for these investments to fail to keep up with inflation in the short run, but, over the long run, both the prices of these assets and the income they generate have more than kept up with inflation.

The risk associated with inflation is not so much with the level of inflation, since investments tend to be priced in the market to yield returns that account for anticipated inflation and give investors the real returns that are commensurate with their risk levels. The risk is with respect to *unanticipated* changes in inflationary expectations. But these changes can sometimes be beneficial as well. For instance, nobody anticipated in the early 1980s the speed with which President Reagan's tax and economic policies brought inflation rates down. Investors in long-term bonds reaped a capital appreciation windfall as interest rates fell in concert with inflation rates.

However, the level of inflation is also important, since tax rates are applied to nominal yields, not real yields, so effective real tax rates rise as interest rates rise.

Inflation as Tax – Inflation is effectively a form of tax. It is an indirect tax, but no less real than the income tax investors pay directly to the government. For instance, if investors earn 7% on an investment when inflation is progressing at 4%, their actual or real return is less than 3%. In other words, they can now buy only roughly 3% more than they could before they invested, and the result does not even reflect the direct income taxes yet.

The real inflation-adjusted return on investment is computed using the following formula:

r = (R-i)/(1-i)
where r is the real inflation-adjusted rate of return;
R is the nominal rate of return; and
i is the inflation rate.

The logic of this is straightforward. For each dollar invested today at, say, 7% annually, investors will have $1.07 next year. If inflation progresses at, say, 4% annually, investors will need $1.04 next year to buy what could be bought for a dollar today. The real inflation-adjusted increase in their wealth per dollar invested is equal to $1.07/$1.04, which is equal to 1.028846. In other words, the real return on investment is 2.8846%. If 7% is substituted for R and 4% for i in the equation above for r (the real rate of return), r is equal to 2.8846%, as the example demonstrates.

In this case, the 4% inflation rate is equivalent to a whopping 58.79% tax on the 7% nominal return (0.5879 x 7% = 4.1154%; 7% - 4.1154% = 2.8846%).

Interaction of the Inflation Tax and the Income Tax – Income taxes are paid on nominal returns, not real returns. Consequently, as inflation rates increase, real effective income tax rates also increase.

For example, assume an investor's marginal income-tax rate is 36% and the inflation rate is zero. In this case, the real return on an investment would be equal to the nominal return. An investment earning, say, 3% ordinary interest income before tax would provide a real after-tax return of 1.92% (3% x 0.36 = 1.08%; 3% - 1.08% = 1.92%).

Now assume that inflation is 4% instead of zero percent and that the nominal return on investment is correspondingly higher, say 7.12%. Checking the formula above, the real return is still 3% before tax. Assuming that ordinary interest income comprises the return, the nominal after-tax rate of return is 4.5568% [7.12% x (1 - 0.36)]. Applying the formula above once again to this nominal after-tax rate of return of 4.5568%, a real after-tax rate of return of 0.53538% is derived, or just slightly more than just a one-half-of-one-percent real increase in wealth. As was shown above, in the absence of inflation, the same 3% real before-tax rate of return was worth almost 2% in real terms after tax.

The real effective tax rate of 36% in a zero inflation environment becomes an effective tax rate of over 82% on the 3% real return in a 4% inflation environment (3% - 0.53538% = 2.46462% taxed away; 2.46462% ÷ 3% = 82.154% effective real tax rate). In fact, assuming that real before-tax rates of return remain at 3%, the 36% tax rate on nominal returns effectively becomes over a 100% tax rate on real returns when inflation reaches 5.64% or higher.

The total effective tax rate (combining both the inflation tax and the income tax) must be measured relative to the nominal return. In the example above, investors in the 36% tax bracket earning nominal returns of 7.12% in a 4% inflation environment end up with just slightly more than a half of a percent increase in their real after-tax wealth. The effective tax rate on their nominal returns is 92.48% (7.12% - 0.53538% = 6.58462% taxed away; 6.58462% ÷ 7.12% = 92.48% effective real tax rate on nominal returns).

If the return on investment is composed of both ordinary and capital elements, the analysis becomes more difficult. The actual real after-tax rate of return will depend not only on the ordinary income tax rate but also on the capital gains tax rate, as well as the timing of recognition of gains and the length of the investment horizon.

Interest Rate Risk – Interest rate risk is really two different risks – called **capital value risk** and **reinvestment risk** – that reflect two different sides to the interest rate risk coin. **Capital value risk** arises from the behavior of bond prices in response to changes in interest rates. Whenever interest rates rise, the prices of previously issued bonds (offering lower interest payments) will fall. This has nothing to do with the creditworthiness

Chapter 30 – Investment Risk

Figure 30.1

Years to a bond's maturity	The approximate market price of a $1,000 par value bond paying $80 annual interest, 8%) when interest rates increase to:		
	9%	10%	11%
5 years	$960	$923	$887
25 years	$901	$817	$746

of the issuer; it simply reflects the fact that bonds are currently being issued that pay higher rates of interest than paid by the older bonds. In order to sell the older bonds, their prices will have to fall. As the prices of bonds fall, their current yields to investors rise. So the prices of the previously issued bonds will have to fall sufficiently to make them attractive to buyers who could purchase the newly issued bonds paying higher interest rates. If investors expect market interest rates to rise, they might want to avoid purchasing long-term bonds unless they think the current price already reflects the market's anticipation of rising interest rates. Similar to inflation, it is *unanticipated* changes in interest rates that present a risk. Generally, the longer a bond has to maturity, the greater will be the price drop for any increase in interest rates.

The price of a bond in secondary markets is a function of its coupon yield, the time it has to maturity, and the movement of market interest rates since it was first issued. Basically, interest rates and bond prices move in opposite directions. When interest rates drop, bond prices increase; and when interest rates increase, bond prices drop.

- *Premium Bond* – A premium bond is one that sells for a price greater than its par value. Bonds will sell at a premium whenever interest rates fall below the coupon rate on the bond.

- *Discount Bond* – A discount bond sells in secondary markets at less than its par value. This occurs whenever market interest rates exceed the bond's coupon rate.

There are two times when investors can be fairly certain a bond will sell at close to its par value: first, when it is just issued (unless it is a zero-coupon bond) and, second when it is about to mature. What happens between those dates depends not only on the direction of interest rates but also on the magnitude of interest rate changes. The larger the change in interest rates, the larger will be the swing in bond prices.

According to Figure 30.1, if an investor wants to reduce the price volatility of a bond portfolio, the investor should shorten the maturities. For any given increase in interest rates, the price volatility of a five-year bond is much less than the price volatility of a 25-year bond. Generally, longer-term bonds provide higher coupons (interest payments) to compensate investors for this added volatility. For most individual investors, however, the slight increase in interest income is generally not worth the increase and risk due to added price volatility.

Of course, if interest rates fall, the market value of the bond will increase. Figure 30.2 shows the approximate market values of an 8% coupon bond (paying interest semiannually) for various assumed market interest rates ranging from 2% to 14% and for various terms to maturity ranging from one to 50 years. The relationship is called the whip because the market values of the bond vary more for longer terms and for greater changes in market rates of interest than for shorter terms and smaller changes in interest rates. The market values carve out a picture that is very much like the cracking of a whip, with very little movement close to the handle (near term and small change in interest rates), but very large movement toward the tip (long terms and large changes in interest rates).

The value of bonds varies inversely with interest rates. Stocks and other property may also be affected by general interest rates.

Reinvestment risk is the other side of the interest rate risk coin. If interest rates rise, investors in shorter-term notes and bonds can profitably reinvest at higher rates and avoid the capital value loss associated with longer-term investments. However, if interest rates fall, then the shorter-term note and bond owners will have to reinvest at lower rates when they could have locked in higher rates by originally buying longer-term bonds.

Inventory Risk – Inventory risk is the possibility that price changes, obsolescence, or other factors will shrink the value of a company's inventory. For example, oil

Figure 30.2

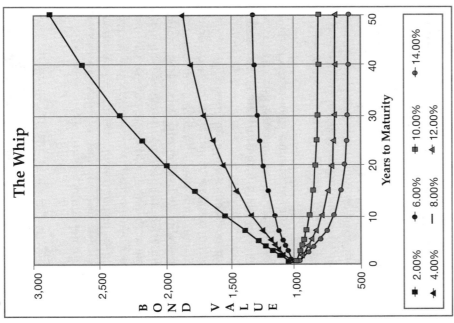

tariff is believed by most economists to be one of the principal factors precipitating the Great Depression of the 1930s. Since then, congress has passed NAFTA and other free-trade legislation that has had both adverse effects for some industries and positive effects for others. The only thing that remains the same in the area of law and regulation is that it constantly changes.

Liquidity Risk – Liquidity risk is related to **bid-ask spread risk** and **depth of market risk**. The possibility of not being able to sell an asset at a relatively known value, when one wants to, adds an element of risk to an investment. Generally, savings accounts, money market funds, and other assets that can be quickly converted into cash are considered highly liquid. Many bond issues are less liquid because, first, they may suffer from depth of market risk, and second, they are subject to greater capital value risk and so cannot be converted to cash at a highly certain value if interest rates change. On the other extreme, collectibles, most real estate, IRAs, and deferred annuities are considerably less liquid, as they either do not have ready markets or place restrictions on access to cash values. Listed stocks are readily marketable, but are considered less liquid than, say CDs, in the sense that the value at which they can be sold or converted to cash is much less certain because of market price fluctuations. Of course, stocks traded over the counter are even less liquid, since they have more bid-ask spread risk and depth of market risk than listed stocks.

Longevity Risk – This is the risk that a person will live longer than the period his income can support.

Management Risk – Management risk is related to **agency risk**. In the case of companies, the risk is related to the poor judgment or malfeasance of a company's professional management. In the case of professional investment managers, the majority of actively managed funds under-perform broad market benchmarks. Even though a fund has beaten the market in the past, there are no guarantees it will continue to do so. A star manager may leave or lose his touch. Individuals who stick with poorly run funds risk substantial under performance, which can compound over time. Investors in index mutual funds avoid management risk.

Market Risk – This is the most familiar of all risks. It is the day-to-day fluctuations in a stock's price. It is also referred to as volatility. Market risk applies mainly to stocks and options. As a whole, stocks tend to perform well during a bull market and poorly during a bear market – volatility is not so much a cause but an effect of certain market forces. Volatility is a measure of risk because it refers to the behavior, or temperament, of

companies, whose reserves are essentially their inventory, and refiners, who may have substantial amounts of oil in process, can be greatly affected by changes in the price of crude oil or of the retail prices of gasoline or other petroleum derivative products.

Legislative/Regulatory/Tax Risk – Statutes, regulations, and tax laws in effect today may be extinct tomorrow or new regulations or laws may be enacted. For example, the long-term capital gains tax rate has been changed 6 times in the last 20 years. The introduction of Individual Retirements Accounts (IRAs) in 1974 gave investors a tax-advantaged vehicle to help them save for retirement. Initially, anyone with earned income could open one, contribute up to $2,000 annually, and then take a full deduction on that amount. Years later, the tax code was amended, placing certain limitations on deductibility, thereby detracting from IRAs' tax benefits. Conversely, in 1997, Congress enhanced the traditional IRA, introduced two new variations – the Roth IRA and the Education IRA – and lowered the tax rate on long-term capital gains. Changes in the banking regulations were certainly partly responsible for the S&L crisis of the 1980s and 1990s and have indubitably changed the landscape in the financial services industries. The Smoot-Hawley an investment rather than the reason for this behavior. Because market movement is one reason why people can make money from stocks, volatility is important for returns, and the more unstable the investment, the more chance its value can move dramatically either way.

More broadly, the term market risk is sometimes used to encompass all the political, economic, geographic, and other forces that can influence the financial markets and affect the return of most assets. **Economic risk** is the term for the uncertainty of broad economic variables such as economic growth levels, inflation, interest rates, foreign exchange rates, import-export prices, etc. The general market environment, such as periods of bull and bear markets, may exert influence on the performance of individual securities. But some companies will be more vulnerable to market risk than others. A high exchange rate, for example, will hit electronic and electrical equipment manufacturers who target export markets, more than food retailers who target the domestic market, because a high exchange rate will make those electrical goods more expensive in foreign markets.

But it is not conclusive. A really efficient company in the electronics sector may suffer less than an inefficient food retailer. Most investors are familiar with market risk, as the media gives a great deal of attention to the performance of the stock market. It is important to remember that this risk may affect virtually every asset class to some extent.

Measurement Risk – Measurement risk is the risk associated with the collection and accuracy of financial data and with the proper use and application of that data for estimating future company or security values.

Political Risk – Political risk includes **legislative/regulatory/tax risk** that government legislation or action will have an adverse affect on investment. This can be in the form of high taxes, prohibitive licensing, or the appointment of individuals or regulators whose policies interfere with investment growth. Political risks also include wars, changes in government leadership, politically-motivated embargoes, and the like.

Purchasing Power Risk – Purchasing power risk is another name for **inflation risk**.

Security Risk – Security risk is a broad risk term encompassing all the risk factors associated with a particular stock, bond, option, or other financial security. For instance, for a bond it may include its default risk, liquidity risk, capital value risk, documentation risk, call risk, and the like.

Size Risk – Size risk is the risk associated with a firm's size. Studies have found that risk and return characteristics vary, systematically, by the size of companies.

Style Risk – Style risk is a term related to whether stocks are classified as value or growth stocks. Studies conducted by Fama and French and others have shown that value stocks and growth stocks have systematically different risk and return profiles, which makes them essentially separate asset classes. During certain times in the business cycle, value stocks may outperform growth stocks and, at other times, growth stocks may outperform value stocks. So style risk arises when investors fail to allocate their portfolio to both classes and, thus, expose themselves to the risk that they are investing in the wrong class at the wrong time. Style risk is also used to describe the risk associated with different management styles of professional managers or advisers

Systematic Risk – Systematic risk is a widespread or economy-wide risk that influences a large number of assets. Examples of systematic risk are political events, inflation, and the business cycle. It is virtually impossible to protect oneself against this type of risk. However, one can manage exposure to such broad risks by allocating one's portfolio among various asset classes that have differing exposures to widespread risk factors.

Tax (Rate) Risk – Investors have to be cautious in changes in tax laws that could make their holdings less valuable.

Timing Risk – Timing risk works two ways. Investors run the risk of investing when security prices hit their peak. They also take the risk that they may need to sell their investments for a loss during a market setback because they need to fund a planned or unplanned expense.

Tracking Risk – Risk associated with failure of managers of indexed funds to accurately, timely, and cost-effectively track and match the underlying index's performance.

Underwriting Risk – Underwriting risk is the risk taken by an investment banker that a new issue of securities purchased outright will not be bought by the public and/or that the market price will drop during the offering period.

Unsystematic (Specific, Diversifiable) Risk – It is risk that does not have wide spread impact, such as the impact an economic recession has on virtually all investment assets. Rather, it is risk that affects a particular company or security, or a very small number of assets. An example is news that affects a specific stock, such as a sudden strike by employees. Diversification is the only way to protect oneself from unsystematic risk.

INVESTMENT RISK MANAGEMENT

Unfortunately, there is really no such thing as a risk-free investment. Even federal government T-bills have a remote risk of default and are subject to at least some inflation risk. In addition, investors that invest short term, always face reinvestment risk, that is, the risk that they will not be able to reinvest at a rate equal to that which they could have locked in originally long term. Risk can never be completely eliminated. However, there are several strategies that may help manage investment risk.

1. *Diversification* – Because each asset class and each specific asset carries its own unique degree of risk, it may be best to diversify money across a range of investments. An appropriate mix of aggressive, moderate, and conservative investments could help balance the overall risk of a portfolio.

2. *Asset Allocation* – Before choosing individual investments, it may be a good idea to determine how much money should be allocated to each asset class – cash, bonds, and stocks (as well as other classes such as real estate, commodities, foreign securities, and the like). By blending one's portfolio, an investor can reduce short term volatility, while maintaining the potential to achieve long term financial goals.

3. *Professional Management* – Many investors have turned to professionally managed products

such as mutual funds, variable annuities, and variable life insurance. Along with offering diversification, each portfolio is closely monitored by an expert manager who makes investment decisions based on careful analysis and thorough research.

Modern portfolio and capital market theory posits that investors who are willing to bear greater investment risk can expect greater returns. However, the theory does not say that all risks will be rewarded. Investors are only rewarded for bearing systematic risks, those risks that cannot be diversified away.

Many of the types or sources of risk described above are diversifiable. The diversifiable risks tend to be those more closely related to specific companies or securities, such as management risk and default risk. However, those risks that are more industry, sector, or asset-class related become more difficult to diversify and require investors to balance those risks by investing in a wide array of sectors or asset classes. Those risks that are economy or market wide, or even world wide, cannot be eliminated entirely, but investors can manage their exposure to such risk by applying the principles of modern portfolio and capital market theory.

Diversification, asset allocation, and portfolio management are discussed in Chapters 37 and 38. Chapter 31, "Measuring Investment Risk" will explain in more detail how to measure these risks in both absolute and relative terms.

CHAPTER ENDNOTES

1. Chapter 31, "Measuring Investment Risk," will address the issues of risk and uncertainty and alternative notions of risk and risk measurements in the investment context.

Chapter 31

MEASURING INVESTMENT RISK

WHAT IS IT?

Measuring investment risk is a critical but difficult aspect of investment planning. This chapter describes and explains the principal risk measures, such as variance and standard deviation, semi-variance and semi-deviation, skewness, kurtosis, correlation and covariance, and beta. A brief review of probability distributions is useful before examining these ways of measuring risk.

Measuring investment returns, including risk-adjusted returns, is discussed in Chapter 33, "Measuring Investment Return." Some performance measures for measuring and managing a portfolio are discussed in Chapter 37, "Portfolio Management and Measurement."

PROBABILITY DISTRIBUTIONS

Of all the ways to describe risk, the simplest and possibly most accurate is "the uncertainty of a future outcome." The anticipated return for some future period is known as the expected return. The actual return over some past period is known as the realized return. The simple fact that dominates investing is that the realized return on an asset with any risk attached to it may be different from what was expected.

Financial economists define volatility as the range of movement (or price fluctuation) from the expected level of return. The more a stock, for example, goes up and down in price, the more volatile that stock is. Because wide price swings create more uncertainty of an eventual outcome, increased volatility can be equated with increased risk. Being able to measure and determine the past volatility of a security is important in that it provides some insight into the riskiness of that security as an investment.

Investors and analysts should be at least somewhat familiar with the study of probability distributions. Since the return an investor will earn from investing is not known, investors must estimate it. An investor may expect the total return on a particular security to be 10% for the coming year, but in truth this is only a point estimate.

To deal with the uncertainty of returns, investors need to think explicitly about a security's distribution of probable total returns. In other words, investors need to keep in mind that, although they may expect a security to return 10%, for example, this is only a one-point estimate of the entire range of possibilities. Given that investors must deal with the uncertain future, a number of possible returns could occur.

In the case of a Treasury bond paying a fixed rate of interest, the interest payment will be made with (almost) 100% certainty, barring a financial collapse of the economy. The probability of occurrence is close to 1.0, because no other outcome is possible (but nothing is ever really certain).

With the possibility of two or more outcomes, which is the norm for common stocks and virtually all other investments, investors must consider each possible likely outcome and assess the probability of its occurrence. The result of considering these outcomes and their probabilities together is a probability distribution consisting of the specification of the likely returns that may occur and the probabilities associated with these likely returns.

Probabilities represent the likelihood of various outcomes and are typically expressed as a decimal (sometimes fractions are used). The sum of the probabilities of all possible outcomes must be 1.0, because they must completely describe all the (perceived) likely occurrences.

How are these probabilities and associated outcomes obtained? In the final analysis, investing for some future period involves uncertainty, and therefore subjective estimates. Although investors may rely heavily on past occurrences (frequencies) to estimate the probabilities, they must adjust these estimates based on the past for any changes expected in the future.

Probability distributions can be either discrete or continuous. With a discrete probability distribution, a probability is assigned to each possible outcome. With a continuous probability distribution an infinite number of possible outcomes exist. The most familiar continuous distribution is the normal distribution depicted by the well-known bell-shaped curve often used in statistics. It is called a two-parameter distribution because one only needs to know the mean and the variance to fully describe the distribution.

To describe the single most likely outcome from a particular probability distribution, it is necessary to calculate its expected value. The expected value is the average of all possible return outcomes, where each outcome is weighted by its respective probability of occurrence. Investors typically use variance or standard deviation, at least as a first approximation, to calculate the total risk associated with the expected return.

STANDARD DEVIATION AND VARIANCE[1]

What is the standard deviation and what relevance does it have?

Technically, the standard deviation is a statistical measure defined as the square root of the variance of returns. The variance of returns is the expected value of the average squared differences from the mean of the distribution.[2] Technicalities aside, it is simply a measure of how much, on average, any particular observation of a randomly distributed variable (in this case, the returns on various asset classes) will differ from the average or mean value of the distribution. Since variance, volatility, and risk, in this context, can be used synonymously, remember that the larger is the standard deviation, the more uncertain is the outcome.

For example, assume balls with numbers ranging from zero to 100 are placed in a sack. If a person picks a ball from the sack, each ball is equally likely to be drawn. If balls are repeatedly picked from the sack, replacing each ball after it is selected, one would expect the average value of the balls selected to be close to 50, since 50 is the average value. If a person had to guess what value will turn up in any particular draw and wanted to minimize the potential error of the guess, the best guess would be 50, the expected or mean value of the possible outcomes. The greatest possible error one can make by guessing the mean (50) is 50, since the minimum and maximum possible values that could actually be drawn are zero or 100. If a person guessed any value other than 50, the error could exceed 50. For example, if a person guessed 20 and the ball actually drawn had the number 100, the error would be 80.

Even though the mean value (50) is the best possible guess, it is not necessarily a good guess in the sense of being anywhere near the value that will actually be drawn. Even though 50 is the best guess, one would expect most picks to differ substantially from 50. As explained above, by guessing 50, the result could still be wrong by as much as 50. What the standard deviation measures is by how much one would expect, on average, any given draw to differ from the best guess of 50.

Suppose that a person knows that the value of a ball drawn from the sack has a value equal to or less than 50. What would then be this person's best guess? Clearly, the answer is 25, since it is the average of the values from zero to 50. By guessing 25, this person could never be off by more than 25. The analysis is similar if a person knows the value of the drawn ball is equal to or greater than 50 before making the guess as to its value. In this case, the best guess is 75, since that is the mean value over the range from 50 to 100. By guessing 75, one could never be wrong by more than 25. Therefore, even when a person does not know whether the ball drawn is either above or below 50, the person does know that if it is above 50, it will be above 50 by an average of 25; if it is below 50, it will be below 50 by an average of 25. In other words, the guesser knows that the best guess of the mean value 50 will differ from the actual number drawn by an average absolute value of 25. For this distribution, 25 is the mean absolute deviation,[3] the usual or average amount by which the values drawn differ from the mean of the distribution, which is closely related to the standard deviation.[4]

It is generally held that investments whose distributions of returns have large standard deviations are riskier than those having smaller standard deviations since the future outcomes are much less certain. This idea is not entirely inappropriate, but it is also not entirely correct, since it does not encompass the entire scope of the issue.

For example, assume now that all the balls with values below 40 and above 60 are thrown out of the sack. The best guess regarding the value of a ball drawn from the sack is still 50, since the mean value has not changed. However, the mean absolute deviation is now just five, not 25 (standard deviation is 5.77). What does this tell a person about the best guess? It tells one nothing about what the best guess should be. It is still 50. What it tells a person is the relative goodness of the best guess. In the first case with numbers ranging from zero to 100, 50 is the best guess, but it is not a very good guess, since the first guess could be wrong by 50. In the second case, with numbers ranging from 40 to 60, the best guess is still 50, and it is a relatively good guess, since a person could be wrong by only 10, and a person would expect to be wrong by only five, on average.

Suppose now that as a ball is drawn from either sack, a person will receive or pay an amount based on the outcome. If the value of the drawn ball exceeds 50, the person will receive the difference between the value on the drawn ball and $50. If the value of the drawn ball is less than 50, the person will have to pay the amount by which the draw is less than $50. Regardless of from which sack the ball is drawn, the expected payoff/payout is $0. However, most people would agree that drawing balls from the sack containing balls numbered from zero to 100 is riskier than drawing balls from the sack with balls numbered from 40 to 60. In this sense, the standard deviation is a good indicator of risk.

However, now suppose the sack containing the balls from 40 to 60 is reconstituted to include only the balls numbered from zero to 20. The expected or mean value is now 10, but the mean absolute deviation is still five. The payoff/payout rules are also now changed to pay the person the amount by which the number on any drawn ball exceeds 10 and for the person to pay back the amount by which the number of any drawn ball falls below 10. In this case, would draws from the sack containing balls numbered zero to 100 still be considered riskier?

No one would say that drawing from the sack containing balls numbered zero to 100 is riskier than drawing from the sack containing balls numbered zero to 20, even though the mean absolute deviation (or standard deviation) of the number of outcomes for the sack containing balls numbered zero to 100 remains 25, or five times greater than the mean absolute deviation of draws from the sack containing balls numbered from zero to 20. Draws from the zero-to-20 sack still have an expected payoff of $0; the person has a 50% chance of losing money on any particular draw, and could lose as much as $10 [ball 0 - 10] if the worst occurs.

In contrast to draws from the zero-to-20 sack, draws from the zero-to-100 sack have an expected payoff of $40 [50 average value of a ball minus 10] and the person has only a 10% chance of losing money on any particular draw [the chance of losing money is limited to balls 0 to 9; 10 is breakeven]. In addition, the maximum potential loss on a draw from the zero-to-100 sack is still $10, exactly the same as the maximum potential loss on a draw from the zero-to-20 sack. Therefore, drawing from the zero-to-100 sack presents one with the possibility of losing, at most, $10 [ball 0 - 10] (the same as drawing from the zero-to-20 sack), only a 10% chance of losing any money (as compared to a 50% chance from the zero-to-20 sack), an expected gain of $40 (as compared to $0 from the zero-to-20 sack), and a maximum potential gain of up to $90 [ball 100 - 10] (as compared to only $10 from the zero-to-20 sack).

Clearly, draws from the zero-to-100 sack are no more risky (in terms of loss) than draws from the zero-to-20 sack, even though the uncertainty regarding the payoff of draws from the zero-to-100 sack as measured by the mean absolute deviation is five times greater than the uncertainty regarding the payoff from the zero-to-20 sack (the standard deviation is 5.006 times larger). Therefore, the standard deviation alone is an incomplete and sometimes misleading indicator of risk. In the area of investment analysis, risk assessment must also include differences in expected values and the downside or loss potentials of the alternative investments.

Consequently, the standard deviation can best be described as a measure of the "goodness" or confidence one can place in a best guess estimate (mean value) of the outcome of a random variable. As applied to investment returns, the expected value may be the best guess of future returns, but if the standard deviation of returns is large, the best guess still may not be a very good guess.

Also, the standard deviation is at best only a partial or incomplete and, sometimes misleading, measure of the riskiness of an investment relative to another investment. In order for standard deviations to take on any real meaning when comparing alternative investments, investors must use standard deviations relative to the investments' expected returns. That is, standard deviations are useful in conjunction with expected returns to measure each investment's return per unit of risk—its return bang per risk buck, so to speak. The standard deviation of equity returns (i.e., S&P stocks and small-capitalization stocks) is greater than the standard deviation of fixed-income investment returns (i.e., corporate and government bonds and Treasury bills) for all investment horizons. However, at longer investment horizons, equities dominate fixed income investments. Despite greater standard deviations, equities can and should be viewed as less risky investments than bonds and Treasury bills for longer investment horizons.

One of the nice characteristics of the standard deviation is that if returns are normally distributed, investors can predict that actual realized returns will fall within one standard deviation above or below the mean about 68% of the time and within 2 standard deviations above or below the mean about 95% of the time. Based on history, investors can expect to earn average annual returns of between 7.7% and 14.9% on a 20-year investment in S&P stocks with about a 68% probability, or odds of two in three. They can expect the average annual returns to range from 4.1% to 18.5% with odds of about 19 out of 20. Investors have only about three chances in 1,000 that the realized average annual compound return would fall outside three standard deviations from the mean (below 0.5% or above 22.1%).

Calculating a standard deviation using probability distributions involves making subjective estimates of the probabilities and the likely returns. However, investors cannot avoid such estimates because future returns are uncertain. The prices of securities are based on investors' expectations about the future. The relevant standard deviation in this situation is the *ex ante* standard deviation and not the *ex post* standard deviation based on past realized returns.

Although standard deviations based on past realized returns are often used as proxies for *ex ante* standard deviations, investors should be careful to remember that the past cannot always be extrapolated into the future without modifications. *Ex post* standard deviations may be convenient, but they are subject to errors.

One important point about the estimation of standard deviation is the distinction between individual securities and portfolios. Standard deviations for well-diversified portfolios tend to be reasonably steady over time and, therefore, historical calculations may be fairly reliable in projecting the future. Moving from well-diversified portfolios to individual securities, however, makes historical calculations much less reliable. Fortunately, the number one rule of portfolio management is to diversify by holding a broad portfolio of securities, and the standard deviations of well-diversified portfolios may be more stable.

One further very important point is that the standard deviation is a measure of the *total* risk of an asset or a portfolio, including therefore both systematic and unsystematic risk. It captures the total variability in the asset's or portfolio's return, whatever the sources of that variability.

For an example of how to calculate the standard deviation, see "How It Is Done – An Example," below.

SEMI-VARIANCE

The use of standard deviation as a measure of risk has been criticized because it considers the possibility of returns above the expected return as well as below the expected return. Investors, however, do not view possible returns above the expected return as an unfavorable outcome. Many investors think that only deviations below the expected return really matter.

Harry Markowitz, the father of modern portfolio theory, recognized this limitation and suggested a measure of downside risk – the risk of realizing an outcome below the expected return – called the semi-variance. The semi-variance is similar to variance except that in making this calculation, no consideration is given to returns above the expected return.[5]

In some cases, investors may be more concerned with the chance that an investment's return will fall below some benchmark or target return, such as T-bill rates, rather than the expected return of the investment. In such cases, investors may use a measure called the downside volatility or semi-volatility. The semi-volatility is computed in exactly the same way as the semi-variance, except that all returns above a benchmark or target return (sometimes called the minimal acceptable rate of return, or mar), such as the risk-free rate, rather than the expected return are ignored.

The square root of the semi-variance is sometimes called the semi-deviation, although there does not appear to be any universally accepted term for this concept. Semi-deviation is to semi-variance as the standard deviation is to variance. The term downside deviation is sometimes used to refer to the square root of the semi-variance, but more frequently seems to be used to refer to the square root of the downside volatility, which is computed with respect to a minimal acceptable rate of return different from the expected return.

Even though semi-variance is conceptually superior to standard deviation, in practice, because of some difficult math problems, most researchers and analysts use the standard deviation as the risk measure of choice. As it turns out, as long as the return distribution is symmetrical (the same shape above and below the mean), then the standard deviation gives exactly the same answers in a portfolio context as the semi-variance. With notable exceptions, stock return distributions do seem to be reasonably symmetrical, especially for longer investment horizons.

However, especially for shorter-term investment horizons and for certain types of investments, such as options and other derivatives, technology stocks, media stocks, telecom stocks, or hedge funds, the distributions may not be normally distributed. In these cases, the standard deviation can be an incomplete and misleading measure of risk, even when used in conjunction with expected returns.

For an example of how to calculate the semi-variance and the semi-deviation, see "How It Is Done – An Example," below.

COVARIANCE AND CORRELATION

The principal conclusion of Harry Markowitz's seminal book, *Portfolio Selection*, which heralded the modern era of modern portfolio and capital market theory, was that portfolios of risky stocks could be put together in such a way that the portfolio as a whole could actually be less risky than any one of the individual stocks in it. This result follows in part from the concept of covariance among securities, or lack of it.

As the term suggests, covariance means varying together. Covariance is a measure of the degree to which two variables move in a systematic or predictable way, either positively or negatively. If two variables move in perfect lockstep, up and down, then they are said to exhibit perfect positive covariance. For example, the pressure and temperature of a fixed volume of gas at sea level exhibit perfect covariance. Double the pressure of a given volume of gas and the temperature will change proportionally, and vice-versa. Or, halve the temperature of a gas and the pressure will also decline proportionally, and vice versa.

Two variables that move perfectly in lockstep, but in opposite directions, are said to exhibit perfect negative covariance. For instance, if one doubles (halves) the pressure on a gas and wants to keep the temperature unchanged, the volume for the gas must increase (decrease) in direct proportion to the change in pressure.

If two variables are completely independent, showing no systematic relationship, their covariance is zero.

Correlation is a standardized version of covariance where values can range from –1 (perfect negative covariance) to +1 (perfect positive covariance). Letting σ_{12} represent the covariance between 2 variables, σ_1 the standard deviation of variable 1, σ_2 the standard deviation of variable 2, and ρ_{12} the correlation of the two variables, the relation between correlation and covariance is as follows:

$$\rho_{12} = \frac{\sigma_{12}}{\sigma_1 \times \sigma_2}$$

Expressed as a function of covariance, covariance is equal to the correlation times the standard deviations of the two variables:

$$\sigma_{12} = \rho_{12} \times \sigma_1 \times \sigma_2$$

Markowitz showed that if investors added stocks that do not exhibit perfect covariance to their portfolio, the total risk of the portfolio as measured by variance or standard deviation would decline. For example, assume an investor holds just one stock, S_1, with a standard deviation of σ_1. Thus, the standard deviation of the investor's initial "portfolio" of one security is σ_1. If the investor sells off part of his interest in S_1 and uses the proceeds to buy another stock, S_2, with a standard deviation of σ_2, the variance per dollar of investment in his portfolio, σ_p^2, is given by the following equation:

$$\sigma_p^2 = (w_1^2 \times \sigma_1^2) + (w_2^2 \times \sigma_2^2) + (2 \times w_1 \times w_2 \times \sigma_{12})$$

Here, σ_{12} is the covariance between S_1 and S_2, and w_i is the proportion of the portfolio invested in stock S_i.

Alternatively, one can express the variance of the portfolio in terms of correlation rather than covariance:

$$\sigma_p^2 = (w_1^2 \times \sigma_1^2) + (w_2^2 \times \sigma_2^2) + (2 \times w_1 \times w_2 \times \rho_{12} \times \sigma_1 \times \sigma_2)$$

Assume, first, for illustration, that the weight invested in each stock is equal, 50%, that the standard deviations of the stocks are equal, $\sigma_1 = \sigma_2$, and that the returns on the two stocks are independent, that is, the covariance and correlation are zero, then, the variance of the portfolio is:

$$\sigma_p^2 = (0.5^2 \times \sigma_1^2) + (0.5^2 \times \sigma_2^2)$$
$$\sigma_p^2 = (0.25 \times \sigma_1^2) + (0.25 \times \sigma_2^2)$$
$$\sigma_p^2 = (0.25 \times \sigma_1^2) + (0.25 \times \sigma_1^2)$$
$$\sigma_p^2 = 0.5 \times \sigma_1^2$$

By splitting the portfolio equally between two independently distributed stocks, the investor cuts the variance of the portfolio in half! In fact, for each additional independent stock added to the portfolio, the variance declines in proportion to the number of stocks, that is

$$\sigma_p^2 = \frac{\sigma_1^2}{n}$$

This equation explains the principle of diversification. By splitting a portfolio into more and more securities, the variance attributable to the nonsystematic (uncorrelated) risks approaches zero as the number of securities increases.

Taking the square root of each side of the equation to derive the standard deviation, one can see that the standard deviation of the portfolio declines by the square root of the number of independently distributed securities in the portfolio:

$$\sigma_p = \frac{\sigma_1}{\sqrt{n}}$$

In other words, the standard deviation of a portfolio split into 100 independently distributed securities is 10 times less than the standard deviation of any one of the securities alone.

Now, assume instead that the investor starts once again with just one stock, S_1, but then splits his portfolio evenly between stock S_1 and stock S_3, which, once again, for illustration, is assumed to have a standard deviation, σ_3, equal to σ_1. However, in this case assume S_3's return is perfectly negatively correlated with S_1's return. Then the variance of the portfolio is:

$$\sigma_p^2 = (0.25 \times \sigma_1^2) + (0.25 \times \sigma_3^2) + (2 \times 0.25 \times \rho_{13} \times \sigma_1 \times \sigma_3),$$

or, since $\rho_{13} = -1$,

$$\sigma_p^2 = (0.25 \times \sigma_1^2) + (0.25 \times \sigma_3^2) - (2 \times 0.25 \times \sigma_1 \times \sigma_3),$$

and now replacing σ_3 with σ_1,

$$\sigma_p^2 = (0.25 \times \sigma_1^2) + (0.25 \times \sigma_1^2) - (2 \times 0.25 \times \sigma_1 \times \sigma_1)$$

$$\sigma_p^2 = (0.25 \times \sigma_1^2) + (0.25 \times \sigma_1^2) - (0.5 \times \sigma_1^2)$$

$$\sigma_p^2 = 0$$

If two securities are perfectly negatively correlated, splitting one's investment equally between the two securities completely eliminates all variability!

Finally, assume instead the investor starts once again with just S_1 in his portfolio, but then puts half his money into security S_4, with a standard deviation equal to S1's and a correlation with S_1 of +1. The variance of the portfolio is, substituting immediately for $\sigma_1 = \sigma_4$ and $\rho_{14} = 1$:

$$\sigma_p^2 = (0.25 \times \sigma_1^2) + (0.25 \times \sigma_1^2) + (2 \times 0.25 \times 1 \times \sigma_1^2)$$

$$\sigma_p^2 = (0.25 \times \sigma_1^2) + (0.25 \times \sigma_1^2) + (0.5 \times \sigma_1^2)$$

$$\sigma_p^2 = \sigma_1^2$$

The portfolio's variance remains unchanged. There is no risk reduction advantage to adding perfectly positively correlated assets to one's portfolio.

In the real world, instances of either perfectly negatively correlated or perfectly positively correlated securities are extremely rare, if not nonexistent. In fact, instances of correlations between securities that are negative at any level do exist, but are relatively few. However, investors do not need negative correlations between securities for them to benefit by adding securities to their portfolio. As long as a security added to a portfolio is not perfectly positively correlated with the existing portfolio, the addition of the security will reduce the portfolio's risk as measured by variance or standard deviation.

This concept is a central principle of modern portfolio and asset allocation theory. As long as there are any classes of assets whose returns are not perfectly correlated with investors' current portfolios, these investors can further reduce the risk of their portfolios by adding securities from those asset classes.

BETA[6]

While standard deviation determines the volatility of a security or fund according to the disparity of its returns over a period of time, beta, another useful statistical measure, determines the volatility, or risk, of a security or fund in relation to that of its index or benchmark. In the single factor Capital Asset Pricing Model, the index or benchmark is the "market" portfolio, often measured by the S&P 500 index. When beta is used to compare funds or to measure an investment manager's performance, the benchmark is frequently the average of the funds in that mutual fund category.

A fund with a beta very close to 1 means the fund's performance closely matches the index or benchmark – a beta greater than 1 indicates greater volatility than the overall market, and a beta less than 1 indicates less volatility than the benchmark. If, for example, a fund has a beta of 1.05 in relation to the S&P 500, the fund has been moving 5% more than the index. Therefore, if the S&P 500 increased 15%, the fund would be expected to increase 15.75%. On the other hand, a fund with a beta of 2.4 would be expected to move 2.4 times more than its corresponding index. If the S&P 500 moved 10%, the fund would be expected to rise 24%, and, if the S&P 500 declined 10%, the fund would be expected to lose 24%.

Investors expecting the market to be bullish may choose funds exhibiting high betas, which increase investors' chances of earning high returns in up markets. If an investor expects the market to be bearish in the near future, the funds that have betas less than 1 are a good choice because they would be expected to decline less in value than the index. For example, if a fund had a beta of 0.5 and the S&P 500 declined 6%, the fund would be expected to decline only 3%. Be aware of the fact that beta by itself is limited and can be skewed due to factors other than the market risk affecting the fund's volatility.

R-SQUARED (R²)

The R-squared of a fund (also called the coefficient of determination) is a measure of what proportion of a security's or portfolio's total variability is explained by its relationship to a benchmark or index and how much is its independent risk unrelated to the benchmark or index. When used in conjunction with ratings of mutual funds or the performance of professional managers it advises investors if the beta of a mutual fund is measured against an appropriate benchmark. Measuring the correlation of a fund's movements to that of an index, R-squared describes the level of association between the fund's volatility and market risk, or more specifically, the degree to which a fund's volatility is a result of the day-to-day fluctuations experienced by the overall market.

R-squared values range between 0 and 100, where 0 represents the least correlation and 100 represents full correlation. If a fund's beta has an R-squared value that is close to 100, the beta of the fund should be trusted. On the other hand, an R-squared value that is close to 0 indicates that the beta is not particularly useful because the fund is being compared against an inappropriate benchmark.

If, for example, a bond fund were judged against the S&P 500, the R-squared value would be very low. A bond index such as the Lehman Brothers Aggregate Bond Index would be a much more appropriate benchmark for a bond fund, so the resulting R-squared value would be higher. Obviously the risks apparent in the stock market are different than the risks associated with the bond market. Therefore, if the beta for a bond were calculated using a stock index, the beta would not be trustworthy.

An inappropriate benchmark will skew more than just beta. Alpha (see Chapter 32) is calculated using beta, so if the R-squared value of a fund is low, it is also wise not to trust the figure given for alpha.

SKEWNESS

Skewness measures the coefficient of asymmetry of a distribution.[7] In contrast with the normal distribution, or bell curve, where both tails of the distribution are symmetrical mirror images of each other, skewed distributions have one tail of the distribution that is longer than the other. Figure 31.1 shows two distributions with equal means and standard deviations, but one has positive skewness and the other has negative skewness.

Figure 31.1

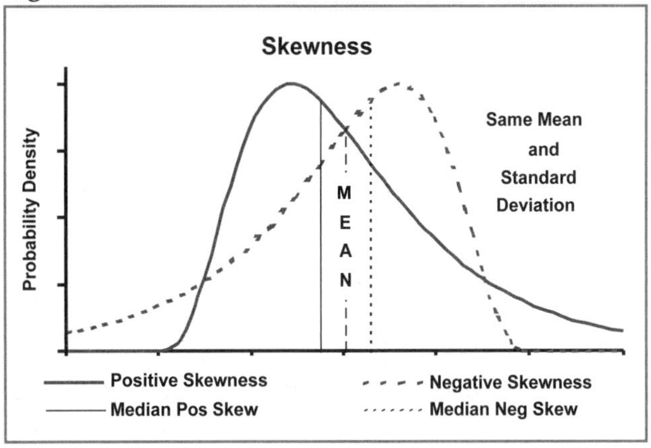

Figure 31.1

If investors base their investment decisions solely upon means and risk as measured by standard deviations, they should be indifferent between these two distributions since the means and standard deviations are equal. However, a risk-averse investor does not like negative skewness. In this case, the investment with negative skewness has a substantial downside tail exposing the investor to low or negative returns below the worst potential returns on the investment with positive skewness. In addition, the investment with positive skewness offers investors the potential for upside returns far above any they could ever expect from the negatively skewed investment.

It would seem almost inescapable that any risk adverse investor would prefer the positively skewed investment to the negatively skewed investment. Although this is in fact true, it may not be quite as evident as it first appears. Figure 31.1 also shows the medians of the two distributions. In symmetric distributions, such as the normal distribution, the mean and median are equal, but in skewed distributions, they are different.

The median is the point where there is a 50% probability that realized returns will fall below (or above) that value. In positively skewed distributions, the median is below the mean. In negatively skewed distributions, the median is above the mean. What this means is that an investor actually has less than a 50% chance of earning the mean return in a positively skewed investment, but more than a 50% chance of earning the mean return on a negatively skewed investment. So although the means and standard deviations of these two investments are identical, an investor actually has a higher chance of earning at least the mean return with the negative skewed investment than with the positively skewed investment. Therefore, although all risk adverse investors will prefer the positively skewed to the negatively skewed investment when their means and standard deviations are identical, it does not mean that they would always prefer a positively skewed investment to a symmetrically distributed investment with the same mean and standard deviation, or other possible combinations of means, standard deviations, and skewness.

For an example of how to calculate skewness, see "How It Is Done – An Example," below.

KURTOSIS

Kurtosis measures the degree of "fatness" in the tails of a distribution. Figure 31.2 shows an example of a symmetric distribution that has a positive coefficient of excess kurtosis relative to a normal distribution.[8] The distributions have equal means and standard deviations.

It is easy to see that risk-averse investors prefer a distribution with low kurtosis (that is, where tails are thin and returns are more likely to fall closer to the mean). Although the extra fatness in the downside tail is exactly matched by the excess fatness in the upside tail, risk averse investors will always weight the potential downside returns heavier than the potential upside returns. Consequently, they will always prefer a lower excess kurtosis. If investors use only means and standard deviations to choose among investments and some of those investments have either positive or negative excess kurtosis, they will be ignoring an important factor in making the best choice.

Figure 31.2

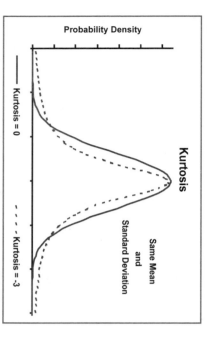

Kurtosis

Same Mean and Standard Deviation

Probability Density

—— Kurtosis = 0
- - - Kurtosis = -3

−100%! Since the mean-variance framework of much of modern portfolio and capital market theory does not account for these factors, it cannot explain this excess return anomaly.

For an example of how to calculate kurtosis, see "How It Is Done – An Example," below.

SKEWNESS AND KURTOSIS COMBINED

Distributions can exhibit both skewness and excess kurtosis. Figure 31.3 shows an example of two negatively skewed distributions, but one also has a positive excess kurtosis.

Figure 31.3

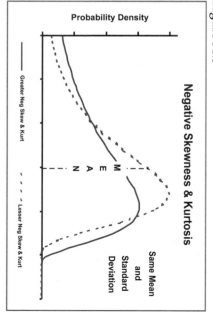

Negative Skewness & Kurtosis

Same Mean and Standard Deviation

Probability Density

MEAN

—— Greater Neg Skew & Kurt
- - - Lesser Neg Skew & Kurt

As soon as skewness begins to be negative the impact of a high excess kurtosis is significant for a risk-averse investor. The most interesting situation is when the return distribution has a negative skewness of -1 (or below) and an excess kurtosis higher than 1. In this case, the probability of having a huge negative return increases dramatically. For a distribution with a skewness of -1 and an excess kurtosis of -5 (technology stocks, media stocks, telecom stocks or hedge funds may have this kind of excess kurtosis level), a mean-variance approach will conclude that an investor will not lose more than -3.5% in the next one day with 99% probability. However, an approach that accounts for skewness and kurtosis gives instead a 99% probability of not losing more than 7.4% in the next one day. The difference is substantial: more than a 100% underestimation of the potential one-day loss when using just the mean-variance approach that ignores skewness and kurtosis.

In conclusion, for optimization, simulation, and investment selection, the investor's approach should account not only for volatility, but also for skewness and kurtosis when the return distribution over the relevant period is likely to be significantly different than the normal distribution.

One of the reasons posited for the small-stock premium being higher than it should be in theory under the mean-variance framework of the capital-asset pricing model is that small cap stocks exhibit greater excess kurtosis and negative skewness than larger stocks. For instance, the risk of total failure and bankruptcy is unquestionably greater for most small business than it is for most large ones. Negative skewness does not get any greater than

Figure 31.4

STANDARD DEVIATION (SD)

Period	Total Return	Deviation (D)	D²	(D / SD)³	(D / SD)⁴
1	-25.0	-29.1	848.3	-10.1977	22.1142
2	-10.0	-14.1	199.5	-1.1632	1.2234
3	-5.0	-9.1	83.3	-0.3136	0.2131
4	-1.0	-5.1	26.3	-0.0556	0.0212
5	0.0	-4.1	17.0	-0.0290	0.0089
6	0.0	-4.1	17.0	-0.0290	0.0089
7	1.0	-3.1	9.8	-0.0126	0.0029
8	1.0	-3.1	9.8	-0.0126	0.0029
9	5.0	0.9	0.8	0.0003	0.0000
10	5.0	0.9	0.8	0.0003	0.0000
11	5.0	0.9	0.8	0.0003	0.0000
12	10.0	5.9	34.5	0.0837	0.0366
13	10.0	5.9	34.5	0.0837	0.0366
14	10.0	5.9	34.5	0.0837	0.0366
15	25.0	20.9	435.8	3.7548	5.8360
16	35.0	30.9	953.3	12.1486	27.9277
Sum	66.0		2,705.8	4.3420	57.4691
Average	4.1		180.4		

Average = 4.1

Median = $(1 + 5) / 2$ = 3.0

Variance = 180.4

Standard Deviation = $\sqrt{180.4}$ = 13.4

Skewness = $\dfrac{16}{(16-1)\,(16-2)}$ × 4.342029

Skewness = 0.076190 × 4.342029

Skewness = 0.330821

Kurtosis = $\dfrac{16\,(16+1)}{(16-1)(16-2)(16-3)}$ × 57.469059 − $\dfrac{3\,(16-1)^2}{(16-2)\,(16-3)}$

Kurtosis = 0.099634 × 57.469059 − 3.708791

Kurtosis = 5.725855 − 3.708791

Kurtosis = 2.017064

HOW IT IS DONE – AN EXAMPLE

The following example will illustrate how to calculate the standard deviation, the semi-variance, skewness, and kurtosis.

Figure 31.4 illustrates calculation of the standard deviation, along with measurements of skewness and kurtosis, in the following steps.

1. Sample total returns for 16 periods are shown, sorted in order of lowest return (biggest loss) to highest return. [Returns have been sorted to help illustrate determination of the median, and to help illustrate calculation of the semi-variance (which follows).] Total returns could be for a single investment, a portfolio of investments, an entire market segment, or the entire market. Total returns could be historical or projected.

Tools & Techniques of Investment Planning

Figure 31.5

Sample Returns

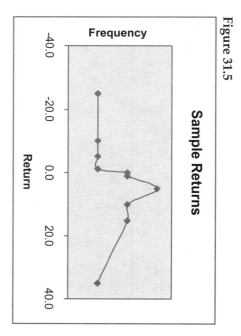

1. Sample total returns for 16 periods are shown here, sorted in order of lowest return (biggest loss) to highest return. [Returns have been sorted to help illustrate determination of the median, and to help illustrate calculation of the semi-variance).] [Total returns could be for a single investment, a portfolio of investments, an entire market segment, or the entire market. Total returns could be historical or projected.]

2. The total return is summed up and then divided by the number of values (or periods) to determine the average return [66.0 ÷ 16 = 4.1].

3. The deviation for each period is determined by subtracting from the total return for each period the average return [e.g., -25.0 - 4.1 = -29.1]. A target return, such as the risk-free rate of return or a return of zero, could be used instead of the average return.

4. Only those deviations with a negative result are then used.

5. The deviation for each period is squared [e.g., $-29.1^2 = 848.3$].

6. The squared deviations for each period are summed up and then divided by the number of values (or periods) used minus one to determine the average squared deviation, or semi-variance [1,210.9 ÷ (8 - 1) = 173.0]. Where the whole universe of values is used instead of just a sample, the number of values may be used instead of the number of values minus one.

7. The square root of the semi-variance is the semi-deviation [$173.0^{\frac{1}{2}} = 13.2$].

8. Skewness and kurtosis are then calculated as shown.

The median is the middle value (for the numbers used); one-half of returns are above the median and one-half of returns are below the median. Where there is an even number of values, as here, the median is equal to one-half the sum of the two middle values [(-1 + 0) ÷ 2 = -0.5]. Note that the median [-0.5] is greater than the average of the values used [-4.9]. This is consistent with the negatively-skewed distribution [-2.396096].

2. The total return is summed up and then divided by the number of values (or periods) to determine the average return [66.0 ÷ 16 = 4.1].

3. The deviation for each period is determined by subtracting from the total return for each period the average return [e.g., -25.0 - 4.1 = -29.1].

4. The deviation for each period is squared [e.g., $-29.1^2 = 848.3$].

5. The squared deviations for each period are summed up and then divided by the number of values (or periods) minus one to determine the average squared deviation, or variance [2,705.8 ÷ (16 - 1) = 180.4]. Where the whole universe of values is used instead of just a sample, the number of values may be used instead of the number of values minus one.

6. The square root of the variance is the standard deviation [$180.4^{\frac{1}{2}} = 13.4$].

7. Skewness and kurtosis are then calculated as shown.

The median is the middle value; one-half of returns are above the median and one-half of returns are below the median. Where there is an even number of values, as here, the median is equal to one-half the sum of the two middle values [(1 + 5) ÷ 2 = 3.0]. Note that the median [3.0] is less than the average [4.1]. This is consistent with the slightly positively-skewed distribution [0.330821]. See also Figure 31.5.

Figure 31.6 illustrates calculation of the semi-variance and semi-deviation, along with measurements of skewness and kurtosis, in the following steps.

1. Sample total returns for 16 periods are shown here, sorted in order of lowest

WHERE CAN I FIND OUT MORE?

1. Brown, Robert A., Ph.D., CFA, "Avoiding 5 Common Mistakes in Overestimating Future Equity Returns," FPA Journal, May 2002.

Figure 31.6

SEMI-VARIANCE

Period	Total Return	Deviation (D)	D²	(D / SD)³	(D / SD)⁴
1	-25.0	-29.1	848.3	-10.8592	24.0470
2	-10.0	-14.1	199.5	-1.2387	1.3303
3	-5.0	-9.1	83.3	-0.3340	0.2317
4	-1.0	-5.1	26.3	-0.0592	0.0231
5	0.0	-4.1	17.0	-0.0309	0.0097
6	0.0	-4.1	17.0	-0.0309	0.0097
7	1.0	-3.1	9.8	-0.0134	0.0032
8	1.0	-3.1	9.8	-0.0134	0.0032
9	5.0				
10	5.0				
11	5.0				
12	10.0				
13	10.0				
14	10.0				
15	25.0				
16	35.0				
Sum	66.0		1,210.9	-12.5795	25.6578
Average	4.1		173.0		

$$\text{Average} = -4.9$$

$$\text{Median} = (-1 + 0) / 2 = -0.5$$

$$\text{Semi-Variance} = 173.0$$

$$\text{Semi-Deviation (SD)} = \sqrt{173} = 13.2$$

$$\text{Skewness} = \frac{8}{(8 - 1)\,(8 - 2)} \times -12.579502$$

$$\text{Skewness} = 0.190476 \times -12.579502$$

$$\text{Skewness} = -2.396096$$

$$\text{Kurtosis} = \frac{8(8 + 1)}{(8 - 1)(8 - 2)(8 - 3)} \times 25.657804 - \frac{3(8 - 1)^2}{(8 - 2)\,(8 - 3)}$$

$$\text{Kurtosis} = 0.342857 \times 25.657804 - 4.9$$

$$\text{Kurtosis} = 3.896961$$

2. Campbell, John Y., "Forecasting U.S. Equity Returns in the 21st Century," Paper presented to the Social Security Advisory Board, August 2001.

3. Diamond, Peter A., "What Stock Market Returns to Expect for the Future: An Update," Paper presented to the Social Security Advisory Board, August 2001.

4. Diamond, Peter A., "What Stock Market Returns to Expect for the Future," Social Security Bulletin, Vol. 63, No. 2, 2000.

5. Evanson, Steven, "Stocks for the Long Run?" Evanson Asset Management, June 2001.

6. Fama, Eugene F., and Kenneth R. French, "The Equity Premium," The Center for Research in Security Prices Working Paper No. 522, The University of Chicago, Graduate School of Business April 2001.

7. Ibbotson, Roger G. and Peng Chen, "The Supply of Stock Market Returns," Ibbotson Associates, Chicago, IL June 2001.

8. Reichenstein, William, "The Investment Implications of Lower Stock Return Prospects," *AAII Journal*, October 2001.

9. Shoven, John B., "What Are Reasonable Long-Run Rates of Return to Expect on Equities," Paper presented to the Social Security Advisory Board, August 2001.

CHAPTER ENDNOTES

1. Standard deviation and variance are discussed as concepts here. Actual calculations of standard deviation and related subjects are rather complex. Do not be concerned with the actual calculations here. Actual calculations of standard deviation and related subjects are discussed in detail later in this chapter, under "How It Is Done – An Example."

2. Variance $\equiv \sigma^2 = E[(R - \mu)^2]$, where σ is the standard deviation, μ is the mean value, R is the return variable, and E is the expectation operator. For continuous distributions, $F(R)$, with probability density function $f(R)$, $\sigma^2 = \int_{\mathbb{R}} (R - \mu)^2 \times f(R) dR$. For discrete distributions, with probabilities p_i for each possible outcome, in the set of all possible outcomes, $\sigma^2 = \sum p_i (R_i - \mu)^2$. Variances and standard deviations are generally estimated based upon historical returns which are computed as follows: $\sigma^2 = \sum (R_i - \mu^*)^2 / (n-1)$, where R_i are each of the historical observations, n is the number of observations, and μ^* is the average return of the observations used to compute the estimate of variance.

3. The mean absolute deviation is the expected value of the absolute value of the differences from the mean: $MAD = E(|R - \mu|)$, where R is the return variable and μ is the expected value of R. It is estimated from data using the formula: $MAD = \sum |R_i - \mu^*| / n$, where Ri is the ith observation of R from the dataset, n is the number of data points in the dataset, and μ^* is the average value of the n observation of R.

4. The standard deviation is actually 28.9 for this distribution, slightly higher than the mean absolute deviation, but closely related. For nonuniform distributions, other than those like picking balls from an urn, the standard deviation is generally considered the better measure of dispersion around the mean of the distribution.

5. Estimates of semi-variance are calculated in the same manner as variances, except only the historical returns below the average return are used in the calculation. Specifically, semi-variance = $\sigma_{sv}^2 = \sum (R_{<\mu*} - \mu^*)^2 / (n^{<\mu} - 1)$, where $R_{<\mu}$ is the ith return less than the average return, μ^*, and $n^{<\mu}$ is the number of observations of Ri that are less than μ^*. Similar to the standard deviation, which is the square root of the variance, the semi-standard-deviation or semi-deviation is the square root of the semi-variance, or σ_{sv}.

6. Beta is described and discussed in more detail in relation to the Capital Asset Pricing Model in Chapter 36, "Asset Pricing Models."

7. To estimate the skewness from sample data use the following formula:

$$S = \frac{n}{(n-1)(n-2)} \sum \left(\frac{R_i - \mu^*}{\sigma} \right)^3$$

Here, σ^* is the sample standard deviation and μ^* is the sample mean.

8. Since the normal distribution has a kurtosis of 3, the measure of kurtosis is generally expressed as the coefficient of excess kurtosis, which is simply K – 3. Therefore, a measure of less than zero means the distribution has skinnier tales and a fatter center than the normal distribution while an excess kurtosis greater than zero means the distribution has fatter tales and a skinnier center than the normal distribution. To estimate the sample coefficient of excess kurtosis from sample data, use the following formula:

$$EK = \frac{n(n+1)}{(n-1)(n-2)(n-3)} \sum \left(\frac{R_i - \mu^*}{\sigma} \right)^4 - \frac{3(n-1)^2}{(n-2)(n-3)}$$

Here, μ^* is the sample mean and σ^* is the sample standard deviation.

Chapter 32

TIME VALUE CONCEPTS

This chapter discusses basic time value concepts. Appendix K discusses how to adjust time value concepts for inflation or growth and for taxes. Chapter 33 discusses related concepts used in measuring investment returns.

WHAT IS IT?

The old adages that "a bird in the hand is worth two in the bush" and "time is money" tersely capture the essence of time value principles.

Whenever people "invest" or "save" money, they are deferring the pleasure of currently consuming what that money could buy now until some later time. However, investors and savers never have any absolute assurance that money which is saved or invested today will be able to purchase consumption goods of comparable value and appeal to the investors in the future as the consumption goods they could have bought today. People die, inflation may erode the purchasing power of the money, and the money may be lost, stolen, embezzled, or simply mismanaged. Thus, investors or savers always bear some risk that they will get less "value" later than the value they have foregone today. As a result, investors and savers will demand two or more "birds in the bush" tomorrow for each "bird" they let out of hand today, depending upon the level of risk associated with giving up the "bird in hand" today. Basically, investors will demand not only a return *of* their money but a return *on* their money with the level of return they demand *on* their money increasing with the risk that it might be worth less tomorrow than it is today.

In addition, time *is* money. The longer is the time that investors postpone their consumption, the greater is the chance something adverse will occur to erode or lessen the value of their investment. Consequently, the longer is the period of time their money is tied up in an investment, the greater is the return they will demand *on* their money as compensation for deferring current consumption.

In order to evaluate alternative investment opportunities or differing financial planning strategies, investors

or their advisers must fully understand time value concepts. Although various basic time value functions are built into the spreadsheet programs on everyone's computer, these functions often have serious limitations and are useless, or worse, subject to misuse, if users do not fully understand the underlying time value concepts and principles. In addition, these built-in functions are often difficult to adapt to the needs of real-world problems unless the users really grasp the underlying time value concepts and mathematics.

This chapter provides an extensive guide to basic time value formulas and concepts, including formulas for computing present values for future lump sums and annuities; future values for present lump sums and annuities; periodic payment values related to present and future lump sums; terms of years or number of periods related to present and future lump sums and annuities; and rate conversions, compounding periods, and effective interest rates. In addition, Appendix K explains how to modify these formulas for inflation-adjusted or growth-adjusted rates of return.

Finally, Appendix K describes how the timing, incidence, and nature of the tax on returns from various types of investment and accumulation vehicles or financial planning strategies and tactics affect an investor's real after-tax wealth accumulation; and (2) provides financial advisers and investors with a conceptual framework for proper time and tax-adjusted financial planning and investment analysis. The use of tax leverage, tax-adjusted time value concepts, and measuring the effect of tax strategies are covered in separate sections.

HOW DOES IT WORK?

Time value analysis is founded on the basic economic premise that value or price today depends on the future cash flows or other tangible benefits that flow from an investment. From this basic premise all other basic time value concepts follow. These basic concepts include that the analysis must:

1. Account for all anticipated cash flows, benefits, and costs;

Tools & Techniques of Investment Planning

2. Properly account for differences in the *timing* of cash flows, benefits, and costs by applying a properly risk-adjusted discount rate; and

3. Thereby evaluate all cash flows, benefits, and costs as of the same point in time.

A number of "short-hand" or "down-and-dirty" approaches to valuation (such as pay-back period analysis) ignore one or more of these basic concepts, but are sometimes useful as a quick, first-cut look at a valuation problem. However, for any serious analysis, short cuts will not work; the analysis must incorporate all of the basic concepts.

The first concept basically states that cash is king. In general, the only thing one can spend is cash or other property that is readily convertible to cash. However, in some cases other tangible benefits must also be counted, such as debt reduction, for instance. If an investor's outstanding debt is reduced in a given period, that investor does not actually receive cash in that period, but the debt reduction is the equivalent of receiving cash. Had the investor received cash instead of having the debt balance reduced and used the cash to pay down the debt, he would have been in exactly the same position.

Time value analysis is so-named because differences in the timing of cash flows matter. The proper risk-adjusted discount rate (or sometimes called hurdle rate) should be the investor's "opportunity cost rate" which is equal to the rate of return the investor could earn on the next best available investment or project of comparable risk.

The purpose of the discount rate is to adjust all the cash flows to the same time period. It really makes no difference whether the time period is today – present value analysis – or some future date – future value analysis – as long as all the cash flows are adjusted to the same date.

WHEN IS THE USE OF THIS TECHNIQUE INDICATED?

Virtually all financial planning and investment analyses involve weighing tradeoffs between dollars today (e.g., investment outlays) versus dollars tomorrow (e.g., investment returns); that is, present value and future value concepts. In addition, most financial planning and investment planning also involves taxes and tax planning as well as adjustments for inflation. Advisers and their clients are presented with innumerable invest-

ment, retirement, insurance, and other financial choices, vehicles, and strategies with widely varying tax rules. Various vehicles and strategies differ not only with respect to the timing of cash flows and tax payments, but also with respect to the character of return for tax purposes and the tax rates applicable to the components of the return.

Time value analyses are required whenever a person is evaluating investment alternatives or financial planning strategies or tactics that involve differences in the timing of cash flows. In other words, time value analysis is required in virtually every investment and financial planning situation.

ADVANTAGES

Properly applied time value analyses have the advantage of being the theoretically correct and complete means to quantitatively evaluating investment alternatives and other financial planning strategies and tactics according to economic principles.

DISADVANTAGES

1. In many cases, accurate assessments of future cash flows, discount factors, and risks are difficult. Even in the simpler analyses, investors or planners implicitly have to make assumptions about future interest rates, inflation rates, tax rates, risks of default, business and economic conditions, and the like. Any quantitative time value analysis is only as good as the estimates that go into the analysis. So all time value analyses are, at best, good guesses about values. Investors and advisers must always keep in mind the level of confidence that they can place in their estimates and temper the reliance and weight they place in the quantitative analyses accordingly.

2. Although the basic principles of time value analysis are relatively simple, in application the analyses can at times become quite complex. In many cases, analyses require several conceptual and computational steps and must incorporate a number of often complicated adjustments, such as for growth factors for payment streams, inflation, and esoteric tax rules. Errors in the application of proper time value formulas or in computations are not uncommon, even in the most sophisticated academic and professional journals. Great care must be taken to assure that time value principles are properly applied and properly computed.

HOW IS IT IMPLEMENTED?

Basic Time Value Formulas

The following sections present basic time value formulas for computing present values, future values, payments for annuities, the number of periods or the term, rates of return, and interest rate conversions, compounding periods, and effective interest rates, with examples. The following formulas will use the following terminology:

PV   =   Present Value – A value today

FV   =   Future Value – A value at some future date

Pmt   =   Level Periodic Payment – Constant dollar amount paid or received at regularly spaced time intervals, such as an annuity payment

r   =   Interest rate or rate of return per period

n   =   Number of periods or the term of the investment or valuation

ln   =   Natural logarithm operator

In general, an annuity is a stream of level periodic payments. (Annuities with payments that increase at a constant growth rate will also be discussed.) An annuity paid at the beginning of each period is known as an annuity due. An annuity paid at the end of each period is known as an ordinary annuity.

Present Value Calculations

Overview

Present value is the value of future cash flows "discounted" at an assumed interest rate or rate of return back from the future to their value today. In other words, when investors calculate a present value, they are determining the amount of money they would have to invest today earning the assumed rate of return (the discount rate used to compute the present value) to be able to exactly reproduce the schedule of cash flows they are valuing.

The discount rate that is used to compute present values and other time adjusted dollar values is extremely important in most cases. It should generally represent the best estimate or guess of the true "opportunity cost" of money for investment opportunities of comparable risk over the time period cash flows are being valued.

In other words, it should represent a rate that is comparable to the rate they could earn on the best alternative use of their money; hence the term, "opportunity cost rate." In certain valuation situations, the term "hurdle rate" is also used to mean essentially the same thing as an opportunity cost rate or discount rate.

Present Value of Future Lump Sum Payment

An investment of a single dollar today at a periodic rate of return of r per period will provide that dollar plus the return, or $(1 + r)$ dollars, at the end of the first period. For each dollar accumulated at the end of the first period, an investor will again have $(1 + r)$ dollars at the end of the second period. So, for each dollar invested at the beginning of the first period, investors will have $(1 + r) \times (1 + r)$, or $(1 + r)^2$ dollars at the end of the second period. At the end of n periods, investors would have $(1 + r)^n$ dollars for each dollar invested at the beginning of the first period.

If investors want to know how much they would have to invest at the beginning of the first period to accumulate just one dollar at the end of n periods, rather than $(1 + r)^n$ dollars, all they have to do is simply divide $1 by $(1 + r)^n$. Thus, to find the present value of FV dollars in n periods, just divide FV by $(1 + r)^n$.

Equation PV1

$$PV = \frac{FV}{(1 + r)^n} = FV \times (1 + r)^{-n}$$

The term $(1 + r)^n$ simply means multiply $(1 + r)$ by itself n times. The term $(1 + r)^{-n}$ simply means the inverse of $(1 + r)^n$, or $1 \div (1 + r)^n$.

Example 1: Your client's child will be attending college in 5 years and she asks you how much she will need to set aside today to pay the first year's tuition and fees. She estimates that if her child attends her alma mater the tuition and fees will be $36,000. Assuming she can earn 5% on the money she invests for this purpose, how much would she need to invest today to meet her child's first year college need?

$$FV = \$36,000$$
$$r = 5\%$$
$$n = 5 \text{ years}$$

$$PV = \frac{\$36,000}{(1 + 5\%)^5} = \frac{\$36,000}{1.27628} = \$28,207$$

[*Using Valuation Tables.* The present value of a future lump sum can also be calculated using the tables for the present value of a future lump sum contained in Appendix A. The factor where the table intersects at 5.0% and 5 years is 0.7835. Multiplying $36,000 by 0.7835 equals $28,206, approximately equal to the answer in the preceding example. Slight differences can result from rounding.]

Present Value of Perpetual Annuity

The British government has issued perpetual bonds called "consuls" in the past. Perpetual bonds pay a fixed periodic payment forever; they never mature. In essence, a bond paying a fixed periodic interest amount is a form of annuity.

Although we do not have any such investments in the United States, for time value purposes the valuation formula of a perpetual bond is very useful. Obviously, if an annuity is paying a fixed amount forever, the annuity payment must just exactly equal the rate of return earned on the investment. When that is the case, the principal amount neither increases nor decreases over time, permitting the principal amount to generate a fixed level periodic payment forever. Therefore, if the original principal amount is PV and the periodic rate of return is r, the periodic payment, Pmt, must be equal to PV x r. Thus, if an investor wants to determine the amount he would have to invest today, PV, for a perpetual annuity that will generate a perpetual periodic payment stream with periodic payments equal to Pmt, the formula would be:

Equation PV2

$$PV = \frac{Pmt}{r}$$

Example 2: A British consul (perpetual bond) pays $50 yearly. If the market rate of interest is 4%, what is the value of the consul?

$$Pmt = \$50$$
$$r = 4\%$$
$$PV = \frac{\$50}{4\%} = \$1,250$$

If the market rate of interest rises to 6%, what will happen to the price of the consul?

$$Pmt = \$50$$
$$r = 6\%$$
$$PV = \frac{\$50}{6\%} = \$833.33$$

A 2 percentage point rise (50% rise from the original 4% to the final 6%) in the market rate of interest will cause a $416.67 (or 33%) decline from the consul's original $1,250 value.

Present Value of Ordinary Annuity

The valuation of an annuity, which is simply a stream of level periodic payments, can be viewed as simply the sum of a whole series of present values of future lump sum values where each future value is equal to the same level amount, Pmt. If the payments occur at the end of each period, the sum of the present values for n periods would look as follows:

Equation PV3

$$PV = \frac{Pmt}{(1+r)^1} + \frac{Pmt}{(1+r)^2} + \frac{Pmt}{(1+r)^3} + ... + \frac{Pmt}{(1+r)^{n-1}} + \frac{Pmt}{(1+r)^n}$$

Or, factoring out the Pmt:

Equation PV4

$$PV = Pmt \times \frac{1}{(1+r)^1} + \frac{1}{(1+r)^2} + \frac{1}{(1+r)^3} + ... + \frac{1}{(1+r)^{n-1}} + \frac{1}{(1+r)^n}$$

This formula is typically written in shorthand version using the summation sign as:

Equation PV5

$$PV = Pmt \times \sum_{j=1}^{n} \frac{1}{(1+r)^j} = Pmt \times \sum_{j=1}^{n}(1+r)^{-j}$$

It is a simple matter to create spreadsheet columns to permit such calculations and sums if the number of periods, n, is not too large. But if n is large, that method is extremely cumbersome, so it would be nice to have a simpler formula for the present value of an annuity. Here is where the formula for a perpetual annuity comes in handy to simplify these expressions.

As was shown in the previous section, the present value of a perpetual annuity paying Pmt per period

Chapter 32 – Time Value Concepts

forever is simply Pmt ÷ r. What will be the value of that perpetual annuity after n periods? Well, at the end of n periods, the annuity will still be paying periodic payments of Pmt forever. Therefore, its value at the end of n periods is the same as its value today, Pmt ÷ r; it never changes.[1]

An annuity paying Pmt per period for n periods can be viewed as a perpetual annuity paying Pmt per period forever minus a perpetual annuity paying Pmt per period forever that starts after n periods. In other words, the present value of an annuity paying Pmt for n periods can be determined by subtracting the present value of a perpetual annuity starting in n years from the present value of a perpetual annuity starting today.

The value of a perpetual annuity starting today is simply Pmt ÷ r as shown in equation PV2. The value in n years of a perpetual annuity is also Pmt ÷ r. However, to determine its value today, this future lump sum value must be discounted back to today as shown previously in equation PV1.

Specifically, the present value of an n-period annuity paying Pmt per period can be written as the value of a perpetual annuity today, less the value of a perpetual annuity in n periods discounted back to today:

Equation PV6

$$PV = \frac{Pmt}{r} - \frac{Pmt}{r} \times (1+r)^{-n}, \text{ if } r \neq 0$$

Example 3: What is the value of an annuity paying $50 at the end of each of 20 years if the market rate of interest is 4%?

Pmt = $50
r = 4%
n = 20

The previous example showed that a British consul (perpetual bond) paying $50 yearly is worth $1,250 if the market rate of interest is 4% ($50 ÷ 4%). The value of a perpetual bond that commences payments of $50 per year in 20 years when the market rate of interest is 4% is still $1,250. However, the value today of the perpetual bond commencing payments in 20 years is determined by discounting the value in 20 years by 4% for 20 years using equation PV1:

PV of perpetual bond starting in 20 years =

$$\frac{\$1,250}{(1+4\%)^{20}} = \frac{\$1,250}{2.191123} = \$570.48$$

Therefore, the value today of an annuity paying $50 at the end of each of 20 years is equal to the value of a perpetual bond commencing payments today less the value today of a perpetual bond commencing payments in 20 years:

PV of 20-year bond = $1,250.00 – $570.48 = $679.52

By factoring out Pmt ÷ r and rearranging terms, one can derive the more commonly used present value formula for an ordinary annuity:

Equation PV7

$$PV = \frac{Pmt}{r} \times \left[1 - (1+r)^{-n}\right] = Pmt \times \left(\frac{1 - (1+r)^{-n}}{r}\right),$$

$$\text{if } r \neq 0$$

Example 4: What is the value of an annuity paying $50 at the end of each of 20 years if the market rate of interest is 4% valued using equation PV7?

Pmt = $50
r = 4%
n = 20

PV of 20-year bond =

$$\$50 \times \frac{[1 - (1+4\%)^{-20}]}{4\%} = \$50 \times \frac{0.543613}{4\%} = \$679.52$$

Obviously, the value computed using equation PV7 is identical to that computed using equation PV6. Which formula one uses is strictly a matter of personal preference.

[*Using Valuation Tables.* The present value of a level ordinary annuity can also be calculated using the tables for the present value of an ordinary annuity contained in Appendix C. The factor where the table intersects at 4.0% and 20 years is 13.5903. Multiplying $50 by 13.5903 equals $679.52, the same as the answer in the preceding example. Slight differences can result from rounding.]

If the discount rate happens to be zero (which can occur in some situations), then neither equation PV6 nor equation PV7 can be used to compute the present value of an annuity. In the case where the discount rate is zero, dividing by zero in the formulas gives one an infinite value, which obviously cannot be correct. But if one looks up at equation PV3 in this section and puts zero in for the discount rate, r, the present value of an annuity paying Pmt per period is simply the sum of the payments. That is, for an n-period annuity:

Equation PV8

$$PV = n \times Pmt, \text{ if } r = 0$$

Present Value of Annuity Due

The present value of a level payment annuity with payments at the beginning of each period for n periods can be viewed as an ordinary annuity for n-1 periods (equation PV3) plus one payment immediately:

Equation PV9

$$PV = Pmt +$$

$$\frac{Pmt}{(1+r)^1} + \frac{Pmt}{(1+r)^2} + \ldots + \frac{Pmt}{(1+r)^{n-2}} + \frac{Pmt}{(1+r)^{n-1}}$$

If one multiplies the terms in the present value of an ordinary annuity for n periods (equation PV4) by (1 + r), the result is the above formula (canceling out one (1 + r) in the denominator of each term):

Equation PV10

$$PV = (1+r) \times Pmt \times$$

$$\left(\frac{1}{(1+r)^1} + \frac{1}{(1+r)^2} + \ldots + \frac{1}{(1+r)^{n-1}} + \frac{1}{(1+r)^n} \right)$$

Therefore, the simple formula for the present value of an n-period annuity due is just the simple formula for the present value of an n-period ordinary annuity (equation PV7) multiplied by (1 + r), or:

Equation PV11

$$PV = Pmt \times \left(\frac{1 - (1+r)^{-n}}{r} \right) \times (1+r), \text{ if } r \neq 0$$

$$PV = n \times Pmt, \text{ if } r = 0$$

Example 5: What is the value of an annuity paying $50 at the beginning of each of 20 years if the market rate of interest is 4%?

One way to value this is to compute the value of an annuity paying $50 per year at the end of each year for 19 years, plus the value of one

payment of $50 immediately. The present value of an annuity paying $50 at the end of each year for 19 years discounted at 4% is:

$$\begin{aligned} Pmt &= \$50 \\ r &= 4\% \\ n &= 19 \end{aligned}$$

$$PV = \$50 \times \frac{[1 - (1 + 4\%)^{-19}]}{4\%} = \$50 \times \frac{0.5253576}{4\%} = \$656.70$$

Adding an immediate payment of $50 to the $656.70 value of the 19-year annuity gives a total present value of $706.70.

Alternatively, the present value of the annuity can be computed by finding the value of a 20-year annuity making payments at the end of each year and multiplying that value by (1 + 4%) (i.e., using equation PV11).

The previous example computed the present value of a 20-year annuity paying $50 per year at the end of each year for 20 years when the market rate of interest is 4%. That value is $679.52. Multiplying this value by (1+4%) gives a value of $706.70 for a 20-year annuity making $50 payments at the beginning of each year.

Obviously, the value computed using equation PV11 is identical to that computed by adding the value of a 19-year annuity with $50 payments at the end of the year and one immediate payment of $50. Once again, which approach one uses is strictly a matter of personal preference.

Example 6: Assume your client, described above, anticipates that it will cost $36,000 for each of the 4 years of her child's college education. In this case, how much will your client have to accumulate by the beginning of her child's first year of college in 5 years to pay the $36,000 cost at the beginning of each of her child's four years of college assuming she can earn 5% on her money?

$$\begin{aligned} Pmt &= \$36,000 \\ r &= 5\% \\ n &= 4 \end{aligned}$$

$$PV = \$36,000 \times \frac{[1 - (1 + 5\%)^{-4}] \times (1 + 5\%)}{5\%}$$

$$PV = \$36,000 \times \frac{0.1772975 \times 1.05}{5\%} = \$134,037$$

Your client will need to accumulate a sum slightly greater than $134,000 by the time her child begins college in 5 years.

[*Using Valuation Tables* – The present value of a level annuity due can also be calculated using the tables for the present value of an annuity due contained in Appendix B. The factor where the table intersects at 5.0% and 4 years is 3.7232. Multiplying $36,000 by 3.7232 equals $134,035, approximately equal to the answer in the preceding example. Slight differences can result from rounding.]

If r = 0, then equation PV11 is undefined (divide by zero error). If r = 0, then equation PV8 is used to find the present value of an annuity with payments at the beginning of each of n period.

Future Value Calculations

Future Value of Present Lump Sum

The future value of a lump sum is just the inverse of the present value. Specifically, if one multiplies both sides of the present value formula (equation PV1) by $(1 + r)^n$ the result is the future value formula:

Equation FV1

$$FV = PV \times (1 + r)^n$$

Example 7: In the example above we determined that your client whose child will be attending college in 5 years and who estimates that the tuition and fees will be $36,000 for each of 4 years of college needs to accumulate about $134,037 in 5 years to meet her goal if she invests at 5%. She tells you that she has $60,000 currently set aside for this purpose and wants to know how much will this $60,000 be worth in 5 years if it is invested at 5%?

$$\begin{aligned} \text{Pmt} &= \$60{,}000 \\ r &= 5\% \\ n &= 5 \text{ years} \end{aligned}$$

$$FV = \$60{,}000 \times (1 + 5\%)^5 = \$60{,}000 \times 1.276282 = \$76{,}577$$

[*Using Valuation Tables* – The future value of a present lump sum can also be calculated using the tables for the future value of a lump sum contained in Appendix D. The factor where the table intersects at 5.0% and 5 years is 1.2763. Multiplying $60,000 by 1.2763 equals $76,578, approximately equal to the answer in the preceding example. Slight differences can result from rounding.]

Future Value of Ordinary Annuity

The future value calculation of an ordinary annuity can be derived directly from the formula for the present value of an ordinary annuity by substituting the present value of a lump sum formula for PV into the present value of the formula for an ordinary annuity and solving for FV. Specifically, the present value of an ordinary annuity is (equation PV7):

$$PV = \text{Pmt} \times \frac{[1 - (1+r)^{-n}]}{r} \quad , \text{ if } r \neq 0.$$

The present value of a future lump sum is (equation PV1):

$$PV = \frac{FV}{(1 + r)^n}$$

Substitute the right-hand-side of the present value of lump sum formula into the present value of the annuity formula and one gets:

$$\frac{FV}{(1 + r)^n} = \text{Pmt} \times \frac{[1 - (1 + r)^{-n}]}{r}$$

Multiply both sides of the equation by $(1 + r)^n$ and one gets the formula for the *future value of an ordinary annuity*:

Equation FV2

$$FV = \text{Pmt} \times \frac{(1 + r)^n - 1}{r} \quad , \text{ if } r \neq 0$$

Example 8: Upon discovering that she will be about $57,500 short of her objective to fund her child's education in 5 years, your client estimates that she might manage to save another $5,000 at the end of each year for the next 5 years to

This will leave your client almost $57,500 short ($134,037 - $76,577 = $57,460) of her objective in 5 years.

meet her goal. Assuming this money is also invested at 5%, to what value would this series of five $5,000 investments grow by the end of the 5-year period?

$$Pmt = \$5,000$$
$$r = 5\%$$
$$n = 5$$

$$FV = \$5,000 \times \frac{[(1 + 5\%)^5 - 1]}{5\%}$$

$$FV = \$5,000 \times \frac{0.27628156}{5\%} = \$27,628$$

So even if your client can manage to save an additional $5,000 each year until her child starts college after 5 years, she will still be about $30,000 ($57,460 - $27,628 = $29,832) short of her $134,037 total goal.

[*Using Valuation Tables* – The future value of a level ordinary annuity due can also be calculated using the tables for the future value of an ordinary annuity contained in Appendix F. The factor where the table intersects at 5.0% and 5 years is 5.5256. Multiplying $27,628, the same as the answer in the preceding example. Slight differences can result from rounding.]

Similar to the present value calculations, the value of equation FV2 is not defined if r = 0 (divide-by-zero error), but in this case, the FV simply equals the sum of the payments made over the n periods:

Equation FV3

$$FV = n \times Pmt, \text{ if } r = 0$$

Future Value of Annuity Due

Analogous to the derivation of the present value of an annuity due formula, the future value of an annuity due formula is just the future value of an ordinary annuity formula multiplied by (1 + r):

FV4

$$FV = Pmt \times \left(\frac{(1 + r)^n - 1}{r} \right) \times (1 + r), \text{ if } r \neq 0$$

[*Using Valuation Tables* – The future value of a level annuity due can also be calculated using the tables for the

future value of an annuity due contained in Appendix E. Assume annual payments of $1,000 at the end of each year for 20 years and an interest rate of 5%. The factor where the table intersects at 5.0% and 20 years is 34.7193. Multiplying $1,000 by 34.7193 equals $34,719.

Once again, the value of equation FV4 is undefined for r = 0, but the value can be computed, as before, by simply multiplying Pmt by number of periodic payments n, as shown in equation FV3.

Annuity Payment Calculations

Overview

The calculation of the level periodic payment for an annuity depends on whether it is computed in reference to a present value (the level periodic amount a given present value can support for n years), a future value (the amount to which level periodic investments would accumulate in n periods), and in reference to whether the payments are to be made at the beginning or end of each period. Each of the level periodic payment formulas can be derived from the corresponding present value and future value annuity formulas previously described by making simple arithmetic adjustments to isolate the payment value on the left-hand side of the equation.

Ordinary Annuity Payment for a Given Present Value

This equation is derived by rearranging equation PV7 to solve for Pmt in terms of the other factors:

Equation Pmt1

$$Pmt = PV \times \left(\frac{r}{1 - (1 + r)^{-n}} \right), \text{ if } r \neq 0$$

Example 9: When your client discovers that saving another $5,000 per year will still not accomplish her goal, she asks you to determine the additional amount she would need to save each year to reach the goal if she earns 5% on her money.

To determine this amount using equation Pmt1, one must first compute the present value of the future shortage using equation PV1. Then this amount can be used in equation Pmt1 to find the required payment.

In the previous example, we determined that your client would still be about $29,832 short of her goal even if she saved another $5,000 per year. The amount she would have to invest today in a lump sum to accumulate this additional $29,832 may be calculated using equation PV1:

$$FV = \$29,832$$
$$r = 5\%$$
$$n = 5 \text{ years}$$

$$PV = \frac{\$29,832}{(1+5\%)^5} = \frac{\$29,832}{1.2762816} = \$23,374$$

So your client would need to invest about $23,375 more today to meet her goal – but she does not have it now! So the question is, what additional amounts invested at the end of each year for the next 5 years are equivalent to $23,374 investing today? Using equation Pmt1, we derive:

$$PV = \$23,374$$
$$r = 5\%$$
$$n = 5 \text{ years}$$

$$FV = \$23,374 \times \frac{5\%}{[1-(1-5\%)^{-5}]}$$

$$Pmt = \$23,374 \times \frac{5\%}{0.2164738} = \$5,399.$$

So, in addition to the $60,000 your client already has invested and earmarked for this objective and the $5,000 per year she had already planned to save each year for the next five years, your client needs to save about an additional $5,400 at the end of the year for the next 5 years to meet the objective of funding her child's college education.

If r = 0, then equation Pmt1 is undefined (divided-by-zero error). If r = 0, then equation Pmt2, derived from equation PV5, is used to find the value of Pmt:

Equation Pmt2

$$Pmt = \frac{PV}{n} \text{ , if } r = 0$$

Annuity Due Payment for a Given Present Value

The formula for determining the periodic payment of an annuity with payments at the beginning of each period is the same as the formula for the ordinary annuity, except that the denominator is multiplied by (1 + r). This equation is just a simple algebraic rearrangement of equation PV11 to solve for Pmt in terms of the other variables.

Equation Pmt3

$$Pmt = PV \times \frac{r}{(1-(1+r)^{-n}) \times (1+r)} \text{ , if } r \neq 0$$

If r = 0, then Pmt is computed using equation Pmt2.

Periodic Payment for a Perpetual Annuity (n = ∞)

This formula is easily derived from equation PV2:

Equation Pmt4

$$Pmt = PV \times r$$

Ordinary Annuity Payment for a Given Future Value

The Pmt for an ordinary annuity based upon the future value is derived in a manner analogous to the case when it is based upon the present value by rearranging equation FV2:

Equation Pmt5

$$Pmt = FV \times \left(\frac{r}{(1+r)^n - 1} \right) \text{ , if } r \neq 0$$

Example 10: In the previous example, we computed the additional amount your client needed to save each year in a two-step process where we first found the present value of the future shortfall, $29,832, using equation PV1 And then found the required annual payments using equation Pmt1. By using equation Pmt5, this payment amount can be derived in a single step.

$$FV = \$29,832$$
$$r = 5\%$$
$$n = 5 \text{ years}$$

$$Pmt = \$29,832 \times \frac{5\%}{[(1-5\%)^5 - 1]}$$

$$Pmt = \$29,832 \times \frac{5\%}{0.27281562} = \$5,399$$

Both approaches derive the same result, but, obviously, using equation Pmt5 requires fewer steps.

Once again, if r=0, then equation Pmt5 is not defined. In this case, Pmt is determined by simply dividing FV by the number of periods n.

Equation Pmt6

$$Pmt = \frac{FV}{n}, \text{ if } r = 0$$

Annuity Due Payment for a Given Future Value

The Pmt for an annuity due given the future value is derived in a manner analogous to the annuity due given the present value by rearranging equation FV4 to solve for Pmt in terms of the other variables. Also, similar to the case where Pmt is determined for ordinary annuities given the future value, if r = 0, Pmt is computed by dividing the future value by the number of periods n, as shown in equation Pmt6.

Equation Pmt7

$$Pmt = FV \times \left(\frac{r}{[(1 + r)^n - 1] \times (1 + r)} \right), \text{ if } r \neq 0$$

Number of Periods or Term Calculations

Overview

Similar to the payment calculations, the calculations to solve for the number of periods (n) for annuities depends on whether n is calculated in reference to a present value or a future value and whether the annuities are ordinary annuities or annuities due. These calculations require the use of the natural logarithm operator, which is built into most spreadsheet programs and financial calculators.

In many, if not most, cases the value of n, the number of periods, will be a non-integer value. Other than in the case of n values calculated using equation N1 below, where n represents the number of periods until a present lump sum investment will grow to a given future lump sum value, a non-integer value for n is misleading and technically inaccurate. In these cases (equations N2 thru N5) which involve solving for the number of periods for an annuity, a non-integer value for n must be adjusted in the manner described in the section below entitled

"Caveat: Final Payment Adjustment When n Is a Non-Integer Value."

Number of Periods for Present Lump Sum Value to Reach Future Value

At times investors wish to know how long it will take for a given lump sum investment to grow to a specified future value given some assumed periodic rate of return. Equation N1 calculates the number of periods until the investors will reach their goal.

Equation N1

$$n = \frac{\ln(FV/PV)}{\ln(1 + r)}, \text{ for } r > -100\%; (FV/PV) > 0$$

The value of n is not defined if the rate of return is less than –100% or the ratio of the future value to the present value is equal to or less than zero.

Example 11: Out of curiosity, your client asks you how long it would take the $60,000 she has earmarked for her child's college education to grow to her goal of $134,037 if she made no further contributions to the fund and continued to earn 5% on her money.

PV	=	$60,000
r	=	5%
FV	=	$134,037

$$n = \frac{\ln(\$134,037 \div \$60,000)}{\ln(1 + 5\%)} = \frac{0.8037713}{0.0487902} = 16.4 \text{ years}$$

Number of Periods Present Value Will Provide Ordinary Annuity Payments

Equation N2 calculates the number of periods a given lump sum investment earning some specified periodic rate of return can sustain a specified level of ordinary annuity payments before the fund is exhausted.

Equation N2

$$n = \frac{\ln(1 - (PV \times r)/Pmt)}{\ln(1 + r)}, \text{ for } r > -100\%; (PV \times r)/Pmt < 1$$

Example 12: Your client receives a $100,000 inheritance and wishes to know how long he could expect to sustain $10,000 annual end-of-year withdrawals if the fund is invested to earn 7%.

$$PV = \$100,000$$
$$r = 7\%$$
$$Pmt = \$10,000$$

$$n = \frac{-\ln[1 - (\$100,000 \times 7\%) \div \$10,000]}{\ln(1 + 7\%)} =$$

$$\frac{1.2039728}{0.0676586} = 17.8 \text{ years}$$

Number of Periods Present Value Will Provide Annuity Due Payments

Equation N3 calculates the number of periods a given lump sum investment earning some specified periodic rate of return can sustain a specified level of annuity due payments before the fund is exhausted.

Equation N3

$$n = \frac{\ln(1 - (PV \times r)/[Pmt \times (1 + r)])}{\ln(1 + r)} ,$$

for r > -100%; (PV x r)/[Pmt x (1 + r)] < 1

Example 13: Your client from the previous example wishes to know how long he could expect to sustain $10,000 annual beginning-of-year withdrawals if the $100,000 fund is invested to earn 7%.

$$PV = \$100,000$$
$$r = 7\%$$
$$Pmt = \$10,000$$

$$n = \frac{-\ln [1 - (\$100,000 \times 7\%) \div [\$10,000 \times (1 + 7\%)]]}{\ln(1 + 7\%)} =$$

$$\frac{1.0619109}{0.0676586} = 15.7 \text{ years}$$

Number of Periods of Ordinary Annuity Payments to Reach Future Value

Equation N4 calculates the number of periods it will take for level end-of-period investments of a given amount earning some specified periodic rate of return to reach a desired future accumulated value.

Equation N4

$$n = \frac{\ln\{[(FV \times r)/Pmt] + 1\}}{\ln(1 + r)} ,$$

for r > -100%; (FV x r)/Pmt > -1

Example 14: Your client is hoping to buy an oceanfront vacation/retirement home and figures he will need $50,000 for the down payment and closing costs. If he can save $7,500 at the end of each year, how long will it take him to reach his goal? What if he earns 6% on his investments?

$$FV = \$50,000$$
$$r = 6\%$$
$$Pmt = \$7,500$$

$$n = \frac{-\ln \{[(\$50,000 \times 6\%) \div \$7,500] + 1\}}{\ln(1 + 6\%)} =$$

$$\frac{0.3364722}{0.0582689} = 5.77 \text{ years}$$

Number of Periods of Annuity Due Payments to Reach Future Value

Equation N5 calculates the number of periods it will take for level beginning-of-period investments of a given amount earning some specified periodic rate of return to reach a desired future accumulated value.

Equation N5

$$n = \frac{\ln \{[(FV \times r)/[Pmt \times (1 + r)]] + 1\}}{\ln(1 + r)} ,$$

for r > -100%; (FV x r)/[Pmt x (1 + r)] > -1

Example 15: Your client, from the previous example, who is hoping to buy an ocean-front vacation/retirement home, now asks you to determine how long it would take to accumulate the $50,000 for the down payment and closing costs if he saves $7,500 at the beginning of each year and he earns 6% on his investments?

$$
\begin{aligned}
FV &= \$60{,}000 \\
r &= 6\% \\
Pmt &= \$7{,}500
\end{aligned}
$$

$$
n = \frac{\ln\left(\left((\$50{,}000 \times 6\%) \div [\$7{,}500 \times (1 + 6\%)]\right) + 1\right)}{\ln(1 + 6\%)} =
$$

$$
\frac{0.3201675}{0.0582689} = 5.49 \text{ years}
$$

Caveat: Final Payment Adjustment When n Is a Non-Integer Value

Be careful, a non-integer value for the number of periods (n) may not mean what you think it means!

The formulas for computing the number of periods for annuities may provide non-integer values. However, annuities are discreet, equal-interval, periodic payment series. What does it mean if the solution to n is 7.25 periods? If one solves for the number of periods using the NPER function of EXCEL, for example, and similar functions in other spreadsheets, the results will be the same as those presented in equations N1 through N5.

Consider an example to illustrate the issues. Suppose a client wants to know how many years it will take to accumulate $100 if she saves $5 each year at the end of the year and earns 10% on her investment.

Applying equation N4, one gets the result that n is 11.52670461 years, just slightly over half a year more than 11 years exactly. Does that mean your client will actually accumulate $100 in just over 11 and one-half years? Probably not.

To show this, compute first how much your client will accumulate by the end of 11 years exactly. Applying equation FV2, one gets a future value of $92.6558353. Then if that amount accumulates for just over half a year (0.52670461 years) using equation FV1, the result is:

$$
92.6558353 \times (1.1)^{0.52670461} = 97.4259
$$

Therefore, at the end of 11.52670461 years your client *will not* have accumulated $100. This means the solution (that n = 11.52670461) computed using equation N1 does *not* mean that your client needs to make 11 end-of-period payments and then wait for about an additional half year for the balance to grow to $100. Your client will still be $2.5741 short. So what *does* the value of n = 11.52670461 mean?

Let us first calculate how much would your client accumulate by the end of year 12 if we assume she does not make any further payments after her payment at the end of year 11. To compute this value, just multiply the balance at the end of year 11, 92.6558353, by 1.1; the result is:

$$
92.6558353 \times 1.1 = 101.9214188
$$

This result is *more* than the $100 your client is seeking, so the correct value for the number of periods *is* between 11.52670461 and 12 years, *not* the result given by the formula for n. Why is that?

This result is a mathematical anomaly attributable to the fact that the formulas solve for the number of periods in what is really a discreet sequence of payments. However, it is highly unlikely that one would actually hit the future value target right on one of these discreet intervals. These formulas for n, and the various spreadsheet functions, such as NPER in EXCEL, calculate the number-of-period values by implicitly splitting each period into infinitesimally small intervals with corresponding infinitesimally small payments. When these very small payments for very small intervals are accumulated over one full period, the accumulation is exactly the same as if you made one full regular payment for one full regular interval. Thus, the accumulated value computed at each discreet interval is exactly the same as the regular calculation. But if the result of the calculation includes a partial interval, such as the 11.52670461 years previously described, then the *formula effectively assumes the investor makes one final additional partial payment related to the partial period.* In other words, in the case described above, the formula assumes that your client will make 11 end-of-year payments of $5 and then one additional final, or twelfth, payment of some lesser amount at the end of the final partial year, that is, in 11.52670461 years.

Let Nres represent the final partial period and Pmt_{Nres} represent the final partial payment. If the annuity is an ordinary annuity, the formula for computing the final partial payment implicitly assumed to be paid at the end of the final partial period is (using equation FV2'):

Equation Pmt8

$$
Pmt_{Nres} = Pmt \times \left(\frac{(1 + r)^{Nres} - 1}{r}\right)
$$

Putting the appropriate values into the formula, the result is:

$$Pmt_{Nres} = 5 \times \frac{[(1 + 10\%)^{0.5267046 1} - 1]}{10\%} = 2.5741$$

So the formulas for given here and the functions built into most spreadsheet programs, will derive the value of 11.52670461 for n in this case by implicitly assuming that the investor will make 11 full payments of $5 at the end of each full year and then one final (twelfth) partial payment of $2.5741 just past halfway through the twelfth year (0.52670461% of the way through the year).

Checking to see if this is correct, start with the balance at the end of 11.52670461 years, as computed above, $97.4259, add the final residual payment of $2.5741 just calculated, and the result is $100, the target future value.

The problem with this non-integer valued partial-period calculation is that your client probably was not planning to make a final partial payment part way through the twelfth year to reach her $100 goal. In fact, she probably would not have known that such a partial payment was implicitly required and, even if she did know, she almost certainly would not know the value of this necessary final partial payment. So how does one work around this problem when the formulas involving discrete-period annuities derive a non-integer number of periods?

In this case the answer is fairly easy. As was previously determined, if your client let her balance at the end of year 11 accumulate at 10%, her balance will reach $100 before the end of the year 12, without her having to make any further partial or full payments.

One can use equation N1 to determine the final partial year by putting the value of $92.6558353 accumulated by the end of year 11 in for PV, $100 in for FV, and 10% in for r and solving for the final residual period:

$$Nres = \frac{\ln(100 \div 92.6558353)}{\ln(1 + 10\%)} = \frac{0.076278253}{0.09531018} = 0.8$$

The result is 0.8 years. If your client makes annual payments of $5 at the end of each year for 11 years, she will accumulate $100 in 11.8 years, with no requirement to make any partial payments in the final partial year.

This term of 11.8 years is probably the term most people assume they are getting when they solve for the number of periods, n, for an annuity and the result is a non-integer value. This is only logical, since most people are completely unaware that the various spreadsheet

functions that compute the number of periods virtually always implicitly compute the value of the partial period by assuming that the investor will make a final partial payment as well. In other words, the built-in spreadsheet functions, such as *EXCEL's NPER* function, typically *understate* the actual time that it will take to accumulate a given sum. In most cases, of course, most people using these built-in spreadsheet functions have no clue that the value of n is computed by assuming they will make a final partial payment and, therefore, they make the logical, but incorrect, assumption that the number derived from the function is the actual term until they will reach their accumulation goal – without making any final partial payment.

Another problem arises with some other built-in functions. For instance, Hewlett-Packard's excellent financial calculator, the *hp 12C*, gives 12 as the value of n for this problem. Hewlett-Packard's solution to the non-integer-value difficulty is to round the result up to the next highest integer. However, this value overstates the actual number of periods until investors would reach their accumulation goals. In addition, by rounding up to the next full period, anyone using the calculator would naturally assume it would take 12, not 11, annual payments to reach the goal. However, as was shown above, the goal will be reached in 11.8 years with only 11 annual payments. Hewlett-Packard's solution to the problem not only overstates the term until investors will reach their target, but also has them believing they would have already exceeded their goal! Therefore, as was shown above, the "correct" answer is neither 11.52670461 as given by *EXCELS's NPER* function nor 12 as given by *Hewlett-Packard's HP 12C* calculator, but rather 11.8.

In the case described above, we were able to adjust the results so that no final partial payment was required. Unfortunately, in some cases a final partial payment cannot be avoided.

What if the value we computed for the accumulation at the end of year 12 without any further payments (at the end of year 12) had been $99 rather than about $101.92? In other words, what if the investment earnings alone in year 12 on the balance at the end of year 11 were not sufficient to reach the future value target before the end of year 12?

In cases such as this, investors will require one final partial payment at the end of the last year, rather than a full payment, to reach the target. If the accumulated value at the end of year 12 had been $99, as hypothesized above, a full $5 payment at the end of year 12 would shoot investors $4 over their mark. An investor only needs to contribute one last partial payment of $1 at the end of year 12 to reach the $100 targeted amount.

When one computes non-integer values for n using the formulas given above or spreadsheet functions, the methodology that has been suggested here to adjust the value of n to a more realistic number gives one two possible outcomes. Either the result will be a non-integer period, such as 11.8 years in the case above, but with no partial final payment, or an integer period, such as 12 years, but with a final partial payment, such as $1. Every time one derives a non-integer value for n in an annuity calculation, one of these two outcomes is inevitable.

In all the cases where the investment earnings in the last period are not sufficient to reach the goal before the end of the last period, the actual number of periods, n, necessary to reach the target are really integer values, but the investor is required to make one final partial payment. In all the cases where the investment earnings in the last period are more than sufficient to reach the accumulation target before the end of the next full period, the actual n will be a non-integer value, but the investor will not have to make a final partial payment.

For instance, assume that the rate of return used in the above case is 9.5% rather than 10%. In this case, the number of periods until an investor reaches the $100 target (using equation N4) is 11.73178565 years, rather than the 11.52670461 years calculated when the rate of return was assumed to be 10%. The balance at the end of year 11 (using equation FV2) is 90.19259141 and if this balance is accumulated at 9.5% for one more full year (multiplying by 1.095), the result is 98.7608759. Therefore, in this case, the investor not only does not reach the $100 goal by 11.73178565 years, but also does not even reach the goal by 12 full years, unless he makes one additional final partial payment of $1.2391124 at the end of year 12. In this case, the "correct" answer to how many years it takes to accumulate $100 is exactly 12 years with 11 full $5 payments at the end of each of the first 11 years and one final partial payment of about $1.24 at the end of year 12.

In the case when investors are dealing with annuities due and the annuity formula determines that n is a non-integer value, the formula for calculating the final partial payment is as follows (using equation PV11):

Equation Pmt9

$$Pmt_{Nres} = Pmt \times (1 - (1 + r)^{-Nres}) \times (1 + r)$$

In contrast with ordinary annuities, the final partial payment for annuities due is not assumed to be paid at the very end of the non-integer number of periods, but rather at the beginning of the final partial period. For illustration, assume the annuity described above was an annuity due rather than an ordinary annuity, all else remaining the same.

In this case, n is computed using equation N5 and the result is 10.87073735 years. Using equation FV4, the balance at the end of year 10 would be $87.65583531. The implicit final partial payment at the beginning of year 11 (end of year 10) computed using equation Pmt9 is $4.38018747. Adding these two values together, the balance at the beginning of year 11 (end of year 10) is $92.03602278. If this amount is accumulated for the final partial period of 0.87073735 years using equation FV1, the result, as expected, is $100.

However, once again this is an unrealistic scenario. If the balance at the end of year 10 were only $87.65583531, why would anyone who is investing $5 per year until they reach $100 ever choose to invest only $4.38 dollars at the beginning of year 11? They would not. They would expect to contribute $5, just as in every other year. So if an annual contribution of $5 is added to the balance at the end of year 10, the result is $92.65583531. Equation N1 can be used to determine how long it would now take for the balance of $92.65583531 to grow to $100. The result is another 0.8 years. So the "correct" answer as to how long it would take for a person investing $5 at the beginning of each year (with no final partial payments) to accumulate $100 is 10.8 years, not 10.87073735. In other words, investors making 11 $5 contributions at the beginning of each year (in years 0 through 10) could expect to accumulate $100 in 10.8 years.

Rate-Of-Return Calculations

Rate of Return Required for Lump Sum Present Value to Reach Future Value

The rate of return earned on a lump sum present value investment that grows to a given future value in n years can be derived from equation FV1 using simple algebra to isolate r:

Equation R1

$$R = (FV / PV)^{1/n} - 1$$

Example 16: Once again, out of curiosity your client asks you what rate of return she would have to earn on the $60,000 she has earmarked for her child's college education so that it would grow to her goal of $134,037 at the end of 5 years.

$$PV = \$60,000$$
$$n = 5$$
$$FV = \$134,037$$

$$R = (\$134,037 \div \$60,000)^{1/5} - 1 = 17.44\%$$

Rate of Return on Annuities

There is no reduced-form analytical equation to solve for the rate of return on an annuity. Numerical methods, trial-and-error methods, or built-in spreadsheet or calculator algorithms must be employed to compute this value. The *RATE* function in Microsoft® *EXCEL* and similar functions in other spreadsheets and calculators can be used to compute these values. Alternatively, the "Solver" add-in to Microsoft® *EXCEL, Quattro Pro, Lotus,* and other spreadsheets may be employed to "back-solve" for the rate-of-return value when the rate-of-return value is an input value to a spreadsheet calculation using one of the above, or other more involved, annuity formulas in a spreadsheet.

Rate Conversions, Compounding Periods, and Effective Interest Rates

Frequently, financial planners and investors need to convert a rate quoted for one interval into an equivalent rate for another interval or to convert a rate determined for one compounding period into an equivalent rate for another compounding period.

For instance, most mortgages are generally paid monthly and the compounding period is also generally monthly. However, interest rates are almost always quoted in annual terms.

To understand interest-rate conversions, a few terms must be defined.

First, let

c = The number of compounding periods per year
r_c = The rate per compounding period
p = The number of payment periods per year

r_p = The rate per payment period
r_{sa} = The stated annual rate
r_{ea} = The effective annual rate

The values of the number of compounding periods, c, and for the number of payment periods, p, are often the same, but they need not be.

Stated Annual Rate

The "stated annual rate" is usually defined as the compounding rate per period times the number of compounding periods per year. That is:

Equation R2

$$r_{sa} = c \times r_c$$

Generally, of course, the calculation actually goes the other way where one knows the stated annual rate and wants to find the compounding period rate:

Equation R3

$$r_c = \frac{r_{sa}}{c}$$

For example, if the stated annual rate is 9% and the number of compounding periods per year is 12, then the compounding period rate is 0.75% (9% ÷ 12).

Effective Annual Rate

The "effective annual rate" is the rate one is really effectively paying over a year's time on a loan with more than one compounding period per year. This value will virtually always be higher than the stated annual rate, unless there is only one compounding period per year. The formula for the effective annual rate is determined as follows:

Equation R4

$$r_{ea} = (1 + r_c)^c - 1$$

In the case where the stated rate is 9% and the number of compounding periods per year is 12, the compounding period rate is 0.75% (9% ÷ 12). Thus, the effective annual rate is about 9.381%, not the stated rate of 9%.

$$r_{ea} = (1 + 0.0075)^{12} - 1 = 9.3807\%$$

In general, when one is working with a series of periodic payments, the interest rate or rate of return one uses must be the effective payment period interest rate or rate of return. To find the effective rate per payment period in the case when c, the number of compounding periods per year, and p, the number of payment periods per year, are different, one first determines the effective annual rate using equation R4 and then applies equation R5 to compute the effective rate per payment period:

Equation R5

$$r_p = (1 + r_{ea})^{1/p} - 1$$

For example, if, given the circumstances described above, payments were to be made quarterly, all other factors remaining the same, the rate per payment period would be about 2.267%:

$$r_p = (1 + 0.093807)^{1/4} - 1 = 2.267\%$$

Equivalent Annuities/Loan Payments

Occasionally, advisers or investors will want to know what annuity payments or loan payments for one set of payment periods is exactly equivalent to another set of annuity payments or loan payments for another set of payment periods, assuming the overall term of the annuity or loan is unchanged.

For example, assume the facts described above apply to a three-year loan: the stated rate is 9% and the compounding period is monthly. Assuming the amount borrowed is $30,000, what quarterly payments would be required to pay the loan off in 3 years?

Equation Pmt1 is used to compute the required periodic payment. Set PV equal to $30,000, r equal to r_p (2.267%), and n equal to 12 (3 years x 4 Pmts per year). The result is $2,883.50.[3]

What if one wanted to determine what the periodic payment would be if payments were semiannual rather than quarterly?

First find the rate per period for two payment periods per year using equation R5:

$$r_p = (1 + 0.093807)^{1/2} - 1 = 4.5852284\%$$

Then, once again plug the corresponding values into equation Pmt1 (PV = $30,000; r_p = 4.5852284; n = 6) to derive the result of $5,832.36.

The result is more than twice the quarterly amount, since one will have to pay more interest as payments are deferred longer. Specifically, the first semiannual payment includes all the interest one would have to pay on two quarterly payments, plus the additional interest accrued since no payment was made at the end of the first quarter.

WHERE CAN I FIND OUT MORE?

1. Frank Fabozzi, Fixed Income Mathematics: Analytical and Statistical Techniques (Chicago, IL: Irwin Professional Publishers, 1996).

2. David Spaulding, Measuring Investment Performance: Calculating and Evaluating Investment Risk and Return (New York, NY: McGraw-Hill, 1997).

3. Robert Rachlin, Return on Investment Manual: Tools and Applications for Managing Financial Results (Armonk, NY: Sharpe Professional, 1997).

4. Arefaine Yohannes, The Irwin Guide to Risk and Reward (Chicago, IL: Irwin Professional Publishers, 1996).

5. Birrer & Carrica, Present Value Applications for Accountants and Financial Planners (New York, NY: Quorum Books, 1990).

6. Charles Akerson, The Internal Rate of Return in Real Estate Investments (Chicago, IL: American Inst. of Real Estate Appraisers, 1988).

7. David Leabigh, A Pocket Guide to Finance (Fort Worth, TX: Dryden Press, 1996).

8. Calculator Analysis for Business and Finance (New York, NY: McGraw-Hill).

9. HP-12C Owner's Handbook and Problem-Solving Guide (Hewlett-Packard Co.).

CHAPTER ENDNOTES

1. The value of a perpetual annuity will never change, given that the market rate of interest on alternative investments with similar risk characteristics never changes, which is unlikely. But market valuation of a perpetual bond using market rates of interest is different than determining what payment a perpetual bond with a stated rate of interest, r, for example, would be. The payment is determined by reference to the stated rate. Obviously, when valuing any annuity, if you assume the interest rate will change during the payout period, you have to value each subperiod of the annuity stream based upon the interest rate assumed for that subperiod.

2. The formula for computing the final partial payment for annuities due when n is determined to be a non-integer value is provided later in this section.

3. Actual value is $2,883.494423, but the amount has been rounded up to $2,883.50.

Chapter 33

MEASURING INVESTMENT RETURN

WHAT IS IT?

An analytical method of comparison is an objective way to assess the relative risks and potential rewards from alternative investments. Although the ultimate decision as to which (if any) investment should be made may be subjective, the assessment should initially be based on both factual and measurable information.

The techniques discussed in this chapter are all based on the time value of money concept. The general principles of present value and future value, discussed in Chapter 32, "Time Value Concepts," may be sufficient in themselves to evaluate the return on a particular investment. But, in many cases, the more sophisticated approaches described below may be appropriate or necessary.

HOW DOES IT WORK?

This chapter will examine five comparative techniques commonly used to evaluate alternative investment opportunities. All of these devices have the same goal: they are designed to measure the return on an investor's principal. This is the concept of return on investment (ROI).

1. *Net Present Value (NPV)* is the difference between the present value of all future benefits of an investment and the present value of all capital contributions. This method measures the tradeoff between the cash invested (outflows) and the benefits projected (inflows).

2. *Internal Rate of Return* is that discount rate at which the present value of all the future benefits an investor will receive from an investment exactly equals the present value of all the capital contributions the investor will be required to make. IRR is generally used to compare the *effective* interest rates of two or more investments, particularly with non-matching or irregular cash flows.

3. *Modified Internal Rates of Return* are IRR methods that adjust cash flows for realistic assumptions

regarding reinvestment rates, borrowing rates, and the like.

4. *Pay Back Period* measures the relative periods of time needed to recover the investor's capital (income received after the pay back period will be considered gain).

5. *Cash on Cash*, as its name implies, analyzes an investment by dividing the annual cash flow by the amount of the cash investment in order to determine the cash return on the cash invested.

ADVANTAGES

1. These methods of comparison offer a way to measure the potential return on alternative investment choices in a logical and consistent manner.

2. The use of mathematics (assuming the accuracy of the input) balances an investor's natural inclination to play a hunch by introducing objectivity into the decision-making process.

3. The use of more than one comparative method will help the investor more effectively recognize and evaluate risk/reward parameters.

DISADVANTAGES

1. There are a number of unknowns in the measurement process. For instance, an investor can only estimate or project how much money will be received from a given investment and when that cash inflow and outflow will occur. There is no way to completely guarantee either the amount or timing of cash flows.

   These uncertainties, though drawbacks, should not preclude the use of analytical techniques. There is no single technique that can be applied to every case. The method that most closely reflects the investor's perception of how return should be measured is the one that should be used. It is important that the chosen method be used *consistently*. In many cases, more than one analytical technique should be used in order to corroborate the results of the other approaches.

2. Undue reliance on mathematical quantitative evaluation techniques, as noted in the previous chapter, may create a false sense of security. Such excessive reliance can both hinder the investor's ability to utilize appropriate subjective analytical skills and inhibit the consideration of external factors that may affect the viability of the investment.

3. It is possible that a particular investment may not be adequately or properly quantified by any of the evaluation techniques discussed here; an investor may not have objective tools available.

4. It is often difficult to know which measuring device to select. The use of an inappropriate technique will often result in drawing an inappropriate conclusion.

5. In practice it is often difficult to obtain accurate and comprehensive data.

WHEN IS THE USE OF THIS TECHNIQUE INDICATED?

The five techniques discussed in this chapter are all useful when an investor wants to compare alternative investments that are seemingly similar with respect to risk and it is desirable to distinguish the investments by measuring their relative rewards in terms of: (1) timing – when and/or how often cash must be invested in and/or may be taken out of the investment; and (2) quantity – the rate of interest the investment will earn or the rate at which it will grow.

A second reason for the use of these return-on-investment techniques is to evaluate one particular investment in comparison with a safe alternative, such as a U.S. Treasury Note. Used in this manner, the safe alternative serves as a benchmark to determine whether the potential reward from the investment under consideration is sufficient relative to the associated risks.

RATE OF RETURN CONCEPTS

Rate of return means different things in different contexts, depending upon a host of factors. Consequently, financial economists and investors use a wide variety of terms to describe returns in these different contexts, such as *total return, holding-period return, annualized return, simple return, compound return, arithmetic average return, geometric average return, time-weighted return, dollar-weighted return, nominal return, real (inflation-adjusted) return, risk-adjusted return, after-tax return, taxable-equivalent return, internal rate of return,* and various *modified internal rate of return* measures. Although financial professionals do not always define and use these terms in exactly the same way, the following descriptions are commonly accepted definitions for the various measures.

Total Return

The term total return means the total gain or loss over a specified period relative to an initial dollar investment at the beginning of the period. All investments potentially have some combination of six components or sources of return for which a proper analysis must account:

- Cash inflows from the investment (outflows to the investment); plus (minus)

- Price or capital appreciation (price or capital depreciation); plus (minus)

- Debt amortization (negative amortization); plus (minus)

- Tax shelter (tax payments); plus (minus)

- Other tangible property or boot received (paid); plus (minus)

- Intangible but measurable benefits or services received (paid), if any.

In addition, since the ultimate goal of investing is to enhance real future wealth, investors cannot ignore the potential erosion of their future purchasing power as a result of inflation.

Cash flows in the form of interest payments, dividends, rents, royalties, and the like are the most obvious and ubiquitous source of return. Also, for many investments, changes in the market value of the investment each period, such as a stock's price increase or decrease, are part of the investor's total return for each period. When an investment is leveraged through the use of borrowing, the analysis must account for changes in the debt balance. If an investment generates a net cash flow of $100, but the investor's debt is also reduced (debt amortization) during the period by $10, the investor is in fact $110 wealthier than at the start of the period.

Although total returns are frequently computed without accounting for taxes, investors can use and spend only the amount they get to keep after paying taxes. Consequently, any income, capital gain, personal property, or other tax payments attributable or allocable to the investment reduce the investor's total return. Conversely, if interest payments on debt used to finance investments are tax-deductible or the investment generates depreciation deductions, real estate tax deductions, or other tax deductions, the tax savings so generated each period increase the investor's return above and beyond the amount measured solely by cash flow, price changes, and debt reduction.

If an investor receives any other tangible property or boot, such as shares of stock in lieu of cash interest payments, the total return includes the market value of the property or boot received. Finally, the total return must include the value of any intangible but measurable benefits received. For example, if an investor purchases a commercial office building and in the transaction receives an easement for a private access road, the market or use value of the easement for each period should be included in the total return.[1]

To compute the *rate* of return on investment for any period one simply divides the total return by the investor's *equity* in the investment at the beginning of the period.

An investor's equity in an investment at any point in time is the sum of all cash contributions, plus debt amortization, plus price appreciation or less price depreciation. For example, assume an investor purchases a residential rental unit for $100,000 with an initial cash outlay of $20,000 and borrowing of $80,000. The investor's initial equity is $20,000 (the amount of cash paid, not the total purchase price of the property). After one year, the investor's net operating cash flow (after debt-repayment) is $5,000, the debt balance has been reduced by $1,500, and the market value of the property has risen to $102,500. Net tax savings (on interest and depreciation deductions in excess of taxable rental income) equal $1,000. The investor's total return for the year is $10,000 ($5,000 cash flow + $1,500 debt reduction + $2,500 price appreciation + $1,000 net tax savings), which is a 50% return on the initial $20,000 equity investment. At the end of the year, the investor's equity in the investment has increased to $24,000 ($20,000 original equity + $1,500 debt reduction + $2,500 price appreciation). Each year or period of evaluation may generate a different rate of return (as both the return for the time period, and the underlying equity, may change). Consequently, different measures of the rate of return are often used to generalize the results or performance of an investment over a number of holding periods.

Holding-Period Return

The holding-period return is simply the total return for a specified period over which an investment is held. For instance, suppose a person invested $1,000 in the S&P 500 index at the beginning of 1997 and held the investment for 5 years until the end of 2001 while reinvesting the cash flows. This investor would have accumulated about $1,662.45 by the end of 2001 (ignoring expenses).[2] The 5-year holding-period return is $662.45 ($1,662.45 - $1,000) and the 5-year holding-period rate of return is 66.245% ($662.45 / $1,000). In contrast, if the dividends were not reinvested, the value of the stocks would have grown to about $1,550.03 at the end of 2001 and total dividend payments over all 5 years would have totaled about $85.96, for a cumulative holding-period return of $635.99 ($550.03 + $85.96) and a holding-period rate of return of about 63.6%. The larger value for the first holding-period return is attributable to the earnings on reinvested dividends within the holding period (the market having risen during this period).[3]

Annualized Returns

Since comparing investment returns over different holding periods is difficult, the standard practice is to express returns in annualized terms. One may express the annualized return in one of two ways – as a *simple* or a *compound* annual return. Which expression is the better measure depends on the context in which it is used, as is described below. Two closely related terms that are also applicable in these contexts are the *arithmetic average annual return* and the *geometric average annual return*.

Simple and Arithmetic Average Annual Returns

Investors compute the *simple annual return* by dividing the holding-period return by the number of years in the holding period. Essentially, the simple annual return is the rate of return computed by stretching or shrinking the holding period to be equal to just one year and stretching or shrinking the holding-period return proportionately. As a result, it computes the annual rate as if the holding period were actually one year without assuming any reinvestment of principal and interest. For instance, in the example above, the annualized return for the S&P 500 investment earning a 66.245% 5-year holding-period rate of return is 13.25% (66.245% / 5). In other words, by shrinking the holding period from five years to just one year, the rate of return similarly shrinks to just one fifth its original value of 66.245% to 13.25%.

If the holding-period is less than a year, say a month, then the simple annual return of the 1-month holding-period return is determined by dividing the 1-month holding-period return by 1/12 – in other words, by multiplying or stretching the period by a factor of 12. For example, suppose an investor pays \$9,925 for a T-bill maturing at \$10,000 in three months. The 3-month (1/4th year) holding-period return is \$75 and the 3-month holding-period rate of return is 0.756% (\$75 / \$9,925). Since the holding period must be stretched by four times its original length to equal a year, the simple annual rate of return is equal to four times the 3-month holding-period rate of 0.756%, or about 3.024% (0.756% × 4).

The *arithmetic average return* corresponds conceptually to the simple return, only applied to a series of holding-period returns. If investors want to find the arithmetic average annual return of a series of 1-year holding-period returns they simply sum the 1-year holding-period returns and divide by the number of years of returns. For example, if an investment earns 10%, –5%, and 15% over three years, the arithmetic average annual rate of return is 6.67% [(10% – 5% + 15%) / 3 = 6.67%].

Compound and Geometric Average Annual Returns

In contrast with the simple annual return, one computes the *compound annual return* by assuming earnings and principal are being reinvested rather than by stretching or contracting the holding period. Investors calculate the compound annual return of an n-year holding-period rate of return by adding one to the holding-period return, taking the nth root of this sum, and subtracting one.

For example, the 3-month T-bill described earlier has a 3-month holding-period rate of return of 0.756%. The compound annual rate of return is the annual rate investors would earn if they could continue to reinvest the earnings and principal at a 3-month holding-period rate of 0.756% for each of the next three 3-month periods. If this were the case, each initial dollar of investment would grow to \$1.03058 [(1.00756)⁴] by the end of one year. With this assumption, the compound annual rate of return is about 3.06% (1.03058 – 1 ≈ 3.06%), which is *greater* than the simple annual rate of 3.024%, as computed above.

The compound annual rate of return for the S&P 500 index investment with a 66.245% 5-year holding-period rate of return is 10.7% [(1.66245)^{1/5} – 1 = 1.107 – 1 = 10.7%]. In other words, in this case the compound annual rate of return is the annual rate of return that, if principal and cash flows were reinvested each year at this rate, would provide a 66.245% holding-period return over a 5-year period. This 10.7% compound annual rate is about 2.55% *less* than the simple annual rate of 13.25% computed above.

The geometric average return is related to the compound return in the same manner as the arithmetic average return is related to the simple return. To calculate the geometric average annual return for a series of 1-year holding-period returns, add one to each period's return, compute the product of these sums over all periods, extrapolate the nth root of the product, where n is the number of years, and subtract one.[4] For example, the 3-year accumulation of $1 invested as described above (earning 10%, -5%, and 15%) with earnings and principal reinvested is 1.20175 [(1+10%) x (1-5%) x (1+15%)]. Taking the third root of 1.20175 and subtracting one, the resulting geometric average annual return is 6.32% [(1.20175)$^{1/3}$ – 1 = 1.0632 – 1 = 6.32%)]. This result is *less* than the simple annual rate of 6.67%.

Simple Versus Compound and Arithmetic Versus Geometric

As the examples above demonstrate, simple (arithmetic average) annual rates differ from compound (geometric average) annual rates. Is there a systematic relationship and is one measure better than another?

First, for any investment providing a net positive return over a given holding period, the simple annual rate is always equal to or greater than the compound annual rate if the reference holding period is greater than a year and always equal to or less than the compound annual rate if the holding period is less than a year. Similarly, for any series of (on average, positive) annual holding-period returns, the arithmetic average annual return is always equal to or greater than the geometric average annual return. In addition, the greater is the variability of the annual holding-period returns, the larger the difference will be.

The logic of these results may not be immediately apparent, but, if one thinks about it, it takes a lower return to achieve the same terminal value if one assumes that cash flows are reinvested and compounded.

Second, whether one measure is better than another depends upon how one intends to use it. If the objective is to measure historical performance as, for example, to compare the past performance of two different mutual funds, then the compound or geometric average returns are the better measures. If one is looking to estimate future returns based upon historical performance, the simple or arithmetic average returns are the better measures for estimating returns in any given future year. This is because, in general, the simple or arithmetic average is an unbiased estimate of expected future returns for a single year. However, if investors are attempting to estimate the average annual rate at which they could expect their money to grow over a period of years in the future, the compound or geometric average returns are the ideal measures. In general, using the simple or arithmetic average return to estimate expected future average returns over a number of years would lead to significant overestimations of future wealth accumulations (because, as noted above, the arithmetic average tends to be higher than the geometric, and the difference is magnified by increased variability).

The reason for this is demonstrated by a simple example. Suppose a person invests $100 and earns a 100% return the first year and a negative 50% return the second year. This investor has an average annual rate of return of 25%, right? [(100% - 50%) / 2 = 25%]. Wrong! The investment grows from $100 to $200 when it earns a 100% return the first year and then falls back to $100 when it loses 50% of the $200 accumulated investment the second year. The investor starts with $100 and ends with $100 two years later, so the actual average annual return is zero% (the geometric average annual return), not 25% (the arithmetic average annual return)! Although this is an extreme example, the effect is generally the same, albeit to a lesser degree, in all other cases.[5]

Nominal and Real (Inflation-Adjusted) Returns

Nominal returns are simply the actual returns earned over a given period computed without accounting for changes in the purchasing power of the dollar (inflation). The inflation-adjusted or real rate of return represents the return adjusted for changes in the general level of the prices of goods and services that investors could purchase if they liquidated their investments. The real rate of return is computed by dividing one plus the nominal rate of return by one plus the inflation rate, and then subtracting one:

$$\text{Real Rate of Return} = \frac{(1 + \text{Nominal Rate of Return}) - 1}{(1 + \text{Inflation Rate})} = \frac{(\text{Nominal Rate} - \text{Inflation Rate})}{(1 + \text{Inflation Rate})}$$

For example, an investor buys 100 shares of XYZ Corp. for $10,000 and holds the shares for 5 years. During the 5-year period, the stock pays no dividends but grows to a value of $17,623.42. The nominal 5-year holding-period rate of return is 76.2342% ($7,623.42 / $10,000). Now assume that the general level of prices has increased by 21.6653% over the 5-year period. The real 5-year holding-period rate of return is 44.8517% [(1.762342) / (1.216653) – 1].

Investors must use care when adjusting real holding-period returns to real annualized returns. For instance, the *simple* annual *real* return computed by dividing the 44.8517% real 5-year holding-period return by 5 years is 8.9703%. However, if, instead, one first computes the *simple* annual *nominal* return by dividing the 5-year *nominal* holding-period return of 76.2342% by 5 years and then computes the *simple* annual inflation rate by dividing the 5-year holding-period inflation rate of 21.6653% by 5 years, the results are 15.4468% and 4.3306%, respectively. Computing the *simple* annual *real* rate of return using these rates results in a value of 10.6522% (1.154468 / 1.043306 – 1), not 8.9703%! So which is the "real" *simple* annual real return?

In contrast, if one computes the *compound* annual *real* return from the 5-year real holding-period rate of return of 44.8517%, the result is 7.6923% [(1.448517)^{1/5} – 1]. If, instead, one first finds the *compound* annual *nominal* return from the 5-year nominal holding-period rate of return of 76.2342% and then the *compound* annual *nominal* inflation rate from the 21.6653% 5-year holding-period inflation rate, the results are 12% [(1.762342)^{1/5} –1] and 4% [(1.216653)^{1/5} – 1], respectively. Now, using these two annual rates to compute the *compound* annual *real* rate of return also gives a result of 7.6923% (1.12 / 1.04 – 1).

Therefore, annualizing real holding-period returns using the *compound-return* methodology is consistent, regardless of whether one first computes the real holding-period return and then annualizes that real holding-period return or first annualizes the nominal holding-period return and holding-period inflation rate and then computes the real return. In contrast, if one is using the simple-return methodology, one will derive different annualized real returns, depending upon the order of the computations. Although there is no definitive consensus on which order of computations is the correct methodology for computing the simple annual real rate of return, the authors strongly favor first calculating the real holding-period rate of return and then deriving the simple annual real rate of return. Computing the simple annual real return in this way has the theoretical advantage of starting the determination with the conceptually correct real holding-period return and also the practical advantage of requiring one less step in the calculations.

Internal Rate of Return and Net Present Value

The internal rate of return and the net present value (NPV) are essentially two-sides of the same coin. To understand the internal rate of return, one must first understand net present value. Net present value is simply the current value of a stream of cash flows discounted at some appropriate rate of return representing the investor's opportunity cost rate (best alternative rate). For example, assume an investor's opportunity cost rate is 6%. Assume also that the investor is contemplating a 3-year investment involving a $1,000 cash outlay at the beginning of year 1, a $2,000 cash outlay at the beginning of year 2, a $1,000 cash withdrawal at the beginning of year 3, and a terminal value of $2,236.75 at the end of year 3 (beginning of year 4). What is the net present value of this investment, after the value of each cash flow item is discounted for its appropriate time period?

$$NPV = \frac{-\$1,000}{(1.06)^0} - \frac{\$2,000}{(1.06)^1} + \frac{\$1,000}{(1.06)^2} + \frac{\$2,236.75}{(1.06)^3}$$

$$= \frac{-\$1,000}{1} - \frac{\$2,000}{1.06} + \frac{\$1,000}{1.1236} + \frac{\$2,236.75}{1.910}$$

$$= -\$1,000 - \$1,886.79 + \$890.00 + \$1,878.02 = -\$118.77$$

The net present value is – $118.77. A negative net present value means that this investment does not earn the investor's required 6% rate of return. However, it is important to note that the key aspect of evaluating an investment in terms of NPV is whether it is positive or negative (whether it earns more or less than the investor's required rate of return). The *magnitude* of the NPV is not necessarily a valid way to select between two different investment choices (selecting between investment options is covered in greater detail later in this chapter).

So what annual rate of return does this investment earn? The rate of return that equates the NPV to zero is the annual rate of return earned by the investment. That rate of return is called the internal rate of return. The following table shows that 3.823% is the internal rate of return.

$$NPV = \frac{-\$1,000}{(1.03823)^0} - \frac{\$2,000}{(1.03823)^1} + \frac{\$1,000}{(1.03823)^2} + \frac{\$2,236.75}{(1.03823)^3}$$

$$= \frac{-\$1,000}{1} - \frac{\$2,000}{1.03823} + \frac{\$1,000}{1.07792} + \frac{\$2,236.75}{1.11913}$$

$$= -\$1,000 - \$1,926.36 + \$927.71 + \$1,998.65 = -\$0.00$$

Net present values and internal rates of return are essential tools for measuring investment returns and comparing and analyzing alternative investments. How these tools are used to measure returns and in investment analysis is discussed in considerable detail later in this chapter.

Time–Weighted and Dollar–Weighted Annual Returns

The time-weighted annual return is the geometric (compounded) annual return measured on the basis of periodic market valuations of assets. This is the preferred method for evaluating the performance of investment managers because it eliminates the impact of cash contributions and disbursements (inflows and outflows). However, in principle it requires valuations to be made on the occasion of each cash flow. Approximations to this measure can be obtained by prorating cash flows to successive valuation points or by computing internal rates of return between valuation points. If there are no interim cash flows, the time-weighted return, compounded annually, determines the ending value of an investment.

In contrast, the dollar-weighted annual return is the rate of return that discounts a portfolio's terminal value and interim cash flows back to its initial value. It is equivalent to a portfolio's internal rate of return. The dollar-weighted return can be misleading for purposes of comparative performance measurement, because it is influenced by the timing and magnitude of contributions and disbursements that are beyond the control of the portfolio manager. However, if investors want to compute the average annual return they actually have earned on an investment over a given period where they have made cash withdrawals and/or contributions during that period, they should use the dollar-weighted return (internal rate of return) method.

A simple example can demonstrate the difference. Above, the discussion described a 3-year investment that had 1-year holding-period returns of 10%, -5%, and 15%. The geometric average annual return or time–weighted return is computed by compounding these returns over the three-year period, resulting in a geometric or time-weighted average annual return of 6.32%, as shown earlier. However, assume that a person invests $1 the first year, another $2 the second year, and withdraws $1 the third year. In this case, the dollar-weighted return is equivalent to the internal rate of return (which will be discussed further below) of a $1 outflow at the beginning of the 1st year, a $2 outflow at the start of the 2nd, a $1 inflow at the beginning of the 3rd year, and a $2.24 withdrawal at the end of the 3rd year (the terminal value). This series of cash flows has an internal rate of return (a dollar-weighted annual return) of only 3.87% (as compared to the 6.32% time-weighted annual return). This makes sense, since the greatest amount of money was deposited in the 2nd year (when the 1-year return was negative) and less money was invested during the years of positive returns. As a result, the negative returns received a greater dollar-weight than the positive returns (in comparison to equal weightings under the time-weighted return), resulting in a lower dollar-weighted than the time-weighted annual return.

After–Tax Return and Taxable–Equivalent Return

What investors get to keep after paying taxes is what matters. Virtually all financial planning issues and investment choices involve tax considerations. The real value of any financial planning strategy or tactic or investment choice relates to the real spendable dollars that each option provides relative to the alternatives. For instance, nominal yields on taxable bonds are virtually uniformly higher than returns on tax-free municipals of comparable maturity. However, for some taxpayers in high tax brackets, the tax-free yields of municipal bonds are higher than the after-tax yields from taxable bonds, so the tax-free municipals are the preferable investment.

If it is assumed that the investment return is entirely currently taxable, then the after-tax return (also called the *tax-free-equivalent return*) is simply equal to the before-tax return less the taxes on the return. Specifically, if the tax rate is assumed to be t and the before-tax rate of return is r, then the after-tax return, rat, is:

$$rat = r \times (1 - t).$$

For example, investors earning 6% before tax, whose tax rate on that income is 28%, will earn 4.32% after tax [6% × (1 − 28%) = 4.32%].

The taxable-equivalent return is the reverse of the after-tax return; representing the before-tax return (r) an investor would have to earn to equal, after tax (t), the return on a tax-free investment (rat):

$$r = rat / (1 - t).$$

Although these formulas are frequently used to compute after-tax returns, they are often not an accurate measure. Only a relatively small class of investments, such as money market funds, bank accounts, and the like provide investment returns that are entirely currently taxable. Other investments, such as stocks, real estate, and the like provide some combination of currently taxable income and income, return, or gain on which tax is deferred. In addition, a whole host of vehicles such as qualified retirement plans, commercial annuities, life insurance, Section 529 plans, Coverdell educational savings accounts, and the like provide unique tax incentives that cannot be accounted for using the simple formulas above.

In many financial planning and investment situations, not only the level of taxation but also the timing of taxation is a critical factor. Between two investments providing identical before-tax returns and identical total tax burdens, the one that defers some or all of the taxation to a later date is generally preferable.

Appendix K, "Additional Time Value Concepts," has an extensive discussion of after-tax returns and the concept of tax leverage and describes the tax-adjusted time-value tools financial advisers and investors must understand to properly handle financial and investment plans. That appendix discusses the tools necessary to account for the five most-prevalent types of after-tax returns and tax leverage, ranging from nondeductible fully currently taxable vehicles, such as T-bills, on one end of the spectrum, through stocks and other income and appreciation assets in the middle of the spectrum, to tax-deductible, fully tax-deferred vehicles, such as IRC Section 401(k) plans on the other end of the spectrum.

Risk–Adjusted Returns

Risk-adjusted return measures were developed to help investors gauge how much return they were getting per unit of risk. Both volatility (level of risk) and return are combined in one measure, permitting a rank ordering of investments. Investments ranking high on a risk-adjusted return scale demonstrated a favorable trade-off between risk and reward: either the returns were high enough to compensate for the additional risk taken, or, the returns may not have been extraordinarily high, but the risk taken was much lower than expected.

Various popular methods exist to measure an investment's risk-adjusted return. Some use standard deviation; others use beta. Risk-adjusted returns are most appropriate when used in "apples to apples" comparisons. Measures using standard deviation, for example, should compare funds in the same category or peer group. Beta relates a fund's volatility to a benchmark – usually the S&P 500 Index – so it is important to use an appropriate benchmark for a fair comparison.

These risk-adjusted return measures are discussed in greater detail in Chapter 31, "Measuring Investment Risk."

HOW IS IT IMPLEMENTED

Before examining these five comparative techniques, it may help to review a number of rate of return concepts. See "Rate of Return Concepts," on page 294.

An examination of the five comparative techniques for evaluating alternative investment opportunities [(1) net present value (NPV), (2) internal rate of return (IRR), (3) modified internal rate of return (MIRR), (4) pay back period, and (5) cash on cash] follows.

I. Net Present Value

Net present value is an extension of the present value concepts discussed in the previous chapter. Present value is the amount that must be invested now to produce a given future value. For instance, if an investor can invest money at 10%, the investor must have $1,000 now in order to have it grow to $1,100 one year from now. $1,000 is the present value of $1,100 to be received in one year. Obviously, the present value is affected by (1) the interest (investment analysts call this the discount) rate, as well as (2) the length of the investment period.

Present value is a simple means of comparing two investments. For example, an investor is considering an investment of $1,000 that will pay $1,200 three years from now. The investor can also invest the $1,000 in an alternative investment of equal risk and earn 10% on the money. Which investment should the investor make?

An easy way to compare the investments is to compute the present value of the $1,200 payable three years from

now at a 10% discount rate. The present value of the first investment is only $902; the present value of $1,000 in hand today is, obviously, $1,000. Therefore, from a pure present value standpoint, the proposed investment for $1,200 in three years is inferior to the alternative of simply investing the $1,000 at 10%.

Net present value is the net difference between (a) the present value of all future benefits to be realized from an investment and (b) the present value of all capital contributions into the investment. A negative net present value should result in an almost automatic rejection of the investment. A positive net present value indicates that the investment is worth further consideration since the present value of the stream of dollars that will be recovered exceeds the present value of the stream of dollars that will be paid out.

The difficulty is determining what discount rate should be used in computing the present values of the cash inflows and cash outflows. Usually this discount rate will be the minimal acceptable rate of return, found by determining the cost of capital or, as in the example above, determining the rate an alternative investment of similar quality/risk can earn. In the example above, the rate was 10%. Once this reinvestment rate is determined, it can be used as the discount factor to compute the present value of the money invested and the present value of the expected return.

These present value amounts are then netted against each other. If the result is positive, the investment will exceed the reinvestment rate and should be considered. If the net present value is a negative number and falls short of the reinvestment rate, the investment under consideration should be rejected.

Chapter 33 – Measuring Investment Return

To the extent that a proposed investment yields a positive net present value, the investment provides a potential cushion for safety. It may also allow the investor to incur certain additional costs (such as attorney's, accountant's, or financial planner's fees in connection with the analysis of the investment) and still achieve the desired reinvestment rate.

An example of the use of net present value analysis may be helpful.

Assume that at the beginning of the year an individual has been shown an investment opportunity requiring a lump sum outlay of $10,000. Currently the funds he would use for this investment are in a money market fund earning 6% annually, net after taxes. The investment proposal projects the following after-tax cash flows at the end of each year.

Year	Amount Received
1	$ 2,000
2	1,500
3	750
4	500
5	10,000
Total Receipts	$14,750

Based solely on net present value analysis, should he make the investment?

The first step in the analysis would be to determine the appropriate reinvestment rate. In this example, the investor currently is earning a net after tax return of 6% in what he believes is a safe investment. To warrant any further consideration, this proposed investment must have at least a positive net present value based on the benchmark reinvestment rate of 6%.

Does the proposed investment meet/beat that benchmark? The stream of dollars projected to be received from the proposed investment has a present value of $11,720 assuming a 6% discount rate. The net present value is a positive $1,720 (the difference between the present value of the future stream of cash inflows, $11,720, and the $10,000 present value of the lump sum outflow of $10,000). (See below regarding how to compute net present value.) Therefore, the proposal does deserve further consideration.

But what if the investor demands a rate of return from the proposed investment higher than his benchmark rate of 6% in order to compensate for the additional risk? If he sets a 15% rate as his minimum, the stream of dollars projected to be received from the proposed investment has a present value of only $8,624. The net present value is a *negative* $1,376 (the difference between the present value of the future stream of cash inflows, $8,624, and the $10,000 present value of the lump sum outflow of $10,000). (See below regarding how to compute net present value.) Therefore, the proposal would be rejected based upon the requirement of a 15% reinvestment rate.

What discount rate, when applied to the expected stream of cash inflows from the proposed investment, has a present value exactly equal to the $10,000 lump sum investment (a net present value of $0)? That discount rate is 10.5%. This computation illustrates the concept of Internal Rate of Return, discussed more fully below.

How to Compute Net Present Value

A. Lump Sum Investment, Single Future Receipt

Assume an individual makes a lump sum investment at the beginning of year one of $10,000. The expected return on this investment is $15,000 (after tax) to be received as a single amount at the end of year five. The investor's discount rate (for an alternative safe investment) is 6% after tax. What is the net present value of the investment under consideration?

To compute the net present value of the investment, the following basic steps are necessary:

1. Compute the present value of the $10,000 investment. Since only one payment is required (immediately at the beginning of the cash flow period), the present value of that payment would be $10,000.

2. Compute the present value of the $15,000 future amount to be received (at the end of year five) using the 6% discount rate. Refer to the Present Value Table in Appendix A. The applicable factor for the present value of $1 at the end of 5 years, using a 6% discount rate, is 0.7473. This factor is multiplied by the $15,000 amount to be received in the future. The present value is therefore $11,210 ($15,000 x 0.7473). [Calculating the present value of a lump sum using a formula, rather than a table factor, is discussed in Chapter 32.]

3. Subtract the present value of the $10,000 lump sum investment ($10,000) from the present value of the $15,000 single payment to be received

($11,210). The net amount is +$1,210; a positive net present value. [Note that if the $15,000 were not received until the end of seven years, the present value of the receipt would be only $9,977 ($15,000 x 0.6651 discount factor), resulting in a negative net present value of $23.]

B. Lump Sum Investment, Multiple Future Receipts

Assume an individual makes a lump sum investment at the beginning of year one of $10,000, the present value of which is $10,000 [Step (1)].

The expected return on this investment (received at each year end) and the present value of each receipt, discounted at 6%, are as follows [Step 2]:

Year	Amount Received	PV @ 6%
1	$ 2,000	$ 1,887
2	1,500	1,335
3	750	630
4	500	396
5	$10,000	$7,473
	$14,750	$11,721
Total Receipts		

[The present value amounts in this table were computed using the Present Value Table in Appendix A and applying the factors to each particular cash flow as seen in the prior example. Computations made using different tables or software may vary slightly due to rounding differences, including the number of decimal places that factors are rounded.]

The net present value is therefore $1,721 ($11,721 present value of the future flow of receipts, less $10,000 present value of the lump sum investment) [Step 3].

C. Multiple Investments, Multiple Future Receipts

Continuing the above example, assume that instead of one $10,000 investment at the beginning of year one, there will be two $5,000 payments, one at the beginning of year one, and the other at the beginning of year two. The present value of the investment, using the same 6% discount rate would be computed as follows [Step 1].

	Year	Payment	PV @ 6%
[Beginning]	1	$ 5,000	$ 5,000
[Beginning]	2	5,000	4,717
Total Payments		$10,000	$ 9,717

When multiple investment payments are required over a period of time, the present value of these payments

must be determined. In this example, the present value of the first $5,000 investment is $5,000. The present value of the second $5,000 is $4,717, $5,000 multiplied by the present value factor of 0.9434 (since the payment is made at the beginning of the second year, the present value factor for the end of the first year is appropriate). If it is assumed the present value of the receipts are the same as above, $11,721 [Step 2], then the net present value of this investment is $2,004 ($11,721 – $9,717) [Step 3]. This larger net present value is logical in this case, since, for an equivalent series of cash inflows, it is better to make the outflows/payments later rather than earlier, due to the time value of money.

II. Internal Rate of Return

In the discussion of the concept of net present value (NPV), it was defined as the difference between the present value of all future benefits to be realized from an investment and the present value of all capital contributions into the investment. The discount (interest) rate at which these two present values will be equal is the Internal Rate of Return (IRR) of the investment.

Stated in other terms, in computing IRR, the interest rate sought is that rate at which inflows of cash, discounted to present value, will equal the original (and subsequent, if applicable) principal contributions. It is a method of determining what percentage rate of return estimated cash inflows would provide based on a known investment (cash outflow). Actually, even the cash outflow must sometimes be estimated.

Internal rate of return is really the same as a present value computation except that the discount rate is either not known or not given. The financial advisor is therefore attempting to find that rate which will discount the future cash inflows so that they will precisely equal the investor's initial (and subsequent, if applicable) investment(s).

Confused? Here's an example.

Assume a client is considering the purchase of a $100,000 unit of a limited partnership. The full $100,000 is due at the beginning of the year. It is estimated that, after taxes, she should be receiving the following cash inflows at the end of each year.

End of Year	In-Flow
1	$ 10,000
2	10,000
3	120,000

Figure 33.1

Outflows	Amount Paid	Present Value of Amount Paid @			
	8%	10%	12.9%	20%	
Year 1	-$100,000	-$100,000	-$100,000	-$100,000	(Beginning of year)
Inflows	**Amount Received**	**Present Value of Amount Received @**			
	8%	10%	12.9%	20%	
Year 1	$ 10,000	$ 9,259	$ 9,091	$ 8,857	$ 8,333 (End of year)
2	10,000	8,573	8,264	7,845	6,944
3	120,000	95,260	90,158	83,387	69,444
Total of Present Value of Inflows		$113,092	$107,513	$100,089	$84,721
Net Present Value (NPV)		$ 13,092	$ 7,513	$ 89	-$15,279

A NPV analysis of this investment, looking at several alternative rates of return, would look as presented in Figure 33.1.

At an 8% rate, this investment has a positive net present value of $13,092. That is, if $100,000 was invested at 8% (for example, in a certificate of deposit), the present value of the future cash inflow should be $100,000. But, in the investment above, the present value of the expected cash inflows was actually $113,092, $13,092 higher than it should be at 8%. Therefore, it is obvious that the investment is generating a significantly higher rate of return than 8%.

At a 10% rate, this investment has a positive net present value of $7,513. Again, if $100,000 was invested at 10%, the present value of the future cash inflow should be $100,000. Since the present value of the expected cash inflows is actually $107,513, it appears that the investment is generating a higher rate of return than 10% as well.

At a 20% rate, this investment has a negative net present value of $15,279 – the present value of the expected cash inflows is only $84,721, compared to the $100,000 present value that would be anticipated if the investment actually earned 20%. Therefore, the investment must be generating a lower rate of return than 20%.

What is the actual rate of return on this investment? Clearly it lies somewhere between 10% and 20%. The exact rate is equivalent to the internal rate of return. The internal rate of return of the investment is approximately 12.9%. That is, the present value of the cash outflows ($100,000) is roughly equal to the present value of the cash inflows ($100,089) when discounted at a 12.9% rate.

How to Compute Internal Rate of Return

In an earlier example it was assumed a client was considering the purchase of a $100,000 unit of a limited partnership, and that, after taxes, she should be receiving the following cash inflows:

End of Year	In-Flow
1	$ 10,000
2	10,000
3	120,000

In manually computing the IRR of this investment, the first step is to compute the NPV using a preliminary estimate of the IRR. If the first computation results in a positive NPV, a second calculation, using a higher discount rate, will be necessary. If a negative NPV is computed, the recalculation will require a lower discount rate. The process continues until a NPV of $0 is reached (i.e., the rate at which the present value of the cash outflows equals the present value of the cash inflows).

The chart in Figure 33.2 provides an example of the series of iterative computations that might be necessary.

If 8% is used as the initial (test) discount rate, a positive net present value is found, and therefore a higher discount rate should be tried. On the second attempt, using 10%, there is still a positive NPV, although it is closer to $0 as the internal rate of return is approached. The third computation, using 20%, yields a negative NPV. Therefore, the IRR must be between 10% and 20%.

After several attempts, a rate of 12.9% is tried, which results in a positive NPV of only $89. It's getting close. For most planning purposes, this would be close enough. To do the job more accurately and efficiently, a business calculator or computer could be used, which can repeat this iterative process hundreds of times for total accuracy in a matter of seconds.

Figure 33.2

Outflows	Amount Paid	8%	Present Value of Amount Paid @ 10%	20%	12.9%
Year 1	-$100,000	-$100,000	-$100,000	-$100,000	-$100,000 (Beginning of year)

Inflows	Amount Received	8%	Present Value of Amount Received @ 10%	20%	12.9%
Year 1	$10,000	$9,259	$9,091	$8,333	$8,857 (End of year)
2	10,000	8,573	8,264	6,944	7,845
3	120,000	95,260	90,158	69,446	83,387
Total of Present Value of Inflows		$113,092	$107,513	$84,721	$100,089
Net Present Value (NPV)		$ 13,092	$ 7,513	-$15,279	$ 89

Project Cash Flows

Year	A	B	C	D	E
0	($1,000)	($1,000)	($1,000)	($1,000)	($1,000)
1	100	50	(200)	200	600
2	100	50	(200)	200	600
3	1,100	1,215	1,793	869	(55)
IRR	10%	10%	10%	10%	10%

Each project has a 10% IRR.

Project A earns 10%, but also pays out $100, or 10% of the initial $1,000 investment, each year. Therefore, the unrecovered investment earning 10% remains at $1,000 each year, which is similar to a 10% coupon bond purchased at par value.

Project B, in contrast, is similar to a bond that has been purchased at a discount. It earns 10% on the initial $1,000 investment, but it only pays out $50 each year. Therefore, Project B's unrecovered investment increases each year.

Year	Unrecovered Investment	Earnings @ 10% IRR	(Pay-in) Payout	Increase (Decrease) In Unrecovered Investment
0-1	$1,000	$100.00	$50.00	$50.00
1-2	1,050	105.00	50.00	55.00
2-3	1,105	110.50	1,215.50	(1,105.00)
3	0			

Project B is the same as Project A with all but $50 of the yearly cash flows essentially reinvested in the project at 10%. These implicitly reinvested earnings increase the unrecovered investment and earn the 10% IRR rate.

Project C has an even greater increasing unrecovered investment over time, as additional deposits are made to the investment and no withdrawals are taken.

Year	Unrecovered Investment	Earnings @ 10% IRR	(Pay-in) Payout	Increase (Decrease) In Unrecovered Investment
0-1	$1,000	$100.00	$(200.00)	$300.00
1-2	1,300	130.00	(200.00)	330.00
2-3	1,630	163.00	1,793.00	(1,630.00)
3	0			

Shortcomings of the IRR Method

What are the shortcomings of the IRR? There are several, but to some extent the shortcomings arise from widespread misconceptions and misunderstandings about the theoretical underpinnings as well as the proper application of the method, even among the most elite and sophisticated investors and investment advisers. Consequently, although IRR is one of the most commonly used tools; it is also the least understood and most misapplied method of evaluating alternative investments.

One of the most common misconceptions, even appearing in many, if not most, of the finance and investment textbooks used by the leading business schools, is that the IRR method inherently assumes that the cash flows from an investment being evaluated are implicitly reinvested at the computed internal rate of return of the investment itself. This is decidedly *not* the case, but this generally held misconception is one of the principal reasons the IRR is often misapplied.

The fact is that the IRR assumes that the cash flows are *not* reinvested, at *any* rate. Rather, it assumes cash flows from an investment are consumed when paid and never enter the analysis again. If it were assumed they are reinvested at the IRR, they would not be, or should not be, shown as cash flows.

The reality is that the IRR measures the rate of return on the *unrecovered* investment over time. Cash flows from an investment represent money taken out of the investment. Over time, only the investor's as-yet-unrecovered investment implicitly continues to earn the IRR. The following example shows five alternative investments and demonstrates the point. In each case, only the unrecovered investment earns the IRR; cash flows received back from the investments do not subsequently earn anything.

cash flow patterns, and/or investment terms, they must *explicitly* account for the differences in cash flows, otherwise *they*, not the IRR method, *are* implicitly assuming cash flows are reinvested at the IRR. When reinvestment at the IRR is not realistic, the IRR method, improperly used, leads to poor choices *among* investments.

For instance, an investor is offered an immediate annuity paying $5,092.61 per year for 20 years for an initial investment of $50,000. He computes the IRR and finds that it is 8%. Whether he spends the cash flows or reinvests them is immaterial; the IRR method does not care. Whatever rate he might earn by reinvesting the cash flows paid to him does not change the return on the investment in the annuity. The annuity investment is earning 8%, and that is a fact regardless of whether or not and at what rate the cash outflows are reinvested.

Now, however, assume he is also offered another annuity that will pay him $6,021.02 per year for 15 years for the same $50,000 initial investment. He computes the IRR for this annuity and finds that it is 8.5%. Is this the better deal? Not necessarily, even though it is, in fact, paying a half a percent more on his investment.

The 8.5%, 15-year annuity might be the better deal if he could reinvest part or all of the $928.41 annual difference in cash flows for the first 15 years so that he could at least match the cash flows he would otherwise receive for the last five years of the 8%, 20-year annuity. But if he cannot, the 8% annuity would be the better deal, even though it really is paying one-half percent less on his money, because of the inadequate return that will be earned in the final 5 years, compared to the continued 8% growth available in the first scenario.

Assume the investor feels he could earn 5% by reinvesting the difference in cash flows in an investment with the same level of safety and security as the annuity. The $928.41 annual difference invested each year at 5% would grow to $20,033.81 in 15 years. If this amount continues to earn 5%, he could withdraw $4,627.31 each year for the next 5 years before exhausting the fund. But that is $465.30 per year less than he would receive from the 8%, 20-year annuity, despite the fact that the investor applied all of his excess growth savings to the side investment at 5%. So he would be worse off investing in the 8.5%, 15-year annuity than if he invested in the 8%, 20-year annuity.

Obviously, if his best alternative investment with the same level of safety and security earns only 5%, then both of these annuities are good investments for him. The IRR of either one is greater than his opportunity cost

Since none of the earnings (or original investment) are taken out of Project C until the end, all of the implicit earnings are essentially reinvested in the project at 10%.

Project D has a decreasing unrecovered investment over time.

Year	Unrecovered Investment	Earnings @ 10% IRR	(Pay-in) Payout	Increase (Decrease) In Unrecovered Investment
0-1	$1,000	$100.00	$200.00	($100.00)
1-2	900	90.00	200.00	(110.00)
2-3	790	79.00	869.00	(790.00)
3	0			

In this case, the project throws off cash flows that are more than the implicit earnings each year, thereby reducing the unrecovered investment over time and, as a result, the implicit earnings.

Project E has decreasing and, ultimately, negative unrecovered investment over time.

Year	Unrecovered Investment	Earnings @ 10% IRR	(Pay-in) Payout	Increase (Decrease) In Unrecovered Investment
0-1	$1,000	$100.00	$600.00	($500.00)
1-2	500	50.00	600.00	(550.00)
2-3	(50)	(5.00)	(55.00)	50.00
3	0			

Project E can actually be viewed as a combination of investment and loan since it requires the investor to contribute additional dollars at the end to pay back early withdrawals in excess of the remaining unrecovered investment. Since there are no explicit payments on the loan, except to pay off the entire amount at the end, the implicit loan does, in fact, charge interest at a rate equal to the 10% IRR.

Although it is true that *if* the cash flows were reinvested at the IRR, the computed IRR would not change, this misconception about the IRR and reinvestment of cash inflows leads to errors in the application of the method. In some cases, it does not matter at what rate an investor can reinvest cash flows; in other cases, it makes all the difference in the world.

Specifically, when investors want to know what rate of return they will earn on an investment, their potential reinvestment rate for the cash flows is immaterial, generally. The IRR is the rate of return they will earn on the investment itself.

However, when investors want to use the IRR to compare investments that involve different initial outlays, rate or hurdle rate of 5%. If he had $100,000 to invest and was limited to a $50,000 investment in each annuity, it would be reasonable to invest in both of them. However, if he ranked the annuities based on their IRRs in order to choose between them, he would have made the wrong choice. Later in the chapter, it is explained how to properly use the IRR to compare investments.

In addition to it being often misunderstood and misapplied, the IRR method has other real weaknesses, but they can be overcome with proper use of the method. These limitations include:

- As described above, investors cannot use an IRR method (unless modified, as discussed below) to compare (directly) mutually exclusive investments, particularly when they have different time periods and cash flow timings (the investment with the highest IRR is not necessarily the best investment among a mutually exclusive set);

- The unmodified IRR method does not consider realistic (or sometimes, *any*) reinvestment rates for positive cash flows or realistic borrowing rates for negative cash flows over the holding period;

- An investment project may have multiple IRRs; and

- Solving for the IRR often requires a series of iterative calculations to determine the IRR since, for many types of IRR calculations, there is no single, closed-end formula to compute the IRR. However, financial calculators and computer software programs (such as the common spreadsheet) have built-in functions that are adequate to solve for the IRR in most cases.

Let us start with the problem of multiple IRRs. The other issues will be discussed in later sections of this chapter.

How can an investment have more than one IRR?

Let us prove it first and then explain why. Figure 33.3 shows an admittedly odd hypothetical investment that has four IRRs. The investment involves an initial pay-in of $1,000, a payout of $4,700, another pay-in of $8,277.50, another payout of $6,356.75, and then one last pay-in of $1,828.78. As the table shows, if this cash flow stream is discounted at -5%, 10%, 25%, and 40%, in each case the net present value is zero. By definition, an IRR is a discount rate that equates the net present value of the cash flows to zero, so these rates are all IRRs.

Potentially, an investment has as many different real IRRs as there are changes in the sign, or direction, of the cash flows over time. In most cases when there is a single initial investment or a series of investment deposits (pay-ins), and, subsequently, a series of cash disbursements/returns (payouts) from the investment, there is only one distinct IRR, since there is only one change in the direction of cash flows. However, if the investment involves a series of pay-in deposits mixed over time with a series of payout returns, then each time the cash flow stream changes from pay-ins to payouts, or vice versa, there could potentially be more IRRs.

One problem with multiple IRRs is that it is not always easy to find them all and most software solutions will find just one, or refuse to solve for any at all if there could be more than one IRR. Regardless of the initial guess or seed one picks to start the search for multiple IRRs, the calculator or software program may home in on a particular IRR, even if it happens to be the one furthest away from the initial guess. There is generally no assurance that picking a seed closer to one of the IRRs than the others will cause the solution algorithm to find the nearest IRR. Consequently, even if it is known that there is more than one IRR, after one is found, changing the guess or seed to find the next IRR will not always be successful with the use of calculator or computer solvers, unless the entire process is undertaken manually. Finding each successive IRR tends to become increasingly difficult.[6]

In addition, just because there could be several distinct real IRRs does *not* mean that there actually *are* several distinct real IRRs. In some cases, some of the IRRs are in the realm of imaginary numbers: those odd numbers that involve the square root of -1. Although such numbers have real-world significance in the arena of physics and electronics, for example, they have no practical significance in the realm of finance and investments.

Even if one finds all the real IRRs, the question remains: which is the right one? Mathematically, they are all correct, but which is the correct one financially? Suppose one finds that an investment has two IRRs, -10% and +25%. If one invests in the project, is the investor losing 10% or making 25%? Perhaps both? Could the investor be both making 25% and losing 10%, thereby averaging 7.5%? Hardly!

The only way to solve the dilemma is to use one of the modified IRR methods discussed in the next section. Depending on how the investor actually will handle the cash flows from the project, it can be determined which IRR is in fact closer to the rate the investor will

Figure 33.3

MULTIPLE INTERNAL RATES OF RETURN

	Period 0	Period 1	Period 2	Period 3	Period 4
Cash Flow	(1,000.00)	4,700.00	(8,227.50)	6,356.75	(1,828.78)
Interest -5%	1.00000	1.05263	1.10803	1.16635	1.22774
PV CF	(1,000.00)	4,947.37	(9,116.34)	7,414.22	(2,245.23)
Cum. PV CF	(1,000.00)	3,947.37	(5,168.98)	2,245.23	0.00
Interest 10%	1.00000	0.90909	0.82645	0.75131	0.68301
PV CF	(1,000.00)	4,272.73	(6,799.59)	4,775.92	(1,249.06)
Cum. PV CF	(1,000.00)	3,272.73	(3,526.86)	1,249.06	0.00
Interest 25%	1.00000	0.80000	0.64000	0.51200	0.40960
PV CF	(1,000.00)	3,760.00	(5,265.60)	3,254.66	(749.06)
Cum. PV CF	(1,000.00)	2,760.00	(2,505.60)	749.06	0.00
Interest 40%	1.00000	0.71429	0.51020	0.36443	0.26031
PV CF	(1,000.00)	3,357.14	(4,197.70)	2,316.60	(476.04)
Cum. PV CF	(1,000.00)	2,357.14	(1,840.56)	476.04	0.00

actually earn on the investment. The added bonus of learning about modified IRR methods is that they are also necessary whenever a person wants to compare or rank investment alternatives, one against another. The proper procedures for applying net present value analyses and internal rate of return methods when comparing or ranking investments is discussed in the last section of this chapter.

III. Modified Internal Rate of Return Methods

As a result of the problems inherent in the use of the regular IRR method, a number of modified IRR methods have been devised to circumvent the problems. These modified methods adjust the cash flows of the investment to account for reinvestment, borrowings, setting up sinking funds to cover later cash outflows, and the like.

Debates have raged in the financial and investment community as to which is the best method. The debates are quite surprising since the answer to that question is quite simple and obvious. The best method is that which most closely approximates how, in fact, an investor is most likely to handle the cash flows of the investment. Any idea that a one-size-fits-all approach to the problem is the right method is off the mark. None of the modified methods is the best approach all of the time and each of the modified methods is the best approach some of the time. The following discussion explains and demonstrates the application of five different modified IRR methods that may be suitable depending on the nature of the cash flows and how the investor plans to handle them.

The *IRR-reinvestment-rate* method is used to solve the problem of *intermediate cash inflows* by making specific assumptions about how those cash inflows will be reinvested. For example, Figure 33.4 shows the case where the initial investment is $10,000. The investor expects to receive annual cash inflows of $2,000 per year for five years, at which time he expects to sell or liquidate the investment for $11,000 (receiving a total of $13,000 in the fifth year). For simplicity, it is assumed all cash flows are at the end of each year. The regular, unadjusted IRR for this investment is 21.31%.

The investor expects to be able to reinvest the cash inflows at 10% over the five-year period. If he wants to compare this investment with other potential investments, which probably will have a different cash flow pattern over the five-year period, he has to account for the intermediate cash flows. If he expects to reinvest the cash flows at 10%, he can take each of the cash inflows and accumulate them at 10% until the end of the fifth year (the future value of each cash inflow grown at the reinvestment rate from payout until the end of year 5). By making this adjustment he converts the cash flow stream from the original series of six cash flows in years 0 through 5 into just two cash flows: his initial $10,000

Figure 33.4

IRR-REINVESTMENT-RATE METHOD

Reinvestment Rate: 10.00%

Years	0	1	2	3	4	5
	Investment			Cash Flow		
Amounts	($10,000)	$2,000	$2,000	$2,000	$2,000	$2,000
					@10%	2,200
				@10%		2,420
			@10%			2,662
		@10%				2,928
FV of CFs						$12,210
Net Sale Proceeds						$11,000
	Adjusted Cash Flows with Reinvestment					
Totals	($10,000)	$0.00	$0.00	$0.00	$0.00	$23,210

Unadjusted IRR on Original Cash Flows = 21.31%
IRR-Reinvestment-Rate with Adjusted Cash Flows = 18.34%

investment in year 0 and the sales or liquidation value of $11,000 plus the $12,210 accumulated balance of his reinvested cash flows, or $23,210, in year 5. The IRR-reinvestment-rate with adjusted cash flows is 18.34% – this is the IRR for a single initial deposit in year 0 of $10,000 and a final $23,210 inflow at the end of year 5.

If the investor were instead planning to consume $500 of the intermediate cash flows each year and to reinvest only the remaining $1,500 of each annual cash inflow, the appropriate way to adjust the cash flows under this method would be to leave $500 of the yearly cash inflows where they are each year and to accumulate only the $1,500 he plans to actually reinvest. In this case, the cash flow stream would be adjusted to show a $10,000 initial investment and cash inflows of $500 in years 1 through 4. Then in the fifth year, the total cash inflow would be composed of $11,000 from sales proceeds, $2,000 from the fifth year cash inflow, and $7,658 from the accumulated value of the $1,500 reinvested in years 1 through 4 at 10%, for a total of $20,658. The IRR of this cash flow stream is 18.94% – more than when all the cash flows are reinvested, but still less, of course (since the reinvestment rate is lower than the pure unmodified IRR), than when none of the cash flows are assumed to be reinvested.

The *IRR-safe-rate* method is used to solve the problem of *additional cash outflows* (or additional investments

required after the initial investment in year 0) by assuming additional funds are set aside up-front as a sinking fund that is treated as part of initial year-0 investment to cover later cash outflows. This method is demonstrated in Figure 33.5. In this case the initial investment is $30,000, but the project requires additional outlays of $11,000 in year 1, $10,000 in year 2, and subsequent outlays decreasing each year by $1,000 to $7,000 in year 5. In year 5, the investor expects to sell the investment for $140,000. This is the type of cash flow pattern one might see in developing rental or commercial real estate or in bringing a new drug to market. In each case, one would expect a number of years of continuing cash outlays while the real estate is being cleared, the buildings are built, and tenants are found, or while the drug is researched, developed, and tested. However, once the property is completed and rented or the drug is ready for market, the building or rights to the drug can be sold for large amounts.

In this case, the *IRR-safe-rate* method is an appropriate IRR method if the investor plans to set aside enough capital at the beginning to assure that he can make the cash outlays when they are needed in future years. If the investor assumes he can invest the sinking fund at a safe rate of 8%, the additional amount he would need to set aside the first year to cover the later year's cash outlays is $36,546 (determined by summing each future required cash outlay discounted by the 8% investment rate). By

Tools & Techniques of Investment Planning

Figure 33.5

IRR-SAFE-RATE METHOD

Safe Rate: 8.00%

Years	0	1	2	3	4	5
	Investment	**Cash Flow from Operations**				
Amounts	($30,000)	($11,000)	($10,000)	($9,000)	($8,000)	($7,000)
	(10,185) @8%	@8%				
	(8,573)	@8%				
	(7,144)		@8%			
	(5,880)			@8%		
	(4,764)				@8%	
Net Sales Proceeds						$140,000
Totals	($66,546)	$0.00	$0.00	$0.00	$0.00	$140,000

Adjusted Cash Flows with Sinking Fund

Unadjusted IRR on Original Cash Flows = 19.05%
IRR-Safe-Rate with Adjusted Cash Flows = 16.04%

---

doing so, the investor converts the original cash flow stream into just two cash flows: an initial total outlay of $66,546 in year 0 and a $140,000 cash inflow in year 5. Before adjusting the cash flows, the IRR was 19.05%. After the adjustment, the IRR fell to 16.04% (because some funds were specifically invested at a much lower rate (8%) for a period of time).

The *IRR-safe-rate* method and the *IRR-reinvestment-rate* methods may be combined, if appropriate. This method would typically be used when cash flows continue to be flowing out for several years and then change to inflows during the term of the investment. Figure 33.6 shows how this method may be employed. In this case cash flows out through year 2 of the project and then becomes positive until year 5 when the investment is assumed to be sold for $140,000. If the investor plans to set aside a sinking fund invested at a safe rate of 6% to cover the additional cash outflows in years 1 and 2 and also expects to be able to reinvest the cash inflows in years 3 and 4 at 8%, he can convert the original cash flow stream once again into just two cash flows in year 0 and year 5. The IRR of the unadjusted cash flows is 20.60%. After adjusting the cash flows, the IRR is 19.05%.

The *IRR-borrowing-rate* method solves the problem of *later cash outflows* by assuming money will be *borrowed* to cover future cash outflows and will be repaid out of later cash inflows. Figure 33.7 demonstrates the use of this method.

In this case the investor expects ongoing cash outflows through the first 3 years of the project. Instead of setting money aside up front to cover these later cash outflows, this investor plans to borrow money as needed from a line of credit and then repay the loans out of future cash inflows. The investor's borrowing rate is 12%. The $10,000 borrowed in year 3, plus interest, is repaid in year 4 out of the $20,000 cash inflow in that year, leaving $8,800. This remaining $8,800 cash inflow in year 4 is then applied to reduce the outstanding balance of the amount borrowed from year 2, leaving a remaining balance yet to be repaid of $16,288. This amount plus the entire $20,000 borrowed in year 1, plus the accruing interest are carried forward to year 5 at 12%. After applying the $20,000 cash inflow from operations in year 5 against this loan balance, the remaining balance is $29,713. This remaining amount is repaid from the net sale proceeds.

By applying this methodology, the investor has once again converted the cash flow stream from one involving a number of different payouts and pay-ins over a number of years into just two cash flows at the very beginning and the very end of the investment period.

The IRR before adjusting the cash flows is 17.08%. After adjusting the cash flows, the IRR jumps to 18.16%. What this result shows is the benefit of financial leverage. Any time a person can borrow at a rate less than the rate the person is earning on an investment, borrowing to finance part of the investment will increase return

Figure 33.6

				IRR-SAFE-RATE-REINVESTMENT-RATE METHOD		

Safe Rate: 6.00%
Reinvestment Rate: 8.00%

Years	0	1	2	3	4	5
	Investment			Cash Flow from Operations		
Amounts	($50,000)	($11,000)	($10,000)	$6,000	$8,000	$10,000
	(10,377)	@6%			@8%	8,640
	(8,900)		@6%	@8%		6,998
PV of CFs	($19,277)					
FV of CFs						$15,638
Net Sale Proceeds						$140,000
			Adjusted Cash Flows with Sinking Fund			
Totals	($69,277)	$0.00	$0.00	$0.00	$0.00	$165,638

Unadjusted IRR on Original Cash Flows	=	20.60%
IRR-Safe-Rate-Reinvestment-Rate with Adjusted Cash Flows	=	19.05%

because the person is earning more on the amount he borrows than he is paying to borrow it. Conversely, any time a person reinvests cash flows at a rate less than the unmodified IRR on the investment, the modified IRR will be less than the unmodified IRR because the person is now earning less on this part of the investment than on the underlying investment itself, which reduces the overall return on the total investment.

The *Adjusted Rate of Return (ARR)* is the last modified IRR method that will be described here. The modified IRR methods described so far calculate the actual rate of return earned by an investor who really intends to handle cash flows in the manner applied by the chosen method. In contrast, the adjusted rate of return method does not.

The adjusted rate of return is the method preferred by many leading tax and investment specialists, especially in real estate. It seems to be preferred largely because its proponents believe that a one-size-fits-all method is an appropriate approach to modified IRR analyses. However, any methodology that adjusts cash flows in a manner starkly different than how the cash is actually likely to flow will derive IRR results that have as much bearing to the real IRR as the adjusted cash flows have to the real cash flows. In other words, one cannot pretend that cash is going to flow one way when it is actually going to flow another way and expect the results one gets from those assumptions to have any resemblance to actual values.

The whole point of time value analysis is that the amount and timing of cash flows matters. If a person moves a cash flow from one period to another in his methodology when the cash flow is not actually going to move from one period to another, the IRR computed will be distorted. The more a modified IRR method moves or adjusts cash flows in a manner that does not reflect the underlying reality, the greater will be the distortion and the more useless or worthless the results derived from the method employed.

The ARR is applied in the following manner:

1. discount all cash flows into the project (negative cash flows or investments into the project) at a safe rate of return back to period 0 (find the PV of the pay-ins);

2. compound all cash flows out of the project (positive cash flows or returns of investment) at a safe rate to the end of the holding period (find the FV of the cash flows from the project); and

3. The ARR is the discount rate that equates the PV of cash flows into the project with the discounted FV of cash flows out of the project.

Figure 33.8 shows each of the methods discussed in this section, as they would be applied to a common set of cash flows (including an additional method shown in pieces but not explicitly demonstrated thus far, the

Figure 33.7

IRR-BORROWING-RATE METHOD

Borrowing Rate: 12.00%

Years	0	1	2	3	4	5
	Investment	Cash Flow from Operations				
Amounts	($100,000)	($20,000)	($20,000)	($10,000)	$20,000	$20,000
			@12%	@12% (11,200)		
		@12%		$8,800		
				(25,088)		
				(16,288)	(18,243)	
					$1,757	
					(31,470)	
					(29,713)	
Net Sale Proceeds						$260,000
Totals	($100,000)	$0.00	$0.00	$0.00	$0.00	$230,287

Adjusted Cash Flows with Reinvestment

Unadjusted IRR on Original Cash Flows = 17.08%
IRR-Borrowing-Rate with Adjusted Cash Flows = 18.16%

IRR-Borrow/Reinvestment Rate Method, which merges the already-covered IRR-Borrow and IRR-Reinvestment methods). To show how the results differ for each modified IRR method, the rate for all types of adjustments is the same, 6%, regardless of whether the adjustment is for reinvestment, borrowing, or for a sinking fund invested at a safe rate.

The great disparity in the computed IRRs – ranging from 14.4% to 30.66% – using the various methods for the same original cash flows, proves how important it is to use the appropriate method for the circumstances. Using an inappropriate method may lead an investor to rejecting an investment that is really an acceptable investment, or worse, accepting an investment that is really unacceptable.

It is perfectly possible that the same investment could be acceptable to one investor yet unacceptable to another, even if their opportunity cost rates or hurdle rates are identical. For example, assume two investors have identical hurdle rates of 22% for the investment shown in Figure 33.8. However, for investor 1, the *IRR-safe-rate* method most closely approximates how he will handle the cash flows from the investment while, for investor 2, the *IRR-safe-rate/reinvestment-rate* method better describes how he would handle the cash flows of the investment. In this case, the investment is acceptable to investor 1, since it earns 25.18% in his circumstances, but is unacceptable to investor 2, since it earns only 20.44% in his circumstances.

IV. Pay Back Period

Pay back period analysis is a time value of money concept. This method compares alternative investments by measuring the length of time required to recover the original investment. From this perspective, the investment that returns the original capital in the shortest period of time is the best investment.

The major flaw in this analytical technique is obvious: taken to its extreme, an indiscriminate investor would choose a deal requiring a $10,000 investment which paid back $15,000 in one year rather than an alternative which required the same capital outlay but returned $25,000 in two years. In other words, this method fails to capture the potentially extremely favorable returns that may accrue under one investment beyond the end point of the pay back period of another investment choice.

V. Cash on Cash

Cash on cash analysis, as its name implies, focuses on the *amount* of cash generated by the investment. It ignores both taxes and the potential gain from any sale.

Figure 33.8

IRR-ADJUSTED RATE METHOD COMPARED WITH OTHER ADJUSTED IRR METHODS

Method	Years	0	1	2	3	4	5	IRR
Unadjusted IRR Method	Pay-ins Cash Inflows	$(2,000.00) 0.00	$(2,000.00) 1,000.00	$(2,000.00) 2,000.00	$0.00 2,500.00	$0.00 2,500.00	$0.00 2,000.00	
	Net CFs	$(2,000.00)	$(1,000.00)	$0.00	$2,500.00	$2,500.00	$2,000.00	26.99%
IRR-Adjusted Rate Method	PV of All Negative Cash Flows	$(2,000.00) (1,886.79) (1,779.99)	$(2,000.00) 6%	($2,000.00) 6%				
	FV of All Positive Cash Flows		$1,000.00	$2,000.00 6%	$2,500.00 6%	$2,500.00 6%	$2,000.00 2,650.00 2,809.00 2,382.03 1,262.48	
	Adjusted CFs	$(5,666.78)	$0.00	$0.00	$0.00	$0.00	$11,103.51	14.40%
IRR-Safe-Rate Method	PV of Net Pay-Ins	$(2,000.00)	$(1,000.00) (943.40) 6%					
	Adjusted CFs	$(2,943.40)	$0.00	$0.00	$2,500.00	$2,500.00	$2,000.00	25.18%
IRR-Borrow Rate Method		$(2,000.00)	$(1,000.00) 6%		$2,500.00 (1,123.60)	$2,500.00	$2,000.00	
	Adjusted CFs	$(2,000.00)	$0.00	$0.00	$1,376.40	$2,500.00	$2,000.00	30.66%
IRR-Safe/ Reinvestment Rate Method		$(2,000.00)	$(1,000.00) (943.40) 6%		$2,500.00 6%	$2,500.00 6%	$2,000.00 2,650.00 2,809.00	
	Adjusted CFs	$(2,943.40)	$0.00	$0.00	$0.00	$0.00	$7,459.00	20.44%
IRR-Borrow/ Reinvestment Rate Method		$(2,000.00)	$(1,000.00) 6%		$2,500.00 (1,123.60) 1,376.40 6%	$2,500.00 6%	$2,000.00 2,650.00 1,546.52	
	Adjusted CFs	$(2,000.00)	$0.00	$0.00	$0.00	$0.00	$6,196.52	25.38%

To compute cash on cash return, divide the annual cash flow by the cash investment. For example, let us assume that a woman plans to invest $10,000 in the stock of Z-Rocks Corp. Each year she would receive a dividend of $1,000, and she expects to receive $15,000 upon the sale of the stock in three years.

She is considering an alternative investment for the $10,000, Eye-B-Em Stock, which yields a cash distribution of only $600 per year, but which she believes will be worth $25,000 at the end of the three-year investment period. Under the cash on cash method her return on the first investment is 10% per year ($1,000 dividend divided by the $10,000 investment), while the return on the alternative is only 6% per year ($600 divided by the $10,000 investment).

Using only the cash on cash method to evaluate the investments, she would choose the Z-Rocks stock, because of the higher annual dividend. However, if she had compared the investments by looking at their relative internal rates of return or adjusted rates of return, she would probably have chosen the alternative. Ultimately, which is appropriate depends upon her needs and plans for use of the cash inflows from the investments.

VI. Using Analytical Methods to Compare Investments

The net present value method or the unmodified IRR method should virtually always give the same accept or reject decision regarding an investment when the investment is evaluated independently of other investments. For example, for investors whose opportunity cost rate or hurdle rate is 15%, all investments with an IRR above 15% will also have positive net present values (and thus should be acceptable). Conversely, all investments with positive net present values will have IRRs in excess of 15% (and thus should still be acceptable). Investments with IRRs less than 15% will also yield net present values that are negative, and should be unacceptable.

Independent Versus Mutually Exclusive Investments

If an investor is comparing investments and trying to choose the best among a number of investment alternatives, picking the investment with the highest NPV or the highest IRR may not lead to the best investment.

As long as investments are evaluated independently, the NPV and unmodified IRR will work just fine in determining whether an investment is acceptable or unacceptable. Two projects are considered independent if the acceptance or rejection of one project has no bearing on the acceptability or feasibility of investing in the other project. However, if the investments cannot be evaluated independently and an investor cannot choose to invest in both alternatives at the same time, then the NPV method and/or the IRR method must be applied in a more involved manner to determine the better alternative.

Two investments that are *not* independent are said to be mutually exclusive. That is, they are mutually exclusive if the acceptance of one project precludes the acceptance of the other.

Example 1. A plot of land can be used for farming or as the site for an office complex, but not for both.

Example 2. Corporate money allocated to payroll increases cannot be used to finance an advertising campaign.

Example 3. Like the annuity investor described earlier, the choice is between two annuities and the investor may choose to invest in one, or the other, or neither, but not both.

Table A shows the forecasted cash flows from two investment projects. The project with highest ranking relative to an independent standard (the NPV or IRR) is not necessarily the best alternative if the projects are mutually exclusive.

TABLE A

Year	Project 1	Project 2
0	($1,000.00)	($1,000.00)
1	400.00	0.00
2	400.00	0.00
3	400.00	0.00
4	400.00	0.00
5	400.00	0.00
6	400.00	0.00
7	400.00	0.00
8	1,400.00	5,960.00
Annual Return	40%	25%

If evaluated independently, project 1 is acceptable if the investor's alternative rate on the use of funds is less than 40%. Project 2 is acceptable if the alternative rate on the use of funds is less than 25%.

However, if the two investments are evaluated as mutually exclusive investments, *Project 1 may not be superior to Project 2.*

Table B presents a terminal value analysis of projects 1 and 2 assuming a 10% cash reinvestment rate. The investor is better off after the eight years by about $385.65 if he invests in Project 2 rather than in Project 1, despite Project 1's much higher rate of return. This result occurs because of the relatively low cash reinvestment rate.

As was explained earlier, the IRR is earned on the un-recovered investment. Project 1 correctly earns 40%, but it pays out all of its earnings. Therefore, the unrecovered investment remains at $1,000 and the cash flows can only be reinvested at 10%, not 40%. In contrast, Project 2 earns 25% on an ever-increasing unrecovered investment, since it makes no cash payments until the end of year eight. In the meantime, the implicit earnings are effectively being reinvested in the project and earning

25%. As Table B demonstrates, earning 40% on $1,000 for eight years while reinvesting the earnings at only 10% is less profitable than investing an initial amount of $1,000 at 25%, but implicitly reinvesting all the earnings at that same 25% rate.

TABLE B

TERMINAL VALUES
10% Reinvestment Rate

	Project 1				Project 2
Year	Reinvest Fund Before Cash Flow	Earnings On Reinvest Fund	Cash Flow	Reinvest Fund After Cash Flow	Cash Flow
0	N/A	N/A	($1,000)	N/A	($1,000)
1	$0.00	$0.00	400	$ 400.00	0.00
2	400.00	40.00	400	840.00	0.00
3	840.00	84.00	400	1,324.00	0.00
4	1,324.00	132.40	400	1,856.40	0.00
5	1,856.40	185.64	400	2,442.04	0.00
6	2,442.04	244.20	400	3,086.24	0.00
7	3,086.24	308.62	400	3,794.86	0.00
8	3,794.86	379.49	1,400	5,574.35	5,960.00

Difference in terminal values $ 385.65

Which investment is actually better depends critically on the assumed reinvestment rate. In this example, for reinvestment rates that are less than 12.22%, Project 2 is superior. Alternatively, if reinvestment rates are greater than 12.22%, Project 1 is superior.

Before proceeding on, let us consider another measure closely related to net present value. Net present value is the difference between the discounted benefits and the discounted costs of a project. If the present value of the benefits exceeds the present value of the costs, the project is an acceptable investment.

The *Discounted Accounting Return Ratio (DARR)* is the ratio of discounted benefits to discounted costs (also called the *Discounted Profitability Index or DPI*). It is a measure of the PV of benefits to the PV of the costs of an investment relative to each dollar of investment. A related value, called the *Undiscounted Accounting Return Ratio (UARR)*, or *Undiscounted Profitability Index (UPI)*, is essentially a version of the payback method described earlier.

Figure 33.9 presents an example of three projects, B, C, and D, with cash flows and both the DPI and UPI for each investment.

The decision rule when using the DPI is simple: a project is acceptable when the ratio is greater than one. It gives exactly the same accept and reject decisions as the net present value method.

The DPI is introduced because it is sometimes beneficial to view the feasibility of investments in relative terms (per dollar of investments), rather than in absolute terms, as is the case with the DPI's sister method, the net present value method.

Incremental Analysis Methodology

When evaluating mutually exclusive investments or comparing any two or more investments to determine the better or best among the alternatives, the traditional NPV and IRR evaluation methods are up to the task, but they must be applied incrementally. They have to be applied following the three basic rules, which state that the analysis must:

Figure 33.9

	DISCOUNTED PROFITABILITY INDEX (DPI)							
		Project B		Project C		Project D	
Year	10% Discount Factor	Undis-counted	Discounted	Undis-counted	Discounted	Undis-counted	Discounted
0	1.00000	($1,000)	($1,000)	($1,000)	($1,000)	($1,500)	($1,500)
1	0.90909	500	455	200	182	700	636
2	0.82645	300	248	300	248	515	426
3	0.75131	200	150	500	376	285	214
4	0.68301	700	478	700	478	700	478
5	0.62092	0	0	0	0	375	233
UPI		1.700		1.700		1.717	
DPI			1.331		1.284		1.325

1. Take account of all costs and all sources of return;

2. Give more weight to early cash flows than later ones (time-value weighting); and

3. Standardize choices (compare apples with apples), which means they must account for differences in:

- Initial outlays;

- Holding periods;

- Cash flow payouts;

- Risk levels; and

- Time perspective.

Standardizing the choices means that if the initial outlays are different, the analysis must account for in the analysis. If the length or term of one investment is different than another investment, the analysis must account for how cash that is generated by the investment that tends first will be reinvested until the end of the term of the second investment. If the cash flow streams are different, the analysis must account for how those differences in cash flows will be handled. If the risk levels are different, appropriately different discount rates or hurdle rates must be employed for each of the investments. Finally, each of the investments or projects must be evaluated as of the same point in time. If a present value is used to evaluate one investment, present values must be used to evaluate all investments. It really makes no difference whether the investments are evaluated as of today. They could be evaluated as of a future date, such as the end of the term of the longest project. However, if one project is evaluated as of a future date, all the others must be evaluated as of that same future date.

An incremental analysis is applied as follows when one is using the NPV method, the DPI method, or the IRR method.

First, each of the investments in the comparison must be evaluated as if they were independent investments by applying any of the traditional NPV, DPI, or unmodified IRR methods (bearing in mind that, due to different risk levels, they may have different hurdle rates for initial rejection). Any investment that is unacceptable when evaluated as a completely independent investment can be disregarded from further consideration.

Second, for ease of analysis, the surviving investment alternatives are sorted by the size of the initial outlay, from smallest to largest. (This is not really necessary, but it makes the process less confusing.)

Third, starting with the investments with the smallest and next to smallest initial outlays, the investments are compared head-to-head based upon the NPV, DPI, or IRR of the additional or incremental investment in the larger outlay investment over the smaller outlay investment. The winner of the comparison goes on to challenge the next larger outlay project until all investments have been challenged and the winner determined.

The basic premise behind the incremental analysis is that, when one is selecting between two mutually exclusive investments (e.g., B and D), the mutually exclusive project involving the larger initial outlay (D) can be evaluated as if it were a package of two separate projects. The cash flows of the investment with the smaller outlay (B) are subtracted period by period from the cash flows of the larger outlay investment (D), leaving a residual or incremental series of cash flows in the larger outlay investment. Therefore, since cash flows are carved out of the larger investment (D) that exactly match the cash flows of the smaller investment (B), those cash flows negate each other and one is left with just the difference in cash flows between the two investments, which can then be evaluated.

The fourth and final step at each stage of the incremental analysis is to apply the NPV, DPI, or IRR analysis to the incremental cash flows. The decision rule is simple. If, after applying the chosen methodology, the incremental project (D−B) is an acceptable investment in its own right, then the larger outlay project is the better investment. If the incremental investment in the larger outlay investment is rejected by the application of the chosen methodology, then the smaller outlay project is the better investment. By design, the cash flows of the larger project (D) are segregated into two separate cash flow pools. One of the pools is exactly equal to the cash flows from the smaller investment (B) and the other is equal to the difference in cash flows between the larger and smaller investment (D−B). Since the B pool of D obviously matches the real B project dollar for dollar, only the difference pool of cash flows, or the incremental investment in D over B, matters. If the D−B pool is an acceptable investment in its own right, then by selecting D, the investor gets everything he would have had by investing in B plus a profitable additional investment.

Figure 33.10 shows an example applying the incremental analysis to two projects B and D and using the DPI criteria to pick the winner. The analysis assumes an alternative rate of 10%.

Figure 33.10

INCREMENTAL ANALYSIS OF PROJECTS B AND D

Year	10% Discount Factor	Project B Cash Flow	Project B Discounted	Project D Cash Flow	Project D Discounted	Project D-B Cash Flow	Project D-B Discounted
0	$0	$(1,000)	$(1,000)	$(1,500)	$(1,500)	$(500)	$(500)
1	0.90909	500	455	700	636	200	182
2	0.82645	300	248	515	426	215	178
3	0.75131	200	150	285	214	85	64
4	0.68301	700	478	700	478	0	0
5	0.62092	0	0	375	233	375	233
UPI		1.700		1.717		1.750	
DPI			1.331		1.325		1.314

Project B has the greater DPI, so if the investments were ranked by their DPI, project B would be the winner. However, Project D is the superior project. Although Project B has a DPI (1.331) that is greater than Project D's DPI (1.325), the incremental investment in Project D is itself still an acceptable investment (DPI 1.314). Therefore, given a mutually exclusive choice between B and D the investor would be better off choosing D despite B's higher DPI.

A terminal value comparison (see Figure 33.11) confirms that D is superior to B. Since D involves a $500 greater initial outlay than project B, Project B must be supplemented with a side fund of $500 to account for the money that otherwise would have been invested in Project D if Project D had been the selected investment. With a reinvestment rate of 10%, the future values of D's cash flows are $251.58 greater than Project B's.

The following section presents an evaluation or comparison of five mutually exclusive investments using the IRR method in an incremental analysis. Once again, a hurdle rate or opportunity cost of 10% is assumed for the analyses. The five projects F through J have the following cash flows.

Projected Cash Flows of Potential Projects

Project/Year	F	G	H	I	J
0	($1,100)	($1,500)	($2,100)	($2,400)	($2,400)
1	400	550	1,000	1,120	200
2	440	700	1,100	1,000	200
3	444	633	760	1,079	3,156

Each project is first evaluated independently to weed out those that might be unacceptable before comparing them to the others.

Figure 33.11

TERMINAL VALUE COMPARISON OF PROJECTS B AND D

Initial Outlay	PROJECT B $1,000 (Outlay B) + $500 Side Fund				PROJECT D $1,500 (Outlay D)			
Year	Side Fund Begin of Year Bal.	Earnings on Side Fund 10%	Cash Flow	Side Fund End of Year Bal.	Side Fund Begin of Year Bal.	Earnings on Side Fund 10%	Cash Flow	Side Fund at end of Year
1	$500.00	$50.00	$500.00	$1,050.00	$0.00	$0.00	$700.00	$700.00
2	1,050.00	105.00	300.00	1,455.00	700.00	70.00	515.00	1,285.00
3	1,455.00	145.50	200.00	1,800.50	1,285.00	128.50	285.00	1,698.50
4	1,800.50	180.05	700.00	2,680.55	1,698.50	169.85	700.00	2,568.35
5	2,680.55	268.05	0.00	2,948.61	2,568.35	256.84	375.00	3,200.19

Terminal Values .... $2,948.61 .... $3,200.19
Difference in terminal values .... $ 251.58

Project F

Year	Cash Flow	PV @ 6%	PV @ 8%	PV @ 10%
0	(1,100)	(1,100)	(1,100)	(1,100)
1	400	377	370	364
2	440	392	377	364
3	444	373	352	334
PV of Cash Flows:		42	(1)	(38)

IRR of Project F is 8%: Unacceptable

Project G

Year	Cash Flow	PV @ 10%	PV @ 12%	PV @ 14%
0	(1,500)	(1,500)	(1,500)	(1,500)
1	550	500	491	482
2	700	579	558	539
3	633	476	451	427
PV of Cash Flows:		55		(52)

IRR of Project G is 12%: Acceptable if Independent

Project H

Year	Cash Flow	PV @ 17%	PV @ 18%	PV @ 19%
0	(2,100)	(2,100)	(2,100)	(2,100)
1	1,000	855	847	840
2	1,100	804	790	777
3	760	475	463	451
PV of Cash Flows:		34	0	(32)

IRR of Project H is 18%: Acceptable if Independent

Project I

Year	Cash Flow	PV @ 15%	PV @ 16%	PV @ 17%
0	(2,400)	(2,400)	(2,400)	(2,400)
1	1,120	974	966	957
2	1,000	756	743	731
3	1,079	709	691	674
PV of Cash Flows:		39	0	(38)

IRR of Project I is 16%: Acceptable if Independent

Project J

Year	Cash Flow	PV @ 14%	PV @ 15%	PV @ 16%
0	(2,400)	(2,400)	(2,400)	(2,400)
1	200	175	174	172
2	200	154	151	149
3	3,156	2,130	2,075	2,022
PV of Cash Flows:		59	0	(57)

IRR of Project J is 15%: Acceptable if Independent

When each of the five projects, F through J, is evaluated independently, all but Project F are acceptable given a hurdle rate of 10%. The following table presents the independent rankings based upon their IRRs.

Summary of Independent Rankings

Project	IRR	Rank	Decision (10% Hurdle Rate)
H	18%	1	Acceptable
I	16%	2	Acceptable
J	15%	3	Acceptable
G	12%	4	Acceptable
F	8%	5	Unacceptable

As the subsequent analyses will show, Project H has the highest IRR, 18%, but it would not be the the best investment if these five projects were not independent (that is, if they were mutually exclusive and the investor could choose one, and only one, of these alternatives).

Rather, Project J is the best alternative. The following pair-wise comparisons lead to the selection of Project J as the best alternative despite the fact that both Projects H and I have higher IRRs. The pair-wise comparisons begin with an incremental analysis of H relative to G, which are the two lowest outlay projects with an acceptable independent IRR.

Incremental Analysis (H - G)

Year	Cash Flows H	G	(H - G)	Present Value of (H - G) 30%	36%	40%
0	(2,100)	(1,500)	(600)	(600)	(600)	(600)
1	1,000	550	450	346	331	321
2	1,100	700	400	237	216	204
3	760	633	127	58	50	46
Present Value of Cash Flows:				41	(3)	(29)

IRR of the incremental investment (H-G) is about 36%, which is acceptable; therefore H is superior to G.

It is probably not surprising that H beats G soundly, earning a whopping 36% on the $600 additional investment in H over the investment in G, since H has an independent IRR of 18% and G's independent IRR is just 12%. Next, the winner of round 1, H, is compared to the next higher outlay project, I.

Incremental Analysis (I - H)

Year	Cash Flows I	H	(I -H)	Present Value of (I - H) 4%	5%	6%
0	(2,400)	(2,100)	(300)	(300)	(300)	(300)
1	1,120	1,000	120	115	114	113
2	1,000	1,100	(100)	(92)	(91)	(89)
3	1,079	760	319	284	276	268
Present Value of Cash Flows:				7	(1)	(8)

IRR of the incremental investment (I-H) is about 5%, which is unacceptable; therefore I is not superior to H (i.e., I is rejected and H is retained as the best yet project).

Project H wins again! Project I involves a greater outlay than project H, so if an investor picked project I, he would be making an incremental investment in Project I of $300 above the amount otherwise invested in project H. Since cash flows from I have been carved out to exactly match the cash flows of Project H, that part of the investment in project I is assumed to earn 18%, exactly what Project H earns. However, the additional $300 invested in project I only earns about 5%. Therefore, the investor would be better off choosing to invest in Project H and to instead invest the additional $300 at his alternative rate of 10%, which is 5% more than he would earn on that money if he chose to invest in Project I.

Finally, Project H is compared to its last remaining competitor, Project J.

Incremental Analysis (J - H)

	Cash Flows			Present Value of (J - H)		
Year	J	H	(J-H)	10%	11%	12%
0	(2,400)	(2,100)	(300)	(300)	(300)	(300)
1	200	1,000	(800)	(727)	(721)	(714)
2	200	1,100	(900)	(744)	(730)	(717)
3	3,156	760	2,396	1,800	1,752	1,705
Present Value of Cash Flows:				29	1	(26)

IRR of the incremental investment (J-H) is about 11%, which is acceptable; therefore J is superior to H.

It may seem feasible that Project J could be superior to Project H, despite Project H's higher IRR, because Project J involves an additional outlay of $300 that need only earn more than the 10% hurdle rate to be an acceptable investment. The analysis has been constructed so that the first $2,100 of Project J's investment and the corresponding cash flows exactly matches Project H's investment and cash flows. Therefore, this portion of Project J's investment exactly matches Project H's performance. The additional $300 investment in Project J then produces incremental cash flows that are in themselves acceptable relative to the hurdle rate of 10%. Based upon the incremental analysis, the first $2,100 of the investment in Project J matches Project H's 18% rate of return. The additional $300 invested in Project J earns about 11%, which is still greater than the hurdle rate. In other words, Project J exactly matches Project H's performance with an additional kicker of about an 11% return on the additional $300 investment.

So, despite Project H's 3% advantage in IRR when evaluated independently, Project J is still the better investment.

The reason for this apparent contradiction is that the IRR is an annual rate of return on the *unrecovered* investment in Project J. Although Project J earns only a 15% rate of return on investment, versus 18% for Project H, the funds invested in Project J earn the 15% rate of return for a longer period of time than the funds earn the 18% rate of return in Project H. An investor in Project H earns 18%, but recovers the investment relatively quickly and then may reinvest those cash flows at only 10%. In contrast, since the payout in Project J comes later, an investor makes up for the lower 15% internal rate of return by effectively earning it for a longer period.

The discount rate, hurdle rate, alternative rate, or opportunity cost rate (whatever it is called) plays a critical role in the battle for investment dollars. Table NPV shows the results of using different discount rates in conjunction with the NPV method in an incremental analysis of Projects F through G. For discount rates below 11% (the rate earned on the incremental investment in Project J over Project H), Project J wins the right to the investor's money. But for discount rates above 11%, Project H jumps to the lead.

Table NPV
NPV of Projects F, G, H, I, and J Assuming Various Alternative Rates of Return

Hurdle Rate	F	G	H	I	J
0%	184.00	383.00	760.00	799.00	1,156.00*
5%	63.59	205.54	506.63	505.78	698.15*
10%	(39.14)	54.09	289.18	255.30	318.26*
12%	(76.06)	(0.34)	210.72*	165.20	184.39
15%	(127.53)	(76.23)	101.04*	39.52	0.26
18%	(174.78)	(145.91)	0.02*	(79.95)	(166.03)

* The superior investment if the projects are mutually exclusive.

WHERE CAN I FIND OUT MORE?

1. Frank Fabozzi, *Fixed Income Mathematics: Analytical and Statistical Techniques* (Chicago, IL: Irwin Professional Publishers, 1996).

2. David Spaulding, *Measuring Investment Performance: Calculating and Evaluating Investment Risk and Return* (New York, NY: McGraw-Hill, 1997).

3. Robert Rachlin, *Return on Investment Manual: Tools and Applications for Managing Financial Results* (Armonk, NY: Sharpe Professional, 1997).

4. Arefaine Yohannes, *The Irwin Guide to Risk and Reward* (Chicago, IL: Irwin Professional Publishers, 1996).

5. Birrer & Carrica, *Present Value Applications for Accountants and Financial Planners* (New York, NY: Quorum Books, 1990).

6. Charles Akerson, *The Internal Rate of Return in Real Estate Investments* (Chicago, IL: American Inst. of Real Estate Appraisers, 1988).

7. David Leahigh, *A Pocket Guide to Finance* (Fort Worth, TX: Dryden Press, 1996).

8. *Calculator Analysis for Business and Finance* (New York, NY: McGraw-Hill).

9. *HP-12C Owner's Handbook and Problem-Solving Guide* (Hewlett-Packard Co.).

QUESTIONS AND ANSWERS

Question – What is meant by sensitivity analysis?

Answer – In any quantitative analysis, it is necessary to make a number of assumptions and predictions (and at times, just some guesstimates). These inputs include: (1) yields, (2) rates of inflation, (3) growth rates, (4) effective tax rates, and (5) timing of inflows and outflows.

Obviously, these variables, by definition, cannot be predicted with certainty. Therefore, it is important to determine the sensitivity of the results of the analysis to fluctuations (upward or downward) in any of the variables relevant to decision-making. Sensitivity analysis can be defined as a procedure by which relevant variables are changed one at a time to determine the effect on the overall results.

Sensitivity analysis utilizes the mathematical methods of comparison discussed above. It enables the planner to ascertain which assumptions or predictions must be most-closely-monitored, emphasized, or modified, in order to obtain the most realistic or accurate conclusion possible.

Sensitivity analysis can be used to establish parameters of potential results such as worst down-side risk, highest upside potential, and most probable result. Once the worst case, best case and most probable scenarios have been developed, the investor can then make subjective judgments as to whether or not the investment is appropriate.

Question – In analyzing the viability of a real estate investment, how does one determine what rental revenues, expenses, and final selling price to use in the analytical computations?

Answer – Forecasting revenues, expenses, and final selling price in a real estate investment involves a multiplicity of factors, such as: (1) market demand for the specific location, (2) price and availability of comparable properties, (3) technological and other factors which may result in a greater or lesser property value, (4) government restrictions on alternative uses, and (5) neighborhood influences. The determination of what values to use will be based primarily on available historical data that will require modifications based on expected future trends.

Question – How can a planner help an investor determine how long to hold an investment?

Answer – The internal rate of return and adjusted rate of return concepts can be used to mechanically determine the most desirable holding period. For instance, IRR analysis could be used to ascertain the rate if the investment were held for 5 years, 6 years, 7 years, etc. Mathematically, the number of years that produces the highest IRR would be the one selected.

Some investment analysts ask, "What would the incremental effect be if the investment were held one additional year?" This one-year-more concept is often called the marginal method. It compares the benefit of waiting one more year to the benefit of investing the cumulative benefits received in an alternative investment.

Basing the decision solely on the mathematical results of this marginal analysis, it will make sense to remain in the original investment for at least one more year as long as the marginal IRR is greater than what the investor can receive from an alternative investment.

CHAPTER ENDNOTES

1. In some cases such intangibles might be capitalized for accounting purposes and booked as a separate asset or liability or as an adjustment to the initial investment or basis. However, from an economic standpoint, such benefits or services should be included in return measurements at the time when, otherwise, money would be paid for these benefits or services had they not been included as part of the deal.

2. Data from *Stocks, Bonds, Bills, and Inflation 2002 Yearbook* (Chicago, IL: Ibbotson Associates).

3. Whenever cash returns, such as dividends, interest, or rent, are not reinvested, but rather withdrawn during the holding period, the holding-period rate of return computed by adding all cash returns to the capital appreciation over the holding period will mismeasure the actual return. The error will be greater the longer

the time period between non-reinvestment of cash income and the end of the holding period. Similarly, any other additions or withdrawals of principal other than at the beginning or end of the holding period will distort the calculation of the actual holding-period return. Adjustments for such cash withdrawals or additions are discussed under "III. Modified Internal Rate of Return Methods."

4. Geometric average annual return = $\left(\prod_{i=1}^{n}(1+r_i) \right)^{\frac{1}{n}} - 1$.

5. If, on average, the returns are negative over the period of consideration, the effect is a mirror image on the negative side of zero. The

geometric average annual return will be greater than the arithmetic average annual return (but still smaller in absolute value).

6. There is a procedure based upon Sturm's Theorem for determining both how many IRRs are within the realm of real numbers and for finding partitions within the overall range of possible rates within which one and only one of the real IRRs can be found. By restricting searches within these ranges, each and every real IRR generally can be found. The technical details of this method are far beyond the scope of this discussion. See, for example, Stephen G. Kellison, *Fundamentals of Numerical Analysis*, Richard D. Irwin, Inc. or almost any other text on Numerical Methods.

Chapter 34

MEASURING YIELD

WHAT IS IT?

Yield measures the annual (or semi-annual, or some other time period) rate of return on an investment in fixed-income securities (securities that offer a stated rate of return). In evaluating fixed-income investments such as corporate or government bonds, the investor is faced with a variety of measures of investment return or yield: current yield; yield-to-maturity; yield-to-call; after-tax yield; taxable equivalent yield; and realized compound yield.

This chapter presents the basics of bond prices and describes these measures of yield. It also explains advanced topics such as duration and convexity. Finally, this chapter examines the special categories of U.S. Treasury bills (short-term government securities) and convertible bonds.

Fixed–Income Terminology

The terminology associated with fixed-income investing provides a foundation for understanding the differences between seemingly similar yields and ultimately for managing fixed-income investments (i.e., bonds).

Bonds represent debt. The *issuer* of the bond is borrowing funds. The original purchaser of the bond is effectively making a loan to the issuer. The *principal* of the bond is the amount the issuer borrows and promises to repay. The principal is also referred to as the face value or par value of the bond. Bonds are usually issued in $1,000 increments and have a specified *maturity date* on which the issuer promises to repay the principal.

The *coupon rate* is the interest rate the issuer promises to pay each period on the borrowed funds. The term "coupon" comes from the fact that bonds were formerly issued in "bearer"-form (where the interest and principal were payable to the bearer, or holder, regardless of the person it was originally issued to). With the original bearer-form bonds, the individual or agent in possession of the bond would literally clip a coupon off of the bond and send it in to receive each interest payment. The coupon would note the amount of a specific inter-

est payment and date the payment was due. There was generally one coupon for each interest payment due.

The coupon rate is also known as the *stated rate*. Most bonds pay interest semi-annually; a small number of bonds pay interest annually or quarterly. Bonds that do not have/pay a coupon rate of interest are called zero-coupon bonds.

Example 1: Palmetto Enterprises, Inc. issues bonds with a total face value of $10,000,000 on July 1, 2006. The bonds pay a coupon rate of 3.5% semi-annually and mature in 5 years on June 30, 2011. Purchasers of each $1,000 bond will receive cash interest payments of $35 every six months, on December 31 and June 30. The company will pay each $1,000 bondholder $35 in interest on each of these dates and promises to repay the $1,000 at maturity.

Bond Pricing

While a bond has a specified face value, the bond cannot necessarily be bought or sold at this price. Circumstances change, and investors will demand different interest rates at different times. Only if the bond offers a coupon rate of return equal to the return then required by investors will it sell for face value. Example 1 presented a bond issued in face value increments of $1,000 and paying interest of 3.5% semi-annually. If a bond investor requires a 3.5% semi-annual rate of return for an investment at this risk level, then $1,000 is a fair price.

But what if a new investor considering a purchase of the bond requires a semi-annual rate of 4% for this bond's level of risk? Since the bond is only paying 3.5% semi-annually, the investor would purchase the bond only if it were offered at a discount from face value.

As with practically any other investment, the current value (selling price) of a bond can be determined by taking the present value of the future cash flows expected to be received:

Tools & Techniques of Investment Planning

Equation 34-1

$$V_0 = \frac{C_1}{(1+r)^1} + \frac{C_2}{(1+r)^2} + \frac{C_3}{(1+r)^3} + ... + \frac{C_n}{(1+r)^n}$$

Here, V_0 is the current value, C is the cash flow for each period (1, 2, 3...), r is the required rate of return, and n is the number of periods. Dividing by $(1 + r)^n$ is the mathematical formula for taking the present value of each cash flow. For example, if an investor expects to receive $1 one year from today and the desired rate of return of 10% (r = 0.10), the present value would be $0.9091 ($1.0/1.1). If the investor expects to receive $1 in two years, the present value would be $0.8264 ($1/1.1²). Rather than using the formula to determine the present value, a present value table for a single sum for each cash flow (see Appendix A), a present value table for an ordinary annuity for the series of cash flows (see Appendix C), or a financial calculator can be used.

In the case of a bond, the cash flows include interest to be received each semi-annual period and the face value to be received at maturity. This can be expressed as:

Equation 34-2

$$V_0 = \frac{C_1}{(1+r)^1} + \frac{C_2}{(1+r)^2} + \frac{C_3}{(1+r)^3} + ... + \frac{C_n}{(1+r)^n} + \frac{Face_n}{(1+r)^n}$$

In this version of the discounted cash flow equation, C represents each periodic coupon payment and Face represents the face or par value of the bond to be received at maturity (n).

For the Palmetto Enterprises bond the cash flows would be as follows:

Semi-annual Period	Cash Flow
1	35.00
2	35.00
3	35.00
4	35.00
5	35.00
6	35.00
7	35.00
8	35.00
9	35.00
10	1,035.00
Total	1,350.00

Note that since the bond matures in five years and there are semi-annual payments, there are ten semi-annual periods. In periods one through nine, the bond investor will receive coupon payments of $35.00 each period. In period ten, the bond investor receives the final interest payment, plus the face value of the bond.

Taking the present value of each cash flow (discounted at the investor's required rate of return, 4% semi-annually) and summing them would produce the following:

Semi-annual Period	Cash Flow	Present Value
1	35.00	33.65
2	35.00	32.36
3	35.00	31.11
4	35.00	29.92
5	35.00	28.77
6	35.00	27.66
7	35.00	26.60
8	35.00	25.57
9	35.00	24.59
10	1,035.00	699.21
Total	1,350.00	959.45

While the bondholder will receive nominal cash flows of $1,350, they are worth just $959.45 in today's dollars given a desired rate of return of 4%. Stated another way, if the bondholder invested $959.45 and achieved a semi-annual rate of return of 4%, the bondholder would have an equivalent total return at the end of the time period as the promised cash flow stream shown above. The fair price of this bond that would satisfy the investor's required rate of return is therefore $959.45. Since this bond has a par value of $1,000.00, it is said to sell at a discount, or 95.945 percent of par. So whenever the market's desired or required rate of return exceeds the bond's coupon rate of interest, the bond will sell at a discount.

The reverse is also true: If the investor required a rate of return of only 3% semi-annually for a bond of this risk level, an investor would be willing to pay more than the $1,000 par value. The fair price would be determined as above, using a 3% discount rate:

Semi-annual Period	Cash Flow	Present Value
1	35.00	33.98
2	35.00	32.99
3	35.00	32.03
4	35.00	31.10
5	35.00	30.19
6	35.00	29.31
7	35.00	28.46
8	35.00	27.63
9	35.00	26.82
10	1,035.00	770.14
Total	1,350.00	1,042.65

The bond would need to sell at a premium, or 104.265 percent of par. At this price, the bondholder would expect to earn 3% semi-annually. Note, however, that the investor receives the coupon rate of interest in cash in all cases.

Let's summarize the present value of the bond given the various desired rates of return:

Desired Semi-annual Rate of Return	Present Value of Bond
4.0%	$ 959.45
3.5%	$1,000.00
3.0%	$1,042.65

This exercise illustrates the important principle that bond prices and returns are inversely related; all else being equal, the higher the desired rate of return, the lower the value of the bond to the investor. This makes sense, as a rational investor that wishes to achieve a certain rate of return, and will contractually receive precisely the stated rate of interest from the bond, can only achieve the desired return by purchasing the underlying bond at a discount or premium – such that the *total return*, at the end of the period, will be adjusted by the gain or loss on the face value of the bond to achieve this goal.

In practice, the required rate of return is not that of a single investor, but of all investors in aggregate – the market rate of interest. This is the rate of return that market participants require in order to purchase a particular bond or other offerings that are functionally equivalent. All investors will generally be purchasing a bond based upon the market rate of interest because, in the aggregate, any bond that is over-priced relative to the market rate of interest will not be sold until the seller lowers the price, while any bond that is underpriced will be quickly snatched up by market participants until the seller realizes the price can be raised. The market rate of interest is equivalent to the yield realized if the bond is purchased on the open market and is held to its maturity date – and is generally called the *yield-to-maturity*.

Assume now that the investor purchases the above bond for $1,042.65, which is the price available in the open market. Knowing the semi-annual interest payments, the face value, and the number of payments (as these are all stated quite clearly on the bond), Equation 34-2 can be solved for r, the required rate of return. This tells what rate of interest is required by the market. In this case, the required rate of return is 3% semi-annually. This is the expected rate of return from the investment or its yield-to-maturity.

More formally, the yield-to-maturity can be defined as the rate of return that will make the net present value (present value of future cash flows minus the initial investment) of investing in the bond zero – assuming:

- The bond is held to maturity;

- All promised interest and principal payments are received when due; and

- Coupon payments can be reinvested at the same rate of interest.

Equation 34-3

$$\frac{\text{Present Value of}}{\text{Future Cash Flows}} \\ \frac{-\ \text{Initial Investment}}{\text{Net Present Value}}$$

The mathematically-inclined reader will note that when the net present value is zero, the yield is equal to, and also known as, the internal rate of return.

For example, as shown above, if the semi-annual yield or internal rate of return is 4%, both the price of a five-year $1,000 bond with a coupon rate of 3.5% and the present value of the future cash flows is $959.45, and the net present value is zero ($959.45 - $959.45 = $0). And, if the semi-annual yield or internal rate of return is 3%, both the price of a five-year $1,000 bond with a coupon rate of 3.5% and the present value of the future cash flows is $1,042.65, and the net present value is zero ($1,042.65 - $1,042.65 = $0).

A much more complex and important question is, "How do investors arrive at the desired or required rate of return?" In the next section, the factors that underlie the market's required rate of return are examined.

Market Interest Rates

The market rate of return is determined by a variety of factors at any given time. There are two primary components to the required rate of return: the risk-free rate and the risk premium.

A risk-free asset is one whose future return can be predicted with near certainty. The typical example is a 3-month Treasury bill, which is virtually risk-free. As a component of the required rate of return, the risk-free rate of return is that return that would be expected if an investment had virtually no risk. The risk-free rate

Figure 34.1

REUTERS CORPORATE SPREADS FOR INDUSTRIALS AS OF OCTOBER 9, 2003

Rating	1 yr	2 yr	3 yr	5 yr	7 yr	10 yr	30 yr
Aaa/AAA	5	10	15	22	27	30	55
Aa1/AA+	10	15	20	32	37	40	60
Aa2/AA	15	25	30	37	44	50	65
Aa3/AA-	20	30	35	45	53	55	65
A1/A+	30	40	45	58	62	55	70
A2/A	40	50	57	65	65	65	79
A3/A-	50	65	79	85	82	75	90
Baa1/BBB+	60	75	90	97	100	88	108
Baa2/BBB	65	80	88	95	126	107	127
Baa3/BBB-	75	90	105	112	116	121	146
Ba1/BB+	85	100	115	124	130	133	168
Ba2/BB	290	290	265	240	265	210	235
Ba3/BB-	320	395	420	370	320	290	300
B1/B+	500	525	600	425	425	375	450
B2/B	525	550	600	500	450	450	725
B3/B-	725	800	775	800	750	775	850
Caa/CCC	1500	1600	1550	1400	1300	1375	1500

Source: Bonds-online.com

is the amount necessary to properly compensate the lender for the use of his cash before risk is taken into consideration. Expected inflation is a major factor in determining this risk-free rate.

Short of treasury bills though, most investments in bonds (such as corporate bonds) entail at least some degree of risk (such as risk of default). Therefore, a charge must be imposed, in addition to the risk-free rate, to compensate the lender for the risk taken. The additional return that must be paid to compensate investors for such risk is called the risk premium.

One way to assess the risk premium for a bond is to examine the bond's yield spread. The spread is the difference between the bond's yield to maturity and that of a risk-free bond (e.g., a government bond) with otherwise similar underlying characteristics (such as maturity). The spread is measured in basis points, where 100 basis points equals 1%. So if a 20-year U.S. governmental bond were offering a yield of 5.00% and the spread on a AAA-rated corporate bond of the same maturity is 50 basis points, the corporate bond would have a required return (yield to maturity) of 5.50%. Figure 34.1 presents an example of spreads for industrial bonds by maturity and credit rating. Note that for a 10-year industrial bonds rated AAA (the highest rating), a spread of 30 basis points (0.30%) is required, whereas for a CCC-rated bond, (a much lower bond rating, indicating the

investor is taking significant risk) a 1,375 basis point (13.75%) spread is required. Since the bonds are being compared to similar-maturity government bonds, and government bonds are generally considered to be risk-free, the spreads represent the risk premium.

Having reviewed the factors that determine the required return on a bond investment, one must then be sure that the price of the bond reflects those factors. While this should be straightforward, an array of interest rates is quoted by market participants to communicate the price of a single bond. This section is designed to clarify the meaning and distinctions among: coupon rate, yield-to-maturity, after-tax yield, taxable equivalent yield, current yield, realized compound yield, and yield-to-call.

Bond Yields

The coupon rate of interest determines the periodic cash interest payment that will be made by the issuer to the bondholder(s). The yield-to-maturity is the effective rate that the bondholder expects to receive based upon the actual selling price of the bond (which may not necessarily be the same rate the issuer pays in interest and principal repayments). Only if the bond is sold at par value will the coupon rate equal the yield-to-maturity. If the bond is callable (redeemable by the issuer prior to maturity at a predetermined price), then it is also useful for the bondholder to compute the expected *yield-to-call*.

The yield-to-call is the internal rate of return obtained by solving the bond present value equation in Equation 34-2 and using the call price for the principal payment and the number of periods until call for the time to maturity.

Equation 34-4

$$V_0 = \frac{C_1}{(1+r)^1} + \frac{C_2}{(1+r)^2} + \frac{C_3}{(1+r)^3} + \ldots + \frac{C_n}{(1+r)^n} + \frac{Call\ Price_n}{(1+r)^n}$$

As before, V_0 is the selling price of the bond. Now n is the number of periods to the call date and Call Price is the price to be received by the bondholder if the bond is called (the call price usually includes a small "call premium," or slight excess above the face value). Call prices are normally expressed as a percentage of face value. For example, a $1,000 par value bond callable at 102 would have a call price of 102% of the $1,000 par, or $1,020. Using the example, the bond is initially offered at par value of $1,000.00 and is callable at the end of six periods (three years) at 102. V_0 is $1,000, Call Price is $1,020, each coupon payment is $35 and n is 6. Solving for r results in a value of 3.803% semi-annually [r is the discount rate at which the present value of the cash flow to the call date equals the bond purchase price of $1,000, see below]. This is the bond's yield-to-call at issue.

Semi-annual Period	Cash Flow	Present Value
1	35.00	33.72
2	35.00	32.48
3	35.00	31.29
4	35.00	30.15
5	35.00	29.04
6	1,055.00	843.32
Total	1,230.00	1,000.00

It was noted earlier that the rate of return actually realized on a bond investment held to maturity could differ from the expected yield-to-maturity (or yield-to-call). This is due to reinvestment risk. Let's reconsider the case of the $1,000 bond from Example 1. If it is sold at par value, then the expected yield-to-maturity is 3.5% semi-annually. If interest rates subsequently fall to 3% before any coupon payments are received, the investor must reinvest those amounts at only 3%. The bondholder's wealth at the end of the period is $1,401.24.

This is comprised of the accumulated coupon payments reinvested at 3% semi-annually and the principal that is received at maturity. The *realized compound yield* can be found by solving an internal rate of return problem. Here, one uses $1,000 as the initial investment (Present Value[1]) $1,401.24 as the wealth at the end of 10 periods (Future Value, see below), and 10 is the number of periods; solving for the rate of return results in a realized compound yield of 3.43% (see below). This is lower than the expected yield-to-maturity of 3.5% since the interest payments were reinvested at a lower rate.

Semi-annual Period	Cash Flow	Present Value
1	35.00	45.67
2	35.00	44.34
3	35.00	43.05
4	35.00	41.79
5	35.00	40.57
6	35.00	39.39
7	35.00	38.25
8	35.00	37.13
9	35.00	36.05
10	1,035.00	1,035.00
Total	1,350.00	1,401.24

The future value of each payment is calculated by multiplying the cash flow by $(1 + i)$, where n is the remaining number of periods until maturity and i is the reinvestment rate. Thus, the future value for the first period equals $45.67 [$35 x $(1 + 3\%)^9$]. The realized compound yield, r, is then calculated as follows: (FV / PP)$^{1/P}$ – 1, where FV equals the future value of payments, PP equals the purchase price of the bond, and p equals the number of periods. Thus, r equals 3.43% [(1,401.24 / 1,000)$^{1/10}$ – 1].

Since most bonds (other than municipal bonds) are subject to federal income tax, it is also useful to express all of these yields on an after-tax basis:

Equation 34-5

After Tax Yield = Before Tax Yield x (1 – Tax Rate)

If the expected semi-annual yield-to-maturity is 3.5% and the tax rate is 25%, the *after-tax yield* would be 2.625% on a semi-annual basis. In the case of a nontaxable bond (municipal bond), the process can be reversed to determine the *taxable equivalent yield* of a tax-free bond:

Equation 34-6

$$Taxable\ Equivalent\ Yield = \frac{Tax\ Free\ Yield}{(1 - Tax\ Rate)}$$

If a municipal bond has a tax-free yield-to-maturity of 3% and the tax rate is 25%, then the taxable equivalent yield would be 4.0%. In other words, a tax-free bond yielding 3% is equivalent to a taxable bond yielding 4.0% when the investor's tax rate is 25%.

Both to minimize confusion and because bond math is customarily performed using semi-annual rates, all yields have been expressed in semi-annual form. However, although the math is done on a semi-annual basis, bonds are frequently discussed in terms of annual rates. The coupon rate can be converted to an annual rate by simply multiplying by two. So, the 3.5% semi-annual rate bond pays a coupon of 7.0% annually. However, calculating the actual *annualized yield* is slightly more complicated, since the interest must be compounded (interest is earned during the second six months on the interest payment received after the first six months). A compound annualized yield can be obtained as follows:

Equation 34-7

$$Annualized\ Yield = ((1 + Non\ Annualized\ Yield)^n - 1) * 100$$

In this equation, n is the number of compounding periods and Non-Annualized Yield is the periodic yield (such as semi-annual yield) and is expressed in decimal format. So a 3.5% (0.035) semi-annual yield-to-maturity converts to an annualized yield of 7.1225% (a little higher than doubling due to the compounding of interest).

The *current yield* is an approximation as to how much the bondholder is earning from his investment on a current basis – the yield based upon the interest payments received relative to the exact current price of the bond. It is measured as the *annual* coupon interest payment divided by the price of the bond. If the $1,000 bond is sold at par, the current yield would be ($35 x 2) / $1000 or 7.0%. When a bond is sold at par, the annual coupon rate, expected yield-to-maturity, and current yield are all equal. For the earlier bond example, if the current market rate of interest is 3% semi-annually (6.09% effective annual rate) and the bond sells at $1,042.65, the current yield would be 6.71% ($70 / $1,042.65). Note that for a bond sold at a premium, the current yield is less than the coupon rate (7%) because the coupon rate essentially assumes the bond is priced at par, and more than the expected yield-to-maturity (6.1%) because of the lower rate that will be earned on reinvested funds. If the required semi-annual return were 4% (8.16% effective annual rate), then the bond would sell for $959.45. The current yield would be 7.30%. For a discount bond, the current yield is more than the coupon rate (7%) but less than the expected yield-to-maturity (8.16%) (the bond discount boosts the total return as the bond is purchased for $959.45 but will mature at $1,000).

Figure 34.2 presents bond prices as presented in the *Wall Street Journal*.

The Goldman Sachs bond is selling at a discount (96.413%) to par value. As a result, the yield-to-maturity is higher than the promised coupon payment. This bond matures in 30 years and offers a spread or premium over ten-year U.S. Government bonds of 155 basis points. (Remember that a basis point is one hundredth of a percentage point, or 0.01%.) The Valero Energy bond on the other hand is offering a higher coupon rate than is required given its risk and it is therefore selling at a premium. The yield-to-maturity is 6.670% versus a coupon rate of 7.50%. Note that both bonds are long term and offer similar yields to maturity in spite of their differing coupon rates.

Figure 34.2

SELECTED WALL STREET JOURNAL CORPORATE BOND DATA AS OF THURSDAY JULY 13, 2006

Company (ticker)	Coupon	Maturity	Last Price	Last Yield	EST Spread	UST	EST $ Vol (000's)
Goldman Sachs Group (GS)	6.450	May 01, 2036	96.413	6.729	155	10	57,055
Valero Energy Corp (VLO)	7.500	Apr. 15, 2032	110.130	6.670	150	30	50,000

Last Yield is the yield-to-maturity of the bond based upon its last price. EST Spread is estimated spread in basis points over U.S. Treasury Security with maturity listed under UST. EST $ Vol is the total dollar volume of activity in that bond.

Figure 34.3

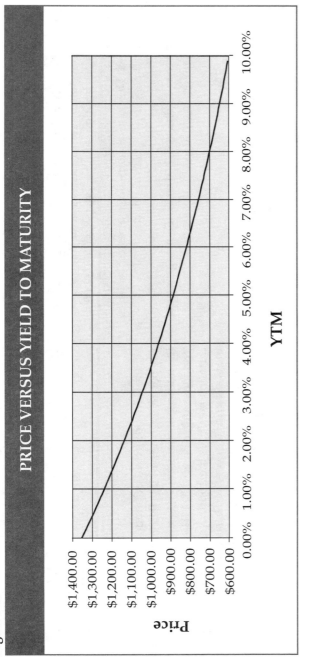

PRICE VERSUS YIELD TO MATURITY

Interest Rate Volatility

As already seen, there is an inverse relationship between interest rates (required returns) and bond prices; when interest rates rise, bond market prices decline. Interestingly, some bonds are more sensitive to changes in interest rates than others. That is, a given change in interest rates results in a greater change in some bond prices than in others. This section will explore some of the factors that affect a bond's sensitivity to interest rates and thus its price volatility.

Figure 34.3 shows the relationship between the yield-to-maturity and the bond price for the sample bond ($1,000 par value, 3.5% semi-annual coupon, and maturing in 5 years).

This relationship between bond yields and bond prices shows that a 1% (relative) change in interest rates (as measured by YTM) produces some relative change in the price of the bond.[2] From the previous example and the above graph, it is known that if the required market rate of interest is 3.5% semi-annually, the bond price should be $1,000.00. If interest rates decline to 3% semi-annually, then the bond price will rise to $1,042.65. This is usually referred to as a 100 basis point change (50 basis points semi-annually = 100 basis points annually) in interest rates (100 basis points = an absolute 1.00%). The price of the bond rose by $42.65, which is 4.265% of the original price. So a 100 basis point (or 1% absolute) decline in annual interest rates (50 basis points or 0.5% semi-annually) caused the price of the bond to change by 4.265% and in the opposite direction (interest rate decline caused a price increase). This is a measure of the bond's volatility. By definition, a more volatile bond

will show a greater change in price for a given change in interest rates.

As an investor in bonds, it is certainly important to understand the potential change in the price of the investment. This factor will be one major determinant in the selection of bonds in which to invest (as it is a major element of risk given that interest rates do in fact fluctuate). Furthermore, the expected volatility of a bond can potentially be used as part of an investment strategy.

Fortunately, a bond's volatility can be estimated using a concept known as duration. Duration is the weighted average time until receipt of all of a bond's cash flows. For the sample bond, the maturity is five years. However, since cash flows occur throughout the bond's life, the weighted average time is less than five years. The duration can be measured precisely by discounting each expected cash flow by the current market rate of interest (4% semi-annually here) and weighting each one by the period in which it occurs:

Semi-annual Period	Cash Flow	Present Value	PV times Period
1	35.00	33.82	33.82
2	35.00	32.67	65.35
3	35.00	31.57	94.70
4	35.00	30.50	122.00
5	35.00	29.47	147.35
6	35.00	28.47	170.84
7	35.00	27.51	192.57
8	35.00	26.58	212.64
9	35.00	25.68	231.13
10	1,035.00	733.73	7337.31
Total	1,350.00	1,000.00	8,607.69

The sum of the present value of each cash flow is $1,000.00 which is the bond's current price given a 3.5% required rate of return. The sum of the present value multiplied by the period in which each cash flow occurs is $8,607.69. Dividing this sum by the current price of the bond ($1,000) produces the duration of 8.6 periods ($8,607.69 / $1,000), or the weighted average time until receipt of the bond's cash flows. Duration is normally expressed in years rather than periods, 4.3 years in this case.

This process can be expressed by the following formula for duration determined in periods:

Equation 34-8

$$Dur = \frac{\sum_{t=1}^{n} \frac{C_t(t)}{(1+i)^t}}{\sum_{t=1}^{n} \frac{C_t}{(1+i)^t}}$$

Where C is each cash flow for time period t. The numerator represents the sum of the present value of each cash flow multiplied by the time period. The denominator represents the sum of each present value (the price). This value may need to be adjusted if the period is not already expressed in terms of years.

Since duration is calculated based upon the current price and current yield-to-maturity, it will change as the price and yield-to-maturity change. The calculated duration is therefore valid only for the current price and yield. This version of duration is more formally known as Macaulay duration, named for Frederick Macaulay, who derived it in a paper published in 1938. As noted above, Macaulay duration is expressed in years, so the Macaulay duration for the example bond is 4.3.

Macaulay duration can also be approximated, avoiding the need to compute all of the present values. The approximation formula is:

Equation 34-9

$$Dur = \frac{1+y}{Y} - \frac{(1+y)+T(c-y)}{c[(1+y)^T-1]+y}$$

Where y is the yield-to-maturity, c is the coupon rate, and T is the time to maturity. For the sample bond, using y = .035, c = .035, and T = 10 (all in periods) yields an approximation for duration of 8.6 periods or 4.3 years.

Take this one step further to measure the interest rate sensitivity of a bond. Divide Macaulay duration (in

periods) by one plus the periodic (semi-annual in this case) yield-to-maturity.

Equation 34-10

$$D = \frac{Macaulay\ Duration}{1+y}$$

Where D is modified duration and y is the yield-to-maturity per period (the annual yield-to-maturity divided by the number of compounding periods per year). For the previous sample bond, 4.3/1.035 equals 4.15. Modified duration measures the approximate relative change in the bond price for every 100 basis point (1%) change in *annual* interest rates. Since there is an inverse relationship in bond yields and prices, the change (Δ) in the price of a bond can be expressed as:

Equation 34-11

$$\frac{\Delta P}{P} = -D(\Delta y) \text{ or } \frac{\Delta P}{P} = \frac{Macaulay\ Duration\ (\Delta y)}{1+y}$$

Where Δy is the change in annual yield in decimal form. So for the bond at hand, a decline in semi-annual interest rates from 3.5% to 3% is a move of 50 basis points semi-annually or 100 basis points annually. In decimal form this is 0.01 (1%). A decrease of 100 basis points on an annual basis should cause the bond price to change by approximately -4.15*(-.01) = +0.0415 or +4.15%. This is close to the observed price increase of the sample bond above, from $1,000.00 to $1,042.65 (which was 4.265%).

Note that duration provides only an approximation of the percentage change in price for a given (absolute) change in interest rates. Duration, as formulated here, measures the slope of a straight-line tangent to the curve presented in Figure 34.3 at a semi-annual yield of 3.5% and a price of $1,000.00. Note also that, in fact, the relationship shown in Figure 34.3 is *not* a straight line but a curve. As one moves along any particular tangent line (where the slope of the line represents duration) from the intersection/starting point (i.e., a more substantial interest rate change), the curvilinear relationship 'curves' away and the distance between the tangent line and the actual relationship curve increases. This represents the "error" of the estimate under the duration formula (the tangent line) from the actual effect of an interest rate change (the relationship curve). As a result of the curvature of the relationship, duration is a fairly accurate predictor for very small changes in interest rates, but not for larger changes – even the 100 basis point change presented here partially revealed the inaccuracy.

As a further check of understanding duration, consider the special case of zero-coupon bonds. Investors in "Zeroes" (as this type of bond is often labeled) receive no periodic interest payments.[3] Instead, the interest accrues from the purchase date and is received along with the principal at maturity. Since the desired rate of return is always greater than zero, zero-coupon bonds will always sell at a discount.

Example 2: TRR Financial Enterprises is raising debt to fund a business acquisition. In order to preserve cash flow while integrating this new business, TRR decides to issue zero-coupon bonds with a total face value of $5,000,000. Each $1,000 bond matures in 5 years. Given the risk level of TRR and current market conditions, investors desire a 4% semi-annual rate of return on their investment.

Pricing a zero-coupon bond is easier than pricing a coupon bond, since there is only one cash flow involved. The investor will receive $1,000 at maturity in five years. The present value of $1,000 over 10 semi-annual periods at a 4% semi-annual rate is $675.56 – the price that investors would buy this bond when initially issued. This is 67.556% of par value and a substantial discount to $1,000.

How would an investor calculate the duration of a zero-coupon bond? In this and only this special case, one can see that the duration is exactly equal to the remaining life of the bond. For a 5-year zero-coupon bond that is currently priced at $675.56 and is expected to return $1,000 at maturity, the duration is calculated as follows:

Present value of the (single) cash flow = $675.56

Time to maturity = 5.

So, according to Equation 34-8, duration equals 5 x (675.56) / (675.56) = 5. Therefore, the duration of a zero-coupon bond is identical to its remaining life. This is logical, as duration is the average weighted time to receive the cash flows of a bond – if the only cash flow occurs 5 years from now, then the average weighted time is the average of one number – the time to maturity, or 5 years.

Across all bonds, a higher duration equates to higher bond price volatility. Since volatility is directly related to duration, one can infer that zero-coupon bonds are more volatile than other bonds of the same maturity, all

else being equal. Further, bonds with a longer maturity (hence a longer duration) are more volatile than bonds of shorter maturity.

Because the relationship between interest rates and bond prices is curvilinear, as noted earlier, one can modify the measure of duration to predict bond volatility more precisely. Recall from Figure 34.3 and the discussion above that duration measures the slope of a line tangent to the curve at a particular point. However, the relationship between price and yield itself is curvilinear – this phenomenon is called *convexity*. Convexity is a measure of the curvature of the relationship between bond yields and prices. Specifically, convexity can help explain the movement in bond prices that is not accounted for by duration. Convexity is determined by taking the duration computation one step further and multiplying (PV times t) by (t+1):

Semi-annual Period	Cash Flow	Present Value	PV times Period	(PV times t) times (t+1)
1	35.00	33.82	33.82	67.63
2	35.00	32.67	65.35	196.04
3	35.00	31.57	94.70	378.82
4	35.00	30.50	122.00	610.01
5	35.00	29.47	147.35	884.07
6	35.00	28.47	170.84	1,195.85
7	35.00	27.51	192.57	1,540.54
8	35.00	26.58	212.64	1,913.72
9	35.00	25.68	231.13	2,311.25
10	1,035.00	733.73	7,337.31	80,710.41
Total	1,350.00	1,000.00	8,607.69	89,808.33

The total of the last column is divided by the price of the bond times the number of compounding periods squared times (one plus y) squared.

Convexity for this bond is therefore: 89,808.33 / ((1,000.00 * 4) (1.035)²) or 20.9593.

Incorporating these factors together, the price change in a bond using both duration and convexity can be measured as:

Equation 28-12

$$\frac{\Delta P}{P} = -D\,(\Delta y) + \frac{1}{2}\;Convexity\,(\Delta y)^2$$

For the bond, the change in price for a 100 basis point decline in interest rates can be measured as (-4.15(-.01) + 0.5 x 20.9593 x (0.0001) = 0.0425 or 4.25%. Recall that the bond in question actually increased in value 4.265%. Although the expected change did not fully anticipate

Tools & Techniques of Investment Planning

the actual change, it was substantially closer than the initial estimate of 4.15% based upon modified duration alone. Note that convexity is always a good thing for the bond investor, regardless of whether interest rates rise or fall. If interest rates fall, convexity augments the increase in the price of the bond. If interest rates rise, convexity dampens the decline in the price. This is evident in the original example: a 100 basis point decline in rates caused the bond price to increase to $1,042.65, or 4.265%; a 100 basis point increase in rates caused the bond price to decline to $959.45, or (only) 4.055%. It is important to remember that due to convexity the price change for a rise in interest rates is not equal to the (opposite-direction) price change for an equivalent decline in interest rates. Therefore, when evaluating the potential consequences of interest rate changes, both effects should be evaluated separately – particularly for large interest rate changes, where the impact of the curvilinear nature of the relationship (i.e., convexity) is larger.

The combination of duration and convexity allow us to predict movements in the bond's value for certain expected changes in interest rates.

Special Cases

U.S Treasury Bills are short-term securities issued for 13, 26, and 52 week periods. They are issued on a discount basis (non-interest paying zero-coupon bonds), in increments of $1,000 face value. The price quotes for Treasury bills are somewhat unusual compared to other fixed-income investments and warrants some explanation. Consider the following quote from the U.S. Treasury web site (www.publicdebt.treas.gov):

Term:	182-Day
Issue Date:	09-28-2000
Maturity Date:	03-29-2001
Discount Rate:	5.985%
Investment Rate:	6.258%
Price Per $100:	96.974
CUSIP:	912795FZ9

Treasury bill prices are quoted in terms of the Discount Rate, sometimes called a bank discount rate. The price is derived by computing the discount based upon a 360-day year and the maturity in days of the bill:

$$100 - ((182/360) \times (5.985\% \times 100)) = 96.974$$

However, to evaluate the bill compared to other fixed-income investments, examine the annualized yield-to-maturity rather than the discount rate. The Treasury refers to this as the Investment Rate or equivalent coupon

yield. To compute the yield-to-maturity on a Treasury bill, calculate the internal rate of return for a single period, with a present value of 96.974 and a future value (par) of 100.000. The resulting rate is 3.1204%, which is the yield-to-maturity for a 182-day period. The annualized rate listed by the Treasury is 3.1204% x 365/182 or 6.258%.[4] This is not a compounded rate.

Convertible bonds allow the investor to exchange the bond for a pre-specified amount of another security, typically a common stock.[5] While the size of the U.S. market for convertibles is dwarfed by the markets for equities and nonconvertible bonds, it is a market that continues to grow in size and importance along with the growth in related derivative securities (for example, options).

Why do investors purchase convertible bonds? In short, convertibles offer much of the upside potential of an equity security *and* the downside protection of a bond. The upside portion of this interesting combination stems from the fact that the holder has the right to surrender the bond in exchange for a fixed number of shares of the common stock, which rise in value if the shares appreciate. The downside protection is a result of the combination of two factors. First, the bondholder need not acquire the stock if its price does not rise. Second, provided the issuer remains solvent, the investor can hold the bond to maturity and collect its face value at maturity or sell it to another investor in the interim period.

Convertible bonds pay the coupon rate of interest semi-annually on the face amount of the security. So a convertible bond with a $1,000 face value and a coupon rate of 5.5% will pay $27.50 (i.e., ½ x .055 x $1,000) twice each year. In addition, assume this convertible bond can be converted into 16 2/3 shares of common stock. In this case the *conversion ratio* is 16.667 and implies a *conversion price* of $60, which is simply the face value ($1,000) divided by the conversion ratio (16.667). To summarize, the convertible investor has the right to acquire 16.667 shares for each $1,000 bond by surrendering the bond for this pre-specified number of shares of the common stock.

In assessing the potential risk of a convertible investment, the prospective investor must break this hybrid investment vehicle into its two components and examine each in turn. Convertibles are called hybrid securities because they have both equity and fixed-income characteristics.

If the current price of the stock of the issuer is $50 and the investor could elect to surrender the bond today in exchange for 16 2/3 shares, then clearly the convertible could not be priced less than $833.33 (16 2/3 shares x $50 per share) in today's market because investors would simply buy and convert it, thereby reaping an immediate (arbitrage) profit. This amount, $833.33, is known as the convertible's *conversion value*.

One must also consider the fixed-income component alone in the process of assessing the downside risk of this investment. What price would the convertible bond move toward in the event that investors decide today that the common stock has little or no potential to exceed its conversion price? In effect, the convertible bond would then be priced as if it were a straight bond of the issuer. So, if a 20-year (40 coupon payment) straight $1,000 par value bond of this firm with a 5.5% annual coupon rate (payable $27.50 each semiannual period) were priced for a semi-annual yield-to-maturity of 3.5%, the convertible bond would then be priced to yield about the same rate of return.

Using the same approach to value bonds as earlier in this chapter, one could compute its expected market price as the present value of the future stream of interest and principal payments discounted at the appropriate rate (3.5% semi-annually in this case): $839.84. The value of the convertible as a bond alone is called its *bond value*. This indicates a second possible *floor price* to which the convertible could descend. Clearly, the convertible will not be priced in the market below its price as a straight bond because it also contains the conversion option, which has some non-zero market value.

The conclusion of the preceding two-stage analysis is that the minimum price of a convertible is the *greater* of its Bond Value and its Conversion Value. To complete this assessment of the downside risk of a convertible, its *conversion premium* is defined as the percentage difference between its current market price and its theoretical minimum value. Assuming the bond is currently selling for $1,050 its conversion premium would be $210.16 or 25.02% ($210.16/839.84). This is the premium the market is willing to pay for the potential increase in the stock price.

WHERE CAN I FIND OUT MORE?

1. Frank J. Fabozzi, Ed., *The Handbook of Fixed-Income Securities*, 6th Edition (New York, NY: McGraw Hill, 2000).

2. Annette Thau, *The Bond Book*, 2nd Edition (New York, NY: McGraw Hill, 2001).

3. Marilyn Cohen and Nick Watson, *The Bond Bible* (New York, NY: New York Institute of Finance, 2000).

QUESTIONS AND ANSWERS

Question – What is the yield-to-maturity for a bond?

Answer – A bond's yield-to-maturity is the rate of return expected by a bond investor based on the current market price of the bond and promised future interest and principal payments.

Question – What is the relationship between investors' required rates of return and bond prices?

Answer – Bond prices are inversely related to investors' required rates of return: the higher the required rate of return the lower the bond price; the lower the required rate of return the higher the bond price. This relationship is a source of bond price volatility. As interest rates rise (fall), investors' required rates of return increase (decrease) and bond prices fall (rise).

Question – What is Duration?

Answer – Duration measures the weighted average time to maturity for a bond. The duration of a zero-coupon bond is the same as its time to maturity. For bonds paying a coupon rate of interest, the duration will be less than the time to maturity. Duration is useful for assessing the sensitivity of bond prices to changes in interest rates. Prices of bonds with higher (lower) duration will be more (less) sensitive to interest rate changes. Duration is most frequently used to approximate the percentage change in the price of a bond given a 100-basis-point change in interest rates.

Question – Consider the following bond: $1,000 par value; 5 years to maturity; 5% annual coupon, paid semiannually. The market yield for a nonconvertible bond with similar characteristics is 5.5%. What should the price of this bond be? Assume the bond sells for this price. What is its compound yield to maturity? What is its initial current yield?

Answer – The price of the bond should be $978.40. The compound yield to maturity would be 2.75% semiannually; 5.58% annually [(1 + 2.75%)² – 1]. The initial current yield would be 5.11% [$50 / $978.40].

Tools & Techniques of Investment Planning

Period	Cash Flow	Present Value
1	25.00	24.33
2	25.00	23.68
3	25.00	23.05
4	25.00	22.43
5	25.00	21.83
6	25.00	21.24
7	25.00	20.68
8	25.00	20.12
9	25.00	19.58
10	1,025.00	781.46
Total		978.40

CHAPTER ENDNOTES

1. On some financial calculators this initial investment is considered a cash outflow and must be entered as a negative number to solve for the internal rate of return.

2. Throughout the remainder of this discussion, it is important that the distinction between a relative and an absolute percentage change in rates be maintained. For example, when interest rates on a hypothetical bond move from 8% to 9% annually, this would constitute a 12.5% relative change in rates or a 1% absolute (or 100 basis point) change. From this point forward, the parenthetical word "relative" will be omitted when referring to the former type of change. To ensure further clarity, the word absolute or basis points will be explicitly used when referring to changes of the latter type.

3. Why would an investor in a fixed-income instrument purchase a bond that makes no periodic interest payments? One reason, which the reader might now suspect, is that the investor has thereby avoided reinvestment risk. The bond is purchased at a discount to its par value and, barring default, the investor receives the yield-to-maturity in the form of price increases (approaching par) as a rate of return until the bond matures.

4. The Investment Rate will always be higher than the Discount Rate. Given (with the bond example above) a discount amount (price difference) of $1,000 - $969.74 = $30.26 (accrued over the 182 day period); the Discount Rate is essentially the ratio of the discount amount to the par value, or $30.26 / $1,000; the Investment Rate is essentially the ratio of the discount amount to the *purchase* value, or $30.26 / $969.74. Since Treasury Bills are always purchased at a discount, this second ratio will always be lower than the first; the Discount Rate will always be lower than the Investment Rate.

5. While some convertible bonds can be exchanged for preferred stock or other instruments, this brief presentation of convertibles is confined to those that are most common – those that can be converted into the common stock of the bond issuer.

Chapter 35

SECURITY VALUATION

WHAT IS IT?

Security valuation is the use of analytic methods to determine the intrinsic value (as opposed to the observed market price) of a security. The intrinsic value is then compared to the market price to determine whether the security appears attractively priced.

There are several classes of valuation methods for assessing a security's intrinsic value, including:

- Discounted Cash Flow Methods

- Market Based Methods

- Asset Based Methods

The focus of this chapter is valuing equity securities (stock). Equities are most commonly valued using the first two categories: discounted cash flow methods and market based methods. Less often used are asset based methods that entail valuing a company based upon its underlying net assets (assets less liabilities, or book value). Asset based methods are more likely to be used when the company is expected to be liquidated.

DISCOUNTED CASH FLOW METHODS

As with any investment, the intrinsic value of a stock can be determined by calculating the present value of the future cash flows expected to be received:

$$V_0 = \frac{C_1}{(1+r)^1} + \frac{C_2}{(1+r)^2} + \frac{C_3}{(1+r)^3} + ... + \frac{C_n}{(1+r)^n}$$

Here, V_0 is the current value, C is the cash flow for each period (1, 2, 3...), r is the required rate of return, and n is the number of periods. Dividing by $(1+r)^n$ is the mathematical formula for taking the present value of each cash flow. For example, if an investor expects to receive $1 one year from today and has a desired rate of return of 10% (r = 0.10), the present value would be $0.9091 ($1.0/1.1). If the investor expects to receive $1 in two years, the present value would be $0.8265 ($1/1.1²). Rather than using the formula to determine the present

value, a present value table (see Appendix A) can be used to determine the present value of each cash flow or a financial calculator can be used.

Assume an investor is considering investing in an entity that promises a return of $1 per year for three years. At the end of the three years the entity is expected to liquidate and pay the investor an additional $10. If the investor requires a 10% rate of return for this investment, how much is it worth today? The present value would be:

$$V_0 = \frac{\$1}{(1.1)^1} + \frac{\$1}{(1.1)^2} + \frac{\$11}{(1.1)^3}$$

$$= \$0.9091 + \$0.8265 + \$8.2644 = \$10$$

So a fair price for this investment would be $10.00. If the market price were $9, the investment would be undervalued given the investor's expectations and required return. If the investment is purchased for $9, the expected return would be greater than the required return of 10%.[1] If the market price was above $10, the investment would be considered overvalued and the expected return would be less than 10%.

In practice, valuing the cash flows from a stock is not as easy as in this stylized example. Future cash flows must first be estimated. There are several cash flows that can be used in a discounted cash flow approach. Two of the most common are dividends and free cash flow to equity. Dividends are cash flows that are actually distributed by the firm to shareholders. Free cash flow to equity is the cash flow the company generates from its operations after deducting any needed investments in the new assets. Free cash flow to equity may be distributed to shareholders as dividends or kept by the firm for future use. The next section presents discounted dividend valuation and the subsequent section presents discounted free cash flow valuation. Finally, this chapter addresses the use of earnings in place of cash flow in valuation models (termed capitalization of earnings).

It is also important to understand the role of the discount rate (desired or required rate of return) in the present value equations used throughout this chapter. It is the rate at which an investor is indifferent between receiving a smaller amount of money today or a larger amount in the future. In the investment world, this number is highly dependent on the general level of interest rates.

Discounted Dividend Models

As the actual cash flows an investor will receive from stock holdings, dividends are an appropriate cash flow to value. Modifying the general cash flow model to consider the present value of dividends (D):

$$V_0 = \frac{D_1}{(1+r)^1} + \frac{D_2}{(1+r)^2} + \frac{D_3}{(1+r)^3} + ... + \frac{D_n}{(1+r)^n}$$

A share of stock's current value can be determined by forecasting future dividends per share and discounting them back to the current value at the required rate of return, r. Absent evidence to the contrary, a company is generally considered to be a going concern with dividend streams that continue into perpetuity.

That a company will continue paying dividends forever may seem an aggressive assumption. However, the further out in time a dividend occurs, the less it is worth in today's dollars. Consider a stock that is expected to pay a dividend of $1 at the end of each of the next 30 years and assume that an investor requires a 10% rate of return. The present value of each dividend is:

Year	Dividend	Present Value
1	1.00	0.9091
2	1.00	0.8264
3	1.00	0.7513
4	1.00	0.6830
5	1.00	0.6209
6	1.00	0.5645
7	1.00	0.5132
8	1.00	0.4665
9	1.00	0.4241
10	1.00	0.3855
11	1.00	0.3505
12	1.00	0.3186
13	1.00	0.2897
14	1.00	0.2633
15	1.00	0.2394
16	1.00	0.2176
17	1.00	0.1978
18	1.00	0.1799
19	1.00	0.1635
20	1.00	0.1486
21	1.00	0.1351

Year	Dividend	Present Value
22	1.00	0.1228
23	1.00	0.1117
24	1.00	0.1015
25	1.00	0.0923
26	1.00	0.0839
27	1.00	0.0763
28	1.00	0.0693
29	1.00	0.0630
30	1.00	0.0573
Total	30.00	9.4269

In present value terms, each subsequent dividend in the table above is worth incrementally less than the previous dividend. By year 30, the $1 dividend is worth less than six cents in today's dollars.

Only 30 years of dividends were presented in this example; forecasting dividends in perpetuity would be inconvenient, to say the least. Fortunately, the process can be simplified for value estimation. If it is assumed that the dividends are constant forever (as they were for 30 years in the table above), the present value of future dividends can be tersely stated as:

$$V_0 = \frac{D}{r}$$

This is the formula for a no-growth dividend discount model. It is based on the formula for a perpetual annuity (or perpetuity) where the dividend does not increase over time. So, if a company is expected to pay a constant $1 dividend forever and an investor requires a 10% return, the company's intrinsic value is $10 ($1 / 0.10). This is a little higher than the table above, where the dividend was only expected for 30 years.

Will the expected intrinsic value of this security be higher next year? Note that since dividends do not change, the expected price next year will remain $10 unless the required rate of return changes. In this case the expected return is based solely on the dividend to be received each year. The dividend yield (dividend divided by price) would be 10% ($1 / $10), the same as the required rate of return.

Example: Mark Mitchell is considering an investment in a regional utility that has paid the same annual dividend for the past 10 years of $1.25 per share. Mark views this investment as relatively low risk, but lacking in growth. Mark determines that he would be happy to receive a return of 8% per year on such investments. Using the no-growth dividend discount model Mark computes an intrinsic value of $15.62 ($1.25 / 0.08). Mark observes that the current market price is $17.50 and concludes that this is not a satisfactory investment since the market price exceeds his computed intrinsic value.

There are few cases (some utilities and preferred stock issues) in which one can expect a constant, eternal stream of dividends. However, the formula's assumptions can be relaxed to permit a dividend that grows at a constant rate, g:

$$V_0 = \frac{D_1}{r - g}$$

This is the formula for a constant growth dividend discount model (also known as the Gordon Growth Model), where D_1 is next year's expected dividend, r is the investor's required rate of return, and g is the rate at which dividends are expected to grow. Another version of this formula starts with this year's dividend rather than next year's expected dividend:

$$V_0 = \frac{D_0(1+g)}{r - g}$$

This formula is mathematically equivalent to the prior formula since next year's dividend is the same as this year's dividend plus one year of growth.

Assume that a company paid a dividend this past year of $1.00 and that the dividend is expected to grow at a constant rate of 5% per year. The required rate of return is 10%. The intrinsic value of this security would be:

$$V_0 = \frac{D_0(1+g)}{r - g} = \frac{1.00(1.05)}{(0.10 - 0.05)} = \$21$$

Note that adding a growth rate of 5% increased the value of the security from $10 in the no-growth case to $21 in the growth case. This is due to the fact that, not only is next year's dividend expected to grow at 5%, but so are all future dividends. By year 30, the expected dividend will be $4.32.

In this case, the expected price of the security will change next year – assuming the required rate of return and expected growth rate do not change. The value at time one (V_1) would be:

$$V_1 = \frac{D_2}{r - g} = \frac{1.1025}{(0.10 - 0.05)} = \$22.05$$

Why is the price expected to increase from $21.00 to $22.05, an increase of 5%? This is a result of the expected growth rate of 5%. Investors in stocks derive two sources of returns, the dividend yield and the expected growth in share price (appreciation). Rewriting the dividend discount model and using the observed market price, rather than intrinsic value, results in:

$$r = \frac{D_1}{P} + g$$

Here r is the expected return, D_1 is next year's expected dividend, P is the current observed market price, and g is the expected growth rate. So, if a security is expected to pay a dividend next year of $2.00, dividends are expected to grow at 6% per year, and the current price is $40, the expected return would be 11% (5% dividend yield plus 6% growth).

Example: Evelyn Garcia is considering an investment in a large manufacturing company that paid dividends last year of $1.95. Evelyn believes that dividends will grow at 4% per year. Evelyn would like to earn an 11% return on this investment. Using the constant growth dividend discount model, Evelyn computes an intrinsic value of $28.97 [($1.95 x (1 + 0.04)) / (0.11 - 0.04)]. Evelyn observes that the current market price is $26 and concludes that this investment meets her criteria. Based on the current market price, Evelyn expects a return of 11.80% [(($1.95 x (1 + 0.04)) / $26) + 0.04].

What if growth is not expected to be constant? The dividend discount model can be extended to permit two (or more) separate growth rates.

Example: Salazar Ventures, Inc. (SVI) paid a dividend last year of $1.00. An investor who requires a return of 10% expects SVI's dividend to grow 10% a year for the next three years. Subsequently, the growth rate is expected to fall to 5% in perpetuity. To apply a two-stage model, first estimate the dividends for the next three years, and compute their present value:[2]

Year	Dividend	Present Value
1	1.10	1.0000
2	1.21	1.0000
3	1.33	1.0000

The total present value of the first three years (stage 1) of dividends is $3.00. The second stage applies the constant growth dividend model to estimate the value of the stock at the end of year 3:

$$V_3 = \frac{D_3(1+g)}{r-g} = \frac{1.33(1.05)}{(0.10-0.05)} = \$27.93$$

The intrinsic value of SVI's stock at the end of year three is expected to be $27.93.

To determine the value today, discount the $27.93 back to the present for three years at the required return of 10%. This results in a present value of $20.98. Adding the second stage result to the $3.00 (present value of dividends) from stage one results in a total value today of $23.98.

Discounted Free Cash Flow Models

What if a company does not pay dividends? Other discounted cash flow models are available, and are often preferred over dividend-based models even when the company pays dividends. One of the most frequently used discounted cash flow models is based on **free cash flow to equity** rather than dividends. Free cash flow to equity (FCFE) is the company's operating cash flow, less capital investments and debt repayments. While this cash flow is available for distribution as dividends, many companies choose to retain it for future use.

FCFE can be viewed as the cash flow that would be available to an entity that acquired control of the subject company. Even shareholders who buy only a few shares of stock have an interest in the value of a firm on a FCFE basis since the potential exists for some other entity to acquire control of the subject company or for the subject company to begin paying dividends at some future date.

A FCFE model is simply a dividend discount model where the dividend is replaced by FCFE per share:

$$V_0 = \frac{FCFE_1}{r-g}$$

The intrinsic value is denoted by V_0, as before. $FCFE_1$ represents next year's forecast of free cash flow to equity. The required rate of return[3] for an equity investment is r and the estimated growth in FCFE is g.

If a company has estimated FCFE of $3.50 per share next year, is expected to grow its FCFE 3% annually, and requires a return of 12%, the intrinsic value using this model would be $38.89. As with the dividend discount model, the FCFE model can be expanded for multiple growth stages as in the example above, by replacing dividends with FCFE per share. This method is frequently used to value acquisitions including closely held businesses.

Free cash flow to the firm (FCFF) is another alternative that is often used in valuing firms in leveraged buyouts or where the new owner plans to change the capital structure of the acquired firm. Free cash flow to the firm is the cash flow available to all capital providers, including debt and equity holders. It is therefore a broader concept. When valuing equity using free cash flow to the firm, the value obtained is that of the overall enterprise (debt plus equity), not just the value of the equity (stock).

Companies that are able to generate free cash flow (whether FCFE or FCFF) are often viewed as attractive takeover candidates. Free cash flow is also often discussed in company press releases as one metric to evaluate how well the company is doing.

Capitalized Earnings

The previous two sections presented models based on discounting some measure of future cash flows. Another approach is to discount earnings rather than cash flows. This method is related to the market multiple (Price/Earnings) approach that is discussed later and is very often used for public companies. The capitalized earnings method is frequently used to evaluate real estate investments (including real estate investment trusts.) In a capitalized earnings approach, some measure of historic earnings is divided by a capitalization rate (encompassing both the required rate of return for risk and expected growth) to obtain intrinsic value:

$$V_0 = \frac{Earnings}{Capitalization\ Rate}$$

The capitalization rate can be determined by subtracting the expected growth rate from a required rate of return that compensates for risk, as in the previous discounted cash flow models. The required rate of return, however, is not the same as that used in discounted cash flow models. Cash flows such as dividends and free cash flow are available to be spent currently, whereas investors may be unable to access earnings (for example, the company may reinvest them in inventory or other assets). Another approach, used frequently in real estate, is to develop a capitalization rate by looking at similar real estate companies/projects and determining their implied capitalization rate.

Example: Bill Grant wants to value a real estate project that had net operating earnings of $100,000 last year. Net operating earnings are defined as revenues minus all operating expenses. Operating expenses exclude income taxes and interest expense. Bill identifies several other real estate projects that sold recently and are similar in size, expected growth and amenities to the subject property:

Property	(1) Net Operating Income	(2) Sales Price	Effective Capitalization Rate (1)/(2)
A	$150,000	$1,875,000	0.080
B	$200,000	$2,350,000	0.085
C	$180,000	$2,000,000	0.090

On average, the subject companies have a capitalization rate of 0.085 or 8.5%. Bill uses this rate to estimate the intrinsic value of his subject property:

$$V_0 = \frac{Earnings}{Capitalization\ Rate} = \frac{\$100,000}{0.085} = \$1,176,471$$

Care must be taken when using a capitalization of earnings approach since earnings are subject to a great deal of management discretion. Earnings may be overstated (or even understated) and result in an inappropriate estimate of value.

MARKET BASED METHODS

A market-based approach to valuation involves estimating the intrinsic value of a security with reference to the value of other similar securities. This is done by comparing the market price, divided by some fundamental value such as earnings for the subject company, to that of similar peer companies. This method is sometimes referred to as a market multiple, price multiple, or

guideline company method. Several market multiples are commonly used for this comparison:

- Price/Earnings
- Price/Free Cash Flow
- Price/Sales
- Dividend/Price (Dividend Yield)

Note that the last one listed is evaluated inversely to the others. Customarily, investors like to think in terms of dividend yields rather than price as a multiple of dividends.

Price/Earnings Approach

A price/earnings ratio (P/E) is a stock's price per share divided by earnings per share. It is a measure of relative value. A P/E ratio of 15 indicates that the price is 15 times the earnings per share of the company. A high P/E ratio relative to other companies indicates that the company is expensive relative to earnings.

What is the appropriate P/E for a company? The P/E ratio is directly related to the dividend discount model presented earlier. Let's revisit the no-growth dividend discount model from earlier:

$$V_0 = \frac{D}{r}$$

First, let's replace intrinsic value, V_0, with the current observed market price, P:

$$P = \frac{D}{r}$$

A no-growth company is one in which earnings are paid out as dividends to shareholders rather than being reinvested in the company (either because the company simply chooses to or has no opportunities for growth). Therefore, for a no-growth company, earnings are equal to dividends and:

$$P = \frac{E}{r}$$

Where P is the price per share, E is the earnings per share and r is the required rate of return. Now dividing both sides by E results in:

$$\frac{P}{E} = \frac{1}{r}$$

In this modification of the dividend discount model, it can be seen that the P/E ratio for a no-growth company should be equal to one divided by the required rate of return. So, a no-growth company having a required rate of return of 10% (r = 0.10) would have a theoretical P/E ratio of 10 (1 / 0.10). This is also known as a justified or warranted P/E. The intrinsic value of a no-growth company can be assessed by multiplying the justified P/E times the earnings per share:

$$V = Justified\ P/E \quad \times \quad Earnings\ Per\ Share$$

Say that the no-growth company with a justified P/E of 10 has earnings per share of $1.20. Its intrinsic value would be $12.00 (10 × $1.20).

Now let's take a look at a theoretical or justified P/E for a growth company. The formula derived from the dividend discount model is:

$$\frac{P}{E} = \frac{Payout\ Ratio\ (1+g)}{r-g}$$

Where P/E is the current price divided by last year's earnings per share, Payout Ratio is the proportion of earnings paid out as dividends (in decimal form), r is the required rate of return based on risk, and g is the expected growth rate.

A company that pays out 40% (0.40) of its earnings as dividends, is expected to grow at 7% (0.07), and has a required return of 10% (0.10), would have a justified P/E of 14.27 [(0.40 × (1 + 0.07)) / (0.10 - 0.07)]. If last year's earnings were $1.50, the intrinsic value would be $21.40 (14.27 × $1.50).

Since the theoretical P/E formulas are derived directly from the dividend discount model, they will provide the same estimate of intrinsic value as the dividend discount model. Nonetheless, the distinct models are useful in understanding which factors influence P/E ratios.

Two critical factors are risk (which impacts r) and expected growth. A company with higher risk than other companies will have a higher required rate of return and therefore should trade at a lower P/E ratio. On the other hand, a company with a higher growth rate should trade at a higher P/E ratio.

A market multiple or guideline valuation approach uses these concepts to assess the relative value of a subject

company. Assume an investor is comparing a company to three similar peer companies (same industry, similar size, etc.). They have the following P/E ratios:

Company	Price	Earnings Per Share	P/E Ratio
Subject	$20.00	$1.00	20
Company X	$36.00	$2.00	18
Company Y	$24.00	$1.50	16
Company Z	$25.20	$1.80	14

Absent any additional information, it appears that the subject company is overvalued since its price relative to earnings is higher than those of the three peer companies. How much overvalued? If it is assumed that the subject company deserves a P/E multiple equal to the median (i.e., middle, which in this case is the same as the average) multiple of the peers (16), then the intrinsic value would be $16.00 ($1.00 × 16) and the stock could be considered overvalued by $4.00 ($20 - $16).

However, perhaps the subject company does not deserve the same multiple as the peer companies. Why could this be true? Even similar companies have different exposure to risk and growth. If the subject company has a higher growth rate than its peers (or lower risk), it might deserve its higher multiple. A commonly used method of assessing P/E ratios relative to growth is to compute a PEG ratio:

$$PEG = \frac{P}{E} \div g$$

Here, expected growth is in percentage form (e.g., g = 100 × 10% = 10). Adding expected growth to the subject and peer companies yields:

Company	P/E Ratio	Expected Growth	PEG Ratio
Subject	20	10%	2.00
Company X	18	9%	2.00
Company Y	16	8%	2.00
Company Z	14	8%	1.75

Adjusting for growth, it can be seen that the subject company has the same P/E relative to growth as companies X and Y. It would appear that its higher P/E is justified by its higher growth expectations. Company Z appears to be the best value in terms of price relative to earnings and growth.

Care must be taken when using the PEG ratio for several reasons. Expected growth is normally only available for short periods of time (five years). Companies that have a lower but more persistent growth rate may be penalized by the model. Also the PEG formula assumes a linear relationship between growth and P/E ratios, which is not strictly correct. Lastly, the PEG ratio does not consider differences in risk between the companies, which is another major factor in justified P/E ratios.

P/E ratios in general are further limited in that earnings can be subject to differences between companies due to accounting methods and other non-operating reasons that can make companies non-comparable. Ideally, peer companies should be in the same industry, of similar size, and use similar accounting methods. Above all, it is *imperative* to remember that any estimate of future growth is just that—an estimate. No one, even experienced Wall Street analysts can predict the future with certainty.

P/E ratios are not only useful in evaluating companies, but are useful in evaluating the holdings of mutual funds. One metric used to evaluate equity mutual funds is the average (or median) P/E ratio of the underlying stocks.

P/E ratios can also be viewed in an inverse format as E/P. E/P is known as the earnings yield. A company with a P/E of 20 would have an earnings yield of 5%. This is an alternative view of value. Companies with high P/E ratios have low earnings yields and companies with low P/E ratios have high earnings yields.

Price/Free Cash Flow Approach

Another market multiple that can be used to assess intrinsic value is the Price/Free Cash Flow or P/FCFE ratio. A theoretical P/FCFE model can be derived as:

$$\frac{P}{FCFE} = \frac{1+g}{r-g}$$

Where FCFE is free cash flow to equity for the last year. A company with a required return of 10% and growth rate of 5% would have a justified P/FCFE ratio of 21. Practically speaking, a P/FCFE approach involves comparison of a subject company's ratio to those of similar companies to determine if it appears properly valued. As with the P/E ratios, differences may be justified by differences in risk and growth.

Price/Sales Approach

Price to sales (P/S) is yet another multiple that can be used for a relative valuation. A theoretical P/S ratio is:

$$\frac{P}{S} = \frac{Profit\ Margin \times Payout\ Ratio \times (1+g)}{r-g}$$

Profit margin is a company's earnings divided by sales, payout ratio is the portion of earnings paid out as dividends, g is the expected growth rate, and r is the required rate of return. The practical application is the same as with the P/E ratio where the P/S ratio is compared to those of peer companies.

Dividend Yield Approach

Another valuation metric utilizes price per share and dividends. While a dividend multiple (P/D) could be computed, it is more traditional to express relative dividend valuation in terms of dividend yield (D/P). Companies with high dividend yields would indicate a good value (low price relative to dividends). Some investors have a preference for investing in stocks with high dividend yields, especially in light of favorable tax treatment in recent years. Companies with low dividend yields (or zero) are likely to be growth oriented companies that choose to reinvest cash flow in the business. Other investors often favor growth stocks and prefer to defer receipt (and taxation) of income.

ASSET BASED METHODS

A less frequently used approach is to assess the value of a company based on the book value of its assets. Book value is the amount reported on the company's financial statements. A balance sheet shows the assets a company owns and the claims against those assets.

Alpha Beta, Inc.
Balance Sheet
As of December 31, 2006

Cash		$ 500,000
Equipment		2,000,000
Total Assets		$2,500,000
Liabilities		$1,000,000
Stockholders Equity	1,500,000	
Total Liabilities		
And Equity		$2,500,000

Book value (assets minus liabilities) for this firm is $1,500,000. This is also known as stockholders equity – the amount that stockholders have invested over time in the company. If the company has 50,000 total shares outstanding (owned by stockholders), book value per share is $30 ($1,500,000 / 50,000). Most companies sell for more than their book value for a couple of reasons; many of the assets are reported on the balance sheet based at what the company paid for them, which may not reflect their current value. Additionally, most companies are more valuable as a going concern than the sum of their assets minus liabilities. If the value of assets can be determined, the book value can be adjusted. Alternatively, the book value per share can be used to compute a price to book value ratio (P/B) and a relative valuation can be performed as in the market approach presented in the previous section.

WHERE CAN I FIND OUT MORE ABOUT IT?

1. John Stowe, Thomas Robinson, Jerald Pinto, and Dennis McLeavey, *Analysis of Equity Investments: Valuation* (Association for Investment Management and Research, 2002).

2. Shannon P. Pratt, *Valuing a Business*, 4th Edition (New York, NY: McGraw Hill, 2000).

3. Z. Christopher Mercer, "Adjusting Capitalization Rates for the Differences Between Net Income and Net Free Cash Flow," *Business Valuation Review* (December 1992, Vol. 11, No. 4, 201-207).

QUESTIONS AND ANSWERS

Question – What is the difference between a stock's price (market value), intrinsic value, and book value?

Answer – A stock's market value is the observed price trading on the stock market. The intrinsic value is the perceived or underlying value of the stock determined by using a valuation method. Book value is simply the difference between a company's assets and liabilities without regard to its value as an ongoing business.

Question – What are the factors that determine value in a dividend discount model?

Answer – The three factors used to determine intrinsic value in a dividend discount model are the expected dividend, the required return, and expected growth.

Question – What factors impact a company's P/E ratio?

Answer – A P/E ratio is primarily influenced by risk and growth. Higher (lower) risk relative to other compa-

nies should result in a lower (higher) P/E ratio. Higher (lower) expected growth relative to other companies should result in a higher (lower) P/E ratio.

Question – If the information in the table is correct and using the constant growth dividend discount model, what rate of return (r) does the market expect (require) for Verizon? Based on this information what would Verizon's justified P/E multiple be?

Answer – The following information relates to shares of telecom services provider Verizon, Inc. as of July 13, 2006:

Annual dividend (last twelve months)	$1.62
Earnings (last twelve months)	$2.57
Payout ratio (5-year average)	63%
Share price	$31.60
Estimated 5-year growth rate	2.9%

The expected return (r) would equal next year's expected dividend (D_1), divided by the price (P), plus the expected long term growth rate (g): 8.18% $[(1.62 \times (1 + 0.029)) / 31.60) + 0.029]$.

The justified P/E multiple is found by multiplying the payout ratio by one plus the growth rate (g), then dividing the total by the difference between the required return (r) and the growth rate (g): 12.27 $[((0.63 \times (1 + 0.029)) / (0.0818 - 0.029)]$.

Question – Verizon's closest peer company is AT&T, which has a trailing P/E multiple of 17.5 and a payout ratio of 85%. Assuming both will have similar growth rates, what does this say about the market's beliefs for AT&T relative to Verizon (refer to last question)?

Answer – An important factor for P/E ratios, besides growth, is relative risk. If the market is awarding AT&T a higher P/E ratio than Verizon and they have similar growth prospects, it may view AT&T as less risky.

CHAPTER ENDNOTES

1. How much greater? By making V_0=$9 and solving for r, an investor would obtain an expected return of 14.33%. This is known as an internal rate of return, which makes the present value of the future cash flows equal to the initial investment. See Chapter 33, "Measuring Investment Return."

2. Forecasted dividends are rounded to two decimal places.

3. Methods of assessing an appropriate required return on equity are presented in Chapter 36, "Asset Pricing Models."

Chapter 36

ASSET PRICING MODELS

WHAT ARE THEY?

Chapter 35, "Securities Valuation," presented techniques for valuing equity securities (stocks). A key factor in valuing securities is a required rate of return. This chapter presents asset pricing models that help determine the appropriate required rate of return for equity securities. Additionally, this chapter presents valuation models for valuing stock options. Stock options are a type of derivative; a security whose value is derived from equity securities.

PORTFOLIO THEORY AND ASSET PRICING MODELS

Modern portfolio theory suggests that the rate of return required on a security must compensate investors for the risk involved. The theory began with the pioneering work of Harry Markowitz in the 1950s and basically states that given the choice between multiple assets (or portfolios) with equal expected returns, investors prefer the asset (or portfolio) with the lowest risk. Similarly, given the choice between multiple assets (or portfolios) of equal perceived risk, investors prefer the asset (or portfolio) with the highest expected return.

Markowitz Portfolio Theory

Markowitz believed investors expect returns on an asset approximating that asset's average (mean) returns. He defined risk as the variability (standard deviation) of returns. Using these concepts, investors can graph all available portfolios to examine the relationship between risk and return as depicted in Figure 36.1.

The area on and under the curve in Figure 36.1 represents all available portfolios. The curve from point A to point D is called the efficient frontier, and it includes those portfolios with the highest return for a particular level of risk.

Portfolios falling below the efficient frontier are considered inefficient. For example, portfolio E in Figure 36.1 would not be an optimal choice for investors. Portfolio B offers investors the same return as portfolio

Figure 36.1

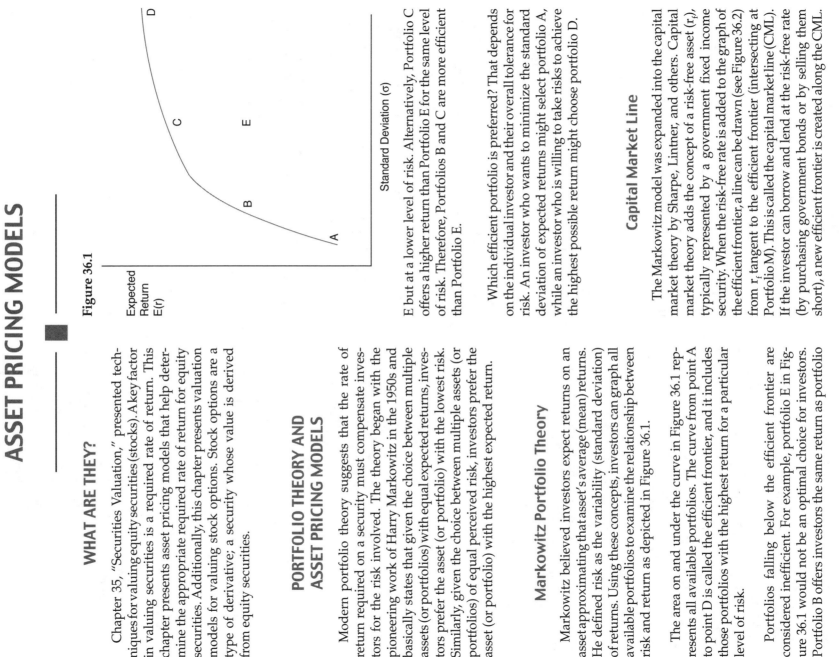

E but at a lower level of risk. Alternatively, Portfolio C offers a higher return than Portfolio E for the same level of risk. Therefore, Portfolios B and C are more efficient than Portfolio E.

Which efficient portfolio is preferred? That depends on the individual investor and their overall tolerance for risk. An investor who wants to minimize the standard deviation of expected returns might select portfolio A, while an investor who is willing to take risks to achieve the highest possible return might choose portfolio D.

Capital Market Line

The Markowitz model was expanded into the capital market theory by Sharpe, Lintner, and others. Capital market theory adds the concept of a risk-free asset (r_f), typically represented by a government fixed income security. When the risk-free rate is added to the graph of the efficient frontier, a line can be drawn (see Figure 36.2) from r_f tangent to the efficient frontier (intersecting at Portfolio M). This is called the capital market line (CML). If the investor can borrow and lend at the risk-free rate (by purchasing government bonds or by selling them short), a new efficient frontier is created along the CML.

Figure 36.2

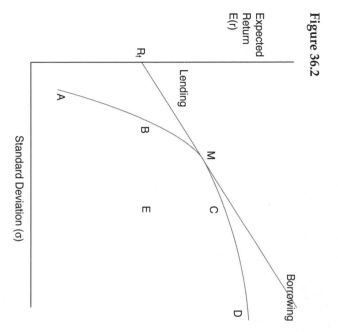

Expected
Return
E(r)

R_f

Lending

M

C

Borrowing

D

A

B

E

Standard Deviation (σ)

Portfolio M represents the market-weighted portfolio of all investable assets (the market portfolio).

An investor wholly invested in the market portfolio could expect the same risk and return as the market portfolio. Investors who put less than 100% in the market portfolio and place the remainder in the risk-free asset (a government security) would have a portfolio with less expected return and risk than the market portfolio.

Investors willing to accept more risk can borrow at the risk-free rate and invest more than 100% (their own money plus the borrowed money) of their assets in the market portfolio. Such a portfolio would have a higher expected return, but higher expected risk than the market portfolio. The expected return from a portfolio can be measured as:

Equation 36-1

$$E(r_p) = r_f + \sigma_p \left[\frac{r_m - r_f}{\sigma_m} \right]$$

where: $E(r_p)$ represents a portfolio's expected return

r_m is the expected return of the market portfolio

The expected return for a portfolio is therefore the risk-free rate plus a premium for the risk of the portfolio, based upon the market risk premium $(r_m - r_f)$ and the risk of the portfolio relative to the risk of the market (as captured by the standard deviations of each). A portfolio with the same risk as the market portfolio would have an expected return equal to that of the market portfolio.

Capital Asset Pricing Model

The capital market line can be applied to individual equity securities by using Beta as a measure of risk instead of standard deviation. Beta measures the risk of an individual security relative to the market. It is determined by running a regression of a security's return against returns on a market index (such as the Standard and Poor's 500). A Beta of 1.0 means the security exhibited the same level of risk as the index over the period measured. A Beta greater (less) than 1.0 indicates higher (lower) risk than the index. Figure 36.3 depicts the security market line, which represents the relationship between expected return and risk measured by Beta.

Figure 36.3

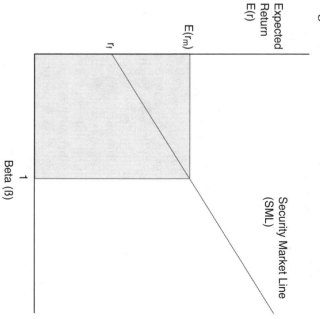

Expected
Return
E(r)

E(r_m)

r_f

Security Market Line
(SML)

1

Beta (β)

The capital asset pricing model (CAPM) states that the expected return on an individual asset (E(r_i)) should be the risk-free rate plus a premium for risk, determined as:

Equation 36-2

$$E(r_i) = r_f + \beta_i (r_m - r_f)$$

The risk premium for an individual security is based on the security's Beta and the overall equity market risk premium $(r_m - r_f)$. Expected market and risk free returns are a matter of judgment. They are often based on historical market returns combined with current market conditions.

Example 1: Cornerstone Electronics, Inc. (CEI) has a Beta of 1.3. Assume that the expected return on the market is 12% and the expected risk-free rate is 4%. Under the CAPM, investors should require a return of:

$$4\% + 1.3\ (12\% - 4\%) = 14.4\%.$$

As one would expect, CEI's higher risk results in a required return higher than that of the market. This required rate of return could then be used to assess the value of the equity using models such as the dividend discount model presented in Chapter 35. Assuming that CEI has an expected growth rate of 6% per year and a current dividend of $2.00, its value under a constant dividend growth model would be:

$$V_0 = \frac{D_0\ (1+g)}{r - g} = \frac{2.00\ (1.06)}{(0.144 - 0.06)} = \$25.24$$

The capital asset pricing model assumes that investors own diversified portfolios. As such, it only accounts for the impact of systematic risk; that is the risk that is common to all market securities and cannot be mitigated by holding diverse securities. Beta captures the relative sensitivity of a particular security to this overall market risk. The CAPM does not consider non-systematic risk, also known as unique risk or diversifiable risk. In a well-diversified portfolio, non-systematic risks of individual securities should offset each other. For example, one stock in the portfolio could be affected by a loss of market share to a major competitor whose stock gains as a result of the change in market share. Since the diversified portfolio owns both, the two offset each other. If a portfolio is not well diversified, the required rate of return computed under the CAPM may not capture all of the risks in that portfolio.

The capital asset pricing model can help estimate the appropriate rate of return for valuing a security. But it should be viewed primarily as a starting point. Why? The CAPM relies on a number of assumptions, and research into the CAPM's ability to explain observed returns has been mixed. An investor should consider whether the required return computed under the CAPM makes sense and satisfies the investor's requirement for return commensurate with the risk of the investment.

The CAPM, in particular the SML, can also be useful in selecting securities for inclusion in a portfolio as is demonstrated in Chapter 38.

Arbitrage Pricing Theory

The capital asset pricing model captures risk in a single factor, the variability of returns relative to a market index (market risk). Arbitrage pricing theory (APT), developed by Stephen A. Ross, introduces multiple risk factors into the assessment of expected returns. Each of the factors can capture different aspects of risk. Unlike the CAPM, the individual factors that influence risk and expected return are not pre-specified. A generic form of an APT model can be specified as:

Equation 31-3

$$E\ (r_i) = a + b_{i1}\ F_1 + b_{i2}\ F_2 + b_{i3}\ F_3 + \ldots + b_{in}\ F_n + \varepsilon$$

Where a is some constant term (such as the risk-free rate), and b_{in} represents the sensitivity of a security to a particular risk factor, F_n.[1]

Investment advisors and analysts can develop their own risk factors for use in an APT model or use those developed in research and practice by others. Burmeister, Roll, and Ross created a model with the following five individual factors, F:[2]

- F_1 Confidence Risk – Unexpected changes in investor's confidence about risk taking, measured as the differential in corporate versus government bond yields.

- F_2 Time Horizon Risk – Unexpected changes in an investors' preference for short versus long-term investments.

- F_3 Inflation Risk – Unexpected changes in inflation.

- F_4 Business Cycle Risk – Unexpected changes in real business activity.

- F_5 Market-Timing Risk – The market return not explained by the other four factors – commonly thought of as market risk, as in the CAPM.

In this model, the constant is represented by the short-term (30 day) Treasury bill rate. Each of the individual risk factors must be measured periodically, as must an individual security's (i) sensitivity to each factor.

Example 2: Dot Murphy, investment advisor, is assessing the expected return for Alpha Enterprises (AE), a large diversified conglomerate. Dot has computed the following coefficients and risk factor components for AE:

Tools & Techniques of Investment Planning

Risk Factor	AE's Coefficient	Price of Risk (F)
Confidence Risk	0.60	2.50%
Time Horizon Risk	0.50	-0.70%
Inflation Risk	-0.40	-4.00%
Business Cycle Risk	1.50	1.50%
Market-Timing Risk	1.10	3.50%

The current Treasury bill rate is 3.0%. Dot computes the expected return on AE as:

$$3.0\% + 0.60 \times 2.50\% + 0.50 \times (-0.70\%) - 0.40 \times (-4.0\%) + 1.5 \times 1.5\% + 1.10 \times 3.50\% = 11.85\%$$

Option Pricing Models

Options are contracts involving the future trade of an underlying asset. In an options contract, only one party is obligated to complete the transaction but must do so only if the other party exercises the option. An option gives the holder (buyer of the option) the right, but not the obligation, to buy the underlying asset (a call option) or sell it (a put option) at a specified price for a given period of time.

The writer (seller of the option) collects a fee for selling the option and must fulfill their side of the contract if the option is exercised. Chapter 35 showed valuation methods for shares of stock. This discussion will demonstrate valuation models for stock options when the current value of the underlying stock is known.

- *Strike Price* – The strike price, also known as the exercise price, is the price at which the holder of the option can buy (or sell) the underlying asset. Usually, there are standardized options contracts with several standardized strike prices available above and below the current market price. If the market price moves above or below this range, new options series are added.

- *Expiration Date* – Standardized equity options cease trading on the third Friday of the indicated expiration month and expire the next day (Saturday.) Further, options are generally available for the two near term months plus two additional months, depending upon the security's designated quarterly cycle.

  Most options traded in the U.S. are American style options, which can be exercised any time on or before the expiration date. By contrast, European style options can only be exercised on the expiration date.

- *Underlying Security* – This is the underlying asset on which the value of the option depends. For standardized equity options, one contract generally represents 100 shares of common stock or American Depository Receipts.

OPTIONS PRICING FUNDAMENTALS

Call Options Pricing

The option seller (writer) charges a fee (premium) to the option purchaser. How is the option premium determined? It is determined by the market, based upon the prospects for the underlying security and the terms of the option. Option value can be broken into two parts: intrinsic value and time value. The option's intrinsic value is the amount by which the current market price

Table 36-1 summarizes the rights and obligations to the parties in an options contract.

Options can be negotiated between two parties, though standardized options are traded on organized exchanges. Option values are determined by several important characteristics: the strike price, the expiration date, and the underlying security.

Table 36-1

	Option Writer (Seller)	Option Holder (Buyer)
Call Option	Must sell the underlying security at the agreed upon price if the option is exercised	May purchase underlying security at agreed upon price if doing so is advantageous
Put Option	Must buy the underlying security at the agreed upon price if the option is exercised	May sell underlying security at agreed upon price if doing so

Table 36-2

XYZ Call Option Premium

Expiration Month	Strike Price					
	100	105	110	115	120	125
July	14.30	11.20	5.50	2.55	1.00	.30
August	14.90	11.50	7.50	4.70	2.50	1.25
October	19.00	13.00	11.70	8.70	5.80	3.80
January	21.60	19.00	13.90	11.60	9.50	7.00

exceeds (in the case of a call option) or falls short of (in the case of a put option) the strike price. Table 36-2 presents some hypothetical American style options prices in early July for XYZ Computers, assuming the current market price is $113.

At a current price of $113, a call option on XYZ with a $100 strike price has an intrinsic value of $13 per share (current market price of $113 less strike price of $100).[3] This is the intrinsic value regardless of the time to expiration. An option that has intrinsic value is known as being "in the money," and the intrinsic value will vary based on the strike price. Table 36-3 presents intrinsic values by strike price for the July XYZ call options.

Table 36-3

Strike Price	Intrinsic Value
100	13.00
105	8.00
110	3.00
115	None
120	None
125	None

Note that strike prices above $113 have no intrinsic value.

The difference between the current option price (premium) and the intrinsic value represents the time value. For the July 100 option, the intrinsic value is $13.00 and the time value is $1.30 ($14.30 – $13.00) (see Table 36-2).

The time value of the option reflects the fact that the underlying price of the security can change before the expiration of the contract. Note that the longer the time to expiration, the higher is the time value. All of the options with a strike price of $100 have an intrinsic value of $13.00. The time values of the options with a strike price of $100 are presented in Table 36-4.

Table 36-4

Expiration Month	Time Value
July	$1.30
August	$1.90
October	$6.00
January	$8.60

The longer the time until expiration, the greater is the likelihood that the option will confer additional value to the holder prior to expiration. Over time, the option's time value will be reduced to zero (known as decaying), and the option value should equal intrinsic value at expiration.

For the call options with a strike price of $125, the intrinsic value is zero. This makes sense because the option holder has the right to buy the underlying security for $125 when it is only worth $113. Therefore the premium for a call option with a strike price above the current stock price is comprised entirely of time value.

Such call options are referred to as "out of the money." Call options with a strike price below the current market price of the underlying security are known as "in the money." Call options with a strike price equal to the current market price are known as "at the money."

While determining the intrinsic value is relatively straightforward, it is difficult to determine what the time value, and hence, total value of the option should be. While an investor can observe the current market prices of the options contracts, the value could be higher or lower. Fortunately, options-pricing models, such as the binomial model and the Black-Scholes model, exist to help us understand what the intrinsic value of an option should be.

The Binomial Model

For simplicity, let's assume that an investor wants to value a European style option; one which can only be exercised at expiration. In order to assess the value of a European stock option today, expectations about

Tools & Techniques of Investment Planning

future prices for the underlying security must be developed. In a binomial model, it is assumed that in the next period (which could be a day, week, month, or year) there are only two outcomes; the underlying stock price goes up by X% or goes down by Y%. The X and Y percentages are the investor's expectations for a particular security. Assume a call option on an underlying security where:

- Current market price of the underlying security is $30 (denoted as S_0).

- Strike price is $30 (denoted as K).

- Time to maturity is 1 year (Denoted as T).

- In one year, the stock price is expected to either increase by 10.25% or decrease by 4.938%.

- The risk free rate of interest is 5.063%.

In one year, it is expected that the stock price (S_1) will be either $33.08 or $28.52, depicted in Figure 36.4.

Figure 36.4

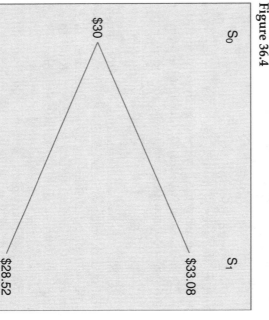

S_0 S_1

$30

$33.08

$28.52

The value of the option at expiration will be the intrinsic value; the excess value of the underlying security over the strike price (there is no remaining time value, and the option cannot be worth less than zero). Therefore, if the price of the underlying security increases to $33.08, the option will be worth $3.08 at expiration. Conversely, if the price of the underlying security falls to $28.52, the option will expire worthless. The expected future value of the call option, C_1, is depicted in Figure 36.5.

In the binomial options pricing model, the current value of an option is the present value of the weighted average of the future call values:

Figure 36.5

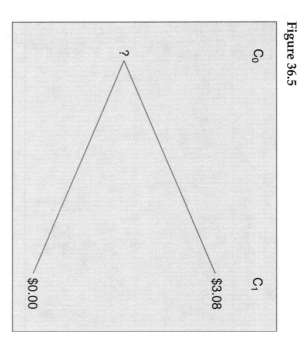

C_0 C_1

?

$3.08

$0.00

Equation 36.4

$$C_0 = \frac{\pi \left(C_1^+\right) + (1 - \pi)\left(C_1^-\right)}{(1 + r)}$$

The risk free rate, r, is the rate for the single period over which the option values are being discounted, and π is the weighting factor. The weighting factor is based upon the potential increase and decrease in the price of the underlying security:

Equation 36.5

$$\pi = \frac{(1 + r) - d}{u - d}$$

The potential downside is represented by d, which is one minus the downside percentage (Y%) in decimal form. For the example, the potential downside is 4.938% or 0.04938, so d is 0.95062. The potential upside is represented by u, which is one plus the upside percentage (X%) in decimal form. For the example, the potential upside is 10.25% or 0.1025, so u is 1.1025. Computing π results in:

$$\pi = \frac{(1 + r) - d}{u - d} = \frac{(1.05063 - 0.95062)}{(1.1025 - 0.95062)} = 0.65848$$

The intrinsic value of the call option today should therefore be:

$$C_0 = \pi \left(C_1^+\right) + (1 - \pi)\left(C_1^-\right) = $$

$$\frac{0.65848\,(3.08) + 0.34152\,(0.00)}{1.05063} = \$1.93$$

Chapter 36 – Asset Pricing Models

Figure 36.6 presents the completed call option diagram, known as a binomial tree.

Figure 36.6

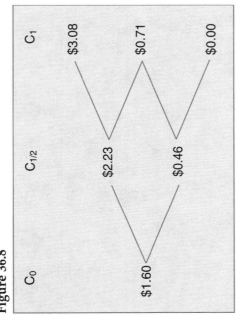

maturity is determined at the far right of the binomial tree. Then each sub-period option value is determined working right to left until the current option value is determined. The resulting binomial option tree is presented in Figure 36.8.

Figure 36.8

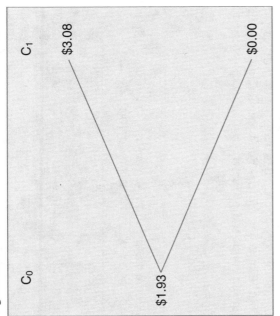

This one-period binomial model is obviously a simplistic version of reality, assuming only two outcomes. The model can be improved and result in better estimates of intrinsic value by breaking the single period into sub-periods. For example, if the one-year period is divided into two six-month periods, a price tree for the underlying stock can be obtained as depicted in Figure 36.7, assuming prices increase by 5% or decrease by 2.5% during each six-month period. Note that this is equivalent to an annual increase of 10.25% and decrease of 4.938%.

Figure 36.7

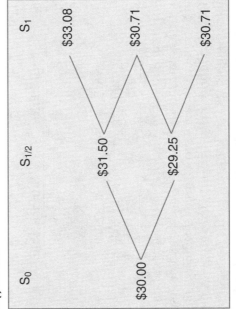

The end result is an option value today of $1.60 versus $1.93 obtained in the single period model. This new value is a better one to use. The more periods that are used in the model, the better the estimate of value is.

Although this demonstration was for a European style option, it can easily be extended for an American style option. The only difference is that an American style option can be exercised during any of the sub-periods. Therefore, the computed option value must be compared to the intrinsic value at each node. If the intrinsic value exceeds the computed value, the intrinsic value is used instead. For example, the computed value of $2.23 in the first sub-period is compared to the intrinsic value of $1.50. In this case, the computed value is greater, and there is no need for an adjustment.

Black–Scholes Model

The binary option pricing model assumes two outcomes and discrete time periods. A mathematical extension of this process to a continuous time period with a wider distribution of outcomes is obtained with the Black-Scholes option pricing model. While mathematically complex, the latter model is useful to examine what factors influence option value. Without going into the details of how it was derived, Fischer Black, Myron Scholes, and Robert Merton developed a formula for pricing call options (Scholes and Merton subsequently won the Nobel Prize in Economics for this work). The theoretical options price is:

There are now three possible ending values. As the number of sub-periods increases, the number of potential ending values increases as well. The process for determining the value of the call option at time 0 (today) is the same as before. First, the intrinsic value at

Tools & Techniques of Investment Planning

Chapter 36 – Asset Pricing Models

Table 36-5

Expiration Month			XYZ Put Option Premium			
	Strike Price					
	100	105	110	115	120	125
July	0.55	1.10	2.25	4.50	8.00	9.50
August	1.60	2.55	4.10	6.20	9.00	12.00
October	3.60	4.70	5.90	8.70	11.60	13.10
January	5.50	7.30	9.20	11.00	13.60	15.50

Equation 36-6

$$C = S \times [N(d_1)] - K \times (e^{-rt}) \times [N(d_2)]$$

$$d_1 = \frac{\ln(S/K) + (r + 0.5 \times \sigma^2) \times t}{\sigma \times \sqrt{t}}$$

$$d_2 = d_1 - (\sigma \times \sqrt{t})$$

Here, S is the current stock price, $N(d_1)$ and $N(d_2)$ represent cumulative probability distributions, K is the option strike price, r is the risk free rate of return, t is the fraction of the year remaining until expiration and σ is the standard deviation of the annual rate of return on the underlying security.

Note that earlier the intrinsic value of a call option was defined as the stock price (S in the formula above) minus the strike price (K in the formula above) but not less than zero. The two components in the Black Scholes formula above are similar, but reflect the theoretical total value of the call option (intrinsic value plus time value). The probability distributions are statistical concepts that consider the range of potential outcomes.

From that model, several things can be derived about the value of the option as it relates to different factors:

- As the value of the underlying stock increases, so does the value of the call option.

- As the time to expiration increases, so does the value of the option.

- As the volatility of the underlying stock increases, so does the value of the option.

- As the strike price increases, the value of the call option decreases.

- As the risk free rate of return increases, the value of the call option increases.

The Black-Scholes formula is based on a European style option and is best used in valuing those types of options.

Put Option Pricing

As noted earlier, the holder of a put option has the right to sell the underlying security at a certain price. Selected put options for a hypothetical XYZ Computers as of early July are presented in Table 36-5.

Intrinsic value for a put option only exists where the strike price exceeds the current market price, and it is measured as the strike price less the current market price (K-S, but not below zero) (see Table 36-6). For the options with a strike price of $120, there would be an intrinsic value of $7 ($120 - $113). With a current price of $113, the options with strike prices of $100, $105, and $110 would have no intrinsic value. The holder of the option would not want to exercise his right to sell something at a price lower than the current market price. The intrinsic value for each strike price is shown in Table 36-6.

Table 36-6

Strike Price	Intrinsic Value
100	None
105	None
110	None
115	$2.00
120	$7.00
125	$12.00

Put options with a strike price below the current market price of the underlying security are referred to as "out of the money." They have no intrinsic value. Put options with a strike price above the current market price of the underlying security are known as "in the money." Put options with a strike price equal to the current market price are known as "at the money."

The time value equals the difference between the current option price (premium) and the intrinsic value. For example, an $8.00 option price minus a $7.00 intrinsic value equals a time value of $1.00 for options above with a strike price of $120 and an expiration month of July. As with a call option, a longer time to maturity equates to greater time value. The observed time values for a strike price of $120 are summarized in Table 36-7.

Table 36-7

Expiration Month	Time Value
July	$1.00
August	$2.00
October	$4.60
January	$6.60

There are several methods available to determine the value of a put option, including variations of the binomial and Black-Scholes models. They can also be valued with reference to the value of call options.

The binomial pricing model for put options is applied in the same manner as for call options (see above). The intrinsic value is determined at maturity based on the excess of the strike price over the value of the underlying security. The put value at each node is computed based on the weighted average of the values for the put option in the upside and downside cases.

The formula for the value of a European put option under the Black-Scholes option pricing model (see above) is:

Equation 36-7

$$P = K\,(e^{-rt})\,[1 - N(d_2)] - S\,[1 - N(d_1)]$$

Intuitively, this is the excess of the strike price over the current stock price, adjusting for the time value of money and a normal distribution of outcomes.

Put options can also be theoretically valued using a concept known as Put-Call Parity. Put-Call Parity is derived from the assumption that puts and calls should be priced relative to the underlying security such that no arbitrage opportunity exists. Theoretically, purchasing a stock and a put option should be an equivalent position to holding cash equal to the exercise price and purchasing a call option (where the put and call options have the same exercise price):

$$S + P = \frac{K}{e^{rt}} + C$$

Here, S is the security's current market price, P is the price of a put option, K is the exercise price (which is being discounted using the risk fee rate) and C is the call price.

Using the example above, if an investor purchases XYZ stock for $113 and a July 110 put option, the investor will profit if the price of IBM rises but is protected with the put option on the downside (if the price falls below $110, the investor will exercise the option and sell for $110). No matter what happens, the investor is ensured of having a value of $110 at expiration. Note that the total investment is $115.25 ($113 plus $2.25).

The investor would be in a similar position if the investor took the present value of the exercise price (PV of $110 over about two weeks at 5% would be about $109.75), invested it at the risk free rate of interest until option expiration and simultaneously purchased a July 110 call option for $5.50. If the underlying security rises in value, the call price will rise accordingly. If the price falls and the call option expires worthless, the investor will be left with $110. Note that the total investment is $115.25 ($109.75 plus $5.50). Therefore Put-Call parity holds for this example.

This is not always the case for real data due to bid-ask spreads and the timing of the quotations. Rearranging the above equation, the theoretical price for a put option is:

$$P = \frac{K}{e^{rt}} + C - S$$

Holding a put option is equivalent to investing the present value of the strike price, purchasing a call option and selling the stock short.

WHERE CAN I FIND OUT MORE ABOUT IT?

1. John Stowe, Thomas Robinson, Jerald Pinto, and Dennis McLeavey, *Analysis of Equity Investments: Valuation* (Association for Investment Management and Research, 2002).

2. *A Practitioner's Guide to Factor Models*, The Research Foundation of The Institute of Chartered Financial Analysts, Association for Investment Management and Research.

3. Harry Markowitz, "Portfolio Selection," *Journal of Finance*, 7, No. 1, March 1952.

3. William F. Sharpe, "Capital Asset Prices: A Theory of Market Equilibrium under Conditions of Risk," *Journal of Finance*, 19, No. 3, September 1964, pp. 425-442.

4. John Lintner, "Security Prices, Risk and Maximal Gains from Diversification," *Journal of Finance*, 20, No. 4, December 1965, pp. 587-615.

5. Stephen Ross, "The Arbitrage Theory of Capital Asset Pricing," *Journal of Economic Theory*, 13, No. 2, December 1976, pp. 341-360.

6. Don M. Chance, *Analysis of Derivatives for the CFA Program* (Charlottesville, VA: Association for Investment Management and Research, 2003).

7. Lawrence G. McMillan, *Options as a Strategic Investment*, 4th Edition (New York, NY: New York Institute of Finance, 2002).

QUESTIONS AND ANSWERS

Question – Under what conditions would an investor choose a portfolio that lies below the efficient frontier?

Answer – None. For any portfolio below the efficient frontier, alternative portfolios are available offering higher returns, lower risk or both.

Question – Given a stock with the following characteristics, use the CAPM and a constant growth dividend discount model to estimate the value of the stock:

Annual dividend per share	$1.00
Expected growth rate	4%
Risk-free rate	5%
Expected market return	11%
Beta	1.5

Answer –

$$E_r = r_f + B(r_m - r_f) = 0.05 + 1.5(0.11 - 0.05) = 0.14 = 14\%$$

$$V_0 = \frac{D_0(1+g)}{r-g} = \frac{1.00(1.04)}{(0.14-0.04)} = \frac{1.04}{0.10} = \$10.40$$

Question – On July 14, 2006, DELL was trading at $21.82 per share and the option prices below were observed. Why is the July $20.00 put priced so cheaply?

Expiration	Strike	Call	Put
July 06	20.00	1.85	0.05
July 06	22.50	0.15	0.85
July 06	25.00	0.05	3.20
August 06	20.00	2.40	0.40
August 06	22.50	0.80	1.45
August 06	25.00	0.20	3.40

Answer – Because on July 14, 2005 there was only one week to expiration and the option was out of the money. The stock would have to fall more than 8.6% to below 19.95 in that week for the option to have value at expiration.

Question – Which of the options for Dell, above, has the greatest time value?

Answer – The total value of an option is comprised of intrinsic value and time value. Time value is the total value less the intrinsic value. For a call option the intrinsic value is the greater of zero and the stock price minus the exercise price. So the intrinsic values for the call options are zero ($22.50 and $25.00 strike) and 1.82 ($20.00 strike). The highest time value for a call is $0.80 for the August $22.50's. For the puts, the intrinsic value is the greater of zero and the exercise price less the stock price. The 20's have no intrinsic value, the $22.50's have $0.68 intrinsic value and the $25.00's have $3.18. The greatest time value is again for the August $22.50's, for which it is $0.77. This also exceeds the highest call option time value and is thus the highest overall.

Question – On the same date, Microsoft traded at $22.36 and the prices below were observed for Microsoft options. Although the prices of both stocks (Dell and Microsoft) were closest to the $22.50 stock price, it was cheaper to buy options on Microsoft than on DELL for that exercise price. This phenomenon was true of both the call and put options. Why?

Expiration	Strike	Call	Put
August 06	20.00	2.50	0.10
August 06	22.50	0.65	0.75
August 06	25.00	0.10	2.65

Answer – From the Black-Scholes model, it can be seen that:

• As the value of the underlying stock increases, so does the value of the call option. Microsoft had a higher stock price, so this cannot be the explanation.

• As the time to expiration increases, so does the value of the option. They both have the same time to expiration, so this cannot be the explanation.

• As the strike price increases, the value of the call option decreases. They both have the same strike price, so this is not the explanation.

- As the risk free rate of return increases, the value of the call option increases. The risk-free rate is the same for both securities, so this is not the explanation.

- As the volatility of the underlying stock increases, so does the value of the option. DELL must be a more volatile stock than Microsoft.

CHAPTER ENDNOTES

1. Note, small b is used for the coefficients here to distinguish them from Beta in the CAPM. Essentially, these small b's represent individual Beta coefficients for each risk Factor.

2. Edwin Burmeister, Richard Roll and Stephen A. Ross, "A Practitioners' Guide to Arbitrage Pricing Theory," in *A Practitioner's Guide to Factor Models*, The Research Foundation of The Institute of Chartered Financial Analysts (Association for Investment Management and Research).

3. Since each options contract denotes 100 shares, the contract has an intrinsic value of $1,300.

Chapter 37

PORTFOLIO MANAGEMENT AND MEASUREMENT

WHAT IS IT?

Previous chapters presented tools and techniques to evaluate specific types of investments such as common stocks, corporate bonds, and government bonds. Next up is the overall investment planning process. This process begins with analyzing an investor's objectives and constraints and ends with evaluating the results of investment decisions. This chapter shows how to develop an investment policy statement to guide the investment process. It also presents return measures useful for evaluating portfolio performance and choosing appropriate asset allocations (the proportion of different asset classes in an investor's portfolio). The final section demonstrates the importance of allocating assets appropriately to meet a client's objectives and constraints. The next chapter presents more advanced topics in asset allocation using modern portfolio theory.

THE INVESTMENT PROCESS

Planning for investments is related to the overall financial planning process. The general steps in the financial planning process are adapted here for the investment planning process:

1. Establishing client-advisor relationships.

2. Gathering client data and determining objectives and expectations.

3. Analyzing the client's financial status, current investments, and special needs.

4. Developing and presenting the Investment Policy Statement.

5. Implementing the investment policy.

6. Monitoring the portfolio.

Note that the first four steps in the process involve gaining an understanding of the client and developing an appropriate investment policy to assist the client in meeting his objectives. The actual decision as to what

investments to purchase comes much later. A planner must know the client before implementing an investment strategy.

Client Lifecycle Analysis

While each client is unique, there are common themes that impact the creation of an investment policy. One of these themes is that people's needs and resources change over time, and an investment policy must first identify these needs and then reflect these changes.

For example, consider Mary. A 25-year old beginning her career, she has no savings and barely earns enough to pay the bills. At this stage, she is probably mostly concerned with setting aside an emergency fund and reducing risks such as the possibility of disability.

When Mary is 35, she is married with children, and earning more. Her husband also works, and they have more disposable income. They can afford to save some of this income for their future needs, which are college for the children and their own retirement.

At 65, Mary and her husband retire and their earned income levels decline dramatically. At this point, they rely on their investments, including retirement plans, to maintain their newfound leisure. Eventually, they will probably want any of their wealth that remains at the time of their death to be passed to their children or charities.

This scenario is familiar to everyone, and is often called the investor life cycle. The investor life cycle is considered to run through three phases:[1]

1. Accumulation phase

2. Consolidation phase

3. Spending phase

During the accumulation phase, the client is accumulating assets: saving and investing for the future. As this is the earliest stage during which investing will occur, there is typically a long time horizon. Clients in this phase are often able to accept more risk since they have time to accumulate wealth. They may therefore prefer a higher risk and return policy, although they have a low level of net worth to be invested. In other cases, clients in the accumulation phase may have more pressing needs. If the client is saving to purchase a home or to build an emergency fund, their time horizon is shorter and risk tolerance may be low despite their long life expectancy.

The consolidation phase occurs when the client's income outpaces expenses and wealth accumulates more rapidly. The client has greater wealth to invest and still has a relatively long time horizon. However, the time horizon shortens over this period to arrive at the spending phase. During this phase, the client typically can tolerate moderate to higher risk in order to achieve higher returns.

The spending phase is when earned income (such as wages) ends and investment income is needed from accumulated retirement and non-retirement funds to meet living expenses. The client typically has a desire for lower risk and higher investment income during this period. Since life expectancies can be long, the time horizon is shorter, but not necessarily short, during this phase.

Figure 37.1

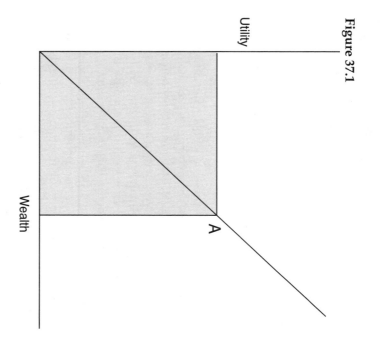

Utility

Wealth

Client Risk Tolerance

A client's willingness to accept investment risk is a function of a number of factors. While most individuals have some degree of risk aversion, some individuals are more tolerant of risk than others. This can be a function of their willingness to undertake risk (for example, based on past experiences) or their ability to take risk (for example, alternative sources of income and/or wealth such as a potential inheritance). A client's time horizon is also relevant. Generally, the longer the investment time horizon, the greater the ability to incur risk.

A useful framework for considering risk tolerance is the economic concept of utility. Utility is the satisfaction that an individual gets from consuming goods and services and, in terms of wealth, the satisfaction conferred by a given level of wealth. Consider Figure 37.1, which shows one possible relationship between wealth and utility. This utility function indicates that as investor wealth increases, the investor's utility increases. Further, there is a linear relationship so that starting at any point such as A, an increase in wealth of $X will increase utility by the same amount as a decrease in wealth of $X will decrease utility. An investor with such a utility function is said to be risk-neutral; neither avoiding nor seeking risk.

Another possible utility function is presented in Figure 37.2. This function shows a convex utility curve, where utility increases at a faster rate as wealth increases. An investor with wealth at point B would be risk seeking, since he would gain more utility for an $X increase in wealth than he would lose utility for an $X decrease in wealth.

Figure 37.2

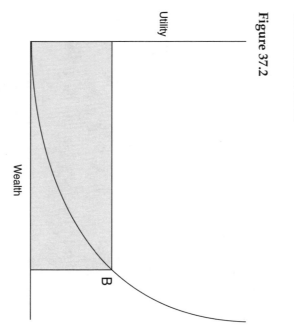

Utility

Wealth

Lastly, Figure 37.3 shows a concave utility function, where utility increases at a slower rate as wealth increases. An investor with wealth at point C will be risk-averse, because as wealth decreases by $X the investor's utility decreases by more than it increases when wealth increases by $X.

356

Figure 37.3

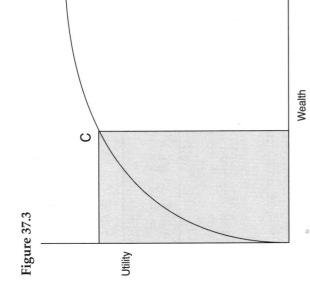

For most goods and services, economists assume diminishing marginal utility – the more a person has of a good, the less satisfaction he gets from each additional unit. If investors have diminishing marginal utility for wealth, they would exhibit the risk-averse utility function presented in Figure 37.3.

One problem with utility is that it cannot be measured, so it is not easy to assess an individual's risk preferences. Additionally, research on the behavior of individuals indicates that these utility functions do not capture the subtlety of human utility functions. In their well-known work on Prospect Theory, Kahneman and Tversky found that investors do not exhibit the same behavior for gains and losses. Kahneman and Tversky performed experiments where individuals were faced with choices such as:

Choice A: Participate in a gamble where there is a 50% chance of winning $1,000 and a 50% chance of winning nothing.

Choice B: Receive $450 with certainty.

They found that individuals exhibit risk aversion behavior when faced with choices involving a sure gain (they tended to take Choice B), but when faced with choices involving a sure loss or a possibility of a loss they exhibit risk seeking behavior. They conclude that individuals' utility functions appear to be concave for gains and convex for losses.

Figure 37.4

	Strongly Agree	Agree	Neutral	Disagree	Strongly Disagree
Earning a high long-term total return that will allow my capital to grow faster than the inflation rate is one of my most important objectives.	5	4	3	2	1
I would like an investment that provides me with an opportunity to defer taxation of capital gains to future years.	5	4	3	2	1
I do not require a high level of current income from my investments.	5	4	3	2	1
I am willing to tolerate some sharp down swings in the return on my investments in order to seek a potentially higher return than would normally be expected from more stable investments.	5	4	3	2	1
I am willing to risk a short term loss in return for a potentially higher long-term rate of return.	5	4	3	2	1
I am financially able to accept a low level of liquidity in my investment portfolio.	5	4	3	2	1
Over what period of time you expect to remain invested in this portfolio?	Short-term (3 years or less)	Intermediate term (4 to 7 years)		Long-term (over 7 years)	

Global Portfolio Allocation Scoring System (PASS) chart used with permission of Dr. William G. Droms, CFA.

Tools & Techniques of Investment Planning

Figure 37.5

Asset Class	Average Return	Standard Deviation	Proportion of years with a loss
Large Stocks (S&P 500)	13.84%	15.40%	20.00%
Government Bonds (10 year)	9.56%	11.62%	16.67%
Treasury Bills (3 month)	6.22%	3.15%	0.00%
Consumer Price Index	4.35%	2.29%	0.00%

Source: Based on data obtained from Global Financial Data, Los Angeles, CA www.globalfindata.com.

While investor's risk tolerance cannot be measured precisely, questionnaires have been developed which provide a good starting point to understanding a client's risk tolerance relative to other investors. Professor William Droms has been a leader in developing risk tolerance questionnaires with his Global Portfolio Allocation Scoring System (PASS), which is designed to categorize investors into risk tolerance categories. Recently Droms and Stauss presented a modified version of his scoring system that considers the interaction of risk tolerance and time horizon. Figure 37.4 presents the questionnaire proposed by Droms and Strauss. The minimum score on this questionnaire is 6 and the maximum 30. Clients with a higher score and longer time horizon will have a higher tolerance for and ability to take risk.

Droms and Stauss stress that the risk tolerance questionnaire is only a starting point in understanding the client in order to develop an appropriate investment policy statement.

THE INVESTMENT POLICY STATEMENT

A client's Investment Policy Statement should be developed in accordance with the client's objectives and constraints. Objectives include the desired return and level of risk that the client is willing and able to take. Constraints are limitations that must be considered in the investment process, such as liquidity, time horizon, taxes, and legal or regulatory restrictions. Lastly, constraints can include unique client circumstances and other self-imposed client preferences.

Determining the objectives for risk and return must be done simultaneously due to their interrelatedness. Generally, the higher the risk, the higher the return investors require. A starting point is to determine the return necessary to meet the investor's objectives. For example, if the investor wants to accumulate $1,000,000 over the next 20 years and can deposit $20,000 at the end

of each year, an 8.8% return is necessary (see Chapter 32, "Time-Value Concepts").

The next issue is whether that return can be achieved at a risk level appropriate for the investor. Risk is often measured as the standard deviation of returns (a measure of total risk). However, individual investors may perceive potential losses to be more important than potential gains. Standard deviation includes both upside and downside deviations.

Consider the historical return data for 1976 through 2005 provided in Figure 37.5. The data exhibit the expected positive relationship of risk and returns. The funds with the highest return had the highest risk measured based on both standard deviation and proportion of years with a loss. Treasury bills represent a risk-free rate of return. The consumer price index represents a level of inflation.

The investor's desired rate of return should be obtainable and consistent with risk tolerance. Financial advisers often present long term historic risk and return data, such as that from www.ibbotson.com or www.globalfinancia-data.com, to clients to demonstrate potential returns and risk. Historic returns do not necessarily predict future returns, but they do provide guidance as to what is possible. If an investor desires a long-term compound return of 15% with a standard deviation of 5% and no negative returns, this is not likely achievable given the historical data. The return exceeds that exhibited by any of the asset classes in the past and the risk is certainly much lower than could likely be achieved for that level of return.

Historical index returns are not achievable since they do not include fees and expenses. Use of index fund return data does consider some fees and expenses. Care must also be taken when using nominal historic returns. Some historical periods had high returns, but high inflation. If current or expected inflation differ at the time the investment policy is being developed, consideration should be given to using real (inflation-adjusted) returns.

The ability to achieve a desired return is also a function of certain constraints. The liquidity constraint is the client's desire to maintain a certain level of liquid assets (such as cash). The time horizon constraint relates to the timing of expected withdrawals. A long time horizon generally allows the investor to accept more risk. If the investor has particular needs (or desires) for cash at particular dates (such as for a second home purchase), this must be factored into the investment policy. Since taxes can have a significant impact on net investment returns, any tax constraints should be considered. If the account is tax-deferred, there is more investment flexibility (except that municipal bonds would not be appropriate). If the account is taxable, tax favored investment returns such as long-term gains and dividends should be considered. Any legal or regulatory constraints should be examined. For example, if the client has a trust, the trust document must be examined. Further, the need to adhere to state law "prudent man/prudent investor" provisions must be considered. Some clients have unique circumstances or preferences that can lead to constraints on the investment policy. For example, the investor may wish to avoid tobacco or military-industrial stocks or may prefer mutual funds to individual securities.

Once the client's objectives and constraints are determined, they should be put in writing as an Investment Policy Statement to guide asset allocation and security selection for the client's accounts.

Return Measures for Portfolio Evaluation

Previous chapters have shown a variety of return measures such as holding-period returns and internal rates of return. Which of these is appropriate when evaluating portfolio performance? Further, should the performance be compared to the risk-free rate or some other benchmark such as a market index?

Let's look at a hypothetical example. Assume an investor deposits $100,000 in a professionally managed account. One year later, the account has grown in value to $120,000 and the investor withdraws $30,000 (remaining value $90,000). At the end of the second year, the account value is $99,000. No other additions or withdrawals were made. During the same two years, the risk-free rate remained constant at 6% and a relevant benchmark earned 18% the first year and 12% the second.

The investor's return could be measured as the holding-period return over the two years:

$$R_H = \frac{MV_E - MV_0 + D}{MV_0}$$

Where R_H is the holding-period return

MV_E is the market value of the account at the end

MV_0 is the market value at the beginning and

D is the net distributions during the time period (contributions minus withdrawals)

For this investor the holding-period return is:

$$R_H = \frac{MV_E - MV_0 + D}{MV_0} = \frac{99,000 - 100,000 + 30,000}{100,000}$$

$$= 0.29 \; or \; 29\%$$

This return measure informs the investor that they have earned 29% over the holding period, but since the holding period is two years, it is not that useful in comparing to benchmarks or prior periods. Return measures are usually expressed on an annual basis.

The holding-period return could be computed for each year individually. The holding period return for year one is:

$$R_H = \frac{MV_E - MV_0 + D}{MV_0} = \frac{90,000 - 100,000 + 30,000}{100,000}$$

$$= 0.20 \; or \; 20\%$$

The holding-period return in year two is:

$$R_H = \frac{MV_E - MV_0 + D}{MV_0} = \frac{99,000 - 90,000}{90,000}$$

$$= 0.10 \; or \; 10\%$$

So the investor earned 20% in the first year and 10% in the second. These annual returns can be compared to the benchmark since there were no withdrawals or deposits during the year, only at the beginning or end of the year. Year one returns of 20% beat the benchmark by 2% and returns in year two trailed the benchmark by the same 2%. Note that, had there been interim withdrawals or deposits, holding-period returns for sub-periods would need to be calculated.

Having beaten the index one year and trailed it the next by a similar amount, how should the manager's performance be evaluated? The simple average of the holding period returns is 15% for both the manager and the benchmark. However, the simple average does not adequately capture the performance during the two-year period.

To measure the geometric average performance of the account over the period, the internal rate of return for the portfolio can be computed over the two-year time period. Using a financial calculator with the following inputs:

Cash Flow Time Zero   (100,000)
Cash Flow Time One   30,000
Cash Flow Time Two (Value)   99,000

Solving for the internal rate of return yields 15.62%. (See Chapter 33, "Measuring Investment Risk.") The internal rate of return is also known as a dollar-weighted return. The investor earned more than the simple average of 15% in this instance due to the timing of the withdrawal. By withdrawing funds after the 20% return and before the lower 10% return, the investor earned a higher average return. Note, however, that since the dollar-weighted return is an internal rate of return, it implicitly assumes that cash flows are re-invested at the same rate.

While the dollar-weighted return may measure the return to the investor, it does not measure the performance of the portfolio manager. The decision to withdraw funds was made by the investor and should not be included in the manager's evaluation.

Instead, a time-weighted return is used. The time-weighted return is measured as:

$$R_p = [(1 + R_1)(1 + R_2)(1 + R_3)...(1 + R_N)]^{1/N} - 1$$

It measures the geometric return, excluding the impact of contributions and withdrawals, over the period. As such, it is an appropriate measure of the portfolio manager's performance. For this example, the time-weighted return would be:

$$R_p = [(1 + R_1)(1 + R_2)(1 + R_3)...(1 + R_N)]^{1/N} - 1$$

$$= [(1.20)(1.10)]^{1/2} - 1 = 14.89\%$$

In this case, the portfolio manager's performance was an average annual return of 14.89% over the two years. This is slightly less than the simple average and quite a bit less than the dollar-weighted average that included the impact of the investor's withdrawal. It can also be compared to the benchmark index by calculating the time-weighted benchmark return of $[(1.18)(1.12)]^{1/2} - 1 = 14.96$. Doing so, it is discovered that although the magnitudes of the outperformance in year 1 and under-performance in year 2 were equal, the manager's annual returns over the entire period fell slightly behind those of the benchmark. Fortunately, the difference turned out to be minimal.

Risk-Adjusted Performance Measures

The return earned is only one component of portfolio performance. Another important component is the amount of risk taken to achieve the return. Portfolio performance can and should (assuming risk-averse investors) be evaluated on a risk-adjusted basis. In risk-adjusted measures, return is compared to the portfolio's riskiness. A high return relative to risk is desirable. In this section, four types of risk-adjusted returns are examined: the Sharpe ratio, the Treynor ratio, the information ratio, and Jensen's alpha.

The Sharpe ratio measures the excess return of a portfolio relative to risk and is computed as:

$$Sharpe\ Ratio = \frac{R_p - R_f}{O_p}$$

The numerator represents a portfolio's excess return over the risk-free rate. The denominator measures the portfolio's risk as the standard deviation of portfolio returns (total risk).[2] If the Sharpe Ratio is negative, the portfolio's return was lower than the risk-free rate. The higher the Sharpe Ratio, the better the performance.

For this example, the following is used: a risk-free rate of 6%, the portfolio's time-weighted return of 14.89% annually and standard deviation of 7.07%, and the benchmark return and standard deviation of 14.96% and 4.24%, respectively.[3] Plugging in these numbers gives the portfolio a Sharpe ratio of 1.26 [(14.89 - 6.00) / 7.07]. By comparison, the benchmark index has a Sharpe ratio of 2.11 [(14.96-6.00) / 4.24]. The benchmark's much higher Sharpe ratio indicates that it was much less risky than the portfolio given their similar returns.[4]

The Treynor ratio also measures the excess return relative to risk but measures risk as Beta:

$$Treynor\ Ratio = \frac{R_p - R_f}{\beta_p}$$

As with the Sharpe ratio, a positive number indicates greater returns than the risk-free rate and a higher ratio is preferred. If it is assumed the portfolio had a Beta of 1.2, a Treynor ratio is derived of 7.41 [(14.89 - 6.00) / 1.2]. Typically, the portfolio Beta is measured against the benchmark, so the benchmark should have a Beta of 1.0 and a resulting Treynor ratio of 8.96 [(14.96-6.00) / 1.00]. This measure also shows the manager produced worse risk-adjusted returns than the benchmark. Note, however, that if the Beta of a portfolio differs significantly from that of the benchmark it could signal that the chosen benchmark is inappropriate because it does not reflect the manager's style (or that the manager is inappropriate because he doesn't follow the investment guidelines).

Using the risk-free rate as the hurdle rate for determining the excess return may not be a high enough hurdle for some. An alternative is to calculate an information ratio, which measures excess return relative to the benchmark portfolio:

$$Information\ Ratio\ =\ \frac{R_p - R_B}{\sigma_{Excess}}$$

The risk measure is the standard deviation of the excess return. For this portfolio, excess return is -0.07% [14.89 - 14.96]. The standard deviation of excess return is 2.83%, yielding an information ratio of -0.02. The negative information ratio is another sign that this manager has not performed well.

Jensen's alpha is another risk-adjusted performance measure. However, it is measured quite differently:

$$\alpha = R_p - [R_f + \beta_p (R_m - R_f)]$$

Alpha is measured as the portfolio's return in excess of that predicted by the capital asset pricing model (see Chapter 36, "Asset Pricing Models"). An alpha of zero indicates that the portfolio earned its expected rate of return given its risk (measured as Beta). A positive alpha indicates that the portfolio manager has added value. Given this example, alpha equals -1.86 [14.89 - {6.00 + 1.2 x (14.96 - 6.00)}]. The negative alpha indicates this portfolio manager has not performed as well as predicted by the capital asset pricing model.

Note that for risk-adjusted measures using Beta, a diversified portfolio is assumed. Standard deviation measures total risk and does not assume a diversified portfolio. The Sharpe and Treynor ratios will provide similar rankings for well diversified portfolios.

Selecting an Appropriate Benchmark

It has been described how to measure portfolio results compared to a benchmark. An equally important consideration is which benchmark to use. The most frequently cited benchmark is the S&P 500 index, but this may not be appropriate for every investor as it consists only of large-cap U.S. stocks, which may not be similar to the investor's portfolio.

Appropriate benchmark selection should follow naturally from the investment planning process. Once the client's preferences, constraints, risk tolerance, and

return requirements are established and a mix of assets is selected to accomplish these goals, a benchmark should be chosen that reflects the same goals. For example, if the client's asset allocation is 50% large-cap stocks and 50% intermediate-term bonds, the benchmark should have a similar construction. A single benchmark that contains the same proportions of each asset would be acceptable, as would a combination of two separate single-asset class benchmarks. In some cases, the choice may depend on whether the investor has chosen separate equity and fixed income managers or whether a single investment manager is responsible for the entire account. Complex allocations may even require construction of a custom benchmark.

While the terms "benchmark" and "index" are often substituted for each other, an appropriate benchmark could be a published index, a custom composite of assets or indexes, or a peer group of similar funds or managers. Regardless of which type of benchmark is chosen, the CFA Institute and other global investment bodies generally agree that it should meet the following criteria:

1. *Representative of the asset class or mandate* – An investor in small-cap stocks should not choose a manager who invests in S&P 500 names, nor should they compare their small-cap manager to that index.

2. *The benchmark should be investible* – This means that the investor should be able to invest in the benchmark as an alternative to hiring an active manager. There is no sense in comparing performance to a benchmark that could not be reasonably matched (such as a market-weighted portfolio of all the real estate in the world.)

3. *Should be constructed in a disciplined and objective manner* – Some managers believe the benchmark should be easy to beat so their performance looks better. The investor may prefer a tougher standard. The benchmark should have neither bias.

4. *Formulated from publicly available information.*

5. *Acceptable by the manager as the neutral position* – The manager should be comfortable with comparisons to the benchmark.

6. Consistent with the investor's status regarding taxes, time horizon, etc.

Figure 37.6

Asset Class	Average Return	Sharpe Ratio	Proportion of years with a loss
Large Stocks (S&P 500)	13.84%	0.49	20.00%
Government Bonds (10 year)	9.56%	0.29	16.67%
Treasury Bills (3 month)	6.22%	0.00	0.00%
Consumer Price Index	4.35%	- 0.63	0.00%

In short, the benchmark should reflect both the client's needs and the manager's style. Otherwise, either the manager or the benchmark was not selected well.

Risk–Adjusted Measures and Investment Policy

Risk-adjusted measures can be useful in setting investment policy for a client and in explaining the importance of asset allocation to the client. Based on the historical data presented earlier, the return versus risk data provided in Figure 37.6 can be computed. Sharpe ratios were computed using average returns relative to Treasury bills and the standard deviation of returns for the asset class. Notice that although large stocks have a high level of risk, they have the highest risk-adjusted return. Government bonds have the next highest risk-adjusted return.

To demonstrate the importance of diversification among asset classes, five portfolios are formed as presented in Figure 37.7 and the same measures computed. The equity portion of the portfolio consists of large stocks.

Figure 37.7

Asset Class	Average Return	Sharpe Ratio	Proportion of years with a loss
90% Equity 10% Fixed Income	13.24%	0.50	20.00%
75% Equity 25% Fixed Income	12.35%	0.51	20.00%
50% Equity 50% Fixed Income	10.86%	0.51	13.33%
25% Equity 75% Fixed Income	9.38%	0.46	3.33%
10% Equity 90% Fixed Income	8.48%	0.36	3.33%

The fixed income portion of the portfolio consists of equal weights of government bonds and Treasury bills. By creating portfolios with asset classes that are not perfectly correlated, the overall risk has been reduced and the risk-adjusted returns are higher than could be obtained with any single asset class.

This example is based on a simple portfolio formation that did not consider the correlations of the asset classes or the appropriateness of the individual asset classes. The next chapter examines asset allocation and portfolio construction using advanced techniques including Modern Portfolio Theory and Monte Carlo simulation.

WHERE CAN I FIND OUT MORE ABOUT IT?

1. *AIMR Benchmarks and Performance Attribution Subcommittee Report* (Charlottesville, VA: CFA Institute, August 1998), www.cfainstitute.org.

2. John L. Maginn and Donald L. Tuttle, *Managing Investment Portfolios: A Dynamic Process*, 2nd Edition (Charlottesville, VA: CFA Institute, 1990).

3. William G. Droms and Steven N. Stauss, "Assessing Risk Tolerance for Asset Allocation," *Journal of Financial Planning*, March 2003.

4. Daniel Kahneman and Amos Tversky, "Prospect Theory: An Analysis of Decision Under Risk," *Econometrica*, March 1997, Vol. 47, No. 2.

QUESTIONS AND ANSWERS

Question – Would an investor be likely to prefer a manager who generates an alpha of 2.0% and has a portfolio Beta of 1.0 or one who generates an alpha of 1.0% and has a portfolio Beta of 2.0?

Answer – The risk-averse investor should prefer the manager who generates higher alpha, as that manager is earning returns in excess of those expected given the level of risk taken on. However, it would be desirable to have additional information about the level of returns and the composition of the portfolio.

Question – Jose's small-cap investment manager has produced returns that lag the benchmark S&P 500 index. What should Jose do?

Answer – The S&P 500 index is an inappropriate benchmark for a small-cap portfolio. Jose must first decide whether he wants to invest in small cap stocks or large cap stocks. In the case of the former, he should compare his manager to a different index, such as the Russell 2000. In the latter case, he should hire a manager who follows a large cap strategy.

Question – A consultant wants to evaluate the performance of a large-cap investment manager and has collected the risk and return information below. Calculate and evaluate the manager's Sharpe Ratio, Treynor Ratio, Information Ratio, and Alpha.

Manager's 10-year annualized return	11.7%
S&P 500 10-year annualized return	9.0%
Risk-free rate	5.0%
Manger's 10-year standard deviation of returns	21.3%
S&P 500 10-year standard deviation of returns	16.2%
Manger's Beta (relative to S&P 500)	1.2
Standard deviation of manager's excess returns	2.0%

Answer – The ratios are calculated as follows:

Sharpe Ratio = (11.7 – 5.0) / 21.3 = 0.31

Treynor Ratio = (11.7 – 5.0) / 1.2 = 5.6

Information Ratio = (11.7 – 9.0) / 2.0 = 1.35

Alpha = 11.7 – (5.0 + 1.2 x [9.0 – 5.0]) = 1.9%

The Sharpe and Treynor Ratios can only be evaluated with respect to those earned by other managers.

The Information Ratio is positive, which indicates that the manager outperformed the benchmark. It is also greater than one, which suggests the additional risk taken was less than the incremental return generated.

The 1.9% Alpha shows that the manager beat the benchmark performance, relative to the additional risk the manager took, by 1.9% annually. This is a good performance.

CHAPTER ENDNOTES

1. More than three phases are possible. In Maginn and Tuttle (see "Where Can I Find Out More About It?" above), a gifting phase is included. A pre-accumulation phase when income is less than or equal to expenses can also be imagined. We focus on what we consider to be the three main phases for purposes of investment policy.

2. The denominator can also be measured as the standard deviation of the excess return rather than the standard deviation of the portfolio return.

3. Obviously, the two years of data are insufficient to generate statistically meaningful measures for return and standard deviation, but it is assumed that the two years were typical of those generated over a longer period for purposes of this illustration.

4. There is no standard level of Sharpe or Treynor ratios that are good versus bad. The level of the ratio is dependent upon the time period and data source used. They should be evaluated relative to similar ratios computed for the same time period and in a similar manner.

ASSET ALLOCATION AND PORTFOLIO CONSTRUCTION

WHAT IS IT?

Asset allocation involves selecting the proportions of various types of assets to include in a portfolio. Proper asset allocation improves a portfolio's risk-adjusted return. The asset allocation decision is a prelude to selecting individual securities or funds for portfolio inclusion.

ASSET ALLOCATION

The relationship of return and risk is an important investment planning concept. Generally, riskier investments must offer a higher potential return to compensate for the added risk. However, combining two or more risky assets can actually reduce the risk of the overall portfolio, as long as the assets are not highly correlated. Highly correlated assets tend to move in the same direction and at a similar magnitude, while assets that are not highly correlated do not. Investors can use non-highly correlated assets to build portfolios with more favorable risk/return relationships.

Consider four potential investments that have the following expected returns for next year depending on three possible economic environments, each of which is equally likely to occur:

Economic Environment	Expected Returns			
	Asset A	Asset B	Asset C	Asset D
Strong	6%	15%	20%	5%
Normal	6%	10%	10%	10%
Weak	6%	5%	0%	15%
Expected Return	6%	10%	10%	10%
Variability	+/- 0%	+/- 5%	+/-10%	+/-5%

Expected return is the asset's average return under all three business conditions. Variability (risk) is simply the range of potential outcomes relative to the expected return. Note that Asset A is a risk free asset, with an expected return of 6% and no variability. Assets B, C, and D all offer an expected return of 10% but at different levels of risk. Assets B and D are equally risky, while Asset C is riskiest. For a risk-averse investor, Assets B

and D appear preferable to C because they offer lower variability for the same expected return. The choice between A, B, and D depends on whether the higher return of B or D is sufficiently enticing for the investor to take on the risk relative to A.

However, the investor doesn't have to choose only one asset. Instead, let's take a look at three potential portfolios where an equal amount of two assets (50% of each) is purchased. Note that all three portfolios offer the same 10% expected return as the individual assets.

Business Conditions	Expected Returns		
	Portfolio BC	Portfolio CD	Portfolio BD
Strong	17.5%	12.5%	10.0%
Normal	10.0%	10%	10.0%
Weak	2.5%	7.5%%	10.0%
Expected Return	10.0%	10.0%	10.0%
Variability	+/- 7.5%	+/- 2.5%	+/-0%

The variability of Portfolio BC is the average variability of assets B and C. This portfolio does not achieve any reduction in risk because Assets B and C are perfectly correlated (a correlation coefficient of 1.0). They both do well in strong business conditions and poorly in weak conditions.

The expected variability of Portfolio CD is less than the variability for each of the individual assets. This portfolio would be preferred to individual assets B, C, and D since it offers the same expected return but lower risk. This is because assets C and D are perfectly negatively correlated. One asset is always up when the other is down.

Similarly, the Portfolio BD offers the same expected return as assets B, C, and D, but no variability. Again, this is due to the fact that B and D are negatively correlated. In fact, this portfolio offers a higher return for the same expected risk as Asset A, making it the most preferable portfolio for a risk-averse investor.

By combining assets that are not highly correlated together in portfolios, the investor can achieve a more favorable risk/return relationship. It is not necessary for assets to be negatively correlated to achieve this benefit. Small positive correlations (assets that occasionally, but not always, move in the same direction) also reduce risk.

Modern Portfolio Theory and Asset Allocation

The ability to reduce risk for a given level of return is a fundamental principal of modern portfolio theory (MPT). Properly constructed portfolios of assets that are not highly correlated achieve the highest possible return for a given level of risk. MPT measures risk as standard deviation of returns. The standard deviation for a portfolio of assets can be determined as:

$$\sigma_p = \sqrt{\sum_{i=1}^{N} w_i^2 \sigma_i^2 + \sum_{i=1}^{N}\sum_{j=1}^{N} w_i w_j \sigma_i \sigma_j Corr_{ij}}$$

The standard deviation for the portfolio, p, is based upon the weights, w, and standard deviation of each asset, σ, in the portfolio and the correlation between all pairs of assets, i and j. For a two-asset portfolio, this can be expressed more simply as:

$$\sigma_p = \sqrt{w_1^2 \sigma_1^2 + w_2^2 \sigma_2^2 + 2 w_1 w_2 \sigma_1 \sigma_2 Corr_{1,2}}$$

Now consider two assets with the following expected returns, standard deviations, and correlation:

	Asset	
	A	B
Expected Return	10.00%	6.00%
Standard Deviation	20.00%	5.00%
Correlation	0.2	

The low correlation between A and B indicates that there should be a benefit from combining these assets in a portfolio. Consider the following potential portfolios, with varying weights of A and B in the portfolio:

Portfolio	Asset A	Asset B	Expected Return	Standard Deviation
1	0	100.00%	6.000%	5.00%
2	10.00%	90.00%	6.400%	5.28%
3	20.00%	80.00%	6.800%	6.20%
4	30.00%	70.00%	7.200%	7.53%
5	40.00%	60.00%	7.600%	9.09%
6	50.00%	50.00%	8.000%	10.78%
7	60.00%	40.00%	8.400%	12.55%
8	70.00%	30.00%	8.800%	14.38%
9	80.00%	20.00%	9.200%	16.23%
10	90.00%	10.00%	9.600%	18.11%
11	100.00%	0.00%	10.000%	20.00%

The expected return is always the weighted average return of the underlying assets. For example, for portfolio 6 the expected return is 8% [((0.5 x 10%) + (0.5 x 6%)]. The standard deviation of each portfolio is based upon the standard deviation formula for the two-asset portfolio above.

Note that portfolios 1 and 11 represent the individual assets. For a risk adverse investor, note that relative to portfolio 1, portfolio 2 offers a 6.7% higher return [(6.4% / 6%) - 1] but has only a 5.6% [(5.28% / 5%) - 1] increase in standard deviation. The return/risk can also be computed, which is 1.20 [6% / 5%] for portfolio 1 and 1.212 [6.4% / 5.28%] for portfolio 2. Portfolio 2 offers a greater return relative to risk compared to portfolio 1. Similarly at the other end of the spectrum, moving from portfolio 11 to portfolio 10, there is a reduction in return of 4% (1 – (9.6% / 10%)], but a 9.4% reduction [1 – (18.11% / 20%)] in standard deviation. The relationship between risk and return for these portfolios is demonstrated in Figure 38.1. An investor could choose the combination of assets A and B which provides them with their desired return while maintaining an acceptable level of risk.

Figure 38.1

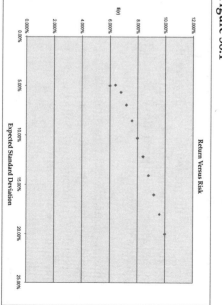

Return Versus Risk

Expected Standard Deviation

Portfolios of more than two assets make the math more complex, but the basic concepts are the same. Adding assets with low or negative correlations to the rest of the portfolio improves the return/risk relationship.

Overall portfolio asset allocation decisions are made using the expected returns, standard deviation, and correlations between asset classes, rather than individual assets. An asset class is a group of securities with similar characteristics. Broadly speaking, the major asset classes include stocks, bonds, real estate, cash, commodities, and international investments. Within each asset class, however, there can be various gradations that sometimes constitute their own asset class. For example, an investor may consider growth stocks and value stocks to be separate asset classes. Likewise, treasury bonds can differ greatly from high-yield bonds in terms of their risk and return. It makes sense to consider these subsets of broad asset classes when forming a portfolio. Commercial asset allocation software packages have varying numbers of asset classes available.

Asset allocation strategies must also consider the appropriateness of each asset class for the particular investor or account. For example, municipal bonds would likely be excluded as an asset class for non-taxable or tax deferred accounts.

Using asset allocation software and the expected returns, standard deviations, and correlations of the asset classes, the advisor should attempt to generate an "efficient frontier" of potential portfolios. The efficient frontier represents those portfolios with the highest expected return for a given level of expected risk as depicted in Figure 38.2.

Figure 38.2

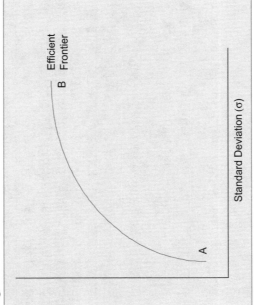

curves for each investor could be drawn. Indifference curves represent the different combinations of risk and return to which an investor is indifferent. Optimally an investor would select the investor's highest indifference curve that touches the efficient frontier as depicted in Figure 38.3. This represents the point of highest utility for the investor.

Figure 38.3

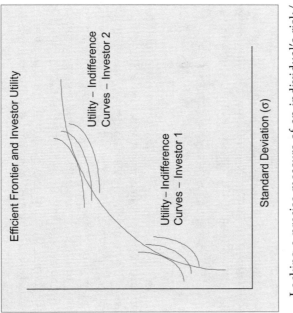

Portfolio A on the efficient frontier might represent a portfolio concentrated in short-term fixed income securities such as Treasury Bills. Portfolio B might represent a portfolio concentrated in risky securities such as emerging market equities. As with the simplified example for assets A and B above, the efficient frontier can be used to present to a client potential portfolios based on upon their desired returns or the level of risk they are willing to take.

Efficient frontiers can easily be generated based upon historic relationships between asset classes or expected relationships. The challenge is determining which point on the efficient frontier should be selected for a particular client. Theoretically, if the utility (satisfaction) that an investor obtains from different levels of returns relative to risk could be measured, a set of indifference

Lacking a precise measure of an individual's risk/return preferences, advisors typically use judgment to select an appropriate point on the efficient frontier based on some measure of the investor's risk tolerance (see Chapter 36, "Asset Pricing Models"). One approach involves classifying investors as conservative, intermediate, or aggressive. The investor is then placed in the relevant section of the efficient frontier as shown in Figure 38.4.

Figure 38.4

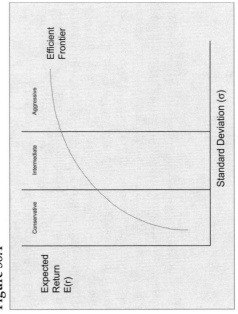

Additional degrees of risk tolerance can also be used. Some advisors use a scale such as:

- Aggressive Growth
- Growth
- Growth and Income
- Income
- Safety

The categories including growth are typically concentrated in equities, with a large portion of the expected return derived from appreciation. Income, by contrast, typically includes investments such as bonds where the current yield is an important component of return. Note that when constructing a portfolio based on a client's investment policy statement, the advisor should include the constraints and preferences (see Chapter 37, "Portfolio Management and Measurement") in determining an appropriate allocation.

Strategic Asset Allocation

A strategic asset allocation can be thought of as the long-range plan for a portfolio. Taking into consideration the long-range return requirements and risk tolerance, allocations to various asset classes are developed as described above. The strategic allocation typically is not altered to take into account short-term issues such as current market conditions (perceived current relative value of different asset classes). Instead, assets are periodically rebalanced to conform to the original allocation.

This rebalancing is necessary since the asset classes will have different returns. For example, over the long term equities usually have a higher return than bonds. If the strategic allocation is 50% stocks and 50% bonds and stocks have a higher return, over time, the portfolio will have a greater than 50% position in stocks. To bring the allocation back to the overall strategic allocation, enough stocks would have to be sold and bonds purchased to get back to the 50/50 allocation. Note that if dividends and interest are reinvested in the same asset class or held in cash, this will also impact the rebalancing. An advantage to rebalancing within a strategic asset allocation is that it enforces a discipline to sell the best performing asset classes and buy the lowest performing (buy low, sell high). Alternatively, a momentum investing strategy would suggest no rebalancing – letting the winners run.

Example

Consider an investor who has created a strategic asset allocation of 30% bonds, 30% commodities, and 40%

stocks, and who has set a guideline that the portfolio will be rebalanced when any asset class varies from the strategic allocation by more than 500 basis points (5%). Over the next five years, the assets exhibit the following return pattern:

Year	Bonds	Commodities	Stocks
1	2.43%	13.54%	4.91%
2	4.34%	20.25%	10.88%
3	4.10%	38.59%	28.68%
4	10.25%	-15.94%	-22.10%
5	8.44%	-21.44%	-11.89%

How frequently will the portfolio be rebalanced? How will strategic rebalancing affect the ending value of the portfolio relative to letting the winners run?

First, let's consider an initial portfolio of $1 million that is allowed to run:

Year-end	Bonds	Commodities	Stocks	Total
0	300,000	300,000	400,000	1,000,000
1	307,290	340,620	419,640	1,067,550
2	320,626	409,596	465,297	1,195,519
3	333,772	567,658	598,744	1,500,175
4	367,984	477,174	466,422	1,311,579
5	399,042	374,868	410,964	1,184,873

The ending value of the portfolio is $1,184,873.

Now let's consider the percentage of the portfolio in each asset for the period:

Year-end	Bonds	Commodities	Stocks	Total
0	30%	30%	40%	100%
1	29%	32%	39%	100%
2	27%	34%	39%	100%
3	22%	38%	40%	100%
4	28%	36%	36%	100%
5	34%	32%	35%	100%

At the end of year 1, the allocations are 29% bonds, 32% commodities, and 39% stocks. No allocation has drifted by more than 500 basis points from the strategic goal, so no rebalance is necessary. The same applies at the end of year 2.

At the end of year 3, however, the allocation to bonds has fallen by 800 basis points relative to the strategic allocation, and the allocation to commodities has risen by 800 basis points. According to the guidelines, the portfolio needs to be rebalanced. Doing so results in the following adjustments:

Chapter 38 – Asset Allocation And Portfolio Construction

Year-end	Bonds	Commodities	Stocks	Total
3	450,052	450,052	600,070	1,500,175
4	496,183	378,314	467,454	1,341,951
5	538,061	297,203	411,874	1,247,138

Note that by letting this newly rebalanced portfolio run, the ending value of $1,247,138 is $62,265 higher than the original ending value. However, going forward, the percentage of assets changes as follows:

Year-end	Bonds	Commodities	Stocks	Total
3	30%	30%	40%	100%
4	37%	28%	35%	100%
5	43%	24%	33%	100%

Once again, at the end of year 4 there is an imbalance of more than 500 basis points – this time there is too high an allocation to bonds. The portfolio must be rebalanced a second time at the end of year 4, to the following allocations:

Year-end	Bonds	Commodities	Stocks	Total
4	402,585	402,585	536,780	1,341,951
5	436,564	316,271	472,957	1,225,792

After the new rebalancing is completed and the final year elapses, the ending value of the portfolio is still $40,919 better than would have been achieved from letting the assets run from year 1 on. However, it is $21,346 *lower* than it would have been if the second rebalancing had not been done. This is because in year 5 bonds continued to do well, while stocks and commodities continued to fall.

Since there is no way of knowing in advance whether the trends will continue or reverse in a given year, it is generally best to decide in advance how frequently to rebalance in order to retain the desired level of risk for the client's portfolio.

Tactical Asset Allocation

In contrast to strategic allocation, tactical asset allocation attempts to capitalize on changing market conditions. In a tactical asset allocation, the overall asset allocation is frequently adjusted to take advantage of perceived opportunities in the current market. For example, in a high interest rate environment, the advisor may shift the asset allocation to favor long-term bonds. If U.S. equities are perceived to be undervalued, the advisor may overweight them. The rewards of tactical asset allocation depend on the advisor's ability to predict which asset classes will perform best in the near term. Strategic asset allocation is generally a low turnover investment strategy, while tactical asset allocation generally results in high turnover.

Example

The investor starts with the same $1 million portfolio and strategic allocation guidelines as in the previous example. However, the advisor is given discretion to shift the allocation tactically once per year as long as the starting allocations are within 500 basis points of each asset's strategic goal. The advisor decides to follow a momentum strategy that overweights the previous year's top-performing asset by 500 basis points and underweights the worst-performing asset by 500 basis points. The resulting performance is as follows:

	Bonds	Commodities	Stocks	Total
Beginning of year 1	300,000	300,000	400,000	1,000,000
Performance	2.43%	13.54%	4.91%	
End of year 1	307,290	340,620	419,640	1,067,550
New allocation	25%	35%	40%	
Beginning of year 2	266,888	373,643	427,020	1,067,550
Performance	4.34%	20.25%	10.88%	
End of year 2	278,470	449,305	473,480	1,201,255
New allocation	25%	35%	40%	
Beginning of year 3	300,314	420,439	480,502	1,201,255
Performance	4.10%	38.59%	28.68%	
End of year 3	312,627	582,687	618,310	1,513,624
New allocation	25%	35%	40%	
Beginning of year 4	378,406	529,768	605,449	1,513,624
Performance	10.25%	-15.94%	-22.10%	
End of year 4	417,193	445,323	471,645	1,334,161
New allocation	35%	30%	35%	
Beginning of year 5	466,956	400,248	466,956	1,334,161
Performance	8.44%	-21.44%	-11.89%	
End of year 5	506,367	314,435	411,435	1,232,238

The manager's tactical rebalancing results in a higher ending value than either the untouched portfolio or the one that was strategically rebalanced. However, the $6,446 improvement over strategic rebalancing may not have justified the higher trading costs from larger and more frequent allocation adjustments.

Controlling Volatility

Asset allocation is a means of controlling the volatility that is inherent in investment returns. Some investors may have a high degree of risk tolerance and desire to achieve the maximum possible return regardless of risk. Other investors may not sleep well at night with volatile portfolio values. Even investors who think they can tolerate risk may have circumstances where volatility can impair their ability to maintain a certain standard of living. Take for example a long-term historical return on large stocks of 10% and a long term inflation rate of 3%. An investor has $1,000,000 at retirement and desires to withdraw the maximum amount possible each year while maintaining the purchasing power of the portfolio each year and not running out of money during any foreseeable life expectancy. One might naively assume that the investor could withdraw 7% each year starting with $70,000 the first year (and increasing the dollar amount by inflation in each subsequent year). Unfortunately, it turns out that is not possible unless there is no volatility in returns. If the stock market achieved 10% returns each and every year it would be possible, but with volatility the maximum safe withdrawal rate is much lower. In fact, studies have shown that the maximum safe withdrawal rate given historic volatility of returns for a stock is less than 4%.

As noted in previous sections, creating a diversified portfolio with assets that are not highly correlated can reduce the volatility of an investment portfolio. Time also moderates volatility. If an investor has a long time horizon before investment withdrawals are to begin, the impact of volatility is dampened over time. Additionally, volatility can be managed using hedging strategies and options strategies such as a covered call (selling a call option on a currently held investment). A covered call sells some of the upside and reduces the potential downside (from the collection of the option premium), reducing the standard deviation of the portfolio. Downside risk can also be reduced through the purchase of put options. Hedging and option strategies are described in more detail in Chapter 41.

Monte-Carlo Simulation

Expected returns and standard deviation are not necessarily constant over time. Nor is the return in an individual period predictable. Returns in each asset class are probabilistic. Investors may also make periodic deposits and withdrawals, further increasing the difficulty of predicting long-term returns and risk. If an investor desires a particular level of retirement income, what is the assurance that this level of income is likely to be obtained?

Monte-Carlo simulation assesses the likelihood of an expected outcome. In a Monte-Carlo simulation, a computer program randomly chooses returns from an expected distribution of returns for each period (perhaps rebalancing the asset allocation if required under the strategy). Each run results in an ending expected portfolio value. The process is run many times (perhaps 1,000), to achieve a distribution of ending values. This process can help assess the probability of achieving a certain value or income in the future (including the possibility that an individual will outlive his retirement assets).

Example

As noted in the prior section, volatility has a significant impact on the ability of a client to make desired retirement withdrawals during retirement. The impact of volatility on the sustainability of retirement distributions can be demonstrated using Monte-Carlo simulation. Assume that an investment adviser has the following market expectations:

	Expected Long-Term Arithmetic Average Return	Expected Long-Term Standard Deviation of Returns
Stocks	9.0%	20.0%
Bonds	5.5%	9.0%

Expected long-term correlation of stocks and bonds is 0.20.

Consider a retired client who has a $1,000,000 portfolio. The client would like to withdraw as much as possible each year with that amount increasing for inflation. Ideally the client would like to withdraw about $40,000 (4% of the initial portfolio amount) adjusted for inflation each year. Using one Monte-Carlo simulation software (MC-Retire – www.effsols.com) using a 9% expected return for stocks, 20% expected standard deviation for stocks, and 3% inflation, the probability of success (the ability to withdraw $40,000 each year adjusted for inflation over the next 30 years without running out of money) can be computed. Running one million iterations, the Monte-Carlo simulation reveals that there is about an 80% probability of success with a 100% stock portfolio. In other words, in 20% of the 30 year time periods the client would run out of money within 30 years (not an attractive scenario for most clients). The software can also be run to output the maximum safe initial withdrawal given a certain desired probability of success. Let's say a client wants to be 95% certain not to run out of money. Monte-Carlo simulation reveals that the maximum safe withdrawal amount is about 2.6% ($26,000 rather than $40,000). Running the Monte-Carlo simulation with a 100% bond portfolio reveals that there is a 66% probability of success at withdrawing $40,000. Conversely, to achieve a 95% probability of success with bonds, the maximum safe initial withdrawal rate is about 2.9%. While the expected return on stocks was higher than that of bonds, bonds had a lower volatility. The probably of success was lower than for a stock only portfolio, but the sustainable withdrawal was higher. However, neither the stock only nor the bond only portfolios are very attractive.

By creating a portfolio of these two asset classes that are not highly correlated, the sustainability of withdrawals can be improved. Take a portfolio of 50% stocks and 50% bonds. From the above data, the expected return on the portfolio would be 7.75% with a standard deviation of 11.76%. Running Monte-Carlo simulation reveals that the combined portfolio would have an 86.5% probability of succeeding with a 4% withdrawal rate. To achieve a 95% probability of success the maximum safe withdrawal rate would be about 3.3%. The diversified portfolio outperforms both the stock only and bond only portfolios, once again demonstrating the advantages of asset allocation in controlling volatility. Note, however, that the diversified portfolio has a lower expected return than the stock only portfolio and the average expected wealth accumulation would be lower than a stock only portfolio. This is consistent with using a higher equity allocation during the pre-retirement years and switching to a more diversified portfolio during retirement years for risk adverse clients.

The preceding example was for illustrative purposes only. Each Monte Carlo software is presumably unique. Calculated results may vary.

INDIVIDUAL SECURITY SELECTION

Once the asset allocation decision has been made, the next step is to select individual securities (stocks, bonds, etc.) or mutual funds within each asset class. As with the overall asset allocation strategy, this can be either passive or active. In a passive approach, the advisor selects broad diversified portfolios (such as index mutual funds or exchange-traded index funds) representing each asset class. In an active approach, the advisor selects individual securities or traditional, actively managed mutual funds within each asset class that are expected to outperform their peers. The active approach requires more frequent monitoring, security selection, and buy/sell decisions. The choice between the active and passive approaches depends upon an advisor's beliefs about market efficiency and the advisor's ability to select, in advance, better performing securities or funds. Efficient markets generally assume rational behavior by

market participants and a number of anomalies have been shown to occur. A study of behavioral finance can help the advisor understand investor behavior both in selecting investment strategies and educating clients to avoid some common pitfalls.

Market Efficiency

The Efficient Market Theory (EMT) hypothesizes that securities markets process information efficiently. This implies that new information about a security is quickly (almost instantaneously) reflected in its price.

In order for a market to be efficient, certain conditions must be met. These include a large number of profit maximizing investors competing in the market and a free, random flow of information. When these conditions are present, the market is assumed to be efficient.

Beginning with the first point, a large number of profit-seeking market participants ensures that no trader is able to manipulate the market. If a participant tries to drive the price of a security too high or too low, other investors will recognize the mispricing and sell or buy to offset the rogue trader. Note that this does not imply that prices will always adjust immediately to the "correct" price. Rather, the efficient market theory requires only an equal likelihood that prices are either too high or too low (no bias that would allow investors to earn excess returns).

An efficient market requires that news flow be random and freely available. If positive or negative announcements can be consistently predicted, a trader can take advantage of them. As long as the timing is uncertain, all traders have an equal opportunity to profit or lose from a given speculation.

Given a market with many traders, a quick reaction to information is generally a given. Still, there could be other factors limiting an investor's ability to trade. For example, exchange rules put in place after the 1987 market crash include "circuit breakers" that halt trading when the market is up or down more than a certain amount. It has been argued that these rules reduce efficiency, as investors are prevented from fully responding to important events.

Strong Form EMT

In its strong form, efficient market theory posits that all information, whether public or not, is reflected in security prices. In other words, this is a perfect market assumption. In a strong-form efficient market, no participants would be able to consistently perform better than the market other than by random luck.

Semi-Strong Form EMT

The semi-strong form of efficient market theory states that all public information is reflected in stock prices. This includes prices of securities, security volume data, financial reports, press releases, statements of company officers, newspaper articles, and the work of sell-side securities analysts, as well as many other types of information.

Weak Form EMT

To be weak form efficient, security prices need reflect only market data, such as historical trade prices, volume, and order size. In a weak form efficient market, an investor could use fundamental analysis tools such as financial statement analysis and other fundamental information to glean information that has not been efficiently priced. This information could then be used to outperform the market. However, technical analysis (charting of security price and volume data) would still fail to provide consistent out-performance, because it relies on market data.

EMT Anomalies

There are a number of research studies that show that some basic fundamental strategies can result in an investor out-performing the market. These are known as EMT anomalies.

Stocks paying high dividend yields have been shown to perform better over time than low dividend yield stocks. Similarly, stocks with low price/book, price/sales, and price/earnings ratios have been found to outperform those stocks with higher price multiples.

The market appears to over and under react to news. Sometimes it takes several quarters for news to be fully reflected in stock prices and, in other cases, news causes an overreaction that is later corrected. Studies have been done showing that the market overreacts, and others indicate that there is persistent under-reaction. Note that unless an investor can predict whether the market reaction to news will be too much or not enough, the efficient market hypothesis would hold.

Some research has demonstrated a "January effect" under which the market tends to perform better in January. Some of this effect may be explained by the timing of tax selling. Late in the year, investors who want to minimize taxes will sell stocks that have gone down in order to incur a capital loss. Under the tax rules, if the investor desires to repurchase the security, he must wait 30 days, which can cause buying in January.

Shares of firms with small market capitalization (the size effect) or few dedicated analysts (the neglect effect) tend to perform better than others. In some ways, this is not so much an anomaly as a validation of the efficient market theory. Few analysts or a small market cap could reduce buyers' willingness to take a chance on such names. As a result, the first requirement of an efficient market – that there be many participants – is violated.

The Value Line effect is a finding that stocks ranked highest by Value Line have been found to outperform the market in certain periods. This is considered to be an efficient market anomaly, because this consistent outperformance should be recognized by the market and reflected in the stock price as soon as the ranking is published.

The existence of the various anomalies calls into question the relative efficiency of the markets. The research studies that uncovered these anomalies relate to particular time periods and, of course, do not guarantee they will work in future periods. In addition, identifying anomalies should cause traders to act on them, which in turn helps to achieve a greater level of market efficiency.

Behavioral Finance

Behavioral finance involves the study of how investors make decisions. Investors often use mental shortcuts or demonstrate biases in their decision making. Understanding these concepts can assist the advisor in understanding market behavior and anomalies and helping clients make better decisions. Some investment managers and mutual funds attempt to exploit these behavioral issues in making securities investments. This section explores some common behavioral finance issues.

Mental Accounting. Investors (and consumers) have been shown to have "categories of money" such that all dollars are not equivalent. They categorize money into buckets. Imagine that a ticket to a hockey game is purchased for $100. When the individual arrives for the game, he discovers that he has lost his ticket. Question 1 – Does he spend another $100 to purchase another ticket? Consider another example where the individual has not yet purchased a ticket. When he arrives for the game, he discovers that he has lost $100 in the parking lot. Question 2 – Does he spend another $100 to purchase a ticket? Belsky and Gilovich (1999) find that most people answer no to Question 1 but yes to question 2 since in the first situation $200 would be charged to the entertainment "mental account." In the investment arena, clients may be inclined to mentally view money differently depending upon the source, such as inheritance versus earned money, or principal versus capital gains.

Confirmation Bias. People tend to search for and select information which confirms their beliefs. This is a dangerous bias that can lead to bad investment decisions. For example, in evaluating an individual security for investment, the advisor or client may examine a half dozen analysts' reports and select the one that confirms his prior beliefs (buy, sell, or hold). Of course, the analyst writing the report may have used confirmation bias in evaluating data for purposes of reaching his recommendation based on other relationships the analyst may have with the company. Advisors need to be aware of the potential existence of this bias in evaluating reports of others and in making their own evaluations. An independent, objective frame of mind should be strived for.

Optimism/Overconfidence. People tend to believe that they are better than average (while everyone wants to be – by definition, they cannot all be above average). For example, in a survey of British drivers, 95% of them felt they were above average. Analysts, investors, and advisors may be overconfident in their abilities to forecast company earnings, future growth rates, investment returns, and similar future events. Overconfidence can be reduced by considering many different possibilities or alternatives.

Loss Aversion/Framing. Individuals are generally willing to take more risk to avoid a certain loss, but are conservative in locking in gains and avoiding risk. Aversion to losses also results in a reluctance of investors to sell losing investments. They may feel they can "avoid" the loss by not selling the investment, even though the investment has declined in value.

Herding. Individuals may engage in herding behavior. This can be demonstrated with financial analysts who forecast earnings for a company. Analysts may want to stay with the herd by having a forecast that

is similar to the forecast of other analysts. Having a forecast that is much higher or lower than the "herd" can result in being out on a limb if the analyst is wrong. If an individual is wrong, but in with the herd there is no loss in reputation.

Use of Heuristics. Individuals often use heuristics (shortcuts) in making decisions. These include representativeness, availability, and anchoring. In representativeness, individuals make judgments based on similar past events. Availability involves making decisions based on how recent or vivid information is. For example, they may view the market more positively if recent returns have been positive even though market returns may actually exhibit some reversion to the mean. Similarly, they may become increasingly pessimistic if the market has declined recently. Anchoring involves individuals anchoring on a current number such as a stock price or returns and make adjustments from that number, rather than making an independent assessment of potential outcomes. These simple shortcuts ease decision making but can result in bad investment decision, such as buying investments that have recently increased in value rather than buying those that have recently declined.

Active Security Selection

If an active security selection strategy is chosen, there are two basic approaches: a top-down approach and a bottom-up approach. In a top-down approach, the advisor performs an analysis of the global and domestic economy. Based on this economic analysis, the advisor selects industries or sectors that are expected to do well under those economic conditions. Lastly, the advisor selects the best securities within those industries or sectors, perhaps based on fundamental characteristics such as earnings, cash flow, growth prospects, and risk.

In a bottom-up approach, the advisor starts at the individual security level, identifying the "best" companies according to some predefined criteria. These criteria can be based on relative valuation, fundamental analysis, or technical analysis. Chapter 39 explores fundamental and technical analysis in more detail. Chapter 33 presents valuation models useful in selecting equity securities, while Chapter 34, "Measuring Yield," presents similar models for fixed income securities.

WHERE CAN I FIND OUT MORE ABOUT IT?

1. *2005 Yearbook, Stocks, Bonds, Bills and Inflation* (Chicago, IL: Ibbotson Associates, 2005).

2. Harold Evensky, *Wealth Management*, (New York, NY: McGraw Hill, 1997).

3. James O'Shaughnessy, *What Works On Wall Street*, 2nd Edition (New York, NY: McGraw Hill, 1998).

4. John Stowe, Thomas Robinson, Jerald Pinto and Dennis McLeavey, *Analysis of Equity Investments: Valuation* (Charlottesville, VA: Association for Investment Management and Research, 2002).

5. Willam P. Bengen, Conserving Client Portfolios During Retirement, (Denver, Colorado: FPA Press, 2006).

6. Gary Belsky and Thomas Gilovich, *Why Smart People Make Big Money Mistakes-And How to Correct Them*, (New York, NY: Simon & Schuster, 1999).

QUESTIONS AND ANSWERS

Question – How does asset allocation reduce the risk of holding multiple risky securities?

Answer – Asset allocation looks for risky securities that behave differently from each other (have low or negative correlation.) If the overall portfolio has some assets that rise when others fall, the overall returns will be more stable (less risky).

Question – What is an advantage to controlling volatility (risk) and how can volatility be controlled?

Answer – Reducing the volatility of a portfolio can make clients feel more comfortable with their portfolio and improve the sustainability of retirement withdrawals. Volatility can be reduced through diversification, time, and the use of hedging/option strategies.

Question – Edwin Jackson is a portfolio manager who relies on in-depth research to select stocks. He examines a firm's competitiveness and position within its industry, and then evaluates management's performance using such measures as operating margin, return on equity, and its efficiency in keeping inventory and collecting accounts receivable. In a semi-strong form efficient market, are Jackson's efforts useful?

Answer – In a semi-strong form efficient market, all public information would be reflected in the stock price. This includes all of the measures Jackson uses in his investment process. Therefore, his work would be unlikely to add significant value. (Note however that there is a chicken and egg phenomenon, because if Jackson and others like him become discouraged and quit their jobs as analysts, the market would become less efficient.)

Question – A client who is willing to take more risk with the portion of his portfolio that came from recent capital gains than the amount related to his or her original principal is exhibiting what type of behavioral finance issue?

Answer – The client is using mental accounting where they are maintaining capital gains in one mental account and principal in another.

Chapter 39

INVESTMENT STRATEGIES

WHAT IS IT?

This chapter explores strategies used to select individual securities and time their purchase or sale.

Passive investment strategies implicitly assume markets are efficient, and that, therefore, reducing investment trading and research costs is more important than pursuing "market out-performance." A passive approach typically involves purchasing a basket of securities that represent a market index and holding them for the long term (perhaps with periodic rebalancing). A passive approach typically does not focus on individual security selection.

By contrast, active management strategies either assume the market is inefficient or that inefficiencies within the market can be profitably exploited. A great deal of time and effort is expended in security selection and the timing of purchases and sales.

SECURITY SELECTION

Active security selection usually involves fundamental analysis, technical analysis, or both. Fundamental analysis examines company-specific factors such as profitability, risk, relative valuation, and growth prospects. Technical analysis studies market information such as price and volume to identify important trends and opportunities.

Fundamental Analysis

Many managers use fundamental analysis techniques to identify securities they believe are mispriced. Fundamental analysis can be employed using either a top-down or a bottom-up philosophy (see Chapter 38, "Asset Allocation and Portfolio Construction").

Top-down managers begin with an overview of the entire economy and market. The idea behind such research is that one must first understand where the overall economy is headed in order to identify the asset classes, economic sectors, and, ultimately, securities that are expected to outperform. In a top down approach, the final step is typically to examine the fundamentals of a particular company whose securities are of interest.

Bottom-up analysts often call themselves stock-pickers. They attempt to identify the best securities and the price at which to buy them, regardless of sector or industry considerations. Bottom-up analysts typically begin by examining company fundamentals, often by screening large databases of securities for information the analyst finds attractive. Only after they have identified securities of interest do they consider the prospects for the industry, sector, and economy.

Some investors blend both top-down and bottom-up approaches in an attempt to add value across the spectrum.

Company Fundamentals

In order to understand some of the fundamental factors analysts look for, first some basic company financial information is presented. There are three important financial statements on which analysts focus: (1) the balance sheet; (2) the income statement; and (3) the statement of cash flows. There are other financial statements (such as a statement of owners' equity), schedules, and footnotes that are also useful in understanding the three primary statements.

The balance sheet reflects the company's financial position as of a particular date. Figure 39.1 presents a basic balance sheet for a hypothetical electronics retailer. The balance sheet presents the company's resources (assets) and the claims against those resources (liabilities and equity). The resources must always equal the claims (hence the term balance sheet).

The balance sheet heading indicates that the company has a calendar year end and that all numbers are denominated in millions. The balance sheets as of year-end 2004 and 2005 are both presented. The company's assets are classified either as current or long-term. Current assets are expected to be used up in a single operating cycle, typically one year. Non-current assets have a lifetime that spans multiple operating cycles.

Figure 39.1

HOWARD'S ELECTRONIC RETAILERS, INC.
BALANCE SHEET
AS OF DECEMBER 31
(IN MILLIONS OF DOLLARS)

	2004	2005
Cash	$ 10	$ 15
Accounts Receivable	50	60
Inventory	100	120
Current Assets	160	195
Property, Plant and Equipment	640	730
Accumulated Depreciation	(300)	(330)
Total Assets	$ 500	$ 595
Accounts Payable	$ 40	$ 45
Accrued Expenses	30	38
Current Liabilities	70	83
Long Term Debt	200	240
Total Liabilities	270	323
Common Stock	100	115
Retained Earnings	130	157
Total Equity	230	272
Total Liabilities and Equity	$ 500	$ 595

U.S. accounting conventions list assets in order of how quickly they can be converted into cash. Not surprisingly, therefore, cash is normally the first asset presented. The balance sheet cash account includes cash on hand, in banks, and other short-term deposits (such as certificates of deposits).

Accounts receivable represents money the company is owed by its customers for goods or services that have been provided. For example, when a doctor provides services and bills the patient at a later date, an accounts receivable balance is created from the time the service is performed until the bill is paid.

Inventory is the unsold merchandise and materials on hand at the end of the year.

Property, plant, and equipment are long-term fixed assets of the company such as buildings, equipment,

vehicles, and furniture. These assets are not used up in a single year, but rather benefit the company over time. Generally accepted accounting principles (GAAP) require that companies report the costs associated with money earned in the same period the money is earned, a concept known as the matching principle. Since a factory, for example, helps a company earn money for many years, GAAP requires that the cost of the factory be spread over many years. When the company earns money later, the relevant factory costs are recognized at the same time.

The cost a company recognizes for a fixed asset in the future period is called depreciation. Essentially, depreciation is an estimation of the economic wear and tear on the fixed assets over time.

Total assets are the sum of current and noncurrent assets. For Howard's Electronic Retailers, Inc. (HERI), there were total assets of $500 million at the end of 2004 and $595 million at the end of 2005.

Liabilities are also classified as current or noncurrent. Just as assets are listed in order of how quickly they are likely to be turned into cash or used up, liabilities are listed in the order they are expected to be paid.

Accounts payable represent the amounts owed to suppliers. Accrued expenses represent additional expenses payable to others, such as employees, the government, or landlords.

Long-term debt represents amounts due to creditors, such as banks. For example, when a company buys vehicles, it may choose to finance their purchase. In a way, financing long-lasting assets with liabilities that are paid off over time is the economic (as opposed to accounting) version of the matching principle.

Equity represents the amount owners have invested in a business, either initially or by reinvesting the company's earnings. Common stock represents the amounts paid into the company when the stock was first sold to shareholders. Retained earnings are the earnings accumulated in the company (not paid out to shareholders as dividends) since inception.

The income statement shows how profitable a company was during a particular time period. Figure 39.2 presents income statements for HERI. Typically three years of the income statement are presented in a company's annual report. For HERI, income statements for December 31, 2003, 2004, and 2005 are provided.

Figure 39.2

HOWARD'S ELECTRONIC RETAILERS, INC. INCOME STATEMENT FOR THE YEAR ENDED DECEMBER 31 (IN MILLIONS OF DOLLARS)			
	2003	**2004**	**2005**
Revenues	$750	$800	$900
Cost of Goods Sold	560	600	713
Gross Profit	190	200	187
Operating Expenses	100	120	130
Operating Income	90	80	57
Interest Expense	18	18	18
Pre-Tax Income	72	62	39
Income Tax Expense	21	19	12
Net Income	$51	$43	$27
Shares Outstanding (millions)	100	100	102
Earnings Per Share	$0.51	$0.43	$0.26

As discussed earlier, the matching principle requires that revenues be reported when earned and expenses when incurred. This does not necessarily coincide with when the cash is received or paid. As a result, the third important financial statement, the cash flow statement, presents the cash received and paid out during the period. Figure 39.3 presents the cash flow statement for HERI.

Cash flow is important because it is necessary to pay employees, suppliers, creditors, and, ultimately, owners. The cash flow statement is divided into three sections; operating cash flows, investing cash flows, and financing cash flows. Operating cash flows relate to operating the business. Investing cash flows relate to investments in long-term assets. Financing cash flows relate to financing the company, such as issuing/repaying debt, issuing/repurchasing shares, and paying dividends.

Generally, it is preferable to have strong, positive operating cash flows that can be used to invest in long-term assets and repay capital providers (debt and equity).

Figure 39.3

HOWARD'S ELECTRONIC RETAILERS, INC. STATEMENT OF CASH FLOWS FOR THE YEAR ENDED DECEMBER 31 (IN MILLIONS OF DOLLARS)			
	2003	**2004**	**2005**
Operating			
Net Income	$51	$43	$27
Plus Depreciation	25	25	30
Change in Working Capital	(20)	10	(17)
Operating Cash Flow	56	78	40
Investing			
Capital Expenditures	(60)	(70)	(90)
Investing Cash Flow	(60)	(70)	(90)
Financing			
Borrowing	0	0	40
Issuance of Stock	0	0	15
Financing Cash Flow	0	0	55
Total Cash Flow	(4)	8	5
Beginning Cash	6	2	10
Ending Cash	$2	$10	$15

The top line of the income statement, revenues, is the total amount received (or due) from customers for goods and services provided during the period. Cost of goods sold represents the cost of those goods (or services), such as materials and labor used directly in delivering the goods (or services). The difference between revenues and cost of goods sold is called gross profit. Gross profit is a basic measure of how the company is doing. The higher the gross profit, the better.

Operating expenses are other expenses incurred in the operation of a business, such as overhead. Operating income is the subtotal reflecting gross profit minus operating expenses.

Interest expense is the interest paid to creditors for the use of their money during the period. Pre-tax income is the subtotal that includes operating and non-operating (financing) results. Income tax is the amount owed on the reported income. Net income, commonly termed "the bottom line," is the overall net profit during the period. When net income is divided by the number of shares of stock outstanding, the result is known as earnings per share (EPS). EPS allows each investor to determine his share of net income.

Figure 39.4

Category	Ratio	Formula
Liquidity & Solvency	Current Ratio	$\dfrac{\text{Current Assets}}{\text{Current Liabilities}}$
	Debt Ratio	$\dfrac{\text{Total Liabilities}}{\text{Total Assets}}$
	Times Interest Earned	$\dfrac{\text{Earning Before Interest and Taxes}}{\text{Interest Expense}}$
Efficiency	Accounts Receivable Turnover	$\dfrac{\text{Sales}}{\text{Average Accounts Receivable}}$
	Inventory Turnover	$\dfrac{\text{Cost of Goods Sold}}{\text{Average Inventory}}$
	Total Asset Turnover	$\dfrac{\text{Sales}}{\text{Average Total Assets}}$
Profitability	Net profit margin	$\dfrac{\text{Net Income}}{\text{Sales}}$
	Return on assets	$\dfrac{\text{Net Income}}{\text{Average Total Assets}}$
	Return on equity	$\dfrac{\text{Net Income}}{\text{Average Total Equity}}$
Price Multiples	Price/Earnings	$\dfrac{\text{Price Per Share}}{\text{Earnings Per Share}}$
	Price/Book Value	$\dfrac{\text{Price Per Share}}{\text{Book Value Per Share}}$
	Price/Operating Cash Flow	$\dfrac{\text{Price Per Share}}{\text{Operating Cash Flow Per Share}}$

Recent accounting scandals have highlighted the importance of paying attention to the cash flow statement. Some companies abuse and pervert accounting guidelines to overstate net income. If a company has rising net income but declining operating cash flow, this is a warning sign and the company should be scrutinized carefully.

Company Ratios

In order to evaluate how a company is doing over time and relative to other companies in the industry, financial performance and position must be compared.

Since comparisons between companies of different sizes or growth rates can be difficult, analysts often create ratios to remove the impact of size differences. Ratios can be categorized as: liquidity and solvency, efficiency, profitability, and price multiples. Some common ratios in each of these categories are presented in Figure 39.4.

Liquidity and solvency ratios show the ability of a company to pay short- and long-term obligations, respectively. HERI has a current ratio of 2.35 (195/83) indicating that it has $2.35 of current assets for every $1.00 of current liabilities. When the current ratio is greater than one, current assets are sufficient to satisfy current liabilities. A company with a higher current ratio is less likely to default on its payments, but an extremely high current ratio may indicate the company is not using its resources efficiently.

HERI's debt ratio is 54.29% (323/595), indicating that a little more than half of its assets are financed with liabilities. In terms of solvency, a lower number would indicate lower financial risk. However, debt can be beneficial if the company can use the debt-financed assets to earn more than it pays in interest.

Times interest earned measures whether the company earns enough operating income to make its interest payments. HERI has a times interest earned ratio of 3.17 (57/18), meaning it can cover its interest slightly more than 3 times.

Efficiency ratios provide insight into how well the company is managing various activities. Accounts receivable turnover indicates how quickly the company collects money owed by its customers. A high number means the company collects its receivables quickly. HERI has an accounts receivable turnover ratio of 16.36 [900 / ((50 + 60) / 2)]. On average, this means it takes 22.31 days (365/16.36) on average to collect receivables. Similarly, inventory turnover measures how often the company turns over its inventory. HERI turned over its inventory 6.48 times per year [713 / ((100 + 120) / 2)] (equivalent to 56.33 days of inventory on hand [365 / 6.48]). Total asset turnover indicates the companies overall efficiency. HERI has a total asset turnover ratio of 1.64 times. This indicates that HERI generates $1.64 in sales for every $1.00 invested in assets.

Profitability ratios indicate the company's relative profitability. HERI's net profit margin of 3.0% (271/900) indicates that it earns $3.00 for every $100.00 in revenue. HERI has a return on assets ratio of 4.93% [27 / ((500 + 595) / 2)] indicating that it earns $4.93 of profits for every $100.00 invested in assets. Lastly, HERI's return on equity is 10.76% [27 / ((230 + 272) / 2)], indicating that it earned $10.76 in profits for every $100.00 invested by the owners.

The price multiples indicate the relative valuation of the company by the market. A low ratio indicates a low valuation relative to some fundamental measure, and could indicate that the company is a bargain or that investors expect it to do poorly. A high ratio could indicate overvaluation or high expected future growth. The price earnings (P/E) ratio is the price per share relative to earnings per share. The price to book (P/B) ratio is the price share divided by book value (stockholders' equity) per share. Price to operating cash flow is the price per share relative to operating cash flow per share. Assuming a price of $4.00 per share for HERI, its price multiples are:

P/E   15.38 [4 / .26]
P/B   1.50 [4 / (272 / 102)]
P/OCF   10.20 [4 / (40 / 102)]

The company is selling for 15.38 times earnings, 1.5 times book value (accounting basis for equity), and 10.20 times operating cash flow. These measures can be compared to peer companies and the overall market to assess the company's relative valuation.

Example

Landstar System, Inc. provides transportation services, mainly truckload transportation over medium distances. The company does not own its own vehicles, but instead uses technology to match loads sourced by commissioned agents with drivers who provide their own vehicle. As a result, Landstar's fixed asset base is relatively small.

An investor looking at Landstar in early 2006 might find the following information in the company's annual report:

Year ended December 31

(in thousands of dollars)	2005	2004	2003
Total revenue	2,520,523	2,021,282	1,597,791
Net income	119,956	71,872	50,700
Cash flow from operating activities	6,529	49,744	53,396

At first glance, the investor is pleased with the company's rapid revenue growth rate (24.7% in 2005 and 26.5% in 2004). In addition, net profit margins (net income divided by total revenue) have risen from 3.2% in 2003 to 3.6% in 2004 and 4.8% in 2005. However, each year the cash flow has fallen even though the company reported higher income. The investor looks at the cash flow statement and determines that rising receivables have been the culprit.

A look at the footnotes to the financial statements provides this explanation:

Included in revenue at the global logistics segment for the 2005 and 2004 fiscal years was $275,929,000 and $63,790,000, respectively, of revenue related to disaster relief efforts for the storms that impacted the United States. These emergency transportation services were provided primarily under a contract between Landstar Express America, Inc. and the United States Department of Transportation/Federal Aviation Administration (the "FAA")....

Included in accounts receivable at December 31, 2005 was trade accounts receivable due from various departments of the United States Government of $226,057,000, which includes $215,250,000 in trade receivables from disaster relief services provided under the contract with the FAA. The decrease in cash provided by operating activities was primarily due to an increase in trade receivables resulting in large part from revenue related to the emergency transportation services provided under the FAA contract. The financing of a portion of this $215,250,000 receivable from the FAA with borrowings under the Company's revolving credit agreement is the primary reason for the increase in long term debt....

The FAA contract expires December 31, 2006.

So, the investor was able to use ratios and fundamental analysis to spot a potential problem, which could then be tracked to its source using other information. If the 10K had not disclosed this information, the investor could have tried calling management to ask for an explanation.

However, as is often the case, the answer has led to more questions. The investor can feel more confident about the company's ability to collect the receivables (the US Government is a reliable customer) and can easily explain the falling cash flow in spite of rising income. In fact, the March quarter 10Q shows $97 million in cash flow against $24 million net income, as a good portion of the disaster relief receivables were collected. However, the information also reveals that a large portion of the growth depended on severe weather that may not happen again. Furthermore, with the contract expiring in 2006 it is unclear that the company would benefit even in the event that severe weather did strike again.

Fundamental Screening

Since there are more than 10,000 potential public company investments to consider, advisors are unable to examine the financial statements and ratios in detail for each company. Therefore, the process often begins by screening a large database of securities to find a small number that have desirable attributes. For example, a value manager may look for companies with relatively low price multiples but strong profitability and growing

cash flows. The database could be screened to select companies that meet these criteria. The smaller sample of companies that is produced can then be analyzed in more detail.

Technical Analysis

Technical analysis assumes that fundamental information is reflected in market data such as price and trading volume and, therefore, the analyst can focus on charts of such data to make investment decisions. This does not necessarily mean that markets are perfectly efficient. For example, if markets react slowly to new information, this can be found by looking at the trend in a price chart and making an investment decision based on this trend. Technical analysis includes a study of charts depicting trends in price and volume and indicators as to when a trend is expected to continue or reverse. While many view technical analysis as the antithesis of fundamental analysis, some analysts view them as complementary tools. Technical analysts can benefit by understanding how fundamentals may be driving trends and fundamental analysts can benefit from using trend information to time buy and sell decisions.

Charting

In its simplest form, technical analysis involves preparing a chart of past price and volume data. Figure 39.5 presents a typical bar chart for Dell Computer.

Figure 39.5

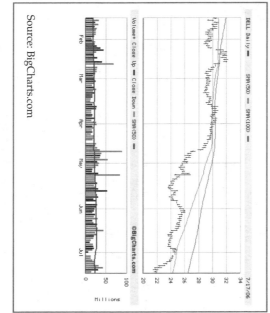

Source: BigCharts.com

The top portion of the chart depicts price information. Each bar on the graph summarized a day's trading activity: showing the open, high, low and closing prices.

Figure 39.6 shows one such daily bar. This bar depicts the opening price with a horizontal line to the left, the closing price with a horizontal line to the right. The vertical bar depicts the range of prices for the day from the low (bottom) to the high (top).

Figure 39.6

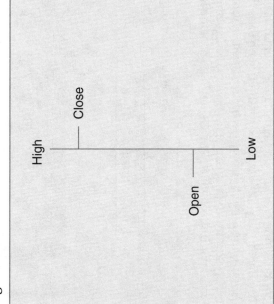

The price trend for the day appears to be up. In technical analysis, a trend is generally considered to continue until a reversal signal or pattern emerges in the chart. One such signal compares the price to a moving average of price over some period. The solid line in the price area within Figure 39.5 is a moving average of the last 50 days of prices. A reversal of the short-term trend is signaled when the price crosses the moving average line. When the price falls below the moving average it is considered a sell signal. When the price rises above the moving average it generates a buy signal.

Some technical analysts believe that certain patterns in prices signal a trend reversal. One such pattern is a head and shoulders top, depicted in Figure 39.7.

Figure 39.7

The jagged line in Figure 39.7 represents a summary of the price action. The line with an arrow is added to show the point at which a sell signal would be generated. This is termed the neckline. When a price chart forms a head and shoulders pattern, the analyst watches as the right shoulder is formed to see if the price falls below the neckline, which would be a sell signal.

The bottom portion of Figure 39.5 provides vertical bars depicting daily volume information. In technical analysis, trading volume is used to confirm signals generated by price data. For example, a decreasing volume pattern with each subsequent peak (left shoulder, head, right shoulder) accompanying the head and shoulders pattern confirms the strength of the sell signal. It indicates that fewer people are willing to buy as the pattern develops.

Support and resistance are two important concepts in technical analysis. Consider the price pattern in Figure 39.8. The arrow indicates a support line. Each time the price falls to this line, it rebounds indicating that buyers are coming into the security at that price.

Figure 39.8

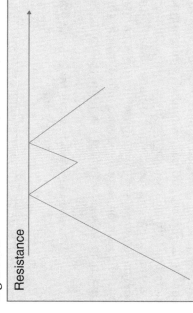

Figure 39.9 presents a resistance level pattern. Resistance levels indicate a point at which sellers step in to sell at a particular price, driving the price down.

Figure 39.9

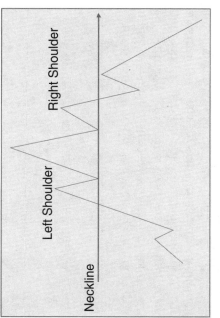

Support (resistance) levels may be useful in indicating target purchase (sale) prices. Care must be taken when using support and resistance levels since the support and resistance lines can be broken (for example due to new fundamental news). Breaking a support or resistance line can indicate that a new trend is forming.

Overall Market Analysis

In addition to charting individual securities, technical analysis involves the evaluation of overall security markets. Technical indicators can be used to determine the trend in the overall market and evaluate when it is desirable to make an investment in a particular asset class or alter asset allocation. Technical analysis of security markets can include the use of sentiment indicators, flow of funds indicators, and market structure indicators.

Sentiment indicators are used to evaluate the overall bullishness or bearishness of the market. Commonly used sentiment indicators include the volatility index, put/call ratio, short-interest ratio, and insider trading activity.

Volatility Index. The CBOE Volatility Index® (VIX®) is a measure of market expectations of near-term volatility derived from S&P 500 stock index option prices (www.cboe.com). According to the Chicago Board Options Exchange:

"VIX is based on real-time option prices, which reflect investors' consensus view of future expected stock market volatility. During periods of financial stress, which are often accompanied by steep market declines, option prices – and VIX – tend to rise. The greater the fear, the higher the VIX level. As investor fear subsides, option prices tend to decline, which in turn causes VIX to decline. It is important to note, however, that past performance does not necessarily indicate future results." (www.cboe.com, Frequently Asked Questions, as of July 23, 2006).

Figure 39.10 demonstrates the relationship of the VIX and the S&P 500 index in recent periods.

Put/Call Ratio. The CBOE also presents daily data on the ratio of put options to call options for equities, indices, and their total (equity plus indices). The ratio is the daily volume of puts options divided by the daily volume of call options. The lower the ratio the more bullish market participants are and the higher the ratio the more bearish market participants are. However,

Figure 39.10

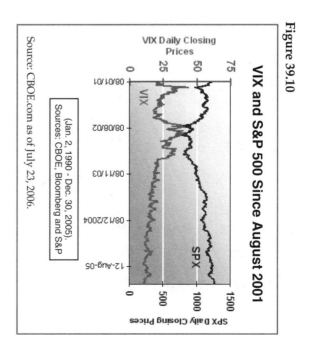

VIX and S&P 500 Since August 2001

Source: CBOE.com as of July 23, 2006.

sentiment indicators such as this are contrary indicators, bullishness of market participants gives a bearish signal for the market and bearishness of market participants gives a bullish signal for the market. This accounts for overconfidence of market participants at market tops and pessimism at market bottoms. Figure 39.11 presents CBOE Total Put/Call ratio data as of July 21, 2006.

Figure 39.11

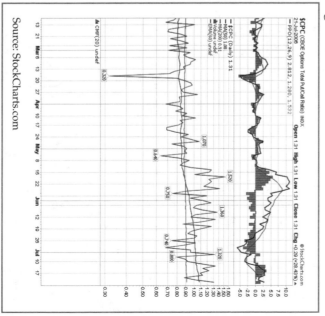

Source: StockCharts.com

Short Interest Ratio. The short interest ratio measures the volume of short sales for an index or security relative to average volume. This is a contrary sentiment ratio, since a high ratio indicates a high level of short activity and is considered bullish, whereas a low ratio is considered bearish.

Insider Trading. While the overall market is often wrong at market tops and bottoms, insiders have been found to be right at tops and bottoms. High insider buying relative to insider selling is therefore a bullish sentiment indicator. Low insider buying relative to selling is bearish.

Flow of funds indicators are used to assess the prospects for inflows or outflows of cash into the market or sectors. Flow of funds analysis also involves examining trends of sources of cash, such as the cash positions of large investors such as mutual funds and pension funds. For example, mutual fund data can be obtained from the Investment Company Institute. Flow of funds analysis involves examining potential demands for cash, such as new public offerings, and overall liquidity in the economy.

Market structure indicators examine charts of market indices for patterns and trends in both prices and volume (as with individual stocks discussed earlier). Market indices that are subject to analysis include the Dow Jones Industrial Average, S&P 500 Composite, Dow Jones Transportation Average, Dow Jones Utility Average, the NASDAQ, and Russell indices. Other market structure indicators include those that examine market breadth. Market breadth measures the extent to which issues underlying the indices are participating in the market trend. A market trend is stronger when more issues are participating. A popular measure of market breadth is the Advance/Decline line, which measures the number of issues advancing in excess of those declining. An increasing advance/decline line is positive for the overall market.

TIMING OF INVESTMENT PURCHASES AND SALES

In addition to selecting the right individual securities for purchase, the advisor must decide on the right price and the timing of the purchase and subsequent sale. Valuation of stocks and bonds is covered in Chapter 33, "Measuring Investment Returns," and Chapter 34, "Measuring Yield." This section explores purchase and sale strategies.

Market Timing

Market timing attempts to anticipate the market's broad direction and individual security prices, but the focus is usually on the broader market. Investors who believe stocks are too expensive will favor other asset classes. Those who believe stocks are cheap will sell other asset classes to buy more stocks.

The timing can be based on economic trends, stock prices, or valuation levels. For example, when stocks are above their normal P/E multiple range, this may be an indicator to reduce stock holdings. Similarly, when an individual security is at the high (low) end of its normal valuation range, this may be a sell (buy) indicator. Technical charts of market indices and individual securities can be useful in generating buy and sell signals in a market timing strategy.

Buy and Hold

In contrast to market timing, a buy and hold strategy does not attempt to anticipate moves in the market or even individual securities. Rather, such a strategy relies on the notion that a well-planned investment policy will result in a portfolio that best meets an investor's risk and return profile. Buy and hold strategies tend to be long-term oriented, whereas market timing strategies are short-term in nature.

One advantage of a buy and hold strategy is that it reduces transaction costs. Another is its simplicity. A disadvantage of a buy and hold strategy is that it can distort an investor's asset allocations. Consider an investor who decided in January 1996 that her appropriate asset allocation was 50% stocks and 50% bonds. She makes a single decision to buy the assets in those proportions and promptly forgets about it. By year-end 1999, stocks have vastly outperformed bonds. Because of this relative difference in performance, stocks now comprise two thirds of her portfolio. She has unintentionally changed her asset allocations to favor stocks – just before the stock market crashes and bonds enjoy several years of superior performance.

A buy and hold strategy implies that only one investment decision is made (to buy). Occasionally, however, passive market timing strategies such as rebalancing will be described as "buy and hold." It could be argued that one decision is made to "buy" the chosen allocation, and the later adjustments simply conform to the original strategy. It is important to understand which definition of "buy and hold" a particular pundit may espouse.

Passive Investing or Indexing

Passive investment strategies seek to mimic the returns on a benchmark index, such as the Standard & Poor's 500. The goal of a passive investment manager is not to beat the benchmark index, but rather to match it as closely as possible. But if no attempt is made to provide returns superior to the benchmark, why should an investor choose a passive strategy?

The main advantage of passive investing is reduced cost. Since benchmark index constituents change only occasionally, trading costs are lower than with most actively managed strategies. Also, active strategies require skilled analysts and managers. There is no need for active security selection in a passive indexing strategy.

One way to construct a passive portfolio is to simply buy and hold the securities in the index, at their appropriate weightings. This method is known as replication, and its main advantage is low tracking error with the index. However, replication can be difficult to accomplish for many reasons. For one thing, in small portfolios replication is likely to require owning partial shares. Furthermore, investment flows, such as new investment, withdrawals, or dividends, would require the proceeds to be distributed to buy or sell tiny amounts of each stock in the index. An alternative is the use of index mutual funds or exchange-traded index funds.

A second means of constructing an indexed portfolio is sampling. Under this strategy, several securities are chosen in such a way as to be representative of the overall index. Doing so reduces trading costs and the need to buy small quantities of many stocks. However, it increases specific security risk and is unlikely to track the benchmark well.

WHERE CAN I FIND OUT MORE ABOUT IT?

1. More information on financial analysis and ratios can be found on Tom Robinson's Financial Education blog at www.financial-education.com.

2. John J. Murphy, *Technical Analysis of the Financial Markets* (New York, NY: New York Institute of Finance, 1999).

3. Martin J. Pring, *Technical Analysis Explained*, 4th Edition (New York, NY: McGraw-Hill, 2002).

QUESTIONS AND ANSWERS

Question – What are the differences between fundamental and technical analysis?

Answer – Fundamental analysis involves an examination of underlying company and industry fundamentals, such as financial statements and ratios, whereas technical analysis examines only market information, such as price and volume.

Question – An investment advisor examines the overall economy and selects the industry he feels will perform best over the coming five-year period. He then screens a database of securities to find companies in this industry. Finally, he narrows down the list of companies in the industry by focusing on companies that have a low price relative to earnings, but stable and positive returns on equity. What investment strategy is being followed?

Answer – This advisor is following a top-down, fundamental strategy. Further, the fundamental screens appear to be a value (versus a growth) approach.

Question – A company's stock price has been below its 50-day moving average for some time. The price for the last few days has moved above the moving average line. Further, volume is increasing. What type of technical signal is generated?

Answer – The fact that the price has moved above the moving average from the bottom would generate a buy signal. This is reinforced by the fact that volume is increasing with the price increase.

Question – What would a high put/call ratio indicate?

Answer – A high put/call ratio indicates a high level of put option volume relative to call option volume. This signals pessimism for market participants, which is considered to be bullish for the market.

Chapter 40

FORMULA INVESTING

WHAT IS IT?

Formula investing is a strategy that seeks to limit the role of emotions in investing by adhering to a strict set of rules. Typically, formula investment strategies involve making fixed periodic investments through "dollar cost averaging" or "dividend reinvestment plans." These two strategies can effectively lower the average cost of both equity and fixed-income securities in fluctuating markets. Other formula investing techniques, such as "bond laddering" and "bond barbell strategies," are designed to minimize risk of interest rate fluctuations.[1]

DOLLAR COST AVERAGING

Dollar cost averaging is a simple strategy practiced by many investors who may not even realize it. The strategy is to simply make regular, periodic investments in a security without regard to price. 401(k) investors who automatically invest a certain amount each paycheck are practicing dollar cost averaging. The premise behind dollar cost averaging is to take advantage of market fluctuations to buy more shares when prices are low and fewer when prices are high.

Contrast an investment strategy where an investor purchases the same number of shares of a mutual fund each month with a dollar cost averaging strategy where an investor purchases the same dollar amount of a mutual fund each month. An investor has approximately $1,000 of discretionary income each month and would like to purchase shares of a mutual fund that is currently selling for $10 per share. Consider the following two strategies:

- Strategy A - Purchase 100 shares per month; and

- Strategy B - Purchase $1,000 per month.

The price for each month of the year and the results of each strategy are presented in Figure 40.1. Under Strategy A, the investor has 1,200 shares at the end of the year with an average cost of $10.583 ($12,700 cost / 1,200 shares). The value of the 1,200 shares is $13,200.00 at the final price of $11.00/share ($11 x 1,200 shares), and there is an unrealized gain of $500.00 ($13,200 value - $12,700 cost). Under Strategy B, the investor has 1,141.914 shares with an average cost of $10.509 ($12,000 cost / 1,141.914 shares). The value of the shares is $12,561.05 ($11 x 1,141.914 shares) and there is an unrealized gain of $561.05 ($12,561.05 value - $12,000 cost). By purchasing more shares when the price is low and fewer shares when the price is high, the investor lowered his average cost basis with Strategy B. Consequently, the investor

Figure 40.1

Month	Mutual Fund Share Price	Strategy A – Shares Purchased	Strategy A – Total Cost	Strategy B – Shares Purchased	Strategy B – Total Cost
1	$10.00	100	$1,000.00	100.000	$1,000.00
2	$11.00	100	$1,100.00	90.909	$1,000.00
3	$11.00	100	$1,100.00	90.909	$1,000.00
4	$10.50	100	$1,050.00	95.238	$1,000.00
5	$10.00	100	$1,000.00	100.000	$1,000.00
6	$9.50	100	$950.00	105.263	$1,000.00
7	$9.00	100	$900.00	111.111	$1,000.00
8	$10.00	100	$1,000.00	100.000	$1,000.00
9	$11.00	100	$1,100.00	90.909	$1,000.00
10	$12.00	100	$1,200.00	83.333	$1,000.00
11	$12.00	100	$1,200.00	83.333	$1,000.00
12	$11.00	100	$1,100.00	90.909	$1,000.00
Total		**1,200**	**$12,700**	**1,141.914**	**$12,000**

Figure 40.2

Month	Mutual Fund Share Price	Strategy A – Shares Purchased	Strategy A – Total Cost	Strategy B – Shares Purchased	Strategy B – Total Cost
1	$10.00	100	$1,000.00	100.000	$1,000.00
2	$10.10	100	$1,010.00	99.010	$1,000.00
3	$10.20	100	$1,020.00	98.039	$1,000.00
4	$10.30	100	$1,030.00	97.087	$1,000.00
5	$10.40	100	$1,040.00	96.154	$1,000.00
6	$10.50	100	$1,050.00	95.238	$1,000.00
7	$10.60	100	$1,060.00	94.340	$1,000.00
8	$10.70	100	$1,070.00	93.458	$1,000.00
9	$10.80	100	$1,080.00	92.593	$1,000.00
10	$10.90	100	$1,090.00	91.743	$1,000.00
11	$11.00	100	$1,100.00	90.909	$1,000.00
12	$11.10	100	$1,110.00	90.090	$1,000.00
Total		1,200	$12,660	1,138.661	$12,000

finished with greater investment gains of $561.05 vs. $500.00) on the amounts actually invested. Furthermore, the investor maintained a predictable investment outlay – he was not struck with the need to find additional funds for investment in months when the share price was higher.

Dollar cost averaging worked well in this example because prices were fluctuating up and down. What if prices were always trending up?

Figure 40.2 shows the impact of the two strategies in a continuous uptrend. In this case, Strategy A has an average cost of $10.55 ($12,660 cost / 1,200 shares), a value of $13,320 ($11 x 1,200 shares), and an unrealized gain of $660 ($13,320 value - $12,660 cost). Strategy B has an average cost of $10.54 ($12,000 / 1,138.661 shares), a value of $12,639.14 ($11 x 1,138.661 shares), and an unrealized gain of 639.14 ($12,639.14 value - $12,000 cost). Note that the dollar cost averaging Strategy B resulted in the lower average cost, but not the maximum gain in this case.

Dollar cost averaging strategy can also be compared to an initial lump sum purchase. For example, assume that Andrea, a 30-year old with limited investments, earns a $12,000 bonus received at the end of January. She has a choice of investing the entire amount in an S&P 500 index fund at one time or spreading the investment evenly over the next 12 months. Each share in the fund currently sells for $9.12. If she invests the entire lump sum at once, she can purchase just over 1,315.8 shares. She is not sure whether the market will rise or fall over the next 12 months and decides to spread the investment over the course of the year.

Here are the month-end values for the fund purchases Andrea makes:

Month	Fund	Shares
January	$9.12	109.6
February	$9.16	109.2
March	$8.15	122.7
April	$8.86	112.9
May	$9.36	106.8
June	$8.80	113.6
July	$8.56	116.8
August	$8.41	118.9
September	$8.48	117.9
October	$9.16	109.2
November	$9.64	103.7
December	$9.75	102.6
Total:		**1,343.9**

At the end of the year, she has about 1,344 shares, 28 more than she would have purchased had she bought them all up front (1,344 – 1,316). At the final price of $9.75/share, her investment has grown to $13,103 ($9.75 x 1,344 shares) instead of $12,829 ($9.75 x 1,316 shares) – an additional $274. The reason is that, as the market fell early in the year, she was able to buy a larger number of shares each month (at a lower cost). For example, when the market was at 815 in March she bought nearly 123 shares in the fund. When the market briefly rallied to 936 in May, she purchased only 107 shares at the higher price. Because she was able to take advantage of market fluctuations, she ended the year with more than 2% of additional value than she would have had by investing as a lump sum up-front.

Dollar cost averaging works best when markets are declining or fluctuating, as the investor is able to buy more shares when prices fall (and purchases fewer shares when prices are higher). In this sense, it is a contrarian strategy. Dollar cost averaging does not work in a steadily rising market, as the investor would be better off buying as much as possible at the lower initial price than to pay more each month for a smaller number of shares. Since markets do tend to rise over the long term, it would usually not make sense for Andrea to spread her investment over years rather than months. However, over a span of months, it is quite possible that Andrea will have the opportunity to make purchases at lower prices.

Even though Andrea has a long time horizon and should buy as much in the early years as possible, she must currently make a decision about investing a specific amount of available cash. By spreading the investment over 12 months, she is able to benefit from market fluctuations (since the market did occasionally decline) and at least ensure that she does not (accidentally) invest all of her money at a market peak. It also allows her to establish an investing discipline.

The consequences of investing at a market peak instead of dollar cost averaging can be quite substantial. For example, assume the returns from the above example occurred in reverse order, such that the market started at 9.75 and finished at 9.12. The results of this scenario are as follows:

Month	Fund	Shares
January	$9.75	102.6
February	$9.64	103.7
March	$9.16	109.2
April	$8.48	117.9
May	$8.41	118.9
June	$8.56	116.8
July	$8.80	113.6
August	$9.36	106.8
September	$8.86	112.9
October	$8.15	122.7
November	$9.16	109.2
December	$9.12	109.6
Total:		**1,343.9**

At the end of the year, Andrea still has about 1,344 shares through a dollar cost averaging program. However, in this case the total shares in the end are worth only $12,256 (1,343.9 shares x $9.12/share). But if Andrea had made a lump-sum investment of her $12,000, she would have only been able to purchase about 1,231 shares at the high price of $9.75/share – at the end of the term, this would have only been worth $11,225 (1,230.8 shares x $9.12/share)! In the first case of a fluctuating but rising market, Andrea's dollar cost averaging strategy allowed her to end the year with an extra 2% of additional value – in the latter case, she enjoys an extra $1,031, or over 9% of additional value!

For many investors, dollar cost averaging is as much a matter of necessity as of choice. For those that do not have a lump sum available to invest, dollar cost averaging becomes the de facto strategy simply because they make purchases as cash becomes available to invest.

DIVIDEND REINVESTMENT

Dividend reinvestment plans (DRIPs) allow shareholders to take dividends in the form of additional shares rather than cash. Many companies with dividend reinvestment plans allow shareholders to purchase shares commission-free (or with a minimal transaction fee) through their dividend reinvestment plan, and others offer shareholders discounted share prices in return for reinvesting dividends.

At their simplest, dividend reinvestment plans are a form of dollar cost averaging. Instead of accepting a cash dividend, the dividend is reinvested at the then-prevailing price. For the investor, the most basic advantage relates to cash planning. Why should an investor accept dividends if he doesn't need the income for many years? By reducing costly transaction fees and commissions, the investor is able to put more of his investment dollars to work over the long run and earn more. For plans that allow discounted purchases or other perquisites for shareholders, the advantages can be even greater.

FIXED-INCOME STRATEGIES

Just as with equity investments, bonds are subject to risk. Likewise, bond investors share the desire to maximize their return for a given level of risk.

For risk adverse investors, there are ways to reduce the risk of investing in bonds. For example, an investor who does not want to face any default risk could limit investments to U.S. government bonds. If a somewhat greater return is sought, investing in a diversified portfolio of corporate bonds might be appropriate.

Diversification reduces the negative impact of any single bond defaulting by reducing the amount invested in any particular bond. Risk can also be reduced (although not eliminated) when investing in individual bonds through strategies such as immunization (see below).

As with any investment, bond investments can be actively managed or left alone. A passive approach usually entails selecting a portfolio of bonds to match an investor's preferences toward factors such as time horizon, tax status, and risk, and simply holding the portfolio until maturity. A passive approach often assumes that markets are relatively efficient and that superior returns cannot be obtained by timing the market or continuously looking for mispriced assets. However, care should still be taken in selecting the bonds to include in the portfolio. As with all investments, individual assets and the portfolio as a whole should be examined for appropriateness. The passive approach can also involve techniques such as immunization (see below) and laddering (see below) to reduce portfolio risk over time.

An active approach, on the other hand, generally assumes that markets are less than efficient and that superior (to the passive approach) returns can be generated through market timing and asset selection. Active management can involve analyzing particular bonds and sectors or forecasting anything from interest rates to inflation to economic outlook – looking for mispriced securities and seeking to avoid areas that (in the investor's opinion) may decline in value. This will usually result in more active trading or swapping of bonds within the portfolio, and may require substantial additional investments of time for research and analysis. Passive and active strategies are not always mutually exclusive; some techniques have elements of both and can be useful to all investors.

Immunization

One fixed-income risk reducing strategy is known as immunization. Immunization involves selecting a bond or portfolio of bonds such that interest rate movements result in bond price fluctuations (interest rate risk) and cash flows for reinvestment (reinvestment risk) that offset one another. It was noted in earlier chapters that these two risks move in opposite directions. If interest rates rise, interest rate risk causes the value of the bond to drop, but the investor earns more on any coupon payments that are reinvested. On the other hand, if rates decline, the value of the bond rises, but less is earned from reinvestment.

Macaulay duration measures the point in time when these two risks precisely offset each other.[2] If an investor purchases a bond and sells it when it reaches its duration (as calculated upon purchase), any loss in bond value caused by an increase in interest rates should be offset by the increase in the reinvestment earnings of interest payments. Similarly, if interest rates decline, the loss in reinvested earnings should be offset by an increase in the value of the bonds. By matching the duration of the bond to the investment horizon, interest rate and reinvestment risk can be offset.

Immunization can be accomplished easily using zero coupon bonds, since their maturity is their duration. No computations are necessary. Additionally, zero coupon bonds naturally have no reinvestment risk related to interest payments, since there are no interest payments. If an investor purchases a zero coupon bond and holds it to maturity, the investor will receive his expected yield to maturity (provided there is no default).

Ladder Portfolio

As noted earlier, reinvestment risk is a concern when receiving periodic payments such as interest. Reinvestment risk related to interest payments can be eliminated or reduced by using zero coupon bonds or an immunization strategy (see above). Reinvestment risk also occurs when bonds mature earlier than the investor needs the proceeds – for example, when no bonds are available that match the investment horizon, or when other bonds seem to present a better investment opportunity based upon other factors (e.g., various forecasts or a discovery based upon analysis and research).

One option might be to purchase very long-term bonds (using immunization or duration, see above) to secure the long-term expected return. The danger in this strategy is that long-term bonds are more sensitive to changes in interest rates than shorter-term bonds. If it turns out that the investor must use the money for an emergency or chooses to retire early, the investor may be stuck at an inopportune time with depressed bond prices in the face of a rising interest rate environment.

Another option is to create a laddered portfolio. In a laddered portfolio, an investor invests in an assortment of bonds with staggered maturities. For example, the investor can structure a portfolio where 10% of the bonds mature each year. The bonds would not all mature in the same interest rate environment. If rates rise, the value of the portfolio may fall, but the investor does not need to sell bonds that haven't yet matured. If cash is needed, the investor can reinvest the proceeds of the maturing bonds at the new (higher) interest rate.

If interest rates fall, the investor will reinvest the proceeds at a lower rate, but only for 10% of the portfolio (and the longer maturity bonds would rise in value.) With a laddered portfolio, the proceeds of maturing bonds would be reinvested in new bonds with a maturity later than those currently in the portfolio.

A bond ladder reduces interest rate risk by staggering maturities among several bonds (each of which repre-

Figure 40.3

Maturity	Yield	Amount Invested	Purpose
3 month	1.0%	$10,000	Emergency fund
2 year	1.8%	$10,000	Hedge against rising rates
3 year	2.3%	$10,000	Higher yield hedge
5 year	3.3%	$10,000	Yield
10 year	4.4%	$10,000	Yield
15 year	4.5%	$20,000	Planned tuition payment
16 year	4.6%	$22,000	Planned tuition payment
17 year	4.6%	$24,000	Planned tuition payment
18 year	4.7%	$26,000	Planned tuition payment
20 year	4.8%	$10,000	Yield
25 year	5.0%	$20,000	Yield, hedge against falling rates
30 year	5.2%	$30,000	Yield, retirement and hedge against falling rates

sents a rung on the ladder). For a long-term investor, this ends up being similar to a dollar cost averaging strategy. Shorter maturities cushion interest rate (i.e., bond price) risks, while the fact that only a portion of the bonds mature in a given period reduces reinvestment risk. If rates should rise, the maturing bonds can be used to buy bonds offering a higher yield.

Perhaps a greater reason for using a bond ladder is that it enables the investor to match cash flows with planned expenditures. If the investor knows tuition payments will be due each semester for four years, beginning in 15 years, he can buy bonds maturing at exactly the right times to make the tuition payments. Alternatively, a retired investor can plan a laddered bond portfolio to include regularly maturing bonds that provide the cash necessary for annual living expenses.

Bond ladders also work for unplanned expenses. For example, if the investor loses his job, maturing bonds can be used to supplement lost income. Figure 40.3 presents an example of a bond ladder using treasury bonds of various maturities.

Barbell Strategy

A barbell strategy offers another means of balancing the risks in a bond portfolio. While a ladder portfolio may stagger holdings across all maturities, the barbell places heavy weights on very long and very short maturities, with no position in intermediate-term securities. Because it requires only long and short maturities, one advantage of the barbell is that it can be established with fewer bonds, reducing complexity and transaction costs. A disadvantage is that the investor may be unable to match maturities with cash needs as effectively.

A barbell allows the investor to create a fairly effective hedge against both interest rate and reinvestment risk, simply and at low cost. If rates go up, the short portion of the barbell can be reinvested at the higher rate and help offset losses in the longer maturity. If rates decline, the long maturity gains make up for the lower interest rate available for reinvestment of the short maturity portion. Figure 40.4 provides an example of a barbell.

A barbell strategy can also be appropriate based upon the current shape of the yield curve and expected changes in interest rates. A barbell strategy can also result in a portfolio with the same duration as a bullet strategy (a single bond maturity), but with higher convexity. Convexity measures the curvature of the relationship between bond yields and prices.[3] Positive convexity is always a good thing for the bond investor, regardless of whether interest rates rise or fall. If interest rates fall, then convexity will augment the rise in the price of the bond. Interestingly, if interest rates rise, convexity will dampen the decline in the price.

Figure 40.4

Maturity	Yield	Amount Invested	Purpose
3 month	1.0%	$50,000	Emergency fund and hedge against rising rates
30 year	5.2%	$50,000	Long-term needs and profit from falling rates

WHERE CAN I FIND OUT MORE ABOUT IT?

1. Frank J. Fabozzi, Ed., *The Handbook of Fixed-Income Securities*, 6th Edition (New York, NY: McGraw Hill, 2000).

2. Annette Thau, *The Bond Book*, 2nd Edition (New York, NY: McGraw Hill, 2001).

3. Marilyn Cohen and Nick Watson, *The Bond Bible* (New York, NY: New York Institute of Finance, 2000).

QUESTIONS AND ANSWERS

Question – An investor is convinced that the stock market will fall in the current year, but rise over the long term. She has a lump sum available to invest. How can she take advantage of her beliefs about the market?

Answer – She can dollar cost average by investing equal amounts over the course of the coming year. If she is wrong and the market rises, she will have taken advantage of lower prices early. If she is correct about the market falling, she will buy more shares at the lower prices later in the year. In this manner, she is able to mitigate the risk of being wrong while still enjoying some benefit if she is correct.

Question – Bob Boomer started his family late and was able to amass a large portfolio due to his low expenses. However, he now faces the prospect of 3 children going to college over a 10-year period, immediately followed by his own retirement. Of the strategies discussed in this chapter, which would be most appropriate for the fixed-income portion of his portfolio?

Answer – Boomer could structure a bond ladder that matches his needs in terms of his future cash inflows and outflows.

CHAPTER ENDNOTES

1. See LeClair, "Ladders and Barbells", Bob LeClair's Finance and Markets Newsletter, 10.11.2003 at http://www.leimberg-services.com.

2. For further discussion of Macaulay duration, see Chapter 34, "Measuring Yield."

3. For further discussion of convexity, see Chapter 34, "Measuring Yield."

Chapter 41

HEDGING AND OPTION STRATEGIES

WHAT ARE THEY?

The Chicago Board Options Exchange defines hedging as "a conservative strategy used to limit investment loss by effecting a transaction that offsets an existing position." In essence, hedging is a form of investment insurance, which, like traditional life, property, and casualty, or liability insurance, transfers risk from one person or entity to another. And, just like traditional insurance, hedging involves tradeoffs. Hedgers may have to pay a "premium" or be otherwise willing to forego potential investment returns to shift risk.

Quite frankly, as many possible hedging strategies exist as the creative mind can structure. In addition, what one investor may perceive as a risky strategy, another may perceive as being a hedge, depending on each investor's circumstances, other investment holdings, view, forecast of future events, and/or perception of market conditions.

Investors may employ hedging strategies and tools to reduce risk, or even "immunize" their investment holdings in stocks, bonds and other debt instruments, commodities, futures, and other investments against almost any conceivable risk, including market risk, sector or industry risk, company or business-specific risk, purchasing power risk, currency risk, interest rate risk, country-specific risk, reinvestment risk, liquidity risk, callability risk, default or credit risk, selection risk, management or agency risk, etc.

The scope of these hedging strategies and tools ranges from those employed at the portfolio level to the asset class, sector, or industry level, to the individual security or investment instrument level. The time frame for employing hedging strategies may range from same-day or overnight to years.

Hedging strategies are sometimes employed for special or unusual circumstances, such as to protect the current value of stock subject to restrictions on sale from a decrease in value before the restriction expires. Some institutional investors adopt computer-aided hedging strategies, called "portfolio insurance" techniques, as part of an ongoing portfolio policy and objective to assure at least a minimum portfolio return in both up and down markets and from year to year. The same tools and strategies used for conservative hedging purposes are also employed—many argue aggressively, or even speculatively, rather than defensively—by "hedge funds" that attempt to capitalize on what their managers see as market imperfections or as opportunities to beat the market using market timing or business cycle sector-rotation techniques.

Hedging involves "tools" (certain investment instruments) and "techniques" (strategies). In the techniques or strategies area, first and foremost are the fundamental principles of sound investing—diversification and asset allocation. Investors can usually eliminate nearly all of the company-specific risk of stocks, the security-specific risk of individual investment instruments, selection risk, and country-specific risk by diversifying and investing in a large number of securities within a given asset class, sector, or industry, and across a number of countries. This reduces the amount invested in any particular aspect of the portfolio, and, accordingly, the potential loss that might be experienced in proportion to the total portfolio.

Similarly, investors can further reduce their exposure to loss within a given asset class, sector, or industry by allocating portions of their portfolio among different assets or asset classes whose returns are not highly correlated (or are even inversely correlated) with each other. This reduces the odds that several aspects of the portfolio might experience declines at once (and in fact may increase the odds that one element is increasing while another is experiencing losses). In general, investors should consider allocating their investments among domestic and foreign stocks, short-, intermediate-, and long-term bonds and other debt instruments, real estate, commodities, etc. and the subclasses within each larger asset class to minimize these types of risks

Many of the "tools" involved in hedging are "derivative" securities, such as options contracts, forward and futures contracts, and other derivatives that are essentially just variations or combinations of regular options and forward or futures contracts. How these tools are used to accomplish hedging objectives involves concepts that are discussed in more detail below in the section entitled, "HOW IS IT DONE?"

WHEN IS THE USE OF SUCH DEVICES INDICATED?

Because hedging tools and techniques are virtually unlimited in choices and flexibility, the situations in which hedging might be involved also become nearly limitless. But some of the more popular or frequent situations where hedging tools and techniques might be indicated include:

1. Investors want to protect current security values from price decline when they must make quick decisions with limited information. In many situations, investors can protect portfolio appreciation by using measured and well-reasoned strategies and fundamental portfolio and investment management techniques after a thorough examination of all relevant facts. Yet, large declines in value too often occur when investors do not have adequate time to fully digest the reliable information and to sort through the rumors and untruths, while waiting for the release of the true facts. While non-taxable accounts can sell without concern over taxes, hedging strategies may provide investors holding highly appreciated positions with security against loss until they have the time they need to evaluate all relevant information and then later decide whether to hold the security (with no taxable sale), or to sell (and incur the applicable taxes).

2. An investor is uncomfortable with a large percentage of value in a single stock—that is, a concentrated portfolio—but does not wish to sell and trigger capital gains taxes at the present time.

3. An investor has a large holding that is facing an almost certain dramatic movement up or down, but the question is which? For instance, the stock of a company facing a major litigation will almost certainly decline dramatically if the company loses the suit and increase significantly if it wins the suit. Investors can set up hedges that will protect them from serious loss (or even protect gains) regardless of the outcome of the suit.

4. An investor may own a large position in a stock that has trading restrictions due to initial public offering (IPO) lock-up provisions, or trading restrictions imposed by the government or the company due to insider status or other factors.

5. An individual with a short life expectancy due to advanced age or illness (or as spousal beneficiary of a marital trust) may wish to protect against a decrease in stock or equity portfolio value (to protect the value of the assets for heirs), but may not wish to sell because the appreciated positions would receive a step-up in basis at death (but would incur substantial capital gains taxes if sold before death).

6. An individual may be in need of liquidity for a new home purchase, payments to creditors, or other cash flow needs, but does not wish to trigger capital gains taxes. By entering into a hedge strategy, the minimum value of the appreciated position can be fixed, providing an asset that can serve as collateral for loans.

7. Investment advisers, trust officers, investment managers, or other fiduciaries responsible for other people's money want to meet their fiduciary duty to protect the value of the total portfolio—this can be facilitated by diversifying and hedging against declines in value of their clients' investments. The duty to diversify and hedge appreciated or concentrated holdings (and the duty to recommend diversification and hedging) is not the focus of this chapter. But recent cases provide an excellent fact pattern for an overview of the claims that can arise in the area of the financial adviser's duty to diversify or recommend hedging strategies.

Hedging may allow this investor to control the risk of loss in a position that may have substantial value now, but may not when it is allowed to be sold.

In the Levy case[2], which does not involve a testamentary trust or the Prudent Investor Rule being adopted by many states, the plaintiff received stock in Corning Inc. through a stock merger with his privately owned company. The Corning stock represented $8 million in value but was restricted from sale for one year. The plaintiff, on several occasions, made it very clear to the defendant—an investment adviser and trust company—that he wanted his Corning stock to be protected from a decline in value during the restriction period, if possible. The defendant held itself out to the public and to the plaintiff as having sophisticated wealth management and financial planning expertise. The plaintiff alleged that the defendant said that hedging the downside risk of the restricted stock was not possible. The plaintiff later learned from another investment firm that hedging the restricted stock was possible and the plaintiff then implemented a hedging strategy (using a combination of put options and call options to provide a floor and ceiling value on the stock) with another investment firm. But he took this action only after suffering losses in Corning stock prior to the time the new hedge was in place. The case settled before trial.

While the Levy case involved an investment adviser's duty to hedge, the investment advisory firm held itself out as a broader wealth management firm that provided financial planning counsel and services. Therefore, Levy is good food for thought for all financial planners and investment advisers.

Not only is the duty to diversify a necessary standard to evaluate, but there is also a growing persuasion that, in making the diversification decision, advisers must consider all reasonable methods of diversification and risk reduction. As fiduciary expert George Crawford says, "This tool [hedging strategies] is now so widely used that it should be in every fiduciary's tool kit, even if used only carefully and sparingly. Like any other tool, it can be used, or misused."[3]

HOW IS IT DONE?

Fundamental Investment Principles

Although not traditionally considered a "hedging" strategy, per se, simply employing the sound investment fundamentals of diversification and asset allocation, whenever possible, is the best way for investors to reduce the risk of their investments. Although any individual company's stock value and price volatility is related to both industry and overall market factors, the single biggest contributor to an individual stock's price volatility is its individual business risk. Overall market and industry factors may explain 20 to 40% of a typical firm's price volatility, but the remaining 60 to 80% is generally attributable to factors unique to the company. A company's business risk is *unsystematic* risk that investors can eliminate by diversifying into many companies rather than just one or a few. On the average, the losses sustained on the stocks of companies that (unexpectedly) perform poorly for their own peculiar

reasons will be offset by comparable gains on the stocks of other companies that (unexpectedly) perform well for their own unique reasons. By diversifying into a number of companies, investors will earn the average return for the group, but with considerably less average return volatility than that associated with any single company within the group. In fact, the greater the extent that these assets are non-correlated (or inversely correlated), the better the odds that multiple positions will not experience declines simultaneously. The same basic ideas and rules apply to bonds, commodities, futures, real estate, and other investment assets and asset classes.

Even broad diversification within a sector, industry, or asset class still exposes investors to sector, industry, or asset-class risk factors as well as market-wide risk factors—what are called systematic risk factors. But investors can manage the level of their exposure to *systematic* risk factors by diversifying across sector, industry, or asset classes—the process of asset allocation and portfolio management. Different sectors, industries, and asset classes tend to respond differently to changing economic conditions, periods in the business cycle, and various economic, social, political, and other major events. In other words, the values of investments associated with different asset classes are imperfectly correlated. Using the principles of asset allocation and portfolio management, investors can diversify across asset classes to minimize the risk in their portfolios from individual sector, industry, and asset class risks and to derive an overall portfolio exposure to market-wide risk and volatility that is consistent with their risk tolerance and risk and return objectives. When investors can fully employ these fundamental investment principles, the need to hedge investments in any particular security, group of securities, industry, or asset class becomes negligible and the cost to engage in such hedges is generally prohibitive, relative to the minimal benefits potentially gained.[4]

But in some cases investors cannot or do not wish to fully exploit these fundamental investment principles. At any given time, for whatever reasons, investors might have a "concentrated portfolio" (a portfolio that is over-invested in a particular security or asset class and, therefore, overexposed to risks associated with that investment) that they cannot (e.g., trading restrictions) or choose not (e.g., expectations about positive future performance) to "fix" using the fundamental principles of investment and portfolio management - these investors should consider hedging strategies.

For instance, the principal investment of the owner of a small closely held import-export business dealing principally with just two foreign countries is his closely held business. Generally, such people will be grossly under-diversified and therefore exposed to business, industry, foreign currency, and country-specific risk factors that they cannot easily diversify away or mitigate through diversification and asset allocation. But such a person may be able to engage in hedging operations both outside and inside of his business to hedge his business, industry, currency, and country risks.

Here is a real-world example. In 1996, MFS (a telecom company) was acquired by WorldCom in a $12 billion all-stock, tax-free merger. David McCourt, who was CEO of RCN, a publicly traded cable/telephone company, was a large investor in MFS and sat on the new MFS board of directors. Before hedging his stock in the new MFS WorldCom, his 812,000 shares were valued at roughly $25 million. McCourt was acquainted with the management of WorldCom but did not know it well enough to place a substantial portion of his net worth at risk, which would be dependent on their success in running WorldCom. As a previously cited investment company president has put it in facing the same situation, "Today we have all our eggs in one basket, but we own the basket; if we take your stock, we'd still be all in one basket, but you'd own the basket, and that's an enormous difference!"[5]

McCourt had a similar view. "I wanted to protect my holding because when you sell something for stock, and you don't know the people, it's a smart way to manage the investment."[6]

McCourt protected his $25 million position in MFS WorldCom by entering into a "cashless collar" (also called a zero-premium collar, described below). McCourt sold call options, which could obligate him to sell his 812,308 shares at $64 a share, giving up any appreciation above that price for a period of five years from the option date of June 19, 1997. McCourt used the funds received from that transaction to purchase put options that gave him the right, for five years, to sell his shares at $28 a share, protecting himself from a decline in the share price below $28.[7]

Therefore, McCourt's investment could fluctuate between $28 and $64 a share for five years, but no more or less. If the price rose above $64, he could be *obligated* to sell the shares at that price and if the price fell below $28 he would be *permitted* to sell the shares at that price. In total value terms, his $25 million in MFS WorldCom could fluctuate between $22.75 million and $52 million in value. He guaranteed the protection of 91% of his $25

million investment (minimum value of $22.75 million), while reserving the right to achieve just over 100% appreciation on his investment, but no more ($52 million), for a five-year period.

As it happened, WorldCom appreciated nearly 300% after McCourt implemented the collar strategy. If the call option had been exercised, McCourt would have been entitled to $52 million.

But as of June 2002, the stock had declined substantially. It was worth less than 10% ($2.5 million) of the original $25 million in value as compared with the floor of the collar, which was 91% ($22.75 million) of the original $25 million in value. The hedge appears to have been a very smart play for McCourt, as evidenced by the dramatic decline in WorldCom stock the last few years. [But note this trade-off: if the hedge had not been in place and McCourt had timed the sale of his stock right, McCourt could have sold his stock for nearly 300% of the original $25 million.]

Value of WorldCom stock with hedge:	$22.75 million
6/2002 Value of WorldCom stock without hedge:	$2.50 million ($2 a share)
Value Protected by hedging strategy	$20.25 million

In a bit of irony, McCourt went on to say that, if he had known WorldCom management at the time of his hedge as well as he knew them a few months later, he would never have used options to protect his investment. Fortunately for McCourt, he did not know them well and placed the hedge. While WorldCom stock had a very strong performance in the bull market up through 1999, making the option hedge look like a bad bet, the stock plummeted in 2000, 2001, and 2002, making his hedge quite valuable.

McCourt's position in MFS WorldCom was a concentrated holding, which likely represented a majority of McCourt's net worth. But just because an appreciated holding does not represent a majority of value does not mean it might not be worth hedging or protecting. Sometimes hedging will depend on an investor's ability to accept long-term declines in value in relation to the investor's anticipated goals and cash flow or liquidity needs in the future.

Example: Some institutional portfolios, trust funds, college endowment funds, charitable foundation funds, and others employ hedging strategies called "portfolio insurance" techniques to set floors or minimums on the amount the funds earn over any given period. These funds typically have reasonably predictable required outlays and want to assure that they can meet these obligations without eating into the principal of the funds. They are willing to forego some upside earnings potential in order to prevent losses below some specified level. Although they generally employ the fundamentals of modern investment, asset allocation, and portfolio theory to structure their "base" portfolios, they will use options and futures contracts and options contracts on futures contracts on broad-based market and asset-class indexes and other strategies to hedge against declines in value below their designated limit.

Also, in less volatile markets, investors generally can rebalance their portfolios periodically and incrementally with an eye towards minimizing the tax consequences and transactions costs of rebalancing by matching recognition of gains and losses while not deviating too substantially from their preferred risk/return profile. But in more volatile markets, investors' portfolios may quickly deviate from their preferred mix among asset classes and expose them to market and asset-class risk levels that they deem unacceptable. Making adjustments all at once to move back to their preferred asset mix and risk/return profile may be difficult and expensive as well as disadvantageous for tax purposes. Sales of assets in those asset classes that have appreciated substantially and where the investor is overexposed may result in large realizations of gains (and a subsequent tax bill) that the investor may not be able to easily offset with sales of loss assets without also incurring substantial transactions costs. In such cases, the investors can enter into temporary hedging positions in options and/or financial futures that are long positions in those asset classes that are underweighted in their portfolios and short positions in those asset classes that are overweighted in their portfolios and buy time to make tax-and-cost-efficient transactions in the underlying securities to rebalance to their preferred asset mix.

So even when investors employ the fundamentals of modern investment and portfolio theory to construct a risk/return profile that meets their objectives, at times, they may still wish or need to engage in hedging operations.

Sales, Stop-Loss Orders, and Short Sales

In many cases, simply closing out or selling a position is the best decision when an investor finds it necessary to diversify a security or asset class. Often investors can also sell loss assets in their portfolio to offset gains and neutralize the tax effects. But investors overexposed in a security or asset class cannot always be sure that they will recognize the need to rebalance or that they will have sufficient time to "manage" the sale of the position and offsetting loss positions before the appreciated position declines in value. In addition, after the unprecedented gains of the 1990s, even with the market declines of the past few years, many investors are still sitting on substantially appreciated positions where it is often difficult to find offsetting loss positions within their portfolios.

Two relatively simple techniques that investors have to protect themselves from loss in these situations are stop-loss orders and short sales.

Stop-Loss Orders

Stop-loss orders are generally good-till-cancelled or standing orders with brokers to sell (or buy) a security held long (short) if the price moves below (above) a specified value. For instance, if an investor owns (is short) a stock currently worth $100, he could place a stop-loss order with his broker to sell (buy) the stock if it falls (rises) to $90 ($110). In most (but not all) cases, the investor can rest assured that if the price moves adversely, he will lose only about $10.

But the problems with stop-loss orders are three-fold. First, and this is relatively minor, but important nonetheless, the investor has to or should reassess and reset the stop-loss orders as the value of the position changes. For instance, if the investor owns the stock with a market price of $100 and a stop-loss of $90, and the market price moves to $110, he should consider resetting the stop-loss order (e.g., at $100) to protect the increased gain.

Second, and this is an important consideration in most cases, the broker will actually sell the position if the market price hits the stop-loss price. Therefore, the investor will be liable for tax on any gains realized. In many cases, investors wish to hedge against losses without realizing gains and paying tax—if that is the case, stop-loss orders are generally not a viable choice of strategy.

Third and, perhaps, most importantly, investors have no assurance that trades triggered by their stop-loss orders will take place at a price that is anywhere close to their stop-loss trigger price. For instance, in the great crash of October 1987, many investors who had stop-loss orders in place discovered, much to their chagrin, that their trades had taken place at prices 10, 20, or 30% or more below their stop-loss price. In such volatile market situations, the stop-loss orders enter the queue for trades with all the other market orders and may not be executed until the market price has declined far below the stop-loss price. In such markets, large transactions by large institutional investors frequently precipitate or foreshadow the decline in value. If they place their market orders before the security hits an investor's stop-loss price, the market price may move right through (or "gap" through) the stop-loss price before the institutions' and other investors' transactions are cleared, leaving the trades for investors with stop-loss orders to take place after much of the market move (and investment loss) has already occurred.[8]

Short Sales

A short-sale strategy involves selling securities borrowed from a third party. In general, the investor's broker or custodian arranges to borrow the securities from the margin account of one of its other customers. While short-sellers maintain their short position, they must reimburse the lenders for any dividends or interest paid on the borrowed securities.[9] If the securities decline in value, the short-seller may then purchase the securities on the open market at a lower price than the initial sales price. The short-seller returns the purchased stock to the third party and pays tax on the gain (difference between the initial sales price and subsequent purchase price) at long-term or short-term capital gain tax rates, depending on the holding period. If the short-seller closes out the short position by buying the securities after they have appreciated in value, the loss is treated as long-term or short-term capital loss.

Short Sales Against the Box

Investors use short sales for hedging purposes when they sell short "against the box." This means that they sell short securities that they also hold long in their portfolio. This technique offers perfect inverse correlation because gains or losses on the long position are perfectly matched by losses or gains on the short position. As long as an investor maintains both the long and short position, the economic value of the investor's position cannot change. The investor is perfectly immunized against loss on the long position, but also foregoes any possibility of further gain while the short against the box is in place.

Originally, this strategy was used primarily for tax timing purposes. An investor that had an appreciated position that he wanted to sell but didn't want to incur a taxable gain for could enter into a short sale against the box. This allowed the investor to perfectly hedge and thus completely avoid any further price changes (equivalent to the situation if the position had been sold outright and the investor simply no longer owned the security) without requiring the investor to declare the taxable gain (because the position was still open). Ultimately, the investor could opt to close out the position at some future point of his choosing. Doing this allowed the investor to defer the tax bill until the position was closed, possibly shift the income to a year that would be more favorable in light of tax laws or other taxable events, but eliminate all risk in the meantime (as though the position had been sold). Unfortunately, short sales against the box now are treated for income tax purposes as constructive sales, making them much less attractive for hedging purposes. Although investors can still use this technique to prevent economic loss on an appreciated position indefinitely, they generally will have to realize their gain and pay tax on the appreciated long position in the tax year in which they enter into the short sale against the box. Investors step-up the basis of their long position by the amount of the realized gain and start a new holding period for the long position, just as if they had actually sold and then repurchased the securities. If they later close out the short position by delivering the securities they hold long, losses and gains on the long and short positions will cancel out, so they will incur no further taxable consequences. But if they later close out the short position by purchasing new securities in the market for delivery, rather than by delivering the securities they hold long, they will recognize long-term or short-term gain or loss on the short position, depending upon the holding period of the short position. (See the discussion of the constructive sale rules under "What Are the Tax Implications?" below.)

Short Sales of Close Substitutes

In light of the currently unfavorable constructive sale rules for short selling against the box, an investor can, alternatively, select a short sale involving securities of a company in the same industry, which has a close, but not perfect, correlation to the securities the investor wants to protect. In general, even if closely correlated, short sales of a different company's securities will not be treated as a constructive sale.[10] For example, an investor who has a very significant holding in Dell Computer might sell short a similar amount of Gateway Computer. But as discussed above, the individual business risk is generally greater than the industry or market risk. So, any time correlation is not perfect, a hedging strategy can fail. Gateway's stock could soar while Dell's stock plummets, putting the investor in double jeopardy. Simply stated, investors cannot use short-selling strategies to hedge perfectly against company-specific events such as fraud or massive liability, unless they short that specific company's securities.

Short Sale of Exchange-Traded Funds

The strategies described above allow investors to avoid company-specific risk (on at least one side of the position). In recent years, the markets have introduced exchange-traded index funds (ETFs) that permit investors to buy long or sell short certain baskets of stocks (such as the basket of stocks that comprise an index like the S&P 500 or NASDAQ 100). This can provide investors with a more broadly diversified correlation (or inverse correlation) for market and industry or asset class risks. For example, the investor mentioned in the previous section could sell short the S&P Computer Technology sector to hedge against his position in Dell. This would not protect him from the company-specific risks for Dell, but it would eliminate most of the company-specific risks of Gateway and ensure perhaps better protection from the sector risks of Dell, as compared to when Gateway was used for the short side of the position.

Selling a Forward Contract or Futures Contract

A forward contract is a contract negotiated privately or traded over-the-counter to deliver a security at a specific time in the future, at a specific price. Also, with the recent advent of single-stock listed futures contracts on an ever-increasing number of companies, investors can now sell standardized futures contracts on many companies. Since these futures and forward contracts are substantially identical property, the use of this hedging strategy will trigger the constructive sale rules. (See the discussion of the constructive sale rules under "What Are the Tax Implications?" below.)

Example: Adams owns 1,000 shares of Z stock, currently valued at $100 per share. He contracts with Burrows to deliver 1,000 shares of Z stock, at $101 per share in three months.

Offsetting Notional Principal Contract or Equity Swap

An offsetting notional principal contract is one where the holder of a security or bundle of securities agrees to pay substantially all of the investment yield (interest, dividends, etc.) and appreciation from the security or the bundle of securities for a specified period. Generally, in return, the investor receives interest based upon an interest rate index, such as the LIBOR rate, or a bond index, such as the 20-year U.S. Treasury bond index. In addition, the investor generally is also reimbursed for substantially any loss of value in the security or bundle of securities. This arrangement should run afoul of the constructive sale rules, since it is essentially equivalent to the sale of the stock at its current price and the purchase of the bond index.

Example: Johnson owns 1,000 shares of XYZ stock, valued at $100 per share. She contracts with Masters as follows: Any dividends on the stock and any appreciation in value will be delivered to Masters. In return, Masters will pay Johnson interest on $100,000 based upon the LIBOR rate and will reimburse Johnson for any drop in the value of XYZ stock value below $100 per share.

Pre-Paid Forward Sale

A pre-paid forward sale is a risk management strategy suitable for investors whose primary goal is to monetize a concentrated equity position without incurring an immediate tax liability. The pre-paid forward sale may be appropriate for investors who have legal restrictions or practical limitations on selling their stock (e.g., restricted or unregistered stock, or stock with a low cost basis).

Investors may receive an up-front payment of 75% to 95% of the value of their stock rather than the traditional payment for the full contract amount at the time the contract matures. Generally, the investor making the forward sale has no obligations to the counterparty until the expiration of the transaction. The amount of the up-front payment may be affected by several factors, including the term of the transaction (generally, more discount of the upfront payment with longer terms), the level of an investment's upside potential (less discount or even a premium if the upside potential is substantial), prevailing interest rates (more discount with higher interest rates), and other market conditions. Essentially, this is a variation of the equity swap.

since the investor selling the stock in the forward sale effectively transfers all potential appreciation or loss on the stock (payable at the end of the contract term when the stock is transferred) for the interest or other investment income or returns he will earn by investing the up-front payment.

Final Note

What these hedging techniques have in common is that the owner of the securities continues to hold the securities. All, or most, risk of loss—and opportunity for gain—on the securities is transferred from the owner to someone else. The owner has effectively disposed of the securities, while retaining nominal ownership. They also have the unfortunate consequence (generally) of triggering the constructive sale rules (but see the section entitled, "What Are the Tax Implications?" for a discussion of one method to circumvent the constructive sale rules in certain circumstances).

Options, Futures, and Other Derivatives

Given the limitations, risks, and adverse tax consequences (under the constructive sale rules) of stop-loss orders, short sales, and other essentially short-sale equivalents, many investors have turned to options, futures, and other derivative instruments to achieve their hedging objectives. To understand why, one must understand derivative instruments and markets.

Derivatives are so named because they "derive" their value in reference to the value of some other security or property. These instruments do not represent an ownership interest in the security or property. Rather, they provide investors with the *right* or *obligation* to buy or sell securities or property or to receive payments based upon the performance of some underlying security or property some time in the future. The number of new derivative instruments being introduced into the markets and the growth in the volume of trading in these markets has been tremendous. This almost revolutionary evolution provides investors with an ever-increasing arsenal for hedging an ever-expanding list of risks. The prevalence and usefulness of these instruments in hedging operations, as well as the risks associated with the misuse or misapplication of these instruments, makes it imperative that financial advisers and investors understand the fundamental nature of these instruments and their relation to markets. This is vital for anyone that seeks to successfully employ these tools in hedging strategies.

Nature of the Derivatives Markets

In contrast with the stock market or other markets trading ownership interests or claims on real or personal property, the derivatives markets are "zero-sum" games or markets. A zero-sum game is one in which the average gain and loss of all participants in the game is zero. For example, since 1926, the "average" investor (i.e., the average result amongst all investors) in the S&P 500 index of stocks has earned about 10.5% (compounded) per year, ignoring transactions costs. But the "average" investor in every options, futures, or other derivatives market, for however long all of these the markets have existed, *by design*, has earned exactly 0%, ignoring transactions costs.

The reason for the difference between the derivatives and the stock markets is that the market for stocks is, on average, a long market. That is, it represents ownership in the productive capacity of the economy, which has a positive value. So, although some investors may sell short shares of the market, the average position must represent a long position in the productive capacity of the economy. As knowledge grows, technology advances, and labor productivity improves, the entire economy grows (i.e., experiences *real* growth after inflation), providing more, on average, for everyone. Therefore, it is a positive-sum game.

In contrast, derivative securities do not represent, on balance, any ownership interest in anything. They are essentially side bets on economic values and, as such, have a total economic value of zero.[11] For example, suppose two farmers disagree about what the price of a bushel of wheat will be in 9 months. One thinks it will be less than $3, while the other thinks it will be more than $3. The one who thinks it will be less than $3 says he is willing to put his money where his mouth is and bet that it will be less than $3. He proposes that they agree today that the must sell, and the other farmer must buy, 500 bushels of his wheat in 9 months for $3 per bushel (which would be higher than he expects the price to actually be, producing a "profit" for him). The other farmer takes him up on his bet. If the farmer proposing the bet is right and the price of wheat is less than $3 per bushel in 9 months, he wins the bet and pockets the difference between the market price (less than $3) and the $3 target price of the bet.

Their bet neither creates nor destroys any wheat. It does not have any effect on the price of wheat whatsoever.[12] If the price of wheat rises above $3 per bushel, say to $4, the farmer who wins the bet and buys the 500 bushels for $3 will realize a quick $500 gain ($1 per bushel times 500 bushels) when he turns around and sells the wheat for $4. The farmer losing the bet will forfeit exactly $500 by selling the 500 bushels of wheat for $3 per bushel, when he could otherwise have sold it for $4 per bushel. Of course, they could just settle up by having the farmer losing the bet pay the winner $500 in cash. So, one farmer's gain is the other farmer's loss—the bet is a zero-sum game.

The farmers' bet is essentially a forward contract. All of the forward and futures contracts on the various commodities and financial instruments are just variations on this simple example. For every long position where someone agrees to buy a given amount of some commodity or financial instrument for a given price at a specified time in the future there must be an equal and offsetting short position where someone agrees to sell under the same terms.

Although described as zero-sum games, the derivatives markets are actually negative-sum games, since each side of every transaction pays commissions and/or other transactions costs.

If investing in these derivative instruments is a losing proposition on average, the question naturally arises as to why such markets exist and why anyone would invest in them. A good question!

The answer is risk asymmetry—different risk tolerances and capacities. Two parties can enter opposite sides of a transaction with each having the perception that the position reduces his risk. For instance, assume instead that the "bet" is between the farmer and the local baker. The farmer is willing to agree to sell the wheat in 9 months for $3 per bushel because he knows that amount will be sufficient for him to recoup his costs and still make an acceptable profit. He can rest assured that he can continue his farming the next year. Sure, he would like to sell at $4 if the price is that high, but he would gladly give up the additional $1 per bushel to insure that he still gets the $3 even if the price falls to $2. Conversely, the baker would love to buy the wheat at $2 per bushel if the price is that low, but he also would gladly pay the extra $1 to insure that he can buy the wheat at $3 per bushel even if the price rises to $4. For the farmer, the risk is that prices will fall; for the baker, that prices will rise; so they are both better off agreeing to set the price in advance to eliminate their risk. Both are willing to give up potential gains to reduce their risk.

The derivatives markets would not be nearly as immense and diverse as they are if it were not also for differences in investors' risk tolerance and capacity to bear risk. Just as some people like to bet the horses or play blackjack in Vegas, some investors are willing to speculate on the values of derivative securities, even though they are neither producers nor users of the products. In fact, the vast majority of the positions in the futures markets, for instance, are closed out prior to the expiration of the contracts by buying or selling offsetting positions. These investors provide both liquidity and depth to the markets, making them more efficient at pricing or valuing the underlying assets and the cost of risk transfer.

Therefore, basically the derivatives markets are risk transfer mechanisms. As such, they add to overall economic efficiency by reducing and transferring risks and promoting more efficient planning and production throughout the economy. Although investing in derivatives is a zero-sum game (or negative-sum game, after transactions costs), the derivatives markets as a whole add value to the economy.

Options markets, like futures markets, are also a zero-sum game (or negative-sum game after transactions costs). Similar to futures contracts, options contracts deal with the delivery of a specified amount of some financial instrument, commodity, or other property at a specified price (called the strike or exercise price) on (or before, depending on the type of contract) some specified future date. Also similar to the futures markets, for each "long" position there is an equal and opposite "short" position. The principal distinction is that options give one side of the position the *right, but not the obligation*, to buy or sell and the other side the *obligation* to sell or buy if the other side exercises his right. In futures markets, both sides of the transaction have the obligation to either buy or sell depending on whether they are "long" or "short" in the transaction (but only if the position is still "open" at the time of exercise—as mentioned above, the vast majority of futures contracts are closed out before this).

Derivatives are highly leveraged instruments. For example, on November 31, 2003, the underlying notional value of an S&P 500 A.M. index option was $1056.77. The premium for a March 2004 call with a strike price of $1,050 was $40.30 ($6.77 intrinsic value and $33.53 speculative premium). If the price of the underlying index had risen to $1,100, say, at expiration in March 2004, the call option would have been worth $50. This represents a $9.70 gain on the option above the initial $40.30 investment, or a 24% return for the 3½-month period until expiration. If an investor had paid $1,056.77 to buy the underlying index directly, the gain would have been $43.33. This represents just a 4.1% return, or about 6 times less than the return on the option, for the same period and based upon the movement of the same underlying investment.

This leverage is one feature that makes options and other derivatives such good hedging vehicles (and also such appealing speculative instruments, for those that are so inclined). The markets are generally rather liquid and investors can take offsetting positions with just pennies on the dollar relative to the securities held long. Consequently, they provide investors with a great deal of flexibility. But the leverage is inherently risky and investors may lose all of their initial investment, or more, depending upon the type of hedge and the instruments they use. Therefore, misuse of these instruments for hedging purposes can lead to severe losses, far in excess of the original risk that was meant to be hedged. A discussion of all the features and characteristics of derivatives is beyond the scope of this chapter. Readers can get further details regarding the features and characteristics of stock options, financial futures, and commodity futures in Chapters 13, 14, and 15, respectively.

Finally, the proliferation of derivative instruments stems from a desire to "span" the market and to provide vehicles capable of hedging many different types of risk in addition to potential losses in appreciated positions. For instance, one particular type of financial futures contract, the interest-rate swap, permits investors with variable interest rates on their assets and fixed interest obligations to exchange the variable interest for fixed interest. Equity swaps trade returns on an equity index for returns on another equity index or a bond or interest rate index or security. By entering into an equity swap, investors who are long on the index (or close substitutes) can essentially replace part or all of their exposure to loss on the equity position by exchanging the returns on a specified amount of the equity index for, say, interest payments tied to the 20-year Treasury bond index. Effectively, they change the composition of their portfolio and their risk/return profile without actually having to sell part or all of their position in the index. Currency futures permit investors to hedge currency risks; new swap derivatives permit investors to replace variable or fixed rate payments with inflation-adjusted payments; and the list goes on and on.

Options, Spanning, and Synthetics

The concept of spanning is important to understanding hedging and is related to the concept of creating "synthetic" securities. A market or security is "spanned" if investors can combine derivatives in that market or on that security to reproduce the risk and return char-

acteristics of the underlying market or security. In other words, investors can create or exactly reproduce the returns on that market or security by creating "synthetic" markets or securities. When this is possible, investors can also create "synthetic" derivatives of each of the derivatives of that market or security by combining positions in the market or security together with some combination of the other derivatives in that market or on the security.

The benefit of spanning is that it makes markets more efficient, since investors will exploit price differentials in the "synthetics" relative to the underlying market or security through arbitrage and force all the instruments into price conformity. Consequently, the derivatives become even better and more reliable instruments for hedging.

To see how this works, consider the following profit profiles for two option contracts. Figures 41.1 and 41.2 show the profit profiles for call options and put options, respectively.

A profit profile shows the gain or loss an investor would realize on the option position for different prices of the underlying stock at *expiration* of the option. In Figures 41.1 and 41.2, the price of the stock at the initiation of the option is assumed to be $50. The exercise price of the option is also $50, or at the money. For ease of illustration, the option premium is assumed to be $10 for both the call and the put (which usually would not be the case in actuality).

Figure 41.1

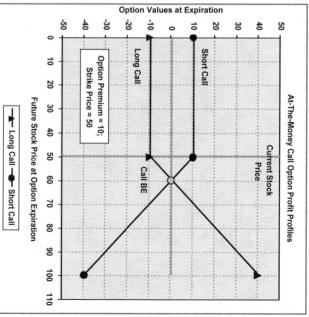

Figure 41.2

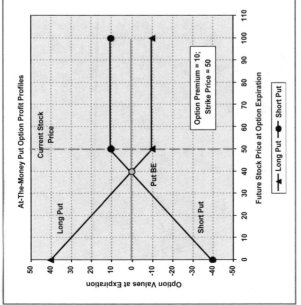

At-The-Money Put Option Profit Profiles

Option Premium = 10;
Strike Price = 50

— Long Put   ● Short Put

Option Values at Expiration

Future Stock Price at Option Expiration

fectly matches the original premium earned when the call was written). At prices above $60 for the stock, the short call's profit profile shows ever-increasing losses. In contrast with the long call, the loss on a short call position is potentially unlimited. The gain on the short call is limited to the premium of the call option when it is written.

If an investor *buys* a call option giving him the right to buy the stock, he is *long* in the call. If the investor *writes* a call, collects the premium, and is obligated to sell the stock if the buyer exercises the option, he is *short* in the call. Analogously, if the investor buys a put giving him the right to sell the stock, he is long in the put. If he writes a put, collects the premium, and is obligated to buy the stock if the buyer exercises the put, he is short in the put.

The long call position is equivalent to buying just the upside potential of the stock above the exercise price. For each dollar that the stock price exceeds the exercise price, the long call will increase by one dollar at expiration—perfect positive correlation. Therefore, the long call's profit profile is potentially unlimited. For each dollar the stock price falls below the exercise price, the option is worth the same amount—zero—so the investor can lose no more than the $10 premium he paid for the call. In this case, the investor will break even if the stock price rises to $60 (when the stock appreciates enough for the investor to recover the initial premium cost of the option).

If the long call is equivalent to buying the upside potential of the stock, the short call position must be equivalent to selling the upside potential of the stock. So the profit profile of the short call position shows the investor making $10 (the call premium) if the price of the stock remains below the exercise price of $50. As the price of the stock rises above $50, the short call's profit declines on a dollar-for-dollar basis with increases in the price of the underlying stock—perfect negative correlation. At $60 for the stock, the short call position just breaks even (the loss on the price appreciation per-

The profit profile of the long put position is equivalent to buying the upside gain potential of a short position in the underlying stock. In this respect it is analogous to the long call position with respect to a long position in the stock. As the price of the stock falls below the exercise price, the profit profile of the long put increases dollar-for-dollar with decreases in the price of the stock—perfect negative correlation (or perfect positive correlation with a short stock). The profit potential is limited only by the fact that the stock price cannot fall below zero. For each dollar the stock price ends up above the exercise price, the put option is worth the same amount—zero—so the investor can lose no more than his put premium of $10. The stock price has to fall to $40 for the investor to break even on the long put.

Similar to the short call, the short put position is equivalent to selling the upside gain potential of a short position in the stock. If the stock price is above the exercise price, the investor pockets the $10 premium as profit. But if the stock price falls below the exercise price, the profit profile of the short put declines dollar-for-dollar with declines in the value of the underlying stock—perfect positive correlation (or perfect negative correlation with the short stock). The investor will break even if the stock price falls to $40 and he could lose up to $40 if the stock price were to fall all the way to zero.

Figure 41.3 now shows how a combination of a long call and short put has essentially the same profit profile as the underlying stock.

Line LC + SP is derived by adding the adding the profit profiles of the long call and short put together. The gain or loss on the LC + SP position is exactly the same as the gain or loss on the stock. So holding the LC + SP position is essentially equivalent to creating a "synthetic" stock.[13] Any combination of a long call and a short put at the same exercise price, even if different than the current market price, together with a corresponding investment in the risk-free asset to keep the total investment amount equivalent, will be technically equivalent to owning the stock outright. Similarly, a combination of a short call and a long put, together with the corresponding investment in the risk-free asset, will be equivalent to a short sale of the underlying stock.

Figure 41.3

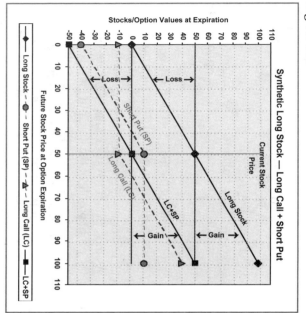

Synthetic Long Stock — Long Call + Short Put

Legend: Long Stock — Short Put (SP) — Long Call (LC) — LC+SP

Stocks/Option Values at Expiration

Future Stock Price at Option Expiration

Labels: Loss, Loss, Gain, Gain, Current Stock Price, Long Stock, Short Put (SP), Long Call (LC), LC+SP

Figure 41.5

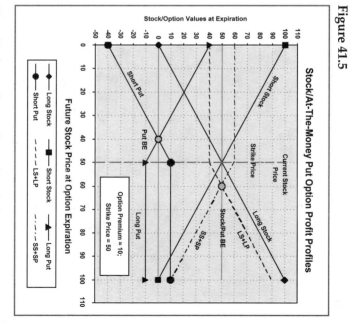

Stock/At-The-Money Put Option Profit Profiles

Legend: Long Stock — Short Stock — Short Put — Long Put — LS+LP — SS+SP

Stock/Option Values at Expiration

Future Stock Price at Option Expiration

Option Premium = 10; Strike Price = 50

Labels: Short Put, Short Stock, Long Stock, Strike Price, Current Stock Price, Put BE, Long Put, Stock/Put BE, SS+SP, LS+LP

Figure 41.4

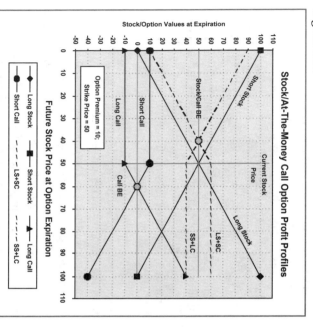

Stock/At-The-Money Call Option Profit Profiles

Legend: Long Stock — Short Stock — Long Call — Short Call — LS+SC — SS+LC

Stock/Option Values at Expiration

Future Stock Price at Option Expiration

Option Premium = 10; Strike Price = 50

Labels: Short Stock, Short Call, Long Call, Stock/Call BE, Current Stock Price, Long Stock, Call BE, LS+SC, SS+LC

This is evidenced in Figure 41.3 above by the fact that the two lines (Long Stock and LC+SP) have equivalent slopes—that is, for any particular change in the price of the stock, there is an equivalent change in the value of the investor's position, regardless of whether he holds the stock or the options.

Figures 41.4 and 41.5 now show the profit profiles of combinations of the options and holdings of the underlying stock.

For reference, the profit profiles of the naked options are shown at the bottom of the graphs. Line LS + SC in

Figure 4 shows the profit profile of a long position in the stock combined with a short position in the call—called a "covered call" position. Notice, that the profit profile of the long stock + short call position is exactly the same as the profit profile of the short put position shown in Figure 41.2. The LS + SC or covered call position is a synthetic short put.[14]

The SS + LC line of Figure 41.4 is a combination of a short position in the underlying stock and a long call. The profit profile of this combined position is equivalent to the profit profile of the long put position shown in Figure 41.2, so the SS + LC position is a synthetic long put.

The LS + LP line of Figure 41.5 is a combination of a long position in the underlying stock and a long put position on the stock that has a profit profile identical to that of the long call position in Figure 1. This combination is a synthetic long call position.

Finally, line SS + SP of Figure 41.5 is a combination of a short position in the stock and a short put position which has a profit profile identical to the short call position shown in Figure 41.1. The SS + SP combination is a synthetic short call position.

Obviously, these are not the only combinations of these instruments that investors can create. For instance, instead of buying an at-the-money call option, investors can buy long calls with exercise prices that are either in- or out-of-the-money. By buying an out-of-the-money call, they purchase only some of the upside potential above the current market price of the stock, rather than all of it. Various combinations of long and short calls and long and short puts with different exercise prices can permit investors to buy or sell almost any component part of the underlying security's profit profile over a given term. In addition, investors can buy and sell long and short positions in puts and calls with different terms to expiration to buy or sell components of the underlying security's profit profile that essentially begin and end at different times in the future. The possible strategies and hedging opportunities are nearly endless, so the Option Strategies section below will discuss some of the more commonly used combinations.

Option Premiums

The amount one pays for an option is called the option's *premium*. The premium is composed of two elements: the intrinsic value and the speculative value. Each of these values can fluctuate over time based on many factors.

The intrinsic value of an option is simply the amount by which the option's strike price is in-the-money. For example, if an investor owns a call option with a strike price of $45 when the market price of the underlying security is $50, the intrinsic value is $5. In the case of a put option on the same stock, the intrinsic value of the put option is $5 if the strike price is $55 and the market price of the underlying security is $50. Essentially, the intrinsic value of the option is the profit that could be realized if the option was exercised immediately, and the underlying stock was sold at fair market value (disregarding the cost of the option). If the option's strike price is at- or out-of-the-money, the intrinsic value is $0. Of course, the intrinsic value changes throughout the term until the option expires, as the market price of the underlying security fluctuates. At, or just before, expiration of the option, the intrinsic value and the premium become one and the same, since the speculative value of the premium disappears.

The speculative value of the premium is a function of several variables: (1) the volatility of the price of the underlying security; (2) the length of the remaining term until the option expires; (3) the dividend payout rate and the timing of dividend payments, if any; (4) the level of the risk-free rate appropriate to the remaining term until the option expires; and (5) how far in- or out-of-the-money the strike price is.

The underlying security's price volatility is a factor because the prices of more volatile securities are more likely to move into a range where the option is in (or

further in) -the-money. So, all else being equal, the speculative value for more volatile securities will be greater than that for less volatile securities. In addition, if the underlying security's volatility increases (decreases) during the term until the option expires, the speculative premium will also increase (decrease).

The longer the term until the option expires, the greater the likelihood that the option will move into (or deeper into) the money. Consequently, all else being equal, speculative value diminishes as the option approaches its expiration date.

The prices of stocks paying dividends tend to decrease by the amount of dividends paid per share when the stock goes ex-dividend. Consequently, the stock's intrinsic value will decrease by the amount of the dividend, yet the option-holder does not receive the dividend. Therefore, the speculative value for call options on stocks paying higher dividends tends to be lower than that on stocks paying low or no dividends, if all else is equal—the speculative value is less because a call option will repeatedly lose intrinsic value due to dividends, reducing the upside potential for the investor. For put options, on the other hand, the effect is just the opposite.

If the risk-free (opportunity cost) rate is lower, the present value of future potential benefits is higher. Therefore, the speculative value will be greater when interest rates are lower. Conversely, a higher risk-free rate means that the investor may have attractive gains available from risk-free options and will demand a greater return (i.e., spend less for the option via a reduced speculative premium) to compensate for the risk of the option.

Finally, the deeper an option is in- or out-of-the-money, the less likely it is that its status will change substantially (i.e., from out-of-the-money to in-the-money, or vice-versa), so the speculative value tends to diminish as the stock price moves further away from the strike price. The speculative premium approaches a value of zero asymptotically as the stock price moves further and further from the strike price.

Generally, there are two kinds of options available for most investors: American options and European options. The difference between the two is that American options can be exercised before the expiration date, whereas European options cannot. But since option premiums always include at least some speculative value until just before they expire, investors holding American options will almost always be better off if they sell the options rather than exercise them, if they wish to close out the position before the expiration date. But the investor does need to factor in the transaction cost of selling the option in the open market, including the implications of the bid/ask spread.

Option Strategies

The discussion above described the profit profiles for long call, short call, long put, and short put positions but did not elaborate on the strategic reasons for taking these positions. The following discussion will briefly explain the strategic opportunities these positions present alone before addressing how to use them in various combinations to achieve various objectives. Keep in mind that options can be written or bought on individual securities and futures contracts, sector, industry, or asset class indexes or futures contracts, or broad-based market indexes or futures contracts—so investors can use them for speculative or risk hedging purposes at each of those levels within their portfolios. Also, listed options generally expire in less than a year, but long-term options, called LEAPS, have terms of up to 2 years and 8 months from issue (and warrants may have expiration dates of 5 to 7 years or longer). Also, options written and traded over the counter can have terms of almost any duration to which the parties to the transaction agree.

Long Call

In general, the purchase of a naked call option[15] is a bullish strategy employed when an investor thinks the market will rise significantly in the relative short term (before expiration of the option). Generally, the more bullish the investor's perspective, the higher the exercise or strike price he may want for the call. Premiums decline as the strike price rises, so bullish investors potentially can still gain considerably while putting less money at risk—or can create greater leverage by purchasing a greater quantity of lower-premium options. The profit potential is theoretically unlimited and rises as the market rises. The break-even point at expiration is the strike price plus the premium. The downside risk is limited to the premium paid and generally no margin is required.

An investor also can use long calls as an effective and flexible defensive strategy when the asset allocation mix of a portfolio diverges from a preferred position. An investor can use long calls to quickly and relatively inexpensively increase the effective portfolio weights in those asset classes that are underweighted until the investor can rebalance the portfolio with sales or purchases of

Short Call

Shorting calls (i.e., writing calls) is appropriate if an investor's strategic view is relative certainty that the market will not rise and he is unsure or unconcerned about whether it will fall. Investors who are quite confident in their view should write at-the-money calls or even in-the-money calls. If they are less certain of their view, they should write out-of-the-money calls. The upside gain on the position is limited to the premium received if the market price of the underlying stock is at or below the strike price. The downside risk is unlimited (unless the short call is covered—sees "Covered Call" below), Losses on the position worsen as the market price of the stock rises. An investor, who likes the idea of the strategy, but not the potentially unlimited downside risk, might be interested in a bear spread (described below). Since this is a short position, margin is always required to assure performance in the event the option is exercised. Figure 41.1 (shown earlier) illustrates the profit profile of a short call.

Long Put

Investors with a bearish perspective on market conditions for the underlying asset and who expect the market value of the underlying asset to fall significantly over the term of the option should consider buying puts. In general, investors with more bearish perspectives should look for lower exercise prices to minimize their outlay (or increase their leverage) while still expecting sufficient price movement to make a profit on the put (in a similar manner to the bullish investor in a long call). The maximum profit potential of a long put is equal to the entire strike price of the stock less the premium paid (which would apply if the value of the stock went to $0). The break-even point at expiration is equal to the original stock price minus the premium paid. Maximum losses are limited to the premium paid (which the investor will incur if the market price of the underlying asset is equal to or above the strike price at expiration). Investing in a long put requires no margin. Figure 41.2 (shown earlier) illustrates the profit profile of a long put.

Short Put

Selling a put is a moderately bullish strategy when investors are virtually certain that the market will not

the securities in the portfolio. Figure 41.1 (shown earlier) illustrates the profit profile of a long call.

Chapter 41 – Hedging and Option Strategies

go down (much, if at all), but they are unsure or unconcerned about whether it will rise. If investors are concerned about whether it will rise. If investors are very bullish, then they should consider selling puts with strike prices that are more in-the-money to get the larger premiums. The profit potential is limited to the premium received. The breakeven point at expiration is the strike price less the premium. Margin is always required to help secure the investor's obligation to sell under the contract. Potential loss is almost unlimited (almost, since the underlying price cannot fall below zero)—the maximum loss is the strike price of the contract minus the premium received. If this basic strategy is appealing, but the potential downside risk is unacceptable, investors may prefer a bull spread (described below). Figure 41.2 (shown earlier) illustrates the profit profile of a short put.

Covered Call

A covered call is a long position in the stock combined with a short call. As described above, it has the same profit profile and characteristics as a short put. Figure 41.4 (shown earlier) illustrates the profit profile for a covered call—line LS + SC.

For most investors, this relatively neutral position is employed to increase income when they expect the market price of the underlying stock to fluctuate within a fairly narrow range over the term of the option. It tends to work best when the investor expects short-term price weakness due to company-specific factors, or industry or sector or even overall factors, but has a generally optimistic forecast in the longer term. The upside potential at expiration of the option is limited to the strike price minus the market price of the stock (when the option is purchased) plus the premium received on the sale of the call. Essentially, upside appreciation potential on the stock is sold for immediate cash. The downside potential is large—the investor is still long on the underlying stock, which can experience a decline limited only by the fact that it cannot drop below $0. But the investor will retain the premium of the written call to slightly mitigate such a loss. But the most serious potential "loss" could be the opportunity lost if the market price of the stock rises sharply. Margin is always required.[16]

Protective Put

A protective put is a long position in a stock combined with a long position in a put. If the stock and put are acquired at the same time, it is called a married put. The protective put position has the same profit profile and

characteristics of a long call. Figure 41.5 (shown earlier) illustrates the profit profile at expiration of a protective call—line LS + LP.

The protective put is a strategy employed when investors hold a stock long, generally with gains, and are bearish regarding the relatively short-term prospects for the market price of the stock. The put protects the value of the stock, while not preventing the position from benefiting in the event of a market rise. The profit potential is unlimited, being the ordinary return on the stock minus the fixed premium paid for the put option. The downside risk is limited to the premium paid for the put if the stock position is entirely hedged by puts, since the gains on the puts will offset the stock losses as the market falls. No margin is required.

Bull Spread

The bull spread is a moderately bullish strategy investors may employ when they are fairly certain that the market will not fall but want to cap the risk of loss. To reduce the cost of limiting the downside risk, investors sell an offsetting position that also limits their upside potential. It is a conservative strategy for investors who think that the market is more likely to rise than to fall.

Investors may implement the bull spread in two different ways:

1. *Bull Spread–Call* – Investor buys an in-the-money call (typically) and sells an out-of-the-money call (typically) with strike prices roughly equally spaced below and above the current market price of the stock. More aggressive or confident investors can set the strike prices higher.

2. *Bull Spread–Put* – Investor buys an out-of-the-money put (typically) and sells an in-the-money put option (typically) with strike prices roughly equally spaced below and above the market price of the stock. More aggressive or confident investors can set the strike prices higher.

In these examples, the current stock price is assumed to be 50, the lower strike price is 45, and the higher strike price is 55. The profit profiles for the call-based bull spread and the put-based bull spread are nearly identical, but the initial outlay for the two positions differs considerably. The initial net premium for the call-based bull spread is $4.44; the put-based bull spread generates a net premium of -$5.27.[17] The upside potential is limited in each case. For the call-based bull spread, it is limited to

Figure 41.6

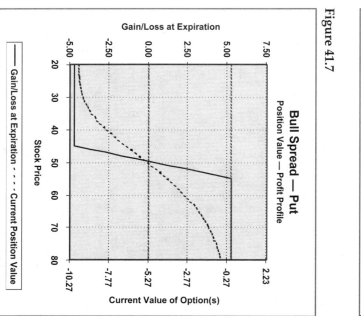

Bull Spread — Call

Position Value — Profit Profile

Gain/Loss at Expiration

Stock Price

— Gain/Loss at Expiration   - - - Current Position Value

Current Value of Option(s)

Figure 41.7

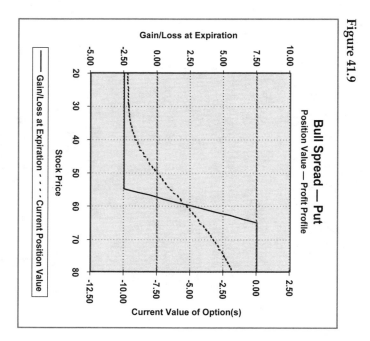

Bull Spread — Put

Position Value — Profit Profile

Gain/Loss at Expiration

Stock Price

— Gain/Loss at Expiration   - - - Current Position Value

Current Value of Option(s)

Figure 41.8

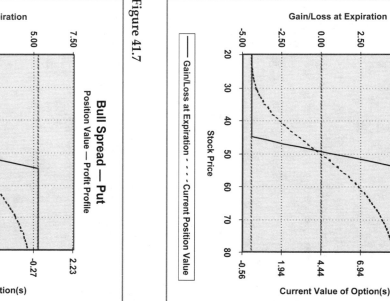

Bull Spread — Call

Position Value — Profit Profile

Gain/Loss at Expiration

Stock Price

— Gain/Loss at Expiration   - - - Current Position Value

Current Value of Option(s)

Figure 41.9

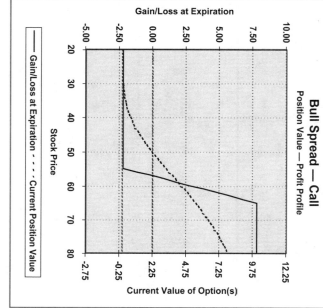

Bull Spread — Put

Position Value — Profit Profile

Gain/Loss at Expiration

Stock Price

— Gain/Loss at Expiration   - - - Current Position Value

Current Value of Option(s)

The higher the investor sets the strike prices relative to the current market price, the greater is the investor's upside potential and the lesser is the investor's maximum possible loss. But the break-even point also moves higher. For example, using the same parameters as for Figures 41.6 and 41.7, except that the strike prices are set at 55 and 65, instead of 45 and 55, the call-based bull spread and put-based bull spread profit profiles are as shown in Figures 41.8 and 41.9, respectively.

the difference in the strike prices, $10, less the net initial payout for the options, $4.44, or $5.46; for the put-based bull spread, it is limited to the net initial pay-in, or $5.27. The downside risk is also limited in both cases. For the call-based bull spread, the maximum potential loss is the net initial payout, or $4.44; for the put-based bull spread, the maximum potential loss is the difference between the strike prices, $10, less the net initial pay-in, $5.27, or $4.73. In this case, the break-even stock price is approximately equal to the current stock price.

Bear Spread

The bear spread is the moderately bearish analog to the vertical bull spread. Investors may employ this strategy when they think that the market will not rise, but they want to limit their risk of loss. To reduce the cost of limiting the risk of loss, investors sell an offsetting position that also limits their potential gain. It is a conservative strategy for investors who think that the market is more likely to fall than rise.

Investors may implement the bear spread in two different ways:

1. *Bear Spread–Call* – Investor sells an in-the-money call (typically) and buys an out-of-the-money call (typically) with strike prices roughly equally spaced below and above the current market price of the stock. More aggressive or confident investors can set the strike prices lower.

2. *Bear Spread–Put* – Investor sells an out-of-the-money put (typically) and buys an in-the-money put option (typically) with strike prices roughly equally spaced below and above the market price of the stock. More aggressive or confident investors can set the strike prices lower.

In these examples, the current stock price is assumed to be 50, the lower strike price is 40, and the higher strike price is 50 (i.e., an aggressive bear spread). The profit profiles for the call-based bear spread and the put-based

bear spread are nearly identical, but the initial outlay for the two positions differs considerably. The initial net premium for the call-based bear spread is -$5.83 (net amount investor receives); the put-based bear spread generates a net premium of $3.87 (net amount investors pays). The upside potential is limited in each case. For the put-based bear spread, it is limited to the difference in the strike prices, $10, less the net initial payout for the options, $3.87, or $6.13; for the call-based bear spread, it is limited to the net initial pay-in, or $5.83. The downside risk is also limited in both cases. For the put-based bear spread, the maximum potential loss is the net initial payout, or $3.87; for the call-based bear spread, the maximum potential loss is the difference between the strike prices, $10, less the net initial pay-in, $5.83, or $4.17. In this case, the break-even stock price is approximately equal to $46.

Collar

A collar is a hedging strategy whereby an investor who wishes to minimize potential loss in the value of a long equity position sells an out-of-the-money covered call option and uses the premium received to reduce or offset the cost of an out-of-the-money put option, thus limiting the investor's downside risk. But the downside protection comes at the expense of foregoing some potential upside gains. The maturity of a collar can range from several months to several years, and both options may (or may not) mature simultaneously. If the call option is written in the OTC market, the investor can negotiate the strike price and premium so that

Figure 41.11

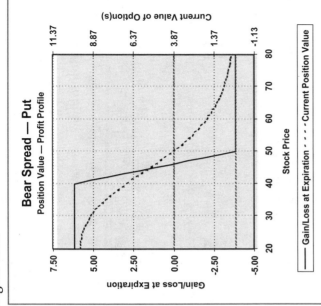

Bear Spread — Put
Position Value — Profit Profile

— Gain/Loss at Expiration · · · Current Position Value

Figure 41.10

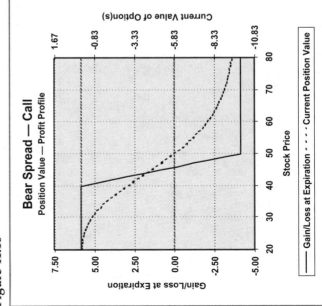

Bear Spread — Call
Position Value — Profit Profile

— Gain/Loss at Expiration · · · Current Position Value

the investor's out-of-pocket cost for the put and call options is reduced to zero—a zero-premium collar. In many cases, investors can pick out-of-the-money puts and calls on listed options exchanges whose premiums also come close to zeroing out. Investors who have legal restrictions or practical limitations on selling their stock (e.g., restricted or unregistered stock, or stock with a low cost basis) may find collars especially useful.[18] The collar has a profit profile very similar to the vertical bull spread.

Figure 41.12 shows the profit profile of a collar where the current stock price is 50, and the strike prices on the short call and long put are 60 and 45, respectively.

Although infrequently used, investors could also create a short collar to hedge against adverse price movements when they are short in an equity position. To create a short collar that is analogous to the long collar shown in Figure 41.12, sell a call with a strike price of 45 and buy a put with a strike price of 60. The profit profile will be similar to that of a bear spread.

Figure 41.12

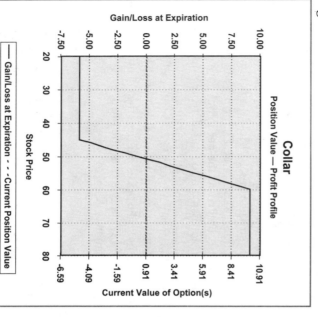

Collar
Position Value — Profit Profile

— Gain/Loss at Expiration   - - -Current Position Value

investors think that the market will be less volatile, they can sell a straddle and profit if the price does not move outside of a given range.

The long straddle is created by buying a call option and a put option with the same strike price; usually, at the money. The upside potential of the long straddle is unlimited. The largest possible loss is equal to the two premiums paid for the long call and long put. The breakeven point is equal to the strike price plus or minus the sum of the long call and long put premiums (since a movement in either direction brings either the call, or the put, into the money, a straddle investor can profit with a move price in *either* direction beyond the boundaries of the breakeven points).

The short straddle is created by selling a call and a put for the same strike price; usually, at the money. The upside potential is limited to the sum of the two premiums received on the short call and short put. The downside risk is unlimited. The breakeven point is the strike price plus or minus the sum of the short call and short put premiums (where the investor profits as long as the stock price stays *within* the boundaries of the breakeven points).

Figures 41.13 and 41.14 show the profit profile of a long straddle and a short straddle, respectively, where the current stock price and both strike prices are equal to 50.

Figure 41.13

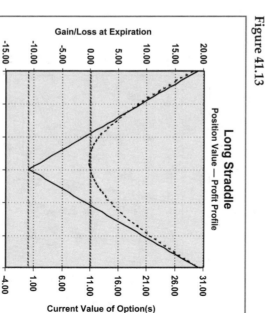

Long Straddle
Position Value — Profit Profile

— Gain/Loss at Expiration   - - -Current Position Value

Straddle

If investors think that the market will be very volatile in the short-term or a company is facing a situation that could greatly impact the stock price, either up or down, such as a ruling in a major lawsuit or the awarding of a major government contract, they can buy a straddle. The long straddle position will reward them if the price moves substantially either up or down. In contrast, if

408

Figure 41.14

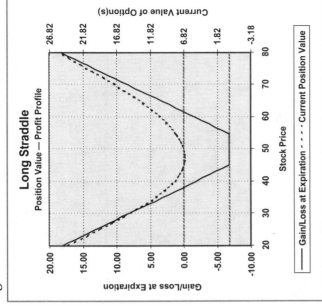

Short Straddle
Position Value — Profit Profile

Current Value of Option(s)

Gain/Loss at Expiration

Stock Price

— Gain/Loss at Expiration · · · Current Position Value

Figure 41.15

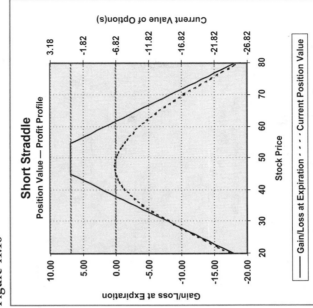

Long Straddle
Position Value — Profit Profile

Current Value of Option(s)

Gain/Loss at Expiration

Stock Price

— Gain/Loss at Expiration · · · Current Position Value

Figure 41.16

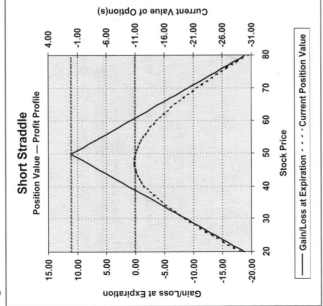

Short Straddle
Position Value — Profit Profile

Current Value of Option(s)

Gain/Loss at Expiration

Stock Price

— Gain/Loss at Expiration · · · Current Position Value

Strangle

Strangles are variations on straddles. Investors use them for the same purposes. But instead of buying or selling an at-the-money call and a put, the investor buys or sells an out-of-the-money call and put. This reduces the premium cost for the long strangle as well as the maximum possible loss (which is equal to the sum of the premiums on the long call and the long put). But it also requires the stock price to move further before the investor breaks even. Similar to the straddle, the upside potential is unlimited.

For the short strangle, the lower premiums reduce the investor's maximum potential gain, which is equal to the sum of the premiums on the short call and the short put. But the range in which the stock price can fluctuate until expiration is wider, so the investor is more likely to make some profit on the position.

Figures 41.15 and 41.16 show the profit profile for a long strangle and a short strangle when the current stock price is 50 and the strike prices on the put and call are 45 and 55, respectively.

long straddle to reduce the net premium paid for the position. The tradeoff is that the butterfly has a limited upside potential.

In the case of the short butterfly, investors add an out-of-the-money long call and an out-of-the-money long put to the at-the-money short call and the at-the-money short put of the short straddle to limit the downside risk. The tradeoff is that the net premium the investor receives is less and, consequently, the maximum upside is less than it would be with a straddle.

Butterfly

Butterflies are another variation on straddles with essentially the same objectives. But they employ two additional out-of-the-money options. When investors create a long butterfly, they add an out-of-the-money short call and an out-of-the-money short put to the at-the-money long call and at-the-money long put of the

Figures 41.17 and 41.18 show the profit profiles of a long butterfly and short butterfly, respectively. In this case, the current price of the stock and the strike price on the two in-the-money options are 50. The strike prices for the out-of-the-money short call and short put are 60 and 40, respectively.

Figure 41.17

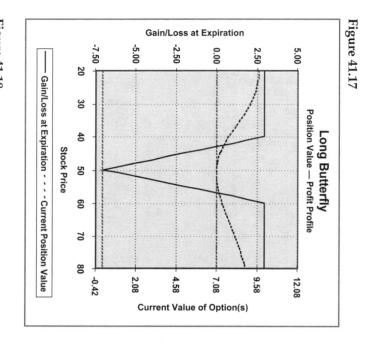

Long Butterfly
Position Value — Profit Profile

Gain/Loss at Expiration

Stock Price

Current Value of Option(s)

— Gain/Loss at Expiration - - - Current Position Value

Figure 41.18

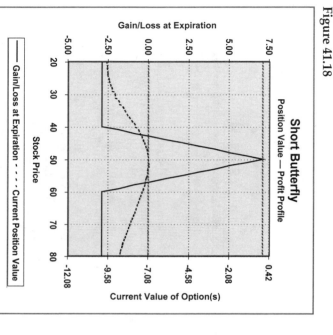

Short Butterfly
Position Value — Profit Profile

Gain/Loss at Expiration

Stock Price

Current Value of Option(s)

— Gain/Loss at Expiration - - - Current Position Value

Calendar Spread

Calendar spreads are also known as time spreads. The most common type of calendar spread consists of opposing positions in two options of the same type (either both puts or both calls) that have the same exercise price, but expire at different times. Investors can create a long (short) time spread position by selling (buying) a short-term call option and buying (selling) a longer-term call option. The investor of the long position would profit when the price of the underlying asset is close to the strike price of the short call at its expiration.

WHAT ARE THE TAX IMPLICATIONS?

Taxes are a key factor in evaluating how to most efficiently minimize risk in taxable portfolios. For hedging strategies, two primary rules govern taxation: (1) the constructive sale rules, and (2) the straddle rules. The constructive sale rules govern when investors initiating a hedge position have to treat the transaction as a sale of the hedged security (i.e., as a taxable event), even though no actual sale has taken place. The straddle rules govern the tax aspects of closing a hedge position, including such issues as tolling or freezing capital gain holding periods and capitalizing the carrying costs (interest expense, commissions, and the like) of the hedge strategy. For most hedging situations, a primary objective is to avoid constructive sale treatment and the requirement to recognize gain (if an actual sale has not occurred). If investors can also avoid the negative aspects of the straddle rules, then the hedging strategy can be a much more tax-efficient strategy.

Constructive Sale Rules

The 1997 Tax Reform Act provides that certain transactions attempting to neutralize future gain and/or loss in a current appreciated stock holding are treated as "constructive sales," which cause recognition of gain, if entered into after June 8, 1997.[19] A constructive sale is a transaction in which the owner of an appreciated security enters into one of the following three transactions:

- A short sale of the same or substantially identical property;

- An offsetting notional principal contract with respect to the same or substantially identical property; or

- A futures or forward contract to deliver the same or substantially identical property[20]

The term "substantially identical" is normally considered to be securities issued by the same issuer, which are commercially identical in all major aspects including dividend provisions. Normally, securities issued by two different issuers are not considered "substantially identical" unless, for example, the companies are merging, are days away from a merged close, and the common stock of each company is trading for all practical intents and purposes as the same security.[21] Correlated pricing (meaning that the prices move virtually in lock-step) in the market is the key test for securities being considered substantially identical.

Initiating a put option purchase is not a constructive sale.

An investor who purchases a put option should not have the transaction treated as a constructive sale, even if the put option is for a stock the put holder already owns. Although the Internal Revenue Service (IRS) has not issued final regulations to clarify what is and is not a constructive sale, the committee report for the applicable 1997 Tax Reform Act code provisions provides some guidance. The committee report suggests that strategies that trigger constructive sale treatment are those that eliminate *nearly all potential gain and loss.*[22] Out-of-the-money put options only reduce some, but not all, of the potential loss and none of the gain, so purchasing a put option on stock already owned should not trigger the constructive sale rules with respect to the stock. But, in theory, if the put option is "deep-in-the-money" when the investor initiates the hedge and, therefore, it is a close proxy for the stock itself, a purchase could trigger a constructive sale or taxable event.[23]

A short sale on stocks or indexes not otherwise owned is not a constructive sale.

A short sale of a stock or stock index that is not otherwise owned by an investor is not a constructive sale because the shorted stock is not substantially identical to securities held long in the investor's portfolio. For example, selling short Ford Motor Company (which is not otherwise owned by the investor) to hedge against a potential decline in a highly appreciated position in GM Motors is not a constructive sale resulting in tax, even though the stocks are in the same industry and their stock prices are correlated (albeit imperfectly). This technique of shorting a different, but price-correlated, stock in the same industry is beneficial for avoiding the constructive sale rules while hedging against market-wide and industry-specific risks. But it is still a considerably less effective hedge (because of the imperfect correlation) than shorting against the box, which is a perfect hedge (because of the perfect correlation), because the investor is still bearing substantial company-specific risk. GM's stock could still decline while Ford's stock remained level or rose due to business factors or circumstances unique to GM (e.g., labor problems, problems with a key component parts supplier, lawsuits, liability, a recall associated with a critical design flaw in a major product line, etc.).

Selling short a stock or stock index already owned is a constructive sale (except for a few limited exceptions for short-term short sales) that triggers tax. Therefore, selling short against the box is a wise hedging strategy generally only if the reasons for hedging the position and keeping the long stock position, rather than just selling the stocks held long, outweigh the cost of accelerating the tax. Investors might wish to consider this strategy in 2008, the last year under current tax rules the 15% maximum capital gains tax rate will apply before reverting to the 20% tax rate of prior law, so as to pay tax at the lower rate and step-up the basis in their shares, especially if they expect to sell the shares in 2009 anyway. This may also be beneficial if the investor seeks to hedge away the risk of a stock that otherwise cannot be sold because of restrictions on the particular account or shares held.

Initiating a non-abusive collar should not be a constructive sale or taxable event.

Creating collars that do not essentially freeze the value of the stock within a relatively tight range ("abusive collars") should not trigger a constructive sale of the underlying stock. Generally, collars are unlikely to be considered abusive if the term of the transaction is three years or less and the difference between the floor and ceiling price of the collar is at least 20%.[24] The Congressional committee report seems to suggest that collars that are not abusive will be grandfathered under the final regulations.[25] The IRS has not issued final regulations covering constructive sales, so investors must cautiously evaluate any hedge that attempts to control both gain and loss.

There are other exemptions from the constructive sale rule, such as short-term hedges relating to shorting the same stock, but for most situations the put option, the short sale against a similar but different stock or index, and the collar are the most often used hedging techniques that can avoid the constructive sale rules. (See Chapter 43, "Taxation of Investment Vehicles," for further discussion of the constructive sale rules.)

Avoiding Constructive Sale Treatment

Investors are required to ignore the constructive sale rules if they close the offsetting position prior to January 30th of the following tax year and they retain their original position for at least 60 days after closing the offsetting position.[26] But investors must "go bare" for that 60 days—that is, without entering into another offsetting position for that 60-day period. If they enter into an offsetting position during that 60-day period, the original constructive sale in the prior year is reinstated. (For more information about the details of this exception, see Chapter 43, "Taxation of Investment Vehicles.")

Example: On May 1 last year, an investor bought 100 shares of ABC Corporation stock for $1,000. On September 3 last year, she sold short 100 shares of ABC stock for $1,600, triggering the constructive sale rules. The investor held both of these positions until January 10 of this year. On that date, she closed the offsetting short position for $1,800 and kept the "long" position open until at least March 11 (at least 60 days). During that 60-day period, the investor did not enter into any other offsetting positions that would reduce risk of loss on the original position. Since the investor met the exceptions to the constructive sale rules, she has no constructive sale for last year. When she closes her short position on January 10, she recognizes a short-term capital loss of $200 for this tax year. Her cost basis for the long position remains at $1,000, but her holding period is now deemed to have started on January 10 of this year.[27]

Example: On May 1 last year, an investor bought 100 shares of ABC Corporation stock for $1,000. On September 3 last year, she sold short 100 shares of ABC stock for $1,600, triggering the constructive sale rules. The investor held both of these positions until January 10 of this year. On that date, she closed her offsetting short position for $1,800. But because of fluctuations in the stock, the investor sells the long position on March 1 (well before the 60-day required holding period ending March 11) for $1,500. The investor has now violated the exceptions to the constructive sale rules and she must recognize the constructive sale of the original position last year (when the constructive sale actually took place), and not in the current year, when she actually sold the stock.

Straddle Rules

Avoiding the constructive sale rules is usually a paramount tax issue when hedging. A second tax issue is whether the hedge is a straddle. While the constructive sale rules apply to transactions that attempt to lock in value within a certain range, eliminating the chance for both gain and loss, the straddle rules are broader and include most situations where a taxpayer is attempting to limit losses on an appreciated security by owning another security. If a hedge is a straddle, numerous tax implications arise with respect to closing out the hedge. The tax impact of a straddle is usually much less onerous than a constructive sale, but the straddle rules are nonetheless a very important tax factor with hedges.

Straddle Defined

The Internal Revenue Code defines a straddle as "offsetting positions with respect to personal property."[28] A taxpayer holds offsetting positions "if there is a substantial diminution of the taxpayer's risk of loss from holding any position with respect to personal property by reason of his holding 1 or more other positions… (whether or not of the same kind)."[29] Therefore, if an investor shorts a stock or buys a put option on a stock held long, that position creates a straddle.

In evaluating if the offsetting positions meet the facts and circumstances test of "intent to substantially limit risk of loss," the Internal Revenue Code provides several tests, which, if met, result in a rebuttable presumption that a straddle exists.[30] These rebuttable presumptions assume a position is a straddle if the hedge involves the same security as the protected security, even if in substantially different form.[31] These tests also presume a straddle exists if the hedge is sold or marketed as an offsetting position (regardless of the name used).[32] But these tests require that there be an inverse relationship in valuation changes between the offsetting positions.[33] The bottom line is that straddle rules will apply to nearly any hedge that reduces the investor's potential for loss on an existing position within his portfolio.

To summarize the basic straddle rules:

A straddle occurs when an investor owns stock (or a call option on the stock) and then enters into an offsetting position such as:

• an option on such stock or substantially identical stock or

- a position with respect to substantially similar or related property (not including stock).

Property is substantially similar or related to stock when the fair market value of the offsetting position primarily reflects the performance of

- a single firm;

- the same industry; or

- the same economic factors (such as interest rates, commodity prices, a stock market index, or foreign currency rates as well as other economic factors).

- In addition, changes in the fair market value of the offsetting positions must be reasonably expected to move inversely to the market value of the position held. The price relationship does not have to be one-to-one. The prices may move as a fraction or multiple of each other. In other words, if appreciated stock is on one side of the position, then a put option on the same stock or substantially similar stock on the other side of the position is a straddle.

Absent final regulations, a straddle does not appear to exist with an offsetting position in substantially similar stock.[34]

Stock acquired before January 1, 1984, is not subject to the straddle rules.[35] For these stocks, investors can purchase puts against stock positions with identical correlation and protection, yet without adverse tax implications under either the constructive sale or straddle rules.

Many other hedge strategies have straddle implications, including selling short or buying puts on an index fund (either broad based or by sector). These strategies can offer higher correlation than hedge strategies employing short sales or puts on a different stock in the same industry as the appreciated stock.

Position	Example	Straddle/Constructive Sale?
Sell Short a Substantially Similar Stock Not Otherwise Owned	Sell Short Ford to Hedge a Position in GM	No/No
Sell Short a Stock Already Owned	Sell Short GM to Hedge a Position in GM	Yes/Yes

Position	Example	Straddle/Constructive Sale?
Purchase of Put Option on Substantially Similar Stock to a Position Owned	Purchase a Put Option on Ford to Hedge a Position in GM	Yes/No
Purchase of Put Option on Stock Already Owned	Purchase a Put Option on GM to Hedge a Position in GM	Yes/No
Non-Abusive Collar on Stock Already Owned	Purchase Put Option and Sell Call Option on GM to Limit Values to a Range	Yes/No

Straddle Rule Tax Implications on Closing the Straddle

If an investor is in a straddle position

- The capital gain holding periods are suspended during the time of the offsets.[36] The holding period of the hedged security remains long-term if it was long-term at the time the investor initiated the hedge; non-long-term hedged securities have their holding periods started anew when the offsetting position (i.e., straddle) is closed. The holding periods for put options or other similar offsetting positions acquired to initiate the hedge remain short-term since they are prevented from becoming long-term by the suspension effect of the straddle.

- Investors may take no current deduction for losses to the extent of any unrealized gain in the offsetting positions.[37] Therefore, losses on a straddle are deferred until unrealized gains on the offsetting position are eliminated or realized. But losses on a straddle in excess of any unrealized gains may still be taken. Any deferred losses are carried forward into the subsequent tax year.

- Investors must capitalize all carrying charges and interest expense (including margin) during the offset period (net of dividends) and add them to the basis of the long stock position. This has the effect of reducing the amount of capital gain when the investor sells the long stock position.[38]

One of the major concerns of the straddle rules are that they may convert what otherwise would have been long-term capital gain into short-term capital gain for tax purposes. For example, assume an investor owns 100 shares of XYZ corp. that he purchased 3 years ago for $50 per share. The stock is now worth $100 per share, so he has a substantial unrealized long-term capital gain. He thinks the company's prospects are good in the long run, but the stock price and the stock's P/E are at their historical highs. Consequently, he fears that the price may decline in the relative short run. If he sells the shares now, he must realize and pay tax on the long-term gain of $5,000. If instead the investor purchases a put option on the stock with an exercise price per share equal to the stock's current market price of $100, he can protect himself from any loss resulting from a downward price adjustment during the term of the hedge.

Suppose the investor purchases the option to create the hedge. The hedge is not treated as a constructive sale, but it is subject to the straddle rules. Now suppose for illustration purposes that the price of the stock falls all the way to the investor's original $50 purchase price by the time the option expires. The investor will have lost the entire $5,000 long-term gain on the stock in his portfolio, but gained $5,000 on the put (less the cost of the put, of course). Now if he closes out the put by either selling the put or buying new shares in the market at $50 to deliver on the put contract for $100 per share, the $5,000 gain (less the cost of the put) will be short-term. Consequently, as a result of the transaction, he would have hedged his economic position (less the cost of the put), but converted what otherwise would have been a long-term gain taxable at the lower capital gains rate into a short-term capital gain taxable at his ordinary income tax rate (assuming he has realized no other offsetting losses in his portfolio).

Of course, he could and generally should avoid this short-term capital gain treatment by delivering the stock he held in his portfolio to satisfy the put. Since the stock delivered in this case would have a long-term holding period, the gain would be taxed as long-term gain. As a result, he would end up having exactly the same amount of money after tax as he otherwise would have had if had he originally sold the stock rather than create the hedge, but less the cost of creating the hedge.

Actually, had he originally sold the stock and then reinvested the after-tax proceeds elsewhere, for instance, at worst in a risk-free asset like T-bills, he would also have the additional after-tax interest income from the T-bills. So the hedge has cost the investor, at a minimum, the amount he paid to buy the put and create the hedge (plus commissions and other transaction costs) plus the after-tax income he could have earned by investing in a risk-free asset.

This example demonstrates two important points. First, investors must carefully assess the tax consequences of hedges that are treated as straddles and how they close out their straddle positions in light of their overall tax situation and objectives. Second, hedges are not free lunches. Hedges have both direct costs and indirect (opportunity) costs that investors must weigh relative to the benefits or objectives they hope to achieve by entering into the hedge transaction.

Economics of Primary Hedging Strategies

After the tax analysis is completed, the basic question is whether the economics merit a hedging strategy considering all relevant taxes (including estate taxes) and the variety of potential price changes for the security or portfolio to be hedged. Several possible outcomes should be modeled, using various rates of appreciation (and potential depreciation) and considering taxation and other economic impacts such as lost opportunities for other investments, dividend income, and transaction costs.

Conclusion

The decision-making process for diversification and risk management of highly appreciated securities and portfolios is becoming more prevalent and more complex. While the sale decision is usually simplest, investors and investment advisors should evaluate the alternatives, including hedging strategies for possible use. Hedging strategies can be utilized to effectively manage risk, with favorable (or at least potentially avoiding unfavorable) tax treatment. In the limited situations where hedging strategies are appropriate, the same diligent attention that is given to evaluation and implementation of hedges must be given to proper management and monitoring of hedges.

WHERE CAN I FIND OUT MORE?

The American Stock Exchange, L.L.C.
A Subsidiary of the NASDAQ-AMEX Market
An NASD Company
86 Trinity Place
New York, NY 10006 USA
1-800-THE-AMEX
(212) 306-1000
www.amex.com

Chicago Board Options Exchange, Inc.
400 South LaSalle Street
Chicago, IL 60605 USA
1-877-THE-CBOE
(312) 786-5600
www.cboe.com

International Securities Exchange L.L.
60 Broad Street
26th Floor
New York, NY 10004 USA
(212) 943-2400
www.iseoptions.com

Pacific Exchange, Inc.
Options Marketing
301 Pine Street
San Francisco, CA 94104 USA
1-877-PCX-PCX1
(415) 393-4028
www.pacificex.com

Philadelphia Stock Exchange, Inc.
1900 Market Street
Philadelphia, PA 19103 USA
1-800-THE-PHLX
(215) 496-5404
www.phlx.com

The Options Clearing Corporation
One North Wacker Drive
Chicago, IL 60606 USA
1-800-537-4258
(312) 322-6200
www.optionsclearing.com

The Options Industry Council
1-888-OPTIONS
www.888options.com

High-net-worth Investors and Listed Options, Chicago Board Options Exchange

www.ffstudies.org—Foundation for Financial Studies

www.twenty-first.com—Twenty-First Securities Corporation (Go to the Academic Press)

www.occ.treas.gov/handbook/invmgt.pdf—Office of the Comptroller of Currency (Handbook for Investment Management).

www.occ.treas.gov/handbook/deriv.pdf—Office of the Comptroller of Currency (Handbook for Risk Management of Financial Derivatives).

CHAPTER ENDNOTES

1. *High-net-worth Investors and Listed Options*, Chicago Board Options Exchange, p. 23.

2. The 1997 New York case of *Levy v. Bessemer* is an example of the fact patterns that are becoming more prevalent (No. 97 Civ. 1785, 1997 U.S. Dist. WL 431079 (S.D.N.Y. July 30, 1997). Defendant's motion to dismiss for the plaintiff's failure to state a claim upon which relief could be granted was denied. In the original complaint by the plaintiff, claims of negligence, negligent misrepresentation, breach of fiduciary duty, breach of the duty to supervise, breach of contract, and fraud were alleged. The only claim dismissed by the court was the breach of contract claim.

3. Summarizing the key argument found in one of the seminal papers on a fiduciary's duty to hedge. George Crawford, "A Fiduciary Duty to Use Derivatives," 1 *STAN. J.L. BUS & FIN.* 307 (1995). For a complete discussion of the duty of fiduciaries to hedge, Crawford's paper is an excellent overview. See also, "A Trust Fiduciary's Duty to Implement Capital Preservation Strategies Using Financial Derivatives Techniques," Randall H. Borkus, 36 REAL PROP., PROB. & TR.J. 150 (2001).

4. But as the flexibility for hedging increases, tools such as index options are developing that provide investors the opportunity to hedge against even broad, systematic market risk in a way that still involves trade-offs, but may be cost-effective.

5. "Reflections on Portfolio Management after 25 Years," Robert W. Jeffrey, *Journal of Investing*, 2001.

6. Elizabeth MacDonald, "WorldCom Director Uses Exotic Play to Hedge Stake," *The Wall Street Journal*, October 15, 1997.

7. Due to a subsequent split in WorldCom stock, his 812,308 shares eventually increased to 1,218,462 shares.

8. There are technically two types of stop-loss orders – a stop-market order, and a stop-limit order. A stop-market order converts into a regular market order and executes a sale (purchase) as soon as the price of the security falls (rises) to the stop level. A stop-limit order actually utilizes two prices – a stop price, and a limit price. When the value of the security reaches the stop price, the order converts into a regular limit order, and thus will only actually execute a sale (purchase) as long as the price is above (below) the level of the limit order. For example, if a security is at $100, an investor might enter a stop-limit order with a stop of $90 and a limit of $88 (in fact, the limit price can be higher, lower, or equal to the stop price). In this case, if the security drops below the price of $90, the order will immediately become a limit order at $88. If the price moved to $90 slowly, the limit order will likely execute immediately around $90 (since this is higher than $88). But if the stock gapped down and fell precipitously from $91 to $87, the stop-limit will convert to a limit, but will not actually execute the sale until the price rises back above $88. This ensures that the investor will not sell the security at the very bottom of a short-term precipitous drop; But this also means that the underlying limit order may never be executed (if which case the investor will have gained no value from the protection strategy. Consequently, stop-limit orders should be used with caution, particularly if the investor is concerned about a sudden sharp decline in the stock price.

9. Caveat for investors with margin accounts: brokers generally may lend securities held long in their customers' margin accounts to other customers wishing to sell such securities short. They may not even notify a customer that his securities are being lent. In general, this would not pose a serious problem. If an investor wishes to sell securities that have been lent, the broker simply

borrows someone else's securities and uses them to replace those that had been lent. For tax purposes, the investor is treated as if he had never lent the securities. But under current tax law, payments received in lieu of dividends that qualify for the preferential capital gains tax rate, are *not* treated as qualifying dividends. In other words, investors who lend stock will have the cash payments they receive in lieu of qualifying dividends taxed at their ordinary income tax rate as ordinary interest-type investment income, not at the lower rate for qualifying dividends. Brokers may have to make adjustments to their margin account agreements to account for this differential tax treatment. This may require investors who sell stock short to make in-lieu-of-dividend payments that are actually greater than the actual dividend payments to compensate the lender for the additional tax on the payments. The status of this issue is ongoing – at the time of publication, the last IRS discussion on this issue was covered in IRS Notice 2003-67.

10. Short sales of close substitutes also appear to avoid tax treatment as a straddle. See the discussion of the tax rules for straddles in the section entitled, "What Are the Tax Implications?"

11. The fact that the sum or total value of all positions in all derivatives markets is zero, does not mean that the functioning of the derivatives markets provides no value to the economy, as will be explained later.

12. The existence of a futures market can have an effect on the prices of the underlying commodities by making the markets more efficient and reducing risk, as will be discussed later.

13. Generally, the call premium for a call will be greater than the premium for a put with the same exercise price and term, so the investor will generally end up paying a net premium for the position. In addition, the position must account for the opportunity cost of funds. If the net premium for the position is actually $3, for example, the investor must add the value of an additional $47 investment in the risk-free asset (generally T-bills) to equal the $50 amount he would otherwise have to spend to buy the stock directly. The combined option position together with the T-bill investment is technically equivalent to the long stock position.

14. Keep in mind that, theoretically, the "synthetics" also include investments in the "risk-free" asset (i.e., T-bills) equating the outlays. Also, from a practical perspective the "synthetics" are never quite identical to the actual securities because of differences in margin requirements, tax rules, commissions and other transactions costs.

15. Call options are often referred to as "naked" or "covered" – the label refers to whether the investor has a corresponding open position in the underlying stock or asset. See the section entitled "Covered Call" later in this chapter.

16. Although margin is always required for a covered call, and IRA accounts cannot use margin, some custodians do allow an investor to write covered calls (or sometimes cash-secured calls) in an IRA account (i.e., the option writing doesn't actually utilize any margin borrowing). But doing this improperly risks disqualification of the IRA account.

17. The negative premium means that the investor received the net amount, rather than paid it. The position value line shows what the net premium would be for various initial prices of the stock assuming all other factors being the same. The position values are computed based upon a 9-month (270-day) term until expiration, a stock price standard deviation of 33% per year, a 4% annualized risk-free rate, and a 3% annualized dividend rate. The individual option values were estimated using

Merton's continuous-dividend version of the Black-Scholes option-pricing model.

18. In this case, since the stock often cannot be sold because of the restriction, the investor can sell the put to recover the value of the decrease in the stock (which will reflect its intrinsic and speculative value), rather than simply exercising the put. But in the event that the stock rises, the call will be exercised against the investor – who may still be unable to sell the stock to the call option holder because of restrictions. In this case, the investor can sometimes purchase stock on the open market to immediately sell to the call holder. But this will create an instant loss as the stock is purchased at market value and sold for the (lower) strike price of the call. Alternatively, the investor could sell short the stock, but may be subject to the short-selling-against-the-box rules. Consequently, the best choice may be for the investor to purchase an offsetting call option to close out the position.

19. The 1997 Tax Act added IRC Section 1259, titled "Constructive Sales Treatment for Appreciated Financial Positions."

20. IRC Sec. 1259(c).

21. Treas. Reg. §1.1233-1(d)(1).

22. Committee Report on P.L. 105-34 (Taxpayer Relief Act of 1997).

23. According to the Chicago Board Options Exchange (CBOE), a put option is in-the-money if the strike price is greater than the market price of the underlying security. If the put option strike price is significantly higher than the market price of the underlying stock, the put option trades somewhat like the stock itself and is considered "deep-in-the-money." Because deep-in-the-money puts correlate *very* closely with the price movements of the underlying stock (far more than out-of-the-money puts), there is a risk that the deep-in-the-money put could be considered substantially identical property that triggers a constructive sale. Future regulations may deem a deep-in-the-money put as an abusive hedging transaction that is not grandfathered.

24. This generalization may not apply if the collar is used to hedge a stock with very high volatility, so more conservative investors may wish to wait until the IRS releases regulations before relying on this guidance.

25. H.R. Conf. Rep. No. 105-220, at p. 514 (1997).

26. IRC Sec. 1259(c)(3).

27. IRC Sec. 1233(b)(2).

28. IRC Sec. 1092(c) (1).

29. IRC Sec. 1092(c)(2)(a).

30. IRC Sec. 1092(c)(3).

31. IRC Secs. 1092(c)(3)(A)(i), 1092(c)(3)(A)(ii).

32. IRC Sec. 1092(c)(3)(A)(iv).

33. IRC Sec. 1092(c)(3)(A).

34. "Stock offset by another position (other than an option) in substantially similar or related stock…does not constitute a straddle." Joint Committee of Taxation's General Explanation of the Tax Provisions of the Deficit Reduction Act of 1984 at p. 309.

35. IRC Sec. 1092.

36. Treas. Reg. §1.1092(b)-2T(a). Security positions that are long-term prior to the creation of the straddle maintain their long-term nature when the straddle is unwound.

37. IRC Sec. 1092(a)(1)(A).

38. IRC Sec. 263(g).

Chapter 42

LEVERAGING INVESTMENT ASSETS

WHAT IS IT?

Leveraging is the use of techniques that permit investors to control or benefit from an investment with a given dollar value while using less than that given dollar value of the investor's own money. Essentially, as the name implies, it is similar to the action of a lever that permits a person to move a boulder larger than he could move with his hands alone. Leveraging permits investors to control more or larger investment assets than they could control with their own equity alone.

Essentially, there are three types of leverage:

1. Financial leverage

2. Inherent leverage

3. Tax leverage

Financial leverage is the use of borrowed funds to supplement the investor's own dollar investment (equity) to increase the scale of investment. For example, an investor can purchase stocks, bonds, and other marketable securities, real estate, business assets, and the like using some combination of investor and borrowed funds. If the investment return on the asset exceeds the interest rate paid on the loan, the investor's return on his equity will rise above the return on the underlying asset (positive leverage). Conversely, if the return on the asset is less than the interest rate paid on the loan, the investor's return will fall below the return on the underlying asset (reverse or negative leverage). Investors may be able to deduct the interest expense against investment income on their tax returns, subject to limitations. (See "What Are the Tax Implications?" below.)

Inherent leverage (which is often also referred to as financial leverage, although it involves no borrowing) refers to the leverage inherently created by the investment asset itself. Generally, no borrowed funds are involved. For instance, derivative securities such as options contracts and futures contracts require investors to deposit only a fraction of the value of the assets underlying the contract. Similar to financial leverage, if the value of the underlying asset moves

the right way, investors' returns are potentially much greater than the returns they would earn by taking a similar position directly in the underlying assets themselves, and vice versa.

Tax leverage is similar to the concept of financial leverage, except that the money is implicitly borrowed from the government rather than from an actual lender. These implicit loans are created when the U.S. government (and/or other tax entities) provides tax incentives for employing various tools and techniques (e.g., IRAs) that allow taxpayers to defer the payment of taxes. Generally, if a taxpayer remains in the same tax bracket, the taxpayer will pay the deferred taxes in full at a later date, but with no increase or adjustment for the lapse in time. In other words, the ability to defer the payment of tax is essentially an interest-free loan from the government. In some situations, such as when an investor moves into a higher tax bracket, the amount of tax that must ultimately be repaid may be greater than the amount originally deferred. But even in this case the investor may still benefit. The tax leverage involved is essentially equivalent to a subsidized or below-market discount loan rather than a fully interest-free loan. In some other cases, the amount of tax paid in the future may be less than the amount of tax originally deferred. This is essentially equivalent to an interest-free loan where part of the debt is forgiven. (See "Questions and Answers," below, for additional discussions on tax leverage.)

Securities traded on organized exchanges or in the over-the-counter market are subject to minimum investor equity requirements, called margin requirements, as set by the Federal Reserve Board's Regulation T. These rules apply to the amount of equity investors must have and maintain in both securities purchased with financial leverage (e.g., stocks) and those that are inherently leveraged (e.g., futures contracts). These limitations apply regardless of the source of borrowing – brokerage firm, bank, or even family members. The National Association of Securities Dealers (NASD), the New York Stock Exchange (NYSE), and other exchanges have their own rules that generally match the Reg. T requirements, but which may be more restrictive.

If investors borrow money to leverage their investments from their brokerage firm, or trade in securities with inherent leverage, they must set up a margin account. The minimum portion of the purchase price that the customer must deposit is called the initial margin and is the customer's initial equity in the account. Subsequently, investors must maintain a specified minimum level of equity relative to the market value of the investment called the maintenance margin. The maintenance margin requirement is generally lower than the initial margin requirement. If an investor's margin falls below the required maintenance level, the brokerage firm will issue a margin call requiring the investor to deposit additional funds within a specified period of time. If the investor fails to do so, the brokerage firm will sell the assets and close out the investor's position. Brokerage firms may have their own margin requirements that are more restrictive than those spelled out in Reg. T or the NYSE or NASD guidelines. (See "Questions and Answers," below, for further discussion of margin requirements and how margin accounts operate.)

Margin requirements or borrowing limitations for real estate, business assets, private placements, non-publicly-traded limited partnership interests, and other non-exchange-traded investments are generally not subject to regulation. The equity requirements are generally determined by mutual agreement among the parties to the transaction and the lenders.

HOW DOES IT WORK?

The operations of a commercial bank provide a good illustration of the day-to-day use of leverage. The owners of the bank use their own funds to provide approximately 10% of the bank's assets. For simplicity, assume that the bank obtains the balance of its cash needs through the following sources:

	COST
Checking accounts	0%-3%
Savings accounts	4%-6%
Certificates of Deposit	5%-7%

If these funds (90% of which are someone else's money) are lent or invested at a 14% average return, it is easy to see how the bank makes money.

Leveraging also enables an investor to purchase a larger asset than his own available funds will permit. For example, if an individual wishes to purchase a $100,000 real estate investment that he expects to appreciate by 20% over the next year, but he has only $20,000 available to invest, the individual would leverage the investment by borrowing the other $80,000 he needs for the investment.

The application of leveraging to personal financial planning can best be explained by way of an example. Assume an investor wishes to purchase undeveloped land at a price of $50,000. The investor believes he can have the zoning for the property changed within a year, allowing him to sell the land for $75,000. The investor has arranged with his bank to borrow $40,000 of the purchase price for the needed one year at a fixed rate of 5%, with all interest payable at the end of the one-year term. The investor will therefore be required to invest only $10,000 of his own funds. In deciding whether to invest $50,000 of his own funds or to invest only $10,000 and borrow the balance under the terms provided by the bank, the investor would make the following analysis:

Purchase Price: $50,000
Expected Sale Price: $75,000
Holding Period: one year
Investor's Tax Bracket: 28%

	No Leverage	Financing
(1) Initial Equity	$50,000	$10,000
(2) Loan Principal	—	40,000
(3) Sales Price	75,000	75,000
(4) Gain on Sale [(3) - (1) - (2)]	25,000	25,000
(5) Interest Cost [.05 × (2)]	—	2,000
(6) Tax on Sale [.28 × (4)]	7,000	7,000
(7) Tax benefit of interest [.28 × (5)]	—	560
(8) Net Return [(4) - (5) - (6) + (7)]	18,000	16,560
Return on Investor's Equity [(8)/(1)]	$18,000 $50,000 = 36%	$16,560 $10,000 = 166%

In evaluating whether leveraging is appropriate for this investment, the investor must review not only the potential rewards of leveraging, but also the associated risks. What if he is not able to obtain the expected zoning change and can sell the property in one year for only $35,000? The investor must still repay the bank the $40,000 borrowed plus the interest of $2,000. The results of this investment would look like this:

Purchase Price: $50,000
Sale Price: $35,000
Holding Period: one year
Investor's Tax Bracket: 28% (loss on sale will be a capital loss, offsetting other gains of investor.)

	No Leverage	Financing
(1) Initial Equity	$50,000	$10,000
(2) Loan Principal	—	40,000
(3) Sales Price	35,000	35,000
(4) Gain on Sale [(3) - (1) - (2)]	(15,000)	(15,000)
(5) Interest Cost [.05 x (2)]	—	2,000
(6) Tax Benefit of loss [.28 x (4)]	4,200	4,200
(7) Tax benefit of interest [.28 x (5)]	—	560
(8) Net Loss [(4) - (5) + (6) + (7)]	(10,800)	(12,240)
Return on Investor's Equity [(8)/(1)]	(10,800) / $50,000 = -22%	(12,240) / $10,000 = -122%

This example illustrates the concept of "negative leverage," the risk that the investment will not generate enough cash income to pay off the debt. The result could be the loss of the entire investment, including not only the capital put into the investment, but also the cash needed to repay the borrowed money.

Even if the investor can afford to lose only $10,000, if he believes the risk of loss is small, then leveraging may still make sense. However, a loss in such a case could be devastating to the investor, if he can sell the land for only $35,000. Where will he get the $12,240 to cover his net loss?

WHEN IS THE USE OF THIS TECHNIQUE INDICATED?

1. When the investor does not have the available cash to finance the purchase of a particular asset.

2. When the investor can borrow money at a rate lower than the expected return on an investment. Leveraged debt should be incurred only when the investment will earn more than the cost of borrowing.

3. When the investment itself can generate sufficient "cash flow" to cover "debt service" (the annual cost of interest and any principal payable on the debt).

4. Where the goal of the investment is long-term appreciation rather than a current return, and the investor has other available resources to cover the annual cost of debt service.

5. During periods of high inflation. At such times, borrowing money enables an investor to purchase an asset immediately. The appreciation in that asset offsets the effects of inflation. The investor can pay off the debt in the future with dollars that have been "cheapened" by the effects of inflation.

ADVANTAGES

1. Leveraging makes it possible to purchase an asset the investor might not otherwise be able to afford.

2. Leveraging may significantly increase the return on the investor's equity.

3. When used to obtain depreciable property, leveraging increases the tax benefits to the investor. This is because depreciation may be based on the full purchase price of the asset, and not just the amount of the investor's equity. For example, if David Kurt purchased an office building costing $100,000 (exclusive of land), his depreciation will be computed on the full $100,000, even though he may have used only $20,000 of his own funds.

4. Leveraging permits the investor to spread a limited amount of available funds throughout a number of investments. This enhanced diversification adds to the safety of principal.

5. The creditor will have an interest in the financial soundness of the investment. In order to protect that interest, before a loan is made, most lenders will make an independent investigation of the underlying value of the property and the borrower's ability to pay both interest and principal. This may provide the investor with an objective evaluation of the appropriateness of the venture.

DISADVANTAGES

1. "Reverse leverage" is the most serious disadvantage of borrowing money to purchase an investment. Reverse leverage means that the cost of servicing the debt (both interest and principal) exceeds the total return (both cash flow and appreciation). For example, if the annual debt service for a $100,000

loan is $15,000 and the annual cash flow from the investment is only $8,000, the investor must fund the $7,000 shortfall from other income or assets.

2. If the primary purpose of the investment is to obtain appreciation, and there is little or no current income generated, the annual debt service payment requirements may place significant cash flow pressures on the investor.

3. Leveraging automatically increases the risks of an investment since the debt must be repaid, regardless of the return the investor receives.

4. The creditor, as a "partner" in the venture, may impose certain restrictions on the investor. For example, a bank may limit the amount of salary that can be paid to the sole shareholder of a corporation borrowing funds to finance the purchase of a new manufacturing facility. Similarly, a brokerage firm lending money to a customer to help him purchase securities may require him to provide other securities as collateral. Therefore, the cost of this "margin account" is not only the interest on the borrowed funds, but also the limitations on the free use of the securities used as additional collateral.

5. Borrowing to finance the purchase of an investment asset may restrict an individual's ability to borrow for other purposes. Other potential creditors may determine that the individual cannot safely handle any further indebtedness.

HOW IS IT IMPLEMENTED?

Once it is determined that an investment may be appropriate for leveraging:

1. *Determine the investor's borrowing capacity* – No matter how much the investor may want to borrow, prospective lenders will impose limitations on the amount they are willing to lend.

2. *Determine the appropriate amount of leverage* – The factors that should be examined include:

   a) The availability of future funds to meet debt service requirements. An investor's borrowing should be limited to his ability to meet debt payments as they come due. The future funds needed may be derived from the cash flow of the investment itself ("self-funding") or from outside sources such as

other investments, the investor's personal income, or other borrowed funds.

   b) The spread between the expected return on the investment and the cost to borrow. The higher the expected rate of return, the greater the advantage of leverage (and therefore the greater the risk the investor should be willing to take). For example, if the investor expects to earn 20% on his money and it costs him only 14% to borrow, he would tend to borrow more than if the money cost him 18%. The 2% spread between the 18% cost to borrow and the 20% expected return may still make leveraging worthwhile, but the spread is *only* 2%. In other words, there is little margin for error. With the 6% spread between 14% and 20%, even if the return on the investment drops 3% below the projected 20%, the investor still has positive leverage.

   c) The greater the tax advantages of borrowing (all other things being equal), the more the investor should borrow. Subject to limitations imposed by the tax law on deductions and other tax benefits relating to investment property (see Chapter 43, "Taxation of Investment Vehicles"), the investor receives the same type and level of tax benefits from borrowed funds as he does from the use of his own capital. Therefore, financial leveraging is also tax leveraging. For example, an investor who purchases an office building for $100,000 of his own funds receives depreciation deductions based on that amount. He obtains neither financial nor tax leverage. But if the same individual had purchased a $500,000 building using his $100,000 and $400,000 of borrowed money, his depreciation deductions would be five times higher.

3. *Determine the alternative sources for leverage borrowing* – Such alternatives might include (a) bank financing (either secured by the investment property, other personal assets, or possibly unsecured), (b) margin borrowing from a brokerage house (secured by the investor's portfolio of securities), (c) the cash value of insurance policies, (d) seller financing (often called "purchase-money" financing), and (e) borrowing from friends and family.

WHAT ARE THE TAX IMPLICATIONS?

Interest paid on debt to finance investments may be tax deductible, but the deduction is subject to limitations. In a nutshell, interest paid on debt to finance investments (other than passive activity investments) is deductible only to the extent of net investment income. Net investment income means the excess of investment income over investment expenses associated with the investments producing the income. Investment income includes dividends, interest, royalties, rents (except from passive activities), net short-term and long-term capital gains, and ordinary income gains from the sale of investment property.

However, under the tax rules until 2010, taxpayers may include dividends and long-term capital gains qualifying for the reduced rate (maximum rate of 15%) in the computation of their net investment income only if they elect to forgo the reduced rate on those dividends and gains. Normally this is not a good choice, because the interest expense not deductible by reason of this limitation may be carried over indefinitely and applied against net investment income in future years. Effectively, interest expense is deductible only to the extent of investment interest income on instruments such as bonds and other categories of ordinary income.

Borrowing may still make sense in two circumstances. If the lending rate is less than the dividend coupon rate, this is a positive after-tax leverage position for the investor. If the investment interest expense for the year exceeds the net investment income (computed by excluding the qualifying dividends and long-term capital gains), investors may choose to include in net investment income just so much of their qualifying dividends and long-term capital as is necessary to zero-out the investment interest expense. Investors who have substantial income from bond portfolios may also be able to borrow up to the amount that generates interest expense that when aggregated with existing investment interest equals the investment income from the bonds alone.

Another strategy is to borrow against the personal residence. Such interest is not deductible as investment interest even though the proceeds of the loan may be traced to the acquisition of investment property. However, a deduction may be available for qualified residence interest.[1] (See Chapter 43, "Taxation of Investment Vehicles," for a more complete discussion of the investment interest expense limitation and other investment tax issues.)

WHERE CAN I FIND OUT MORE?

1. *Tax Facts on Investments* (formerly *Tax Facts 2*) (Cincinnati, OH: The National Underwriter Company, updated annually).

2. Lilian Chew, *Managing Derivative Risks: The Use and Abuse of Leverage* (Chichester, NY: Wiley, 1996).

3. David Sirota, *Essentials of Real Estate Investment* (Chicago, IL: Dearborn Real Estate Education, 2004).

4. Friedman and Harris, *Keys to Investing in Real Estate* (Hauppauge, NY: Barron's, 2000).

5. Lawrence Gitman, *Personal Financial Planning with Financial Planning Software and Worksheets* (Mason, OH: South-Western/Thomson Learning, 2004).

QUESTIONS AND ANSWERS

Question – What is a margin account?

Answer – A margin account enables an investor to use unencumbered securities to borrow cash that in turn is used to purchase additional securities. Essentially, a margin account with a broker is one that provides loans secured by stocks and other securities held by the brokerage firm.

Question – What are the advantages of a margin account?

Answer – A margin account enables an investor to borrow cash readily, with a minimum of paperwork and without the need to sell or transfer stocks to finance the loan. The investor pays a competitive rate of interest to the broker on this "secured loan."

Borrowing funds to purchase stocks may increase the size of the profit the investor may realize beyond what would be possible if only personal funds were used. This is a classic example of the enhancement of purchasing power available through leveraging; by buying more stocks with the additional money borrowed from the brokerage firm, the investor increases his potential gain as well as possible dividends.

Example: Assume an investor buys 750 shares of the Martin-Stephans Corporation at $50 a share. He uses his own money and pays $37,500.

Assume the stock appreciates $10 a share. It is then worth a total of $45,000, for a gain of $7,500. If the investor had used leverage through a margin account, the gain could have been increased significantly. For instance, he could have bought one-third more shares at a 75% margin. Although he would still have invested $37,500 of his own money for 750 shares, he can borrow $12,500 to purchase an additional 250 shares. If the 1,000 share total appreciates $10 a share, his profit is $10,000. As a result of leveraging, his profit has increased by $2,500 (before the after-tax interest cost of borrowing the $12,500).

Question – How does a maintenance margin call work?

Answer – First, a simple example. If a customer buys $100,000 of securities on Day 1, Regulation T would require the customer to deposit a margin of 50%, or $50,000, in payment for the securities. As a result, the customer's equity in the margin account is $50,000, and the customer has received a margin loan of $50,000 from the firm. Assume that on Day 2 the market value of the securities falls to $60,000. Under this scenario, the customer's margin loan from the firm would remain at $50,000, and the customer's account equity would fall to $10,000 ($60,000 market value less $50,000 loan amount). However, the minimum maintenance margin requirement for the account is 25%, meaning that the customer's equity must not fall below $15,000 ($60,000 market value multiplied by 25%). Since the required equity is $15,000, the customer would receive a maintenance margin call for $5,000 ($15,000 less existing equity of $10,000). Because of the way the margin rules operate, if the firm liquidated securities in the account to meet the maintenance margin call, it would need to liquidate $20,000 of securities ($5,000 maintenance margin ÷ 25% maintenance margin).

Here are a few more examples, showing Long Market, Short Market, Debit Balance, Credit Balance, and Equity numbers for various situations. Equity is defined as the Long Market Value plus the Credit Balance, less any Short Market Value and Debit Balance. (The Current Market Value of securities is the Long Market value less the Short Market value.) The Credit Balance is cash – money that is left over after everything is paid and all margin requirements are satisfied.

In the first example, a customer buys $100,000 worth of some stock on margin. The 50% margin requirement (Regulation T) can be met with either stock or cash. To satisfy the margin requirement with cash, the customer must deposit $50,000 in cash. The account will then appear as follows; the "Equity" reflects the cash deposit:

Long Market	Short Market	Credit Balance	Debit Balance	Equity
$100,000	$0	$50,000	$50,000	$50,000

To satisfy the margin requirement with stock, the customer must deposit marginable stock with a loan value of $50,000, i.e., a value of $100,000 ($50,000 maintenance margin call ÷ 50% initial margin). The account will then appear as follows; the $200,000 of long market consists of $100,000 stock deposited to meet Regulation T and $100,000 of the stock purchased on margin:

Long Market	Short Market	Credit Balance	Debit Balance	Equity
$200,000	$0	$0	$100,000	$100,000

Here's a new example. What happens if the account looks like this?

Long Market	Short Market	Credit Balance	Debit Balance	Equity
$20,000	$0	$0	$17,000	$3,000

The maintenance requirement calls for an equity position that is 25% of $20,000, which is $5,000, but the equity is only $3,000. Because the equity is less than 25% of the market value, a maintenance margin call is triggered. The call is for the difference between the requirement and actual equity, which is $5,000 - $3,000, or $2,000. To meet the call, either $2,000 of cash or $4,000 ($2,000 maintenance margin call ÷ 50% initial margin) of stock must be deposited. Here is what would happen if the account holder deposits $2,000 in cash; note that the cash deposit pays down the loan.

Long Market	Short Market	Credit Balance	Debit Balance	Equity
$20,000	$0	$0	$15,000	$5,000

Here is what would happen if the account holder deposits $4,000 of stock:

Long Market	Short Market	Credit Balance	Debit Balance	Equity
$24,000	$0	$0	$17,000	$7,000

Ok, now what happens if the account holder does not meet the call? To meet the maintenance margin requirement, the brokerage firm must sell four times the amount of the call ($2,000 maintenance margin call ÷ 25% maintenance margin = $8,000). So stock in the amount of $8,000 will be sold and the account will look like this:

Long Market	Short Market	Credit Balance	Debit Balance	Equity
$12,000	$0	$0	$9,000	$3,000

In the case of short sales, Regulation T imposes an initial margin requirement of 150%. This sounds extreme, but the first 100% of the requirement can be satisfied by the proceeds of the short sale, leaving just 50% for the customer to maintain in margin (so it looks much like the situation for going long). To maintain a short position, rule 2520 requires a margin of $5 per share or 30% of the current market value (whichever is greater).

Assume a person shorts $10,000 worth of stock. The investor must have securities with a loan value of at least $5,000 to comply with Regulation T. In this example, to keep things simple, the customer deposits cash. So the Credit Balance consists of the $10,000 in proceeds from the short sale plus the $5,000 Regulation T deposit. Remember that market value is long market value minus short market value, and because the customer owns no securities long in this example, the "long market" value is zero, making the market value of the account negative.

Long Market	Short Market	Credit Balance	Debit Balance	Equity
$0	$10,000	$15,000	$0	$5,000

What about being short against the box? When an individual is long on a stock position and then shorts the same stock, a separate margin requirement is applicable. When shorting a position that is long in an account, the margin requirement is 5% of the market value of the underlying stock. Let's say the original stock holding of $100,000 was purchased on margin (with a corresponding 50% requirement). And the same holding is sold short against the box, yielding $100,000 of proceeds that is shown in the Credit Balance column, plus a cash deposit of $5,000. The account would look like this:

	Long Market	Short Market	Credit Balance	Debit Balance	Equity
Initial position	$100,000			$50,000	$50,000
Sell short	$0	$100,000	$105,000	$100,000	$5,000
Net	$100,000	$100,000	150,000	$105,000	$55,000

Question – What are the some of the risks involved with margin trading?

Answer – There are a number of risks that all investors need to consider in deciding to trade securities on margin. These risks include the following:

• Investors can lose more funds than they deposit in the margin account. A decline in the value of securities that are purchased on margin may require investors to provide additional funds to the firm that has made the loan to avoid the forced sale of those securities or other securities in their account.

• The firm can force the sale of securities in investors' accounts. If the equity in the account falls below the maintenance margin requirements under the law – or the firm's higher "house" requirements – the firm can sell the securities in the account to cover the margin deficiency. Investors will also be responsible for any shortfall in the account after such a sale.

• The firm can sell investors' securities without contacting the investors. Some investors mistakenly believe that a firm must contact them for a margin call to be valid, and that the firm cannot liquidate securities in their accounts to meet the call unless the firm has contacted them first. This is not the case. As a matter of good customer relations, most firms will attempt to notify their customers of margin calls, but they are not required to do so.

• Investors are not entitled to an extension of time on a margin call. While an extension of time to meet initial margin requirements may be available to customers under certain conditions, a customer does not have a right to the extension. In addition, a customer does not have a right to an extension of time to meet a maintenance margin call.

Question – How do margin requirements vary among different securities?

Answer – Margin requirements tend to vary somewhat depending upon each brokerage firm's own "house" rules, but competition tends to keep them quite close to Regulation T requirements and the NASD guidelines.

Question – What is a concentrated account?

Answer – An account is considered to be concentrated when one position accounts for a significant proportion of the entire balance in the account. Brokerage firms typically require higher margins for greater concentrations or larger balances of concentrated accounts, which vary from firm to firm.

Question – What is a pattern day trader?

Answer – Investors are considered pattern day traders if they trade 4 or more times in 5 business days and their day-trading activities are greater than 6% of their total trading activity for that same five-day period.

A brokerage firm also may designate an investor as a pattern day trader if it knows or has a reasonable basis to believe that the investor is a pattern day trader. For example, if the firm provided day trading training to an investor before opening his account, it could designate the investor as a pattern day trader.

Question – What are the margin requirements for a pattern day trader?

Answer – A pattern day trader must maintain minimum equity of $25,000 on any day that the customer day trades. The required minimum equity must be in the account prior to any day-trading activities. If the account falls below the $25,000 requirement, the pattern day trader will not be permitted to day trade until the account is restored to the $25,000 minimum equity level.

The rules permit a pattern day trader to trade up to four times the maintenance margin excess in the account as of the close of business of the previous day. If a pattern day trader exceeds the day-trading buying power limitation, the firm will issue a day-trading margin call to the pattern day trader. The pattern day trader will then have, at most, five business days to deposit funds to meet this day-trading margin call. Until the margin call is met, the day-trading account will be restricted to day-trading buying power of only two times maintenance margin excess based on the customer's daily total trading commitment. If the day-trading margin call is not met by the fifth business day, the account will be further restricted to trading only on a cash available basis for 90 days or until the call is met.

In addition, the rules require that any funds used to meet the day-trading minimum equity requirement or to meet any day-trading margin calls remain in the pattern day trader's account for two business days following the close of business on any day when the deposit is required.

Effectively, for stock investments, this means pattern day traders can trade up to four times their maintenance margin in excess of $25,000 as of the close of business of the previous day.

It is important to note that the brokerage firm may impose a higher minimum equity requirement and/or may restrict trading to less than four times the day trader's maintenance margin excess.

Question – How is tax leverage created?

Answer – Typically, tax leverage is created in one or both of two ways: (1) by postponing the tax on earnings or benefits; and/or (2) by providing tax incentives that in effect reduce or subsidize the up-front cost of the investment.

Question – What are some of the tools and techniques that create tax leverage by postponing the tax on earnings or benefits?

Answer – Typical examples of the types of vehicles that postpone the tax on earnings or benefits are Series EE savings bonds, life insurance, annuities, pension and profit-sharing plans, ESOPs, stock-bonus plans, IRAs (traditional, Roth, SEP, and SIMPLE), IRC Section 401(k) plans, IRC Section 403(b) plans, and certain types of nonqualified deferred compensation plans. However, the most prevalent type of tax-deferral vehicle is appreciating assets, such as stocks or real estate. Under the current tax laws, the tax on capital gains is deferred until the gain is recognized, usually when the asset is sold.

In addition, techniques that may be employed to defer full recognition of capital gains even beyond the time of disposal include the use of installment sales, IRC Section 1031 like-kind exchanges, private annuities, and, in the case of personal residences, the lifetime gain exclusion provisions. IRC Section 1035 provides similar nonrecognition treatment for qualifying life insurance exchanges. Certain other transfers of life insurance policies between related parties also avoid recognition. In the area of corporate securities, recapitalizations, reorganizations, mergers, and acquisitions, there is an assortment of provisions allowing nonrecognition treatment.

Life insurance, capital gains, and Roth IRAs are special cases. In the case of life insurance, if the proceeds are paid in the form of death benefits, in effect the tax loan associated with the earnings on the cash value is generally completely forgiven. In the case of appreciated assets that are held at death, the step-up in basis effectively cancels the tax loan. [However, a modified carryover basis is scheduled to replace a step-up in basis in 2010.] Also, in the case of charitable gifts of appreciated property where the appreciation qualifies as long-term capital gain, the donor is generally able to take a deduction for the entire amount of the gift without recognizing or paying tax on the gain. (There may be alternative-minimum-tax implications, however.) Once again, the tax loan is essentially forgiven. Similarly, qualified distributions from Roth IRAs can be received tax-free.

Question – What are some of the tools and techniques that create tax leverage by providing up-front tax incentives?

Answer – Up-front tax incentives come from three sources: (1) acceleration (immediate deductibility) of expenses that would normally be deducted against later income; (2) tax deductibility or excludability of the initial payment or investment itself; or (3) direct tax credits or subsidies.

1. *The Acceleration Principle* – Examples of the acceleration principle include immediate expensing of up to $108,000 (as indexed, in 2006) per year for personal property under IRC Section 179, intangible drilling and development costs in oil and gas programs, accelerated expensing of certain pre-production period expenses in drilling and mining operations, a host of acceleration allowances for small farmers, and immediate expensing associated with certain research and development costs. Except for IRC Section 179 expensing (essentially the small business owner's tax shelter), acceleration of expenses is associated with what used to be called tax shelters and what are now known as passive activities. The passive-activity loss rules now severely restrict the use of the accelerated expenses to shelter income from other nonpassive activity sources. Therefore, with one notable exception, the acceleration principle is not as important a factor in the evaluation of tools and techniques employing tax leverage as before, except with respect to managing a client's portfolio of passive-activity investments.

    However, the acceleration principle does enter, in part, into any decisions regarding depreciable or amortizable property where the allowable depreciation or amortization deductions may exceed actual economic deterioration

or obsolescence. In these cases, the excess of the allowable deductions over the true economic deterioration or obsolescence creates tax leverage by reducing reported income below actual economic income. In most cases, this tax loan is repaid when the asset is later disposed of for more than its remaining basis (for a gain) or continues to generate income beyond its tax depreciable or amortizable life.

The notable exception mentioned earlier is in the area of charitable giving and, in particular, with respect to charitable remainder trusts. Charitable remainder trusts permit taxpayers to take an immediate tax deduction for property that will not pass to the charity until some later date.

2. *Tax Deductibility or Excludability* – A large number of tools and techniques permit tax deductibility or excludability of the up-front costs or investment. The most notable examples include contributions to qualified pension and profit-sharing plans, ESOPs, stock-bonus plans, Keogh plans, certain IRAs (traditional, SEP, and SIMPLE), IRC Section 401(k) plans, and IRC Section 403(b) tax-deferred annuities. Other examples of excludability include the gain on Series EE savings bonds that are exchanged for Series HH bonds, salary deferrals under certain types of nonqualified deferred compensation plans, the gain on exercise of incentive stock options, and built-in gain on distributions of employer stock from ESOPs and stock-bonus plans. In these cases, taxation of the benefit is deferred until the income is received or gains are realized by sale or taxable disposition of the stock or bond.

3. *Tax credits and subsidies* – Tax credits are a direct reduction of tax. The amount of the tax benefit is generally the same for every taxpayer regardless of the taxpayer's tax bracket. The premier example was the 10% investment tax credit for qualifying investments in business personal property. Like in so many other areas, tax policy on the investment tax credit has varied and the investment tax credit has currently fallen from favor. However, other tax credits survive. Examples include the low-income housing credit, certain credits for research and development expenditures, the childcare credit, and job creation credits. Tax credits are especially lucrative tax incentives since the interest-free tax loan

(deferred tax) is typically forgiven in whole or in part if the taxpayer meets certain qualifying criteria or holding-period requirements. In some cases, tax credits are potentially subject to recapture (being added back to the amount of tax due on a later return).

Direct subsidies are unusual, but examples include low-interest mortgages in certain types of low-income housing projects and special development loans for preserving wetlands or ecological landscaping. Also included are various subsidies to farmers (such as for not growing crops). Indirect subsidies include loan guarantees and minimum rent guarantees for low-income housing, farm price supports, tariffs and import quotas, and the like. The effects of indirect subsidies are generally difficult to measure and are frequently ignored in formal analyses. However, even if ignored, their presence should not be forgotten.

Question – How is tax leverage like financial leverage with interest-free borrowing?

Answer – If a person in a 33.3% combined federal and state tax bracket invests $1,000 for one year at a fully taxable 10% rate of return, she will have $1,066.70 after tax at the end of the year. The after-tax rate of return is 6.67%.

Now suppose the investor can borrow $500 at 0% interest and add it to her $1,000 investment. This $1,500 total investment will earn $150 before tax. The investor must pay $500 plus $0 interest back to the lender, so the investor is left with $1,150 before tax, or $1,100 after tax. The investor has increased the after-tax return on her equity from 6.67% to 10% through the use of financial leverage.

Assume the investor elects instead, to invest in the same instrument but inside a deductible IRA. Since the contribution to the IRA is tax-deductible, the investor will have $1,500 to invest before tax (assuming the contribution is also deductible for state tax purposes) for each $1,000 she would otherwise have to invest after tax [$1,500 x (1 - 33.3%) = $1,000]. The $1,500 investment inside the IRA will earn $150 before tax and have a balance of $1,650. If the investor now withdraws the money from the IRA (assuming no 10% early withdrawal penalty) she will pay a 33.3% tax on the entire amount, or $550 in tax, leaving her with $1,100 after tax. The result is exactly the same 10% after-tax rate of return she would earn by borrowing $500 (the amount of tax deferred on her original investment in the IRA) interest free.

Question – What is a "leveraged lease"?

Answer – A leveraged lease is one in which the lessor finances a portion of the purchase price of the leased property with debt. Sometimes this debt is "nonrecourse." This means that the borrower has no personal liability. A nonrecourse loan is secured by specific assets of the borrower. For example, in many real estate financing transactions, the lender may look only to the property itself as security for the loan.

CHAPTER ENDNOTES

1.	IRC Sec. 163(h)(3).

Chapter 43

TAXATION OF INVESTMENT VEHICLES

WHY TAXES ARE IMPORTANT TO THE INVESTOR

An investor must consider income taxes (federal, state, and local) as part of the cost of any investment. The objective of financial and investment planning is to maximize the utility of invested capital in order to accomplish financial and personal goals. Consequently, investors must attempt to minimize the tax element of the investment cost in a manner that is consistent with those goals. An understanding of the basic concepts of the income tax law is therefore essential.

The complexity of the federal income tax law (not to mention the various state and local income tax laws) is almost overwhelming. Only qualified tax specialists should give specific tax advice. But advisers and investors must both have a working knowledge of (1) the issues involved in the acquisition and disposition of an investment, (2) the issues relating to income and expenses during the period the investment is held, (3) the federal income tax rate structure, and (4) some other selected investment tax topics. This chapter will focus on these four broad areas and subdivide them as follows:

1. Acquisition and Disposition Issues

   a) Basis (including the "at risk" rules)

   b) Business, energy, and rehabilitation tax credits

   c) Timing of reporting gain or loss upon disposition

   d) Character of gain or loss upon disposition

2. Issues relating to income and expenses while the investment is held

   a) "Income" defined

   b) Character of income or loss

   c) Deductible expenses

   d) Timing of recognition of income and expenses

3. The Federal income tax rate structure

   a) Income tax rates

   b) Capital gain tax rates

   c) Qualified dividend income

   d) Alternative minimum tax

   e) The "kiddie" tax

4. Selected Investment Tax Issues

   a) Original issue and market discounts and premiums

   b) Short-sale rules

   c) Wash-sale rules

   d) Constructive-sale rules

   e) Straddle rules

ACQUISITION AND DISPOSITION ISSUES

Basis

Basis is a key concept to the investor because it is the starting point for determining the amount of gain or loss on a sale or other disposition of property. It is also the measure of the maximum amount of depreciation or amortization allowable for certain types of assets.

An investor's original basis in a purchased asset is its cost. The cost of property is the amount the investor paid for it in cash or other property. For example, if Bob buys a rental property for $100,000 cash, his original basis in the acquired property is $100,000.

When property other than (or in addition to) cash is used to acquire an investment, and the transaction does not qualify as a tax-free exchange, the cost (basis) of the property acquired is the sum of (1) any cash paid *plus* (2) the fair market value of any property given in exchange for the property. For instance, if Bob purchased the rental property for $10,000 cash plus IBM stock worth $90,000, Bob's original basis in the rental property would be $100,000 [the sum of (1) the $10,000 cash paid plus (2 the $90,000 fair market value of the stock].

Typically, when an investor exchanges one property for another, the market value of the property given up and the market value of the property received will be approximately equal. The fair market value of both properties will, as a practical matter, usually be ascertained by reference to the property whose value is most easily determined. In the example in the previous paragraph, it is easy to determine Bob's basis in the rental property since Bob paid for the property with cash ($10,000) and publicly traded IBM stock ($90,000), the value of which can be easily found.

When property is acquired subject to a mortgage or other debt, the basis of the property is not merely the amount of the investor's equity in the property. The taxpayer can use as the basis: the total of (1) the cash, (2) the value of other property paid, and (3) the total amount of the debt. For example, if Rich buys a $1,000,000 apartment house, paying $250,000 in cash and borrowing the remaining $750,000, his basis in the property is the full $1,000,000.

At Risk Rules

An investor's ability to create basis through the use of debt is limited by the at risk rules. These rules provide that losses are deductible only to the extent the investor is personally at risk.

The at risk rules limit deductions for borrowing that attempt to be characterized as at risk for tax purposes when there is no actual economic risk to the investor. For instance, assume Georgia wants to purchase a $100,000 interest in an oil drilling venture. She intends to invest $20,000 of her own funds while borrowing the $80,000 balance. The bank providing the loan to Georgia has agreed to make a nonrecourse loan to her. In other words, the bank has no recourse to any of Georgia's other assets other than her interest in the oil drilling venture and will rely solely on the value of that property as its collateral for the debt. In the event Georgia cannot repay the loan, the bank cannot look to Georgia's other assets to cover the unpaid balance. Since the most Georgia can lose on

her investment is $20,000 in cash, her deductions will be limited to that $20,000 (plus the amount of income generated from the investment).

The at risk rules cover essentially all investment activities except for real estate acquired before 1987. With respect to real estate subject to the at risk rules, qualified nonrecourse financing is treated as an additional amount at risk. Qualified financing is generally defined as borrowings (except convertible debt) from persons or entities actively engaged in the business of lending money (such as banks), and not loans or mortgages from the former owner of the property. Loans from or guaranteed by a federal, state, or local government agency will also qualify.

Aside from real estate investments, the at risk rules apply to the following examples of activities engaged in by an individual for the production of income:

1. Holding, producing, or distributing motion picture films or videotapes.

2. Farming.

3. Exploring for or exploiting oil and gas reserves or geothermal deposits.

4. Leasing of depreciable personal property.

An investor is considered at risk to the extent of:

1. Cash invested; *plus*

2. The basis of property invested; *plus*

3. Amounts borrowed for use in the investment that are secured by the investor's assets (other than the property used in the investment activity); *plus*

4. Amounts borrowed to the extent the investor is personally liable for repayment; *plus*

5. When the investment is made in partnership form—

   a) The investor-partner's undistributed share of partnership income, *plus*

   b) The investor-partner's proportionate share of partnership debt, to the extent he is personally liable for its repayment.

An investor is not considered at risk with respect to nonrecourse debt (other than qualified nonrecourse financing as described above) used to finance the activity, or to finance the acquisition of property used in the activity, or with respect to any other arrangement for the compensation or reimbursement of any economic loss. For example, if Georgia is able to obtain commercial insurance against the risk that the oil drilling fund will not return her original $20,000 cash investment, she would not be considered at risk to the extent of that insurance coverage.

Losses limited by the at risk provisions are not lost; instead, these amounts may be carried over and deducted in subsequent years (but only if the investor's at risk amount is sufficiently increased).

The benefit of previously deducted losses must be recaptured when the investor's at risk amount is reduced below zero. For example, assume Tania's loss deductions from her interest in an oil drilling venture total $5,000 through the end of last year. Her basis in the venture at the end of last year (after the deductions) was $1,000. In the current year Tania received $3,000 in cash distributions. That distribution reduces Tania's basis by $3,000 to -$2,000.

Since an investor cannot have a negative basis in an investment for tax purposes, Tania must recapture (i.e., report as income) the $2,000 of prior year deductible losses in order to bring her basis up to zero. In addition, Tania will not be able to deduct any losses from the venture in the current year because she has a zero basis.

Property Acquired From a Decedent

Under current law, when an investor dies (in any year *other than* 2010) the beneficiary of his property does not carry over (substitute) the decedent's basis as his own (the rules for property inherited from a decedent dying *in 2010* are explained below). Instead, the basis of property acquired from or passing from a decedent is the fair market value of the property as of the date of (1) the investor's death, or (2) the federal estate tax alternate valuation date if the estate's executor elects that date (typically six months after the date of death). Therefore, if the value of an investment held until death has increased from the date of its acquisition, the potential gain (or loss in the case of a decrease in value) is never recognized for income tax purposes. An increase in the property's basis to its federal estate tax value is called a step up in basis.

Note that this stepped up basis is obtained even though no one pays income tax on the intervening appreciation.

For example, if an individual had purchased stock that cost $10,000 and that had a fair market value of $50,000 at the time of his death, his beneficiary would receive a $50,000 basis for the stock. The $40,000 appreciation in the value of the stock would never be subjected to income tax. If the beneficiary then sold the property for $55,000, the taxable gain would be only $5,000 ($55,000 amount realized minus $50,000 basis).

But a step up in basis is not available for property that is income in respect of a decedent (IRD). IRD is income that a decedent was entitled to that was not included in taxable income in the year of death or a prior year. Some examples of IRD include qualified plans, IRAs, deferred compensation, and installment sale payments. IRD is included in income as received by the person receiving payments. A deduction may be available for income tax purposes for the estate tax attributable to the amount includable in income.

An executor or administrator may elect the alternate valuation method only if the election will decrease (1) the value of the gross estate and also (2) the amount of the federal estate tax imposed. Generally, an election to use the alternate valuation date means that the gross estate will include the property at its fair market value as of six months after the decedent's death. But if the estate distributes, sells, exchanges, or otherwise disposes of any property within six months after the decedent's death, the value of the property at that disposition date becomes the alternate value.

Example: Assume property purchased for $10,000 is worth $50,000 on the date of a widower's death. Assume that the executor sells the asset for $45,000 three months after the death. If the executor elects to use the alternate valuation date, the valuation date for this property would be the date of its sale. The property's basis becomes $45,000.

The estate realizes no tax gain or loss because the $45,000 amount realized on the sale is equal to the property's $45,000 basis.

As a result of the Economic Growth and Tax Relief Reconciliation Act of 2001 (EGTRRA 2001), the stepped up basis at death rules are repealed for property acquired from a decedent after December 31, 2009. Note, however, that this repeal is scheduled to remain in effect for only one year. (All of the provisions of EGTRRA 2001 are subject to a sunset provision that, in effect, revokes the entire Act, including this repeal of stepped up basis.) For property inherited during 2010, modified carryover basis rules apply. The recipient of the property will receive a basis equal to the lesser of the adjusted basis in the hands of the decedent or the fair market value of the property as of the date of death. Under these rules, a partial basis step up is allowed, which is limited to $1,300,000 and an additional $3,000,000 in the case of a surviving spouse. The determination of which assets will receive the step up is discretionary in the sole control of the executor or administrator of the estate.

Property Acquired by Gift

When property is acquired by lifetime gift and the donee sells the property for a gain, the general rule is that the property in the hands of the donee has the same basis (subject to an adjustment discussed below) it had in the hands of the donor. This is called a substituted or carryover basis. The donee of the gift—the new owner—computes the basis by referring to the basis in the hands of the donor. In other words, the donor's basis is carried over to the donee. The result of this carryover is that gain will not escape tax forever but merely be deferred. The gain remains deferred only until the donee disposes of the property in a taxable transaction.

Example: Assume that Alex purchases stock for $3,000. After it appreciates in value to $9,000, he gives it to Sara. The basis of the stock in Sara's hands for determining gain on a later sale by Sara is still $3,000. Therefore, if she sells it for $10,000, she has a $7,000 gain.

When the donor's basis carries over to the donee, it is subject to an adjustment for any gift taxes paid on the net appreciation in the value of the gift (but not above the amount of the gift tax paid). For instance, in the example in the paragraph above, if the gift tax were $1,500, the donee's basis would be the $3,000 carryover basis plus a $1,000 adjustment, a total of $4,000.

The addition to basis is computed according to the following formula:

$$\frac{\text{Net Appreciation in Value of Gift}}{\text{Value of Gift at Transfer}} \times \text{Gift Tax Paid}$$

= Gift Tax Adjustment to Basis

In our example, the computation would be

$$\frac{\$9,000 - \$3,000}{\$9,000} \times \$1,500$$

= $1,000 Adjustment to $3,000 Carryover Basis

The basis rule for determining loss on the sale of property acquired by gift is different from the rule for determining the amount of the gain on the sale. For purposes of determining the amount of a loss, the basis of the property in the hands of the donee is the lesser of (1) the donor's basis or (2) the fair market value of the property at the time of the gift. The purpose of this special provision is to prevent investors from gaining a tax benefit by transferring property with a built-in loss to persons who could take better advantage of tax losses.

Assume, for instance, that in the example above the value of the stock at the time of the gift was only $1,000. If Alex sold the stock, he would have a capital loss of $2,000 ($3,000 basis−$1,000 amount realized). If Alex had other capital losses of at least $3,000 but no capital gains, the $2,000 loss would be of no immediate tax benefit to him. Were it not for the special provision, Alex might give the stock to his father who had capital gains. If his father were allowed to use Alex's $3,000 basis, his father could sell the stock, take a $2,000 loss, and obtain the tax benefit from the loss that Alex himself could not have used. For this reason, the father, in determining his loss on the sale, must use as his basis the $1,000 fair market value of the property at the time of the gift, since that is lower than Alex's $3,000 basis. If Alex's father sold the property for $900, he would only recognize a $100 loss on the sale ($900 proceeds less $1,000 basis). If Alex's father sold the property at a time when it was worth only $1,200 (or any other amount between the $1,000 fair market value at the date of the gift or the $3,000 carryover basis), he would recognize no gain or loss.

General Business Tax Credits

A credit is a dollar-for-dollar reduction in the investor's tax. The energy, rehabilitation, and low-income tax credits are Congressional incentives to encourage investment in certain types of property used in a trade or business, including rental property.

The energy credit is a percentage of the taxpayer's qualified investment in energy property and is generally limited to 10%. This category includes solar energy and geothermal property. The rehabilitation credit is available for expenditures incurred to rehabilitate buildings that are certified historic structures or were initially placed in service before 1936. The credit is limited to 10% of qualified rehabilitation expenditures for buildings that are not certified historic structures. Rehabilitation expenditures for buildings that qualify as certified historic structures are eligible for a credit of 20%. A credit is also available for investment in certain low-income housing (see Chapter 20, "Real Estate").

The energy, rehabilitation, and low-income housing credits are aggregated with certain other credits to form the general business credit. The amount of the general business credit that may offset income taxes in any one year is limited.

The energy and rehabilitation tax credits are not without cost. The investor must reduce basis for purposes of computing both future depreciation deductions and gain or loss upon the sale or other taxable disposition of the asset.

The investor must reduce the property's basis by:

1. 50% of the business energy tax credit; and

2. 100% of the rehabilitation credits.

Upon early disposition of property for which the investor claimed an energy or rehabilitation credit, and that also reduced the investor's tax liability, the investor must recapture some or all of the investment credit (i.e., report as an additional tax). But if the investor holds the property for at least five full years from the date he placed it in service, the credit is not subject to recapture. Likewise, early dispositions triggered by the investor's death or by a tax-free transfer to a corporation in exchange for its stock will not result in recapture.

If recapture is required, the investor must add to his tax a portion of the credit as indicated in the following table:

If Disposition Occurs Before the End of	Percentage of Investment Credit to be Recaptured
1 Year	100%
2 Years	80%
3 Years	60%
4 Years	40%
5 Years	20%

This recapture has the effect of increasing the investor's basis in the property (which was previously reduced when the credit was claimed). This adjustment to basis is treated as if it were made immediately before the disposition.

But the low-income housing credit is subjected to a 15-year recapture period rather than the 5-year schedule above. For additional information on the rehabilitation credit and the low-income housing credit, see Chapter 20, "Real Estate."

Timing of Reporting Gain or Loss upon Disposition

The ability to time the reporting of gain or loss is critical to enhancing the success of the investor. Deferring income until a later year, particularly a year in which the investor is in a lower tax bracket, or accelerating a deduction into a year in which the taxpayer has a great deal of income can significantly enhance the after-tax return from an investment.

The problems of determining the correct year to report income or take deductions flow from the requirement that income must be reported on the basis of annual periods. Although a few exceptions exist, as a general rule investors must report income and claim deductions according to annual accounting periods.

Most individuals are cash basis taxpayers. An investor (i.e., one who reports income as it is received and who takes deductions as expenses are paid) generally will recognize a gain or loss from the disposition of an asset at the time the transaction is closed. The mere signing of an agreement to sell does not trigger the recognition of gain or loss. A transaction is not closed until the seller transfers title to the property in exchange for cash or other proceeds.

Installment Sales

An investor can defer the recognition of gain until the actual receipt of cash or other property in exchange for the asset sold. The key ingredient in an installment sale is that the seller will receive at least one payment in a year after the year of sale.

The installment sale provisions are particularly important to an investor who has sold an asset for a substantial profit and has received a cash down payment and note from the purchaser for the balance due. Usually, these notes are not readily transferable. Without the installment sale rules, the investor would incur a large tax in one year even if he does not have sufficient cash from the transaction to pay the tax. Installment sales are also indicated when an investor wants to sell property to another party who does not have enough liquid assets to pay for the property in a lump sum at closing. Installment sales are an important estate as well as financial planning tool and are used to shift wealth within the family unit as well as to protect appreciating assets from creditors.

The basic rules for installment sale reporting include the following:

1. A seller of property can defer as much or as little as desired and can set payments to fit his financial needs. Even if the seller receives payments in the year of sale, he may still use the installment method for the unpaid balance.

2. The seller does not have to receive any payments in the year of sale. An investor may contract to have payments made to him at the time when it is most advantageous (or the least disadvantageous).

3. Installment sale treatment is automatic unless the investor affirmatively elects *not* to have installment treatment apply. No special election is required.

4. The contract may provide that the installment note receivable is independently secured (such as with a letter of credit obtained from a bank) without triggering the recognition of income when the note is secured.

The tax law imposes several limitations on the use of the installment sale method of accounting for gain on the sale of property. One such limitation is that taxpayers may not use the installment sale method for the sale of stock or securities that are traded on an established securities market.

As a final note on installment sales, strict rules govern the use of the installment method for sales between related parties.

Character of Gain or Loss

The effect of having the gain from the sale of property treated as a capital gain rather than ordinary income can be substantial. Investors can use capital losses only to offset capital gains and a limited amount of ordinary income (no more than $3,000 per year—although unused capital losses may be carried forward and utilized in future years).

Investors determine the amount of capital gain or loss upon a taxable sale or exchange by computing the difference between the sales price or proceeds received and the investor's tax basis (usually his cost) in the capital asset. Certain provisions of the tax law require taxpayers to treat part of the gain as ordinary income, such as those provisions dealing with original issue discount and depreciation recapture.

With certain limited exceptions, all securities held by investors are considered capital assets. Most other assets held for investment purposes or for the production of income are also considered capital assets. In general, the following rules apply to the treatment of capital gains and losses:

1. *Net capital gain* (i.e., the excess of long-term capital gains over short-term capital losses) is determined by first separating the long-term capital gains and losses into three tax-rate groups. These groups are: (a) the 28% group, which generally includes collectibles gain and IRC Section 1202 gain; (b) the 25% group (i.e., IRC Section 1250 gain); and (c) the remainder group, consisting of long-term capital gains and losses not falling under (a) or (b). Any net short-term capital losses are then applied to reduce any net gain from the 28% group, 25% group, and remainder group in that order.

2. *Adjusted net capital gain* (i.e., net capital gain reduced, but not below zero) by the sum of unrecaptured IRC Section 1250 gain *plus* the 28% rate gain and then *plus* as his own—through 2008—qualifying dividend income). The reduced capital gains tax rate applies only to the adjusted net capital gain.

3. Taxpayers may use capital losses first to offset any capital gains. They are allowed to offset net capital losses against ordinary income on a dollar-for-dollar basis, but only to the extent of $3,000 per year ($1,500 in the case of married taxpayers filing separately).

4. Taxpayers may carry forward indefinitely any excess capital losses (from (3), above) and use them to offset future tax years' capital gains and up to $3,000 per year of ordinary income.

Holding Period

A capital asset falls into its category of short-term or long-term based upon the time the investor holds

INCOME AND EXPENSES WHILE THE INVESTMENT IS HELD

Income Defined

Tax law defines income in very broad terms. Income includes all income from whatever source derived that is not specifically excluded by a section of the Internal Revenue Code. The implication is that if an item is considered something other than a return of an investor's capital, it will be taxable unless otherwise specifically excluded by a provision in the Internal Revenue Code. The Supreme Court has defined income as "gains received from capital, from labor, or from both combined, provided it be understood to include profit gained through a sale or conversion of capital assets."

Common items realized by an investor that are specifically enumerated by the Internal Revenue Code as income include: (1) gains derived from dealings in property; (2) interest; (3) rents; (4) royalties; (5) dividends; (6) annuities; and (7) income from an interest in an estate or trust.

Note that the tax is levied only on income. The distinction in answering the question of whether an item is income lies between the terms "income" and "capital." An investor may recover, income tax free, his capital investment in an asset.

Among the very few items common to an investor specifically excluded from income by the Internal Revenue Code are: (1) interest on certain governmental obligations (e.g., many municipal bonds); (2) certain improvements by the lessee on the lessor's property; (3) generally, death proceeds received under a life insurance contract.

Whose income is it? This is an important issue that investors must resolve. An individual may have to report and pay tax on income that he never receives, but that someone else receives. Income is taxed to the person who: (1) earns it; (2) creates the right to receive it; (3) owns or controls the property that is the source of the income; or (4) has the right to control who will enjoy the benefit of it.

The tax rule governing income shifting is known as the "assignment of income doctrine." According to this doctrine, although one individual may shift income to another individual (which may create gift tax problems), the burden of income taxation will not change. The person who earns the income—or owns or controls the source of the income—is deemed to have

it. The calculation of the holding period begins on the day after the investor acquires the property. The same date in each successive month is considered the first day of a new month. The holding period includes the date on which the property is sold or exchanged. If property is acquired on the last day of a month, the holding period begins on the first day of the following month.

The specific holding periods are as follows: (1) short-term—held for one year or less—and (2) long-term—held for more than one year. Special rules apply in the case of gains or losses of: (1) regulated futures contracts; (2) nonequity option contracts; (3) foreign currency contracts; (4) short sales; (5) wash sales; (6) tax straddles; (7) constructive sales; and (8) constructive ownership transactions.

The tax law permits tacking of a holding period in the case of gifts, tax-free exchanges, and certain other nontaxable exchanges. Tacking means an investor may add the holding period of the prior owner to his own. For instance, if Sara gives Lara stock that Sara bought three years ago, Lara's holding period would include the three years that Sara held the stock, as well as the period Lara actually holds the stock.

When a person acquires an asset through bequest or inheritance, the recipient automatically and immediately treats the property as having a long-term holding period. This rule applies even if the decedent held the asset for less than one year. For example, assume Sam purchased shares of stock one month before his death. Sam's heir, Sandi, could sell the shares four months after Sam's death and still obtain long-term treatment on any gain.

Many investors buying stocks, bonds, mutual funds, or other investments have multiple holdings of the same types of assets. It, therefore, becomes necessary to be able to identify each separate share or unit of a multiple investment so that the investor can determine each share's own basis and holding period. Record keeping, documentation, and an information retrieval system are therefore all important tools for the sophisticated investor.

If an investor is unable to adequately identify the lot from which securities are sold or transferred, the investor must use the first-in, first-out (FIFO) method. This means that the investor will be deemed to have sold the securities in the order in which he acquired them. In some cases involving mutual fund shares, the tax law allows the investor to use an average basis method for ascertaining both tax basis and holding period.

received it and then passed it on to its actual recipient. For example, if an attorney directs a client to pay his fee to the attorney's mother, or a wealthy investor who owns an office building directs that all tenants pay rent directly to his widowed sister, the tax liability will not shift, despite the shift in income.

Although merely assigning *income* will not shift the burden of taxation, an assignment of an *income-producing asset* will cause the income derived from that asset to be taxed to the assignee. For example, if an individual makes a gift of securities or any other income producing property to his son, the son will be responsible for tax on the income produced by that property after the transfer.

To accomplish income shifting tax objectives, the owner must transfer the property before the income is actually earned and the transfer must be complete and bona fide. In addition, to shift the burden of income tax (as well as to remove it from the transferor's estate), the transferor must retain no control over either the property or the income it produces.

Character of Income or Loss

Under current tax law, it is necessary to distinguish among (1) earned income or losses (such as salary, or active business income or losses); (2) investment income (such as interest, dividends, royalties, and annuities); and (3) passive activity income or losses. These separate categories of income are important, since an investor may not use passive activity losses (and credits) to offset earned income or investment income. (Taxpayers may offset losses from active business endeavors against income from other active businesses, investment income, or passive activity income.) The passive activity loss limitations apply to estates and trusts, personal service corporations, and pass-through entities such as partnerships and S corporations, in generally the same manner as they apply to individuals. Passive activity losses of closely-held C corporations (where five or fewer shareholders own more than 50% of the stock value) can offset trade or business (earned) income, but not investment income of the corporation.

Taxpayers may carry forward disallowed passive activity losses and credits and treat them as deductions and credits from passive activities in the next taxable year. Taxpayers may deduct suspended *losses* from a passive activity in full when the taxpayer disposes of his entire interest in the passive activity in a fully taxable transaction. Taxpayers may not claim suspended *credits* in full in the year the taxpayer disposes of the interest in a passive activity. Rather they carry forward such credits until the taxpayer may use them to offset tax liability from passive income. But upon a fully taxable disposition of a passive activity, a taxpayer may elect to increase the basis of property immediately before the transaction by an amount equal to the portion of any suspended credit that reduced the basis of the property for the taxable year in which the credit arose.

Passive Activity Income or Loss

In general, the term passive activity means any activity that involves the conduct of any trade or business in which the taxpayer has an interest but does not materially participate. The definition of passive activity generally includes any rental activity of either real or tangible personal property regardless of whether the individual materially participates. With respect to equipment leasing, short-term rental to certain users (where the lessor provides substantial services) is an active business rather than a passive activity. In general, working interests in oil and gas property held directly or indirectly via a pass-through entity where the investor's liability is not limited (e.g., general partnership) will be treated as an active trade or business, not a passive activity.

Material Participation Defined – In general, a taxpayer will be treated as materially participating in an activity only if the taxpayer is involved in the operations of the activity on a regular, continuous, and substantial basis. Substantial and bona fide management decision-making by an individual may constitute material participation. For example, if an individual performs managerial services on a full-time basis and the success of the business is dependent upon the exercise of business judgment by an individual, such services would constitute material participation. This test applies regardless of whether an individual owns an interest in the activity directly or through a pass-through entity such as a general partnership or an S corporation. Limited partnership interests are generally treated as not materially participating.

Net Investment Income Defined – Net investment income is not treated as passive activity income and, therefore, investors cannot offset this income with passive activity losses. Net investment income means (1) gross income from interest, dividends, annuities, or royalties not derived in the ordinary course of a trade or business; less (2) expenses (other than interest) that are clearly and directly allocable to such gross income; less (3) interest expense properly allocable to such gross income; plus (4) gains from the disposition of property generating the interest, dividend, royalty, etc. income; less (5) losses from the disposition of property generating the interest, dividend, royalty, etc. income. Investment income earned within a pass-through entity, such as a partnership or S corporation, retains its character when reported to each investor in the entity. Investors cannot use this income to reduce the passive activity losses that pass through to each investor.

Treatment of Former Passive Activity – If an activity is a former passive activity for any taxable year and has suspended losses or credits from prior years when the activity was passive, the investor may offset the current year's income from that activity with the suspended losses and the suspended credits may offset any current year's regular tax liability allocable to that activity. Any remaining suspended losses or credits continue to be treated as derived from a passive activity. Such losses and credits can be used to offset income or tax from that activity in years after it changed from passive to active, as well as income or tax from other passive activities.

Dispositions of an Entire Interest in a Passive Activity – Upon the taxable disposition (including abandonment) of an entire interest in a passive activity (or former passive activity), any suspended losses from the activity are no longer treated as passive activity losses and are allowable as a deduction against the taxpayer's income in the following order: (1) income or gain from the passive activity for the taxable year (including any gain recognized on the disposition); (2) net income or gain for the taxable year from all passive activities; (3) any other income or gain.

When an interest in a passive activity is transferred upon the death of the taxpayer, suspended losses may be deducted against income, but only to the extent such losses exceed the amount by which the basis of the interest in the activity is stepped-up at the taxpayer's death. Investors who dispose of an entire interest in a passive activity using an installment sale may deduct suspended losses each year based on the ratio of the gain recognized each year to the total gain on the sale.

If a person disposes of an interest in a passive activity by gift, the basis of the interest to the transferee is increased by the amount of the suspended losses generated from the interest. Such suspended losses added to the transferee's basis are not allowed as a deduction in any taxable year. The increase in basis will, of course, reduce the gain (or possibly increase the loss) from the ultimate taxable sale by the transferee.

Special Rules for Rental Real Estate – Where an individual owns an interest in rental real estate in which he actively participates, the individual may deduct up to $25,000 ($12,500 in the case of married taxpayers filing separately) of such losses or claim an equivalent amount of credits from the rental activity each year, regardless of the general limitations imposed on passive activities. This $25,000 annual allowance is reduced by 50% of the taxpayer's adjusted gross income (determined without regard to passive activity losses, taxable social security benefits, or IRA deductions) that exceeds $100,000 ($50,000 for married taxpayers filing separately). Consequently, the special $25,000 allowance is fully phased-out for taxpayers with adjusted gross income greater than $150,000 ($75,000 for married taxpayers filing separately).

Taxpayers may carry over any losses in excess of the $25,000 (or the reduced allowable amount) from rental real estate where there is active participation as suspended passive activity losses. Taxpayers may use such losses in computing the $25,000 allowable amount in subsequent years in which the investor actively participates in the rental real estate activity.

The requirement for active participation is less stringent than the test for material participation used in distinguishing a passive activity from an active interest in a trade or business. Generally, less personal involvement will be required. But an individual can never be considered to actively participate in a rental property during a period where neither the individual nor the individual's spouse has at least a 10% interest in the property. Except as provided in regulations, a limited partnership interest in real estate does not qualify as active participation.

In the case of the rehabilitation and low-income housing credits (but not losses), the $25,000 allowance applies on a credit equivalent basis, regardless of whether the individual actively participates in the rental real estate activity. Even if the interest is in a limited partnership, the credits may be claimed (up to the $25,000 credit equivalent). The phaseout of the credit equivalent for rehabilitation credits, regardless of when the property was placed in service, starts at adjusted gross income of $200,000, rather than $100,000. Similarly, with respect to property placed in service prior to 1990, phaseout of the $25,000 credit equivalent for the low-income housing tax credit starts at adjusted gross income of $200,000, rather than $100,000. With respect to property placed in service after 1989, there is no phaseout of the $25,000 credit equivalent for the low-income housing tax credit.

Deductible Expenses

A deduction is permitted for many of the investment expenses incurred by an investor. These expenses fall into two major categories: (1) interest paid on amounts borrowed in order to acquire or hold taxable investments; and (2) other expenses paid in connection with the production of income.

Deductibility of Interest

Subject to some complex rules and limitations, investors may deduct interest paid or accrued within the taxable year on indebtedness. Interest can be defined as the compensation allowed by law or fixed by the parties for the use of money. Tax law allows no interest deduction, regardless of the label given to a particular payment, unless the investor has incurred (1) a valid obligation, (2) to pay a fixed or determinable sum of money, (3) in return for the use of money.

Sometimes mortgages contain penalty clauses if the mortgagor prepays the loan. These penalty payments are for the use of money and are therefore—as payments for the privilege of prepaying mortgage indebtedness—deductible as interest.

Points may also be considered interest. Points are premiums in addition to the stated interest rate that borrowers pay to obtain a loan. This additional charge is a percentage of the loan amount. Points are assessed and paid at the inception of the loan. If the borrower paid the fee as compensation for the use of money, it is interest and therefore deductible. Typically, borrowers deduct points ratably over the term of the loan; yet, if certain requirements are met, borrowers can deduct points in the year paid. On the other hand, if all or a part of the charge was for services provided by the lending institution to the investor, such as appraisal fees, that portion is not interest.

If one person pays the interest on another person's debt, the person paying the interest may not deduct the interest; only the person who is liable for the debt may claim the interest deduction. When there is joint- and- several liability (such as when a husband and wife are joint obligors or co-makers of a note), the obligation to pay the interest extends to each co-debtor, so each co-debtor may deduct whatever portion of the interest he pays.

Rules Limiting the Deductibility of Interest – Under current law, essentially all the interest expenses of an individual investor (other than interest incurred in the ordinary course of a trade or business in which the individual materially participates) are subject to one or more limitations. These limitations can be most easily described by the categories to which the debt is properly allocable. These categories include (1) passive activity interest, (2) investment interest, and (3) personal interest. Generally, the allocation of interest is based on the use of the proceeds of the underlying debt. Any interest expense properly allocable to a passive activity is added to other passive activity expenses in determining the annual limitation on the deductibility of passive activity losses (discussed above).

Investment interest generally includes interest expense paid on indebtedness properly allocable to property held for investment (other than passive activity investments). Investment interest is deductible only to the extent of net investment income.

Investment interest generally includes interest expense (1) allocable to the production of portfolio income (dividends, interest, royalties, etc.); (2) allocable to a trade or business in which the investor does not materially participate (unless the activities are treated as a passive activity, in which case the interest expense is subject to the passive activity loss limitations); or (3) allocable to the portfolio income of a passive activity.

Net investment income means the excess of investment income over investment expenses. Investment income includes portfolio income (except from passive activity investments), net short-term and long-term capital gains, and ordinary income gains from the sale of investment property (other than passive activity investment property). Investment expenses include expenses (except interest) related to these sources of investment income.

Investors may carry over annual interest deductions that are disallowed solely due to the investment interest expense limitation indefinitely and deduct them against investment income in future years.

Individuals, estates and trusts are not allowed to deduct personal interest paid or accrued during the taxable year. Personal interest is defined to include all interest *except*: (1) interest expense incurred or continued in connection with the conduct of a trade or business; (2) investment interest expense; (3) interest expense taken into account in computing a taxpayer's income or losses from passive activities; (4) qualified residence interest (see below); (5) interest on qualified educational loans (see below); or (6) interest payable resulting from allowable extensions of payments of estate tax (on the value of reversionary or remainder interests in property).

With respect to mortgage debt incurred after October 13, 1987, taxpayers may deduct interest on mortgage acquisition indebtedness up to a total of $1 million ($500,000 in the case of married taxpayers filing separately) covering up to two homes. Acquisition indebtedness is debt incurred to finance the purchase or improvement of no more than two qualified residences. Taxpayers must reduce the amount of acquisition indebtedness upon which the interest deduction is computed by the amount of their principal payments. Taxpayers cannot increase acquisition indebtedness by refinancing unless they use the additional debt they received from the refinancing for additional improvements.

In addition to interest on acquisition indebtedness, taxpayers may deduct interest on home equity indebtedness of up to $100,000 ($50,000 for married taxpayers filing separately). Home equity indebtedness must be secured by the same two qualified residences as the acquisition indebtedness. But there is no limitation on the use of the home equity indebtedness funds.

Interest on qualified residence debt incurred prior to October 14, 1987 is treated as acquisition indebtedness that is not subject to the $1,000,000 limitation, and is deductible in full. In other words, such amounts are grandfathered under the post-October 14, 1987 rules. But the amount of pre-October 14, 1987 debt reduces (but not below zero) the amount of the $1,000,000 limitation on acquisition indebtedness incurred after October 13, 1987 (but does not reduce the amount of home equity debt that taxpayers can incur after that date). Any refinancing of pre-October 14, 1987 acquisition indebtedness that extends the term of the debt beyond the original term or exceeds the principal amount of the original debt will no longer qualify under the grandfather provision. But the interest on a debt with a balloon type principal payment requirement is deductible for the term of the first refinancing of such acquisition indebtedness, not to exceed 30 years.

Taxpayers with modified adjusted gross income (MAGI) up to certain limits may deduct interest payments due and paid on loans for qualified educational expenses. For these purposes, modified adjusted gross income is computed after applying the Social Security inclusion, moving expenses, and passive loss rules, but without regard either to the student loan interest deduction, the exclusion for amounts received in redemption of qualified education savings bonds, the foreign earned income exclusion and foreign housing exclusion, and amounts excluding sources from possessions or Puerto Rico.

Qualified educational expenses include tuition, fees, room and board, and related expenses. The maximum deduction is $2,500. No deduction is allowed for an individual who is claimed as a dependent on another taxpayer's return.

If MAGI exceeds certain limits, the deduction for interest on education loans is reduced. Single tax-payers may take no deduction if their MAGI is in excess of $65,000 and the amount of the deduction is reduced proportionately if MAGI is between $50,000 and $65,000. Married taxpayers filing jointly may take no deduction if their MAGI is in excess of $130,000 and the amount of the deduction is reduced proportionately if MAGI is between $100,000 and $130,000. Married taxpayers filing separately may take no such deduction.

Taxpayers may not deduct interest that would otherwise be deductible if it is allocable to a class of income wholly exempt from tax (e.g., municipal bonds). The rationale is that if the taxpayer entirely excludes the income items from gross income, it is not necessary or appropriate to permit any interest deduction. This rule makes it difficult for an investor borrowing money for investment purposes to deduct interest on those loans if he also holds tax-exempt bonds for investment.

The tax law provides a number of other limitations on the deduction of interest that are of importance to investors. One such restriction is imposed on interest investors incur to purchase or carry market discount bonds (i.e., bonds purchased after original issue at a price below both its redemption price and its original issue price, because of an increase in the interest rates available on newly issued alternative investments). Such interest is not currently deductible to the extent the investor has deferred the recognition of current income. The investor may claim the interest deduction at the time he reports the market discount income, which is essentially the unreported interest that has accrued on the bond from the date of purchase until the date of disposition.

A similar restriction is imposed on interest expenses investors incur in financing non-interest-bearing short-term obligations such as Treasury bills. If the investor acquired the short-term obligation through a loan, the net interest expense is not deductible to the extent of the ratable portion of the bond discount attributable to the current year (the disallowed interest is, however, deductible upon the disposition of the bond). Interest is currently deductible if the investor elects to include the discount as income in the taxable year it is earned.

Deductibility of Investment Expenses Other than Interest

Many expenses investors incur are deductible (subject to the 2% floor on miscellaneous itemized deductions) if they meet certain requirements.

The requirements are that the investor must incur these expenses (1) for the production or collection of income; or (2) for the management, conservation, or maintenance of property held for the production of income; or (3) in connection with the determination, collection, or refund of any tax. Additionally, an investor's expenses must be (1) ordinary and necessary, (2) paid or incurred in the taxable year, and (3) expenses rather than capital expenditures. An expense is considered ordinary if it normally occurs or is likely to occur in connection with an investment similar to the one for which an expense deduction is claimed.

Common deductible investment-related expenses include (1) rental expenses of a safe deposit box used to store taxable securities; (2) subscriptions to investment advisory services; (3) investment counsel fees (whether or not the advice is followed); (4) custodian's fees; (5) service charges in connection with a dividend reinvestment plan; (6) service, custodial, and guaranty fees charged by the issuer of mortgage backed pass-through certificates; (7) bookkeeping services; (8) office expenses such as rent, water, telephone, stamps, and stationary incurred in connection with investment activities; (9) secretarial services relating to the management of rental property and investment record keeping; (10) premiums paid for an indemnity bond required for issuance of a new stock certificate to replace lost, stolen, destroyed, or mislaid certificates; and (11) fees incurred for tax advice (including (a) preparation of income tax returns, (b) cost of tax books used in preparing tax returns, (c) tax advice from attorneys and accountants, (d) legal fees for obtaining a letter ruling from the IRS, and (e) legal or accounting fees contesting a tax deficiency or claiming a refund (whether or not successfully).

But deductible investment related expenses of individuals are only deductible to the extent they exceed 2% of the taxpayer's adjusted gross income (AGI). For example, if on's deductible investment related expenses equal $4,500 in a year in which his AGI is $200,000, his allowable deduction for such expenses is limited to $500 ($4,500 – $4,000 [2% x $200,000]).

Common investment-related expenses that investors may not deduct (because they are personal or because they are not ordinary and necessary) also include travel to attend shareholders' meetings. An investment related expense need not be essential in order for it to be considered necessary. But it must be one that the investor reasonably believes is appropriate and helpful. Generally the courts will not question the investor's determination. The standard of what is or is not both ordinary and necessary depends on the situation in the community where the issue arises. If most investors in the same situation would have incurred the same expenditure, the taxpayer would satisfy the ordinary and necessary tests.

It is essential that an expense be paid or incurred in the taxable year (see "Timing and Recognition of Income and Expenses," below).

To be deductible, an expense must meet one additional major test—it must not be a capital expenditure. If an outlay is an expense, the taxpayer can deduct it immediately. If an outlay is considered the cost or part of the cost of an asset, the taxpayer must capitalize it. This means that the investor must add the outlay to the basis in the asset. If the asset is depreciable or amortizable, this increased basis will result in additional deductions over the life of the asset. The investor may otherwise use the increased basis to lower the gain or increase the loss upon a sale or other taxable disposition of the investment.

Common expenditures that are considered capital in nature and are, therefore, not currently deductible include: (1) brokers' commissions and fees in connection with acquiring investments (these are added to the basis of the property); (2) selling expenses (these are offset against selling price in determining capital gains and losses); and (3) expenses to defend, acquire, or perfect title to property (these are added to the basis of the property).

Timing of Recognition of Income and Expenses

Cash basis taxpayers report income in the year that they receive it and, generally, deduct expenses in the year that they pay it. The cash basis method is therefore essentially an "in and out of pocket" method of reporting. Items do not have to be received or paid in cash; receipts and payments in property are income and deduction items to the extent of the fair market value of the property received or paid.

Accrual basis taxpayers report income when they earn it, even if they do not receive the cash income until a subsequent tax year. Generally, accrual basis

Chapter 43 – Taxation Of Investment Vehicles

taxpayers deduct an expense when their liability for payment has become fixed and determinable. Most individuals are cash basis taxpayers. The following discussion will focus on the application of the general rules applicable to cash basis investors and four of the major exceptions.

Cash basis investors generally will include interest, royalty, dividend, and other investment income, as well as gains from the sale of investments, in gross income in the year in which they receive cash or other property. Cash basis investors generally will deduct interest and other expenses they incur in connection with their investments, as well as losses from the sale of investments, from gross income in the year in which they pay cash or other property. Thus, they may deduct interest expense, investment advisory fees, and other deductible expenses in the year paid. But generally they deduct losses on the sale of securities on the trade date (even if delivery and receipt of the proceeds occurs in the following year). Some exceptions to the general rules governing cash basis investors follow.

Constructive Receipt

Under the doctrine of constructive receipt, an investor must include an item in gross income even though he does not actually take possession, if the item is (1) credited to his account, (2) set apart for him, or (3) otherwise made available so that he can obtain it at his own volition without any substantial conditions or restrictions. Therefore, income is taxable if the investor can take it when he wants it.

The purpose of the doctrine is to prevent investors from determining at will the year in which they will report income. Without the doctrine of constructive receipt, investors could postpone the taxability of income until the year in which they chose to reduce the item to their actual possession. For example, taxpayers must report interest credited to their bank savings accounts regardless of whether they withdraw the interest or leave it on deposit.

Constructive receipt will not apply if the taxpayer's control of the income is restricted in some meaningful manner. For instance, an investor will not be considered to have constructively received money or other property if (1) it is only conditionally credited, (2) it is indefinite in amount, (3) the payor has no funds, (4) the money is available only through the surrender of a valuable right, or (5) receipt is subject to any other substantial limitation or restriction. The doctrine of constructive receipt is

particularly important to individuals whose employers have enhanced their financial security through nonqualified deferred compensation arrangements.

Economic Benefit

The economic benefit theory states that when employees receive from their employers a benefit that is the equivalent of cash, the employees are currently taxed on the value of that benefit. The most common example is where executives receive group term life insurance coverage in excess of the amount excludable from federal income tax. The employees must include in income an amount (computed from government tables) that represents the economic benefit they receive when their employer makes premium payments. The term insurance provided in a split-dollar arrangement and the incidental life insurance coverage employers sometimes provide in their qualified retirement plans are other examples of currently reportable economic benefits.

There is an important difference between the doctrine of constructive receipt and the economic benefit theory. The constructive receipt doctrine requires the inclusion of income when taxpayers have an unrestricted choice—that is, whether to take or not to take income set apart for them or credited to their account. This theory is concerned with the issue of when income is realized by the taxpayer.

Conversely, the economic benefit theory requires taxpayers to report income even if they cannot take the income. Under the economic benefit theory, all that is necessary to trigger taxation is that employees receive from their employer a benefit that is the equivalent of cash—that is, something with a (1) current, (2) real, and (3) measurable value. The economic benefit theory is concerned with whether the taxpayer has enjoyed a present benefit from his employer capable of measurement and subject to tax. This theory is concerned with the issue of what income is.

Restricted Property

An employer often transfers property to an employee in connection with the performance of services. A business may give or sell stock or other property to a key employee but withhold, by separate agreement, significant rights. For example, an employer may transfer stock to an employee but restrict the employee's right to vote the stock or sell it. The idea is that the employer will withhold (restrict) property rights until the employee has performed certain specified services. If the employee fails to achieve the goal or meet the specified requirements, the employee may forfeit his right to the stock or other property.

Suppose an employer pays a bonus to an executive in the form of company stock. Assume the ownership of this stock is subject to certain restrictions, including a provision that if the employee leaves the company within a 5-year period he will forfeit the stock and will receive no compensation. Such property is appropriately called restricted stock or restricted property.

If an employer gave an employee property with no restrictions, the entire value of the property would constitute current compensation income. For instance, an employee who receives a bonus of 100 shares of his employer's stock currently selling for $200 a share realizes $20,000 of income. But, if certain requirements are met, an employer can compensate an employee in a manner that delays the tax until the employee is given full rights in the property.

The general rules governing restricted property (the IRC Section 83 rules) provide that employees will report transfers of restricted property as income in the first tax year in which the employees' rights are (1) not subject to any substantial risk of forfeiture and (2) transferable free of this risk. In other words, employees will not be subject to tax on restricted property as long as their rights to that property are forfeitable (subject to a substantial risk of forfeiture) and not transferable by them free of such risk. (This means that if employees should sell or give the property away, the recipients of the property must also be under a substantial risk that they (the new owner) would forfeit the property if the employees failed to satisfy the conditions necessary to obtain full ownership.)

Substantial risk of forfeiture means that rights in transferred property are conditioned, directly or indirectly, upon the future performance (or refraining from performance) of substantial services by any person or upon the occurrence of a condition related to the purpose of the transfer. In addition, there must be a realistic and substantial possibility of forfeiture if the specified condition is not satisfied. The following examples illustrate common situations that probably would *not* be considered substantial restrictions: (1) a consulting contract with a retiring executive that called for only occasional services at the executive's discretion, (2) a requirement that an employee must return the property if he commits a felony, or (3) a noncompetition provision (since this is largely within the employee's control).

What happens when the restrictions expire? At the lapse of the restrictions, the employee must generally include in income the value of the property at that time. Sometimes an employer will remove restrictions in stages so that an employee may "earn out" of the restrictions.

But the employee has a choice—he can elect to have the value of the restricted property taxed to him immediately in the year he receives it (even though it remains nontransferable or subject to a substantial risk of forfeiture.) If an employee makes this election within 30 days of receipt of the property, the general restricted property rules do not apply. Any appreciation in the value of the property is treated as capital gain rather than as compensation. The employee pays no tax at the time the risk of forfeiture expires (and will pay no tax until the property is sold or otherwise disposed of in a taxable exchange). But if the property is later forfeited, no deduction is allowed for the loss.

An employee who makes this election must be willing to pay ordinary income tax on the fair market value of the property in the year he receives the stock or other property. He is gambling that the value of the property will increase considerably before the restrictions lapse (in which case he may be eligible to pay tax on any realized gain as capital gain). He is also gambling that he will not forfeit the stock before he is able to sell or dispose of it without restriction.

Another exception to the strict rule of includability of the fair market value of the property (upon the lapse of restrictions) concerns restrictions that affect value. This exception pertains to value-affecting restrictions, which, by their terms, will never lapse. For instance, if an employee may sell restricted property only at book value and that restriction, by its terms, will never lapse, that amount will be treated as the property's fair market value.

An employer's compensation deduction will be allowed at the time the employee recognizes income from restricted property. The amount of the deduction will be the same as the amount of income recognized by the employee.

Prepaid Deductions

In certain situations, cash basis investors can control the year in which they will take deductions. They can, for instance, prepay certain taxes and take the deduction in the year of payment even though the expenses relate to future years. This ability to time deductions is limited. For example, taxpayers cannot deduct the payment of multiple years' prepaid rent and insurance premiums in the year of payment. They generally must spread the deductions over the period covered by the prepayment if the deduction of the prepayment would materially distort income.

Special rules apply to the deductibility of interest expense for all taxpayers, whether they use the cash basis or the accrual method of accounting. A cash basis investor must deduct prepaid interest over the period of the loan to the extent the interest represents the cost of using the borrowed funds during each taxable year in the period. Generally, investors must deduct points paid on an investment loan ratably over the term of the loan. An investor on the accrual method of accounting accrues interest ratably over the loan period. This means the accrual method investor must deduct the interest ratably even if he prepays the interest.

THE FEDERAL INCOME TAX RATE STRUCTURE

Tax planning is such an important part of investment planning that advisers and investors need to have a complete understanding of the federal income tax rate structure. This section will discuss the federal income tax rate structure, the alternative minimum tax, and the "kiddie tax" on unearned (investment) income of children under age 18.

Ordinary Income Tax Rates

The income tax rates are applied to a taxpayer's taxable income, which can be defined as the amount of income that remains after a taxpayer subtracts all deductions and exemptions from gross income. For income tax rates, see Appendix I.

Capital Gain Tax Rates

For long-term capital gains properly taken into account after May 5, 2003 and before 2011, the 10% and 20% rates on capital gain are reduced to 5% (0% in 2008) and 15%, respectively. These rates apply for both the regular tax and the alternative minimum tax (AMT). In addition, gain from an installment sale that would have qualified for the 10% or 20% rates will now qualify for the 5% or 15% rate on payments collected after May 5, 2003 and before 2011. But the 25% rate on unrecaptured IRC Section 1250 gain and the 28% rate on collectibles and qualified small-business stock (IRC Section 1202 stock) still apply.

After 2010, the capital gain tax rates and rules are scheduled to revert to the old rates. Consequently, when planning for investment horizons beyond 2010, investors should know the rates and rules that will apply at that time under current law. (In the case of qualified 5-year gain—that is, adjusted net capital gain from capital assets held more than five years before their sale, and where the 10% rate had been reduced to 8% and the 20% rate had been reduced to 18%—note that the 8%/18% rates have been repealed.[1])

Qualified Dividend Income

Effective for tax years beginning after 2002 and before 2011, dividends received by an individual shareholder from certain corporations are generally taxed at the same rates that apply to long-term capital gains (see above).[2] Dividends received on common and preferred stock should qualify for the lower rates. Furthermore, dividends received by an S corporation, partnership, or LLC (if the LLC is taxed as a partnership or disregarded entity) should be eligible for the lower rates to the extent the dividends are ultimately taxed to individual (noncorporate) owners. These rates apply for both regular-tax and alternative-minimum-tax (AMT) purposes.[3]

For purposes of these rules, qualified dividend income means dividends received during the tax year from domestic corporations and qualified foreign corporations. A qualified foreign corporation is a corporation that is incorporated in a U.S. possession, or that is eligible for benefits of a comprehensive income tax treaty with the United States that the IRS determines is satisfactory for purposes of the IRC qualified dividend income rules, and that includes an exchange of information program. Corporations whose stock of American Depository Receipts (ADRs) is readily tradable on an established U.S. securities market also are qualified foreign corporations. But qualified foreign corporations do not include foreign personal holding companies, foreign investment companies, and passive foreign investment companies.

Exclusions

Several types of dividend income are specifically excluded from the definition of qualified dividend income, including the following:

1. Dividends received on the stock are not eligible for the reduced rates if the shareholder does not

hold the share of stock for more than 60 days during the 121-day period beginning 60 days before the "ex-dividend date" (i.e., the first date following the declaration of a dividend on which the buyer of a stock will not be entitled to receive the next dividend).[4] In the case of preferred stock, the share of stock must be held for more than 90 days during the 181-day period beginning 90 days before the ex-dividend date;

2. Dividends on any share of stock to the extent that the taxpayer is under an obligation (whether pursuant to a short sale or otherwise) to make related payments with respect to positions in substantially similar or related property;

3. Any amount taken into account as investment income under IRC Section 163(d)(4)(B) (which treats qualified dividend income as investment income if elected by the taxpayer) allowing the dividend to support a deduction for investment interest;

4. Dividends from corporations that are exempt from tax under IRC Sections 501 and 521;

5. Amounts that are allowed as a deduction under IRC Section 591 relating to dividends paid by mutual savings banks; and

6. Dividends paid on employer securities held by an employee stock ownership plan (ESOP).

Payments in lieu of dividends (e.g., dividends paid on stock that a broker has loaned to a customer, where the dividends are paid to the short sale buyer before the short sale is closed) are not eligible for the reduced dividend rates.

Dividends from Mutual Funds and REITs

With some restrictions, dividends received from regulated investment companies (RICs or mutual funds) are eligible for the reduced dividend rates. In the case of mutual funds, what currently comes out as dividends normally is made up of different types of income: interest, short-term capital gains, and dividends received from various stock investments. The interest income and short-term capital gains still will be taxed at the ordinary income rates; only the actual dividends included in the distributions will be eligible for the lower rates. Therefore, dividends from money market funds will

generally be entirely ineligible for the lower dividend tax rates. If at least 95% of a RIC's gross income (other than long-term capital gains) is qualifying dividend income, the RIC will be able to designate 100% of its ordinary income dividends as qualifying for the lower dividend rates.

Most REIT dividends are not eligible for the reduced rate.[5] The 15% tax rate applies to REIT dividends that are attributable to: (1) dividends received by the REIT from non-REIT corporations (e.g., taxable REIT subsidiaries); and (2) income that was subject to tax by the REIT at the corporate level. REIT capital gain dividends are taxed at a maximum rate of 25% to the extent of unrecaptured IRC Section 1250 gains, and at a maximum rate of 15% thereafter.[6]

Alternative Minimum Tax

The tax law imposes an alternative minimum tax (AMT) so that individuals with substantial economic income will not be able to avoid a tax liability by using exclusions, deductions, and credits. The AMT attempts to broaden the taxable income base to insure that most investors will incur at least some tax liability. Because the actual tax liability of taxpayers is the greater of the regular tax and the AMT, any cuts in the regular tax that lowers taxpayers' regular tax liability below their AMT liability are not actual cuts in taxes.

But the number of taxpayers now paying AMT has grown rapidly and will continue to grow. Experts estimate that the number of AMT affected taxpayers will rise from about 2.4 million in 2003 to 35.5 million in 2010. Among the most important reasons for the expanding impact of the AMT is that AMT tax brackets and exemptions are not indexed for inflation, unlike other income tax items. Also, while certain credits—the child credit, the adoption credit, dependent child-care credit, and the HOPE and Lifetime Learning credits—have been allowed for AMT purposes for the past few years, they are not allowed for taxable years beginning after 2003.

AMT Computation

Individuals pay alternative minimum tax to the extent that it exceeds their regular tax liability. If the tax computed under the AMT formula does not exceed the investor's regular tax, the AMT does not apply. For 2006, alternative minimum tax is computed as follows:

- Taxable income (from Form 1040)
+/- Certain adjustments to taxable income (listed below)
+ Tax-preference items (described below)
= Alternative-minimum-taxable income (AMTI)
- Exemption: **Joint Return**
    $62,550 – 25% (AMTI – $150,000) **or**
    Single Return
    $42,500 – 25% (AMTI – $112,500) **or**
    Married Filing Separately
    $31,275 – 25% (AMTI – $75,000)
= Alternative-minimum-tax base
× **26% of first $175,000^{7} plus 28% of amount > $175,000**
= Tentative minimum tax before the foreign-tax credit
- Credit for foreign taxes
= Tentative minimum tax
- Regular tax (reduced by foreign-tax credit only)
= Alternative-minimum-tax liability

In 2006, the Congress continued the process of one-year band-aids to the growing politically sensitive topic of AMT relief by extending the enhanced AMT exemption for one more year over the baseline amount, and in fact increasing the amount. Unless Congress acts to extend such relief in future years, in subsequent years, the exemption amounts revert to the lower 2000 levels—$45,000, $33,750 and $22,500 for married taxpayers filing jointly, single taxpayers, and married taxpayers filing separately, respectively. Also, for years before 2011, the maximum tax rate on net capital gains (including qualifying dividends) is reduced from 20% to 15% for alternative-minimum-tax purposes. Corresponding reductions are made for those taxpayers in the 10% or 15% ordinary income tax brackets to 5%.

Adjustment to Taxable Income

The adjustments to taxable income include the following:

1. For property placed in service after 1986, adjust depreciation deductions to conform to special (less favorable) depreciation rules used for AMT purposes.

2. Adjust mining exploration and development costs, circulation expenditures, and research and development expense deductions to conform to special (less favorable) AMT amortization rules.

3. Recompute gains or losses on the sale of property to reflect the special depreciation rules used for AMT purposes.

4. Adjust long-term contracts entered into after February 28, 1986 using the percentage-of-completion method for purposes of the AMT.

5. Calculate net operating loss (NOL) deductions under special (less favorable) AMT rules and limit NOL to no more than 90% of AMT income. Certain AMT operating losses generated or taken as carry forwards in 2001 or 2002 can offset up to 100% of AMT income.

6. Add back certain itemized deductions allowable in computing regular taxable income. In addition, the medical expense deduction is subject to a 10% floor under the AMT as compared to a 7.5% of AGI floor used in computing regular taxable income. For purposes of this adjustment item, one does not take into account the phaseout of itemized deductions for certain upper income.

7. Add the excess of the fair market value of any incentive stock option (ISOs) stock received over the option exercise price (the bargain element) into AMTI in the year of exercise. When the taxpayer subsequently sells the option stock, the taxpayer may subtract the bargain element amount computed and added to AMTI in a previous year from AMTI computed in the year of sale.

8. Taxpayers may not use passive activity losses in determining AMTI, except to the extent the taxpayer is insolvent.

Tax Preferences

The tax preferences that taxpayers must add back when computing AMTI include:

1. The excess of accelerated depreciation or ACRS deductions over straight-line depreciation on real property placed in service before 1987 (to the extent not taken into account in computing the adjustment to taxable income discussed above).

2. Percentage depletion in excess of cost basis.

3. Accelerated depreciation on depreciable personal property placed in service before 1987 that is leased (to the extent not taken into account in computing the adjustment to taxable income discussed above).

4. Amortization of certified pollution control facilities.

5. Certain excess intangible drilling costs.

6. Tax-exempt interest on certain private activity bonds issued after August 7, 1986.

7. Use of the installment method by dealers in personal property.

8. For dispositions of IRC Section 1202 stock after May 5, 2003 and before January 1, 2009, taxpayers need to treat only 7%, rather than the previous 28% or 42%, of the amount excluded from gross income under IRC Section 1202 (gains on sales of certain small business stock), as a preference item for AMT purposes.

Alternative Minimum Tax Credit

Individuals can take a credit against their regular tax liability in years in which their regular tax exceeds their computed alternative minimum tax. The amount of the credit is based on the amount of alternative minimum tax paid in excess of the regular tax computed in prior years. The credit is not available to the extent the prior years' AMT was attributed to excess percentage depletion, tax-exempt interest, or non-AMT itemized deductions. The credit is limited to the amount necessary to reduce the regular tax to the amount of AMT computed for the year in which the credit is claimed.

Tax Planning for the AMT

The existence of the alternative minimum tax places a premium on planning techniques. With the availability of the AMT credit, it is less critical to undertake some of the more drastic planning concepts when the taxpayer will be able to use the AMT credit within a year or two after the AMT tax would be due. Here are some planning ideas and considerations:

In order to avoid or minimize the effect of the AMT:

1. Determine the maximum amount of deductions or losses that an investor can claim before becoming subject to the AMT. Once an investor reaches the point where the AMT applies, any additional deductions will yield at most a 26% (or 28% as determined by AMT) tax benefit.

2. An investor can reduce or eliminate tax preference items by: (a) electing to capitalize excess intangible drilling costs, mining exploration expenses, and research and experimentation expenses, and amortize them over the permissible AMT periods; (b) electing the AMT or straight-line methods of computing depreciation; or (c) considering an early disposition (in the year of exercise) of stock acquired through the exercise of an Incentive Stock Option.

When it has been determined that the investor will be subject to the AMT:

1. The investor should consider deferring current year deductions (which will be of minimal value because of the AMT) and save them for a future year when they will be more valuable, by: (a) postponing charitable contributions; (b) postponing elective medical treatments; or (c) delaying making estimated state tax payments.

2. The investor should consider accelerating ordinary income, since it will be taxed at no greater than the AMT rate. This can be accomplished, for example, by exercising options under an Incentive Stock Option Plan (ISO) and selling the stock within the same year. (This has the double advantage of qualifying the ordinary income from the accelerated sale of the ISO for the maximum AMT tax rate and eliminating the ISO as a tax preference item.)

The Impact of Capital Gains

Although not included in the list of tax preferences or tax adjustments, capital gains and qualifying dividends can play a significant, yet not well understood, role in the alternative minimum tax. While capital gains and qualifying dividends are taxed for AMT purposes at the same favorable rate they are taxed for regular tax purposes, they may still contribute indirectly to the creation of AMT in some circumstances.

First, capital gains increase the taxable income from which the alternative minimum taxable income is

Chapter 43 – Taxation Of Investment Vehicles

computed. For certain ranges of income, it may phase out a part of the AMT exemption applicable to the taxpayer. Depending on the amount of other ordinary income and the proportion of adjustments and preferences relative to regular taxable income, recognition of capital gains may cause the AMT. Second, large capital gains generally create a large state income-tax liability, which itself is a tax adjustment in computing AMT in the year paid.

The "Kiddie Tax"—Unearned Income of Certain Minor Children

The net unearned income of a child who has not reached age 18 by year-end and who has at least one parent alive at year-end is subjected to a special tax computation.[8] Unearned income means income from sources other than wages, salaries, professional fees, and other amounts received as compensation for personal services actually rendered. The tax payable by the child on the net unearned income is essentially the additional amount of tax that the parent would have had to pay if the net unearned income of the child were included in the parent's taxable income. Effectively, the minor children's unearned income is taxed at the parent's highest marginal federal tax rate for the type of investment income involved.

If the parents have two or more minor children with unearned income to be taxed at the parents' marginal tax rate, all of the children's applicable unearned income will be added together and the tax calculated. The tax is then allocated to each child based on the child's pro-rata share of the unearned income.

There are three levels of a minor's unearned income involved in the calculation of the tax on such income:

1. Generally, a minor child's unearned income is exempt from tax up to the amount of the child's standard deduction. (The standard deduction of a child claimed as a dependent is limited to the greater of (a) $850 (in 2006) or (b) the sum of $300 (in 2006) and the amount of his earned income, not to exceed the regular standard deduction amount for the year ($5,150 in 2006). After the first $850 (in 2006) is used to offset the child's unearned income, any excess is available to offset earned income of the child).

2. The next $850 (in 2006) of unearned income is taxable at the child's bracket.

3. Unearned income in excess of the first $1,700 (in 2006) is taxed to the child at the appropriate parent's rate.

In addition to the limitation on their standard deductions, children that may be claimed as dependents on a parent's return may not claim a personal exemption.

The kiddie tax rules apply regardless of the source of the children's assets producing the unearned income. It does not matter whether the children used their own earned income to purchase the investment assets producing the income, or received the assets (or funds) as an inheritance or a gift from grandparents, parents, or other sources.

Parents may elect to include their children's unearned income over $1,700 (in 2006) on their own return, thus avoiding the necessity of filing a return for each child. The election is available if the child has income of more than $850 (in 2006) but less than $8,000 (in 2006), all of which is from interest and dividends. But an additional tax is imposed equal to $85 (in 2006) or 10% of the income over $850 (in 2006), whichever is less, for each child to whom the election applies.

In the case of unmarried parents, the parent whose taxable income is used in computing the tax on the unearned income of the minor child is the custodial parent. In the case of parents who are married but filing separately, the marginal rate of the parent with the greater taxable income will be used in the calculation.

The tax impact of the kiddie tax rules is potentially greatest with respect to investment income, such as interest, that is taxed as ordinary income. If the children would be in the 10% or 15% tax bracket, the children's ordinary investment could be taxed at a rate as high as 35%, depending upon the parent's income tax bracket.

With respect to qualifying dividends and long-term capital gains, the maximum impact of the kiddie tax rules is to raise the tax rate from 5% to 15%. This will occur only if the children's total income would put them in the 10% or 15% federal income tax brackets and the parents are in a higher tax bracket. If the children would be in a federal tax bracket that is greater than the 15% bracket, the kiddie tax will have no impact at all, since the tax rate on qualifying dividends and long-term capital gains will be 15% for both the parents and the children.

Tools & Techniques of Investment Planning

445

SELECTED INVESTMENT TAX ISSUES

Original Issue and Market Discounts and Premiums[9]

Discounts

Original issue discount (OID) arises when corporate or governmental borrowers originally issue bonds or notes (or other similar debt instruments) at a price that is less than the stated redemption price at maturity (i.e., par or face value). The extreme example is zero coupon bonds that borrowers issue at deep discounts from the redemption value at maturity. The difference between the issue price (the original buyer's initial basis in the bond) and the redemption price is the original issue discount. But a de minimis exception provides that the discount can be ignored if it less than 1/4 of 1% (0.0025) of the stated redemption price multiplied by the number of complete years to maturity.[10]

Purchasers or lenders must include the amount of OID in income as it accrues over the life of the debt instrument.[11] The purpose of the OID rules is to prevent purchasers of OID bonds from deferring tax on the interest they are implicitly earning each year until the bonds mature, or until the owners sell, exchange, or otherwise dispose of the bonds. For deep discount bonds, this means that bondholders may have tax liability that exceeds the actual cash interest income from the bonds.

For bonds issued after April 4, 1994, bondholders must accrue the OID at a constant rate (explained below). Bondholders may use accrual periods of different lengths provided that no accrual period is longer than one year. Generally, if the bond pays some periodic interest, the accrual period is equal to the period between interest payments. Interest payments may occur either on the first day or final day of an accrual period.[12]

In many, if not most, cases, an accrual period may span two taxable years of the bondholder. Bondholders apportion to each taxable year the amount of OID in the accrual period spanning the two tax years by ratably allocating the period's accrued discount to each day in the period. For instance, if the accrual period is the three months from November 1 to January 31 and the OID accruing in that three-month period is $184, the bondholder would allocate $2 to each day in this 92 day period ($184 / 92). Thus, a calendar year taxpayer would include $122 (61 days in November and December x $2) of this period's OID in income for the current tax year

and $62 (31 days in January x $2) in the subsequent tax year. These OID allocation rules apply to both accrual basis and cash basis taxpayers.[13]

Bondholders add the amount of OID taken into income each period to their basis in the bond. The constant rate method requires bondholders to accrue interest on the bond at its yield to maturity. The yield to maturity is the rate that equates the issue price to the present value of all scheduled cash interest payments on the bond, if any, plus the present value of the redemption.

Example: On February 1, 2004, XYZ Corp. issues 5-year bonds with a redemption value of $10,000 and a stated interest rate of 4.5%. The bonds pay interest of $225 semiannually on January 31 and July 31 each year. The subscription or issue price is $9,000. Since the original issue discount—$1,000—is greater than the de minimis amount (0.0025 x $10,000 x 5 = $125), the OID rules apply to the bondholders.

The yield to maturity (with semiannual compounding and 6-month accrual periods) is equal to the rate that equates $9,000 with (1) the present value of 10 semiannual cash interest payments of $225, plus (2) the present value of the $10,000 redemption value payable in five years. The 6-month rate that satisfies this condition is 3.449% (6.899% annual rate, or 7.018% effective annual rate). Therefore, the schedule of principal values, cash interest, taxable interest, and OID interest would be as follows over the 5-year period until maturity:

Date	Current Basis (Basis$_{t-1}$ + OID$_t$)	Stated (Cash) Interest	Imputed (Taxable) Interest (Basis$_{t-1}$ x 3.449%)	OID Interest (Imputed Interest – Stated Interest)
2/1/2004	9,000.00	—	—	—
8/1/2004	9,085.44	225.00	310.44	85.44
2/1/2005	9,173.83	225.00	313.39	88.39
8/1/2005	9,265.27	225.00	316.44	91.44
2/1/2006	9,359.86	225.00	319.59	94.59
8/1/2006	9,457.71	225.00	322.85	97.85
2/1/2007	9,558.94	225.00	326.23	101.23
8/1/2007	9,663.66	225.00	329.72	104.72
2/1/2008	9,771.99	225.00	333.33	108.33
8/1/2008	9,884.06	225.00	337.07	112.07
2/1/2009	10,000.00	225.00	340.94	115.94

Since the beginning and end of the accrual periods do not coincide with the calendar year, bondholders must compute their reportable

OID interest income by ratably allocating the OID on a daily basis. Taxpayers will report the cash interest payments in the year they actually receive them whereas accrual basis taxpayers will also have to apportion the cash interest income to the year in which it accrues.

The number of days from August 1 to January 31 of the following year is 184 and the number of days from August 1 to December 31 each year is 153. Therefore, bondholders must include 153/184 of the OID for the accrual period ranging from August 1 to January 31 to the period from August 1 to December 31 each year and 31/184 of the OID to the following year. Therefore the schedule of taxable interest income for a taxpayer would look as follows:

Date	Stated (Cash) Interest	OID Interest	Total Taxable Interest
2/1/04 – 7/31/04	225.00	85.44	310.44
8/1/04 – 12/31/04	0.00	153/184 x 88.39 = 73.50	73.50
Total 2004	**225.00**	**158.94**	**383.94**
1/1/05 – 1/31/05	225.00	31/184 x 88.39 = 14.89	239.89
2/1/05 – 7/31/05	225.00	91.44	316.44
8/1/05 – 12/31/05	0.00	153/184 x 94.59 = 78.65	78.65
Total 2005	**450.00**	**184.98**	**634.98**
1/1/06 – 1/31/06	225.00	31/184 x 94.59 = 15.94	240.94
2/1/06 – 7/31/06	225.00	97.85	322.85
8/1/06 – 12/31/06	0.00	153/184 x 101.23 = 84.17	84.17
Total 2006	**450.00**	**197.96**	**647.96**
1/1/07 – 1/31/07	225.00	31/184 x 101.23 = 17.06	242.06
2/1/07 – 7/31/07	225.00	104.72	329.72
8/1/07 – 12/31/07	0.00	153/184 x 108.33 = 90.08	90.08
Total 2007	**450.00**	**211.86**	**661.86**
1/1/08 – 1/31/08	225.00	31/184 x 108.33 = 18.25	243.25
2/1/08 – 7/31/08	225.00	112.07	337.07
8/1/08 – 12/31/08	0.00	153/184 x 115.94 = 96.41	96.41
Total 2008	**450.00**	**226.73**	**676.73**
1/1/09 – 1/31/09	225.00	31/184 x 115.94 = 19.53	244.53
Total 2009	**225.00**	**19.53**	**244.53**

Market discounts or premiums in bond prices arise as a result of fluctuations in market rates of interest or changes in the borrower's credit rating after the bond is originally issued. If bondholders sell, exchange, or otherwise dispose of an OID bond before maturity, they determine their gain or loss in reference to their adjusted basis. Generally, the gain or loss is treated as long-term or short-term capital gain or loss, depending upon the bond owner's holding period.[14]

Example: The bondholder in the previous example sells the bond on September 30, 2006 for $9,100. From the first table above, the bondholder's adjusted basis in the bond on August 1, 2006 is $9,457.71. September 30, 2006 is 61 days into the next 184-day accrual period. The OID for the next accrual period is $326.23, so the amount allocable to the 61-day period is 61/184 x $326.23 = $108.15. The bondholder must include this amount in income for the year and increase his basis accordingly. Therefore, the bondholder's adjusted basis in the bond on September 30, 2006 is $9,565.86 and the bondholder realizes a $465.86 long-term capital loss on the sale ($9,565.86 – $9,100).

How does the new bondholder treat the purchase? If a bond was originally issued at par, the market discount is the amount by which the stated redemption price exceeds the taxpayer's basis in the bond immediately after its acquisition.[15] If the bond was originally issued at a discount and later purchased on the market for less than the original issue price increased by the amount of original issue discount accruing since issue up to the date of purchase, the difference is market discount.[16] Therefore, a person who purchases a bond that was originally issued at a discount measures the market discount or premium not by reference to the redemption value, but by reference to the basis adjusted for OID. Similar to original issue discounts, if the total market discount is less than 1/4 of 1% (.0025) of the stated redemption price at maturity (or, if the bond was issued at a discount of the issue price increased by original issue discount accruing since issue to the date of purchase) multiplied by the number of complete years until maturity, it is treated as if there is no market discount.[17]

In general, investors do not include market discount in income until they sell or dispose of the bond. But if they purchase a bond that was originally issued at a discount, they must continue to accrue the OID at a constant rate over the remaining term until the bond matures or until they sell or dispose of the bond, just as if they were the original bondholders. They must include the OID in income as it accrues and increase their bases accordingly.

Example: The investor who purchased the bond on September 30, 2006 from the original bondholder for $9,100 (at a $465.86 market discount) holds the bond to maturity. The bondholder's adjusted basis at maturity will be $9,534.14 ($9,100 plus the accrued OID until maturity).

Although an investor who buys a bond at a market discount generally does not have to accrue the market discount over the remaining term of the bond, upon the sale, exchange, redemption, or other disposition of the bond for a price in excess of the bondholder's adjusted basis, the investor must treat as ordinary interest income any gain up to the amount of the market discount. Any gain in excess of the market discount is treated as long-term or short-term capital gain, depending upon the investor's holding period. If the amount received is less than the investor's adjusted basis, the loss is treated as long-term or short-term capital loss, depending upon the investor's holding period.

Example: If the investor who purchased the bond on September 30, 2006 at a $465.86 market discount holds the bond to maturity, the difference between his adjusted basis of $9,534.14 and the $10,000 redemption price, $465.86, is exactly equal to the market discount. Therefore, the investor must report this entire amount as interest income on his tax return for that year.

Assume instead that the investor sells the bond on January 31, 2008 for $9,950. From the first table above, the investor's adjusted basis would be $9,306.13 ($9,771.99 less the $465.86 market discount). Once again, the first $465.86 of the gain is treated as ordinary interest income, but the amount in excess of $9,771.99, that is, $178.01, is treated as long-term capital gain.

Investors may make an election to include market discount as it accrues on bonds and notes other than tax-exempt obligations purchased before May 1, 1993, short-term obligations, U.S. Savings Bonds, or certain obligations arising from installment sales of property.[18] In general, deferring the tax on market discounts until disposition of the bond is preferable. But investors may wish to make the election if they have insufficient investment income to absorb all of their investment interest expense on borrowing to finance their investments. Once an investor makes this election, it applies to all obligations having market discount (other than tax-exempt obligations purchased before May 1, 1993, short-term obligations, certain obligations arising from installment sales of property, or U.S. Savings Bonds)

acquired by the taxpayer in the tax year of the election, and any future years (whether or not using borrowed funds) unless the investor petitions the IRS to revoke the election.[19]

If an investor elects to accrue market discount, the default method is to accrue the discount on a ratable basis. Investors determine the daily accrual under the ratable accrual method by dividing the total market discount on the bond by the number of days after the date of acquisition up to and including the date of maturity. Alternatively, an investor may elect to use the constant yield method, similar to the original issue discount rules, with respect to particular bonds and notes. Once elected, the constant yield election is irrevocable with respect to that particular bond. But investors may use the ratable method with respect to any other market discount bonds, unless they choose separately for each bond to apply the constant yield method.[20]

Premiums

In general, investors recover both original issue and market premiums (amounts paid in excess of the face or redemption value of a bond), as part of their basis in the bond. If the investor sells, redeems, or otherwise disposes of the bond for more (less) than it originally cost the investor, the gain (loss) is treated as long-term or short-term capital gain (loss), depending on the investor's holding period.

Investors are willing to pay premiums for bonds when the interest being paid by the bond is greater than the current market rate of interest on bonds of similar quality and risk. Essentially, investors will bid up the price until the yield to maturity on their investment in the bond equals the market rate. But the premium creates an unfavorable tax-timing and conversion problem. Investors pay tax at their ordinary income tax rates as the interest is paid on the bond but have to wait until they dispose of or redeem the bond to recover their premium. In addition, the gain or loss relative to their cost is capital, not ordinary, in nature. Consequently, if investors hold bonds until maturity and redeem them at par, they will treat the amount of the premium as a long-term capital loss. Instead of offsetting interest income taxable at the investor's ordinary rate, the loss usually will offset capital gains that are generally taxed at a more favorable rate than interest income. Consequently, not only is the recovery of the premium delayed, but investors will typically recover less in taxes than they paid earlier on the portion of the interest payments attributable to the premium.

As a result of this generally adverse tax treatment with respect to premiums, the tax law permits investors to elect to amortize premiums over the remaining life of the bonds (or, in some cases, until an earlier call date).[21] For bonds acquired after December 31, 1987, an electing taxpayer applies the part of the premium attributable to the year as an offset to interest payments received on the bond to which the premium is attributable.[22]

The amount of the bond premium amortizable in any year is determined by the issue date of the bond.

- If the bond was issued before September 28, 1985, taxpayers may use any reasonable method, including the straight line or ratable method.

- If the bond was issued after September 27, 1985, the taxpayers must use the constant yield to maturity method analogous to the OID rules.[23]

Investors must reduce their bases in the bonds by the amount of premium that is applied to reduce interest payments each year.[24]

The election to amortize applies to all taxable bonds that the investor owns at the beginning of the first year to which the election applies and to all bonds acquired thereafter. Investors may revoke the election only with the consent of the IRS.[25]

Although a bondholder can *elect* to amortize premiums on taxable bonds, premiums on tax-exempt bonds *must* be amortized. For tax-exempt bonds acquired on or after March 2, 1998, a bondholder amortizes bond premium under the same rules that apply to taxable bonds. But in the case of tax-exempt bonds, bond premium in excess of qualified stated interest is treated under a separate rule. If the bond premium allocable to an accrual period exceeds the qualified stated interest allocable to the accrual period, the excess is a nondeductible loss.

Short–Sale Rules

Short sales occur when investors agree to sell property they do not own (or own but do not wish to sell). They make this type of sale in two steps.

1. They sell short. They borrow property and deliver it to a buyer.

2. They close the sale. At a later date, they either buy identical property and deliver it to the lender or make delivery out of property that they held at the time of the sale.

Investors do not realize gain or loss until delivery of property to close the short sale. They will have a capital gain or loss if the property used to close the short sale is a capital asset.

Exception if Property Becomes Worthless – A different rule applies if the property sold short becomes substantially worthless. In that case, the investor must recognize gain as if the short sale were closed when the property became substantially worthless.

Exception for Constructive Sales – Entering into a short sale may cause investors to be treated as having made a constructive sale of property. In that case, they will have to recognize gain on the date of the constructive sale. For details, see "Constructive Sale Rules," below.

Short–Term or Long–Term Capital Gain or Loss

As a general rule, investors determine whether they have short-term or long-term capital gain or loss on a short sale by the amount of time they actually hold the property eventually delivered to the lender to close the short sale.

Example: Even though Jim does not own any stock of the Ace Corporation, he contracts to sell 100 shares of it, which he borrows from his broker. After 13 months, when the price of the stock has risen, Jim buys 100 shares of Ace Corporation stock and immediately delivers them to his broker to close out the short sale. His loss is a short-term capital loss because his holding period for the delivered property is less than one day.

Special Rules – Special rules may apply to gains and losses from short sales of stocks, securities, and commodity and securities futures (other than certain straddles) if investors held or acquired property substantially identical to that sold short. But if the amount of property they sold short is more than the amount of that substantially identical property, the special rules do not apply to the gain or loss on the excess.

Gains and Holding Period – If investors held the substantially identical property for 1 year or less on the date of the short sale, or if they acquired the substantially identical property after the short sale and by the date of closing the short sale, then:

Rule 1: Their gain, if any, when they close the short sale is a short-term capital gain, and

Rule 2: The holding period of the substantially identical property begins on the date of the closing of the short sale or on the date of the sale of this property, whichever comes first.

Losses – If, on the date of the short sale, investors held substantially identical property for more than 1 year, any loss they realize on the short sale is a long-term capital loss, even if they held the property used to close the sale for 1 year or less. Certain losses on short sales of stock or securities are also subject to wash-sale treatment. For more information, see "Wash Sale Rules," below.

Mixed Straddles – Under certain elections, investors can avoid the treatment of loss from a short sale as long term under the special rule. These elections are for positions that are part of a mixed straddle. See "Other Elections" under "Mixed Straddles," below, for more information about these elections.

Reporting Substitute Payments

If any broker transferred an investor's securities for use in a short sale, or similar transaction, and received certain substitute dividend payments on the investor's behalf while the short sale was open, that broker must give the investor a Form 1099–MISC or a similar statement, reporting the amount of these payments. Form 1099–MISC must be used for those substitute payments totaling $10 or more that are known on the payment's record date to be in lieu of an exempt-interest dividend, a capital gain dividend, a return of capital distribution, or a dividend subject to a foreign tax credit, or that are in lieu of tax-exempt interest. Investors do not treat these substitute payments as dividends or interest. Instead, they report the substitute payments shown on Form 1099–MISC as "Other income" on line 21 of Form 1040.

Substitute payment – A substitute payment means a payment in lieu of:

1. Tax-exempt interest (including OID) that has accrued while the short sale was open, and

2. A dividend, if the ex-dividend date is after the transfer of stock for use in a short sale and before the closing of the short sale.

Payments in Lieu of Dividends – If investors borrow stock to make a short sale, they may have to remit to the lender payments in lieu of the dividends distributed while they maintain their short position. They can deduct these payments only if they hold the short sale open at least 46 days (more than 1 year in the case of an extraordinary dividend as defined below) and they itemize deductions. They deduct these payments as investment interest on Schedule A (Form 1040).

If investors close the short sale by the 45th day after the date of the short sale (1 year or less in the case of an extraordinary dividend), they cannot deduct the payment in lieu of the dividend that they make to the lender. Instead, they must increase the basis of the stock used to close the short sale by that amount. To determine how long a short sale is kept open, do not include any period during which the investor holds, has an option to buy, or is under a contractual obligation to buy substantially identical stock or securities.

If an investor's payment is made for a liquidating distribution or nontaxable stock distribution, or if he buys more shares equal to a stock distribution issued on the borrowed stock during his short position, the investor has a capital expense. The investor must add the payment to the cost of the stock sold short.

Exception – If investors close the short sale within 45 days, the deduction for amounts they pay in lieu of dividends will be disallowed only to the extent the payments are more than the amount that they receive as ordinary income from the lender of the stock for the use of collateral with the short sale. This exception does not apply to payments in place of extraordinary dividends.

Extraordinary Dividends – If the amount of any dividend investors receive on a share of preferred stock equals or exceeds 5% (10% in the case of other stock) of the amount realized on the short sale, the dividend they receive is an extraordinary dividend.

Wash Sale Rules

Investors cannot deduct losses from sales or trades of stock or securities in a wash sale. A wash sale occurs when investors sell or trade stock or securities at a loss and within 30 days before or after the sale investors

1. buy substantially identical stock or securities,

2. acquire substantially identical stock or securities in a fully taxable trade, or

3. acquire a contract or option to buy substantially identical stock or securities.

If the loss was disallowed because of the wash sale rules, the investor adds the disallowed loss to the cost of the new stock or securities. The result is the investor's basis in the new stock or securities. This adjustment postpones the loss deduction until the disposition of the new stock or securities. The holding period for the new stock or securities begins on the same day as the holding period of the stock or securities sold.

Example: Sue buys 100 shares of X stock for $1,000. She sells these shares for $750 and within 30 days from the sale she buys 100 shares of the same stock for $800. Because Sue bought substantially identical stock, she cannot deduct her loss of $250 on the sale. But she adds the disallowed loss of $250 to the cost of the new stock, $800, to obtain her basis in the new stock, which is $1,050.

Example: Sara is an employee of a corporation that has an incentive pay plan. Under this plan, she is given 10 shares of the corporation's stock as a bonus award. Sara includes the fair market value of the stock in her gross income as additional pay. She later sells these shares at a loss. If she receives another bonus award of substantially identical stock within 30 days of the sale, Sara cannot deduct her loss on the sale.

Options and Futures Contracts

The wash sale rules apply to losses from sales or trades of contracts and options to acquire or sell stock or securities. They do not apply to losses from sales or trades of commodity futures contracts and foreign currencies. See "Coordination of Loss Deferral Rules" and "Wash Sale Rules" under "Straddles," below, for information about the tax treatment of losses on the disposition of positions in a straddle. Losses from the sale, exchange, or termination of a securities future contract to sell generally are treated in the same manner as losses from the closing of a short sale.

Warrants

The wash sale rules apply if investors sell common stock at a loss and, at the same time, buy warrants for common stock of the same corporation. But if investors sell warrants at a loss and, at the same time, buy common stock in the same corporation, the wash sale rules

apply only if the warrants and stock are considered substantially identical.

Substantially Identical

In determining whether stock or securities are substantially identical, investors must consider all the facts and circumstances in their particular case. Ordinarily, stocks or securities of one corporation are not considered substantially identical to stocks or securities of another corporation. But they may be substantially identical in some cases. For example, in reorganization, the stocks and securities of the predecessor and successor corporations may be substantially identical.

Similarly, bonds or preferred stock of a corporation are not ordinarily considered substantially identical to the common stock of the same corporation. But where the bonds or preferred stock are convertible into common stock of the same corporation, the relative values, price changes, and other circumstances may make these bonds or preferred stock and the common stock substantially identical. For example, preferred stock is substantially identical to the common stock if the preferred stock

1. is convertible into common stock,

2. has the same voting rights as the common stock,

3. is subject to the same dividend restrictions,

4. trades at prices that do not vary significantly from the conversion ratio, and

5. is unrestricted as to convertibility.

More or Less Stock Bought than Sold

If the number of shares of substantially identical stock or securities investors buy within 30 days before or after the sale is either more or less than the number of shares they sold, the investors must determine the particular shares to which the wash sale rules apply. Investors do this by matching the shares bought with an equal number of the shares sold. Match the shares bought in the same order that an investor bought them, beginning with the first shares bought. The shares or securities so matched are subject to the wash sale rules.

Example: Joe bought 100 shares of M stock on September 24 for $5,000. On December 21, he bought 50 shares of substantially identical stock for $2,750. On December 28, he bought 25 shares of substantially identical stock for $1,125. On January 4 the following year Joe sold for $4,000 the 100 shares he bought the past September. He has a $1,000 loss on the sale. But because he bought 75 shares of substantially identical stock within 30 days of the sale, he cannot deduct the loss ($750) on 75 shares. Joe can deduct the loss ($250) on the other 25 shares. The basis of the 50 shares bought on the past December 21 is increased by two-thirds (50 ÷ 75) of the $750 disallowed loss. The new basis of those shares is $3,250 ($2,750 + $500). The basis of the 25 shares bought on the past December 28 is increased by the rest of the loss to $1,375 ($1,125 + $250).

Example: John bought 100 shares of M stock on September 24. On February 1 the following year he sold those shares at a $1,000 loss. On each of the 4 days from February 12–15 he bought 50 shares of substantially identical stock. John cannot deduct his $1,000 loss. He must add half the disallowed loss ($500) to the basis of the 50 shares bought on February 12. Add the other half ($500) to the basis of the shares bought on February 13.

Loss and Gain on Same Day

Loss from a wash sale of one block of stock or securities cannot be used to reduce any gains on identical blocks sold the same day.

Example: During 2000, Bill bought 100 shares of X stock on each of three occasions. He paid $158 a share for the first block of 100 shares, $100 a share for the second block, and $95 a share for the third block. On December 23, 2005, Bill sold 300 shares of X stock for $125 a share. On January 6, 2006, he bought 250 shares of identical X stock. He cannot deduct the loss of $33 a share on the first block because within 30 days after the date of sale he bought 250 identical shares of X stock. In addition, Bill cannot reduce the gain realized on the sale of the second and third blocks of stock by this loss.

Dealers

The wash sale rules do not apply to a dealer in stock or securities if the loss is from a transaction made in the ordinary course of business.

Short Sales

The wash sale rules apply to a loss realized on a short sale if investors sell, or enter into another short sale of, substantially identical stock or securities within a period beginning 30 days before the date the short sale is completed and ending 30 days after that date. For purposes of the wash sale rules, a short sale is considered complete on the date the short sale is entered into, if:

1. On that date, an investor owns stock or securities identical to those sold short (or by that date the investor enters into a contract or option to acquire that stock or those securities), and

2. The investor later delivers the stock or securities to close the short sale.

Otherwise, a short sale is not considered complete until the property is delivered to close the sale. This treatment also applies to losses from the sale, exchange, or termination of a security's futures contract to sell.

Example: On June 2, Sonya buys 100 shares of stock for $1,000. She sells short 100 shares of the stock for $750 on October 6. On October 7, she buys 100 shares of the same stock for $750. Sonya closes the short sale on November 17 by delivering the shares bought on June 2. She cannot deduct the $250 loss ($1,000 - $750) because the date of entering into the short sale (October 6) is considered the date the sale is complete for wash sale purposes and she bought substantially identical stock within 30 days from that date.

Residual Interests in a REMIC

The wash sale rules generally will apply to the sale of an investor's residual interest in a real estate mortgage investment conduit (REMIC) if, during the period beginning 6 months before the sale of the interest and ending 6 months after that sale, the investor acquires any residual interest in any REMIC or any interest in a taxable mortgage pool that is comparable to a residual interest.

How to Report

Report a wash sale or trade on line 1 or line 8 of Schedule D (Form 1040), whichever is appropriate. Show the full amount of the loss in parentheses in column (f). On the next line, enter "Wash Sale" in column (a) and the amount of the loss not allowed as a positive amount in column (f).

Constructive-Sale Rules

In 1997 Congress expanded the Internal Revenue Code by adding IRC Section 1259, titled "Constructive Sales Treatment for Appreciated Financial Positions." The section says that when investors enter into certain transactions involving an "appreciated financial position in stock," a partnership interest, or certain debt instruments, they have, in effect, made a sale.

History

In general, a gain or loss is taken into account for tax purposes when realized. A gain or loss generally is realized, with respect to a capital asset, at the time the asset is sold, exchanged, or otherwise disposed of. Investors generally do not have to pay taxes on "paper" gains—they only have to pay taxes when they actually sell a stock and "realize" the gain on the sale.

Prior to the Taxpayer Relief Act of 1997, transactions designed to reduce or eliminate risk of loss on stock or financial assets generally did not cause income realization. For example, a taxpayer could lock in gains on securities by entering into a "short sale against the box" (i.e., when the taxpayer owns securities that are the same as, or substantially identical to, securities borrowed and sold short).

Example: Frank owns 1,000 shares of XYZ stock, with a cost basis of $30/share. The shares are now trading for $90 a share. Frank would like to lock in his gains on this stock, but does not really want to sell the shares and face a large tax liability. So, instead of selling, Frank goes "short" on 1,000 shares of XYZ. Since Frank has not sold the original stock, he pays no taxes on his "paper" gain since the gain is not yet "realized" by sale or other disposition.

By executing the "short sale against the box," Frank has taken virtually all of his cash out of the stock (via the short sale), but is now protected against any future

losses on the shares. If the stock goes up, his "long" position increases, but his "short" position decreases. If the stock goes down, his "long" position increases, but his "short" position decreases. So Frank has, in effect, locked in his gain and received his cash without selling any of the shares or creating a taxable transaction. Of course, Frank will have to cover the short position sometime in the future, but he may be able to manipulate his finances in such a way that the future gain will have less tax impact (such as being used to offset a substantial capital loss in the future). This is an example of a "short sale against the box."

Under prior law, the form of the transaction was respected for income tax purposes, and the investor was not required to recognize any gains on the substantially identical property at the time of the short sale. Pursuant to rules that allowed specific identification of securities delivered on a sale, Frank could obtain open transaction treatment by identifying the borrowed securities as the securities delivered. When it was time to close out the borrowing, the taxpayer could choose to deliver either the securities held or newly purchased securities. The Code only provided rules to prevent investors from using short sales against the box to accelerate losses or to convert short-term capital gains into long-term capital gains, or long-term capital losses into short-term capital losses.

In addition, under prior law, investors could also lock in gains on certain property by entering into offsetting positions in the same or similar property. Under the straddle rules, when investors realized a loss on one offsetting position in actively traded personal property, they generally could deduct this loss only to the extent that the loss exceeded the unrecognized gain in the other positions in the straddle. In other words, investors were prevented from taking losses equal to the gains in the offsetting straddle positions, but they were not forced to realize the gains until they closed out the offsetting positions. In addition, rules similar to the short-sale rules prevented investors from changing the tax characteristics of gains and losses recognized on the offsetting positions in a straddle.

In other words, under prior law, investors could employ methods that would allow them to lock in gains on, and hedge the risk in, a financial position without actually selling the position.

Current Tax Law

Investors are treated as having made a constructive sale when they enter into certain transactions involving an appreciated financial position (defined later) in stock, a partnership interest, or certain debt instruments. Investors must recognize gain as if the position were disposed of at its fair market value on the date of the constructive sale. This gives them a new holding period for the position that begins on the date of the constructive sale. Then, when investors close the transaction, they reduce their gain (or increase their loss) by the gain recognized on the constructive sale.

Constructive Sales

Investors are treated as having made a constructive sale of an appreciated financial position if they

1. enter into a short sale of the same or substantially identical property;

2. enter into an offsetting notional principal contract relating to the same or substantially identical property;

3. enter into a futures or forward contract to deliver the same or substantially identical property (including a forward contract that provides for cash settlement); or

4. acquire the same or substantially identical property (if the appreciated financial position is a short sale, an offsetting notional principal contract, or a futures or forward contract).

Related Parties

Investors are also treated as having made a constructive sale of an appreciated financial position if a person related to them enters into a transaction described above with a view toward avoiding the constructive sale treatment. Related parties include

1. Members of the investor's family. This includes only brothers and sisters, half-brothers and half-sisters, spouse, ancestors (parents, grandparents, etc.), and lineal descendants (children, grandchildren, etc.).

2. A partnership in which an investor directly or indirectly owns more than 50% of the capital interest or the profits interest.

3. A corporation in which an investor directly or indirectly owns more than 50% in value of the outstanding stock.

4. A tax-exempt charitable or educational organization that is directly or indirectly controlled, in any manner or by any method, by the investor or by a member of the investor's family, whether or not this control is legally enforceable.

Example: On May 1, April bought 100 shares of ABC Corporation stock for $1,000. On September 3, she sold short 100 shares of ABC stock for $1,600 (the classic "short against the box"). She made no other transactions involving ABC stock for the rest of the year and the first 30 days of the following year (we'll discuss the importance of this statement a bit later). April's short sale is treated as a constructive sale of an appreciated financial position because a sale of her ABC stock on the date of the short sale would have resulted in a gain. Therefore, she is required to recognize a $600 short-term capital gain from the constructive sale for the tax year in which the sale took place. In addition, she is required to begin a new holding period in her ABC stock that starts on September 3 and her basis in these ABC shares would be increased to $1,600.

Example: On January 10, Ian "shorts" 200 shares of XYZ Corporation stock for $5,000. On August 15 of the same year, he "goes long" 200 shares of XYZ stock for $3,500. Ian made no other transactions in XYZ stock for the rest of the year, and the first 30 days of the following year (again, the relevance of this statement will be discussed later). His "long" position will be treated as a constructive sale, and he will be required to recognize a short-term gain in the amount of $1,500 for the tax year in which the constructive sale took place. The new holding period for his short position will begin August 15, and his new basis for his short position will be $3,500.

The objective of this second example is to show that the rules work either way. An appreciated financial position could be a "long" position or a "short" position.

Exception for Nonmarketable Securities

A contract for sale of any stock, debt instrument, or partnership interest that is not a marketable security is not a constructive sale if it settles within 1 year of the date an investor enter into it.

Exception for Certain Closed Transactions

Transactions in which all of the following conditions are true are not treated as a constructive sale:

1. An investor closed the transaction before the end of the 30th day after the end of his tax year.

2. An investor held the appreciated financial position throughout the 60-day period beginning on the date he closed the transaction.

3. An investor's risk of loss was not reduced at any time during that 60-day period by holding certain other positions.

If a closed transaction is reestablished in a substantially similar position during the 60-day period beginning on the date the first transaction was closed, this exception still applies if the reestablished position is closed before the end of the 30th day after the end of the investor's tax year in which the first transaction was closed and, after that closing, (2) and (3) above are true.

In other words, investors are required to ignore the constructive sale rules if they close the offsetting position prior to January 30th of the following tax year, and they retain their original position for at least 60 days after closing the offsetting position. In addition, they are prohibited from entering into any other type of offsetting position for that same 60-day period.

The examples above included the statement the investor "made no other transactions in the stock for the rest of the year and the first 30 days of the following year." As a result of the closed-transaction rules it may be possible with the proper moves for investors to overcome the constructive sale rules. (See Chapter 41, "Hedging and Option Strategies," for a discussion of these techniques.)

Appreciated Financial Position

This is any interest in stock, a partnership interest, or a debt instrument (including a futures or forward contract, a short sale, or an option) if disposing of the interest would result in a gain. But an appreciated financial position does not include the following:

1. Any position from which all of the appreciation is accounted for under mark to market rules, including IRC Section 1256 contracts (regulated futures contract, foreign currency contract, nonequity option, dealer equity option, or dealer securities futures contract).

2. Any position in a debt instrument if

    a) The position unconditionally entitles the holder to receive a specified principal amount,

    b) The interest payments (or other similar amounts) with respect to the position are payable at a fixed rate or a variable rate described in Treasury Section 1.860G–1(a)(3) of the regulations, and

    c) The position is not convertible, either directly or indirectly, into stock of the issuer (or any related person).

3. Any hedge with respect to a position described in (2).

Certain Trust Instruments Treated as Stock

For the constructive sale rules, an interest in an actively traded trust is treated as stock unless substantially all of the value of the property held by the trust is debt that qualifies for the exception to the definition of an appreciated financial position (explained in (2) above).

Sale of Appreciated Financial Position

A transaction treated as a constructive sale of an appreciated financial position is not treated as a constructive sale of any other appreciated financial position, as long as an investor continues to hold the original position. But if an investor holds another appreciated financial position and disposes of the original position before closing the transaction that resulted in the constructive sale, the investor is treated as if, at the same time, he constructively sold the other appreciated financial position.

Straddle Rules

A straddle is any set of offsetting positions on personal property. For example, a straddle may consist of a purchased option to buy and a purchased option to sell on the same number of shares of the security, with the same exercise price and period.

Personal Property – This is any property of a type that is actively traded. It includes stock options and contracts to buy stock, but generally does not include stock.

Straddle Rules for Stock – Although stock is generally excluded from the definition of personal property when applying the straddle rules, it is included in the following two situations:

1. The stock is part of a straddle in which at least one of the offsetting positions is

   a) an option to buy or sell the stock or substantially identical stock or securities,

   b) a securities futures contract on the stock or substantially identical stock or securities, or

   c) a position on substantially similar or related property (other than stock).

2. The stock is in a corporation formed or availed of to take positions in personal property that offset positions taken by any shareholder.

Position – A position is an interest in personal property. A position can be a forward or futures contract, or an option. An interest in a loan that is denominated in a foreign currency is treated as a position in that currency. For the straddle rules, foreign currency for which there is an active interbank market is considered to be actively traded personal property.

Offsetting Position – This is a position that substantially reduces any risk of loss investors may have from holding another position. But if a position is part of a straddle that is not an identified straddle (described later), they do not treat it as offsetting to a position that is part of an identified straddle.

Presumed Offsetting Positions – Two or more positions will be presumed to be offsetting if

1. the positions are established in the same personal property (or in a contract for this property), and the value of one or more positions varies inversely with the value of one or more of the other positions;

2. the positions are in the same personal property, even if this property is in a substantially changed form, and the positions' values vary inversely as described in the first condition;

3. the positions are in debt instruments with a similar maturity, and the positions' values vary inversely as described in the first condition;

4. the positions are sold or marketed as offsetting positions, whether or not the positions are called a straddle, spread, butterfly, or any similar name; or

5. the aggregate margin requirement for the positions is lower than the sum of the margin requirements for each position if held separately.

Related Persons – To determine if two or more positions are offsetting, investors will be treated as holding any position that their spouses hold during the same period. If investors take into account part or all of the gain or loss for a position held by a flow-through entity, such as a partnership or trust, they are also considered to hold that position.

Loss Deferral Rules

Generally, investors can deduct a loss on the disposition of one or more positions only to the extent that the loss is more than any unrecognized gain on offsetting positions. Unused losses are treated as sustained in the next tax year.

Unrecognized Gain – This is

1. the amount of gain investors would have had on an open position if they had sold it on the last business day of the tax year at its fair market value, and

2. the amount of gain realized on a position if, as of the end of the tax year, gain as been realized, but not recognized.

Example: On July 1 Dave entered into a straddle. On December 16 he closed one position of the straddle at a loss of $15,000. On December 31 the end of his tax year, Dave has an unrecognized gain of $12,750 in the offsetting open position. On his return for the year, his deductible loss on the position he closed is limited to $2,250 ($15,000 - $12,750). He must carry forward to the following year the unused loss of $12,750.

Exceptions – The loss deferral rules do not apply to

1. a straddle that is an identified straddle at the end of the tax year,

Chapter 43 – Taxation Of Investment Vehicles

2. certain straddles consisting of qualified covered call options and the stock to be purchased under the options,

3. hedging transactions, and

4. straddles consisting entirely of IRC Section 1256 contracts (but see "Identified Straddle," next).

Identified Straddle – Losses from positions in an identified straddle are deferred until investors dispose of all the positions in the straddle. Any straddle (other than a straddle described in (2) or (3) above) is an identified straddle if all of the following conditions exist:

1. Investors clearly identified the straddle on their records before the close of the day on which they acquired it.

2. All of the original positions that investors identify were acquired on the same day.

3. All of the positions included in item (2) were disposed of on the same day during the tax year, or none of the positions were disposed of by the end of the tax year.

4. The straddle is not part of a larger straddle.

Qualified Covered Call Options and Optioned Stock – A straddle is not subject to the loss deferral rules for straddles if *both* of the following are true:

1. All of the offsetting positions consist of one or more qualified covered call options and the stock to be purchased from the investor under the options.

2. The straddle is not part of a larger straddle. But see "Special Year-End Rule," later, for an exception.

Qualified covered call options are any options investors grant to purchase stock they hold (or stock they acquire in connection with granting the option), but only if all of the following are true:

1. The option is traded on a national securities exchange or other market approved by the Secretary of the Treasury.

2. The option is granted more than 30 days before its expiration date.

3. The option is not a deep-in-the-money option.

4. The investor is not an options dealer who granted the option in connection with his activity of dealing in options.

5. Gain or loss on the option is capital gain or loss.

A deep-in-the-money option is an option with a strike price lower than the lowest qualified benchmark (LQB). The strike price is the price at which the option is to be exercised. The LQB is the highest available strike price that is less than the applicable stock price. But the LQB for an option with a term of more than 90 days and a strike price of more than $50 is the second highest available strike price that is less than the applicable stock price. Strike prices are listed in the financial section of many newspapers.

The availability of strike prices for equity options with flexible terms does not affect the determination of the LQB for an option that is not an equity option with flexible terms.

The applicable stock price for any stock for which an option has been granted is

1. the closing price of the stock on the most recent day on which that stock was traded offset before the date on which the option was granted, or

2. the opening price of the stock on the day on which the option was granted, but only if that price is greater than 110% of the price determined in (1).

If the applicable stock price is $25 or less, the LQB will be treated as not less than 85% of the applicable stock price. If the applicable stock price is $150 or less, the LQB will be treated as not less than an amount that is $10 below the applicable stock price.

Example: On May 13 Andy held XYZ stock and he wrote an XYZ/September call option with a strike price of $120. The closing price of one share of XYZ stock on May 12 was $130.25. The strike prices of all XYZ/ September call options offered on May 13 were as follows: $110, $115, $120, $125, $130, and $135. Because the option has a term of more than 90 days, the LQB is $125, the second highest strike price that is less than $130.25, the applicable stock price. The call option is a deep-in-the-money option because its strike price is lower than the LQB.

Tools & Techniques of Investment Planning

457

Therefore, the option is not a qualified covered call option, and the loss deferral rules apply if Andy closed out the option or the stock at a loss during the year.

Capital Loss on Qualified Covered Call Option – If investors hold stock and they write a qualified covered call option on that stock with a strike price less than the applicable stock price, they treat any loss from the option as long-term capital loss if, at the time the loss was realized, gain on the sale or exchange of the stock would be treated as long-term capital gain. The holding period of the stock does not include any period during which the investors are the writers of the option.

Special Year-End Rule – The loss deferral rules for straddles apply if all of the following are true:

1. The qualified covered call options are closed or the stock is disposed of at a loss during any tax year.

2. Gain on disposition of the stock or gain on the options is includable in gross income in a later tax year.

3. The stock or options were held less than 30 days after the closing of the options or the disposition of the stock.

How to Report Gains and Losses (Form 6781)

Investors report each position (whether or not it is part of a straddle) on which they have unrecognized gain at the end of the tax year and the amount of this unrecognized gain in Part III of Form 6781. They use Part II of Form 6781 to figure their gains and losses before entering these amounts on Schedule D (Form 1040). They should include a copy of Form 6781 with their income tax return.

Coordination of Loss Deferral Rules and Wash Sale Rules

Rules similar to the wash sale rules apply to any disposition of a position or positions of a straddle. The rules work as follows. First apply Rule 1, explained next, and then apply Rule 2. But Rule 1 applies only if stocks or securities make up a position that is part of the straddle. If a position in the straddle does not include stock or securities, use Rule 2.

Rule 1 – Investors cannot deduct a loss on the disposition of shares of stock or securities that make up the positions of a straddle if, within a period beginning 30 days before the date of that disposition and ending 30 days after that date, they acquired substantially identical stock or securities. Instead, the loss will be carried over to the following tax year, subject to any further application of Rule 1 in that year. This rule will also apply if they entered into a contract or option to acquire the stock or securities within the time period described above. See "Loss Carryover," later, for more information about how to treat the loss in the following tax year.

Dealers – For dealers in stock or securities, this loss treatment will not apply to any losses they sustained in the ordinary course of their business.

Example: Bruce is not a dealer in stock or securities. On December 2 he bought stock in XX Corporation (XX stock) and an offsetting put option. On December 13 there was $20 of unrealized gain in the put option and he sold the XX stock at a $20 loss. By December 16, the value of the put option had declined, eliminating all unrealized gain in the position. On December 16, Bruce bought a second XX stock position that is substantially identical to the XX stock he sold on December 13. At the end of the year there is no unrecognized gain in the put option or in the XX stock. Under these circumstances, the $20 loss will be disallowed for the current tax year under Rule 1 because, within a period beginning 30 days before December 13, and ending 30 days after that date, Bruce bought stock substantially identical to the XX stock he sold.

Rule 2 – Investors cannot deduct a loss on the disposition of less than all of the positions of a straddle (their loss position) to the extent that any unrecognized gain at the close of the tax year in one or more of the following positions is more than the amount of any loss disallowed under Rule 1:

1. successor positions,

2. offsetting positions to the loss position, or

3. offsetting positions to any successor position.

Successor Position – A successor position is a position that is or was at any time offsetting to a second position, if both of the following conditions are met:

Chapter 43 – Taxation Of Investment Vehicles

1. The second position was offsetting to the loss position that was sold.

2. The successor position is entered into during a period beginning 30 days before, and ending 30 days after, the sale of the loss position.

Example: On November 1 Connie entered into offsetting long and short positions in non-IRC Section 1256 contracts. On November 12 she disposed of the long position at a $10 loss. On November 14, she entered into a new long position (successor position) that is offsetting to the retained short position, but that is not substantially identical to the long position disposed of on November 12. Connie held both positions through year-end, at which time there was $10 of unrecognized gain in the successor long position and no unrecognized gain in the offsetting short position. Under these circumstances, the entire $10 loss will be disallowed for the current tax year because there is $10 of unrecognized gain in the successor long position.

Example: The facts are the same as in the previous example, except that at year end Connie has $4 of unrecognized gain in the successor long position and $6 of unrecognized gain in the offsetting short position. Under these circumstances, the entire $10 loss will be disallowed for the current tax year because there is a total of $10 of unrecognized gain in the successor long position and offsetting short position.

Example: The facts are the same as in the first example above, except that at year end Connie has $8 of unrecognized gain in the successor long position and $8 of unrecognized loss in the offsetting short position. Under these circumstances, $8 of the total $10 realized loss would be disallowed for current tax year because there is $8 of unrecognized gain in the successor long position.

Loss Carryover – If investors have a disallowed loss that resulted from applying Rule 1 and Rule 2, they must carry it over to the next tax year and apply Rule 1 and Rule 2 to that carryover loss. For example, a loss disallowed in 2007 under Rule 1 will not be allowed in 2008, unless the substantially identical stock or securities (which caused

the loss to be disallowed in 2007) were disposed of during 2008. In addition, the carryover loss will not be allowed in 2008 if Rule 1 or Rule 2 disallows it.

Example: The facts are the same as in the example under Rule 1 above. On December 31 Connie sells the second XX stock at a $20 loss and there is $40 of unrecognized gain in the put option. Under these circumstances, she cannot deduct for that tax year either the $20 loss disallowed in that tax year or the $20 loss she incurred for the December 31 sale of XX stock. Rule 1 does not apply because the substantially identical XX stock was sold during the year and no substantially identical stock or securities were bought within the 61-day period. But Rule 2 does apply because there is $40 of unrecognized gain in the put option, an offsetting position to the loss positions.

Capital Loss Carryover – If the sale of a loss position would have resulted in a capital loss, investors treat the carryover loss as a capital loss on the date it is allowed, even if they would treat the gain or loss on any successor positions as ordinary income or loss. Likewise, if the sale of a loss position (in the case of IRC Section 1256 contracts) would have resulted in a 60% long-term capital loss and a 40% short-term capital loss, investors treat the carryover loss under the 60/40 rule, even if they would treat any gain or loss on any successor positions as 100% long-term or short-term capital gain or loss.

Exceptions – The rules for coordinating straddle losses and wash sales do not apply to the following loss situations:

1. loss on the sale of one or more positions in a hedging transaction,

2. loss on the sale of a loss position in a mixed straddle account—see the discussion later on the mixed straddle account election,

3. loss on the sale of a position that is part of a straddle consisting only of IRC Section 1256 contracts.

Holding Period and Loss Treatment Rules

The holding period of a position in a straddle generally begins no earlier than the date on which the straddle ends

459

Tools & Techniques of Investment Planning

(the date investors no longer hold an offsetting position). This rule does not apply to any position investors held more than 1 year before they established the straddle. But see Exceptions, later.

Example: On March 6, 2005, Patti acquired gold. On January 4, 2006, she entered into an offsetting short gold forward contract (nonregulated futures contract). On April 1, 2006, she disposed of the short gold forward contract at no gain or loss. On April 8, 2006, she sold the gold for a gain. Because the gold had been held for 1 year or less before the offsetting short position was entered into, the holding period for the gold begins on April 1, 2006, the date the straddle ended. Gain recognized on the sale of the gold will be treated as short-term capital gain.

Loss Treatment – Treat the loss on the sale of one or more positions (the loss position) of a straddle as a long-term capital loss if both of the following are true:

1. Investors held (directly or indirectly) one or more offsetting positions to the loss position on the date they entered into the loss position.

2. Investors would have treated all gain or loss on one or more of the straddle positions as long-term capital gain or loss if they had sold these positions on the day they entered into the loss position.

Exceptions – The special holding period and loss treatment for straddle positions does not apply to positions that

1. constitute part of a hedging transaction,

2. are included in a straddle consisting only of IRC Section 1256 contracts, or

3. are included in a mixed straddle account (Election C), discussed later.

Mixed Straddles – Special rules apply to a loss position that is part of a mixed straddle and that is a non-IRC Section 1256 position. A mixed straddle is a straddle

1. that is not part of a larger straddle,

2. in which all positions are held as capital assets,

3. in which at least one (but not all) of the positions is an IRC Section 1256 contract, and

4. for which the mixed straddle election (Election A, discussed later) has not been made.

Investors treat the loss as 60% long-term capital loss and 40% short-term capital loss, if all of the following conditions apply:

1. Gain or loss from the sale of one or more of the straddle positions that are IRC Section 1256 contracts would be considered gain or loss from the sale or exchange of a capital asset.

2. The sale of no position in the straddle, other than an IRC Section 1256 contract, would result in a long-term capital gain or loss.

3. The investor has not made a straddle-by-straddle identification election (Election B) or mixed straddle account election (Election C), both discussed later.

Example: On March 1 Diana entered into a long gold forward contract. On July 15 she entered into an offsetting short gold regulated futures contract. She did not make an election to offset gains and losses from positions in a mixed straddle. On August 9 Diana disposed of the long forward contract at a loss. Because the gold forward contract was part of a mixed straddle and the disposition of this non-IRC Section 1256 position would not result in long-term capital loss, the loss recognized on the termination of the gold forward contract would be treated as a 60% long-term and 40% short-term capital loss.

Mixed Straddles

If investors disposed of a position in a mixed straddle and made one of the elections described in the following discussions, they report their gain or loss as indicated in those discussions. If investors do not make any of the elections, they report their gain or loss in Part II of Form 6781. If they disposed of the IRC Section 1256 component of the straddle, they enter the recognized loss (line 10, column (h)) or their gain (line 12, column (f)) in Part I of Form 6781, on line 1. They do not include it on line 11 or 13 (Part II).

Mixed Straddle Election (Election A) – Investors can elect out of the marked to market rules for all IRC Section 1256 contracts that are part of a mixed straddle. Instead, the gain and loss rules for straddles will apply to these contracts. But if they make this election for an option on an IRC Section 1256 contract, the gain or loss treatment discussed earlier under "Options" will apply, subject to the gain and loss rules for straddles.

Investors can make this election if

1. at least one (but not all) of the positions is an IRC Section 1256 contract, and

2. each position forming part of the straddle is clearly identified as being part of that straddle on the day the first IRC Section 1256 contract forming part of the straddle is acquired.

If investors make this election, it will apply for all later years as well. It cannot be revoked without the consent of the IRS. If they made this election, they should check box A of Form 6781. They do not report the IRC Section 1256 component in Part I.

Other Elections – Investors can avoid the 60% long-term capital loss treatment required for a non-IRC Section 1256 loss position that is part of a mixed straddle, described earlier, if they choose either of the two following elections to offset gains and losses for these positions:

1. *Election B* – Make a separate identification of the positions of each mixed straddle for which they are electing this treatment (the straddle-by-straddle identification method).

2. *Election C* – Establish a mixed straddle account for a class of activities for which gains and losses will be recognized and offset on a periodic basis.

These two elections are alternatives to the mixed straddle election. Investors can choose only one of the three elections. They use Form 6781 to indicate their election choice by checking box A, B, or C, whichever applies.

Straddle-by-Straddle Identification Election (Election B) – Under this election, investors must clearly identify each position that is part of the identified mixed straddle by the earlier of

1. the close of the day the identified mixed straddle is established, or

2. the time the position is disposed of.

If investors dispose of a position in the mixed straddle before the end of the day on which the straddle is established, this identification must be made by the time they dispose of the position. Investors are presumed to have properly identified a mixed straddle if independent verification is used.

The basic tax treatment of gain or loss under this election depends on which side of the straddle produced the total net gain or loss. If the net gain or loss from the straddle is due to the IRC Section 1256 contracts, gain or loss is treated as 60% long-term capital gain or loss and 40% short-term capital gain or loss. Investors enter the net gain or loss in Part I of Form 6781 and identify the election by checking box B.

If the net gain or loss is due to the non-IRC Section 1256 positions, gain or loss is short-term capital gain or loss. Investors enter the net gain or loss on Part I of Schedule D and identify the election.

For the specific application of the rules of this election, see Treasury Regulation Section 1.1092(b)-T.

Example: On April 1, Jackie entered into a non-IRC Section 1256 position and an offsetting IRC Section 1256 contract. She also made a valid election to treat this straddle as an identified mixed straddle. On April 8, she disposed of the non-IRC Section 1256 position at a $600 loss and the IRC Section 1256 contract at an $800 gain. Under these circumstances, the $600 loss on the non-IRC Section 1256 position will be offset against the $800 gain on the IRC Section 1256 contract. The net gain of $200 from the straddle will be treated as 60% long-term capital gain and 40% short-term capital gain because it is due to the IRC Section 1256 contract.

Mixed Straddle Account (Election C) – Investors may elect to establish one or more accounts for determining gains and losses from all positions in a mixed straddle. They must establish a separate mixed straddle account for each separate designated class of activities.

Generally, investors must determine gain or loss for each position in a mixed straddle account as of the close of each business day of the tax year. They offset the net IRC Section 1256 contracts against the net non-IRC Section 1256 positions to determine the "daily account net gain or loss." If the daily account amount is due to non-IRC Section 1256 positions, the amount is treated as short-term capital gain or loss. If the daily account amount is due to IRC Section 1256 contracts, the amount gain or loss is treated as 60% long-term and 40% short-term capital gain or loss. On the last business day of the tax year, investors determine the "annual account net gain or loss" for each account by netting the daily account amounts for that account for the tax year. The "total annual account net gain or loss" is determined by netting the annual account amounts for all mixed straddle accounts that they had established.

The net amounts keep their long-term or short-term classification. But no more than 50% of the total annual account net gain for the tax year can be treated as long-term capital gain. Any remaining gain is treated as short-term capital gain. Also, no more than 40% of the total annual account net loss can be treated as short-term capital loss. Any remaining loss is treated as long-term capital loss.

The election to establish one or more mixed straddle accounts for each tax year must be made by the due date (without extensions) of the investor's income tax return for the immediately preceding tax year. If investors begin trading in a new class of activities during a tax year, they must make the election for the new class of activities by the later of either

1. the due date of their return for the immediately preceding tax year (without extensions), or

2. 60 days after they entered into the first mixed straddle in the new class of activities.

Investors make the election on Form 6781 by checking box C and then attach Form 6781 to their income tax return for the immediately preceding tax year, or file it within 60 days, if that applies. They should report the annual account net gain or loss from a mixed straddle account in Part II of Form 6781. In addition, they must attach a statement to Form 6781 specifically designating the class of activities for which a mixed straddle account is established.

For the specific application of the rules of this election, see Treasury Regulation Section 1.1092(b)-4T.

Interest Expense and Carrying Charges Relating to Mixed Straddle Account Positions – Investors cannot deduct interest and carrying charges that are allocable to any positions held in a mixed straddle account. They should treat these charges as an adjustment to the annual account net gain or loss and allocate them proportionately between the net short-term and the net long-term capital gains or losses.

CHAPTER ENDNOTES

1. The Tax Increase Prevention and Reconciliation Act of 2005 (TIPRA) extends the sunset provisions of JGTRRA 2003 by two years. JGTRRA 2003 originally repealed IRC Secs. 1(h)(2), 1(h)(9). When the 5%/15% rates "sunset" after 2010, the 8%/18% rates will, once again, be effective. JGTRRA 2003, Sec. 107 as modified by TIPRA 2005.

2. The reduction in rates for dividends does not apply to corporate taxpayers. As under prior law, corporations will generally be entitled to a dividends received deduction of 70% or more of qualifying dividend income.

3. IRC Sec. 1(h)(11).

4. See Ann. 2004-11 2004-10 IRB 581; IRS News Release IR-2004-22 (2-19-2004). See also the 2003 edition of Publication 550 (Investment Income and Expenses), pp. 2, 19-20, at: www.irs.gov.

5. Available data indicates that in 2003, about one third of REIT dividends qualified for the lower 15% tax rate. National Association of Real Estate Investment Trusts, *REITs and the New Tax Law: Questions and Answers*, at: www.nareit.com.

6. National Association of Real Estate Investment Trusts, *REITs and the New Tax Law: Questions and Answers*, at: www.nareit.com.

7. $87,500 for married taxpayers filing separately.

8. TIPRA 2006 modified the kiddie tax to set the age limitation at minors under the age of 18; however, it will not apply if such minor is married and files a joint return. Some relief is available for beneficiaries of qualified disability trusts, as such income distributions to a minor are recharacterized for this purpose as earned income regardless of the actual character of the income.

9. The discussion addresses the discount and premium rules for debt instruments with a fixed stated rate. For rules applying to variable rate debt instruments and debt instruments that provide for contingent payments, see Treas. Reg. §1.1272-1(b)(2).

10. IRC Sec. 1273(a). For example, a corporation could issue a 20-year bond with a $10,000 par or redemption value at a price as low as $9,500 and buyers could ignore the discount. ($10,000 x 0.0025 = $25; $25 x 20 years = $500).

11. Similar rules apply to tax-exempt municipal bonds with original issue discount with respect to the accrual of OID and adjustment of basis. But the OID accruing each period is tax exempt, just like the cash interest payments.

12. Treas. Reg. §1.1272-1(b)(1).

13. *Gaffney v. Comm*, TC Memo 1997-249.

14. Gain on the sale, exchange, or retirement of a bond is treated as ordinary income to the extent of unaccrued original issue discount if at the time of original issue there existed an intention to call the bond prior to maturity. According to final regulations, an intention to call exists only if there is an agreement not provided for in the debt instrument that the issuer will redeem the instrument prior to maturity. Treas. Reg. §1.1271-1(a)(1). This rule is not applicable to publicly offered bonds. Treas. Reg. §1.1271-1(a)(i).

15. IRC Sec. 1278(a)(2).

16. IRC Sec. 1278(a)(2)(B).

17. IRC Sec. 1278(a)(2)(C).

18. IRC Sec. 1278(b).

19. IRC Sec. 1278(b)(3).

20. IRC Sec. 1276(b)(2).

21. IRC Sec. 171.

22. IRC Sec. 171(e). Prior to this, amortized premiums were deductions, not offsets.

23. IRC Sec. 171(b)(3).

24. IRC Sec. 1016(a)(5); Treas. Reg. §1.1016-5(b).

25. IRC Sec. 171(c)(2); Treas. Reg. §1.171-4.

Chapter 44

TAX–EFFICIENT INVESTMENT STRATEGIES

The following tax-efficient investment strategies are discussed here: comparing investments with taxable and tax-free yields; comparing investments with ordinary income, capital gain, and/or qualified dividends; controlling the timing of recognition of capital gain or loss; and tax considerations in selecting mutual funds.

For more on the taxation of investments, see Chapter 43, "Taxation of Investment Vehicles." Investment strategies for tax-advantaged accounts are discussed in Chapter 45.

TAX EXEMPT EQUIVALENT (TAXABLE EQUIVALENT YIELD)

Some bonds are taxable while others are not. It is useful to convert a taxable yield to an after-tax yield, and to convert a tax exempt yield to a taxable equivalent yield (or tax exempt equivalent). Then comparisons can be made between taxable and nontaxable yields on an equivalent basis.

Since most bonds (other than municipal bonds) are subject to federal income tax, it is useful to express these yields on an after-tax basis:

After Tax Yield = Before Tax Yield x (1 – Tax Rate)

If the expected semi-annual yield-to-maturity is 3.5% and the tax rate is 25%, the after-tax yield would be 2.625% on a semi-annual basis [3.5% x (1 - 25%) = 2.625%].

In the case of a non-taxable bond (municipal bond), the process can be reversed to determine the tax exempt equivalent (or taxable equivalent yield) of a tax exempt bond:

Tax Exempt Equivalent =
Tax Exempt Yield ÷ (1 – Tax Rate)

If the expected semi-annual yield-to-maturity is 2.625% and the tax rate is 25%, the tax exempt equivalent (or taxable equivalent yield) would be 3.5% on a semi-annual basis [2.625% ÷ (1 - 25%) = 3.5%].

Appendix G contains tables for tax exempt equivalents. For example, if the tax exempt yield is 3.00% and the tax rate is 20%, then the tax exempt equivalent (or taxable equivalent yield) from the table is 3.75%. This is verified by using the formula above: 3.00% ÷ (1 - 20%) = 3.75%.

Conversely, if the taxable yield is 3.75% and the tax rate is 20%, then the after-tax yield (the tax exempt yield) from the table is 3.00%. This is verified by using the formula above: 3.75% x (1 - 20%) = 3.00%.

Example. Two bonds are available for investment. The tax rate is 20%. The first bond is taxable and has a yield of 5.31%. The second bond is nontaxable and has a yield of 4%. The after-tax yield of 5.31% is 4.25% (the tax exempt yield), which is greater than 4%. Therefore, looking only at yield, the first bond is preferable. Other factors, such as risk, should also be taken into consideration.

Measuring yield is discussed in detail in Chapter 34.

ORDINARY INCOME, CAPITAL GAIN, AND QUALIFIED DIVIDENDS

Favorable tax rates exist for capital gains and qualified dividends. Capital gain and qualified dividends are generally taxed at a maximum rate of 15%. On the other hand, ordinary income is currently taxed at a maximum rate of 35%. In addition, the taxation of capital appreciation of property can generally be postponed until the property is sold. (For more on the taxation of ordinary income, capital gain, and qualified dividends, see Chapter 43, "Taxation of Investment Vehicles.") Favorable tax rates and tax deferral generally improve the after tax bottom line.

If $1,000 is placed in a tax-free investment and grows at 5% for 20 years, the future value of the investment is:

$$FV = PV \times (1 + r)^n$$

$$FV = \$1,000 \times (1 + .05)^{20} = \$2,653$$

If $1,000 is placed in an investment that has annual income of 5% and is taxed at an ordinary income tax rate of 28%, the future value of the investment in 20 years is:

$$FV = PV \times (1 + (r \times (1 - t_d))$$

$$FV = \$1{,}000 \times (1 + (.05 \times (1 - .28))^{20} = \$2{,}029$$

This is less than with the tax-free investment. For comparison purposes, a 5% income or growth rate has been used for each investment; however, a taxable investment will generally have a higher rate of return than a tax-free investment.

The following formula from Appendix K can be used to calculate the future value of an investment where part of the returns will be taxed currently as ordinary income or qualified dividends and part will be taxed on distribution as capital gains:

FVat4

$$FV = PV \times \left[(1 + ar)^n - t_d \times \left(g \times r \times \left(\frac{(1 + ar)^n - 1}{ar} \right) + b \right) \right],$$
if $ar \neq 0$

$$FV = PV \times (1 - t_d \times b), \text{ if } ar = 0$$

where: ar = The accumulation rate after tax on the currently taxable component of return (usually ordinary income), but before tax on the accumulating and tax-deferred capital gains or tax-deferred income component of return

 = $(g \times r) + ((1 - t_o) \times (1 - g) \times r)$

 = $r \times [1 - \{(1 - g) \times t_o\}]$

r = The total before-tax rate of return

g = The proportion of total before-tax return, r, attributable to tax-deferred capital gain (or tax-deferred income)

t_o = The tax rate on the currently taxable ordinary income component of return

t_d = The tax rate on the long-term capital gain (or the tax-deferred) component of investment return

b = The built-in gain or tax-deferred return proportion of the investment, PV, or the periodic payment, Pmt, if any

n = Years until distribution

For example, assume the investment grows at 5% (r), the proportion of taxable gains is 85% (g), the ordinary income tax rate is 28% (t_o), the capital gain tax rate is 15% (t_d), and the built-in gain is 0 (b).

$$ar = (g \times r) + ((1 - t_o) \times (1 - g) \times r)$$

$$ar = (.85 \times .05) + ((1 - .28) \times (1 - .85) \times .05) = 4.790\%$$

$$(1 + ar)^n = (1 + 4.790\%)^{20} = 254.916\%$$

$$FV = \$1{,}000$$

$$FV = \$1{,}000 \times \left[254.916\% - .15 \times \left(.85 \times .1 \times \left(\frac{254.916\% - 1}{4.790\%} \right) + 0 \right) \right]$$

$$FV = \$1{,}000 \times 2.343 = \$2{,}343$$

This is more than with the ordinary income investment with no capital gains.

For example, assume the side fund grows at 5% (r), the proportion of taxable gains is 85% (g), the qualified dividend rate is 20% (t_o), the capital gain tax rate is 20% (t_d), and the built-in gain is 0 (b).

$$ar = (g \times r) + ((1 - t_o) \times (1 - g) \times r)$$

$$ar = (.85 \times .05) + ((1 - .20) \times (1 - .85) \times .05) = 4.888\%$$

$$(1 + ar)^n = (1 + 4.790\%)^{20} = 259.702\%$$

$$FV = \$1{,}000 \times$$

$$\left[259.702\% - .15 \times \left(.85 \times .1 \times \left(\frac{259.702\% - 1}{4.888\%} \right) + 0 \right) \right]$$

$$FV = \$1{,}000 \times 2.389 = \$2{,}389$$

This is more than with the capital gain property with ordinary income investment because of the favorable qualified dividend tax rate.

TIMING OF CAPITAL GAIN OR LOSS

A person who owns capital property may be able to control when gain or loss is recognized for tax purposes. In general, gain is not recognized until property is sold. There are certain ways to control the timing of such recognition and, thus, manage taxation.

Deferring recognition of gain on investments such as stock or bonds can be accomplished using a buy and hold strategy; gain is not recognized until the bond or security is sold. When stocks or bonds are sold, gain can be minimized by selling stocks or bonds with the highest basis relative to sales price. In the same year, stocks or bonds might also be sold at a loss to offset the gain.

Accelerating recognition of loss on investments such as stock or bonds can be accomplished by selling the stock or bond. However, the recognition of a loss may not be allowed currently where the sale is between certain related persons, or where the investor holds/or acquires certain other positions in the property being sold at a loss. Wash sales and straddles are discussed in Chapter 43, "Taxation of Investment Vehicles."

Certain tangible property, such as real estate, can be exchanged for other property in a like-kind exchange. The effect of a like-kind exchange is generally to defer the taxation that would otherwise have occurred upon disposition of the first property until the like-kind property is sold. Some gain may be recognized at the time of the like-kind exchange if cash or other property that is not like-kind property is also received in the exchange, or if a party to the exchange is relieved of liability for a debt.

Like-kind exchange treatment is also available for life insurance and annuities.

Gain on sale of property (other than marketable securities, certain real estate, and inventory) may also be deferred through installment sales and private annuities. In general, recognition of gain is deferred until installment or annuity payments are received.

MUTUAL FUNDS

Just as different investments may be taxed differently, an investor can invest in mutual funds with different tax characteristics. One factor to be considered in selecting a mutual fund is the expected tax treatment of distributions from the fund. In addition, sale by the investor of shares in the mutual fund is generally a taxable event.

In many ways, an investor in a mutual fund is taxed the same as if the investor invested in the investments owned by the mutual fund. If the mutual fund has tax-free income from municipal bonds, the mutual fund investor treats distributions of such income as tax-free. If the mutual find has ordinary income such as interest income, the mutual fund investor treats distributions of such income as ordinary income. And if the mutual fund has qualified dividends or capital gains, the mutual fund investor treats distributions of such amounts as qualified dividends or capital gain.

Therefore, an investor can select a mutual fund that complements the investor's tax objectives. If the investor wants tax-free income, a mutual fund that invests in municipal bonds might be appropriate (income is free of federal tax and gains are taxed as capital gain). If the investor wants higher current income and a preferred tax rate, a mutual fund that emphasizes stocks that pay qualified dividends with some capital gains might be chosen.

If the investor wants long-term capital gains, the investor might choose a mutual fund that invests in stocks with tax management. Such a fund emphasizes minimizing current taxation by avoiding interest, dividends, and realized capital gains. Capital gain recognition is minimized or postponed using a buy and hold strategy. The turnover ratio for a fund's assets may be useful in determining how well the fund does this. When the fund sells stocks, the fund may minimize the gain by selecting stocks with the highest basis relative to sales price. The fund may also sell stocks at a loss to offset the capital gain.

When an investor sells, exchanges (including switching between funds managed by the same company), or redeems a mutual fund share, the investor generally has a capital gain. The gain is generally long-term if the investor owned the mutual fund for more than one year. For more on tax strategies when buying or selling mutual funds, see Chapter 16, "Mutual Funds."

However, different treatment generally applies when an individual retirement account (IRA) or retirement plan is invested in a mutual fund. In the case of an IRA or retirement plan, taxation is generally deferred until distributions are made from the IRA or retirement plan. Therefore, an IRA owner or retirement plan investor can have distributions reinvested in the mutual fund and there is no current taxation of such reinvested distributions. In addition, such an IRA owner or plan participant can generally roll over the IRA or retirement account to another mutual fund without being taxed on the rollover. However, all distributions from the IRA or retirement account are generally taxed at ordinary income tax rates. (Qualified distributions from Roth IRAs are not subject to income tax. Nor are distributions of nondeductible contributions by any IRA or qualified plan.) Thus, there may be a trade-off between the tax benefits of an IRA or qualified plan (possibly a tax deduction, tax deferral, and/or tax-free distribution) and the forgoing of special capital gain or qualified dividend treatment. See Chapter 45, "Investment Strategies for Tax-Advantaged Accounts."

Chapter 45

INVESTMENT STRATEGIES FOR TAX–ADVANTAGED ACCOUNTS

This chapter uses many of the time-value concepts and formulas presented in Chapter 32 and Appendix K, "Time Value Concepts," to evaluate a number of investment strategies for tax-advantaged accounts. The topics addressed here include determining when a Roth IRA is better than a traditional IRA; when to convert traditional IRAs into Roth IRAs; how other IRAs and qualified plans compare to traditional IRAs and Roth IRAs; measuring the effects of tax leverage by comparing alternative investments; evaluating which assets should be inside, and which outside, of tax-advantaged retirement plans; and distributions of employer securities with net unrealized appreciation.

ROTH IRA VS. TRADITIONAL IRA

Deductible contributions can be made to traditional IRAs. Nondeductible contributions can be made to either traditional IRAs or Roth IRAs. Deductible contributions to traditional IRAs and nondeductible contributions to Roth IRAs may be subject to phaseout based on adjusted gross income. In addition, earnings in an IRA accumulate without any current taxation. Assuming contributions can be made to either a traditional IRA or a Roth IRA, is it better to contribute to a traditional IRA or a Roth IRA?

This question may take on more importance now that employer-sponsored 401(k) plans may permit participants to elect to make nondeductible contributions to Roth IRA sub-accounts within the 401(k) plan rather than the regular deductible contributions to the traditional tax-deferred account. The elective deferral limit for 401(k) plans is $15,000 (in 2006) and participants over the age of 49 can make additional "catch-up" contributions of up to $5,000 (in 2006). Therefore, the maximum potential elective deferral limit for 401(k) plans are about four times larger than the maximum contribution limits for traditional IRAs and Roth IRAs. The following discussion will address the question of investing in Roth IRAs versus regular IRAs, but the same general analysis would apply with respect to making before tax deductible contributions to the traditional 401(k) account versus after tax nondeductible contributions to a 401(k) Roth IRA sub-account.

The tax rules for distributions from a Roth IRA are generally more favorable than those from a traditional IRA. Qualified distributions from a Roth IRA can be received tax-free. Qualified distributions generally include distributions received after age 59½ or death, on account of disability, or for certain first-time home purchases. Even if distributions are not qualified, distributions from a Roth IRA are generally treated as made from contributions first, and contributions are received tax-free. On the other hand, distributions from a traditional IRA are taxable except to the extent that portions of the distributions are attributable to nondeductible contributions. Furthermore, distributions from a traditional IRA are treated as made from earnings and contributions on a pro-rata basis.

In addition, distributions from a Roth IRA can generally be stretched out longer than distributions from a traditional IRA. Under the required minimum distribution rules, distributions from a traditional IRA must generally start at age 70½; distributions from a Roth IRA can be delayed until after death. Where the spouse is the sole beneficiary and elects to treat the IRA as his or her own, distributions can generally be delayed until the surviving spouse reaches age 70½ (traditional IRA) or dies (Roth IRA).

Nondeductible v. Nondeductible – Since the tax rules for distributions from a Roth IRA are more favorable than those from a traditional IRA, it is better to make nondeductible contributions to a Roth IRA, rather than nondeductible contributions to a traditional IRA.

Deductible v. Nondeductible – Whether it is better to make deductible contributions to a traditional IRA or nondeductible contributions to a Roth IRA depends on the circumstances. Let's use some of the time-value concepts and formulas presented in Chapter 32 and Appendix K to evaluate deductible contributions to a traditional IRA versus nondeductible contributions to a Roth IRA.

Assume a taxpayer can contribute $1,000 (PV) before tax to a traditional IRA on a deductible basis, or to a Roth IRA on a nondeductible basis. Assume either IRA will grow at a 5% rate (r) for 20 years (n) and then be distributed (the Roth distribution is qualified), and that

Tools & Techniques of Investment Planning

467

the tax rate at time of contribution (t_c) and at distribution (t_d) is 28%.

The formula for the future after tax value of the Roth IRA in 20 years is:

$$FV = PV \times (1 - t_c) \times (1 + r)^n$$

$$FV = \$1,000 \times (1 - 0.28) \times (1 + 0.05)^{20} = \$1,910$$

Here, since the taxpayer is making nondeductible contributions, the tax is paid up front, reducing the after tax contribution to the Roth IRA to $720 [$1,000 × (1 - 0.28)]. This $720 then grows at a 5% rate to $1,910 in 20 years. There is no tax at distribution because the distribution is qualified.

The formula for the future after tax value of the traditional IRA in 20 years is:

$$FV = PV \times (1 + r)^n \times (1 - t_d)$$

$$FV = \$1,000 \times (1 + 0.05)^{20} \times (1 - 0.28) = \$1,910$$

Here, since the taxpayer is making deductible contributions, the contribution to the traditional IRA is $1,000. This $1,000 then grows at a 5% rate to $2,653 in 20 years. After paying tax, $1,910 is left [$2,653 × (1 - 0.28)], the same as with the Roth IRA.

Note that the tax equivalent amount that the taxpayer can contribute to the traditional IRA on a deductible basis can also be calculated by dividing the amount contributed to the Roth IRA by one plus the tax rate at the time of contribution [$720 ÷ (1 + 0.28) = $1,000]. Where the tax-equivalent amount will not fit inside the traditional IRA will be discussed below.

Where tax equivalent amounts are contributed to a traditional IRA on a deductible basis or to a Roth IRA on a nondeductible basis and the tax rates stay the same from the time of contribution to the time of distribution, both IRAs produce the same result. Of course, if the distribution from the Roth IRA was not qualified, the Roth IRA would be worth only $1,577 [$720 + ($1,910 – $720) × (1 - .28)] after tax, and the traditional IRA would produce the better result. Obviously, tax-free qualified distributions are important to the Roth IRA results.

Where the taxpayer contributes tax equivalent amounts to a traditional IRA on a deductible basis and the tax rates go down from the time of contribution to the time of distribution, the traditional IRA produces the better result. For example, assume the tax rate at time of distribution is 25% instead of 28%. Then, the result for the traditional IRA is:

$$FV = \$1,000 \times (1 + 0.05)^{20} \times (1 - 0.25) = \$1,990$$

The future value of the traditional IRA, $1,990, is now $80 greater than the future value of the Roth IRA, $1,910.

Where the taxpayer contributes tax equivalent amounts to a traditional IRA on a deductible basis or to a Roth IRA on a nondeductible basis and the tax rates go up from the time of contribution to the time of distribution, the Roth IRA generally produces the better result. For example, assume the tax rate at time of distribution is 30% instead of 28%. Then, the result for the traditional IRA is:

$$FV = \$1,000 \times (1 + 0.05)^{20} \times (1 - 0.30) = \$1,857$$

The future value of the traditional IRA, $1,857, is now $53 less than the future value of the Roth IRA, $1,910.

Up to now, it has been assumed that tax equivalent amounts can be placed into the traditional IRA on a deductible basis and the Roth IRA on a nondeductible basis. However, assume the contribution limit for traditional IRAs and Roth IRAs is $4,000. If $4,000 is contributed to the Roth IRA, the tax equivalent amount $5,556 [$4,000 ÷ (1 + .28 tax rate at contribution)] cannot be contributed to the deductible traditional IRA.

In this situation, for comparison purposes, $4,000 should be placed into the traditional IRA and an additional amount (see below) placed in a side fund. The future value of the $4,000 Roth IRA will then be compared to the sum of the future value of the $4,000 traditional IRA and the future value of the side fund.

Once again, assume either IRA will grow at a 5% rate (r) for 20 years (n) and then be distributed (the Roth distribution is qualified), and that the tax rate at time of contribution (t_c) and at distribution (t_d) is 28%. Here, the future after tax value of the Roth IRA in 20 years is:

$$FV = \$5,556 \times (1 - .28) \times (1 + 0.05)^{20} = \$10,613$$

With the Roth IRA, the taxpayer is making nondeductible contributions, so the tax is paid up front, reducing the after tax contribution to the Roth IRA to $4,000 [$5,556 × (1 - 0.28)]. This $4,000 then grows at a 5% rate to $10,613 in 20 years. There is no tax at distribution because the distribution is qualified.

Chapter 45 – Investment Strategies For Tax-Advantaged Accounts

If the side fund can effectively be placed in another tax-advantaged account (such as a Section 401(k) plan) that has the same tax characteristics as a deductible traditional IRA (i.e., deductible contributions and taxable distributions), then the side fund could effectively be treated as part of the traditional IRA and the comparisons of future value made the same as above. In this situation, for comparison purposes, $4,000 should be placed in the traditional IRA and $1,556 [($5,556 - $4,000)] placed in a side fund. The future value of the $4,000 Roth IRA will then be compared to the sum of the future value of the $4,000 traditional IRA and the future value of the $1,556 side fund.

Here, the future after tax value of the traditional IRA (with equivalently treated side fund) in 20 years is:

$$FV = \$5,556 \times (1 + 0.05)^{20} \times (1 - 0.28) = \$10,613$$

Here, since deductible contributions are being made, the contribution to the traditional IRA is $4,000, with $1,556 being contributed to a side fund with the same tax characteristics as the traditional IRA – a total of $5,556 [$4,000 ÷ (1 + .28 tax rate at contribution)]. This $5,556 then grows at a 5% rate to $14,742 in 20 years. After paying tax, $10,613 is left [$14,742 × (1 - 0.28 tax rate at distribution)], the same as with the Roth IRA.

If the side fund is taxed differently than the traditional IRA, the future value of the traditional IRA and the future value of the side fund should be calculated separately and the two values should be added together. In this situation, for comparison purposes, $4,000 should be placed in the traditional IRA and $1,120 [($5,556 - $4,000) x (1 - 0.28)] placed in a side fund. [The extra $1,556 is reduced to an $1,120 after tax contribution to the side fund in this case.] The future value of the $4,000 Roth IRA will then be compared to the sum of the future value of the $4,000 traditional IRA and the future value of the $1,120 side fund.

Here, the future after tax value of the traditional IRA in 20 years is:

$$FV = \$4,000 \times (1 + 0.05)^{20} \times (1 - 0.28) = \$7,641$$

Here, since deductible contributions are being made, the contribution to the traditional IRA is $4,000 (with $1,556 being contributed to a side fund). This $4,000 then grows at a 5% rate to $19,613 in 20 years. After paying tax, $7,641 is left [$10,613 x (1 - 0.28 tax rate at distribution)], less than with the Roth IRA. However, the future value of the side fund must be added to the value of the traditional IRA.

If the side fund grows at the same 5% as the IRAs and is tax-free, the future value of the side fund is:

$$FV = PV \times (1 + r)^n$$

$$FV = \$1,120 \times (1 + 0.05)^{20} = \$2,972$$

The sum of the future value of the traditional IRA ($7,641) and the future value of the side fund ($2,972) equals $10,613, the same as the future value of the Roth IRA.

If the side fund grows at the same 5% as the IRAs and is then taxed at 28%, the future value of the side fund is:

$$FV = PV + [\{(PV \times ((1 + r)^n)) - PV\} \times (1 - t_f)]$$

$$FV = \$1,120 + [\{[(\$1,120 \times ((1 + 0.05)^{20})) - \$1,120\} \times (1 - 0.28)] = \$2,453$$

The sum of the future value of the traditional IRA ($7,641) and the future value of the side fund ($2,453) equals $10,094, less than the future value of the Roth IRA by $519. The tax on the side fund has reduced the benefit of the traditional IRA and side fund combination.

If growth in the side fund is taxed annually at 28%, the future value of the side fund is:

$$FV = PV \times (1 + (r \times (1 - t_d))^n$$

$$FV = \$1,120 \times (1 + (.05 \times (1 - .28))^{20} = \$2,272$$

The sum of the future value of the traditional IRA ($7,641) and the future value of the side fund ($2,272) equals $9,913, less than the future value of the Roth IRA.

The following formula from Appendix K can be used to calculate the future value of the side fund where part of the returns will be taxed currently as ordinary income or qualified dividends and part will be taxed on distribution as capital gains:

FVat4

$$FV = PV \times \left[(1 + ar)^n - t_d \times \left(g \times r \times \left(\frac{(1 + ar)^n - 1}{ar} \right) + b \right) \right],$$

if ar ≠ 0

$$FV = PV \times (1 - t_d \times b), \text{ if } ar = 0$$

where: ar = The accumulation rate after tax on the currently taxable component of return (usually ordinary income), but before tax on the accumulating and tax-

Tools & Techniques of Investment Planning

469

deferred capital gains or tax-deferred income component of return

$= (g \times r) + (1 - t_o) \times (1 - g) \times r$

$= r \times (1 - (1 - g) \times t_o);$

r = The total before-tax rate of return;

g = The proportion of total before-tax return, r, attributable to tax-deferred capital gain (or tax-deferred income);

t_o = The tax rate on the currently taxable ordinary income component of return;

t_d = The tax rate on the long-term capital gain (or the tax-deferred) component of investment return;

b = The built-in gain or tax-deferred return proportion of the investment, PV, or the periodic payment, Pmt, if any; and

n = Years until distribution.

For example, assume the side fund grows at 5% (r), the proportion of taxable gains is 85% (g), the ordinary income tax rate is still 28% (t_o), the capital gain tax rate is 20% (td), and the built-in gain is 1 (b).

$$ar = (g \times r) + (1 - t_o) \times (1 - g) \times r$$

$$ar = (0.85 \times 0.05) + ((1 - 0.28) \times (1 - 0.85) \times 0.05) = 4.790\%$$

$$(1 + ar)^n = (1 + 4.790\%)^{20} = 254.916\%$$

$$FV = \$1,120 \times$$

$$\left[254.916\% - .2 \times \left(85 \times .051 \times \left(\frac{254.916\% - 1}{4.790\%} \right) + 1 \right) \right]$$

$$FV = \$1,120 \times 2.074 = \$2,323$$

The sum of the future value of the traditional IRA ($7,641) and the future value of the side fund ($2,323) equals $9,964, less than the future value of the Roth IRA.

Any reduction in tax rate between the time of contribution and the time of distribution generally works to the benefit of the traditional IRA. Any increase in tax rate between the time of contribution and the time of distribution generally works to the benefit of the Roth IRA.

Distributions from IRAs (and qualified plans and annuities) before age 59½ or death are subject to a 10% penalty tax to the extent the distribution is includable in income, unless an exception applies. Important exceptions include distributions made on account of disability and distributions that are part of a series of substantially equal periodic payments. If the penalty tax applies, reduce the future value of any IRAs being compared by an additional 10% of the amount of the distribution includable in income. (Note that qualified distributions from Roth IRAs generally include only distributions received after age 59½ or death, on account of disability, or for certain first-time home purchases.)

In the end, the best way to determine whether it is better to make deductible contributions to a traditional IRA or nondeductible contributions to a Roth IRA is to compare the future value of the Roth IRA to the future value of the traditional IRA (and side fund where appropriate).

CONVERTING TRADITIONAL IRA TO ROTH IRA

A traditional IRA (as well as a SEP IRA or a SIMPLE IRA) can be rolled over or converted to a Roth IRA in a taxable event. (A SIMPLE IRA cannot be rolled over until the individual has participated in the SIMPLE IRA for more than two years.) However, for tax years before 2010, the conversion cannot be made if the taxpayer's adjusted gross income exceeds $100,000 for the year, or if the individual is married and files a separate return. These limitations do not apply after 2009. Qualified plans, tax-sheltered annuities, and eligible IRC Section 457 government plans can be converted to a Roth IRA indirectly by rolling such plan over to a traditional IRA and then converting the traditional IRA to a Roth IRA. After 2007, qualified plans, tax-sheltered annuities, and eligible IRC Section 457 government plans can be converted to a Roth IRA directly (subject to the separate return and income limitations).

Should a traditional IRA be converted to a Roth IRA? A person making the conversion is trading the immediate taxation of the traditional IRA for the future favorable taxation of the Roth IRA. Whether it makes sense to convert a traditional IRA to a Roth IRA depends on the circumstances. The methodology for making the decision is similar to that used in evaluating whether deductible contributions should be made to a traditional IRA or nondeductible contributions made to a Roth IRA (see above).

The tax rules for distributions from a Roth IRA are generally more favorable than those from a traditional

IRA. Qualified distributions from a Roth IRA can be received tax-free. Qualified distributions generally include distributions received after age 59½ or death, on account of disability, or for certain first-time home purchases. Even if distributions are not qualified, distributions from a Roth IRA are generally treated as made from contributions first, and contributions are received tax-free. On the other hand, distributions from a traditional IRA are taxable except to the extent of nondeductible contributions. Furthermore, distributions from a traditional IRA are treated as made from earnings and contributions on a pro-rata basis.

In addition, distributions from a Roth IRA can generally be stretched out longer than distributions from a traditional IRA. Under the required minimum distribution rules, distributions from a traditional IRA must generally start at age 70½; distributions from a Roth IRA can be delayed until after death. Where the spouse is the sole beneficiary and elects to treat the IRA as her own, distributions can generally be delayed until the spouse reaches age 70½ (traditional IRA) or dies (Roth IRA).

A person converting a traditional IRA to a Roth IRA can pay the tax on conversion from inside the traditional IRA or outside the IRA. It generally makes sense to pay the tax from outside the traditional IRA; the payment of taxes from inside the IRA reduces the amount in the IRA.

Assume an individual has a traditional IRA worth $100,000, all contributions to the IRA have been deductible, either IRA will grow at a 5% rate (r) for 20 years (n) and then be distributed (the Roth distribution is qualified), and that the tax rate at time of contribution (t_c) and at distribution (t_d) is 28%.

Assuming the tax on conversion is paid outside the IRA, the formula for the future after tax value of the Roth IRA in 20 years is:

$$FV = PV \times (1 + r)^n$$

$$FV = \$100,000 \times (1 + 0.05)^{20} = \$265,330$$

Here, the $100,000 Roth IRA grows at a 5% rate to $265,330 in 20 years. There is no tax at distribution because the distribution is qualified.

Comparatively, if the conversion is not made, the formula for the future after tax value of the traditional IRA in 20 years is:

$$FV = PV \times (1 + r)^n \times (1 - t_f)$$

$$FV = \$100,000 \times (1 + 0.05)^{20} \times (1 - 0.28) = \$191,037$$

Here, the $100,000 traditional IRA grows at a 5% rate to $265,330 in 20 years. After paying tax, $191,037 is left [$265,330 x (1 - 0.28)], less than with the Roth IRA.

However, if the conversion is not made, taxes equal to $28,000 ($100,000 x 0.28 tax rate at time of proposed conversion) have been saved. For comparison purposes, an amount equal to this should be placed in a side fund. If the side fund grows at the same 5% as the IRAs and is tax-free, the future value of the side fund is:

$$FV = PV \times (1 + r)^n$$

$$FV = \$28,000 \times (1 + 0.05)^{20} = \$74,292$$

The sum of the future value of the traditional IRA ($191,037) and the future value of the side fund ($74,292) equals $265,329, effectively the same as the future value of the Roth IRA.

Assuming the tax on conversion is paid inside the IRA, the formula for the future after tax value of the Roth IRA in 20 years is:

$$FV = PV \times (1 - t_c) \times (1 + r)^n$$

$$FV = \$100,000 \times (1 - 0.28) \times (1 + 0.05)^{20} = \$191,037$$

Here, the tax is paid out of the IRA, reducing the tax contribution to the Roth IRA to $720,000 [$100,000 x (1 -0.28)]. This $720,000 then grows at 5% rate to $191,037 in 20 years. There is no tax at distribution because the distribution is qualified.

Comparatively, if the conversion is not made, the formula for the future after tax value of the traditional IRA in 20 years is:

$$FV = PV \times (1 + r)^n \times (1 - t_f)$$

$$FV = \$100,000 \times (1 + 0.05)^{20} \times (1 - 0.28) = \$191,037$$

Here, the $100,000 traditional IRA grows at a 5% rate to $265,330 in 20 years. After paying tax, $191,037 is left [$265,330 x (1 - 0.28)], the same as with the Roth IRA.

As with the comparison of deductible contributions to a traditional IRA with nondeductible contributions to a Roth IRA (see above), results with changes in tax rates from time of contribution to time of distribution can be made. Also, the side fund may be calculated assuming different tax patterns (e.g., tax-free, tax-deferred, taxed annually, with different amounts of capital gain, etc.).

Any reduction in tax rate between the time of conversion and the time of distribution generally works to the benefit of the traditional IRA. Any increase in tax rate between the time of conversion and the time of distribution generally works to the benefit of the Roth IRA. Any tax on the side fund reduces the benefit of the traditional IRA and side fund combination.

In the end, the best way to determine whether it makes sense to convert a traditional IRA to a Roth IRA is to compare the future value of the Roth IRA to the future value of the traditional IRA (and side fund where appropriate).

OTHER IRAS AND QUALIFIED PLANS

In addition to deductible contributions to traditional IRAs, deductible or excludable contributions may also be made to SEP IRAs, SIMPLE IRAs, qualified plans, tax-sheltered annuities, and eligible IRC Section 457 government plans. The taxation of such retirement accounts generally follows that for a traditional IRA [i.e., deductible/excludable contributions with distributions taxable on a pro-rata basis to the extent of nondeductible/nonexcludable contributions (if any)]. Therefore, comparisons can generally be made for these other IRAs and qualified plans in the same manner as described for traditional IRAs above.

Employers can make matching contributions to certain plans (e.g., SIMPLE IRAs and 401(k) plans). The employee contributes to the plan on a deductible/excludable basis, and the employer matches part or all of the employee's contribution, also on a deductible/excludable basis. Where an employee is eligible for such matching contributions, the employee should generally place making contributions to such a plan at the top of her list. In addition to the regular tax benefits for such plans, the employee receives a matching contribution from the employer that the employee would not otherwise have.

MEASURING THE EFFECTS
OF TAX LEVERAGE

Comparing Alternative Investments

Figure 45.1 compares the after-tax accumulations in an environment of unchanging tax rates over investment

horizons ranging from five to 45 years of investments with various degrees of tax leverage.

The before tax rate of return for each investment is assumed to be 10%. The investor is assumed to be in a 35% tax bracket for ordinary income. At one end of the tax leverage spectrum (no tax leverage) is a $1,000 after-tax investment in a nondeductible, fully taxable investment, such as a bond purchased at par. At the other end of the tax leverage spectrum is the corresponding before tax investment of $1,538.46 [$1,000 ÷ (1 - 0.35)] in a fully tax deductible, fully tax deferred vehicle such as a contribution to an IRC Section 401(k) plan, deductible IRA, a qualified pension plan, profit-sharing plan, IRC Section 403(b) TDA, SEP or SAR-SEP IRA, or SIMPLE IRA. Three intermediate types of tax leveraged investments are also included.

The first intermediate type of partially tax leveraged investment is a nondeductible $1,000 investment in a stock portfolio or equity mutual fund. Equity investments are tax leveraged because the tax on gains is deferred until gains are realized. The realized long-term gains are generally taxed at a lower rate than ordinary investment income or interest. In addition, under the new law, qualifying dividends, themselves currently become a tax preferred form of income, generally taxed at a maximum rate of 15%.

To help illustrate the impact of the new tax rates on dividend income and long-term capital gains, Figure 45.1 shows the after tax accumulation for an investment in a stock portfolio first using the old tax rules and then using the new tax rules, assuming, in each case, that the tax rates would remain unchanged over the entire investment horizon. Clearly, some prospectively appreciating assets, such as real estate, fall in between, with the income (rents, for example) not qualifying for the preferential tax rate on qualifying dividends, but potentially with some of any capital gains qualifying for the 15% rate and some (unrecaptured IRC Section 1250 depreciation, for instance) still being taxed at the old 25% rate.

Using the old rules, the returns on this equity (stock or mutual fund) investment are computed using the following assumptions. First, 70% of the total 10% return (or 7%) is assumed to be attributable to capital appreciation and the remaining 30% of the 10% return (or 3%) is assumed to be attributable to dividend income. These percentages are approximately equal to the long-term compound return and appreciation/income proportions of the returns on the S&P 500 stock index. Second, the realized capital gains are taxed at a rate of 20% for investment horizons of five years or less and 18% for investment horizons longer than five years.

Chapter 45 – Investment Strategies For Tax-Advantaged Accounts

Figure 45.1

COMPARATIVE TAX-LEVERAGE ANALYSIS
ENDING AFTER-TAX VALUES ON A $1,000 INVESTMENT EARNING 10-PERCENT BEFORE TAX

Investment	Investment Horizon (Years)								
	5	10	15	20	25	30	35	40	45
Fully Taxable[1]	1,370	1,877	2,572	3,524	4,828	6,614	9,062	12,416	17,011
Tax-Free ROR[a]	6.50%	6.50%	6.50%	6.50%	6.50%	6.50%	6.50%	6.50%	6.50%
Stock[2] (Old Rules)[3][c]	1,451	2,166	3,249	4,912	7,465	11,385	17,401	26,638	40,816
Tax-Free ROR	7.74%	8.03%	8.17%	8.28%	8.37%	8.45%	8.50%	8.55%	8.59%
% Increase[b]	5.9%	15.4%	26.3%	39.4%	54.6%	72.1%	92.0%	114.5%	139.9%
Stock[2] (New Rules)[4][d]	1,514	2,326	3,606	5,626	8,814	13,844	21,779	34,301	54,058
Tax-Free ROR	8.65%	8.81%	8.93%	9.02%	9.10%	9.15%	9.20%	9.24%	9.27%
% Increase	10.5%	23.9%	40.2%	59.7%	82.6%	109.3%	140.3%	176.3%	217.8%
Tax-Deferred Annuity[5][cd]	1,397	2,036	3,065	4,723	7,393	11,692	18,617	29,769	47,729
Tax-Free ROR	6.91%	7.37%	7.75%	8.07%	8.33%	8.54%	8.71%	8.85%	8.97%
% Increase	2.0%	8.5%	19.2%	34.0%	53.1%	76.8%	105.4%	139.8%	180.6%
Roth IRA[6][e]	1,611	2,594	4,177	6,727	10,835	17,449	28,102	45,259	72,890
Tax-Free ROR	10.00%	10.00%	10.00%	10.00%	10.00%	10.00%	10.00%	10.00%	10.00%
% Increase	17.5%	38.2%	62.4%	90.9%	124.4%	163.8%	210.1%	264.5%	328.5%
401(k)[7][e]	1,611	2,594	4,177	6,727	10,835	17,449	28,102	45,259	72,890
Tax-Free ROR	10.00%	10.00%	10.00%	10.00%	10.00%	10.00%	10.00%	10.00%	10.00%
% Increase	17.5%	38.2%	62.4%	90.9%	124.4%	163.8%	210.1%	264.5%	328.5%

[1] The entire 10-percent return is assumed to be subject to an ordinary income tax rate of 35-percent each year.

[2] Capital appreciation is assumed to comprise 70-percent (and dividend income, 30-percent) of the total 10-percent stock return. The proportion of portfolio gains assumed to be realized each year due to portfolio turnover is 0-percent. The remainder of the gain is realized and taxed at the end of the investment horizon.

[3] Dividend income is taxed at 35-percent and realized long-term capital gains are taxed at 20-percent for 5-year or shorter periods and 18-percent for investment horizons longer than 5 years.

[4] Dividend income is taxed at 15-percent and realized long-term capital gains are taxed at 15-percent.

[5] The tax rate on all returns is 35-percent and the payment of tax is deferred until the end of the investment horizon.

[6] The distributions are assumed to be qualifying distributions so that all returns are received tax free.

[7] The before-tax equivalent, $1,538, of $1,000 after-tax contribution is assumed to accumulate at a tax-deferred rate of 10-percent. At the end of the investment horizon, the entire balance (the $1,538 contribution plus accumulated earnings) is taxed at a rate of 35-percent.

[a] The "Tax-Free ROR" is the rate the investor would have to earn on an entirely tax-free return investment to equal the after-tax return earned on the given investment for the given horizon.

[b] The "% Increase" is the amount, in percentage terms, by which a given investment's after-tax accumulation exceeds the fully taxable investment's accumulation for a given investment horizon.

[c] Under the old rules, the Stock investment outperformed the Tax-Deferred Annuity investment for investment horizons under about 26 years. For periods exceeding 26 years, the Tax-Deferred Annuity was superior on an after-tax basis.

[d] Under the new rules, the Stock investment outperforms the Tax-Deferred Annuity investment for investment horizons under about 76 years. For periods exceeding 76 years, the Tax-Deferred Annuity is superior on an after-tax basis.

[e] The after-tax results are exactly the same for a $1,000 investment in a tax-free Roth IRA as they are for an equivalent before-tax contribution of $1,538 in a fully deductible, fully tax-deferred investment, such as a 401(k) plan, if the investor's tax rate on ordinary income remains the same over the investment horizon.

Tools & Techniques of Investment Planning

473

Under the new rules, capital appreciation still comprises 70% (and dividend income, 30%) of the stock portfolio's total return. Otherwise, the dividend-income component of return is taxed at the maximum rate of 15% and the long-term gains are taxed at the maximum rate of 15%.

The second intermediate type of partially tax-leveraged investment is a $1,000 after tax contribution to a commercial annuity (or nondeductible traditional IRA). This type of investment enjoys complete tax deferral on investment earnings, but all earnings are ultimately taxed at ordinary income tax rates. It is assumed that no 10% early withdrawal penalties or other penalties or surrender charges apply at the end of the investment horizon. Also, although commercial annuities typically have higher expense rates and fees than other types of investments, it is assumed that this investment and all the other comparison investments earn 10% before tax per year, effectively, net of expenses.

Finally, Figure 45.1 shows the accumulation of a $1,000 after tax contribution to a Roth IRA. It is assumed that withdrawals at any given investment horizon would be qualified distributions and, therefore, free of all income tax or penalties.

Implications and Conclusions

1. *Fully tax deductible, fully tax deferred vehicles still the best after tax –*

Clearly, absent any tax penalties for early withdrawals or any change in tax rates, the fully deductible, fully tax deferred IRC Section 401(k)-type investment is superior to all other accumulation vehicles, except the Roth IRA investment. The after-tax accumulation for the IRC Section 401(k) investment and the Roth IRA investment are equal for every investment horizon if the investor's tax rate on ordinary income remains the same throughout the investment horizon. In other words, a before tax contribution to a tax deferred investment vehicle such as a IRC Section 401(k) plan or profit-sharing plan, etc. is equivalent to making the corresponding after tax investment into a tax free account if the investor's tax rate on ordinary income remains the same over the investment horizon.

The amount by which the IRC Section 401(k) and Roth IRA investment outperform the others increases significantly with the length of the investment horizon. For example, at 15 years, the IRC Section 401(k) and the Roth IRA provide 62.4% more after tax wealth than a fully taxable investment. The annuity, the stock investment using the old rules, and the stock investment using the new rules provide only 19.2%, 26.3%, and 40.2% more after tax wealth than the fully taxable investment, respectively. At 30 years, the increase in the after tax wealth (compared to the fully taxable alternative) provided by the IRC Section 401(k), Roth IRA, stock (new rules), annuity, and stock (old rules) is 163.8, 163.8, 109.3, 76.8, and 72.1%, respectively.

Planning point: Even with tax rates at 15% on both capital gains and dividend income (or even 5% or 10% for lower-income investors), as compared to 35% with respect to distributions from qualified type plans, the qualified type plans where contributions are tax deductible and returns are entirely tax deferred generally are still the better investment. As Figure 45.1 shows, investing after tax dollars in qualifying dividend paying equities or mutual funds with substantial appreciation (capital gain) potential will still accumulate less after tax for any given investment horizon than making either the corresponding before tax contribution to a tax-deferred vehicle, such as an IRC Section 401(k) plan, profit-sharing plan, or traditional IRA, or the equivalent after tax contribution to a tax free vehicle, such as a Roth IRA or an IRC Section 529 plan that will be used for qualified education expenses.

In fact, the tax advantage of making before tax contributions to qualified-type plans, such as IRC Section 401(k) plans, profit-sharing plans, IRC Section 403(b) plans, SEP IRAs, or SIMPLE IRAs, or to traditional IRAs is sufficiently great that it will overcome the 10% penalty for early withdrawals after a certain break-even period. In other words, the illiquidity associated with contributions to these types of plans because of the 10% early withdrawal penalty is limited to a certain break-even period. The break-even period is a function of several variables including: (a) the rate of return earned on the investment; (b) the proportions of the return attributable to ordinary income, dividends, and capital gains; (c) the tax rates applicable to ordinary income, dividends, and capital gains on the outside investment; and (d) the tax rate applicable to the distribution from the plan.

However, if tax rates remain as low as 15% (or lower) on both capital gains and qualifying dividend income, the break-even periods would be considerably longer than they used to be. For investors who prefer equity investments that qualify for the 15% or lower tax rates on dividend income and capital gains, contributions to qualified type plans now must be considered, in this sense, comparatively less liquid than they used to be.

Chapter 45 – Investment Strategies For Tax-Advantaged Accounts

2. *Stock investments under old and new tax rule –*

Not surprisingly, the stock fund investment, under the old tax rules and even more so under the new tax rules, outperforms the fully taxable investment by an ever increasing margin as the investment horizon lengthens. What this demonstrates is the potentially gross error of ignoring the type of investment a client is most likely to make when evaluating potential after tax accumulations outside of tax favored retirement plans. Very few investors are likely to invest in fully taxable investments outside of their retirement plans. Mutual funds and stock type investments, real estate, and other capital appreciating assets are far more likely to be the investment vehicles of choice. Using the assumption that investments outside of retirement plans are fully taxable may be plain and simple, but may be wrong, plain and simple. This point is driven home even further by comparing the performance of the stock fund type of investment to the commercial annuity type of investment.

3. *Stock investments versus annuity investments –*

For longer investment horizons, the nondeductible, fully tax deferred commercial annuity type of investment outperforms the stock fund investment. However, for shorter accumulation periods, the stock fund type of investment is superior after tax. Under the old tax rules for dividends and capital gains, the crossover point is about 26 years. Under the new tax rules, the crossover point increases to over 76 years. What this means in practical terms is that even if one can earn essentially the same before tax returns after expenses inside a commercial annuity as one could earn, say, by investing directly in an S&P 500 index fund, the annuity would still be the better choice under the new tax law rules only if an investor plans to invest for more than 76 years before amounts will be withdrawn. Since total expense charges for annuities typically range from at least 0.75 to 2.5 percentage points more per year than for an S&P 500 index fund, the potential for earning essentially the same return after expenses inside the annuity as outside is virtually nil. Consequently, the actual crossover point, taking account of actual expense differences, is considerably longer than 76 years -- maybe even never!

EXAMPLE: GEORGE'S RETIREMENT PLANS

Assume a client, George age 35, wants to see what the retirement planning numbers would be if, investing outside of qualified type retirement plans:

- He funds for a 25-year payout period after retirement;

- Inflation before and after retirement is assumed to be 4%;

- His after tax income objective is $20,000 per year in current dollars, or starting at age 65, $65,000 per year [$20,000 x (1.04)^{30}], increasing each year by an assumed 4% rate of inflation;

- His required annual investments during the accumulation phase are computed on the basis of equal annual real (inflation adjusted) payments; and

- His tax rate on ordinary income is 28%, both before and after retirement, and the tax rate on capital gains, when realized, is 20%.

It probably would be unrealistic for George to assume that he would earn more than about 10% before tax during the accumulation. Assuming that long-term before tax rates of return for various asset classes are similar to the long-term average compound rate since 1926[1], his portfolio might look something like the following (assuming the portfolio is rebalanced each year to keep the relative asset weights constant):

George's Portfolio During Accumulation Phase

Asset class	Portfolio Weight	Rate of Return	Weighted ROR	Capital Gain %	Weighted CG ROR
Small stocks/ aggressive growth	30%	13.00%	3.90%	95%	3.71%
S&P-type stocks	45%	11.00%	4.95%	70%	3.47%
Corporate bonds	15%	5.75%	0.86%	0%	0.00%
T-bill/money-market fund	10%	4.00%	0.40%	0%	0.00%
Total portfolio			**10.1125%**	**70.9023%**	**7.1700%**

Assuming that George should invest somewhat more conservatively during the retirement/liquidation phase, George's retirement portfolio might be structured as follows.

George's Portfolio During Retirement Phase

Asset class	Portfolio Weight	Rate of Return	Weighted ROR	Capital Gain %	Weighted CG ROR
Small stocks/ aggressive growth	15%	13.00%	1.95%	95%	1.85%
S&P-type stocks	35%	11.00%	3.85%	70%	2.70%
Corporate bonds	35%	5.75%	2.01%	0%	0.00%
T-bill/money-market fund	15%	4.00%	0.60%	0%	0.00%
Total portfolio			**8.4125%**	**54.0565%**	**4.5475%**

Chapter 45 – Investment Strategies For Tax-Advantaged Accounts

Figure 45.2

FUTURE VALUES OF INVESTMENT DURING ACCUMULATION PHASE

1	2	3	4	5	6	7	8
Year of pmt	FV factor before tax on gain	Capital gain factor	Inflated payment factor	FV of payment before tax on gain	Capital gain on payment	Total FV of payments before tax on gains	Total capital gains
	Eq. FVbt4	Eq. FVCG	@4%	Col 2 x Col 4	Col 3 x Col 4	Sum Col 5	Sum Col 6
1	14.3630	10.3151	1.0000	14.3630	10.3151	14.3630	10.3151
2	13.1423	9.3728	1.0400	13.6680	9.7477	28.0310	20.0628
3	12.0253	8.5106	1.0816	13.0066	9.2051	41.0376	29.2679
4	11.0033	7.7217	1.1249	12.3772	8.6858	53.4147	37.9537
5	10.0681	6.9998	1.1699	11.7782	8.1887	65.1930	46.1424
6	9.2124	6.3392	1.2167	11.2083	7.7127	76.4012	53.8551
7	8.4294	5.7349	1.2653	10.6659	7.2564	87.0671	61.1115
8	7.7130	5.1818	1.3159	10.1497	6.8189	97.2169	67.9305
9	7.0574	4.6758	1.3686	9.6586	6.3992	106.8754	74.3296
10	6.4576	4.2128	1.4233	9.1912	5.9961	116.0666	80.3258
11	5.9088	3.7891	1.4802	8.7464	5.6089	124.8131	85.9346
12	5.4066	3.4015	1.5395	8.3232	5.2365	133.1362	91.1711
13	4.9471	3.0468	1.6010	7.9204	4.8780	141.0567	96.0491
14	4.5266	2.7222	1.6651	7.5371	4.5327	148.5938	100.5818
15	4.1419	2.4253	1.7317	7.1724	4.1998	155.7662	104.7816
16	3.7899	2.1535	1.8009	6.8253	3.8784	162.5915	108.6600
17	3.4678	1.9049	1.8730	6.4950	3.5678	169.0865	112.2278
18	3.1730	1.6774	1.9479	6.1807	3.2674	175.2673	115.4952
19	2.9033	1.4692	2.0258	5.8816	2.9764	181.1489	118.4716
20	2.6566	1.2787	2.1068	5.5970	2.6941	186.7459	121.1657
21	2.4308	1.1045	2.1911	5.3262	2.4200	192.0721	123.5857
22	2.2242	0.9450	2.2788	5.0684	2.1534	197.1405	125.7391
23	2.0352	0.7991	2.3699	4.8232	1.8937	201.9637	127.6328
24	1.8622	0.6655	2.4647	4.5898	1.6404	206.5535	129.2731
25	1.7039	0.5434	2.5633	4.3677	1.3928	210.9212	130.6659
26	1.5591	0.4316	2.6658	4.1563	1.1505	215.0775	131.8164
27	1.4266	0.3293	2.7725	3.9552	0.9130	219.0326	132.7294
28	1.3053	0.2357	2.8834	3.7638	0.6796	222.7964	133.4090
29	1.1944	0.1501	2.9987	3.5817	0.4500	226.3781	133.8590
30	1.0929	0.0717	3.1187	3.4083	0.2236	229.7864	134.0826

George could expect each dollar (adjusted upward for inflation) invested each year during the 30-year accumulation period to grow to the following future values (assuming beginning of year payments), as shown in Figure 45.2.

What Figure 45.2 shows is the amount George can expect to accumulate by the end of the 30-year accumulation period for each dollar of initial investment. The values are computed assuming that each subsequent annual investment increases at the rate of inflation (4%) and that all annual investments are invested as shown in the portfolio allocations above for the accumulation phase. The result is that he can expect to accumulate about $229.7864 dollars per dollar of initial investment with about $134.0826 of accumulated, but untaxed capital gains.

Next, compute the present value of his desired retirement income stream. After computing the future

Figure 45.3

	1	2	3	4	5	6	7
				PRESENT VALUES OF RETIREMENT INCOME			
	Year of Payout	After-tax FV factor	PV factor (1/FV factor)	Inflation factor	Inflation-adjusted retirement income	PV dollar value	Total PV dollar value
		Eq. FVat4	Eq. PVat4	@4%	Col 4 x $65,000	Col 5 x Col 3	Sum Col 6
	1	0.9475	1.0554	1.0000	65,000.00	68,601.15	68,601.15
	2	1.0164	0.9838	1.0400	67,600.00	66,507.90	135,109.05
	3	1.0904	0.9171	1.0816	70,304.00	64,476.19	199,585.24
	4	1.1698	0.8549	1.1249	73,116.16	62,504.45	262,089.70
	5	1.2550	0.7968	1.1699	76,040.81	60,591.11	322,680.81
	6	1.3464	0.7427	1.2167	79,082.44	58,734.62	381,415.43
	7	1.4446	0.6922	1.2653	82,245.74	56,933.47	438,348.90
	8	1.5499	0.6452	1.3159	85,535.57	55,186.14	493,535.04
	9	1.6630	0.6013	1.3686	88,956.99	53,491.17	547,026.21
	10	1.7844	0.5604	1.4233	92,515.27	51,847.12	598,873.32
	11	1.9146	0.5223	1.4802	96,215.88	50,252.56	649,125.88
	12	2.0545	0.4867	1.5395	100,064.51	48,706.10	697,831.98
	13	2.2045	0.4536	1.6010	104,067.09	47,206.39	745,038.37
	14	2.3656	0.4227	1.6651	108,229.78	45,752.10	790,790.47
	15	2.5384	0.3939	1.7317	112,558.97	44,341.91	835,132.38
	16	2.7240	0.3671	1.8009	117,061.33	42,974.57	878,106.95
	17	2.9231	0.3421	1.8730	121,743.78	41,648.83	919,755.79
	18	3.1368	0.3188	1.9479	126,613.53	40,363.48	960,119.27
	19	3.3662	0.2971	2.0258	131,678.07	39,117.34	999,236.62
	20	3.6124	0.2768	2.1068	136,945.20	37,909.26	1,037,145.88
	21	3.8767	0.2580	2.1911	142,423.00	36,738.11	1,073,883.99
	22	4.1603	0.2404	2.2788	148,119.92	35,602.81	1,109,486.80
	23	4.4648	0.2240	2.3699	154,044.72	34,502.28	1,143,989.08
	24	4.7915	0.2087	2.4647	160,206.51	33,435.50	1,177,424.57
	25	5.1422	0.1945	2.5633	166,614.77	32,401.45	1,209,826.02

value of George's retirement savings per dollar of initial investment, it is known from the analysis above that the beginning balance for financing his retirement income will have about 58.351% ($134.0826/$229.7864) of the balance attributable to as-yet-untaxed built-in gains. Therefore, when computing the total required to finance his desired retirement income, this ratio can be used in the present value formula.

George needs to accumulate a balance of about $1.21 million ($1,209,826) at the beginning of his retirement to finance his desired retirement income (see Figure 45.3). (This balance includes about $706,000 of as-yet-untaxed accumulated capital gains – 58.35% x $1,210,530 = $705,946 – which will be recognized and taxed as the balance is withdrawn to finance his retirement income.) It is already known from the analysis above that he can expect to accumulate about $229.7864 for each dollar of initial annual investment over the accumulation period. Therefore, the required initial annual investment necessary to finance his desired retirement income may be determined by dividing $1,209,826 by $229.7864. The result is $5,265.

Therefore, George needs to start saving about $5,265 this year and increase his investment each year by 4% for the next 30 years, to accumulate enough (outside qualified-type plans) to pay the real after-tax equivalent of $20,000 today for 25 years, beginning when he turns age 65.

Tools & Techniques of Investment Planning

WHICH ASSETS SHOULD BE IN RETIREMENT PLANS?

The Issue

Many investors have undoubtedly accumulated sizeable sums in their retirement plans and IRAs. These same investors have also frequently accumulated considerable investment balances outside their qualified plans and IRAs.

Typically, a well-diversified and properly managed portfolio of investments will include some allocation of funds in a variety of asset classes such as domestic and foreign stocks, large- and small-capitalization stocks, value and growth stocks, foreign and domestic bonds, short- and long-term bonds, real estate, commodities, collectibles, etc. Given that an investor has some kind of optimal mix of assets that meets his risk and return objectives, the following question usually arises. Which of these assets should be invested inside qualified plans and IRAs and which should be invested outside qualified plans and IRAs?

Conventional wisdom has often suggested that it is best to acquire the currently taxable income-generating assets, such as bonds, first within qualified plans and IRAs because this income will be sheltered from current taxation within the plan. In contrast, a large portion of the return on growth-oriented investments, such as stocks and stock mutual funds, is already sheltered, since the gains are not generally recognized and taxed until the assets are sold. In addition, long-term gains are taxed at a lower rate than ordinary investment income when the gains are realized outside of qualified plans and IRAs. The gains on growth oriented investments held within qualified plans and IRAs are ultimately taxed at ordinary income tax rates. When investors hold these types of investments within qualified plans and IRAs, they forfeit the favorable tax treatment on the gains. The logic appears sound, but is it?

Clearly, it would never be advantageous to invest nondeductible dollars, such as amounts one might contribute to a nondeductible IRA, if growth comprises the entire return on the investment. The investor would be giving up return that is entirely tax-deferred, and ultimately taxed at a favorable capital gains rate, for return that is also entirely tax-deferred, but ultimately taxed at ordinary income tax rates. However, very few investments provide all of their return in the form of capital appreciation. In many cases, appreciating assets also provide some element of currently taxable dividend

or interest-type income. So, is there some level of growth versus income and/or some length of time, where the benefit of having the entire return sheltered from current tax within a qualified plan or IRA more than compensates for the loss of the capital gains tax rate on the growth portion of the return outside the plan, given that part of the investment's return will be subject to current taxation outside the plan? How would that be measured?

Furthermore, even if growth comprises an investment's entire return, chances are not good that the investor will hold that same investment for an indefinitely long period. If an investor wants to change the investment at some point, for whatever reason, he must generally sell it, recognize the gain, and pay the capital gains tax. Investments can be bought and sold within a qualified plan or IRA without current recognition of gains or current taxation. So qualified plans and IRAs give investors more flexibility to change their investments, rebalance their portfolios, and the like, without having to currently recognize gains and pay tax as a result of the transactions.

But this may not be quite as disadvantageous as it first appears. Through astute management of the timing of transactions and the matching of loss positions with gain positions in one's portfolio, one can minimize the impact of taxes on gains through offsetting loss transactions. This is not always possible, but it is possible frequently enough to greatly ameliorate the overall problem.

If one is considering tax-deductible contributions inside qualified plans and IRAs, then the problem becomes more difficult. For every $1 an investor may contribute before tax to a qualified plan or deductible IRA, he will have only (1-t) $1 to invest outside the plan, assuming his marginal tax rate is t. Will the $1 invested in a highly appreciating asset entirely tax-deferred inside the plan – and ultimately taxed at ordinary income-tax rates – accumulate more after tax when it is ultimately withdrawn, than (1-t) $1 invested outside the plan where the gain component will ultimately be taxed at the more favorable capital-gain rate?

Deductible Contributions

The following example sets the stage for answering the question of which type of asset is better suited to investment within a qualified plan or IRA.

Assume that the optimal portfolio mix includes some combination of both growth assets, such as stocks or mutual funds, and income assets, such as bonds or

Chapter 45 – Investment Strategies For Tax-Advantaged Accounts

Figure 45.4

	Name	Growth Asset	Income Asset
Total before-tax rate of return:	I	11.000%	7.000%
Growth % of total return:	g	85.0%	0.0%
Ordinary income-tax rate:	t	31.0%	Same
LT capital-gains tax rate:	tg	20.0%	Same
Number of years:	N	20	Same
Are plan contributions deductible?		Yes	Same
Accumulation rate outside plan: (before capital-gains tax)	ar	10.489%	4.830%
FVAT $1 in Growth Asset inside plan:		5.563	
-FVAT $1 Income Asset Inside plan:		(2.670)	
Difference inside plan:			2.893
FVAT of $1 in Income Asset outside plan:		2.569	
-FVAT of $1 in Growth Asset outside plan:		(6.219)	
Difference outside plan:			(3.650)
Total after-tax difference:			(0.757)
% Gain (Loss):			(75.70%)

bond funds. To determine whether it is better to invest the income assets or the growth assets within the plan, the investor should compare the amounts the investor would ultimately expect to accumulate after tax by shifting some portion of growth assets from outside the plan to inside the plan and the equivalent portion of income assets from inside the plan to outside the plan. Since it makes no difference what the exact dollar amount being shifted is, the analysis can be performed based upon shifting just a single dollar.[2]

Figure 45.4 presents the calculations based upon the time-value formulas presented in Chapter 32 and Appendix K, "Time Value Concepts." The growth asset is assumed to be a stock or mutual fund type of investment with characteristics similar to the S&P 500 index. The assumed average annual compound rate of return is 11%. In recent decades, the proportion of the S&P 500 index's return attributable to growth has averaged about 85%. This means that if this investment were held outside of the plan, about 85% of the 11% total return would be entirely tax-deferred and ultimately taxable at a 20% long-term capital-gains tax rate. The remaining 15% of the 11% total return is assumed to be currently taxable ordinary dividend-type income. The investor's combined ordinary dividend-type income. The investor's combined ordinary tax rate is assumed to be 31%.

The income asset is assumed to a bond-fund-type investment paying 7% in currently taxable ordinary interest income with no appreciable growth potential.

Based upon the formulas presented in Chapter 32, and the other assumptions presented here, the growth investment would be expected to grow at an accumulation rate of about 10.148% (not including tax on capital gains ultimately payable when the asset is sold) if held outside the plan. Similarly, the income investment would be expected to grow at an accumulation rate of about 4.83% if held outside the plan.

Now, assuming the investor has heeded the general advice that one should invest income assets inside the plan and growth assets outside the plan, what would the impact be of shifting just one dollar of an income investment inside the plan with a growth investment inside the plan? In order to do so, one would also have to include the impact of the corresponding shift from growth investment outside the plan to income investment outside the plan.

The impact will obviously depend on how long the investor expects the money to stay within the plan before the investor withdraws and consumes it. For this illustration, let us assume 20 years. The results will also depend on whether the dollars contributed to the plan are before-tax or after-tax dollars. In this case, it is assumed contributions to the plan are tax-deductible.

Using the formulas from Chapter 32 and Appendix K, the future value after tax of a $1 growth investment inside the plan is $5.563. The future value after tax of the income investment the investor has to give up in order to increase growth investment inside the plan is $2.67. Therefore, shifting $1 from the income investment to the growth investment inside the plan would increase future after-tax wealth by $2.893.

Tools & Techniques of Investment Planning

However, the objective is to keep the asset allocation between the growth asset and the income asset the same in the overall portfolio while increasing (decreasing) the amount of the growth asset (income asset) invested in the plan and decreasing (increasing) the amount of the growth asset (income asset) invested outside the plan. If the investor is going to keep the overall asset allocation unchanged, the investor has to exactly match the shift between the assets inside the plan with an equal but opposite shift between the assets outside the plan.[3]

Once again using the formulas derived in Chapter 32 and Appendix K, the future after-tax value of a $1 income investment outside the plan is $2.569. The future after-tax amount given up by shifting $1 of investment from the growth investment outside the plan is $6.219. So the net effect of shifting this amount from the growth investment to the income investment outside the plan is a loss of $3.650.

The investor would gain 2.893 by shifting $1 from the income investment to the growth investment within the plan but lose $3.650 by completing the corresponding shift of investment outside the plan, for a net loss of $0.757, or 75.70% on every dollar so shifted.

Under these assumptions, the investor should invest the plan dollars first in the income investment. For each dollar the investor shifts away from the income investment to the growth investment inside the plan, the investor will be poorer after tax by about $0.757 in 20 years.

There are so many variables that it is impossible to know whether any strong generalizations can be applied. But in this case, the conventional wisdom seems to be supported.

How would the results of the analysis change if the period of analysis changed? How would the results change if the capital-gain proportion of the growth asset were different? What if the client's ordinary income-tax rate is higher, or lower, than 31%?

DISTRIBUTIONS OF EMPLOYER SECURITIES WITH NET UNREALIZED APPRECIATION

Overview

The gain on employer securities with net unrealized appreciation is excluded when computing tax on lump-sum distributions.[4] Net unrealized appreciation (NUA) is the difference between the value of the stock when credited to the participant's account and its fair market value on the date of the distribution. NUA typically arises with stock bonus plans and employee stock ownership plans.

Taxation

Unrealized appreciation is taxed as long-term capital gain even if the participant sells the securities immediately after the distribution. Currently, the gains on most investment assets held for more than 12 months are taxed at a rate of 15% (5% for gain that would as ordinary income be taxed at 15% or 10%). Under Notice 98-24,[5] any amount of net unrealized appreciation (excluding amounts included in the recipient's basis at the time of the distribution) that occurred while the plan held the securities will be treated as long-term gain subject to the 15% (5%) rate when it is ultimately realized in a subsequent taxable transaction. For appreciation that occurs after the plan distributes the securities, however, the actual period the recipient held the securities after the distribution determines whether the long-term gain rate applies to that portion of gain.

Planning

Generally, only if the participant anticipates an immediate sale of the securities and intends to elect lump-sum-averaging tax treatment, might it be better to have the trustee sell stocks and distribute cash. The proceeds will be included in and benefit from lump-sum averaging calculation. However, most unrealized appreciation on employer stock is currently taxed at maximum rate of 15%. Adjusted total taxable amount in excess of $30,583 is subject to tax at a rate in excess of 15%. Consequently, it will only pay to have the trustee sell the stocks and distribute cash if the value of the stocks and cash distributions does not exceed $30,583 in total. If sale of stocks will not follow immediately, it is virtually always better to take the distribution of stock and defer taxation of the net unrealized appreciation until the stocks are ultimately sold.

CHAPTER ENDNOTES

1. Based on data from Stocks, Bonds, Bills, and Inflation 2002 Yearbook (Chicago, IL: Ibbotson Associates).

2. This may not be entirely correct, since if very large amounts are involved, some portion of the ultimate distribution may be taxed at one rate and the rest taxed at another rate, if the total amount spans tax brackets.

3. Note that the analysis does not assume that the investor actually shifts the assets, which might incur transactions costs and recognition of gains on the sale and purchase of assets that would be necessary to rebalance the portfolio outside the plan. Rather, it is asking the question whether having had one more dollar of growth asset inside the plan rather than outside the plan, with the same overall asset allocation, would have increased expected future after-tax wealth or reduced future after-tax wealth. Suppose it is determined that having had one more dollar of growth asset inside the plan rather than outside the plan would have enhanced one's future after-tax wealth. The

question of whether or not it would be profitable to actually buy and sell assets, incur transactions costs, and pay tax on recognition of gains on transactions outside the plan to achieve this shift in the balance of growth and income assets held inside and outside the plan is a separate analysis. In essence, the analysis asks the question of whether or not the investor should have had the alternative allocation inside and outside the qualified plan from the onset.

4. IRC Sec. 402(e)(4).

5. 1998-1 CB 929.

PRESENT VALUE OF LUMP SUM
(The use of this table is explained in Chapter 32)

YEARS	3.0%	3.5%	4.0%	4.5%	5.0%	5.5%	6.0%
1	0.9709	0.9662	0.9615	0.9569	0.9524	0.9479	0.9434
2	0.9426	0.9335	0.9246	0.9157	0.9070	0.8985	0.8900
3	0.9151	0.9019	0.8890	0.8763	0.8638	0.8516	0.8396
4	0.8885	0.8714	0.8548	0.8386	0.8227	0.8072	0.7921
5	0.8626	0.8420	0.8219	0.8025	0.7835	0.7651	0.7473
6	0.8375	0.8135	0.7903	0.7679	0.7462	0.7252	0.7050
7	0.8131	0.7860	0.7599	0.7348	0.7107	0.6874	0.6651
8	0.7894	0.7594	0.7307	0.7032	0.6768	0.6516	0.6274
9	0.7664	0.7337	0.7026	0.6729	0.6446	0.6176	0.5919
10	0.7441	0.7089	0.6756	0.6439	0.6139	0.5854	0.5584
11	0.7224	0.6849	0.6496	0.6162	0.5847	0.5549	0.5268
12	0.7014	0.6618	0.6246	0.5897	0.5568	0.5260	0.4970
13	0.6810	0.6394	0.6006	0.5643	0.5303	0.4986	0.4688
14	0.6611	0.6178	0.5775	0.5400	0.5051	0.4726	0.4423
15	0.6419	0.5969	0.5553	0.5167	0.4810	0.4479	0.4173
16	0.6232	0.5767	0.5339	0.4945	0.4581	0.4246	0.3936
17	0.6050	0.5572	0.5134	0.4732	0.4363	0.4024	0.3714
18	0.5874	0.5384	0.4936	0.4528	0.4155	0.3815	0.3503
19	0.5703	0.5202	0.4746	0.4333	0.3957	0.3616	0.3305
20	0.5537	0.5026	0.4564	0.4146	0.3769	0.3427	0.3118
21	0.5375	0.4856	0.4388	0.3968	0.3589	0.3249	0.2942
22	0.5219	0.4692	0.4220	0.3797	0.3418	0.3079	0.2775
23	0.5067	0.4533	0.4057	0.3634	0.3256	0.2919	0.2618
24	0.4919	0.4380	0.3901	0.3477	0.3101	0.2767	0.2470
25	0.4776	0.4231	0.3751	0.3327	0.2953	0.2622	0.2330
26	0.4637	0.4088	0.3607	0.3184	0.2812	0.2486	0.2198
27	0.4502	0.3950	0.3468	0.3047	0.2678	0.2356	0.2074
28	0.4371	0.3817	0.3335	0.2916	0.2551	0.2233	0.1956
29	0.4243	0.3687	0.3207	0.2790	0.2429	0.2117	0.1846
30	0.4120	0.3563	0.3083	0.2670	0.2314	0.2006	0.1741
31	0.4000	0.3442	0.2965	0.2555	0.2204	0.1902	0.1643
32	0.3883	0.3326	0.2851	0.2445	0.2099	0.1803	0.1550
33	0.3770	0.3213	0.2741	0.2340	0.1999	0.1709	0.1462
34	0.3660	0.3105	0.2636	0.2239	0.1904	0.1620	0.1379
35	0.3554	0.3000	0.2534	0.2143	0.1813	0.1535	0.1301
36	0.3450	0.2898	0.2437	0.2050	0.1727	0.1455	0.1227
37	0.3350	0.2800	0.2343	0.1962	0.1644	0.1379	0.1158
38	0.3252	0.2706	0.2253	0.1878	0.1566	0.1307	0.1092
39	0.3158	0.2614	0.2166	0.1797	0.1491	0.1239	0.1031
40	0.3066	0.2526	0.2083	0.1719	0.1420	0.1175	0.0972
41	0.2976	0.2440	0.2003	0.1645	0.1353	0.1113	0.0917
42	0.2890	0.2358	0.1926	0.1574	0.1288	0.1055	0.0865
43	0.2805	0.2278	0.1852	0.1507	0.1227	0.1000	0.0816
44	0.2724	0.2201	0.1780	0.1442	0.1169	0.0948	0.0770
45	0.2644	0.2127	0.1712	0.1380	0.1113	0.0899	0.0727
46	0.2567	0.2055	0.1646	0.1320	0.1060	0.0852	0.0685
47	0.2493	0.1985	0.1583	0.1263	0.1009	0.0807	0.0647
48	0.2420	0.1918	0.1522	0.1209	0.0961	0.0765	0.0610
49	0.2350	0.1853	0.1463	0.1157	0.0916	0.0725	0.0575
50	0.2281	0.1791	0.1407	0.1107	0.0872	0.0688	0.0543

Appendix A – Present Value of Lump Sum

PRESENT VALUE OF LUMP SUM (continued)

YEARS	6.5%	7.0%	7.5%	8.0%	8.5%	9.0%	9.5%
1	0.9390	0.9346	0.9302	0.9259	0.9217	0.9174	0.9132
2	0.8817	0.8734	0.8653	0.8573	0.8495	0.8417	0.8340
3	0.8278	0.8163	0.8050	0.7938	0.7829	0.7722	0.7617
4	0.7773	0.7629	0.7488	0.7350	0.7216	0.7084	0.6956
5	0.7299	0.7130	0.6966	0.6806	0.6650	0.6499	0.6352
6	0.6853	0.6663	0.6480	0.6302	0.6129	0.5963	0.5801
7	0.6435	0.6227	0.6028	0.5835	0.5649	0.5470	0.5298
8	0.6042	0.5820	0.5607	0.5403	0.5207	0.5019	0.4838
9	0.5674	0.5439	0.5216	0.5002	0.4799	0.4604	0.4418
10	0.5327	0.5083	0.4852	0.4632	0.4423	0.4224	0.4035
11	0.5002	0.4751	0.4513	0.4289	0.4076	0.3875	0.3685
12	0.4697	0.4440	0.4199	0.3971	0.3757	0.3555	0.3365
13	0.4410	0.4150	0.3906	0.3677	0.3463	0.3262	0.3073
14	0.4141	0.3878	0.3633	0.3405	0.3191	0.2992	0.2807
15	0.3888	0.3624	0.3380	0.3152	0.2941	0.2745	0.2563
16	0.3651	0.3387	0.3144	0.2919	0.2711	0.2519	0.2341
17	0.3428	0.3166	0.2925	0.2703	0.2499	0.2311	0.2138
18	0.3219	0.2959	0.2720	0.2502	0.2303	0.2120	0.1952
19	0.3022	0.2765	0.2531	0.2317	0.2122	0.1945	0.1783
20	0.2838	0.2584	0.2354	0.2145	0.1956	0.1784	0.1628
21	0.2665	0.2415	0.2190	0.1987	0.1803	0.1637	0.1487
22	0.2502	0.2257	0.2037	0.1839	0.1662	0.1502	0.1358
23	0.2349	0.2109	0.1895	0.1703	0.1531	0.1378	0.1240
24	0.2206	0.1971	0.1763	0.1577	0.1412	0.1264	0.1133
25	0.2071	0.1842	0.1640	0.1460	0.1301	0.1160	0.1034
26	0.1945	0.1722	0.1525	0.1352	0.1199	0.1064	0.0945
27	0.1826	0.1609	0.1419	0.1252	0.1105	0.0976	0.0863
28	0.1715	0.1504	0.1320	0.1159	0.1019	0.0895	0.0788
29	0.1610	0.1406	0.1228	0.1073	0.0939	0.0822	0.0719
30	0.1512	0.1314	0.1142	0.0994	0.0865	0.0754	0.0657
31	0.1420	0.1228	0.1063	0.0920	0.0797	0.0691	0.0600
32	0.1333	0.1147	0.0988	0.0852	0.0735	0.0634	0.0548
33	0.1252	0.1072	0.0919	0.0789	0.0677	0.0582	0.0500
34	0.1175	0.1002	0.0855	0.0730	0.0624	0.0534	0.0457
35	0.1103	0.0937	0.0796	0.0676	0.0575	0.0490	0.0417
36	0.1036	0.0875	0.0740	0.0626	0.0530	0.0449	0.0381
37	0.0973	0.0818	0.0688	0.0580	0.0489	0.0412	0.0348
38	0.0914	0.0765	0.0640	0.0537	0.0450	0.0378	0.0318
39	0.0858	0.0715	0.0596	0.0497	0.0415	0.0347	0.0290
40	0.0805	0.0668	0.0554	0.0460	0.0383	0.0318	0.0265
41	0.0756	0.0624	0.0516	0.0426	0.0353	0.0292	0.0242
42	0.0710	0.0583	0.0480	0.0395	0.0325	0.0268	0.0221
43	0.0667	0.0545	0.0446	0.0365	0.0300	0.0246	0.0202
44	0.0626	0.0509	0.0415	0.0338	0.0276	0.0226	0.0184
45	0.0588	0.0476	0.0386	0.0313	0.0254	0.0207	0.0168
46	0.0552	0.0445	0.0359	0.0290	0.0235	0.0190	0.0154
47	0.0518	0.0416	0.0334	0.0269	0.0216	0.0174	0.0140
48	0.0487	0.0389	0.0311	0.0249	0.0199	0.0160	0.0128
49	0.0457	0.0363	0.0289	0.0230	0.0184	0.0147	0.0117
50	0.0429	0.0339	0.0269	0.0213	0.0169	0.0134	0.0107

PRESENT VALUE OF LUMP SUM (continued)

YEARS	10.0%	10.5%	11.0%	11.5%	12.0%	12.5%	13.0%
1	0.9091	0.9050	0.9009	0.8969	0.8929	0.8889	0.8850
2	0.8264	0.8190	0.8116	0.8044	0.7972	0.7901	0.7831
3	0.7513	0.7412	0.7312	0.7214	0.7118	0.7023	0.6931
4	0.6830	0.6707	0.6587	0.6470	0.6355	0.6243	0.6133
5	0.6209	0.6070	0.5935	0.5803	0.5674	0.5549	0.5428
6	0.5645	0.5493	0.5346	0.5204	0.5066	0.4933	0.4803
7	0.5132	0.4971	0.4817	0.4667	0.4523	0.4385	0.4251
8	0.4665	0.4499	0.4339	0.4186	0.4039	0.3897	0.3762
9	0.4241	0.4071	0.3909	0.3754	0.3606	0.3464	0.3329
10	0.3855	0.3684	0.3522	0.3367	0.3220	0.3079	0.2946
11	0.3505	0.3334	0.3173	0.3020	0.2875	0.2737	0.2607
12	0.3186	0.3018	0.2858	0.2708	0.2567	0.2433	00.2307
13	0.2897	0.2731	0.2575	0.2429	0.2292	0.2163	0.2042
14	0.2633	0.2471	0.2320	0.2178	0.2046	0.1922	0.1807
15	0.2394	0.2236	0.2090	0.1954	0.1827	0.1709	0.1599
16	0.2176	0.2024	0.1883	0.1752	0.1631	0.1519	0.1415
17	0.1978	0.1832	0.1696	0.1572	0.1456	0.1350	0.1252
18	0.1799	0.1658	0.1528	0.1409	0.1300	0.1200	0.1108
19	0.1635	0.1500	0.1377	0.1264	0.1161	0.1067	0.0981
20	0.1486	0.1358	0.1240	0.1134	0.1037	0.0948	0.0868
21	0.1351	0.1229	0.1117	0.1017	0.0926	0.0843	0.0768
22	0.1228	0.1112	0.1007	0.0912	0.0826	0.0749	0.0680
23	0.1117	0.1006	0.0907	0.0818	0.0738	0.0666	0.0601
24	0.1015	0.0911	0.0817	0.0734	0.0659	0.0592	0.0532
25	0.0923	0.0824	0.0736	0.0658	0.0588	0.0526	0.0471
26	0.0839	0.0746	0.0663	0.0590	0.0525	0.0468	0.0417
27	0.0763	0.0675	0.0597	0.0529	0.0469	0.0416	0.0369
28	0.0693	0.0611	0.0538	0.0475	0.0419	0.0370	0.0326
29	0.0630	0.0553	0.0485	0.0426	0.0374	0.0329	0.0289
30	0.0573	0.0500	0.0437	0.0382	0.0334	0.0292	0.0256
31	0.0521	0.0453	0.0394	0.0342	0.0298	0.0260	0.0226
32	0.0474	0.0410	0.0355	0.0307	0.0266	0.0231	0.0200
33	0.0431	0.0371	0.0319	0.0275	0.0238	0.0205	0.0177
34	0.0391	0.0335	0.0288	0.0247	0.0212	0.0182	0.0157
35	0.0356	0.0304	0.0259	0.0222	0.0189	0.0162	0.0139
36	0.0323	0.0275	0.0234	0.0199	0.0169	0.0144	0.0123
37	0.0294	0.0249	0.0210	0.0178	0.0151	0.0128	0.0109
38	0.0267	0.0225	0.0190	0.0160	0.0135	0.0114	0.0096
39	0.0243	0.0204	0.0171	0.0143	0.0120	0.0101	0.0085
40	0.0221	0.0184	0.0154	0.0129	0.0107	0.0090	0.0075
41	0.0201	0.0167	0.0139	0.0115	0.0096	0.0080	0.0067
42	0.0183	0.0151	0.0125	0.0103	0.0086	0.0071	0.0059
43	0.0166	0.0137	0.0112	0.0093	0.0076	0.0063	0.0052
44	0.0151	0.0124	0.0101	0.0083	0.0068	0.0056	0.0046
45	0.0137	0.0112	0.0091	0.0075	0.0061	0.0050	0.0041
46	0.0125	0.0101	0.0082	0.0067	0.0054	0.0044	0.0036
47	0.0113	0.0092	0.0074	0.0060	0.0049	0.0039	0.0032
48	0.0103	0.0083	0.0067	0.0054	0.0043	0.0035	0.0028
49	0.0094	0.0075	0.0060	0.0048	0.0039	0.0031	0.0025
50	0.0085	0.0068	0.0054	0.0043	0.0035	0.0028	0.0022

PRESENT VALUE OF LUMP SUM (continued)

YEARS	14.0%	15.0%	16.0%	17.0%	18.0%	19.0%	20.0%
1	0.8772	0.8696	0.8621	0.8547	0.8475	0.8403	0.8333
2	0.7695	0.7561	0.7432	0.7305	0.7182	0.7062	0.6944
3	0.6750	0.6575	0.6407	0.6244	0.6086	0.5934	0.5787
4	0.5921	0.5718	0.5523	0.5337	0.5158	0.4987	0.4823
5	0.5194	0.4972	0.4761	0.4561	0.4371	0.4190	0.4019
6	0.4556	0.4323	0.4104	0.3898	0.3704	0.3521	0.3349
7	0.3996	0.3759	0.3538	0.3332	0.3139	0.2959	0.2791
8	0.3506	0.3269	0.3050	0.2848	0.2660	0.2487	0.2326
9	0.3075	0.2843	0.2630	0.2434	0.2255	0.2090	0.1938
10	0.2697	0.2472	0.2267	0.2080	0.1911	0.1756	0.1615
11	0.2366	0.2149	0.1954	0.1778	0.1619	0.1476	0.1346
12	0.2076	0.1869	0.1685	0.1520	0.1372	0.1240	0.1122
13	0.1821	0.1625	0.1452	0.1299	0.1163	0.1042	0.0935
14	0.1597	0.1413	0.1252	0.1110	0.0985	0.0876	0.0779
15	0.1401	0.1229	0.1079	0.0949	0.0835	0.0736	0.0649
16	0.1229	0.1069	0.0930	0.0811	0.0708	0.0618	0.0541
17	0.1078	0.0929	0.0802	0.0693	0.0600	0.0520	0.0451
18	0.0946	0.0808	0.0691	0.0592	0.0508	0.0437	0.0376
19	0.0829	0.0703	0.0596	0.0506	0.0431	0.0367	0.0313
20	0.0728	0.0611	0.0514	0.0433	0.0365	0.0308	0.0261
21	0.0638	0.0531	0.0443	0.0370	0.0309	0.0259	0.0217
22	0.0560	0.0462	0.0382	0.0316	0.0262	0.0218	0.0181
23	0.0491	0.0402	0.0329	0.0270	0.0222	0.0183	0.0151
24	0.0431	0.0349	0.0284	0.0231	0.0188	0.0154	0.0126
25	0.0378	0.0304	0.0245	0.0197	0.0160	0.0129	0.0105
26	0.0331	0.0264	0.0211	0.0169	0.0135	0.0109	0.0087
27	0.0291	0.0230	0.0182	0.0144	0.0115	0.0091	0.0073
28	0.0255	0.0200	0.0157	0.0123	0.0097	0.0077	0.0061
29	0.0224	0.0174	0.0135	0.0105	0.0082	0.0064	0.0051
30	0.0196	0.0151	0.0116	0.0090	0.0070	0.0054	0.0042
31	0.0172	0.0131	0.0100	0.0077	0.0059	0.0046	0.0035
32	0.0151	0.0114	0.0087	0.0066	0.0050	0.0038	0.0029
33	0.0132	0.0099	0.0075	0.0056	0.0042	0.0032	0.0024
34	0.0116	0.0086	0.0064	0.0048	0.0036	0.0027	0.0020
35	0.0102	0.0075	0.0055	0.0041	0.0030	0.0023	0.0017
36	0.0089	0.0065	0.0048	0.0035	0.0026	0.0019	0.0014
37	0.0078	0.0057	0.0041	0.0030	0.0022	0.0016	0.0012
38	0.0069	0.0049	0.0036	0.0026	0.0019	0.0013	0.0010
39	0.0060	0.0043	0.0031	0.0022	0.0016	0.0011	0.0008
40	0.0053	0.0037	0.0026	0.0019	0.0013	0.0010	0.0007
41	0.0046	0.0032	0.0023	0.0016	0.0011	0.0008	0.0006
42	0.0041	0.0028	0.0020	0.0014	0.0010	0.0007	0.0005
43	0.0036	0.0025	0.0017	0.0012	0.0008	0.0006	0.0004
44	0.0031	0.0021	0.0015	0.0010	0.0007	0.0005	0.0003
45	0.0027	0.0019	0.0013	0.0009	0.0006	0.0004	0.0003
46	0.0024	0.0016	0.0011	0.0007	0.0005	0.0003	0.0002
47	0.0021	0.0014	0.0009	0.0006	0.0004	0.0003	0.0002
48	0.0019	0.0012	0.0008	0.0005	0.0004	0.0002	0.0002
49	0.0016	0.0011	0.0007	0.0005	0.0003	0.0002	0.0001
50	0.0014	0.0009	0.0006	0.0004	0.0003	0.0002	0.0001

PRESENT VALUE OF ANNUITY DUE

(The use of this table is explained in Chapter 32)

YEARS	3.0%	3.5%	4.0%	4.5%	5.0%	5.5%	6.0%
1	1.0000	1.0000	1.0000	1.0000	1.0000	1.0000	1.0000
2	1.9709	1.9662	1.9615	1.9569	1.9524	1.9479	1.9434
3	2.9135	2.8997	2.8861	2.8727	2.8594	2.8463	2.8334
4	3.8286	3.8016	3.7751	3.7490	3.7232	3.6979	3.6730
5	4.7171	4.6731	4.6299	4.5875	4.5459	4.5052	4.4651
6	5.5797	5.5151	5.4518	5.3900	5.3295	5.2703	5.2124
7	6.4172	6.3286	6.2421	6.1579	6.0757	5.9955	5.9173
8	7.2303	7.1145	7.0021	6.8927	6.7864	6.6830	6.5824
9	8.0197	7.8740	7.7327	7.5959	7.4632	7.3346	7.2098
10	8.7861	8.6077	8.4353	8.2688	8.1078	7.9522	7.8017
11	9.5302	9.3166	9.1109	8.9127	8.7217	8.5376	8.3601
12	10.2526	10.0016	9.7605	9.5289	9.3064	9.0925	8.8869
13	10.9540	10.6633	10.3851	10.1186	9.8633	9.6185	9.3838
14	11.6350	11.3027	10.9856	10.6829	10.3936	10.1171	9.8527
15	12.2961	11.9205	11.5631	11.2228	10.8986	10.5896	10.2950
16	12.9379	12.5174	12.1184	11.7395	11.3797	11.0376	10.7122
17	13.5611	13.0941	12.6523	12.2340	11.8378	11.4622	11.1059
18	14.1661	13.6513	13.1657	12.7072	12.2741	11.8646	11.4773
19	14.7535	14.1897	13.6593	13.1600	12.6896	12.2461	11.8276
20	15.3238	14.7098	14.1339	13.5933	13.0853	12.6077	12.1581
21	15.8775	15.2124	14.5903	14.0079	13.4622	12.9504	12.4699
22	16.4150	15.6980	15.0292	14.4047	13.8212	13.2752	12.7641
23	16.9369	16.1671	15.4511	14.7844	14.1630	13.5832	13.0416
24	17.4436	16.6204	15.8568	15.1478	14.4886	13.8750	13.3034
25	17.9355	17.0584	16.2470	15.4955	14.7986	14.1517	13.5504
26	18.4131	17.4815	16.6221	15.8282	15.0939	14.4139	13.7834
27	18.8768	17.8904	16.9828	16.1466	15.3752	14.6625	14.0032
28	19.3270	18.2854	17.3296	16.4513	15.6430	14.8981	14.2105
29	19.7641	18.6670	17.6631	16.7429	15.8981	15.1214	14.4062
30	20.1885	19.0358	17.9837	17.0219	16.1411	15.3331	14.5907
31	20.6004	19.3920	18.2920	17.2889	16.3724	15.5337	14.7648
32	21.0004	19.7363	18.5885	17.5444	16.5928	15.7239	14.9291
33	21.3888	20.0689	18.8735	17.7889	16.8027	15.9042	15.0840
34	21.7658	20.3902	19.1476	18.0229	17.0025	16.0751	15.2302
35	22.1318	20.7007	19.4112	18.2468	17.1929	16.2370	15.3681
36	22.4872	21.0007	19.6646	18.4610	17.3742	16.3906	15.4982
37	22.8323	21.2905	19.9083	18.6660	17.5469	16.5361	15.6210
38	23.1672	21.5705	20.1426	18.8622	17.7113	16.6740	15.7368
39	23.4925	21.8411	20.3679	19.0500	17.8679	16.8047	15.8460
40	23.8082	22.1025	20.5845	19.2297	18.0170	16.9287	15.9491
41	24.1148	22.3551	20.7928	19.4016	18.1591	17.0461	16.0463
42	24.4124	22.5991	20.9931	19.5661	18.2944	17.1575	16.1380
43	24.7014	22.8349	21.1856	19.7235	18.4232	17.2630	16.2245
44	24.9819	23.0627	21.3708	19.8742	18.5459	17.3630	16.3062
45	25.2543	23.2828	21.5488	20.0184	18.6628	17.4578	16.3832
46	25.5187	23.4954	21.7200	20.1563	18.7741	17.5477	16.4558
47	25.7754	23.7009	21.8847	20.2884	18.8801	17.6329	16.5244
48	26.0247	23.8994	22.0429	20.4147	18.9810	17.7137	16.5890
49	26.2667	24.0912	22.1951	20.5356	19.0772	17.7902	16.6500
50	26.5017	24.2766	22.3415	20.6513	19.1687	17.8628	16.7076

PRESENT VALUE OF ANNUITY DUE (continued)

YEARS	6.5%	7.0%	7.5%	8.0%	8.5%	9.0%	9.5%
1	1.0000	1.0000	1.0000	1.0000	1.0000	1.0000	1.0000
2	1.9390	1.9346	1.9302	1.9259	1.9217	1.9174	1.9132
3	2.8206	2.8080	2.7956	2.7833	2.7711	2.7591	2.7473
4	3.6485	3.6243	3.6005	3.5771	3.5540	3.5313	3.5089
5	4.4258	4.3872	4.3493	4.3121	4.2756	4.2397	4.2045
6	5.1557	5.1002	5.0459	4.9927	4.9406	4.8897	4.8397
7	5.8410	5.7665	5.6938	5.6229	5.5536	5.4859	5.4198
8	6.4845	6.3893	6.2966	6.2064	6.1185	6.0330	5.9496
9	7.0888	6.9713	6.8573	6.7466	6.6392	6.5348	6.4334
10	7.6561	7.5152	7.3789	7.2469	7.1191	6.9952	6.8753
11	8.1888	8.0236	7.8641	7.7101	7.5613	7.4177	7.2788
12	8.6890	8.4987	8.3154	8.1390	7.9690	7.8052	7.6473
13	9.1587	8.9427	8.7353	8.5361	8.3447	8.1607	7.9838
14	9.5997	9.3577	9.1258	8.9038	8.6910	8.4869	8.2912
15	10.0138	9.7455	9.4892	9.2442	9.0101	8.7861	8.5719
16	10.4027	10.1079	9.8271	9.5595	9.3042	9.0607	8.8282
17	10.7678	10.4466	10.1415	9.8514	9.5753	9.3126	9.0623
18	11.1106	10.7632	10.4340	10.1216	9.8252	9.5436	9.2760
19	11.4325	11.0591	10.7060	10.3719	10.0555	9.7556	9.4713
20	11.7347	11.3356	10.9591	10.6036	10.2677	9.9501	9.6496
21	12.0185	11.5940	11.1945	10.8181	10.4633	10.1285	9.8124
22	12.2850	11.8355	11.4135	11.0168	10.6436	10.2922	9.9611
23	12.5352	12.0612	11.6172	11.2007	10.8098	10.4424	10.0969
24	12.7701	12.2722	11.8067	11.3711	10.9629	10.5802	10.2209
25	12.9907	12.4693	11.9830	11.5288	11.1041	10.7066	10.3341
26	13.1979	12.6536	12.1469	11.6748	11.2342	10.8226	10.4376
27	13.3924	12.8258	12.2995	11.8100	11.3541	10.9290	10.5320
28	13.5750	12.9867	12.4414	11.9352	11.4646	11.0266	10.6183
29	13.7465	13.1371	12.5734	12.0511	11.5665	11.1161	10.6971
30	13.9075	13.2777	12.6962	12.1584	11.6603	11.1983	10.7690
31	14.0587	13.4090	12.8104	12.2578	11.7468	11.2737	10.8347
32	14.2006	13.5318	12.9166	12.3498	11.8266	11.3428	10.8947
33	14.3339	13.6466	13.0155	12.4350	11.9001	11.4062	10.9495
34	14.4591	13.7538	13.1074	12.5139	11.9678	11.4644	10.9996
35	14.5766	13.8540	13.1929	12.5869	12.0302	11.5178	11.0453
36	14.6870	13.9477	13.2725	12.6546	12.0878	11.5668	11.0870
37	14.7906	14.0352	13.3465	12.7172	12.1408	11.6118	11.1251
38	14.8879	14.1170	13.4154	12.7752	12.1897	11.6530	11.1599
39	14.9792	14.1935	13.4794	12.8289	12.2347	11.6908	11.1917
40	15.0650	14.2649	13.5390	12.8786	12.2763	11.7255	11.2207
41	15.1455	14.3317	13.5944	12.9246	12.3145	11.7574	11.2472
42	15.2212	14.3941	13.6460	12.9672	12.3498	11.7866	11.2715
43	15.2922	14.4524	13.6939	13.0067	12.3823	11.8134	11.2936
44	15.3588	14.5070	13.7385	13.0432	12.4123	11.8380	11.3138
45	15.4214	14.5579	13.7800	13.0771	12.4399	11.8605	11.3322
46	15.4802	14.6055	13.8186	13.1084	12.4653	11.8812	11.3490
47	15.5354	14.6500	13.8545	13.1374	12.4888	11.9002	11.3644
48	15.5873	14.6916	13.8879	13.1643	12.5104	11.9176	11.3785
49	15.6359	14.7305	13.9190	13.1891	12.5303	11.9336	11.3913
50	15.6816	14.7668	13.9479	13.2122	12.5487	11.9482	11.4030

PRESENT VALUE OF ANNUITY DUE (continued)

YEARS	10.0%	10.5%	11.0%	11.5%	12.0%	12.5%	13.0%
1	1.0000	1.0000	1.0000	1.0000	1.0000	1.0000	1.0000
2	1.9091	1.9050	1.9009	1.8969	1.8929	1.8889	1.8850
3	2.7355	2.7240	2.7125	2.7012	2.6901	2.6790	2.6681
4	3.4869	3.4651	3.4437	3.4226	3.4018	3.3813	3.3612
5	4.1699	4.1359	4.1024	4.0696	4.0373	4.0056	3.9745
6	4.7908	4.7429	4.6959	4.6499	4.6048	4.5606	4.5172
7	5.3553	5.2922	5.2305	5.1703	5.1114	5.0538	4.9976
8	5.8684	5.7893	5.7122	5.6370	5.5638	5.4923	5.4226
9	6.3349	6.2392	6.1461	6.0556	5.9676	5.8820	5.7988
10	6.7590	6.6463	6.5370	6.4311	6.3282	6.2285	6.1317
11	7.1446	7.0148	6.8892	6.7678	6.6502	6.5364	6.4262
12	7.4951	7.3482	7.2065	7.0697	6.9377	6.8102	6.6869
13	7.8137	7.6500	7.4924	7.3406	7.1944	7.0535	6.9176
14	8.1034	7.9230	7.7499	7.5835	7.4235	7.2698	7.1218
15	8.3667	8.1702	7.9819	7.8013	7.6282	7.4620	7.3025
16	8.6061	8.3938	8.1909	7.9967	7.8109	7.6329	7.4624
17	8.8237	8.5962	8.3792	8.1719	7.9740	7.7848	7.6039
18	9.0216	8.7794	8.5488	8.3291	8.1196	7.9198	7.7291
19	9.2014	8.9451	8.7016	8.4700	8.2497	8.0398	7.8399
20	9.3649	9.0952	8.8393	8.5964	8.3658	8.1465	7.9380
21	9.5136	9.2309	8.9633	8.7098	8.4694	8.2414	8.0248
22	9.6487	9.3538	9.0751	8.8115	8.5620	8.3256	8.1016
23	9.7715	9.4649	9.1757	8.9027	8.6446	8.4006	8.1695
24	9.8832	9.5656	9.2664	8.9845	8.7184	8.4672	8.2297
25	9.9847	9.6566	9.3481	9.0578	8.7843	8.5264	8.2829
26	10.0770	9.7390	9.4217	9.1236	8.8431	8.5790	8.3300
27	10.1609	9.8136	9.4881	9.1826	8.8957	8.6258	8.3717
28	10.2372	9.8811	9.5478	9.2355	8.9426	8.6674	8.4086
29	10.3066	9.9422	9.6016	9.2830	8.9844	8.7043	8.4412
30	10.3696	9.9974	9.6501	9.3255	9.0218	8.7372	8.4701
31	10.4269	10.0474	9.6938	9.3637	9.0552	8.7664	8.4957
32	10.4790	10.0927	9.7331	9.3980	9.0850	8.7923	8.5183
33	10.5264	10.1337	9.7686	9.4287	9.1116	8.8154	8.5383
34	10.5694	10.1707	9.8005	9.4562	9.1354	8.8359	8.5560
35	10.6086	10.2043	9.8293	9.4809	9.1566	8.8542	8.5717
36	10.6442	10.2347	9.8552	9.5030	9.1755	8.8704	8.5856
37	10.6765	10.2621	9.8786	9.5229	9.1924	8.8848	8.5979
38	10.7059	10.2870	9.8996	9.5407	9.2075	8.8976	8.6087
39	10.7327	10.3095	9.9186	9.5567	9.2210	8.9089	8.6183
40	10.7570	10.3299	9.9357	9.5710	9.2330	8.9191	8.6268
41	10.7791	10.3483	9.9511	9.5839	9.2438	8.9281	8.6344
42	10.7991	10.3650	9.9649	9.5954	9.2534	8.9361	8.6410
43	10.8174	10.3801	9.9774	9.6058	9.2619	8.9432	8.6469
44	10.8340	10.3937	9.9886	9.6150	9.2696	8.9495	8.6522
45	10.8491	10.4061	9.9988	9.6233	9.2764	8.9551	8.6568
46	10.8628	10.4173	10.0079	9.6308	9.2825	8.9601	8.6609
47	10.8753	10.4274	10.0161	9.6375	9.2880	8.9645	8.6645
48	10.8866	10.4366	10.0235	9.6435	9.2928	8.9685	8.6677
49	10.8969	10.4448	10.0302	9.6489	9.2972	8.9720	8.6705
50	10.9063	10.4524	10.0362	9.6537	9.3010	8.9751	8.6730

Appendix B – Present Value of Annuity Due

PRESENT VALUE OF ANNUITY DUE (continued)

YEARS	14.0%	15.0%	16.0%	17.0%	18.0%	19.0%	20.0%
1	1.0000	1.0000	1.0000	1.0000	1.0000	1.0000	1.0000
2	1.8772	1.8696	1.8621	1.8547	1.8475	1.8403	1.8333
3	2.6467	2.6257	2.6052	2.5852	2.5656	2.5465	2.5278
4	3.3216	3.2832	3.2459	3.2096	3.1743	3.1399	3.1065
5	3.9137	3.8550	3.7982	3.7432	3.6901	3.6386	3.5887
6	4.4331	4.3522	4.2743	4.1993	4.1272	4.0576	3.9906
7	4.8887	4.7845	4.6847	4.5892	4.4976	4.4098	4.3255
8	5.2883	5.1604	5.0386	4.9224	4.8115	4.7057	4.6046
9	5.6389	5.4873	5.3436	5.2072	5.0776	4.9544	4.8372
10	5.9464	5.7716	5.6065	5.4506	5.3030	5.1633	5.0310
11	6.2161	6.0188	5.8332	5.6586	5.4941	5.3389	5.1925
12	6.4527	6.2337	6.0286	5.8364	5.6560	5.4865	5.3271
13	6.6603	6.4206	6.1971	5.9884	5.7932	5.6105	5.4392
14	6.8424	6.5831	6.3423	6.1183	5.9095	5.7147	5.5327
15	7.0021	6.7245	6.4675	6.2293	6.0081	5.8023	5.6106
16	7.1422	6.8474	6.5755	6.3242	6.0916	5.8759	5.6755
17	7.2651	6.9542	6.6685	6.4053	6.1624	5.9377	5.7296
18	7.3729	7.0472	6.7487	6.4746	6.2223	5.9897	5.7746
19	7.4674	7.1280	6.8178	6.5339	6.2732	6.0333	5.8122
20	7.5504	7.1982	6.8775	6.5845	6.3162	6.0700	5.8435
21	7.6231	7.2593	6.9288	6.6278	6.3527	6.1009	5.8696
22	7.6870	7.3125	6.9731	6.6648	6.3837	6.1268	5.8913
23	7.7429	7.3587	7.0113	6.6964	6.4099	6.1486	5.9094
24	7.7921	7.3988	7.0442	6.7234	6.4321	6.1668	5.9245
25	7.8351	7.4338	7.0726	6.7465	6.4509	6.1822	5.9371
26	7.8729	7.4641	7.0971	6.7662	6.4669	6.1951	5.9476
27	7.9061	7.4906	7.1182	6.7831	6.4804	6.2060	5.9563
28	7.9352	7.5135	7.1364	6.7975	6.4919	6.2151	5.9636
29	7.9607	7.5335	7.1520	6.8099	6.5016	6.2228	5.9697
30	7.9830	7.5509	7.1656	6.8204	6.5098	6.2292	5.9747
31	8.0027	7.5660	7.1772	6.8294	6.5168	6.2347	5.9789
32	8.0199	7.5791	7.1872	6.8371	6.5227	6.2392	5.9824
33	8.0350	7.5905	7.1959	6.8437	6.5277	6.2430	5.9854
34	8.0482	7.6005	7.2034	6.8493	6.5320	6.2462	5.9878
35	8.0599	7.6091	7.2098	6.8541	6.5356	6.2489	5.9898
36	8.0700	7.6166	7.2153	6.8582	6.5386	6.2512	5.9915
37	8.0790	7.6231	7.2201	6.8617	6.5412	6.2531	5.9929
38	8.0868	7.6288	7.2242	6.8647	6.5434	6.2547	5.9941
39	8.0937	7.6338	7.2278	6.8673	6.5452	6.2561	5.9951
40	8.0997	7.6380	7.2309	6.8695	6.5468	6.2572	5.9959
41	8.1050	7.6418	7.2335	6.8713	6.5482	6.2582	5.9966
42	8.1097	7.6450	7.2358	6.8729	6.5493	6.2590	5.9972
43	8.1138	7.6478	7.2377	6.8743	6.5502	6.2596	5.9976
44	8.1173	7.6503	7.2394	6.8755	6.5510	6.2602	5.9980
45	8.1205	7.6524	7.2409	6.8765	6.5517	6.2607	5.9984
46	8.1232	7.6543	7.2421	6.8773	6.5523	6.2611	5.9986
47	8.1256	7.6559	7.2432	6.8781	6.5528	6.2614	5.9989
48	8.1277	7.6573	7.2442	6.8787	6.5532	6.2617	5.9991
49	8.1296	7.6585	7.2450	6.8792	6.5536	6.2619	5.9992
50	8.1312	7.6596	7.2457	6.8797	6.5539	6.2621	5.9993

Appendix C

PRESENT VALUE OF ORDINARY ANNUITY

(The use of this table is explained in Chapter 32)

YEARS	3.0%	3.5%	4.0%	4.5%	5.0%	5.5%	6.0%
1	0.9709	0.9662	0.9615	0.9569	0.9524	0.9479	0.9434
2	1.9135	1.8997	1.8861	1.8727	1.8594	1.8463	1.8334
3	2.8286	2.8016	2.7751	2.7490	2.7232	2.6979	2.6730
4	3.7171	3.6731	3.6299	3.5875	3.5460	3.5051	3.4651
5	4.5797	4.5151	4.4518	4.3900	4.3295	4.2703	4.2124
6	5.4172	5.3286	5.2421	5.1579	5.0757	4.9955	4.9173
7	6.2303	6.1145	6.0021	5.8927	5.7864	5.6830	5.5824
8	7.0197	6.8740	6.7327	6.5959	6.4632	6.3346	6.2098
9	7.7861	7.6077	7.4353	7.2688	7.1078	6.9522	6.8017
10	8.5302	8.3166	8.1109	7.9127	7.7217	7.5376	7.3601
11	9.2526	9.0016	8.7605	8.5289	8.3064	8.0925	7.8869
12	9.9540	9.6633	9.3851	9.1186	8.8633	8.6185	8.3838
13	10.6350	10.3027	9.9856	9.6829	9.3936	9.1171	8.8527
14	11.2961	10.9205	10.5631	10.2228	9.8986	9.5896	9.2950
15	11.9379	11.5174	11.1184	10.7395	10.3797	10.0376	9.7122
16	12.5611	12.0941	11.6523	11.2340	10.8378	10.4622	10.1059
17	13.1661	12.6513	12.1657	11.7072	11.2741	10.8646	10.4773
18	13.7535	13.1897	12.6593	12.1600	11.6896	11.2461	10.8276
19	14.3238	13.7098	13.1339	12.5933	12.0853	11.6077	11.1581
20	14.8775	14.2124	13.5903	13.0079	12.4622	11.9504	11.4699
21	15.4150	14.6980	14.0292	13.4047	12.8212	12.2752	11.7641
22	15.9369	15.1671	14.4511	13.7844	13.1630	12.5832	12.0416
23	16.4436	15.6204	14.8568	14.1478	13.4886	12.8750	12.3034
24	16.9355	16.0584	15.2470	14.4955	13.7986	13.1517	12.5504
25	17.4131	16.4815	15.6221	14.8282	14.0939	13.4139	12.7834
26	17.8768	16.8904	15.9828	15.1466	14.3752	13.6625	13.0032
27	18.3270	17.2854	16.3296	15.4513	14.6430	13.8981	13.2105
28	18.7641	17.6670	16.6631	15.7429	14.8981	14.1214	13.4062
29	19.1885	18.0358	16.9837	16.0219	15.1411	14.3331	13.5907
30	19.6004	18.3920	17.2920	16.2889	15.3725	14.5337	13.7648
31	20.0004	18.7363	17.5885	16.5444	15.5928	14.7239	13.9291
32	20.3888	19.0689	17.8736	16.7889	15.8027	14.9042	14.0840
33	20.7658	19.3902	18.1476	17.0229	16.0025	15.0751	14.2302
34	21.1318	19.7007	18.4112	17.2468	16.1929	15.2370	14.3681
35	21.4872	20.0007	18.6646	17.4610	16.3742	15.3906	14.4982
36	21.8323	20.2905	18.9083	17.6660	16.5469	15.5361	14.6210
37	22.1672	20.5705	19.1426	17.8622	16.7113	15.6740	14.7368
38	22.4925	20.8411	19.3679	18.0500	16.8679	15.8047	14.8460
39	22.8082	21.1025	19.5845	18.2297	17.0170	15.9287	14.9491
40	23.1148	21.3551	19.7928	18.4016	17.1591	16.0461	15.0463
41	23.4124	21.5991	19.9931	18.5661	17.2944	16.1575	15.1380
42	23.7014	21.8349	20.1856	18.7235	17.4232	16.2630	15.2245
43	23.9819	22.0627	20.3708	18.8742	17.5459	16.3630	15.3062
44	24.2543	22.2828	20.5488	19.0184	17.6628	16.4578	15.3832
45	24.5187	22.4955	20.7200	19.1563	17.7741	16.5477	15.4558
46	24.7754	22.7009	20.8847	19.2884	17.8801	16.6329	15.5244
47	25.0247	22.8994	21.0429	19.4147	17.9810	16.7137	15.5890
48	25.2667	23.0912	21.1951	19.5356	18.0772	16.7902	15.6500
49	25.5017	23.2766	21.3415	19.6513	18.1687	16.8628	15.7076
50	25.7298	23.4556	21.4822	19.7620	18.2559	16.9315	15.7619

PRESENT VALUE OF ORDINARY ANNUITY (continued)

YEARS	6.5%	7.0%	7.5%	8.0%	8.5%	9.0%	9.5%
1	0.9390	0.9346	0.9302	0.9259	0.9217	0.9174	0.9132
2	1.8206	1.8080	1.7956	1.7833	1.7711	1.7591	1.7473
3	2.6485	2.6243	2.6005	2.5771	2.5540	2.5313	2.5089
4	3.4258	3.3872	3.3493	3.3121	3.2756	3.2397	3.2045
5	4.1557	4.1002	4.0459	3.9927	3.9406	3.8897	3.8397
6	4.8410	4.7665	4.6938	4.6229	4.5536	4.4859	4.4198
7	5.4845	5.3893	5.2966	5.2064	5.1185	5.0330	4.9496
8	6.0888	5.9713	5.8573	5.7466	5.6392	5.5348	5.4334
9	6.6561	6.5152	6.3789	6.2469	6.1191	5.9952	5.8753
10	7.1888	7.0236	6.8641	6.7101	6.5613	6.4177	6.2788
11	7.6890	7.4987	7.3154	7.1390	6.9690	6.8052	6.6473
12	8.1587	7.9427	7.7353	7.5361	7.3447	7.1607	6.9838
13	8.5997	8.3577	8.1258	7.9038	7.6910	7.4869	7.2912
14	9.0138	8.7455	8.4892	8.2442	8.0101	7.7862	7.5719
15	9.4027	9.1079	8.8271	8.5595	8.3042	8.0607	7.8282
16	9.7678	9.4466	9.1415	8.8514	8.5753	8.3126	8.0623
17	10.1106	9.7632	9.4340	9.1216	8.8252	8.5436	8.2760
18	10.4325	10.0591	9.7060	9.3719	9.0555	8.7556	8.4713
19	10.7347	10.3356	9.9591	9.6036	9.2677	8.9501	8.6496
20	11.0185	10.5940	10.1945	9.8181	9.4633	9.1285	8.8124
21	11.2850	10.8355	10.4135	10.0168	9.6436	9.2922	8.9611
22	11.5352	11.0612	10.6172	10.2007	9.8098	9.4424	9.0969
23	11.7701	11.2722	10.8067	10.3711	9.9629	9.5802	9.2209
24	11.9907	11.4693	10.9830	10.5288	10.1041	9.7066	9.3341
25	12.1979	11.6536	11.1469	10.6748	10.2342	9.8226	9.4376
26	12.3924	11.8258	11.2995	10.8100	10.3541	9.9290	9.5320
27	12.5750	11.9867	11.4414	10.9352	10.4646	10.0266	9.6183
28	12.7465	12.1371	11.5734	11.0511	10.5665	10.1161	9.6971
29	12.9075	12.2777	11.6962	11.1584	10.6603	10.1983	9.7690
30	13.0587	12.4090	11.8104	11.2578	10.7468	10.2737	9.8347
31	13.2006	12.5318	11.9166	11.3498	10.8266	10.3428	9.8947
32	13.3339	12.6466	12.0155	11.4350	10.9001	10.4062	9.9495
33	13.4591	12.7538	12.1074	11.5139	10.9678	10.4644	9.9996
34	13.5766	12.8540	12.1929	11.5869	11.0302	10.5178	10.0453
35	13.6870	12.9477	12.2725	11.6546	11.0878	10.5668	10.0870
36	13.7906	13.0352	12.3465	11.7172	11.1408	10.6118	10.1251
37	13.8879	13.1170	12.4154	11.7752	11.1897	10.6530	10.1599
38	13.9792	13.1935	12.4794	11.8289	11.2347	10.6908	10.1917
39	14.0650	13.2649	12.5390	11.8786	11.2763	10.7255	10.2207
40	14.1455	13.3317	12.5944	11.9246	11.3145	10.7574	10.2472
41	14.2212	13.3941	12.6460	11.9672	11.3498	10.7866	10.2715
42	14.2922	13.4524	12.6939	12.0067	11.3823	10.8134	10.2936
43	14.3588	13.5070	12.7385	12.0432	11.4123	10.8379	10.3138
44	14.4214	13.5579	12.7800	12.0771	11.4399	10.8605	10.3322
45	14.4802	13.6055	12.8186	12.1084	11.4653	10.8812	10.3490
46	14.5354	13.6500	12.8545	12.1374	11.4888	10.9002	10.3644
47	14.5873	13.6916	12.8879	12.1643	11.5104	10.9176	10.3785
48	14.6359	13.7305	12.9190	12.1891	11.5303	10.9336	10.3913
49	14.6816	13.7668	12.9479	12.2122	11.5487	10.9482	10.4030
50	14.7245	13.8007	12.9748	12.2335	11.5656	10.9617	10.4137

PRESENT VALUE OF ORDINARY ANNUITY (continued)

YEARS	10.0%	10.5%	11.0%	11.5%	12.0%	12.5%	13.0%
1	0.9091	0.9050	0.9009	0.8969	0.8929	0.8889	0.8850
2	1.7355	1.7240	1.7125	1.7012	1.6901	1.6790	1.6681
3	2.4869	2.4651	2.4437	2.4226	2.4018	2.3813	2.3612
4	3.1699	3.1359	3.1024	3.0696	3.0373	3.0056	2.9745
5	3.7908	3.7429	3.6959	3.6499	3.6048	3.5606	3.5172
6	4.3553	4.2922	4.2305	4.1703	4.1114	4.0538	3.9975
7	4.8684	4.7893	4.7122	4.6370	4.5638	4.4923	4.4226
8	5.3349	5.2392	5.1461	5.0556	4.9676	4.8820	4.7988
9	5.7590	5.6463	5.5370	5.4311	5.3282	5.2285	5.1317
10	6.1446	6.0148	5.8892	5.7678	5.6502	5.5364	5.4262
11	6.4951	6.3482	6.2065	6.0697	5.9377	5.8102	5.6869
12	6.8137	6.6500	6.4924	6.3406	6.1944	6.0535	5.9176
13	7.1034	6.9230	6.7499	6.5835	6.4235	6.2698	6.1218
14	7.3667	7.1702	6.9819	6.8013	6.6282	6.4620	6.3025
15	7.6061	7.3938	7.1909	6.9967	6.8109	6.6329	6.4624
16	7.8237	7.5962	7.3792	7.1719	6.9740	6.7848	6.6039
17	8.0216	7.7794	7.5488	7.3291	7.1196	6.9198	6.7291
18	8.2014	7.9451	7.7016	7.4700	7.2497	7.0398	6.8399
19	8.3649	8.0952	7.8393	7.5964	7.3658	7.1465	6.9380
20	8.5136	8.2309	7.9633	7.7098	7.4694	7.2414	7.0248
21	8.6487	8.3538	8.0751	7.8115	7.5620	7.3256	7.1016
22	8.7715	8.4649	8.1757	7.9027	7.6446	7.4006	7.1695
23	8.8832	8.5656	8.2664	7.9845	7.7184	7.4672	7.2297
24	8.9847	8.6566	8.3481	8.0578	7.7843	7.5264	7.2829
25	9.0770	8.7390	8.4217	8.1236	7.8431	7.5790	7.3300
26	9.1609	8.8136	8.4881	8.1826	7.8957	7.6258	7.3717
27	9.2372	8.8811	8.5478	8.2355	7.9426	7.6674	7.4086
28	9.3066	8.9422	8.6016	8.2830	7.9844	7.7043	7.4412
29	9.3696	8.9974	8.6501	8.3255	8.0218	7.7372	7.4701
30	9.4269	9.0474	8.6938	8.3637	8.0552	7.7664	7.4957
31	9.4790	9.0927	8.7331	8.3980	8.0850	7.7923	7.5183
32	9.5264	9.1337	8.7686	8.4287	8.1116	7.8154	7.5383
33	9.5694	9.1707	8.8005	8.4562	8.1354	7.8359	7.5560
34	9.6086	9.2043	8.8293	8.4809	8.1566	7.8542	7.5717
35	9.6442	9.2347	8.8552	8.5030	8.1755	7.8704	7.5856
36	9.6765	9.2621	8.8786	8.5229	8.1924	7.8848	7.5979
37	9.7059	9.2870	8.8996	8.5407	8.2075	7.8976	7.6087
38	9.7327	9.3095	8.9186	8.5567	8.2210	7.9089	7.6183
39	9.7570	9.3299	8.9357	8.5710	8.2330	7.9191	7.6268
40	9.7791	9.3483	8.9511	8.5839	8.2438	7.9281	7.6344
41	9.7991	9.3650	8.9649	8.5954	8.2534	7.9361	7.6410
42	9.8174	9.3801	8.9774	8.6058	8.2619	7.9432	7.6469
43	9.8340	9.3937	8.9886	8.6150	8.2696	7.9495	7.6522
44	9.8491	9.4061	8.9988	8.6233	8.2764	7.9551	7.6568
45	9.8628	9.4173	9.0079	8.6308	8.2825	7.9601	7.6609
46	9.8753	9.4274	9.0161	8.6375	8.2880	7.9645	7.6645
47	9.8866	9.4366	9.0235	8.6435	8.2928	7.9685	7.6677
48	9.8969	9.4448	9.0302	8.6489	8.2972	7.9720	7.6705
49	9.9063	9.4524	9.0362	8.6537	8.3010	7.9751	7.6730
50	9.9148	9.4591	9.0417	8.6580	8.3045	7.9778	7.6752

PRESENT VALUE OF ORDINARY ANNUITY (continued)

YEARS	14.0%	15.0%	16.0%	17.0%	18.0%	19.0%	20.0%
1	0.8772	0.8696	0.8621	0.8547	0.8475	0.8403	0.8333
2	1.6467	1.6257	1.6052	1.5852	1.5656	1.5465	1.5278
3	2.3216	2.2832	2.2459	2.2096	2.1743	2.1399	2.1065
4	2.9137	2.8550	2.7982	2.7432	2.6901	2.6386	2.5887
5	3.4331	3.3522	3.2743	3.1993	3.1272	3.0576	2.9906
6	3.8887	3.7845	3.6847	3.5892	3.4976	3.4098	3.3255
7	4.2883	4.1604	4.0386	3.9224	3.8115	3.7057	3.6046
8	4.6389	4.4873	4.3436	4.2072	4.0776	3.9544	3.8372
9	4.9464	4.7716	4.6065	4.4506	4.3030	4.1633	4.0310
10	5.2161	5.0188	4.8332	4.6586	4.4941	4.3389	4.1925
11	5.4527	5.2337	5.0286	4.8364	4.6560	4.4865	4.3271
12	5.6603	5.4206	5.1971	4.9884	4.7932	4.6105	4.4392
13	5.8424	5.5831	5.3423	5.1183	4.9095	4.7147	4.5327
14	6.0021	5.7245	5.4675	5.2293	5.0081	4.8023	4.6106
15	6.1422	5.8474	5.5755	5.3242	5.0916	4.8759	4.6755
16	6.2651	5.9542	5.6685	5.4053	5.1624	4.9377	4.7296
17	6.3729	6.0472	5.7487	5.4746	5.2223	4.9897	4.7746
18	6.4674	6.1280	5.8178	5.5339	5.2732	5.0333	4.8122
19	6.5504	6.1982	5.8775	5.5845	5.3162	5.0700	4.8435
20	6.6231	6.2593	5.9288	5.6278	5.3527	5.1009	4.8696
21	6.6870	6.3125	5.9731	5.6648	5.3837	5.1268	4.8913
22	6.7429	6.3587	6.0113	5.6964	5.4099	5.1486	4.9094
23	6.7921	6.3988	6.0442	5.7234	5.4321	5.1668	4.9245
24	6.8351	6.4338	6.0726	5.7465	5.4509	5.1822	4.9371
25	6.8729	6.4641	6.0971	5.7662	5.4669	5.1951	4.9476
26	6.9061	6.4906	6.1182	5.7831	5.4804	5.2060	4.9563
27	6.9352	6.5135	6.1364	5.7975	5.4919	5.2151	4.9636
28	6.9607	6.5335	6.1520	5.8099	5.5016	5.2228	4.9697
29	6.9830	6.5509	6.1656	5.8204	5.5098	5.2292	4.9747
30	7.0027	6.5660	6.1772	5.8294	5.5168	5.2347	4.9789
31	7.0199	6.5791	6.1872	5.8371	5.5227	5.2392	4.9824
32	7.0350	6.5905	6.1959	5.8437	5.5277	5.2430	4.9854
33	7.0482	6.6005	6.2034	5.8493	5.5320	5.2462	4.9878
34	7.0599	6.6091	6.2098	5.8541	5.5356	5.2489	4.9898
35	7.0700	6.6166	6.2153	5.8582	5.5386	5.2512	4.9915
36	7.0790	6.6231	6.2201	5.8617	5.5412	5.2531	4.9929
37	7.0868	6.6288	6.2242	5.8647	5.5434	5.2547	4.9941
38	7.0937	6.6338	6.2278	5.8673	5.5452	5.2561	4.9951
39	7.0997	6.6380	6.2309	5.8695	5.5468	5.2572	4.9959
40	7.1050	6.6418	6.2335	5.8713	5.5482	5.2582	4.9966
41	7.1097	6.6450	6.2358	5.8729	5.5493	5.2590	4.9972
42	7.1138	6.6478	6.2377	5.8743	5.5502	5.2596	4.9976
43	7.1173	6.6503	6.2394	5.8755	5.5510	5.2602	4.9980
44	7.1205	6.6524	6.2409	5.8765	5.5517	5.2607	4.9984
45	7.1232	6.6543	6.2421	5.8773	5.5523	5.2611	4.9986
46	7.1256	6.6559	6.2432	5.8781	5.5528	5.2614	4.9989
47	7.1277	6.6573	6.2442	5.8787	5.5532	5.2617	4.9991
48	7.1296	6.6585	6.2450	5.8792	5.5536	5.2619	4.9992
49	7.1312	6.6596	6.2457	5.8797	5.5539	5.2621	4.9993
50	7.1327	6.6605	6.2463	5.8801	5.5541	5.2623	4.9995

FUTURE VALUE OF LUMP SUM

(The use of this table is explained in Chapter 32)

YEARS	3.0%	3.5%	4.0%	4.5%	5.0%	5.5%
1	1.0300	1.0350	1.0400	1.0450	1.0500	1.0550
2	1.0609	1.0712	1.0816	1.0920	1.1025	1.1130
3	1.0927	1.1087	1.1249	1.1412	1.1576	1.1742
4	1.1255	1.1475	1.1699	1.1925	1.2155	1.2388
5	1.1593	1.1877	1.2167	1.2462	1.2763	1.3070
6	1.1941	1.2293	1.2653	1.3023	1.3401	1.3788
7	1.2299	1.2723	1.3159	1.3609	1.4071	1.4547
8	1.2668	1.3168	1.3686	1.4221	1.4775	1.5347
9	1.3048	1.3629	1.4233	1.4861	1.5513	1.6191
10	1.3439	1.4106	1.4802	1.5530	1.6289	1.7081
11	1.3842	1.4600	1.5395	1.6229	1.7103	1.8021
12	1.4258	1.5111	1.6010	1.6959	1.7959	1.9012
13	1.4685	1.5640	1.6651	1.7722	1.8856	2.0058
14	1.5126	1.6187	1.7317	1.8519	1.9799	2.1161
15	1.5580	1.6753	1.8009	1.9353	2.0789	2.2325
16	1.6047	1.7340	1.8730	2.0224	2.1829	2.3553
17	1.6528	1.7947	1.9479	2.1134	2.2920	2.4848
18	1.7024	1.8575	2.0258	2.2085	2.4066	2.6215
19	1.7535	1.9225	2.1068	2.3079	2.5270	2.7656
20	1.8061	1.9898	2.1911	2.4117	2.6533	2.9178
21	1.8603	2.0594	2.2788	2.5202	2.7860	3.0782
22	1.9161	2.1315	2.3699	2.6337	2.9253	3.2475
23	1.9736	2.2061	2.4647	2.7522	3.0715	3.4262
24	2.0328	2.2833	2.5633	2.8760	3.2251	3.6146
25	2.0938	2.3632	2.6658	3.0054	3.3864	3.8134
26	2.1566	2.4460	2.7725	3.1407	3.5557	4.0231
27	2.2213	2.5316	2.8834	3.2820	3.7335	4.2444
28	2.2879	2.6202	2.9987	3.4297	3.9201	4.4778
29	2.3566	2.7119	3.1187	3.5840	4.1161	4.7241
30	2.4273	2.8068	3.2434	3.7453	4.3219	4.9840
31	2.5001	2.9050	3.3731	3.9139	4.5380	5.2581
32	2.5751	3.0067	3.5081	4.0900	4.7649	5.5473
33	2.6523	3.1119	3.6484	4.2740	5.0032	5.8524
34	2.7319	3.2209	3.7943	4.4664	5.2533	6.1742
35	2.8139	3.3336	3.9461	4.6673	5.5160	6.5138
36	2.8983	3.4503	4.1039	4.8774	5.7918	6.8721
37	2.9852	3.5710	4.2681	5.0969	6.0814	7.2501
38	3.0748	3.6960	4.4388	5.3262	6.3855	7.6488
39	3.1670	3.8254	4.6164	5.5659	6.7048	8.0695
40	3.2620	3.9593	4.8010	5.8164	7.0400	8.5133
41	3.3599	4.0978	4.9931	6.0781	7.3920	8.9815
42	3.4607	4.2413	5.1928	6.3516	7.7616	9.4755
43	3.5645	4.3897	5.4005	6.6374	8.1497	9.9967
44	3.6715	4.5433	5.6165	6.9361	8.5572	10.5465
45	3.7816	4.7024	5.8412	7.2482	8.9850	11.1266
46	3.8950	4.8669	6.0748	7.5744	9.4343	11.7385
47	4.0119	5.0373	6.3178	7.9153	9.9060	12.3841
48	4.1323	5.2136	6.5705	8.2715	10.4013	13.0653
49	4.2562	5.3961	6.8333	8.6437	10.9213	13.7838
50	4.3839	5.5849	7.1067	9.0326	11.4674	14.5420

FUTURE VALUE OF LUMP SUM (continued)

YEARS	6.0%	6.5%	7.0%	7.5%	8.0%	8.5%
1	1.0600	1.0650	1.0700	1.0750	1.0800	1.0850
2	1.1236	1.1342	1.1449	1.1556	1.1664	1.1772
3	1.1910	1.2079	1.2250	1.2423	1.2597	1.2773
4	1.2625	1.2865	1.3108	1.3355	1.3605	1.3859
5	1.3382	1.3701	1.4026	1.4356	1.4693	1.5037
6	1.4185	1.4591	1.5007	1.5433	1.5869	1.6315
7	1.5036	1.5540	1.6058	1.6590	1.7138	1.7701
8	1.5938	1.6550	1.7182	1.7835	1.8509	1.9206
9	1.6895	1.7626	1.8385	1.9172	1.9990	2.0839
10	1.7908	1.8771	1.9672	2.0610	2.1589	2.2610
11	1.8983	1.9992	2.1049	2.2156	2.3316	2.4532
12	2.0122	2.1291	2.2522	2.3818	2.5182	2.6617
13	2.1329	2.2675	2.4098	2.5604	2.7196	2.8879
14	2.2609	2.4149	2.5785	2.7524	2.9372	3.1334
15	2.3966	2.5718	2.7590	2.9589	3.1722	3.3997
16	2.5404	2.7390	2.9522	3.1808	3.4259	3.6887
17	2.6928	2.9170	3.1588	3.4194	3.7000	4.0023
18	2.8543	3.1067	3.3799	3.6758	3.9960	4.3425
19	3.0256	3.3086	3.6165	3.9515	4.3157	4.7116
20	3.2071	3.5236	3.8697	4.2479	4.6610	5.1120
21	3.3996	3.7527	4.1406	4.5664	5.0338	5.5466
22	3.6035	3.9966	4.4304	4.9089	5.4365	6.0180
23	3.8197	4.2564	4.7405	5.2771	5.8715	6.5296
24	4.0489	4.5331	5.0724	5.6729	6.3412	7.0846
25	4.2919	4.8277	5.4274	6.0983	6.8485	7.6868
26	4.5494	5.1415	5.8074	6.5557	7.3964	8.3401
27	4.8223	5.4757	6.2139	7.0474	7.9881	9.0490
28	5.1117	5.8316	6.6488	7.5759	8.6271	9.8182
29	5.4184	6.2107	7.1143	8.1441	9.3173	10.6528
30	5.7435	6.6144	7.6123	8.7550	10.0627	11.5583
31	6.0881	7.0443	8.1451	9.4116	10.8677	12.5407
32	6.4534	7.5022	8.7153	10.1174	11.7371	13.6067
33	6.8406	7.9898	9.3253	10.8763	12.6760	14.7632
34	7.2510	8.5092	9.9781	11.6920	13.6901	16.0181
35	7.6861	9.0623	10.6766	12.5689	14.7853	17.3796
36	8.1473	9.6513	11.4239	13.5115	15.9682	18.8569
37	8.6361	10.2786	12.2236	14.5249	17.2456	20.4598
38	9.1543	10.9467	13.0793	15.6143	18.6253	22.1988
39	9.7035	11.6583	13.9948	16.7853	20.1153	24.0857
40	10.2857	12.4161	14.9745	18.0442	21.7245	26.1330
41	10.9029	13.2231	16.0227	19.3976	23.4625	28.3543
42	11.5570	14.0826	17.1443	20.8524	25.3395	30.7644
43	12.2505	14.9980	18.3444	22.4163	27.3666	33.3794
44	12.9855	15.9729	19.6285	24.0975	29.5560	36.2167
45	13.7646	17.0111	21.0025	25.9048	31.9204	39.2951
46	14.5905	18.1168	22.4726	27.8477	34.4741	42.6352
47	15.4659	19.2944	24.0457	29.9363	37.2320	46.2592
48	16.3939	20.5485	25.7289	32.1815	40.2106	50.1912
49	17.3775	21.8842	27.5299	34.5951	43.4274	54.4574
50	18.4202	23.3067	29.4570	37.1898	46.9016	59.0863

FUTURE VALUE OF LUMP SUM (continued)

YEARS	9.0%	9.5%	10.0%	10.5%	11.0%	11.5%
1	1.0900	1.0950	1.1000	1.1050	1.1100	1.1150
2	1.1881	1.1990	1.2100	1.2210	1.2321	1.2432
3	1.2950	1.3129	1.3310	1.3492	1.3676	1.3862
4	1.4116	1.4377	1.4641	1.4909	1.5181	1.5456
5	1.5386	1.5742	1.6105	1.6474	1.6851	1.7234
6	1.6771	1.7238	1.7716	1.8204	1.8704	1.9215
7	1.8280	1.8876	1.9487	2.0116	2.0762	2.1425
8	1.9926	2.0669	2.1436	2.2228	2.3045	2.3889
9	2.1719	2.2632	2.3579	2.4562	2.5580	2.6636
10	2.3674	2.4782	2.5937	2.7141	2.8394	2.9699
11	2.5804	2.7137	2.8531	2.9991	3.1518	3.3115
12	2.8127	2.9715	3.1384	3.3140	3.4985	3.6923
13	3.0658	3.2537	3.4523	3.6619	3.8833	4.1169
14	3.3417	3.5629	3.7975	4.0464	4.3104	4.5904
15	3.6425	3.9013	4.1772	4.4713	4.7846	5.1183
16	3.9703	4.2719	4.5950	4.9408	5.3109	5.7069
17	4.3276	4.6778	5.0545	5.4596	5.8951	6.3632
18	4.7171	5.1222	5.5599	6.0328	6.5436	7.0949
19	5.1417	5.6088	6.1159	6.6663	7.2633	7.9108
20	5.6044	6.1416	6.7275	7.3662	8.0623	8.8206
21	6.1088	6.7251	7.4003	8.1397	8.9492	9.8350
22	6.6586	7.3639	8.1403	8.9944	9.9336	10.9660
23	7.2579	8.0635	8.9543	9.9388	11.0263	12.2271
24	7.9111	8.8296	9.8497	10.9823	12.2392	13.6332
25	8.6231	9.6684	10.8347	12.1355	13.5855	15.2010
26	9.3992	10.5869	11.9182	13.4097	15.0799	16.9491
27	10.2451	11.5926	13.1100	14.8177	16.7386	18.8982
28	11.1671	12.6939	14.4210	16.3736	18.5799	21.0715
29	12.1722	13.8998	15.8631	18.0928	20.6237	23.4948
30	13.2677	15.2203	17.4494	19.9926	22.8923	26.1967
31	14.4618	16.6662	19.1943	22.0918	25.4104	29.2093
32	15.7633	18.2495	21.1138	24.4114	28.2056	32.5684
33	17.1820	19.9832	23.2252	26.9746	31.3082	36.3137
34	18.7284	21.8816	25.5477	29.8069	34.7521	40.4898
35	20.4140	23.9604	28.1024	32.9367	38.5749	45.1461
36	22.2512	26.2366	30.9127	36.3950	42.8181	50.3379
37	24.2538	28.7291	34.0040	40.2165	47.5281	56.1268
38	26.4367	31.4584	37.4043	44.4392	52.7562	62.5814
39	28.8160	34.4469	41.1448	49.1053	58.5593	69.7782
40	31.4094	37.7194	45.2593	54.2614	65.0009	77.8027
41	34.2363	41.3027	49.7852	59.9589	72.1510	86.7500
42	37.3175	45.2265	54.7637	66.2545	80.0876	96.7263
43	40.6761	49.5230	60.2401	73.2113	88.8972	107.8498
44	44.3370	54.2277	66.2641	80.8984	98.6759	120.2525
45	48.3273	59.3793	72.8905	89.3928	109.5302	134.0816
46	52.6767	65.0204	80.1795	98.7790	121.5786	149.5009
47	57.4177	71.1973	88.1975	109.1508	134.9522	166.6936
48	62.5852	77.9611	97.0172	120.6117	149.7969	185.8633
49	68.2179	85.3674	106.7190	133.2759	166.2746	207.2376
50	74.3575	93.4773	117.3909	147.2698	184.5648	231.0699

Tools & Techniques of Investment Planning

Appendix D – Future Value of Lump Sum

FUTURE VALUE OF LUMP SUM (continued)

YEARS	12.0%	12.5%	13.0%	13.5%	14.0%	14.5%
1	1.1200	1.1250	1.1300	1.1350	1.1400	1.1450
2	1.2544	1.2656	1.2769	1.2882	1.2996	1.3110
3	1.4049	1.4238	1.4429	1.4621	1.4815	1.5011
4	1.5735	1.6018	1.6305	1.6595	1.6890	1.7188
5	1.7623	1.8020	1.8424	1.8836	1.9254	1.9680
6	1.9738	2.0273	2.0820	2.1378	2.1950	2.2534
7	2.2107	2.2807	2.3526	2.4264	2.5023	2.5801
8	2.4760	2.5658	2.6584	2.7540	2.8526	2.9542
9	2.7731	2.8865	3.0040	3.1258	3.2519	3.3826
10	3.1058	3.2473	3.3946	3.5478	3.7072	3.8731
11	3.4785	3.6532	3.8359	4.0267	4.2262	4.4347
12	3.8960	4.1099	4.3345	4.5704	4.8179	5.0777
13	4.3635	4.6236	4.8980	5.1874	5.4924	5.8140
14	4.8871	5.2016	5.5348	5.8877	6.2613	6.6570
15	5.4736	5.8518	6.2543	6.6825	7.1379	7.6222
16	6.1304	6.5833	7.0673	7.5846	8.1372	8.7275
17	6.8660	7.4062	7.9861	8.6085	9.2765	9.9929
18	7.6900	8.3319	9.0243	9.7707	10.5752	11.4419
19	8.6128	9.3734	10.1974	11.0897	12.0557	13.1010
20	9.6463	10.5451	11.5231	12.5869	13.7435	15.0006
21	10.8038	11.8632	13.0211	14.2861	15.6676	17.1757
22	12.1003	13.3461	14.7138	16.2147	17.8610	19.6662
23	13.5523	15.0144	16.6266	18.4037	20.3616	22.5178
24	15.1786	16.8912	18.7881	20.8882	23.2122	25.7829
25	17.0001	19.0026	21.2305	23.7081	26.4619	29.5214
26	19.0401	21.3779	23.9905	26.9087	30.1666	33.8020
27	21.3249	24.0502	27.1093	30.5414	34.3899	38.7033
28	23.8839	27.0564	30.6335	34.6644	39.2045	44.3153
29	26.7499	30.4385	34.6158	39.3441	44.6931	50.7410
30	29.9599	34.2433	39.1159	44.6556	50.9502	58.0985
31	33.5551	38.5237	44.2010	50.6841	58.0832	66.5227
32	37.5817	43.3392	49.9471	57.5265	66.2148	76.1685
33	42.0915	48.7566	56.4402	65.2925	75.4849	87.2130
34	47.1425	54.8512	63.7774	74.1070	86.0528	99.8588
35	52.7996	61.7075	72.0685	84.1115	98.1002	114.3384
36	59.1356	69.4210	81.4374	95.4665	111.8342	130.9174
37	66.2318	78.0986	92.0243	108.3545	127.4910	149.9005
38	74.1797	87.8609	103.9874	122.9824	145.3397	171.6360
39	83.0812	98.8436	117.5058	139.5850	165.6873	196.5232
40	93.0510	111.1990	132.7815	158.4289	188.8835	225.0191
41	104.2171	125.0989	150.0431	179.8169	215.3272	257.6469
42	116.7231	140.7362	169.5487	204.0921	245.4730	295.0057
43	130.7299	158.3283	191.5901	231.6446	279.8392	337.7815
44	146.4175	178.1193	216.4968	262.9166	319.0167	386.7598
45	163.9876	200.3842	244.6414	298.4103	363.6791	442.8400
46	183.6661	225.4322	276.4447	338.6957	414.5942	507.0518
47	205.7060	253.6113	312.3825	384.4197	472.6373	580.5743
48	230.3907	285.3127	352.9923	436.3163	538.8066	664.7576
49	258.0376	320.9768	398.8813	495.2190	614.2395	761.1474
50	289.0022	361.0989	450.7358	562.0736	700.2330	871.5138

FUTURE VALUE OF LUMP SUM (continued)

YEARS	15.0%	16.0%	17.0%	18.0%	19.0%	20.0%
1	1.1500	1.1600	1.1700	1.1800	1.1900	1.2000
2	1.3225	1.3456	1.3689	1.3924	1.4161	1.4400
3	1.5209	1.5609	1.6016	1.6430	1.6852	1.7280
4	1.7490	1.8106	1.8739	1.9388	2.0053	2.0736
5	2.0114	2.1003	2.1924	2.2878	2.3864	2.4883
6	2.3131	2.4364	2.5652	2.6996	2.8398	2.9860
7	2.6600	2.8262	3.0012	3.1855	3.3793	3.5832
8	3.0590	3.2784	3.5115	3.7589	4.0214	4.2998
9	3.5179	3.8030	4.1084	4.4355	4.7854	5.1598
10	4.0456	4.4114	4.8068	5.2338	5.6947	6.1917
11	4.6524	5.1173	5.6240	6.1759	6.7767	7.4301
12	5.3503	5.9360	6.5801	7.2876	8.0642	8.9161
13	6.1528	6.8858	7.6987	8.5994	9.5964	10.6993
14	7.0757	7.9875	9.0075	10.1472	11.4198	12.8392
15	8.1371	9.2655	10.5387	11.9737	13.5895	15.4070
16	9.3576	10.7480	12.3303	14.1290	16.1715	18.4884
17	10.7613	12.4677	14.4265	16.6722	19.2441	22.1861
18	12.3755	14.4625	16.8790	19.6733	22.9005	26.6233
19	14.2318	16.7765	19.7484	23.2144	27.2516	31.9480
20	16.3665	19.4608	23.1056	27.3930	32.4294	38.3376
21	18.8215	22.5745	27.0336	32.3238	38.5910	46.0051
22	21.6447	26.1864	31.6293	38.1421	45.9233	55.2061
23	24.8915	30.3762	37.0062	45.0076	54.6487	66.2474
24	28.6252	35.2364	43.2973	53.1090	65.0320	79.4969
25	32.9190	40.8742	50.6578	62.6686	77.3881	95.3962
26	37.8568	47.4141	59.2697	73.9490	92.0918	114.4755
27	43.5353	55.0004	69.3455	87.2598	109.5892	137.3706
28	50.0656	63.8004	81.1342	102.9666	130.4112	164.8447
29	57.5755	74.0085	94.9271	121.5006	155.1893	197.8136
30	66.2118	85.8499	111.0647	143.3707	184.6753	237.3763
31	76.1435	99.5858	129.9456	169.1774	219.7636	284.8516
32	87.5651	115.5196	152.0364	199.6293	261.5187	341.8219
33	100.6998	134.0027	177.8826	235.5626	311.2072	410.1863
34	115.8048	155.4431	208.1226	277.9639	370.3366	492.2236
35	133.1755	180.3141	243.5035	327.9974	440.7006	590.6683
36	153.1519	209.1643	284.8991	387.0369	524.4337	708.8019
37	176.1247	242.6306	333.3319	456.7035	624.0761	850.5623
38	202.5434	281.4515	389.9984	538.9102	742.6505	1020.6748
39	232.9249	326.4837	456.2981	635.9140	883.7541	1224.8098
40	267.8636	378.7211	533.8687	750.3785	1051.6674	1469.7717
41	308.0431	439.3165	624.6264	885.4467	1251.4842	1763.7261
42	354.2496	509.6071	730.8129	1044.8271	1489.2662	2116.4713
43	407.3871	591.1443	855.0511	1232.8960	1772.2268	2539.7655
44	468.4951	685.7273	1000.4098	1454.8172	2108.9499	3047.7187
45	538.7694	795.4437	1170.4795	1716.6843	2509.6504	3657.2624
46	619.5848	922.7147	1369.4610	2025.6875	2986.4839	4388.7149
47	712.5225	1070.3491	1602.2694	2390.3113	3553.9159	5266.4579
48	819.4009	1241.6049	1874.6552	2820.5674	4229.1599	6319.7495
49	942.3111	1440.2617	2193.3466	3328.2695	5032.7003	7583.6994
50	1083.6577	1670.7035	2566.2155	3927.3581	5988.9133	9100.4393

Appendix E

FUTURE VALUE OF ANNUITY DUE
(The use of this table is explained in Chapter 32)

YEARS	3.0%	3.5%	4.0%	4.5%	5.0%	5.5%
1	1.0300	1.0350	1.0400	1.0450	1.0500	1.0550
2	2.0909	2.1062	2.1216	2.1370	2.1525	2.1680
3	3.1836	3.2149	3.2465	3.2782	3.3101	3.3423
4	4.3091	4.3625	4.4163	4.4707	4.5256	4.5811
5	5.4684	5.5502	5.6330	5.7169	5.8019	5.8881
6	6.6625	6.7794	6.8983	7.0192	7.1420	7.2669
7	7.8923	8.0517	8.2142	8.3800	8.5491	8.7216
8	9.1591	9.3685	9.5828	9.8021	10.0266	10.2563
9	10.4639	10.7314	11.0061	11.2882	11.5779	11.8754
10	11.8078	12.1420	12.4864	12.8412	13.2068	13.5835
11	13.1920	13.6020	14.0258	14.4640	14.9171	15.3856
12	14.6178	15.1130	15.6268	16.1599	16.7130	17.2868
13	16.0863	16.6770	17.2919	17.9321	18.5986	19.2926
14	17.5989	18.2957	19.0236	19.7841	20.5786	21.4087
15	19.1569	19.9710	20.8245	21.7193	22.6575	23.6411
16	20.7616	21.7050	22.6975	23.7417	24.8404	25.9964
17	22.4144	23.4997	24.6454	25.8551	27.1324	28.4812
18	24.1169	25.3572	26.6712	28.0636	29.5390	31.1027
19	25.8704	27.2797	28.7781	30.3714	32.0660	33.8683
20	27.6765	29.2695	30.9692	32.7831	34.7193	36.7861
21	29.5368	31.3289	33.2480	35.3034	37.5052	39.8643
22	31.4529	33.4604	35.6179	37.9370	40.4305	43.1118
23	33.4265	35.6665	38.0826	40.6892	43.5020	46.5380
24	35.4593	37.9499	40.6459	43.5652	46.7271	50.1526
25	37.5530	40.3131	43.3117	46.5706	50.1135	53.9660
26	39.7096	42.7591	46.0842	49.7113	53.6691	57.9891
27	41.9309	45.2906	48.9676	52.9933	57.4026	62.2335
28	44.2188	47.9108	51.9663	56.4230	61.3227	66.7114
29	46.5754	50.6227	55.0849	60.0071	65.4388	71.4355
30	49.0027	53.4295	58.3283	63.7524	69.7608	76.4194
31	51.5028	56.3345	61.7015	67.6662	74.2988	81.6775
32	54.0778	59.3412	65.2095	71.7562	79.0638	87.2248
33	56.7302	62.4532	68.8579	76.0303	84.0670	93.0771
34	59.4621	65.6740	72.6522	80.4966	89.3203	99.2514
35	62.2759	69.0076	76.5983	85.1640	94.8363	105.7652
36	65.1742	72.4579	80.7022	90.0413	100.6281	112.6373
37	68.1594	76.0289	84.9703	95.1382	106.7095	119.8873
38	71.2342	79.7249	89.4091	100.4644	113.0950	127.5361
39	74.4013	83.5503	94.0255	106.0303	119.7998	135.6056
40	77.6633	87.5095	98.8265	111.8467	126.8398	144.1189
41	81.0232	91.6074	103.8196	117.9248	134.2318	153.1005
42	84.4839	95.8486	109.0124	124.2764	141.1933	162.5760
43	88.0484	100.2383	114.4129	130.9138	150.1430	172.5727
44	91.7199	104.7817	120.0294	137.8500	158.7002	183.1192
45	95.5015	109.4840	125.8706	145.0982	167.6852	194.2457
46	99.3965	114.3510	131.9454	152.6726	177.1194	205.9842
47	103.4084	119.3883	138.2632	160.5879	187.0254	218.3684
48	107.5406	124.6018	144.8337	168.8594	197.4267	231.4336
49	111.7969	129.9979	151.6671	177.5030	208.3480	245.2175
50	116.1808	135.5828	158.7738	186.5357	219.8154	259.7594

FUTURE VALUE OF ANNUITY DUE (continued)

YEARS	6.0%	6.5%	7.0%	7.5%	8.0%	8.5%
1	1.0600	1.0650	1.0700	1.0750	1.0800	1.0850
2	2.1836	2.1992	2.2149	2.2306	2.2464	2.2622
3	3.3746	3.4072	3.4399	3.4729	3.5061	3.5395
4	4.6371	4.6936	4.7507	4.8084	4.8666	4.9254
5	5.9753	6.0637	6.1533	6.2440	6.3359	6.4290
6	7.3938	7.5229	7.6540	7.7873	7.9228	8.0605
7	8.8975	9.0769	9.2598	9.4464	9.6366	9.8306
8	10.4913	10.7319	10.9780	11.2298	11.4876	11.7512
9	12.1808	12.4944	12.8164	13.1471	13.4866	13.8351
10	13.9716	14.3716	14.7836	15.2081	15.6455	16.0961
11	15.8699	16.3707	16.8885	17.4237	17.9771	18.5492
12	17.8821	18.4498	19.1406	19.8055	20.4953	21.2109
13	20.0151	20.7673	21.5505	22.3659	23.2149	24.0989
14	22.2760	23.1822	24.1290	25.1184	26.1521	27.2323
15	24.6725	25.7540	26.8881	28.0772	29.3243	30.6320
16	27.2129	28.4930	29.8402	31.2580	32.7502	34.3207
17	29.9057	31.4101	32.9990	34.6774	36.4502	38.3230
18	32.7600	34.5167	36.3790	38.3532	40.4463	42.6655
19	35.7856	37.8253	39.9955	42.3047	44.7620	47.3370
20	38.9927	41.3490	43.8652	46.5525	49.4229	52.4891
21	42.3923	45.1016	48.0057	51.1190	54.4568	58.0356
22	45.9958	49.0982	52.4361	56.0279	59.8933	64.0537
23	49.8156	53.3546	57.1767	61.3050	65.7648	70.5832
24	53.8645	57.8877	62.2490	66.9779	72.1059	77.6678
25	58.1564	62.7154	67.6765	73.0762	78.9544	85.3546
26	62.7058	67.8569	73.4838	79.6319	86.3508	93.6947
27	67.5281	73.3326	79.6977	86.6793	94.3388	102.7437
28	72.6398	79.1642	86.3465	94.2553	102.9659	112.5620
29	78.0582	85.3749	93.4608	102.3994	112.2832	123.2147
30	83.8017	91.9892	101.0730	111.1544	122.3459	134.7730
31	89.8898	99.0335	109.2182	120.5659	133.2135	147.3137
32	96.3432	106.5357	117.9334	130.6834	144.9506	160.9203
33	103.1838	114.5255	127.2588	141.5596	157.6267	175.6836
34	110.4348	123.0347	137.2369	153.2516	171.3168	191.7017
35	118.1209	132.0969	147.9135	165.8205	186.1021	209.0813
36	126.2681	141.7482	159.3374	179.3320	202.0703	227.9382
37	134.9042	152.0269	171.5610	193.8569	219.3159	248.3980
38	144.0585	162.9736	184.6403	209.4712	237.9412	270.5968
39	153.7620	174.6319	198.6351	226.2565	258.0565	294.6825
40	164.0477	187.0480	213.6096	244.3008	279.7810	320.8156
41	174.9505	200.2711	229.6322	263.6983	303.2435	349.1699
42	186.5076	214.3537	246.7765	284.5507	328.5830	379.9343
43	198.7580	229.3517	265.1209	306.9670	355.9496	413.3137
44	211.7435	245.3246	284.7493	331.0645	385.5056	449.5304
45	225.5081	262.3357	305.7518	356.9694	417.4260	488.8255
46	240.0986	280.4525	328.2244	384.8171	451.9001	531.4607
47	255.5645	299.7469	352.2701	414.7534	489.1321	577.7198
48	271.9584	320.2954	377.9990	446.9349	529.3427	627.9110
49	289.3359	342.1796	405.5289	481.5300	572.7701	682.3684
50	307.7560	365.4863	434.9860	518.7197	619.6717	741.4548

Appendix E – Future Value of Annuity Due

FUTURE VALUE OF ANNUITY DUE (continued)

YEARS	9.0%	9.5%	10.0%	10.5%	11.0%	11.5%
1	1.0900	1.0950	1.1000	1.1050	1.1100	1.1150
2	2.2781	2.2940	2.3100	2.3260	2.3421	2.3582
3	3.5731	3.6070	3.6410	3.6753	3.7097	3.7444
4	4.9847	5.0446	5.1051	5.1662	5.2278	5.2900
5	6.5233	6.6189	6.7156	6.8136	6.9129	7.0134
6	8.2004	8.3426	8.4872	8.6340	8.7833	8.9349
7	10.0285	10.2302	10.4359	10.6456	10.8594	11.0774
8	12.0210	12.2971	12.5795	12.8684	13.1640	13.4663
9	14.1929	14.5603	14.9374	15.3246	15.7220	16.1300
10	16.5603	17.0385	17.5312	18.0387	18.5614	19.0999
11	19.1407	19.7522	20.3843	21.0377	21.7132	22.4114
12	21.9534	22.7236	23.5227	24.3517	25.2216	26.1037
13	25.0192	25.9774	26.9750	28.0136	29.0949	30.2207
14	28.3609	29.5402	30.7725	32.0600	33.4054	34.8110
15	32.0034	33.4416	34.9497	36.5313	38.1899	39.9293
16	35.9737	37.7135	39.5447	41.4721	43.5008	45.6362
17	40.3013	42.3913	44.5992	46.9317	49.3959	51.9993
18	45.0185	47.5135	50.1591	52.9645	55.9395	59.0942
19	50.1601	53.1222	56.2750	59.6308	63.2028	67.0051
20	55.7645	59.2638	63.0025	66.9970	71.2651	75.8257
21	61.8733	65.9889	70.4028	75.1367	80.2143	85.6606
22	68.5319	73.3529	78.5430	84.1311	90.1479	96.6266
23	75.7898	81.4164	87.4973	94.0698	101.1741	108.8536
24	83.7009	90.2459	97.3471	105.0522	113.4133	122.4868
25	92.3240	99.9143	108.1818	117.1877	126.9988	137.6878
26	101.7231	110.5012	120.0999	130.5974	142.0786	154.6369
27	111.9682	122.0938	133.2099	145.4151	158.8173	173.5351
28	123.1354	134.7877	147.6309	161.7887	177.3972	194.6067
29	135.3075	148.6875	163.4940	179.8815	198.0209	218.1015
30	148.5752	163.9078	180.9434	199.8740	220.9132	244.2981
31	163.0370	180.5741	200.1378	221.9658	246.3236	273.5074
32	178.8003	198.8236	221.2516	246.3772	274.5292	306.0758
33	195.9824	218.8068	244.4767	273.3518	305.8374	342.3895
34	214.7108	240.6885	270.0244	303.1588	340.5896	382.8793
35	235.1247	264.6489	298.1268	336.0954	379.1644	428.0254
36	257.3760	290.8855	329.0395	372.4905	421.9825	478.3633
37	281.6298	319.6146	363.0434	412.7070	469.5106	534.4901
38	308.0665	351.0730	400.4478	457.1462	522.2667	597.0714
39	336.8825	385.5200	441.5926	506.2515	580.8261	666.8496
40	368.2919	423.2394	486.8518	560.5129	645.8269	744.6524
41	402.5282	464.5421	536.6370	620.4718	717.9779	831.4024
42	439.8457	509.7686	591.4007	686.7263	798.0655	928.1287
43	480.5218	559.2916	651.6408	759.9376	886.9626	1035.9785
44	524.8588	613.5193	717.9049	840.8360	985.6385	1156.2310
45	573.1861	672.8987	790.7954	930.2288	1095.1688	1290.3125
46	625.8628	737.9191	870.9749	1029.0079	1216.7473	1439.8135
47	683.2805	809.1164	959.1724	1138.1587	1351.6996	1606.5070
48	745.8657	887.0774	1056.1896	1258.7703	1501.4965	1792.3704
49	814.0837	972.4448	1162.9086	1392.0462	1667.7711	1999.6079
50	888.4412	1065.9220	1280.2995	1539.3161	1852.3359	2230.6779

FUTURE VALUE OF ANNUITY DUE (continued)

YEARS	12.0%	12.5%	13.0%	13.5%	14.0%	14.5%
1	1.1200	1.1250	1.1300	1.1350	1.1400	1.1450
2	2.3744	2.3906	2.4069	2.4232	2.4396	2.4560
3	3.7793	3.8145	3.8498	3.8854	3.9211	3.9571
4	5.3528	5.4163	5.4803	5.5449	5.6101	5.6759
5	7.1152	7.2183	7.3227	7.4284	7.5355	7.6439
6	9.0890	9.2456	9.4047	9.5663	9.7305	9.8973
7	11.2997	11.5263	11.7573	11.9927	12.2328	12.4774
8	13.7757	14.0921	14.4157	14.7468	15.0853	15.4317
9	16.5487	16.9786	17.4197	17.8726	18.3373	18.8142
10	19.6546	20.2259	20.8143	21.4204	22.0445	22.6873
11	23.1331	23.8791	24.6502	25.4471	26.2707	27.1220
12	27.0291	27.9890	28.9847	30.0175	31.0887	32.1997
13	31.3926	32.6126	33.8827	35.2048	36.5811	38.0136
14	36.2797	37.8142	39.4175	41.0925	42.8424	44.6706
15	41.7533	43.6660	45.6717	47.7750	49.9804	52.2928
16	47.8837	50.2493	52.7391	55.3596	58.1176	61.0203
17	54.7497	57.6554	60.7251	63.9681	67.3941	71.0132
18	62.4397	65.9873	69.7494	73.7388	77.9692	82.4551
19	71.0524	75.3608	79.9468	84.8286	90.0249	95.5561
20	80.6987	85.9058	91.4699	97.4154	103.7684	110.5568
21	91.5026	97.7691	104.4910	111.7015	119.4360	127.7325
22	103.6029	111.1152	119.2048	127.9162	137.2970	147.3987
23	117.1552	126.1296	135.8315	146.3199	157.6586	169.9165
24	132.3339	143.0208	154.6195	167.2081	180.8708	195.6994
25	149.3339	162.0234	175.8501	190.9162	207.3327	225.2208
26	168.3740	183.4013	199.8406	217.8249	237.4993	259.0228
27	189.6989	207.4515	226.9499	248.3662	271.8892	297.7261
28	213.5827	234.5079	257.5834	283.0306	311.0937	342.0414
29	240.3327	264.9464	292.1992	322.3748	355.7869	392.7824
30	270.2926	299.1897	331.3151	367.0304	406.7370	450.8809
31	303.8477	337.7135	375.5160	417.7145	464.8202	517.4036
32	341.4294	381.0526	425.4631	475.2409	531.0350	593.5721
33	383.5210	429.8092	481.9033	540.5335	606.5199	680.7851
34	430.6635	484.6604	545.6808	614.6405	692.5727	780.6439
35	483.4631	546.3679	617.7493	698.7520	790.6729	894.9823
36	542.5987	615.7889	699.1867	794.2185	902.5071	1025.8997
37	608.8305	693.8875	791.2109	902.5730	1029.9981	1175.8002
38	683.0101	781.7485	895.1983	1025.5553	1175.3378	1347.4362
39	766.0914	880.5920	1012.7041	1165.1403	1341.0251	1543.9594
40	859.1423	991.7910	1145.4856	1323.5693	1529.9086	1768.9785
41	963.3594	1116.8899	1295.5288	1503.3861	1745.2358	2026.6254
42	1080.0825	1257.6262	1465.0775	1707.4783	1990.7089	2321.6311
43	1210.8124	1415.9544	1656.6676	1939.1228	2270.5481	2659.4126
44	1357.2299	1594.0737	1873.1643	2202.0394	2589.5648	3046.1724
45	1521.2175	1794.4579	2117.8057	2500.4498	2953.2439	3489.0124
46	1704.8836	2019.8902	2394.2504	2839.1455	3367.8381	3996.0642
47	1910.5896	2273.5015	2706.6330	3223.5652	3840.4754	4576.6385
48	2140.9804	2558.8141	3059.6252	3659.8815	4379.2820	5241.3960
49	2399.0180	2879.7909	3458.5065	4155.1005	4993.5215	6002.5434
50	2688.0202	3240.8898	3909.2423	4717.1741	5693.7545	6874.0572

FUTURE VALUE OF ANNUITY DUE (continued)

YEARS	15.0%	16.0%	17.0%	18.0%	19.0%	20.0%
1	1.1500	1.1600	1.1700	1.1800	1.1900	1.2000
2	2.4725	2.5056	2.5389	2.5724	2.6061	2.6400
3	3.9934	4.0665	4.1405	4.2154	4.2913	4.3680
4	5.7424	5.8771	6.0144	6.1542	6.2966	6.4416
5	7.7537	7.9775	8.2068	8.4420	8.6830	8.9299
6	10.0668	10.4139	10.7720	11.1415	11.5227	11.9159
7	12.7268	13.2401	13.7733	14.3270	14.9020	15.4991
8	15.7858	16.5185	17.2847	18.0859	18.9234	19.7989
9	19.3037	20.3215	21.3931	22.5213	23.7089	24.9587
10	23.3493	24.7329	26.1999	27.7551	29.4035	31.1504
11	28.0017	29.8502	31.8239	33.9311	36.1802	38.5805
12	33.3519	35.7862	38.4040	41.2187	44.2445	47.4966
13	39.5047	42.6720	46.1027	49.8180	53.8409	58.1959
14	46.5804	50.6595	55.1101	59.9653	65.2607	71.0351
15	54.7175	59.9250	65.6488	71.9390	78.8502	86.4421
16	64.0751	70.6730	77.9792	86.0680	95.0217	104.9306
17	74.8364	83.1407	92.4056	102.7403	114.2659	127.1167
18	87.2118	97.6032	109.2846	122.4135	137.1164	153.7400
19	101.4436	114.3797	129.0329	145.6280	164.4180	185.6880
20	117.8101	133.8405	152.1385	173.0210	196.8474	224.0256
21	136.6316	156.4150	179.1721	205.3448	235.4384	270.0307
22	158.2764	182.6014	210.8013	243.4869	281.3618	325.2369
23	183.1679	212.9776	247.8076	288.4945	336.0105	391.4843
24	211.7930	248.2140	291.1049	341.6035	401.0425	470.9811
25	244.7120	289.0883	341.7627	404.2722	478.4305	566.3773
26	282.5688	336.5024	401.0323	478.2212	570.5223	680.8528
27	326.1041	391.5027	470.3779	565.4810	680.1116	818.2234
28	376.1697	455.3032	551.5121	668.4475	810.5228	983.0680
29	433.7452	529.3117	646.4391	789.9481	965.7121	1180.8816
30	499.9570	615.1616	757.5038	933.3188	1150.3874	1418.2580
31	576.1005	714.7474	887.4494	1102.4962	1370.1510	1703.1096
32	663.6656	830.2670	1039.4858	1302.1255	1631.6697	2044.9315
33	764.3655	964.2697	1217.3684	1537.6881	1942.8770	2455.1178
34	880.1703	1119.7129	1425.4911	1815.6519	2313.2136	2947.3414
35	1013.3458	1300.0269	1668.9946	2143.6493	2753.9142	3538.0096
36	1166.4977	1509.1912	1953.8937	2530.6862	3278.3478	4246.8116
37	1342.6224	1751.8218	2287.2256	2987.3897	3902.4239	5097.3739
38	1545.1657	2033.2733	2677.2239	3526.2999	4645.0745	6118.0487
39	1778.0906	2359.7570	3133.5220	4162.2139	5528.8286	7342.8585
40	2045.9542	2738.4781	3667.3907	4912.5924	6580.4960	8812.6302
41	2353.9974	3177.7946	4292.0172	5798.0391	7831.9803	10576.3562
42	2708.2470	3687.4017	5022.8301	6842.8661	9321.2465	12692.8275
43	3115.6340	4278.5460	5877.8812	8075.7621	11093.4733	15232.5931
44	3584.1292	4964.2733	6878.2911	9530.5793	13202.4232	18280.3117
45	4122.8985	5759.7170	8048.7705	11247.2637	15712.0736	21937.5741
46	4742.4834	6682.4318	9418.2315	13272.9512	18698.5575	26326.2890
47	5455.0059	7752.7808	11020.5009	15663.2625	22252.4734	31592.7469
48	6274.4068	8994.3857	12895.1561	18483.8299	26481.6333	37912.4963
49	7216.7179	10434.6474	15088.5027	21812.0994	31514.3336	45496.1957
50	8300.3756	12105.3509	17654.7181	25739.4575	37503.2469	54596.6350

Appendix F

FUTURE VALUE OF ORDINARY ANNUITY
(The use of this table is explained in Chapter 32)

YEARS	3.0%	3.5%	4.0%	4.5%	5.0%	5.5%
1	1.0000	1.0000	1.0000	1.0000	1.0000	1.0000
2	2.0300	2.0350	2.0400	2.0450	2.0500	2.0550
3	3.0909	3.1062	3.1216	3.1370	3.1525	3.1680
4	4.1836	4.2149	4.2465	4.2782	4.3101	4.3423
5	5.3091	5.3625	5.4163	5.4707	5.5256	5.5811
6	6.4684	6.5502	6.6330	6.7169	6.8019	6.8881
7	7.6625	7.7794	7.8983	8.0192	8.1420	8.2669
8	8.8923	9.0517	9.2142	9.3800	9.5491	9.7216
9	10.1591	10.3685	10.5828	10.8021	11.0266	11.2563
10	11.4639	11.7314	12.0061	12.2882	12.5779	12.8754
11	12.8078	13.1420	13.4864	13.8412	14.2068	14.5835
12	14.1920	14.6020	15.0258	15.4640	15.9171	16.3856
13	15.6178	16.1130	16.6268	17.1599	17.7130	18.2868
14	17.0863	17.6770	18.2919	18.9321	19.5986	20.2926
15	18.5989	19.2957	20.0236	20.7841	21.5786	22.4087
16	20.1569	20.9710	21.8245	22.7193	23.6575	24.6411
17	21.7616	22.7050	23.6975	24.7417	25.8404	26.9964
18	23.4144	24.4997	25.6454	26.8551	28.1324	29.4812
19	25.1169	26.3572	27.6712	29.0636	30.5390	32.1027
20	26.8704	28.2797	29.7781	31.3714	33.0660	34.8683
21	28.6765	30.2695	31.9692	33.7831	35.7193	37.7861
22	30.5368	32.3289	34.2480	36.3034	38.5052	40.8643
23	32.4529	34.4604	36.6179	38.9370	41.4305	44.1118
24	34.4265	36.6665	39.0826	41.6892	44.5020	47.5380
25	36.4593	38.9499	41.6459	44.5652	47.7271	51.1526
26	38.5530	41.3131	44.3117	47.5706	51.1135	54.9660
27	40.7096	43.7591	47.0842	50.7113	54.6691	58.9891
28	42.9309	46.2906	49.9676	53.9933	58.4026	63.2335
29	45.2188	48.9108	52.9663	57.4230	62.3227	67.7114
30	47.5754	51.6227	56.0849	61.0071	66.4388	72.4355
31	50.0027	54.4295	59.3283	64.7524	70.7608	77.4194
32	52.5028	57.3345	62.7015	68.6662	75.2988	82.6775
33	55.0778	60.3412	66.2095	72.7562	80.0638	88.2248
34	57.7302	63.4532	69.8579	77.0303	85.0670	94.0771
35	60.4621	66.6740	73.6522	81.4966	90.3203	100.2514
36	63.2759	70.0076	77.5983	86.1640	95.8363	106.7652
37	66.1742	73.4579	81.7022	91.0413	101.6281	113.6373
38	69.1594	77.0289	85.9703	96.1382	107.7095	120.8873
39	72.2342	80.7249	90.4091	101.4644	114.0950	128.5361
40	75.4013	84.5503	95.0255	107.0303	120.7998	136.6056
41	78.6633	88.5095	99.8265	112.8467	127.8398	145.1189
42	82.0232	92.6074	104.8196	118.9248	135.2318	154.1005
43	85.4839	96.8486	110.0124	125.2764	142.9933	163.5760
44	89.0484	101.2383	115.4129	131.9138	151.1430	173.5727
45	92.7199	105.7817	121.0294	138.8500	159.7002	184.1192
46	96.5015	110.4840	126.8706	146.0982	168.6852	195.2457
47	100.3965	115.3510	132.9454	153.6726	178.1194	206.9842
48	104.4084	120.3883	139.2632	161.5879	188.0254	219.3684
49	108.5406	125.6018	145.8337	169.8594	198.4267	232.4336
50	112.7969	130.9979	152.6671	178.5030	209.3480	246.2175

Appendix F – Future Value of Ordinary Annuity

FUTURE VALUE OF ORDINARY ANNUITY (continued)

YEARS	6.0%	6.5%	7.0%	7.5%	8.0%	8.5%
1	1.0000	1.0000	1.0000	1.0000	1.0000	1.0000
2	2.0600	2.0650	2.0700	2.0750	2.0800	2.0850
3	3.1836	3.1992	3.2149	3.2306	3.2464	3.2622
4	4.3746	4.4072	4.4399	4.4729	4.5061	4.5395
5	5.6371	5.6936	5.7507	5.8084	5.8666	5.9254
6	6.9753	7.0637	7.1533	7.2440	7.3359	7.4290
7	8.3938	8.5229	8.6540	8.7873	8.9228	9.0605
8	9.8975	10.0769	10.2598	10.4464	10.6366	10.8306
9	11.4913	11.7319	11.9780	12.2298	12.4876	12.7512
10	13.1808	13.4944	13.8164	14.1471	14.4866	14.8351
11	14.9716	15.3716	15.7836	16.2081	16.6455	17.0961
12	16.8699	17.3707	17.8885	18.4237	18.9771	19.5492
13	18.8821	19.4998	20.1406	20.8055	21.4953	22.2109
14	21.0151	21.7673	22.5505	23.3659	24.2149	25.0989
15	23.2760	24.1822	25.1290	26.1184	27.1521	28.2323
16	25.6725	26.7540	27.8881	29.0772	30.3243	31.6320
17	28.2129	29.4930	30.8402	32.2580	33.7502	35.3207
18	30.9057	32.4101	33.9990	35.6774	37.4502	39.3230
19	33.7600	35.5167	37.3790	39.3532	41.1463	43.3655
20	36.7856	38.8253	40.9955	43.3047	45.7620	48.3770
21	39.9927	42.3490	44.8652	47.5525	50.4229	53.4891
22	43.3923	46.1016	49.0057	52.1190	55.4568	59.0356
23	46.9958	50.0982	53.4361	57.0279	60.8933	65.0537
24	50.8156	54.3546	58.1767	62.3050	66.7648	71.5832
25	54.8645	58.8877	63.2490	67.9779	73.1059	78.6678
26	59.1564	63.7154	68.6765	74.0762	79.9544	86.3546
27	63.7058	68.8569	74.4838	80.6319	87.3508	94.6947
28	68.5281	74.3326	80.6977	87.6793	95.3388	103.7437
29	73.6398	80.1642	87.3465	95.2553	103.9659	113.5620
30	79.0582	86.3749	94.4608	103.3994	113.2832	124.2147
31	84.8017	92.9892	102.0730	112.1544	123.3459	135.7730
32	90.8898	100.0335	110.2182	121.5659	134.2135	148.3137
33	97.3432	107.5357	118.9334	131.6834	145.9506	161.9203
34	104.1838	115.5255	128.2588	142.5596	158.6267	176.6836
35	111.4348	124.0347	138.2369	154.2516	172.3168	192.7017
36	119.1209	133.0969	148.9135	166.8205	187.1021	210.0813
37	127.2681	142.7482	160.3374	180.3320	203.0703	228.9382
38	135.9042	153.0269	172.5610	194.8569	220.3159	249.3980
39	145.0585	163.9736	185.6403	210.4712	238.9412	271.5968
40	154.7620	175.6319	199.6351	227.2565	259.0565	295.6825
41	165.0477	188.0480	214.6096	245.3008	280.7810	321.8156
42	175.9505	201.2711	230.6322	264.6983	304.2435	350.1699
43	187.5076	215.3537	247.7765	285.5507	329.5830	380.9343
44	199.7580	230.3517	266.1209	307.9670	356.9496	414.3137
45	212.7435	246.3246	285.7493	332.0645	386.5056	450.5304
46	226.5081	263.3357	306.7518	357.9694	418.4260	489.8255
47	241.0986	281.4525	329.2244	385.8171	452.9001	532.4607
48	256.5645	300.7469	353.2701	415.7534	490.1321	578.7198
49	272.9584	321.2954	378.9990	447.9349	530.3427	628.9110
50	290.3359	343.1796	406.5289	482.5300	573.7701	683.3684

Appendix F – Future Value of Ordinary Annuity

FUTURE VALUE OF ORDINARY ANNUITY (continued)

YEARS	9.0%	9.5%	10.0%	10.5%	11.0%	11.5%
1	1.0000	1.0000	1.0000	1.0000	1.0000	1.0000
2	2.0900	2.0950	2.1000	2.1050	2.1100	2.1150
3	3.2781	3.2940	3.3100	3.3260	3.3421	3.3582
4	4.5731	4.6070	4.6410	4.6753	4.7097	4.7444
5	5.9847	6.0446	6.1051	6.1662	6.2278	6.2900
6	7.5233	7.6189	7.7156	7.8136	7.9129	8.0134
7	9.2004	9.3426	9.4872	9.6340	9.7833	9.9349
8	11.0285	11.2302	11.4359	11.6456	11.8594	12.0774
9	13.0210	13.2971	13.5795	13.8684	14.1640	14.4663
10	15.1929	15.5603	15.9374	16.3246	16.7220	17.1300
11	17.5603	18.0385	18.5312	19.0387	19.5614	20.0999
12	20.1407	20.7522	21.3843	22.0377	22.7132	23.4114
13	22.9534	23.7236	24.5227	25.3517	26.2116	27.1037
14	26.0192	26.9774	27.9750	29.0136	30.0949	31.2207
15	29.3609	30.5402	31.7725	33.0600	34.4054	35.8110
16	33.0034	34.4416	35.9497	37.5313	39.1899	40.9293
17	36.9737	38.7135	40.5447	42.4721	44.5008	46.6362
18	41.3013	43.3913	45.5992	47.9317	50.3959	52.9993
19	46.0185	48.5135	51.1591	53.9645	56.9395	60.0942
20	51.1601	54.1222	57.2750	60.6308	64.2028	68.0051
21	56.7645	60.2638	64.0025	67.9970	72.2651	76.8257
22	62.8733	66.9889	71.4028	76.1367	81.2143	86.6606
23	69.5319	74.3529	79.5430	85.1311	91.1479	97.6266
24	76.7898	82.4164	88.4973	95.0698	102.1741	109.8536
25	84.7009	91.2459	98.3471	106.0522	114.4133	123.4868
26	93.3240	100.9143	109.1818	118.1877	127.9988	138.6878
27	102.7231	111.5012	121.0999	131.5974	143.0786	155.6369
28	112.9682	123.0938	134.2099	146.4151	159.8173	174.5351
29	124.1354	135.7877	148.6309	162.7887	178.3972	195.6067
30	136.3075	149.6875	164.4940	180.8815	199.0209	219.1015
31	149.5752	164.9078	181.9434	200.8740	221.9132	245.2981
32	164.0370	181.5741	201.1378	222.9658	247.3236	274.5074
33	179.8003	199.8236	222.2516	247.3772	275.5292	307.0758
34	196.9824	219.8068	245.4767	274.3518	306.8374	343.3895
35	215.7108	241.6885	271.0244	304.1588	341.5896	383.8793
36	236.1247	265.6489	299.1268	337.0954	380.1644	429.0254
37	258.3760	291.8855	330.0395	373.4905	422.9825	479.3633
38	282.6298	320.6146	364.0434	413.7070	470.5106	535.4901
39	309.0665	352.0730	401.4478	458.1462	523.2667	598.0714
40	337.8825	386.5200	442.5926	507.2515	581.8261	667.8496
41	369.2919	424.2394	487.8518	561.5129	646.8269	745.6524
42	403.5282	465.5421	537.6370	621.4718	718.9779	832.4024
43	440.8457	510.7686	592.4007	687.7263	799.0655	929.1287
44	481.5218	560.2916	652.6408	760.9376	887.9626	1036.9785
45	525.8588	614.5193	718.9049	841.8360	986.6385	1157.2310
46	574.1861	673.8987	791.7954	931.2288	1096.1688	1291.3125
47	626.8628	738.9191	871.9749	1030.0079	1217.7473	1440.8135
48	684.2805	810.1164	960.1724	1139.1587	1352.6996	1607.5070
49	746.8657	888.0774	1057.1896	1259.7703	1502.4965	1793.3704
50	815.0837	973.4448	1163.9086	1393.0462	1668.7711	2000.6079

Tools & Techniques of Investment Planning

FUTURE VALUE OF ORDINARY ANNUITY (continued)

YEARS	12.0%	12.5%	13.0%	13.5%	14.0%	14.5%
1	1.0000	1.0000	1.0000	1.0000	1.0000	1.0000
2	2.1200	2.1250	2.1300	2.1350	2.1400	2.1450
3	3.3744	3.3906	3.4069	3.4232	3.4396	3.4560
4	4.7793	4.8145	4.8498	4.8854	4.9211	4.9571
5	6.3528	6.4163	6.4803	6.5449	6.6101	6.6759
6	8.1152	8.2183	8.3227	8.4284	8.5355	8.6439
7	10.0890	10.2456	10.4047	10.5663	10.7305	10.8973
8	12.2997	12.5263	12.7573	12.9927	13.2328	13.4774
9	14.7757	15.0921	15.4157	15.7468	16.0853	16.4317
10	17.5487	17.9786	18.4197	18.8726	19.3373	19.8142
11	20.6546	21.2259	21.8143	22.4204	23.0445	23.6873
12	24.1331	24.8791	25.6502	26.4471	27.2707	28.1220
13	28.0291	28.9890	29.9847	31.0175	32.0887	33.1997
14	32.3926	33.6126	34.8827	36.2048	37.5811	39.0136
15	37.2797	38.8142	40.4175	42.0925	43.8424	45.6706
16	42.7533	44.6660	46.6717	48.7750	50.9804	53.2928
17	48.8837	51.2493	53.7391	56.3596	59.1176	62.0203
18	55.7497	58.6554	61.7251	64.9681	68.3941	72.0132
19	63.4397	66.9873	70.7494	74.7388	78.9692	83.4551
20	72.0524	76.3608	80.9468	85.8286	91.0249	96.5561
21	81.6987	86.9058	92.4699	98.4154	104.7684	111.5568
22	92.5026	98.7691	105.4910	112.7015	120.4360	128.7325
23	104.6029	112.1152	120.2048	128.9162	138.2970	148.3987
24	118.1552	127.1296	136.8315	147.3199	158.6586	170.9165
25	133.3339	144.0208	155.6195	168.2081	181.8708	196.6994
26	150.3339	163.0234	176.8501	191.9162	208.3327	226.2208
27	169.3740	184.4013	200.8406	218.8249	238.4993	260.0228
28	190.6989	208.4515	227.9499	249.3662	272.8892	298.7261
29	214.5827	235.5079	258.5834	284.0306	312.0937	343.0414
30	241.3327	265.9464	293.1992	323.3748	356.7869	393.7824
31	271.2926	300.1897	332.3151	368.0304	407.7370	451.8809
32	304.8477	338.7135	376.5160	418.7145	465.8202	518.4036
33	342.4294	382.0526	426.4631	476.2409	532.0350	594.5721
34	384.5210	430.8092	482.9033	541.5335	607.5199	681.7851
35	431.6635	485.6604	546.6808	615.6405	693.5727	781.6439
36	484.4631	547.3679	618.7493	699.7520	791.6729	895.9823
37	543.5987	616.7889	700.1867	795.2185	903.5071	1026.8997
38	609.8305	694.8875	792.2109	903.5730	1030.9981	1176.8002
39	684.0101	782.7485	896.1983	1026.5553	1176.3378	1348.4362
40	767.0914	881.5920	1013.7041	1166.1403	1342.0251	1544.9594
41	860.1423	992.7910	1146.4856	1324.5693	1530.9086	1769.9785
42	964.3594	1117.8899	1296.5288	1504.3861	1746.2358	2027.6254
43	1081.0825	1258.6262	1466.0775	1708.4783	1991.7089	2322.6311
44	1211.8124	1416.9544	1657.6676	1940.1228	2271.5481	2660.4126
45	1358.2299	1595.0737	1874.1643	2203.0394	2590.5648	3047.1724
46	1522.2175	1795.4579	2118.8057	2501.4498	2954.2439	3490.0124
47	1705.8836	2020.8902	2395.2504	2840.1455	3368.8381	3997.0642
48	1911.5896	2274.5015	2707.6330	3224.5652	3841.4754	4577.6385
49	2141.9804	2559.8141	3060.6252	3660.8815	4380.2820	5242.3960
50	2400.0180	2880.7909	3459.5065	4156.1005	4994.5215	6003.5434

FUTURE VALUE OF ORDINARY ANNUITY (continued)

YEARS	15.0%	16.0%	17.0%	18.0%	19.0%	20.0%
1	1.0000	1.0000	1.0000	1.0000	1.0000	1.0000
2	2.1500	2.1600	2.1700	2.1800	2.1900	2.2000
3	3.4725	3.5056	3.5389	3.5724	3.6061	3.6400
4	4.9934	5.0665	5.1405	5.2154	5.2913	5.3680
5	6.7424	6.8771	7.0144	7.1542	7.2966	7.4416
6	8.7537	8.9775	9.2068	9.4420	9.6830	9.9299
7	11.0668	11.4139	11.7720	12.1415	12.5227	12.9159
8	13.7268	14.2401	14.7733	15.3270	15.9020	16.4991
9	16.7858	17.5185	18.2847	19.0859	19.9234	20.7989
10	20.3037	21.3215	22.3931	23.5213	24.7089	25.9587
11	24.3493	25.7329	27.1999	28.7551	30.4035	32.1504
12	29.0017	30.8502	32.8239	34.9311	37.1802	39.5805
13	34.3519	36.7862	39.4040	42.2187	45.2445	48.4966
14	40.5047	43.6720	47.1027	50.8180	54.8409	59.1959
15	47.5804	51.6595	56.1101	60.9653	66.2607	72.0351
16	55.7175	60.9250	66.6488	72.9390	79.8502	87.4421
17	65.0751	71.6730	78.9792	87.0680	96.0217	105.9306
18	75.8364	84.1407	93.4056	103.7403	115.2659	128.1167
19	88.2118	98.6032	110.2846	123.4135	138.1664	154.7400
20	102.4436	115.3797	130.0329	146.6280	165.4180	186.6880
21	118.8101	134.8405	153.1385	174.0210	197.8474	225.0256
22	137.6316	157.4150	180.1721	206.3448	236.4384	271.0307
23	159.2764	183.6014	211.8013	244.4869	282.3618	326.2369
24	184.1679	213.9776	248.8076	289.4945	337.0105	392.4843
25	212.7930	249.2140	292.1049	342.6035	402.0425	471.9811
26	245.7120	290.0883	342.7627	405.2722	479.4305	567.3773
27	283.5688	337.5024	402.0323	479.2212	571.5223	681.8528
28	327.1041	392.5027	471.3779	566.4810	681.1116	819.2234
29	377.1697	456.3032	552.5121	669.4475	811.5228	984.0680
30	434.7452	530.3117	647.4391	790.9481	966.7121	1181.8816
31	500.9570	616.1616	758.5038	934.3188	1151.3874	1419.2580
32	577.1005	715.7474	888.4494	1103.4962	1371.1510	1704.1096
33	664.6656	831.2670	1040.4858	1303.1255	1632.6697	2045.9315
34	765.3655	965.2697	1218.3684	1538.6881	1943.8770	2456.1178
35	881.1703	1120.7129	1426.4911	1816.6519	2314.2136	2948.3414
36	1014.3458	1301.0269	1669.9946	2144.6493	2754.9142	3539.0096
37	1167.4977	1510.1912	1954.8937	2531.6862	3279.3478	4247.8116
38	1343.6224	1752.8218	2288.2256	2988.3897	3903.4239	5098.3739
39	1546.1657	2034.2733	2678.2239	3527.2999	4646.0745	6119.0487
40	1779.0906	2360.7570	3134.5220	4163.2139	5529.8286	7343.8585
41	2046.9542	2739.4781	3668.3907	4913.5924	6581.4960	8813.6302
42	2354.9974	3178.7946	4293.0172	5799.0391	7832.9803	10577.3562
43	2709.2470	3688.4017	5023.8301	6843.8661	9322.2465	12693.8275
44	3116.6340	4279.5460	5878.8812	8076.7621	11094.4733	15233.5931
45	3585.1292	4965.2733	6879.2911	9531.5793	13203.4232	18281.3117
46	4123.8985	5760.7170	8049.7705	11248.2637	15713.0736	21938.5741
47	4743.4834	6683.4318	9419.2315	13273.9512	18699.5575	26327.2890
48	5456.0059	7753.7808	11021.5009	15664.2625	22253.4734	31593.7469
49	6275.4068	8995.3857	12896.1561	18484.8299	26482.6333	37913.4963
50	7217.7179	10435.6474	15089.5027	21813.0994	31515.3336	45497.1957

TAX EXEMPT EQUIVALENTS

TAX EXEMPT YIELDS	15%	16%	17%	18%	19%	20%	21%	22%	23%
3.00	3.53	3.57	3.61	3.66	3.70	3.75	3.80	3.85	3.90
3.25	3.82	3.87	3.92	3.96	4.01	4.06	4.11	4.17	4.22
3.50	4.12	4.17	4.22	4.27	4.32	4.38	4.43	4.49	4.55
3.75	4.41	4.46	4.52	4.57	4.63	4.69	4.75	4.81	4.87
4.00	4.71	4.76	4.82	4.88	4.94	5.00	5.06	5.13	5.19
4.25	5.00	5.06	5.12	5.18	5.25	5.31	5.38	5.45	5.52
4.50	5.29	5.36	5.42	5.49	5.56	5.63	5.70	5.77	5.84
4.75	5.59	5.65	5.72	5.79	5.86	5.94	6.01	6.09	6.17
5.00	5.88	5.95	6.02	6.10	6.17	6.25	6.33	6.41	6.49
5.25	6.18	6.25	6.33	6.40	6.48	6.56	6.65	6.73	6.82
5.50	6.47	6.55	6.63	6.71	6.79	6.88	6.96	7.05	7.14
5.75	6.76	6.85	6.93	7.01	7.10	7.19	7.28	7.37	7.47
6.00	7.06	7.14	7.23	7.32	7.41	7.50	7.59	7.69	7.79
6.25	7.35	7.44	7.53	7.62	7.72	7.81	7.91	8.01	8.12
6.50	7.65	7.74	7.83	7.93	8.02	8.13	8.23	8.33	8.44
6.75	7.94	8.04	8.13	8.23	8.33	8.44	8.54	8.65	8.77
7.00	8.24	8.33	8.43	8.54	8.64	8.75	8.86	8.97	9.09
7.25	8.53	8.63	8.73	8.84	8.95	9.06	9.18	9.29	9.42
7.50	8.82	8.93	9.04	9.15	9.26	9.38	9.49	9.62	9.74
7.75	9.12	9.23	9.34	9.45	9.57	9.69	9.81	9.94	10.06
8.00	9.41	9.52	9.64	9.76	9.88	10.00	10.13	10.26	10.39
8.25	9.71	9.82	9.94	10.06	10.19	10.31	10.44	10.58	10.71
8.50	10.00	10.12	10.24	10.37	10.49	10.63	10.76	10.90	11.04
8.75	10.29	10.42	10.54	10.67	10.80	10.94	11.08	11.22	11.36
9.00	10.59	10.71	10.84	10.98	11.11	11.25	11.39	11.54	11.69
9.25	10.88	11.01	11.14	11.28	11.42	11.56	11.71	11.86	12.01
9.50	11.18	11.31	11.45	11.59	11.73	11.88	12.03	12.18	12.34
9.75	11.47	11.61	11.75	11.89	12.04	12.19	12.34	12.50	12.66
10.00	11.76	11.90	12.05	12.20	12.35	12.50	12.66	12.82	12.99
10.25	12.06	12.20	12.35	12.50	12.65	12.81	12.97	13.14	13.31
10.50	12.35	12.50	12.65	12.80	12.96	13.13	13.29	13.46	13.64
10.75	12.65	12.80	12.95	13.11	13.27	13.44	13.61	13.78	13.96
11.00	12.94	13.10	13.25	13.41	13.58	13.75	13.92	14.10	14.29
11.25	13.24	13.39	13.55	13.72	13.89	14.06	14.24	14.42	14.61
11.50	13.53	13.69	13.86	14.02	14.20	14.38	14.56	14.74	14.94
11.75	13.82	13.99	14.16	14.33	14.51	14.69	14.87	15.06	15.26
12.00	14.12	14.29	14.46	14.63	14.81	15.00	15.19	15.38	15.58
12.25	14.41	14.58	14.76	14.94	15.12	15.31	15.51	15.71	15.91
12.50	14.71	14.88	15.06	15.24	15.43	15.63	15.82	16.03	16.23
12.75	15.00	15.18	15.36	15.55	15.74	15.94	16.14	16.35	16.56
13.00	15.29	15.48	15.66	15.85	16.05	16.25	16.46	16.67	16.88
13.25	15.59	15.77	15.96	16.16	16.36	16.56	16.77	16.99	17.21
13.50	15.88	16.07	16.27	16.46	16.67	16.88	17.09	17.31	17.53
13.75	16.18	16.37	16.57	16.77	16.98	17.19	17.41	17.63	17.86
14.00	16.47	16.67	16.87	17.07	17.28	17.50	17.72	17.95	18.18
14.25	16.76	16.96	17.17	17.38	17.59	17.81	18.04	18.27	18.51
14.50	17.06	17.26	17.47	17.68	17.90	18.13	18.35	18.59	18.83
14.75	17.35	17.56	17.77	17.99	18.21	18.44	18.67	18.91	19.16
15.00	17.65	17.86	18.07	18.29	18.52	18.75	18.99	19.23	19.48

Appendix G – Tax Exempt Equivalents

TAX EXEMPT EQUIVALENTS (continued)

TAX EXEMPT YIELDS	24%	25%	26%	27%	28%	29%	30%	31%	32%
3.00	3.95	4.00	4.05	4.11	4.17	4.23	4.29	4.35	4.41
3.25	4.28	4.33	4.39	4.45	4.51	4.58	4.64	4.71	4.78
3.50	4.61	4.67	4.73	4.79	4.86	4.93	5.00	5.07	5.15
3.75	4.93	5.00	5.07	5.14	5.21	5.28	5.36	5.43	5.51
4.00	5.26	5.33	5.41	5.48	5.56	5.63	5.71	5.80	5.88
4.25	5.59	5.67	5.74	5.82	5.90	5.99	6.07	6.16	6.25
4.50	5.92	6.00	6.08	6.16	6.25	6.34	6.43	6.52	6.62
4.75	6.25	6.33	6.42	6.51	6.60	6.69	6.79	6.88	6.99
5.00	6.58	6.67	6.76	6.85	6.94	7.04	7.14	7.25	7.35
5.25	6.91	7.00	7.09	7.19	7.29	7.39	7.50	7.61	7.72
5.50	7.24	7.33	7.43	7.53	7.64	7.75	7.86	7.97	8.09
5.75	7.57	7.67	7.77	7.88	7.99	8.10	8.21	8.33	8.46
6.00	7.89	8.00	8.11	8.22	8.33	8.45	8.57	8.70	8.82
6.25	8.22	8.33	8.45	8.56	8.68	8.80	8.93	9.06	9.19
6.50	8.55	8.67	8.78	8.90	9.03	9.15	9.29	9.42	9.56
6.75	8.88	9.00	9.12	9.25	9.38	9.51	9.64	9.78	9.93
7.00	9.21	9.33	9.46	9.59	9.72	9.86	10.00	10.14	10.29
7.25	9.54	9.67	9.80	9.93	10.07	10.21	10.36	10.51	10.66
7.50	9.87	10.00	10.14	10.27	10.42	10.56	10.71	10.87	11.03
7.75	10.20	10.33	10.47	10.62	10.76	10.92	11.07	11.23	11.40
8.00	10.53	10.67	10.81	10.96	11.11	11.27	11.43	11.59	11.76
8.25	10.86	11.00	11.15	11.30	11.46	11.62	11.79	11.96	12.13
8.50	11.18	11.33	11.49	11.64	11.81	11.97	12.14	12.32	12.50
8.75	11.51	11.67	11.82	11.99	12.15	12.32	12.50	12.68	12.87
9.00	11.84	12.00	12.16	12.33	12.50	12.68	12.86	13.04	13.24
9.25	12.17	12.33	12.50	12.67	12.85	13.03	13.21	13.41	13.60
9.50	12.50	12.67	12.84	13.01	13.19	13.38	13.57	13.77	13.97
9.75	12.83	13.00	13.18	13.36	13.54	13.73	13.93	14.13	14.34
10.00	13.16	13.33	13.51	13.70	13.89	14.08	14.29	14.49	14.71
10.25	13.49	13.67	13.85	14.04	14.24	14.44	14.64	14.86	15.07
10.50	13.82	14.00	14.19	14.38	14.58	14.79	15.00	15.22	15.44
10.75	14.14	14.33	14.53	14.73	14.93	15.14	15.36	15.58	15.81
11.00	14.47	14.67	14.86	15.07	15.28	15.49	15.71	15.94	16.18
11.25	14.80	15.00	15.20	15.41	15.63	15.85	16.07	16.30	16.54
11.50	15.13	15.33	15.54	15.75	15.97	16.20	16.43	16.67	16.91
11.75	15.46	15.67	15.88	16.10	16.32	16.55	16.79	17.03	17.28
12.00	15.79	16.00	16.22	16.44	16.67	16.90	17.14	17.39	17.65
12.25	16.12	16.33	16.55	16.78	17.01	17.25	17.50	17.75	18.01
12.50	16.45	16.67	16.89	17.12	17.36	17.61	17.86	18.12	18.38
12.75	16.78	17.00	17.23	17.47	17.71	17.96	18.21	18.48	18.75
13.00	17.11	17.33	17.57	17.81	18.06	18.31	18.57	18.84	19.12
13.25	17.43	17.67	17.91	18.15	18.40	18.66	18.93	19.20	19.49
13.50	17.76	18.00	18.24	18.49	18.75	19.01	19.29	19.57	19.85
13.75	18.09	18.33	18.58	18.84	19.10	19.37	19.64	19.93	20.22
14.00	18.42	18.67	18.92	19.18	19.44	19.72	20.00	20.29	20.59
14.25	18.75	19.00	19.26	19.52	19.79	20.07	20.36	20.65	20.96
14.50	19.08	19.33	19.59	19.86	20.14	20.42	20.71	21.01	21.32
14.75	19.41	19.67	19.93	20.21	20.49	20.77	21.07	21.38	21.69
15.00	19.74	20.00	20.27	20.55	20.83	21.13	21.43	21.74	22.06

TAX EXEMPT EQUIVALENTS (continued)

TAX EXEMPT YIELDS	33%	34%	35%	36%	37%	38%	39%	40%	41%
3.00	4.48	4.55	4.62	4.69	4.76	4.84	4.92	5.00	5.08
3.25	4.85	4.92	5.00	5.08	5.16	5.24	5.33	5.42	5.51
3.50	5.22	5.30	5.38	5.47	5.56	5.65	5.74	5.83	5.93
3.75	5.60	5.68	5.77	5.86	5.95	6.05	6.15	6.25	6.36
4.00	5.97	6.06	6.15	6.25	6.35	6.45	6.56	6.67	6.78
4.25	6.34	6.44	6.54	6.64	6.75	6.85	6.97	7.08	7.20
4.50	6.72	6.82	6.92	7.03	7.14	7.26	7.38	7.50	7.63
4.75	7.09	7.20	7.31	7.42	7.54	7.66	7.79	7.92	8.05
5.00	7.46	7.58	7.69	7.81	7.94	8.06	8.20	8.33	8.47
5.25	7.84	7.95	8.08	8.20	8.33	8.47	8.61	8.75	8.90
5.50	8.21	8.33	8.46	8.59	8.73	8.87	9.02	9.17	9.32
5.75	8.58	8.71	8.85	8.98	9.13	9.27	9.43	9.58	9.75
6.00	8.96	9.09	9.23	9.38	9.52	9.68	9.84	10.00	10.17
6.25	9.33	9.47	9.62	9.77	9.92	10.08	10.25	10.42	10.59
6.50	9.70	9.85	10.00	10.16	10.32	10.48	10.66	10.83	11.02
6.75	10.07	10.23	10.38	10.55	10.71	10.89	11.07	11.25	11.44
7.00	10.45	10.61	10.77	10.94	11.11	11.29	11.48	11.67	11.86
7.25	10.82	10.98	11.15	11.33	11.51	11.69	11.89	12.08	12.29
7.50	11.19	11.36	11.54	11.72	11.90	12.10	12.30	12.50	12.71
7.75	11.57	11.74	11.92	12.11	12.30	12.50	12.70	12.92	13.14
8.00	11.94	12.12	12.31	12.50	12.70	12.90	13.11	13.33	13.56
8.25	12.31	12.50	12.69	12.89	13.10	13.31	13.52	13.75	13.98
8.50	12.69	12.88	13.08	13.28	13.49	13.71	13.93	14.17	14.41
8.75	13.06	13.26	13.46	13.67	13.89	14.11	14.34	14.58	14.83
9.00	13.43	13.64	13.85	14.06	14.29	14.52	14.75	15.00	15.25
9.25	13.81	14.02	14.23	14.45	14.68	14.92	15.16	15.42	15.68
9.50	14.18	14.39	14.62	14.84	15.08	15.32	15.57	15.83	16.10
9.75	14.55	14.77	15.00	15.23	15.48	15.73	15.98	16.25	16.53
10.00	14.93	15.15	15.38	15.63	15.87	16.13	16.39	16.67	16.95
10.25	15.30	15.53	15.77	16.02	16.27	16.53	16.80	17.08	17.37
10.50	15.67	15.91	16.15	16.41	16.67	16.94	17.21	17.50	17.80
10.75	16.04	16.29	16.54	16.80	17.06	17.34	17.62	17.92	18.22
11.00	16.42	16.67	16.92	17.19	17.46	17.74	18.03	18.33	18.64
11.25	16.79	17.05	17.31	17.58	17.86	18.15	18.44	18.75	19.07
11.50	17.16	17.42	17.69	17.97	18.25	18.55	18.85	19.17	19.49
11.75	17.54	17.80	18.08	18.36	18.65	18.95	19.26	19.58	19.92
12.00	17.91	18.18	18.46	18.75	19.05	19.35	19.67	20.00	20.34
12.25	18.28	18.56	18.85	19.14	19.44	19.76	20.08	20.42	20.76
12.50	18.66	18.94	19.23	19.53	19.84	20.16	20.49	20.83	21.19
12.75	19.03	19.32	19.62	19.92	20.24	20.56	20.90	21.25	21.61
13.00	19.40	19.70	20.00	20.31	20.63	20.97	21.31	21.67	22.03
13.25	19.78	20.08	20.38	20.70	21.03	21.37	21.72	22.08	22.46
13.50	20.15	20.45	20.77	21.09	21.43	21.77	22.13	22.50	22.88
13.75	20.52	20.83	21.15	21.48	21.83	22.18	22.54	22.92	23.31
14.00	20.90	21.21	21.54	21.88	22.22	22.58	22.95	23.33	23.73
14.25	21.27	21.59	21.92	22.27	22.62	22.98	23.36	23.75	24.15
14.50	21.64	21.97	22.31	22.66	23.02	23.39	23.77	24.17	24.58
14.75	22.01	22.35	22.69	23.05	23.41	23.79	24.18	24.58	25.00
15.00	22.39	22.73	23.08	23.44	23.81	24.19	24.59	25.00	25.42

Appendix G – Tax Exempt Equivalents

TAX EXEMPT EQUIVALENTS (continued)

TAX EXEMPT YIELDS	42%	43%	44%	45%	46%	47%	48%	49%	50%
3.00	5.17	5.26	5.36	5.45	5.56	5.66	5.77	5.88	6.00
3.25	5.60	5.70	5.80	5.91	6.02	6.13	6.25	6.37	6.50
3.50	6.03	6.14	6.25	6.36	6.48	6.60	6.73	6.86	7.00
3.75	6.47	6.58	6.70	6.82	6.94	7.08	7.21	7.35	7.50
4.00	6.90	7.02	7.14	7.27	7.41	7.55	7.69	7.84	8.00
4.25	7.33	7.46	7.59	7.73	7.87	8.02	8.17	8.33	8.50
4.50	7.76	7.89	8.04	8.18	8.33	8.49	8.65	8.82	9.00
4.75	8.19	8.33	8.48	8.64	8.80	8.96	9.13	9.31	9.50
5.00	8.62	8.77	8.93	9.09	9.26	9.43	9.62	9.80	10.00
5.25	9.05	9.21	9.38	9.55	9.72	9.91	10.10	10.29	10.50
5.50	9.48	9.65	9.82	10.00	10.19	10.38	10.58	10.78	11.00
5.75	9.91	10.09	10.27	10.45	10.65	10.85	11.06	11.27	11.50
6.00	10.34	10.53	10.71	10.91	11.11	11.32	11.54	11.76	12.00
6.25	10.78	10.96	11.16	11.36	11.57	11.79	12.02	12.25	12.50
6.50	11.21	11.40	11.61	11.82	12.04	12.26	12.50	12.75	13.00
6.75	11.64	11.84	12.05	12.27	12.50	12.74	12.98	13.24	13.50
7.00	12.07	12.28	12.50	12.73	12.96	13.21	13.46	13.73	14.00
7.25	12.50	12.72	12.95	13.18	13.43	13.68	13.94	14.22	14.50
7.50	12.93	13.16	13.39	13.64	13.89	14.15	14.42	14.71	15.00
7.75	13.36	13.60	13.84	14.09	14.35	14.62	14.90	15.20	15.50
8.00	13.79	14.04	14.29	14.55	14.81	15.09	15.38	15.69	16.00
8.25	14.22	14.47	14.73	15.00	15.28	15.57	15.87	16.18	16.50
8.50	14.66	14.91	15.18	15.45	15.74	16.04	16.35	16.67	17.00
8.75	15.09	15.35	15.63	15.91	16.20	16.51	16.83	17.16	17.50
9.00	15.52	15.79	16.07	16.36	16.67	16.98	17.31	17.65	18.00
9.25	15.95	16.23	16.52	16.82	17.13	17.45	17.79	18.14	18.50
9.50	16.38	16.67	16.96	17.27	17.59	17.92	18.27	18.63	19.00
9.75	16.81	17.11	17.41	17.73	18.06	18.40	18.75	19.12	19.50
10.00	17.24	17.54	17.86	18.18	18.52	18.87	19.23	19.61	20.00
10.25	17.67	17.98	18.30	18.64	18.98	19.34	19.71	20.10	20.50
10.50	18.10	18.42	18.75	19.09	19.44	19.81	20.19	20.59	21.00
10.75	18.53	18.86	19.20	19.55	19.91	20.28	20.67	21.08	21.50
11.00	18.97	19.30	19.64	20.00	20.37	20.75	21.15	21.57	22.00
11.25	19.40	19.74	20.09	20.45	20.83	21.23	21.63	22.06	22.50
11.50	19.83	20.18	20.54	20.91	21.30	21.70	22.12	22.55	23.00
11.75	20.26	20.61	20.98	21.36	21.76	22.17	22.60	23.04	23.50
12.00	20.69	21.05	21.43	21.82	22.22	22.64	23.08	23.53	24.00
12.25	21.12	21.49	21.88	22.27	22.69	23.11	23.56	24.02	24.50
12.50	21.55	21.93	22.32	22.73	23.15	23.58	24.04	24.51	25.00
12.75	21.98	22.37	22.77	23.18	23.61	24.06	24.52	25.00	25.50
13.00	22.41	22.81	23.21	23.64	24.07	24.53	25.00	25.49	26.00
13.25	22.84	23.25	23.66	24.09	24.54	25.00	25.48	25.98	26.50
13.50	23.28	23.68	24.11	24.55	25.00	25.47	25.96	26.47	27.00
13.75	23.71	24.12	24.55	25.00	25.46	25.94	26.44	26.96	27.50
14.00	24.14	24.56	25.00	25.45	25.93	26.42	26.92	27.45	28.00
14.25	24.57	25.00	25.45	25.91	26.39	26.89	27.40	27.94	28.50
14.50	25.00	25.44	25.89	26.36	26.85	27.36	27.88	28.43	29.00
14.75	25.43	25.88	26.34	26.82	27.31	27.83	28.37	28.92	29.50
15.00	25.86	26.32	26.79	27.27	27.78	28.30	28.85	29.41	30.00

INVESTMENT CHARACTERISTICS MATRIX AND INVESTMENT PRIORITY VALUATOR

All investment alternatives ("tools") possess certain important functional characteristics. These characteristics include:

(1) Liquidity

(2) Tax Advantages

(3) Current Income

(4) Security (Safety)

(5) Substantial Appreciation Potential

(6) Moderate Appreciation (Inflation Hedge).

The degree to which any investment will perform these functions may vary dramatically. For example, an investment such as a money market fund may provide a great degree of liquidity, but has no potential for substantial appreciation. On the other hand, an individual retirement plan may have outstanding tax advantages, but provides no current income to investors until withdrawals are made upon retirement.

This appendix provides the financial planner with two useful devices for comparing and analyzing the performance of investment alternatives:

(1) The *Investment Characteristics Matrix* provides a basic appraisal of how well the investment tools discussed in this volume might be expected to perform each of the six functional characteristics listed above.

(2) The *Investment Priority Valuator* uses the Investment Characteristic Matrix to provide the financial planner with a simple method of incorporating the investor's individual goals and priorities into the comparative analysis process.

The *Investment Characteristics Matrix* provides a rating for each of the six functional characteristics for each investment alternative. The highest rating given is a five (5). The lowest possible rating is a one (1).

Liquidity is an extremely important characteristic. A higher rating is given to an investment which can be readily converted to cash-in-hand without any loss in value. If the immediate sale of the investment is difficult and will result in a sacrifice in cash proceeds, a lower rating is warranted.

For example, money market funds and certificates of deposit, especially short term certificates, are considered highly liquid. Publicly traded stocks and bonds are easily converted to cash, but the value at the time of sale may not be worth what the investor had hoped for. Real estate will generally receive a low liquidity rating because of the difficulty in obtaining the full value of real property in a "forced sale" situation.

The more an investment utilizes certain benefits available in the tax law to enhance the investor's return, the higher the rating it receives in the *tax advantage* category. Individual retirement accounts, Keogh plans, and municipal bonds are obviously rated the highest. Common stocks, for example, receive a moderate rating because of the potential for capital gain treatment (generally net long-term capital gains are taxed at a maximum rate of 15%). Money market funds and certificates of deposit, which have no tax advantages, receive the lowest rating.

Higher ratings for *current income* are given to those investments that provide both the highest amount and greatest certainty of providing regular cash flow to investors (without regard to tax benefits). Annuities, corporate bonds and mortgage backed securities receive the highest rank in this category. Collectibles, commodities, and unimproved real estate, for instance, receive the lowest rating. These investments provide the investor with no income on a regular, recurring basis.

The risk of loss of capital invested is the primary criterion in evaluating the security or safety of an investment. Generally, investments that are guaranteed or otherwise secured by the federal government are considered the most secure. U.S. Government securities (such as Treasury notes and bonds) and FDIC-insured certificates of deposit are in this category. Highly rated (AAA) municipal bonds are considered relatively safe. The more speculative investments, such as commodities and financial futures, usually receive low ratings for security.

An investment that is more likely to have a rapid or extreme increase in market value is considered to have *substantial appreciation potential*. Investments that receive high ratings in this category tend to be more speculative and therefore less secure. These include collectibles, commodities, gold and other precious metals, and exploratory oil and gas investments.

Certificates of deposit, corporate bonds, municipal bonds, and other fixed income assets are examples of investments with little or no potential for appreciation. These "fixed dollar" investments will in fact lose value in periods of high inflation, even though the face value will remain secure.

An investment is considered to provide *moderate appreciation* (and therefore a hedge against inflation) if it is likely that the value of the investment will increase (at least moderately) during a period of inflation, but will not reduce substantially during a deflationary period. An investment receiving a high rating in this category tends to hold its value because of such factors as limited supply (e.g., real estate), variable income potential (e.g., variable IRAs and mutual funds), and general ability to fluctuate with market conditions (e.g., growth oriented common stocks). Fixed income investments, such as certificates of deposit, and corporate and municipal bonds, which do not react positively to inflationary conditions, receive lower ratings.

The *Investment Priority Valuator* enables the financial planner to make a comparative analysis of alternative investments based upon the investor's own valuation of the importance of each of the six functional criteria of the *Investment Characteristics Matrix*. Each characteristic of each alternative investment is given two ratings: (1) Importance, and (2) Performance.

Importance is the personal value given by the investor to each of the functional criteria. The values for Importance can range from one (1), for a characteristic of little importance to the investor, to five (5) for a criterion of utmost importance to the investor.

The *Performance* value is the rating ascribed in the *Investment Characteristics Matrix* to each functional criterion for each investment type. (Alternatively, the financial planner and investor can modify these ratings based on information more appropriate to the investor's individual circumstances.)

The following steps should be followed in using the *Investment Priority Valuator*:

(1) For each characteristic, insert the investor's Importance rating under the "Importance" column for all of the investments. (The same Importance rating for a particular characteristic should be used for all of the investment alternatives.)

(2) For each investment, insert the Performance ratings (from the *Investment Characteristics Matrix* or as otherwise determined) under the "Performance" column for each characteristic.

(3) Multiply the Importance rating by the Performance rating for each characteristic of each investment and insert the result in the appropriate space under the "Value" columns.

(4) Add the computed values for each characteristic of each investment. For each investment, insert the total amount in the "Total Value" column.

(5) Compare the "Total Value" computed for each alternative investment. The investments with the highest total values are most likely to fulfill the investor's investment goals.

The final exhibit of this appendix provides an example of a completed *Investment Priority Valuator*, using the Performance ratings from the *Investment Characteristics Matrix* and the following Importance ratings of the investor:

Liquidity = 4

Tax Advantage = 4

Current Income = 3

Security = 5

Substantial Appreciation Potential = 2

Moderate Appreciation (Inflation Hedge) = 5

Based on these priorities, the investments receiving the highest ratings are Real Estate Investment Trusts

Appendix H – Investment Matrix and Valuator

(REITs)—equity (80), common stocks (77), convertible securities (75), annuities (75), individual retirement accounts—variable (73), Keogh plans—variable (73), real estate—commercial (73), real estate—apartments (73), Real Estate Investment Trusts (REITs)—hybrid (73) and municipal bonds (72).

The investments receiving the lowest ratings (and therefore are least appropriate based on the investor's goals) are commodities (47), individual retirement accounts—fixed (59), Keogh plans—fixed (59), life insurance—variable (60), Real Estate Mortgage Investment Conduits (REMICs)—regular interests (60), and financial futures (60).

INVESTMENT CHARACTERISTICS MATRIX

	Liquidity	Tax Advantage
Annuities	2	4
Certificates of Deposit	5	1
Collectibles	2	3
Commodities	1	3
Common Stocks	4	3
Convertible Securities	4	3
Corporate Bonds	4	2
Financial Futures	4	2
Gold & Other Precious Metals	3	3
Individual Retirement Accounts — Fixed	1	5
Individual Retirement Accounts — Variable	1	5
Keogh (HR-10) Plans — Fixed	1	5
Keogh (HR-10) Plans — Variable	1	5
Life Insurance — Whole Life	2	4
Life Insurance — Interest Sensitive Whole Life	2	4
Life Insurance — Universal	2	4
Life Insurance — Variable	2	4
Money Market Funds	5	1
Mortgage Backed Securities	4	3
Municipal Bonds	4	5
Mutual Funds (Balanced Fund)	4	3
Oil & Gas (Balanced Program)	1	4
Preferred Stock	4	3
Puts & Calls	4	3
Real Estate — Apartments	2	4
Real Estate — Commercial	2	4
Real Estate — Unimproved Land	2	2
Real Estate Investment Trusts (REITs) — Equity	4	3
Real Estate Investment Trusts (REITs) — Mortgage	4	3
Real Estate Investment Trusts (REITs) — Hybrid	4	3
Real Estate Mortgage Investment Conduits (REMICs) — Regular Interest	4	2
Real Estate Mortgage Investment Conduits (REMICs) — Residual Interest	3	2
U.S. Government Securities	4	2

INVESTMENT CHARACTERISTICS MATRIX

Current Income	Security (Safety)	Substantial Appreciation Potential	Moderate Appreciation (Inflation Hedge)
4	4	2	3
3	5	1	1
1	2	4	4
1	1	4	3
2	3	4	4
3	3	4	3
4	4	1	1
1	1	4	4
1	3	4	4
1	5	1	1
1	4	3	4
1	5	1	1
1	4	3	4
1	4	2	2
1	3	3	4
1	4	3	3
3	2	4	3
4	5	1	1
3	4	1	1
3	4	1	1
3	3	3	3
1	2	4	3
2	3	2	2
2	3	4	3
1	3	4	4
3	3	4	4
3	3	4	4
3	3	4	4
3	3	2	2
3	4	3	3
3	3	1	1
3	5	3	3

Appendix H – Investment Matrix and Valuator

INVESTMENT PRIORITY VALUATOR

I = Importance; P = Performance

	Liquidity					Tax Advantage				
	I	x	P	=	Value		I	x	P	=	Value
Annuities	4		2		8		4		4		16
Certificates of Deposit	4		5		20		4		1		4
Collectibles	4		2		8		4		3		12
Commodities	4		1		4		4		3		12
Common Stocks	4		4		16		4		3		12
Convertible Securities	4		4		16		4		3		12
Corporate Bonds	4		4		16		4		2		8
Financial Futures	4		4		16		4		2		8
Gold & Other Precious Metals	4		3		12		4		3		12
Individ. Retirement Accounts — Fixed	4		1		4		4		5		20
Individual Retirement Accounts — Variable	4		1		4		4		5		20
Keogh (HR-10) Plans — Fixed	4		1		4		4		5		20
Keogh (HR-10) Plans — Variable	4		1		4		4		5		20
Life Insurance — Whole Life	4		2		8		4		4		16
Life Insurance — Int. Sens. W. L.	4		2		8		4		4		16
Life Insurance — Universal	4		2		8		4		4		16
Life Insurance — Variable	4		2		8		4		4		16
Money Market Funds	4		5		20		4		1		4
Mortgaged Backed Securities	4		4		16		4		3		12
Municipal Bonds	4		4		16		4		5		20
Mutual Funds (Balanced Fund)	4		4		16		4		3		12
Oil & Gas (Balanced Program)	4		1		4		4		4		16
Preferred Stock	4		4		16		4		3		12
Puts & Calls	4		4		16		4		3		12
Real Estate — Apartments	4		2		8		4		4		16
Real Estate — Commercial	4		2		8		4		4		16
Real Estate — Unimproved Land	4		2		8		4		2		8
Real Estate Investment Trusts (REITs) — Equity	4		4		16		4		3		12
Real Estate Investment Trusts (REITs) — Mortgage	4		4		16		4		3		12
Real Estate Investment Trusts (REITs) — Hybrid	4		4		16		4		3		12
Real Estate Mortgage Investment Conduits (REMICs) — Regular Interest	4		4		16		4		2		8
Real Estate Mortgage Investment Conduits (REMICs) — Residual Interest	4		3		12		4		2		8
U.S. Government Securities	4		4		16		4		2		8

INVESTMENT PRIORITY VALUATOR

I = Importance; P = Performance

Current Income			Security (Safety)			Substantial Appreciation Potential			Moderate Appreciation (Inflation Hedge)			Total Value
I x	P	= Value	I x	P	= Value	I x	P	= Value	I x	P	= Value	Value
3	4	12	5	4	20	2	2	4	5	3	15	75
3	3	9	5	5	25	2	1	2	5	1	5	65
3	1	3	5	2	10	2	4	8	5	4	20	61
3	1	3	5	1	5	2	4	8	5	3	15	47
3	2	6	5	3	15	2	4	8	5	4	20	77
3	3	9	5	3	15	2	4	8	5	3	15	75
3	4	12	5	4	20	2	1	2	5	1	5	63
3	1	3	5	1	5	2	4	8	5	4	20	60
3	1	3	5	3	15	2	4	8	5	4	20	70
3	1	3	5	5	25	2	1	2	5	1	5	59
3	1	3	5	4	20	2	3	6	5	4	20	73
3	1	3	5	5	25	2	1	2	5	1	5	59
3	1	3	5	4	20	2	3	6	5	4	20	73
3	3	9	5	4	20	2	2	4	5	2	10	61
3	4	12	5	3	15	2	3	6	5	4	20	68
3	3	9	5	4	20	2	3	6	5	3	15	68
3	3	9	5	3	15	2	4	8	5	3	15	60
3	3	9	5	2	10	2	1	2	5	1	5	65
3	1	3	5	3	15	2	1	2	5	1	5	67
3	2	6	5	2	10	2	4	8	5	1	5	72
3	2	6	5	3	15	2	4	8	5	3	15	73
3	1	3	5	3	15	2	4	8	5	3	15	73
3	3	9	5	3	15	2	4	8	5	4	20	62
3	3	9	5	3	15	2	2	4	5	2	10	66
3	3	9	5	4	20	2	3	6	5	3	15	64
3	3	9	5	3	15	2	1	2	5	1	5	73
3	3	9	5	5	25	2	1	2	5	3	15	73
3	1	3	5	4	20	2	3	6	5	3	15	62
3	4	12	5	4	20	2	4	8	5	4	20	80
3	3	9	5	3	15	2	2	4	5	2	10	66
3	3	9	5	3	15	2	3	6	5	3	15	73
3	3	9	5	4	20	2	1	2	5	1	5	60
3	3	9	5	3	15	2	3	6	5	3	15	65
3	3	9	5	5	25	2	1	2	5	1	5	65

INVESTMENT PRIORITY VALUATOR

I = Importance; P = Performance

	Liquidity			Tax Advantage		
	I	x P	= Value	I	x P	= Value
Annuities						
Certificates of Deposit						
Collectibles						
Commodities						
Common Stocks						
Convertible Securities						
Corporate Bonds						
Financial Futures						
Gold & Other Precious Metals						
Individ. Retirement Accounts — Fixed						
Individual Retirement Accounts — Variable						
Keogh (HR-10) Plans — Fixed						
Keogh (HR-10) Plans — Variable						
Life Insurance — Whole Life						
Life Insurance — Int. Sens. W. L.						
Life Insurance — Universal						
Life Insurance — Variable						
Money Market Funds						
Mortgaged Backed Securities						
Municipal Bonds						
Mutual Funds (Balanced Fund)						
Oil & Gas (Balanced Program)						
Preferred Stock						
Puts & Calls						
Real Estate — Apartments						
Real Estate — Commercial						
Real Estate — Unimproved Land						
Real Estate Investment Trusts (REITs) — Equity						
Real Estate Investment Trusts (REITs) — Mortgage						
Real Estate Investment Trusts (REITs) — Hybrid						
Real Estate Mortgage Investment Conduits (REMICs) — Regular Interest						
Real Estate Mortgage Investment Conduits (REMICs) — Residual Interest						
U.S. Government Securities						

INVESTMENT PRIORITY VALUATOR

I = Importance; P = Performance

Current Income			Security (Safety)			Substantial Appreciation Potential			Moderate Appreciation (Inflation Hedge)			Total
I	x P	= Value	I	x P	= Value	I	x P	= Value	I	x P	= Value	Value

Appendix I

INCOME TAX
Individuals, Estates and Trusts
(Tax Years Beginning in 2006)

Col. 1 Taxable Income $	Separate Return Tax on Col. 1 $	Rate on Excess %	Joint Return Tax on Col. 1 $	Rate on Excess %	Single Return Tax on Col. 1 $	Rate on Excess %	Head of Household Tax on Col. 1 $	Rate on Excess %	Trusts and Estates Tax on Col. 1 $	Rate on Excess %
0	0	10.0	0	10.0	0	10.0	0	10.0	0	15.0
2,050	205	10.0	205	10.0	205	10.0	205	10.0	308	25.0
4,850	485	10.0	485	10.0	485	10.0	485	10.0	1,008	28.0
7,400	740	10.0	740	10.0	740	10.0	740	10.0	1,722	33.0
7,550	755	15.0	755	10.0	755	15.0	755	10.0	1,771	33.0
10,050	1,130	15.0	1,005	10.0	1,130	15.0	1,005	10.0	2,596	35.0
10,750	1,235	15.0	1,075	10.0	1,235	15.0	1,075	15.0	2,841	35.0
15,100	1,888	15.0	1,510	15.0	1,888	15.0	1,728	15.0	4,364	35.0
30,650	4,220	25.0	3,843	15.0	4,220	25.0	4,060	15.0	9,806	35.0
41,050	6,820	25.0	5,403	15.0	6,820	25.0	5,620	25.0	13,446	35.0
61,300	11,883	25.0	8,440	25.0	11,883	25.0	10,683	25.0	20,534	35.0
61,850	12,020	28.0	8,578	25.0	12,020	25.0	10,820	25.0	20,726	35.0
74,200	15,478	28.0	11,665	25.0	15,108	28.0	13,908	25.0	25,049	35.0
94,225	21,085	33.0	16,671	25.0	20,715	28.0	18,914	25.0	32,057	35.0
106,000	24,971	33.0	19,615	25.0	24,012	28.0	21,858	28.0	36,179	35.0
123,700	30,812	33.0	24,040	28.0	28,968	28.0	26,814	28.0	42,374	35.0
154,800	41,075	33.0	32,748	28.0	37,676	33.0	35,522	28.0	53,259	35.0
168,275	45,522	35.0	36,521	28.0	42,122	33.0	39,295	28.0	57,975	35.0
171,650	46,703	35.0	37,466	28.0	43,236	33.0	40,240	33.0	59,156	35.0
188,450	52,583	35.0	42,170	33.0	48,780	33.0	45,784	33.0	65,036	35.0
336,550	104,418	35.0	91,043	35.0	97,653	35.0	94,657	35.0	116,871	35.0

Corporations†
(Tax Years Beginning in 2006)

Col. 1 Taxable Income	Tax on Col. 1	Rate on Excess
-0-	-0-	15%
$ 50,000	7,500	25%
$ 75,000	13,750	34%
$ 100,000	22,250	39% *
$ 335,000	113,900	34%
$ 10,000,000	5,150,000	35%
$ 15,000,000	6,416,000	38% **
$ 18,333,333	——	35%

† Personal Service Corporations are taxed at a flat rate of 35%.

* A 5% surtax is imposed on income above $100,000 until the benefit of the 15 and 25% tax rates has been canceled. Thus, taxable income from $100,001 to $335,000 is taxed at the rate of 39%.

** Corporations with taxable income over $15,000,000 are subject to an additional tax of the lesser of 3% of the excess over $15,000,000 or $100,000. Thus, taxable income exceeding $18,333,333 is taxed at 35%. See Ann. 93-133, 1993-32 IRB 12.

Appendix J

MILLION DOLLAR GOAL GUIDE
20 Years
To reach $1,000,000

I have now	I need	My money has to earn (OR)	If the money I have now earns 5%, it will be worth	Shortfall	Return needed to meet goal if $10,000 invested annually (OR)	If the annual investment earns 5%, I need to invest each year
$ 20,000	$980,000	21.48%	$ 53,066	$946,934	13.28%	$27,274
40,000	960,000	17.46%	106,132	893,868	12.82%	25,746
60,000	940,000	15.10%	159,198	840,802	12.33%	24,217
80,000	920,000	13.46%	212,264	787,736	11.81%	22,689
100,000	900,000	12.20%	265,330	734,670	11.25%	21,160
120,000	880,000	11.18%	318,396	681,604	10.64%	19,632
140,000	860,000	10.33%	371,462	628,538	9.98%	18,103
160,000	840,000	9.60%	424,528	575,472	9.26%	16,575
180,000	820,000	8.95%	477,594	522,406	8.46%	15,047
200,000	800,000	8.38%	530,660	469,340	7.57%	13,518
220,000	780,000	7.86%	583,725	416,275	6.56%	11,990
240,000	760,000	7.40%	636,791	363,209	5.39%	10,461
260,000	740,000	6.97%	689,857	310,143	4.01%	8,933
280,000	720,000	6.57%	742,923	257,077	2.33%	7,404
300,000	700,000	6.20%	795,989	204,011	.19%	5,876
320,000	680,000	5.86%	849,055	150,945	**	4,348
340,000	660,000	5.54%	902,121	97,879	**	2,819
360,000	640,000	5.24%	955,187	44,813	**	1,291
380,000	620,000	4.96%	1,008,253	(8,253)	**	**
400,000	600,000	4.69%	1,061,319	(61,319)	**	**
420,000	580,000	4.43%	1,114,385	(114,385)	**	**
440,000	560,000	4.19%	1,167,451	(167,451)	**	**
460,000	540,000	3.96%	1,220,517	(220,517)	**	**
480,000	520,000	3.74%	1,273,583	(273,583)	**	**
500,000	500,000	3.53%	1,326,649	(326,649)	**	**

*Figures courtesy of Financial Planning Toolkit.

Tools & Techniques of Investment Planning

Appendix K

ADDITIONAL TIME VALUE CONCEPTS

Chapter 14 discusses basic time value concepts. This appendix discusses how to adjust time value concepts for inflation or growth and for taxes.

ADJUSTING FOR INFLATION OR GROWTH FACTORS

Overview

Often investment analyses and other financial planning problems involve adjustments for inflation or for expected systematic increments or decrements of payments or cash flows over time. For example, when planning for how much one must accumulate for retirement it is common to assume that the amount needed each year in retirement will increase as a result of inflation. The annuity formulas presented earlier will compute the present value of a series of level payments for a specified number of years, but how does one compute the present value if the payments are assumed to be increasing at some constant rate rather than remaining level?

Actually, the formulas given in Chapter 32 are generally still perfectly applicable, with some slight modification, if one substitutes inflation-adjusted or growth-adjusted rates for nominal rates.

Inflation/Growth–Adjusted Rate of Return

The inflation- or growth-adjusted rate of return, ρ, is defined as follows, where r is the nominal rate of return and i is the inflation or growth factor:

Equation RIA

$$\rho = \left(\frac{1+r}{1+i} \right) - 1 = \left(\frac{r-i}{1+i} \right)$$

Example 1: Our client earns 12% on her investment for the year. However, inflation for the year is 4%. What is her real inflation-adjusted rate of return?

For each $100 invested, your client has $112 in nominal terms at the end of the year. However, the purchasing power of that $112 has declined by 4% as a result of inflation. Therefore, the real inflation-adjusted value of each dollar invested is only $112 ÷ 1.04 = $107.69 (using equation PV1 from Chapter 32). So her real inflation-adjusted return is only 7.69%.

Applying equation RIA, one derives the same result:

$$\rho = (12\% - 4\%) \div (1.04) = 7.69\%.$$

Inflation/Growth Adjusted ROR, PVs and FVs

Equation PV1 computes the present value of a future value. However, if the future value is expressed in current dollars and one expects inflation during the intervening period, one must first inflate the future value by the anticipated inflation using equation FV1 (from Chapter 32) before computing the present value investment required today to reach the future inflated value. In other words, one must compute the required present value in a two-step procedure.

However, the calculation can take just one step by using an inflation-adjusted rate of return where both the present value and future value are expressed in current dollars.

Example 2: Recall, your client's child will be attending college in 5 years and she asked you how much she will need to set aside today to pay the first year's tuition and fees. If the current tuition and fees are $36,000, and inflation for college costs averages 6% over the next five years, she will need to accumulate $48,176, not just $36,000 (using equation FV1). Assuming she earns 5% on the money she invests for this purpose, she will need to invest $37,747 today (using equation PV1), not just $28,207, to meet her child's first year college need.

However, the amount can be computed directly using just one equation with the inflation-adjusted rate of return of –0.9434% [(5% - 6%) ÷ 1.06] and the $36,000 goal expressed in today's dollars.

$$PV = \frac{\$36,000}{(1 - 0.9434\%)^5} = \frac{\$36,000}{0.953712} = \$37,747$$

Inflation/Growth Adjusted ROR and Annuities

The inflation/growth-adjusted rate becomes much more useful when dealing with calculations involving annuities. For inflation-adjusted ordinary annuities where the payment is assumed to grow at i% per period, the present value can be computed by adjusting equation PV4 (from Chapter 32) for the growth of payments as follows:

Equation PV4'

$$PV = Pmt \times \left[\frac{(1+i)^0}{(1+r)^1} + \frac{(1+i)^1}{(1+r)^2} + \frac{(1+i)^2}{(1+r)^3} + ... + \frac{(1+i)^{n-1}}{(1+r)^n} \right]$$

Multiplying inside the bracket and dividing outside the bracket by (1 + i) one derives the following formula:

$$PV = Pmt \times \left[\frac{(1+i)^1}{(1+r)^1} + \frac{(1+i)^2}{(1+r)^2} + \frac{(1+i)^3}{(1+r)^3} + ... + \frac{(1+i)^{n-1}}{(1+r)^{n-1}} + \frac{(1+i)^n}{(1+r)^n} \right] \times \frac{1}{(1+i)}$$

Substituting (1 + ρ) for (1 + r) ÷ (1 + i), the result is:

$$PV = Pmt \times \left[\frac{1}{(1+\rho)^1} + \frac{1}{(1+\rho)^2} + \frac{1}{(1+\rho)^3} + ... + \frac{1}{(1+\rho)^{n-1}} + \frac{1}{(1+\rho)^n} \right] \times \frac{1}{(1+i)}$$

With ρ substituted for r, this formula is identical to the formula used to derive equation PV7 (from Chapter 32) for

the present value of an ordinary annuity, except that it is multiplied by 1 + (1+i). Therefore, the equation for computing *the present value of an inflation-adjusted ordinary annuity with payments increasing at the rate of i% per period* is:

Equation PV7'

$$PV = Pmt \times \left(\frac{1 - (1+\rho)^{-n}}{\rho} \right) \times (1+i)^{-1}, \text{ if } \rho \neq 0$$

$$PV = Pmt \times n \times (1+i)^{-1}, \text{ if } \rho = 0$$

Through similar algebraic manipulations and substitutions of equation PV11, (from Chapter 32) the formula derived for *the present value of an inflation-adjusted annuity due* is:

Equation PV11'

$$PV = Pmt \times \left(\frac{1 - (1+\rho)^{-n}}{\rho} \right) \times (1 + \rho), \text{ if } \rho \neq 0$$

$$PV = Pmt \times n, \text{ if } \rho = 0$$

Example 3: Example 6 (from Chapter 32) computed the present value of your client's four beginning-of-year college cost payments at the time her daughter begins college, assuming that the annual cost would be $36,000. Example 2 showed that if college costs were assumed to inflate at the rate of 6% per year for the 5 years until your client's child starts college, the first-year cost would be $48,176, not just $36,000. It also computed the growth-adjusted rate of return, –0.9434%, assuming a 5% nominal rate of return and a 6% rate of inflation for college costs. Assuming that college costs continue to rise at a 6% rate after your client's daughter begins college, how much will your client have to accumulate by the beginning of her child's first year of college in 5 years to pay the 4-year cost if she can earn 5% on her money?

$$Pmt = \$48,176$$
$$\rho = -0.9434\%$$
$$n = 4$$

$$PV = \$48,176 \times \frac{[1 - (1 - 0.9434\%)^{-4}] \times (1 - 0.9434\%)}{-0.9434\%}$$

$$PV = \$48,176 \times \frac{-0.0386431 \times 0.990566}{-0.9434\%} = \$195,474$$

Your client will need to accumulate a sum of almost $200,000 ($195,474) by the time her child begins college in 5 years, not just $134,000 as determined in Example 6 when inflation was ignored.

Example 4: What is the total amount your client would need to invest today to reach her goal of $195,474 in 5 years?

You could compute this amount by discounting the $195,474 target determined in Example 3 at 5% for 5 years using equation PV1. The result is $153,160.

Alternatively, you could compute the amount required today by realizing that the present value of a 4-year annuity due commencing at the end of 5 years is equal to the value of a 9-year annuity due commencing today less the value of a 5-year annuity due commencing today.

Using equation PV11 with n = 9, ρ = −0.9434%, and Pmt = $36,000 (you would use the current college cost value since the analysis starts from today), the present value of a 9-year inflation-adjusted annuity is $336,621. Similarly, using equation PV11 with n = 5, ρ = −0.9434, and Pmt = $36,000, the present value of a 4-year inflation-adjusted annuity is $183,461. The difference is $153,160.

This 2-step calculation derives exactly the same result as was determined by using the 3-step process of (1) inflating the $36,000 payment for 5 years of inflation at 6% to derive the first-year college cost figure, (2) calculating the present value in 5 years of a 4-year inflation-adjusted annuity due, and (3) computing the present value today (5 years earlier) of the amount determined in step 2.

The formulas for computing the future value of inflation-adjusted annuities due and ordinary annuities can be derived by similar manipulations and adjustments of equations FV2 and FV4 (from Chapter 32). The *future value of an inflation-adjusted ordinary annuity* is:

Equation FV2'

$$FV = Pmt \times (1 + i)^{n-1} \times \left(\frac{(1+\rho)^n - 1}{\rho} \right), \text{ if } \rho \neq 0$$

$$FV = Pmt \times n \times (1 + i)^{n-1}, \text{ if } \rho = 0$$

The *future value of an inflation-adjusted annuity due* can be determined by simply multiplying the future value of the ordinary annuity by (1 + r):

Equation FV4'

$$FV = Pmt \times (1 + i)^{n-1} \times \left(\frac{(1+\rho)^n - 1}{\rho} \right) \times (1 + r), \text{ if } \rho \neq 0$$

$$FV = Pmt \times n \times (1 + i)^{n-1} \times (1 + r), \text{ if } \rho = 0$$

An alternative form is sometimes preferred, expressed only in terms of ρ and i, by multiplying $(1 + i)^{n-1}$ in front of the equation by (1 + i) and dividing (1 + r) at the end of the equation by (1 + i) to derive:

Equation FV4"

$$FV = Pmt \times (1 + i)^n \times \left(\frac{(1+\rho)^n - 1}{\rho} \right) \times (1 + \rho), \text{ if } \rho \neq 0$$

$$FV = Pmt \times n \times (1 + i)^n, \text{ if } \rho = 0$$

The formulas to compute Pmt amounts for inflation-adjusted annuities can be derived from equations PV7, PV11, FV2, and FV4 (from Chapter 32). Equation Pmt1' shows the formula for computing *the initial payment amount for an inflation-adjusted ordinary annuity based upon a given present value*:

Equation Pmt1'

$$Pmt \times \left(\frac{\rho}{1 - (1+\rho)^{-n}} \right) \times (1 + i), \text{ if } \rho \neq 0$$

$$Pmt = \frac{PV}{n} \times (1 + i), \text{ if } \rho = 0$$

Equation Pmt3' shows the formula for computing *the initial payment amount for an inflation-adjusted annuity due based upon a present value*:

Equation Pmt3'

$$Pmt = PV \times \left(\frac{\rho}{1 - (1+\rho)^{-n}} \right) \times \frac{1}{(1+\rho)}, \text{ if } \rho \neq 0$$

$$Pmt = \frac{PV}{n}, \text{ if } \rho = 0$$

Equations Pmt5' and Pmt7' show the corresponding formulas for computing *the initial payment for inflation-*

adjusted ordinary annuities and annuities due based upon a future value:

Equation Pmt5'

$$Pmt = FV \times \left(\frac{1}{(1+i)^{n-1}}\right) \times \left(\frac{\rho}{(1+\rho)^{n-1}}\right), \text{ if } \rho \neq 0$$

$$Pmt = \frac{FV}{n} \times \left(\frac{1}{(1+i)^{n-1}}\right), \text{ if } \rho = 0$$

Equation Pmt7'

$$Pmt = FV \times \left(\frac{1}{(1+i)^{n}}\right) \times \left(\frac{\rho}{(1+\rho)^{n}-1}\right) \times \frac{1}{(1+\rho)}, \text{ if } \rho \neq 0$$

$$Pmt = \frac{FV}{n} \times \left(\frac{1}{(1+i)^{n}}\right), \text{ if } \rho = 0$$

Example 5. Example 4 determined that your client needs $153,160 invested today to meet her child's 4-year education costs starting in 5 years assuming your client invests to earn 5% and that college costs increase at 6% per year. Your client already has set aside $93,160 for this purpose, so she is currently $60,000 short. She anticipates that her income will increase at 4% per year. She wishes to know how much she would need to save at the end of each year until the beginning of her child's last year of college (8 years), assuming that she increases the amount saved by 4% each year. (This would permit her to keep the yearly payment equal to a fixed percentage of her growing earnings.)

$$
\begin{aligned}
PV &= \$93,160 \\
r &= 5\% \\
I &= 4\% \\
n &= 8 \text{ years}
\end{aligned}
$$

$$\rho = (5\% - 4\%) \div (1 + 4\%) = 0.96154\%$$

Equation Pmt1' calculates the initial yearly amount:

$$Pmt = \$93,160 \times \frac{0.96154\% \times (1 + 4\%)}{1 - (1 + 0.96154\%)^{-8}}$$

$$Pmt = \$93,160 \times \frac{0.0096154 \times 1.04}{0.0736986}$$

$$Pmt = \$93,160 \times = \$12,641$$

Beginning with $60,000 and adding subsequent investments starting at $12,641 at the end of the first year that increase each year by 4% (i.e. $12,641 × (1.04) = $13,147 the second year, etc.), your client will be able to finance her child's education over the period until the child commences her senior year in college.

ADJUSTING FOR TAXES

Overview

Bottom line: what investors get to keep after tax is what matters. Virtually all financial planning issues and investment choices involve tax considerations. The real value of any financial planning strategy or tactic or investment choice relates to the real spendable dollars the strategy or tactic or investment choice provides relative to the alternatives. For instance, nominal yields on taxable bonds are virtually uniformly higher than returns on tax-free municipals of comparable maturity. However, for some taxpayers in high tax brackets, the tax-free yields of municipal bonds are higher than the after-tax yields from taxable bonds, so the tax-free municipals are a preferable investment.

If it is assumed that the investment return is entirely currently taxable, then the after-tax return is simply equal to the before-tax return less the taxes on the return. Specifically, if the tax rate is assumed to be t and the before-tax rate of return is r, then the after-tax return, r_{at}, is:

$$r_{at} = r \times (1 - t)$$

For example, investors earning 6% before tax, whose tax rate on that income is 30%, will earn 4.2% after tax [6% × (1 − 30%) = 4.2%].

Although this formula is frequently used to compute after-tax returns, it is often not an accurate measure. Only a relatively small class of investments, such as money market funds, bank accounts, and the like, provide investment returns that are entirely currently taxable. Other investments, such as stocks, real estate, and the like provide some combination of currently taxable income and income, return, or gain on which tax is deferred. In addition, a whole host of vehicles, such as qualified retirement plans, commercial annuities, life insurance, IRC Section 529 plans, and the like, provide unique tax incentives that cannot be accounted for using the simple formula above.

In many financial planning and investment situations, not only the level of taxation but also the timing of taxation is a critical factor. Between two investments providing identical before-tax returns and identical total tax burdens, the one that defers some or all of the taxation to a later date is preferable.

For instance, the tax incentives associated with qualified plans and IRAs are hard to beat. With tax-deductible contributions and tax-deferred accumulations, it adds up fast. But qualified plans, IRC Section 401(k) plans, SEP IRAs, traditional IRAs, Roth IRAs, IRC Section 403(b) TDAs, and SIMPLE IRAs are not the only tax-preferred accumulation vehicles, nor are they necessarily the best for all circumstances. These tax-favored plans have their limitations as well. In order to assess whether one tax-favored investment is superior to another, advisers and investors need quantitative tools to measure the tax effects, and to weigh the trade-offs.

The most prevalent type of tax-deferral vehicle is not qualified plans, IRAs, and the like, but rather appreciating assets. Under our current tax laws, the tax on capital gains is deferred until the gain is recognized, usually when the asset is sold. Also, long-term gains are usually taxed at a lower rate than ordinary income.

Furthermore, techniques may be employed to defer full recognition of capital gains even beyond the time of disposal including the use of installment sales, IRC Section 1031 like-kind exchanges, private annuities, and, in the case of personal residences, the lifetime gain exclusion provisions. Section 1035 provides similar nonrecognition treatment for qualifying life insurance exchanges. Certain other transfers of life insurance policies between related parties also avoid recognition. In the area of corporate securities, there is an assortment of provisions allowing nonrecognition treatment, including recapitalizations, reorganizations, mergers, and acquisitions.

Life insurance and capital gains are special cases. In the case of life insurance, if the proceeds are paid in the form of death benefits, in effect the tax loan associated with the earnings on the cash value is generally completely forgiven. If amounts are withdrawn from the cash value during the insured-owner's lifetime through policy loans, there is generally no income taxation on amounts withdrawn, even if the amounts withdrawn are attributable to investment earnings inside the policy. If amounts are withdrawn directly, not through policy loans, then the earnings will generally be subject to tax.

In the case of appreciated assets that are held at death, the step-up in basis effectively cancels the tax loan.[1] Also,

in the case of charitable gifts of appreciated property where the appreciation qualifies as long-term capital gain, the donor is generally able to take a deduction for the entire amount without recognizing or paying tax on the gain. Once again, the tax loan is essentially forgiven.

The optimal use of tax-advantaged tools and techniques is a major wealth-accumulation principle and objective. Tax advantage in the form of deferred taxes helps to finance wealth accumulation and to reduce the rate at which wealth is depleted. The use of various tax-preferred tools and techniques should not proceed without careful consideration of the trends in tax policy. What looks like a favorable arrangement today can quickly change with changes in the tax laws.

The following sections will explain the concept of tax leverage and describe the tax-adjusted time value tools financial advisers must understand to properly serve their clients' financial planning needs. The following sections discuss the tools necessary to account for the 5 most-prevalent types of tax leverage, ranging from nondeductible fully currently taxable vehicles, such as T-bills, on one end of the spectrum to tax-deductible, fully tax-deferred vehicles, such as IRC Section 401(k) plans, on the other end of the spectrum.

Tax Leverage

Any strategy or technique that defers taxes that would otherwise be paid currently creates what is called tax leverage. Tax leverage is similar to the concept of financial leverage, where an investor borrows money to help finance an investment. When financial leverage is successfully employed, the rate of return earned from the investment exceeds the cost of borrowing. The borrowing works like a lever to increase the earning power of the investor's equity. The return on equity rises above the return rate actually paid by the investment because the return includes not only the amount earned on the investment, but also the differential between the investment return and the borrowing rate on the portion of the investment that was financed.

Example 6: If $1,000 is invested for one year at a fully taxable 10% rate of return, an investor in a 50%[2] combined federal, state, and local tax bracket will have $1,050 after tax at the end of the year. In other words, his after-tax rate of return is 5%.

Suppose the investor can borrow $1,000 at 6%, which is equivalent to 3% after tax assum-

Tools & Techniques of Investment Planning

ing the interest is deductible. This $2,000 total investment will earn $200 before tax. The investor must pay $1,000 plus $60 back to the lender, so the investor is left with $1,140 before tax, or $1,070 after tax. The investor has increased the after-tax return on his equity from 5% to 7% through the use of financial leverage.

The problem with financial leverage is the risk the investment will earn less than the cost of borrowing. This negative leverage reduces the investor's return below what it would have been without borrowing. Of course, if the loan were interest-free, the risk of negative leverage would be very small. Any positive return at all from the investment would produce positive leverage. But who would lend at a 0% rate? The U.S. government, for one.

Example 7: The investor in the previous example now borrows $1,000 at 0% interest, rather than 6%. At the end of the year he now will have $1,200 before tax after paying off the debt. At his 50% tax rate, he will take home $1,100. His after-tax rate of return on equity doubles from 5% to 10%.

How does the government get into the 0% lending business? The government does it by providing tax incentives for employing various tools and techniques that allow taxpayers to defer the payment of taxes. The deferred taxes are the equivalent of a loan. Generally, if tax rates remain constant and the taxpayer remains in the same tax bracket, the taxpayer will pay the deferred taxes in full at a later date, but with no increase or adjustment for the lapse in time. In other words, the ability to defer the payment of tax is essentially an interest-free loan from the government.

Example 8: Assume the government institutes a new program permitting taxpayers to contribute before-tax dollars to accounts to fund Special Pre-Olympic Recruiting and Training Schools (SPORTS) for athletically gifted children. Under this program, taxes on both contributions and on earnings are deferred until money is withdrawn to pay for the approved school's tuition. When the money is withdrawn to pay tuition, the amount withdrawn is then subject to tax.

Assume the taxpayer from our previous examples elects to contribute $2,000 before tax to a SPORTS account earning a 10% rate of return. At the end of the first year, the taxpayer withdraws the entire balance of $2,200 to pay the taxpayer's oldest child's tuition at one of the government-approved SPORTS schools during the child's summer vacation. At a 50% tax rate, the taxpayer is left with $1,100 after tax.

Had the taxpayer not invested in the SPORTS account, the taxpayer would have had only $1,000 after tax available for investment outside the SPORTS account and would have accumulated only $1,050 after tax. By using the SPORTS account, the results are exactly the same as in the previous example where the investor borrowed $1,000 interest-free. The taxpayer has essentially received an interest-free loan of $1,000 from the government and has raised his after-tax rate of return, as before, from 5% to 10%.

Tax-favored investments that permit tax-deductible contributions and defer tax on earnings, such as pension plans, profit-sharing plans, and deductible IRAs, are essentially equivalent to nondeductible investments whose earnings are received tax-free. In the SPORTS account example above, the investment in the SPORTS account is equivalent to investing the taxpayer's $1,000 after-tax amount at 10% tax-free.

Of course, this relationship holds only as long as the taxpayer's tax rate remains the same. In some situations, the amount of tax that ultimately must be repaid may be greater than the amount originally deferred. For instance, this may occur as a result of tax penalties for early withdrawals or an increase in tax rates generally. But even in this case, the client may benefit. The tax leverage involved is then still essentially equivalent to a subsidized or below-market discount loan rather than a fully interest-free loan. In some other cases, the amount of tax paid in the future may be less than the amount of tax originally deferred. This is essentially equivalent to an interest-free loan where part of the debt is forgiven. Some of these types of situations are discussed later.

Since tax leverage may arise from up-front deductions, tax-deferred earnings, or both, there are several variations of the time value formulas for computing the future value of single payments in tax-leveraged situations. The principal factors in the analysis are:

r = The assumed before-tax rate of return

t_c = The client's current marginal tax rate

t_f = The client's assumed future marginal tax rate

n = The number of years in the planning horizon

P = The amount available for tax-leveraged investment

Up-Front Deductions or Exclusions

Assume the situation being investigated involves up-front deductions or exclusions, such as would be the case if one were comparing investments outside of an IRC Section 401(k) plan with voluntary tax-excludable salary-reduction contributions to an IRC Section 401(k) plan. In this case, your client would have only $(1-t_c)$ dollars to invest *outside* the plan for each dollar that could be invested *inside* the plan. In other words, by foregoing the elective deferrals, your client would only have the opportunity to invest his after-tax dollars outside the IRC Section 401(k) plan. By electing to defer salary into the IRC Section 401(k) plan, he would have a greater number of before-tax dollars earning money inside the IRC Section 401(k) plan.

In contrast, if your client were comparing nondeductible contributions to an IRA to an investment outside the IRA, he would have $1 available after tax to invest outside the nondeductible IRA for each $1 available after tax for investment inside the nondeductible IRA. In either case, your client would still have only $(1-t_c)$ dollars to invest for each $1 that otherwise would be available, for example, to invest in a deductible IRA or IRC Section 401(k) plan.

Tax Status of Initial Investment	Amount Invested	
	Inside Plan	Outside Plan
Tax Deductible	$P	$P × (1 − t_c)
Non-Tax Deductible	$P × (1 − t_c)	$P × (1 − t_c)

Example 9: Your client, who is in a 28% combined state and federal tax bracket[3], is considering increasing IRC Section 401(k) contributions by $1,000. Since contributions are tax deductible, the entire $1,000 will go into the plan. In contrast, if the client does not make the $1,000 elective deferral into the plan, the amount is taxable. The client will have only $720 after tax of the $1,000 before tax remaining ($1,000 x 0.28 = $280 tax) to invest outside the plan.

Tax–Deferred Earnings or Benefits

A tax-leveraged vehicle may or may not provide tax-deferred earnings, but most do. If the earnings are entirely tax-deferred, the total before-tax amount accumulated within the plan is simply equal to the future value of PV dollars compounded using the before-tax return:

Equation FVbt1

$$FV(before\ tax) = PV(before\ tax) \times (1 + r)^n$$

Example 10: Your client, described in the previous example, is earning 10% on amounts invested in the IRC Section 401(k) plan. If your client continues to earn 10%, how much will your client accumulate before tax in 8 years? First, calculate that $(1 + .10)^8$ equals 2.143589. Therefore, the total before-tax accumulation will be $2,143.59 [$1,000 x 2.143589].

If the initial contribution to the plan was tax deductible or excludable, the entire accumulation (initial contribution plus accumulated earnings) will be subject to tax when the amounts are withdrawn. In this case, the total after-tax accumulation for PV dollars of contributions is determined by subtracting the tax payable on the total amount from the total before-tax accumulation:

Equation FVat1

$$FV\ (after\ tax) = PV\ (before\ tax) \times (1 + r)^n \times (1 - t_f)$$

Example 11: Your client, described in the previous example expects to be in a 35% tax bracket in eight years. Disregarding any penalty taxes that may apply if your client withdraws the funds at that time, your client's total after-tax accumulations will be (1 − 0.35) x $2,143.59 = $1,393.33.

The tax-deductible amount one needs to invest in a tax-deferred plan to reach a specified future after-tax value is computed by simply rearranging equation FVat1 to isolate PV on the left-hand side of the equation:

Equation PVat1

$$PV\ (before\ tax) = \frac{FV\ (after\ tax)}{(1 + r)^n \times (1 - t_f)}$$

The formula for the future after-tax value of a series of level end-of-period tax-deductible contributions to a plan where investment earnings are tax deferred is:

Equation FVAEat1

$$FV\ (after\ tax) = Pmt\ (before\ tax) \times \left(\frac{(1 + r)^n - 1}{r}\right) \times (1 - t_f),$$

if $r \neq 0$

FV (after tax) = Pmt (before tax) × n × (1 − t_f), if r = 0

The formula for the *future after-tax value of before-tax annuity due payments* is computed simply by multiplying the right-hand side of equation FVAEat1 by (1 + r):

Equation FVABat1

FV (after tax) = Pmt (before tax) ×

$$x \ (1 + r) \times (1 - t_f), \text{ if } r \neq 0$$

FV (after tax) = Pmt (before tax) × (1 − t_f), if r = 0

The formula for determining the Pmt(before tax) that one needs to invest each period to reach a specified future after-tax value, is simply the desired FV(after tax) divided by the multiplier of Pmt(before tax) in equation FVAEat1 or equation FVABat1, as appropriate.

The formula to determine the present before-tax value one needs to invest in a tax-deductible, tax-deferred plan to generate after-tax ordinary annuity payments is:

Equation PVAEat1

$$PV \ (before \ tax) = Pmt \ (after \ tax) \times \left(\frac{1 - (1 + r)^{-n}}{r \times (1 - t_f)} \right), \text{ if } r \neq 0$$

$$PV \ (before \ tax) = Pmt \ (after \ tax) \times n \times \frac{n}{(1 - t_f)}, \text{ if } r = 0$$

The present before-tax value one needs to invest to generate level after-tax annuity due payments is equal to equation PVAEat1 multiplied by (1 + r):

Equation PVABat1

$$PV \ (before \ tax) = Pmt \ (after \ tax) \times \left(\frac{1 - (1 + r)^{-n}}{r \times (1 - t_f)} \right) \times (1 + r),$$

if r ≠ 0

$$PV \ (before \ tax) = Pmt \ (after \ tax) \times \frac{n}{(1 - t_f)}, \text{ if } r = 0$$

Once again, the formula for determining the Pmt(after tax) that can be supported by a specified present before-tax value is simply PV(before tax) divided by the multiplier of Pmt(after tax) in equations PVAEat1 or PVABat1, as appropriate.

Nondeductible Contributions and Tax-Deferred Earnings

Some vehicles permit investors to make after-tax payments to tax-deferred accounts, such as non-deductible contributions to nondeductible IRAs and to commercial annuities. If the initial contribution to the plan is not tax deductible, tax must be applied only to the accumulated earnings (that is, the growth and income), not the entire accumulation, when the funds are withdrawn.

The total before-tax earnings for each $1 contribution are equal to the total accumulated value less the initial investment of $1: [(1 + r)^n − 1]. The total after-tax return on each dollar of earnings accumulated within the plan is computed by subtracting the amount of tax that is due from the total before-tax earnings: $[(1 + r)^n - 1] \times (1 - t_f)$. The total after-tax accumulation for each $1 contribution is the total after-tax return plus $1: $[(1 + r)^n - 1] \times (1 - t_f) + 1$. Rearranging and simplifying terms we derive the formula for the future after-tax value of a lump sum after-tax present value investment:

Equation FVat2

$$FV \ (after \ tax) = PV(after \ tax) \times [[(1 + r)^n \times (1 - t_f)] + t_f],$$

if r ≠ 0

FV (after tax) = PV(after tax), if r = 0

Example 12: Assume your client, described in the previous three examples, was considering a nondeductible investment in an IRA rather than the tax-deductible contribution to an IRC Section 401(k) plan. Since the IRA contribution is not tax deductible, your client will have only $720 to invest from $1,000 of pretax income (assuming a 28% tax rate at time of contribution). The total net amount your client would accumulate in 8 years, assuming a 10% annual rate of return and a 35% tax rate at the time of withdrawal, is $720 × [(1 + .10)^8 × (1 − 0.35)) + 0.35] = $1,255.20.

The *present after-tax value one needs to invest to accumulate a specified future after-tax value in a nondeductible, tax-deferred plan is:*

Equation PVat2

$$PV \ (after \ tax) = \frac{FV \ (after \ tax)}{[(1 + r)^n \times (1 - t_f)] + t_f}, \text{ if } r \neq 0$$

PV (after tax) = FV (after tax), if r = 0

Appendix K – Additional Time Value Concepts

The formula for the *future after-tax value of a series of end-of-period nondeductible contributions to a plan where investment earnings are tax deferred* is the same as equation FVAEat1, substituting Pmt (after tax) for Pmt (before tax) and adding the term $n \times t_f$:

Equation FVAEat2

$$FV\ (after\ tax) = Pmt\ (after\ tax) \times \left[\left(\frac{(1+r)^n - 1}{r}\right) \times (1 - t_f) + (n \times t_f)\right], \text{if } r \neq 0$$

$$FV\ (after\ tax) = Pmt\ (after\ tax) \times n, \text{if } r = 0$$

The formula for the *future after-tax value of beginning-of-period nondeductible contributions to a plan where investment earnings are tax deferred* is the same as equation FVBEat1, substituting Pmt (after tax) for Pmt (before tax) and adding the term $n \times t_f$:

Equation FVABat2

$$FV\ (after\ tax) = Pmt\ (after\ tax) \times \left[\left(\frac{(1+r)^n - 1}{r}\right) \times (1+r) \times (1 - t_f) + (n \times t_f)\right], \text{if } r \neq 0$$

$$FV\ (after\ tax) = Pmt\ (after\ tax) \times n, \text{if } r = 0$$

The formula for determining the Pmt(after tax) that one needs to invest each period to accumulate a specified future after-tax value is simply FV(after tax) divided by the multiplier of Pmt(after tax) in equations FVAEat2 or FVABat2, as appropriate.

The *present after-tax value one needs to invest in a non-deductible, tax-deferred investment to generate a series of periodic level after-tax ordinary annuity payments* cannot be simplified to a single reduced-form equation similar to the future after-tax value formula. Instead, one must calculate the present after-tax value of each separate periodic payment using equation PVat2 with Pmt(after tax) replacing FV(after tax) and then summing these separate present values to derive the total:

Equation PVAEat2

$$PV\ (after\ tax) = Pmt\ (after\ tax) \times$$

$$\sum_{j=1}^{n} \frac{1}{[(1+r)^j \times (1 - t_f)] + t_f}, \text{if } r \neq 0$$

$$PV\ (after\ tax) = Pmt\ (after\ tax) \times n, \text{if } r = 0$$

Similar to earlier formulations, the formula for determining the Pmt(*after tax*) that can be supported by a specified present after-tax value is simply PV(after tax) divided by the multiplier of Pmt(after tax) in equations PVAEat2 or PVABat2, as appropriate.

The future after-tax value that would be accumulated by investing a present after-tax value in a fully taxable investment (no tax deferral on earnings) is determined by assuming the income is subject to tax when earned. That is, for each r dollars of return, the after-tax return is $r \times (1 - t)$ (ignoring, for the time being, any capital gain component). Therefore, the *future after-tax value of a present after-tax value invested in a fully taxable investment* is:

$$FVat3: FV(after\ tax) = PV(after\ tax) \times [1 + r \times (1 - t_f)]^n$$

Example 13: If your client invested $720 in a fully taxable investment earning 10% before tax (assuming your client stays in the 28% tax bracket until the end of the eighth year), in 8 years your client will have $1,255.71 [$720 x {1 + (0.10 x (1 – 0.28))}]^8].

The *present after-tax value one needs to invest to accumulate a specified future after-tax value in a nondeductible, fully taxable investment* is:

Equation PVat3

$$PV\ (after\ tax) = \frac{FV\ (after\ tax)}{[1 + r \times (1 - t_f)]^n}$$

The formula for the *future after-tax value of a series of end-of-period nondeductible contributions to a plan where investment earnings are currently taxable* is:

Equation FVAEat3

$$FV\ (after\ tax) = Pmt\ (after\ tax) \times \left(\frac{[1 + r \times (1 - t_f)]^n - 1}{r \times (1 - t_f)}\right),$$
$$\text{if } r \times (1 - t_f) \neq 0$$

$$FV\ (after\ tax) = Pmt\ (after\ tax) \times n, \text{if } r = 0$$

The formula for the *future after-tax value of a series of beginning-of-period nondeductible contributions to a plan where investment earnings are currently taxable* is:

Equation FVABat3

$$FV\ (after\ tax) = Pmt\ (after\ tax) \times \left(\frac{[1 + r \times (1 - t_t)]^n - 1}{r \times (1 - t_t)} \right)$$

$$\times [1 + r \times (1 - t_t)], if\ r \times (1 - t_t) \neq 0$$

$$FV\ (after\ tax) = Pmt\ (after\ tax) \times n, if\ r = 0$$

The formula for determining the Pmt(after tax) that one needs to invest each period to accumulate a specified future after-tax value is simply FV(after tax) divided by the multiplier of Pmt(after tax) in equations FVAEat3 or FVABat3, as appropriate.

The formula to determine the present before-tax value one needs to invest in a nondeductible currently fully taxable investment to generate after-tax ordinary annuity payments is:

Equation PVAEat3

$$PV\ (after\ tax) = Pmt\ (after\ tax) \times \left(\frac{1 - [1 + r \times (1 - t_t)]^{-n}}{r \times (1 - t_t)} \right),$$

$$if\ r \neq 0$$

$$PV\ (after\ tax) = Pmt\ (after\ tax) \times n, if\ r = 0$$

The formula to determine the *present before-tax value* one needs to invest in a nondeductible currently fully taxable investment to generate level after-tax annuity due payments is:

Equation PVABat3

$$PV\ (after\ tax) = Pmt\ (after\ tax) \times \left(\frac{1 - [1 + r \times (1 - t_t)]^{-n}}{r \times (1 - t_t)} \right)$$

$$\times [1 + r \times (1 - t_t)], if\ r \neq 0$$

$$PV\ (after\ tax) = Pmt\ (after\ tax) \times n, if\ r = 0$$

Similar to earlier formulations, the formula for determining the Pmt(after tax) that can be supported by a specified present after-tax value is simply PV(after tax) divided by the multiplier of Pmt(after tax) in equations PVAEat3 or PVABat3, as appropriate.

Applying the Formulas

Example 14: Let us suppose your client wishes to know how much better off he would be if he increased his IRC Section 401(k) contribution by $1,000. Assuming an 8% interest rate, a 28% tax bracket both now and in the future, and a 15-year planning horizon, the after-tax amounts inside and outside the plan are as follows:

Total after tax from plan
$$P \times (1 - t_f) \times (1 + r)^n$$
$$\$1,000 \times (1 - 0.28) \times (1.08)^{15}$$
$$\$1,000 \times 0.72 \times 3.17217 = \qquad \$2,283.96$$

Total after tax outside plan
$$P \times (1 - t_f) \times \{1 + [r \times (1 - t_t)]\}^n$$
$$\$1,000 \times (1 - 0.28) \times \{1 + [0.08 \times (1 - 0.28)]\}^{15}$$
$$\$1,000 \times 0.72 \times \{1 + 0.0576\}^{15}$$
$$\$1,000 \times 0.72 \times 2.31644 = \qquad \$1,667.84$$
$$Difference = \qquad \$616.12$$

Your client will have about $616 more after tax by increasing the contribution to the IRC Section 401(k) plan rather than investing outside the plan. This represents about a 37% after-tax increase over the fully taxable outside investment.

Example 15: Your client now wishes to know if it would still be better to invest the extra amount in the plan if the plan balance is taxed at a higher rate when he withdraws it. Assuming your client's tax rate increases to 35% and assuming a worst-case scenario that it will increase only just before he withdraws the money from the plan (that is, the earnings on the outside investment enjoy the lower 28% tax rate throughout the period), the comparison is:

Total after tax from plan
$$P \times (1 - t_f) \times (1 + r)^n$$
$$\$1,000 \times (1 - 0.35) \times (1 + 0.08)^{15}$$
$$\$1,000 \times 0.65 \times 3.17217 = \qquad \$2,061.91$$

Total after tax outside plan
$$(same\ as\ previous\ example) = \qquad \$1,667.84$$
$$Difference = \qquad \$394.07$$

Even if the tax rate increases from 28% to 35%, your client is still almost $395 better off investing inside the plan. This represents almost a 24% advantage, despite the increase in tax rates.

Example 16: Your client complains that investment options and potential rates of return are limited within the investment options available from the IRC Section 401(k) plan (presently yielding 8%) and feels that he could earn 10% if he had more control over the investments. You suggest that making contributions to a nondeductible traditional IRA with a different custodian might be better than investing in the IRC Section 401(k). However, compared with each dollar invested in the IRC Section 401(k), your client would have only 72 cents (1 – 0.28 tax rate) to invest in the IRA. The question is whether the tax-deferred accumulation at the higher 10% rate within the IRA would more than compensate for the loss of deductibility. Assuming the tax rate in 15 years remains at 28%, the after-tax amounts are as follows:

Total after tax from IRC Section 401(k) plan
(from Example 30) = $2,283.96

Total after tax in IRA plan

$P \times (1 - t_c) \times \{[(1+r)^n \times (1 - t_f)] + t_f\}$
$1,000 \times 0.72 \times \{[(1.10)^{15} \times 0.72] + 0.28\}$
$1,000 \times 0.72 \times \{[(4.17725 \times 0.72) + 0.28]$
$1,000 \times 0.72 \times (3.00762 + 0.28)$
$1,000 \times 0.72 \times 3.28762 = \qquad$ $2,367.09

Difference = \qquad ($83.13)

If your client can earn two% more per year by investing in the nondeductible traditional IRA rather than the IRC Section 401(k), he will be slightly better off investing the money in the IRA, even though the contribution to the IRA is nondeductible. The results would favor the IRA even slightly more if tax rates increased during or at the end of the 15-year period.

Example 17: Your client now wants to know if he should make all contributions to the nondeductible traditional IRA rather than to the IRC Section 401(k) from now until retirement (15 years).

At some point, further contributions to the IRA would be unproductive. In some future year, the compound value of the additional 2% return for the fewer remaining years would not be sufficient to compensate for the loss of the tax deductibility of the contributions. Your client asks you to determine in what year he should shift back to the IRC Section 401(k). You could recalculate the values for each year and determine in which year the difference turns positive.

Adding Capital Gains or Partially Tax-Deferred Income

Assets that promise substantial capital appreciation, such as growth stocks and real estate, or that permit tax on some portion of investment earnings to be deferred, are themselves tax-leveraged investments. Gains generally are not taxed until they are recognized, usually at the time of sale or liquidation.

Ironically, given the widespread use of these types of assets, the tax-leverage associated with capital gains is largely ignored when evaluating and comparing alternative strategies. Perhaps it is ignored because of the difficulty of prospectively measuring the possible gains. However, the tax-leverage of capital gains can provide very sizable benefits. Failure to account properly for the tax-advantage of potential capital gains or other forms of tax-deferred investment earnings may lead to comparative overvaluation of alternative tax-leveraged techniques and lead to improper decisions. For instance, if you proceed as if the outside (taxable) investments are immediately taxable when comparing the benefit of additional contributions to a IRC Section 401(k) plan, IRA, or the like, you will overestimate the benefit of the tax-free build-up type investment. You must consider the tax-deferred capital appreciation on the outside investments when comparing the investment alternatives.

Ignoring the capital gain component of returns could be especially critical in the current tax environment. Under current law, the long-term capital gain tax rate for most investment assets generally is capped at 15%. Even if the current legislation sunsets and the tax law reverts to prior rules, the maximum long-term capital gain tax rate on most investment assets will be 20% or less. We may even see lower capital gains rates in future years.

A lower capital gains tax rate would significantly enhance tax benefits since, in effect, part of the tax loan would be forgiven. In addition, with many of the other tax-leveraged tools and techniques, capital appreciation is irrelevant since all income and gains are taxed alike. For example, generally any capital appreciation on assets in qualified plans, IRAs, and IRC Section 401(k) plans, life insurance, annuities, and the like is ultimately taxed at ordinary rates (even if there is a preferential capital gains rate for gains on investments held outside these vehicles).

Although the formula for projecting the after-tax return from capital gain assets is somewhat more complicated than those previously presented, it is not incomprehensible. The following equation calculates the future after-tax value of a PV dollar investment in a vehicle with a tax-deferred capital gain or tax-deferred return component of total return:

Equation FVat4

$$FV \text{ (after tax)} = PV \times$$

$$\left[(1 + ar)^n - t_d \times \left(g \times r \times \left(\frac{(1 + ar)^n - 1}{ar} \right) + b \right) \right], \text{ if } ar \neq 0$$

$$FV \text{ (after tax)} = PV \times (1 - t_d \times b), \text{ if } ar = 0$$

where:

ar = The accumulation rate after tax on the currently taxable component of return (usually ordinary income), but before tax on the accumulating and tax-deferred capital gains or tax-deferred income component of return

= $(g \times r) + (1 - t_o) \times (1 - g) \times r$

= $r \times (1 - (1 - g) \times t_o)$

r = The total before-tax rate of return

g = The proportion of total before-tax return, r, attributable to tax-deferred capital gain (or tax-deferred income)

t_o = The tax rate on the currently taxable ordinary income component of return

t_d = The tax rate on the long-term capital gain (or the tax-deferred) component of investment return

b = The built-in gain or tax-deferred return proportion of the investment, PV, or the periodic payment, Pmt, if any

The first part of equation FVat4 is familiar in form. It is the same as the before-tax future value of an entirely tax-deferred investment earning ar% instead of r%, as shown earlier in equation FVbt1.

Equation FVbt4

$$FV \text{ (before cap – gain tax)} = PV \times (1 + ar)^n$$

The accumulation rate, ar, is composed of two parts. The first part, (g × r), is the capital gain (or tax-deferred) component of the total return. This is the part of the return that is not subject to tax until the asset is sold or liquidated.

The second part of the accumulation rate, ar, is the after-tax income component of the total return. The portion of the total return, r, that is subject to current taxation is (1 – g) × r. The amount left after paying tax on the currently taxable return component of total return is determined by multiplying this component of return by (1 – t_o). Therefore, the first part of equation FVat4 is the total accumulated value of an investment of PV dollars in n years (assuming reinvestment of after-tax income) before taxation of the accumulated capital gain or tax-deferred return component of total return.

The second part of equation FVat4 is the tax on the accumulated capital gain or tax-deferred return component of total return. Equation FVCG shows the total accumulated gain or total tax-deferred return component of total return for a lump sum investment of PV dollars. Multiplying the accumulated gains or deferred return component by the tax rate on deferred return or long-term capital gains, t_d, gives the total tax on the tax-deferred return or capital gains at the time of sale or liquidation of the investment. Finally, t_d × b is the tax paid upon sale or liquidation on the built-in gain or total tax-deferred return per initial dollar of PV or Pmt. For example, if one is computing the future after-tax value of an investment of $100,000 in a stock portfolio, where $40,000 of the current balance is attributable to as yet untaxed capital appreciation, then b equals 40% ($40,000 ÷ $100,000).

Equation FVCG

Total tax – deferred return

$$= PV \times \left[g \times r \times \left(\frac{(1 + ar)^n - 1}{ar} \right) + b \right], \text{ if } ar \neq 0$$

Total tax – deferred return = PV × b, if ar = 0

For example, suppose a client wishes to determine the after-tax future value of a fully tax-deferred investment such as salary reduction contributions to a SEP IRA plan. In this case, set g equal to 1, since the entire return is tax deferred, set t_d equal to t_p since the tax-deferred return is taxed at the investor's future ordinary income tax rate, and set b = 1, since the entire present value is a before-tax amount subject to tax upon liquidation. As a result of these assumptions, the accumulation rate, ar, equals

Equation FVat4 is really a generic formula that can be used in virtually any tax-leveraged analysis.

the before-tax rate of return, r. When these values are substituted into equation FVat4, the resulting equation is the same as equation FVat2.

In contrast, assume the investment vehicle is one where the return is fully currently taxable and where PV is an after-tax contribution. In this case, no portion of the return is attributable to appreciation or is tax deferred, so g and b are set to 0, and ar then equals $r \times (1 - t_f)$. The result is the same as shown in equation FVat3 for the total future after-tax value from a fully taxable investment.

Example 18: In Example 16, we found that your client would be better off investing in a nondeductible IRA rather than in an IRC Section 401(k) plan if that client can earn 2% more by directing investments in the IRA. Would your client enjoy even greater success if he instead invests the funds outside the IRA in growth stocks earning a 10% total return that is composed of 2.5% dividend yield and 7.5% capital growth?

No, not generally. The IRA and the growth stock each earn 10% total return, but the IRA's return is entirely tax-deferred. Only 75% of the stock's return is tax-deferred.

However, what if the tax rate on capital gains is reduced and the tax rate on ordinary income increased? Assuming the tax rate on capital gains is capped at 20% and your client's tax rate on ordinary income increases to 36%, would the stock investment outside the IRA be preferable?

To put the stock investment in the least favorable light possible, assume the tax changes take effect right after the investment is made. In this case, the income portion of the stock investment return is immediately subjected to the higher tax rate.

<u>Total after tax in IRA plan</u>
$$P \times (1 - t_c) \times \{[(1 - t_f) \times (1 + r)^n] + t_f\}$$
$$\$1{,}000 \times 0.72 \times \{[0.64 \times (1.10)^{15}] + 0.36\}$$
$$\$720 \times [(0.64 \times 4.17724816942) + 0.36]$$
$$\$720 \times (2.67344 + 0.36)$$
$$\$720 \times 3.03344 = \qquad \$2{,}184.08$$

<u>Total after tax in stock</u>
$$ar = (g \times r) + ((1 - t_c) \times (1 - g) \times r)$$
$$ar = (0.75 \times 0.10) + (0.64 \times 0.25 \times 0.1)$$
$$ar = 0.09100$$
$$(1 + ar)^n = 1.09100^{15} = 3.69293$$
$$t_d = 0.20$$

$$\$720 \times (3.69293 - (0.20 \times 0.075 \times (2.69293 \div 0.09100)))$$
$$\$720 \times (3.69293 - 0.44389)$$
$$\$720 \times 3.2490 = \qquad \$2{,}339.31$$
$$\text{Difference} = \qquad (\$155.23)$$

In this case, your client is better off investing in the stock *outside* the IRA. The additional after-tax gain is about 21.6% of the $720 initial investment or about 7% more than the after-tax accumulation using the IRA.

Example 19: Your client's balance in a stock account is $25,000. His basis is $15,000, so the built-in gain in gain proportion, b, is $10,000 ÷ $25,000, or 40%. Assume the stocks are expected to return an average of 11% (r) per year on a compound basis and that about 80% (g) of this return is expected to be attributable to capital appreciation. Assume also that your client's marginal tax rate on ordinary income is expected to be 35% and the tax rate on long-term capital gains is expected to be 20%. If your client plans to liquidate the stock account in 12 years to pay college tuitions for his children, how much money after tax should he expect to accumulate?

$$b = \$10{,}000 \div \$25{,}000 = 0.4$$
$$ar = (0.8 \times 0.11) + ((1 - 0.35) \times (1 - 0.8) \times 0.11)$$
$$ar = 0.088 + (0.65 \times 0.2 \times 0.11) = 0.088 + 0.0143$$
$$ar = 0.1023$$
$$(1 + ar)^n = (1.1023)^{12} = 3.2180863$$
$$ATFV\$1 = 3.2180863 -$$
$$(0.2 \times (0.4 + 0.8 \times 0.11 \times (2.2180863 \div 0.1023)))$$
$$ATFV\$1 = 2.75648$$

$$FV \text{ after tax of } \$25{,}000 = \$25{,}000 \times 2.75648 = \$68{,}912$$

Now suppose instead that the income return on the stocks is qualified dividend income taxed at a maximum rate of 15% and that the capital gains will also be taxed at a maximum rate of 15%. In this case the future after-tax value is determined as follows:

$$b = \$10{,}000 \div \$25{,}000 = 0.4$$
$$ar = (0.8 \times 0.11) + ((1 - 0.15) \times (1 - 0.8) \times 0.11)$$
$$ar = 0.088 + (0.85 \times 0.2 \times 0.11) = 0.088 + 0.0187$$
$$ar = 0.1067$$
$$(1 + ar)^n = (1.1067)^{12} = 3.375662$$
$$ATFV\$1 = 3.375662 -$$
$$(0.15 \times (0.4 + 0.8 \times 0.11 \times (2.375662 \div 0.1067)))$$
$$ATFV\$1 = 3.0218$$

$$FV \text{ after tax of } \$25{,}000 = \$25{,}000 \times 3.0218 = \$75{,}544$$

Now, suppose further that you advise your client that the 15% tax rate on qualifying dividends and capital gains is scheduled to expire after 4 years, with the tax rates reverting to the old rules. In the event this occurs, what would be the after-tax accumulation if the 15% tax regime applies in the first 4 years and the old tax regime where dividend income is taxed at ordinary income tax rates (35%) and the 20% (18% 5 year holding period) applies to capital gains? You advise your client that essentially all of his long-term gains should qualify for the 18% 5-year-holding-period rate.

From above, the accumulation rate, ar, for the first 4 years is 10.67%, so using equation FVat4, the accumulation over the first 4 years before paying the capital gains tax is

FV 4 yrs. before CG tax = $25,000 × $(1.1067)^4$
= $25,000 × 1.5001 = $37,502

The accumulated but as yet untaxed capital gains at the end of year 4 are computed using equation FVCG:

Capital gains yr. 4
= $25,000 × (0.4 + 0.8 × 0.11 × (0.5001 ÷ 0.1067))
= $25,000 × 0.812452 = $20,311.30

Therefore, the built-in gain, b, after 4 years is
$20,311.30 ÷ $37,502 = 54.16%.

To find the final after-tax accumulation in 12 years, the balance after 4 years, $37,502, must be accumulated for another 8 years applying the 35% rate for investment income and the 18% rate for capital gains using equation FVat4. As was shown above, the accumulation rate, ar, under this regime is 10.23%.

The future value before capital gain tax
= $37,502 × $(1.1023)^8$
= $37,502 × 2.17971
= $81,743

The accumulated gain
= $37,502 × (0.5416 + 0.8 × 0.11 × (1.17971 ÷ 0.1023))
= $37,502 × 1.5564 = $58,368

The tax on long-term gain
= $58,368 × 0.18 = $10,506

The after-tax accumulation
= $81,743 – $10,506 = $71,237

Not surprisingly, the value falls between the $68,912 computed applying the old tax rules over the entire period and the $75,544 computed applying the new tax rules over the entire period.

Example 20: In Example 19, what is the effective after-tax rate of return (or tax-free-equivalent rate of return) earned by your client over the 12 year period in the case (1) where investment income is taxed at 35% and capital gains are taxed at 20% and he accumulates $68,912 after tax and (2) in the case where investment income and capital gains are taxed at 15% and he accumulates $75,544 after tax?

Using equation R1 $[r = (FV \div PV)^{1/n} - 1]$ to compute the rates of return, the results for cases (1) and (2) are:

(1) $r = (\$68{,}912 \div \$25{,}000)^{1/12} - 1 =$ $2.7565^{1/12} - 1 = 1.0882 - 1 = 8.82\%$;

(2) $r = (\$75{,}544 \div \$25{,}000)^{1/12} - 1 =$ $3.0218^{1/12} - 1 = 1.0965 - 1 = 9.65\%$

Investing under the tax assumptions of scenario (1) or (2) are equivalent to investing in tax-free investments paying 8.82% or 9.65%, respectively.

Present Value Formula

Equation PVat4 presents the after-tax, future value formula for an investment where both ordinary and capital gain or tax-deferred income elements comprise the total return. In the same fashion as any other future value formula, the inverse of equation FVat4 is the present value formula, that is PV formula = 1 ÷ FV formula. Equation PVat4 is the present value formula for finding the amount that would have to be invested today to accumulate some specified desired after-tax future value.

Equation PVat4

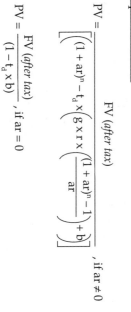

$$PV = \frac{FV\ (after\ tax)}{\left[(1+ar)^{-n} - t_d \times \left(g \times r \times \left(\dfrac{(1+ar)^n - 1}{ar}\right) + b\right)\right]}, \text{ if } ar \neq 0$$

$$PV = \frac{FV\ (after\ tax)}{(1 - t_d \times b)}, \text{ if } ar = 0$$

Appendix K – Additional Time Value Concepts

Example 20: Your client, described in Example 19, has determined that he will probably need about $120,000 to finance his children's education in 12 years. As shown in Example 19, (assuming a 35% tax rate on ordinary income and 20% tax rate on capital gains) he can expect the $25,000 he has set aside already to accumulate to $68,912 after tax in 12 years. How much would he have to add to his stock account today to accumulate the extra $51,088 after tax in 12 years?

Since the additional new investment would not have any built-in gain when invested today, b should be set at zero. From Example 20, ar is equal to 10.23% and $(1.1023)^{12}$ is equal to 3.2180863, so the after-tax future value factor for a $1 investment, ATFV$1, is:

$$ATFV\$1 = 3.2180863 - (0.2 \times (0.8 \times 0.11 \times (2.2180863 \div 0.1023)))$$

$$ATFV\$1 = 2.8365$$

PV to reach $51,088 after tax = $51,088 \div 2.8365 = $18,011

The additional amount your client would have to set aside today to meet the additional college-financing need 12 years from now would be about $18,000.

Future Value of Annuity Formulas

Similar to any other annuity formula, the formula for the future value after tax of an annuity is simply the sum of the future after-tax values of each of the level periodic investments or payments. *The future after-tax value of ordinary annuity payments is:*

FVAEat4

$$FV_{(after\ tax)} = Pmt \times \left[\left(\frac{(1+ar)^n - 1}{ar}\right) \times \left(1 - t_d \times \frac{g \times r}{ar}\right) + n \times t_d \times \left(\frac{g \times r}{ar} - b\right)\right], \text{ if } ar \neq 0$$

$$FV_{(after\ tax)} = Pmt \times n \times (1 - t_d \times b), \text{ if } ar = 0$$

The built-in gain (b) in this case is measured with respect to the periodic payments, Pmt. In most cases, b will be equal to 0, since amounts invested periodically to accumulate some future value are usually after-tax dollars. However, if one is calculating the amount one would accumulate after tax by contributing $10,000 before-tax each year to an IRC Section 401(k) plan, for instance, b would be set equal to 1, t_d and t_b would be set equal to the investor's anticipated future tax rate on ordinary income, and ar would be set equal to the before-tax rate of return r.

This formula appears daunting but becomes less so when broken into its component parts. The future value before capital gain tax of annuity due payments can be broken into its component parts as follows. *The future value before paying the tax on capital gains or tax-deferred returns of ordinary annuity payments is:*

Equation FVAEbt4

$$FV_{(before\ tax)} = Pmt \times \left(\frac{(1+ar)^n - 1}{ar}\right), \text{ if } ar \neq 0$$

$$FV_{(before\ tax)} = Pmt \times n, \text{ if } ar = 0$$

The total accumulated gains or total tax-deferred return is:

Equation FVAECG

Total tax – deferred return =

$$Pmt \times \left\{\frac{g \times r}{ar} \times \left[\left(\frac{(1+ar)^n - 1}{ar}\right) - n\right] + n \times b\right\}, \text{ if } ar \neq 0$$

Total tax – deferred return = Pmt × n × b, if ar = 0

Therefore, the tax on the accumulated gains or tax-deferred return is:

Equation FVAECGtax

Total tax on deferred return =

$$Pmt \times t_d \left\{\frac{g \times r}{ar} \times \left[\left(\frac{(1+ar)^n - 1}{ar}\right) - n\right] + n \times b\right\}, \text{ if } ar \neq 0$$

Total tax on deferred return = Pmt × n × t_d × b, if ar = 0

The future after-tax value of level annuity due payments is:

Equation FVABat4

FV (*after tax*) = Pmt x

$$\left[\left(\frac{(1+ar)^n - 1}{ar}\right) \times (1+ar) \times \left(1 - t_d \times \frac{g \times r}{ar}\right) + n \times t_d \times \left(\frac{g \times r}{ar} - b\right)\right],$$

if ar ≠ 0

FV (*after tax*) = Pmt x n x (1 − t_d x b), if ar = 0

The *future value before paying the tax on capital gains or tax-deferred returns of annuity due payments is:*

Equation FVABbt4

FV (*before tax*) = Pmt x $\left(\dfrac{(1+ar)^n - 1}{ar}\right) \times (1+ar)$, if ar ≠ 0

FV (*before tax*) = Pmt x n, if ar = 0

The total accumulated gains or total tax-deferred return is:

Equation FVABCG

Total tax – deferred return = Pmt x

$$\left\{\frac{g \times r}{ar} \times \left[\left(\frac{(1+ar)^n - 1}{ar}\right) \times (1+ar) - n\right] + n \times b\right\}, \text{ if } ar \neq 0$$

Total tax – deferred return = Pmt x n x b, if ar = 0

Therefore, the tax on the accumulated gains or tax-deferred return is:

Equation FVABCGtax

Total tax on deferred return = Pmt x t_d x

$$\frac{g \times r}{ar} \times \left[\left(\frac{(1+ar)^n - 1}{ar}\right) \times (1+ar) - n\right] + n \times b, \text{ if } ar \neq 0$$

Total tax on deferred return = Pmt x n x t_d x b, if ar = 0

Just as in prior cases, the formula for determining the periodic payment, Pmt, is derived by dividing FV(*after tax*) by the multiplier of Pmt in equations FVAEat4 or FVABat4, as appropriate.

Present Value of Annuity Formulas

The formulas for determining the present value amount one needs to invest today to generate after-tax

ordinary annuity payments cannot be simplified to a reduced form similar to the future value annuity equations. In order to compute the present value of a series of periodic after-tax payments, one must use equation PVAt4 to compute the present value of each periodic payment separately and then sum them to derive the total amount one needs to invest today to generate the given series of payments. Therefore, the *present value of a series of ordinary annuity payments is:*

Equation PVAEat4

PV = Pmt (*after tax*) x t_d x

$$\sum_{j=1}^{n}\left\{(1+ar)^{-j} - t_d \times \left[g \times r \times \left(\frac{(1+ar)^n - 1}{ar}\right) - b\right]\right\}^{-1},$$

if ar ≠ 0

$$PV = \frac{Pmt\ (\textit{after tax}) \times n}{(1 - t_d \times b)}, \text{ if } ar = 0$$

The *present value of annuity due payments is:*

Equation PVABat4

PV = Pmt (*after tax*) x t_d x

$$\sum_{j=0}^{n-1}\left\{(1+ar)^{-j} - t_d \times \left[g \times r \times \left(\frac{(1+ar)^j - 1}{ar}\right) - b\right]\right\}^{-1},$$

if ar ≠ 0

$$PV = \frac{Pmt\ (\textit{after tax}) \times n}{(1 - t_d \times b)}, \text{ if } ar = 0$$

Once again, the formula for determining the periodic payment, Pmt, is derived by dividing PV by the multiplier of Pmt(*after tax*) in equations PVAEat4 or PVABat4, as appropriate.

Inflation/Growth Adjusted Formulas

Inflation/Growth Adjusted Rate of Return

The tax-adjusted time value formulas can be modified to include inflation or growth adjustments in a manner analogous to the discussion earlier. Simply substituting ar for r in equation RIA, one derives the inflation- or growth-adjusted accumulation rate, ρ. That is, where all variables are as defined earlier:

Appendix K – Additional Time Value Concepts

Equation ARIA

$$\rho = \frac{1+ar}{1+i} = \frac{ar-1}{1+i}$$

Inflation/Growth-Adjusted Payment Streams

Investment and financial planning applications often involve payment streams that are adjusted for anticipated inflation or growth. For instance, when ascertaining how much a person needs to accumulate for retirement, the analysis usually makes some assumption about how much the cost of living will increase each year during retirement and increases the required annual income accordingly. Analogously, when determining how much a person needs to save each year for retirement, the analysis often assumes that payments will increase each year in relation to the anticipated growth in the investor's salary.

The future after-tax value of a series of ordinary annuity payments increasing (or decreasing) each year at i% (i ≠ 0) per year is:

Equation FVAEat5

FV (*after tax*) = Pmt x

$$\left\{ (1+i)^{n-1} \times \left(\frac{(1+\rho)^n - 1}{\rho} \right) \times \left(1 - t_d \times \frac{g \times r}{ar} \right) + t_d \times \left(\frac{g \times r}{ar} - b \right) \times \left(\frac{(1+i)^n - 1}{i} \right) \right\} , \text{ if } \rho \neq 0$$

if ρ = 0

$$\left\{ (1+i)^{n-1} \times n \times \left[1 - t_d \times \frac{g \times r}{ar} \right] + t_d \times \left(\frac{g \times r}{ar} - b \right) \times \left(\frac{(1+i)^n - 1}{i} \right) \right\} ,$$

$$\left\{ (1+i)^n \times n \times \left(1 - t_d \times \frac{g \times r}{ar} \right) + t_d \times \left(\frac{g \times r}{ar} - b \right) \times \left(\frac{(1+i)^n - 1}{i} \right) \right\} ,$$

if ρ ≠ 0

Similar to equations PVAEat4 and PVABat4, the present value of the investment necessary to generate inflation/growth-adjusted after-tax annuity payments cannot be expressed in a simple reduced-form equation. Rather, the present value of the total investment is equal to the sum of the present values of each inflation/growth-adjusted after-tax payment computed separately. The ordinary annuity payment formula is:

Equation PVAEat5

PV = Pmt (*after tax*) x

$$\sum_{j=1}^{n-1} (1+i)^{j-1} \times \left\{ (1+ar)^j - td \times \left[g \times r \times \left(\frac{(1+ar)^j - 1}{ar} \right) - b \right] \right\}$$

if ar ≠ 0

$$PV = \frac{Pmt \ (after \ tax)}{(1 - t_d \times b)} \times \left(\frac{(1+i)^n - 1}{i} \right) , \text{ if } ar = 0$$

The annuity due payment formula is:

Equation PVABat5

PV = Pmt (*after tax*) x

$$\sum_{j=0}^{n-1} (1+i)^{j-1} \times \left\{ (1+ar)^j - td \times \left[g \times r \times \left(\frac{(1+ar)^j - 1}{ar} \right) - b \right] \right\}^{-1} ,$$

if ar ≠ 0

$$PV = \frac{Pmt \ (after \ tax)}{(1 - t_d \times b)} \times \left(\frac{(1+i)^n - 1}{i} \right) , \text{ if } ar = 0$$

CHAPTER ENDNOTES

1. Under current law, the step-up in basis at death is scheduled to be largely eliminated in 2010. However, that same legislation is also scheduled to "sunset" with estate tax and step-up basis rules reverting to 2001 law after 2010. At this time it is impossible to be sure whether the law will be permitted to expire or whether it will be extended beyond 2010. Most experts expect that at least some of the current law rules will be extended beyond 2010, but have doubts about whether the step-up basis rules will be largely phased-out.

2. A 50% tax rate is used to simplify the numbers and better illustrate the concepts. Under the current tax regime, a 50% tax rate would be rare even if one combined the highest federal, state, and local tax rates.

Similarly, the future after-tax value of annuity due payments increasing (or decreasing) each year at i% (i ≠ 0) per year is:

Equation FVABat5

FV (*after tax*) = Pmt x

$$\left\{ (1+i)^n \times \left(\frac{(1+\rho)^n - 1}{\rho} \right) \times (1+p) \times \left(1 - t_d \times \frac{g \times r}{ar} \right) + t_d \times \left(\frac{g \times r}{ar} - b \right) \times \left(\frac{(1+i)^n - 1}{i} \right) \right\} , \text{ if } \rho \neq 0$$

FV (*after tax*) = Pmt x

3. Under the 2003 tax act, the tax rate changes scheduled for future years have been accelerated into 2003. In addition, the maximum tax rate on certain dividend income and on long-term capital gains for most common investment instruments has been cut to 15%. The examples in this chapter were calculated using tax rates that may or may not be actual tax rates at any point in time. However, the general principles and concepts presented in these examples do not change with changes in tax rates, although the relative after-tax returns certainly do. For instance, under new law, many equity investments qualify for a 15% tax on dividend income and for a maximum long-term capital gain rate of 15% and so these investments become relatively better after-tax investments than they were previously. However, these tax benefits still do not generally outweigh or overcome the tax advantages of making either after-tax contributions to a tax-free investment, such as a Roth IRA, or before-tax contributions to a tax-deferred investment, such as a 401(k) plan.

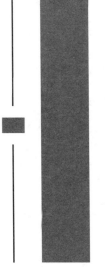

GLOSSARY

ACCELERATION CLAUSE. The clause in a note, bond, or mortgage giving the creditor (mortgagee) the right to demand, upon default of the debtor (mortgagor), the immediate payment of the unpaid balance of the loan or mortgage.

ACCRUED INTEREST. Interest accrued on a bond or other debt obligation since the last interest payment was made. The buyer of a bond pays the market price plus accrued interest. Exceptions include bonds that are in default and income bonds.

AMORTIZE. To pay off a debt by periodic payments set aside for the purpose, or to allocate the cost of an asset over its life.

ANNUAL EXCLUSION. A federal gift tax exclusion of $10,000 (as indexed; $11,000 in 2004) allowed to the donor each year for each donee, provided the gift is one of a present interest (that is, the donee must be given an immediate right to possession or enjoyment of the property interest).

ANNUAL REPORT. The formal financial statement issued yearly by a corporation.

ANNUITY. A series of payments of a fixed amount for a specified number of years.

ASKED PRICE. The price at which securities are offered to potential buyers; or the price sellers offer to take.

ASSESSED VALUE. Value assigned to property by a public body for property tax purposes.

ASSIGNMENT. The act of transferring any interest in property to another party. The one who transfers the right is the "assignor;" the receiver of the right is the "assignee."

BALANCE SHEET. A statement of the financial position of a business entity at a given time, disclosing the assets, liabilities, and invested capital.

BALLOON PAYMENT. The balance due on a debt instrument at maturity that is in excess of a regular principal payment.

BANKRUPTCY. The condition of a business or individual that has been declared insolvent (unable to pay debts) by a court proceeding and whose financial matters are being administered by the court through a receiver or trustee.

BEAR. Someone who believes that the stock market will decline. See Bull.

BEAR MARKET. A declining market. See Bull Market.

BEARER BOND. A bond that does not have the owner's name registered on the books of the issuing company and that is payable to the holder. See Coupon Bond, Registered Bond.

BENEFICIARY. The recipient of funds, property, or other benefits from an insurance policy, will, or other settlement. The individual or entity entitled to the beneficial interest of a trust.

BID PRICE. The price buyers offer to pay for securities; the price at which sellers may dispose of them.

BIG BOARD. A popular term for the New York Stock Exchange.

BLUE CHIP. A company known nationally for the quality and wide acceptance of its products or services, and for its ability to earn income and pay dividends.

BLUE LIST. The trade offering sheets of bond dealers, which list dealers' offerings of municipal bonds for sale all over the country.

BOND. An IOU or promissory note of a corporation or governmental body, usually issued in multiples of $1,000 or $5,000. A bond is evidence of a debt on which the issuer usually promises to pay the bondholders a specified amount of interest for a specified length of time, and to repay the loan on the expiration date.

549

Tools & Techniques of Investment Planning

BOOK VALUE. The net amount (i.e., cost minus accumulated depreciation) at which an asset appears on the books of a company.

BROKER. An agent who handles the public's orders to buy and sell securities, commodities, or other property. For this service a commission is charged.

BULL. A person who believes that the stock market will rise. See Bear.

BULL MARKET. An advancing market. See Bear Market.

CALL. The process of redeeming a bond or preferred stock issue before its scheduled maturity. Sometimes used to refer to a "call option" (see below).

CALL OPTION. An option to buy (or "call") shares of stock at a specified price for a set period of time.

CAPITAL GAIN or CAPITAL LOSS. Profit or loss from the sale of a capital asset. A capital gain is either short-term or long-term. Capital gain is short-term if the asset was held for 1 year or less; the gain is long-term if the asset was held for more than 1 year. This more-than-1-year period necessary to qualify a capital gain as long-term is often referred to as the "long-term capital gain holding period." *Net long-term capital gain* (i.e., the excess of long-term capital gains over short-term capital losses) is taxed at special 5% and 15% tax rates. (See Chapter 43, "Taxation of Investment Vehicles.")

CAPITAL STOCK. All shares representing ownership of a business, including preferred and common. See Common Stock, Preferred Stock.

CAPITALIZATION. The total amount of all the securities issued by a corporation.

CASH FLOW. The amount of cash generated over time from an investment, usually after any tax effects.

CERTIFICATE. The actual piece of paper that is evidence of ownership of stock in a corporation, or of other intangible property.

CHARITABLE DEDUCTION. A deduction allowed for a reportable gift to a charitable organization.

CLOSING. The conclusion or consummation of a real estate transaction where all documents are signed and a deed or land contract, etc., is transferred.

COMMERCIAL PAPER. Unsecured, short-term promissory notes of large firms, usually issued in denominations of $1 million or more.

COMMON STOCK. Securities that represent an ownership interest in a corporation.

CONGLOMERATE. A corporation that has diversified its operations usually by acquiring enterprises in widely varied industries.

CONVERTIBLE. A bond, debenture, or preferred share that may be exchanged by the owner for common stock or another security, usually of the same company, in accordance with the terms of the issue.

CORPORATION. A legal unit organized under state laws that has a continuous life span independent from its ownership. In the event of dissolution, its owners are not responsible for its debt (beyond the amount of their original investment). Corporations can raise capital by issuing securities.

COUPON. Evidence of interest due on a bond, usually every six months. With a bearer bond, the coupon is detached from the bond and presented for payment of interest to the issuer's agent or the bondholder's bank. In the case of a registered bond, the issuing corporation will mail a check for the semiannual interest to the owner of record on each interest payment date.

COUPON BOND. A bond with interest coupons attached. The coupons are removed ("clipped") as they come due and are presented by the holder for payment of interest. See Bearer Bond, Registered Bond.

COUPON RATE. The stated rate of interest on a bond.

COVERED OPTION. An option on stock is covered if the individual who, on exercise of the option, would be required to sell the stock owns the subject stock. Thus, a call option is "covered" if the writer of the call owns the subject stock; a put is "covered" if the purchaser of the put option (who by exercising the put elects to sell his stock) owns the subject stock.

CUMULATIVE PREFERRED. A preferred stock having a provision that if one or more dividends are omitted, the omitted dividends must be paid in full before dividends may be paid on the company's common stock.

Glossary

CURRENCY RISK. The potential gain (or loss) on an investment denominated in a foreign currency due to fluctuations in exchange rates.

CURRENT YIELD. The percentage relation of the annual interest received to the current price of a bond, or other debt obligation.

DEALER. A person or firm acting as a principal in buying and selling securities.

DEBENTURE. A promissory note backed by the general credit of a company and usually not secured by a mortgage or lien on any specific property. See Bond.

DEBT SERVICE. The amount of cash needed to cover periodic mortgage payments or bond interest, including interest and principal.

DEFAULT. Failure to pay principal or interest promptly when due.

DISCOUNT. The amount by which a preferred stock or bond may sell below its par value. Also used as a verb to mean "takes into account" (e.g., "the price of the stock has discounted the expected dividend cut"). See Premium.

DIVIDEND. A payment made from earnings to the stockholders of a corporation. It is authorized by the board of directors and paid among the shares outstanding. In the case of common shares, payment is made on a pro rata basis; however, preferred shares may be entitled to a specific dividend rate that is different from that paid common shareholders.

DIVIDEND YIELD. The ratio of the current dividend to the current price of a share of stock.

DOLLAR COST AVERAGING. A system of buying securities at regular intervals with a fixed dollar amount of capital.

DOMICILE. A location legally regarded as the main place of residence of an individual or business entity.

DONEE. The recipient of a gift. The term also is used to refer to the recipient of a power of appointment.

DONOR. The person who makes a gift. The term also refers to the person who grants a power of appointment to another.

EARNINGS PER SHARE (EPS). The earnings available to common stockholders divided by the number of common shares outstanding. It is considered to be a measure of how well a company is doing by its common shareholders.

ESTATE. An interest in real property. All assets owned by an individual.

ESTATE TAX. A tax imposed upon the right of a person to transfer property at death. This type of tax is imposed not only by the federal government, but also by a number of states.

EURODOLLAR INVESTMENTS. Time deposits denominated in U.S. dollars, but held in banks headquartered outside the United States or in foreign branches of U.S. banks.

EXPIRATION DATE. The last day on which an option (call or put) can be exercised.

EXTRA DIVIDEND. A dividend in the form of stock or cash in addition to the regular or usual dividend a company has been paying.

FIDUCIARY. A person occupying a position of trust, (e.g., an executor, administrator, or trustee).

FLOATING-RATE BOND. A bond on which the interest rate is adjusted, usually every six months, for the subsequent six months, according to a formula based on the then prevailing interest rates. The prime rate, federal funds rate, commercial paper rate, and Treasury bill rates are frequently used indices.

GENERAL OBLIGATION BOND. A municipal bond backed by the general taxing power of its issuer.

GIFT. Property or property rights or an interest gratuitously passed on or transferred for less than an adequate and full consideration in money or money's worth to another – whether the transfer is in trust or otherwise, direct or indirect.

GOVERNMENT BONDS. Obligations of the United States Government; regarded as the highest grade issues in existence.

GROWTH STOCK. Stock of a company with a record of rapid growth in earnings.

INCOME STATEMENT. A statement that summarizes the revenues and expenses of a business for a specified period of time.

INDENTURE. A written agreement under which bonds and debentures are issued, setting forth maturity date, interest rate, and other terms.

IN-THE-MONEY. Description of a *call* option when the stock price is above the striking price of the call. Description of a *put* option when the stock price is below the striking price of the put.

INTERVIVOS TRUST. A trust created during the settlor's lifetime. It becomes operative during one's lifetime as opposed to a trust under a will, which does not become operative until the settlor dies.

INTEREST. Payments a borrower pays a lender for the use of money. A corporation pays interest on its bonds to its bondholders. See Bond.

INVESTMENT. The use of money for the purpose of making more money in order to gain income, increase capital, or both.

INVESTMENT COMPANY. See Mutual Fund.

JOINT TENANCY. The holding of property by two or more persons in such a manner that, upon the death of one, the survivor or survivors take the entire property.

LESSEE. The party to whom a lease is granted.

LESSOR. The party who grants a lease.

LEVERAGE. The use of funds borrowed at a fixed rate in an attempt to reinvest them at a higher rate. Borrowing against the established equity. The term is also used with investments that offer enhanced return without increased investment, such as options and warrants, even without borrowing.

LIEN. A claim against property that has been pledged or mortgaged to secure the performance of an obligation. A bond may be secured by a lien against specific property owned by the company issuing the bonds.

LIMIT ORDER. An order to purchase or sell securities at a set price determined by the customer.

LISTED STOCK. The stock of a company that is traded on an organized securities exchange.

LIQUID ASSETS. Cash or assets that can readily be converted into cash without a serious loss of capital.

LOAD. The portion of the offering price of shares of a mutual fund that covers sales commissions and all other costs of distribution. A load incurred on purchase is a "front-end" load. See No-Load Fund. For "back-end" load and "level" load, see Chapter 16 (Mutual Funds).

MARGIN. The buying of stocks or bonds on credit (known as "buying on margin").

MARKETABILITY. The ease or difficulty with which a security or other asset can be sold in the secondary market.

MARKET ORDER. An order by a customer to buy or sell securities at the best obtainable price.

MARKET PRICE. In the case of a security, the market price is usually considered the last reported price at which a stock or bond has been sold.

MATURITY. The date on which a loan, bond, or debenture comes due and is to be paid off.

MODIFIED ENDOWMENT CONTRACT (MEC). A life insurance policy that has failed the seven-pay test of IRC section 7702A. Distributions (including loans) from a MEC are taxed less favorably than distributions from a life insurance policy that has met the requirements of the seven-pay test.

MONEY MARKET. Financial markets in which funds are borrowed or loaned for short periods, typically less than one year.

MONEY MARKET FUND. A type of mutual fund that invests in short-term government securities, commercial paper, and repurchase agreements.

MORTGAGE. A pledge of property designated as security for a loan.

MORTGAGE BOND. A bond backed by a lien on a specific property.

MORTGAGEE. One who lends funds on the security of specific property (mortgage).

MORTGAGOR. The borrower who uses specific property as collateral for a loan.

MUNICIPAL BOND. A bond issued by a state or a political subdivision, such as a county, city, town, or village. The interest paid on many municipal bonds is exempt from federal income taxes and state and local income taxes within the state of issue.

MUTUAL FUND. An investment company that uses the proceeds from the sale of its shares in order to invest in the securities of other companies.

NET ASSET VALUE. A term used in connection with mutual funds, meaning "net asset value per share" – i.e., the total market value of all securities owned by the fund minus liabilities, divided by the number of fund shares outstanding.

NEW ISSUE. Securities offered to the public for the first time.

NO-LOAD FUND. A mutual fund on which no sales commission is paid.

ODD LOT. An amount of a security less than the established "round lot." See Round Lot.

OVER THE COUNTER. Unlisted securities; those not traded on a major exchange.

PAR VALUE. The nominal or face value of a bond (or a stock).

PARTNERSHIP. An association of two or more individuals to carry on a business for profit. The life span of the partnership is directly linked to that of the owners. Technically, if a partner dies, the partnership has ended. A partnership raises money based on the personal credit available to the owners.

PAY OUT RATIO. The percentage of earnings paid out in the form of dividends.

PORTFOLIO. Securities held by an individual or institution. A portfolio may consist of bonds, stocks, or other securities of various types of institutions.

PREFERRED STOCK. A class of stock with a claim on the company's earnings before payment may be made on the common stock, and that is usually entitled to priority over common stock if the company liquidates.

PREMIUM. The amount by which a bond (or preferred stock) may sell above its par value.

PRICE-EARNINGS RATIO. The price of a share of stock divided by earnings per share for a 12-month period. For example, a stock selling for $20 with

earnings per share of $2 is said to be selling for a price-earnings ratio of 10 to 1.

PRIMARY MARKET. The market for new issues of stocks or bonds.

PRINCIPAL. The property comprising the estate or fund that has been set aside in trust, or from which income is expected to accrue (corpus).

PROPRIETORSHIP. A type of business owned by one person (also known as a "sole proprietorship"). It raises money based on the owner's personal credit.

PROSPECTUS. A document issued for the purpose of describing a new security issue.

PROXY. Written authorization given by a shareholder to someone else to represent him and vote his shares at a stockholders' meeting.

PUT OPTION. An option to sell (or "put") a particular security at a specified price within a designated period of time.

RATING. A formal opinion by an outside professional service on the credit reputation of an issuer and the investment quality of its securities.

REAL ESTATE INVESTMENT TRUST (REIT). An organization similar to a mutual fund in which investors pool funds that are invested in real estate or used to make construction or mortgage loans.

REFUNDING. Redeeming an existing bond issue by selling a new bond issue, usually at terms more favorable to the issuer.

REGISTERED BOND. A bond that is registered on the books of the issuing company in the name of the owner. It can be transferred only when endorsed by the registered owner. See Bearer Bond, Coupon Bond.

REIT. See Real Estate Investment Trust.

REVENUE BOND. A municipal bond backed by revenues produced from a particular project, such as a turnpike. See General Obligation Bond.

REVOCABLE TRUST. A trust that can be changed or terminated during the grantor's lifetime and the property recovered.

ROUND LOT. A unit of trading, or multiple thereof. On the NYSE the unit of trading is generally 100 shares in stocks and $10,000 par value in the case of bonds.

SECONDARY MARKET. Where existing issues are bought and sold. It may be either an over-the-counter market or through an organized exchange.

SERIAL BOND. A part of an issue that matures in relatively small amounts at periodic stated intervals. See Term Bond.

SETTLEMENT DATE. The date on which money and securities are exchanged (usually three business days after the trade was executed, or one day for government securities and listed options).

SINKING FUND. Money set aside by the issuer to be used to retire a bond issue.

SPREAD. The difference between what a dealer pays for a security and the price at which he offers to sell it.

SPECIALIST. A member of a stock exchange whose function is to maintain an orderly market in certain stocks. Each specialist is responsible for specific issues and must make a market in those issues.

STANDARD DEDUCTION. The amount set forth in the Internal Revenue Code that may be deducted (along with personal exemptions) by a taxpayer who does *not* itemize.

STOCK DIVIDEND. A dividend paid in shares of stock rather than cash.

STOCK EXCHANGE. A central market place where securities are traded.

STRIKING PRICE. The price at which an option can be exercised.

SYNDICATE. A group of investment bankers and/or banks that underwrite a bond or stock issue and offer it for public sale.

SYSTEMATIC WITHDRAWAL. An arrangement where a mutual fund automatically liquidates sufficient shares to pay an investor a predetermined amount of money at regular intervals.

TAX CREDIT. A direct reduction of income tax liability based on items such as investments, child care, energy conservation, and foreign taxes.

TAX SHELTER. A tax avoidance transaction as classified by the IRS (i.e., a "listed transaction").

TAXABLE YEAR. A 12-month period (usually the calendar year in the case of individuals) that is used in the calculation of taxable income.

TERM BOND. Part of a bond issue that has a single maturity. See Serial Bond.

TRANSFER AGENT. A professional agency (typically a bank) employed by a corporation to handle the issuance and transfer of securities, payment of dividends, and maintenance of books of the corporation.

UNDERWRITER. The investment banker (or bankers) who buys the entire issue of securities from the issuer and then sell the securities to individual and institutional investors.

VARIABLE ANNUITY. An annuity contract under which the annuity holder has the ability to allocate the annuity premiums among several available investment choices. The annuity holder, not the company issuing the contract, assumes the investment risk associated with the investment decisions.

WARRANT. A right or option to buy a stated number of shares of stock at a specified price over a given period of time. It is usually of longer duration than a call option.

WARRANTY DEED. A deed by which a grantor conveys and guarantees good title to real property; the safest form of deed for the buyer.

YIELD. Also known as return. The dividends or interest paid by a company expressed as a percentage of the current price. A stock with a current market value of $25 per share paying dividends at a rate of $2.50 is said to return 10% ($2.50 ÷ $25.00).

YIELD TO MATURITY. The average annualized rate of return that an investor will receive if a bond is held until its maturity date. It differs from "yield" or "current yield" in that it takes into consideration the increase to par of a bond bought at a discount, and the decrease to par of a bond bought at a premium.

ZERO COUPON BOND. A bond that pays no interest during the life of the bond and that is normally issued at a substantial discount from par. The face amount of the bond, when it is paid at maturity, includes the payment of interest.

INDEX

Index